ECONOMICS

CAMPBELL R. McCONNELL
PROFESSOR OF ECONOMICS
UNIVERSITY OF NEBRASKA
FIFTH EDITION

ECONOMICS

PRINCIPLES, PROBLEMS, AND POLICIES

McGRAW-HILL BOOK COMPANY

NEW YORK ST. LOUIS SAN FRANCISCO DÜSSELDORF
JOHANNESBURG KUALA LUMPUR LONDON MEXICO
MONTREAL NEW DELHI PANAMA RIO DE JANEIRO
SINGAPORE SYDNEY TORONTO

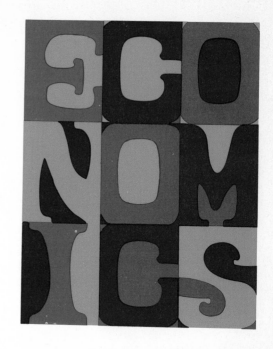

ECONOMICS

Library of Congress Catalog Card Number 75-37867

07-044893-0

2 3 4 5 6 7 8 9 0 DODO 7 9 8 7 6 5 4 3 2

This book was set in Vega Light by York Graphic Services, Inc., and printed and bound by R. R. Donnelley & Sons Company. The designer was Betty Binns; the drawings were revised by B. Handelman Associates, Inc. The editors were Jack R. Crutchfield, Michael Elia, and Edwin Hanson. Robert R. Laffler and Matt Martino supervised production.

TO MEM

CONTENTS

6

CURRENT DOMESTIC ECONOMIC PROBLEMS

PREFACE

The fifth edition of *Economics* embodies a very substantial revision and thereby contributes significantly to the metamorphosis which this book has experienced since its publication in 1960. Although the fifth edition bears only a modest resemblance to the first, the basic purpose remains the same: to introduce the beginning economics student to those principles essential to an understanding of fundamental economic problems and the policy alternatives society may utilize to contend with these problems. It is hoped that the ability to reason accurately and objectively about economic matters and the development of a lasting interest in economics will be two valuable by-products of this basic objective. Furthermore, my intention remains that of presenting the principles and problems of economics in a straightforward, logical fashion. To this end great stress has been put upon clarity of presentation and organization.

THE FIFTH EDITION

This edition incorporates many changes; some of the more significant ones are summarized here in order of descending importance.

First, two new chapters have been added. Chapter 37 is on urban economics. Although it is problem-oriented and deals with such questions as urban sprawl, transportation, the ghettos, urban renewal, and pollution, the chapter is built upon the framework of the economics of agglomeration. My goal is to explain, rather than merely assert, the problems of the cities. Chapter 40 discusses the economics of the war industry, hopefully in a balanced and unemotional way. Student interest in both of these subjects is quite intense, and I have tried to take full advantage of the many opportunities to apply both micro- and macroanalysis.

Chapter 6 has been extensively reworked to emphasize the simple analytics of spillover effects. Greater emphasis has also been given to the three basic functions of government: resource allocation, stabilization, and income redistribution. Both of these changes help provide an analytical point of reference which is used repeatedly in later chapters. The introduction of the elements of benefit-cost analysis helps make the revised Chapter 6 more objective with respect to the appropriate economic role of government.

Chapter 19 is no longer merely a summary chapter. In addition to providing a synthesis of macrotheory and stabilization policies, the chapter now contains a thorough explanation of the monetarist debate and a discussion and analysis of the Nixon Administration's "New Economic Policy." Chapter 44 incorporates the international aspects of the New Economic Policy—the floating of the dollar and the tariff surcharge.

In Chapter 22 the debate over the desirability of rapid growth has a new orientation toward the environment and human values rather than the United States–Soviet Union growth race of earlier editions. In Chapter 32 the discussion of wage determination includes important new material on the minimum wage as an antipoverty device; there also is a new discussion of investment in human capital which ties into the explanation of wage differentials. Chapter 35 on the monopoly problem has been extensively reorganized; it now picks up more of the "new industrial state" debate and deals explicitly with conglomerates. The examination of income inequality in Chapter 38 includes a section on President Nixon's family assistance plan and a discussion of the problem of devising an income maintenance plan which effectively and efficiently deals with poverty and simultaneously sustains incentives to work. New material on consumer protection has been added to Chapter 7. Chapter 9 has been considerably revised in terms of the Tax Reform Act of 1969. Most of the theory chapters—both micro and macro—have been rewritten to clarify technical points or applications.

Users of the fourth edition will discover a multitude of other changes. Indeed, few chapters have escaped some rewriting, revisions of content, organizational changes, or updating. Reasons for this extensive revision are both general (the innumerable changes in the economic milieu of the past several years) and specific (the solicited and volunteered criticisms of users of the fourth edition).

PRODUCT DIFFERENTIATION

In terms of content I feel this text embraces a number of departures in content and organization which distinguish it from other books in the field.

1. The principles course usually fails to provide students with a comprehensive and meaningful definition of economics. To remedy this shortcoming, one complete chapter (Chapter 2) is devoted to a careful statement and development of the economizing problem and an exploration of its implications. The foundation thereby provided should be helpful in putting the many particular subject areas of economics into proper perspective.

2. There is a rather apparent intellectual lag among economists in their discussions of the economic functions of government. Government is an integral and increasingly important component of modern capitalism. Its economic role, therefore, should not be treated piecemeal or as an afterthought. This text attempts to overcome these difficulties by introducing economic functions of government early and according them systematic treatment in philosophical (Chapter 6), factual (Chapter 9), and controversial (Chapter 41) terms.

3. This volume puts considerable emphasis upon the crucial topic of economic growth. Chapters 20, 21, and 22 are devoted to economic growth in an advanced economy, namely, the United States. Chapter 45 employs the conceptual framework of Chapter 20 in treating the obstacles to economic growth that plague the underdeveloped countries. An important segment of Chapter 46 concerns the growth record and prospects of Soviet Russia's command economy. Beyond this it will be found that the chapters on price theory pay special attention to the implications that the various market structures have for technological progress.

4. It is understandable that the elusiveness of general equilibrium analysis eminently qualifies this topic for omission at the principles level. The result, however, is a grievous shortcoming of most introductory courses. A sincere effort is made in this book to remedy the deficiency. Specifically, an entire chapter (Chapter 5) is devoted to the notion of the price system, and another chapter (Chapter 34) explicitly outlines the nature and significance of general equilibrium analysis.

5. This volume forgoes the presentation of necessarily sketchy descriptions of a number of alternative economic systems in favor of a detailed discussion of the Soviet economy and the challenge it poses for the Free World. I feel this emphasis upon the Soviet system is more vital, more timely, and decidedly more interesting to students.

6. I have purposely given considerable attention to microeconomics in general and to the theory of the firm in particular. There are several reasons for this emphasis. In the first place, the concepts of microeconomics are difficult for most beginning students. Short expositions usually compound these difficulties by raising more questions than they answer. Second, a majority of economists now agree that we possess the fiscal and monetary tools necessary for the maintenance of near-full employment. This tends to shift the economic spotlight back to the question of resource allocation, and ultimately to the operation of the price system. Finally, I have coupled analysis of the various market structures with a discussion of the social implications of each. The impact of each market arrangement upon price and output levels, resource allocation, and the rate of technological advance is carefully assessed.

7. Part 6 provides a broad spectrum of chapters on current socioeconomic problems. As most students see it, this is where the action is. I have sought to guide the action along logical lines through the application of appropriate analytical tools. My bias in Part 6 is in favor of inclusiveness; each instructor can effectively counter this bias by omitting those chapters he feels to be less relevant for his particular students.

8. The imaginative use of a multicolor format permits great flexibility in the functional use of color and in the fifth edition is a feature of considerable esthetic merit.

ORGANIZATION AND CONTENT

In terms of organization, this book has been written with the conviction that the basic prerequisite of an understandable economics text is the logical arrangement and clear exposition of subject matter. This concern with organization is most evident in Part 1, which centers upon the step-by-step development of a comprehensive and realistic picture of American capitalism. This coherent group of introductory chapters is substituted for the traditional smattering of more or less unrelated background topics that ordinarily introduce the student to the study of economics.

Throughout this volume the exposition of each particular topic and concept is directly related to the level of difficulty which in my experience the average student is likely to encounter. It is for this reason that national income accounting, microeconomics, and to a lesser degree, employment theory are purposely accorded comprehensive and careful treatments. Simplicity in these instances is correlated with comprehensiveness, not brevity. Furthermore, my experience suggests that in the treatment of each basic topic—employment theory, money and banking, international economics, and so forth—it is highly desirable to couple analysis and policy. A three-step development of basic analytical tools is employed: (1) verbal description and illustration, (2) numerical examples, and (3) graphic presentation based upon these numerical illustrations.

The material is organized around seven basic topics: (1) an introduction to American capitalism; (2) national income, employment, and fiscal policy; (3) money and monetary policy; (4) American economic growth; (5) economics of the firm and resource allocation; (6) current domestic economic problems; and (7) international economics, the underdeveloped countries, and the Soviet economic challenge.

Part 1 is designed to introduce the method and subject matter of economics and to develop the ideological framework and the factual characteristics of American capitalism. This group of chapters develops in an orderly fashion the overall picture of how our

economy operates. After an introduction to the methodology of economics in Chapter 1, an entire chapter is devoted to defining and explaining the economizing problem. Chapters 3 to 5 develop the capitalistic ideology and the notion of the most fundamental institution of capitalism—the price system. Early emphasis upon the price system is designed to provide the necessary orientation for the detailed treatment of pricing found in Part 5 and to contribute to an understanding of the national income analysis of Part 2 and, more specifically, the topics of inflation and deflation. Chapter 6 introduces government as a basic economic component of modern capitalism; government's economic functions are systematically explained and evaluated. Upon this superstructure of a mixed public-private economy, Chapters 7 to 9 add the factual information concerning the household, business, and government aggregates of the economy, thereby making our mixed capitalism model much more realistic. However, instructors who wish to minimize institutional material may choose to omit Chapters 7 through 9.

Part 2 treats national income analysis and fiscal policy. Chapter 10 on national income accounting reflects my conviction that this difficult topic merits detailed treatment. Chapter 11 employs the national income measures in describing the last five decades of American business cycle experience. This I feel is an important undertaking for college sophomores who, fortunately, have grown up amidst the virtually unabated prosperity of the last thirty years. The next four chapters are devoted to neo-Keynesian employment theory, fiscal policy, and the public debt.

Part 3 emphasizes the balance sheet approach to money and banking. This approach seems most in accord with the goal of providing the student with an analytical tool needed in reasoning through, as opposed to memorizing, the economic impact of the various basic banking transactions. Just as fiscal policy is linked directly to income theory in Part 2, monetary policy immediately follows the discussion of money and banking. The first half of the book is completed with Part 4 on American economic growth and problems related thereto.

For reasons already noted, the treatment of pricing and resource allocation in Part 5 is purposely detailed. Throughout Chapters 27 to 30 emphasis is placed upon the social implications of the various market structures. What is the significance of each market structure for price and output levels, resource allocation, and technological progress? Emphasis in the discussion of distribution—Chapters 31 to 33—is generally in accord with the relative quantitative importance of the various market shares in our economy. I have not belabored the analysis of interest, rent, and profits where, it seems to me, economic analysis leaves much to be desired. Chapter 34 provides a simple and, it is hoped, revealing discussion of general equilibrium and an introduction to input-output analysis.

Part 6 deals with domestic issues: the monopoly problem, the farm problem, the problems of the cities, the economics of inequality and poverty, labor relations and collective bargaining, the economic problems associated with war and defense, and social balance. In each of these chapters an attempt has been made to (1) describe the historical and factual background of the problem, (2) analyze its causes and effects, (3) explore government policy, and (4) offer a thought-provoking discussion of public policy alternatives. As noted, instructors may choose to use the chapters of Part 6 selectively.

The first three chapters of Part 7 survey international trade and finance with some rigor. Chapter 45 explores the very crucial problems surrounding the efforts of the underdeveloped countries to achieve economic growth. Finally, Chapter 46 offers a relatively comprehensive discussion of the Soviet economy, emphasizing its planning processes and its growth prospects.

End-of-chapter summaries provide a concise, pointed recapitulation of each chapter. Much thought has gone into the end-of-chapter questions. Though purposely intermixed, these questions are of three general types. Some are designed to highlight the main points of each chapter. Others are "open-end" discussion or thought questions. Wherever pertinent, numerical problems which require the student to derive and manipulate key concepts and relationships are employed. Numerical problems are stressed in

those chapters dealing with national income accounting and analysis, money and banking, and price theory. Some optional "advanced analysis" questions have been added to certain theory chapters as a new feature of the fifth edition. These problems usually involve the stating and manipulation of certain basic concepts in equation form. The bibliographical references at the end of each chapter are designed to provide both breadth and depth for the ambitious student. Yet care has been taken to see that these references are not beyond the grasp of the average college sophomore.

ORGANIZATIONAL ALTERNATIVES

Though economics instructors are in general agreement as to the basic content of a principles of economics course, there are considerable differences of opinion as to what particular arrangement of material is best. The structure of this book is designed to provide considerable organizational flexibility. And I am happy to report that users of prior editions have informed me that they accomplished substantial rearrangements of chapters with little sacrifice of continuity. Though I have chosen to move from macro- to microeconomics, there is no reason why the introductory material of Part 1 cannot be followed immediately by the microanalysis of Part 5. Similarly, in my judgment money and banking can best be taught after, rather than before, national income analysis. Those who disagree will encounter no problems by preceding Chapter 10 with Chapters 16, 17, and 18. Furthermore, some instructors will prefer to intersperse the microeconomics of Part 5 with the problems chapters of Part 6. This is easily accomplished. Chapter 36 on the farm problem may follow Chapter 27 on pure competition; Chapter 35 on the social control of monopoly may follow Chapters 28 to 30 on imperfect competition. Chapter 39 on labor unions and collective bargaining may either precede or follow Chapter 32 on wages, and Chapter 38 on income inequality may follow Chapters 32 and 33 on the distributive shares of national income.

Those who teach the typical two-semester course and who feel comfortable with the book's organization will find that, by putting the first four parts in the first semester and Parts 5 through 7 in the second, the material is divided both logically in terms of content and quite satisfactorily in terms of quantity and level of difficulty between the two semesters. For a course based on three quarters of work I would suggest Chapters 1 through 15 for the first quarter, 16 through 34 for the second, and 35 through 46 for the third. Finally, those interested in the one-semester course will be able to discern several possible groups of chapters that will be appropriate to such a course. Tentative outlines for three one-semester courses, emphasizing macroeconomics, microeconomics, or a survey of micro and macro theory, follow this preface on page xxv.

SUPPLEMENTS

The fifth edition of *Economics* is accompanied by a variety of useful supplements.

A new fourth edition of *Economic Issues: A Book of Readings* has been prepared, and I am sufficiently immodest to feel that it embodies some distinctive features which make it a valuable supplement for this or any other standard principles of economics textbook.

Students have found Professor Robert C. Bingham's *Study Guide* to be an extremely valuable aid. Professor Bingham's *Economic Concepts* provides carefully designed programmed materials for all the key analytical areas of the principles course.

In addition to the *Study Guide* and *Economic Concepts* Professor Bingham has prepared a new supplement, *Economics, Mathematically Speaking* to accompany the fifth edition. This supplement translates the verbal-tabular-graphical development of theory found in *Economics* into the language of mathematics. The uniqueness of this supplement lies in its specific orientation to the principles course. I am certain that those instructors who prefer a more quantitative approach will find *Economics, Mathematically Speaking* to be of the same high levels of quality and usefulness as Professor Bingham's other supplements.

My *Instructor's Manual* includes some comments of a pedagogical character and, more important, is a reservoir of objective and essay questions.

The *Test File* of questions which was introduced with the fourth edition is available in a slightly enlarged form. The file contains the multiple-choice questions from the *Instructor's Manual* which can be arranged in any desired sequence and efficiently employed in constructing an examination. The *Test File* was received most enthusiastically by adopters of the fourth edition, but somewhat less ecstatically by the publisher, who provides the *File* without charge to users of *Economics.* I am particularly pleased that other authors have accorded the *Test File* the most sincere form of flattery.

Both color and black-and-white transparencies for overhead projectors accompany the text.

DEBTS

It has been more than a decade since the first edition of *Economics* was published. Its acceptance, which was most generous from the start, has expanded with each edition. An important by-product of this widespread acceptance is that many teachers and students have been kind enough to give me the benefit of their criticisms and suggestions.

I must restate my debt to the reviewers of the original manuscript: L. S. Van Scoyoc of Bowling Green State University, John Auten of Rice Institute, J. J. Kaufman of Pennsylvania State University, Raymond W. Ritland of Auburn University, and Howell E. Jones of Bethany College. I owe a special debt to Prof. Arthur M. Okun of The Brookings Institution, who contributed much to both the content and organization of this text.

The second and third editions benefited from the counsel and criticisms of Professors Clayton Hall and Fred Picard of Ohio University, David G. Brown of the University of North Carolina, Carl Stern of Randolph-Macon, Kenneth O. Alexander of Michigan Technical University, James M. Cahill of Manhattan College, Ira Castles of Delta State College, Edward Coen of the University of Minnesota, Kalman Goldberg of Bradley University, Keith D. Evans of San Fernando Valley State College, Will Lyons of Franklin and Marshall College, Ray Marshall of the University of Texas, Glenn L. Simpson of Colorado State University, Janet L. Weston of the University of Illinois, and Simon N. Whitney of Rutgers University.

Many of the changes embodied in the fourth edition reflect the wisdom of Professors Donald C. Darnton of Virginia Polytechnic Institute, Robert P. Fairbanks of Northern Illinois University, E. C. Griffith of Washington and Lee University, John P. Henderson of Michigan State University, Richard J. Kiesewetter of American River College, Edward Kittrell of Northern Illinois University, George Powell of Pennsylvania Military College, and Jack W. Skeels of Northern Illinois University.

Perceptive reviews by Ira C. Castles of Delta State College, Frank J. Bonello and Frank J. Jones of Notre Dame, John W. Dorsey of Maryland, and Robert Horton of Purdue were invaluable in preparing the present edition. Kenneth E. Boulding of Colorado and Murray L. Weidenbaum of Washington University contributed instructive reviews of the new chapter on the war industry. Charles Lamphear of Nebraska, Hugh O. Nourse of Illinois, Robert J. Saunders of Kent State, and Douglas M. Brown of Northeastern provided most helpful reviews of the new chapter on urban economics.

Through all five editions I have unashamedly exploited the brainpower of a number of present and former University of Nebraska colleagues, including Robert C. Bingham, Wallace C. Peterson, Clemens B. Thoman, Ernst W. Kuhn, and Harry M. Trebing. Last, but not least, my daughter Lauren provided ample cheap labor in preparation of the index.

It is obvious that in a very real sense "my" book has become a collective endeavor. But, as tradition demands, I accept sole responsibility for all errors of omission and commission.

CAMPBELL R. McCONNELL

THREE SUGGESTED OUTLINES FOR ONE-SEMESTER COURSES

OPTION ONE: One-semester Course Emphasizing Macroeconomics

1 THE NATURE AND METHOD OF ECONOMICS
2 AN INTRODUCTION TO THE ECONOMIZING PROBLEM
3 PURE CAPITALISM AND THE CIRCULAR FLOW
23 THE MARKET STRUCTURES OF AMERICAN CAPITALISM
4 THE MECHANICS OF INDIVIDUAL PRICES: DEMAND AND SUPPLY
24 DEMAND, SUPPLY, AND ELASTICITY: SOME APPLICATIONS
26 SUPPLY AND THE COSTS OF PRODUCTION (OPTIONAL)
27 PRICE AND OUTPUT DETERMINATION: PURE COMPETITION (OPTIONAL)
28 PRICE AND OUTPUT DETERMINATION: PURE MONOPOLY (OPTIONAL)
5 THE FIVE FUNDAMENTAL QUESTIONS AND THE PRICE SYSTEM
6 MIXED CAPITALISM AND THE ECONOMIC FUNCTIONS OF GOVERNMENT
7 THE FACTS OF AMERICAN CAPITALISM: HOUSEHOLDS
8 THE FACTS OF AMERICAN CAPITALISM: BUSINESSES
9 THE FACTS OF AMERICAN CAPITALISM: GOVERNMENT
10 NATIONAL INCOME ACCOUNTING
11 THE BUSINESS CYCLE: UNEMPLOYMENT AND INFLATION
12 THE BACKGROUND AND ANALYTICAL TOOLS OF EMPLOYMENT THEORY
13 THE EQUILIBRIUM LEVELS OF OUTPUT, EMPLOYMENT, AND INCOME
14 THE ECONOMICS OF FISCAL POLICY
15 FISCAL POLICY AND THE PUBLIC DEBT
16 MONEY AND BANKING IN AMERICAN CAPITALISM
17 HOW BANKS CREATE MONEY
18 THE FEDERAL RESERVE BANKS AND MONETARY POLICY
19 ECONOMIC STABILITY: THEORY AND POLICY
20 THE SIMPLE ANALYTICS OF ECONOMIC GROWTH
21 ECONOMIC GROWTH: THE AMERICAN EXPERIENCE
22 GROWTH IN AMERICAN CAPITALISM: COSTS, PROBLEMS, AND POLICIES

OPTION TWO: One-semester Course Emphasizing Microeconomics

1 THE NATURE AND METHOD OF ECONOMICS
2 AN INTRODUCTION TO THE ECONOMIZING PROBLEM

OPTION THREE: One-semester Survey of Micro and Macro Theory

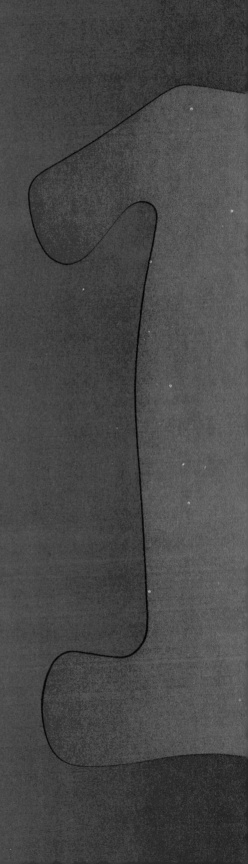

AN INTRODUCTION TO AMERICAN CAPITALISM

1

THE NATURE AND METHOD OF ECONOMICS

Man, unfortunate creature, is plagued with wants. He wants, among other things, love, social recognition, and the material necessities and comforts of life. Man's striving to improve his material well-being, to "make a living," is the concern of economics. More specifically, economics is the study of man's behavior in producing, exchanging, and consuming the material goods and services he wants. Most of us think of economics in terms of specific problems—balancing the household budget, labor disputes, farm surpluses, taxes, debt, inflation, unemployment. Although limited, this thinking is not incorrect. These specific problems are fragments or signs of the larger problem of man's attempt to satisfy his material wants.

It is tempting to seek out immediately answers and solutions to specific problems of current interest. But this would be precipitate; certain preliminary matters must be discussed first. In particular, we must know the answers to these questions:

1. Of what importance or consequence is the study of economics?
2. How should we study economics—what are the proper procedures? Stated in more technical terms, what is the character of the methodology of economics?
3. What specific problems, limitations, and pitfalls might we encounter in studying economics?

These topics will occupy our attention in this introductory chapter.

THE AGE OF THE ECONOMIST

Is economics a discipline of consequence? Is the study of economics an endeavor worthy of one's time and effort? Over three decades ago John Maynard Keynes (1883–1946)—clearly the most influential economist of this century—offered a telling response:

> The ideas of economists and political philosophers, both when they are right and when they are wrong, are more powerful than is commonly understood. Indeed the world is ruled by little else. Practical men, who believe themselves to be quite exempt from any intellectual influences, are usually the slaves of some defunct economist.

The ideologies of the modern world which compete for the minds of men have been shaped in substantial measure by the great economists of the past—Adam Smith, John Stuart Mill, David Ricardo, Karl Marx, and John Maynard Keynes.[1] And it is currently commonplace for world leaders to receive and invoke the advice and policy prescriptions of economists; "the political economist is now a fixture in the high councils of government."[2] To illustrate: The President of the United States benefits from the ongoing counsel of his Council of Economic Advisors. The broad spectrum of economic issues with which political leaders must contend, and on which they must assume some tenable posture, is suggested by the contents of the annual *Economic Report of the President:* unemployment and inflation, economic growth and productivity, taxation and public expenditures, poverty and income maintenance, the balance of payments and the international monetary system, labor-management relations, the farm problem, manpower development and training, competition and antitrust, to enumerate only a few.

These comments correctly imply that a basic understanding of economics is essential if we are to be well-informed citizens. Most of the specific problems of the day have important economic aspects, and we in a democracy make the ultimate decisions in meeting those problems. Should America maintain the price of gold in the face of great strains upon the international monetary system? Should we continue to subsidize farmers? Should we wage a war on poverty? And if so, what specific programs will alleviate poverty most efficiently? Why is inflation bad? What can be done about it? Does technological progress or automation threaten to create large pools of permanently unemployed workers? What are the economic implications of war? And of disarmament? Intelligence at the polls requires that we have a basic working knowledge of economics.

[1] Either of the following two volumes—Robert Heilbroner, *The Worldly Philosophers,* 3d ed. (New York: Simon and Schuster, Inc., 1967), or Daniel R. Fusfeld, *The Age of the Economist* (Chicago: Scott, Foresman and Company, 1966)—will provide the reader with a fascinating introduction to the historical development of economic ideas.

[2] Walter W. Heller, *New Dimensions of Political Economy* (New York: W. W. Norton & Company, Inc., 1967), p. 14.

Economics is also a vital discipline for somewhat more mundane and immediate reasons. Economics is of practical value in business. An understanding of the overall operation of the economic system puts the businessman in a better position to formulate his policies. For example, if he understands the causes and consequences of inflation, he is better equipped during inflationary periods to make intelligent decisions concerning his enterprise than he might be otherwise. Indeed, more and more economists are appearing on the payrolls of large corporations. Their job? To gather and interpret economic information upon which rational business decisions can be made. Also, economics gives the individual as worker and income receiver some insights as to how he might make himself more secure against the effects of inflation and unemployment. How can one "hedge" against the reduction in the purchasing power of the dollar which accompanies inflation? What occupations are most immune to unemployment?

In spite of its practical benefits, however, the reader must be forewarned that economics is an academic, not a vocational, subject. Unlike accounting, advertising, corporation finance, and salesmanship, economics is not a how-to-make-money area of study.[3] A knowledge of economics may be helpful in running a business or in managing one's personal finances, but this is not its primary objective. In economics, problems are examined from the social, not from the individual, point of view. The production, exchange, and consumption of goods and services are discussed from the viewpoint of society as a whole, not from the standpoint of one's own bankbook.

METHODOLOGY

What do economists do? What are their goals? What procedures do they employ? The title of this volume—*Economics: Principles, Problems, and Policies*—contains a thumbnail answer to the first two questions. Economists are concerned with the derivation

[3] An economist has been defined as an individual with a Phi Beta Kappa key on one end of his watch chain and with no watch on the other.

of economic *principles* which are useful in the formulation of *policies* designed to solve economic *problems.* The procedure employed by the economist is summarized in Figure 1·1. The economist must first ascertain and gather the facts which are relevant to consideration of a specific economic problem. This aspect of his job is sometimes called "descriptive economics." The economist then puts his collection of facts in order and summarizes them by "distilling out" a principle, that is, by generalizing about the way individuals and institutions actually behave. Deriving principles from facts is called "economic theory" or "economic analysis." Finally, the general knowledge of economic behavior which economic principles provide can then be used in formulating policies, that is, remedies or solutions, for correcting or avoiding the problem under scrutiny. This final aspect of the field is sometimes called "applied economics" or "policy economics."

Still using Figure 1·1 as a point of reference, let us now examine this three-step procedure in more detail.

Descriptive economics

All sciences are empirical. All sciences are based upon facts, that is, upon observable and verifiable behavior of certain data or subject matter. In the physical sciences the factual data are inorganic. As a social science, economics is concerned with the behavior of individuals and institutions engaged in the production, exchange, and consumption of goods and services.

The first major step, then, in investigating a given problem or a specific segment of the economy is to gather the facts. This can be an infinitely complex task. The world of reality is cluttered with a myriad of interrelated facts. The economist therefore must use discretion in fact gathering. He must distinguish economic from noneconomic facts and then determine which economic facts are relevant and which are irrelevant for the specific problem under consideration. But even when this sorting process has been completed, the relevant economic facts may appear diverse and unrelated.

Economic theory

A conglomeration of facts is relatively useless; mere description is not enough. To be meaningful, facts must be systematically arranged, interpreted, and generalized upon. This is the task of economic theory or analysis. Principles and theories—the end result of economic analysis—bring order and meaning to a number of facts by tying these facts together, putting them in correct relationship to one another, and generalizing upon them. "Theories without facts

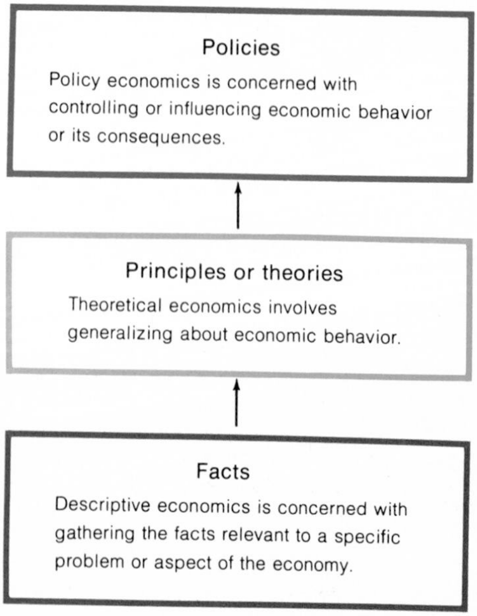

Policies
Policy economics is concerned with controlling or influencing economic behavior or its consequences.
Principles or theories
Theoretical economics involves generalizing about economic behavior.
Facts
Descriptive economics is concerned with gathering the facts relevant to a specific problem or aspect of the economy.

FIGURE 1·1 THE RELATIONSHIP BETWEEN FACTS, PRINCIPLES, AND POLICIES IN ECONOMICS

In studying any problem or segment of the economy the economist must first gather the relevant facts. These facts must then be systematically arranged, interpreted, and generalized upon. These generalizations are useful not only in explaining economic behavior, but also in predicting and therefore controlling future events.

may be barren, but facts without theories are meaningless."[4]

The interplay between the levels of fact and theory is more complex than Figure 1·1 indicates. Principles and theories are meaningful statements drawn from facts, but facts, in turn, serve as a constant check on the validity of principles already established. Facts—how individuals and institutions actually behave in producing, exchanging, and consuming goods and services—change with time. This makes it essential that economists continuously check existing principles and theories against the changing economic environment. The history of economic ideas is strewn with once-valid generalizations about economic behavior which were rendered obsolete by the changing course of events.

Terminology A word on terminology is essential at this juncture. Economists talk about "laws," "principles," "theories," and "models." These terms all mean essentially the same thing: generalizations, or statements of regularity, concerning the economic behavior of individuals and institutions. The term "economic law" is a bit misleading because it implies a high degree of exactness, universal application, and even moral rightness. So to a lesser degree does the term "principle." And some people incorrectly associate the term "theory" with idle pipe dreams and ivory-tower hallucinations, divorced from the facts and realities of the world. The term "model" has much to commend it. A model is a simplified picture of reality, an abstract generalization of how the relevant data actually behave. In this book these four terms will be used synonymously. The choice of terms in labeling any particular generalization will be governed by custom or convenience here. Hence, the relationship between the price of a product and the quantity consumers purchase will be called the "law" of demand, rather than the theory or principle of demand, because it is customary to so designate it.

These comments on terminology raise two points which merit further consideration: First, economic principles (laws, theories, or models) are *generalizations,* and second, they are *abstractions.*

Generalizations Economic principles are generalizations and, as such, subject to exceptions and to quantitatively imprecise statement. Economic facts are usually diverse; some individuals and institutions act one way and some another. Hence, economic principles are frequently stated in terms of averages or statistical probabilities. For example, when economists say that the average household earned an income of about $9,400 in 1969, they are making a generalization. It is recognized that some households earned much more and a good many others much less. Yet this generalization, properly handled and interpreted, can be very meaningful and useful. Or an economist may conclude that 95 percent of the time—95 chances out of 100—consumers will increase their purchases of a product when its price falls. Five percent of the consumers constitute an exception to the general rule.

The main reason for the inexactness of economic principles is the fact that the economist cannot conduct controlled experiments—he does not have a laboratory in which he can create simplified and controlled conditions. The laboratory of the social sciences is the real world, where the specific aspects of human behavior we wish to examine cannot be readily isolated from the social and cultural milieu. The chemist can "make other things equal" in his controlled experiments; the economist cannot.

The "other things equal" assumption Unable to make other things equal in their analyses, economists do the next best thing: They *assume* other things are equal in isolating certain data for analysis. To illustrate: In analyzing the relationship between the price of product X and the amount of X purchased, economists assume that of all the factors influencing the amount of X purchased, only its price varies. To cut the problem down to size, they must assume that all other factors which might influence the amount of X purchased are unchanged or "equal." In this way

[4]Kenneth E. Boulding, *Economic Analysis: Microeconomics,* 4th ed. (New York: Harper & Row, Publishers, Incorporated, 1966), p. 5.

economists can isolate the relationship between price and quantity demanded from all sorts of real-world complications. However, in applying the resulting generalization—consumers buy more of X at a low price than they do at a high price—to a real-world situation, exceptions may be encountered. Why? Because other things are not often equal in the real world. For example, an increase in incomes—another consideration which, in addition to a price change, will cause the amount of X purchased to alter—may complicate the application of the general conclusion about the relationship between the price of X and the amount of X purchased. The economist may find that, although the price of X has risen, the quantity demanded has *increased* contrary to his generalization. This does not make the generalization invalid, but rather means that peculiar circumstances—higher incomes—have entered this particular application of the principle to upset its accuracy. It is merely an exception to the rule, and in economics such exceptions may be rather frequent. Economics is admittedly an inexact science.

Abstractions Economic principles, or theories, are necessarily abstractions. They do not embody the full bloom of reality. The very process of sorting out noneconomic and irrelevant facts in the fact-gathering process involves abstracting from reality. Unfortunately, the abstractness of economic theory prompts the uninformed to identify theory as something which is impractical and unrealistic. This is nonsense! As a matter of fact, economic theories are practical for the simple reason that they are abstractions. The level of reality is too complex to be very meaningful. Economists theorize in order to give meaning to a maze of facts which would otherwise be confusing and useless and to put facts into a more usable, practical form. Thus to generalize is to abstract; generalization for this purpose is practical, and therefore so is abstraction. An economic theory is a model—a simplified picture or map—of some segment of the economy. This enables us to better understand reality because it avoids the details of reality. Finally, theories—*good* theories—are grounded on facts and therefore are realistic. Theories which do not fit the facts are simply not good theories.

Graphic expression Theories, or models, can be expressed in many ways. For example, the physicist and chemist illustrate their theories by building Tinker-Toy arrangements of multicolored wooden balls that represent protons, neutrons, and so forth, held in proper relationship to one another by wires or sticks. Economists are not so lucky as to have theories that lend themselves to such tangible demonstrations. Economic models must take the form of verbal description, numerical tables, mathematical equations, or graphs. The last are particularly helpful and will be used throughout this book. Most of the principles we shall encounter will explain the relationship between just two sets of economic facts, for example, the relationship between the price of a specific product and the quantity of it which consumers buy. Simple two-dimensional graphs are a convenient and clear way of summarizing and manipulating these relationships.

As shown in Figure 1·2, graphs are drawn on squared paper divided into four quarters, or quadrants, by a horizontal axis and a vertical axis, which intersect at right angles. The point of intersection is called the *origin*. Each axis has a scale of numerical values. On the vertical axis, all values above the origin are positive, and all values below are negative. On the horizontal axis, values to the right of the origin are positive; those to the left are negative. The point of intersection, that is, the origin, designates zero. Though the vertical and horizontal scales in Figure 1·2 measure the same numerical values, this need not be the case. Each unit on the vertical axis may measure $1, while the same distance on the horizontal axis denotes 1,000 bushels of corn.

In elementary economics we are virtually always concerned with the relationship between two sets of economic facts the values of which are positive. Hence, we are concerned with the upper right-hand quarter of the chart where both scales measure positive values.

Now let us explore an example or two to illustrate

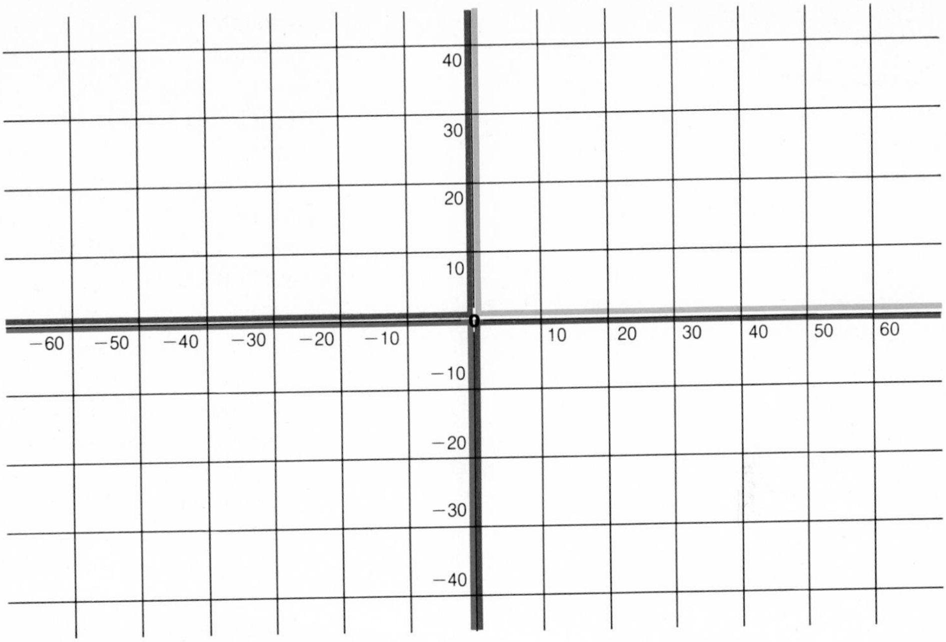

FIGURE 1·2 ECONOMIC PRINCIPLES CAN BE EXPRESSED GRAPHICALLY

Two-dimensional graphs are a convenient way of presenting and manipulating relationships between data. The relationship between two sets of economic data with positive numerical values is shown in the upper right quadrant of the chart.

the construction and interpretation of graphs. Suppose detailed factual investigation reveals that the relationship between the price of corn per bushel and the amount farmers are willing to produce and offer for sale per year is as shown in Table 1·1.

How can this be shown graphically? Simply by putting the two sets of facts—product price and quantity supplied—on the two axes of the chart and locating the five combinations of price-quantity supplied shown in Table 1·1. Convention or convenience dictates which set of facts goes on the vertical axis and which on the horizontal axis. By convention, economists put "price" on the vertical and "quantity" on the horizontal axis, as indicated in Figure 1·3. The five price-quantity combinations are plotted on the chart by drawing perpendiculars from the appropriate points on the two axes. For example, in plotting the $5–12,000-bushel combination, perpendiculars must be drawn across from the vertical (price) axis at $5 and up from the horizontal (quantity-supplied) axis at 12,000 bushels. Their point of intersection locates the $5–12,000-bushel combination on the graph. The same procedure locates the other four price-quantity combinations. If it is assumed that the same general relationship between price and quantity supplied will prevail at all points between the five graphed, a line or curve can be drawn to connect these points. In this instance the two sets of data

TABLE 1·1 THE QUANTITIES OF CORN FARMERS WILL SUPPLY AT VARIOUS PRICES (*hypothetical data*)

Price per bushel	Bushels supplied per year
$5	12,000
4	10,000
3	7,000
2	4,000
1	1,000

are *directly related;* that is, price and quantity supplied move in the same direction. As price increases, the quantity supplied increases. As price declines, so does the quantity supplied. When two sets of data are directly related, they will always graph as an upsloping line or curve, such as *SS* in Figure 1·3.

Now suppose fact gathering reveals that the price of corn and the quantity which consumers will buy per year are related in the manner shown in Table 1·2. These data indicate that consumers will demand more corn when its price is low than they will when the price is high; that is, price and quantity are *inversely related.* If price increases, the amount purchased will decline. If price declines, the quantity purchased will increase. An inverse relationship will always graph as a downsloping line or curve, such as *DD* in Figure 1·4.

In Chapter 4 we will combine the laws of supply and demand in constructing a model of a market and use this model to explain product price and output.

Dangers of models When properly constructed and interpreted, economic models are invaluable tools. But we must be aware of certain potential dangers in deriving and applying these models.

1. The fundamental danger in constructing an eco-

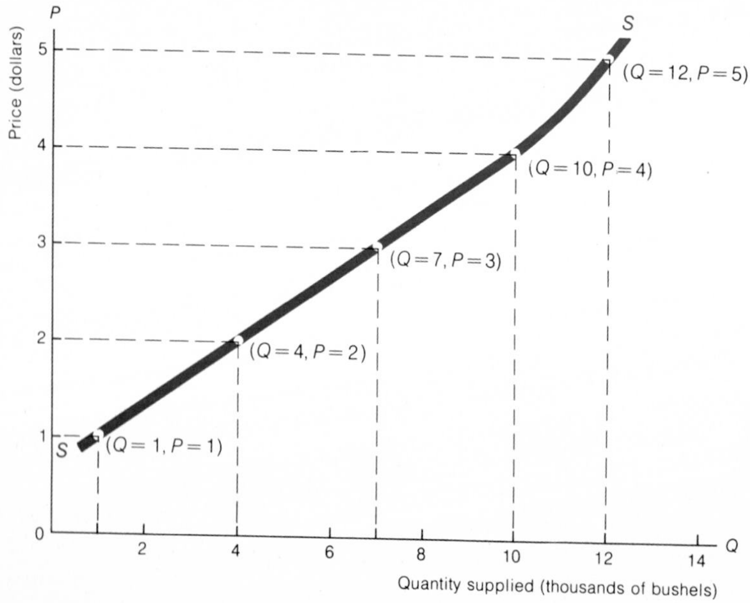

FIGURE 1·3 RELATIONSHIP BETWEEN PRICE AND QUANTITY SUPPLIED

Two sets of economic data which are directly related, such as price and quantity supplied, graph as an upsloping curve (*SS*).

TABLE 1·2 THE QUANTITIES OF CORN CONSUMERS WILL PURCHASE AT VARIOUS PRICES (*hypothetical data*)

Price per bushel	Bushels demanded per year
$5	2,000
4	4,000
3	7,000
2	11,000
1	16,000

nomic model or principle is that the economist might fail to distinguish correctly between relevant and irrelevant facts. If the economist "boils out" some relevant facts, the resulting principle may be a disjointed, misleading, and, at best, incomplete analytical tool. A related difficulty stems from the possibility that an overzealous economist might abstract from too many facts and construct a model which is hyperabstract and truly out of touch with reality.

2. In applying economic models, we must always recognize them for what they are—useful first approximations. It is easy, but dangerous, to slip into the practice of becoming so enthusiastic about logical clarity that we forget such models are simply rough outlines of reality. There may be many omissions between a simplified economic model and reality.

3. We must be on guard in applying economic models so as not to impute any ethical or moral qualities to them. Economic models are the analytical tools of the economist, and, as such, they are ethically neutral. Because they are constructed of facts, economic models afford general statements about "what is," not indications of "what ought to be." Figure 1·3 does not tell us that farmers *should* supply more corn at higher prices than at lower prices, but rather that they *actually do.* Economic models are not tin gods to be worshiped as an end in themselves, or as a compendium of ethically desirable results. Instead, they should be recognized for what they are—a means to an end, a summary of factual data.

Policy economics

Of what value are economic principles? The answer is twofold. There is first the matter of explanation for explanation's sake—economic principles help to explain to us why certain events occur the way they do. Through economic principles we can comprehend why prices change, how surpluses and shortages of products arise, what causes depression and unemployment, and so forth. Our curiosity concerning these and similar phenomena can be satisfied through the development of economic principles to serve as tools for the understanding of reality.

Apart from pure explanation, economic principles can also be extremely valuable as predictive devices, and prediction is the prerequisite of control. If an undesirable event can be predicted by the application of an economic principle, we may be able to influence or control that event.

Or if we cannot control an event, at least we gain from prediction invaluable time to prepare for adjusting to its consequences. Ability to predict a rainstorm does not give us control over the weather, but it does permit us to prepare for it by carrying a raincoat and umbrella.

Values It is evident that value judgments—opinions as to what is desirable or undesirable—come into the picture at this juncture. Descriptive economics and economic theory are both concerned with facts—the former immediately and the latter once removed. Policy economics necessarily entails value judgments as to the desirability of certain events. When operating at this level, economists are no longer functioning as scientists, but rather as policy makers. They are dealing not only with facts, but also with values.

An example or two will help at this point. Our previously noted principle of consumer behavior is the basis for one illustration: "Consumers generally buy more of a product at a low price than they do at a high price." Suppose a clothing merchant finds that

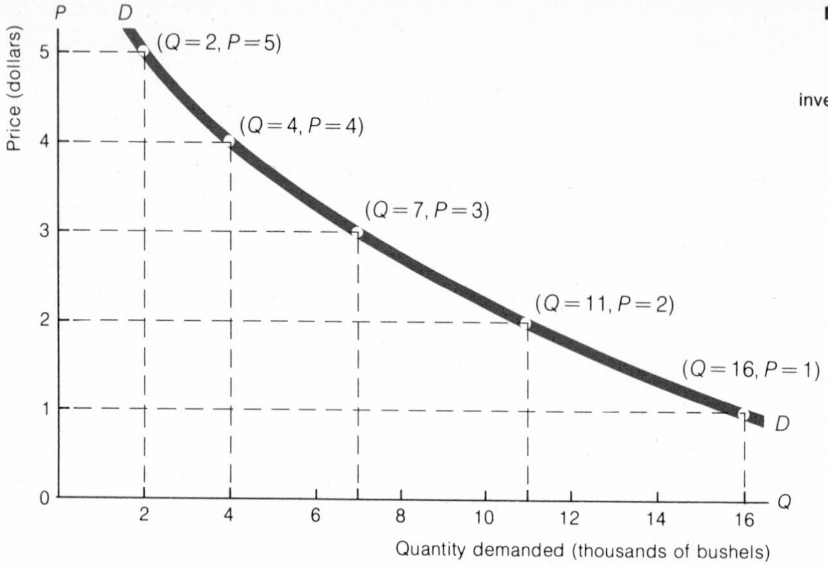

FIGURE 1·4 RELATIONSHIP BETWEEN PRICE AND QUANTITY DEMANDED

Two sets of economic data which are inversely related, such as price and quantity demanded, graph as a downsloping curve (*DD*).

he is greatly overstocked with summer clothing at a time when shipments of fall and winter clothing are due. The merchant has the problem of ridding himself of his undesired surplus stock of summer wear. Our principle of consumer behavior helps the merchant to solve this problem by predicting for him how consumers will react to price changes. In particular, the principle predicts that the merchant will be able to increase his sales and "move" the surplus by lowering prices. The merchant, formulating his price policies accordingly, "runs a sale." The surplus disappears.

A second example, of greater consequence to the economy as a whole, involves the fundamental principle that, within certain limits, there is a direct relationship between total spending and the level of employment in the economy. "If total spending increases (decreases), the volume of employment will rise (fall)." This principle can be invaluable to government in determining its economic policies. For example, if government economists note that available statistics indicate an actual slackening of total expenditures, the principle will permit them to predict the undesirable consequence of unemployment. Aware of this anticipated result, public officials are now in a position to set in motion certain government policies designed to bolster total spending and head off expected unemployment. In short, we must be able to predict in order to effectively control. Economic principles help make prediction possible.

Economic goals of American capitalism It is important at this point that we note and reflect upon a number of economic goals or values which are widely, though not universally, accepted in our society. These goals may be briefly listed as follows:

1. ***Economic growth*** The production of more and better goods and services, or, more simply stated, a higher standard of living, is desired.
2. ***Full employment*** Suitable jobs should be available for all who are willing and able to work.
3. ***Price stability*** Sizable upswings or downswings

in the general price level, that is, inflation and deflation, should be avoided.

4. Economic freedom Businessmen, workers, and consumers should enjoy a high degree of freedom in their economic activities.

5. An equitable distribution of income No groups of citizens should face stark poverty while others wallow in luxury.

6. Economic security Provision should be made for those who are chronically ill, disabled, handicapped, aged, or otherwise dependent.

Now this list of widely accepted goals provides the basis for several significant points. First, note that this or any other statement of basic economic goals inevitably entails problems of interpretation. What are "sizable" changes in the price level? What is a "high degree" of economic freedom? What is an "equitable" distribution of income? Although most of us might accept the above goals as generally stated, we might also disagree very substantially as to their specific meanings and hence as to the types of policies needed to attain these goals. It is noteworthy that, although goals 1 to 3 are subject to reasonably accurate measurements, the inability to quantify goals 4 to 6 undoubtedly contributes to any controversy over their specific meaning.

Second, certain of these goals are complementary in that to the extent one goal is achieved, some other goal or goals will also tend to be realized. For example, the achieving of full employment (goal 2) obviously means the elimination of unemployment, a basic cause of low incomes (goal 5) and economic insecurity (goal 6). Furthermore, considering goals 1 and 5, it is generally agreed that the sociopolitical tensions which may accompany a highly unequal distribution of income are tempered to the extent that most incomes rise absolutely as a result of economic growth.

Third, some goals may be conflicting or mutually exclusive. Currently a number of highly regarded economists argue that those forces which further the attainment of economic growth and full employment may be the very same forces which cause inflation. That is, to some degree goals 1 and 2 may conflict with goal 3. Other economists are reluctantly concluding that to some extent economic growth and full employment (goals 1 and 2) may conflict with economic freedom (goal 4). They contend that rapid growth and continuous full employment may require an expanding role for government and that this will inevitably impinge upon the free choices of businessmen, workers, and consumers.

This leads us to a fourth point: When basic goals do conflict, society is forced to develop a system of priorities for the objectives it seeks. To illustrate: If full employment and price stability are to some extent mutually exclusive, that is, full employment entails some inflation and price stability entails some unemployment, society must decide upon the relative importance of these two goals. Suppose the relevant choice is between, say, a 3 percent annual increase in the price level accompanied by full employment on the one hand, and a perfectly stable price level with 5 percent of the labor force unemployed on the other. Which is the better choice? Or how about a compromise goal in the form of, say, a 1 percent increase in the price level each year with 4 percent of the labor force out of work? There is obviously ample room for disagreement here.

There would admittedly be disagreement among individuals in our society as to the priorities to be assigned these six goals, or, for that matter, as to whether this is a "correct" list in the first place.[5] Now, finally, we must keep in mind that other societies can, and do, have substantially different goals. Soviet society—or perhaps more accurately the Soviet state—puts relatively greater emphasis upon goals 1 and 2 and, our experts tell us, has at times done a better job of achieving these goals than we have (Chapter 46). A good part of the explanation of the success of the Soviet Union in achieving rapid growth and full employment is that they attach a much lower priority than we do to other goals. In particular, Soviet disregard for economic freedom allows the use of policies for achieving full employment and rapid growth which would be completely unacceptable in

[5] For example, we will discover in Part 7 that the realization of balance in our international trade and finance is an important national goal. Furthermore, the improvement of the physical environment is a goal of increasing significance (Chapter 37).

our society. In short, other societies assign different weights or priorities to various goals, and these differing priorities may permit these other societies to do a better job in achieving certain of these objectives.

Formulating economic policy The creation of specific policies designed to achieve the broad economic goals of our society is no simple matter. A brief examination of the basic steps in policy formulation is in order.

1. The first step is to make a clear statement of goals. If we seek "full employment," do we mean that everyone between, say, eighteen and sixty-five years of age has a job? Or do we mean that everyone who wants to work has a job? Should we allow for some "normal" unemployment caused by workers' voluntarily changing jobs?

2. Next we must state and recognize the possible effects of alternative policies designed to achieve the goal. This entails a clear-cut understanding of the economic impact, benefits, costs, and political feasibility of alternative programs. Thus, for example, economists currently debate the relative merits and demerits of fiscal policy (changing government spending and taxes), monetary policy (altering the supply of money), or direct controls (public control of wages and prices) as alternative means of achieving and maintaining full employment.

3. We are obligated to both ourselves and future generations to look back upon our experiences with chosen policies and evaluate their effectiveness; it is only through this type of evaluation that we can hope to improve policy applications. Did a given change in taxes or the supply of money alter the level of employment to the extent originally predicted? If not, why not?

One final point: The formulation of economic policy is greatly complicated by the fact that our economy is a dynamic, changing organism. We must therefore not expect once-and-for-all answers to basic economic problems, but rather short-run adjustments which may rapidly become obsolete. What is correct policy today may be rendered inappropriate tomorrow by a rapidly changing economic milieu.

PITFALLS TO STRAIGHT THINKING

Our discussion of the economist's procedure has, up to this point, skirted some of the problems and pitfalls frequently encountered in deriving and applying economic principles. Some of these difficulties—for example, problems of terminology and bias—are almost self-evident. Indeed, they are so obvious that we tend to overlook them, which makes explicit comment imperative. Other difficulties, particularly those which take the form of logical pitfalls, are rather complex and most conducive to faulty economic reasoning.

Terminology

It is extremely important in studying any science to understand its terminology, but this is particularly so in the social sciences. There are three specific reasons why a clear, objective grasp of relevant terms will prove to be half the battle in understanding many aspects of economics:

1. The economic terminology to which we are exposed in newspapers and popular magazines is sometimes emotionally loaded. The writer—or more frequently the particular interest group he represents—may have a cause to further or an ax to grind, and his terms will be slanted to solicit the support of the reader. Hence, we may find a governmental irrigation project in the Great Plains region called "creeping socialism" by its opponents and "intelligent democratic planning" by its proponents. We must be prepared, therefore, to discount such terminology in achieving objectivity in the understanding of important economic issues.

2. It is embarrassing to admit that economists are often guilty of dual terminology—the unfortunate practice of using two or more labels to designate the same thing. In part, this is a matter of historical accident. It is also the result of economic inquirers discovering that two different theories or explanations are actually the same. The dual labels persist after the theories have been merged. For example, the terms "economic resources," "productive services," and "factors of production" have identical meanings.

Similarly, in probing the causes of depression, we hear some authorities laying the blame at the door of "underconsumption," while others cite "oversaving" as the villain. The beginner who is not familiar with the definitions of these terms may envision a basic conflict of views. Actually, "oversaving" and "underconsumption," properly defined, refer essentially to the same phenomenon.

3. It is important to keep in mind that no scientist is obligated to use commonsense or man-in-the-street definitions of his terms. He may find it convenient and essential to define his terms in such a way that they are clearly at odds with the definitions held by laymen in everyday speech. So long as the economist is explicit and consistent in his definitions, he is on safe ground. A typical example: The term "investment" to John Q. Citizen is associated with the buying of bonds and stocks in the securities market. How often have we heard someone talking of investing in General Motors stock or government bonds? But to the economist, "investment" means the purchase of real capital assets such as machinery and equipment, or the construction of a new wing on a factory building, not the purely financial transaction of swapping cash or part of a bank balance for a neatly engraved piece of paper. As a matter of fact, we shall discover in Chapter 10 that what the layman calls "investment" is a swapping of assets or a form of saving, as the economist sees it.

Bias and preconceptions

The beginning student in chemistry or physics traditionally knows little or nothing about the subject matter of these fields at the outset. He starts from scratch with a blank but, supposedly, clear mind. Not so in the social sciences in general or in economics in particular. For a variety of reasons the budding economist ordinarily launches into his field of study with a bundle of preconceptions about the operation of our economy and its component parts. Such issues as the farm problem, the public debt, the legitimate functions of labor unions, big business versus competition, the nature and operation of our tax system, and the like are everyday topics of conversation. Unless we live in a void, most of us have some *preconceived notions* on these issues. Unfortunately, all too often these preconceptions are flatly wrong or, at best, partially true; in other cases they are hopelessly biased. Thus as neophyte economists—in contrast to physicists or chemists—we start at a disadvantage in our search for truth, and our task in learning economics is doubled: we must recognize and "unlearn" misguided preconceptions, and we must supplant these inaccuracies with valid concepts and generalizations.

These observations contain an urgent plea for objectivity in studying economics. Economic principles can become a vice rather than a valuable analytical tool if, in using them, we are obsessed with a point of view. By approaching them from the angle or viewpoint of, say, management or labor, we jeopardize much of the value these principles hold for us. Dissociating ourselves from any particular viewpoint—whether that of the workingman, the businessman, or the farmer—will pay us dividends, because such associations can imperceptibly undermine our reason and hopelessly color our conclusions. Objectivity is an obvious prerequisite to the successful pursuit of scientific truth. This objectivity is most likely to be achieved when a *social point of view* is embraced. "How does this policy or action affect the economy (society) as a whole and *all* its relevant parts?" is a question much superior to "How does this policy or action affect me as a businessman or laborer?" We must keep an open mind in pursuing economic knowledge.

Fallacy of composition: macro and micro

Many of the false preconceptions people have about economics are attributable to the fallacy of composition. This is the fallacy of contending that "what is true for the individual or part is necessarily also true for the group or whole." This is a logical fallacy; it is not correct. The validity of a particular generalization for an individual or part does not necessarily ensure its accuracy for the group or whole.

A noneconomic example may help: You are watching a football game on a sunny autumn afternoon.

The home team executes an outstanding play. In the general excitement, you leap to your feet to get a better view. *Generalization:* "If you, *an individual,* stand, then your view of the game is improved." But does this also hold true for the group—for everyone watching the game? Certainly not! If everyone stands to watch the play, everyone—including you—is likely to have the same or even a worse view than he had when seated!

Now an illustration from economics: An *individual* farmer who is fortunate enough to realize a bumper crop is likely to find that his resulting income is larger than usual. This is a correct generalization. Does it apply to farmers as a *group?* Possibly not, for the simple reason that to the individual farmer, crop prices will not be influenced (reduced) by his bumper crop, because each farmer is producing a negligible fraction of the total farm output. But to farmers as a group, prices vary inversely with total output.[6] Thus, as all farmers realize bumper crops, the total output of farm products rises, thereby depressing prices. If price declines overbalance the unusually large output, farm incomes *fall.*

In a sense, these comments on the fallacy of composition boil down to this: There are two essentially different levels of analysis at which the economist may derive laws concerning economic behavior. The level of *macroeconomics* is concerned either with the economy as a whole or with the basic subdivisions or aggregates—such as government, households, and businesses—which make up the economy. An aggregate is a collection of specific economic units which are treated *as if* they were one unit. Thus, we might find it convenient to lump together the sixty-two million households in our economy and treat them as if they were one huge unit. In dealing with aggregates, macroeconomics is concerned with obtaining an overview, or general outline, of the structure of the economy and the relationships between the major aggregates which constitute the economy. No attention is given to the specific units which make up the various aggregates. It is not surprising, then, to find that macroeconomics entails discussions of such magnitudes as *total* output, the *total* level of employment, *total* income, *total* expenditures, the *general* level of prices, and so forth, in analyzing various economic problems. The problems of unemployment and inflation, by the way, are the primary topics of macroeconomics. In short, macroeconomics examines the forest, not the trees. It gives us a bird's-eye view of the economy.

On the other hand, *microeconomics* is concerned with *specific* economic units and a *detailed* consideration of the behavior of these individual units. When operating at this level of analysis, the economist figuratively puts an economic unit, or very small segment of the economy, under the microscope to observe the details of its operation. Here we talk in terms of an individual industry, firm, or household and concentrate upon such magnitudes as the output of a *specific* product, the number of workers employed by a single firm, the revenue or income of a particular firm or household, the expenditures of a given firm or family, the price of a particular product, and so forth. In microeconomics we examine the trees, not the forest. Microeconomics is useful in achieving a worm's-eye view of some very specific component of our economic system.

The basic point is this: The fallacy of composition reminds us that *generalizations which are valid at one of these levels of analysis may or may not be valid at the other.*

Prosperity and depression

Closely related to the fallacy of composition is the fact that notions or ideas which are valid during prosperity may be invalid during depression, or vice versa. Some economic principles rest upon a specific presupposition concerning the phase of the business cycle; the validity of a given principle may depend upon the existence of good times or bad times. For example, the economist deems thrift or saving as economically beneficial and therefore desirable during periods of prosperity involving sharp inflation. Why? Because, as we shall discover, a high level of saving will tend to reduce inflationary pressure. Yet during periods of depression, the economist is

[6] This assumes there is no government price fixing.

equally correct in generalizing to the effect that saving is an economic vice, the reason being that too much saving is the immediate cause of unemployment or depression.

Cause and effect

The discovery of cause-and-effect relationships is an important and difficult part of any science. The absence of controlled experimentation adds significantly to the woes of the social scientist in isolating such cause-effect relationships. It is therefore exceedingly important to warn against grasping at straws in constructing cause-effect sequences. In particular, beware of the *post hoc, ergo propter hoc* or "after this, therefore, because of this" fallacy—the incorrect notion that simply because one event precedes another, the first is necessarily the cause of the second.

A classic example clearly indicates the fallacy inherent in such reasoning. Suppose that early each spring the medicine man of a native tribe performs his ritual by cavorting around the village in a green costume. A week or so later the trees and grass turn green. Can we safely conclude that event A, the medicine man's gyrations, has caused event B, the landscape's turning green? Day follows night, but this doesn't mean that night is the cause of day!

Furthermore, causation in economics rarely resides in a simple, single event. Example: Many people believe that the stock market crash of 1929 caused the Great Depression of the 1930s. Although there is an element of accuracy in this statement, it is basically incorrect. The Depression and the stock market crash itself were the *results* of a number of more fundamental forces within the economy (see Chapter 11). A more complex illustration: Economists have found a positive correlation between education and income. In general, people with more education earn higher incomes than do people with less education. But are the higher incomes of the "more educated" attributable solely to education? Or in fact do these people simply have more intelligence, greater motivation, or better family connections and therefore would have earned higher incomes even if they had not elected to pursue more education? Upon reflection seemingly simple cause-effect relationships—"more education produces more income"—may prove to be only partially correct and therefore misleading.

In short, cause-and-effect relationships are typically not self-evident in economics; the economist must look carefully before he leaps to the conclusion that event A caused event B. Certainly the simple fact that A preceded B is not sufficient to warrant any such conclusion.

Effect of expectations

The anticipations, or expectations, of consumers and businesses are frequently of great importance in economics. This is so because the widespread anticipation of an event can prompt behavior which may cause the expected event to become a reality. For example, if consumers and businessmen suspect that inflation lies on the economic horizon, they may increase their current levels of spending to "beat" expected higher prices. But increased outlays are likely to cause the anticipated inflation to materialize. Such was the case at the start of the Korean conflict. Conversely, if the economy expects a siege of unemployment, its natural reaction is to retrench on spending. Building a nest egg of savings seems to be a logical means of financing ourselves through an anticipated economic slump. But increasing savings means less spending, and this is likely to cause expected unemployment to become a reality. Similarly, if speculators expect the price of a stock to dip, they will attempt to sell that stock before the decline occurs. The resulting increased offerings of that stock relative to the demand for it will then cause the value of that stock to nosedive.

In short, what people think will happen has a vital influence upon what actually does occur in the economy.

Intentions versus realizations

It is also important to recognize that what consumers or business firms attempt or intend to do may be considerably at odds with what they are actually able

to accomplish or realize. In our own experience we may plan to wage a campaign of hard work and frugality each summer vacation in order to provide adequate finances for school expenses, but at summer's end we find we have managed to save considerably less than we had originally planned. Events can drastically alter plans. As a matter of fact, the very attempt to achieve a given goal may create certain circumstances which prevent the attainment of that objective. For example, we shall find in Chapter 13 that if the economy attempts to achieve too high a rate of saving, unemployment will result. Unemployment means lower incomes, and this in turn undermines the ability to save. The attempt to save too much may create a situation in which the economy can actually save little or nothing at all. Plans on the one hand and accomplishments on the other may be very different things.

Logical explanations and social practice

Economics is concerned with both describing and explaining human behavior. Explanations in economics, however, occasionally fall short of logical standards. Thus, some explanations in the following chapters will not be "logical" but will, nevertheless, expound the actual operation of our economic units in terms of current social or business practice. For example, we might consider a more logical system of practices and regulations under which our monetary and banking system could operate than that currently employed. It would be misleading, however, to devote our efforts to an understanding of such a logical masterpiece, since it is out of touch with reality. Of course, our system might be of great value as a guide to reform. Or we might later question the logic of classifying the construction of private residential housing as investment goods rather than as consumer goods. After all, housing is generally bought by individual consumers just as automobiles, bread, and shoes are purchased. Yet, for good reasons of their own, government statisticians classify private housing as an investment good. For us to learn it otherwise—despite the apparent logic of the situation—would be flatly incorrect. In short, we will occasionally find ourselves relying upon that's-the-way-it-is explanations in which logic is subservient to business or social practice. Fortunately, this kind of explanation is not encountered with great frequency.

Economic quackery

A final general warning: The field of economics is, and always has been, a fertile ground for quacks and charlatans. While few feel capable of offering aid and advice to the nuclear physicist or research chemist, a great many people envision themselves as unrecognized geniuses in economics and politics. The world abounds with self-styled economists who stand ready to cure the world's ills with seemingly simple changes in the structure, legal framework, or ideology of our economy. Some half-baked schemes are frequently appealing in their directness and simplicity, and the task of undermining such schemes is not easy. The ideas of the quack chemist or physicist can be taken to the laboratory and quickly tested for validity. But no clear-cut testing ground is available for rapidly exposing the remedies of economic quacks. (However, one quite obvious earmark of a quack is his eagerness to engage in the highly unscientific practice of generalizing from a single, isolated case rather than from a carefully gathered broad base of empirical evidence.)

The economist's job is made even more difficult by the fact that hard scraping and manipulating will uncover statistics that "prove" just about any point desired![7] Thus, quack schemes often achieve considerable popular support before they are exposed and relegated to the scrap heap as nonsense or half-truths.

We should be foolish to accept medical advice for the treatment of cancer from our milkman or corner grocer. We should be silly if we let an automobile mechanic advise us on dental work. We ought to be equally hesitant to accept the economic analyses and remedies offered by untrained but highly vocal ama-

[7]One can spend a profitable and highly entertaining evening with Darrell Huff's *How to Lie with Statistics* (New York: W. W. Norton & Company, Inc., 1954).

teurs. Let us remember that answers to major economic problems are rarely self-evident or clear-cut. If they were, the given problem would in all likelihood have been solved and forgotten long ago. The best answers to complex economic problems rarely present themselves in terms of blacks and whites, but rather as varying shades of gray. Easy answers do not often go hand in hand with complex questions.

SUMMARY

1. Economics is studied for several reasons: *a.* It provides valuable knowledge concerning man's social environment and his behavior; *b.* it equips a democratic citizenry to render fundamental decisions intelligently; *c.* although not a vocational discipline, economics may provide the businessman with valuable information.

2. Economics is based upon facts concerning the activities of individuals and institutions in producing, exchanging, and consuming goods and services. The task of descriptive economics is the gathering of those economic facts which are relevant to a particular problem or specific segment of the economy.

3. These facts are then studied, arranged, and generalized upon. The resulting generalizations are called "principles," "theories," or "models." The derivation of these principles is the task of economic theory.

4. Economic principles have several noteworthy characteristics. First, they are generalizations and, as such, are subject to exceptions and elude quantitatively precise statement. Further, economic principles are models of reality and are hence abstract; their usefulness depends upon this abstraction. Finally, economic principles often can be conveniently expressed on two-dimensional graphs.

5. In deriving and applying principles, the economist must *a.* not omit any relevant facts, *b.* recognize that principles are simplified models of reality, and *c.* take care not to impute any moral qualities to these principles.

6. Economic principles are particularly valuable as predictive devices; they are the bases for the formulation of economic policy designed to solve problems and control undesirable events.

7. Economic growth, full employment, price stability, economic freedom, equity in the distribution of income, and economic security are all widely accepted economic goals in our society. Some of these goals are complementary; others are mutually exclusive.

8. There are numerous pitfalls in studying economics which the beginner may encounter. Some of the more important chuckholes strewn along the road to economic understanding are *a.* terminological difficulties, *b.* biases and erroneous preconceptions, *c.* the fallacy of composition, *d.* the fact that the validity of some economic ideas may depend upon the stage of the business cycle, *e.* the difficulty of establishing clear cause-effect relationships, *f.* the fact that expectations may influence actual events, *g.* the fact that intentions and accomplishments may be at odds, *h.* possible discrepancies between logic and social practice, and finally, *i.* the ever-present threat of economic quackery.

QUESTIONS AND STUDY SUGGESTIONS

1. "The trouble with economics is that it is not practical. It has too much to say about theory and not enough to say about facts." Critically evaluate.

2. Define descriptive economics, economic theory, and policy economics, and explain the relationships between the three.

3. Analyze and explain the following quotation:[8]

Facts are seldom simple and usually complicated; the-

[8]Henry Clay, *Economics for the General Reader* (New York: The Macmillan Company, 1925), pp. 10–11.

oretical analysis is needed to unravel the complications and interpret the facts before we can understand them . . . the opposition of facts and theory is a false one; the true relationship is complementary. We cannot in practice consider a fact without relating it to other facts, and the relation is a theory. Facts by themselves are dumb; before they will tell us anything we have to arrange them, and the arrangement is a theory. Theory is simply the unavoidable arrangement and interpretation of facts, which gives us generalizations on which we can argue and act, in the place of a mass of disjointed particulars.

4. "As is the case with other sciences, economics is not content with merely descriptive knowledge. Economics tries to discern general patterns of uniformity in human behavior." Explain.

5. Of what significance is the fact that economics is not a laboratory science? What problems may be involved in deriving and applying economic principles?

6. "Like all scientific laws, economic laws are established in order to make successful prediction of the outcome of human actions."[9] Explain.

7. "Abstraction . . . is the inevitable price of generality . . . indeed abstraction and generality are virtually synonyms."[10] Explain.

8. Briefly explain the use of graphs as a means of presenting economic principles. What is an inverse relationship? How does it graph? What is a direct relationship? How does it graph? Graph and explain the relationships one would expect to find between ***a.*** the number of inches of rainfall per month and the sale of umbrellas, ***b.*** the amount of tuition and the level of enrollment at a university, and ***c.*** the size of a university's athletic scholarships and the number of games won by its football team. In each case cite and explain how considerations other than those specifically mentioned might upset the expected relationship.

9. To what extent would you accept the six economic goals stated and described in this chapter? What priorities would you assign to them? It has been said that we seek simply four goals: progress, stability, justice, and freedom. Is this list of goals compatible with that given in the chapter?

[9]Oskar Lange, "The Scope and Method of Economics," *Review of Economic Studies*, vol. 13, 1945–1946, p. 20.

[10]George J. Stigler, *The Theory of Price* (New York: The Macmillan Company, 1947), p. 10.

10. Analyze each of the following specific goals in terms of the six general goals stated on pages 11–12, and note points of conflict and compatibility: ***a.*** Conservation of natural resources and the lessening of environmental pollution, ***b.*** increasing leisure, and ***c.*** protection of American producers from foreign competition. Indicate which of these specific goals you favor and justify your position.

11. Interpret and explain the following quotation.[11] Do you agree with this view?

> In comparison with the free economy, the Russian system shows elements of decided strength. Its power to . . . carry out plans without opposition gives it an advantage that may overcome grave handicaps in other respects. If we reject this system, as we most decidedly do, we must found our rejection on our attachment to freedom, not on economic grounds. . . . We want freedom, and we are willing to pay an economic price for it, by sacrificing the larger output that we might have in a forced draft economy.

12. Interpret Figure 22·4 on page 388, indicating the nature of the public policy dilemma it illustrates. Which of the choices posed by the curve do you prefer? Why?

13. Explain and give an illustration of ***a.*** the fallacy of composition and ***b.*** the "after this, therefore, because of this" fallacy. Why are cause-and-effect relationships difficult to isolate in the social sciences? Distinguish clearly between macroeconomics and microeconomics.

14. "Economists should never be popular; men who afflict the comfortable serve equally those who comfort the afflicted and one cannot suppose that American capitalism would long prosper without the critics its leaders find such a profound source of annoyance."[12] Interpret and evaluate.

SELECTED REFERENCES

*McConnell, Campbell R. (ed.): *Economic Issues: A Book of Readings*, 4th ed. (New York: McGraw-Hill Book Company, 1972), readings 1 and 2.

[11]Henry C. Wallich, *The Cost of Freedom* (New York: Harper & Row, Publishers, Incorporated, 1960), p. 48.

[12]John Kenneth Galbraith, *American Capitalism*, rev. ed. (Boston: Houghton Mifflin Company, 1956), p. 49.

* *Economic Issues* is a book of readings that emphasizes current economic problems and controversies. It is especially designed to supplement this text and will be listed as the first reference item following most chapters, with relevant readings indicated.

Boulding, Kenneth E.: *Economics as a Science* (New York: McGraw-Hill Book Company, 1970).

Keynes, J. M.: *The Scope and Method of Political Economy,* 4th ed. (New York: The Macmillan Company, 1930).

Krupp, Sherman Roy (ed.): *The Structure of Economic Science* (Englewood Cliffs, N.J.: Prentice-Hall, Inc., 1966).

Lange, Oskar: "The Scope and Method of Economics," *Review of Economic Studies,* vol. 13, 1945–1946, pp. 19–32.

Laurent, Robert D.: "Models as Economic Tools," *Business Conditions* (Federal Reserve Bank of Chicago, November 1970), pp. 9–15.

Stigler, George J.: *The Theory of Price* (New York: The Macmillan Company, 1947), chap. 1.

2

AN INTRODUCTION TO THE ECONOMIZING PROBLEM

The primary objective of this chapter is to introduce and explore certain fundamental considerations which constitute the foundation of economic science.

But we must be more specific. We shall first seek to introduce a more sophisticated definition of economics. No longer can we content ourselves with the mere statement that economics is concerned with man's behavior in making a living, or that economics has to do with the production, exchange, and consumption of goods and services. These accurate, but not particularly revealing, facts concerning the nature of economics must give way to a comprehensive understanding of the economizing problem. To this end, we shall illustrate, extend, and modify the sophisticated definition of economics by the use of so-called production possibilities tables. We shall then restate and discuss the economizing problem in terms of certain practical questions. Finally, we shall survey briefly the different ways in which institutionally and ideologically diverse economies go about solving the economizing problem.

THE FOUNDATION OF ECONOMICS

Two fundamental facts provide a foundation for the field of economics. It is imperative that we carefully state and fully understand these two facts, since everything that follows in our study of economics depends directly or indirectly upon them. The first fact is this: *Society's material wants, that is, the material wants of its citizens and institutions, are virtually unlimited or insatiable.* Secondly: *Economic resources are limited or scarce.*

Unlimited wants

Let us systematically examine and explain these two facts in the order stated. In the first statement, precisely what do we mean by "material wants"? We mean, first, the desires consumers have to obtain and use various *goods* and *services* which give pleasure or satisfaction.[1] An amazingly wide range of products

[1] This leaves a variety of wants—recognition, status, love, and so forth—for the other social sciences to worry about.

fills the bill in this respect: houses, automobiles, toothpaste, pencils, onions, sweaters, and the like. In short, innumerable products which we sometimes classify *as necessities* (food, shelter, clothing) and *luxuries* (perfumes, yachts, mink coats) are all capable of satisfying human wants. Needless to say, that which is a luxury to Smith may be a necessity to Jones, and what is a commonplace necessity today may have been a luxury a few short years ago.

But services may satisfy our wants as much as tangible products. A repair job on our car, the removal of our appendix, a haircut, and even legal advice have in common with goods the fact that they satisfy human wants. As a matter of fact, on reflecting, we realize that we buy many goods, for example, automobiles and washing machines, for the services they render. The differences between goods and services are often less than they seem to be at first.

Material wants also include the desires which businesses and units of government seek to satisfy. Businesses want factory buildings, machinery, trucks, warehouses, and so forth. Government, reflecting the collective wants of its citizenry or goals of its own, seeks highways, schools, hospitals, and military hardware.

As a group, these material wants are, for practical purposes, *insatiable,* or *unlimited.*[2] This means simply that material wants for goods and services are incapable of being completely satisfied. A simple experiment will help to verify this point: Suppose we are asked to list those goods and services we want but do not now possess. If we take time to ponder our unfilled material wants, chances are our list will be impressive. And over a period of time, our wants seem to multiply so that, as we fill some of the wants on the list, at the same time we add new ones. Material wants, like rabbits, have a high reproduction rate. This is particularly so in the United States, where the relatively rapid introduction of new products whets our appetites, and extensive advertising tries to persuade us that we need countless items we might not otherwise consider buying. Not too many years ago, the desire for television, air conditioners, stereophonic phonographs, and tubeless tires was nonexistent. Furthermore, we cannot stop with simple satisfaction: upon acquiring a Ford or Chevrolet, we become interested in owning a Cadillac or a Lincoln.

In short, we may say that at any point in time the individuals and institutions which constitute society have innumerable unfulfilled material wants. Some of these wants—food, clothing, shelter—have biological roots. But some are also influenced by the conventions and customs of society: the specific kinds of food, clothing, and shelter we seek are frequently determined by the general social and cultural environment in which we live. Over time, wants change and multiply, abetted by the development of new products and by extensive advertising and sales promotion.

Finally—although we may be getting ahead of ourselves—let us emphatically add that the overall end or objective of all economic activity is the attempt to satisfy these diverse material wants.

Scarce resources

Consider now the second fundamental fact: *Economic resources are limited or scarce.* What do we mean by "economic resources"? In general, we are referring to all the natural, human, and man-made resources that go into the production of goods and services. This obviously covers a lot of ground: factory and farm buildings and all sorts of equipment, tools, and machinery used in the production of manufactured goods and agricultural products; a variety of transportation and communication facilities; innumerable types of labor; and, last but not least, land and mineral resources of all kinds. There is an apparent need for a simplified classification of such resources, which we shall meet with the following categories: (1) *property* resources—land or raw materials and capital; (2) *human* resources—labor and entrepreneurial ability.

[2] It should be mentioned in passing that the fallacy of composition is relevant here. Our wants for a *particular* good or service can obviously be satisfied; that is, over a short period of time we can get sufficient amounts of toothpaste or beer. Certainly one appendicitis operation is par for the course. But goods *in general* are another story. Here we do not, and cannot, get enough. We shall have more to say about the satisfying of wants for specific goods in Chapter 25.

What does the economist mean by *land?* Much more than the layman. Land refers to all natural resources—all "free gifts of nature" which are usable in the productive process. Such resources as arable land, forests, mineral and oil deposits, and water resources come under this general classification. What about *capital?* Capital, or investment goods, has a variety of meanings attached to it. The one that is correct for our purposes refers to all man-made aids to production, that is, all tools, machinery, equipment, and factory, storage, transportation, and distribution facilities used in producing goods and services and getting them to the ultimate consumer. Capital goods ("tools") differ from consumer goods in that the latter satisfy wants directly, whereas the former do so indirectly by facilitating the production of consumable goods. We should note especially that the term "capital" as here defined does not refer to money. True, businessmen and economists often talk of "money capital," referring to money which is available for use in the purchase of machinery, equipment, and other productive facilities. But money, as such, produces nothing; hence, it is not to be considered as an economic resource. *Real capital*—tools, machinery, and other productive equipment—is an economic resource; *money* or *financial capital* is not.

Labor is a broad term which the economist uses in referring to all man's physical and mental talents usable in producing goods and services (with the exception of a special set of human talents—entrepreneurial ability—which, because of their special significance in a capitalistic economy, we choose to consider separately). Thus the services of a ditch-digger, retail clerk, machinist, teacher, and nuclear physicist all fall under the general heading of labor.

Finally, what can be said about this special human resource which we label *entrepreneurial ability,* or, more simply, *enterprise?* We shall give the term a specific meaning by assigning four related functions to the entrepreneur.

1. The entrepreneur takes the initiative in combining the resources of land, capital, and labor in the production of a good or service. Both a sparkplug and a catalyst, the entrepreneur is at once the driving force behind production and the agent who combines the other resources in what he hopes will be a profitable venture.

2. He has the chore of making basic business-policy decisions, that is, those nonroutine decisions which set the course of a business enterprise.

3. The entrepreneur is an innovator—he is the one who attempts to introduce on a commercial basis new products, new productive techniques, or even new forms of business organization.

4. The entrepreneur is obviously a risk bearer. This is apparent from a close examination of his other three functions. The entrepreneur in a capitalistic system has no guarantee that he will make a profit. The reward for his time, efforts, and abilities may be attractive profits or immediate losses and eventual bankruptcy. In short, the entrepreneur risks not only his time, effort, and business reputation, but his invested funds and those of his associates or stockholders.

We shall see shortly how these resources are provided for business institutions in exchange for money income. The income received from supplying property resources—raw materials and capital equipment—is called *rental* and *interest income.* The income accruing to those who supply labor is called simply *wages* and includes salaries and various wage and salary supplements in the form of bonuses, commissions, royalties, and so forth. Entrepreneurial income is called *profits,* which, of course, may be a negative figure—that is, losses.

These four broad categories of economic resources, or *factors of production* as they are often called, leave room for debate when it comes to classifying specific resources. For example, suppose you receive a dividend on some General Motors stock which you may be fortunate enough to own. Is this an interest return for the capital equipment which the company was able to buy with the money you provided in buying GM stock? Or is this return a profit which compensates you for the risks involved in purchasing corporate stock? What about the earnings of a one-man general store where the owner is both the entrepreneur and the labor force? Are his earnings to be considered as wages or profit income? The answer to both queries is "Some of each." The

important point is this: Although we might quibble about classifying a given flow of income as wages, rent, interest, or profits, all income can be listed without too much arbitrariness under one of these general headings.

All economic resources, or factors of production, have one fundamental characteristic in common: *Economic resources are scarce or limited in supply.* Without a doubt, our economy possesses extremely large amounts of arable land, mineral deposits, capital equipment, and labor. These are, however, not infinitely large supplies; they have limits. A civilian labor force of 83 million workers may seem extremely large, but it is not an infinite amount. World War II, for example, reminded us of just how scarce labor actually is. Critical shortages of semiskilled and skilled labor constituted a formidable obstacle in the production of vitally needed armaments. Much the same can be said for the other factors of production.

One additional point: These economic resources—land, labor, capital, and entrepreneurial ability—are obviously the *means* by which we produce goods and services in trying to satisfy material wants. Consumption in the broadest sense of the term—that is, fulfilling the material wants of the institutions and individuals which make up society—is the objective of economic activity. We are now pointing out that the means of attaining the goal of consumption are our available supplies of various economic resources. And these resources, though perhaps abundant in the absolute sense, are scarce in relation to the demand for them in the production of goods and services.

ECONOMICS DEFINED

Recalling that wants are unlimited and resources are scarce, economics can be defined as *the social science concerned with the problem of using or administering scarce resources* (*the means of producing*) *so as to attain the greatest or maximum fulfillment of society's unlimited wants* (*the goal of producing*). Economics is concerned with "doing the best with what we have." If our wants are virtually unlimited and our resources are scarce, we cannot conceivably satisfy all of society's material wants. The next best thing is to achieve the greatest possible satisfaction of these wants. Economics is without a doubt a science of efficiency—efficiency in the use of scarce resources.

Precisely what is meant by *efficiency* as economists use the term? It means something akin to, but not identical with, the term "efficiency" as used in engineering. The mechanical engineer tells us that a steam locomotive is only "60 percent efficient" because a large part—some 40 percent—of the energy in its fuel is not transformed into useful power but is wasted through friction and heat loss. The maximum output of usable power is not derived from the inputs of fuel.

Economic efficiency is also concerned with *inputs* and *outputs*. Specifically, it is concerned with the relationship between the units of scarce resources which are put into the process of production and the resulting output of some wanted product; economic efficiency has to do with inputs of scarce resources and outputs of useful products.

We must recognize that the emphasis or priority placed upon various material wants differs between societies. Capitalist-type systems, for example, the United States, tend to put relatively greater stress upon the satisfaction of the wants of households; the ultimate objective of production is generally regarded as consumption by individuals. Communist-type economies put relatively greater stress upon the production of capital and military goods, which presumably enhance the power and prestige of the national state.

Full employment and full production

Economic efficiency is achieved when full employment and full production are realized or, stated negatively, when unemployment and underemployment are avoided. A worker is clearly unemployed when he is involuntarily out of work. This is the man who is standing in a relief line or a bread line or

waiting to pick up his unemployment compensation check. This is a case of *apparent unemployment* or simply *unemployment;* the worker obviously has no job connection. On the other hand, a worker may have a job but in a sense still be "unemployed." For example, a worker who is harvesting wheat by hand or cutting a lawn with a pair of scissors is "partially unemployed." In this case, however, it is a matter of *disguised unemployment* or, more simply, *underemployment.* The worker has a job but simply is not being employed efficiently. The *un*employed worker who has no job and the *under*employed worker who has a job but is producing in a highly inefficient manner differ more in degree than in kind. Both entail the relatively inefficient use of resources. The point is this: There are two major aspects of economic efficiency. On the one hand, there is the *full-employment* problem—the problem of providing jobs for all who are able and willing to work. On the other hand, there is the closely related *full-production* or resource-allocation problem—the problem of using employed resources in the most efficient manner. These two facets of economic efficiency are of such importance as to merit further comment.

Eliminating unemployment Economic efficiency requires, first, that available resources be actually utilized in the production of goods and services rather than allowed to lie idle. An unused locomotive is of zero efficiency. The same can be said for unemployed resources. Unutilized resources—both human and property—obviously mean waste and inefficiency. Unemployment is the height of economic inefficiency; when society fails to put its available resources into the productive process, it obviously realizes no output at all.

Note that we specify that all *available* resources should be employed. Each society has certain established customs and practices which determine what particular resources are available for employment. For example, legislation and custom provide that children and the very aged should not be employed. Also, we should not employ all our farmland every year; it is desirable for productivity to allow land to lie fallow periodically. Furthermore, society wants to avoid complete utilization and rapid exhaustion of particularly scarce resources in order to conserve them as long as possible. In short, society wants to employ only those resources that are available for employment and whose current employment is desirable.

In Part 2 we shall discover that in a capitalistic economy it is the volume of total spending which determines the level at which resources are employed. If buyers are willing and able to spend in large amounts in satisfying their wants, entrepreneurs will respond by employing large amounts of resources in producing goods and services to fulfill these wants. Conversely, a meager volume of spending will mean unemployment.

Eliminating underemployment But the full employment of all available resources is not sufficient for the attainment of economic efficiency. Society also seeks full production; that is, the production of goods must be carried out with a proper assignment or allocation of available resources and with use of the best available production techniques. In other words, society wants to get the maximum amount of goods and services produced with its limited inputs of employed resources. For example, if society's wants include both wheat and space probes, it would obviously entail an inefficient or uneconomical allocation of resources to assign astrophysicists and mathematicians to farming and experienced farmers to space research centers. Nor should we want Iowa's farmland planted to cotton and Alabama's to corn when experience indicates that the opposite assignment would provide the nation substantially more of both products from the same amount of land. We also want to use the best production methods; for example, other things being equal, a given volume of resources will produce more corn when crop rotation is employed as a technique of production. To plant the same acres to corn year after year will wear out the soil and eventually result in a relatively small output. By employing the same amounts of land, capital, labor, and entrepreneurial resources and by practicing the technique of crop rotation, a larger output of corn can be realized.

Production possibilities table

The nature of the economizing problem can be brought into even clearer focus by the use of a production possibilities table.[3] This ingenious device reveals the core of the economizing problem: A full-employment, full-production economy cannot have an unlimited output of goods and services.

We make several specific assumptions to set the stage for our illustration.

1. Let us assume that the economy is operating at full employment and achieving full production. Neither *un*employment nor *under*employment exists.

2. Let us assume that the available supplies of the factors of production are fixed. But, of course, they can be shifted or reallocated, within limits, between different uses; for example, an unskilled laborer can work on a farm, on an automobile assembly line, or in a munitions factory.

3. Let us assume that the technological state of the arts is constant; that is, technology does not change during the course of our analysis.

The second and third assumptions are another way of saying that we are looking at our economy at some specific point in time, or over a very short period of time. Over a relatively long period it would clearly be unrealistic to rule out technological advances and the possibility that resource supplies might vary. In short, we assume full employment and full production, fixed resources, and a fixed technology.

To simplify our illustration further, let us suppose that our economy is producing just two products—for example, drill presses and bread—instead of the innumerable goods and services actually produced. Bread is symbolic of *consumer goods,* that is, those goods and services which directly satisfy our wants; drill presses are symbolic of *capital goods,* that is, those goods which satisfy our wants *indirectly* by permitting more efficient production of consumer goods.

Now is it not evident from the assumptions we have made that our economy is faced with a very fundamental choice? Our total supplies of resources are limited. Thus the total amounts of drill presses and bread that our economy is capable of producing are limited. Limited resources mean a limited output. A choice must be made as to what quantities of each product society wants produced. Since resources are limited in supply and fully employed, any increase in the production of drill presses will necessitate the shifting of resources away from the production of bread. And the reverse holds true: If we choose to step up the production of bread, needed resources must come at the expense of drill-press production. Society cannot have its cake and eat it, too. This is the essence of the economizing problem.

Let us generalize by noting in Table 2·1 some alternative combinations of drill presses and bread which our economy might conceivably choose. Though the data in this and ensuing tables are hypothetical, the points illustrated are of tremendous practical significance. At alternative A, our economy would be devoting all its resources to the production of drill presses, that is, capital goods. At alternative E, all our resources would be devoted to the production of bread, that is, consumer goods. Both these alternatives are clearly unrealistic extremes: any economy typically strikes a balance in dividing its total output between capital and consumer goods. As we move from alternative A to E, we step up the production of consumer goods (bread). How? By shifting resources away from capital goods production. Re-

TABLE 2·1 PRODUCTION POSSIBILITIES OF BREAD AND DRILL PRESSES WITH FULL EMPLOYMENT, 1972 (*hypothetical data*)

Type of product	Production alternatives				
	A	B	C	D	E
Bread (in hundred thousands)	0	1	2	3	4
Drill presses (in thousands)	10	9	7	4	0

[3] Paul A. Samuelson, *Economics,* 8th ed. (New York: McGraw-Hill Book Company, 1970), pp. 17–27.

membering that consumer goods directly satisfy our wants, any movement toward alternative E looks tempting. In making this move, society increases the current satisfaction of its wants. But there is a cost involved. This shift of resources catches up with society over time as its stock of capital goods dwindles—or at least ceases to expand at the current rate—with the result that the efficiency of future production is impaired. In short, in moving from alternative A toward E, society is in effect choosing "more now" at the expense of "much more later." In moving from E toward A, society is choosing to forgo current consumption. This sacrifice of current consumption frees resources which can now be used in stepping up the production of capital goods. By building up its stock of capital in this way, society can anticipate more efficient production and, therefore, greater consumption in the future.

The important point is this: *At any point in time, a full-employment, full-production economy must sacrifice some of product X to obtain more of product Y.* The basic fact that economic resources are scarce prohibits such an economy from having more of both X and Y.

FIGURE 2·1 THE PRODUCTION POSSIBILITIES CURVE

Each point on the production possibilities curve represents some maximum output of any two products. Society must choose which product-mix it desires: more drill presses means less bread, and vice versa.

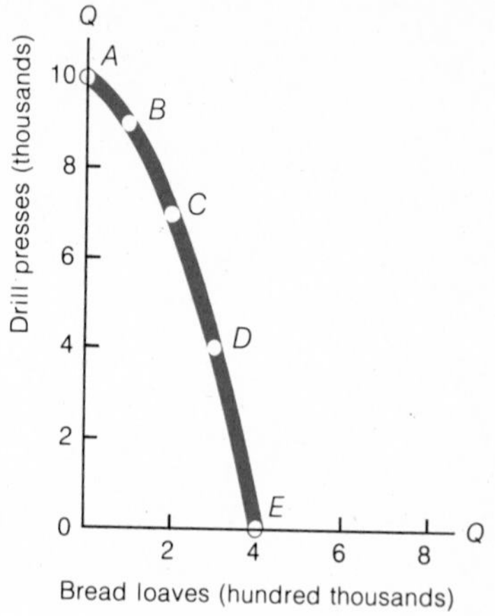

Production possibilities curve

To ensure our understanding the production possibilities table, let us view these data graphically. We employ a simple two-dimensional graph, putting the output of drill presses on the vertical axis and the output of bread on the horizontal axis, as in Figure 2·1. Following the plotting procedure discussed in Chapter 1, we can locate the "production possibilities" or "transformation"[4] curve, as shown in Figure 2·1.

Optimum product-mix

We know that each point on the production possibilities curve represents some maximum output of the two products. To realize the various combinations of bread and drill presses which fall on the production possibilities curve, society must achieve full employment and full production. All combinations of bread and drill presses on the curve represent maximum quantities attainable only as the result of the most efficient use of all available resources.

But now a final question arises: If all outputs on the production possibilities curve reflect full employment and full production, which combination will society prefer? This is a subjective question—a moral issue—and the economist as a social scientist possesses no superior judgment or insight on this matter. For example, the Soviet Union has put great emphasis upon the rapid industrialization of its society. The United States, on the other hand, puts a relatively high priority upon satisfying the material wants of consumers. In terms of the production possibilities curve, the government of the Soviet Union has purposely chosen a "many drill presses—few loaves of

[4]Why "transformation"? Because in moving from one alternative to another, say from *B* to *C*, we are in effect transforming drill presses into bread by shifting resources from the production of the former to the production of the latter.

bread'' product-mix as its goal and has implemented its achievement through central planning. In comparison the individuals and institutions of the United States have selected a ''few drill presses—many loaves of bread'' product-mix, an output objective which has been implemented largely through a system of markets and prices. Which of these goals is ''best''? Is point *B* or point *D* superior in Figure 2·1? This, to repeat, is a nonscientific matter; it reflects the values of society as expressed by its control group—the dictatorship, the party, the electorate, the citizenry, the individual institutions, or some combination thereof. What the economist can say is that if a society's production possibilities are as in Table 2·1 *and* if that society seeks the product-mix indicated by, say, alternative B, it is using its resources inefficiently if it only realizes a total output comprised of $8\frac{7}{8}$ units of drill presses and $\frac{9}{10}$ unit of loaves of bread. And he can also say that the society cannot hope to achieve a national output of $9\frac{1}{2}$ units of drill presses and $1\frac{3}{8}$ units of loaves of bread with its available resources. These are quantitative matters. But, although he may have opinions as an individual, the economist as a social scientist cannot say that combination B is ''better'' or ''worse'' than combination D. This is purely a qualitative matter.

Law of increasing costs

We have stressed that resources are scarce relative to the virtually unlimited wants which these resources could be used to satisfy. As a result, choices among alternatives must be made. Specifically, more of X (drill presses) means less of Y (bread). The *amount* of Y which must be forgone or given up to get another unit of X is the cost of X. In the technical jargon of the economist, the *opportunity cost* of any product is the amount of alternative products which must be forgone. Hence, in moving from possibility A to B in Table 2·1 we find that the cost, or opportunity cost, of 1 unit of bread is 1 unit of drill presses. But as we now pursue the concept of cost through the additional production possibilities—B to C, C to D, and so forth—an important economic principle is revealed to us. In moving from alternative A to alternative E, the sacrifice or cost of drill presses involved in getting each additional 100,000 units of bread increases. Hence, in moving from A to B, just 1 unit of drill presses is sacrificed for 1 more unit of bread; but going from B to C involves the sacrifice of 2 units of drill presses for 1 more of bread; then 3 of drill presses for 1 of bread; and finally 4 for 1. Why does the sacrifice of drill presses increase as we get more bread? The answer to this query is rather complex. But, simply stated, it amounts to this: *Economic resources are not completely adaptable to alternative uses.* As we attempt to step up bread production, resources which are less and less adaptable to agriculture must be induced, or ''pushed,'' into that line of production. If we start at A and move to B, we can first pick resources whose productivity of bread is greatest in relation to their productivity of drill presses. But as we move from B to C, C to D, and so forth, those resources which are highly productive of bread become increasingly scarce. To get more bread, resources whose productivity in drill presses is great in relation to their productivity in bread will be needed. It will obviously take more and more of such resources—and hence an increasingly great sacrifice of drill presses—to achieve a given increase of 1 unit in the production of bread. This lack of flexibility, or adaptability, on the part of resources and the resulting increase in the sacrifice of one good that must be made in the acquisition of more and more units of another good are sometimes termed the *law of increasing costs,* costs in this case being stated as sacrifices of goods and not in terms of dollars and cents. The reader should (1) verify that the law of increasing costs also holds true in moving from alternative E to alternative A and (2) explain how the shape (concave in relation to the origin) of the production possibilities curve in Figure 2·1 reflects this law.

SOME MODIFICATIONS

It is of signal importance to understand what happens when the three assumptions underlying the preceding explanation are released.

Unemployment and underemployment

The first assumption was that our economy is characterized by full employment and full production. How would our analysis and conclusions be altered if idle resources were available or if employed resources were used inefficiently? With full employment and full production, our five alternatives represent a series of maximum outputs; that is, they illustrate what combinations of drill presses and bread might be produced when the economy is operating at its full capacity. With *un*employment or *under*employment, the economy would obviously be producing less than each alternative shown in Table 2·1.

Graphically, a situation of unemployment or underemployment can be illustrated by a point *inside* the original production possibilities curve, which has been reproduced in Figure 2·2. Point U is such a point. Here the economy is obviously falling short of the various maximum combinations of bread and drill presses reflected by all the points *on* the production possibilities curve. The broken arrows in Figure 2·2 indicate three of the possible paths back to full employment and full production. A movement toward full employment and full production will obviously entail a greater output of one or both products. And there are points *outside* the production possibilities curve which would be superior to any point on the curve; but such points are unobtainable, given the current supplies of resources and technology. The production barrier of full employment prohibits the production of any combination of capital and consumer goods lying outside the production possibilities curve.

It is interesting to note that in beginning to produce war goods for World War II the United States found itself with considerable unemployment. Hence, our economy was able to accomplish the production of an almost unbelievably large quantity of war goods and at the same time increase the volume of consumer goods output.[5] The Russians, on the other hand, entered World War II at almost capacity production; that is, they were operating close to full employment. Therefore, their military preparations entailed a considerable shifting of resources from the production of civilian goods and a concomitant drop in the standard of living.[6]

[5]There did occur, however, rather acute shortages of specific types of consumer goods.

FIGURE 2·2 UNEMPLOYMENT AND THE PRODUCTION POSSIBILITIES CURVE

Any point inside the production possibilities curve, such as *U*, indicates unemployment or underemployment. By moving toward full employment and full production, the economy can produce more of either or both of the two products, as the arrows indicate.

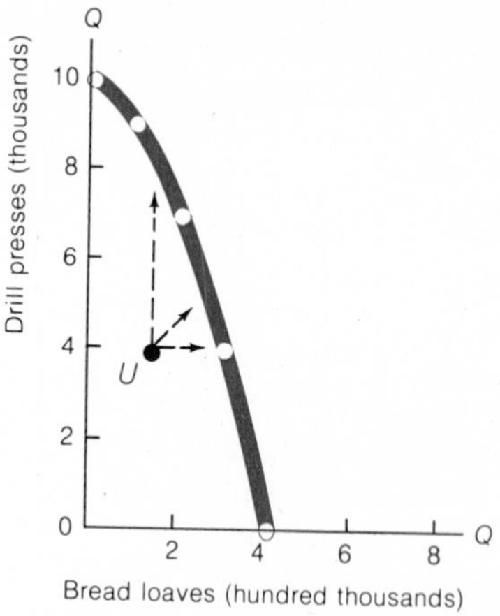

A growing economy

What happens to the production possibilities curve when we drop the remaining assumptions that the quantity and quality of resources and technology are fixed? The answer is: The production possibilies curve will shift position; that is, the potential total output of the economy will change.

Expanding resource supplies Now let us drop the simplifying assumption that our total supplies of land,

[6]Needless to say, it is sheer folly to leap to the conclusion that this contrast illustrates the desirability of unemployment at the outbreak of hostilities!

TABLE 2·2 PRODUCTION POSSIBILITIES OF BREAD AND DRILL PRESSES WITH FULL EMPLOYMENT, 1992 (*hypothetical data*)

Type of product	Production alternatives				
	A′	B′	C′	D′	E′
Bread (in hundred thousands)	0	2	4	6	8
Drill presses (in thousands)	14	12	9	5	0

labor, capital, and entrepreneurial ability are fixed. Common sense tells us that over a period of time the rapidly growing population which we have in the United States will bring about significant increases in the supplies of labor and entrepreneurial ability.[7] Historically, our stock of capital has increased at a remarkable, though unsteady, rate. And although we are depleting some of our oil and mineral deposits, new sources are constantly being discovered. The drainage of swamps and the development of irrigation programs add to our supply of arable land. Assuming continuous full employment and full production, the net result of these increased supplies of the factors of production will be the ability to produce more of both drill presses and bread. Thus in, say, 1992, the production possibilities of Table 2·1 may be obsolete, having given way to those shown in Table 2·2. Note that the greater abundance of resources results in a greater output of one or both products at each alternative; economic growth has occurred.

But note this important point: Such a favorable shift in the production possibilities curve does not guarantee that the economy will operate at a point on that new curve. The economy might fail to realize its new potentialities. Some 83 million jobs will give us full employment at the present time, but ten years from now our labor force, because of a growing population, will be much larger, and 83 million jobs will not be sufficient for full employment. In short, the production possibilities curve may shift, but the economy may fail to produce at a point on that curve.

[7] This is not to say that population growth as such is always desirable. In Chapter 45 we shall discover that overpopulation is a constant drag upon the living standards of many underdeveloped countries. In advanced countries overpopulation can have adverse effects upon the environment and the quality of life.

Technological advance Our final simplifying assumption was that technology was constant. Simple observation tells us that technology has progressed with amazing rapidity over a long period of time. What does an advancing technology entail? New and better goods and improved ways of producing these goods. For the moment, let us think of technological advance as entailing simply improvements in capital facilities—more efficient machinery and equipment. How does such technological advance alter our earlier discussion of the economizing problem? In this way: Technological advance, by improving productive effi-

FIGURE 2·3 ECONOMIC GROWTH AND THE PRODUCTION POSSIBILITIES CURVE

The expanding resource supplies and technological advances which characterize a growing economy move the production possibilities curve outward and to the right. This permits the economy to enjoy larger quantities of both types of goods.

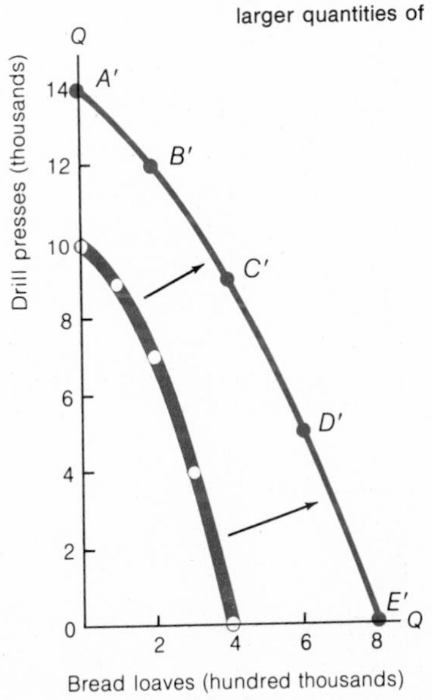

ciency, allows society to produce more goods with a fixed amount of resources. As with increases in resource supplies, technological advance permits the production of more drill presses and more bread.

What happens to the production possibilities curve of Figure 2·2 when the supplies of resources increase or an improvement in technology occurs? The curve shifts outward and to the right, as illustrated by the thin curve in Figure 2·3. *Economic growth can be defined as a rightward shift of the production possibilities curve; it is the result of increases in resource supplies and technological progress.* The consequence of growth is that our full-employment economy can enjoy a greater output of both bread and drill presses.

On Figure 2·2 the student should pencil in two new production possibilities curves: one to show the situation where a better technique for producing drill presses has been developed, the technology for producing bread being unchanged, and the other to illustrate an improved technology for bread, the technology for producing drill presses being constant.

Present choices and future possibilities

You may have anticipated this important point in the foregoing paragraphs: *An economy's current choice of position on its production possibilities curve is a basic determinant of the future location of that curve.* To illustrate this notion, let us designate the two axes of the production possibilities curve as "goods for the future" and "goods for the present," as in Figure 2·4*a* and *b*. By "goods for the future" we refer to such things as capital goods, research and education, and preventive medicine, which obviously tend to increase the quantity and quality of property resources, enlarge the stock of technological information, and improve the quality of human resources. By "goods for the present" we mean pure consumer goods in the form of foodstuffs, clothing, transistor radios, automobiles, power mowers, and so forth.

Now suppose there are two economies, Alphania and Betania, which at the moment are identical in every respect, except that Alphania's current (1972) choice of position on its production possibilities curve strongly favors "present goods" as opposed to "fu-

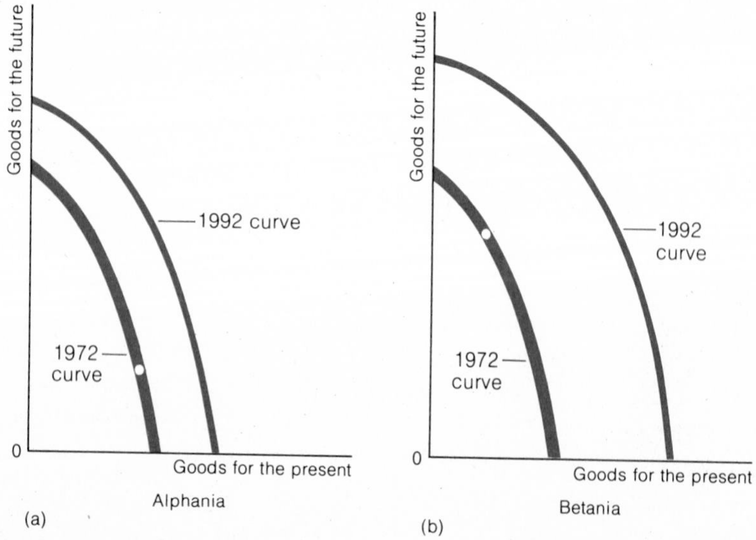

FIGURE 2·4 AN ECONOMY'S PRESENT CHOICE OF POSITION ON ITS PRODUCTION POSSIBILITIES CURVE HELPS DETERMINE THE CURVE'S FUTURE LOCATION

A current choice favoring "present goods," as rendered by Alphania in (*a*), will cause a modest rightward shift of the curve. A current choice favoring "future goods," as rendered by Betania in (*b*), will result in a greater rightward shift of the curve.

ture goods.'' The dot in Figure 2·4*a* indicates this choice. Betania, on the other hand, renders a current (1972) choice which stresses large amounts of ''future goods'' and lesser amounts of ''present goods'' (Figure 2·4*b*). Now, all other things being the same, we can expect the future (1992) production possibilities curve of Betania to be further to the right than that of Alphania. That is, by currently choosing an output which is more conducive to technological advance and to increases in the quantity and quality of property and human resources, Betania will tend to achieve greater economic growth than will Alphania, whose current choice of output puts less emphasis upon those goods and services which cause the production possibilities curve to shift rightward.

ECONOMIZING: FIVE FUNDAMENTAL QUESTIONS

In order to provide a broad understanding of the essence of the economizing problem, the preceding discussion is pitched at a fairly abstract level. Let us now be more practical and examine some of the specific questions or problems that any economic system must answer in attempting to use its scarce resources to achieve the maximum satisfaction of society's material wants. Basically, there are Five Fundamental Questions which must be answered in attempting to achieve and maintain efficiency in the use of scarce resources.

What is to be produced

Society must somehow decide what collection of goods and services will most fully satisfy its wants. This decision concerning the composition of total output must be consistent with the production possibilities currently facing the economy. Choosing a combination of capital and consumer goods lying *inside* the production possibilities curve entails economic inefficiency in the form of unemployment. Seeking a combination *outside* the current production possibilities curve is unrealistic; society is obviously setting its sights on an unattainable target.

Actually, the basic question of determining what is to be produced can be divided into two closely related subquestions: First, what goods and services are to be produced? Second, in what quantities does society want these goods produced?

Consider the first subquestion: What goods and services should be produced? Answering this entails, in effect, the setting up of a list of goods and services which society deems important enough to produce. How should society apportion its scarce resources among those products which it is capable of producing? Should our list include bread? Drill presses? Fords? Cadillacs? Color television? Mink coats? Buggy whips? Football stadiums? An ABM system? Society must somehow decide what items to include in—and what items to exclude from—the list of goods that are to be produced.

But this decision is only half the battle. Once society has decided what to produce, somehow it must then assign proper weights to each of the items on the list. Without asking how this decision has been reached, suppose society has decided that bread, drill presses, Fords, and football stadiums are the items from the above list which it actually wants to produce. The fact that resources are scarce tells us that society cannot produce unlimited amounts of the goods on this list. Society must now decide *how many* loaves of bread, *how many* drill presses, *how many* Fords, and *how many* football stadiums it wants in its total output. Society must not only decide the relative amounts of capital and consumer goods to be produced—the question posed in our production possibilities illustrations—but it must also determine the specific quantities of each type of capital goods and each type of consumer goods that will best fulfill society's material wants. Even in relatively primitive economies these decisions can become complex.

Remember, too, that in deciding the relative amounts of capital and consumer goods to be produced, society is of necessity weighing the relative merits of future, as opposed to current, want fulfillment. More resources devoted to technological re-

search and to the expansion of the economy's capital facilities means fewer available for the production of goods for current consumption. The choice here is between more now or much more later. By cutting back on research and on the expansion of our productive facilities, society can produce a greater current output. But sacrificing some current consumption in order to free resources for research and capital expansion will mean an expanded output in the future.

These two subquestions—what goods shall we produce? in what quantities?—have been considered in a very simplified way in our analysis of the production possibilities tables. We solved—or dodged!—the first by assuming the economy had somehow decided to produce only bread and drill presses.

The answer to the second subquestion entails society's choosing which one of the five alternatives—A, B, C, D, or E—yields the highest level of satisfaction. Thus the perennial question of consumer goods versus capital goods is part of the larger question of deciding the specific composition of the total output. The vital question of civilian versus war goods falls under the same general heading.

Organizing production

Hand in glove with our decision as to the composition of total output is another query: *How should this total output be produced?* This major question can also be broken into parts.

1. How does society steer resources into industries producing goods that we want produced and, conversely, keep resources away from industries producing goods wanted in very small amounts or not at all?

2. What firms in the various industries are to do the producing, and how are they to obtain the needed resources?

3. What is the most efficient combination of resources for each firm to use in producing a given level of output? More subtly, what is the best technology to use in production?

All these questions center upon the goal of achieving full production from society's available resources. A reminder: Although the question of organizing production is spelled out here in terms of an industrially advanced economy, similar questions would be pertinent for a primitive or underdeveloped economy.

Distributing output

The third basic decision comes close to home: *How is society to divide or ration the total output among the various economic units which comprise our economic system?* How should the total output of consumer goods be shared by the various households in our economy? Similarly, how should any additions to our stock of capital equipment included in our total output be apportioned to the various industries and the individual firms in those industries? What part of total output should be given over to government? In short, the question of how the total output is to be distributed among households, businesses, and government must somehow be answered by society. Obviously, these questions involve not only economics but also politics and ethics.

Level of resource use

Society is obligated to determine the degree to which its economic resources are to be utilized. This decision is more complex than it first appears. Two related subquestions are involved:

1. To what degree is society *willing* to utilize its human and property resources?

2. To what extent is society actually *able* to employ its resources? Let us briefly explore these subquestions in the order stated.

A society which seeks to maximize the immediate fulfillment of its material wants must be willing to utilize its human and property resources to a very high degree. For human resources this means that both men and women must enter the labor force at an early age, retire at a very old age, and work long hours with few holidays and vacations in the intervening span of years. This obviously means little leisure. And leisure, after all, is a source of satis-

faction—a part of our standard of living. What good is a stereo set or golf clubs if one has no time to use them? In all economies the decision as to how the time at the disposal of human resources is to be divided between production and leisure is influenced by sociocultural factors. The mores and customs of society are important in determining what percentage of the population is to work, the number of work hours, and, as a matter of fact, the intensity of labor.

The problem of resource conservation is primary in discussing the willingness of society to utilize its property resources currently. The nature of this decision can best be envisioned in terms of nonrenewable natural resources such as petroleum, natural gas, and a host of mineral deposits. The current rapid exploitation of these resources makes for a high output now but at the same time lessens the ability of the economy to produce in the future. A lower current rate of utilization would spread more evenly over time the output of goods and services whose production is dependent upon these resources. A less obvious facet of the conservation problem has to do with the overall deterioration of the physical environment; high levels of resource use—high levels of industrial production—are a serious challenge to nature's limited capacity to absorb wastes.

Having determined the level of resource utilization which it desires, society must then achieve that level of resource use. Society must avoid the involuntary idleness of its human and property resources. Involuntary idleness is the height of economic inefficiency. To be efficient, any economic system must somehow provide for high and stable levels of employment. We shall discover in Part Two of this book that one of the basic defects of modern capitalism lies in the fact that it does not guarantee economic stability—full employment accompanied by a stable level of prices. Unemployment—actual or potential—is generally recognized as the greatest domestic problem which American capitalism currently faces. Inflation can be an equally potent adversary.

In a primitive Robinson Crusoe economy there is no problem of achieving full employment. The consumer and the producer are one and the same. Thus the producer, if he so desires, can spend all his waking hours in an effort to fulfill his material wants. Though we cannot pause at this point for lengthy explanations, it must be emphasized that the problem of achieving full employment is not so simple a task in such modern industrial societies as American capitalism. Here producers and consumers—sellers and buyers—have different identities, and their decision making is linked only imperfectly by the use of money in buying and selling both goods and resources. Hence, although consumers on the one hand and producers on the other bóth desire full employment, their nonidentity raises the possibility that inconsistencies in their spending and producing decisions may lead to unemployment. If the spending of buyers is deficient in amount, producers will not find it advantageous to employ all the economy's available resources. Why hire resources to produce goods that no one will buy? Conversely, too much spending will result in price inflation. In between lies some specific level of spending that will give the economy full employment with relatively stable prices. The point is this: Nothing guarantees that an industrially advanced economy—particularly a capitalistic economy—will operate at a point on its production possibilities curve. Finally, it is also worth noting that an economy with an expanding population and labor force must provide more and more jobs each year to sustain full employment; the status quo with respect to the level of employment is not enough in a growing economy.

Flexibility

To achieve the maximum fulfillment of society's material wants over time, the economy must be flexible and adaptable to change. Modern economies are far from static, unchanging things. Indeed, their basic feature is *change*. What changes? Several things: consumer tastes, the supplies of resources, and technology. Why does our basic objective of efficiency in the use of scarce resources demand that the economy be adaptable to such changes? Because a changing technology, changes in consumer tastes, and variations in resource supplies imply significant reallocations of our resources in order to

preserve efficiency in their use. The collection of goods and services which maximizes consumer satisfactions today will fail to do so tomorrow if consumer wants have changed in the meantime. The collection of goods and services which pleased your grandparents in the 1920s will simply not be acceptable to you in the 1980s. Put more bluntly, we should not be particularly happy if today's output provided for large quantities of buggy whips and mustache cups at the expense of stereophonic phonographs, transistor radios, and ballpoint pens. Similarly, changing resource supplies and the development of improved techniques of production will call for changes in the combinations of resources used in the production of given products if efficiency is to be maintained. And, needless to say, flexibility is a basic prerequisite of such sudden economic transformations as those entailed by the shift from peace to war and, for that matter, from war to peace.

We should keep constantly in mind that scarcity of economic resources lurks behind all five of these Fundamental Questions and their component parts; the Five Questions are merely a breakdown of the basic economizing problem of scarce resources and unlimited wants. Also the apparent interrelatedness of these questions is almost self-evident, as we shall see in the following chapters, where we shall attempt to describe in detail how a capitalistic economy answers these questions. Indeed, it is difficult to treat the Five Questions independently of one another—they demand simultaneous treatment.

THE "ISMS"

If we lived in an isolated, one-man economy—a Robinson Crusoe economy—the answers we would provide to our list of questions would be relatively simple. But when millions of diverse and interdependent economic units exist, no simple answers to these queries present themselves. How is our society, for example, to strike a mutually acceptable balance between the business tycoon's demand for a Cadillac, the Negro's demand for improved housing, the schoolchild's demand for bubble gum and roller skates, and the housewife's demand for an automatic washer? Certainly no simple answer can be expected. And, to complicate matters, we know that answers which are acceptable today may not be acceptable tomorrow. The preferences of economic units change over time, and so do productive techniques, supplies of resources, and standards of equity in distributing output. In short, there are no final, once-and-for-all answers of a universal nature to the questions which constitute the economizing problem.

Furthermore, we must recognize that *various societies have established different output goals and utilize different institutions and methods of organizing their resources in trying to fulfill these goals.* Generally speaking, a survey of modern, industrially advanced economies suggests there are two fundamentally different philosophies concerning the means of achieving the best answers to the Five Fundamental Questions. At the one extreme, emphasis is put upon private ownership of resources, the freedom of individual economic units to make those choices which they feel are most appropriate in terms of their own specific objectives, and the use of a market system as a coordinating mechanism. The other extreme stresses public ownership of property resources and central economic planning by government, the presumption being that the exercise of authoritarian power by the state in the functioning of the economy will result in greater efficiency than the sum of free economic choices by individual economic units. The former philosophy crudely describes the core of *pure,* or *laissez faire, capitalism;* the latter, the basic tenet of authoritarian socialism, or *communism.* Between these two hypothetical extremes can be arrayed an infinite number of variations and compromises. There is, strictly speaking, an unlimited number of production goals and ways of attempting to achieve maximum fulfillment of any society's particular goals from its scarce resources.

Table 2·3 summarizes the fundamental assumptions, institutional characteristics, and basic methods employed in achieving efficiency in the use of resources which are associated with pure capitalism, communism, and an intermediate hybrid—liberal so-

TABLE 2·3 THE "ISMS" AND THE ECONOMIZING PROBLEM

Economic system	Underlying assumption	Institutional characteristics	Method of solving economizing problem
Pure, or laissez faire, capitalism	Each economic unit decides what choices and policies are best for it; such choices will prove to be in the social interest.	Private ownership of resources and business institutions; freedom of choice for consumers, resource suppliers, and enterprisers.	Emphasis upon a system of free, competitive markets—virtually no governmental planning or control.
Liberal, or democratic, socialism	Some governmental intervention is needed to improve upon the choices and policies of individual economic units.	Mixture of public and private ownership and public and private decision making.	Mixture of loose governmental planning and regulation of basic industry; reliance on system of markets and prices in other segments of economy.
Communism, or authoritarian socialism	The state is in the best position to know what choices and policies are beneficial for the economy as a whole and for its component parts.	Public ownership and control of the bulk of industry and agriculture; severe restriction of individual choices when in conflict with state-determined objectives.	Governmental plans are established by central planning authority; heavy reliance on government directives; some reliance on a price system to implement the plans.

cialism. While students of comparative economic systems might quibble a bit about these descriptions, all would agree with the basic point emphasized by the table. And that point is: There are no unique or universally accepted answers to the Five Fundamental Questions. Various societies, having different cultural and historical backgrounds, different mores and customs, and contrasting ideological frameworks—not to mention resources which differ both quantitatively and qualitatively— supply significantly different answers to the Five Questions. Russia, the United States, and Great Britain, for example, are all—in terms of their accepted goals, ideology, technologies, resources, and culture—attempting to achieve efficiency in the use of their respective resources. The best method for answering the Five Questions in one economy may be inappropriate for another economic system.

Table 2·3 is couched in terms of industrially advanced or "mature" economies. We shall discover in Chapter 45 that many nations of the world have underdeveloped economies. These *traditional* economies are characterized by feudalistic remnants of the Middle Ages. In these systems answers to the Five Fundamental Questions are shrouded in custom, habit, and tradition, all of which tend to perpetuate the status quo. In pursuing economic development traditional economies must face the basic question as to which model of Table 2·3 will result in growth and simultaneously be consistent with other economic and noneconomic goals.

The ensuing four chapters undertake to explain how in the so-called *mixed capitalism* of the United States, which stands at some intermediate position between pure capitalism and liberal socialism in Table 2·3, decisions are made about the objectives of the econ-

omy, how production is to be organized, and how output is to be distributed. Chapter 3 discusses the institutional framework of capitalism and provides a very general picture of the operation of pure, or laissez faire, capitalism. Chapter 4 explains the mechanics of supply and demand as price- and output-determining forces. The role of markets and prices in answering the Five Fundamental Questions is the topic of Chapter 5. Government is brought into the picture in Chapter 6, enlarging our picture of pure capitalism to one of mixed capitalism.

SUMMARY

1. The science of economics centers upon two basic facts: First, human material wants are virtually unlimited; second, economic resources are scarce.
2. Economic resources may be classified as property resources—materials and capital—or as human resources—labor and entrepreneurial ability.
3. Economics is concerned with the problem of administering scarce resources in the production of goods and services for the fulfillment of the material wants of society. Both the full employment and the full production of available resources are essential if this administration is to be efficient.
4. At any point in time a full-employment, full-production economy must sacrifice the output of some types of goods and services to achieve increased production of others.
5. Over time, technological advance and increases in the quantity and quality of human and property resources permit the economy to produce more of all goods and services. Society's choice as to the composition of current output is a determinant of the future location of the production possibilities curve.
6. Any economy faces Five Fundamental Questions in attempting to use its scarce resources to achieve the maximum fulfillment of its material wants. They are: *a.* What goods and services do we want to produce and in what specific amounts? *b.* How is production to be organized in getting these goods and services produced? *c.* How will this output of goods and services be distributed among the various economic units which make up the economic system? *d.* What must an economy do to obtain and maintain the full employment of its available resources? *e.* How does an economy provide the internal flexibility or adaptability required to maintain efficiency in the use of its resources?
7. The various economic systems of the world differ in their ideologies and also in their approaches in answering the Five Fundamental Questions.

QUESTIONS AND STUDY SUGGESTIONS

1. "Economics is the study of the principles governing the allocation of scarce means among competing ends when the objective of the allocation is to maximize the attainment of the ends."[8] Explain. Why is the problem of unemployment a part of the subject matter of economics?

2. "Wants aren't insatiable. I can prove it. I get all the coffee I want to drink every morning at breakfast." Critically analyze. Explain: "Goods and services are scarce because resources are scarce."

3. What are economic resources? What are the major functions of the entrepreneur?

4. Comment on the following statement from a newspaper article: "Our junior high school serves a splendid hot meal for 35 cents without costing the taxpayers anything, thanks in part to a government subsidy."

5. "Economics is concerned with two problems. One has to do with achieving full employment of the economy's available resources. The other has to do with allocating employed resources among various possible uses. Both aspects emphasize efficiency in the use of resources." Explain.

[8] George J. Stigler, *The Theory of Price* (New York: The Macmillan Company, 1947), p. 12.

6. The following is a production possibilities table for war goods and civilian goods:

Type of product	Production alternatives				
	A	B	C	D	E
Automobiles (in millions)	0	2	4	6	8
Guided missiles (in thousands)	30	27	21	12	0

a. Show these production possibilities data graphically. What do the points on the curve indicate? How does the curve reflect the law of increasing costs? Explain.

b. Label point *G* inside the curve. What does it indicate? Label point *H* outside the curve. What does this point indicate? What must occur before the economy can attain the level of production indicated by point *H?*

c. Upon what assumptions is the production possibilities curve based? Be specific. What happens when each of these assumptions is released?

d. Suppose improvement occurs in the technology of producing guided missiles but not in the production of automobiles. Draw the new production possibilities curve. Now assume that a technological advance occurs in producing automobiles but not in producing guided missiles. Draw the new production possibilities curve. Finally, draw a production possibilities curve which reflects technological improvements in the production of both products.

7. "The present choice of position on the production possibilities curve is a major factor in economic growth." Explain.

8. State and thoroughly discuss the Five Fundamental Questions which all economies face. Why must an economy be adaptable to change in order to maintain efficiency in the use of scarce resources? Contrast the means by which pure capitalism, democratic socialism, and communism attempt to answer the Five Questions.

9. "Economics is . . . neither capitalist nor socialist: it applies to every society. Economics would disappear only in a world so rich that no wants were unfulfilled for lack of resources. Such a world is not imminent and may be impossible, for time is always limited."[9] Carefully evaluate and explain these statements. Do you agree that conceptually time is an economic resource?

10. Explain: "It is in the nature of all economic problems that absolute solutions are denied us."

SELECTED REFERENCES

Economic Issues, 4th ed., reading 3.

Galbraith, John K.: *American Capitalism,* rev. ed. (Boston: Houghton Mifflin Company, 1956), chap. 2.

Heilbroner, Robert L.: *The Worldly Philosophers,* 3d ed. (New York: Simon & Schuster, Inc., 1967), chap. 2.

Knight, Frank H.: *The Economic Organization* (New York: Harper & Row, Publishers, Incorporated, 1965), chap. 1.

Mundell, Robert A.: *Man and Economics* (New York: McGraw-Hill Book Company, 1968), chap. 1.

[9] Joseph P. McKenna, *Intermediate Economic Theory* (New York: Holt, Rinehart and Winston, Inc., 1958), p. 2.

PURE CAPITALISM AND THE CIRCULAR FLOW

The task of the present chapter is to describe the capitalist ideology and to explain how pure, or laissez faire, capitalism operates. Strictly speaking, pure capitalism has never existed and probably never will. Why, then, do we bother to consider the operation of such an economy? Because it gives us a workable *first approximation* of how modern American capitalism functions, and approximations or models, when properly handled, can be very useful. In other words, pure capitalism constitutes a simplified model which we shall then modify and adjust to correspond more closely to the reality of American capitalism.

In explaining the operation of pure capitalism, we shall discuss:

1. The institutional framework and basic assumptions which make up the capitalist ideology.
2. Certain institutions and practices common to all modern economies.
3. Capitalism and the circular flow of income.
4. How product and resource prices are determined.
5. The market system and the allocating of economic resources.

The first three topics constitute the present chapter; the latter two, Chapters 4 and 5.

CAPITALIST IDEOLOGY

Unfortunately, there is no neat and universally accepted definition of capitalism to aid us in our present task. We are therefore required to examine in some detail the basic tenets of capitalism to acquire a comprehensive understanding of what pure capitalism entails. In short, the framework of capitalism embodies the following institutions and assumptions: (1) private property, (2) freedom of enterprise and choice, (3) self-interest as the dominant motive, (4) competition, (5) reliance upon the price system, and (6) a limited role for government. Let us explore these characteristics to ensure our understanding them.

Private property

Under a capitalistic system, the means of production—that is, scarce resources—are owned by private individuals and private institutions as opposed to government. Private property, coupled with the freedom to negotiate binding legal contracts, permits private persons or businesses to obtain, control, employ, and dispose of economic resources as they see fit. The institution of private property is sustained over time by the *right to bequeath,* that is, by the right of a property owner to designate the recipient of his property at the time of death.

Needless to say, there are broad legal limits to this right of private ownership. For example, the use of one's resources for the production of narcotics is prohibited by legislation. Nor is public ownership nonexistent. Even in pure capitalism, recognition is given to the fact that public ownership of certain "natural monopolies" may be essential to the achievement of efficiency in the use of resources.

Freedom of enterprise and choice

Closely related to private ownership of property is freedom of enterprise and choice. Capitalism charges its component parts with the responsibility of making certain choices, which are registered and made effective through the free markets of the economy.

Freedom of enterprise means that under pure capitalism, private business enterprises are free to obtain economic resources, to organize these resources in the production of a product of the firm's own choosing, and to sell this product in the markets of their choice. No artificial obstacles or restrictions imposed by government or other producers block an entrepreneur's choice to enter or leave a particular industry.

Freedom of choice means that owners of property resources and money capital can employ or dispose of these resources as they see fit. It also means that laborers are free to enter any of those lines of work for which they are mentally and physically qualified. Finally, it means that consumers are at liberty, within the limits of their money incomes, to buy that collection of goods and services which they feel is most appropriate in satisfying their wants. Freedom of consumer choice may well be the most profound of these freedoms. The consumer is in a particularly strategic position in a capitalistic economy; in a sense, the consumer is sovereign. The range of free choices for suppliers of human and property resources is circumscribed by the choices of consumers. The consumer ultimately decides what the capitalistic economy should produce, and resource suppliers must make their free choices within the boundaries thereby delineated. Resource suppliers and businesses are not really "free" to produce goods and services consumers do not desire.

Again, broad legal limitations prevail in the expression of all these free choices.

Role of self-interest

Since capitalism is individualistic, it is not surprising to find that the primary driving force of such an economy is the promotion of one's self-interest; each economic unit attempts to do what is best for itself. Hence, entrepreneurs aim at the maximization of their firms' profits or, as the case might be, the minimization of losses. And, other things being equal, owners of property resources attempt to achieve the highest price obtainable from the rent or sale of these resources. Given the amount and irksomeness of the effort involved, those who supply human resources will also attempt to obtain the highest possible incomes from their employment. Consumers, in purchasing a given product, will seek to obtain it at the lowest price. In short, capitalism presumes self-interest as the fundamental *modus operandi* for the various economic units as they express their free choices. The motive of self-interest gives direction and consistency to what might otherwise be an extremely chaotic economy.

Although self-interest is the basic motive underlying the functioning of capitalism, there are exceptions to the rule: Businesses and individuals do not always

act in their own self-interest. Altruistic motives are part of the makeup of economic units. Yet self-interest is the best single statement of how economic units actually behave.

Competition

Freedom of choice exercised in terms of promoting one's own monetary returns provides the basis for competition, or economic rivalry, as a fundamental feature of capitalism. Competition, as economists see it, entails

1. The presence of large numbers of independently acting buyers and sellers operating in the market for any particular product or resource.
2. The freedom of buyers and sellers to enter or leave particular markets.

Let us briefly explore these two related aspects of competition:

1. The essence of competition is the widespread diffusion of economic power among the individual units—businesses and households—which comprise the economy. In particular, when a large number of buyers and sellers are present in a market, no one buyer or seller will be able to demand or offer a quantity of the product sufficiently large to noticeably influence its price. Let us examine this statement in terms of the selling or supply side of the product market.

We have all observed that, when a product becomes unusually scarce, its price will skyrocket. For example, an unseasonable frost in Florida may seriously curtail the output of citrus crops and raise the price of orange juice. Similarly, if a single producer, or small group of producers acting together, can somehow control or restrict the total supply of a product, he can raise its price to his own advantage. By controlling supply, the producer can "rig the market" on his own behalf. Now the essence of competition is that there are so many sellers that each, *because he is contributing an almost negligible fraction of the total supply,* has virtually no control over the supply or, therefore, over the product price.

For example, suppose there are 10,000 farmers, each of whom is supplying 100 bushels of corn in the Kansas City grain market at some particular time when the price of corn happens to be $2 per bushel. Could a single farmer, who happens to be dissatisfied with the existing price, cause an artificial scarcity of corn and thereby boost the price above $2? The answer is obviously "No." Farmer Jones, by restricting his output from 100 to 75 bushels, exerts virtually no effect upon the total supply of corn. In fact, he only reduces total supply from 1,000,000 to 999,975 bushels. This obviously is not much of a shortage! Supply is virtually unchanged, and, therefore, the $2 price persists. In brief, competition means that each seller is providing a drop in the bucket of total supply. The individual seller can make no noticeable dent in total supply; hence, he cannot *as an individual producer*[1] manipulate product price. This is what is meant when it is pointed out that an individual competitive seller is "at the mercy of the market."

The same rationale applies to the demand side of the market. Buyers are plentiful and act independently. Thus no single buyer can manipulate the market to his advantage.

The important point is this: The widespread diffusion of economic power underlying competition controls the use and limits the potential abuse of that power. Economic rivalry prevents economic units from wreaking havoc upon one another as they attempt to further their self-interests. Competition imposes limits upon expressions of self-interest by buyers and sellers. Competition is a basic regulatory force in capitalism.

2. Competition also assumes that it is a simple matter for producers to enter (or leave) a particular industry; there are no artificial legal or institutional obstacles to prohibit the expansion (or contraction) of specific industries. This aspect of competition is prerequisite to the flexibility which is essential if an economy is to remain efficient over time. Freedom of entry is necessary if the economy is to adjust

[1]Of course, if a number of farmers simultaneously restricted their production, the resulting change in total supply could no longer be ignored, and price would rise. Competition (a large number of sellers) implies the impossibility of such collusion.

appropriately to changes in consumer tastes, technology, or resource supplies. This matter will receive detailed treatment in Chapter 5.

Markets and prices

Private property, freedom of choice, and self-interest are all basic features of capitalism. But the basic coordinating mechanism of such an economy is the market or price system. *Capitalism is a market economy.* The decisions rendered by the buyers and sellers of products and resources are made effective through a system of markets. The preferences of sellers and buyers are registered on the supply and demand sides of various markets, and the outcome of these choices is a system of product and resource prices. These prices are guideposts upon which resource owners, entrepreneurs, and consumers make and revise their free choices in furthering their self-interests. Just as competition is the controlling mechanism, so a system of markets and prices is a basic organizing force. The price system is an elaborate communications system through which innumerable individual free choices are recorded, summarized, and balanced against one another. Those who obey the dictates of the price system are rewarded; those who ignore it are penalized by the system. Through this communications system, society renders its decisions concerning what the economy should produce, how production can be efficiently organized, and how the fruits of productive endeavor are to be distributed among the individual economic units which make up capitalism.

Not only is the price system the mechanism through which society renders decisions concerning how it allocates its resources and distributes the resulting output, but it is through the price system that these decisions are implemented and carried out. However, a word of caution: Economic systems based upon the ideologies of socialism and communism also depend upon price systems, but not to the same degree or in the same way as does pure capitalism. The socialistic and communistic societies use markets and prices primarily to implement the decisions made wholly or in part by a central planning authority. In capitalism, the price system functions both as a device for rendering innumerable choices of free individuals and businesses and as a mechanism for implementing or carrying out these decisions.

In Chapters 4 and 5 we shall analyze the mechanics and the operation of a capitalistic price system.

Limited government

A competitive capitalist economy is thought to be conducive to a high degree of efficiency in the use or allocation of its resources. Hence, there is allegedly little real need for governmental intervention in the operation of such an economy beyond its aforementioned role of imposing broad legal limits upon the exercise of individual choices and the use of private property. The historical development of the concept of pure capitalism as a self-regulating and self-adjusting type of economy precludes any significant economic role for government. As we shall see shortly, capitalism in practice has not been self-regulating to the degree economists once supposed. But for the moment, at least, our analysis will exclude government. Chapter 6 will elaborate the functions of government in present-day mixed capitalism.

OTHER CHARACTERISTICS

Private property, freedom of enterprise and choice, self-interest as a motivating force, competition, and reliance on a price system are all institutions and assumptions which are more or less exclusively associated with pure capitalism. In addition, there are certain institutions and practices which are characteristic of all modern economies. They are (1) the use of an advanced technology and large amounts of capital goods, (2) specialization, and (3) the use of money. Specialization and an advanced technology are prerequisites to the efficient employment of any economy's resources. The use of money is a permissive characteristic which allows society more

easily to practice and reap the benefits of specialization and of the employment of advanced productive techniques.

Extensive use of capital goods

All modern economies—whether they approximate the capitalist, socialist, or communist ideology—are based upon an advanced technology and the extensive use of capital goods. Under pure capitalism it is competition, coupled with freedom of choice and the desire to further one's self-interest, which provides the means for achieving a rapid rate of technological advance. The capitalistic framework is felt to be highly effective in harnessing incentives to develop new products and improved techniques of production. Why? Because the monetary rewards derived therefrom accrue directly to the innovator. Pure capitalism therefore presupposes the extensive use and rapid development of complex capital goods: tools, machinery, large-scale factories, and facilities for storage, transportation, and marketing.

Why are the existence of an advanced technology and the extensive use of capital goods important? Because the most direct method of producing a product is usually the least efficient.[2] Even Robinson Crusoe avoided the inefficiencies of direct production in favor of "roundabout production." It would be ridiculous for a farmer—even a backyard farmer—to go at production with his bare hands. Obviously, it pays huge dividends in terms of more efficient production and, therefore, a more abundant output, to fashion tools of production, that is, capital equipment, to aid in the productive process. The best way of getting water out of a well is not to dive in after it!

But there is a catch involved. As we recall our discussion of the production possibilities curve and the basic nature of the economizing problem, it is evident that, with full employment and full production, resources must be diverted from the production of consumer goods in order to be used in the production of capital goods. We must currently tighten our belts as consumers to free resources for the production of capital goods which will increase productive efficiency and permit us to have a greater output of consumer goods at some future date.

[2] Remember that consumer goods satisfy wants directly, while capital goods do so indirectly through the more efficient production of consumer goods.

Specialization

The extent to which society relies upon specialization is astounding. The vast majority of consumers produce virtually none of the goods and services they consume and, conversely, consume little or nothing of what they produce. The hammer-shop laborer who spends his life stamping out parts for jet engines may never "consume" an airplane trip. The assembly-line worker who devotes eight hours a day to the installation of windows in Chevrolets may not own a car, or if he does, it may be a Ford. Few households seriously consider any extensive production of their own food, shelter, and clothing. Many a farmer sells his milk to the local creamery and then buys oleomargarine at the Podunk general store. Society learned long ago that self-sufficiency breeds inefficiency. The Jack-of-all-trades may be a very colorful individual, but he is certainly lacking in efficiency.

In what specific ways might human specialization—*the division of labor*—enhance productive efficiency? First, specialization permits individuals to take advantage of existing differences in their abilities and skills. If caveman A is strong, swift afoot, and accurate with a spear, and caveman B is weak and slow, but patient, this distribution of talents can be most efficiently utilized by making A a hunter and B a fisherman. Second, even if the abilities of A and B are identical, specialization may prove to be advantageous. Why? Because by devoting all his time to a single task, the doer is more likely to develop the appropriate skills and to discover improved techniques than when apportioning his time between a number of diverse tasks. One learns to be a good hunter by hunting! Finally, specialization—devoting all one's time to, say, a single task—obviously avoids the loss of time which is entailed in shifting from one job to another. For all these reasons the division of

labor results in greater productive efficiency in the use of human resources.

Specialization also is desirable on a regional basis. Oranges could be grown in Nebraska, but because of the unsuitability of the land, rainfall, and temperature, the costs involved would be exceedingly high. Florida could probably achieve some success in the production of wheat, but for similar reasons, such production would be a relatively costly business. As a result, Nebraskans produce those products—wheat in particular—for which their resources are best adapted, and Floridians do the same, producing oranges and other citrus fruits. In so doing, both produce surpluses of their specialties. Then, very sensibly, Nebraskans and Floridians swap some of their surpluses. Specialization permits each area to put its best foot forward, that is, to turn out those goods which its resources can most efficiently produce. In this way both Nebraska and Florida can enjoy a larger amount of both wheat and oranges than would otherwise be the case. In short, human and geographical specialization are both essential in achieving efficiency in the use of resources.

Specialization and comparative advantage[3]

These simple illustrations make very plausible the contention that specialization is economically desirable because it results in more efficient production. Indeed, the point is almost self-explanatory. But, because the concept of specialization is so vital to an understanding of the production and exchange processes of modern economies, let us tackle a couple of more exacting illustrations of the gains which accrue from specialization. Our examples will be simplified to make the principles involved as clear as possible.

Comparative costs Let us pursue our Nebraska-Florida example of specialization at a more sophisticated level, relying upon an already familiar concept—the production possibilities table—as a basic analytical device. Suppose production possibilities data for the Nebraska and Florida economies are as in Tables 3·1 and 3·2 respectively.

You will immediately sense that these production possibilities tables are "different" from those of Chapter 2 in that we here assume *constant costs* rather than increasing costs. In other words, each state must give up a constant, rather than an increasing, amount of one product in securing constant increments of the other product. This simplification will expedite our discussion without impairing the overall validity of our conclusions. The effects of increasing costs will be noted later (Chapter 42) when we discuss international specialization.

The basic truth which we wish to reveal is that *specialization and trade are mutually beneficial or "profitable" to the two states (individuals, regions, nations) if the comparative costs of the two products within the two states differ.* What is the comparative cost of oranges and wheat in Nebraska? Table 3·1 tells us that 5 tons of oranges must be forgone or sacrificed to produce 20 tons of wheat. Or more simply, it costs 1 ton of oranges to get 4 tons of wheat in Nebraska ($1O = 4W$). Remember that because of our constant-cost assumption, this comparative-cost relationship will not change as we expand the output of either product. Similarly, we find in Table 3·2 that at a cost of 10 tons of oranges Floridians can obtain 30 tons of wheat, that is, in Florida the comparative-cost ratio for the two products is $1O$ equals $3W$. The comparative cost of the two products

TABLE 3·1 NEBRASKA PRODUCTION POSSIBILITIES TABLE (*hypothetical data; in tons*)

Product	Production alternatives			
	A	B	C	D
Wheat	0	20	40	60
Oranges	15	10	5	0

[3]This section may be skipped by instructors who wish to defer any detailed treatment of comparative advantage to Part 7 on international economics.

TABLE 3·2 FLORIDA PRODUCTION POSSIBILITIES TABLE (*hypothetical data; in tons*)

Product	Production alternatives			
	A	B	C	D
Wheat	0	30	60	90
Oranges	30	20	10	0

within the two states is clearly different. Economists describe this situation by saying that Florida has a comparative-cost advantage, or more simply, comparative advantage, in oranges; that is, Florida must forgo less wheat (3 tons) to get 1 ton of oranges than is the case in Nebraska where a ton of oranges costs 4 tons of wheat. Comparatively speaking, oranges are cheap in Florida. Nebraska, on the other hand, has a comparative (cost) advantage in wheat. Whereas it costs $\frac{1}{3}$ ton of oranges to get 1 ton of wheat in Florida, by comparison 1 ton of wheat only costs $\frac{1}{4}$ ton of oranges in Nebraska. Comparatively speaking, wheat is cheap in Nebraska. Given these comparative-cost differences, we now want to demonstrate that, if both states specialize according to their comparative advantage, they can achieve a larger total output of oranges and wheat than otherwise! That is, they can get a larger total output with the same total input of resources through specialization and thereby obviously will be allocating their scarce resources more efficiently.

Terms of trade Given Florida's cost ratio of 1*O* equals 3*W*, it stands to reason that Floridians would be pleased to specialize in oranges, if they could obtain *more than* 3 tons of wheat for a ton of oranges through trade with Nebraska. Similarly, recalling Nebraska's 1*O* equals 4*W* cost ratio, it will be advantageous to Nebraskans to specialize in wheat, provided they can get 1 ton of oranges for *less than* 4 tons of wheat. Suppose through negotiation the two states agree upon an exchange rate of 1 ton of oranges for $3\frac{1}{2}$ tons of wheat.[4] Note that these *terms of trade* will be mutually beneficial in that both states can "do better" through trade than they can at home. Floridians get $3\frac{1}{2}$ tons of wheat by sending 1 ton of oranges to Nebraska, whereas they can only get 3 tons of wheat by reallocating resources from oranges to wheat production at home. It would cost Nebraskans 4 tons of wheat to obtain 1 ton of oranges by reallocating their domestic resources, whereas 1 ton of oranges can be obtained through trade with Florida at the smaller cost of only $3\frac{1}{2}$ tons of wheat.

Gains from specialization and trade In order to pinpoint the size of the gains in total output from specialization and trade, let us assume that before specialization and trade, production alternative B was the optimum product-mix for each state. That is, Nebraskans preferred 20 tons of wheat and 10 tons of oranges (Table 3·1) and Floridians preferred 30 tons of wheat and 20 tons of oranges (Table 3·2) to all other alternatives available within the respective state economies. Both states now specialize according to comparative advantage, Nebraska producing 60 tons of wheat and no oranges (alternative D) and Florida producing no wheat and 30 tons of oranges (alternative A). Utilizing our 1*O* equals $3\frac{1}{2}W$ terms of trade, assume that Nebraska exchanges 35 tons of its wheat for 10 tons of Florida oranges. Nebraskans will now have 25 tons of wheat and 10 tons of oranges, while Floridians will thus obtain 35 tons of wheat and 20 tons of oranges. As compared with their optimum product-mixes prior to specialization and trade, both states now enjoy the same amount of oranges and 5 additional tons of wheat! These extra 10 tons of wheat, equally divided between the two state economies in this instance,[5] represent the *gains from specialization and trade.*

The crucial point is that *resource allocation has been improved through specialization according to*

[4] In Chapter 42 we will find that market forces—supply and demand—will determine the rate at which the two products are exchanged.

[5] We will discover in Chapter 42 that different terms of trade would result in a different division of the 10 tons of wheat between the two states.

comparative advantage. This is obviously so, because the same total inputs of resources have resulted in a larger total output. By having Nebraska and Florida allocate all their resources to wheat and oranges respectively, the same total inputs of resources have given rise to more output, indicating that resources are being more efficiently utilized or allocated.

We might envision the gains from trade from a slightly different vantage point. In Chapter 2 we learned that an expansion of resource supplies or technological progress would permit an economy (state or national) to penetrate its current production possibilities boundary and obtain an output superior to any that was currently available to it. *Although the domestic production possibilities boundaries of the two states have not actually been pushed to the right, we have in specialization and trade discovered a means of circumventing the constraints of the production possibilities curve. In short, the economic effects of specialization and trade between states (regions, nations) are tantamount to having more or better resources or to achieving technological progress.*

Technical postscript: The absolute levels of real costs are not important to this analysis and its conclusions. For example, we might compare the prespecialization optimum product-mixes for Nebraska and Florida (the B alternatives in Tables 3·1 and 3·2) and find that the resulting outputs are being produced with the same total inputs of resources in the two states. This obviously suggests that Florida's resources are absolutely more productive in both oranges *and* wheat. Despite this, specialization and trade will still be advantageous to both parties. All that matters is that the comparative-cost ratios differ!

It should be emphasized that specialization and an advanced technology go hand in hand. Specialization and technological advance reinforce one another. Nebraskans and Floridians are more likely to discover better techniques for producing wheat and oranges when specializing than they would if each state divided its resources between the two products. Specialization encourages technological advance, and technological advance in turn stimulates greater specialization.

Disadvantages One final word: Serious reflection on this matter of geographical and human specialization reveals certain drawbacks. For example, the monotony and drudgery of specialized work are well known. Imagine the boredom of our previously mentioned assembly-line worker who is still putting windows in Chevrolets. Second, specialization and mutual interdependence vary directly with one another. The less each of us produces for himself, the more we are dependent upon the output of others. The less wheat produced in Florida, the greater is that state's dependence upon Nebraska wheat. For the economy as a whole, it is not surprising to discover what profoundly serious consequences may stem from a transportation strike or, on a more localized basis, from the breakdown of an assembly line. A third problem centers upon the exchanging of the surpluses which specialization entails. An examination of this problem leads us into a discussion of the use of money in the economy.

Use of money

Virtually all economies, advanced or primitive, are money-using. Money performs a variety of functions (see Chapter 16), but first and foremost it is a medium of exchange.

In our Nebraska-Florida example it was necessary for Nebraskans to trade 35 tons of wheat for 10 tons of Florida's oranges if both states were to share in the benefits of specialization. If trade were prohibited for some reason, gains from specializing according to comparative advantage might be lost to society. Why? Because consumers want a wide variety of products and, in the absence of trade, would tend to devote their human and material resources to many diverse types of production. If exchange could not occur or was very inconvenient to transact, Nebraska and Florida would be forced to be more self-sufficient, and the advantages of specialization would not be realized. *In short, a convenient means of exchanging goods is a prerequisite of specialization.*

Now exchange can, and sometimes does, occur on the basis of bartering, that is, swapping goods for

goods. But bartering as a means of exchange can pose serious problems for the economy. Specifically, exchange by barter requires a *coincidence of wants* between the two transactors. In our example, we assumed that Nebraskans had excess wheat to trade and that they wanted to obtain oranges. And we assumed Floridians had excess oranges to swap and that they wanted to acquire wheat. So exchange occurred. But if this coincidence of wants did not exist, trade would be stymied. Let us pose such a problem.

Suppose Nebraska does not want any of Florida's oranges but is interested in buying potatoes from Idaho. Ironically enough, Idaho wants Florida's oranges but not Nebraska's wheat. And, to complicate matters, suppose that Florida wants some of Nebraska's wheat but none of Idaho's potatoes. The situation is summarized in Figure 3·1.

In no case do we find a coincidence of wants. Trade by barter would be difficult. To overcome such a stalemate, modern economies use *money,* which is simply a convenient social invention for facilitating the exchange of goods and services. Historically, cattle, cigarettes, shells, stones, pieces of metal, and many other diverse commodities have been used, with varying degrees of success, as a medium for facilitating exchange. But to be money, an item needs to pass only one test: *It must be generally acceptable by buyers and sellers in exchange.* Money is socially defined; whatever society accepts as a medium of exchange is money. Most modern economies, for reasons made clear in Chapter 16, find it convenient to use pieces of paper as money. We shall assume that this is the case with the Nebraska-Florida-Idaho economy; they use pieces of paper which they call "dollars" as money. Can the use of paper dollars as a medium of exchange overcome the stalemate we have posed?

FIGURE 3·1 MONEY FACILITATES TRADE WHERE WANTS DO NOT COINCIDE

By the use of money as a medium of exchange, trade can be accomplished, as indicated by the arrows, despite a noncoincidence of wants. By facilitating exchange, the use of money permits an economy to realize the efficiencies of specialization.

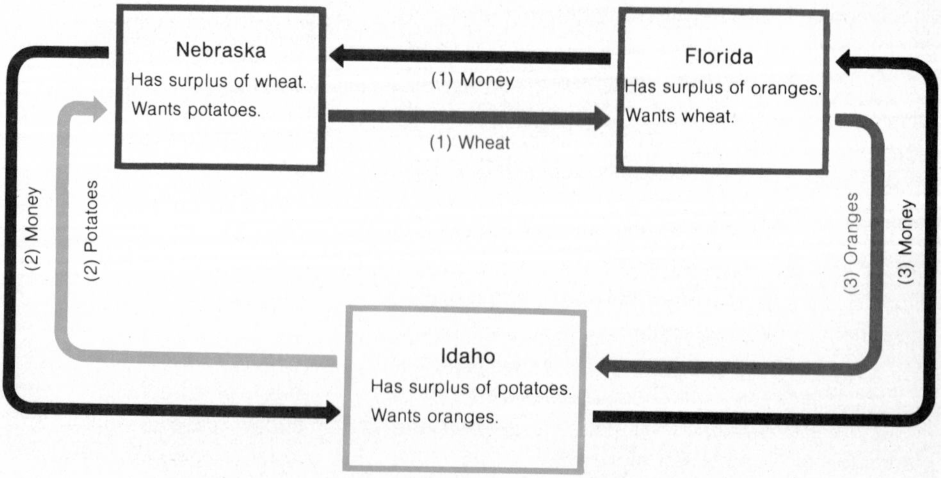

Obviously it can, with trade occurring in this way:

1. Floridians can exchange money for some of Nebraska's wheat.

2. Nebraskans can take the money realized from the sale of wheat and exchange it for some of Idaho's potatoes.

3. Idahoans can then exchange the money received from the sale of potatoes for some of Florida's surplus oranges.

These transactions are shown by the arrows in Figure 3·1.

The willingness to accept paper money (or any other kind of money, for that matter) as a medium of exchange has permitted a three-way trade which allows each state to specialize in one product and obtain the other product(s) its residents desire, despite a noncoincidence of wants. Barter, resting as it does upon a coincidence of wants, would have impeded this exchange and in so doing would have induced the three states not to specialize. Of course, the efficiencies of specialization would then have been lost to those states. Strange as it may first seem, two exchanges—surplus product for money and then money for a wanted product—are simpler than the single product-for-product exchange which bartering entails! Indeed, in this example, product-for-product exchange would not be likely to occur at all.

A final example: Imagine a Detroit laborer producing crankshafts for Oldsmobiles. At the end of the week, instead of receiving a brightly colored piece of paper endorsed by the company comptroller, or a few pieces of paper neatly engraved in green and black, the laborer receives from the company paymaster four Oldsmobile crankshafts. Inconvenient as this is, and with no desire to hoard crankshafts, the laborer ventures into the Detroit business district, intent upon spending his hard-earned income on a basket of food, a suit of clothes, a baseball game, a haircut, and, in anticipation of a late return, a box of candy to pacify his wife. Needless to say, he is faced with some inconvenient and time-consuming trading, and he might not be able to negotiate any exchanges at all. Finding a clothing merchant who has a suit which meets his approval and who happens to be in the market for an Oldsmobile crankshaft is a formidable task. And, even if he locates a barber in need of a crankshaft, how is the barber going to make change for the laborer's haircut? Examples such as this make it evident that money is one of the great social inventions of man!

This, then, is the ideology of pure capitalism, the institutions peculiar to it, and the institutions it shares in common with alternative economic systems.

CIRCULAR FLOW OF INCOME

Our discussion has pointed out the role of markets and prices as a mechanism for the tabulation and communication of the decisions of individual economic units. In pure capitalism, the free decisions of businesses and households concerning what the economy should produce, how production should be organized, and how total output should be distributed are thus rendered effective through a system of markets and prices.

The next logical step in this discussion is to examine in some detail the nature of markets and prices. The remainder of this chapter is devoted to a general overview of the market system of pure capitalism for the purpose of pinpointing the two basic types of markets of pure capitalism and noting the character of the transactions which occur therein. Chapter 4 presents a rather detailed examination of how specific prices are actually determined in pure capitalism. Then Chapter 5 provides a more rigorous discussion of how pure capitalism goes about answering the Five Fundamental Questions through the workings of the price system.

Circular flow models

How does pure capitalism work? Several answers can be offered, depending upon the amount of detail one desires.

Real flows In a barter economy households, which directly or indirectly (through their ownership of business corporations) own all economic resources, supply these resources to businesses as is shown in the upper loop of Figure 3·2. (Let us for the mo-

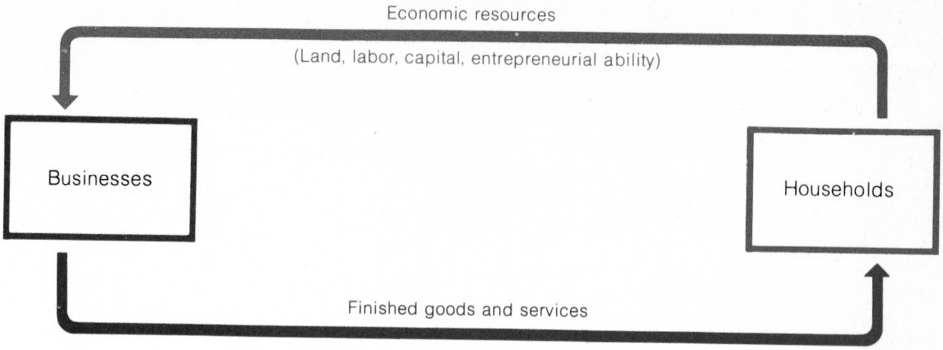

FIGURE 3·2 THE OPERATION OF A BARTER ECONOMY

In a nonmonetary, or barter, economy households supply their economic resources (upper loop) and receive finished goods and services (lower loop) in return.

ment think of businesses simply as organizational charts, that is, institutions on paper apart from the capital, raw materials, labor, and entrepreneurial ability which breathe life into them and make them "going concerns.") Businesses, of course, will want resources, because these are the means by which goods and services are produced. In return for making their resources available for use by businesses, households will receive payments in kind; that is, they will be paid in terms of the goods and services they have helped produce. This flow of payments is shown in the lower loop of Figure 3·2. Of course, households, being paid in terms of crankshafts, shoes, doughnuts, and so forth, will face some difficult exchange problems in swapping goods for goods with one another in seeking to satisfy their various wants. In any event this simple picture of the economy does accurately locate the main *real* flows, that is, the flow of resources and the flow of goods and services which occur in a capitalistic economy.

Money flows To circumvent problems of inconvenience in bartering, virtually all economies are money-using. How does our circular flow picture change as we progress from a barter to a monetary economy? The fact that money is a medium of exchange suggests that money is used as a go-between to facilitate the exchanges of resources and products which occur between businesses and households. In Figure 3·3, the upper loop shows a counterclockwise flow of resources accompanied by a clockwise flow of money payments of income in the form of wages, rent, interest, and profits. These income payments are made in the acquisition of resources and are looked upon as costs to the business firms making them. Note, incidentally, that in economics we treat profits—the expense involved in retaining the firm's supply of entrepreneurial ability—as a cost of production.

But money income received from the sale of resources does not, as such, have real value. Consumers cannot eat or wear coins and paper money. Households will want to obtain a share of the fruits of production by spending their money incomes. Indeed, money income received by a household for the resources it supplies constitutes dollar claims against the total output it helped produce. Households exercise these claims by spending their money incomes—all their incomes, let us assume—on the goods and services of their choice. The clockwise

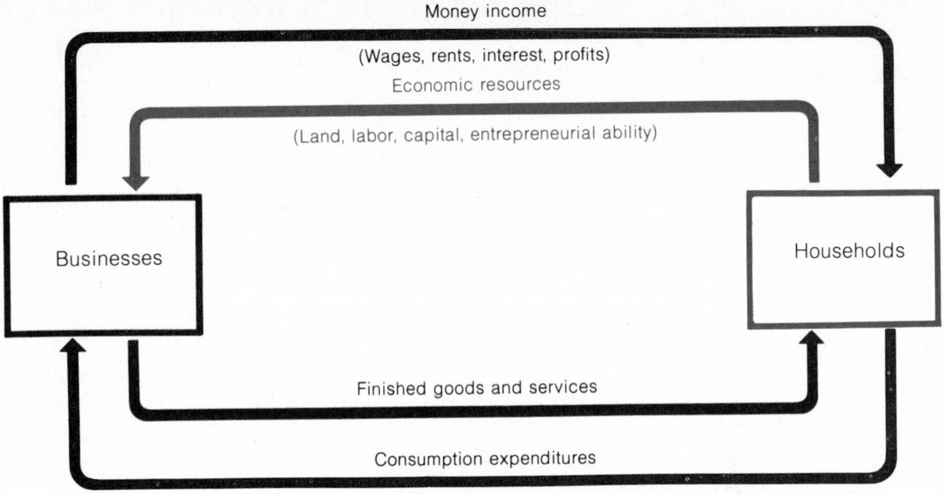

FIGURE 3·3 THE OPERATION OF A MONETARY ECONOMY

In a money-using economy households exchange their economic resources for money income (upper loop), which can then be spent on finished goods and services (lower loop).

flow of consumption expenditures and the counterclockwise flow of goods and services shown in the lower loop of Figure 3·3 reflect the exchange of income for products. From the viewpoint of businesses, the flow of consumption expenditures coming from households is receipts or revenue.

In other words, in a monetary economy, households, as resource owners, sell their resources to businesses and, as consumers, spend the money income received therefrom in buying goods and services. Businesses must buy resources in order to produce goods and services; their finished products are then sold to households in exchange for consumption expenditures or, as businesses view it, receipts. The net result is a counterclockwise real flow of economic resources and finished goods and services and a clockwise money flow of income and consumption expenditures. These flows are simultaneous and repetitive.

Real flows, money flows, and markets Figure 3·4 adds a final step to our circular flow picture. The cost-income and resource flows of the upper loop and the goods-expenditure flows of the lower loop of Figure 3·3 pass through markets where money is exchanged for resources and for goods and services. In the upper loop of Figure 3·4, income payments and resources flow through resource markets. Here households supply resources at certain existing market prices and receive money income in return from businesses that buy or demand these resources. Obviously, the amount of money income flowing through the resource markets and into the hands of households will depend upon the quantities of the various resources supplied by households and the prices at which they are sold. Similarly, in the lower loop, consumer expenditures and goods and services pass through product markets. The size of these consumption flows will depend upon the quantities of

the various goods and services purchased and the prices at which they sell. In other words, there are two basic types of markets in a capitalistic economy—resource markets and product markets. Businesses are on the buying or *demand* side of the resource markets, and households, as resource owners and suppliers, are on the selling or *supply* side. In the product market, these positions are reversed; households, as consumers, are on the buying or demand side, and businesses are on the selling or supply side. Each group of economic units both buys and sells.

Note that the specter of scarcity haunts these transactions. Because households have only limited amounts of resources to supply to businesses, the money incomes of consumers will be limited. This means that each consumer's income will go only so far. A limited number of dollars obviously will not permit the purchase of all the goods and services which the consumer might like to buy. The consumer is handicapped by limited money income; he necessarily operates under a *budget restraint.* Similarly, because resources are scarce, the output of finished goods and services is also necessarily limited. Scarcity permeates our entire discussion.

Limitations

There are certain noteworthy shortcomings and omissions inherent in the circular flow overview of the workings of pure capitalism:

1. This simple model ignores the transactions which

FIGURE 3·4 RESOURCE AND PRODUCT MARKETS IN A MONETARY ECONOMY

The prices paid for the use of land, labor, capital, and entrepreneurial ability are determined in the resource market shown in the upper loop. Businesses are on the demand side and households on the supply side of this market. The prices of finished goods and services are determined in the product market located in the lower loop. Households are on the demand side and businesses on the supply side of this market.

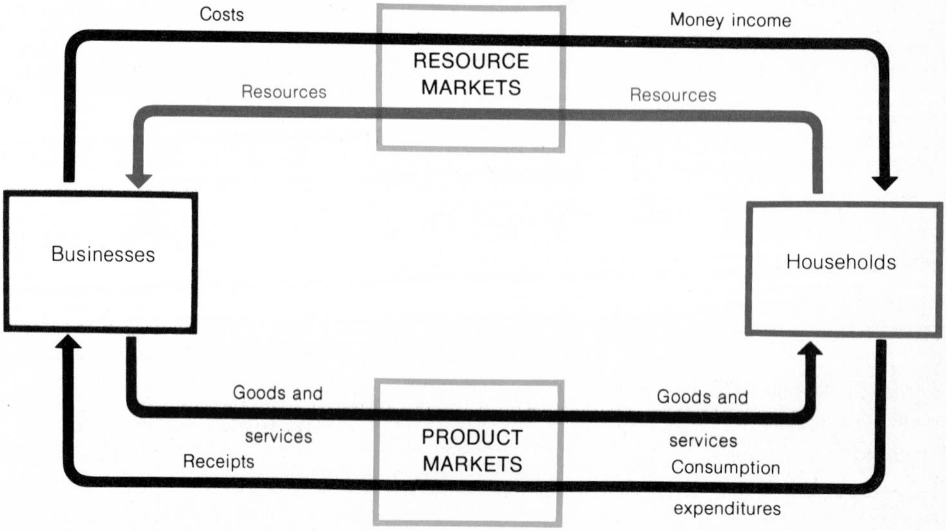

occur *within* the business and household sectors of the economy. For example, the sales of processed materials to manufacturers, parts to fabricators, and finished products to wholesalers and then to retailers are all ignored. This is not a crucial defect, however. At this stage of our discussion, these intrabusiness and intrahousehold transactions are not vital to our understanding of how pure capitalism operates.

2. We must acknowledge that the circular flow model does not reflect the myriad of facts and details about specific households, specific businesses, and specific resource and product markets. Indeed, the main virtue of the circular flow model is that it lays bare the fundamental operations of pure capitalism without ensnaring the viewer in a maze of details. We seek here a view of the whole forest; the examination of specific trees will come later.

3. The circular flow model makes no mention of the economic role of government. The reason? The institutions of pure capitalism would allegedly give rise to a self-contained, self-regulating economy in which government's role would be minor. In Chapter 6 the circular flow will be modified to reflect the economic functions of government in the mixed capitalism which now characterizes the American economy.

4. This model assumes that households spend exactly all their money income and that, therefore, the flows of income and expenditure are constant in volume. In real terms this means that the levels of output and employment are constant. Part 2 of this book is concerned with the causes and effects of fluctuations in income and output flows.

5. Our discussion of the circular flow assumes the existence of certain resource and product prices, but it does not explain how resource and product prices are actually determined. This is the task to which we turn in the ensuing chapter: How are resource and product prices determined in a purely capitalistic economy?

SUMMARY

1. The capitalistic system is characterized by the private ownership of resources and the freedom of individuals to engage in the economic activities of their choice as a means for advancing their material well-being. Self-interest is the driving force of such an economy, and competition functions as a regulatory or control mechanism. Capitalistic production is not organized in terms of a government plan but rather features the price system as a means of organizing and making effective the myriad of individual decisions which determine what is produced, the methods of production, and the sharing of output. Indeed, government plays a minor and relatively passive role.

2. Specialization according to the principle of comparative advantage and an advanced technology based on the extensive use of capital goods are features common to all modern economies. Functioning as a medium of exchange, money circumvents the problems entailed in bartering and thereby permits greater specialization.

3. An overview of the operation of the capitalistic system can be gained through the circular flow of income. This simplified model locates the product and resource markets and presents the major income-expenditure flows and resources-output flows which constitute the lifeblood of the capitalistic economy.

QUESTIONS AND STUDY SUGGESTIONS

1. "Capitalism may be characterized as an automatic self-regulating system motivated by the self-interest of individuals and regulated by competition."[6] Explain and evaluate.

[6]Howard R. Bowen, *Toward Social Economy* (New York: Holt, Rinehart and Winston, Inc., 1948), p. 249.

2. Explain how the price system is a means of communicating and implementing decisions concerning the allocation of the economy's resources.

3. What advantages result from "roundabout" production? What problem is involved in increasing a full-employment, full-production economy's stock of capital goods? Illustrate this problem in terms of the production possibilities curve.

Does an economy with unemployed resources face the same problem?

4. What are the advantages of specialization in the use of human and material resources? Be specific.

5. Dr. Johnson is an outstanding administrator. He is also an excellent teacher, better than anyone else on the staff. Yet the university employs Johnson as dean of his college rather than as a teacher. Explain in terms of the principle of comparative advantage how the university's choice might entail the most efficient use of its labor resources.

6. Foreigners frequently point out that, comparatively speaking, Americans are very wasteful of food and other material goods and very conscious of and overly economical in their use of time. Can you provide an explanation for this observation?

7. The following are production possibilities tables for Japan and Hawaii. Assume that prior to specialization and trade, the optimum product-mix for Japan is alternative D and for Hawaii alternative C.

Product	Japan's production alternatives					
	A	B	C	D	E	F
Radios (in thousands)	100	80	60	40	20	0
Pineapples (in tons)	0	20	40	60	80	100

Product	Hawaii's production alternatives					
	A	B	C	D	E	F
Radios (in thousands)	75	60	45	30	15	0
Pineapples (in tons)	0	30	60	90	120	150

a. Are comparative-cost conditions such that the two nations should specialize? If so, what product should each produce?

b. What is the total gain in radio and pineapple output which results from this specialization?

c. What are the limits of the terms of trade? Suppose the actual terms of trade are 1 unit of radios for 1½ units of pineapples and that 60 units of radios are exchanged for 90 units of pineapples. What are the gains from specialization and trade for each nation?

d. Can you conclude from this illustration that specialization according to comparative advantage results in the more efficient use of world resources? Explain.

8. What problems does barter entail? Be precise. Indicate the economic significance of money as a medium of exchange; explain and illustrate.

9. "Money is the only commodity that is good for nothing but to be gotten rid of. It will not feed you, clothe you, shelter you, or amuse you unless you spend or invest it. It imparts value only in parting."[7] Explain this statement.

10. Describe the operation of pure capitalism as portrayed by the circular flow of income. Emphasize the fact of scarcity throughout your discussion.

SELECTED REFERENCES

Economic Issues, 4th ed., reading 4.

Bowen, Howard R.: *Toward Social Economy* (New York: Holt, Rinehart and Winston, Inc., 1948), chaps. 1–5.

Ebenstein, William: *Today's Isms,* 6th ed. (Englewood Cliffs, N.J.: Prentice-Hall, Inc., 1970), chap. 3.

Heilbroner, Robert L.: *The Making of Economic Society* (Englewood Cliffs, N.J.: Prentice-Hall, Inc., 1962), chaps. 2–4.

Loucks, William N., and William G. Whitney: *Comparative Economic Systems,* 8th ed. (New York: Harper & Row, Publishers, Incorporated, 1969), chap. 2.

Monsen, R. Joseph, Jr.: *Modern American Capitalism: Ideologies and Issues* (Boston: Houghton Mifflin Company, 1963).

[7]Federal Reserve Bank of Philadelphia, "Creeping Inflation," *Business Review,* August 1957, p. 3.

THE MECHANICS OF INDIVIDUAL PRICES: DEMAND AND SUPPLY

The much-simplified analysis of the operation of pure capitalism presented at the conclusion of Chapter 3 assumed that resources and goods and services sell for certain given prices. This permitted us to sidestep the fundamental question to which we now turn: How are prices "set," or determined, in pure capitalism? The answer is easy to state but a bit more difficult to understand. In short, prices are determined in the product market by the interaction of the supply decisions of competing businesses and the demand decisions of competing households. In the resource market, the demand decisions of competing businesses coupled with the supply decisions of competing households determine prices. Our immediate objective is to verify these answers. In doing so we shall concentrate on the product market, then shift our attention later in the chapter to the resource market. The immediate task is to explain the mechanics of prices. How does the interaction of demand and supply decisions set product and resource prices?

DEMAND

The term *demand* has a very definite meaning to the economist. *Demand* is defined as *a schedule which shows the various amounts of a product which consumers are willing and able to purchase at each specific price in a set of possible prices during some specified period of time.*[1] Demand simply portrays a series of alternative possibilities which can be set down in tabular form. As our definition of demand indicates, we usually view demand from the vantage point of price; that is, we read demand as showing the amounts consumers will buy at various possible prices. It is equally correct and sometimes more meaningful to view demand from the reference point of quantity. That is, instead of asking what quantities can be sold at various prices, we can ask what prices can be gotten from consumers for various quantities

[1] In adjusting this definition to the resource market, simply substitute the word "resource" for "product" and "business" for "consumer."

of a good. Table 4·1 is a hypothetical demand schedule for a single consumer who is purchasing bushels of corn.

This tabular portrayal of demand reflects the relationship between the price of corn and the quantity that our mythical consumer would be willing and able to purchase at each of these prices. Note that we say willing and *able,* because willingness alone is not effective in the market. I may be willing to buy a Cadillac, but if this willingness is not backed by the ability to buy, that is, by the necessary dollars, it will not be effective and, therefore, not reflected in the market. In Table 4·1, if the price of corn in the market happened to be $5 per bushel, our consumer would be willing and able to buy 10 bushels per week; if it were $4, he would be willing and able to buy 20 bushels per week; and so forth.

The demand schedule in and of itself does not tell us which of the five possible prices will actually exist in the corn market. As we have already said, this depends on demand *and supply.* Demand, then, is simply a tabular statement of a buyer's plans, or intentions, with respect to the purchase of a product.

Note that to be meaningful the quantities demanded at each price must relate to some specific time period—a day, a week, a month, and so forth. To say that "a consumer will buy 10 bushels of corn at $5 per bushel" is vague and meaningless. To say that "a consumer will buy 10 bushels of corn *per week* at $5 per bushel" is clear and very meaningful.

TABLE 4·1 AN INDIVIDUAL BUYER'S DEMAND FOR CORN (*hypothetical data*)

Price per bushel	Quantity demanded per week
$5	10
4	20
3	35
2	55
1	80

Law of demand

A fundamental characteristic of demand is this: As price falls, the corresponding quantity demanded rises, or, alternatively, as price increases, the corresponding quantity demanded falls. In short, there is an *inverse* relationship between price and quantity demanded. Economists have labeled this inverse relationship the *law of demand.* Upon what foundation does this law rest? There are many levels on which the case can be argued, but it is sufficient for our purposes to rest the case on common sense and simple observation.[2] People ordinarily *do* buy more of a given product at a low price than they do at a high price. To consumers, price is an obstacle which deters them from buying. The higher this obstacle, the less of a product they will buy; the lower the price obstacle, the more they will buy. In other words, a high price discourages consumers from buying, and a low price encourages them to buy. The simple fact that businessmen have sales is concrete evidence of their belief in the law of demand. Bargain, or sales, days are based on the law of demand.

The law of demand can also be explained in terms of the substitutability of products for one another. There are usually (but not always) a number of reasonably good substitutes for any particular product. Hence, an increase in the price of this product will make consumers substitute other products for it. A decline in the price of the given product will induce customers to substitute it for other products. To be more specific, if the price of butter goes up, consumers substitute oleomargarine and therefore purchase less butter at the higher price. If the price of butter declines, consumers substitute butter for oleomargarine, thereby purchasing more butter at the lower price.

The demand curve

This inverse relationship between product price and quantity demanded can be presented on a simple two-dimensional graph measuring quantity demanded

[2]Common sense and simple observation will give way to more sophisticated explanations in Chapter 25.

on the horizontal axis and price on the vertical axis.[3] From Chapter 1, we recall that the process involved is simply that of locating on the graph those five price-quantity possibilities shown in Table 4•1. We do this by drawing perpendiculars from the appropriate points on the two axes. Thus in plotting the "$5-price-10-quantity-demanded" possibility, we must draw a perpendicular from the horizontal (quantity) axis at 10 to meet a perpendicular drawn from the vertical (price) axis at $5. If this is done for all five possibilities, the result is a series of points as shown in Figure 4•1. Each of these points represents a specific price and the corresponding quantity which the consumer will choose to purchase at that price. Now, assuming the same inverse relationship between price and quantity demanded at all points between the ones graphed, we can generalize on the inverse relationship between price and quantity demanded by drawing a curve to represent *all* price–quantity-demanded possibilities within the limits shown on the graph. The resulting curve is called a *demand curve* and is labeled *DD* in Figure 4•1. It slopes downward and to the right because the relationship it portrays between price and quantity demanded is inverse. The law of demand—people buy more at a low price than they do at a high price—is reflected in the downward slope of the demand curve.

What is the advantage of graphing our demand schedule? After all, Table 4•1 and Figure 4•1 contain exactly the same data and reflect the same relationship between price and quantity demanded. The advantage of graphing is that it permits us to represent clearly a given relationship—in this case the law of demand—in a much simpler way than we could if we were forced to rely upon verbal and tabular presentation. A single curve on a graph, if understood, is simpler to state *and to manipulate* than tables and lengthy verbal presentations would be. Graphs are invaluable tools in economic analysis, as

[3] Putting price on the vertical axis and quantity demanded on the horizontal axis is a matter of convention; we do it for the same reason the mathematician makes *X* the unknown quantity in his equations.

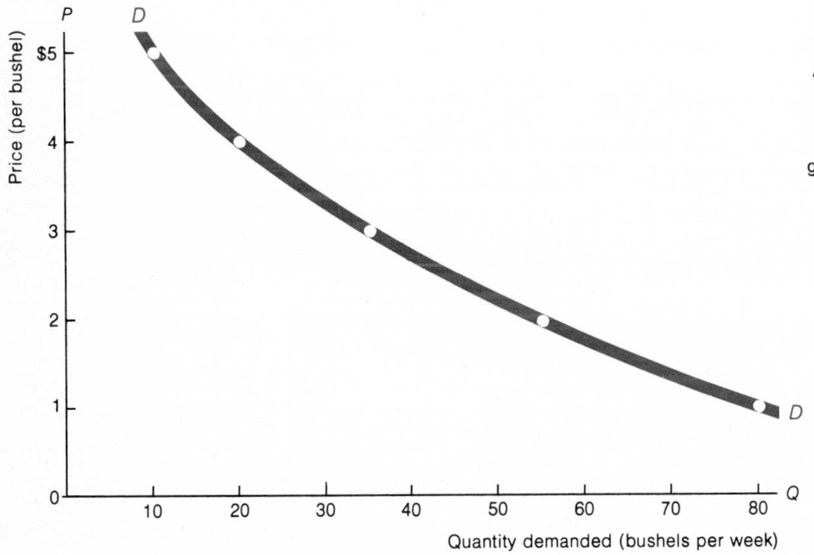

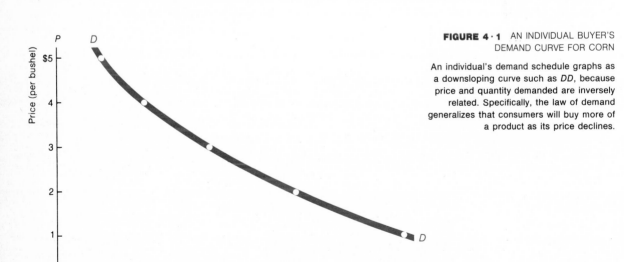

FIGURE 4 • 1 AN INDIVIDUAL BUYER'S DEMAND CURVE FOR CORN

An individual's demand schedule graphs as a downsloping curve such as *DD*, because price and quantity demanded are inversely related. Specifically, the law of demand generalizes that consumers will buy more of a product as its price declines.

TABLE 4·2 MARKET DEMAND FOR CORN, THREE BUYERS (*hypothetical data*)

Price per bushel	Quantity demanded, first buyer		Quantity demanded, second buyer		Quantity demanded, third buyer		Total quantity demanded per week
$5	10	+	12	+	8	=	30
4	20	+	23	+	17	=	60
3	35	+	39	+	26	=	100
2	55	+	60	+	39	=	154
1	80	+	87	+	54	=	221

has been previously indicated. They permit simple expression and handling of ofttimes complex relationships.

Individual and market demand

Until now we have been dealing in terms of just one consumer. The assumption of competition makes us consider a situation in which a large number of buyers are in the market. The transition from an *individual* to a *market* demand schedule can be accomplished by the simple process of summing the quantities demanded by each consumer at the various possible prices. If there were just three buyers in the market, as is shown in Table 4·2, it would be a simple chore to determine the total quantities demanded at each price. Figure 4·2 shows the same summing procedure graphically, using only the $3 price to illustrate the adding-up process.

Competition, of course, entails many more than

FIGURE 4·2 THE MARKET DEMAND CURVE IS THE SUM OF THE INDIVIDUAL DEMAND CURVES.

Graphically the market demand curve (*D* total) is found by summing horizontally the individual demand curves (D_1, D_2, and D_3) of all consumers in the market.

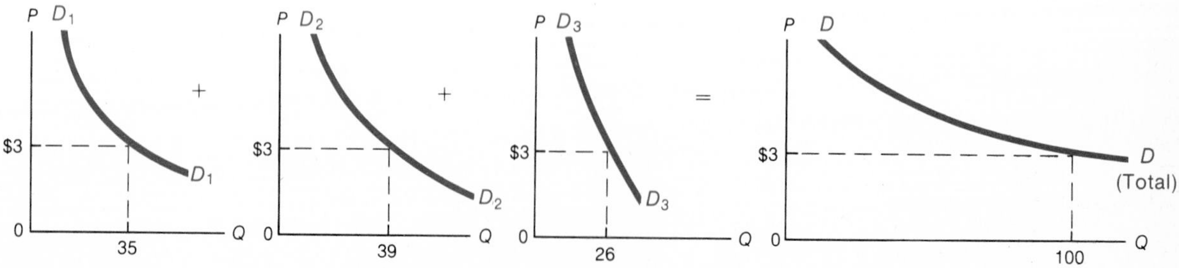

three buyers of a product. So—to avoid a lengthy addition process—let us suppose there are 200 buyers of corn in the market, each of whom chooses to buy the same amount at each of the various prices as our original consumer does. Thus, we can determine market demand by multiplying the quantity-demanded data of Table 4•1 by 200, as in Table 4•3.

Curve D_1 in Figure 4•3 indicates this market demand curve for the 200 buyers.

Determinants of demand

When the economist constructs a demand curve such as D_1 in Figure 4•3, he makes the assumption that price is the most important determinant of the amount of any product purchased. But he is aware that factors other than price can and do affect purchases. Thus, in locating a given demand curve such as D_1, the economist must also assume that "other things are equal"; that is, the nonprice determinants of the amount demanded are conveniently presumed to be constant. When these nonprice determinants of demand do in fact change, the location of the demand curve will shift to some new position to the right or left of D_1.

What are the major nonprice determinants of market demand? The basic ones are (1) the tastes or preferences of consumers, (2) the number of consumers in the market, (3) the money incomes of consumers, (4) the prices of related goods, and (5) consumer expectations with respect to future prices and incomes.

Changes in demand

What happens if one or more of the determinants of demand should change? We know the answer: A change in one or more of the determinants will change the demand schedule data in Table 4•3 and therefore the location of the demand curve in Figure 4•3. Such a change in the demand schedule data, or, graphically, a shift in the location of the demand curve, is designated as a *change in demand.*

More specifically, if consumers become willing and able to buy more of this particular good at each possible price than is reflected in column 4 of Table 4•3, an *increase in demand* has occurred. In Figure 4•3 this increase in demand is reflected in a shift of the demand curve to the right, for example, from D_1 to D_2. Conversely, a *decrease in demand* occurs when, because of a change in one or more of the determinants, consumers buy less of the product at each possible price than is indicated in column 4 of Table 4•3. Graphically, a decrease in demand entails a shift of the demand curve to the left, for example, from D_1 to D_3 in Figure 4•3.

TABLE 4•3 MARKET DEMAND FOR CORN, 200 BUYERS (*hypothetical data*)

(1) Price per bushel	(2) Quantity demanded per week, single buyer		(3) Number of buyers in the market		(4) Total quantity demanded per week
$5	10	×	200	=	2,000
4	20	×	200	=	4,000
3	35	×	200	=	7,000
2	55	×	200	=	11,000
1	80	×	200	=	16,000

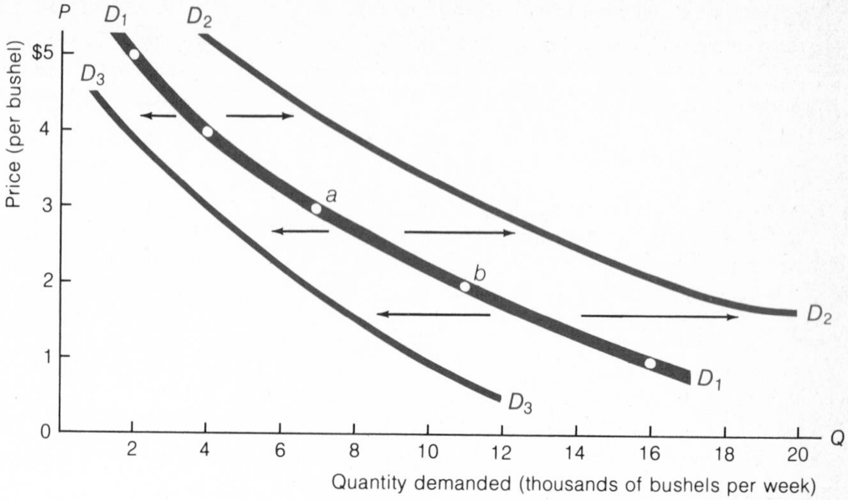

FIGURE 4·3 CHANGES IN THE DEMAND FOR CORN

A change in one or more of the determinants of demand—consumer tastes, the number of buyers in the market, money incomes, the prices of other goods, or consumer expectations—will cause a change in demand. An increase in demand shifts the demand curve to the right, as from D_1D_1 to D_2D_2. A decrease in demand shifts the demand curve to the left, as from D_1D_1 to D_3D_3. A change in the quantity demanded involves a movement, caused by a change in the price of the product under consideration, from one point to another—as from *a* to *b*—on a fixed demand curve.

Let us now examine the effect upon demand of changes in each of the aforementioned determinants.

1. Tastes A change in consumer tastes favorable to this product—possibly prompted by advertising or fashion changes—will mean that more will be demanded at each price; that is, demand will increase. An unfavorable change in consumer preferences will cause demand to decrease, shifting the curve to the left.

2. Number of buyers It is equally obvious that an increase in the number of consumers in a market—brought about perhaps by improvements in transportation or by population growth—will constitute an increase in demand. Fewer consumers will be reflected by a decrease in demand.

3. Income The impact of changes in money income upon demand is a bit more complex. For most commodities, a rise in income will cause an increase in demand. Consumers typically buy more shoes, steaks, stereos, and Scotch as their incomes increase. Conversely, the demand for such products will decline in response to a fall in incomes. Commodities whose demand varies *directly* with money income are called superior, or *normal,* goods.

Although most products are normal goods, there are a few exceptions. Examples: As incomes increase beyond some point, the amounts of bread or potatoes or cabbages purchased at each price may be less because the higher incomes now allow consumers to buy more high-protein foods such as dairy products and meat. Similarly, rising incomes may cause the demands for hamburger and oleomargarine to

decline as wealthier consumers switch to T-bones and butter. Goods whose demand varies *inversely* with a change in money income are called *inferior* or "poor man's" goods.

4. Prices of related goods Whether a given change in the price of a related good will increase or decrease the demand for the product under consideration will depend upon whether the related good is a substitute for or a complement to it. For example, butter and oleomargarine are *substitute,* or competing, goods. When the price of butter rises, consumers will purchase a smaller amount of butter, and this will cause the demand for oleomargarine to increase. Conversely, as the price of butter falls, consumers will buy larger quantities of butter, causing the demand for oleomargarine to decrease. To generalize: When the price of one good and the demand for another good are *directly* related, the two products are substitute goods. So it is with Schlitz and Budweiser, sugar and saccharin, Chevrolets and Fords, tea and coffee, and so forth.

But other pairs of products are *complementary* goods; they "go together." If the price of gasoline falls and, as a result, you drive your car more, this extra driving will increase your demand for motor oil. Conversely, an increase in the price of gasoline will diminish the demand for motor oil. Thus gas and oil are jointly demanded; they are complements. And so it is with ham and eggs, Scotch and soda, phonographs and records, golf clubs and golf balls, and so forth. Whenever the price of one good and the demand for another are *inversely* related, we can say that the two commodities are complements.

Many pairs of goods, of course, are not related at all—they are *independent* goods. For such pairs of commodities as, for example, butter and golf balls, potatoes and automobiles, bananas and wristwatches, we should expect that a change in the price of one would have little or no impact upon the demand for the other.

5. Expectations Consumer expectations of higher future prices may prompt them to buy now in order to "beat" the anticipated price rises, and, similarly, the expectation of rising incomes may induce consumers to be less tightfisted in their current spending. Conversely, expectations of falling prices and income will tend to decrease the current demand for products.

We might summarize by saying that an increase in the demand for product X—the decision of consumers to buy more of X at each possible price—can be caused by (1) a favorable change in consumer tastes, (2) an increase in the number of buyers in the market, (3) a rise (fall) in income if X is a normal (inferior) good, (4) an increase (decrease) in the price of related good Y if Y is a substitute for (complement to) X, and (5) expectations of future increases in prices and incomes. Conversely, a decrease in the demand for X can be associated with (1) an unfavorable change in tastes, (2) a decrease in the number of buyers in the market, (3) a rise (fall) in income if X is an inferior (normal) good, (4) an increase (decrease) in the price of related good Y if Y is complementary to (a substitute for) X, and (5) expectations of future price and income declines.

Changes in quantity demanded

A change in demand must not be confused with a change in the quantity demanded. We have noted that a *change in demand* refers to a shift in the entire demand curve either to the right (an increase in demand) or to the left (a decrease in demand). The consumer's state of mind concerning his purchases of this product has been altered. The cause: a change in one or more of the determinants of demand. As used by economists, the term "demand" refers to a schedule or curve; therefore, a change in demand must mean that the entire schedule has changed or that the curve has shifted its position.

In contrast, a *change in the quantity demanded* designates the movement from one point to another point—from one price-quantity combination to another—on a fixed demand curve. The cause of a change in the quantity demanded is a change in the price of the product under consideration. In Table

4·3 a decline in the price asked by suppliers of corn from $5 to $4 will increase the quantity of corn demanded from 2,000 to 4,000 bushels.

Figure 4·3 is helpful in making the distinction between a change in demand and a change in the quantity demanded. The shift of the demand curve D_1 to either D_2 or D_3 entails changes in demand. But the movement from point *a* to point *b* on curve D_1 is a change in the quantity demanded.

The reader should decide whether a change in demand or a change in the quantity demanded is involved in each of the following illustrations:

1. Consumer incomes rise, with the result that more jewelry is purchased.
2. A barber raises the price of haircuts and finds that his volume of business declines.
3. The price of Fords goes up, and, as a consequence, the sales of Chevrolets increase.

SUPPLY

Supply may be defined as *a schedule which shows the various amounts of a product which a producer is willing and able to produce and make available for sale in the market at each specific price in a set of possible prices during some specified time period.*[4] This schedule portrays a series of alternative possibilities, such as those shown in Table 4·4 for a single producer. Let us suppose that our producer, in this case, is a farmer producing corn, the demand for which we have just considered. Our definition of supply indicates that supply is usually viewed from the vantage point of price. That is, we read supply as showing the amounts producers will offer at various possible prices. It is more useful and quite correct in some instances to view supply from the reference point of quantity. Instead of asking what quantities will be offered at various prices, we can ask what prices will be required to induce producers to offer various quantities of a good.

[4]In talking of the resource market, our definition of supply reads: a schedule which shows the various amounts of a resource which its owners are willing to supply in the market at each possible price in a series of prices during some period of time.

TABLE 4·4 AN INDIVIDUAL PRODUCER'S SUPPLY OF CORN (*hypothetical data*)

Price per bushel	Quantity supplied per week
$5	60
4	50
3	35
2	20
1	5

Law of supply

It will be immediately noted that Table 4·4 shows a *direct* relationship between price and quantity supplied. As price rises, the corresponding quantity supplied rises; as price falls, the quantity supplied also falls. This particular relationship is called the *law of supply.* It simply tells us that producers are willing to produce and offer for sale more of their product at a high price than they are at a low price. Why? This again is basically a commonsense matter.

Price, we recall, is a deterrent from the consumer's standpoint. The obstacle of a high price means that the consumer, being on the paying end of this price, will buy a relatively small amount of the product; the lower the price obstacle, the more the consumer will buy. The supplier, on the other hand, is on the receiving end of the product's price. To him, price is an inducement or incentive to produce and sell a product. The higher the price of the product, the greater the incentive to produce and offer it in the market.

You will also remember that the law of demand was explainable on the basis of product substitution. When the price of product X rises, consumers tend to substitute other goods for it, therefore buying less of X. When the price of X declines, consumers buy more of X, substituting it for other products. The direct relationship between price and quantity supplied can also be explained on the basis of substituta-

bility. In many instances the resources and productive techniques used by a supplier are readily adaptable to a variety of products. A farmer's land and capital, for example, may be of about equal efficiency in producing corn, wheat, soy beans, milo, and so forth. As the market price of one of these products—say, corn—rises, the farmer will shift his resources from other commodities to corn because it pays him to produce more corn when the price goes up.

A simple example may help at this point. Suppose a farmer has just 2 acres of land. He finds from experience that these 2 acres are equally prolific in the production of corn and wheat. Specifically, he has found that each acre is capable of producing *either* 20 bushels of wheat *or* 20 bushels of corn. Suppose, too, that no matter how our farmer decides to apportion his 2 acres between wheat and corn, his total costs of production are always the same—say $25. To begin, let us say that the price of corn is $1 per bushel and that of wheat is $2 per bushel. The farmer will obviously plant all his land to wheat, producing 40 bushels. Total revenue will be $80 (= 40 × $2) and profits will be $55 (= $80 – $25). The output of corn, the crop in which we are particularly interested, will be zero. To plant any corn at a price of $1 per bushel will necessarily result in profits of less than $55. But what if the market price of corn rises to $3, while the price of wheat remains at $2? It would now be profitable for the farmer to shift all his resources to corn, that is, to substitute corn for wheat production. By doing so, his total revenue will be increased to $120 (= 40 × $3) and his profits to $95 (= $120 – $25). Although this example is greatly simplified, the basic point is clear: It is profitable to substitute the production of relatively high-priced for the production of relatively low-priced goods by shifting resources accordingly. Given the $2 price of wheat, no corn will be produced when its price is $1 per bushel, but 40 bushels will be forthcoming when its price is $3. Product substitution explains this direct relationship between the price of corn and the quantity supplied.

In practice, this substitution may be more complex and time-consuming than our illustration implies: very different products whose production requires radically different methods and resources may be in-

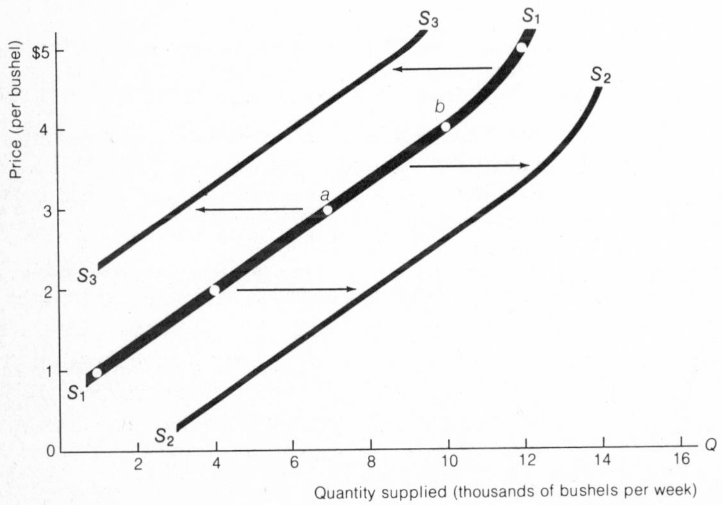

FIGURE 4·4 CHANGES IN THE SUPPLY OF CORN

A change in one or more of the determinants of supply—productive techniques, resource prices, the prices of other goods, price expectations, or the number of sellers in the market—will cause a change in supply. An increase in supply shifts the supply curve to the right, as from S_1S_1 to S_2S_2. A decrease in supply is shown graphically as a movement of the curve to the left, as from S_1S_1 to S_3S_3. A change in the quantity supplied involves a movement, caused by a change in the price of the product under consideration, from one point to another—as from *a* to *b*—on a fixed supply curve.

TABLE 4·5 MARKET SUPPLY OF CORN, 200 PRODUCERS (*hypothetical data*)

(1) Price per bushel	(2) Quantity supplied per week, single producer		(3) Number of sellers in the market		(4) Total quantity supplied per week
$5	60	×	200	=	12,000
4	50	×	200	=	10,000
3	35	×	200	=	7,000
2	20	×	200	=	4,000
1	5	×	200	=	1,000

volved. The process may well necessitate the shifting of resources between different producers. The basic conclusion, however, still holds true.

The supply curve

As in the case of demand, it is convenient to present graphically the concept of supply. Our axes in Figure 4·4 are the same as those in Figure 4·3, except for the obvious change of "quantity demanded" to "quantity supplied." The graphing procedure is the same as that previously explained, but of course the quantity data and relationship involved are different. The market supply data graphed in Figure 4·4 as S_1 are shown in Table 4·5, which assumes there are 200 suppliers in the market having the same supply schedules as the producer previously portrayed in Table 4·4.

Determinants of supply

In constructing a supply curve the economist assumes that price is the most significant determinant of the quantity supplied of any product. But, as with the demand curve, the supply curve is anchored on the "other things are equal" assumption. That is, the supply curve is drawn on the supposition that certain nonprice determinants of the amount supplied are given and do not change. If any of these nonprice determinants of supply do in fact change, the location of the supply curve will be altered.

The basic nonprice determinants of supply are (1) the technique of production, (2) resource prices, (3) prices of other goods, (4) price expectations, and (5) the number of sellers in the market. To repeat: A change in any one or more of these determinants will cause the supply curve for a product to shift to either the right or the left. A shift to the right, from S_1 to S_2 in Figure 4·4, designates an *increase in supply:* producers are now offering more of the product at each possible price. A shift to the left, S_1 to S_3 in Figure 4·4, indicates a *decrease in supply:* suppliers are offering less at each price.

Changes in supply

Let us consider the effect of changes in each of these determinants upon supply.

1 and 2. The first two determinants of supply—technology and resource prices—are the two components of production costs. And the relationship between production costs and supply is an intimate one. (As a matter of fact, in Chapter 27 we shall find that cost and supply data are synonymous.) For our present purposes, it is sufficient to note that anything which serves to lower production costs, that is, a technological improvement or a decline in resource prices, will increase supply. With lower costs, busi-

nessmen will find that it is profitable to offer a larger amount of the product at each possible price. An increase in the price of resources (a deterioration of technology being unlikely) will cause a decrease in supply; that is, the supply curve will shift to the left.

3. Changes in the prices of other goods can also shift the supply curve for a product. A decline in the price of wheat may cause a farmer to produce and offer more corn at each possible price. Conversely, a rise in the price of wheat may make farmers less willing to produce and offer corn in the market.

4. Expectations concerning the future price of a product can also affect a producer's current willingness to supply that product. It is difficult, however, to generalize concerning the way the expectation of, say, higher prices will affect the present supply curve of a product. Farmers might withhold some of their current corn harvest from the market, anticipating a higher corn price in the future. This will cause a decrease in the current supply of corn. On the other hand, in many types of manufacturing, expected price increases may induce firms to expand production immediately, causing supply to increase.

5. Finally, given the scale of operations of each firm, the larger the number of suppliers, the greater will be market supply. As more firms enter an industry, the supply curve will shift to the right. The smaller the number of firms in an industry, the less the market supply will be. This means that as firms leave an industry, the supply curve will shift to the left.

Changes in quantity supplied

The distinction between a change in supply and a change in the quantity supplied parallels that between a change in demand and a change in the quantity demanded. A *change in supply* is involved when the entire supply curve shifts. An increase in supply shifts the curve to the right; a decrease in supply shifts it to the left. The cause of a change in supply is a change in one or more of the determinants of supply. The term "supply" is used by economists to refer to a schedule or curve. A change in supply therefore must mean that the entire schedule has changed or that the curve has shifted.

A *change in the quantity supplied,* on the other hand, refers to the movement from one point to another point on a stable supply curve. The cause of such a movement is a change in the price of the specific product under consideration. In Table 4·5 a decline in the price of corn from $5 to $4 decreases the quantity of corn supplied from 12,000 to 10,000 bushels.

Shifting the supply curve from S_1 to S_2 or S_3 in Figure 4·4 obviously entails changes in supply. The movement from point *a* to point *b* on S_1, however, is merely a change in the quantity supplied.

The reader should determine which of the following involves a change in supply and which entails a change in the quantity supplied:

1. Because production costs decline, producers sell more automobiles.
2. The price of wheat declines, causing the number of bushels of corn sold per month to increase.
3. Fewer oranges are offered for sale because their price has decreased in retail markets.

SUPPLY AND DEMAND: MARKET EQUILIBRIUM

We may now put the concepts of supply and demand together to see how the interaction of the buying decisions of households and the selling decisions of producers will determine the price of a product and the quantity which is actually bought and sold in the market. In Table 4·6 columns 1 and 2 reproduce the market supply schedule for corn (from Table 4·5), and columns 2 and 3 the market demand schedule for corn (from Table 4·3). Note that in column 2 we are using a common set of prices. We assume competition—the presence of a large number of buyers and sellers.

Now the question to be faced is this: Of the five[5] possible prices at which corn might sell in this market, which will actually prevail as the market price for corn? Let us derive our answer through the simple process of trial and error. For no particular reason,

[5]Of course, there are many possible prices; our simple example shows only five of them.

TABLE 4·6 MARKET SUPPLY AND DEMAND FOR CORN (*hypothetical data*)

(1) Total quantity supplied per week	(2) Price per bushel	(3) Total quantity demanded per week	(4) Surplus (+) or shortage (−) (arrows indicate effect on price)
12,000	$5	2,000	+10,000↓
10,000	4	4,000	+ 6,000↓
7,000	3	7,000	0
4,000	2	11,000	− 7,000↑
1,000	1	16,000	−15,000↑

we shall start with an examination of $5. Could this be the prevailing market price for corn? The answer is "No," for the simple reason that producers are willing to produce and supply to the market some 12,000 bushels of corn at this price while buyers, on the other hand, are only willing to take 2,000 bushels off the market at this price. In other words, the relatively high price of $5 encourages farmers to produce a great deal of corn, but that same high price discourages consumers from taking the product off the market. Other products appear as "better buys" when corn is high-priced. The result in this case is a 10,000-bushel *surplus* of corn in the market. This surplus, shown in column 4, is simply the excess of quantity supplied over quantity demanded at the price of $5. Practically put, corn farmers would find themselves with unwanted inventories of output.

Could a price of $5—even if it existed temporarily in the corn market—persist over a period of time? Certainly not. The very large surplus of corn would prompt competing sellers to bid down the price in order to encourage buyers to take this surplus off their hands. Suppose price gravitates down to $4. Now the situation has changed considerably. The lower price has encouraged buyers to take more of this product off the market and, at the same time, has induced farmers to use a smaller amount of resources in producing corn. The surplus, as a result, has diminished to 6,000 bushels. Because a surplus still exists, competition among sellers will once again bid down the price of corn. We can conclude then that prices of $5 and $4 will be unstable, because they are "too high." The market price for corn must be something less than $4.

To avoid letting the cat out of the bag before we have a full appreciation of how supply and demand determine product price, let us now jump to the other end of our price column and examine $1 as the possible market price for corn. It is evident that at this price, quantity demanded is in excess of quantity supplied by 15,000 units. This relatively low price discourages farmers from devoting their resources to corn production; the same low price encourages consumers to attempt to buy more corn than would otherwise be the case. Corn is a "good buy" when its price is relatively low. In short, there is a 15,000-bushel *shortage* of corn. Can this price of $1 persist as the market price? No. Competition among buyers will bid up the price to something greater than $1. In other words, at a price of $1, many consumers who are willing and able to buy at this price will obviously be left out in the cold. Many potential consumers, in order to ensure that they will not have to do without, will express a willingness to pay some price in excess of $1 to ensure getting some of the available corn. Suppose this competitive bidding up

of price by buyers boosts the price of corn to $2. This higher price obviously has reduced, but not eliminated, the shortage of corn. For $2, farmers are willing to devote more resources to corn production, and some buyers who were willing to pay $1 for a bushel of corn will choose not to buy corn at a price of $2, deciding to use their incomes to buy other products or maybe to save more of their incomes. But a shortage of 7,000 bushels still exists at a price of $2. We can conclude that competitive bidding among buyers will push market price to some figure greater than $2.

By trial and error we have eliminated every price but $3. So let us now examine it. At a price of $3, *and only at this price,* the quantity which farmers are willing to produce and supply in the market is identical with the amount consumers are willing to buy. As a result, there is neither a shortage nor a surplus of corn at this price. We have already seen that a surplus causes price to decline and a shortage causes price to rise. With neither a shortage nor a surplus at $3, there is no reason for the actual price of corn to move away from this price. The economist calls this price the *equilibrium price,* equilibrium meaning ''in balance'' or ''at rest.'' At $3, quantity supplied and quantity demanded are in balance; hence $3 is the only stable price of corn under the supply and demand conditions shown in Table 4•6. Or, stated differently, the price of corn will be established where the supply decisions of producers and the demand decisions of buyers are mutually consistent. Such decisions are consistent with one another only at a price of $3. At any higher price, suppliers want to sell more than consumers want to buy; at any lower price, consumers want to buy more than producers are willing to offer for sale. Discrepancies between supply and demand intentions of sellers and buyers, respectively, will prompt price changes which subsequently will bring these two sets of plans into accord with one another.

A graphic analysis of supply and demand should yield the same conclusions. Figure 4•5 puts the

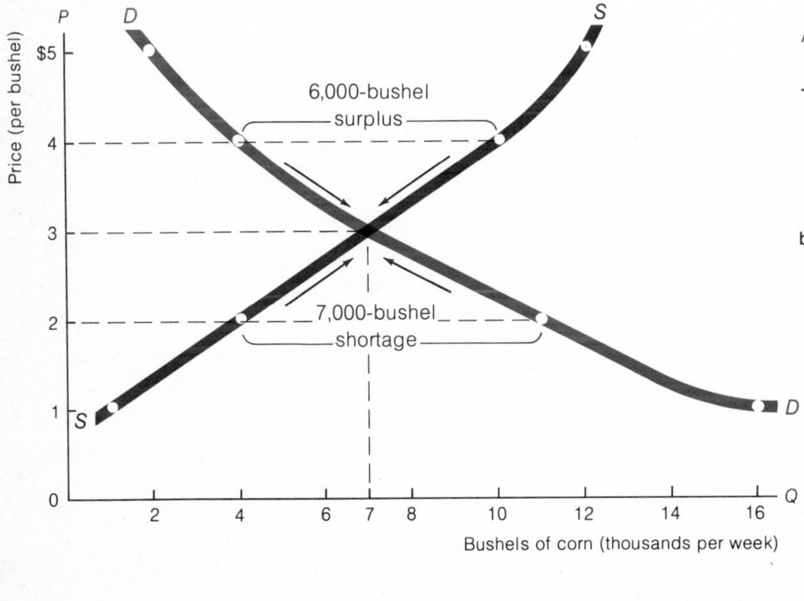

FIGURE 4•5 THE EQUILIBRIUM PRICE AND QUANTITY FOR CORN AS DETERMINED BY MARKET DEMAND AND SUPPLY

The intersection of the downsloping demand curve *D* and the upsloping supply curve *S* indicates the equilibrium price and quantity, $3 and 7,000 bushels in this instance. The shortages of corn which would exist at below-equilibrium prices, for example, 7,000 bushels at $2, drive price up and in so doing increase the quantity supplied and reduce the quantity demanded until equilibrium is achieved. The surpluses which above-equilibrium prices would entail, for example, 6,000 bushels at $4, push price down and therby increase the quantity demanded and reduce the quantity supplied until equilibrium is achieved.

market supply and market demand curves for corn on the same graph, the horizontal axis now reflecting both quantity demanded and quantity supplied. A close examination of this diagram clearly indicates that at any price above the equilibrium price of $3, quantity supplied will exceed quantity demanded. This surplus will cause a competitive bidding down of price by sellers eager to relieve themselves of their surplus. The falling price will cause less corn to be offered and will simultaneously encourage consumers to buy more. Any price below the equilibrium price will entail a shortage; that is, quantity demanded will exceed quantity supplied. Competitive bidding by buyers will push the price up toward the equilibrium level. And this rising price will simultaneously bring forth a greater supply from producers and ration buyers out of the market, thereby causing the shortage to vanish. Graphically, the intersection of the supply curve and the demand curve for the product will indicate the equilibrium point. In this case, as we know, equilibrium price and quantity are $3 and 7,000 bushels.

Rationing function of prices

The ability of the competitive forces of supply and demand to establish a price where supply and demand decisions are synchronized is sometimes called the *rationing function* of prices. In this case, the equilibrium price of $3 clears the market, leaving no burdensome surplus for the sellers and no inconvenient shortage for the potential buyers. The composite of freely made individual buying and selling decisions sets this price which clears the market. In effect, the market mechanism of supply and demand says this: Any buyer who is willing and able to pay $3 for a bushel of corn will be able to acquire one; those who are not, will not. Similarly, any seller who is willing and able to produce bushels of corn and offer them for sale at a price of $3 will be able to do so successfully; those who are not, will not. Were it not that competitive prices automatically bring supply and demand decisions into consistency with one another, some type of administrative control by government would be necessary to avoid or control the shortages or surpluses which might otherwise occur. We shall see in a later chapter some of the administrative problems involved when government steps into the picture and establishes a legal price higher or lower than the equilibrium price. Such *supported prices* and *ceiling prices* rob the price mechanism of its rationing ability, thereby making it necessary for government to assume responsibility for balancing quantity demanded and quantity supplied. The important point is that free, competitive prices automatically synchronize buying and selling decisions and "clear the market"; this is the rationing function of prices.

Changes in supply and demand

It was noted earlier that demand might change because of fluctuations in consumer tastes or incomes, changes in consumer expectations, or variations in the prices of related goods. On the other hand, supply might vary in response to changes in technology or in resource prices. Our analysis would be incomplete if we did not stop to consider the effect of changes in supply and demand upon equilibrium price.

To keep our thinking on the straight and narrow, let us first analyze the effects of a change in demand, assuming that supply is conveniently constant. Suppose now that demand increases, as shown in Figure 4·6*a*. What is the effect upon price? Noting that the new intersection of the supply and demand curves is at a higher point on both the price and quantity axes, we can conclude that an increase in demand, other things (supply) being equal, will have a *price-increasing effect* and a *quantity-increasing effect*. (The value of graphic analysis now begins to become apparent; we need not fumble with figures in determining the effect on price and quantity but only compare the new with the old point of intersection on the graph.) A decrease in demand, as illustrated in Figure 4·6*b*, reveals *price-decreasing* and *quantity-decreasing effects*. Price falls, and quantity also declines. *In brief, we find a direct relationship between a change in demand and the resulting changes in both equilibrium price and quantity.*

Let us reverse the procedure and analyze the effect of a change in supply on price, assuming that de-

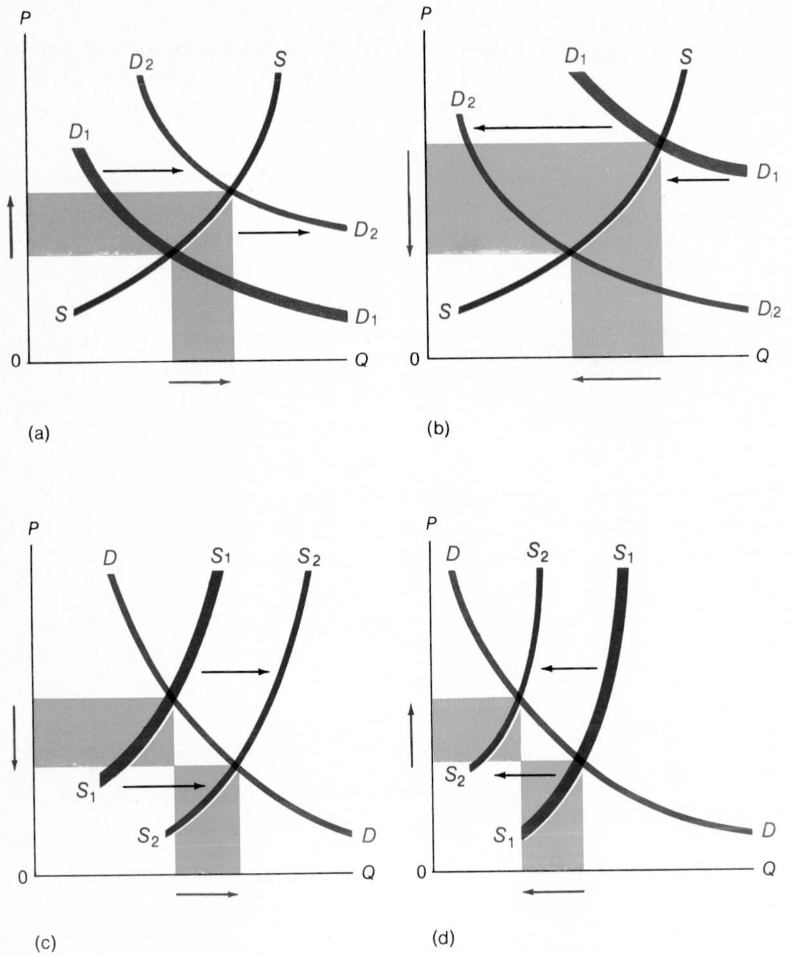

FIGURE 4·6 CHANGES IN DEMAND AND SUPPLY AND THE EFFECTS ON PRICE AND QUANTITY

The increase in demand of (*a*) and the decrease in demand of (*b*) indicate a direct relationship between a change in demand and the resulting changes in equilibrium price and quantity. The increase in supply of (*c*) and the decrease in supply of (*d*) show an inverse relationship between a change in supply and the resulting change in equilibrium price, but a direct relationship between a change in supply and the accompanying change in equilibrium quantity.

mand is constant. If supply increases, as in Figure 4·6*c*, the new intersection of supply and demand is obviously at a lower price. Equilibrium price falls; equilibrium quantity, however, increases. If supply decreases, on the other hand, this will tend to increase product price. Figure 4·6*d* illustrates this situation. Here price increases but quantity declines. In short, an increase in supply has a *price-decreasing* and a *quantity-increasing effect.* A decrease in supply has a *price-increasing* and a *quantity-decreasing effect. There is an inverse relationship between a change in supply and the resulting change in equilibrium price, but the relationship between a change in supply and the resulting change in equilibrium quantity is direct.*

Obviously, a host of more complex cases might arise, involving changes in both supply and demand. Two cases are possible when it is supposed that

supply and demand change in *opposite directions.* Assume first that supply increases and demand decreases. What effect does this have upon equilibrium price? This example couples two price-decreasing effects, and the net result will be a price fall greater than that which would result from either change taken in isolation. How about equilibrium quantity? Here the effects of the changes in supply and demand are opposed: The increase in supply tends to increase equilibrium quantity, but the decrease in demand tends to reduce the equilibrium quantity. The direction of the change in quantity depends upon the relative sizes of the changes in supply and demand. The second possibility is for supply to decrease and demand to increase. Two price-increasing effects are involved here. We can predict an increase in equilibrium price greater than that caused by either change taken separately. The effect upon equilibrium quantity is again indeterminate, depending upon the relative size of the changes in supply and demand. If the decrease in supply is relatively larger than the increase in demand, the equilibrium quantity will be less than it is initially. But if the decrease in supply is relatively smaller than the increase in demand, the equilibrium quantity will increase as a result of these changes. The reader should trace through these two cases graphically to verify for himself the conclusions we have outlined.

What if supply and demand change in the *same direction?* Suppose first that supply and demand both increase. What is the effect upon equilibrium price? It depends. Here we must compare two conflicting effects upon price—the price-decreasing effect of the increase in supply and the price-increasing effect of the increase in demand. If the increase in supply is of greater magnitude than the increase in demand, the net effect will be for equilibrium price to decrease. If the opposite holds true, equilibrium price will increase. The effect upon equilibrium quantity is certain: Increases in supply and in demand both have quantity-increasing effects. This means that equilibrium quantity will increase by an amount greater than that which either change would have entailed in isolation. In the second place, a decrease in both supply and demand can be subjected to similar analysis. If the decrease in supply is greater than the decrease in demand, equilibrium price will rise. If the reverse holds true, equilibrium price will fall. Because decreases in supply and demand both have quantity-decreasing effects, it can be predicted with certainty that equilibrium quantity will be less than that which prevailed initially.

Incidentally, the possibility that supply and demand will both change in a given period of time is not particularly unlikely. As a matter of fact, a single event might simultaneously affect both supply and demand. For example, a technological improvement in cheese production might lower both the supply of and the demand for fluid milk.

Needless to say, special cases might arise where a decrease in demand and a decrease in supply, on the one hand, and an increase in demand and an increase in supply, on the other, cancel out. In both these cases, the net effect upon equilibrium price will be zero; price will not change. The reader should again work out these more complex cases in terms of supply and demand curves to verify all these results.

The resource market

What about the shape of the supply and demand curves in the resource market? As in the product market, resource supply curves are typically upsloping, and resource demand curves are typically downsloping. Why?

Resource supply curves generally slope upward, that is, they reflect a *direct* relationship between resource price and quantity supplied, because it is in their own interests for resource owners to supply more of a particular resource at a high price than at a low price. High income payments in a particular occupation or industry encourage households to supply more of their human and property resources. Low income payments discourage resource owners from supplying resources in this particular occupation or industry and, as a matter of fact, encourage them to supply their resources elsewhere.

On the demand side, businesses tend to buy less of a given resource as its price rises, and they tend

to substitute other relatively low-priced resources for it. Entrepreneurs will find it profitable to substitute low- for high-priced resources. More of a particular resource will be demanded at a low price than at a high price. The result? A downsloping demand curve for the various resources.

In short, just as the supply decisions of businesses and the demand decisions of consumers determine prices in the product market, so the supply decisions of households and demand decisions of businesses set prices in the resource market.

SUMMARY

1. Demand refers to a schedule which summarizes the willingness of buyers to purchase a given product during a specific time period at each of the various prices at which it might be sold. According to the law of demand, consumers will ordinarily buy more of a product at a low price than they will at a high price. Therefore, the relationship between price and quantity demanded is inverse; demand graphs as a downsloping curve.

2. Changes in one or more of the basic determinants of demand—consumer tastes, the number of buyers in the market, the money incomes of consumers, the prices of related goods, and consumer expectations—will cause the market demand curve to shift. A shift to the right is an increase in demand; a shift to the left, a decrease in demand. A change in demand is to be distinguished from a change in the quantity demanded, the latter involving the movement from one point to another point on a fixed demand curve because of a change in the price of the product under consideration.

3. Supply is a schedule showing the amounts of a product which producers would be willing to offer in the market during a given time period at each possible price at which the commodity might be sold. The law of supply says that producers will offer more of a product at a higher price than they will at a low price. As a result, the relationship between price and quantity supplied is a direct one, and the supply curve is upsloping.

4. A change in production techniques, resource prices, the prices of other goods, price expectations, or the number of sellers in the market will cause the supply curve of a product to shift. A shift to the right is an increase in supply; a shift to the left, a decrease in supply. In contrast, a change in the price of a given product will result in a change in the quantity supplied, that is, a movement from one point to another on a given supply curve.

5. Under competition, the interaction of market demand and market supply will adjust price to that point at which the quantity demanded and the quantity supplied are equal. This is the equilibrium price. The corresponding quantity is the equilibrium quantity. Equilibrium price and equilibrium quantity will change in response to a change in demand or supply.

6. The ability of market forces to synchronize selling and buying decisions so as to eliminate potential surpluses or shortages is sometimes termed the "rationing function" of prices.

7. A change in either demand or supply will cause equilibrium price and quantity to change. There is a direct relationship between a change in demand and the resulting changes in equilibrium price and quantity. Though the relationship between a change in supply and the resulting change in equilibrium price is inverse, the relationship between a change in supply and equilibrium quantity is direct.

8. The concepts of supply and demand are also applicable to the resource market.

QUESTIONS AND STUDY SUGGESTIONS

1. Define demand. Explain the law of demand. Why does a demand curve slope downward? What are the determinants of demand? What happens to the demand curve when each of these determinants changes? Distinguish between a change in demand and a change in the quantity demanded, noting the cause(s) of each.

2. Critically evaluate: "In comparing the two equilibrium

positions in Figure 4·6*a* I note that a larger amount is actually purchased at a higher price. This obviously refutes the law of demand."

3. Define supply. Explain the law of supply. Why does the supply curve slope upward? What are the determinants of supply? What happens to the supply curve when each of these determinants changes? Distinguish between a change in supply and a change in the quantity supplied, noting the cause(s) of each.

4. Explain the following news dispatch from Hull, England: "The fish market here slumped today to what local commentators called 'a disastrous level'—all because of a shortage of potatoes. The potatoes are one of the main ingredients in a dish that figures on almost every café menu—fish and chips."

5. Suppose the total demand for wheat and the total supply of wheat per month in the Kansas City grain market are as follows:

Thousands of bushels demanded	Price per bushel	Thousands of bushels supplied	Surplus (+) or shortage (−)
90	\$1.70	70	________
85	1.80	72	________
80	1.90	73	________
75	2.00	75	________
70	2.10	77	________
65	2.20	79	________
60	2.30	81	________
55	2.40	83	________

a. What will be the market or equilibrium price? What is the equilibrium quantity? Using the surplus-shortage column, explain why your answers are correct.

b. Using the above data, graph the demand for wheat and the supply of wheat. Be sure to label the axes of your graph correctly. Label equilibrium price "*P*" and equilibrium quantity "*Q*."

c. Why will \$1.80 not be the equilibrium price in this market? Why not \$2.30?

d. Now suppose that the government establishes a ceiling price of, say, \$1.90 for wheat. Explain carefully the effects of this ceiling price. Demonstrate your answer graphically. What might prompt government to establish a ceiling price?

e. Assume now that the government establishes a supported price of, say, \$2.20 for wheat. Explain carefully the effects of this supported price. Demonstrate your answer graphically. What might prompt the government to establish this price support?

f. "Legally fixed prices strip the price mechanism of its rationing function." Explain this statement in terms of your answers to 5*d* and 5*e*.

6. What effect will each of the following have upon the demand for product B?

a. Product B becomes more fashionable.

b. The price of product C, a good substitute for B, goes down.

c. Consumers anticipate declining prices and falling incomes.

d. There is a rapid upsurge in population growth.

7. What effect will each of the following have upon the supply of product B?

a. A technological advance in the methods of producing B.

b. A decline in the number of firms in industry B.

c. An increase in the prices of resources required in the production of B.

d. The expectation that the equilibrium price of B will be lower in the future than it is currently.

e. A decline in the price of product A, a good whose production requires substantially the same techniques and resources as does the production of B.

8. Explain and illustrate graphically the effect of:

a. An increase in income upon the demand curve of an inferior good.

b. A drop in the price of product S upon the demand for substitute product T.

c. A decline in income upon the demand curve of a normal good.

d. An increase in the price of product J upon the demand for complementary good K.

9. "In the corn market, demand often exceeds supply and supply sometimes exceeds demand." "The price of corn rises and falls in response to changes in supply and demand." In which of these two statements are the terms "supply" and "demand" used correctly? Explain.

10. "Surpluses drive prices up; shortages drive them down." Do you agree?

11. How will each of the following changes in demand and/or supply affect equilibrium price and equilibrium

quantity in a competitive market; that is, do price and quantity *rise, fall, remain unchanged,* or are the answers *indeterminate,* depending upon the magnitudes of the shifts in supply and demand? You should rely on a supply and demand diagram to verify answers.

a. Supply decreases and demand remains constant.
b. Demand decreases and supply remains constant.
c. Supply increases and demand is constant.
d. Demand increases and supply increases.
e. Demand increases and supply is constant.
f. Supply increases and demand decreases.
g. Demand increases and supply decreases.
h. Demand decreases and supply decreases.

12. "Prices are the automatic regulator that tends to keep production and consumption in line with each other." Explain.

13. *Advanced analysis:* Assume that the demand for a commodity is represented by the equation $Q_d = 12 - 2P$ and supply by the equation $Q_s = 2P$, where Q_d and Q_s are quantity demanded and quantity supplied respectively and P is price. Using the equilibrium condition $Q_s = Q_d$, solve the equations to determine equilibrium price. Now determine equilibrium quantity. Graph the two equations to substantiate your answers.

SELECTED REFERENCES

Boulding, Kenneth E.: *Economic Analysis: Microeconomics,* 4th ed. (New York: Harper & Row, Publishers, Incorporated, 1966), chaps. 8, 10, 11.

Henderson, Hubert: *Supply and Demand* (Chicago: The University of Chicago Press, 1958), chap. 2.

5

THE FIVE FUNDAMENTAL QUESTIONS AND THE PRICE SYSTEM

We saw in Chapter 3 that the capitalist ideology makes clear the importance of freedom of enterprise and choice. Consumers are at liberty to buy what they choose; businesses, to produce and sell what they choose; and resource suppliers to make their property and human resources available in whatever occupations they choose. Upon reflection, we might wonder why such an economy does not collapse in complete chaos. If consumers want bread, businesses choose to produce automobiles, and resource suppliers want to offer their services in manufacturing shoes, it would seem that production would be deadlocked because of the obvious inconsistency of these free choices.

Fortunately, two other features of capitalism—a system of markets and prices and the force of competition—provide the coordinating and organizing mechanisms which overcome the potential chaos posed by freedom of enterprise and choice. The competitive price system is a mechanism both for communicating the decisions of consumers, producers, and resource suppliers to one another and for synchronizing those decisions toward consistent production objectives.

Armed with an understanding of individual markets and prices gained from Chapter 4, we are now in a position to analyze the operation of the price system. More specifically, in this chapter we first want to understand how the price system operates as a mechanism for communicating and coordinating individual free choices. Deferring the full-employment question until Part Two, we want to see how the price system answers the other four Fundamental Questions. How does the price system (1) determine what is to be produced, (2) organize production, (3) distribute total output, and (4) adapt itself to change? Then, secondly, we want to evaluate the operation of the market economy.

FRAMEWORK OF THE PRICE SYSTEM

If we could suddenly "freeze" a purely capitalist economy at some point in time, here is what we should find:

1. Households, as consumers, have a variety of material wants. For all practical purposes, these wants are unlimited. Possessing a limited money income derived from the sale of limited amounts of resources at its disposal, each household seeks to purchase that combination of goods and services which will give it the greatest satisfaction. These various consumer wants in effect are tallied on the demand side of the product market. The demand schedule or curve for each product communicates to producers how much competing consumers would purchase of that product at various prices. The demand curve for each product is downsloping, because consumers find it to their advantage to substitute low-priced for high-priced products. Because of the large number of consumers buying each product, no one significantly influences actual product prices.

2. Competing business institutions stand on the supply side of the product market. Their goal is to maximize profits. In so doing, they must decide what product will be most profitable to produce, in what quantity it will be most profitable to produce it, and what combination of resources will produce the desired output at the least cost. For the business sector as a whole, these decisions, which in effect indicate the willingness of businesses to produce and offer various products, are reflected in product supply curves. These supply curves are upsloping, indicating that, other things being equal, businesses will profit by substituting the production of high-priced for the production of low-priced goods. Together with the product demand curves which mirror consumer preferences, these supply curves will establish an equilibrium price for all those products which consumers might want and which businesses might be willing to supply.

3. Businesses require resources in accomplishing production. As we noted in Chapter 4, businesses will minimize their costs and, other things being equal, maximize their profits by substituting low-priced resources for high-priced resources; this means that resource demand curves will be downsloping. These resource demand curves will communicate to resource suppliers how much of each resource businesses will be willing to employ at various possible resource prices.

4. Finally, households as resource suppliers offer the land, labor, capital, and entrepreneurial talents which they own to businesses. The decisions of competing resource suppliers are reflected in resource supply curves. These curves are generally upsloping, reflecting the fact that households seek the greatest return from the sale of their resources. The upsloping nature of these curves implies that households not only want but within limits are able to shift resources from low-paying to high-paying lines of employment.

In brief, the product demand intentions of households and the product supply decisions of businesses will determine a series of product prices. Similarly, the resource demand decisions of businesses and the resource supply decisions of households will establish a series of resource prices.

ECONOMIC CHOICES, SCARCITY, AND SUBSTITUTABILITY

It is evident that our picture of the price system merely envisions a series of interrelated choices on the part of households as consumers and resource suppliers and businesses as producers and resource users. These choices are based upon the fact of scarcity and influenced by considerations of substitutability.

Society is faced with the problem of making economic choices because resources are scarce. If resources were infinitely abundant in relation to the demand for them, the economizing problem would dissolve in a sea of affluence. Consumers would not have to choose between various products; abundance would make it possible for every consumer to have any type and any amount of goods and services he desired. The same would be true for businesses in their use of resources to carry on production. But unfortunately, this describes economic utopia, not economic reality; in real life, resources, and therefore products, are relatively scarce. Hence, consumers with money incomes lim-

ited by their sales of scarce resources are forced to choose between relatively scarce commodities. And businesses, possessing limited money receipts from the sale of relatively scarce products, must choose between scarce resources in carrying on their productive efforts. Indeed, the presence of the basic theme of scarcity in our picture of the price system is mirrored in the very fact that products and resources have price tags on them! Only when something is scarce in relation to the demand for it will it command a price in the market.

How does substitutability come into the picture? Within limits, both resources and products are versatile. Consumer wants can usually be satisfied with various goods. The want for a trip from New York to Chicago can be satisfied by purchasing a car, a train ticket, a plane ticket, or a bus ticket. Hunger can be satisfied by a wide variety of foods—a bowl of rice, a hamburger, or a sirloin steak. And so it is with producing specific products. Resources, within limits dictated by technology, are substitutable for one another. Various resource combinations can be employed in the production of most products. The nature of both the supply and demand choices in a market economy is strongly influenced by substitutability. The demand curve for a product is downsloping because consumers will substitute other products for any particular product whose price happens to rise. And producers tend to substitute alternative resources for that resource whose price rises. Upsloping product and resource supply curves also imply substitutability. Producers tend to substitute high-priced for low-priced products in formulating their production intentions. And resource suppliers shift their human and property resources from low-paying to high-paying employments.

This, of course, is not to say that substitutability is perfect. It obviously is not. A bowl of rice is not a perfect substitute for a sirloin steak. Yet within limits the possibility of substitution exists in both the product and resource market. Indeed, if substitutability did not exist, businesses would have no choices to make in hiring resources to produce specific goods. And if resources were not versatile, households would have no choices to make in supplying them. Similarly, if various products were not substitutable, households would have no problem of choice in spending their incomes.

Thus we may say that economic choices must be rendered because resources, and therefore products, are scarce. The particular choices rendered by businesses and households depend upon:

1. The prices of resources and products as indicators of relative scarcities.
2. The possibilities of substituting between resources, on the one hand, and products, on the other.

The interrelationship between scarcity and substitution is even more intimate than we have suggested. For example, if a product becomes particularly scarce, its price as an index of its relative scarcity will rise. This will signal buyers to substitute other products for the now higher-priced product. This substitution will rechannel consumer purchases away from this particularly scarce product toward others less scarce. Substitution eases this particularly acute scarcity by, in effect, transferring consumer purchases to other substitutable products. Through substitutability, society alters its choices so as to use less of particularly scarce products and resources and more of less scarce ones. By substituting, society conserves most on those products and resources which are most scarce.

OPERATION OF THE PRICE SYSTEM

Now with this point-in-time picture of the price system before us and with the significance of scarcity and substitutability in the making of economic choices clearly in mind, let us examine in some detail the manner in which the competitive price system would answer the Fundamental Questions.

Determining what is to be produced

Given the product and resource prices established by competing buyers and sellers in both the product and resource markets, how would a purely capitalistic economy decide the types and quantities of goods

to be produced? Remembering that businesses are motivated to seek profits and avoid losses, we can generalize that those goods and services which can be produced at a profit will be produced and those whose production entails a loss will not. And what determines profits or the lack of them? Two things:

1. The total receipts which a firm gets from selling a product.
2. The total costs of producing it.

Both total receipts and total costs are price-times-quantity figures. Total receipts are found by multiplying product price by the amount of the product sold. Total costs are found by multiplying the price of each resource used by the amount employed and summing the costs of each.

Economic profits To say that those products which can be produced profitably will be produced and those which cannot will not is only an accurate generalization if the meaning of economic costs is clearly understood. In order to grasp the full meaning of costs, let us once again think of businesses as simply organizational charts, that is, businesses "on paper," distinct and apart from the capital, raw materials, labor, and entrepreneurial ability which make them going concerns. In order to become actual producing concerns, these "on paper" businesses must secure all four types of resources. The payments which must be made to secure and retain the needed amounts of these resources are *economic costs.* The per unit size of these costs will be determined by supply and demand conditions in the resource market. Now the point to note is that—like land, labor, and capital—entrepreneurial ability is a scarce resource and consequently has a price tag on it. Costs therefore must include not only wage and salary payments to labor and interest and rental payments for capital and land, but also payments to the entrepreneur for the functions he performs in organizing and combining the other resources in the production of some commodity. The cost payment for these contributions by the entrepreneur is called a *normal profit.* Hence, a product will be produced only when total receipts are large enough to pay wage, interest, rental, and normal profit costs. Now if total receipts from the sale of a product more than cover all production costs, including a normal profit, the remainder will accrue to the entrepreneur as the risk taker and organizing force in the going concern. This return above costs is called a *pure,* or *economic, profit.* It is not an economic cost, because it need not be realized in order for the business to acquire and retain entrepreneurial ability.

Profits and expanding industries A few hypothetical examples will explain more concretely how the price system determines what is to be produced. Suppose that the most favorable relationship between total revenue and total cost in producing product X occurs when the firm's output is 15 units. Assume, too, that the best combination of resources to use in producing 15 units of X entails 2 units of labor, 3 units of land, 1 of capital, and 1 of entrepreneurial ability, selling at prices of $2, $1, $3, and $3, respectively. Finally, suppose that the 15 units of X which these resources produce can be sold for $1 per unit. Will firms enter into the production of product X? Yes, they will. A firm producing product X under these conditions will be able to pay wage, rent, interest, and normal profit costs of $13 [= (2 × $2) + (3 × $1) + (1 × $3) + (1 × $3)]. The difference between total revenue of $15 and total costs of $13 will be an economic profit of $2.

This economic profit is evidence that industry X is a prosperous one. Such an industry will tend to expand as new firms, attracted by these above-normal profits, are created or shift from less profitable industries. But the entry of new firms will be a self-limiting process. As new firms enter industry X, the market supply of X will increase relative to the market demand. This will lower the market price of X to the end that economic profits will in time disappear. The market supply and demand situation prevailing when economic profits become zero will determine the total amount of X produced.

Losses and declining industries But what if the initial market situation for product X were less favorable? Suppose conditions in the product market initially were such that the firm could sell the 15 units

of X at a price of just 75 cents per unit. Total revenue would be \$11.25 (= 15 × 75 cents). After paying wage, rental, and interest costs of \$10, the firm would yield a below-normal profit of \$1.25. In other words, losses of \$1.75 (= \$11.25 − \$13) would be incurred. Certainly firms would not be attracted to this unprosperous industry. On the contrary, if these losses persisted, entrepreneurs would seek the normal or economic profits offered by more prosperous industries. This means that existing firms in industry X would in time go out of business entirely or migrate to other industries where normal or better profits prevail. However, as this happens, the market supply of X will fall relative to the market demand, thereby raising product price to the end that losses will in time disappear. Industry X will then stabilize itself in size. The market supply and demand situation that prevails at that point where economic profits are zero will determine the total output of product X.

"Dollar votes" The important role of consumer demand in determining the types and quantities of goods produced must be emphasized. Consumers, unrestrained by government and possessing money incomes from the sale of resources, spend their dollars upon those goods which they are most willing and able to buy. These expenditures are in effect "dollar votes" by which consumers register their wants through the demand side of the product market. If these votes are great enough to provide a normal profit, businesses will produce that product. An increase in consumer demand, that is, an increase in the dollar votes cast for a product, will mean economic profits for the industry producing it. These profits will signal the expansion of that industry and increases in the output of the product. A decrease in consumer demand, that is, fewer votes cast for the product, will result in losses and, in time, contraction of the adversely affected industry. As firms leave the industry, the output of the product declines. In short, the dollar votes of consumers play a key role in determining what products profit-seeking businesses will produce. As noted in Chapter 3, the capitalistic system is sometimes said to be characterized by *consumer sovereignty* because of the strategic role of consumers in determining the types and quantities of goods produced.

Market restraints on freedom From the viewpoint of businesses, we now see that firms are not really "free" to produce what they wish. The demand decisions of consumers, by making the production of some products profitable and others not, restrict the choice of businesses in deciding what to produce. Businesses must synchronize their production choices with consumer choices or face the penalty of losses and eventual bankruptcy.

Much the same holds true with respect to resource suppliers. The demand for resources is a *derived demand*—derived, that is, from the demand for the goods and services which the resources help produce. There is a demand for auto workers only because there is a demand for automobiles. More generally, in seeking to maximize the returns from the sale of their human and property resources, resource suppliers are prompted by the price system to make their choices in accord with consumer demands. If only those firms which produce goods wanted by consumers can operate profitably, only those firms will demand resources. Resource suppliers will not be "free" to allocate their resources to the production of goods which consumers do not value very highly. The reason? There will be no firms producing such products, because consumer demand is not sufficient to make it profitable to do so. In short, consumers register their preferences on the demand side of the product market, and producers and resource suppliers respond appropriately in seeking to further their own self-interests. The price system communicates the wants of consumers to business and resource suppliers and elicits appropriate responses.

Organizing production

How is production to be organized in a market economy? This fundamental question, we recall, is composed of three subquestions:

1. How should resources be allocated among specific industries?

2. What specific firms should do the producing in each industry?

3. What combinations of resources—what technology—should each firm employ?

The preceding section has answered the first subquestion. The price system steers resources to those industries whose products consumers want badly enough to make their production profitable. It simultaneously deprives unprofitable industries of scarce resources. If all firms had sufficient time to enter prosperous industries and to leave unprosperous industries, the output of each industry would be large enough for the firms to just make normal profits. If total industry output at this point happens to be 1,500 units and the most profitable output for each firm is 15 units, as in our previous example, the industry will obviously be made up of 100 competing firms.

The second and third subquestions are closely intertwined. In a competitive market economy, the firms which do the producing are those which are willing and able to employ the economically most efficient technique of production. And what determines the most efficient technique? Economic efficiency depends upon:

1. Available technology, that is, the alternative combinations of resources or inputs which will produce the desired output.

2. The prices at which the needed resources can be obtained.

The combination of resources which is most efficient economically depends not only upon the physical or engineering data provided by available technology but also upon the relative worth of the required resources as measured by their market prices. Thus, a technique which requires just a few physical inputs of resources to produce a given output may be highly *in*efficient economically if the required resources are valued very highly in the market. In other words, economic efficiency entails getting a given output of product with the smallest input of scarce resources, when both output and resource inputs are measured in dollars-and-cents terms. In short, that combination of resources which will produce, say, $15 worth of product X at the lowest possible money cost is the most efficient.

Table 5·1 will help illustrate these points. Suppose there are three different techniques by which the desired $15 worth of product X can be produced. The quantity of each resource required by each technique and the prices of the required resources are shown in Table 5·1. By multiplying the quantities of the various resources required by the resource prices in each of the three techniques, the total cost of producing $15 worth of X by each technique can be determined. It can be concluded that technique No. 2 is economically the most efficient of the three, for the simple reason that it is the least costly way of producing $15 worth of X. Technique No. 2 permits

TABLE 5·1 TECHNIQUES FOR PRODUCING $15 WORTH OF PRODUCT X (*hypothetical data*)

Resource	Technique No. 1	Technique No. 2	Technique No. 3	Price per unit of resource
Labor	4	2	1	$2
Land	1	3	4	1
Capital	1	1	2	3
Entrepreneurial ability	1	1	1	3
Total cost of $15 worth of X	$15	$13	$15	

society to obtain $15 worth of output by using up a smaller amount of resources—$13 worth—than would be used up by the two alternative techniques. Technique No. 2 is the most efficient, because it gives society $15 worth of output for an input of $13 worth of resources; the alternative techniques entail an input of $15 worth of resources for the same amount of output.

But what guarantees that technique No. 2 will actually be used? After all, techniques No. 1 and No. 3 entail a normal profit and thereby will permit firms to survive, at least for the moment. The answer to this question can be stated as follows.

1. Technique No. 2 allows the user an economic profit of $2. And firms seeking to further their own interests can be expected to employ techniques which permit them to realize the greatest profits. Firms will *want* to use the most efficient technique; it yields the greatest profit.

2. Competition will literally *force* firms to use the most efficient technique. The firm that fails to employ the least costly method of production will find that other existing firms or new firms coming into the industry will adopt the least costly technique. This leads to an increase in supply and hence to a reduction in the price of X. This will turn the normal profit of the inefficient firm into losses unless it switches to the most efficient technique. Thus, the competitive price system makes the adoption of the most efficient production techniques a condition of survival.

We must emphasize that a change in either technology or resource prices may cause the firm to shift from the technology now employed. For example, if the price of labor falls to 50 cents, technique No. 1 will be superior to technique No. 2. That is, businesses will find that they can lower their costs by shifting to a technology which involves the use of more of that resource whose price has fallen. This shift in techniques illustrates why resource demand curves are downsloping. In this case, a decline in the price of labor prompts businesses to shift to a technique employing more labor and less land. The reader should verify that a new technique involving 1 unit of labor, 4 of land, 1 of capital, and 1 of entrepreneurial ability will be preferable to all three techniques listed in Table 5·1, assuming the resource prices given there.

Distributing total output

The price system enters the picture in two ways in solving the problem of distributing total output. Generally speaking, any given product will be distributed to consumers on the basis of their ability and willingness to pay the existing market price for it. If the price of X is $1 per unit, those buyers who are able and willing to pay that price will get a unit of this product; those who are not, will not. This, we recall, is the rationing function of equilibrium prices.

What determines a consumer's ability to pay the equilibrium price for X and other available products? The size of his money income. And money income in turn depends upon the types and quantities of the various property and human resources which the income receiver supplies and the prices which they command in the resource market. Thus, resource prices play a key role in determining the size of each household's claim against the total output of society. Within the limits of a consumer's money income, his willingness to pay the equilibrium price for X determines whether or not some of this product is distributed to him. And this willingness to buy X will depend upon his preference for X in comparison with available close substitutes for X and their relative prices. Thus, product prices play a key role in determining the expenditure patterns of consumers.

We should emphasize that there is nothing particularly ethical about the price system as a mechanism for distributing the output of pure capitalism. Those households which manage to accumulate large amounts of property resources by inheritance, through hard work and frugality, through business acumen, or by crook will receive large incomes and thus command large shares of the economy's total output. Others which offer only those labor resources which are valued low by the price system will receive meager money incomes and small portions of total output. The price system is impersonal, and if money

incomes are very unequally distributed, a very unequal distribution of the fruits of production will follow (see Chapter 38).

Providing for flexibility

In order to ensure efficiency in the administration of its resources over a period of time, an economy must be flexible. That particular allocation of resources which is *now* the most efficient for a *given* pattern of consumer tastes, for a *given* range of technological alternatives, and for *given* supplies of resources can be expected to become obsolete and inefficient as consumer preferences change, new techniques of production are discovered, and resource supplies alter over time. Can the market economy negotiate adjustments in resource uses appropriate to such inevitable changes and thereby remain efficient? Furthermore, in addition to being permissive of, or adaptable to, such changes, is the market economy conducive to changes in technology and the stock of capital which are crucial to economic growth and a higher standard of living?

Is the price system adaptable to change? Let us suppose a change occurs in consumer tastes. Specifically, let us say that consumers decide they want more shoes and fewer shirts than the economy is currently providing. Will the price system communicate this change to businesses and resource suppliers and prompt appropriate adjustments?

The assumed change in consumers' tastes will be communicated to producers through an increase in the demand for shoes and a decline in the demand for shirts. This means that shoe prices will rise and shirt prices will fall. Now, assuming firms in both industries are enjoying precisely normal profits prior to these changes in consumer demand, higher shoe prices will mean economic profits for the shoe industry, and lower shirt prices will entail losses for the shirt industry. Self-interest induces new competitors to enter the prosperous shoe industry. Losses will in time force firms to leave the depressed shirt industry. As a matter of fact, some firms leaving the shirt industry might enter the shoe industry. But in all probability, most firms entering the shoe industry will be newly created and those leaving the shirt industry will become permanently defunct.

In any event, the prosperous shoe industry will expand, and the unprosperous shirt industry will contract. But these adjustments, we recall, are both self-limiting. The expansion of the shoe industry will continue only to the point at which the resulting increase in the market supply of shoes brings shoe prices back down to a level at which normal profits again prevail. Similarly, contraction in the shirt industry will persist until the accompanying decline in the market supply of shirts brings shirt prices up to a level at which the remaining firms can receive a normal profit. The crucial point to note is that these adjustments in the business sector are completely appropriate to the assumed changes in consumer tastes. Society—meaning consumers—wants more shoes and fewer shirts, and that is precisely what it is getting as the shoe industry expands and the shirt industry contracts.

But this analysis proceeds on the assumption that resource suppliers are agreeable to these adjustments. Will the price system prompt resource suppliers to reallocate their human and property resources from the shirt to the shoe industry, thereby permitting the output of shoes to expand at the expense of shirt production? The answer is "Yes."

The economic profits which initially follow the increase in demand for shoes will not only provide that industry with the inducement to expand but will also give it the added receipts with which to obtain the resources essential to its growth. Higher shoe prices will permit firms in that industry to pay higher prices for resources, thereby drawing resources from what are now less urgent alternative employments. Willingness and ability to employ more resources in the shoe industry will be communicated back into the resource market through an increase in the demand for resources. Substantially the reverse occurs in the adversely affected shirt industry. The losses which the decline in consumer demand initially entails will cause a decline in the demand for resources in that

industry. Workers and other resources released from the contracting shirt industry can now find employment in the expanding shoe industry. As a matter of fact, the increased demand for resources in the shoe industry will mean higher resource prices in that industry than those being paid in the shirt industry, where declines in resource demand have lowered resource prices. The resulting differential in resource prices will provide the incentive for resource owners to further their self-interests by reallocating their resources from the shirt to the shoe industry. And this, of course, is the precise shift needed to permit the shoe industry to expand and the shirt industry to contract.

The ability of the price system to communicate changes in such basic data as consumer tastes and to elicit appropriate responses from both businesses and resource suppliers is sometimes called the *directing* or *guiding function* of prices. By affecting product prices and profits, changes in consumer tastes direct the expansion of some industries and the contraction of others. These adjustments carry through to the resource market as expanding industries demand more resources and contracting industries demand fewer. The resulting changes in resource prices guide resources from the contracting to the expanding industries. In the absence of a price system, some administrative agency, presumably a governmental planning board, would have to undertake the task of directing business institutions and resources into specific lines of production.

Analysis similar to that outlined above would indicate that the price system would adjust appropriately to similar fundamental changes—for example, to changes in technology and changes in the relative supplies of various resources.

Is the price system conducive to change? Adjusting to given changes is one thing; inducing changes, particularly desirable changes, is something else again. Is the competitive price system congenial to technological improvements and capital accumulation, the interrelated changes which lead to greater productivity and a higher level of material well-being for society? This is not an easy question to answer. We state our reply at this point without stopping for qualifications and modifications (see Chapter 30).

The ideology of pure capitalism, with its emphasis upon the competitive price system, is quite a fertile environment for technological advance. Competition provides the *opportunity* for entrepreneurs to introduce new techniques and new products, unimpeded by the artificial barriers which a noncompetitive environment might entail. The competitive price system also furnishes the *incentive* for technological advance. The introduction of cost-cutting techniques provides the innovating firm with a temporary advantage over its rivals. Lower production costs mean economic profits for the pioneering firm. By passing a part of its cost reduction on to the consumer through a lower product price, the innovating firm can achieve a sizable increase in sales and lucrative economic profits at the expense of rival firms. And remember, because the monetary rewards of the successful introduction of a new technique will accrue to the innovating firm, the price system will be very effective in harnessing individual incentives in the cause of technological advance.

Looking at technological advance from the social point of view, we should note that the innovating firm's economic profits will be a temporary phenomenon. Other firms can also adopt the new cost-reducing technique. Indeed, as we have seen, they will be forced to do so. Why? Because by price cutting, the innovating firm will turn the once-normal profits of its competitors into losses. This is of considerable significance: it is in this fashion that the competitive price system communicates the technological improvements of one firm to all other firms in that industry. Rivals must follow the lead of the most progressive firm or suffer the immediate penalty of losses and the eventual pain of bankruptcy.

We should note that the lower product price which the technological advance permits will cause the innovating industry to expand. This expansion may be the result of existing firms expanding their rates of output or of new firms entering the industry under the lure of the economic profits initially created by

a technological advance. This expansion, that is, the diversion of resources from nonprogressive to progressive industries, is as it should be. Sustained efficiency in the use of scarce resources demands that resources be continually reallocated from industries whose productive techniques are relatively less efficient to those whose techniques are relatively more efficient.

But technological advance typically entails the use of increased amounts of capital goods. Can the price system provide the capital goods upon which technological advance relies? More specifically, can the entrepreneur as an innovator command through the price system the resources necessary to produce the machinery and equipment upon which technological advance depends?

Obviously, he can. If society registers dollar votes for capital goods, the product market and resource market will adjust to these votes by producing capital goods. In other words, the price system acknowledges dollar voting for both consumer and capital goods. Indeed, the relative sizes of these two types of dollar voting determine how a market economy will divide its total output between consumer goods, which satisfy wants directly, and capital goods, which satisfy wants indirectly through the more efficient production of consumer goods.

But who will register votes for capital goods? First, the entrepreneur as a receiver of profit income can be expected to apportion a part of his income to the accumulation of capital goods. By so doing he can achieve an even greater profit income in the future if his innovation proves successful. Furthermore, by paying a rate of interest, entrepreneurs can borrow portions of the incomes of other households and use these borrowed funds in casting dollar votes for the production of more capital goods.

In practice, the process of technological advance and capital accumulation is much more complex than envisioned here (see Chapter 12). The important point for present purposes is that the market economy provides the opportunity and incentive for technological advance and the means for providing the capital goods which such advance typically presumes.

Competition, control, and the "invisible hand"

Though the price system is the organizing mechanism of pure capitalism, it is essential to recognize the role of competition as the mechanism of control in such an economy. The market mechanism of supply and demand communicates the wants of consumers (society) to businesses and through businesses to resource suppliers. It is competition, however, which forces businesses and resource suppliers to make appropriate responses. To illustrate: The impact of an increase in consumer demand for some product will raise that good's price above the wage, rent, interest, and normal profit costs of production. The resulting economic profits in effect are a signal to producers that society wants more of the product. It is competition—in particular, the ability of new firms to enter the industry—that simultaneously brings an expansion of output and a lowering of price back to a level just consistent with production costs. However, if the industry was not competitive, but dominated by, say, one huge firm which was able to prohibit the entry of potential competitors, that firm could enjoy economic profits by preventing the expansion of the industry.

But competition does more than guarantee responses appropriate to the wishes of society. It is competition which forces firms to adopt the most efficient productive techniques. In a competitive market, the failure of some firms to use the least costly production technique means their eventual elimination by other competing firms who do employ the most efficient methods of production. Finally, we have seen that competition provides an environment conducive to technological advance.

A very remarkable aspect of the operation and the adjustments of a competitive price system is that a curious and important identity is involved—the identity of private and social interests. That is, firms and resource suppliers, seeking to further their own self-interest and operating within the framework of a highly competitive market system, will simultaneously, as though guided by an "invisible hand," [1]

[1] Adam Smith, *The Wealth of Nations* (New York: Modern Library, Inc., originally published in 1776), p. 423.

promote the public or social interest. For example, we have seen that given a competitive environment, business firms use the least costly combination of resources in producing a given output because it is in their self-interest to do so. To act otherwise would be to forgo profits or even to risk bankruptcy over a period of time. But at the same time it is obviously also in the social interest to use scarce resources in the least costly, that is, most efficient, manner. To do otherwise would be to produce a given output at a greater cost or sacrifice of alternative goods than is really necessary. Furthermore, in our more-shoes–fewer-shirts illustration, it is self-interest, awakened and guided by the competitive price system, which induces the very responses appropriate to the assumed change in society's wants. Businesses seeking to make higher profits and to avoid losses, on the one hand, and resource suppliers pursuing greater monetary rewards, on the other, negotiate the very changes in the allocation of resources and therefore the composition of output which society now demands. The force of competition, in other words, controls or guides the self-interest motive in such a way that it automatically, and quite unintentionally, furthers the best interests of society.

AN EVALUATION OF THE PRICE SYSTEM

Is the price system the best means of deciding how total output is to be determined, how production of that output should be organized, and how total output should be distributed? This is a complex question; any complete answer necessarily leaps the boundary of facts and enters the realm of values. This means there is no scientific answer to the query. The very fact that there exist many competing ways of allocating scarce resources is ample evidence of disagreement as to the effectiveness of the price system.

The case for the price system

1. The basic economic argument for the price system is that it leads to an efficient allocation of resources. The competitive price system, it is argued, guides resources into the production of those goods and services most wanted by society. It forces the use of the most efficient techniques in organizing resources for production, and it is conducive to the development and adoption of new and more efficient production techniques. In short, proponents of the price system argue that the "invisible hand" will in effect harness self-interest so as to provide society with the greatest output of wanted goods from its available resources. This, then, suggests the maximum economic efficiency.

2. The major noneconomic argument for the price system is its great emphasis upon personal freedom. The price system permits—indeed, it thrives upon—freedom of enterprise and choice. Entrepreneurs and workers are not herded from industry to industry to meet the production targets established by some omnipotent governmental agency. On the contrary, they are free to further their own self-interests, subject, of course, to the rewards and penalties imposed by the price system itself.

The case against the price system

The case against the price system is somewhat more complex. Critics of the market economy base their position on the following points:

1. They argue that capitalistic ideology is conducive to the demise of its main controlling mechanism—competition. The alleged weakening of competition as a control mechanism comes from two basic sources.

On the one hand, though desirable from the social point of view, competition is most irksome to the individual producer subject to its rigors. It is allegedly inherent in the free, individualistic environment of the capitalistic system that the profit-seeking entrepreneur will attempt to break free of the restraining force of competition in trying to better his position. Combination, conspiracy, cutthroat competition, and sheer productive efficiency are all means to the end of reducing competition and escaping its regulatory powers.

On the other hand, the very technological advance which the price system fosters has contributed to the decline of competition. Modern technology typically

requires (*a*) the use of extremely large quantities of real capital, (*b*) large markets, (*c*) a complex, centralized, and closely integrated management, and (*d*) large and reliable sources of raw materials. Such an operation implies the need for producers who are large-scale not only in the absolute sense but also in relation to the size of the market. In other words, the achievement of maximum productive efficiency through the employment of the best available technology often requires the existence of a small number of large firms rather than a large number of small ones.

To the degree that competition declines, the price system will be weakened as a mechanism for efficiently allocating resources. Producers and resource suppliers will be less subject to the will of consumers; the sovereignty of producers and resource suppliers will then challenge and weaken the sovereignty of consumers. The "invisible hand" identity of private and social interest will begin to lose its grip.

2. Critics also challenge the assertion that the price system provides the goods most wanted by society. This criticism has several roots. First, to the extent that a weakening of competition, as discussed above, lessens consumer sovereignty, the price system becomes less proficient in allocating resources in precise accord with the wishes of consumers.

Second, critical socialists contend that the price system allows the more efficient, or more cunning, entrepreneurs to accumulate vast amounts of property resources, the accumulation process being extended through time by the right to bequeath. This, in addition to differences in the amount and quality of human resources supplied by various households, causes a highly unequal distribution of money incomes in a market economy. The result is that families differ greatly in their ability to express their wants in the market. The wealthy have more dollar votes than the poor. Hence, it is concluded that the price system allocates resources to the production of frivolous luxury goods for the rich at the expense of the output of necessities for the poor. A country that[2]

> . . . spends money on champagne before it has provided milk for its babies is a badly managed, silly, vain, stupid, ignorant nation. . . . The only way in which such a nation can make itself wealthy and prosperous is by good housekeeping: that is by providing for its wants in order of their importance, and allowing no money to be wasted on whims and luxuries until the necessities have been thoroughly served.

In the third place, critics point out that the price system sometimes fails to register all the costs and benefits associated with the production of certain goods and services. That is, consumer demand only embodies the satisfactions which accrue to individual consumers who purchase goods and services; it does not reflect the fact that the purchase of such services as polio shots and chest x-rays yields widespread benefits or satisfactions to the community (society) as a whole. Similarly, the supply decisions of producers hinge upon the costs which they must bear and do not reflect certain costs associated with production which might accrue to society as a whole. The serious environmental pollution which has characterized the production of many industries illustrates such costs. The point is this: Where demand and supply do not accurately reflect all the benefits and all the costs of production, the price system cannot be expected to bring about an allocation of resources which best satisfies the wants of society.

A final argument is this: The price system tabulates only individual wants. There are many wants involving goods and services which cannot be financed by individuals as such. For example, such goods and services as education, highways, and national defense cannot be purchased in desired amounts by households on an individual basis. They can only be consumed economically on a social, or collective, basis. The price system, it is argued, is incapable of registering such social, or collective, wants.

3. The price system has also been criticized for its failure to adjust rapidly to drastic changes in society's production objectives. There is allegedly a persistent time lag between society's production targets and the actual pattern of resource allocation provided by the price system. Even in a highly competitive market economy, the occupational and geographic mobility

[2]George Bernard Shaw, *The Intelligent Woman's Guide to Socialism and Capitalism* (New York: Brentano's, Inc., 1928), pp. 50–55. Used by permission of the Public Trustee and the Society of Authors.

of human resources will be far from perfect. Laborers are hesitant to sever social ties and move to a strange community to take a new job. Such a move may also be costly, particularly if the worker must equip himself with new skills. And property resources are usually reallocated through the price system with even less rapidity. In short, the tardy adjustment of the pattern of resource use to changes in the structure of demand is a persistent source of inefficiency.

4. Finally, the price system is widely recognized as an imperfect mechanism for providing the continuous full employment of the economy's resources. The problem of unemployment will be analyzed in detail in Part 2.

Which of these two positions is correct? To a degree both are. The several criticisms of the market economy are reasonably accurate and certainly too serious to ignore. On the other hand, we cannot judge an issue by the number of arguments pro and con. The basic economic argument for the price system—that it tends to provide an efficient allocation of resources—is not easily undermined. In practice, the price system is—or at least can be—reasonably efficient.

Relevance, realism, and the price system

Does the price system of American capitalism function in the same fashion as the price system discussed in this chapter? In principle, yes; in detail, no. Our discussion of the price system provides us with a working model—a first approximation—of the actual price system of American capitalism. Our analysis presents a much-simplified, yet useful, picture of the real thing.

Specifically, there are two basic differences between the price system as pictured in this chapter and the actual price system of American capitalism:

1. In many product and resource markets, competition clearly has been supplanted by a few giant business corporations and huge labor unions. Competition is simply not as vigorous in practice as our discussion of the price system presumed. This means that the decisions of businesses and resource suppliers are less than perfectly synchronized with those of consumers and that changes in the production goals of society are less precisely communicated throughout the economy. Giant business and labor groups in American capitalism have the power to resist the dictates of consumer sovereignty and, as a matter of fact, will usually find it personally advantageous to do so.

2. Another major difference between our model price system and the market system of American capitalism lies in the economic role of government in the latter. In contrast with the passive, limited government envisioned in the ideology of pure capitalism, the government of American capitalism is an active and integral component of the economy. In particular, the economy of the United States has taken cognizance of the elements of truth which permeate the noted criticisms of the price system. Through government, society has taken steps to correct these shortcomings. Hence, government pursues policies designed not only to preserve and bolster competition, but also to adjust certain inequities fostered by the price system, to speed on occasion the reallocation of resources, and to help maintain full employment. It is with these and related economic functions of government that the ensuing chapter is concerned.

Is our analysis of the price system realistic? Does it provide a workable description of the price system of American capitalism? One scholar has recently provided a meaningful reply to these questions:[3]

> For all the new quality of twentieth-century industrial society, the great principles of self-interest and competition, however watered down or hedged about, still provide basic rules of behavior which no economic organization can afford to disregard entirely . . . the laws of the market can be discerned . . . if we look beneath the surface.

SUMMARY

1. In a market economy, the interacting decisions of competing buyers and sellers will determine a system of product and resource prices at any given point in time.

[3]Robert L. Heilbroner, *The Worldly Philosophers,* 3d ed. (New York: Simon & Schuster, Inc., 1967), pp. 53–54.

2. The relative scarcity of economic resources makes the operation of any economy a matter of choosing between alternatives. At any point in time, these choices depend upon the relative scarcity of resources and products. Over time, the degree to which these choices are altered in a market economy as product and resource prices change depends upon the willingness and ability of consumers to make substitutions among products and the willingness and ability of producers to make substitutions among resources. Substitutability tends to relieve particular scarcities of resources and products.

3. Those products whose production and sale yield total receipts sufficient to cover all costs, including a normal profit, will be produced. Those whose production will not yield a normal profit will not be produced.

4. Economic profits designate an industry as prosperous and signal its expansion. Losses mean an industry is unprosperous and result in a contraction of that industry. Industrial expansion and contraction are self-limiting processes. As expansion increases market supply relative to market demand, the price of a product falls to the point where all economic profits disappear. As contraction decreases market supply relative to market demand, the resulting increase in product price eliminates losses and makes the industry normally profitable once again.

5. Consumer sovereignty dominates a competitive market economy. The penalty of losses and lure of profits force both businesses and resource suppliers to channel their efforts in accordance with the wants of consumers.

6. Competition forces firms to use the least costly and therefore the most economically efficient productive techniques.

7. The price system plays a dual role in distributing total output among individual households. The prices commanded by the quantities and types of resources supplied by each household will determine the number of dollar claims against the economy's output each household receives. Given consumer tastes, product prices are of fundamental importance in determining consumer expenditure patterns. Within the limits of each household's money income, consumer preferences and the relative prices of products determine the distribution of total output.

8. The competitive price system can communicate changes in consumer tastes to resource suppliers and entrepreneurs, thereby prompting appropriate adjustments in the allocation of the economy's resources. The competitive price system also provides an environment conducive to technological advance and capital accumulation.

9. Competition, the primary mechanism of control in the market economy, will foster an identity of private and social interests; as though directed by an "invisible hand," competition harnesses the self-interest motives of businesses and resource suppliers so as to simultaneously further the social interest.

10. The basic virtue of the price system is its continuing emphasis upon efficiency. It produces what consumers want through the use of the most efficient techniques. Operation and adjustments of the price system are automatic in the sense that they are the result of individual, decentralized decisions, not the centralized decisions of government.

11. Criticisms of the price system are several: *a.* The controlling mechanism, competition, tends to weaken over time; *b.* inherent income inequalities, inability to register collective wants, and the exclusion of certain costs and satisfactions from supply and demand prevent the price system from producing that collection of goods most wanted by society; *c.* the price system reallocates resources sluggishly and imperfectly to changes in the structure of demand; *d.* the competitive price system does not guarantee continued full employment.

12. The price system of American capitalism differs from the competitive price system in that the former is characterized by *a.* giant corporations and unions in certain product and resource markets and *b.* government intervention in the economy to correct the major defects of the price system. Yet the competitive price system does provide a working model whereby we can understand the price system of American capitalism.

QUESTIONS AND STUDY SUGGESTIONS

1. Describe in detail how the price system answers the Five Fundamental Questions.

2. Why must economic choices be made? How do scarcity and substitutability influence the rendering of economic choices? Be specific.

3. "The capitalistic system is a profit and loss economy." Carefully analyze and explain the significance of this statement.

4. Define and explain the significance of "dollar voting," "consumer sovereignty," and the "invisible hand."

5. What is the directing or guiding function of the competitive price system? Contrast the guiding function with the rationing function discussed in Chapter 4.

6. "Production methods which are inferior in the engineering sense may be the most efficient methods in the economic sense." Explain.

7. Evaluate and explain the following statements:

a. "The most important feature of capitalism is the absence of a central economic plan."

b. "Competition is the indispensable disciplinarian of the market economy."

8. Explain fully the meaning and implications of the following quotation:[4]

> The beautiful consequence of the market is that it is its own guardian. If output prices or certain kinds of remuneration stray away from their socially ordained levels, forces are set into motion to bring them back to the fold. It is a curious paradox which thus ensues: the market, which is the acme of individual economic freedom, is the strictest taskmaster of all. One may appeal the ruling of a planning board or win the dispensation of a minister; but there is no appeal, no dispensation, from the anonymous pressures of the market mechanism. Economic freedom is thus more illusory than at first appears. One can do as one pleases in the market. But if one pleases to do what the market disapproves, the price of individual freedom is economic ruination.

[4] Ibid., p. 42.

9. Assume that a business firm finds that its profits will be at a maximum when it produces $40 worth of product A. Suppose also that each of the three techniques shown in the following table will produce the desired output.

Resource	Technique No. 1	Technique No. 2	Technique No. 3	Price per unit of resource
Labor	5	2	3	$3
Land	2	4	2	4
Capital	2	4	5	2
Entrepreneurial ability	4	2	4	2

a. Given the resource prices shown above, which technique will the firm choose? Why?

b. Assume now that a new technique, technique No. 4, is developed. It entails the use of 2 units of labor, 2 of land, 6 of capital, and 3 of entrepreneurial ability. Given the resource prices in the table, will the firm adopt the new technique? Explain your answer.

c. Suppose now that the price of labor falls to $1.50 per unit, all other resource prices being unchanged. What technique will the producer now choose? Explain.

d. "The price system causes the economy to conserve most in the use of those resources which are particularly scarce in supply. Resources which are scarcest relative to the demand for them have the highest prices. As a result, producers use these resources as sparingly as is possible." Evaluate this statement. Does your answer to question 9*c* bear out this contention? Explain.

10. Interpret and explain the following quotation in terms of Table 5·1:[5]

> Soviet industrialization has taken place against the background of an abundance of manpower. . . . It was therefore economically sensible for them to use labor lavishly, substituting it whenever possible for capital goods, and bringing in more workers whenever it was possible by doing so to squeeze a bit more output out of existing enterprises. The result of such a policy was

[5] Robert W. Campbell, "Problems of United States–Soviet Economic Comparisons," in Joint Economic Committee, *Comparisons of the United States and Soviet Economies* (Washington: Government Printing Office, 1960), p. 26.

to make output per worker low, but it was still the correct thing to do in the light of the abundance of labor.

Output per Soviet worker is considerably lower than output per American worker. Does this necessarily mean that the Soviet economy is inefficient and wasteful as compared to the United States economy? Explain.

11. What are the major criticisms of the price system? Carefully evaluate these criticisms.

SELECTED REFERENCES

Economic Issues, 4th ed., reading 7.

Boulding, Kenneth E.: *Economic Analysis: Microeconomics,* 4th ed. (New York: Harper & Row, Publishers, Incorporated, 1966), chap. 6.

Heilbroner, Robert L.: *The Worldly Philosophers,* 3d ed. (New York: Simon & Schuster, Inc., 1967), chap. 3.

Klaasen, Adrian (ed.): *The Invisible Hand* (Chicago: Henry Regnery Company,1965).

Leeman, Wayne A. (ed.): *Capitalism, Market Socialism, and Central Planning* (Boston: Houghton Mifflin Company, 1963), chaps. 1, 2, 9–11.

6

MIXED CAPITALISM AND THE ECONOMIC FUNCTIONS OF GOVERNMENT

We now begin the move from our abstract working model of pure capitalism to a discussion of American capitalism. In so doing we inject a significant dose of reality into our analysis.

All real-life economies are "mixed"; government and the price system share the function of answering the Five Fundamental Questions. Yet the various economies of the world differ drastically in the particular blend of government direction and market direction which they embody (see Table 2·3). The economy of Soviet Russia, the topic of the final chapter of this book, leans heavily toward a centrally planned economy. American capitalism, on the other hand, is predominantly a market economy. Yet the economic functions of government—Federal, state, and local—are of considerable significance. In American capitalism a number of strategic economic decisions are rendered, not by individuals as such, but collectively through government. A rough indicator of the relative importance of the market and government in American capitalism is the fact that currently about four-fifths of the total output of the economy is provided by the market system, the remaining one-fifth being produced under the sponsorship of government. In short, the economy of the United States can be accurately described as *mixed capitalism.* Our economy holds *generally* to the capitalist ideology outlined in Chapter 3 and relies primarily upon the price system, the rudiments and functioning of which were outlined in Chapters 4 and 5. Government, however, assists and modifies the functioning of the price system in a variety of significant ways.

ECONOMIC FUNCTIONS OF GOVERNMENT

The economic functions of government are many, and they are varied. As a matter of fact, the economic role of government is so broad in scope that it is virtually impossible to establish an all-inclusive list of its economic functions. We shall employ the following breakdown of government's economic activities as a pattern for our discussion, recognizing that some overlapping is unavoidable.

First, some of the economic functions of government are designed to strengthen and facilitate the operation of the price system. The two major activities of government in this area are

1. Providing the legal foundation and a social environment conducive to the effective operation of the price system
2. Maintaining competition

Through a second group of functions, government supplements and modifies the operation of the price system. There are three major functions of government here. They involve:

3. The redistributing of income and wealth
4. Adjusting the allocation of resources so as to alter the composition of the national output
5. Stabilizing the economy, that is, controlling unemployment and inflation caused by the business cycle and promoting economic growth

While this fivefold breakdown of government's functions is a useful way of analyzing the economic role of government, we shall find that most government activities and policies have *some* impact in all these areas. For example, a program to redistribute income to the poor affects the allocation of resources to the extent that the poor buy somewhat different goods and services than do wealthier members of society. A decline in, say, government military spending for the purpose of lessening inflationary pressures also tends to reallocate resources from public to private uses.

Let us briefly consider the first two functions of government and then analyze the redistributive, allocative, and stabilization roles of government in more detail.

LEGAL AND SOCIAL FRAMEWORK FOR THE PRICE SYSTEM

Government assumes the task of providing the legal framework and certain basic services prerequisite to the effective operation of a market economy. The necessary legal framework involves such things as providing for the legal status of business enterprises, defining the rights of private ownership, and providing for the enforcement of contracts. Government also establishes legal "rules of the game" to govern the relationships of businesses, resource suppliers, and consumers with one another. Through legislation, government is enabled to referee economic relationships, detect foul play, and exercise authority in imposing appropriate penalties. The basic services provided by government include the use of police powers to maintain internal order, provision of a system of standards for measuring the weight and quality of products, and establishment of a monetary system to facilitate the exchange of goods and services.

The Pure Food and Drug Act of 1906 and its various amendments provide an excellent example of how government has strengthened the operation of the price system. This act sets rules of conduct to govern producers in their relationships with consumers. It prohibits the sale of adulterated and misbranded foods and drugs, requires the net weights of products to be specified on their containers, establishes quality standards which must be stated on the labels of canned foods, and prohibits deceptive claims on patent-medicine labels. These measures all prevent fraudulent activities on the part of producers and, simultaneously, increase the public's confidence in the integrity of the price system. In later chapters we shall discuss similar legislation pertaining to labor-management relations and the relations of business firms to one another.

It is worth noting that resource allocation will be altered and, in general, improved upon by this type of governmental activity. Supplying a medium of exchange, ensuring the quality of products, defining ownership rights, and enforcing contracts tend to increase the volume of exchange. This widens markets and permits greater specialization in the use of both property and human resources. Such specialization, we saw in Chapter 3, means a more efficient allocation of resources.

MAINTAINING COMPETITION

Competition is the basic regulatory mechanism in a capitalistic economy. It is the force which subjects producers and resource suppliers to the dictates of

buyer or consumer sovereignty. With competition it is the supply and demand decisions of *many* sellers and buyers which determine market prices. This means that individual producers and resource suppliers can only adjust to the wishes of buyers as tabulated and communicated by the price system. Profits and survival await the competitive producers who obey the price system; losses and eventual bankruptcy are the lot of those who deviate from it. With competition, buyers are the boss, the market is their agent, and businesses their servant.

The growth of monopoly drastically alters this situation. What is monopoly? Broadly defined, it is the situation wherein the number of sellers becomes small enough for each seller to influence total supply and therefore the price of the commodity being sold. What is its significance? Simply this: When monopoly supplants competition, sellers can influence, or "rig," the market in terms of their own self-interests. Through their ability to influence total supply, monopolists can create artificial shortages of products and thereby enjoy higher prices and, very frequently, persistent economic profits. This is obviously in direct conflict with the interests of consumers. Monopolists are not regulated by the will of society as competitive sellers are. Producer sovereignty supplants consumer sovereignty to the degree that monopoly supplants competition. The result is that resources are allocated in terms of the profit-seeking interests of monopolistic sellers rather than in terms of the wants of society as a whole. In short, monopoly tends to cause a misallocation of economic resources.

In the United States the government has controlled monopoly primarily in two ways. First, in the case of "natural monopolies"—that is, in industries wherein technological and economic realities rule out the possibility of competitive markets—the government has created public commissions to regulate prices and service standards. Transportation, communications, and electric and other utilities are illustrations of regulated industries. At local levels of government, public ownership of electric and water utilities is quite common. But, secondly, in the vast majority of markets efficient production can be attained with a high degree of competition. The Federal government has therefore enacted a series of antimonopoly or antitrust laws, beginning with the Sherman Act of 1890, for the purpose of maintaining and strengthening competition as an effective regulator of business behavior. The regulatory commissions and antitrust will be examined in detail in Chapter 35.

Even if the legal foundation of capitalistic institutions is assured and competition is maintained, there will still be a need for certain additional economic functions on the part of government. *The market economy at its best has certain biases and shortcomings which compel government to supplement and modify its operation.*

REDISTRIBUTION OF INCOME

The price system is an impersonal mechanism, and the distribution of income to which it gives rise may entail more inequality than society desires. The market system yields very large incomes to those whose labor, by virtue of inherent ability and acquired education and skills, commands high wages. Similarly, those who possess valuable capital and land receive large property incomes. But others in our society have less ability and have received modest amounts of education and training. And these same people typically have accumulated or inherited no property resources. Hence, their incomes are very low. Furthermore, many of the aged, the physically and mentally handicapped, and widows with dependent children earn only very small incomes or, like the unemployed, no incomes at all through the price system. In short, the price system entails considerable inequality in the distribution of money income and therefore in the distribution of total output among individual households. Poverty amidst overall plenty in American capitalism has become a major economic and political issue.

Government has assumed the responsibility of ameliorating income inequality in our society. This responsibility is reflected in a variety of policies and programs. *Public assistance programs* provide emergency relief to the destitute, aid to the depen-

dent and handicapped, unemployment compensation to the unemployed. These programs bring income to households which would otherwise have little or none. They achieve this goal by altering the income distribution which the price system provides. Our social security and Medicare programs provide financial support for the retired and aged sick. Other programs involve *direct market intervention,* in which the government alters income distribution by modifying the prices established by the forces of supply and demand. Price supports for farmers and minimum-wage legislation both involve government price fixing designed to aid those whose incomes would otherwise be meager. Finally, the Federal *income tax* is designed to take a greater proportion of the incomes of the rich than of the poor and therefore have a kind of Robin Hood effect upon income distribution. The currently debated *negative income tax* proposal holds that those individuals and families whose incomes fall below specified "poverty levels" should receive payments *from* the government sufficient to bring them up to the poverty line. Despite these and other programs designed to lessen income inequality, we will find in Chapter 38 that there is considerable debate about whether government has sufficiently reduced income inequality and provided a minimum standard of living for all its citizenry.

REALLOCATION OF RESOURCES

The price system of pure capitalism operates in response to decisions made by *individual* consumers and *individual* business firms. In deciding what is to be produced and not produced, the price system reacts to the summation of individual wants and satisfactions. And the specific amounts of various goods produced will depend upon the costs which individual firms must bear in acquiring the resources necessary for production.

Now, as we saw in Chapter 5, competitive markets result in an efficient allocation of resources. For example, in Figure 6·1*a* the resulting equilibrium equates the willingness of consumers to pay for a good (as reflected in the demand curve) and the cost of producing the good (as reflected in the supply curve). That is, at equilibrium the extra or marginal *benefit* (satisfaction) derived from consuming the last unit of output is just equal to the extra or marginal *cost* of producing that last unit. To produce some output short of the equilibrium output Q_e would mean that society is forgoing some output of product X, the benefits from which are worth more than their cost. That is, the production of Q_1 units of output would involve an underallocation of resources to

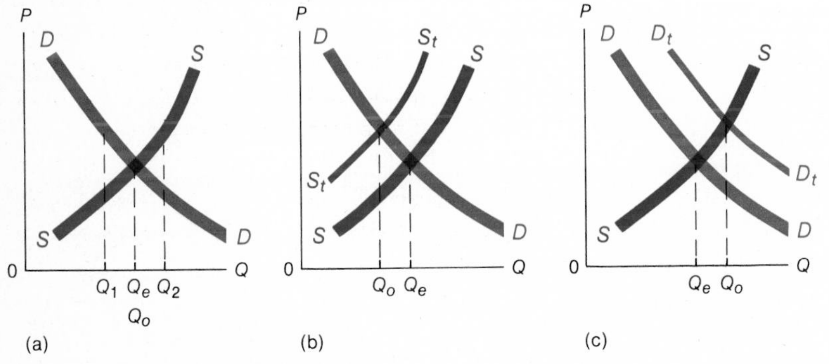

FIGURE 6·1 SPILLOVERS AND THE ALLOCATION OF RESOURCES.

Without spillovers (*a*) the equilibrium output Q_e is also the most efficient, or optimal, output Q_o. But with spillover costs (*b*) resources are overallocated to production; that is, the equilibrium output exceeds the optimum output. Conversely, spillover benefits (*c*) cause an underallocation of resources in that the optimum output exceeds the equilibrium output.

product X; there is a net gain to society in producing all units of X between Q_1 and Q_e. This net gain is obviously forgone if production involves only Q_1 units of output. Similarly, the production of each unit of output in excess of Q_e—for example, all the units between Q_e and Q_2—entails extra or marginal costs in excess of extra or marginal benefits. We know this from the fact that the supply curve (reflecting costs) lies above the demand curve (reflecting benefits) for units in excess of Q_e. The production of units in excess of Q_e would impose net costs upon society. Here the problem is clearly an overallocation of resources to the production of X. The basic point is that in a competitive market system production will take place at that output where the amount of resources allocated to X is "just right" or, more technically put, efficient or optimum. At Q_e there is neither an underallocation (Q_1) or an overallocation (Q_2) to the production of X. It follows that if all markets are competitive an efficient or optimum allocation of resources among all alternative uses will result. Hence, we equate the equilibrium output (Q_e) in Figure 6·1*a* with the optimum output (Q_o).

Spillovers or externalities

But this analysis and its conclusion that competitive markets automatically bring about allocative efficiency rest upon the hidden assumption that all the benefits and costs associated with the production and consumption of each product are fully reflected in the market demand and supply curves. Stated differently, it is assumed that there are no *spillovers* or *externalities* associated with the production or consumption of any good or service. A *spillover*[1] occurs when some of the benefits or costs associated with the production or consumption of a good spill over to third parties, that is, to parties other than the immediate buyer or seller. Spillovers are also termed externalities because they are benefits and costs accruing to some individual or group external to the market transaction.

[1]Spillovers may go by other names—for example, external economies and diseconomies, neighborhood effects, and social benefits and costs.

Spillover costs When the production or consumption of a commodity inflicts costs upon some third party without compensation, there exists a spillover cost. The most obvious examples of spillover or social costs involve environmental pollution. When a chemical manufacturer or meat-packing plant dumps its wastes into a lake or river, the result is that swimmers, fishermen, and boaters—not to mention communities which seek a useable water supply—suffer spillover costs. When a petroleum refinery pollutes the air with smoke or a paint factory creates onerous odors, the community bears spillover costs for which it is not compensated.

How do spillover or social costs affect the allocation of resources? Figure 6·1*b* tells the story. When spillover costs occur—when producers shift some of their costs onto the community—their production costs are lower than would otherwise be the case. That is, the supply curve does not include or "capture" all the costs which can be legitimately associated with the production of the good. Hence, the producer's supply curve, *SS,* understates the total costs of production and therefore lies below the supply curve which would include all costs, S_tS_t. That is, S_tS_t includes the production costs which the polluting firm must bear *plus* the additional costs it would incur if it had properly disposed of its wastes. It is obvious that with S_tS_t the firm would find it profitable to produce output Q_o. This is the optimum output for reasons previously explained. But by polluting, that is, by creating spillover costs, the firm enjoys lower costs and the supply curve *SS*. The result is that the equilibrium output Q_e is larger than the optimum output Q_o. In short, resources are overallocated to the production of the commodity; each unit of output between Q_o and Q_e entails costs (including spillover costs) in excess of benefits; S_tS_t lies above *DD* for all units of output between Q_o and Q_e. Output Q_e fulfills the interest of producers in maximizing profits, but it exceeds output Q_o, which fulfills society's interest in allocating resources efficiently.

Spillover benefits But spillovers also take the form of benefits. The production or consumption of certain

goods and services may confer social or spillover benefits on third parties or the community at large for which payment or compensation is not required. For example, chest x-rays and polio immunization shots result in direct benefits to the immediate consumer. But an early diagnosis of tuberculosis and the prevention of a contagious disease yield widespread and substantial spillover benefits to the entire community. Education is another standard example of spillover benefits. Education entails benefits to individual consumers: "more educated" people generally achieve higher incomes than do "less educated" people. But education also confers sizable benefits upon society; for example, the economy as a whole benefits from a more versatile and more productive labor force, on the one hand, and smaller outlays in the areas of crime prevention, law enforcement, and welfare programs, on the other.

Figure 6•1*c* shows the impact of spillover benefits upon resource allocation. The existence of spillover benefits simply means that the market demand curve, which reflects only private benefits, understates total benefits. The market demand curve fails to capture all the benefits associated with the provision and consumption of goods and services which entail spillover benefits. Thus *DD* in Figure 6•1*c* indicates the benefits which private individuals derive from education; D_tD_t is drawn to include these private benefits *plus* the additional spillover benefits accruing to society at large. Thus, while market demand *DD* and supply *SS* would yield an educational output of Q_e, this output will be less than the optimum output Q_o. That is, if the market took all benefits—private and spillover or social—into account, the output of education would be greater than the market would provide. Comparing D_tD_t and *SS,* we find that for all units of output between Q_e and Q_o the extra or marginal benefits shown by the demand curve exceed the extra or marginal costs embodied in the supply curve. Hence, there is a net benefit to society in having this additional output.

Our discussion of spillover costs and benefits yields two generalizations—two instances of "market failure":

1. When spillover costs are significant, the market will overallocate resources to the production of that good or service. The equilibrium output will exceed that output which entails allocative efficiency.

2. When spillover benefits are important, the market will underallocate resources to that commodity. The equilibrium output will fall short of the optimum output.

Corrective government policy What actions might government take to correct the overallocations and underallocations of resources associated with spillover costs and benefits? In both instances government attempts to "internalize" the external costs and benefits; that is, government follows certain policies designed to cause the market to take into account spillover costs and benefits.

Consider, first, the case of spillover costs. Two basic courses of action are common: Corrective legislation and special taxes.

1. Looking at our examples of air and water pollution, the most direct action is simply to pass *legislation* against it. Cities may pass ordinances which prohibit or control pollution. Such legislation forces potential polluters to bear the costs of more properly disposing of industrial wastes; for example, firms must buy and install smoke-abatement equipment or facilities to purify water which has been contaminated by manufacturing processes. Such action forces potential offenders, under the threat of legal action, to bear *all* the costs associated with their production. In short, legislation can shift the supply curve *SS* toward S_tS_t in Figure 6•1*b,* tending to bring the equilibrium and optimum outputs into equality.

2. A second and less direct action is for government to levy a *special tax* which approximates the spillover costs per unit of output. In effect, through this tax government attempts to shove back onto the offending firm those external or spillover costs which private industry would otherwise avoid. With the added tax costs we again find that producers will have to get a higher price at each possible level of output. This means a decline in supply relative to demand. It is profitable for firms to produce smaller outputs, and resources are freed for alternative uses. The net result will be an improved allocation of resources—an

allocation more consistent with the *total* costs of production. By again shifting the *SS* curve toward S_tS_t, the existing overallocation of resources to this product will be corrected; Q_e will move toward Q_o.

What policies are appropriate for the case of spillover benefits? In the first place, assuming that the spillover or social benefits are not inordinately large when compared with the benefits received by individual purchasers, government can encourage the production of such goods and services by subsidizing their output. Subsidies are simply special taxes in reverse; taxes impose an extra cost on producers, while subsidies provide extra revenue. A unit of government may simply provide an outright bounty to firms for each unit of output they produce. The effect is to internalize the spillover benefits by shifting the *DD* curve of Figure 6·1*c* toward D_tD_t, bringing the equilibrium output into accord with the optimum output. Public subsidization of mass immunization programs and public health clinics are cases in point.

A second policy option arises if spillover benefits are extremely large: Government may simply choose to finance or, in the extreme, own and operate such industries. This option leads us into a discussion of social goods and services.

Social goods and services

There are certain types of goods and services which are produced in grossly insufficient amounts, or possibly not at all, in an economy that relies entirely upon the price system in answering the Five Fundamental Questions. Such products are called *social* or *collective goods.* If society is to obtain social goods in desired amounts, their production must be sponsored, or directly carried on, by government. It is important at the outset to contrast social goods with the *individual,* or *private,* goods which are produced by private enterprises through the price system.

Private goods and social goods The bulk of the goods and services which we consume—for example, loaves of bread, shoes, Fords, transistor radios, suits, and oranges—are private goods. These goods have the following basic characteristics:

1. They are *divisible.* Private goods can be produced in units sufficiently small for individual households to purchase them out of their personal incomes.
2. The satisfactions or benefits from the consumption of private goods are limited almost exclusively to the individual who purchases them; that is, spillover benefits are nonexistent or of modest size. Stated differently, in the case of private goods the *exclusion principle* applies: those who are not willing and able to purchase the good or service through the market are effectively excluded from the benefits or satisfactions such commodities confer. In sum, goods having these two characteristics—divisibility and the exclusion of nonpurchasers from benefits—are called private goods and can be provided in optimum amounts by competitive industries.

But in fact there are certain important goods and services which have contrary characteristics. Social goods and services—national defense, highways, education, police and fire protection, and so forth—differ from private goods and services in one or both of the following ways:

1. Social goods are *indivisible.* They come in such large units that they cannot be readily purchased by individual households or, therefore, profitably produced through the initiative of private industry.
2. Social goods entail large and widespread spillover benefits. Indeed, social goods are in a sense the extreme case of goods which involve social benefits; the benefits from social goods are virtually all spillover benefits. Put differently, the exclusion principle cannot be readily applied to social goods. Once social goods are produced, the associated benefits are available to all; no one can be excluded from those benefits. Because of this fact, private firms will have no incentive to produce such goods. The self-interested individual will not voluntarily pay for a good or service, knowing that he will get the same benefit from the good whether he pays or not. For instance, the benefits from national defense, a flood-control or insect-abatement program, and the provision of police and fire protection or a judiciary system accrue to all who live in the nation or region where the service is rendered. These benefits cannot be effectively withheld; there is no mechanism, com-

parable with the market in the case of private goods, to exclude some particular individuals or groups from the benefits social goods provide.

The inapplicability of the exclusion principle of the market makes it necessary that the production of social goods be sponsored, and sometimes directly undertaken, by government. This production is generally financed through taxes—compulsory levies—imposed upon society or regional beneficiaries as a whole. It is the inapplicability of the exclusion principle that makes tax finance necessary; consumers will ordinarily not make voluntary payments for goods and services whose benefits cannot be denied to them even if they do not help pay for them.

Social goods are thus purchased through the government on the basis of group, or collective, choices in contrast to private goods, which are purchased from private enterprises on the basis of individual choices. More specifically, the types and quantities of the various social goods produced are determined in a democracy by political means, that is, by voting. The quantities of the various social goods consumed are a matter of public policy.[2] These group decisions, made in the political arena, supplement the individual choices of households and businesses in answering the Five Fundamental Questions.

The obvious goal of government in supplying social goods and services is to reallocate resources. Social goods have characteristics which virtually preclude their production by private industry through the price system. Because social goods and services are recognized by society as being a desirable and essential segment of the economy's total output, it is safe to conclude that the price system, by virtue of its failure to provide sufficient resources for their production, misallocates economic resources. A basic economic function of government is the correction of this misallocation. Government must reflect and render effective the group wants of society which by their very nature are incapable of fulfillment through the price system as such.

War and defense goods are perhaps the most outstanding example of social goods. Given the present state of international affairs, no one, short of a pacifist, would question the desirability of assigning *some* portion of the economy's resources for the production of those goods and services necessary for its defense. The goods and services involved come in tremendously large and extremely expensive units. Each modern aircraft, missile, and atomic submarine will bear a price tag involving millions of dollars. The benefits from the production of these goods are obviously widespread and not subject to the exclusion principle. Hence, if war goods are to be a part of the nation's total output, they must be provided through governmental action. The economics of the war industry will be discussed in more detail in Chapter 40.

A final point: While some social goods (for example, war goods) are competitive with the production of private goods, we must note that the production of other social goods is complementary to the private sector. To mention but one of many possible illustrations: The automobile industry could not have achieved the degree of growth and prosperity it has enjoyed were it not for the willingness of Federal, state, and local governments to underwrite a system of quality roads and highways.

Allocating resources to social goods production Precisely how are resources reallocated from the production of private goods to the production of social goods? In a full-employment economy, government is faced with the task of freeing resources from private employment to make them available for the production of social goods. During peacetime, the best means of releasing resources from private uses is to reduce private demand for them. This is accomplished by levying taxes on businesses and households, thereby diverting some of their incomes—some of their potential purchasing power—

[2]There are obvious differences between *dollar voting,* which dictates output in the private sector of the economy, and *political voting,* which determines output in the public sector. The rich man has many more votes to cast in the private sector than does the poor man. In the public sector, each—at least in theory—has an equal say. Furthermore, the children who cast their meager votes for bubble gum and comic books in the private sector are banned by virtue of their age from the registering of social choices.

out of the income-expenditure streams. With lower incomes, businesses and households will be forced to curtail their investment and consumption spending. *In short, taxes tend to diminish private demand for goods and services, which in turn prompts a drop in the private demand for resources.* By diverting purchasing power from private spenders to government, taxes free resources from private uses. Government expenditure of the tax proceeds can then reabsorb these resources and provide social goods and services. For example, corporation and personal income taxes release resources from the production of investment goods—drill presses, boxcars, warehouses—and consumer goods—food, clothing, and television sets. Government expenditures tend to reabsorb these resources in the production of guided missiles, military aircraft, and new schools and highways. Government purposely reallocates resources to bring about significant changes in the composition of the economy's total output.

STABILIZATION

The primary purpose of the governmental functions considered thus far is to alter the allocation of resources or, in other words, to change the composition of the national output. Historically the most recent and in some ways the most important function of government is that of stabilizing the economy—assisting the private economy to achieve both the full employment of resources and a stable price level. Part 2 of this book examines in detail the determinants of employment and the price level in a capitalistic economy. Hence at this point we pause only to outline and assert (rather than fully explain) the stabilization function of government.

The key point is that the level of output depends directly upon total spending or aggregate demand. A high level of total demand means it will be profitable for the various industries to produce large outputs, and this, in turn, will necessitate that both property and human resources be employed at high levels. But we shall find in Part 2 that there are no mechanisms in the capitalistic system to ensure that aggregate demand will be at that particular level which will provide for full employment. Two unhappy possibilities might arise:

1. The level of total demand in the private sector may be too low for full employment. The government's obligation is to somehow augment private demand so that total demand—private *and* public—will be sufficient to generate full employment. How can government do this? The answer is by using the same techniques—government spending and taxes—as it uses to reallocate resources to the production of social goods. Specifically, government should increase its own spending on social goods and services, on the one hand, and reduce taxes in order to stimulate private spending, on the other.

2. The second possibility is that the economy may attempt to spend in excess of its productive capacity. If aggregate demand exceeds the full employment output, the excess demand will have the effect of pulling up the price level. Excessive aggregate demand is inflationary. Government's obligation here is to eliminate the excess spending. It does this primarily by cutting its own expenditures, on the one hand, and raising taxes so as to curtail private spending, on the other.

EVALUATING GOVERNMENT'S ROLE

Thus far we have been content to state the major economic functions of government and to indicate the overall impact of their performance upon the economy. We now turn to the problem of evaluating the economic role of government. Unfortunately, government's economic role is extremely difficult to assess. There are no simple quantitative standards by which the scope and quality of government's performance can be gauged. Any evaluation of the public sector quickly pushes us beyond the boundaries of economic science and into the larger realms of political theory and philosophy. Nevertheless, discussion of the problems involved may turn up some worthwhile insights and explode a few of the more

popular misconceptions about the economic functions of government. In this way each of us may be in a more strategic position to formulate intelligent opinions.[3]

We will consider two general questions:

1. To what extent is there agreement upon the legitimacy of the five stated governmental functions?

2. Do objective standards or guidelines exist for judging the economic worth or efficiency of public-sector decisions?

Desirability of functions

Should government perform the five economic functions we have just discussed? All things considered, there is rather startling agreement that these functions entail tasks which legitimately devolve on government. True, there is a small minority within the United States which espouses the philosophy that that government is best which governs least. At the other extreme, there are those who look upon an expansion of the functions of government as a panacea for any and all the ills of society. Though these groups are highly vocal, it must be emphasized that they are minorities. The vast majority of people are in fairly close agreement that government has an obligation in each of the areas we have discussed.

Beyond these general comments, two more specific points are worth remembering:

1. The economic role of government in American capitalism is not a phenomenon of recent vintage. With the exception of the stabilization function, government has performed all the functions discussed to a greater or lesser degree throughout American economic history.

2. The actions of a democratic government mirror the will of society with reasonable accuracy. This point is so obvious as to be frequently overlooked: A democratic government does essentially what the citizenry wants it to do.[4]

> Government, in the United States, is not an independent entity; it does not possess a will of its own; it is not animated by purposes that are alien to the desires of its citizens. The American government is a creature of the American people; it responds to the pressures that they bring to bear upon it; its policies and its programs, wise or unwise, find their origin in organized demand and depend for their survival upon popular sufferance. . . . It [government] intervenes only when it is forced to intervene. It acts reluctantly, deliberately, and tardily, in response to overwhelming pressures. Criticism of public intervention is criticism, not of dictatorship, but of the results of the democratic process.

Efficiency in government

Men of goodwill may agree that all five of the stated functions of government are legitimate, but they may seriously disagree about the extent to which these functions should be pursued and whether a specific project or program falls within the public sector. Few would question that government has *some* role to play in providing national defense, education, and highways. But there may be substantial disagreement about the size of the public budget for each of these purposes. And there may be controversy about whether certain particular projects—the provision of medical care or electric power, for example—should be within the public sector at all. Such controversy is not surprising. One's view of the proper scope of government is ultimately a matter of personal values and ideology. The relative size of the private and public sectors is only partially an economic question; one's judgment here depends upon one's "politics."

Benefit-cost analysis But recognizing that an individual's position on the proper scope of government in the economy is a subjective matter is not to deny that economics can provide some guidance in formulating a judgment on the proper balance between the private and public sectors. This guidance takes the form of what economists have called *benefit-cost analysis.*

Suppose all available resources are fully employed and the question is "How should resources be allocated between the private and the public sectors?" The basic nature of the economizing problem (Chapter 2) tells us that any decision to use more resources

[3]The ambitious student will do well to compare the philosophies of government presented in Francis M. Bator, *The Question of Government Spending* (New York: Harper & Row, Publishers, Incorporated, 1960), and Henry C. Wallich, *The Cost of Freedom* (New York: Harper & Row, Publishers, Incorporated, 1960).

[4]Clair Wilcox, *Public Policies toward Business,* 3d ed. (Homewood, Ill.: Richard D. Irwin, Inc., 1966), pp. 8–9.

in, say, the public sector will involve both a benefit and a cost. The benefit is the extra satisfaction resulting from the output of more social goods; the cost is the loss of satisfaction associated with the concomitant decline in the production of private goods. Should the resources under consideration be shifted from the private to the public sector? The answer is "Yes" *if* the benefits from the extra social goods exceed the cost resulting from having fewer private goods. The answer is "No" *if* the value or cost of the forgone private goods is greater than the benefits associated with the extra social goods.

But benefit-cost analysis can do more than simply indicate whether a public program is worth undertaking. It can also provide guidance concerning the extent to which a given project should be pursued. Economic questions, after all, are not simply questions of "Yes" or "No," but rather matters of "how much" or "how little." Consider the case of flood control. We note first that the benefits from a flood-control project are largely spillovers and that the exclusion principle is not readily applicable. That is, a flood-control project is basically a social good. Now, should government undertake a flood-control project in a given river valley? And, if so, what is the proper size or scope for the project?

Table 6·1 provides us with the answers. Here we list a series of increasingly ambitious and increasingly costly flood-control plans. To what extent, if at all, should government undertake flood control? In the first place, a quick glance at the most modest plan—plan A—indicates that a flood-control project on this river is economically justifiable because benefits ($6,000) exceed costs ($3,000). Secondly, what is the optimum size or scope for this project? The answer is that plan C—the middle-size reservoir—is the best plan. Why? Because we find in columns 3 and 6 that each progressively more ambitious plan yields extra or marginal benefits in excess of marginal costs down through plan C. Plans A and B are too modest; they entail a failure to realize all *net* benefits. Plans A and B reflect an underallocation of resources to flood control. Plan D imposes *net* costs upon society; marginal costs exceed marginal benefits. The extra costs of going from a medium-size reservoir to the large reservoir are $12,000 (=$30,000 − $18,000), and the resulting extra benefits are only $7,000 (=$32,000 − $25,000). Plan D would entail an overallocation of resources to this flood-control project. Plan C is the most economical; it "pushes" flood control so long as the marginal benefits exceed the marginal costs.

TABLE 6·1 BENEFIT–COST ANALYSIS FOR A FLOOD-CONTROL PROJECT

(1) Plan	(2) Total annual cost of project	(3) Extra or marginal cost	(4) Average annual damage	(5) Total benefit (reduction in damage)	(6) Extra or marginal benefit
Without protection	$ 0		$38,000	$ 0	
A: Levees	3,000	$ 3,000	32,000	6,000	$ 6,000
B: Small reservoir	10,000	7,000	22,000	16,000	10,000
C: Medium reservoir	18,000	8,000	13,000	25,000	9,000
D: Large reservoir	30,000	12,000	6,000	32,000	7,000

Source: Adapted from Otto Eckstein, *Public Finance,* 2d ed. (Englewood Cliffs, N.J.: Prentice-Hall, Inc., 1967), p. 25. Used with permission.

Some implications This elementary discussion of benefit-cost analysis implies several points which are helpful in our thinking about the appropriate scope of the public sector.

1. Benefit-cost analysis explodes the myth that "economy in government" and "reduced government spending" are synonymous. "Economy" is concerned with efficiency in resource use. If a government program yields extra benefits which are less than the extra benefits attainable from alternative private uses—that is, if costs exceed benefits—then the proposed public program should not be undertaken. But if the reverse is true—if benefits exceed costs—then it would be uneconomical or "wasteful" *not* to spend on that governmental program. Economy in government does *not* mean the minimization of public spending; rather it means allocating resources between the private and public sectors until no net benefits can be realized from additional reallocations.

2. A special point must be made with respect to the stabilization function of government. One can argue that, if the economy is experiencing substantial unemployment, public programs can be initiated which benefit society, on the one hand, but entail no costs, on the other. That is, we might construct a production possibilities curve similar to Figure 2·2 with social goods on the vertical axis and private goods on the horizontal axis and put the economy at some unemployment point inside the curve. Now increases in government spending on public projects which move the economy vertically from the unemployment point to a point on the curve entail an increased output of social goods *without* any decline in the availability of private goods. Thus many of the New Deal make-work programs of the Great Depression of the 1930s were labelled as grossly inefficient and wasteful. What could be more inefficient than putting men to work raking leaves, planting trees, and manicuring the roadside at a time when poverty and hunger were widespread? Yet the New Deal projects were quite efficient in the sense that benefits were large as compared with the cost of forgone output. The alternative to New Deal employment during much of the 1930s was unemployment; hence, employment on government projects entailed no real cost in the sense of forgone private production.

3. The application of the benefit-cost principle to the problem of the relative size of the private and public sectors is basically no different than the automatic benefit-cost comparisons which the market makes with respect to the composition of output within the private sector. In our earlier discussion we noted that in the absence of spillovers the competitive market would result in an optimum output of each private good. That is, each private good would be produced so long as the benefits associated with an extra unit exceeded the accompanying costs. In Figure 6·1*a* the market automatically applies benefit-cost analysis and negotiates the production of the optimum output Q_o.

Limitations and problems Benefit-cost analysis is extremely helpful in promoting clear thinking about the public sector and is in fact very useful in actual studies involving projects such as flood control and highway construction. But we must acknowledge that many attempts to apply benefit-cost analysis encounter severe problems and limitations.

In the first place, benefit-cost analysis—as demonstrated in Table 6·1—presumes that benefits and costs can be measured with reasonable accuracy. To the extent that this is not the case, the reliability of benefit-cost analysis as a guide to public spending is diminished. Now the problem is that most of the programs appropriate for the public sector are those which entail large spillover effects. For social goods per se the benefits are almost entirely in the form of spillovers and, in addition, the exclusion principle is inapplicable. In short, benefits are widely diffused and not automatically measured by the dollar yardstick of the market. How does one quantify in dollar terms the decline in the loss of crops and livestock due to flood control? What is the value of the recreational benefits associated with the construction of a reservoir? How does one quantify the total cost of putting, say, several thousand acres of farmland under water? What might be the spillover cost of the reservoir in terms of damage to the ecology of the area?

Consider the possible benefits and costs associated with the construction of a new freeway in a major metropolitan area. In addition to estimating the obvious costs—land purchase and construction costs—the spillover cost of additional air pollution which results from an enlarged flow of traffic must also be estimated. Furthermore, more traffic may call for increased expenditures for traffic police. What about benefits? Improved transportation means a widening of markets, more competition, and a greater opportunity for the community to specialize according to comparative advantage. But what is the monetary value of this benefit? And the freeway may help make more jobs accessible to the central city poor. Again, what is the dollar value of these benefits? Given the suggested difficulties in estimating all the costs and benefits associated with such relatively tangible undertakings as highway and reservoir construction, one can imagine the enormous obstacles in applying benefit-cost analysis to space exploration, foreign aid, or the Head Start program. The point is that the full costs and benefits associated with government programs are not easily calculated, and benefit-cost analysis is frequently difficult, if not impossible, to apply.

Secondly, we must recognize that in practice the allocative, redistributional, and stabilization functions of government are all closely intertwined. A government policy or action specifically designed to, say, reallocate resources from private to public uses will almost invariably affect the distribution of income and have implications for output and price level stabilization. These interactions complicate the making of rational decisions. Consider, once again, our flood-control project. Its purpose is primarily allocative—to increase the output of a specific social good which is worth more than alternative private goods. But the project might have adverse effects in terms of society's distributional and stabilization objectives. Suppose that the taxes to be collected in financing the project are of such a kind that they are paid disproportionately by low-income people. And suppose that the resulting benefits accrue primarily to wealthy farmers and prosperous businessmen. *If* greater equality in income distribution is a high-priority policy objective of society, then presumably the adverse redistributional effects of the project should be taken into account. But how? How can the "cost" of the redistributional impact be measured?

A similar conflict might arise with respect to the stabilization function. Assume the economy is experiencing quite severe inflation as a result of excess aggregate spending. Now, despite the desirability of the flood-control project as indicated by benefit-cost analysis, should the project be initiated in view of the fact that the added spending on flood control will intensify inflationary pressures and promote price level instability? The point is that if a social goods project has adverse implications with respect to society's distributional and stabilization goals, the case for the project is less clear than if these implications were favorable or, at least, substantially neutral. In the context of such possible dilemmas the rendering of rational public policy decisions becomes complex indeed.

TWO ADDENDA

Two final observations are worth appending to this discussion.

A world of imperfections

Despite the limited guidance of benefit-cost analysis, criticism of government inefficiency—by both liberals and conservatives—is frequent and persistent. The public sector is criticized for errors in fact, judgment, and administration. Some critics hold that government has often grossly misjudged the socioeconomic problems of society, failing to recognize and correct important shortcomings of the price system. There is persistent evidence that governmental agencies are bureaucratic, plagued by red tape and wasteful administration. The Pentagon, for example, has been widely criticized for wasteful practices and procedures in obtaining military hardware (Chapter 40). And perhaps worst of all, the interests of society have sometimes been neglected by government in promoting the ends of pressure groups or in the interest of political expediency.

There is no question but that these criticisms are of some substance. But one must keep in mind that the private sector of the economy is by no means perfectly efficient; indeed, government's economic functions are largely attempts to correct the price system's shortcomings. "The relevant comparison is not between perfect markets and imperfect governments, nor between faulty markets and all-knowing, rational, benevolent governments, but between inevitably imperfect institutions."[5] The public sector does not have a monopoly on inefficiency. Within this context the effectiveness of the public sector's performance is not without substantial defenses. At worst one can take the position that it is preferable to have government correct the defects of the price system in an imperfect or partial manner than not at all. Perhaps at best it can be argued that the historical record reveals that government on balance has clearly played a fundamental positive role in fostering the smooth operation and development of American capitalism.

The issue of freedom

We have stressed at several points that any analysis of the proper role of government must go beyond economics. Economists and others have long pondered the nature of the relationship between the role and size of the public sector, on the one hand, and freedom, on the other. While no attempt is made here to explore this issue in depth, it is relevant to indicate the outlines of two divergent views on this question.

Many conservative economists feel that, in addition to the economic costs involved in any expansion of the public sector, there is also a cost in the form of diminished individual freedom. Two basic points constitute this position. First, there is the "power corrupts" argument: "Freedom is a rare and delicate plant. . . . history confirms, that the great threat to freedom is the concentration of power. . . . by concentrating power in political hands, [government] is . . . a threat to freedom."[6] Secondly, one can practice selectivity in the market system of the private sector, using one's income to buy precisely what one chooses and rejecting unwanted commodities. But in the public sector—even assuming a high level of political democracy—conformity and coercion are inherent. If the majority decides in favor of certain governmental actions—to build a reservoir, to establish an old-age insurance program, to provide a guaranteed annual income—the minority must conform. Hence, the "use of political channels, while inevitable, tends to strain the social cohesion essential for a stable society."[7] To the extent that decisions can be rendered selectively by individuals through markets, the need for conformity and coercion is lessened and this "strain" reduced. Proponents of this view argue that (1) the scope of government should be strictly limited and (2) government power should be decentralized.

But liberal economists are skeptical of the conservative position. They hold that the conservative view is based upon what we shall call the *fallacy of limited decisions.* That is, the conservatives implicitly assume that during any particular period of time there is a limited, or fixed, number of decisions to be made in connection with the operation of the economy. Hence, if government makes more of these decisions in performing its stated functions, the private sector of the economy will necessarily have fewer "free" decisions or choices to make. This is held to be fallacious reasoning. By sponsoring the production of social goods, government is in fact *extending* the range of free choice by permitting society to enjoy goods and services which would simply not be available in the absence of governmental provision. One can cogently argue that it is in large measure through the economic functions of government that we have been striving to free ourselves in some measure from ignorance, poverty, disease, crime, discrimination, etc. Note, too, that in providing most social goods, government does not typically undertake production

[5]Otto Eckstein, *Public Finance,* 2d ed. (Englewood Cliffs, N.J.: Prentice-Hall, Inc., 1967), p. 17.

[6]Milton Friedman, *Capitalism and Freedom* (Chicago: University of Chicago Press, 1962), p. 2.

[7]Ibid., p. 23.

itself but rather purchases these goods through private enterprise. When government makes the decision to build an interstate highway, private concerns are given the responsibility for making a myriad of specific decisions and choices in connection with the carrying out of this decision.

Finally, it should be noted that during a depression the number of choices made by private businesses and households is greatly restricted. Why? Because production has been slowed and incomes drastically curtailed. The businessman has fewer choices to make concerning, for example, the types of products and combinations of resources he may use. Indeed, some firms will have to close down and make no decisions at all. The consumer has fewer decisions to make in disposing of his income, because his income is now very small or conceivably nonexistent. Now if government, by increased participation and intervention in the economy, can correct or even alleviate a depression, the number of decisions and choices open to both businesses and consumers will increase. That is, government, by making more decisions concerning the operation of the economy, might restore prosperity, permitting the number of private decisions to increase also. Hence, the number of private and public decisions made in the operation of the economy may, *within limits,* vary in the same direction. A large number of governmental decisions may or may not mean a smaller number of private decisions.

One of America's leading economists has summarized the liberal view in these pointed words:[8]

> Traffic lights coerce me and limit my freedom. Yet in the midst of a traffic jam on the unopen road, was I really "free" before there were lights? And has the algebraic total of freedom, for me or the representative motorist or the group as a whole, been increased or decreased by the introduction of well-engineered stop lights? Stop lights, you know, are also go lights. . . . When we introduce the traffic light, we have, although the arch individualist may not like the new order, by cooperation and coercion created for ourselves greater freedom.

[8]Paul A. Samuelson, "Personal Freedoms and Economic Freedoms in the Mixed Economy," in Earl F. Cheit (ed.), *The Business Establishment* (New York: John Wiley & Sons, Inc., 1964), p. 219.

HOW BIG IS GOVERNMENT?

We end our discussion of the public sector on an empirical note. Precisely how large is government's role in American capitalism? The simplest single indicator of government's economic role is its expenditure on goods and services expressed as a percentage of the economy's total output. Columns 3 and 4 of Table 6·2 suggest that government's role has expanded not only in absolute but also in relative terms. Note, however, that this growth has been somewhat sporadic. Government—Federal, state, and local combined—now accounts for over one-fifth of the total output of American capitalism. How is this long-run expansion of government's economic activities to be explained? Undoubtedly there are many causal factors, but two seem to be of paramount importance. On the one hand, war shifts the production target of the economy drastically in the direction of more social goods and fewer civilian goods. Note the upsurge of government purchases during World War II: in 1944 almost one-half of total output was taken by government. A lesser expansion of government spending accompanied the Korean conflict in 1951. Currently the war in Vietnam necessitates unusually high levels of military spending, keeping government's share of total output considerably above that of four or five decades ago. Note in columns 5 and 6 that were it not for the high level of military spending imposed by the cold war, government's share of total output would be far below the 23 percent of column 4. Furthermore, post–World War II growth in nonmilitary government spending has been modest percentagewise.

A second factor has also contributed to the relative growth of government in the economy: As the incomes of American consumers have risen historically, the pattern of consumer wants has altered in the direction of relatively more social goods and relatively fewer private goods. The members of a relatively poor economy must take their entire incomes in the form of the most urgently needed commodities: food, shelter, and clothing—all private

TABLE 6·2 GOVERNMENT PURCHASES AS A PERCENTAGE OF TOTAL OUTPUT, SELECTED YEARS, 1929–1970

(1) Year	(2) Total output (in billions)	(3) Government purchases of goods and services (in billions)	(4) Government purchases as a percentage of total output, or (3) ÷ (2)	(5) Government nondefense purchases (in billions)	(6) Government nondefense purchases as a percentage of total output, or (5) ÷ (2)
1929	$103	$ 8	8%	$ 7	7%
1933	56	8	14	6	11
1936	82	12	15	7	9
1939	90	13	14	11	12
1941	125	25	20	11	9
1944	210	96	46	9	4
1947	231	25	11	16	8
1951	328	59	18	26	8
1954	365	75	20	34	9
1958	447	94	21	48	11
1962	560	117	21	65	12
1964	632	129	20	79	13
1967	794	180	23	108	14
1970	977	220	23	144	15

Source: U.S. Department of Commerce data. Data for 1970 are preliminary.

goods provided by the private sector of the economy through the price system. But after these basic wants have been largely fulfilled, the growing wealth of society permits it to turn its attention more and more to the satisfaction of somewhat less urgent, but nevertheless important, wants. Many of the wants in this second category entail social goods and services: education, streets and highways, police and fire protection. These goods, produced in minimal amounts in a poor and essentially rural economy, are demanded and provided in increasing amounts as the wealth of the society increases. As a matter of fact, the increasing complexity of a growing economy necessitates—and indeed, economic growth itself depends upon—the provision of social goods and services. The result is a tendency for government to play an increasingly important role in the economy as a provider of these social commodities and services.

Some final words of warning. Table 6·2 both understates and overstates the role of government in American capitalism. It understates government's role because it only reflects the reallocative function. The role of government in providing a legislative framework, in redistributing income, and in stabilizing the economy is not directly reflected in Table 6·2. The importance of the public sector is overstated in that government's role as an owner and operator of business enterprises has not expanded to any significant degree. The job of producing government's increased purchases of social goods and services still lies primarily within the realm of private enterprise. Government sponsors and handles the financing of highways, schools, and war goods, but their actual pro-

duction is carried on by private enterprises. Most of the government's purchases are for goods and services produced by private, profit-guided producers. Production actually undertaken by government itself is relatively small, and its relative growth has been very modest. Consumers now buy relatively fewer goods directly from private enterprises but more goods indirectly from private enterprises through government. Private enterprise has expanded more or less proportionately with the total output of the economy.

We will examine the controversy over the proper size of the public sector in Chapter 41.

SUMMARY

1. The American economy can be described as mixed capitalism. It is primarily a market economy, yet government influences the operation of the price system in a variety of ways.

2. The basic economic functions of government entail *a.* providing a legal and social framework appropriate to the effective operation of the price system, *b.* maintaining competition, *c.* redistributing income, *d.* reallocating resources to adjust for spillovers and provide social goods and services, and ***e.*** stabilizing the economy.

3. The economic role of government is difficult to evaluate. Society generally condones government activity in the five areas outlined above. However, there is considerable disagreement concerning the extent to which government should pursue these functions and whether specific governmental actions fall within the scope of the public sector.

4. Benefit-cost analysis can provide useful guidance regarding the economic desirability and most efficient scope of social goods output. There are serious problems, however, in measuring benefits and costs. Furthermore, the reallocative function of government may be in conflict with redistributive and stabilization objectives.

5. As measured by its purchases, government's economic role has increased historically in both absolute and relative terms. The two major causes of this growth are ***a.*** war and ***b.*** the more than proportionate increase in the public's demand for social goods which has accompanied rising incomes.

QUESTIONS AND STUDY SUGGESTIONS

1. Why is the American economy called "mixed capitalism"? Enumerate and briefly discuss the main economic functions of government.

2. Explain why, in the absence of spillovers, equilibrium and optimum outputs are identical in competitive markets. What divergences arise between equilibrium and optimum output when (*a*) spillover costs and (*b*) spillover benefits are present? How might government correct for these discrepancies?

3. What are the basic characteristics of social goods? Define and explain the significance of the exclusion principle. By what means does government provide social goods?

4. What is benefit-cost analysis? In what ways is it a useful guide to resource allocation? What are its limitations?

5. Carefully evaluate this statement: "The public, as a general rule . . . gets less production in return for a dollar spent by government than from a dollar spent by private enterprise."[9]

6. "The conclusion seems inescapable that pure capitalism . . . would be subject to grave deficiencies and inconsistencies. Such a system would have little chance of survival."[10] Do you agree? Why?

7. "It is conceivable that the Federal government can contribute materially to economic stability and greater efficiency in the use of resources without interfering in the details of business and personal life." Do you agree? Explain.

[9]National Association of Manufacturers, *The American Individual Enterprise System* (New York: McGraw-Hill Book Company, 1946), p. 952.

[10]Howard R. Bowen, *Toward Social Economy* (New York: Holt, Rinehart and Winston, Inc., 1948), p. 321.

8. Carefully evaluate the following statement, and contrast its philosophy with that in question 5:[11]

> The admitted functions of government embrace a much wider field than can be easily included within the ring fence of a restrictive definition . . . it is hardly possible to find any ground of justification common to them all, except the comprehensive one of general expediency; nor to limit the interference of government by any universal rule, save the simple and vague one that it should never be admitted but when the case of expediency is strong.

9. Interpret and evaluate the following quotation:[12]

> Plan or no plan? Everyone believes in planning in the literal sense of the word: and, for that matter, everyone believes that national governments should execute some plans for economic life. No one favors bad planning. Plan or no plan is no choice at all; the pertinent questions turn on particular techniques: Who shall plan, for what purposes, in what conditions, and by what devices? Free market or regulation? Again, this issue is badly posed. Both institutions are indispensable.

What do you feel are the virtues, if any, of government planning? How does the price system "plan"? Explain.

[11] John Stuart Mill, *Principles of Political Economy* (New York: Appleton-Century-Crofts, Inc., 1878), vol. II, p. 392.

[12] Robert A. Dahl and Charles E. Lindblom, *Politics, Economics and Welfare* (New York: Harper & Row, Publishers, Incorporated, 1953), p. 5.

SELECTED REFERENCES

Economic Issues, 4th ed., readings 8 and 9.

Haveman, Robert Henry: *The Economics of the Public Sector* (New York: John Wiley & Sons, Inc., 1970), chaps. 1–5.

Friedman, Milton: *Capitalism and Freedom* (Chicago: The University of Chicago Press, 1962).

Joint Economic Committee, *The Analysis and Evaluation of Public Expenditures: The PPB System,* vols. 1–3 (Washington, 1969).

McKean, Roland N.: *Public Spending* (New York: McGraw-Hill Book Company, 1968).

Phelps, Edmund S. (ed.): *Private Wants and Public Needs,* rev. ed. (New York: W. W. Norton & Company, Inc., 1965).

7

THE FACTS OF AMERICAN CAPITALISM: HOUSEHOLDS

This chapter and the ensuing two are designed to put meat on our bare-boned model of mixed capitalism. We have discussed the three major aggregates of mixed capitalism—business, households, and government—on a very general and somewhat abstract basis. We must now add color to our crude sketch by painting in the factual characteristics of these three major transactors as they function in our American brand of mixed capitalism. In short, we must breathe reality into our abstract model by adding "the facts" of American economic life. The present chapter contributes factual information pertinent to households. The following two chapters do the same for the business and government sectors of the economy. In each case the discussion will focus upon the source of the sector's income or receipts and the manner in which it disposes of that income.

The household sector of American capitalism is currently composed of some sixty-two million households. These households play a dual role: they are the ultimate suppliers of all economic resources and simultaneously the major spending group in the economy. Hence, we shall consider households first as income receivers and second as spenders.

HOUSEHOLDS AS INCOME RECEIVERS

There are two related approaches to studying the facts of income distribution. The *functional distribution* of income is concerned with the manner in which society's money income is divided among wages, rents, interest, and profits. Here total income is distributed according to the function performed by the income receiver. Wages are paid to labor, rents and interest compensate property resources, and profits flow to the owners of corporations and unincorporated businesses. The *personal distribution* of income has to do with the way in which the total money income of society is apportioned among individual

households. A basic understanding of both the functional and the personal distribution of income is essential to understanding the role of households in American capitalism.

Functional distribution of income

The distributive shares of the national income for 1970 were as follows:

	Billions of dollars	Percent of total
Wages and salaries	$599.8	75
Proprietors' income	67.6	8
Corporate profits	76.5	10
Interest	33.5	4
Rents	22.7	3
National income	$800.1	100

Figure 7·1 illustrates the changes that have taken place in the *absolute size* of these shares since 1929. Changes in the *relative shares* of the national income since 1929 are shown in Figure 7·2. Certain generalizations are evident from an examination of these data:

1. It is clear from Figure 7·1 that all the shares of national income tend to expand during prosperity and to decline during depression. *In absolute terms,* none of the major income-receiving classes benefits from bad times. Thus the drastic decline in national income ushered in by the Great Depression of the 1930s affected all income groups adversely. On the other hand, the war-born prosperity of the early 1940s and the postwar boom significantly boosted the incomes of all groups.

2. In terms of the *relative* shares of national income, the outstanding fact shown in Figure 7·2 is the dominant size and high degree of stability of the share going to labor. With exceptions, labor's share of the national income over the last three decades has generally hovered a few percentage points on either side of 70 percent.

3. In contrast to the relative stability of labor's share, corporate profits have proved to be highly unstable over the years. In 1929 corporate profits accounted for about 12 percent of the national income but became a negative figure (losses) during 1932 and 1933. Even since the beginning of World War II, corporate profits have fluctuated substantially in both absolute and percentage terms. Specifically, corporate profits have varied from 10 to 15 percent of the national income in the last two decades.

4. Proprietors' incomes—that is, the incomes of doctors, lawyers, small businessmen, shopkeepers, farmers, and other unincorporated enterprises—have fluctuated between 10 and 20 percent of the national income. As Figure 7·2 indicates, the percentage of national income going to this group has been declining somewhat since the close of World War II. No doubt depressed farm incomes have played a major role in this decline.

5. The relatively small shares of national income accruing to interest and rent receivers merit brief comment. *Interest* has varied considerably as a share of the national income. In 1929 interest receivers got about 7 percent of the national income. Largely because of the drastic decline in national income and the fact that most interest payments are contractually fixed, interest income rose as a share of the national income during the Great Depression of the 1930s. Then in the war years of the early 1940s a burgeoning national income and very low interest rates caused the interest share to fall to less than 2 percent. In recent years the interest share has grown substantially and now stands at about 4 percent. Reasons for this growth are essentially twofold. First, there has been very rapid growth of private debt in the past two or three decades. Secondly, substantial increases in interest rates have occurred since World War II. We will find in Chapter 18 that interest rates are strongly influenced by government monetary policy; recent growth in the interest share is thus a reflection of high interest rate policies. Since the mid-thirties *rents* have fluctuated generally between 3 and 5 percent of the national income.

Personal distribution of income

We defer examination of the empirical details and policy issues relevant to the personal distribution of income until Chapter 38. At this point we simply ask:

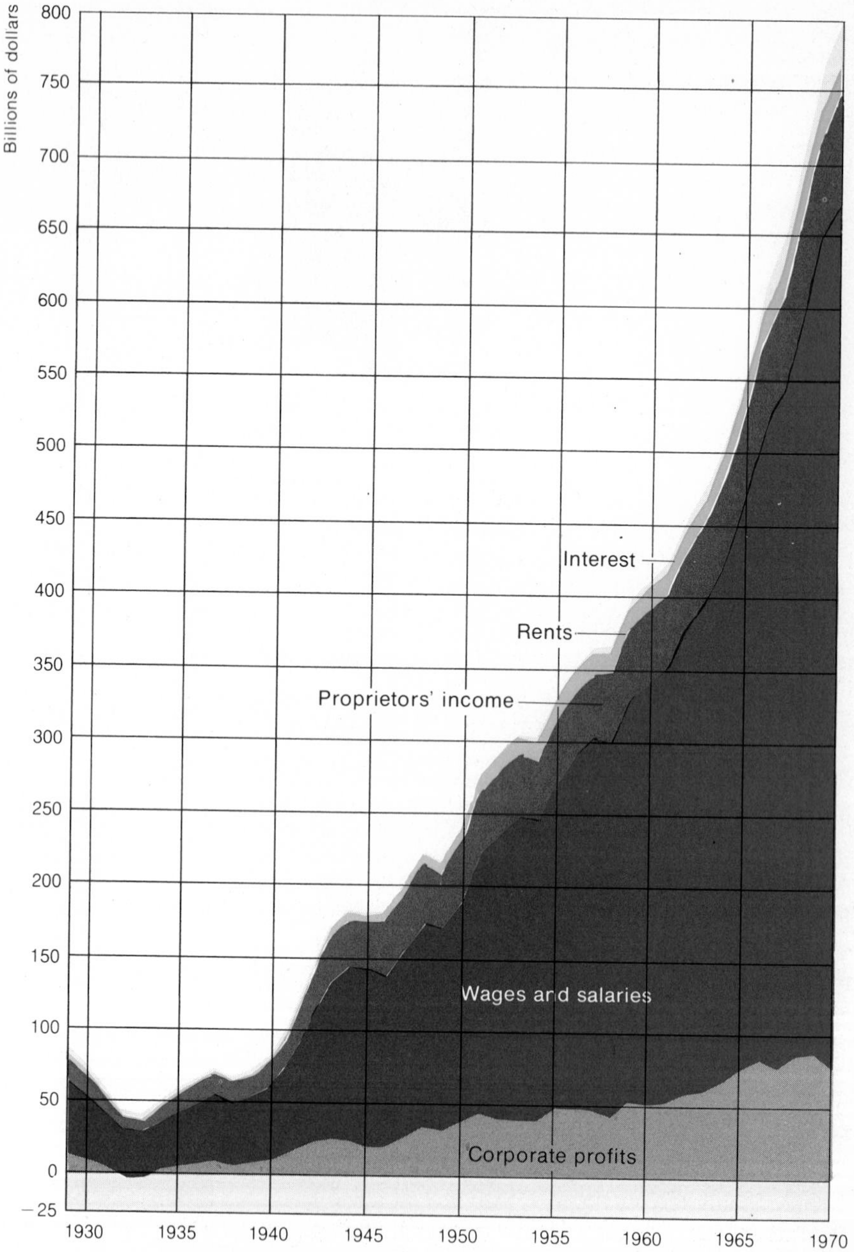

FIGURE 7 · 1 THE FUNCTIONAL DISTRIBUTION OF NATIONAL INCOME IN BILLIONS OF DOLLARS, 1929–1970

All national income shares decrease absolutely during depression and increase absolutely during periods of prosperity and growth. Wages and salaries constitute the largest component of the national income. (U.S. Department of Commerce.)

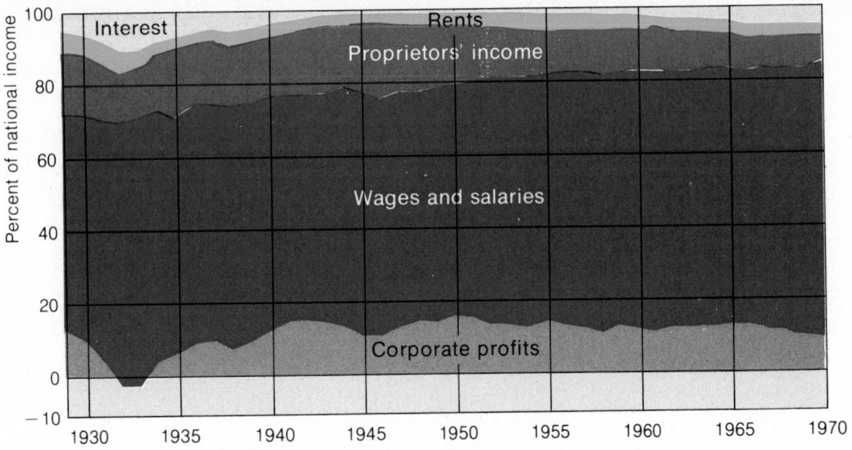

FIGURE 7·2 THE FUNCTIONAL DISTRIBUTION OF NATIONAL INCOME IN PERCENTAGES, 1929–1970

In relative terms the share of national income going to labor has been quite stable over time. Corporate profits have been very unstable, and interest and rental incomes have tended to decline. (U.S. Department of Commerce.)

Why is the personal distribution of money income—the way income is apportioned among households—important in understanding the operation of American capitalism? What impact does the distribution of money income among households have upon the operation of the economy? The manner in which income is distributed among families affects both the *size* and the *composition* of output.

1. The personal distribution of income is a major determinant of how society divides its money income between consumption and saving. We will discover in Chapters 12 and 13 that this division is of utmost significance in determining the levels of output and employment in the economy. Consumption, being a form of spending, induces production and employment. Saving, defined by economists as that part of current income which is not consumed, does not account for production and employment. It follows that a distribution of income which results in a large volume of saving in relation to consumption *may* be conducive to declining levels of production and employment. On the other hand, a distribution which entails a very small volume of saving in relation to consumption will promote high levels of production and employment.

2. The personal distribution of money income goes a long way toward determining the pattern of consumer spending in the economy. A highly unequal distribution of income among individual households results in an expenditure pattern much different from that which a more nearly equal distribution would entail. Generally speaking, the more unequal the distribution of a given total money income, the greater will be the demand for and the output of luxury goods. Businesses, as we have seen, usually find it to their advantage to adjust their outputs to consumer demands. As a consequence, the economy's product-mix is largely geared to the composition of consumer expenditures. And in turn, the economy's product-mix obviously determines the manner in which scarce resources are allocated.

To repeat, the personal distribution of income has

direct and significant consequences for the two major aspects of economic science: (1) the level of resource use and (2) the allocation of resources among alternative uses.

Determinants What determines the amount of money income received by an individual household in, say, a year? Common sense tells us that (1) the quantities of the various human and property resources which a household is able and willing to supply to businesses, (2) the prices which these resources command in the resource market, and (3) the actual level of employment of these resources are the immediate determinants of a household's money income. For the majority of American households, labor service is the only resource supplied. Thus by taking, for example, 2,000 hours of labor service at a wage rate of $3.00 per hour, total money income for the year is found to be $6,000. But the third determinant poses a possible qualification: Though the household may be willing and able to supply 2,000 hours of labor service per year, there is no guarantee that businesses will purchase this amount. Money income depends on the extent to which businesses are willing to employ available supplies of resources. If businesses are only able to use profitably 1,500 of the hours offered, the workers' money income will obviously decline accordingly.

Income and productivity In capitalistic economies, money income is roughly based upon the contribution which a household's resources make to the total production of the economy. Households earn money incomes which are generally in accord with the value of their contributions to total output. If the resources in a household's possession are capable of efficiently producing goods which consumers want, the income earned will be high; if not, it will be low. The prices established by the forces of supply and demand in the resource market roughly gauge the relative worth or "productivity" of the various resources. If a business enterprise pays $2 an hour for unskilled labor and $4 an hour for highly skilled labor, it implies that the skilled labor is twice as productive as unskilled labor. If the market places a high value on the contributions of a resource to production, the supplying household receives a large income. If the market puts a low value on a resource's contribution, the supplying household's income tends to be low.

It is obvious that a distribution of income based upon productivity can result in considerable inequality. The quantity and quality of resources owned by various households and the prices they can command in the resource market can and do vary quite widely. As a glance at Table 38·1 will verify, the lowest 20 percent of all American consumer units in 1969 received only 6 percent of total personal income.

HOUSEHOLDS AS SPENDERS

Having briefly discussed households as income receivers, let us now examine the other side of the coin by viewing households as disposers of income. How do households dispose of the income which they receive? In general terms the answer is simple: A part is given to government in the form of personal taxes, and the remainder is divided between personal consumption expenditures and personal saving. Specifically, here is the way in which households disposed of their total income in 1970.[1]

	Billions of dollars	Percent of total
Personal taxes	$116.2	15
Personal consumption expenditures	616.7	79
Personal saving	50.2	6
Total income	$783.1	100

Figures 7·3 and 7·4 show the absolute and relative importance of personal taxes, consumption expenditures, and personal saving over the last three and a half decades. We note immediately that in absolute

[1]The astute reader will note that the concept of national income, used in discussing households as income receivers, has been supplanted by a different income concept of a somewhat smaller magnitude in analyzing households as disposers of income. Technically, this new "total income" concept is personal income net of consumer interest payments. The distinctions among various income measures will be explored in Chapter 10.

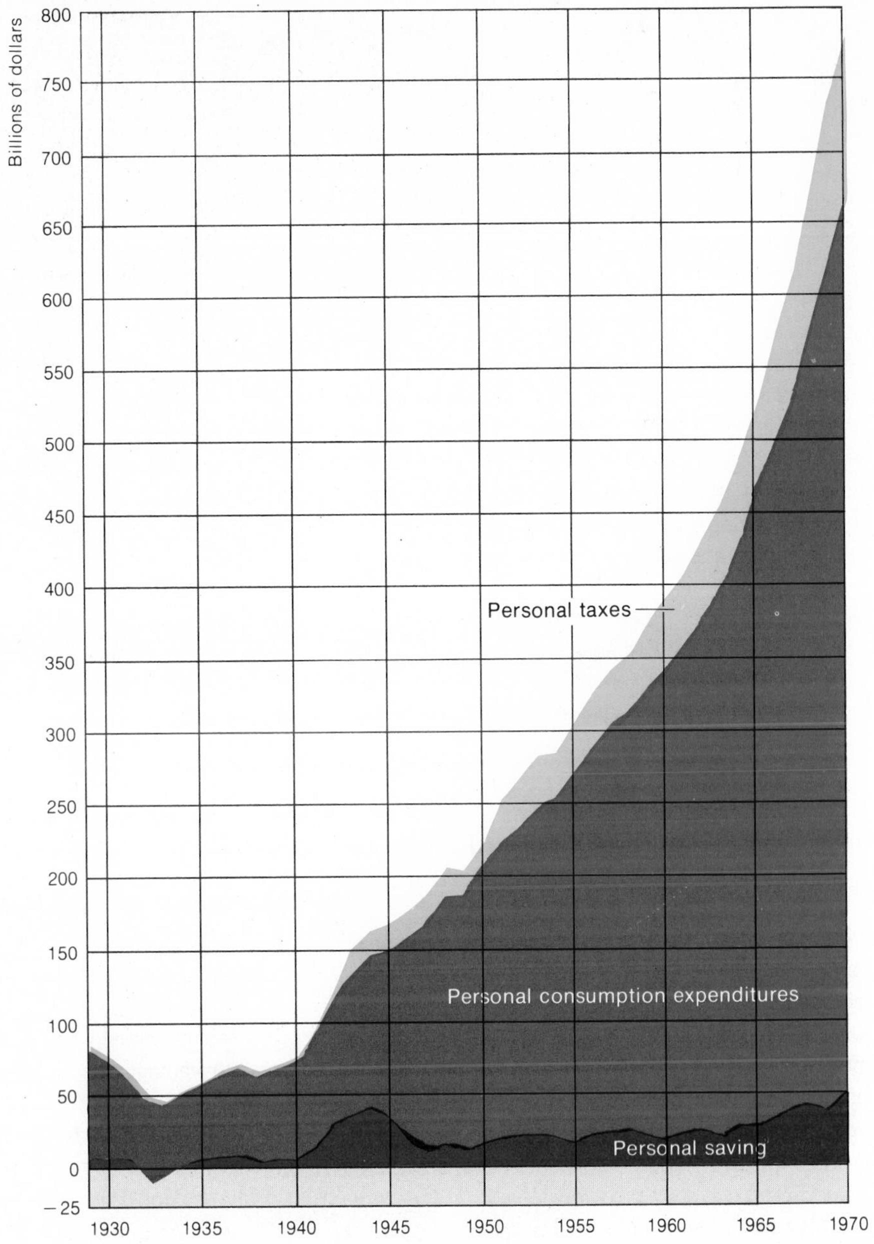

FIGURE 7 · 3 THE DISPOSITION OF INCOME IN BILLIONS OF DOLLARS, 1929–1970

Consumption expenditures, personal tax payments, and personal saving have all increased as personal income has expanded. Increases in personal saving during the early 1940s reflect wartime scarcities of consumer goods and high money incomes. (U.S. Department of Commerce.)

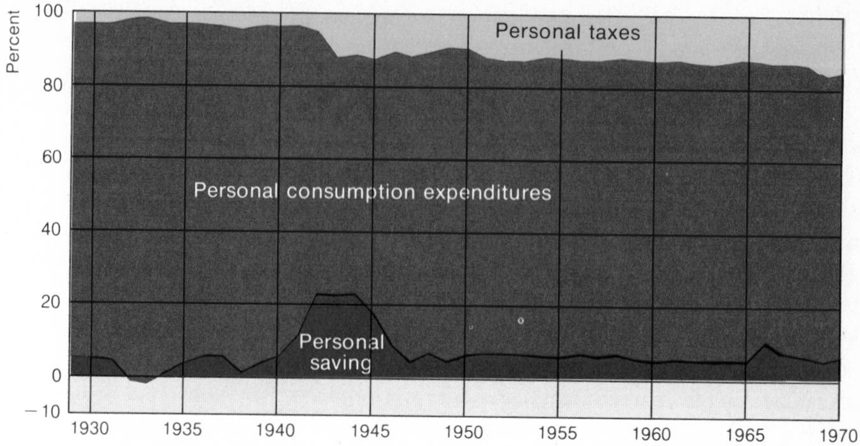

FIGURE 7·4 THE DISPOSITION OF INCOME IN PERCENTAGES, 1929–1970

Currently, personal consumption expenditures account for about 79 percent of total income, personal taxes for 15 percent, and personal saving for 6 percent. (U.S. Department of Commerce.)

terms all three components move with total income. But let us examine each of these components separately.

Personal taxes

Personal taxes, of which the Federal personal income tax is the major component, have risen sharply in both absolute and relative terms since 1941. In 1929, households paid $2.6 billion, or about 3 percent of their $85.9 billion personal income, in personal taxes. In 1970, $116.2 billion, or about 15 percent of that year's $783.1 billion total income, flowed to government as personal taxes. World War II and the financing of vast expenditures on war goods in the postwar era constitute the major explanatory factors. Expanding needs for social goods and services and population growth have also contributed to rising tax bills.

Economists define saving as "not spending"; hence, households have just two choices with their incomes after taxes—to consume or to save.

Personal saving: flows and stocks

Let us first consider the saving component of after-tax income. At the outset we note that "saving" is a slippery term. On one hand, it can refer to that portion of current (this year's) income which is not paid out in taxes or in the purchase of consumer goods but rather flows into bank accounts, insurance policies, bonds and stocks, and other financial assets which represent accumulated savings. On the other hand, the term "saving" is also used in referring to the present size of these financial assets which have been accumulated or stocked over a long period of years. Saving, in brief, can refer to a current flow of income into financial assets or to the accumulated size of such assets. In our discussion, we shall reserve the term "savings" (plural) for designating the accumulation or stock of financial assets held by households. The term "saving" (singular) will designate the portion of current income which flows into, or is added to, this accumulation. Occasionally we shall talk of "accumulated savings" or "the stock of

savings,'' on the one hand, and ''current saving'' or ''the flow of saving,'' on the other, to remind us of the savings-saving distinction.

Why do households want to save? After all, it is ultimately goods and services which satisfy consumer wants, not the pieces of paper which we call checkbooks, savings account books, certificates of deposit, and bonds. The reasons for saving are many and diverse, but they center around *security* and *speculation.* Households save to provide a nest egg for unforeseen contingencies—sickness, accident, unemployment—for retirement from the work force, or simply for the overall financial security of one's family. On the other hand, saving might well occur for speculation. One might channel a part of his income to the purchase of securities, speculating as to increases in their monetary value. Or a household might accumulate funds in bank accounts or as idle dollars in a sugar bowl, speculating as to a change in the purchasing power of those dollars.

The desire or willingness to save, however, is not enough. This willingness must be accompanied by the *ability* to save. And, as we shall discover later (Table 12·1), the ability to save depends basically upon the size of one's income. If income is very low, households may *dissave;* that is, they may consume in excess of their after-tax incomes. They manage this by borrowing and by digging into savings which they may have accumulated in years when their incomes were higher. However, both saving and consumption vary directly with income; as households get more income, they divide it between saving and consumption. Actually, the bulk of the personal saving that occurs in our economy is done by those households in the \$50,000, \$100,000, or higher income brackets. The top 10 percent of the income receivers account for most of the personal saving in our society.

A final point of interest: The bulge in saving during the World War II era (Figure 7·4) was largely ''forced,'' the result of booming prosperity and soaring incomes, on the one hand, and rather severe shortages of certain consumer goods such as automobiles and household appliances, on the other.

Personal consumption expenditures

Figures 7·3 and 7·4 clearly show that the bulk of total income flows from income receivers back into the business sector of the economy as personal consumption expenditures. But note that although consumption has been increasing by large absolute amounts in recent years, it has declined in relative terms. The tendency for income to increase even more sharply than personal consumption expenditures has permitted this to be the case. As with personal taxes and personal saving, the amount of consumption which occurs depends upon the business cycle. The bad times of the thirties caused all three to contract. Yet, as Figure 7·4 shows, consumption actually increased in relative terms during the Depression. For example, during the Depression years of 1932 and 1933, households spent over 98 percent of their income on consumer goods. Currently, households are spending over four times as much as they were during the depth of the Great Depression, but this still only amounts to about 79 percent of income.

Since the size and composition of the economy's total output depend to a very considerable extent upon the size and composition of the flow of consumer spending, it is imperative that we examine how households divide their expenditures among the various goods and services competing for their dollars. Consumer expenditures may be classified in several ways. For example, they may be divided into services and products; and products in turn may be subdivided on the basis of their durability. Thus the U.S. Department of Commerce classifies consumer spending as (1) expenditures on nondurables, (2) expenditures on durables, and (3) expenditures on services. If a product generally has an expected life of one year or more, it is called a ''durable good''; if its life is less than one year, it is labeled ''nondurable.'' Automobiles, refrigerators, washing machines, television sets, and most furniture are good examples of consumer durables. Most food and clothing items are nondurables. Services, of course, refer to the services which lawyers, barbers, mechanics, and so forth provide to consumers.

Statistics show that of the $616.7 billion spent by consumers in 1970, $264.7 billion was for nondurables, $89.4 billion for durables, and $262.6 billion for services. This threefold breakdown is of considerable importance, because it reminds us that a good many consumer outlays are discretionary or postponable. During good times, durable, or "hard," goods are typically traded in or scrapped before they become utterly useless. This is ordinarily the case with automobiles and most major household appliances. But if bad times threaten or begin to materialize, consumers may forgo expenditures on durables, choosing to put up with an old model car and outdated household appliances. When depression threatens, the desire to conserve dollars for the nondurable necessities of food and clothing may cause a radical shrinkage of expenditures on durables. Much the same is true of many services. True, one cannot postpone an operation for acute appendicitis. But education, dental work, and a wide variety of less pressing services can be deferred or, if necessary, forgone entirely. In brief, the durable goods and services segments of personal consumption expenditures are subject to considerably more variation over time than are expenditures on nondurables. As is true of saving, many types of spending on durables and services are expendable during an economic crisis. Table 7·1 provides us with a more detailed look at the composition of personal consumption expenditures.

Consumer protection

In the past decade we have witnessed a soaring interest in consumer protection and knowledge. Consumer ignorance is basically an obstacle to effective competition. If consumers do not know the characteristics and qualities of different products or

TABLE 7·1 THE COMPOSITION OF PERSONAL CONSUMPTION EXPENDITURES, 1970

Types of consumption	Amount (billions of dollars)		Percent of total	
Durable goods		$ 89.4		14
Automobiles and parts	$ 37.4		6	
Furniture and household equipment	38.4		6	
All others	13.6		2	
Nondurable goods		264.7		43
Clothing and shoes	52.3		8	
Food and alcoholic beverages	131.6		21	
Gasoline and oil	22.9		4	
Tobacco, semidurable household furnishings, and others	57.9		10	
Services		262.6		43
Household operations	36.3		6	
Housing	91.9		15	
Transportation	18.1		3	
Personal services, recreation, and others	116.4		19	
Personal consumption expenditures		$616.7		100

Source: U.S. Department of Commerce, *Survey of Current Business*, April, 1970. Details may not add to totals because of rounding.

are unaware of the range of alternative products available to them, they are likely to make inefficient choices. If consumers buy pie and pantyhose—not to mention such complex products as drugs and stereo components—out of ignorance or under the influence of misleading advertising, they will foster a misallocation of resources from quality to shoddy products and thereby experience a decline in their real incomes. Furthermore, as Ralph Nader's indictment of the automobile industry dramatically illustrated, certain products may pose a hazard to the immediate consumer and to others either directly or indirectly through adverse environmental effects.

The Federal government has a long history of involvement in consumer protection. The 1906 Pure Food and Drug Act and the Fair Packaging and Labelling Act of 1969 are obvious and important illustrations. A major purpose of the Federal Trade Commission is to take action against fraudulent and misleading advertising. The 1969 Truth in Lending Act is designed to protect the consumer as a debtor. The act requires lenders to state in concise and uniform language the costs and terms of consumer credit. In particular, the total dollar amount of finance charges on a loan (including interest, investigation fees, credit insurance, and so on) must be explicitly indicated, and interest must be stated as an annual percentage rate.

One can make a good case for the government to establish and enforce standards of quality and safety for potentially hazardous products. Indeed, Federal safety standards for new automobiles have been imposed. In some cases—recall the Thalidomide tragedy and the environmental questions surrounding DDT—government has prohibited or restricted product sales. But some economists envision possible problems in proposals to have government establish product standards on a broad front:[2]

> Despite their beneficial intent, their adoption could in some cases have the undesirable effect of lessening competition among producers—and thus breaching one of the consumer's most effective defenses. The consumer's interest may not be served if so much reliability is required that it adds heavily to the cost. Another possible disadvantage in these restrictions is their effect on the development of new products. Producers may be uncertain about how well potential new products or services can meet published standards requiring reliable performance and freedom from other defects. Such uncertainty, together with the threat of costly damage suits, confiscation of goods, or time-consuming delays in satisfying a multitude of Federal requirements, may inhibit the development of new products and the entry of new firms into the market to compete with established companies.

[2]*Economic Report of the President, 1970,* pp. 97–98.

SUMMARY

1. All three sectors of the economy—households, businesses, and government—receive and spend income. Much can be learned concerning the actual operation of American capitalism by analyzing the sources and uses of the income received by each sector.
2. Insofar as the functional distribution of income is concerned, wages and salaries or labor income currently account for about 75 percent of the national income. Corporate profits account for 10 percent, proprietors' income for 8 percent, and interest and rental income for 4 percent and 3 percent of national income, respectively.
3. The manner in which income is distributed among individual households is a determinant of both the level and the composition of total output.
4. Households divide their total incomes among personal taxes, personal consumption expenditures, and personal saving. Currently about 15 percent of total income is paid to government as personal taxes, 79 percent is spent on consumer goods, and the remaining 6 percent is saved.
5. Since World War II, personal taxes have risen sharply in both absolute and relative terms. The waging of World War II and the need for large armament expenditures in the postwar era have been the major causal factors underlying this upsurge.
6. Personal saving, defined as income which is not spent on consumer goods or in paying taxes, is

directly related to the level of incomes. As income rises, both consumption and saving tend to increase absolutely.

7. In relative terms, personal consumption expenditures increase during bad times and decline during good times. However, in absolute terms consumption varies directly with the level of incomes. Expenditures on durables and the purchase of some services are more postponable than expenditures on nondurables. Since saving can be forgone entirely and indefinitely, personal consumption expenditures tend to be more stable over time than is personal saving.

QUESTIONS AND STUDY SUGGESTIONS

1. Distinguish between the personal distribution of income and the functional distribution of income.

2. What changes have taken place in the absolute and relative size of the major shares of national income? What accounts for these changes? How do you account for the relative stability of labor's share?

3. What implications does the personal distribution of income have for the size and composition of the economy's total output? For resource allocation? Explain.

4. "If we want capitalism, we must also accept inequality of income distribution." Evaluate and explain.

5. What happens to the volumes of consumption and saving as disposable income rises? What is "dissaving"? When is dissaving most likely to occur?

6. Distinguish between consumer durable goods and consumer nondurables. Give examples of each. Why is the demand for durables less stable than that for nondurables?

7. What changes have taken place in the absolute and relative size of personal taxes, personal consumption expenditures, and personal saving over the last four decades? Be specific.

8. Distinguish between saving as a "flow" and as a "stock." How did World War II increase the volume of personal savings?

9. Explain the relationship between "consumer protection" and allocative efficiency.

SELECTED REFERENCES

Economic Issues, 4th ed., reading 10.

Gilbey, Elizabeth Waterman: *A Primer on Economics of Consumption* (New York: Random House, Inc., 1968).

Hicks, J. R., A. G. Hart, and J. W. Ford: *The Social Framework of the American Economy,* 2d ed. (Fair Lawn, N.J.: Oxford University Press, 1955), chap. 17.

Katona, George: *The Mass Consumption Society* (New York: McGraw-Hill Book Company, 1964).

Linder, Staffan B.: *The Harried Leisure Class* (New York: Columbia University Press, 1970).

Preston, Lee E. (ed.): *Social Issues in Marketing* (Glenview, Ill.: Scott, Foresman and Company, 1968), part 4.

8

THE FACTS OF AMERICAN CAPITALISM: BUSINESSES

Private businesses constitute the second major aggregate of American capitalism. This chapter is a factual description of the business segment of the economy. More specifically, the goals of our discussion are fourfold:

1. The major characteristics of the business population will be explored. Emphasis here will be upon the diversity and fluidity of the business population, the various legal forms which private enterprises may assume, and the major industrial classifications.
2. The development of "big business" which has accompanied the development of the American economy will be explored in terms of the causes, the means, and the effects of this growth.
3. The blurring of the line between the private and public sectors of the economy will be noted as will the increasing importance and basic characteristics of the "nonprofit sector."
4. The dual role of businesses as producers and employers will be analyzed in terms of a single firm and then in terms of businesses as a group.

THE BUSINESS POPULATION

To avoid any possible confusion, we preface our discussion of the business population with some comments concerning terminology. In particular, one must distinguish among a plant, a firm, and an industry. A *plant* is a physical establishment in the form of a factory, farm, mine, retail or wholesale store, or warehouse which performs one or more specific functions in the fabrication and distribution of goods and services. A business *firm,* on the other hand, is the business organization which owns and operates these plants. While most firms operate only one plant, many firms own and operate a number of plants. Multiplant firms may be "horizontal," "vertical," or "conglomerate" combinations. For example, without exception, each of the large steel firms of our economy—United States Steel, Bethlehem Steel, Republic Steel, and so forth—are vertical combinations of plants; each firm owns ore and coal mines, limestone quarries, coke ovens, blast fur-

naces, rolling mills, forge shops, foundries, and, in some cases, fabricating shops. The large chain stores in the retail field—for example, A&P, Kroger, Safeway, J. C. Penny—are horizontal combinations in that each plant is at the same stage of production. Other firms are conglomerates; that is, they comprise plants which operate across many different markets and industries. For example, International Telephone and Telegraph, apart from operations implied by its name, is involved through affiliated plants on a large-scale basis in such diverse fields as automobile rentals, hotels, baking products, and education materials and is attempting to acquire additional firms in the insurance, fire-protection equipment, and vending-machine fields (Chapter 35).

An *industry* is a group of firms producing identical, or at least similar, products. Though an apparently simple concept, industries are usually difficult to identify in practice. For example, how are we to identify the automobile industry? The simplest answer is "All firms producing automobiles." But automobiles are heterogeneous products. While Cadillacs and Buicks are similar products, and Buicks and Fords are similar, and Fords and Javelins are similar, and Javelins and Volkswagens are similar, it is clear that Volkswagens and Cadillacs are very dissimilar. At least most buyers think so. And what about trucks? Certainly small pickup trucks are similar in some respects to station wagons. Is it better to speak of the motor vehicle industry rather than of the automobile industry? This matter of delineating an industry becomes all the more complex when it is recognized that most enterprises are multiproduct firms. American automobile manufacturers are also responsible for such diverse products as diesel locomotives, buses, refrigerators, guided missiles, and air conditioners. We pose these questions, not with a view to resolving them, but merely to note that industry classifications are rarely clear-cut and always somewhat arbitrary.

Diversity and fluidity

If we were able to stand back and achieve a broad overview of the business sector of American capitalism, we should be amazed by the phenomenal diversity of its approximately 11.6 million component firms. Indeed, no two business enterprises are exactly alike. At one extreme, you would be impressed by a giant corporation such as General Motors, which in 1969 owned total assets of $15 billion, employed 800,000 people, and realized annual sales of almost $24 billion. At the other end of the scale you could not help being amazed by the extremely large number of "shoestring" enterprises in the form of corner groceries, neighborhood beaneries, and small specialty shops with gross sales of less than $50 per day, and maybe one or two employees and some relatively worthless showcases or counters as their only real capital assets.

The American business population is also very fluid; "here today, gone tomorrow" is a fitting slogan for it. New firms are constantly entering and old firms leaving the business population. In recent years it has been common for some 450,000 to 500,000 new firms to come into existence each year and a somewhat smaller number—say 400,000 or 425,000—to fail every year. Each year—even during periods of prosperity—thousands upon thousands of enterprises fail. And thousands of new ones are started. Average age of all operating firms? About seven or eight years. Although the lion's share of the failures is among the "shoestring" enterprises, it is not uncommon for firms of significant size to slip into the sea of bankruptcy, for example, the Penn Central Railroad. Some people interpret such statistics with alarm. All things considered, however, it is amazing that so many of the small "shoestring" enterprises which are started every year survive and thrive as well as they do.

It should be noted, too, that change also characterizes the types of commodities produced by businesses, the productive techniques employed, the organization and structure of the firms, and the composition of the various industries.

LEGAL FORMS OF BUSINESS ENTERPRISES

The very diverse nature of the business population makes it imperative that we do some classifying. There are many bases for classifying business

firms—legal structure, type of product, and size are common criteria. We shall use all three of these, in varying degrees.

The present emphasis, however, is upon the basic legal forms which businesses might assume: (1) sole proprietorship, (2) partnership, and (3) the corporation. Let us define and outline the advantages and disadvantages associated with each.

Sole proprietorship

A sole proprietorship is simply an individual in business for himself. It is typically "a one-man show." The proprietor owns or obtains the materials and capital equipment used in the operation of his business and personally supervises its operation. Responsibility for the efficient coordination of the resources he owns or can command rests directly upon the proprietor's shoulders.

Advantages Obviously, this extremely simple type of business organization has certain distinct advantages:

1. A sole proprietorship is very easy to organize—there is virtually no legal red tape or expense. The businessman simply acquires the needed facilities and is "in business."

2. The proprietor is his own boss. He has complete freedom of action, and since his own profit income depends upon his enterprise's success, there is a strong and immediate incentive for him to manage the affairs of his business wisely. Furthermore, since the proprietor is sole owner, problems of disagreement and dissension among owners obviously cannot arise.

Disadvantages The sole proprietorship looks very rugged and individualistic. And it clearly is. But the disadvantages of this form of business organization are great:

1. With rare exceptions, the financial resources of a sole proprietorship are insufficient to permit the firm to grow into a large-scale enterprise. Specifically, finances are usually limited to what the proprietor has in his bank account and to what he is able to borrow. Since the mortality rate is very great for proprietorships, commercial banks are not overly eager to extend much credit to them.

2. Being in complete control of an enterprise forces the proprietor to carry out all basic management functions. The proprietor must be a Jack-of-all-trades. He must make all basic decisions concerning, for example, buying, selling, and the acquisition and maintenance of personnel, not to mention the technical aspects which might be involved in producing, advertising, and distributing his product. In short, the potential benefits of specialization in business management are usually inaccessible to the typical small-scale proprietorship.

3. Most important of all, the proprietor is subject to *unlimited liability*. This means that an individual in business for himself risks not only the assets of his firm but also his personal assets. Should the assets of an unsuccessful proprietorship be insufficient to satisfy the claims of creditors, those creditors can file claims against the proprietor's personal property. The stakes are high insofar as individual proprietorships are concerned.

Partnership

The partnership form of business organization is more or less a natural outgrowth of the sole proprietorship. As a matter of fact, partnerships were developed in an attempt to overcome some of the major shortcomings of proprietorships. A partnership is almost self-defining. It is a form of business organization wherein two or more individuals agree to own and operate a business. Usually they pool their financial resources and their business know-how. Similarly, they share the risks and the profits or losses which may accrue to them. There are innumerable variations. In some cases all partners are active in the functioning of the enterprise; in others, one or more partners may be "silent"—that is, they contribute their finances but do not actively participate in the management of the firm.

Advantages What are the advantages of a partnership arrangement?

1. Like the sole proprietorship, it is easy to organize. Although a written agreement is almost invariably involved, legal red tape is not great.

2. Greater specialization in management is made possible, because there are more participants. Managerial functions can be apportioned among the partners in terms of their abilities and training, with increased efficiency as the potential result.

3. Again, because there are several participants, the odds are that the financial resources of a partnership will be less limited than those of a sole proprietorship. Partners can pool their money capital and are usually somewhat better risks in the eyes of bankers.

Disadvantages But the disadvantages cannot be minimized. The partnership often does less to overcome the shortcomings of the proprietorship than first appears and, indeed, raises some new potential problems which the sole proprietorship does not entail.

1. Whenever there are several people participating in management, this division of authority can lead to inconsistent, divided policies or to inaction when action is required. Worse yet, partners may flatly disagree on basic policy. For all these reasons, management in a partnership may be very unwieldy and cumbersome.

2. The finances of partnerships are still limited, although generally superior to those of a sole proprietorship. The financial resources of three or four partners may be such as to restrict severely the potential growth of an enterprise.

3. The continuity of a partnership is very precarious. The withdrawal or death of a partner generally entails the dissolution and complete reorganization of the firm. Needless to say, this may severely disrupt the firm's operations.

4. Finally, unlimited liability plagues a partnership, just as it does a proprietorship. As a matter of fact, each partner is now liable for all business debts incurred, not only as a result of his own management decisions, but also as a consequence of the actions of any other partner. A wealthy partner risks all his riches on the prudence of his partners.

Corporation

Corporations are legal entities, distinct and separate from the individuals who own them. As such, these governmentally created "legal persons" can acquire resources, own assets, produce and sell products, incur debts, extend credit, sue and be sued, and carry on all those functions which any other type of enterprise performs.

Advantages The advantages of the corporate form of business enterprise have catapulted this type of firm into a dominant position in modern American capitalism.

1. The corporation is by far the most effective form of business organization for raising money capital. The corporation features new methods of finance—the selling of stocks and bonds—which allow the firm to tap the savings of untold thousands of households. Through the securities market, corporations can pool the financial resources of extremely large numbers of people. Financing by the sale of securities also has decided advantages from the viewpoint of the purchasers of these securities. First, households can now participate in enterprise and share the expected monetary reward therefrom without having to assume an active part in management. And, in addition, an individual can spread his risks by buying the securities of a variety of corporations. Finally, it is easy for the holder of corporate securities to dispose of his holdings. Organized stock exchanges facilitate the transfer of securities among buyers and sellers. Needless to say, this increases the willingness of savers to buy corporate securities. Furthermore, corporations ordinarily have easier access to bank credit than do other types of business organization. This is the case not only because corporations are better risks but also because they are more likely to provide banks with profitable accounts.

2. Corporations have the distinct advantage of *limited liability.* The owners (stockholders) of a corporation risk only what they paid for the stock purchased. Their personal assets are not at stake if the corporation founders on the rocks of bankruptcy. Creditors can sue the corporation as a legal person, but not

the owners of that corporation as individuals. Once again, this eases the corporation's task in acquiring money capital.

3. As a legal entity, the corporation has a life independent of its owners and, for that matter, of its individual officials. Proprietorships are subject to sudden and unpredictable demise, but, legally at least, corporations are immortal. The transfer of corporate ownership through the sale of stock does not disrupt this continuity which the corporation boasts. In short, corporations have a certain permanence which is lacking in other forms of business organization. This permanence is conducive to long-range planning and growth.

4. Corporations, because of their strategic position in acquiring money capital, typically have the ability to secure more specialized, and therefore more efficient, management than can proprietorships and partnerships.

5. Last but not least is the possible tax advantage which incorporation may give for an enterprise whose net profits are sizable. As we shall find in Chapter 9, the maximum 48 percent marginal tax rate facing a corporation is preferable to the maximum 70 percent marginal rate of the personal income tax.

Disadvantages The corporation's advantages are of tremendous significance and typically override any accompanying disadvantages. Yet the drawbacks of the corporate form of organization merit mentioning.

1. There is some red tape and legal expense in obtaining a corporate charter.

2. From the social point of view, it must be noted that the corporate form of enterprise lends itself to certain abuses. Because the corporation is a legal entity, unscrupulous businessmen sometimes can avoid personal responsibility for questionable business activities by adopting the corporate form of enterprise. And, despite legislation to the contrary, the corporate form of organization has been a cornerstone for the issue and sale of worthless securities. Note, however, that these are potential abuses of the corporate form, not inherent defects.

3. A further possible disadvantage of corporations has to do with the taxation of corporate income. Briefly, that part of corporate income which is paid out as dividends to stockholders is taxed twice—once as a part of corporate profits and again as a part of the stockholders' personal incomes. This disadvantage must be weighed against the previously noted fact that the maximum tax rates on corporate enterprises are less than those which may apply to unincorporated firms.

4. In the sole proprietorship and partnership forms, those who own the real and financial assets of the firm also manage or control those assets.[1] Most observers agree that this is as it should be. But in larger corporations, where the ownership of common stock is widely diffused over thousands or tens of thousands of stockholders, a fundamental cleavage between ownership and control will arise. This divorce of corporate ownership and control is intriguing, because, in theory at least, corporations are organized democratically. Each share of common stock has one vote in electing the firm's board of directors, which has ultimate authority for the operation of the enterprise. The more common stock you own, the more votes you have in selecting the corporation's officials.

How, then, do ownership and control come to be separated? The roots of the cleavage lie in the lethargy of the typical stockholder. Most stockholders simply do not exercise their voting rights or, if they do, merely sign these rights over by proxy to the corporation's present officers. And why not? The average stockholder knows nothing about the efficiency with which "his" corporation is being managed. So long as his dividends are regular and comparable in size to those received by the other members of his golf foursome who also hold common stock in various concerns, he is not troubled by the question of efficient management. And, after all, since the typical stockholder may own only 100 of 150,000 shares of common stock outstanding, his vote "really doesn't make a bit of difference"! Not voting, or the automatic signing over of one's proxy to current corporate officials, typically has the effect of making those officials self-perpetuating.

[1]The silent-partner arrangement is the exception.

The separation of ownership and control is of no fundamental consequence so long as the actions of the control (management) group and the wishes of the ownership (stockholder) group are in accord. The catch lies in the fact that the interests of the two groups are not always identical. For example, management, seeking the power and prestige which accompanies control over a *large* enterprise, may favor unprofitable expansion of the firm's operations, or a conflict of interest can easily develop with respect to current dividend policies. What portion of corporate earnings after taxes should be paid out as dividends, and what amount should be retained by the firm as undistributed profits? More obviously, corporation officials may vote themselves large salaries, pensions, bonuses, and so forth, out of corporate earnings which might otherwise be used for increased dividend payments.

There is no doubt that separation of ownership and control raises important and intriguing questions about the distribution of power and authority, the accountability of corporate managers, and the possibility of intramural conflicts between managers and shareholders. But perhaps a more fundamental question is whether the separation of ownership and control has undesirable consequences for society as a whole. In fact, there is no compelling evidence to suggest that this separation per se is economically harmful: "It would appear . . . that ownership-management separation has no significant economic impact, that is, it affects imperceptibly or not at all the allocation of resources, the rate of capital formation, and the distribution of income."[2]

To incorporate or not to incorporate

Which legal form of enterprise—proprietorship or corporation—is best? Probably the basic determinant of the legal form of enterprise is the amount of funds which a given line of production requires. For example, the corner magazine stand or the small curio or gift shop will have very modest money capital requirements. The only fixed assets which tie up some money capital are a few relatively inexpensive display counters. And the volume of business is so small that the need for "working capital" (funds which bridge the gap between costs and sales receipts) is also minimal. Why go to the cost and trouble of incorporating such a firm when the primary advantage of incorporating—the accessibility of large amounts of money capital through the sale of securities—is actually of little relevance? In contrast, modern technology and a much larger dollar volume of business make incorporation imperative in many lines of production. For example, in most branches of manufacturing—automobiles, steel, fabricated metal products, electrical equipment, household appliances, and so forth—very substantial money requirements for investment in fixed assets and for working capital are involved. The typical manufacturing concern in the United States has about $30,000 worth of capital equipment *per worker!* Given these circumstances, there is little choice. To exist is to incorporate. In brief, the best legal form of business enterprise varies from industry to industry, and the primary determinant of legal form is the money capital requirement of the particular industry.

Actually the American business population is distributed among the three legal forms in the manner indicated in Table 8·1. It is strikingly clear that the

[2] Morton S. Baratz, *The American Business System in Transition* (New York: Thomas Y. Crowell Company, 1970), p. 53.

TABLE 8·1 THE BUSINESS POPULATION BY FORM OF LEGAL ORGANIZATION

Form	Number of firms	Percent of total
Sole proprietorships*	9,126,000	79
Partnerships	906,000	8
Corporations	1,534,000	13
Total	11,566,000	100

* Includes farmers and professional people in business for themselves.
Source: U.S. Department of Commerce. Data are for 1967.

proprietorship form is numerically dominant. Yet corporations, though small in number, are frequently large in size and scale of operations. In fact, corporations account for over 60 percent of the output of all private business enterprises.

INDUSTRIAL DISTRIBUTION OF THE BUSINESS POPULATION

What do the 11.6 million firms which compose the business sector of our economy produce? Table 8·2 measures in several different ways the significance of the various industry classifications. Column 2 indicates the numerical and percentage distribution of the business population among the various industries. Column 3 shows in both absolute and relative terms the portion of the national income originating in the various industries. Column 4 indicates the absolute and relative amounts of employment provided by each industry. Several points in Table 8·2 are noteworthy:

1. The relatively small number of firms in manufacturing account for over one-fourth of national income and total employment. These figures correctly suggest that the American capitalist economy is highly industrialized, characterized by gigantic business corporations in its manufacturing industries.

2. The wholesale and retail industries and the service industries (hotels, motels, personal services, and so forth) are heavily populated with firms and are simultaneously very important sources of employment and incomes in the economy.

3. Note, too, the large number of firms engaged in

TABLE 8·2 INDUSTRY CLASSES: NUMBER OF FIRMS, NATIONAL INCOME ORIGINATING, AND EMPLOYMENT PROVIDED*

(1) Industry	(2) Number of private businesses		(3) Contribution to national income		(4) Full-time workers employed	
	Thousands	Percent	Billions	Percent	Thousands	Percent
Agriculture, forestry, and fisheries	3,411	29	$ 21.9	3	3,606	5
Mining	73	1			623	1
Construction	856	7	42.9	6	3,270	4
Manufacturing	402	4	215.4	30	19,564	26
Wholesale and retail trade	2,528	22	105.2	15	14,778	20
Finance, insurance, and real estate	1,223	11	78.2	11	3,667	5
Transportation, communications, and public utilities	359	3	54.9	7	4,441	6
Services	2,714	23	86.1	12	11,439	16
Government			105.0	15	12,800	17
Rest of world			4.7	1		
Total	11,566	100	$714.3	100	74,188	100

*Column 2 is for 1967; 3 for 1968; and 4 for 1970

Source: Statistical Abstract of the United States, 1970, tables 325, 481, 703.

agriculture but the relative insignificance of agriculture as a provider of incomes and jobs.

4. Table 8·2 reminds us that not all the economy's income and employment originate in private domestic enterprises. Government and foreign enterprises account for about 16 percent of the economy's national income and employ about 17 percent of the labor force.

BIG BUSINESS IN AMERICAN CAPITALISM

Numerically the vast majority of business firms are relatively small; over 80 percent of the total number of business firms in the United States hire less than 10 workers. But the relatively few firms that are large are extremely important, and for this reason American capitalism is sometimes labeled a "big-business" economy.

The major questions to be faced in connection with the existence of big businesses in American capitalism are these:

1. To what degree does big business prevail in the American economy?
2. Why and through what means have businesses sought "bigness"; that is, what are a firm's incentives for and means of growth?
3. What dangers, if any, are posed by the existence of giant business firms?

Extent of bigness

To what degree does big business prevail in our economy? Casual evidence suggests that many of our major industries are dominated by corporate giants which enjoy assets and annual sales revenues calculated in billions of dollars, employ hundreds of thousands of workers, have a hundred thousand or more stockholders, and earn annual profits after taxes running into hundreds of millions of dollars. We have already cited the vital statistics of General Motors, America's largest corporation, for 1969: sales, over $24 *billion;* assets, almost $15 *billion;* employees, about 800,000. Remarkably, there are only 18 or 20 nations in the world with annual national outputs in excess of GM's annual sales! Standard Oil of New Jersey follows with sales of $15 billion and assets of $17.5 billion in 1969. In that year some 42 industrial corporations enjoyed annual sales of over $2 billion; a total of 115 industrial firms realized sales in excess of $1 billion. If we include merchandising and transportation firms, these numbers swell to 52 and 158, respectively. By comparison only 7 state governments had revenues in excess of $2 billion in the same year. More generally, the fact that corporations constituting only 13 percent of the business population produce over 60 percent of the total output hints at the dominant role of large corporations in our economy.

There are data to suggest that historically the concentration of economic power has increased. For example, we note in Table 8·3 that the share of manufacturing assets held by the 100 largest manufacturing firms rose from slightly less than 40 percent in 1929 to almost 50 percent currently. In fact, today the 100 largest firms hold a larger share of total manufacturing assets than the 200 largest firms did some forty years ago. It should be emphasized, how-

TABLE 8·3 SHARE OF MANUFACTURING ASSETS HELD BY THE 100 LARGEST AND 200 LARGEST CORPORATIONS

Year	Share of 100 largest corporations	Share of 200 largest corporations
1929	38.2%	45.8%
1941	38.2	45.1
1950	38.4	46.1
1955	43.0	51.6
1960	45.5	55.2
1965	45.9	55.9
1968	48.8	60.4

Source: Senate Subcommittee on Antitrust and Monopoly, *Economic Concentration,* part 8a (Washington, 1969), p. 173.

ever, that economists debate the meaning and relevance of these and similar data to the issue of concentration; some highly respected economists feel that concentration has not been increasing or, if it has, it has been "at the pace of a glacial drift." It is generally agreed that the American economy *is* highly concentrated and that this concentration is not decreasing.

A final point is that economic concentration is highly uneven among various industries. For example, a look ahead at Table 29•1 reveals a list of industries wherein economic concentration is quite modest. Table 30•1, on the other hand, indicates a number of very basic manufacturing industries wherein economic power is highly concentrated. We shall return to the issues of big business and government policy in later chapters. Let it suffice to say at this point that large corporations do dominate the American business landscape and reasonable grounds do exist for labelling the United States a "big business" economy.

Incentives and means for bigness

What motivates business to grow? The incentives are complex and to some extent overlapping.

1. The desire to achieve greater *productive efficiency* has undoubtedly played a role in the growth of big business. Large firms are frequently in a better position to realize "mass-production economies" than are their small-scale brethren. Yet it seems that the production economies of many mergers—particularly of the conglomerate type—are nil. Furthermore, empirical research indicates that in many important industries the degree of economic concentration has gone beyond the point necessary to attain technically efficient plants.[3]

2. The search for *power* and *prestige* by business leaders has been a factor in the growth of big business. Being the largest employer or controlling the largest quantity of real capital assets in a given industry carries a certain amount of prestige that is generally recognized and much sought for in the business world.

3. *Security* and *assurance of long-run survival* have been factors in the growth of big business. Combination is often effected to "diversify the product line" of a firm as a safeguard against seasonal and cyclical fluctuations in business activity. Diversification also affords some measure of protection against the risk of unfavorable changes in consumer tastes. A multiproduct firm, by not putting all its eggs in one basket, is in a better position to survive the fickleness of consumers. And, of course, the goal of long-run survival prompts firms to branch out into newly developed industries where the prospects of future growth seem to be good. Similarly, combination may serve to ensure a firm of steady and continuing supplies of raw materials, semifinished goods, and product parts.[4]

4. The seeking of *greater financial rewards* has been the dominant factor in the growth of big business. One aspect of this profit seeking has to do with the windfall gains, or promoter's profits, resulting from the immediate combination of several corporations. But of greater significance in the long pull is the enhancement of prospective profits through the demise of competition which combination typically entails.

The means by which once-small firms have evolved into huge industrial giants are essentially twofold. In a relatively few cases—for example, Ford Motor Company and Alcoa (Aluminum Company of America)—gigantic business enterprises have developed primarily through *internal growth,* that is, through the reinvestment of the firm's earnings and the acquisition of additional funds for expansion by floating new issues of securities. However, the vast majority of firms now classified as "big businesses" have relied basically upon some form of business *combination*—mergers, consolidations, or the formation of trusts and holding companies—in achieving

[3]See in particular Joe S. Bain, "Economies of Scale, Concentration, and the Condition of Entry in Twenty Manufacturing Industries," *American Economic Review,* March 1954, pp. 15–39.

[4]The quest for security is a major theme of John Kenneth Galbraith's widely read book, *The New Industrial State* (Boston: Houghton Mifflin Company, 1967).

their present positions of dominance in their respective industries. The important point is that big business is a basic fact of American economic life. It is therefore highly relevant to probe briefly the implications of bigness in the business sector.

Should big business be feared?

This is a knotty question, permitting honest differences of opinion. Two basic schools of thought exist on this issue. We summarize these views here and defer a detailed analysis to Chapter 35.

One school of thought holds that big business is a natural and necessary outgrowth of a progressive industrial economy. In particular, it is argued that modern technology requires (1) the use of extremely large quantities of real capital, (2) wide markets, (3) a complex, closely integrated management, and (4) large and reliable sources of raw materials. Such an operation implies the need for large-scale producers. In short, the achievement of maximum productive efficiency through the employment of the best available technology often presupposes the concentration of economic power. Efficient production is only attainable when business units are large.

Equally competent observers view this situation much differently. Though efficiency may require "bigness" up to a point, it is argued that many American businesses have grown far beyond the size necessary for the achievement of maximum productive efficiency. Indeed, it is pointed out that some industrial giants are inefficient because they are too large; bureaucratic red tape has made them inflexible and unresponsive to fundamental changes in the economy. Furthermore, it is contended that bigness and monopoly power frequently go together. If control of the means of production rests in the hands of a relative few, then the concept of consumer sovereignty may be eroded or substantially supplanted by "producer sovereignty," to the end that resources are no longer allocated in terms of consumer wants. Stated differently, the internal logic of the circular flow model, as introduced in Chapter 3 and developed in Chapter 5, will be disrupted. The "invisible hand" will now fail to function effectively in identifying the private and social interest. Such developments imply fundamental changes in the ideology of pure capitalism.

NEW FORMS?

We tend to view the institutions of our economy on an either-or basis, that is, as profit-seeking private enterprises or governmental agencies. In fact, there exists in American capitalism a sizeable group of institutions which do not fall neatly into either category.

The "nonprofit" sector

The "nonprofit" sector consists of private institutions which are not profit motivated. Specifically, nonprofit organizations include various foundations, mutual insurance companies, Blue Cross and Blue Shield, savings and loan associations, professional societies and trade associations, consumer and farmer cooperatives, private colleges and universities, research institutions, museums and libraries, and so forth. The heterogeneous nature of even this modest listing makes it difficult to generalize with respect to the basic characteristics of nonprofit institutions. However, nonprofit organizations are similar to both the private and public sectors in that they compete with these two sectors for human and property resources. Furthermore, like profit-seeking firms, some of these institutions produce, or sponsor the production of, goods and services which are, or could be, sold in the market. Indeed, some nonprofit institutions—for example, mutual insurance companies and savings and loan associations—provide services which clearly compete with the private sector. A basic difference between the nonprofit and the private sector is that for the former, someone other than the recipient of the product or service pays all or a significant portion of the bill. For example, in making a grant the Ford Foundation directly subsidizes the research work of a scholar and indirectly subsidizes the general public,

which will presumably benefit from the new knowledge thereby produced.

Some observers are quite critical of nonprofit institutions. They contend, on the one hand, that nonprofit organizations are accorded certain legal privileges —exemption from taxes, from social security contributions, and from the obligation to bargain with labor unions—not accorded profit-seeking enterprises. Furthermore, critics allege that many nonprofit institutions are not subject to meaningful criteria of performance; such organizations allegedly escape both the constraints of the market which confront the private sector and the "public interest" mandate which presumably constrains the public sector through the functioning of democratic processes. Defenders of the nonprofit sector contend that these institutions typically provide goods or services which, since they entail substantial social benefits (education, research facilities, health services), are undersupplied by the private sector. Furthermore, the basic virtue of the nonprofit institution may very well lie in the fact that it partially escapes the constraints of both the market and political forces. This allows nonprofit institutions to pursue important objectives and sponsor significant undertakings which both private and public sectors might choose to ignore.

Two points are clear. First, any attempt to construct a realistic model of American capitalism must recognize the growing economic significance of the nonprofit sector. Second, interesting questions concerning the management, control, and economic performance of such organizations can legitimately be raised.[5]

Private-public amalgamation?

Businesses owned and operated by government are not new in the American economy. Municipal governments have traditionally owned and operated electric utilities, water and gasworks, and urban transportation facilities. The Post Office and TVA also come immediately to mind. Yet public enterprises per se are a very small segment of the national economy. Some observers argue, however, that the private and public sectors are becoming increasingly amalgamated. This "merging" of public and private takes at least two forms.

First, there are a number of important industries—the railroads, airlines and bus lines, trucking companies, public utilities, and telephone and telegraph companies—which are "natural monopolies" and therefore governmentally regulated. While the original purpose of this regulation was to protect consumers from the market power of firms in these industries, it is argued that government has in fact shielded these firms from competition. That is, the regulated industries have allegedly become wards of the state and, in effect, "quasi-public" institutions.

Second, recent controversy over the role of the so-called "military-industrial complex" in our society has brought to light the fact that a number of industries are highly dependent upon government markets for their profits and survival. In particular, it is argued that the economic interactions of the Department of Defense and firms supplying military and space hardware are so intimate and detailed that these firms have for all practical purposes lost their identity as distinctly private institutions and have become a part of the public bureaucracy.

The amalgamation argument is controversial and will reoccur for more intensive scrutiny in Chapters 35 and 40. We can assert at this point that economic institutions do not fall neatly into separate boxes marked "private" and "public" but rather are distributed over a private-public continuum.

DUAL ROLE OF BUSINESSES

Businesses, as well as households, play a dual role in American capitalism. On the one hand, businesses are the main fountainhead of the economy's total output of goods and services; almost 85 percent of total output is produced and sold by private enterprises (see Table 8·2). On the other hand, in accomplishing this production, businesses purchase or hire the bulk of the economy's available supplies of

[5]Those who wish to pursue this topic will do well to consult Eli Ginzberg, Dale L. Hiestand, and Beatrice G. Reubens, *The Pluralistic Economy* (New York: McGraw-Hill Book Company, 1965).

resources. In so doing, businesses provide employment and make wage, rent, interest, and profit payments to resource suppliers. In brief, businesses produce and sell goods and thereby acquire money receipts. These money receipts in turn are used to pay the costs of employing the resources necessary in the productive process, not to mention tax revenues. As is true of the household sector, businesses receive and disburse money flows.

Income statement: a single firm

The nature of these flows can best be visualized through the income or profit and loss statement of an individual firm. An income statement is simply an accounting statement which shows the sources of a firm's income or receipts and the manner in which these receipts are allocated or disbursed during any given year. More specifically, an income statement shows how much a firm gets in receipts from its sales of goods and services and how these receipts are apportioned among various production costs and profits. The statement balances because profits (or losses) are the difference between receipts and costs. Table 8·4 presents a simplified income statement for a manufacturing firm. We assume that this concern is a corporation which realizes all its receipts from the sale of a single product to wholesale firms A and B. Sales receipts (net of discounts and rebates) are $100,000.

How are these receipts apportioned between costs and profits? The left side of Table 8·4 provides the answer. Sizable payments for wages and salaries, materials provided by other firms, and interest and rental payments for the use of property resources are typical costs.

Item 5, depreciation, requires some explanation. Most resources—labor services and materials, for example—are used up in the accounting period in which they are purchased. Here the firm's monetary outlays coincide with the use of the particular resource. Capital equipment is a different story, however. A building or piece of machinery may last for many years, even though the actual payment for that machinery may occur entirely in the year of purchase. For example, suppose a $10,000 machine is pur-

TABLE 8·4 INCOME STATEMENT: A SINGLE FIRM (*hypothetical data*)

Allocations			Receipts		
(1) Wages and salaries		$ 35,000	(8) Sales of output		$100,000
(2) Materials		25,000	(a) To firm A	$40,000	
(3) Interest		8,000	(b) To firm B	60,000	
(4) Rents		4,000			
(5) Depreciation		1,000			
(6) Taxes		9,400			
(a) Payroll taxes	$ 3,000				
(b) Indirect business taxes (sales taxes, excises, etc.)	2,000				
(c) Corporate profits taxes	4,400				
(7) Corporate profits (after taxes)		17,600			
(a) Dividends	$10,000				
(b) Undistributed profits	7,600				
		$100,000			$100,000

chased by a firm in 1972. Its estimated life is ten years. Now, if the entire $10,000 cost of this machine were figured in the income statement for 1972 that year's profits would be grossly understated. Indeed, sizable losses might be incurred. Then, in ensuing years, while the machine is actually being used up, profits would be overstated. The machinery would be contributing to output and therefore to receipts, but would entail no cost to the firm. To avoid such arbitrary effects of durable machinery and building purchases upon annual profits and losses, accountants estimate that portion of the value of the machine which will be used up in each year of its estimated ten-year life. This amount, called a "depreciation charge," is then apportioned more or less evenly over the ten-year period. In this way a more accurate picture of annual profits is achieved. Thus, although the actual disbursement for machinery may be made in one year, annual depreciation charges adjust the firm's profits as if the equipment costs occurred evenly over the lifetime of the machinery. In short, the depreciation charge is merely a bookkeeping entry which makes for a more accurate estimate of profits over a period of time.

Table 8·4 also indicates the importance of taxes as a cost of doing business. A corporation will be faced first with payroll taxes, which are contributions made in the financing of the social security programs. Sales and excise taxes are other important expenses. Such taxes are listed as "indirect business taxes" because they are not levied directly upon the firm as such but rather upon the product which the firm produces. Corporate income taxes are levied directly upon the net taxable profits of the corporation. What remains—corporate profits after taxes—is typically divided between dividends paid out to stockholders and undistributed corporate profits or business saving.

Income statement: the business sector

Table 8·5 is a consolidated income statement for the entire business sector of American capitalism for 1969. This is merely a gigantic income statement for all the business firms which make up the business

TABLE 8·5 INCOME STATEMENT: THE BUSINESS SECTOR, 1969 *(in billions of dollars)*

Allocations			Receipts		
(1) Wages and salaries		$404	(8) Sales of output		$794
(2) Interest		31	(a) To consumers	$549	
(3) Rents		22	(b) To other businesses	109*	
(4) Depreciation		79	(c) To government	136	
(5) Taxes		143			
(a) Payroll taxes	$27				
(b) Indirect business taxes	83				
(c) Corporate income taxes	33				
(6) Corporate profits (after taxes)		49			
(a) Dividends	$25				
(b) Undistributed profits	24				
(7) Proprietors' income		67			
		$794			$794

* Includes foreign sales.
Source: Calculated from U.S. Department of Commerce data. Details may not add up to totals because of rounding.

sector of our economy. In most respects, it is similar to the income statement for a single firm.

The importance of the consolidated income statement for the business sector is that it provides us with a picture of the size and composition of the total output provided by the major producing sector of the economy.[6] The receipts side of this consolidated statement tells us that the business sector produced approximately $749 billion worth of goods and services in 1969. The breakdown of these sales indicates in a general way the composition of this output. Some $549 billion, or 69 percent of the business sector's production, was in the form of consumer goods; $109 billion, or 14 percent, in the form of capital goods (machinery, equipment, and buildings) which firms produced and sold to one another; and $136 billion, or 17 percent, in the form of social goods and services (mostly armaments) sold to government.

It should be emphasized that the consolidated income statement leaves out most interbusiness transactions. As a matter of fact, all transactions between businesses, except those where the buying firm is the actual user or consumer of the product, are concealed by the consolidated income statement. This is as it should be if we seek an accurate picture of the size and composition of the business sector's yearly output. The inclusion of "intermediate" transactions between businesses would lead to an exaggeration of the business sector's output. A simple illustration will make this evident. There are likely to be several stages of production in turning out a finished product. In producing a suit, the rancher sells wool to a mill for $10, the mill sells woolen textiles to a manufacturer for $20, the manufacturer sells the finished suit to a wholesaler for $40, the wholesaler sells it to a retailer for $50, and the retailer sells it to you as a consumer for, say, $70. To include all these transactions would tell us that $190 (= $10 + $20 + $40 + $50 + $70) worth of production has occurred in making a suit. But this is nonsense! Only $70 worth of production has occurred. Why? Because the intermediate transactions leading up to the final sale of the product to the consumer are covered, or included, in the $70 selling price. The value of the raw wool, the value of the processing done at the mill, the value of the handling and distributional services performed by the wholesaler and retailer are all included in the $70. To count these intermediate transactions separately would be to exaggerate grossly the output of the business sector. However, we do include sales between businesses when the buying firm is the ultimate user of the product. The production of capital goods, that is, machinery and equipment, by some firms for use by other firms is as much a part of the year's production as is the production of shoes and soap flakes for consumers and of highways and schools for government. To omit these final sales of capital goods would be to understate the year's production.

On the disbursement side of the picture, we see how the businesses allocate their total receipts. In Table 8•5, items 1, 2, 3, 6*a*, and 7—item 7 added to acknowledge that the business sector is composed of both incorporated and nonincorporated businesses—are payments for resources supplied by households. These items, totaling $549 billion, are income payments from the viewpoint of households. Item 4, depreciation, is a bookkeeping adjustment to give us a more accurate picture of business profits. Tax items 5*a*, *b*, and *c*, totaling $143 billion, flow to government. Item 6*b* is that part of business profits which is retained in the business sector; it constitutes business saving. Percentagewise, about 69 percent of business receipts flow as wage, rent, interest, and profit payments to households. Taxes account for about 18 percent. The remaining 13 percent is business saving and depreciation.

The reader will probably have noted that the allocation for materials has been dropped in moving from the single firm's income statement to the consolidated statement for the business sector. The reason again has to do with "intermediate" transactions. For the *individual* firm, relationships with other firms from which it buys materials are important, and such purchases must be listed as disbursements or allocations. But for businesses *as a group*, these transactions are self-canceling; payments from one firm to

[6]For simplicity's sake, we assume that there is no change in inventories to cause a discrepancy between the volume of production and the volume of sales in any given year.

another in the purchase of materials offset one another. The allocation of $25,000 for materials by firm X is offset by $25,000 of receipts flowing to firm Y, the seller of the materials. In other words, the consolidated income statement eliminates or cancels the expenditures and receipts which occur between firms in the business sector and shows only the relationship of the business sector to the household and governmental sectors of the economy. Note that all the allocations shown in Table 8·5 flow to the household sector as income payments, to the governmental sector as taxes, or simply stay in the business sector as undistributed receipts.

SUMMARY

1. The business population of American capitalism is both heterogeneous and fluid.

2. Sole proprietorships, partnerships, and corporations are the major legal forms which business enterprises may assume. Though proprietorships dominate numerically, the bulk of total output is produced by corporations. Corporations have grown to their position of dominance in the business sector primarily because they are *a.* characterized by limited liability and *b.* in a superior position to acquire money capital for expansion.

3. Manufacturing accounts for a larger percentage of national income and employment in American capitalism than does any other industrial classification. The wholesale, retail, and service industries are also major sources of income and employment.

4. Many basic industries in our economy are dominated by a small number of large corporations. Major incentives underlying the growth of these big businesses are *a.* the desire to achieve greater productive efficiency, *b.* the search for power and prestige by business leaders, *c.* security and the assurance of a long-run survival, and *d.* the pursuit of greater financial rewards. Big businesses have developed by means of internal growth and by combination.

5. Economists disagree on the desirability of big businesses. One view holds that big businesses are essential for achieving efficient production. Others contend that many American businesses have grown far beyond the size essential for efficiency in production and have acquired considerable monopoly power as a result of size.

6. Private nonprofit institutions are an increasingly important component of the American economy; some economists envision a growing amalgamation of the private and public sectors.

7. Income statements are useful analytical tools for the economist in that they reveal the sources of income and the disbursement thereof for an individual firm or the business sector as a whole.

QUESTIONS AND STUDY SUGGESTIONS

1. Distinguish clearly between a plant, a firm, and an industry. Why is an "industry" difficult to define in practice?

2. What are the major legal forms of business organization? Briefly state the advantages and disadvantages of each. How do you account for the dominant role of corporations in our economy?

3. Explain and evaluate the separation of ownership and control which characterizes the corporate form of business enterprise. Explain the following statement:[7]

> In the economic realm . . . [a] situation prevails that runs counter to the basic concept of democracy: corporation managers wield far-reaching power over stockholders and employees, and they constantly make decisions affecting the public interest, without any clearly defined responsibility to the public. Whereas in a capitalist democracy political policies are arrived at through processes of consent that begin at the bottom and end at the top, in corporate business economic policies are made from the top and passed on to the bottom.

4. What are the major industries in American capitalism in terms of *a.* the number of firms in operation and *b.* the amount of income and employment provided?

[7] William Ebenstein, *Today's Isms,* 3d ed. (Englewood Cliffs, N.J.: Prentice-Hall, Inc., 1961), p. 166.

5. What factors have motivated the growth of big business in the United States? What are the pros and cons of big business?

6. Explain and evaluate the following statements:
a. "It is the consumer, and the consumer alone, who casts the vote that determines how big any company should be."
b. "The very nature of modern industrial society requires labor, government, and businesses to be 'big' and their bigness renders impossible the functioning of the older, small-scale, simpler, and more flexible capitalist system."[8]
c. "The legal form which an enterprise assumes is dictated primarily by the financial requirements of its particular line of production."

7. What is the nonprofit sector? What are the advantages of nonprofit institutions? How can one measure the efficiency of nonprofit institutions?

8. What is an income statement? Of what value is a consolidated income statement for the business sector? Why does the consolidated income statement exclude all interbusiness transactions except the sale of capital goods to their ultimate users? Why is this desirable?

[8]Eugene O. Golob, *The Isms* (New York: Harper & Row, Publishers, Incorporated, 1954), p. 53.

SELECTED REFERENCES

Economic Issues, 4th ed., readings 11 and 12.

Baratz, Morton S.: *The American Business System in Transition* (New York: Thomas Y. Crowell Company, 1970).

Boulding, Kenneth E.: *Economic Analysis: Microeconomics,* 4th ed. (New York: Harper & Row, Publishers, Incorporated, 1966), chaps. 15 and 16.

Cheit, Earl F. (ed.): *The Business Establishment* (New York: John Wiley & Sons, Inc., 1964).

Hacker, Andrew (ed.): *The Corporation Take-over* (Garden City, N.Y.: Doubleday & Company, Inc., 1965).

Heyne, Paul T.: *Private Keepers of the Public Interest* (New York: McGraw-Hill Book Company, 1968).

McGuire, Joseph W.: *Business and Society* (New York: McGraw-Hill Book Company, 1963).

9

THE FACTS OF AMERICAN CAPITALISM: GOVERNMENT

Current facts characterizing the private sectors of the economy were discussed in Chapters 7 and 8. A factual look at the governmental or public sector of American capitalism is the basic task of the present chapter. Persistent controversy surrounding the scope of government's economic role makes it particularly important that the facts of government be clearly understood and placed in proper perspective.

DUAL ROLE OF GOVERNMENT

Although, as Chapter 6 revealed, there are many ways in which government affects economic life, it is through taxation and expenditures that the functions of government are most directly felt. Indeed, changes in the size and composition of government spending and the volume of tax revenues reflect with a fair degree of accuracy any changes in the size and character of government's role in the economy. It is with the public sector's role as a transactor, that is, as a receiver and disposer of "income," that this chapter is concerned.

One point must be emphasized at the outset. There is a significant difference between the transactions of the private and public sectors of the economy: the former are voluntary, and the latter compulsory. The receipts and expenditures of households and businesses are the result of voluntary decisions by those two aggregates in buying and selling goods and resources. Government tax revenues are the result of compulsory levies: households and businesses have no choice but to pay taxes. To a lesser degree, this compulsion appears on the expenditure side of government's transactions. While no one is compelled to use governmentally provided highways, libraries, or health clinics, all physically and mentally capable children who are within stated age brackets must consume public education or its equivalent.

GROWTH OF GOVERNMENT TAX REVENUES AND EXPENDITURES

Figures 9·1 and 9·2 make clear the growing importance of the public sector of the economy by summarizing the long-term *absolute* growth in government spending and taxation. But this is not all: Government's role as a transactor has also expanded significantly in *relative* terms. In 1929 government expenditures claimed only about 8 percent of total output. By 1939 this figure had expanded to 15 percent. At the peak of the war effort in 1943–1944, government expenditures had expanded to 45 percent of total output. In the postwar era, government expenditures have been about 20 percent of total

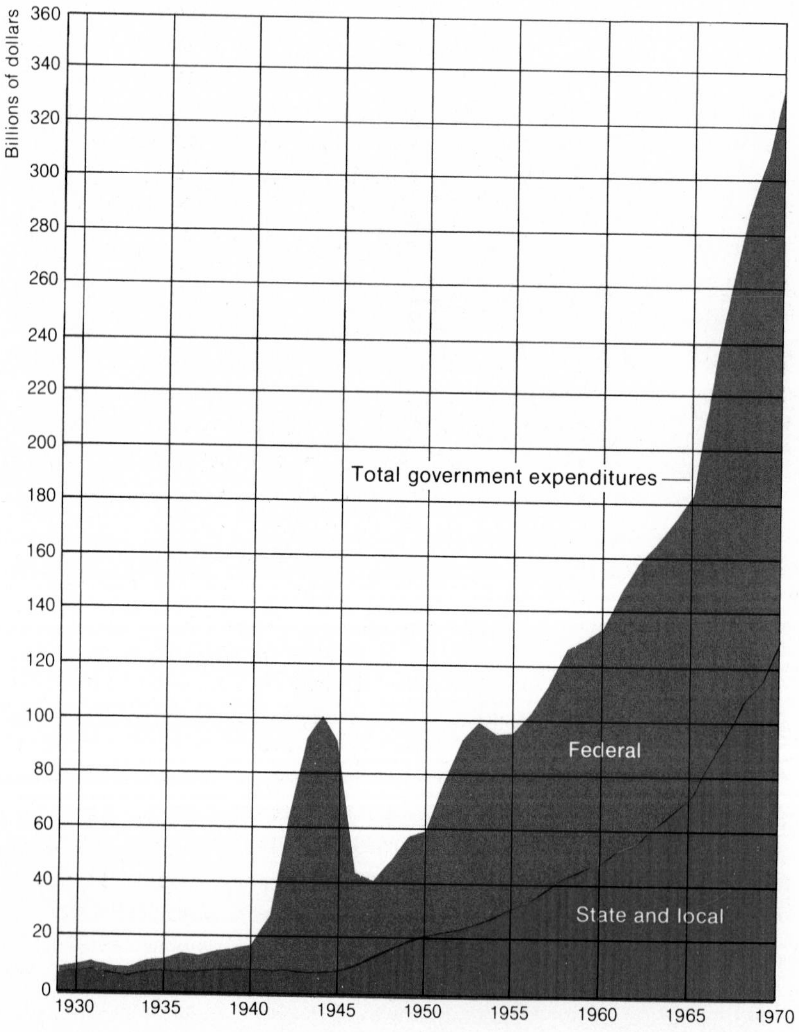

FIGURE 9·1 FEDERAL, STATE, AND LOCAL EXPENDITURES, 1929–1970

Government expenditures have grown both absolutely and as a percentage of total output. Hot and cold wars, population growth, urbanization, and inflation are some of the more important factors underlying this growth. (*Economic Report of the President.*)

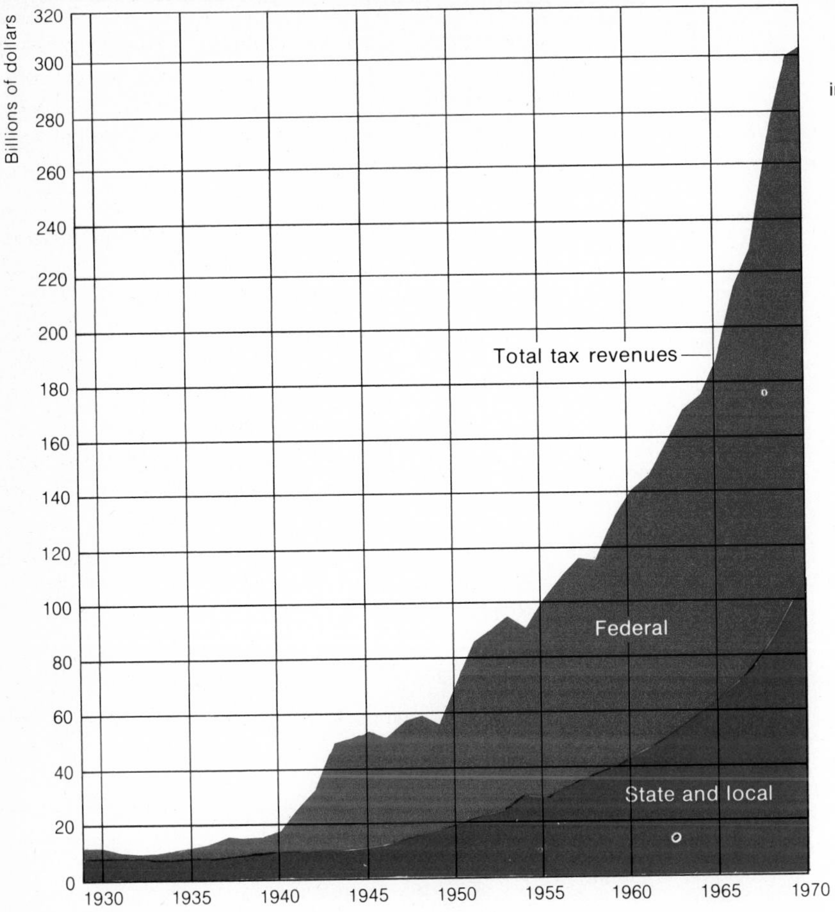

FIGURE 9·2 FEDERAL, STATE, AND LOCAL TAX REVENUES, 1929–1970

Government tax collections have also increased significantly over time, roughly matching the increases in government spending. (*Economic Report of the President.*)

output (see Table 6·1). The 23 percent of total output purchased by government in 1970 was largely financed by an average tax bill of $1,070 presented to every man, woman, and child in the United States!

Some causes

The spectacular growth in government spending and tax collections has a multiplicity of causes. As noted in Chapter 6, root causes center around the desire of the citizenry to correct or alleviate the instability, inefficiency, and inequities which the price system of pure capitalism may foster. But more immediate causes are also abundant:

1. War and defense Hot and cold wars have sustained Federal expenditures at high levels for the past three decades. War, national defense, and military-space research are the major causes of the phenomenal growth of government spending and taxa-

tion which has occurred since 1940. In 1970 expenditures by the Department of Defense were on the order of $80 billion per year.

2. Population growth Population growth has been rapid; there are about twice as many Americans today as there were a scant fifty-five years ago. This obviously means there are more people for whom social goods and services must be provided. Stated differently, even with a constant level of government spending per person, total government spending would have increased dramatically in recent decades.

3. Urbanization and the demand for social goods Not only has the size of our population been an important factor underlying the growth of government, but so has the geographic location of the population. In particular, the fact that our economy has become increasingly urbanized has necessitated massive expenditures on streets, public transportation facilities, police and fire protection, sewers, and so forth. We shall note shortly that, despite rapid growth in spending, state and local governments have experienced great difficulties in meeting these needs adequately. Furthermore, the public has demanded more and better social goods and services to "match" the rising standard of living provided by the private sector of the economy. We want bigger and better highways to accommodate more and better automobiles. We want more and better educational facilities to upgrade the labor force for the more demanding jobs of private industry.

4. Environmental quality Population growth and urbanization have contributed to serious and well-publicized problems of environmental quality. In particular, society has become highly aware that the production and consumption of vast quantities of goods can give rise to serious social or spillover costs in the form of air, water, and land pollution. Government has inherited a central role in coping with these environmental problems.

5. Inflation A rising price level accounts for a considerable portion of the historical rise in government spending. Because of inflation, government has simply had to spend larger and larger amounts for given quantities of goods and services. As a matter of fact, the prices of the goods and services purchased by government have increased more rapidly than have the prices of private consumer and investment goods.

And this list is by no means complete.

As with the business and household sectors of the economy, the receipt and expenditure of government income need not match in any particular year or period of years. Surpluses and deficits—the latter in particular—are not at all uncommon insofar as public finance is concerned. Figures 9·1 and 9·2 tell us, however, that tax collections have *generally* followed the trend of government spending. World War II was a major exception: Federal war expenditures were heavily financed by deficits. Furthermore, since World War II there has been a growing divergence between expenditures and tax revenues for state and local governments.

Purchases versus transfers

Going beyond the trend of government spending, we must also distinguish between two fundamentally different types of governmental outlays.

On the one hand, *government purchases* of goods and services is virtually self-defining. This concept refers to such ordinary governmental purchases as paper clips, typewriter ribbons, automobiles, and school buildings, as well as to such uniquely social goods as jet fighters, atomic submarines, superhighways, and space capsules. Purchases of services include the hiring of clerks, schoolteachers, judges, servicemen, and so forth. Government purchases are often called *exhaustive* in that they directly absorb or employ resources.

Transfer payments, on the other hand, are disbursements for which government currently receives no products or services in return. Most government "welfare" expenditures fall in this classification: for example, social security payments to the aged, unemployment compensation, relief payments, and aid to the handicapped. Some transfer payments, called "subsidies," go to businesses: for example, certain payments to farmers under the current agricultural

program. Because transfer payments rechannel tax revenues back to households and businesses, these payments in effect are "negative taxes." Transfers are frequently labeled *nonexhaustive* because, as such, they do not directly absorb resources.

There is a noteworthy difference between transfer payments and government purchases of goods and services. Through government spending on goods, society tends to reallocate resources from private to social goods consumption. Through transfers, government changes the composition of the output of private goods. If government taxes amount to $10, we can expect purchases of private goods and services to decline by roughly that amount. In purchasing social goods and services with this $10 worth of tax revenue, individuals or groups within the economy, working through government, are in effect negotiating a substitution of social for private goods. Transfer payments are different: Instead of increasing social goods at the expense of private goods, transfers merely tend to "rearrange" private consumption. Though $10 in tax revenues will reduce the private goods consumption of taxpayers by about that amount, households to whom this $10 is transferred can be expected to increase their expenditures on private goods by about $10. But in all probability, the recipients will purchase somewhat different goods than the taxpayers. Hence, transfers alter the composition of private goods production.

This distinction between government purchases and transfer payments is relevant for our discussion of the growth of government. One can argue that transfer payments involve a lesser degree of government intervention in the economy than do government purchases. Because transfers in recent years have been growing more rapidly than government purchases, Figures 9•1 and 9•2 may tend to overstate slightly the expanding role of the public sector.

FEDERAL, STATE, AND LOCAL FINANCE

Let us now examine taxation and expenditures at each level of government, noting first the relative economic significance of the three levels as revealed in Figures 9•1 and 9•2. Federal spending and taxing is significantly greater than the spending and taxing of state and local governments combined. It is also evident, however, that in the last two decades spending and taxing increased rapidly at the state and local levels.

Federal finance

Now for a more detailed look at Federal tax revenues and expenditures. What types of goods and services does the Federal government purchase? And from what sources are taxes collected to finance these outlays? Table 9•1 tells the story for 1971.

Federal expenditures Even a cursory glance at the Federal budget makes painfully clear the economic costs of mobilization and war. The first four categories of spending are the result of past wars, the present cold war, the war in Vietnam, and the desire to head off future wars.

National defense expenditures include outlays to maintain and equip the armed services and to provide military aid to our allies. National defense outlays account for about 36 percent of total Federal expenditures. But even this gigantic outlay belies the economic costs of wars and military preparedness. The next four classes of spending are also closely associated with past wars and national military preparedness. *Veterans' services*—which include GI Bill payments, medical care, disability pay, and pensions to veterans and their dependents—obviously are expenditures resulting from the two world wars, the Korean conflict, and Vietnam. And, since the bulk of the Federal debt of some $390 billion was incurred in financing World War II, the annual payment of *interest* on the public debt also must be considered as a war-born outlay. Furthermore, *international affairs and finance* involve expenditures for the economic and technological development of foreign countries and the costs of administering our foreign affairs. In part, these outlays stem from altruistic motives. But a selfish reason dominates: these expenditures are designed to keep foreign countries

TABLE 9·1 THE FEDERAL BUDGET, 1971

Tax receipts	Billions of dollars	Percent of total
Personal income taxes	$ 88.3	45
Payroll taxes	42.3	22
Corporate income taxes	30.1	15
Excise taxes	16.8	9
Estate and gift taxes	3.7	2
All other	13.0	7
Total receipts	$194.2	100

Expenditures	Billions of dollars	Percent of total
National defense	$ 76.4	36
Veterans' services	10.0	5
Interest on public debt	19.4	9
International affairs and finance	3.6	2
Space research and technology	3.7	2
Income security	55.5	26
Health	14.9	7
Agriculture and rural development	5.3	2
Education and manpower	8.3	4
Commerce and transportation	11.4	5
All other	4.3	2
Total expenditures	$212.8	100

Source: Economic Report of the President. Because of rounding, figures may not add up to totals. Data are estimates.

from turning to communism. Finally, outlays for space research clearly have important implications for national security. As a group, these five expenditure categories account for about $113 billion, or about 54 percent, of total Federal outlays. War and military preparedness carry extremely high price tags. The remaining categories of spending listed in Table 9·1 are largely self-explanatory.

Federal receipts The receipts side of Table 9·1 makes it clear that the Federal government relies on a variety of taxes for revenue. It is equally evident that the *personal income tax, payroll taxes,* and the *corporate income tax* are the basic revenue getters. About 45 cents of each dollar of gross tax revenue collected by the Federal government is in the form of personal income taxes, and 22 cents of each dollar is in the form of payroll taxes. Another 15 cents of each dollar collected is accounted for by the corporate income tax. The remaining 18 cents comes primarily from excises and a variety of other taxes. What is the nature of these major sources of Federal revenue?[1]

Personal income tax The personal income tax is a tax levied on the incomes of households and unincorporated businesses after certain deductions and exemptions have been taken into account.[2] The basic characteristic of this tax is that progressive tax rates are applied to taxable income. The larger your taxable income, the higher the *rate* at which that income is taxed. Progressive tax rates are, in fact, one important means of achieving greater equity in the distribution of income (Chapter 6).

As the personal income tax is applied in the United States, these higher and higher rates apply to the

[1]Our discussion of Federal taxation is based upon the Tax Reform Act of 1969, some provisions of which do not become fully effective until 1973.

[2]The major deductions and exemptions from gross income in determining taxable income are (1) business costs and expenses incurred in earning income, (2) gifts to charitable institutions, (3) interest payments, (4) most other tax payments, and (5) a $750 exemption for the taxpayer and each of his dependents.

increments of income earned and not to total income. For example, a family of four in 1973 would pay no income tax if its income was $4,000[3] or less, because its taxable income would be zero. Assuming no additional deductions or exemptions, the next $1,000 of income earned would be taxed at a rate of 14 percent. Thus, our family of four, earning a $5,000 income, would pay about $140 (14 percent of $1,000) in personal income taxes. The next $1,000 chunk of income would be taxed at a slightly higher rate, 15 percent. In other words, a family of four earning $6,000 would pay $290 in personal income taxes—nothing on the first $4,000, $140 on the next $1,000, and $150 on the next $1,000. Should you be fortunate enough to earn a taxable income of, say, $40,000 per year, you would encounter a tax rate of 48 percent on additional income falling in the next income bracket. And, at the extreme, those who pull down a taxable income in excess of $200,000 per year will find the Federal income tax claiming 70 percent of each taxable dollar earned in excess of $200,000. *Note:* You can never be worse off by making an extra dollar. At least 30 cents of it will be yours.[4]

It is important to note that, although the *marginal tax rate*—the percentage of each *additional* chunk of income received which is paid in taxes—goes up sharply as income increases, the effective or *average tax rate*—the rate of tax paid on one's *total* income—is usually considerably less. Our mythical family, for example, encounters a marginal tax rate of 15 percent on each dollar of income earned between $5,000 and $6,000, but the average rate of taxation is only about 5 percent ($290 divided by $6,000). However, as income rises, the marginal tax rates rise so sharply that even the average tax rate, though less than the marginal tax rate, comes to be large. Using the extreme example, a family receiving a taxable income of $200,000 per year will encounter the peak *marginal* tax rate of 70 percent. The family's Federal income tax bill would be about $110,980, making the *average* tax rate about 56 percent. In all fairness it must be noted that with the aid of a capable lawyer or tax accountant, many wealthy taxpayers take advantage of legal loopholes in the personal income tax. It is doubtful, for example, that those few who fall in the higher tax brackets—where the average rate is, say, 40 or 50 percent—actually pay at a rate in excess of, say, 30 or 35 percent. Indeed, the widely publicized fact that many rich and superrich Americans—some of whom realize annual incomes of $1 million or more!—have legally manipulated their financial affairs so as to pay no taxes at all led to provisions in the Tax Reform Act of 1969 which "catch" ultrahigh income receivers, albeit at low tax rates.

During World War II, the withholding system of collecting the Federal income tax was installed. Under this system, the employer deducts an employee's income taxes from his paycheck and forwards them to the Treasury. Although this method of payment puts the government in the position of a preferred creditor, there are distinct advantages in the withholding system for both the government and the taxpayer. From the government's point of view

1. Income tax evasion is reduced.
2. Tax receipts are more closely attuned to changes in tax rates and size of incomes.
3. The tax is generally easier to administer.

From the taxpayer's point of view, the system in effect puts his income tax bill on the installment plan and makes it somewhat less burdensome to pay.

Corporate income tax The corporate income tax, the Federal government's second major source of revenue, has a relatively simple structure. Any corporation whose annual net earnings are under $25,000 is taxed at a rate of 22 percent. For corporations earning in excess of $25,000 the rate on all dollars earned above the $25,000 mark is 48 percent. For example, a corporation realizing a net annual income of $50,000 would pay $17,500 in corporate income taxes—$5,500 (22 percent of the first $25,000) plus $12,000 (48 percent of the remaining $25,000).

The corporate income tax, as mentioned earlier,

[3] Four exemptions of $750 plus a low-income allowance of $1,000 total $4,000.

[4] Further note: If all the family's income is "earned" income (from wages, salaries, and professional fees) the maximum marginal tax rate is 50 percent, rather than 70 percent.

entails a highly controversial problem—"double taxation." That particular part of the income stream which takes the form of dividends is taxed twice, while other forms of income are taxed but once. All corporate net income is first taxed under the corporate income tax as described above. In addition, that portion of corporate earnings which flows to stockholders is taxed for a second time as personal income. This double taxation of dividends is felt by many economists to be a glaring inequity in the present structure of income taxes. The inequity, however, is at least partially offset by the fact that retained corporate earnings are not subject to tax rates higher than 48 percent.

Sales and excise taxes Commodity or consumption taxes may take the form of sales taxes or excise taxes. The difference between the two is basically one of degree. Sales taxes fall on a wide range of products while excises are taxes on a small, select list of commodities.

The Federal government does not levy a general sales tax; sales taxes are the bread and butter of most state governments. But as Table 9·1 indicates, the Federal government does collect excise taxes imposed upon such commodities as alcoholic beverages, tobacco, gasoline, and trucks.

Payroll and other taxes Social security contributions, or payroll taxes, are the premiums paid on the compulsory insurance plans provided for by existing social security legislation. These taxes are paid by both employers and employees. For the most part, these funds flow into insurance trust funds held by the Federal government. Improvements in, and extensions of, our social security programs have resulted in significant increases in payroll taxes in recent years.

Table 9·1 also shows limited amounts of funds flowing to government as gift and estate taxes and as the result of the sales of various licenses and permits. Conspicuous by its absence is the property tax—the basic source of tax revenue for local units of government.

Federal tax loopholes A basic purpose of the Federal tax system—of the progressive rates of the personal and corporate income taxes in particular—is to make the distribution of income more equitable. But in fact there are important loopholes in the personal and corporate income taxes, that is, provisions which give favorable tax treatment to certain kinds of income. Because these loopholes generally favor high-income recipients, the after-tax distribution of income is less equal than would otherwise be the case (see Table 9·5). Skirting highly technical details, let us briefly mention the three most important loopholes.

1. ***Tax-exempt securities*** Interest income on the bonds of state and local governments is exempt from the Federal income tax. Many high-income people can reduce their income tax liabilities very substantially by availing themselves of this loophole. For example, people in the highest personal income tax bracket can reduce the tax rate on their interest income from 70 to zero percent by switching from savings deposits or corporate bonds to state and local bonds.

2. ***Capital gains*** An individual realizes a capital gain when he sells either securities or property at a higher price than he paid. Provided the gain is long term, that is, that the securities or property have been held for six months or more, one-half the value of the capital gain is tax exempt and the remainder is taxed as ordinary income *or,* at the taxpayer's discretion, at a rate of 50 percent. This means that the maximum tax rate on capital gains is 25 percent, much less than a wealthy taxpayer would pay on other kinds of income.[5]

3. ***Depletion allowances*** The basic loophole in the corporate income tax is that certain extractive industries—mining and petroleum—are allowed to deduct a certain percentage of their sales in determining their taxable income. For example, the petroleum industry can reduce the value of its sales by 22 percent (up to a limit of one-half its taxable income) in determining its taxable income. The rationale for this loophole is that the depletion allowance is necessary to stimulate investment in the highly risky

[5]The Tax Reform Act of 1969 limits this preferential treatment to the first $50,000 of long-term gains. Capital gains in excess of $50,000 are taxed at 35 percent.

business of oil exploration. Whether one accepts the validity of this argument or not, the depletion allowance constitutes a very sizable tax advantage to the petroleum industry.

The basic point to be emphasized is that these and other tax loopholes are means by which high-income people are able to reduce their tax liabilities. The result is that the Federal personal and corporate income taxes are, in practice, much less effective in leveling incomes than might first appear.

State and local finance

State and local governments employ essentially the same types of taxes as are imposed by the Federal government. However, the relative importance of the various taxes and tax rates differs greatly. In particular, while the Federal government finances itself largely through personal and corporate income taxation, state and local governments rely heavily upon sales and property taxes, respectively. And although there is considerable overlapping in the types of expenditures made by the three levels of government, national defense and related outlays account for the majority of Federal expenditures, whereas education, highways, and public welfare lead at state and local levels.

State expenditures and receipts Note in Table 9·2 that the basic sources of tax revenue at the state level are sales and excise taxes, which account for about 51 percent of all state tax revenues. State personal income taxes, which entail much more modest rates than those employed by the Federal government, run a poor second. Taxes on corporate income, property, inheritances, and a variety of licenses and permits constitute the remainder of state tax revenue. On the expenditure side of the picture, the major outlays of state governments are for (1) education and (2) highway maintenance and construction.

It is important to note that the budget statement shown in Table 9·2 contains aggregated data and therefore tells us little about the finances of individual states. States vary tremendously in the types of taxes employed. Thus, although sales and personal income taxes are the major sources of revenue for all state governments combined, five states have no general sales tax and eight do not use the personal income tax. Furthermore, great variations in the size of tax receipts and disbursements exist among the states.

Local expenditures and receipts The receipts and expenditures shown in Table 9·3 are for all units of local government. This includes counties, munici-

TABLE 9·2 CONSOLIDATED BUDGET OF ALL STATE GOVERNMENTS, 1969

Tax receipts	Billions of dollars	Percent of total	Expenditures	Billions of dollars	Percent of total
Sales, excise, and gross receipts taxes	$21.5	51	Education	$12.3	28
Personal income taxes	7.5	18	Highways	10.4	24
Corporate income taxes	3.2	8	Public welfare	6.5	16
Property taxes	1.0	2	Health, hospitals	4.3	10
Death and gift taxes	1.0	2	Natural resources	2.0	4
Licenses, permits, and others	7.7	19	All others	7.8	18
Total receipts	$41.9	100	Total expenditures	$43.4	100

Source: Bureau of the Census, *Government Finances in 1968–69.* Because of rounding, figures may not add up to totals.

TABLE 9·3 CONSOLIDATED BUDGET OF ALL LOCAL GOVERNMENTS, 1969

Tax receipts	Billions of dollars	Percent of total	Expenditures	Billions of dollars	Percent of total
Property taxes	$29.7	85	Education	$34.9	47
Sales and excises	2.5	7	Police, fire, and general government	7.7	10
Personal and corporate income taxes	1.4	4	Public welfare	5.6	8
Licenses, permits, and others	1.2	4	Highways	5.0	7
			Health and hospitals	4.3	6
			All others	15.9	22
Total receipts	$34.8	100	Total expenditures	$73.5	100

Source: Bureau of the Census, *Government Finances in 1968–69.* Because of rounding, figures may not add up to totals.

palities, townships, and school districts. One major source of revenue and a single basic use of revenue stand out: the bulk of the revenue received by local government comes from property taxation; the bulk of local revenue is spent for education. Other less important sources of funds and types of disbursements are self-explanatory.

The gaping deficit shown in Table 9·3 is largely removed when nontax resources of income are taken into account: In 1969 the tax revenues of local governments were supplemented by some $26 billion in intergovernmental grants from Federal and state governments. Furthermore, local governments received an additional $6 billion as proprietary income, that is, as revenue from government-owned liquor stores and utilities.

TAX SHARING: THE HELLER PLAN

A serious fiscal mismatch has evolved in recent years between the Federal government, on the one hand, and state and local governments, on the other. At the risk of oversimplification, the problem is this: Federal tax revenues, derived primarily from personal and corporate income taxes (Table 9·1), generate very substantial amounts of revenue. The progressive rates of these two taxes actually cause the Federal government's tax revenues to rise more rapidly than does the economy's total income. Currently, during prosperous periods growth of the national income automatically (with no increases in personal or corporate income tax rates) brings in some $12 to $15 billion of additional tax revenues each year. We shall find in Chapter 14 that, unless it is somehow offset, this withdrawal of purchasing power can have a depressing effect upon the economy.

On the other hand, state and local tax revenues come primarily from sales and property taxes (Tables 9·2 and 9·3), revenue producers which are much less responsive to economic growth. Indeed, sales and property tax rates have increased sharply in recent years, and it has become increasingly difficult politically to achieve additional increases as means of bolstering state and local tax revenues. Furthermore, state and local governments are frequently faced with constitutional and other legal restraints upon indebtedness. At the same time, many of the nation's most acute socioeconomic problems have resulted in soaring demands upon state and local governments for additional social goods and services (Chapter 37). For example, rapid population growth

and high rates of immigration have put great strains upon the public education systems of most cities. The flight to the suburbs, coupled with burgeoning automobile traffic, has resulted in vast needs for improved highways and streets. A more acute awareness of America's racial problems, particularly as embodied in the ghettos of our cities, makes clear the need for huge outlays on urban renewal, public welfare, and improvements in the quantity and quality of police and fire protection.[6]

Summarizing in the words of one eminent economist:[7]

> The great economic anachronism of our time is that economic growth gives the Federal Government the revenues while, along with population increase, it gives the States and especially the cities the problems. The one unit of government gets the money. . . . The other gets the work.

The question, then, is how to redress this imbalance. One obvious means has been through intergovernmental grants or, more specifically, Federal subsidies to state and local governments. Such grants are now substantial and continue to grow. In 1970, for example, the Federal government made grants of almost $25 billion to state and local governments. But despite their recent growth, these grants have been insufficient to bridge the gap between state and local tax revenues and the expenditures needed to perform their traditional functions adequately and to meet new problems. Furthermore, most Federal grants have been tied to specific programs and are conditional upon matching state and local funds.

Against this background, it was proposed in the early 1960s that the Federal government embark on a new tax-sharing program with the states. More specifically, the *Heller Plan*—named for Walter W. Heller, former chairman of the Council of Economic Advisors under Presidents Kennedy and Johnson—advocates substantial no-strings-attached grants to the states. Although there are many possible variants as to details, presumably these grants would be equal to a certain percentage—say 2 or 3 percent—of the Federal personal income tax receipts and would be distributed to the states on the basis of population.

Proponents argue that the Heller Plan will effectively resolve the fiscal mismatch problem now existing between the various levels of government; the plan will greatly assist state and local governments to meet the acute financial crises now confronting them. Furthermore, the plan is held to be flexible, in that the 2 or 3 percent figure can be altered as needed. Advocates also contend that the plan is politically realistic. Liberals will allegedly support it because it allows the public sector to meet the pressing socio-economic problems we now face. Conservatives will presumably derive some satisfaction from the fact that under the plan, the Federal government is not growing and encroaching upon state and local prerogatives.

But critics point out that state and local governments are more susceptible to graft, corruption, and the padding of payrolls; the Federal government, they argue, can spend money more efficiently than can state or local governments. They also fear that unrestricted Federal grants will supplant, rather than supplement, state and local spending; that is, Federal grants may be used to "finance" state and local tax cuts—or at least defer otherwise necessary tax increases—rather than to meet pressing problems in such areas as education, housing, transportation, and so forth. We can be certain of a continuing dialogue on the whole question of the desirability and character of Federal grants.

APPORTIONING THE TAX BURDEN

The very nature of social goods and services (see Chapter 6) makes it exceedingly difficult to measure precisely the manner in which their benefits are apportioned among individuals and institutions in the economy. It is virtually impossible to determine accurately the amount by which John Doe benefits from military installations, a network of highways, a public

[6] The *Report of the National Advisory Commission on Civil Disorders* (New York: Bantam Books, Inc., 1968), particularly chapters 16 and 17, provides dramatic evidence on the needs and problems of our larger cities.

[7] John Kenneth Galbraith in *Hearings before the Joint Economic Committee on the 1965 Economic Report of the President* (Washington, 1965), p. 14.

school system, and local police and fire protection.

The situation is a bit different on the taxation side of the picture. Statistical studies reveal rather clearly the manner in which the overall tax burden is apportioned. Needless to say, this is a question which affects each of us in a vital way. Although the average citizen is concerned with the overall level of taxes, chances are he is even more interested in exactly how the tax burden is allocated among individual taxpayers.

Benefits received versus ability to pay

Two basic philosophies as to how the economy's tax burden should be apportioned are evident in American capitalism:

Benefits-received principle The *benefits-received principle* of taxation asserts that households and businesses should purchase the goods and services of government in basically the same manner in which other commodities are bought. It is reasoned that those who benefit most from government-supplied goods or services should pay the taxes necessary for their financing. Some social goods are financed essentially on the basis of the benefits principle. For example, gasoline taxes are typically earmarked for the financing of highway construction and repairs. Those who benefit from good roads pay the cost of those roads. Difficulties immediately arise, however, when an accurate and widespread application of the benefits principle is considered:

1. How does one go about determining the benefits which individual households and businesses receive from national defense, education, and police and fire protection? Recall (Chapter 6) that social goods entail widespread social or spillover benefits and that the exclusion principle is inapplicable. Even in the seemingly tangible case of highway finance we find it difficult to measure benefits. Individual car owners benefit in different degrees from the existence of good roads. And those who do not own cars also benefit. Businesses certainly benefit greatly from any widening of their markets which good roads will encourage.

2. The shortcomings of the benefits principle become even more apparent when certain government welfare programs are considered. Relief payments and payments to the physically handicapped would be self-defeating if they were financed on the benefits principle. It would be ridiculous to think of taxing unemployed workers to finance the unemployment compensation payments which they receive. In short, government activities designed to redistribute income preclude the use of the benefits principle in their financing.

Ability-to-pay principle The *ability-to-pay principle* of taxation stands in sharp contrast to the benefits principle. Ability-to-pay taxation rests on the idea that the tax burden should be geared directly to one's financial position. As the ability-to-pay principle has come to be applied in the United States, it contends that individuals and businesses with larger incomes should pay more taxes—both absolutely and relatively—than those with more modest incomes.

What is the rationale of ability-to-pay taxation? Proponents argue that each additional dollar of income received by a household will yield smaller and smaller amounts of satisfaction. It is argued that, because consumers act rationally, the first dollars of income received in any period of time will be spent upon basic high-urgency goods; that is, upon those goods which yield the greatest benefit or satisfaction. Successive dollars of income will go for less urgent goods and finally for trivial goods and services. This means that a dollar taken through taxes from a poor man who has few dollars constitutes a greater sacrifice on his part than does a dollar taken by taxes from the rich man who has many dollars. Hence, to balance the sacrifices which taxes impose on income receivers, it is contended that taxes should be apportioned according to the amount of income one receives.

This is appealing, but problems of application exist here, too. In particular, although we might agree that the household earning $10,000 per year has a greater ability to pay taxes than the household receiving a paltry $3,000, exactly *how much more* ability to pay does the first family have as compared

with the second? There is no scientific way of measuring one's ability to pay taxes. Thus, in practice, the answer hinges upon guesswork, the tax views of the political party in power, expediency, and the urgency with which government needs revenue. As we shall discover in a few moments, the tax structure of our economy is somewhat more in tune with the ability-to-pay principle than with the benefits-received principle.

Progressive, proportional, and regressive taxes

Any discussion of the ability-to-pay and the benefits-received principles of taxation leads ultimately to the question of tax rates and the manner in which tax rates change as one's income increases. Taxes are ordinarily classified as being progressive, proportional, or regressive.

1 A tax is *progressive* if its rate *increases* as income increases. Such a tax claims not only a larger absolute amount, but also a larger fraction or percentage of income as income increases.

2. A *regressive* tax is one whose rate *declines* as income increases. Such a tax takes a smaller and smaller proportion of income as income increases. A regressive tax may or may not take a large absolute amount of income as income expands.

3. A tax is *proportional* when its rate *remains the same,* regardless of the size of income.

Let us illustrate in terms of the personal income tax. Suppose the tax rates are such that everyone pays 10 percent of his income in taxes, regardless of the size of his income. This would obviously be a proportional income tax. But suppose the rate structure is such that the household with an annual taxable income of less than $1,000 pays 5 percent in income taxes, the household realizing an income of $1,000 to $2,000 pays 10 percent, $2,000 to $3,000 pays 15 percent, and so forth.[8] This, as we have already explained, would obviously be a *progressive* income tax. The final case is where the rates decline as taxable income rises: you pay 15 percent if you earn less than $1,000; 10 percent if you earn $1,000 to $2,000; 5 percent if you earn $2,000 to $3,000; and so forth. This is a *regressive* income tax. Generally speaking, progressive taxes are those which bear down most heavily on the rich; regressive taxes are those which hit the poor hardest.

What can we say about the progressivity, proportionality, or regressivity of the major kinds of taxes used in the United States? We have already noted the generally progressive features of the personal and corporate income taxes. At first glance a general sales tax with, say, a 3 percent rate would seem to be proportional. But in fact it is regressive. The reason for its regressivity is that a larger portion of a poor man's income is exposed to the tax than is the case with a rich man; the latter avoids the tax on the part of his income which he saves, while the former is unable to save. Example: "Poor" Smith has an income of $3,000 and spends it all. "Rich" Jones has an income of $6,000 but spends only $4,000 of it. Assuming a 3 percent sales tax applies to the expenditures of each individual, Smith will obviously pay $90 (3 percent of $3,000) in sales taxes, and Jones will pay $120 (3 percent of $4,000). Note that whereas *all* of Smith's $3,000 income is subject to the sales tax, only two-thirds of Jones's $6,000 income is taxed. Thus while Smith pays $90, or 3 percent, of his $3,000 income as sales taxes, Jones pays $120, or just 2 percent, of his $6,000 income. Hence, we conclude that the general sales tax is regressive.

Property taxes and payroll taxes are also regressive. The property tax is regressive for the simple reason that housing is a very large component of consumer spending for low-income households. Property taxes, as a percentage of income, are higher for poor families than for rich families because the poor must spend a larger proportion of their incomes for housing. Payroll taxes are regressive because they apply to only a fixed absolute amount of one's income. For example, in 1972 payroll tax rates were 5.2 percent, but this figure only applies to the first $7,800 of one's income. Thus a person earning exactly $7,800 would pay $406, or 5.2 percent of his total income, while

[8] We refer here to average or effective tax rates, not to marginal tax rates.

someone with twice that income, or $15,600, would also pay $406—his payroll tax rate is only 2.6 percent of his total income.

Shifting and incidence of taxes

Suppose society has decided how it wants the current tax burden to be apportioned among specific households and businesses. Now a complicating factor arises. Taxes do not always stick where the government puts them. Some taxes can be *shifted* among various parties in the economy. It is therefore necessary to locate as best we can the final resting place or *incidence* of the major types of taxes.

Personal income tax The incidence of the personal income tax generally falls on the individual upon whom the tax is levied; little chance exists for shifting. But there might be exceptions to this. Individuals and groups who can effectively control the price of their labor services may be able to shift a part of the tax. For example, doctors, dentists, lawyers, and other professional people who can readily increase their fees may do so because of the tax. Unions might regard personal income taxes as part of the cost of living and, as a result, bargain for higher wages. If they are successful, they may shift a portion of the tax from workers to employers. Generally, however, we can conclude that the individual upon whom the tax is initially levied bears the burden of the personal income tax. The same ordinarily holds true of inheritance taxes.

Corporate income tax The incidence of the corporate income tax is much less certain. The traditional view has it that a firm which is currently charging the profit-maximizing price and producing the profit-maximizing output will have no reason to change price or output when a corporate income tax is imposed. That price and output combination which yields the greatest profit before the tax will still be the most profitable after government takes a fixed percentage of the firm's profits in the form of income taxes. According to this view, the company's stockholders must bear the incidence of the tax in the form of lower dividends or a smaller amount of retained earnings. On the other hand, in recent years many economists have argued that the corporate income tax is shifted in part to consumers through higher prices and to resource suppliers through lower prices. In modern industry, where a small number of firms may control a market, producers may not be in the profit-maximizing position initially. The reason? By fully exploiting their market position currently, monopolistic firms might elicit adverse public opinion and governmental censure. Hence, they may await such events as the imposition of taxes, increases in tax rates, or wage increases by unions to provide an adequate excuse for price increases with less fear of public criticism. When this actually occurs, a portion of the corporate income tax may be shifted to consumers through higher prices.

Both positions are plausible. Indeed, the incidence of the corporate income tax may well be shared by stockholders and the firm's customers and resource suppliers. The consensus seems to be that stockholders bear most of the tax.

Sales and excise taxes Sales and excise taxes are the "hidden taxes" of our economy. They are hidden because such taxes are typically shifted by sellers to consumers through higher product prices. There may be some difference in the shiftability of sales taxes and excises, however. Because a sales tax covers a much wider range of products than an excise, there is little chance for consumers to resist the price boosts which sales taxes entail by reallocating their expenditures to untaxed products.

Excises, however, fall on a relatively short, select list of goods. This means that the possibility of consumers turning to substitute goods and services is greater. For example, an excise tax on theater tickets which does not apply to other types of entertainment might be difficult to pass on to consumers via price increases. Why? Because price boosts might result in considerable substituting of alternative types of entertainment by consumers. From the seller's point of view, the higher price will cause such a marked decline in sales that he will be better off to bear all, or a large portion of, the excise rather than the sharp

decline in sales. With many excises, however, modest price increases have little or no effect on sales. Excises on gasoline, cigarettes, and alcoholic beverages are cases in point. Here there are few good substitute products to which consumers can turn as prices rise. For these commodities, the seller is in a better position to shift the tax.

In general, it is safe to say that the bulk, if not the entire amount, of a sales or excise tax will generally be shifted to the consumer through higher product prices. Later (Chapter 24) we will employ supply and demand analysis as a basis for more sophisticated generalizations as to the shifting and incidence of sales taxes.

Property taxes Many property taxes are borne by the property owner for the simple reason that there is no other party to whom they can be shifted. This is typically true in the case of taxes on land, personal property, and owner-occupied residences. For example, even when land is sold, the property tax is not likely to be shifted. The buyer will tend to discount the value of the land to allow for the future taxes which he will be required to pay on it, and this will be reflected in the price he is willing to offer for the land.

Taxes on rented and business property are a different story. Taxes on rented property can be, and usually are, shifted wholly or in part from the owner to the tenant by the simple process of boosting rents. Business property taxes are treated as a business cost and therefore are taken into account in establishing product price; thus such taxes are ordinarily shifted to the firm's customers.

Table 9·4 summarizes this discussion of the shifting and incidence of taxes.

The American tax structure

As we have seen, the Federal, state, and local governments of the United States employ a variety of taxes. We have concluded that some of these taxes—the personal and corporate income taxes and inheritance taxes—are progressive, whereas others—sales taxes, excises, and property taxes—are for the most part regressive. What is the total picture? A recent estimate—and these figures must be very rough because of the uncertainty of tax incidence—is shown in Table 9·5.

Employing family income as the tax base, column 2 of this table tells us the percentage of income taken by Federal taxes in each of the nine income classes. The progressivity found here reflects the dominant role of the personal and corporate income taxes at the Federal level. Column 3 presents similar data for state and local taxes. Regressivity is evident here, reflecting the predominance of sales and property taxes at the state and local levels. Finally, column

TABLE 9·4 THE PROBABLE INCIDENCE OF TAXES

Type of tax	Probable incidence
Personal income tax	The household or individual upon which it is levied.
Corporate income tax	Disagreement. Some economists feel the firm on which it is levied bears the incidence; others conclude the tax is shifted, wholly or in part, to consumers.
Sales and excise taxes	With exceptions, consumers who buy the taxed products.
Property taxes	Owners in the case of land and owner-occupied residences; tenants in the case of rented property; consumers in the case of business property.

TABLE 9·5 ESTIMATED TAX RATES BY INCOME LEVELS (*taxes as a percentage of income*)

(1) Family income level	(2) Federal taxes	(3) State and local taxes	(4) All taxes, or (2) + (3)
Under $2,000	13.0%	15.1%	28.1%
$2,000–2,999	14.0	12.7	26.7
$3,000–3,999	17.1	12.6	29.7
$4,000–4,999	17.3	11.8	29.1
$5,000–5,999	17.9	11.5	29.4
$6,000–7,499	17.8	10.8	28.5
$7,500–9,999	18.4	10.1	28.5
$10,000–14,999	21.1	9.6	30.6
$15,000 and over	34.9	9.1	44.0

Source: Allocating Tax Burdens and Government Benefits by Income Class (Tax Foundation, Inc., New York, 1967), p. 7. Data are for 1965.

4 sums the two preceding columns and shows the percentage of income taken in Federal, state, and local taxes combined from each of the listed income groups.

Column 4, of course, is the vital one. The overall conclusion is that our total tax system is roughly proportional up to the $15,000 level of income. This range includes the vast bulk of income receivers. While there is obvious progressivity in the "$15,000 and over" class, the often-heard lamentations as to the highly progressive character of our tax structure are simply not accurate insofar as the bulk of American income receivers are concerned.

SUMMARY

1. Historically, government tax receipts and expenditures have grown rapidly both in absolute amounts and relative to the size of the national income. This growth has been particularly marked over the last three decades.

2. Wars and national defense, population growth, urbanization, environmental problems, and inflation have been among the more important causes underlying the growth of government.

3. About 54 percent of all Federal spending is for national defense and related programs. The sum of personal and corporate income taxes and payroll taxes account for over four-fifths of the Federal government's tax revenue.

4. Approximately 51 percent of all state revenue is derived from sales and excise taxes. Education and the construction and maintenance of highways are the major state expenditures, accounting for 28 and 24 percent, respectively, of the total.

5. At the local level of government, property taxes provide about 85 percent of total tax revenue. Education absorbs almost half of local expenditures.

6. The Heller Plan proposes Federal tax sharing with the states to help overcome the severe financial problems of state and local governments.

7. The ability-to-pay principle of taxation is more evident in the American tax structure than is the benefits-received philosophy.

8. Taxes on personal and corporate incomes and

inheritance taxes are progressive. General sales, excise, payroll, and property taxes tend to be regressive.

9. Sales and excise taxes are likely to be shifted; personal income taxes are not. There is disagreement as to whether or not corporate income taxes are shifted. The incidence of property taxes depends primarily upon whether or not the property is owner- or tenant-occupied.

10. Over the income range which includes the bulk of American households, the overall tax structure is roughly proportional.

QUESTIONS AND STUDY SUGGESTIONS

1. Describe the overall changes in government expenditures and taxes which have occurred during the last four decades. How do you account for these changes? Why might it be significant to distinguish between "transfer payments" and "government purchases of goods and services" in evaluating the growth of government expenditures and the impact of this spending upon resource allocation?

2. What is the most important source of revenue and the major type of expenditure at the Federal level? At the state level? At the local level?

3. Briefly describe the mechanics of the Federal personal income and corporate income taxes. Explain why the average or effective personal income tax rate is less than the marginal tax rate.

4. What is the Heller Plan? What arguments are made for and against it?

5. Distinguish clearly between the benefits-received and the ability-to-pay principles of taxation. Which philosophy is more evident in our present tax structure? Justify your answer. To which principle of taxation do you subscribe? Why?

6. Precisely what is meant by a progressive tax? A regressive tax? A proportional tax? Comment upon the progressivity or regressivity of each of the following taxes:
   a. The Federal personal income tax
   b. A 3 percent state general sales tax
   c. A Federal excise tax on playing cards
   d. A municipal property tax on real estate
   e. The Federal corporate income tax
   What is likely to be the incidence of each of these taxes?

7. Comment upon the overall progressivity or regressivity of the American tax structure.

8. Explain and evaluate each of the following statements:
   a. "Any system of public finance should be conceived simply with a view to the maximum social advantage in the long run, and it follows that any tax system . . . should be conceived with the same object."
   b. "No tax on income can be a just tax unless it leaves individuals in the same relative condition in which it found them."
   c. "Because there is no sure definition of the limits to progression, no firm basis of its 'reasonable' use, no protection against its unconscionable abuse, those who uphold the system as a revenue device are playing into the hands of the group that would use progressive taxation as the means of destroying private capitalism and ushering in the collectivist state."
   d. "Even tho it be an open question whether all inequality in wealth and income be unjust, such great degrees of inequality as the modern world shows are regarded as not consonant with canons of justice. Very rich persons should be called to pay taxes not only in proportion to their incomes but more than in proportion."

SELECTED REFERENCES

Economic Issues, 4th ed., readings 13 and 14.

Henderson, William L., and Helen A. Cameron, *The Public Economy* (New York: Random House, Inc., 1969), chaps. 1–15.

Herber, Bernard P.: *Modern Public Finance,* rev. ed. (Homewood, Ill.: Richard D. Irwin, Inc., 1971), chaps. 7–14.

Newman, Herbert E.: *An Introduction to Public Finance* (New York: John Wiley & Sons, Inc., 1968).

Sharp, Ansel M., and Bernard F. Sliger, *Public Finance,* rev. ed. (Austin, Tex.: Business Publications, Inc., 1970), chaps. 13–24.

NATIONAL INCOME, EMPLOYMENT, AND FISCAL POLICY

2

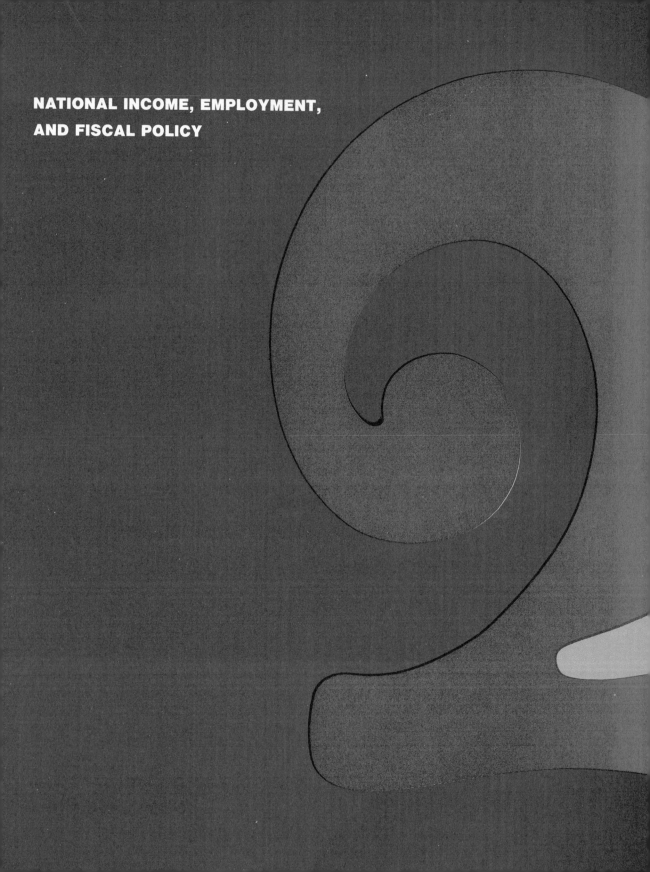

10

NATIONAL INCOME ACCOUNTING

Throughout Part 1 this book has made the flat statement that American capitalism does not consistently provide for the full employment of available resources. Part 1 has also noted that the levels of employment and production depend upon the size of certain flows of expenditures and income. Part 2 now deals at length with the problem of measuring, explaining, and remedying, if need be, the volumes of employment, production, and income in the economy. Specifically, in this chapter we seek an understanding of certain accounting techniques which assist us in gauging the level of production achieved by the economy. In Chapter 11 we take a look at the historical record of American capitalism as reflected in these accounts in order to appraise the past performance of our economy. Then in Chapters 12 and 13 we seek to explain those factors which determine the levels of employment and production in American capitalism. Finally, in Chapters 14 and 15 we explore the problems involved in deriving and applying public policies designed to improve the production performance of the economy.

MEASURING THE ECONOMY'S PERFORMANCE

The present task is that of defining and understanding a group of so-called social or national income accounting concepts which have been designed to measure the overall production performance of the economy. Why do we bother with such a project? Because social accounting does for the economy as a whole what private accounting does for the individual business enterprise or, for that matter, for the household. The individual businessman is vitally interested in knowing how he is doing in his operations, but the answer is not always immediately discernible.

Accurate measurement of the firm's flows of income and expenditures is needed to assess the firm's operations for the current year. With this information before him, the businessman can gauge the economic health of his firm. If things are going well, he can use his accounting data to explain his success. He might find that costs are down or that sales and product prices are up, resulting in large profits. If things are going badly, he can also look to his accounting measures to discover the immediate cause of his plight. And by examining his accounts over a period of time, the businessman can detect growth, stagnation, or decline for his firm and indications of the immediate causes. All this information is invaluable in helping the businessman make intelligent policy decisions.

A system of national income accounting does much the same thing for the economy as a whole: It allows us to keep a finger on the economic pulse of the nation. The various measures which make up our social accounting system permit us to measure the level of production in the economy at some point in time and explain the immediate causes of that level of performance. Further, by comparing the national income accounts over a period of time, we can plot the long-run course which the economy has been following; the growth or decay of the economy will show up in the national income accounts. Finally, the information supplied by the national income accounts provides a basis for the formulation and application of public policies designed to improve the performance of the economy; without the national income accounts, economic policy would be based upon guesswork. In short, national income accounting allows us to keep tab on the economic health of society and to formulate intelligently policies which will improve that health.

GROSS NATIONAL PRODUCT

There are many conceivable measures of the economic well-being of society. It is generally agreed, however, that the best available indicator of an economy's health is its annual total output of goods and services or, as it is sometimes called, the economy's aggregate output. The basic social accounting measure of the total output of goods and services is called the *gross national product* or, simply, GNP. It is defined as *the total market value of all final goods and services produced*[1] *in the economy in one year.* Our definition of GNP is very explicit and merits considerable comment.

GNP is a monetary measure

Note, first, that GNP measures the market value of annual output. GNP is a monetary measure. Indeed, it must be if we are to compare the heterogeneous collections of goods and services produced in different years and get a meaningful idea of their relative worth. Put simply, if the economy produces three oranges and two apples in year 1 and two oranges and three apples in year 2, in which year is society better off? There is no answer to this question until price tags are attached to the various products as indicators of society's evaluation of their relative worth. The problem is resolved in Table 10·1, where it is assumed that the money price of the oranges is 2 cents and the price of apples is 3 cents. It can be concluded that year 2's output is superior to that of year 1. Why? Because society values year 2's output more highly; society is willing to pay more for the collection of goods produced in year 2 than that produced in year 1.

Adjusting GNP for price changes

But you might well object. You have read of inflation in the newspapers. Does this not mean that money prices and therefore the value of the dollar itself will change? You are quite right. The money value of different years' outputs can only be accurately compared if the value of money itself does not change because of inflation or deflation.

Stated differently, inflation or deflation complicates GNP because it is a prices-times-quantity figure. The

[1] We shall see that all goods produced in a particular year may not be sold; some may be added to inventories. Any increase in inventories must be included in determining GNP, since GNP measures all current production regardless of whether or not it is sold.

TABLE 10·1 COMPARING HETEROGENEOUS OUTPUTS BY USING MONEY PRICES (*hypothetical data*)

Year	Annual outputs	Market value
1	3 oranges and 2 apples	3 at 2 cents + 2 at 3 cents = 12 cents
2	2 oranges and 3 apples	2 at 2 cents + 3 at 3 cents = 13 cents

raw data from which the national income accountants estimate GNP are the total sales figures of business firms; these figures obviously embody changes in both the quantity of output and the level of prices. This means that a change in either the quantity of total physical output or the price level will affect the size of GNP. However, it is the quantity of goods produced and distributed to households which affects their standard of living and not the size of the price tags which these goods bear. The hamburger of 1962 which sold for 30 cents yielded the same satisfaction as does an identical hamburger selling for 50 cents in 1972. The problem then is one of adjusting a price-times-quantity figure so it will accurately reflect changes in physical output, not changes in prices.

Fortunately, national income accountants have been able to resolve this difficulty: they deflate GNP for rising prices and inflate it when prices are falling. These adjustments give us a picture of GNP for various years *as if* prices and the value of the dollar were constant.

Inflating and deflating

Some examples will help us understand how GNP figures are adjusted for price changes. First, an exceedingly simple example: Assume our economy produces only one good, product X, and in the amounts indicated in Table 10·2 for years 1, 2, and 3. An examination of columns 1 and 2 tells us that the *money* GNPs for years 2 and 3, as shown in column 4, greatly overstate the increases in *real*

TABLE 10·2 DEFLATING MONEY GNP (*hypothetical data*)

Year	(1) Units of output	(2) Price of X	(3) Price index, percent	(4) Unadjusted, or money, GNP (1) × (2)	(5) Adjusted, or real, GNP (4) ÷ (3)
1	5	$10	100	$ 50	$50 (= $ 50 ÷ 1.00)
2	7	20	100	140	70 (= 140 ÷ 2.00)
3	8	25	250	200	80 (= 200 ÷ 2.50)
4	10	30			
5	11	28			

output occurring in those two years. That is, the monetary measure of production (money GNP) does not accurately indicate the actual changes which have occurred in physical output (real GNP). A considerable portion of the sharp increase in money GNP in years 2 and 3 is due to the drastic inflation shown in column 2, the remainder being due to the changes in physical output shown in column 1. Both increases in physical output and price increases are reflected in the money GNP.

Now the situation facing our social accountants is this: In gathering statistics from the financial reports of businesses and deriving GNP for years 1, 2, and 3, governmental accountants come up with the figures for money GNP shown in column 4. They will not know directly to what extent changes in price, on the one hand, and changes in quantity of output, on the other, have accounted for the given increases in money GNP. Social accountants will not have before them the data of columns 1 and 2, but only the data of column 4. Being resourceful individuals, they attempt to adjust the money GNP figure for price changes. They do this by deriving a general price index which estimates overall changes in the price level. By expressing this index as a decimal and dividing it into money GNP, one can obtain real GNP. In our example, wherein we are dealing with only one product, a simple single-price index number is all that is required. Such a price index is nothing more than *a percentage comparison from a fixed point of reference.* This point of reference, or bench mark, is called the *base year.* By comparing prices in previous and ensuing years with prices in the base year, we can tell how much prices have increased or decreased *relative to* what they were in the base year. Suppose product X sells for $10 in year 1, $20 in year 2, and $25 in year 3. Selecting year 1 as the base year, we can express the prices of product X in years 2 and 3 relative to X's price in year 1 through the formula

$$\text{Price index} = \frac{\text{price in any given year}}{\text{price in base year}} \times 100$$

We multiply the price comparison by 100 in order to express it as a percentage. Using year 2 as the given year, we find that

$$\text{Price index} = \frac{\$20}{\$10} \times 100 = 200 \text{ percent}$$

and for year 3,

$$\text{Price index} = \frac{\$25}{\$10} \times 100 = 250 \text{ percent}$$

For year 1 the index must be 100 percent, since the given year and the base year are identical. In this case,

$$\text{Price index} = \frac{\$10}{\$10} \times 100 = 100 \text{ percent}$$

These index numbers simply tell us that the price of product X in the year 2 was 200 percent of what it was in year 1 and in year 3 it was 250 percent of year 1's price. The index numbers of column 3 can now be used to deflate the inflated money GNP figures of column 4. As already noted, *the simplest and most direct method of deflating is to express these index numbers as hundredths, that is, in decimal form, and divide them into the corresponding money GNP.*[2] Column 5 shows the results. These real GNP figures measure the value of total output in years 1, 2, and 3 as if the price of product X had been constant at $10 throughout the three-year period. Real GNP thus shows the market value of each year's output measured in terms of constant dollars, that is, dollars which have the same value, or purchasing power, as in the base year. Real GNP is clearly superior to money GNP as an indicator of the economy's productive performance over a period of time.

To ensure his understanding of the deflating process, the reader is urged to complete Table 10·2 for years 4 and 5. Second, it is recommended that you rework the entire deflating procedure using year 3 as the base year. You will find, by the way, that in this case you must inflate some of the money GNP

[2]This yields the same result as the more complex procedure of dividing money GNPs by the corresponding index number and multiplying the quotient by 100.

data, just as we have deflated it in our examples.

Table 10·3 provides us with a much more realistic illustration of the inflating and deflating process. Here we are taking actual money GNP figures for selected years and adjusting them with an index of the general price level to obtain real GNP. Note that the base year is 1958. Because the long-run trend has been for the price level to rise, the problem is one of *inflating* the pre-1958 figures. This upward revision of money GNP acknowledges that prices were lower in years prior to 1958 and, as a result, money GNP figures understated the real output of those years. Column 4 indicates what GNP would have been in all these selected years if the 1958 price level had prevailed. However, the rising price level has caused the money GNP figures for the post-1958 years to overstate real output; hence, these figures must be *deflated* as in column 4 in order for us to gauge what GNP would have been in 1961, 1964, and so on, if 1958 prices had actually prevailed. In short, while the money GNP figures reflect both output and price changes, the real GNP figures allow us to make a better estimate of changes in real output, because the real GNP figures, in effect, hold the price level constant. The reader should trace through the computations involved in deriving the real GNP figures given in Table 10·3 and also determine real GNP for years 1937, 1945, and 1964, for which the figures have been purposely omitted.[3]

Double counting

To measure total output accurately, all goods and services produced in any given year must be counted once, but not more than once. Most products go through a series of production stages before reaching a market. As a result, parts or components of most products are bought and sold many times. Hence, to avoid counting several times the parts of products that are sold and resold, GNP only includes the market value of final goods and ignores transactions involving intermediate goods.

By *final goods* we mean goods and services which are being purchased for final use and not for resale or further processing or manufacturing. Transactions involving *intermediate goods,* on the other hand, refer to purchases of goods and services for further processing and manufacturing or for resale. The sale of final goods is included and the sale of intermediate goods is excluded from GNP. Why? Because the value of final goods includes all the intermediate transactions involved in their production. The inclusion of intermediate transactions would involve double counting and an exaggerated estimate of GNP.

An example will clarify this point. Suppose there are five stages of production in getting a Hart, Schaffner & Marx suit manufactured and into the hands of a consumer who, of course, is the ultimate or final user. As Table 10·4 indicates, firm A, a sheep ranch,

[3]Technical footnote: While this discussion of Table 10·3 provides an intuitive understanding of the process of inflating or deflating GNP with appropriate index numbers, a thorough grasp of the rationale for dividing money GNP by an appropriate index to get real GNP calls for further comment. Suppose we want to adjust money GNP for 1972 to real GNP (in 1958 prices) so we can compare the growth of real GNP between 1958 and 1972. We know, first, that money GNP for 1972 (GNP_{1972}) is equal to the physical output in 1972 (Q_{1972}) times the prices (P_{1972}) at which the output sold. That is,

$$GNP_{1972} = Q_{1972} \cdot P_{1972}$$

We also know from the text's discussion of index numbers that the price index for 1972, using 1958 as the base year, equals the ratio of prices in 1972 to prices in 1958. Thus

$$\text{1972 price index} = P_{1972}/P_{1958}$$

The text also directs us to divide money GNP for 1972 by this 1972 price index to get real GNP for 1972, that is, 1972's output measured at 1958 prices:

$$\frac{GNP_{1972}}{P_{1972}/P_{1958}} = \frac{Q_{1972} \cdot P_{1972}}{P_{1972}/P_{1958}}$$

Inverting and multiplying by the fraction or ratio which represents the 1972 index, we get

$$\frac{GNP_{1972}}{P_{1972}/P_{1958}} = (Q_{1972} \cdot P_{1972}) \cdot \frac{P_{1958}}{P_{1972}}$$

The P_{1972} expressions cancel, leaving

$$\frac{GNP_{1972}}{P_{1972}/P_{1958}} = Q_{1972} \cdot P_{1958}$$

That is to say, by dividing the 1972 money GNP (GNP_{1972}) by the 1972 price index (P_{1972}/P_{1958}) we derive real GNP for 1972 or, more specifically, the 1972 output (Q_{1972}) measured in terms of 1958 prices (P_{1958}).

TABLE 10·3 ADJUSTING GNP FOR CHANGES IN THE PRICE LEVEL (*selected years, in billions of dollars*)

(1) Year	(2) Money, or unadjusted, GNP	(3) Price level index,* percent (1958 = 100)	(4) Real, or adjusted, GNP, 1958 dollars
1929	$103.1	50.6	$203.6 (= $103.1 ÷ 0.506)
1933	55.6	39.3	141.5 (= 55.6 ÷ 0.393)
1937	90.4	44.5	
1941	124.5	47.2	263.7 (= 124.5 ÷ 0.472)
1945	211.4	59.7	
1951	328.4	85.6	383.4 (= 328.4 ÷ 0.856)
1958	447.3	100.0	447.3 (= 447.3 ÷ 1.000)
1961	520.1	104.6	497.2 (= 520.1 ÷ 1.046)
1964	632.4	108.8	
1966	749.9	113.9	658.1 (= 749.9 ÷ 1.139)
1967	793.5	117.6	674.6 (= 793.5 ÷ 1.176)
1970	976.5	134.9	724.1 (= 976.5 ÷ 1.349)

* U.S. Department of Commerce implicit price deflators.
Source: U.S. Department of Commerce data; 1970 data are preliminary.

TABLE 10·4 VALUE ADDED IN A FIVE-STAGE PRODUCTIVE PROCESS (*hypothetical data*)

(1) Stage of production	(2) Sales value of materials or product	(3) Value added
		$15
Firm A, sheep ranch	$15	10
Firm B, wool processor	25	20
Firm C, suit manufacturer	45	10
Firm D, clothing wholesaler	55	15
Firm E, retail clothier	70	
Consumer, the final user		$70

provides $15 worth of wool to firm B, a wool processor. Firm A pays out the $15 it receives in wages, rents, interest, and profits. Firm B processes the wool and sells it to firm C, a suit manufacturer, for $25. What does firm B do with this $25? As noted, $15 goes to firm A, and the remaining $10 is used by B to pay wages, rents, interest, and profits for the resources needed in processing the wool. And so it goes. The manufacturer sells the suit to firm D, a clothing wholesaler, who in turn sells it to firm E, a retailer, and then, finally, it is bought for $70 by a consumer, the final user of the product. At each stage, the difference between what a firm has paid for the product and what it receives for its sale is paid out as wages, rent, interest, and profits for the resources used by that firm in helping to produce and distribute the suit.

The basic question is this: How much should we include in GNP in accounting for the production of this suit? Just $70, the value of the final product! Why? Because this figure includes all the intermediate transactions leading up to the product's final sale. It would be a gross exaggeration to sum all the intermediate sales figures and the final sales value of the product in column 2 and add the entire amount, $210, to GNP. This would be a serious case of double counting, that is, counting the final product and the sale and resale of its various parts in the multistage productive process.

There is an alternative means of determining the $70 figure which is to be included in GNP. And this is by the *value-added* method—that is, by summing the value added to the total worth of the product at each step in the productive process. Column 3 summarizes this procedure. Note that this measures the total income derived from the production and sale of the suit. As you might expect, it is easier for the national income accountants to count only final goods than to pursue the value-added method of deriving GNP.

GNP excludes nonproductive transactions

GNP attempts to measure the annual production of the economy. In so doing, the many nonproductive transactions which occur each year must be carefully excluded. Nonproductive transactions are of two major types: (1) purely financial transactions and (2) secondhand sales.

Purely financial transactions in turn are of three general types: public transfer payments, private transfer payments, and the buying and selling of securities. We have already mentioned public transfer payments (Chapter 9). These are the social security payments, relief payments, and veterans' payments which government makes to particular households. These payments are in effect gifts; recipients make no contribution to current production in return for them. Thus, to include them in GNP would be to overstate this year's production. Private transfer payments—for example, a university student's monthly subsidy from home or an occasional gift from a wealthy relative—do not entail production but simply the transfer of funds from one private individual to another. Security transactions, that is, the buying and selling of stock and bonds, are also excluded from GNP. Stock market transactions simply involve the swapping of paper assets. As such, these transactions do not directly involve current production. It should be noted, however, that by getting money from the hands of savers into the hands of spenders, some of these security transactions may indirectly give rise to spending which does account for output.

The reason for excluding secondhand sales from GNP is fairly obvious: Such sales either reflect no *current* production, or they involve double counting. For example, suppose you sell your 1968 Ford to a neighbor. This transaction would be excluded in determining GNP because no current production is involved. The inclusion of the sales of goods produced some years ago in this year's GNP would be an exaggeration of this year's output. Similarly, if you purchased a brand new Ford and resold it a week later to your neighbor, we should still want to exclude the resale transaction from the current GNP. Why? Because when you originally bought the new car, its value was included in GNP. To include its resale value would be to count it twice.

GNP is not an ideal measure

GNP is a reasonably accurate and extremely useful measure of national economic performance. Nevertheless, despite adjustments for price level changes and the careful exclusion of intermediate and nonproductive transactions, it must be recognized that GNP is not an ideal measure of economic welfare. There are several reasons for this:

1. Nonmarket transactions There are certain productive transactions which do not appear in the market. Hence, GNP as a measure of the market value of output fails to include these productive transactions. Standard examples include the productive services of the housewife, the efforts of the carpenter who repairs his own home, or the work of the erudite professor who writes a scholarly but nonremunerative article. Such transactions are not reflected in the profit and loss statements of business firms and therefore escape the national income accountants. However, some very important nonmarket transactions, such as that portion of a farmer's output which the farmer consumes himself, are estimated by national income accountants.

2. Leisure Over a long period of years leisure has increased very significantly. The current average workweek is less than forty hours, whereas as late as the 1920s a sixty-five- or seventy-hour workweek was not uncommon in many industries. Increased leisure has added immeasurably to our well-being. Yet our system of social accounting does not directly take cognizance of this. Nor do the accounts reflect the satisfaction—the "psychic income"—which one might derive from his work.

3. Improved product quality GNP is a quantitative rather than a qualitative measure. It does not accurately reflect improvements in the quality of products. This is a shortcoming: Quality improvement obviously affects economic well-being every bit as much as does the quantity of goods.

4. The composition and distribution of output Changes in the composition and the allocation of total output among specific households may influence economic welfare. GNP, however, reflects only the size of output and does not tell us anything about whether this collection of goods is "right" for society. A switchblade knife and a Beethoven LP record, both selling for $5.95, are weighted equally in the GNP. And, although the point is a matter for vigorous debate (see Chapter 38), some economists feel that a more equal distribution of total output would increase national economic well-being. If these economists are correct, a future trend toward a more nearly equal distribution of GNP would enhance the economic welfare of society. A less nearly equal future distribution would have the reverse effect. In short, GNP measures the size of total output but does not reflect changes in the composition and distribution of output which might also affect the economic well-being of society.

5. GNP and the environment There are undesirable and much publicized "gross national byproducts" which accompany the production and growth of the GNP. These take the form of dirty air and water, automobile junkyards, congestion, noise, and various other forms of environmental pollution. Although we shall defer detailed discussion of the economics of pollution to Chapter 37, it is quite clear that the social costs of pollution affect our economic well-being adversely. These social costs associated with the production of the GNP are not now deducted from total output and, hence, GNP overstates our national economic welfare. Ironically, as GNP increases, so does pollution and the extent of this overstatement. As put by one economist, "The ultimate physical product of economic life is garbage."[4] A rising GNP means more garbage—more environmental pollution. In fact, under existing accounting procedures, when a manufacturer pollutes a river and government spends to clean it up, the cleanup expense is added to the GNP while the pollution is not subtracted!

[4]See the delightful and perceptive essay "Fun and Games with the Gross National Product" by Kenneth E. Boulding, in Harold W. Helfrich, Jr., *The Environmental Crisis* (New Haven: Yale University Press, 1970), p. 162.

6. Per capita output For many purposes the most meaningful measure of economic well-being is per capita output. Because GNP measures the size of total output, it may conceal or misrepresent changes in the standard of living of individual households in the economy. For example, GNP may rise significantly, but if population is also growing rapidly, the per capita standard of living may be relatively constant or may even be declining.

Two sides to GNP

Recognizing the characteristics and the shortcomings of GNP as a measure of output, we now raise this question: How can the market value of any unit of output—or for that matter total output—be measured? How can we measure, for example, the market value of a cashmere sweater?

In two ways: First, we can simply look at how much a consumer, as the final user, spends in obtaining it. Second, we can add up all the wage, rental, interest, and profit incomes created in the production of the sweater. This is simply the value-added approach we spoke of above. These are, indeed, two ways of looking at the same thing. What is spent on a product is received as income by those who contributed to its production. Indeed, the circular flow model previously discussed is based upon this notion. If $20 is spent on the sweater, that is necessarily the total amount of income derived from its production. This equality of the expenditure for a product and the income derived from its production is guaranteed, because profit income serves as a balancing item. Profit—or loss—is the income which remains after wage, rent, and interest incomes have been paid by the producer. If the wage, rent, and interest incomes which the firm must pay in getting the sweater produced are less than the $20 expenditure for the sweater, the difference will be the firm's profits.[5] Conversely, if wage, rent, and interest incomes exceed $20, then profits will be negative, that is, losses will be realized, to balance the expenditure on the product and the income derived from its production.

The same line of reasoning is also valid for the output of the economy as a whole. There are two different ways of looking at GNP: One is to look at GNP as the sum of all the expenditures involved in taking that total output off the market. This is called the *output,* or *expenditures, approach.* The other is to look at it in terms of the income derived or created from the production of the GNP. This is called the *earnings,* or *income,* or *allocations, approach* to the determination of GNP. A closer analysis of these two approaches will reveal that they amount to this: *GNP can be determined either by adding up all that is spent on this year's total output or by summing up all the incomes derived from the production of this year's output.* Putting this in the form of a simple equation, we can say that

The amount spent on this year's total output	=	the money income derived from the production of this year's output

As a matter of fact, this is more than an equation: it is an identity. Buying—that is, spending money —and selling—that is, receiving money income—are actually two aspects of the same transaction. Buying and selling are two sides of the same shield. *What is spent on a product is income to those who have contributed their human and property resources in getting that product produced and to market.*

For the economy as a whole we can expand the above identity to read as in Table 10·5. This summary statement simply tells us that all final goods produced in the American economy are purchased either by the three domestic sectors, households, government, and businesses, or by foreign nations. It also shows us that the total receipts which businesses acquire from the sale of total output are allocated among the various resource suppliers as wage, rent, interest, and profit income. Later we shall explain two additional nonincome allocations of total receipts. Using this summary as a point of reference, let us point out in some detail the meaning and significance of the various types of expenditures and the incomes derived therefrom.

[5]The term "profits" is used here in the accounting sense so as to include both normal profits and economic profits as defined in Chapter 5.

TABLE 10·5 THE INCOME AND OUTPUT APPROACHES TO GNP

Output, or expenditures, approach		Income, or allocations, approach
Consumption expenditures by households plus Government purchases of goods and services plus Investment expenditures by businesses plus Expenditures by foreigners	= GNP =	Wages plus Rents plus Interest plus Profits plus Nonincome charges or allocations

THE EXPENDITURES APPROACH TO GNP

To determine GNP through the expenditures approach, one must add up all types of spending on finished or final goods and services. But our national income accountants have much more sophisticated terms for the different types of spending than the ones we have employed in Table 10·5. We must therefore familiarize ourselves with these terms and their meanings.

Personal consumption expenditures (*C*)

What we have simply called ''consumption expenditures by households'' is ''personal consumption expenditures'' to the national income accountants. It entails expenditures by households on durable consumer goods (automobiles, refrigerators, gas ranges, and so forth), nondurable consumer goods (bread, milk, beer, cigarettes, shirts, toothpaste), and consumer expenditures for services (of lawyers, doctors, mechanics, barbers). We shall use the letter C to designate the total of these expenditures.

Government purchases of goods and services (*G*)

This classification of expenditures includes all governmental spending, Federal, state, and local, on the finished products of businesses and all direct purchases of resources—labor, in particular—by government. However, it excludes all government transfer payments, because such outlays, as previously noted, do not reflect any current production but merely transfer governmental receipts to certain specific households. The letter G will be used to indicate government purchases of goods and services.

Gross private domestic investment (I_g)

This seemingly complicated term refers to all investment spending by American business firms. What is included as investment spending? Basically three things: (1) all final purchases of machinery, equipment, and tools by business enterprises; (2) all construction; and (3) changes in inventories. This obviously entails more than we have imputed to the term ''investment'' thus far. Hence, we must explain why each of these three items is included under the general heading of gross private domestic investment.

The reason for inclusion of the first group of items is apparent. This is simply a restatement of our original definition of investment spending as the purchase of tools, machinery, and equipment. The second item—all construction—merits some explanation. It is clear that the building of a new factory, warehouse, or grain elevator is a form of investment. But why include residential construction as investment rather than consumption? The reason is this: Apartment

buildings are clearly investment goods because, like factories and grain elevators, they are income-earning assets. Other residential units which are rented are for the same reason investment goods. Finally, owner-occupied houses are classified as investment goods because they could be rented out to yield a money income return, even though the owner does not choose to do so. For these reasons all residential construction is considered as investment.

Inventory changes as investment Remembering that GNP is designed to measure total current output, we must certainly make an effort to include in GNP any products which are produced *but not sold* this year. In short, if GNP is to be an accurate measure of total output, it must include the market value of any additions to inventories which accrue during the year. Were we to exclude an increase in inventories, GNP would understate the current year's total output. If businessmen have more goods on their shelves and in their warehouses at the end of the year than they had at the start, the economy has produced more than it has consumed during this particular year. This increase in inventories obviously must be added to GNP as a measure of *current* production.

What about a decline in inventories? This must be subtracted in figuring GNP, because in such a situation the economy sells a total output which exceeds current production, the difference being reflected in an inventory reduction. Some of the GNP taken off the market this year reflects not current production but rather a drawing down of inventories which were on hand at the beginning of this year. And the inventories on hand at the start of any year's production represent the production of previous years. Consequently, a decline in inventories in any given year means that the economy has consumed more than it has produced during the year; that is, society has consumed all of this year's output plus some of the inventories inherited from previous years' production. Remembering that GNP is a measure of the current year's output, we must omit any consumption of past production, that is, any drawing down of inventories, in determining GNP.

Noninvestment transactions We have discussed what investment is; it is equally important to emphasize what investment is not. Specifically, investment does not refer to the transfer of paper assets or secondhand tangible assets. The buying of stocks and bonds is excluded from the economist's definition of investment, because such purchases merely transfer the ownership of existing assets. The same holds true of the resale of existing assets. Investment is the construction or manufacture of *new* capital assets. It is the creation of such earning assets that gives rise to jobs and income, not the exchange of claims to existing capital goods.

Gross versus net investment We have broadened our concepts of investment and investment goods to include purchases of machinery and equipment, all construction, and changes in inventories. Now let us focus our attention on the three modifiers, "gross," "private," and "domestic," which national income accountants see fit to use in describing investment. The second and third terms simply tell us, respectively, that we are talking about spending by private business enterprises as opposed to governmental (public) agencies and that the firms involved are American—as opposed to foreign—firms.

The term "gross," however, cannot be disposed of so easily. *Gross private domestic investment* includes the production of all investment goods—those which are to replace the machinery, equipment, and buildings used up in the current year's production plus any net additions to the economy's stock of capital. In short, gross investment includes both replacement and added investment. On the other hand, we reserve the term *net private domestic investment* to refer only to the added investment which has occurred in the current year. A simple example will make the distinction clear. In 1970 our economy produced about $136 billion worth of capital goods. However, in the process of producing the GNP in 1970, the economy used up some $84 billion worth of machinery and equipment. As a result, our economy added $52 (or $136 minus $84) billion to its stock of capital in 1970. Therefore, *gross* investment was $136 billion in 1970, but *net* investment was only $52 billion. The differ-

ence between the two is the value of the capital used up or depreciated in the production of 1970's GNP.

Net investment and economic growth The relationship between gross investment and depreciation provides a good indicator of whether or not our economy is expanding, static, or declining. Figure 10·1 illustrates these three cases. When gross investment exceeds depreciation, as in Figure 10·1*a,* the economy is obviously expanding in the sense that its productive capacity—as measured by its stock of capital goods—is growing. More simply, net investment is a positive figure in an expanding economy. For example, as noted above, in 1970 gross investment was $136 billion, and $84 billion worth of capital goods were consumed in producing that year's GNP. This meant that our economy ended 1970 with $52 billion more capital goods than it had on hand at the start of the year. Increasing the supply of capital goods, you will recall, is a basic means of expanding the productive capacity of the economy (see Figures 2·3 and 2·4).

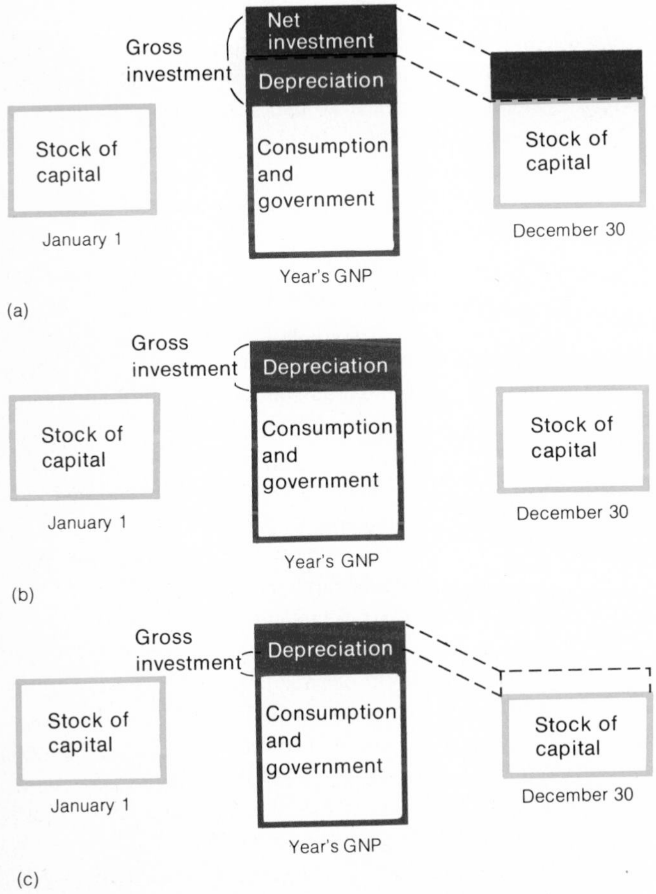

FIGURE 10·1 EXPANDING, STATIC, AND DECLINING ECONOMIES

In an expanding economy (*a*), gross investment exceeds depreciation, which means that the economy is making a net addition to its stock of capital facilities. In a static economy (*b*), gross investment precisely replaces the capital facilities depreciated in producing the year's output, leaving the stock of capital goods unchanged. In a declining economy (*c*), gross investment is insufficient to replace the capital goods depreciated by the year's production. As a result, the economy's stock of capital declines.

A stationary or static economy reflects the situation in which gross investment and depreciation are equal. This means the economy is standing pat; it is producing just enough capital to replace what is consumed in producing the year's output—no more and no less. In 1942, as the United States attempted to push its production of military goods into high gear, our economy approximated this situation. Resources were purposely diverted from the production of capital goods for nonessential industries, and even in essential industries resources were used sparingly for the production of capital goods. Why? Because the wartime emergency demanded astonishing amounts of finished war goods, and the lion's share of our available resources was directed toward attaining that goal. Therefore, it is not surprising that in 1942 gross investment and depreciation were approximately equal at $10 billion. This meant that at the end of 1942 our stock of capital was about the same as at the start of that year. In other words, *net* investment was about zero. Our economy was a stationary one in the sense that its productive facilities failed to expand. Figure 10·1*b* represents the case of a static economy.

The unhappy case of a declining economy arises whenever gross investment is less than depreciation, that is, when the economy consumes more capital in a year than it manages to produce. Under such circumstances net investment will be a negative figure—the economy will be "disinvesting." Depressions foster such circumstances. During bad times, when production and employment are at a low ebb, the nation has a greater productive capacity than it is currently utilizing. Hence, there is little or no incentive to replace depreciated capital equipment, much less add to the existing stock. Depreciation is likely to outweigh gross investment, with the result that the nation's stock of capital is less at the end of the year than it was at the start. This was the case during the heart of the Great Depression. In 1933, for example, gross investment was only $1.4 billion, while the capital consumed during that year was $6.9 billion. Net disinvestment was therefore $5.5 billion. Figure 10·1*c* illustrates the case of a disinvesting, or declining, economy.

We shall use the symbol I to refer to domestic investment spending and attach the subscript g when referring to gross and n when referring to net investment.

Net exports (X_n)

How do American international trade transactions enter into national income accounting? We can best explain it in this way: First, remember that we are trying to add up all spending in American markets which accounts for or induces the output of goods and services in the American economy. A bit of reflection will lead you to the conclusion that spending by foreigners on American goods will account for American output just as will spending by Americans. Hence, we want to add in what foreigners spend on American goods and services—that is, we want to add in the value of American exports—in determining GNP by the expenditures approach. On the other hand, what about spending by Americans on goods and services brought into American markets by foreigners? Obviously this spending induces the output of foreign goods and services. Thus, in determining the GNP for the United States by the expenditures approach, we should want to subtract the value of American imports from total expenditures. Why? Because it accounts for no domestic production.

Rather than treat these two items—American exports and imports—separately, our national income accountants simply take the difference between the two. Hence, *net exports of goods and services* or, more simply, *net exports* is *the amount by which foreign spending on American goods and services exceeds American spending on foreign goods and services.* For example, should foreigners buy $9 billion worth of American exports and Americans buy $7 billion worth of foreign imports in a given year, net exports would be *plus* $2 billion. It must be emphasized that our definition of net exports might result in a negative figure. If foreigners spend $10 billion on American exports and Americans spend $12 billion on foreign imports, our "excess" of foreign spending over American spending is *minus* $2 billion.

The letter X_n will be used to designate net exports.

The four categories of expenditures that we have discussed—personal consumption expenditures (C), government expenditures on goods and services (G), gross private domestic investment (I_g), and net exports (X_n)—are comprehensive. They include all possible types of spending. Added together, they measure the market value of the year's output; they measure GNP.

THE INCOME APPROACH TO GNP

During 1970 total expenditures (that is, $C + I_g + G + X_n$) were \$976.5 billion. How was this \$976.5 billion allocated or distributed as income? It would be most convenient if we could say that the total expenditures upon the economy's annual output flow to households as wage, rent, interest, and profit incomes. Unfortunately, the picture is complicated somewhat by two nonincome charges against the value of total output, that is, against GNP. These are (1) a capital consumption allowance and (2) indirect business taxes.

Depreciation: capital consumption allowance

It was noted in Chapter 8 that the useful life of most capital equipment extends far beyond the year of purchase. Actual expenditures for capital goods and their productive life are not synchronized in the same accounting period. Hence, to avoid gross understatement of profit and therefore of total income in the year of purchase and overstatement of profit and of total income in succeeding years, individual businesses estimate the useful life of their capital goods and allocate the total cost of such goods more or less evenly over the life of the machinery. The annual charge which estimates the amount of capital equipment used up in each year's production is called "depreciation." Depreciation is essentially a bookkeeping entry designed to provide a more accurate statement of profit income and hence total income provided by a firm in each year.

If profits and total income for the economy as a whole are to be stated accurately, a gigantic depreciation charge for the economy as a whole must be made against the total receipts of the business sector. This depreciation charge is called a "capital consumption allowance." Why? Because that is exactly what it is—an allowance for capital goods which have been "consumed" in the process of producing this year's GNP. It is this huge depreciation charge which constitutes the previously noted difference between I_g and I_n. For present purposes, the significance of this charge lies in the fact that it claims a part of the business sector's receipts which is, therefore, not available for income payments to resource suppliers. In real terms, that is, in terms of physical goods and services, the capital consumption allowance tells us in effect that a portion of this year's GNP must be set aside to replace the machinery and equipment used up in accomplishing its production. In other words, all of GNP cannot be consumed as income by society without impairing the economy's stock of productive facilities.

Indirect business taxes

The second complicating nonincome charge arises from the presence of government. Government levies certain taxes—in particular, general sales taxes, excise and business property taxes, license fees, and customs duties—which business firms treat as costs of production and therefore add to the prices of the products they sell. These taxes, as a matter of fact, are called "indirect business taxes" because sales taxes and excises are not levied directly upon the corporation, partnership, or proprietorship as such but rather upon their products or services. Businessmen, knowing the sizes of such levies, pass them on to the consumer in the form of higher prices. We can think of it in this way: A firm produces a product designed to sell at, say, \$1. As we have seen, the production of this item creates an equal amount of wages, rental, interest, and profit income. But now government, in need of revenue to finance its activities, imposes a 2 percent sales tax on all products sold at retail. The retailer simply adds this 2 percent

to the price of the product, raising its price from $1 to $1.02 and thereby shifting the burden of the sales tax to consumers.

Obviously, this 2 percent of total receipts which reflects the tax must be paid out to government before the remaining $1 can be paid to households as wage, rent, interest, and profit incomes. Government, in effect, is a preferred creditor. Furthermore, this flow of indirect business taxes to government is not earned income, because government contributes nothing directly to the production of the good in return for these sales tax receipts. As a matter of fact, in the cases of sales and excise taxes the finished product is being handed to the consumer at the time the tax is levied. In short, we must be careful to exclude indirect business taxes when figuring the total income earned in each year by the factors of production.

Capital consumption allowances and indirect business taxes account for the nonincome allocations listed in Table 10·5. As just noted, what remains is wages, rents, interest, and profits. But for a variety of reasons national income statisticians need a more sophisticated breakdown of wages and profits than we have employed thus far in this discussion.

Compensation of employees

This largest income category comprises primarily the wages and salaries which are paid by businesses and government to suppliers of labor. It also includes an array of wage and salary supplements, in particular payments by employers into social insurance and into a variety of private pension, health, and welfare funds for workers. These wage and salary supplements are a part of the employer's cost of obtaining labor and therefore are treated as a component of his total wage payments.

Rents

Rents are almost self-explanatory. They consist of income payments received by households that supply property resources.

Interest

Interest refers to money income payments which flow from private businesses to the suppliers of money capital. For reasons to be noted later, interest payments made by government and consumers are excluded from interest income.

Proprietors' income

What we have loosely termed "profits" is also broken into two basic accounts by national income accountants: One part is called *proprietors' income* or income of unincorporated businesses and the other *corporate profits.* The former account is largely self-defining. It refers to the net income of sole proprietorships, partnerships, and cooperatives. On the other hand, corporate profits cannot be dismissed so easily, because corporate earnings may be distributed in several ways.

Corporate profits

Generally speaking, three things can be done with corporate profits: First, a part will be claimed by, and therefore flow to, government as *corporate income taxes.* Second, a part of the remaining corporate profits will be paid out to stockholders as *dividends.* Such payments flow to households, which, of course, are the ultimate owners of all corporations. What remains of corporate profits after both corporate income taxes and dividends have been paid is called *undistributed corporate profits.* These retained corporate earnings, along with capital consumption allowances, are invested currently or in the future in new plants and equipment, thereby increasing the real assets of the investing businesses.

Table 10·6 summarizes our detailed discussions of both the expenditure and income approaches to GNP. The reader will recognize that this is merely a gigantic income statement for the economy as a whole. The left-hand side tells us what the economy produced in 1970 and the total receipts derived from that production. The right-hand side indicates how

TABLE 10·6 THE INCOME STATEMENT FOR THE ECONOMY, 1970 (*in billions of dollars*)

Receipts: expenditures approach		Allocations: income approach	
Personal consumption expenditures (C)	$616.7	Capital consumption allowance	$ 84.3
Government purchases of goods and services (G)	220.5	Indirect business taxes	92.1
Gross private domestic investment (I_g)	135.7	Compensation of employees	599.8
Net exports (X_n)	3.6	Rents	22.7
		Interest	33.5
		Proprietors' income	67.6
		Corporate income taxes	37.5
		Dividends	25.2
		Undistributed corporate profits	13.8
Gross national product	$976.5	Gross national product	$976.5

Source: U.S. Department of Commerce data. Because of rounding, figures may not add up to totals.

the income derived from the production of 1970's GNP was allocated. One can determine GNP either by adding up the four types of expenditures on final goods and services or by adding up the nine categories of income which stem from that output's production. Because output and income are two sides of the same coin, the two sums will necessarily match.

OTHER SOCIAL ACCOUNTS

Our discussion thus far has centered upon GNP as a measure of the economy's annual output. However, there are certain related social accounting concepts of equal importance which can be derived from GNP. To round out our understanding of social accounting, it is imperative that we trace through the process of deriving these related concepts. This procedure will also enhance our understanding of how the expenditure and income approaches to GNP dovetail one another. Our plan of attack will be to start with GNP and make a series of adjustments—subtractions and additions—necessary to the derivation of the related social accounts.

Net national product (NNP)

GNP as a measure of total output has an important defect: It tends to give us a somewhat exaggerated picture of this year's production. Why? *Because it fails to make allowance for that part of this year's output which is necessary to replace the capital goods consumed in the year's production.*

Two examples will help make this point clear: First, suppose a farmer starts the year by planting 20 bushels of wheat, realizing a total output of 400 bushels at the end of the year. Is it correct to represent his output for the year as 400 bushels? Certainly not. He would have had 20 bushels available if he had planted nothing at all. His net output for the year is 400 minus 20, or 380 bushels. This is a more accurate measure of the production that has actually occurred this year than is 400 bushels. Second, using hypothetical figures, suppose that on January 1, 1972, the economy had $100 billion worth of capital goods on hand. Assume also that during 1972 $40 billion worth of this equipment and machinery is used up in producing a GNP of $800 billion. Thus, on December 31, 1972, the stock of capital goods

on hand stands at only $60 billion. Is it fair to say that the GNP figure of $800 billion accurately measures this year's output? No. It would be much more accurate to subtract from the year's GNP the $40 billion worth of capital goods which must be used to replace the machinery and equipment consumed in producing that GNP. This leaves a *net* output figure of $800 minus $40, or $760 billion.

In short, a figure for *net* output is a more accurate measure of a year's production than is *gross* output. In our system of social accounting we derive a figure for *net national product* (NNP) by subtracting the capital consumption allowance, which measures the value of the capital used up in a year's production, from GNP. Hence, in 1970:

	Billions
Gross national product	$976.5
Capital consumption allowance	−84.3
Net national product	$892.2

NNP then is simply GNP adjusted for depreciation charges. It measures the total annual output which the entire economy—households, businesses, and governments—might consume without impairing our capacity to produce in ensuing years.

It is a simple matter, by the way, to adjust Table 10·6 from GNP to NNP. On the income side we simply strike out capital consumption allowance. The other eight allocations should add up to an NNP of $892.2 billion. On the expenditure side, one must change *gross* private domestic investment to *net* private domestic investment by subtracting replacement investment as measured by the capital consumption allowance from the former figure. In 1970, a gross investment figure of $135.7 billion less a depreciation charge of $84.3 billion results in a net private domestic investment figure of $51.4 billion and therefore an NNP of $892.2 billion.

National income (NI)

In analyzing certain problems, we are vitally interested in how much income is *earned* by resource suppliers for their contributions of land, labor, capital, and entrepreneurial ability which go into the year's net production or, alternatively stated, how much it costs society in terms of economic resources to produce this net output. The only component of NNP which does not reflect the current productive contributions of economic resources is indirect business taxes. It will be recalled that government contributes nothing to production in return for the indirect business tax revenues which it receives; government is not considered to be a factor of production. Hence, to get a measure of total wage, rent, interest, and profit incomes earned from the production of the year's output, we must subtract indirect business taxes from NNP. The resulting figure is called the *national income.* From the viewpoint of resource suppliers, it measures the incomes they have earned for their current contributions to production. From the viewpoint of businesses, national income measures factor or resources costs; national income reflects the market costs of the economic resources which have gone into the creation of this year's output. In 1970:

	Billions
Net national product	$892.2
Indirect business taxes	−92.1
National income	$800.1

A glance at Table 10·6 shows that national income can also be obtained through the income approach by simply adding up all the allocations with the exception of capital consumption allowances and indirect business taxes. The seven allocations of GNP which remain after the two nonincome charges have been subtracted constitute the national income.

Personal income (PI)

Income *earned* (national income) and income *received* (personal income) are likely to differ, for the simple reason that some income which is earned—social security contributions (payroll taxes), corpo-

rate income taxes, and undistributed corporate profits—is not actually received by households, and, conversely, some income which is received—transfer payments—is not currently earned. Transfer payments, you may recall, are made up of such items as (1) old age and survivors' insurance payments and unemployment compensation, both of which stem from our social security program, (2) relief or welfare payments, (3) a variety of veterans' payments, for example, GI Bill of Rights and disability payments, (4) payments out of private pension and welfare programs, and (5) interest payments paid by government and by consumers.[6]

Obviously in moving from national income as a measure of income earned to personal income as an indicator of income actually received we must subtract from national income those three types of income which are earned but not received and add in income received but not currently earned. This is done as follows:

	Billions
National income (income earned)	$800.1
Social security contributions	−57.1
Corporate income taxes	−37.5
Undistributed corporate profits	−13.8
Transfer payments	+109.3
Personal income (income received)	$801.0

During periods of full employment, national income exceeds personal income. But when unemployment is above normal, as in 1970, PI may exceed NI. This is so because the three subtracted items tend to be small and the added item large during recession. Can you explain why?

[6]Why include interest payments on government bonds as income *not* currently earned, particularly when interest on the bonds of private firms is included in national income as earned income? The rationale underlying the exclusion is this: Most of our present public debt was incurred during World War II. Warbond sales financed the government's purchase of wartime assets, and, unlike the railroad equipment or factories purchasd with the proceeds of private bond sales some ten or twenty years ago, wartime assets of 1940–1944 vintage no longer provide any current services for the economy. Similar, although perhaps less defensible, reasoning underlies the inclusion of interest payments by consumers as a part of transfer payments.

Disposable income (DI)

Disposable income is simply personal income less personal taxes. *Personal taxes* are comprised of personal income taxes, personal property taxes, and inheritance taxes, the first of the three being by far the most important.

Households apportion their disposable income in three ways. The bulk of it is spent on consumer goods. Another significant portion is saved. And, finally, a relatively small amount is paid out as interest. Personal saving can be thought of as a residual; that is, it is the amount of disposable income which remains after consumption and interest outlays have been made out of disposable income. The difference between personal income and disposable income and the division of the latter are shown for 1970:

	Billions
Personal income (income received before personal taxes)	$801.0
Personal taxes	−116.2
Disposable income (income received after personal taxes)	$684.8
Personal consumption expenditures	−616.7
Interest paid by consumers	−17.9
Personal saving	$ 50.2

Households might actually dissave; their consumption and interest outlays may exceed their disposable income as the result of borrowing or drawing down past accumulations of savings. Such was the case in 1933 when saving was a *minus* $0.9 billion.

It is worth noting that just as GNP, NNP, and NI can be derived by adding up their component parts, so can PI and DI. DI is obviously the sum of personal saving, personal consumption expenditures, and personal interest payments. PI is the sum of personal saving, personal consumption expenditures, personal

taxes, and personal interest payments. The reader should employ the figures used in the above calculation of personal saving to verify these points.

For analysis: DI = C + S

A final point: In *explaining* the determination of national income, as opposed to *measuring* its size, economists find it expeditious to treat disposable income as being comprised simply of personal consumption expenditures (C) and personal saving (S). Indeed, economists define saving as "not consuming" or "that part of DI which is not spent on consumer goods." Thus in explaining how the national income is determined in Chapters 12 and 13, we shall suppose households have two choices with respect to their disposable income: to spend or to save.

Relationships between major social accounts

We have derived four new social accounting concepts from GNP: (1) net national product (NNP), the market value of the annual output net of capital consumption allowances, (2) national income (NI), income *earned* by the factors of production for their current contributions to production, or the factor costs entailed in getting the year's total output produced, (3) personal income (PI), income *received* by households before personal taxes, and (4) disposable income (DI), income received by households less personal taxes. The relationships between these concepts are summarized in Table 10·7.

TABLE 10·7 THE RELATIONSHIPS BETWEEN GNP, NNP, NI, PI, AND DI IN 1970

	Billions
Gross national product (GNP)	\$976.5
Capital consumption allowance	−84.3
Net national product (NNP)	\$892.2
Indirect business taxes	−92.1
National income (NI)	\$800.1
Social security contributions	−57.1
Corporate income taxes	−37.5
Undistributed corporate profits	−13.8
Transfer payments	+109.3
Personal income (PI)	\$801.0
Personal taxes	−116.2
Disposable income (DI)	\$684.8
Personal consumption expenditures (C)	−616.7
Interest paid by consumers	−17.9
Personal saving	\$ 50.2

SUMMARY

Figure 10·2 embodies a comprehensive summary and synthesis of all the social accounting measures discussed in this chapter. As a more realistic and more complex expression of the circular flow model of the economy (discussed in Chapter 3), this figure merits careful study by the reader. Starting at the GNP rectangle in the upper left-hand corner, the expenditures side of GNP is shown to the left. For simplicity's sake, we have assumed net exports to be zero. Immediately to the right of the GNP rectangle are the nine income components of GNP and then the various additions and subtractions which are needed in the derivation of NNP, NI, and PI. In the household sector we see the flow of personal taxes out of PI and the division of DI between consumption, personal saving, and personal interest payments. In the government sector the flows of revenue in the form of four basic types of taxes are denoted on the right; on the left, government disbursements take the form of purchases of goods and services and transfers. To simplify, a balanced budget is assumed in the public sector. The position of the business sector is such as to emphasize, on the left, investment expenditures and, on the right, the three major sources of funds for business investment.

The major virture of Figure 10·2 is that it simultaneously portrays the expenditure and income aspects of GNP, fitting the two approaches to one another.

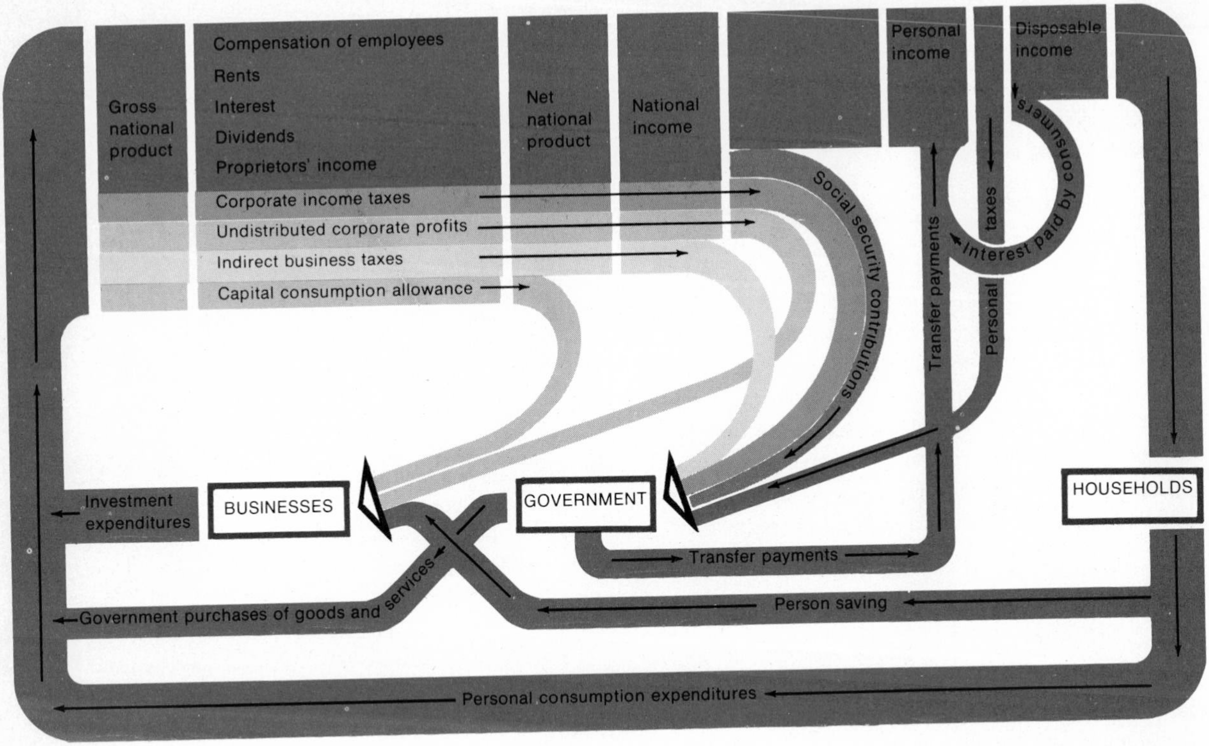

FIGURE 10·2 NATIONAL OUTPUT AND THE FLOWS OF EXPENDITURE AND INCOME

This figure is an elaborate circular flow diagram which fits the expenditures and allocations sides of GNP to one another. The reader should trace through the income and expenditures flows, relating them to the five basic national income accounting measures.

This figure correctly indicates that these flows of expenditure and income are part of a continuous, repetitive process. Cause and effect are intermingled: expenditures give rise to income, and out of this income arise expenditures which again flow to resource owners as income, and so forth.

Finally, the following concise definitions of the most important measures of the economy's performance should be thoroughly understood in studying Figure 10·2:

1. *Gross national product* (GNP) refers to the market value of all final goods and services produced in the economy in a given year.

2. *Net national product* (NNP) is gross national product minus capital consumption allowances (depreciation). NNP may also be found by summing personal consumption expenditures, *net* private domestic investment, government purchases of goods and services, and net exports.

3. *National income* (NI) is the total income *earned*

by resource suppliers for their contributions to the production of GNP. National income also measures the costs of the resources used up in producing GNP. Its magnitude can be derived by subtracting indirect business taxes from NNP or by summing compensation of employees, rents, interest, proprietors' income, corporate income taxes, dividends, and undistributed corporate profits.

4. *Personal income* (PI) is the total income *received* by households during a given year. PI is determined by subtracting from national income that income which is earned but not received (social security contributions, corporate income taxes, and undistributed corporate profits) and adding that income which is received but not earned (transfer payments).

5. *Disposable income* (DI) is the portion of personal income which remains after the payment of personal taxes.

QUESTIONS AND STUDY SUGGESTIONS

1. "National income statistics are a powerful tool of economic understanding and analysis." Explain.

2. Why do national income accountants compare the market value of the total outputs in various years rather than actual physical volumes of production? Explain. What problem is posed by any comparison of the market values of various total outputs? How is this problem resolved?

3. Carefully and completely define *a.* gross national product and *b.* net national product. How do these measures differ?

4. What are final goods? Intermediate goods? What is double counting? Give an example. Why do national income accountants include only final goods in measuring total output?

5. "An economy's output is its income." Do you agree? Explain.

6. What is the difference between gross private domestic investment and net private domestic investment? If you were to determine net national product through the expenditures approach, which of these two measures of investment spending would be appropriate? Explain.

7. Why are changes in inventories included as a part of investment spending? Suppose inventories declined by $1 billion during 1972. How would this affect the size of gross private domestic investment and gross national product in 1972? Explain.

8. Distinguish between an expanding, a static, and a declining economy.

9. "In 1933 net private domestic investment was minus $5.5 billion. This means in that particular year the economy produced no capital goods at all." Do you agree? Explain: "Though net investment can be positive, negative, or zero, it is quite impossible for gross investment to be less than zero."

10. Define net exports. Suppose foreigners spend $7 billion on American exports in a given year and Americans spend $5 billion on imports from abroad in the same year. What is the amount of America's net exports?

11. The following is a list of national income figures for a given year. All figures are in billions. The ensuing question will ask you to determine the major national income measures by both the expenditure and income methods. The answers derived by each approach should be the same.

Personal consumption expenditures	$245
Transfer payments	12
Rents	14
Capital consumption allowance (depreciation)	27
Social security contributions	20
Interest	13
Proprietors' income	31
Net exports	3
Dividends	16
Compensation of employees	221
Indirect business taxes	18
Undistributed corporate profits	21
Personal taxes	26
Corporate income taxes	19
Government purchases of goods and services	72
Net private domestic investment	33
Personal saving	12
Interest paid by consumers	4

a. Using the above data, determine GNP and NNP by both the expenditure and income methods.

b. Now determine NI (1) by making the required subtractions from GNP and (2) by adding up the types of income which comprise NI.

c. Make those adjustments for NI required in deriving PI. Now determine PI by adding up its various components.

d. Make the required adjustments from PI (as determined in 11*c*) to obtain DI. Also determine DI by adding up its component parts.

12. Given the following national income accounting data, compute *a.* GNP, *b.* NNP, and *c.* NI. All figures are in billions.

Compensation of employees	$194.2
U.S. exports of goods and services	13.4
Capital consumption allowance	11.8
Government purchases of goods and services	59.4
Indirect business taxes	12.2
Net private domestic investment	52.1
Transfer payments	13.9
U.S. imports of goods and services	16.5
Personal taxes	40.5
Personal consumption expenditures	219.1

13. The following table shows money GNP and an appropriate price index for a group of selected years. Compute real GNP. Indicate in each calculation whether you are inflating or deflating the money GNP data.

Year	Money GNP, billions	Price level index, percent (1958 = 100)	Real GNP, billions
1943	$191.6	56.8	$______
1947	231.3	74.6	$______
1956	419.2	94.0	$______
1963	590.5	107.2	$______
1969	931.4	128.1	$______

14. Which of the following are actually included in deriving this year's GNP? Explain your answer in each case.

a. Interest on an AT&T bond

b. Social security payments received by a retired factory worker

c. The services of a painter in painting his own home

d. The income of a dentist

e. The money received by Smith when he sells a 1967 Chevrolet to Jones

f. The monthly allowance which a college student receives from home

g. Rent received on a two-bedroom apartment

h. The money received by Wilson when he resells this year's model Plymouth to Wilcox

i. Interest received on government bonds

j. A two-hour decline in the length of the workweek

k. The purchase of an AT&T bond

l. A $2 billion increase in business inventories

m. The purchase of 100 shares of GM common stock

n. The purchase of an insurance policy

o. Wages paid to a domestic servant

p. The market value of a housewife's services

q. The purchase of a Renaissance painting by a public art museum

15. Explain: "A man diminishes the national income by marrying his cook."

SELECTED REFERENCES

Economic Issues, 4th ed., reading 15.

Abraham, William I.: *National Income and Economic Accounting* (Englewood Cliffs, N.J.: Prentice-Hall, Inc., 1969).

Dernburg, Thomas F., and Duncan M. McDougall: *Macroeconomics,* 3d ed. (New York: McGraw-Hill Book Company, 1968), chaps. 1–4.

Edey, Harold C., and Alan T. Peacock: *National Income and Social Accounting* (London: Hutchinson & Co., Publishers, Ltd., 1954).

Shapiro, Edward: *Macroeconomic Analysis,* 2d ed. (New York: Harcourt, Brace & World, Inc., 1970), chaps. 2–5.

U.S. Department of Commerce: *The National Income and Product Accounts of the United States, 1929–1965* (Washington, 1966).

U.S. Department of Commerce: *Survey of Current Business.* July issues contain annual national income data.

11

THE BUSINESS CYCLE: UNEMPLOYMENT AND INFLATION

Emphasis in Part 1 of this book was upon the essentially microeconomic problem of full production. To facilitate our discussion of how American capitalism allocates resources, we assumed that resources would be fully employed. But actual experience indicates that full employment cannot be taken for granted. Hence, in Parts 2 and 3 we seek to explore the problem of achieving and maintaining full employment in American capitalism.

The goals of the present chapter are fourfold. First, we introduce the "macroeconomic trilogy" of growth, full employment, and price stability. Next, we discuss total spending as the immediate determinant of the levels of employment and prices. Thirdly, the meanings and implications of unemployment and price instability are explored. Finally, the major characteristics of the American business cycle are discussed and its history sketched.

THE MACROECONOMIC TRILOGY

The broad spectrum of American economic history reflects quite remarkable economic expansion. Technological progress, rapid increases in productive capacity, and a standard of living which is the envy of the world are strategic facets of the dynamic character of our economy. But our long-run economic growth has not been steady. Rather, it has been interrupted by periods of economic instability. Periods of rapid economic expansion have sometimes been marred by inflation, that is, price instability, and at other times have given way to recession and depression, that is, instability in employment and output. Indeed, on a few occasions we have had the unhappy experience of the price level and unemployment rising simultaneously. In short, secular economic

growth has been interrupted and complicated by both unemployment and inflation.

Needless to say, what society seeks is economic growth *and* full employment *and* price stability, along with other less quantifiable goals (see Chapter 1). The degree to which we have been successful in realizing this macroeconomic trilogy is depicted in detail by the historical record embodied in the national income statistics (see tables inside covers). Aside from a few comments in our historical discussion of the business cycle, we defer any detailed treatment of economic growth until Part 4. In Parts 2 and 3 we concentrate upon the problems involved in achieving full employment and price stability.

SPENDING, EMPLOYMENT, AND THE PRICE LEVEL

Generally speaking, the levels of output and employment, on the one hand, and the level of prices, on the other, have a common determinant. And that determinant is the level of total spending. In a price-directed economy such as American capitalism, businesses produce only those goods which can be sold profitably. Now obviously, if total spending is large, that is, if the demand for goods and services in general is great, businesses will be able to produce and profitably sell a large volume of goods and services. To accomplish a large volume of production, businesses will be required to employ a large volume of resources. And this means high incomes. In brief, a high level of spending will make profitable a large volume of output, and this entails a high level of employment. Conversely, a low level of total spending means that the demand for goods and services in general is depressed. This means, in turn, that the volume of output will be small; few goods and services can be sold profitably. And a small output can be produced with a small amount of resources. A low level of total spending means that resources will be involuntarily unemployed. And, finally, unemployment means low incomes.

Although total spending, on the one hand, and output and employment, on the other, are directly related, this relationship is not completely rigid. When widespread unemployment prevails, a given increase in total spending will have a greater immediate impact[1] upon real output and employment than will that same increase in spending when the economy is operating near, or at, full employment. In particular, price changes loosen the link between changes in spending and the volumes of output and employment as the economy approaches full employment. Let us see exactly how this comes about.

Phase 1: unemployment

Suppose initially that the economy has a large amount of unemployed resources at a time when total spending, for some reason or another, increases. In terms of specific goods, this will mean that demand has increased in relation to supply. As stated in Chapter 4, increases in the demand for specific products will have both a price-increasing and a quantity-increasing effect. During periods of substantial unemployment the price-increasing effect of an increase in demand will tend to be small and the output-increasing effect large. Why? Most obviously, there are large amounts of virtually all types of human and property resources which can be readily employed by firms *at current resource prices* to expand their outputs. Furthermore, the plants of many producers will be operating at less than their designed capacity during a period of unemployment. Hence, an expansion of output may result in a more efficient utilization of existing capital facilities. For both these reasons businesses will find that they can increase their output in response to an increase in consumer demand without any appreciable increase in their unit costs of production or, therefore, in the prices they need receive for their products. During widespread unemployment, an increase in demand will bring forth more or less proportionate increases in output and employment with little or no rise in prices.

[1]Our present discussion is concerned only with the initial impact of a change in spending upon output and employment. Secondary effects will be brought into account in ensuing chapters.

Phase 2: premature inflation

As total spending continues to rise, however, this picture will begin to change. As production expands, supplies of unemployed resources will not vanish simultaneously. Production bottlenecks appear in the form of shortages of certain specific resources, even though unemployment is still generally widespread. As they expand output, firms will find that there are no more idle supplies of, say, skilled labor or technicians or certain metal alloys. Many firms will be forced to hire less qualified labor. In any event, the prices of these fully employed resources will begin to rise as firms, anxious to partake of returning prosperity, scramble to obtain them. Rising resource prices and less efficient labor will mean both that costs rise and, in turn, that producers must receive higher prices for their products. In particular, firms with substantial market power will have some discretion with respect to product prices and will choose to increase them. Labor unions will be quick to take advantage of the improved bargaining position which the decline in unemployment entails, pressing more fervently for wage increases. In addition to the developing scarcities of specific resources, costs will also rise as some firms tend to utilize their plants beyond their most efficient capacities, to man their plants with less productive workers, and to pay premium rates for overtime work. In other words, with moderate unemployment, increases in the demand for products in general will have both price-increasing and output-increasing effects. Prices rise because the unit costs of producers rise.

The inflation just described is called "premature" for the simple reason that it occurs before the economy reaches full employment.

Phase 3: pure inflation

When the economy reaches full employment, prices will begin to rise very sharply as total spending continues to expand. At full employment the economy encounters the production barrier of scarce resources; the economy will be operating at capacity, at a point *on* its production possibilities curve. Businessmen as a group cannot respond to increases in spending by expanding real output. This is aptly termed *demand-pull inflation* by economists: Total demand in excess of society's productive capacity pulls the price level upward. Higher levels of total spending will simply bid up the prices of a fixed real output. At full employment, increases in spending will cause "pure" inflation to set in.

Figure 11·1 summarizes the relationship between the price level, on the one hand, and the levels of output and employment, on the other. The significance of the behavior of the price level as output and employment increase must be emphasized. When unemployment is great and widespread, the initial impact of an increase in total spending will be to bring forth more or less proportionate increases in output and employment (Phase 1). As the economy approaches full employment, however, the price level begins to rise. This means that a part of any increase in total expenditures will be dissipated in the form of higher prices, lessening its impact upon output and employ-

FIGURE 11·1 THE PRICE LEVEL AND THE LEVEL OF EMPLOYMENT

The price level generally begins to rise before full employment is reached. At full employment additional spending tends to be purely inflationary.

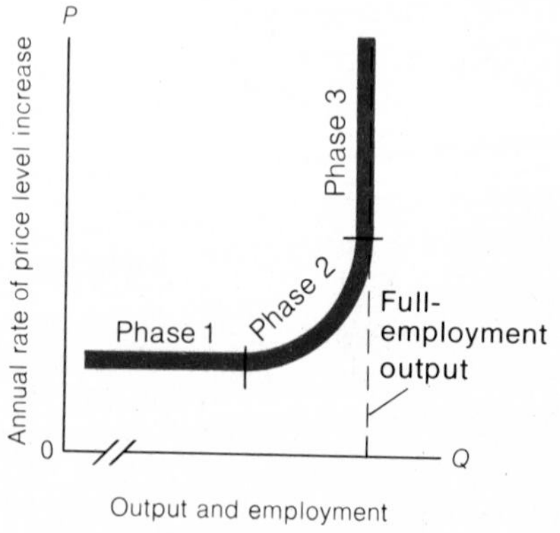

ment (Phase 2). If product X is selling at $1 per unit, a $10 increase in expenditures will induce a 10-unit increase in output. But if the $10 increase in spending causes the price of X to rise to $2 per unit, the resulting increase in output will be just 5 units. As the economy approaches full employment, larger and larger increases in spending are required to increase real output and employment by a given amount. Once at full employment, added spending will simply pull up the price level (Phase 3).

The relationship expressed in Figure 11·1 is only partially reversible. That is, many product and resource prices which are flexible upward as the economy approaches the full-employment output become relatively rigid and inflexible when declines in total spending result in reductions in output and employment. This is primarily the result of monopolistic power—the ability to influence prices—which many businesses and unions possess. Unions can usually resist wage cuts and sometimes secure modest wage boosts even though the total level of spending and therefore output and employment are falling. Monopolistic businesses are equally able to forestall reductions in product prices. Prices that go up during periods of full employment do not necessarily come down—at least all the way—when spending declines and unemployment ensues. It is not surprising that the long-run trend of the price level in American capitalism has been upward. The significance of the downward inflexibility of prices will become evident in Chapter 12.

Now our task is to assess more carefully the meaning and significance of both unemployment and price instability.

UNEMPLOYMENT

When the economist talks of "full employment," he does not mean that 100 percent of the available labor force is working. In a dynamic, free economy a certain amount of unemployment is regarded as normal. At any time there will be some workers who are in the process of voluntarily changing jobs. Some others may be temporarily out of work because of some labor-saving technological improvement or a change in consumer tastes which has adversely affected employment in their industry. Others are temporarily laid off because of seasonality—for example, bad weather in the construction industry—or model changeovers. And there will be some young workers who are looking for their first job. This largely unavoidable minimum of unemployment—often termed frictional unemployment—is estimated at 3 or 4 percent of the labor force for the United States. Full employment therefore exists when 97 or 96 percent of the labor force is employed, that is, when about 3 million of our 83 million civilian labor force is unemployed.

Unemployment statistics, however, can be misleading. For example, statistics for early 1970 indicate that 6 percent of the civilian labor force—5.4 million workers—were out of work. But these figures understate the unemployment problem. First, there were another 1.4 million workers who were working part time because full-time employment was not available to them. Second, there was another group of an estimated 1 million workers who unsuccessfully sought employment and, discouraged by their efforts, dropped out of the labor force. (One must be actively seeking work to be counted as unemployed in government figures.) Thus, actual unemployment may have been closer to 7.8 million or 9 percent of the labor force.

Regardless of the exact interpretation one gives to these statistics, above-normal or "true" unemployment entails great economic and social costs.

Economic costs: the GNP gap

The economic cost of unemployment is obviously forgone output—the goods and services which society could have produced but didn't. For example, the estimated 3.8 million of unemployment in 1964 probably cost the American economy $60 to $70 billion in forgone production.

The cost of a prolonged depression can be astronomical. One scholar has estimated the cost of the Great Depression of the 1930s in these terms:[2]

[2]Sherman J. Maisel, *Fluctuations, Growth, and Forecasting* (New York: John Wiley & Sons, Inc., 1957), p. 18.

A full-employment output for the 1930s would have produced $650 billion additional goods and services in terms of the 1956 price level. Such a sum would have been higher than the material cost of World War II. It would have meant roughly $5,000 more in income for each individual in the United States in that decade, or $20,000 more for the average family. If all resources had been fully employed in this manner, every family could have had a new house, several new cars, and most of the other durable goods it desired.

In more recent years government economists have measured the cost of unemployment in terms of a *GNP gap.* This gap is simply the amount by which the *actual GNP* falls short of *potential GNP.* Potential GNP is determined by assuming that full employment (defined as 4 percent unemployment) is achieved and projecting the economy's "normal" growth rate. Figure 11·2 shows the GNP gap for recent years and underscores the close correlation between the unemployment rate and the GNP gap. Unemployment is indeed costly. The cumulative gap between potential and actual GNP over the 1958–1965 period was $260 billion (measured in 1958 prices) of forgone production!

But aggregate figures are not enough. It is also important to note that the cost of unemployment is unequally distributed. An increase in the unemployment rate from 3 to, say, 6 percent would be more tolerable if every worker's hours of work and wage income were reduced proportionately. But in fact unemployment is borne heavily by teenagers, by women workers, and particularly by minority groups. For example, in 1969 the unemployment rate was only 3.5 percent for the labor force as a whole. But the breakdown of this figure revealed startling inequities. The unemployment rate for Negroes and other minorities was 6.4 percent as compared with 3.1 percent for whites. Unemployment among male workers was 2.8 percent as compared with 4.7 for females. Among all teenagers of labor-force age the unemployment rate was over 12 percent. For black teenagers the figure was over 21 percent![3]

[3]The taxonomy of unemployment is succinctly presented in Betty G. Fishman and Leo Fishman, *Employment, Unemployment, and Economic Growth* (New York: Thomas Y. Crowell Company, 1969).

Noneconomic costs

But unemployment is much more than an economic catastrophe; it is a social catastrophe as well. Depression means idleness. And idleness means loss of skills, loss of self-respect, a plummeting of morale, and sociopolitical unrest. The following commentaries from the unemployed of the 1930s provide important insights into the noneconomic aspects of unemployment:[4]

> The wife works while I look after the home. . . . Any long spell of unemployment leaves you with little to be proud of and much to be ashamed of. Our child is still too young to realize that it is her mother who works. We carefully keep her from knowing it.

> These last few years since I've been out of the mills I don't seem able to take trouble, somehow; I've got no spirit for anything. But I didn't use to be like that.

> My husband is a good man and he does a lot for me in the house. . . . But he is a changed man these last two years. He never complains, but I wish he would. It makes me unhappy to find him becoming quieter and quieter, when I know what he must be feeling. If I had someone to talk to about my troubles I should feel much better. . . . We quarrel far more now than we have ever done in our lives before. We would both rather be dead than go on like this.

It is no exaggeration to say that:[5]

> A job gives hope for material and social advancement. It is a way of providing one's children a better start in life. It may mean the only honorable way of escape from the poverty of one's parents. It helps to overcome racial and other social barriers. In short . . . a job is the passport to freedom and to a better life. To deprive people of jobs is to read them out of our society.

History makes it all too clear that severe unemployment is conducive to rapid and sometimes violent social and political change. Witness the movement

[4]Quotations cited in William H. Beveridge, *Full Employment in a Free Society* (New York: W. W. Norton & Company, Inc., 1945), pp. 243–244. The reader who wants to pursue the sociopolitical implications of prolonged unemployment will do well to consult David A. Shannon (ed.), *The Great Depression* (Englewood Cliffs, N.J.: Prentice-Hall, Inc., 1960).

[5]Henry R. Reuss, *The Critical Decade* (New York: McGraw-Hill Book Company, 1964), p. 133.

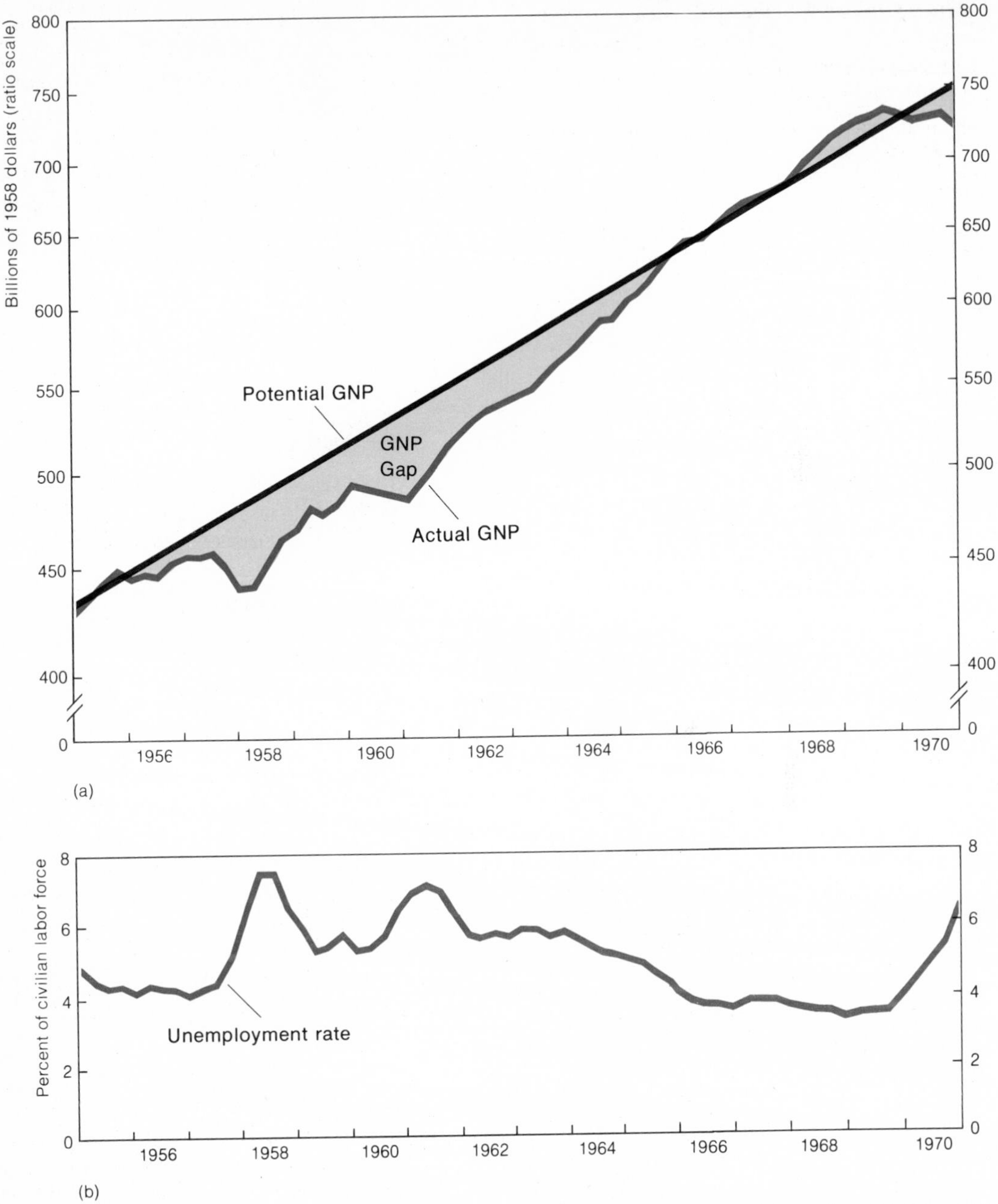

FIGURE 11 · 2 POTENTIAL AND ACTUAL GNP (*a*) AND THE UNEMPLOYMENT RATE (*b*)

The difference between potential and actual GNP is the GNP gap. The GNP gap measures the output which the economy sacrifices because it fails to fully utilize its productive potential. Note that a high unemployment rate means a large GNP gap. (*Economic Report of the President.*)

to the left of American political philosophy during the Depression of the 1930s. The Depression-inspired New Deal was a veritable revolution in American political and economic thinking. Witness also Hitler's ascent to power against a background of unemployment. Furthermore, there can be no question that the heavy concentration of unemployment among blacks and other minorities has been an important cause of the unrest and violence which have plagued American cities in recent years.

PRICE INSTABILITY: INFLATION AND DEFLATION

The problems and costs associated with a changing price level are more subtle than those of unemployment. It is important to note that, unlike unemployment, inflation does *not* entail a direct loss of output. Yet inflation is feared by all of us, criticized by most of us, and not clearly understood by many of us.

What is inflation? Why is it to be feared? *Inflation is a rising general level of prices.* This does not mean, of course, that all prices are necessarily rising. Even during periods of acute inflation some specific prices may be relatively constant and others actually falling. Nor does inflation mean that prices rise evenly or proportionately. Indeed, one of the major sore spots of inflation lies in the fact that prices tend to rise very unevenly. Some spring upward; others rise at a more leisurely pace; others do not rise at all. The fundamental cause of inflation has already been explored. Generally speaking, inflation results when society attempts to spend beyond its capacity to produce.

Deflation is substantially the reverse of inflation—a falling general level of prices. Once again, deflation does not mean that all prices are falling evenly. Falling prices accompany declining levels of output and employment; the cause is a deficiency of total spending.

Redistributive effects

In practice, output and the level of prices typically move together. Inflation is usually associated with an expanding output, and deflation is usually accompanied by a shrinking real output. But in order to isolate the effects of a changing price level upon the distribution of income, let us for the moment assume that real output is constant and at the full-employment level. Assuming the size of the income pie is fixed, how does inflation affect the size of the slices going to different income receivers? At the close of our analysis we shall release this simplification and modify our conclusions accordingly.

Any analysis of the redistributive impact of inflation and deflation demands that we first distinguish carefully between real and money income. *Money income* is simply the number of dollars one receives in his pay envelope. *Real income,* on the other hand, is the amount of goods and services which a consumer can obtain with his money income. A moment's reflection will make clear that one's real income depends upon (1) his money income and (2) the prices which he must pay for the goods and services he purchases.

Fixed-money-income groups With this distinction in mind it is easy to see why inflation arbitrarily penalizes people living on relatively fixed money incomes. Those households whose money incomes lag behind the rising level of product prices will find that their real incomes will deteriorate because of inflation. The purchasing power of each dollar's worth of income they receive will fall as prices rise. And, because they receive about the same number of dollars in their pay envelopes, their standard of living must decline accordingly.

Who are these people? The most obvious cases are pensioners, white-collar workers, civil servants, people living on relief and other transfer payments which remain fixed over substantial periods of time. In particular, elderly people who receive modest and inflexible pensions are the victims of inflation. Some wage earners are hurt by inflation. Those situated in declining industries or without the benefit of strong, aggressive unions may find that the price level skips ahead of their money incomes.

People living on flexible incomes will benefit from inflation. The money incomes of such households will spurt ahead of the price level, or cost of living, with

the result that their real incomes are enhanced. Workers employed in expanding industries and represented by vigorous unions may keep their wage incomes apace with, or ahead of, the rate of inflation. Many businessmen and other profit receivers benefit from inflation. Product prices typically rise faster than do resource prices; that is, business receipts tend to grow at a faster rate than do costs. Thus profit incomes are likely to outdistance the rising tide of inflation.

Debtors and creditors But this is not all. Inflation also redistributes income by altering the relationship between debtors and creditors. Specifically, inflation tends to benefit debtors at the expense of creditors. Suppose you borrow $1,000 from a bank, which you are to repay in two years. If in that period of time the general level of prices were to double, the $1,000 which you repay will have only half the purchasing power of the $1,000 originally borrowed. True, if we ignore interest charges, the same number of dollars are repaid as were borrowed. But because of inflation, each of these dollars will now buy only half as much as it did when the loan was negotiated. As prices go up, the value of the dollar comes down. Thus, because of inflation, the borrower is given "dear" dollars but pays back "cheap" dollars.

Savers Inflation also casts its evil eye upon savers. As prices rise, the real value, or purchasing power, of a nest egg of liquid savings will deteriorate. Savings accounts, insurance policies, annuities, and other fixed-value paper assets which were once adequate to meet rainy-day contingencies or to provide for a comfortable retirement decline in real value during inflation. Mortgage holders and bondholders will be similarly affected. A household's accumulated claims upon the economy's output are worth less and less as prices rise.

On the other hand, these two important exceptions should be noted. First, stock values are flexible and determined by current market conditions; hence, savings in this form will tend to increase in value with, or in some cases ahead of, the general level of prices. Second, so long as the interest rate on savings exceeds the rate of inflation (and this has generally been the case since World War II), the purchasing power of savings will increase rather than diminish. For example, the purchasing power of a $1,000 savings account will increase if the annual interest rate is, say, 5 percent and the annual increase in the price level only 3 percent.

Summary and addenda To summarize: Inflation arbitrarily "taxes" those who receive relatively fixed money incomes and "subsidizes" those who receive flexible money incomes. Inflation benefits debtors at the expense of creditors. Finally, inflation arbitrarily penalizes savers. It should come as no surprise that the effects of deflation are substantially the reverse. *Assuming no change in total output,* those with fixed money incomes will find their real incomes enhanced. Creditors will benefit at the expense of debtors. And savers will find that the purchasing power of their savings has grown as a result of falling prices.

Two final points must be appended to this discussion. First, the fact that any given family is likely to be an income earner, a holder of financial assets, and an owner of real assets simultaneously is likely to cushion the redistributive impact of inflation. For example, if the family owns fixed-value monetary assets (savings accounts, bonds, and insurance policies), inflation will lessen their real value. But that same inflation is likely to increase the real value of any property assets (a house, land) which the family owns. In short, many families are simultaneously hurt and benefited by inflation. All these effects must be considered before we can conclude that the family's net position is better or worse because of inflation. The second point to be reemphasized is that the redistributive effects of inflation *are* arbitrary in that they occur without regard to society's goals and values. Inflation lacks a social conscience and takes from some and gives to others, regardless of whether they be rich, poor, young, old, healthy, or infirm.

Output effects

We have assumed thus far that the economy's real output is fixed at the full-employment level. As a result, the redistributive effects of inflation and defla-

tion have been in terms of some groups gaining absolutely at the expense of others. If the size of the pie is fixed and inflation causes some groups to get larger slices, other groups must necessarily get smaller slices. This is obviously modified somewhat when inflation is accompanied by an expanding real output, as would be the case when the economy is approaching, but has not yet attained, the full-employment output (Phase 2 of Figure 11·1). When the pie is growing, the gains which inflation brings to some will exceed the losses which it imposes upon others. In brief, the redistributive impact of a given amount of inflation will tend to be less adverse when inflation is accompanied by an expansion of real output.

Although mild inflation may be accompanied by an expanding real total output, extreme inflation—"hyperinflation"—might well have adverse effects upon the level of production. There are two main reasons for this. In the first place, as we shall note shortly, hyperinflation may undermine the functioning of the monetary system, forcing the economy to rely upon exchange by barter. And barter, you recall (Chapter 3), inhibits specialization and thereby fosters inefficient production and a declining real output. Secondly, severe inflation encourages speculative, as opposed to productive, activity. Rather than invest in capital equipment, businessmen and savers find that the hoarding of goods and materials and the purchase of nonproductive wealth—jewels, precious metals, real estate, and so forth—are good hedges against inflation and hence more lucrative outlets for one's money.

What about deflation? Falling prices typically go along with depression and a declining total output. Hence, with a rapidly shrinking pie virtually all groups will get a smaller slice. In other words, those on relatively fixed incomes *who are able to hold their jobs* will find that their real incomes rise as a result of deflation. But many of these people may in fact lose their jobs and all their income. Creditors *who are fortunate enough to collect from debtors* will gain. But in fact many debts may not be collectible. And those *who are able to hold on to their savings* as the economy backslides into depression will find the purchasing power of their savings enhanced by lower prices. But, again, some may lose their savings as stock market prices tumble and financial institutions go bankrupt.

In short, during deflation fixed-money-income receivers, creditors, and savers are not likely to be better off in an absolute sense, because in all probability total output will be falling too. But they may be "less worse off" than flexible-income receivers, debtors, and nonsavers.

Creeping inflation

Virtually all economists condemn a sharply rising price level. Economists are divided, however, on the merits and demerits of mild or "creeping" inflation—that is, a 1, 2, or 3 percent annual increase in the price level.

The case for creeping inflation Despite the arbitrary redistributive effects of inflation, some competent economists[6] feel that creeping inflation may very well be desirable because of its expansionary effect upon the economy. Product prices, it is argued, tend to increase ahead of resource prices as the economy approaches full employment. This stimulates money profits and is conducive to additional investment spending, which, in turn, brings the economy closer to full employment. Furthermore, the larger stock of investment goods causes a favorable shift in the production possibilities curve, and economic growth is the result. It is concluded that only under the pressure of a high, inflation-causing level of aggregate demand does American capitalism realize full employment, capacity production, and its maximum growth potential. Mild inflation is allegedly a small price to pay for the attainment of these objectives. It is recognized that mild inflation will tread on the toes of fixed-income receivers, creditors, and savers. But any arbitrary redistributive effects will be more than offset by the benefits which inflation-born in-

[6]See, for example, Alvin H. Hansen, *The American Economy* (New York: McGraw-Hill Book Company, 1957), pp. 45–47, and Sumner H. Slichter, "How Bad Is Inflation?" *Harper's Magazine*, August 1952.

creases in output and employment will bring to the economy as a whole. More fixed-income employees will have jobs, creditors will be more certain of repayment, and prosperity will permit more households to enjoy the luxury of saving. The alternatives, as these economists see it, are full employment and growth accompanied by creeping inflation *or* price stability accompanied by unemployment and the failure of the economy to realize its growth potential. The former choice, they conclude, is far superior to the latter.

The case against creeping inflation But other competent authorities[7] take a dim view of this position. They make two major arguments against creeping inflation. First, they contend that when compounded over the years, the redistributive impact of mild or creeping inflation can be very severe. A 3 percent annual rise in prices will cause the price level to double in about twenty-three years! Second, it is argued that creeping inflation may readily snowball into hyper- or "galloping" inflation. And galloping inflation can precipitate depression. This second argument merits rather detailed consideration.

It is felt that as the economy draws close to the full-employment level, individual segments of the economy will exert pressure to keep their incomes rising ahead of the creeping inflation. But this pressure will cause creeping inflation to get up and run. It happens something like this: As prices persist in creeping upward, people come to expect them to rise further. So rather than let their idle savings and current incomes depreciate, people are induced to "spend now" to beat anticipated price rises. Businesses do the same in buying capital goods. Action on the basis of this "inflationary psychology" simply intensifies the pressure on prices, and inflation feeds upon itself. Furthermore, as the cost of living rises, labor demands and gets higher wages. Indeed, unions may seek wage increases sufficient not only to cover last year's price level increase but also to compensate for the inflation anticipated during the future life of their new collective bargaining agreement. Prosperity is not a good time for businessmen to risk strikes by resisting such demands. Businessmen recoup their rising labor costs by boosting the prices they charge consumers. And for good measure, businesses are likely to jack prices up an extra notch or two to be sure that profit receivers keep abreast or ahead of the inflationary parade. As the cost of living skips merrily upward as a result of these price increases, labor once again has an excellent excuse to demand another round of wage increases. Unions will bargain to recoup declines in real wage incomes resulting from past inflation *and* in anticipation of future rises in the price level. But this triggers another round of price increases. The net effect is a cumulative wage-price inflationary spiral. Wage and price rises feed upon each other, and this helps creeping inflation burst into galloping inflation. Thus, many economists feel that the trouble with a small dose of inflation is that it is not likely to remain small.

But, aside from capricious and disruptive effects upon the distribution of income, why is such hyperinflation to be feared? The answer, curiously enough, is that hyperinflation can lead to a depression. As prices shoot up sharply and unevenly, normal economic relationships are disrupted. Businessmen do not know what to charge for their products. Consumers do not know what to pay. Money becomes "hot," because inflation is rapidly diminishing the purchasing power of the dollar. In the extreme case, inflation may become so severe as to render money virtually worthless. Resource suppliers will want to be paid in kind. Creditors will hide from debtors to escape the repayment of debts with cheap money. Money will cease to do its job as a medium of exchange and a standard of value. Nor will people want to store their wealth in the form of money. The economy will literally be thrown into a state of barter. As inflation increases in severity, businesses may find it more profitable to hoard both materials and finished products, awaiting further price increases. But by further restricting the availability of materials and products relative to the demand for them, such action will merely tend to intensify inflationary pressures. Production and exchange grind toward a halt, and

[7]In recent years the monetary authorities in the United States have generally been opposed to creeping inflation.

the net result is economic, social, and very possibly political chaos. Hyperinflation has precipitated monetary collapse, depression, and sociopolitical disorder. The conclusion? Mild inflation is a very risky foundation for achieving healthy economic progress.

Which view is correct? It is hard to say. Both have proved accurate in specific instances. American economic history reveals that many periods of healthy economic growth have entailed mild inflation. On the other hand, other nations of the world have had mild inflation that got out of control—particularly during wartime—and broke into galloping inflation with disastrous results:[8]

> The inflation in Hungary exceeded all known records of the past. In August, 1946, 828 octillion (1 followed by 27 zeros) depreciated pengös equaled the value of 1 prewar pengö. The price of the American dollar reached a value of 3×10^{22} (3 followed by 22 zeros) pengös. . . . In Germany of 1923 a larger box was needed to carry money to the grocery store than to bring back the groceries bought. . . . Prices rose some 116 times in Japan, 1939 to 1948.

We must settle for the conclusion that creeping inflation can be expansionary but that such inflation may expose the economy to the real risk of galloping inflation, particularly after full employment is achieved.[9]

THE BUSINESS CYCLE

What is the record of American capitalism in providing for stability in output, employment, and the price level? The record is a spotty one. At times the economy has suffered from prolonged periods of underspending. The consequences of such periods have been widespread unemployment, low incomes, and a depressed GNP. At other times the economy has overspent; that is, it has spent in excess of its capacity to produce. The result has been full employment and a high GNP, on the one hand, but inflation—that is, a rising level of prices—on the other. This is not to say United States history has been an uninterrupted series of economic ups and downs. On the contrary, the overall post–World War II record, for example, has been good—much better than economists had dared to hope for at the end of hostilities (see Figure 11·3). Yet even in this period there have been times of inflation and recurring recessions. Thus the economy continues to be plagued by a business cycle.

Generally speaking, the term "business cycle" simply refers to the recurrent ups and downs in the level of economic activity which extend over a period of several years. Individual business cycles vary tremendously in detail. Yet all embody common phases which are variously labeled by different economists. Thus some economists talk of prosperity, recession, depression, and recovery as being the four phases of the business cycle. Others simply distinguish between the phases of expansion and contraction, with upper and lower turning points to divide the two. Still other economists are content to talk merely in terms of the "upswing" and "downswing" of the business cycle.

Despite common phases, specific business cycles vary greatly. (Indeed, some economists prefer to talk of business *fluctuations,* rather than *cycles,* because the latter term implies regularity.) In particular, cycles vary in duration and intensity. The Great Depression of the 1930s seriously undermined the level of business activity for an entire decade. By comparison, the business declines of 1924 and 1927 were minor in both intensity and duration, as our post–World War II recessions also have been. Figure 11·3 provides ample historical evidence as to the existence of the business cycle and its irregularity as to duration and intensity.

Noncyclical fluctuations

It must not be concluded that all changes in business activity are due to the business cycle. On the one hand, there are *seasonal variations* in business activity. For example, the pre-Christmas and pre-Easter buying rushes cause considerable fluctuations each year in the tempo of business activity, particularly

[8]Theodore Morgan, *Income and Employment,* 2d ed. (Englewood Cliffs, N.J.: Prentice-Hall, Inc., 1952), p. 361.

[9]See question 6 at the end of this chapter.

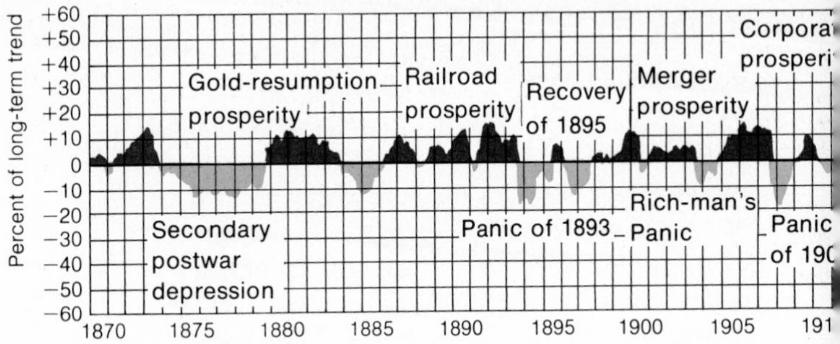

FIGURE 11 · 3 AMERICAN BUSINESS CYCLE EXPERIENCE

The American economy has encountered periods of prosperity and depression. Only minor recessions have occurred since World War II. (Cleveland Trust Company.)

in the retail industry. Agriculture, the automobile industry, construction—indeed, virtually all industries are subject to some degree of seasonality. These seasonal variations complicate the measurement of cyclical fluctuations in business activity. For example, an upswing in retail sales in December may or may not be evidence of a cyclical upswing in business activity. To speak with any degree of certainty, one would have to compare the increase in this December's retail sales with the increase in sales which statistical records for previous Decembers indicate as being normal. If retail sales normally double in December, a tripling of sales in December 1972 would suggest a cyclical upswing in business activity. Conversely, if retail sales for the month fall short of doubling, a cyclical downswing is implied.

Business activity is also subject to a *secular trend.* The secular trend of an economy is its expansion or contraction over a long period of years, for example, 50, 100, or 150 years. We simply note at this juncture that the long-run secular trend for American capitalism has been one of rather remarkable expansion; this growth will be considered in detail in a later chapter. For present purposes the importance of this long-run expansion is that the business cycle involves fluctuations in business activity around a long-run growth trend.

Note that in Figure 11 · 3 cyclical fluctuations are measured as deviations from the long-run trend, a trend that has been persistently upward. Needless to say, the long-run trend may influence the duration and intensity of particular phases of the business cycle.

Diverse impact of cycle

The business cycle is pervasive; it is felt in virtually every nook and cranny of the economy. The interrelatedness of the economy allows few, if any, to escape the cold hand of depression or the fever of inflation. Yet we must keep in mind that various individuals and various segments of the economy are affected in different ways and in different degrees by the business cycle.

Durables versus nondurables Insofar as production and employment are concerned, those industries producing capital goods and consumer durables are typically hit hardest by recession. The construction industry is particularly vulnerable. Output and employment in nondurable consumer goods industries

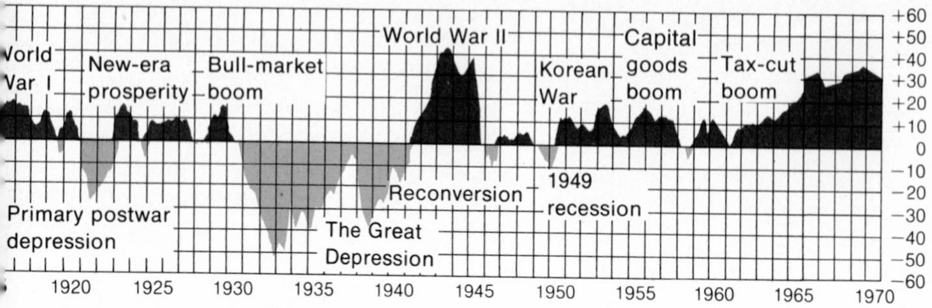

are less sensitive to the cycle. Industries producing housing and commercial buildings, heavy capital goods, farm implements, automobiles, refrigerators, gas ranges, and similar products bear the brunt of bad times. Conversely, these "hard goods" industries seem to be stimulated most by expansion. Two facts go far to explain the vulnerability of hard goods industries to the cycle.

1. Within limits, the purchase of hard goods is postponable. Hence, as the economy slips into bad times, producers forestall the acquisition of more modern productive facilities and the construction of new plants. The business outlook simply does not warrant increases in the stock of capital goods. In all probability the firm's present capital facilities and buildings will still be usable and in excess supply. Except in bad times capital goods are usually replaced before they are completely depreciated; when recession strikes, however, businessmen will patch up their outmoded equipment and make it do. As a result, investment in capital goods will decline sharply. Chances are that some firms, having excess plant capacity, will not even bother to replace all the capital which they are currently consuming. Net investment may be a negative figure.

Much the same holds true for consumer durables. When recession rolls around and the family budget must be trimmed, it is likely that plans for the purchases of durables will first feel the ax. You decide *not* to trade the old jalopy in on a new Belchfire Eight; the little woman is persuaded that she can survive the future without an electronic oven. The household retains its present television set, deferring the purchase of color. And so it goes. Food and clothing—consumer nondurables—are a different story. A family must eat and must clothe itself. These purchases are much less postponable. True, to some extent the quantity and most certainly the quality of these purchases will decline. But not so much as is the case with durables.

2. Most industries producing capital goods and consumer durables are industries of high concentration, wherein a relatively small number of firms dominate the market. As a result, these firms have sufficient monopoly power to resist lowering prices by restricting supply in the face of a declining demand. This means that the impact of a fall in demand centers primarily upon production and employment. The reverse holds true in nondurable, or soft, goods industries, which are for the most part highly com-

petitive and characterized by low concentration. Price declines cannot be resisted in such industries, and the impact of a declining demand falls to a greater extent on prices than upon the levels of production. Figure 11·4 is informative on this point. It shows the percentage declines in price and quantity which occurred in ten selected industries as the economy fell from peak prosperity in 1929 to the depth of depression in 1933. Speaking very generally, high-concentration industries make up the top half of the table and low-concentration industries the bottom half. Note the drastic production declines and relatively modest price declines of the high-concentration industries, on the one hand, and the large price declines and relatively small output declines which took place in the low-concentration industries, on the other.

Incomes and income shares What about incomes? On an industry basis our discussion of the employment and output effects of the cycle correctly implies that those whose livelihood is linked to the production of capital goods and consumer durables are likely to encounter the greatest variations in employment and incomes.[10] Unemployment will loom larger in such industries during bad times than it will elsewhere.

In terms of national income shares, we have seen previously (Figures 7·1 and 7·2) that rent and interest payments are fairly stable over the cycle. Corporate profits, on the other hand, are subject to

[10]Agriculture is a notable exception. The highly competitive nature of this industry makes agricultural incomes very sensitive to the business cycle, despite the fact that it produces nondurables.

FIGURE 11·4 RELATIVE PRICE AND PRODUCTION DECLINES IN TEN INDUSTRIES, 1929–1933

The high-concentration industries shown in the top half of this figure were characterized by relatively small price declines and large declines in output when the economy entered the Great Depression. In the low-concentration industries of the bottom half, price declines were relatively large, and production fell by relatively small amounts. [Gardiner C. Means, *Industrial Prices and Their Relative Flexibility* (Washington, 1953), p. 8.]

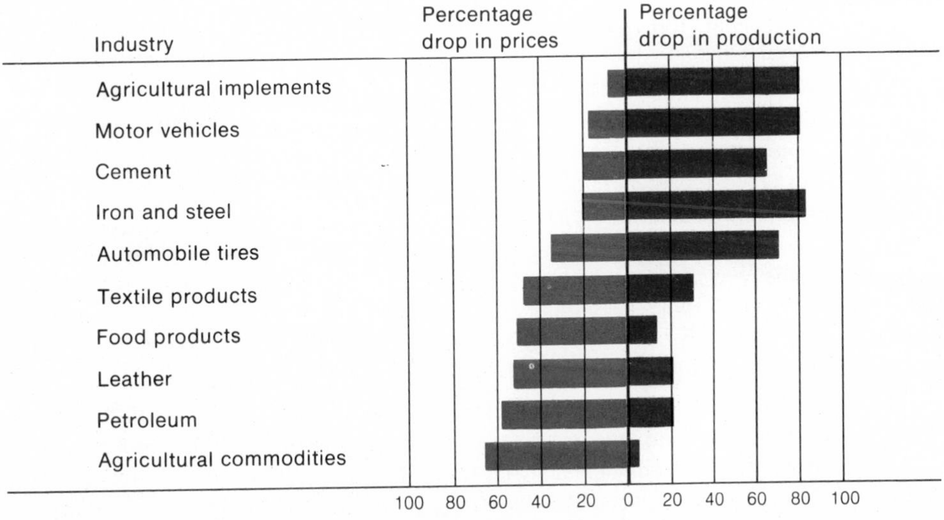

TABLE 11·1 GNP, THE PRICE LEVEL, UNEMPLOYMENT, AND PRODUCTIVITY IN THE 1920s

(1) Year	(2) GNP, billions of current dollars	(3) Real GNP, billions of 1947 dollars	(4) Unemployment, millions	(5) Index of output per man-hour in manufacturing, percent (1939 = 100)	(6) Consumer price index, percent (1947–1949 = 100)
1920	$ 91.6	$102.0	0.6	48.0	85.7
1921	70.0	93.0	4.8	55.2	76.4
1922	74.3	106.6	2.9	60.5	71.6
1923	85.5	119.5	0.7	59.5	72.9
1924	85.1	119.6	2.0	63.4	73.1
1925	93.6	130.3	0.8	67.6	75.0
1926	97.8	137.1	0.5	69.5	75.6
1927	95.8	137.6	1.6	71.3	74.2
1928	98.3	139.7	1.9	75.1	73.3
1929	104.4	149.3	1.6	78.1	73.3

Sources: Columns 2, 3, and 6 are from The National Industrial Conference Board, *The Economic Almanac, 1958* (New York: Thomas Y. Crowell Company, 1958), pp. 71, 394. Columns 4 and 5 are from U.S. Bureau of the Census, *Historical Statistics of the United States: 1789–1945* (1949), pp. 65, 70–71.

considerably more dramatic fluctuations than are the other shares of national income. And, although wage incomes are subject to significant fluctuations in absolute size, labor's relative share of the national income is quite stable over the cycle. During periods of expansion increases in profit incomes usually run ahead of boosts in wage incomes. Similarly, during contraction wage incomes are relatively less flexible than profits. In other words, profit incomes rise and fall more sharply than wage incomes.

BUSINESS CYCLES SINCE 1920

Let us now apply our rudimentary understanding of the business cycle to survey the cyclical experiences of American capitalism since 1920. Such a summary gives us many valuable insights into both the causes and effects of economic fluctuations. The emphasis is upon variations in the different components of total spending.

We shall employ Table 11·1 to substantiate our description of the 1920s. Official U.S. Department of Commerce national income statistics are available starting in 1929 and provide a factual backbone for our discussion of the ensuing four decades. These figures are presented in the inside covers of the book.

The twenties: prosperity

Aside from a sharp but brief depression in 1921 and minor bouts with unemployment in 1924 and 1927, the 1920s were years of booming prosperity. This prosperity was reflected in an expanding GNP and in a level of unemployment which never exceeded 2 million workers in the 1923–1929 period. Furthermore, this growth was cloaked in general price stability (see columns 3, 4, and 6 of Table 11·1).

The major driving force underlying this period of prosperity was a high and prolonged level of investment spending on capital equipment and construction. The following are prominent among the many interrelated causal factors that contributed to this high rate of investment:

1. The strong demand for capital goods World War I had created a backlog of demand for investment goods. Resources simply could not be spared from the production of armaments during the war for the production of investment goods to replace or expand the nation's stock of capital. As a result, the need for capital goods to replace those worn out and rendered obsolete during the war persisted into the 1920s. Investment in machinery and equipment was bolstered by a residential housing boom in the early 1920s.

2. The development of new products and industries The spectacular rise of a group of new and important industries provided both direct and indirect stimuli to investment spending during the twenties. The development of the automobile, electric power, radio, telephone, and electric refrigerator industries all called for tremendous amounts of investment spending in these and related industries. The most notable of these vigorous new industries was the automobile industry. Widespread acceptance of the automobile—annual production increased from 2.2 million in 1920 to 5.5 million by 1929—induced tremendous expansion in the industry. Of greater importance, however, were the secondary effects which the automobile industry had upon a host of related industries. The petroleum, rubber, steel, glass, and textile industries all expanded their facilities enormously to feed parts and materials into the booming auto industry. In addition, an estimated $10 billion was spent on roads and highways during the twenties.

3. Declining labor costs and business optimism The development of mass-production techniques and simultaneous increases in specialization sharply boosted the productivity of labor during the 1920s (see Table 11·1, column 5). Teamed with the relative ineffectiveness of labor unions in boosting wage rates during this era, these productivity increases caused labor costs per unit of output to decline. The resulting expansion of profit margins created an environment of business optimism, and this in turn was also conducive to further investment spending. Furthermore, the stock market boom which accompanied the good times of the decade inflated stock prices, thereby creating conditions very favorable for business borrowing and investing.

But the end of the decade brought an abrupt halt to this vigorous economic growth.

The thirties: the Great Depression

In October of 1929 the stock market collapsed, ushering in the most severe and prolonged depression of modern times. GNP plummeted from $103.1 billion in 1929 to a low of $55.6 billion in 1933. Unemployment rose from 1.6 million to 12.8 million in the same period (lines 5 and 24 of the table on the inside covers).

Just as a high level of investment spending was the backbone of the booming twenties, so a low and sagging level of investment was the major weight that pulled American capitalism into the economic chaos of the thirties. Gross investment spending contracted from $16.2 billion in 1929 to $1.4 billion in 1933 (line 2 of the table)—a 90 percent decline! To a considerable degree the reasons behind this decline in investment spending have their roots in those factors which underlay the high level of investment of the booming twenties.

1. Excess industrial capacity The new industries whose growth underscored the prosperity of the 1920s reached maturity late in that decade. The rapid expansion of these adolescent industries in the twenties occurred at a rate which could not be indefinitely maintained. The markets for these new consumer durables were becoming saturated. Hence, the rate of investment in the automobile and dependent industries began to level off and decline in the early 1930s. Much the same pattern applied to other

industries whose growth had been so vigorous in the 1920s. Overexpansion in the previous decade came home to roost in the 1930s.

2. The decline in residential construction The 1920s was also an era of overbuilding. The high level of construction in the 1920s was partially war-deferred construction; building occurred at a rapid rate in the 1920s to make up for the construction that was forgone during the emergency of World War I. And in part the decline in construction was due to a decline in the rate of population growth during the late twenties. In any event, spending on construction began to level off as early as 1926, residential construction leading the decline. By the late twenties, the construction industry had virtually collapsed.

3. The heavy hand of debt Indebtedness expanded rapidly and became abnormally large as the economy burgeoned in the 1920s. This indebtedness assumed three basic forms: consumer credit, mortgage credit, and indebtedness for stock purchases. The growth of consumer credit—installment buying—had accompanied the development of the various new industries producing consumer durables in the 1920s. The building boom of the 1920s gave rise to heavy mortgage commitments on residential housing and commercial real estate.

The result of this tremendous growth in indebtedness was that by the late twenties much of the income of businesses and households was committed for the payment of interest and principal on past purchases, and hence not available for current expenditures. As expenditures declined, so did incomes and prices. And income declines prompted creditors to liquidate their claims as readily as possible. This was evidenced in a rising tide of business failures and mortgage foreclosures.

4. The stock market crash The most dramatic facet of the Great Depression was the stock market crash of October 1929.[11] The optimism of the prosperous twenties had elevated stock market speculation to something of a national pastime. This speculation had bid up stock prices to the point where they were decidedly out of touch with reality; that is, the prices of stocks were far beyond the profit-making potentials of the issuing firms. The necessary downward adjustment came with a vengeance in 1929. It was sudden, violent, cumulative.[12]

> In that awful last week of October, 1929, the market collapsed. . . . The grim jokes of the period speak for themselves: it was said that with every share of Goldman Sachs you got a complimentary revolver, and that when you booked a hotel room the clerk inquired, "For sleeping or jumping?"

As already noted, many stock purchases had been made on credit. Speculators found themselves hopelessly in debt with only pieces of now worthless paper as reward for their efforts.

The stock market crash had significant secondary effects. Most important was the accompanying unfavorable psychological repercussions; the buoyant optimism of the 1920s gave way to a wave of crippling pessimism. In particular the crashing of stock prices created most unfavorable conditions for acquiring additional money capital for investment or for any other purpose.

5. Shrinking of the money supply Closely allied with the stock market crash and the rapid contraction of indebtedness was a very sharp reduction in the money supply in the early years of the Depression. The money supply of $26.4 billion of 1929 had shrunk to $19.8 billion by 1933 (line 23 of the table on the inside covers). This shrinkage was the result of certain complex forces operating both at home and abroad. In part the shrinkage was tied to the stock market crash and its effect upon the value of bank-held assets. In part it was the result of faulty policies invoked by the monetary authorities. In part it stemmed from the very structure of the banking system—a large number of small and relatively weak banks. The important point for our purposes is that

[11] For a fascinating account of this aspect of the Great Depression read John Kenneth Galbraith's *The Great Crash 1929* (Boston: Houghton Mifflin Company, 1961).

[12] Robert L. Heilbroner, *The Worldly Philosophers,* 3d ed. (New York: Simon & Schuster, Inc., 1967), pp. 226–227.

this drastic reduction in the supply of money contributed to the sharp decline in the volume of spending which characterized the early 1930s.

6. The declining price level Once the contraction of the early 1930s was under way, deflation tended to reinforce that downswing in business activity. Falling product prices discouraged both consumption and investment spending. Consumers were prone to defer their purchases of durables in order to take advantage of anticipated price declines. Businessmen were discouraged from buying capital equipment for substantially the same reasons.

7. Other considerations Though we have touched upon the major considerations underlying the Great Depression, many other factors also entered the picture. For example the enactment of restrictive tariffs, designed to shield domestic workers and their jobs from the rigors of international competition, backfired, dealing a death blow to the already declining volume of international trade. Rather than preserve jobs, higher tariffs only served to reduce trade and further intensify unemployment. Furthermore, drought conditions added materially to the woes of the agricultural segment of the economy in the mid-thirties. All these factors and more combined to turn the booming twenties into the stagnant thirties.

An outstanding feature of the Great Depression was its length. The economy made an abortive recovery in the mid-thirties (1933 to 1937), the "boom" of 1936 and early 1937 falling substantially short of the full-employment mark. This feeble upswing was caused by increases in both consumption and investment spending, but the very modest proportions of the latter caused the Depression to persist. The failure of investment spending to rally sufficiently has many roots. In part this was a backwash of the tremendous exploitation of investment opportunities in the residential and business construction industries during the 1920s. In part it was a carryover of the pessimistic repercussions of the stock market crash. In part investment lagged because of the failure of new investment-stimulating industries comparable to the automobile industry to appear in the thirties. In part investment may have remained depressed in the thirties because of the suspicion and hostility with which many businessmen viewed the controversial reform and recovery measures enacted by the New Deal; the economic intervention embodied in New Deal programs may well have frightened off some private investment outlays. Indeed, some economists came to believe in the late 1930s that the Great Depression was more than a cyclical downswing in business activity. They felt that it was the beginning of an era of persistent or "secular stagnation" in American capitalism. The dynamic, expansive forces of American capitalism were allegedly losing their force, to the end that persistent unemployment was to be the lot of the United States. With unemployment hovering close to 10 million in 1939 (line 24 of the table on the inside covers) the possibility of secular stagnation seemed to be an all-too-accurate viewpoint. But darkening war clouds in Europe were soon to resolve the persistent unemployment of the 1930s.[13]

The forties: prosperity and inflation

Prosperity and inflation were the economic bywords of the 1940–1949 decade. The mobilization of 1940 to 1941 and the all-out war effort of 1942 to 1945 paved the way for a vivid economic contrast with the depressed thirties. War has one great economic virtue—it creates jobs for the unemployed. But governmental expenditures in financing World War II did more than create jobs and boost output; they also gave rise to considerable inflationary pressure. Although this pressure was repressed by direct governmental controls during the war, it broke loose at the cessation of hostilities to boost the price level sharply in the postwar era. We divide this decade into the war years (1940 to 1945) and the postwar years (1946 to 1949). Although prosperity was a main feature of both periods, underlying causal factors differed.

[13]The 1930 depression continues to have a special fascination for economists. See Lester V. Chandler, *America's Greatest Depression: 1929–1941* (New York: Harper & Row, Publishers, Incorporated, 1970).

The war years (1940 to 1945)

The root causes of prosperity in the early forties contrast vividly with those which produced good times in the twenties:

1. The upsurge of military spending Sharp increases in government military spending underlay the upsurge in output and employment which characterized the 1940–1945 period. As line 3 of the table on the inside covers clearly indicates, government spending boomed from a lowly $14 billion in 1940 to a peak of $96.5 billion by 1944. This tremendous expansion in armaments expenditures took many a worker out of the breadline and put him in the employment line of a defense plant.

2. Rising incomes and consumer spending With employment and incomes rising as a result of increased government spending, we should not be surprised to find that consumption spending increased during the war years. It did: the $70.8 billion consumption level of 1940 rose steadily to $119.7 billion by 1945 and was destined to increase even more sharply in the postwar years (line 1 of the table on the inside covers).

3. The rise and forced decline of investment spending The role of investment spending provides an interesting contrast. Investment spurted significantly in 1940 and 1941, basically in response to the increased demand for war goods. Armament production required the use of modern, specialized capital equipment. Furthermore, both defense and civilian industries correctly anticipated future scarcities of capital goods; hence, industry stepped up the level of investment spending accordingly.

But by the end of 1941 the economy was rapidly approaching the full-employment level of production. By 1943 "overfull" employment was achieved; that is, unemployment fell far below the 3 or 4 percent normal unemployment figure (lines 24 and 25 of the table on the inside covers). As a result, further expansion in the production of war and consumer goods had to come at the expense of the production of investment goods. This is precisely what happened. Nonessential investment spending bore the brunt of this cutback. *Net* private domestic investment was negative throughout the height of the war effort in order to free as many resources as possible for the immediate production of war goods (lines 2 and 6 of the table). The nation "lived off its capital" during the 1942–1945 period, as was evidenced by a decline in its accumulated stock of capital.

4. Expansion of the money supply Monetary factors played a significant role in the wartime boom. In the six years between 1939 and 1945 the nation's supply of money almost tripled! The 1939 money supply of about $36.2 billion rose to $102.4 billion by 1945 (line 23). This expansion made possible the tremendous increase in economic activity which the war necessitated.

5. Wartime inflationary pressures By 1943 the American economy had clearly hit the production barrier of full employment. But the total level of spending continued to rise, government and consumption spending leading the way. The inevitable result of spending more and more dollars on a relatively fixed amount of goods is inflation. And war is highly inflationary: it pours money into the pockets of civilians and military personnel but fails to turn out civilian goods at a matching rate.

During the war, however, this inflationary pressure was repressed with considerable success by a bevy of government controls. Price and wage controls were aimed directly at holding the lid on inflation. At the same time, tax increases and intensive war-bond campaigns tried to drain off excessive purchasing power to reduce spending and thereby relieve the pressure on prices. All things considered, these programs were quite successful in postponing inflation until the postwar era. After the war significant increases in the general price level did occur.

The postwar years (1946 to 1949)

As the war drew to a successful close, forecasts of a severe postwar depression clouded the air. Drastic declines in government military spending were ex-

pected to precipitate such a crisis. But, aside from a very mild setback in 1945–1946, prosperity and economic growth persisted into the postwar era. The reasons once again lay in the components of total spending. The drastic $55.3 billion *decline* in government spending which occurred between 1945 and 1946 (line 3 of the table on the inside covers) was largely offset by a $51.8 billion *increase* in private (consumption, investment, and foreign) spending (lines 1, 2, and 4). Aside from a brief recession in 1949, the levels of consumption and investment spending increased in the postwar years to the extent that rather serious inflation resulted.

1. The investment backlog, reconversion, and the housing shortage The desire to replace capital facilities used up during the war years created a large backlog of demand for capital goods. The need to modernize existing capital facilities plus the reconversion to civilian production added to this high level of demand for investment goods. Furthermore, the chronic problem of a housing shortage had reached acute proportions during the war, with the result that the postwar era unleashed a sharp increase in residential construction activity.

2. Government and the climate for investment At the war's end the Federal government passed the Employment Act of 1946, expressing a readiness to take positive steps to correct any serious deviations from full employment. This assurance undoubtedly provided a favorable psychological climate for the resulting high level of investment.

3. Net exports and postwar aid Net exports also jumped sharply in the postwar era as foreign nations, flush with American loans and Marshall Plan dollars, eagerly sought American goods to aid in the reconstruction of their war-torn economies (line 4 of the table).

4. The postwar consumption boom The lion's share of the drop in government military spending was filled by an abrupt increase in consumer spending. As line 1 of the table on the inside covers indicates, consumer spending jumped by almost $24 billion between 1945 and 1946.

A host of factors contributed to the high level of consumption spending which persisted in the postwar years. First, the unavailability of consumer durables during the war meant that consumers emerged from the war with a backlog of demands for automobiles, washing machines, refrigerators, and so forth. Secondly, consumers had the means of financing a high volume of expenditures. Not only were current money incomes at record levels, but consumers had accumulated a huge volume of savings in the form of government bonds and other highly liquid assets during the war. This purchasing power was supplemented by (1) a hasty cut in personal taxes (line 15 of the table), (2) a significant increase in government transfer payments to veterans (line 13), and (3) rapid growth in the volume of consumer credit (line 26). Finally, on top of all this, prices were already rising and showed little sign of falling; it seemed sensible therefore to "spend now" before further price increases occurred. All the factors were present for a consumer spending orgy. And it came to pass.

5. Postwar inflation High levels of spending not only maintained full employment in the postwar era; they also brought rather sharp inflation. Government was able to do a fair job of repressing inflationary pressure during the war. But it was politically impossible to hold the lid on the inflationary kettle once hostilities ended. The Office of Price Administration met a sudden death in 1946. With wartime controls out of the way, the field was clear for open inflation to move into the economic spotlight. Successive rounds of wage and price increases were the order of the day, and the cost of living spiraled ever upward. As a result, the consumer price index, which stood at a relatively innocent 53.9 percent in 1945, had soared to 72.1 percent by 1948 (line 21 of the table). This spending spree leveled off in 1949, and the result was a mild recession. But the Korean conflict in 1950 quickly pushed the vision of depression to one side. Specifically, the Korean hostilities bolstered both

government spending and consumer spending—the former because of the need for increased military outlays and the latter because households anticipated and wanted to "beat" war-born inflation and product shortages. As American capitalism entered the decade of the fifties, inflation was still the major economic problem of the day.

The fifties: economic kaleidoscope

The decade of the 1950s is not easily assessed. On the one hand, the period was generally characterized by overall prosperity and the attainment of an unprecedented level of affluence. On the other hand, there was some inflation, two troublesome recessions, and a weakening of the growth rate late in the decade. Again, the general picture is explainable in terms of the major components of total spending.

The Korean conflict and the 1954 recession We have already noted that the Communist invasion of South Korea in 1950 stimulated anticipatory buying by consumers and businessmen, both of whom expected shortages of goods and materials and inflated prices to result. This was followed in 1951 by a substantial increase in armament spending by the Federal government. The result was a buoyant, expanding economy in the 1950–1953 period. Total spending was high enough to induce substantial increases in real GNP and, in the 1951–1953 period, an unemployment rate of approximately 3 percent of the labor force (lines 20 and 25 of the table). In fact, total spending was sufficiently strong to cause significant inflation; the consumer price index rose from 72.1 in 1950 to 79.5 by 1952 (line 21).

But then came a readjustment. The war-born upsurge in consumer spending was too great to be sustainable, and in 1953 and 1954 consumption expenditures leveled off. Businessmen, having geared their production to the 1951–1952 high levels of consumption, found themselves with overlarge inventories of goods. The resulting cutback in production, coupled with a gradual cutback in Federal military spending as the Korean conflict drew to a close, paved the way for the relatively mild "inventory recession" in 1954.

The 1955–1957 durable goods boom The 1954 recession might have been much more severe in duration and intensity were it not for the fact that long-term investment spending on machinery, equipment, and construction held up during this period. There were several factors at work which contributed to the stability of long-term investment:

1. Technological advances and continued long-term growth in population and incomes bolstered business investment in plant and equipment.
2. Population growth and governmental provision of favorable credit policies sustained the postwar demand for residential construction.
3. The expenditures of state and local governments on schools, highways, and similar social goods continued to expand steadily.

These investment-stimulating factors teamed with a rapidly expanding demand for consumer durables (particularly automobiles) to make 1955 a year of vigorous economic expansion. Substantial growth in consumer credit in 1954 and 1955 (line 26) and the increased demand for furniture and appliances which accompanied the high rate of residential construction were factors in this expansion of consumer spending on durables. Real GNP surged from $407.0 to $438.0 billion between 1954 and 1955. In 1956 and 1957 expenditures for residential housing and automobiles fell rather significantly, and, despite continued strong expenditures for plant and equipment and growing expenditures by state and local governments, the economy plateaued. As a result, although prosperity was sustained in 1956 and 1957, these were years of only modest economic growth. Note (line 25 of table) that unemployment hovered slightly above the normal unemployment mark of 4 percent in the entire 1955–1957 period.

The 1958 recession and recovery Though the 1958 recession was brief—lasting less than a year—it was also the most severe of the several post–World War II recessions. Note (line 20 of table) that real

GNP fell by $5 billion between 1957 and 1958, more than in either the 1954 or 1949 recessions. Unemployment rose to 6.8 percent of the labor force—clearly the highest figure since the end of the war (line 25). The basic cause of this recession was a substantial decline in business investment in machinery and equipment—a decline which was in part a reaction to the leveling of consumer spending in 1956 and 1957. In addition, the enactment of restrictive credit policies by the government in seeking to restrain the price level probably contributed to the downturn by also restraining purchases of housing and consumer durables. Furthermore, the automobile industry was simultaneously plagued by both market saturation and strong foreign competition.

Increased spending on consumer durables, an expansion of residential construction (aided by governmentally eased credit conditions), and increased government spending all underlay recovery in 1959. Increases in state and local government spending stemmed from continually expanding outlays on school and highway construction, whereas increases in Federal spending reflected an intensification of the cold war and, in no small measure, a reaction to Sputnik I.

Lagging growth One of the most distressing features of the fifties was the slowing down of the growth rate during the latter part of the decade. While the average annual growth rate in real GNP in the early postwar period had been on the order of $4\frac{1}{2}$ percent, this figure fell to about $2\frac{1}{2}$ percent in the later 1950s. This sluggishness of the economy was reflected in unemployment figures significantly above the 3 or 4 percent normal unemployment rate (lines 24 and 25) and in a widening GNP gap (Figure 11·2). Virtually all other industrially advanced economies of the world were achieving growth rates superior to that of the United States.

Many explanations were offered for this slowing down of the economy. Some held that the high growth rates of earlier years were a consequence of economic stimuli associated with World War II and Korea, and that in the late fifties the economy was readjusting to a normal and lower growth rate. Others felt that insufficient investment—the result of high interest rates and declining profits—was the cause of the problem. Still others contended that, ironically, the character and pace of technological progress were creating a problem of structural unemployment; automation was creating blocs of technologically unemployed blue-collar workers whose training and skills were inappropriate for reemployment in new expanding white-collar industries (Chapter 22). And, finally, others held that the fiscal system of the Federal government—the economy's primary stabilization device—was actually exerting a contractionary effect on the economy, keeping unemployment above and growth below desired rates. The argument here was that the progressiveness of the Federal tax system was resulting in the withdrawal of more and more purchasing power from the economy each year as the national income expanded; this withdrawal made it increasingly difficult to achieve a level of total spending high enough to maintain full employment and a rapid growth rate. We will have more to say about economic growth (Chapters 20, 21, and 22) and the possibility of a "fiscal drag" (Chapter 14). The point to note at this juncture is that the related problems of slow growth and above-normal unemployment were major concerns as the economy entered the sixties.

The sixties: a mixed bag

Marred in 1959 by the longest steel strike in American history, the recovery from the 1958 recession was neither rapid nor complete. Each of the postwar recessions seemed to have a larger and larger residue of unemployed workers. Newspaper headlines which lamented "creeping inflation" in the early 1950s were speaking of "creeping unemployment" as the 1960s began. Thus in 1960 the economy was marking time in another recession.

The long expansion But then in early 1961 the economy began an unprecedented period of expansion which was to last most of the decade. As is typically the case, several causal factors can be identified.

Perhaps the major factor in this long expansion was the veritable revolution in economic policy which occurred under the Kennedy-Johnson administrations. While discussion of the details is deferred to Chapter 14, in brief this policy called for government to manipulate its tax collections and expenditures in such a way as to stimulate total demand, thereby reducing unemployment and increasing the rate of growth. For example, in 1962 legislation was enacted which provided for a 7 percent tax credit on investment in new machinery and equipment, thereby strengthening incentives to invest. However, despite the fact that unemployment in 1962–1963 was significantly below the 1961 recession level (line 25), the economy was still significantly short of full employment. The major government stimulus to the economy came in 1964 when taxes were cut by some $11 billion. This boosted corporate profits and personal income, stimulating investment and consumer spending in turn. Unemployment fell from 5.2 percent in 1964 to 4.5 percent in 1965.

At this point a second major expansionary force came into play: The escalation of the war in Vietnam. Expenditures for national defense rose from $50 billion in 1965 to $70 billion in 1967. A further $10 billion increase followed in 1968. Simultaneously, the draft claimed more and more young people from the ranks of the unemployed.

There were undoubtedly other factors which contributed to the long expansion. The spending of state and local governments rose steadily and substantially in the 1960s, reflecting acute problems in education, highway construction, urban renewal, and the like. In the private sector, the crucial automobile industry continued to enjoy record-breaking years as the result of suburban growth and the increasing numbers of young people who were reaching driving age. Business investment was stimulated not only by the 1964 tax cut, but also by a rapid rate of technological progress.

As a result of all these stimulative forces the economy achieved full employment and a high rate of economic growth. Quite remarkably, the unemployment rate remained below 4 percent during the entire 1966–1969 period.

A stubborn inflation Prior to the upsurge of military spending in 1965, economic expansion entailed only modest inflation. The consumer price index (line 21) rose from 89.6 in 1961 to only 92.9 in 1964. But then as unemployment fell below 4 percent, price inflation began to accelerate. In fact, the economic demands of Vietnam, imposed upon an already booming economy, brought about the worst inflation in nearly two decades. The consumer price index jumped from 97.2 in 1966 to 116.3 in 1970 (line 21). Initially this inflation was of a "demand-pull" character; that is, rising total demand—spearheaded by government spending—pulled up the price level. But rising prices and the accompanying low level of unemployment generated growing pressure for wage increases. The resulting boosts in wage costs were passed on by businesses to consumers in the form of higher prices, and inflation began to assume more of a "cost-push" character.

An inflationary recession The 1970s began on a sour economic note. In response to the rather alarming inflation of 1966–1969 the Federal government undertook policies in 1969 to restrict total demand and thereby curtail inflation. But the current inflation is proving difficult to restrain. We might speculate that the stubbornness of this inflation results partly from inflationary expectations—a mild "inflationary psychosis"—which has permeated the economy. Labor aggressively seeks substantial wage increases to catch up with past inflation, on the one hand, and in anticipation of future inflation, on the other. Businessmen capitulate to these wage demands because they anticipate that rising costs can be passed on to consumers through price increases. Inflation, thus built into the fabric of behavior, becomes very difficult to halt despite government efforts to restrict total spending.

Ironically, this stubborn inflation was accompanied in 1970 by a sharp increase in unemployment. Unemployment jumped from 3.5 percent in 1969 to 6 percent in early 1971. This growth in unemployment was partially a reflection of public policy; government's efforts to restrict total demand failed to stop inflation but did contribute to a decline in physical

output and employment. Several serious labor disputes—mainly the two-month General Motors strike—and the release of some half million young men from the Armed Forces also contributed to the rise in unemployment. In any event the decade of the 1970s was ushered in by the confusing and paradoxical circumstance of an inflationary recession.

Three observations

Our historical examination of the economic ups and downs of American capitalism yields several noteworthy points:

1. The business cycle is clearly a complex phenomenon. In particular the factors which cause or contribute to prosperity and depression are most diverse. Though the immediate cause of the business cycle is changes in the volume of spending, we find that a host of different factors influence the course of total spending. Such diverse considerations as innovations, changes in the volume of indebtedness, productivity changes, business and consumer expectations, wars, droughts, population changes, and governmental policies at home and abroad all make for variations in total spending and, hence, in the level of economic activity.

2. The variability of investment spending as a component of total spending is also noteworthy. A surging level of investment was the backbone of the prosperous twenties. Similarly, a declining volume of investment ushered in the prolonged depression of the thirties. Sharp increases in investment helped fill the gap left by declining governmental spending at the close of World War II. Our review of recent business cycle experience strongly suggests that the forces which contribute most to economic instability are those which bear upon the decisions of businessmen to invest.

3. Finally, our discussion suggests that, within limits, upswings and downswings in business activity tend to be cumulative. To illustrate: When the nation is at less than full employment, increases in, say, investment spending give rise to increases in output and employment. A higher level of employment means rising incomes, which prompt further increases in spending. Further increases in spending mean still further increases in output, employment, and incomes. The reverse interactions tend to occur as an initial decline in total spending causes the economy to backslide from a full-employment level of performance. Later (Chapter 13) we shall formalize this cumulative character of business fluctuations in the *multiplier* concept.

A "DEPRESSION-PROOF" ECONOMY

Having reviewed the history of the business cycle in some detail, we would be remiss not to raise one final question. What of the future? Is the American economy as vulnerable to the business cycle in the 1970s as it was forty or fifty years ago? Or are we moving toward a more stable "depression-proof" economy?

The majority of expert opinion is that there is no reason why the economy need have a full-fledged depression comparable to the 1930s. Yet relatively mild recessions and inflations, such as those experienced since World War II, will remain a characteristic of American capitalism in the foreseeable future.

There are a number of reasons why economists feel the economy is more stable now than it was several decades ago. Anticipating ensuing chapters, let us note and briefly discuss a few of these stabilizing factors.

Knowledge and public policy

Because of great advances in empirical and theoretical economics, we now possess a vastly superior knowledge of the business cycle—its causes and cures—than was the case a scant three or four decades ago. This knowledge has been reflected increasingly in government policies designed to promote the goal of full employment without inflation. More specifically, we know how to manipulate government spending and tax revenues (fiscal policy) and the supply of money (monetary policy) in such a way as to influence total spending and therefore total output and the price level. Furthermore, the fact that

the Employment Act of 1946 commits the Federal government to invoke these tools to check instability has injected an element of economic confidence into our society which was obvious by its absence a third of a century ago.

Institutional and structural changes

In the past several decades a number of institutional and structural changes have occurred which make the economy less vulnerable to depression and inflation. We mention here only a few of them. First, the economy now contains a number of "built-in stabilizers" which automatically tend to counter or offset changes in the level of economic activity, thereby lessening the cumulative character of these fluctuations. For example, the progressive tax system of the Federal government brings in more tax revenue as the GNP expands, thus dampening a possible inflationary boom. Conversely, tax revenues decline as the level of national income declines. This leaves more income in the hands of households and businesses, so that their spending is largely sustained and the decline in output is cushioned. The unemployment compensation feature of our social security system has the same general effect. Second, our banking system is stronger, as the result not only of improved policies, but also of better systems of insurance and supervision. A virtual collapse of the monetary system such as occurred in the 1930s is extremely unlikely today. Third, in the last three or four decades the structure of American industry and therefore the occupational allocation of the labor force has been away from those industries which are most volatile cyclically. A larger proportion of the work force now has jobs which are somewhat sheltered from cyclical unemployment.

Growth of the public sector

The fact that the public sector has expanded both absolutely and relatively (Table 6·1) has also contributed to economic stability, for the simple reason that government expenditures are not geared to expected profits. State and local expenditures in particular constitute a stable and expanding component of total demand. We shall see in Chapter 37, however, that abrupt changes in military spending have frequently had a destabilizing influence upon the economy.

To sum up: Most economists would agree that, given intelligent use of monetary and fiscal policies, cyclical fluctuations of the magnitude of the Great Depression of the 1930s need never again occur. And the record of the last four decades is quite reassuring (Figure 11·3). On the other hand, mild fluctuations such as the recessions and inflations of the post–World War II era clearly remain as fundamental and costly characteristics of American capitalism. While the business cycle is no longer a roaring lion, neither is it a gentle lamb.

SUMMARY

1. The level of spending determines the levels of output, employment, and incomes in American capitalism. Inflation becomes increasingly severe as the economy approaches full employment; an increase in total spending at full employment tends to boost the price level sharply. The general price level is more flexible upward than downward.

2. It is considered normal for some 3 or 4 percent of the labor force to be unemployed in our economy. The economic cost of unemployment, as measured by the GNP gap, consists of the goods and services which society forgoes when its resources are involuntarily idle. Unemployment is also conducive to a deterioration of national morale and to social and political unrest.

3. Inflation—a rising general level of prices—is caused by excessive spending. Deflation is caused by a deficiency of total spending. Inflation redistributes income at the expense of fixed-income receivers, creditors, and savers. Deflation has substantially the reverse effects.

4. Economists disagree as to the effect which mild inflation may have upon the level of performance achieved by the economy. Some argue that modest inflation is essential in achieving full employment and maximum economic expansion. Another group feels

that over time mild inflation has substantial and undesirable redistributive effects and that it is likely to precipitate hyperinflation and economic collapse by causing a breakdown in the monetary system and diverting otherwise productive energies to speculative activities.

5. Although characterized by common phases—recession, depression, recovery, and prosperity—business cycles vary greatly in duration and intensity.

6. All sectors of the economy are affected by the business cycle, but in varying ways and degrees. The cycle has greater output and employment ramifications in the capital goods and durable consumer goods industries than it does in nondurable goods industries. Over the cycle, price fluctuations are greater in competitive than in monopolistic industries. Profit incomes tend to fluctuate more than do other shares of the national income.

7. Historically, American capitalism has fostered both vigorous expansion and stagnation. An examination of our business cycle experience suggests that *a.* the factors which bear upon total spending and hence output, employment, and the price level are many and varied; *b.* variations in investment play a crucial role in cyclical fluctuations; and *c.* within limits prosperity and depression are cumulative.

8. The development of new knowledge of the cycle and better stabilization policies, coupled with significant institutional and structural changes in the economy, make full-scale depression and extreme inflation highly unlikely in the future.

QUESTIONS AND STUDY SUGGESTIONS

1. Carefully describe the relationship between total spending and the level of resource utilization. Explain the relationship between the price level and increases in total spending as the economy moves from substantial unemployment to moderate unemployment and, finally, to full employment. What is the significance of this relationship?

2. Carefully define "full employment." What is "normal unemployment"? Why is unemployment an economic problem? What is the "GNP gap"? What are the noneconomic effects of unemployment?

3. Distinguish between money income and real income. Explain how an *increase* in one's money income and a *decrease* in his real income might occur simultaneously.

4. Evaluate as accurately as you can the manner in which each of the following individuals would be affected by fairly rapid inflation:

a. a pensioned railroad worker
b. a department-store clerk
c. a UAW assembly-line worker
d. a heavily indebted farmer
e. a retired businessman whose current income is composed entirely from interest on government bonds
f. the owner of an independent smalltown department store

5. "Inflation is a friend on the journey to full employment, but an enemy once the destination is reached." Evaluate and explain. Explain how severe inflation might lead to unemployment.

6. In August 1957, William McChesney Martin, chairman of the Board of Governors of the Federal Reserve System, made the following statement before the Senate Finance Committee:

> There is no validity whatever in the idea that any inflation, once accepted, can be confined to moderate proportions. Once the assumption is made that a gradual increase in prices is to be expected, and this assumption becomes a part of everybody's expectations, keeping a rising price level under control becomes incomparably more difficult than the problem of maintaining stability when that is the clearly expressed goal of public policy. Creeping inflation is neither a rational nor a realistic alternative to stability of the general price level.

Also in 1957, Alvin H. Hansen, noted Harvard economist, made the following comments:[14]

> Periods of rapid growth have usually also been periods

[14] *The American Economy* (New York: McGraw-Hill Book Company, 1957), pp. 45–47.

of moderate price increases. . . . It is not probable that we can achieve in the next twenty years anything like the growth of which we are capable, without some moderate increases in wholesale and consumer prices. . . . Thus I conclude that if in the pursuit of rigid price stability we permit, and even foster, a considerable amount of unemployment, we shall then fail to achieve the growth of which we are capable.

Contrast and evaluate carefully these two points of view. To which do you subscribe?

7. A noted television comedian once defined inflation as follows: "Inflation? That means your money today won't buy as much as it would have during the depression when you didn't have any." Is his definition accurate?

8. What are the major phases of the business cycle? How long do business cycles last? What are seasonal variations and secular trends in business activity? How do they complicate measurement of the business cycle?

9. Why does the business cycle affect durable goods industries more severely than industries producing nondurables? How are the various shares of the national income affected by prosperity and depression?

10. Briefly outline the major factors which contributed to the prosperity of the 1920s. Now explain the basic considerations underlying the Great Depression of the 1930s. What relationships, if any, can you cite between the causes of the booming twenties and the depressed thirties?

11. Explain the extended period of overall prosperity which we have enjoyed since World War II. How do you account for the "long expansion" of the 1960s? What is the likelihood of another Great Depression?

SELECTED REFERENCES

Economic Issues, 4th ed., readings 16, 17, 18, 19, and 20.

Chandler, Lester V.: *America's Greatest Depression: 1929–1941* (New York: Harper & Row, Publishers, Incorporated, 1970).

Economic Report of the President (Washington, 1971).

Fishman, Betty G., and Leo Fishman: *Employment, Unemployment and Economic Growth* (New York: Thomas Y. Crowell Company, 1969).

Haberler, Gottfried: *Prosperity and Depression* (Geneva: League of Nations, 1941), chap. 1.

Silk, Leonard S., and M. Louise Curley: *A Primer on Business Forecasting* (New York: Random House, Inc., 1970).

U.S. Department of Commerce: *Survey of Current Business.* January issues survey the economy's performance in the preceding year.

12

THE BACKGROUND AND ANALYTICAL TOOLS OF EMPLOYMENT THEORY

This and the following chapter are concerned with assessing the ability of a capitalistic economy to achieve the full employment of its resources. If the price system can provide for a reasonably efficient allocation of resources, what is to prevent it from providing for the full utilization of society's available resources?

More specifically, the objectives of the present chapter are threefold: In the first place, we want to understand why for many years economists thought capitalism was capable of providing for virtually uninterrupted full employment. Involved here is a discussion of the so-called classical theory of employment. Second, the shortcomings of the classical theory will be noted and analyzed. Then, finally, the tools of modern employment theory will be introduced and explained. In Chapters 13 and 14 we shall employ these tools to analyze the equilibrium levels of output and employment and extend our analysis to indicate the effects of government policies upon output and employment.

Three simplifying assumptions will greatly facilitate the achievement of these stated objectives:

1. A "closed economy" will be assumed. That is, our discussion will deal with the domestic economy, deferring the complications arising from international trade transactions until later chapters.

2. Government will be ignored until Chapter 14, thereby permitting us in Chapters 12 and 13 to determine whether or not laissez faire capitalism is capable of achieving full employment.

3. Although saving actually occurs in both the business and household sectors of the economy, we shall speak as if all saving were personal saving.[1]

One implication of the second and third assumptions is particularly noteworthy. These two assumptions

[1]When using NNP as our measure of total output, it is accurate to assume that the bulk of the economy's saving is done by households. Table 10·7 shows personal saving at $50.2 billion and undistributed corporate profits as $13.8 billion for 1970. If GNP were employed, however, capital consumption allowances of $84.3 billion would have to be included as a part of business saving, making business saving more than twice as great as personal saving.

permit us to treat NNP, NI, PI, and DI as being equal to one another for the simple reason that all the items which in practice distinguish them from one another are due to government (taxes and transfer payments) and business saving (see Table 10·7). This means that we can readily shift our discussion among these various output and income measures without encountering serious complications which would otherwise arise.

Now the ground is cleared to rephrase our basic question: Is capitalism able to achieve and maintain a full-employment noninflationary total output?

THE CLASSICAL THEORY OF EMPLOYMENT

Answers to this question have varied historically. Until the Great Depression of the 1930s, many prominent economists—now called classical economists[2]—felt that the price system was capable of providing for the full employment of the economy's resources. It was acknowledged that now and then abnormal circumstances would arise in such forms as wars, political upheavals, droughts, speculative crises, gold rushes, and so forth, to push the economy from the path of full employment (see Figure 11·3). But it was contended that when these deviations occurred, automatic adjustments within the price system would soon restore the economy to the full-employment level of output. Though the classical theory of employment is now rejected by the vast majority of economists (including some who earlier were leaders in this school of thought), an analysis of classical thinking will lay a firm foundation for understanding modern employment theory.

The classical theory of employment was grounded on two basic notions. First, it was argued that underspending—that is, a level of spending insufficient to purchase a full-employment output—was most unlikely to occur. Second, even if a deficiency of total spending were to arise, price-wage adjustments would occur so as to ensure that the decline in total spending would not entail declines in real output, employment, and real incomes.

[2]Most notable among the classical economists are John Stuart Mill, F. Y. Edgeworth, Alfred Marshall, and A. C. Pigou.

Say's Law

The classical economists' denial of the possibility of underspending was based upon their faith in Say's Law. Say's Law is the disarmingly simple notion that the very act of producing goods generates an amount of income exactly equal to the value of the goods produced. That is, the production of any output would automatically provide the wherewithal to take that output off the market. Supply creates its own demand.[3] Households, reasoned the classical economists, would only offer their resources on the market if they wanted to consume some good or service the economy was producing. As a matter of fact, the circular flow model of the economy and national income accounting both suggest something of this sort. The income generated from the production of any level of total output would, *when spent,* be just sufficient to provide a matching total demand. Assuming that the composition of output is in accord with consumer preferences, all markets would be cleared of their output. It would seem that all businessmen need do to sell a full-employment output is to produce that output; Say's Law guarantees that there will be sufficient purchasing power for its successful disposal.

Saving: a complicating factor However, there is one obvious omission in this simple application of Say's Law. Although it is an accepted truism that output gives rise to an identical amount of money income (Chapter 10), there is no guarantee that the recipients of this income will spend it all. Some income might be saved (not spent) and therefore not reflected in product demand. Saving would constitute a break, or "leakage," in the income-expenditure flows and therefore undermine the effective operation of Say's Law. Saving is a withdrawal of funds from the income stream which will cause total expenditures to fall short of total output. If households saved a given portion of their incomes, supply would not create its own demand. Saving would cause a deficiency of total expenditures. The consequences?

[3]Attributed to the nineteenth-century French economist J. B. Say.

Unsold goods, cutbacks in production, unemployment, and falling incomes.

Saving, investment, and the interest rate But the classical economists were reluctant to bow to those economists who suggested that such a virtuous act as saving could give rise to underspending and the calamity of depression. Instead, they argued that saving would not really result in a deficiency of total demand, because each and every dollar saved would be invested by businesses. Businessmen, after all, do not plan to sell their entire output to consumers but rather produce a considerable portion of total output in the form of capital goods for sale to one another. In other words, investment spending by businesses is a supplement or addition to the income-expenditure stream. Thus, if businesses as a group intend to invest as much as households want to save, the levels of national output and employment will remain constant. Whether or not the economy could achieve and sustain a level of spending sufficient to provide a full-employment level of output and income therefore would depend upon whether businesses were willing to invest enough to offset the amount households want to save.

Now the classical economists argued that capitalism contained a very special price mechanism—the interest rate—which would guarantee an equality of saving and investment plans and therefore full employment. That is, the interest rate would see to it that dollars which leaked from the income-expenditure stream as saving would automatically reappear as dollars spent on investment goods. The rationale underlying the saving and investment equating adjustments of the interest rate was simple and, if not too carefully scrutinized, very plausible. The classical economists contended that, other things being equal, households normally prefer to consume rather than to save. The consumption of goods and services satisfies human wants; idle dollars do not. Hence, it was reasoned that consumers would save only if someone would pay them a rate of interest as a reward for their thriftiness. The greater the interest rate, the more dollars saved; that is, the saving (supply-of-dollars) curve of households would be upsloping as in Figure 12·1. And who would be inclined to pay for the use of saving? None other than investors—businessmen who seek (demand) money capital to replace and enlarge their plants and their stocks of capital equipment. Because the interest rate is a cost to borrowing businessmen, they will be willing to borrow and invest more at low than at high interest rates. This means that the investment (demand-for-dollars) curve of businesses is downsloping as in Figure 12·1.

Classical economists concluded that the money market, wherein savers supply dollars and investors demand dollars, would establish an equilibrium price for the use of money—an equilibrium interest rate—at which the quantity of dollars saved (supplied) would equal the number of dollars invested (demanded). Saving, said the classicists, does not really constitute a break in the income-expenditure stream or a fatal flaw in Say's Law, because the money market or,

FIGURE 12·1 CLASSICAL VIEW OF THE INTEREST RATE

The classical economists believed that the saving plans of households would be reflected in a supply-of-dollars curve S and the investment plans of businesses in a demand-for-dollars curve I in the money market. The equilibrium interest rate r, the price paid for the use of money, would equate the amounts households and businesses planned to save and invest, thereby guaranteeing a full-employment level of spending.

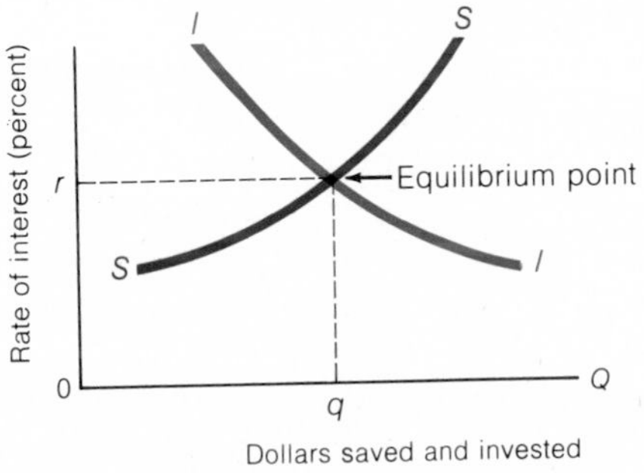

more specifically, the interest rate will guarantee that each and every dollar saved will get into the hands of investors and be spent on capital equipment. Therefore, an increase in thriftiness is not a cause for social concern, because this simply shifts the supply-of-saving curve to the right. Although saving will for a time exceed investment and perhaps cause some temporary unemployment, the surplus of saving will drive the interest rate down to a new and lower equilibrium level. And this lower interest rate will expand the volume of investment spending until it again equals the amount of saving, thereby preserving full employment. In short, changes in the interest rate would guarantee the operation of Say's Law even in an economy in which substantial saving occurs. As the classical economists saw it, the economy was analogous to a gigantic bathtub wherein the volume of water measured the level of output and employment. Any leakage down the drain of saving would be returned to the tub through the spigot of investment. This had to be the case, because the interest rate connected the drainpipe and the spigot!

Price-wage flexibility

The classical economists bolstered their conclusion that full employment is the norm of capitalism with a second basic argument: They argued that the level of output which businessmen can sell depends not only upon the level of total spending but also upon the level of product prices. This meant that even if the interest rate would somehow temporarily fail to equate the amounts which households wanted to save with the investment intentions of businesses, any resulting decline in total spending would be offset by proportionate declines in the price level. That is, \$20 will buy four shirts at \$5, but \$10 will buy the same number of shirts if their price will only fall to \$2.50. Hence, if households somehow managed to succeed in saving more than businesses were willing to invest, the resulting decline in total spending would not result in a decline in real output, real income, and the level of employment *if* product prices declined in proportion to the decline in expenditures. And, according to the classical economists, this is precisely what would happen. Competition among sellers would guarantee it! As declines in product demand became general, competing producers would lower their prices to dispose of accumulating surpluses. Hence, product prices would fall. In other words, the result of saving would be to lower prices; and lower prices, by increasing the value of the dollar, would permit nonsavers to obtain more goods and services with their current money incomes. Saving would therefore simply lower prices, but not output and employment.

"But," ever-present skeptics asked, "doesn't this ignore the resource market? Although businesses can sustain their sales in the face of a declining demand by accepting lower product prices, won't they find it unprofitable to do so? As product prices decline, won't resource prices—particularly wage rates—have to decline significantly to permit businesses to produce *profitability* at the now lower prices?" The classical economists replied that wage rates must and would decline. General declines in product demand would be mirrored in declines in the demand for labor and other resources. The immediate result would be a surplus of labor, that is, unemployment, at the wage rate prevailing prior to these declines in the demand for labor. However, though not willing to employ all workers at the original wage rates, producers would find it profitable to employ additional workers at lower wage rates. The demand for labor, in other words, is downsloping; those workers unable to locate employment at the old higher wage rates could find jobs at the new lower wage rates.

Would workers be willing to accept lower wage rates? Competition among unemployed workers, according to the classical economists, would guarantee it. In competing for scarce jobs, idle workers would bid down wage rates until these rates (wage costs to employers) were so low that employers would once again find it profitable to hire all available workers. This would happen at the new lower equilibrium wage rate. The classical economists therefore concluded that *involuntary unemployment* was impossible. Anyone who was willing to work at the market-determined wage rate could readily find employment. Competition in the labor market ruled out involuntary idleness.

Classical theory and laissez faire

Strictly speaking, each of these price system adjustments—fluctuations in the interest rate, on the one hand, and price-wage flexibility, on the other—seemed fully capable of maintaining full employment in a capitalistic economy. Working together, the classical economists felt, the two adjustment mechanisms made full employment a foregone conclusion. The classical economists came to embrace capitalism as a self-regulating economy wherein full employment was regarded as the norm. Capitalism was capable of "running itself." Government assistance in the operation of the economy was deemed unnecessary—nay, harmful. In an economy capable of achieving both full production and full employment, governmental interference could only be a detriment to its efficient operation.

KEYNESIAN ECONOMICS

One embarrassing fact persistently denied the validity of the classical theory of employment—recurring periods of prolonged unemployment and inflation. While one might explain a minor depression such as the brief downswings of 1924 and 1927 in terms of wars and similar external considerations, serious and prolonged downswings such as the Great Depression were not so easily rationalized. There is a remarkable inconsistency between a theory which concludes that unemployment is virtually impossible and the actual occurrence of a ten-year siege of very substantial unemployment.[4] And so various economists came to criticize both the rationale and the underlying assumptions of classical employment theory. They tried to find a better, more realistic explanation of those forces which determine the level of employment.

[4]It is interesting to note that most of the classical economists stuck to their theoretical guns during the 1930s, arguing that (1) the reluctance of union and business monopolies to accept price and wage cuts, (2) misguided New Deal policies which sought to prevent price-wage declines, and (3) government policies in the area of money and banking which interfered with the operation of the interest rate prevented a quick recovery from the cyclical downswing of the early 1930s.

Finally, in 1936 the renowned English economist, John Maynard Keynes, came forth with a new explanation of the level of employment in capitalistic economies. In his *General Theory of Employment, Interest, and Money*[5] Keynes virtually knocked the props out from under the classical view and, in doing so, touched off a major revolution in economic thinking on the question of unemployment. Although Keynes fathered modern employment theory, many others have since refined and extended his work. In this and the following chapters we are concerned with modern employment theory as it stands today.

Modern employment theory contrasts sharply with the classical position. Its blunt conclusion is that capitalism simply does not contain any mechanisms capable of guaranteeing full employment. The economy, it is argued, might come to rest—that is, reach an aggregate output equilibrium—with either considerable unemployment or severe inflation. Full employment accompanied by a relatively stable level of prices is more of an accident than a norm. Capitalism is not a self-regulating system capable of perpetual prosperity; capitalism cannot be depended upon to "run itself." Furthermore, depressions should not be associated exclusively with external forces such as wars, droughts, and similar abnormalities. Rather the causes of unemployment and inflation lie to a very considerable degree in the failure of certain fundamental economic decisions—in particular, saving and investment decisions—to be completely synchronized in a capitalistic system. Internal in addition to external forces contribute to economic instability.

Modern employment theorists back these sweeping contentions by rejecting the very mechanisms upon which the classical position is grounded—the interest rate and price-wage adjustments.

The unlinking of saving and investment plans

Modern employment theory rejects Say's Law by seriously questioning the ability of the interest rate to synchronize the saving and investment plans of households and businesses. The fact that modern

[5]New York: Harcourt, Brace & World, Inc., 1936.

capitalism is amply endowed with an elaborate money market involving innumerable banking and financial institutions does not diminish this skepticism about the interest rate as a mechanism capable of connecting the saving drain and the investment spigot. Most untenable was the classical contention that businessmen would invest more when households increased their rates of saving. After all, doesn't more saving mean less consumption? Can we really expect businessmen to expand their capital facilities as the markets for their products shrink? More generally, the modern view holds that savers and investors are essentially distinct groups that formulate their saving and investment plans for different reasons which, in each instance, are largely unrelated to the rate of interest.

1. Savers and investors are different groups Who decides the amounts to be saved and invested in a capitalistic economy? (We continue to ignore government in our discussion.) Business organizations of all kinds and descriptions, and in particular corporations, make the vast majority of investment decisions. And who makes the saving decisions? Here the picture is a bit more cluttered. In a wealthy economy such as that of American capitalism, households save substantial amounts—at least when prosperity prevails (table on inside covers, line 19). It is true, of course, that business corporations also do a considerable amount of saving in the form of undistributed corporate profits. The important point is that to a significant degree saving and investment decisions are made by different groups of individuals (see footnote 1 of this chapter).

2. Savers and investors are differently motivated Now the nonidentity of savers and investors would not necessarily be fatal to the classical theory if their decisions were motivated and synchronized by some common factor such as the interest rate. But this is simply not the case. Saving decisions are motivated by several considerations. Some save in order to make large purchases which exceed any single paycheck; households save to make down payments on automobiles or to buy television sets and automatic washers. Some saving is simply for the convenience of having a pool of liquid funds readily available to take advantage of any extraordinarily good buys which one may chance upon. Or saving may occur to provide for the future needs of an individual and his family: households save to provide for the future retirement of the family breadwinner or to expose the offspring to the rigors of a college education. Or saving may be a precautionary, rainy-day measure—a means of protecting oneself against such unpredictable events as prolonged illness and unemployment. Or saving may simply be a deeply ingrained habit that is practiced on an almost automatic basis with no specific purposes in mind.

Regardless of specific motivation, the modern view emphasizes that the total amount which households desire to save is governed primarily by the level of national income, not by the rate of interest.[6] In particular, a higher level of income will mean a high volume of both saving and consumption for households individually and as a group. When income is low, households must spend their entire incomes to achieve an acceptable standard of living; indeed, low incomes may give rise to dissaving. Higher incomes, however, permit households to increase both consumption and the level of saving.

Why do businesses purchase capital goods? The motivation for investment spending, as we shall discover in a few pages, is complex. The interest rate—the cost of obtaining money capital with which to invest—undoubtedly is a consideration in formulating investment plans. But the interest rate is not the most important factor. The rate of profit which businessmen expect to realize on the investment is the really crucial determinant of the amounts businessmen desire to invest. As a matter of fact, some economists

[6]Even if the interest rate were to affect significantly the desire to save, there is no reason why households would necessarily want to save larger amounts at higher interest rates, as the classical economists presumed. To illustrate: If the interest rate is currently 3 percent, a household will need to save $10,000 to provide a retirement income of $300 per year. If the interest rate rises to 6 percent and the household decides that $300 is still a satisfactory retirement income, savings can be cut from $10,000 to only $5,000. A higher interest rate may result in less, not more, saving.

argue that the investment plans of businesses are generally rather insensitive to changes in the interest rate. Furthermore, during the downswing of the business cycle, profit expectations will be so bleak that the level of investment will be low and possibly declining despite substantial reductions in the interest rate. Interest rate reductions are not likely to stimulate investment spending when increases in saving (declines in consumption) make it most sorely needed. Furthermore, if interest rates are relatively low to start with, as they typically are in industrially advanced economies, it simply is not possible for further significant declines to occur.

It is also significant that investors are not entirely dependent upon the current supply of saving in obtaining money capital. We shall find in Chapter 17 that commercial banks do not merely transfer money capital from savers to investors but rather can actually create money by granting loans. This correctly implies that businesses may attempt to invest at a rate in excess of the amount households currently desire to save.

The modern position is that saving and investment plans can be at odds and thereby can result in fluctuations in total output, total income, and the volume of employment. It is largely a matter of chance that households and businesses will desire to save and invest identical amounts. Modern economists have proved themselves better plumbers than their classical predecessors by recognizing that the saving drain and the investment spigot are not connected.

The discrediting of price-wage flexibility

But what of the second aspect of the classical position—the contention that downward price-wage adjustments will eliminate the unemployment effects of a decline in total spending?

1. Price-wage flexibility, modern theorists argue, simply does not exist to the degree necessary for ensuring the restoration of full employment in the face of a decline in total spending. The price system of modern capitalism is no longer a perfectly competitive one; rather it is riddled by market imperfections and circumscribed by practical and political obstacles which work against downward price-wage flexibility. To be specific, monopolistic producers, dominating many important product markets, will have both the ability and the desire to resist falling product prices as demand declines. And in the resource markets strong labor unions are equally persistent in holding the line against wage cuts. In this endeavor they are ably assisted by minimum-wage legislation, public opinion as to what are reasonable and "customary" wage rates, and practical-minded politicians who are well aware of the power of labor at the polls. In short, as a practical matter downward price-wage flexibility cannot be expected to offset the unemployment effects of a decline in total spending.

2. Furthermore, even if price-wage declines accompanied a contraction of total spending, it is doubtful that these declines would help reduce unemployment. The reason? The volume of total money demand cannot remain constant as prices and wages decline. That is, lower prices and wages necessarily mean lower money incomes, and lower money incomes in turn entail further reductions in total spending. The net result is likely to be little or no change in the depressed levels of output and employment.

The modern view points out that the classicists were tripped up in their reasoning by the fallacy of composition. Because any particular group of workers typically buy only a small amount of what they produce, the product and therefore labor demand curves of a single firm can be regarded as independent of any wage (income) changes accorded its own workers. In other words it is correct to reason that a decline in its wage rate will move a *single firm* down its stable labor demand curve and result in more workers hired, that is, more employment. But the same reasoning, argue modern economists, is not applicable to the economy as a whole, to general wage cuts. Why? Because wages are the major source of income in the economy. Widespread wage declines will therefore result in declines in incomes and in the demand for both products and the labor used in producing them. The result is that employers will hire little additional labor (conceivably less labor) after the general wage cuts than they did before. What holds true for a single firm—a wage cut for its

employees will not adversely affect labor demand—does not hold true for the economy as a whole—general wage cuts will lower money incomes and cause the demand for products and labor to decline generally.

To summarize: Modern theorists argue that, in the first place, prices and wages are in fact not flexible downward and, secondly, even if they were, it is doubtful that price-wage declines would alleviate widespread unemployment.

TOOLS OF MODERN EMPLOYMENT THEORY

By rejecting the analysis of the classical economists, we are in effect recognizing that there is no automatic mechanism with the capacity to make full employment the normal state of affairs in a capitalistic system. Yet the question remains: How are the levels of output and employment determined in modern capitalism?

The touchstone of any meaningful answer is that *the amount of goods and services produced and therefore the level of employment depend directly upon the level of total spending.* Subject to the economy's productive potential as determined by the scarce resources available to it, businessmen will produce that level of output which they can profitably sell. Men and machinery are idled when there are no markets for the goods and services they are capable of producing. Total spending, on the one hand, and total output and employment, on the other, vary directly. Therefore in explaining the economy's output-employment levels, we must obviously begin by examining the consumption and investment components of total spending.

CONSUMPTION AND SAVING

In terms of absolute size, consumption is the main component of total spending (Chapter 10). It is therefore of obvious importance to understand the major determinants of consumption spending. Recall (Chapter 10) that economists define personal saving as "not spending" or "that part of DI which is not consumed"; in other words, disposable income equals consumption plus saving. Hence, in examining the determinants of consumption we are also indirectly exploring the determinants of saving.

Income-consumption and income-saving relationships

There are many considerations which influence the level of consumer spending. But common sense and available statistical data both suggest that the most important determinant of consumer spending is income—in particular, disposable income. And, of course, since saving is that part of disposable income which is not consumed, DI is also the basic determinant of personal saving.

As shown in Figure 12•2, national income statistics for the 1929–1970 period indicate that consumption and disposable income are directly related. As income rises, so does consumption; as income falls, so does consumption. We exclude the war years, because the unavailability of certain consumer goods and the strong patriotic appeals to save made consumption abnormally low and saving unusually high. The straight line drawn through these points indicates the general nature of the relationship between consumption and disposable income. The blue 45-degree line is added to the diagram as a point of reference. Because this line bisects the 90-degree angle formed by the vertical and horizontal axes of the graph, each point on the 45-degree line must be equidistant from the two axes. Hence, all the dots falling on the 45-degree line indicate years in which households consumed all their disposable incomes. Points lying below the line indicate years in which disposable incomes exceeded consumption, that is, saving occurred. Those several points which are slightly above the 45-degree line indicate depression years in which households consumed slightly in excess of their disposable incomes, that is, dissaving occurred. The vertical distance of any dot below or above the 45-degree line measures the amount of saving or dissaving in that year.

Figure 12•2 does more than suggest a direct rela-

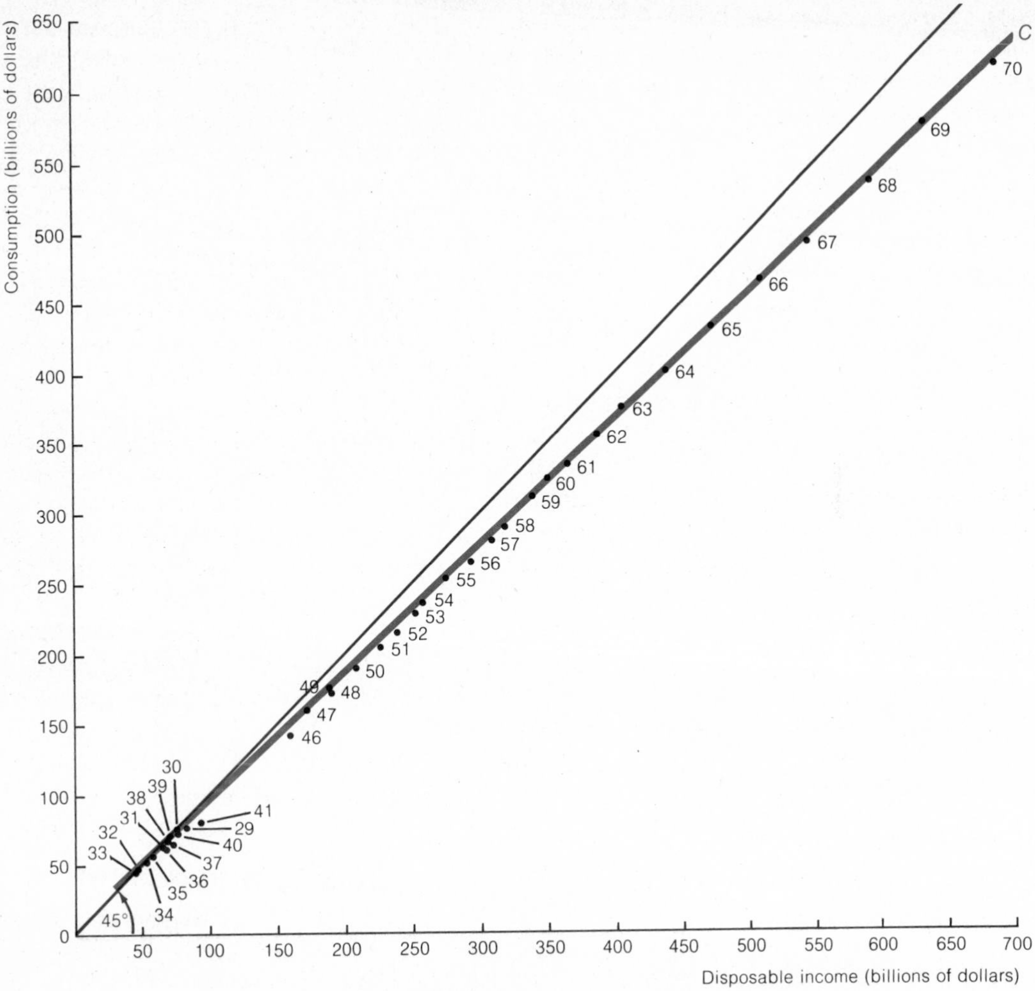

FIGURE 12·2 CONSUMPTION AND DISPOSABLE INCOME, 1929–1970

Each dot in this figure shows disposable income and consumption expenditures in a given year. All points on the 45-degree guideline indicate the situation in which consumption and DI are equal. Thus dots falling below the 45-degree line indicate that saving has occurred; dots above indicate dissaving. The *C* line generalizes on the relationship between consumption and DI. It suggests that households spend a larger portion of a small income than they do of a large income. (U.S. Department of Commerce data.)

tionship between disposable income and consumption. The position of the straight line *C*, which generalizes on the income-consumption relationship, suggests that households will spend a larger portion of a small income than they will of a large income. Or, in terms of saving, the data suggest that households will save a smaller portion of a small income than they will of a large income.

Consumption schedule and saving schedule

Figure 12·2 merely shows the amounts households *actually did consume* (and save) at the various levels of DI which existed over an extended period of years. During this period changes in a good many factors other than the level of DI itself undoubtedly occurred which affected the specific amounts consumed and saved at each of the DI levels. Because of the possible influence of nonincome determinants of consumption and saving, the income-consumption relationship of Figure 12·2 is not particularly useful as an analytic tool. What we need for analytical purposes is an income-consumption relationship—a consumption schedule—which shows the various amounts households will *plan* or *desire to consume* at various possible DI levels over some relatively short period of time in which it is safe to assume nonincome determinants are constant. The consumption schedule, you will note, is similar to the demand schedule discussed in Chapter 4, which shows how much of a particular product a group of buyers intend, or plan, to buy at each of the various possible prices at which the product might sell. The demand schedule was drawn up, remember, on the supposition that nonprice determinants of the amount demanded were constant.

A hypothetical *consumption schedule* of the type we require is shown in columns 1 and 2 of Table 12·1. This schedule is plotted in Figure 12·3*a*. Now while this schedule is a theoretical relationship, it certainly makes sense, in the absence of factual information to the contrary, to draw it so that it embodies the income-consumption relationship of Figure 12·2. The relationship between consumption and DI is direct, and, in addition, households will spend a *larger* proportion of a small DI than of a large DI.

TABLE 12·1 THE CONSUMPTION AND SAVING SCHEDULES (*hypothetical data; columns 1 through 3 in billions*)

(1) Level of output and income (NNP = DI)	(2) Consumption	(3) Saving, or (1) − (2)	(4) Average propensity to consume (APC) (2)/(1)	(5) Average propensity to save (APS) (3)/(1)	(6) Marginal propensity to consume (MPC) Δ(2)/Δ(1)	(7) Marginal propensity to save (MPS) Δ(3)/Δ(1)
$370	$375	$−5	1.01	−.01		
					.75	.25
390	390	0	1.00	0		
					.75	.25
410	405	5	.99	.01		
					.75	.25
430	420	10	.98	.02		
					.75	.25
450	435	15	.97	.03		
					.75	.25
470	450	20	.96	.04		
					.75	.25
490	465	25	.95	.05		
					.75	.25
510	480	30	.94	.06		
					.75	.25
530	495	35	.93	.07		

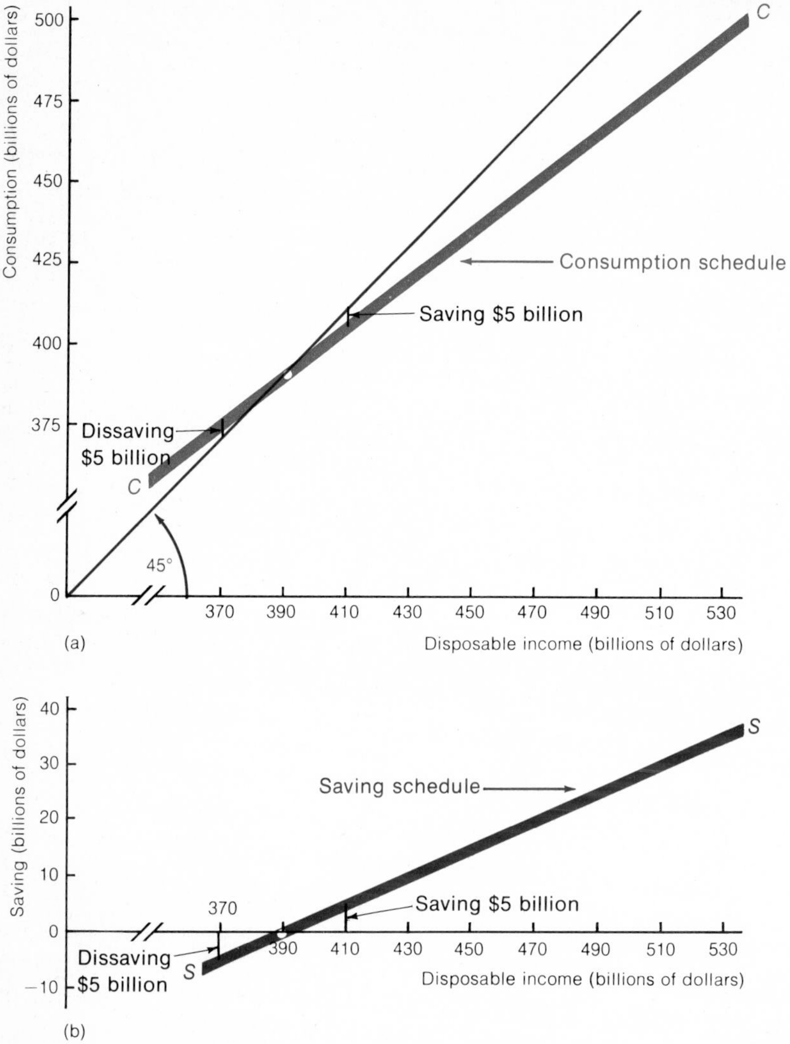

FIGURE 12·3 CONSUMPTION (*a*) AND SAVING (*b*) SCHEDULES

The two parts of this figure show the income-consumption and income-saving relationships graphically. Each point on the 45-degree line in (*a*) indicates an equality of DI and consumption. Therefore, because saving equals DI minus consumption, the saving schedule in (*b*) is found by subtracting the consumption schedule from the 45-degree guideline. Consumers "break even," that is, consumption equals DI (and saving therefore equals zero) at $390 billion for these hypothetical data.

It is a simple task to derive a *saving schedule.* Because disposable income equals consumption plus saving, we need only subtract consumption from disposable income to find the amount saved at each level of DI. Hence, columns 1 and 3 of Table 12·1 constitute the saving schedule. This schedule is plotted in Figure 12·3*b*. Note that there is a direct relationship between saving and DI but that saving constitutes a smaller proportion of a small DI than it does of a large DI. If households consume a smaller and smaller proportion of DI as DI goes up, they must save a larger and larger proportion.

Remembering that each point on the 45-degree line indicates an equality of DI and consumption, we see

that dissaving would occur at the relatively low DI of \$370 billion; that is, households will consume in excess of their current incomes by drawing down accumulated savings or by borrowing. Graphically, the vertical distance the consumption schedule lies *above* the 45-degree line is equal to the vertical distance the saving schedule lies *below* the horizontal axis at the \$370 billion level of output and income (see Figure 12·3*a* and *b*). In this instance these two vertical distances each measure the \$5 billion of *dissaving* which occurs at the \$370 billion income level. At the \$390 billion income level, households will "break even" by spending their entire incomes. Graphically, the consumption schedule cuts the 45-degree line, and the saving schedule cuts the horizontal axis at this income level. At all higher incomes households will plan to save a portion of their income. The vertical distance of the consumption schedule below the 45-degree line measures this saving, as does the vertical distance of the saving schedule above the horizontal axis. For example, at the \$410 billion level of income both these distances indicate \$5 billion worth of saving (see Figure 12·3*a* and *b*).

Average and marginal propensities

Columns 4 to 7 of Table 12·1 point up additional characteristics of the consumption and saving schedules.

That fraction, or percentage, of any given total income which is consumed is called the *average propensity to consume* (APC), and that fraction of any total income which is saved is called the *average propensity to save* (APS). For example, at the \$470 billion level of income in Table 12·1 the APC is 45/47 or about 96 percent, while the APS is obviously 2/47 or about 4 percent. By calculating the APC and APS at each of the nine levels of DI shown in Table 12·1, we find that the APC falls and the APS rises as DI increases. The fraction of total DI which is consumed declines as DI rises, and this makes it necessary for the fraction of DI which is saved to rise as DI rises.

The fact that households consume a certain portion of some given total income—for example, 45/47 of a \$470 billion disposable income—does not guarantee that they will consume the same proportion of any *change* in income which they might receive. The proportion, or fraction, of any change in income which is consumed is called the *marginal propensity to consume* (MPC), marginal meaning "extra." Or, alternatively stated, the MPC is the ratio of a change in consumption to the change in income which brought the consumption change about; that is,

$$\text{MPC} = \frac{\text{change in consumption}}{\text{change in income}}$$

The fraction of any change in income which is saved is called the *marginal propensity to save* (MPS). That is, MPS is the ratio of a change in saving to the change in income which brought it about:

$$\text{MPS} = \frac{\text{change in saving}}{\text{change in income}}$$

Thus, if disposable income is currently \$470 billion and households for some reason find that their incomes rise by \$20 billion, we find that they will consume $^{15}/_{20}$ or $^{3}/_{4}$ and save $^{5}/_{20}$ or $^{1}/_{4}$ of that increase in income (see Table 12·1). In other words the MPC is $^{3}/_{4}$, or 75 percent, and the MPS is $^{1}/_{4}$, or 25 percent. The sum of the MPC and the MPS for any given change in disposable income must always be 1. That is, consuming and saving out of extra income is an either-or proposition; that fraction of any change in income which is not spent is, by definition, saved. Therefore the fraction consumed (MPC) plus the fraction saved (MPS) must exhaust the whole increase in income. In our example 75 percent plus 25 percent equals 100 percent, or 1.

Economists are not in complete agreement as to the exact behavior of the MPC and MPS as income increases. For many years it was presumed that the MPC declined and the MPS increased as income increased. That is, it was felt that a smaller and smaller fraction of increases in income would be consumed and a larger and larger fraction of these increases would be saved. Many economists now feel that the MPC and MPS for the economy as a whole are relatively constant. Statistical data such as those of Figure 12·2 are consistent with this position. We will assume the MPC and MPS to be constant not

only because of this statistical evidence but also because a constant MPC and MPS will simplify our analysis considerably. You will note that for each of the eight \$20 billion income increases shown in Table 12·1, consumption increases by \$15 billion, that is by $^{15}/_{20}$ or $^{3}/_{4}$ of the increase in income, and saving increases by \$5 billion, that is, by $^{5}/_{20}$ or $^{1}/_{4}$ of the increase in income. We assume the MPC and MPS to be constant at $^{3}/_{4}$ and $^{1}/_{4}$, respectively (see columns 6 and 7).[7]

Nonincome determinants of consumption and saving

The level of disposable income is the basic determinant of the amounts households will consume and save, just as price is the basic determinant of the quantity demanded of any product. You will recall that changes in determinants other than price, such as consumer tastes, incomes, and so forth (Chapter 4), will cause the demand curve for a given product to shift location. Similarly, there are certain determinants other than income which might cause households to consume more or less at each possible level of DI and thereby change the locations of the consumption and saving schedules.

1. Stocks of liquid assets Generally speaking, the greater the amounts of liquid assets—private and public bonds, stocks, insurance policies, bank accounts, and so forth—owned by consumers, the greater will be their willingness to consume at each possible level of DI. The ownership of liquid assets makes households feel more secure financially and hence more willing to spend out of current disposable income.

2. Stocks of durable goods on hand If the economy has enjoyed an extended period of prosperity, consumers may find themselves well supplied with various durable goods. That is, the majority of families may own late-model cars, television sets, refrigerators, and other household appliances, all worthy of many years of future service. Hence, for a time many households will be "out of the market" for such products, with the result that consumers are willing to spend less and save more at each possible level of disposable income.

It is relevant to note that the "buying binge" that followed World War II can be largely explained in terms of the prolonged curtailment of durable consumer goods production and the spectacular increases in consumer incomes and liquid asset holdings which occurred during the war years of the early 1940s.

3. Expectations concerning incomes, prices, and product availability Household expectations concerning future prices, money incomes, and the availability of goods may have a significant impact upon current spending and saving. Expectations of rising prices and product shortages tend to trigger more spending and less saving currently. Why? Because it is natural for consumers to seek to avoid paying higher prices or to avoid having to "do without."

[7]The mathematically inclined reader will recognize that the MPC is the numerical value of the slope of the consumption schedule and the MPS is the numerical value of the slope of the saving schedule. The slope of any line can be measured by the ratio of the vertical change to the horizontal change involved in moving from one point to another point on that line. Thus, in the accompanying diagram, if the vertical change is 15 and the horizontal change is 20 between points *A* and *B*, the slope of the line is $^{3}/_{4}$. Now it is evident in the

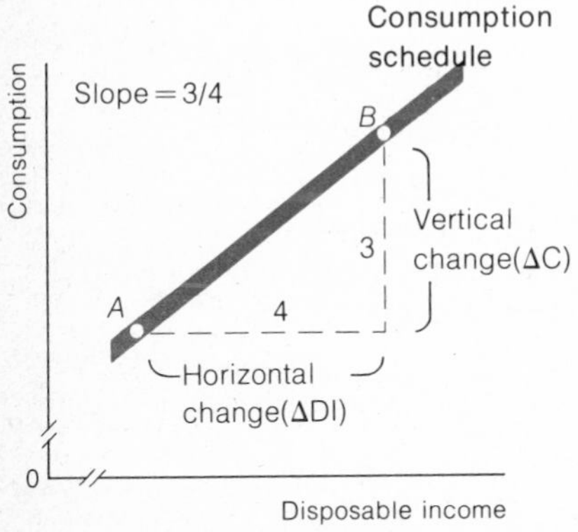

figure that the slope of the consumption schedule between any two points is measured by the change in consumption (the vertical change) relative to the change in income (the horizontal change). And this ratio, change in consumption/change in income, is the fraction of any change in income that is spent; that is, it measures the MPC. Similar reasoning tells us that the MPS measures the slope of the saving schedule.

Expected inflation and expected shortages induce people to "buy now" to escape higher future prices and bare shelves. Anticipated increases in money incomes bolster this tendency. The expectation of rising money incomes in the future tends to make consumers more footloose in their current spending.

Conversely, expected price declines, anticipations of shrinking incomes, and the feeling that goods will be abundantly available may induce consumers to retrench on their consumption and build up their savings.

4. Consumer indebtedness The level of consumer credit can also be expected to affect the willingness of households to consume out of current income. If households are in debt to the degree that, say, 20 or 25 percent of their current incomes are committed to installment payments on previous purchases, consumers may well be obliged to retrench on current consumption in order to reduce their indebtedness. Conversely, if consumer indebtedness is relatively low, households may consume at an unusually high rate by increasing this indebtedness.

5. Attitudes toward thrift Next a catchall item: An economy's general attitude toward frugality will help determine the amount of consumption and saving forthcoming at each possible level of DI. Attitudes toward thrift are governed as much by social and psychological considerations as they are by economic factors. If a society accepts the belief that saving is very virtuous and that "a dollar saved is a dollar earned," saving will tend to be greater and consumption less at each level of disposable income than would be the case where saving was held in lower esteem. There is some evidence to suggest that in the underdeveloped countries attitudes toward thrift are relatively weak, as most households are very anxious to consume in order to emulate the higher living standards of the more advanced nations.

Attitudes toward thrift can be influenced by government policies. During World War II the Federal government waged intensive propaganda campaigns to encourage households to save by buying war bonds. These campaigns—coupled with the hard fact that many consumer durables were unavailable or in scant supply—were fairly successful in boosting the saving schedule and therefore in lowering the consumption schedule. Peacetime government policies may also affect the consumption and saving schedules. By committing itself to policies designed to promote full employment, government may diminish the fear of unemployment and thereby weaken an important motive to save money.

6. Taxation Changes in taxes may shift the consumption and saving schedules through their impact upon disposable income. Like personal saving, taxation is a *non*expenditure use of income; indeed, taxation is sometimes referred to as "public saving." Hence, an increase in taxes will reduce consumption at each level of income as would an increase in saving. Conversely, a reduction in taxes, like a decline in saving, will shift the consumption schedule upward. We will discuss the employment effects of taxes more fully in connection with fiscal policy (Chapter 14).

Two final points are relevant to this discussion. First, the movement from one point to another on a given stable consumption schedule (for example, *A* to *B* on C_0 in Figure 12·4*a*) is called a *change in the amount consumed.* The sole cause of this change in the amount consumed is a change in the level of disposable income. On the other hand, a *change in the consumption schedule* refers to an upward or downward shift of the entire schedule—for example, from C_0 to C_1 or C_2 in Figure 12·4*a*. A relocation of the consumption schedule is obviously caused by changes in any one or more of the nonincome determinants just discussed. A similar terminological distinction applies to the saving schedule in Figure 12·4*b*.

A second related point is that the consumption and saving schedules will necessarily shift in opposite directions. If households decide to consume *more* at each possible level of disposable income, this means that they want to save *less,* and vice versa. Graphically, if the consumption schedule shifts upward from C_0 to C_1 in Figure 12·4, the saving sched-

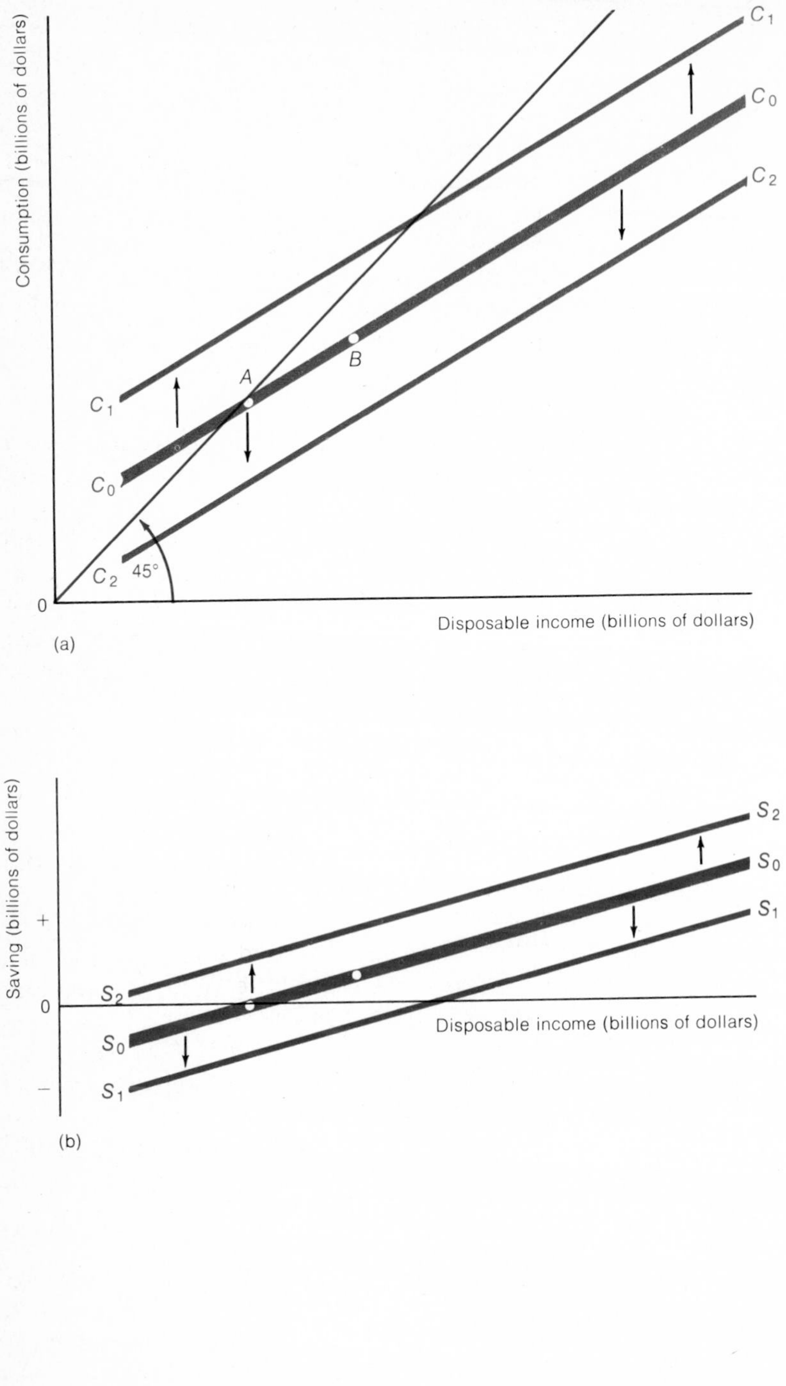

FIGURE 12·4 SHIFTS IN THE CONSUMPTION (*a*) AND SAVING (*b*) SCHEDULES

A change in any one or more of the nonincome determinants will cause the consumption and saving schedules to shift. If households consume more at each level of DI, they are necessarily saving less. Graphically this means that an upshift in the consumption schedule (C_0 to C_1) entails a downshift in the saving schedule (S_0 to S_1). Conversely, if households consume less at each level of DI, they are saving more. A downshift in the consumption schedule (C_0 to C_2) is reflected in an upshift of the saving schedule (S_0 to S_2).

ule will shift downward from S_0 to S_1. Similarly, a downshift in the consumption schedule from C_0 to C_2 means an upshift in the saving schedule from S_0 to S_2.

Economists are in general agreement that the consumption and saving schedules are quite stable. This may be because consumption-saving decisions are strongly influenced by habit or because changes in the nonincome determinants frequently work in opposite directions and therefore tend to be self-canceling.

INVESTMENT

Now let us turn to the second component of private spending. What determines the rate of net investment spending? That is, what determines the amounts businesses want or plan to spend on additional machinery and equipment, new construction, and increases in inventories?

Determinants of investment: profit expectations

The simplest answer to this query is that business investment is based upon the *expected net profits* which businesses hope to realize from such spending. But what are some of the more important factors which influence profit expectations?

1. Technological advance and innovation Innovation—the development of new products and new techniques of production—is a major force underlying the level of investment. By putting innovating firms one jump ahead of competitors, new products frequently entail substantial profits. Realizing this, firms are anxious to invest in the capital equipment needed to produce these new products. Similarly, improved production methods mean lower costs and higher profits, and this too is conducive to a high rate of investment. In short, a rapid rate of innovation is conducive to a high level of investment, and vice versa.

2. Acquisition, maintenance, and operating costs The initial costs of capital goods, along with the estimated costs of operating and maintaining those goods, are obviously important considerations in gauging the profitability of any particular investment. To the extent that these costs are high, expected *net* profits will be low and the level of investment will also be low. If these costs are relatively low, expected net profits and the level of investment will tend to be high. Note that the wage policies of unions affect profit expectations, because wage rates are clearly an operating cost.

3. The interest rate The interest rate is a special type of cost involved in acquiring capital goods. Interest is a cost payment which investors must make in acquiring the money capital needed to negotiate the purchase of real capital. The higher this cost, the less the expected net profit on investment and hence the lower the level of investment. The lower the interest cost, the greater the expected profits and thus the higher the level of investment spending.

4. Government policies There is little doubt that taxes affect profit expectations and the level of investment. Businessmen look to estimated profits *after taxes* in making their investment decisions. Taxes, as an added cost of doing business, tend to dampen profit expectations and retard investment spending.

The impact of government expenditures upon the profit expectations of private firms is difficult to assess. In some cases government spending, by stimulating particular firms and industries and by alleviating depressed business conditions, improves profit expectations. On the other hand, certain types of government spending—for example, the development of public power—allegedly cause the profit expectations of private power producers to deteriorate, thereby retarding investment.

5. The stock of capital goods on hand Just as the stock of consumer goods on hand affects household consumption-saving decisions, so the stock of

capital goods on hand influences expected profits from additional investment in a given industry. To the extent that a given industry is well stocked with productive facilities and inventories of finished goods, investment will be retarded in that industry. The reason is obvious: Such an industry will be amply equipped to fulfill present and future market demand at prices which yield mediocre profits. If an industry has enough productive capacity or even excess productive capacity, profit expectations and further investment in that industry will not be appealing.

6. Expectations We noted earlier that business investment is based upon *expected* profits. Capital goods are durable—they may have a life expectancy of ten or twenty years—and thus the profitability of any capital investment will depend upon businessmen's expectations of the *future* sales and *future* profitability of the product which the capital helps produce. To some significant degree the expectations of businessmen are a projection of current business conditions. If business is currently good, businessmen will tend to be optimistic about the future and will be quite willing to invest at a high level. Poor current business conditions will be conducive to dismal expectations with respect to future profits and therefore a low level of investment.

TABLE 12·2 THE INVESTMENT SCHEDULE (*hypothetical data; in billions*)

(1) Level of output and income	(2) Investment, I_n	(3) Investment, I'_n
$370	$20	$10
390	20	12
410	20	14
430	20	16
450	20	18
470	20	20
490	20	22
510	20	24
530	20	26

Investment and income

In order to compare the investment decisions of businesses with the consumption-saving plans of households, we want to express investment plans in terms of the level of disposable income or NNP. That is, we want to construct an *investment schedule* which shows the amounts which businessmen as a group plan or intend to invest at each of the various possible levels of income or output. Such a schedule will mirror the investment plans or intentions of businessmen in the same way the consumption and saving schedules reflect the consumption and saving plans of households.

We shall assume in our analysis that business investment is geared to long-term profit expectations as influenced by such considerations as technological progress, population growth, and so forth, and therefore is autonomous or independent of the level of current income. In particular, our discussion will presume that the same amount of investment spending—say $20 billion—will be forthcoming at every level of income as reflected in columns 1 and 2 of Table 12·2 and I_n in Figure 12·5. This assumed independence of investment and the level of income is admittedly a simplification. A higher level of current income may well have a modest impact upon investment; a higher level of business activity may induce some investment spending on capital facilities as suggested by columns 1 and 3 of Table 12·2 and I'_n in Figure 12·5. Our simplification, however, is not too severely at odds with reality and will greatly facilitate later analysis.

Instability of investment

In contrast to consumption, investment is unstable. Proportionately investment is the most volatile component of private spending (see Figure 12·6). Some of the more important factors which explain this variability are as follows:

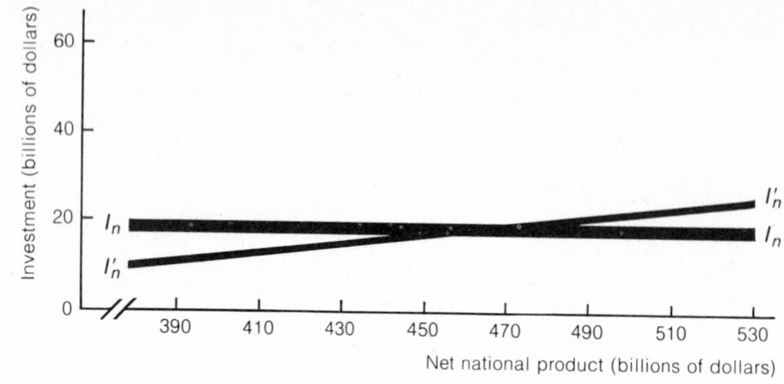

FIGURE 12·5 THE INVESTMENT SCHEDULE: TWO POSSIBILITIES

Our discussion will be facilitated by employing the investment schedule I_n, which assumes that the investment plans of businessmen are independent of the current level of income. Actually the investment schedule may be slightly upsloping, as suggested by I'_n.

1. Durability Because of their durability, capital goods have a rather indefinite useful life. Within limits, purchases of capital goods are discretionary and therefore postponable. Older equipment or buildings can be scrapped and entirely replaced, on the one hand, or patched up and used for a few more years, on the other. Optimism about the future may prompt businessmen to replace their older facilities, that is, to modernize their plants, and this obviously means a high level of investment. A slightly less optimistic view, however, may lead to very small amounts of investment as older facilities are repaired and kept in use.

FIGURE 12·6 INSTABILITY OF INVESTMENT

Private investment spending has varied sharply over time and therefore has been a major cause of fluctuations in total spending, total output, employment, and the price level.

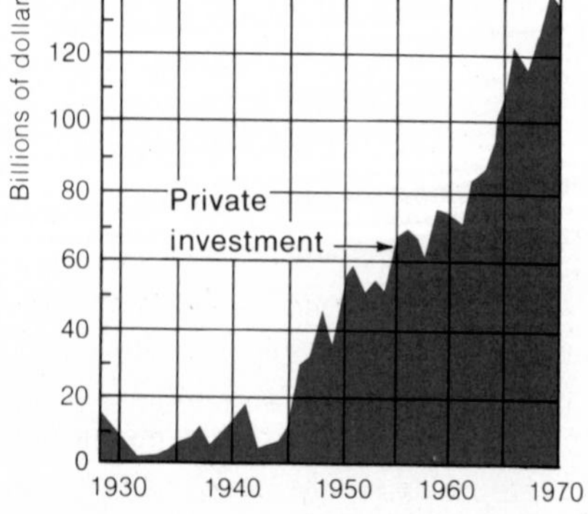

2. Irregularity of innovation We have noted that technological progress is a major determinant of investment. New products and new processes provide a major stimulus to investment. However, history suggests that major innovations—railroads, electricity, automobiles, and so forth—occur quite irregularly, and when they do occur, these innovations induce a vast upsurge or "wave" of investment spending which in time recedes. To illustrate: The widespread acceptance of the automobile in the 1920s not only brought about substantial increases in investment in the automobile industry itself, but, as mentioned in our treatment of the prosperous twenties, also induced tremendous amounts of investment in such related industries as steel, petroleum, glass, and rubber, not to mention public investment in streets and highways. But when investment in these related industries was ultimately completed—that is, when

they had created capital facilities sufficient to meet the needs of the automobile industry—total investment leveled off.

3. Variability of profits We know that businessmen invest only when they feel it will be profitable to do so and that, to a significant degree, the expectation of future profitability is influenced by the size of current profits. Current profits, however, are themselves highly variable (Figures 7•1 and 7•2). Hence the variability of profits contributes to the volatile nature of the incentive to invest. Furthermore, the instability of profits may also cause investment fluctuations, because profits are a major source of funds for business investment. American businesses tend to prefer this internal source of financing to increases in external debt or stock issue. In short, expanding profits give businessmen both greater incentives and greater means to invest; declining profits have the reverse effects. The fact that actual profits are variable adds to the instability of investment.

4. Variability of expectations We have already discussed how the durability of capital equipment results in the making of investment decisions upon the basis of *expected* net profits. Now, while there is a tendency for businessmen to project current business conditions into the future, it is equally true that expectations are sometimes subject to radical revision when some event or combination of events suggests a significant change in future business conditions. What kinds of events make business confidence so capricious? Changes in the domestic political climate, cold-war developments, changes in population growth and therefore in anticipated market demand, court decisions in key labor or antitrust cases, legislative actions, strikes, changes in governmental economic policies, and a host of similar considerations may give rise to waves of business optimism or pessimism.

The stock market merits specific comment in this regard. Businessmen frequently look to the stock market as an index or barometer of the overall confidence of society in future business conditions; a rising "bull" market signifies public confidence in the business future, whereas a falling "bear" market implies a lack of confidence. The stock market, however, is a highly speculative market, and initially modest changes in stock prices can be seriously intensified by less-informed participants who jump on the bandwagon by buying when prices begin to rise and by selling when stock prices start to fall. Recall our discussion in Chapter 11 of the important psychological repercussions of the 1929 stock market crash. Furthermore, by affecting the relative attractiveness of new capital as opposed to purchasing ownership claims (stock) to existing capital facilities, upsurges and slumps in stock values also affect the level of investment.

For these and similar reasons it is quite correct to associate most fluctuations in output and employment with changes in investment spending rather than changes in consumption. In terms of Figure 12•5 we can think of this volatility as being reflected in frequent and substantial upward and downward shifts in the investment schedule.

SUMMARY

1. Classical employment theory envisioned laissez faire capitalism as being capable of providing virtually continuous full employment. This analysis was based on Say's Law and the assumption of price-wage flexibility.

2. The classical economists argued that because supply creates its own demand, general overproduction was impossible. This conclusion was held to be valid even when saving occurred, because the interest rate would automatically synchronize the saving plans of households and the investment plans of businesses.

3. Classical employment theory also held that even if temporary declines in total spending were to occur, these declines would be compensated for by downward price-wage adjustments to the end that real output, employment, and real income would not decline.

4. Modern employment theory rejects the notion that the interest rate would equate saving and investment by pointing out that savers and investors are

substantially different groups who make their saving and investment decisions for different reasons—reasons which are largely unrelated to the interest rate.

5. Modern economists discredit price-wage flexibility on both practical and theoretical grounds. They argue that *a.* union and business monopolies, minimum-wage legislation, and a host of related factors have virtually eliminated the possibility of substantial price-wage reductions and *b.* price-wage cuts will lower total income and therefore the demand for labor.

6. The basic tools of modern employment theory are the consumption, saving, and investment schedules, which show the various amounts households intend to consume and save and businesses plan to invest at the various possible income-output levels.

7. The locations of the consumption and saving schedules are determined by such factors as *a.* the amounts of liquid assets owned by households, *b.* the stocks of durables consumers have on hand, *c.* expectations of future income, future prices, and product availability, *d.* the relative size of consumer indebtedness, *e.* overall attitudes toward thrift, and *f.* taxation. The consumption and saving schedules are relatively stable.

8. The *average* propensities to consume and save show the proportion or fraction of any level of *total* income that is consumed and saved. The *marginal* propensities to consume and save show the proportion or fraction of any *change* in total income that is consumed or saved.

9. The immediate determinant of investment spending is net profit expectation. This expectation is influenced by such objective factors as *a.* technological advance, *b.* the acquisition, maintenance, and operating costs of real capital, *c.* the interest rate, *d.* government policies, *e.* the stocks of capital on hand, and *f.* expectations of future business conditions.

10. The durability of capital goods, the irregular occurrence of major innovations, profit volatility, and the variability of expectations all contribute to the high degree of instability of investment spending.

QUESTIONS AND STUDY SUGGESTIONS

1. What is Say's Law? Explain the classical economists' conclusion that Say's Law would prevail even in an economy where substantial saving occurred. What arguments have modern economists used to undermine the classical view that Say's Law would result in sustained full employment?

2. "Unemployment can be avoided so long as businesses are willing to accept lower product prices, and workers to accept lower wage rates." Critically evaluate.

3. Define *a.* the average propensities to consume and save and *b.* the marginal propensities to consume and save. How do these two sets of concepts differ? Why must the sum of the MPC and the MPS equal 1?

4. What are the basic determinants of the consumption-saving schedules? Of your own level of consumption? What are the basic determinants of investment? Why is the investment schedule less stable than the consumption-saving schedules?

5. Explain precisely what relationships are shown by *a.* the consumption schedule, *b.* the saving schedule, and *c.* the investment schedule.

6. Complete the following table:

Level of output and income (NNP = DI)	Consumption	Saving
$240	$______	$−4
260	______	0
280	______	4
300	______	8
320	______	12
340	______	16
360	______	20
380	______	24
400	______	28

a. Show the consumption and saving schedules graphically.
b. Determine the average propensity to consume and the average propensity to save for each level of income.
c. Now determine the MPC and MPS for each change in the income level.
d. Locate the break-even point. How is it possible for households to dissave at very low income levels?
e. If the proportion of total income which is consumed decreases and the proportion which is saved increases as income rises, explain both verbally and graphically how the MPC and MPS can be relatively constant at various levels of income.

7. Explain how each of the following will affect the consumption and saving schedules or the investment schedule:
a. A decline in the amount of government bonds which consumers are holding
b. The threat of limited, nonnuclear war, leading the public to expect future shortages of consumer durables
c. A decline in the interest rate
d. A sharp decline in stock prices
e. An increase in the rate of population growth
f. The development of a significantly cheaper method of manufacturing pig iron from ore
g. The announcement that the social security program is to be expanded in terms of both coverage and size of benefits
h. The expectation that mild inflation will persist in the next decade
i. The end of the war in Vietnam

8. Explain why an upshift in the consumption schedule necessarily involves an equal downshift in the saving schedule.

9. *Advanced analysis:* Linear equations for the consumption and saving schedules take the general form $C = a + bY$ and $S = -a + (1 - b)Y$, where C, S, and Y are consumption, saving, and national income respectively. The constant a represents the vertical intercept, and b is the slope of the consumption schedule.
a. Use the following data to substitute specific numerical values into the consumption and saving equations.

National income (Y)	Consumption (C)
\$ 0	\$ 80
100	140
200	200
300	260
400	320

b. What is the economic meaning of b? Of $(1 - b)$?

SELECTED REFERENCES

Economic Issues, 4th ed., reading 21.

Dillard, Dudley: *The Economics of John Maynard Keynes* (Englewood Cliffs, N.J.: Prentice-Hall, Inc., 1948), chaps. 1, 2, and 12.

Lekachman, Robert: *The Age of Keynes* (New York: Random House, Inc., 1966).

Peterson, Wallace C.: *Income, Employment, and Economic Growth,* rev. ed. (New York: W. W. Norton & Company, Inc., 1967), chap. 4.

Sirkin, Gerald: *Introduction to Macroeconomic Theory,* 3d ed. (Homewood, Ill.: Richard D. Irwin, Inc., 1970), chaps. 2–5.

Stewart, Michael: *Keynes and After* (Baltimore: Penguin Books, Inc., 1967).

13

THE EQUILIBRIUM LEVELS OF OUTPUT, EMPLOYMENT, AND INCOME

This chapter is both a continuation and an expansion of Chapter 12. We seek, first, to use the consumption, saving, and investment schedules developed in Chapter 12 to explain the equilibrium levels of output, income, and employment. Next, we analyze changes in the equilibrium level of NNP. Until government is added to our discussion in Chapter 14, we retain the simplifying assumptions of Chapter 12 which permitted us to equate NNP and DI.

We now have before us all the analytical tools necessary to explain the equilibrium levels of output, employment, and income. By *equilibrium output* we refer to that level of total output which, once achieved, will be sustained. It exists where the flow of income created by the production of the output gives rise to a level of total spending sufficient to clear the product market of that output. In pursuing the important task of determining and explaining the equilibrium level of output, two closely interrelated approaches—the *aggregate demand–aggregate supply* (or $C + I_n =$ NNP) approach and the *saving-equals-investment* (or $S = I_n$) approach—will be employed. Both will be discussed tabularly and graphically.

AGGREGATE DEMAND–AGGREGATE SUPPLY APPROACH

Let us first discuss the aggregate demand–aggregate supply approach, using both simple arithmetic data and graphic analysis.

Tabular analysis

Table 13·1 merely brings together the income-consumption and income-saving data of Table 12·1 and the simplified income-investment data of columns 1 and 2 in Table 12·2.

This table is in many respects similar to Table 4·6, the supply and demand table for a specific product. You will recall that the demand schedule shows the

TABLE 13·1 DETERMINATION OF THE EQUILIBRIUM LEVELS OF EMPLOYMENT, OUTPUT, AND INCOME: THE PRIVATE SECTOR (*hypothetical data*)

(1) Possible levels of employment,* millions	(2) Aggregate supply (output and income)† (NNP = DI), billions	(3) Consumption, billions	(4) Saving, billions	(5) Investment, billions	(6) Aggregate demand ($C + I_n$), billions	(7) Tendency of employment, output, and incomes
40	$370	$375	$−5	$20	$395	Increase
45	390	390	0	20	410	Increase
50	410	405	5	20	425	Increase
55	430	420	10	20	440	Increase
60	450	435	15	20	455	Increase
65	470	450	20	20	470	Equilibrium
70	490	465	25	20	485	Decrease
75	510	480	30	20	500	Decrease
80	530	495	35	20	515	Decrease

* In later chapters on economic growth we will find that employment need not vary proportionately with output.
† If government is ignored and it is assumed that all saving occurs in the household sector of the economy, NNP as a measure of aggregate supply is equal to NI, PI, and DI. This means that households receive a DI equal to the value of total output.

amount consumers plan to purchase and the supply schedule the amount producers plan to offer at various prices. The equilibrium price was located at the point where the quantity demanded and the quantity supplied were equal. Barring revisions in the buying plans of consumers or the selling plans of producers, price and the corresponding amount exchanged would not vary from their equilibrium levels. This same general type of reasoning can be applied to *aggregate* demand and *aggregate* supply with three notable differences. First, because total output is composed of heterogeneous goods, it is essential to state total supply in money terms rather than physical units. Second, the equilibrating factor is obviously the level of output and income rather than price. Third, and most important, it is quite accurate to regard the forces of supply and demand as playing equally important roles in determining the price of an individual product; changes in either supply or demand can alter equilibrium price. But in the case of aggregate equilibrium it is correct to envision aggregate demand as the crucial determining variable or force to which the level of aggregate supply (NNP) adjusts. We should regard the aggregate supply schedule—the set of production intentions of businesses—as fixed and the actual amount produced by businessmen as responding to shifts in aggregate demand.

Column 2 of Table 13·1 is in effect the total, or aggregate, supply schedule for the economy. It indicates the various possible levels of total output—that is, the various possible NNPs—which the business sector of the economy might produce. *Producers are willing to offer each of these nine levels of output on the expectation that they will receive an identical amount of receipts of income from its sale.* That is, the business sector will produce $370 billion worth of output, thereby incurring $370 billion worth of

wage, rent, interest, and profit costs, only if they expect that this output can be sold for $370 billion worth of receipts. Some $390 billion worth of output will be offered if businesses feel this output can be sold for $390 billion. And so it is for all the other possible levels of output.

The total, or aggregate, demand schedule is shown in column 6 of Table 13•1. It shows the total amount which will be spent at each possible output-income level. In dealing with the private sector of the economy the aggregate demand schedule simply shows the amount of consumption and net investment spending ($C + I_n$) which will be forthcoming at each output-income level. We use net rather than gross investment because we are employing NNP rather than GNP as a measure of total output.

Now the question is this: Of the nine possible levels of NNP indicated in Table 13•1, which will be the equilibrium level? That is, which level of total output will the economy be capable of sustaining? The answer is: The equilibrium level of output is that output whose production will actually create total spending just sufficient to purchase that output. In other words, the equilibrium level of NNP is where the total quantity of goods supplied (NNP) is precisely equal to the total quantity of goods demanded ($C + I_n$). Examination of the aggregate supply schedule of column 2 and the aggregate demand schedule of column 6 indicates that this equality exists only at the $470 billion level of NNP. This is the only level of output at which the economy is willing to spend precisely the amount necessary to take that output off the market. Here the annual rates of production and spending are in balance. There is no overproduction which results in a piling up of unsold goods and therefore cutbacks in the rate of production, nor is there an excess of total spending which draws down inventories and prompts increases in the rate of production. In short, there is no reason for businessmen to vary from this rate of production—this is therefore the equilibrium NNP.

To enhance our understanding of the meaning of the equilibrium level of NNP, let us examine other possible levels of NNP to see why they cannot be sustained. For example, at the $410 billion level of NNP businesses would find that if they produced this output, the income created by this production would give rise to $405 billion in consumer spending. Supplemented by $20 billion of investment, the total quantity demanded ($C + I_n$) would be $425 billion, as shown in column 6. The economy obviously provides an annual rate of spending more than sufficient to purchase the current $410 billion rate of production. Because businessmen are producing at a lower rate than buyers are taking goods off the shelves, an unintended decline in business inventories will occur. Businessmen will adjust to this happy state of affairs by stepping up production. And a higher rate of output will mean more jobs and a higher level of total income. In short, if the total quantity of goods demanded exceeds the total quantity supplied, the latter will be driven upward. By making the same comparisons of NNP (column 2) and $C + I_n$ (column 6) at all other levels of NNP below the $470 billion equilibrium level, it will be found that the economy wants to spend in excess of the level at which businesses are willing to produce. The excess of total spending at all these levels of NNP will drive NNP upward to the $470 billion level.

The reverse holds true at all levels of NNP above the $470 billion equilibrium level. That is, businesses will find that the production of these total outputs fails to generate the levels of spending needed to take them off the market. Being unable to recover the costs involved in producing these outputs, businesses will cut back on their production. To illustrate: At the $510 billion level of output businessmen will be disappointed to find that their productive efforts have not generated enough spending to permit the sale of that output. Of the $510 billion worth of income which this output creates, $480 billion is received back by businesses as consumption spending. Though supplemented by $20 billion worth of investment spending, the total quantity demanded ($500 billion) falls $10 billion short of the $510 billion quantity supplied. Inventories of goods pile up, and businesses react to this unintended accumulation of unsold goods by cutting back on the rate of production. This decline in NNP will mean fewer jobs and a decline in total income. The reader should verify

that deficiencies of total spending exist at all other levels of NNP in excess of the $470 billion level.

The equilibrium level of NNP exists where the total quantity supplied, measured by NNP, and the aggregate quantity demanded, $C + I_n$, are equal. Any excess of total spending over total output will drive the latter upward. Any deficiency of total spending will pull NNP downward.

Graphic analysis

The same analysis can be readily envisioned through a simple graph. In Figure 13·1 the 45-degree line (which was merely a guideline in Chapter 12's discussion of consumption and saving) now represents the economy's aggregate supply schedule. Let us see why this is so. By definition, each point on the aggregate supply schedule will indicate (on the vertical axis) the amount which the business community must receive back as total spending, or total revenue from business' point of view, in order to be induced or motivated to produce the corresponding level of national output (on the horizontal axis). Now, if we make the quite obvious and realistic assumption that the business community will produce or supply that national output whose value is equal to anticipated spending (receipts), we get a series of points equidistant from the two axes of Figure 13·1—that is, we get the 45-degree line for the aggregate supply schedule. We are simply saying that profit-seeking

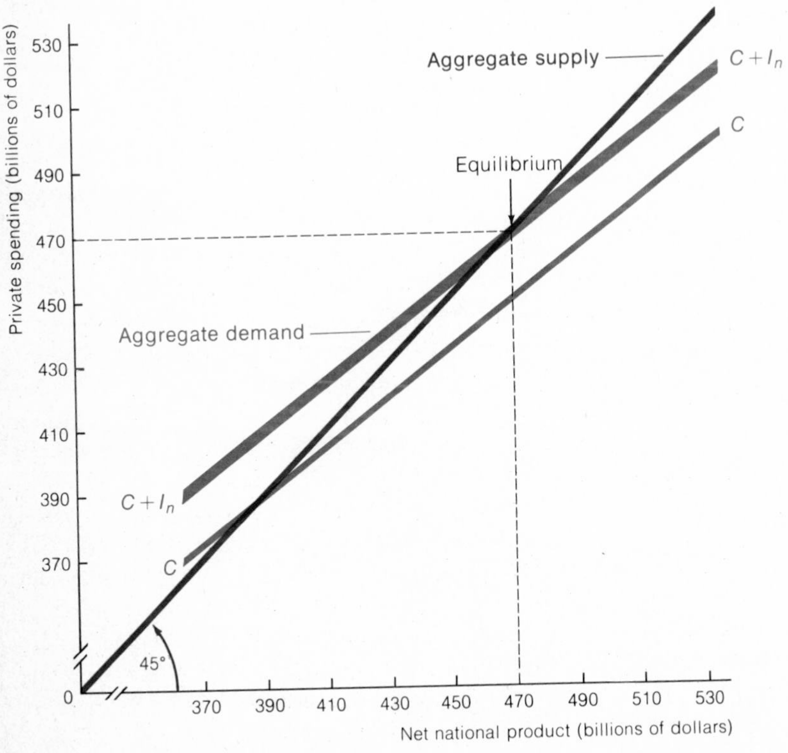

FIGURE 13·1 THE AGGREGATE DEMAND–AGGREGATE SUPPLY APPROACH TO THE EQUILIBRIUM NNP

The aggregate supply schedule is the 45-degree line, because business will produce any given level of NNP only when they expect a level of total spending ($C + I_n$) just sufficient to dispose of that output. The equilibrium level of NNP is determined by the intersection of this aggregate supply schedule with the $C + I_n$, or aggregate demand, schedule. Only at this point are the production and purchasing plans of the economy consistent with one another.

businessmen in the aggregate will be willing to undertake the production of, for example, a \$430 billion national output only if anticipated expenditures are \$430 billion. That is, businessmen will offer any level of NNP only if they expect $C + I_n$ to be just sufficient to clear that output off the national market. Similarly, businessmen will produce and offer a \$450 billion output if they expect $C + I_n$ to be \$450. If businessmen expected total spending to be greater or less than \$450 billion, they would find it profitable to offer an equally larger or smaller national output.[1] Thus, a series of points—a line—equidistant from the total output (NNP) axis and the total spending $(C + I_n)$ axis will summarize the aggregate supply plans of business. Being equidistant from the two axes, this line is necessarily the 45-degree line. We conclude that the 45-degree line is the aggregate supply schedule. This schedule shows the various outputs which businesses will offer at each of the various levels of spending that might prevail.

To get the $C + I_n$ or aggregate demand schedule in Figure 13·1, we simply graph the consumption schedule of Figure 12·3*a* and add to it vertically the constant \$20 billion amount from Figure 12·5, which, we assume, businesses will want to invest at each possible level of NNP. More directly, we can plot the $C + I_n$ data of column 6 in Table 13·1.

The question: What is the equilibrium level of NNP? The answer: That NNP at which the aggregate quantity demanded and the aggregate quantity supplied are equal. And this must be where the aggregate supply schedule (the 45-degree line) and the aggregate demand schedule $(C + I_n)$ intersect. Because our graphed schedules are based on the data of Table 13·1, we once again find the equilibrium output to be at the \$470 billion level. It is evident from Figure 13·1 that no levels of NNP above the equilibrium level are sustainable, because $C + I_n$ falls short of NNP. For example, at the \$510 NNP level $C + I_n$ is only \$500. Inventories of unsold goods rise to undesired levels. This unhappy state of affairs will prompt businesses to readjust their production sights downward in the direction of the \$470 billion output level. Conversely, at all possible levels of NNP less than the \$470 billion level, the economy desires to spend in excess of what businesses are producing. $C + I_n$ exceeds the value of the corresponding output. At the \$410 billion NNP, for example, $C + I_n$ totals \$425 billion. Inventories decline as the rate of spending exceeds the rate of production, prompting businessmen to raise their production sights in the direction of the \$470 billion NNP. Unless there is some change in the consumption-saving plans of households or the investment plans of businesses, the \$470 billion level of NNP will be sustained indefinitely.

[1] Quite nonsensical results follow if one experiments with lines lying below or above the 45-degree line. In the accompanying figure, line 1 suggests that the business community would be willing to produce, for example, a \$430 billion national output if total expenditures were expected to be only \$390! Surely it is ridiculous to suggest that businessmen will purposely produce \$40 billion of output in excess

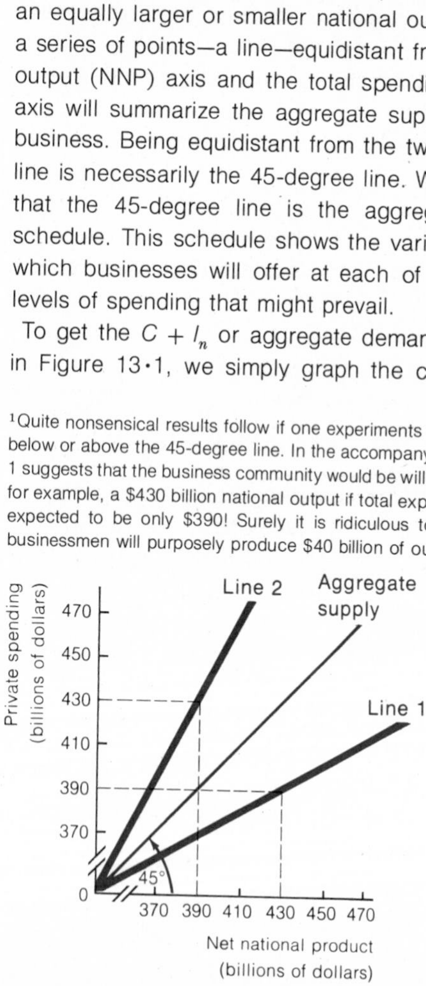

of what they anticipate can be sold. Similarly, line 2 implies that businessmen will produce, for example, only \$390 billion of national output when they anticipate total expenditures of \$430 billion. This suggests that the business community will purposely forgo the production of \$40 billion of salable output.

SAVING-EQUALS-INVESTMENT APPROACH

The aggregate demand–aggregate supply approach to the determination of NNP has the advantage of spotlighting total spending as the immediate determinant of the levels of output, employment, and income. Though the $S = I_n$ approach is less direct, it does have the advantage of giving emphasis to the reason $C + I_n$ and NNP are unequal at all levels of output except the equilibrium level.

Tabular analysis

The saving schedule (columns 2 and 4) and the investment schedule (columns 2 and 5) of Table 13·1 are pertinent. Our $C + I_n =$ NNP approach has just led us to conclude that all levels of NNP less than \$470 billion are unstable because the corresponding $C + I_n$ exceeds these NNPs, driving them upward. A comparison of the amounts households and businesses want to save and invest at each of the below-equilibrium NNP levels explains the excesses of total spending. In particular, at each of these relatively low NNP levels businesses desire to invest more than households plan to save. For example, at the \$410 billion level of NNP, households will save only \$5 billion, thereby spending \$405 of their \$410 billion incomes. Supplemented by \$20 billion of business investment, total spending ($C + I_n$) is obviously \$425 billion. Total spending exceeds NNP by \$15 billion (= \$425 − \$410) *because* the amount businesses desire to invest at this level of NNP exceeds the amounts households plan to save by \$15 billion. It is the fact that a very small "leakage" of saving at this relatively low income level will be more than compensated for by the relatively high level of investment spending which causes $C + I_n$ to exceed NNP and induce the latter upward.

Similarly, all levels of NNP above the \$470 level are also unstable, because here NNP exceeds $C + I_n$. The reason for this insufficiency of total spending lies in the fact that at all NNP levels above \$470 billion households will attempt to save in excess of the amount businesses desire to invest. That is, the saving leakage is not compensated for by the level of investment. For example, households will choose to save at the high rate of \$30 billion at the \$510 billion NNP. Businesses, however, will only invest \$20 billion at this NNP. This \$10 billion excess of saving over investment will cause total spending to fall \$10 billion short of the value of total output. And this deficiency will cause NNP to decline.

Again we verify that the equilibrium NNP is at the \$470 billion level. It is only at this point that the saving desires of households and the investment plans of businesses are equal. And only when businesses and households attempt to invest and save at equal rates will $C + I_n =$ NNP. Only here will the annual rates of production and spending be in balance; only here will unplanned changes in inventories be absent. One can think of it in this way: If saving were zero, consumer spending would always be sufficient to clear the market of any given NNP; that is, consumption would equal NNP. But saving can and does occur, causing consumption to fall short of NNP. Hence, only when businesses are willing to invest at the same rate at which households attempt to save will the amount by which consumption falls short of NNP be precisely compensated for.

Graphic analysis

The $S = I_n$ approach to determining the equilibrium NNP can be readily demonstrated graphically. In Figure 13·2 we have merely combined the saving schedule of Figure 12·3*b* and the simplified investment schedule of Figure 12·5. The numerical data for these schedules are repeated in columns 2, 4, and 5 of Table 13·1. It is evident that the equilibrium level of NNP is at \$470 billion, where the saving and investment schedules intersect. Only here do households and businesses plan to save and invest at the same rates; therefore, only here will NNP and $C + I_n$ be equal. At all higher levels of NNP households will attempt to save at a rate higher than businesses are willing to invest. This causes $C + I_n$ to fall short of NNP, driving the latter downward. At the \$510 billion NNP, for example, saving of \$30 billion will exceed investment of \$20 billion by \$10 billion, with the result that $C + I_n$ is \$500 billion—\$10 billion short of NNP. At all levels of NNP below the \$470 billion equilibrium level, businesses will desire to invest at a rate in excess of the amount households plan to save. The result is that $C + I_n$ exceeds NNP, driving the latter upward. To illustrate: At the \$410 level of NNP the \$5 billion leakage of saving is more than compensated for by the \$20 billion businesses desire to invest. The result is that $C + I_n$ exceeds NNP by \$15 billion, inducing businesses to produce a larger NNP.

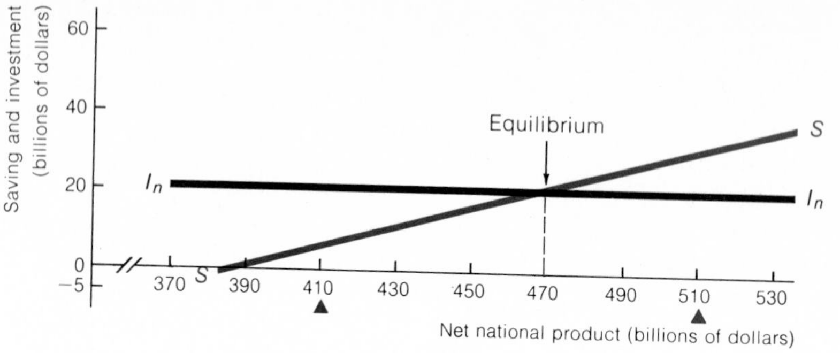

FIGURE 13·2 THE SAVINGS-EQUALS-INVESTMENT APPROACH TO THE EQUILIBRIUM NNP

A second approach is to view the equilibrium NNP as determined by the intersection of the saving (*S*) and investment (I_n) schedules. Only at the point of equilibrium will households plan to save the amount businesses want to invest. It is the consistency of these plans which causes NNP and $C + I_n$ to be equal.

PLANNED VERSUS ACTUAL SAVING AND INVESTMENT

We have emphasized that because savers and investors are essentially different groups and are differently motivated, discrepancies in saving and investment can occur and these differences bring about changes in the equilibrium NNP. Now we must recognize that in another sense saving and investment must always be equal to one another! This apparent contradiction concerning the equality of saving and investment is resolved when we distinguish between *planned* or *intended* saving and investment (which need not be equal) and *actual* or *realized* saving and investment (which by definition must be equal). The catch essentially is that actual investment consists of both intended and unintended investment (unintended changes in inventory investment), and the latter functions as a balancing item which always equates the actual amounts saved and invested in any period of time.

Consider, for example, the $490 billion above-equilibrium NNP (Table 13·1). What would happen if businesses produced this output, thinking they could sell it? At this level households save $25 billion of their $490 billion DI, so consumption is only $465 billion. *Intended* investment is $20 billion; that is, businessmen want to buy $20 billion worth of capital goods. This means aggregate demand ($C + I_n$) is $485 billion, and sales therefore fall short of production by $5 billion. This extra $5 billion of goods is obviously retained by businesses as an *unintended* or involuntary increase in inventories. It is unintended because it results from the failure of total spending to take total output off the market. Remembering that national income accounts include changes in inventories as a part of investment, we note that actual or *realized* investment of $25 billion ($20 intended or planned *plus* $5 unintended or unplanned) equals *realized* saving of $25 billion, even though *intended* saving exceeds *intended* investment by $5 billion. Businessmen, obviously not anxious to accumulate unwanted inventories at this annual rate, will react by cutting back on production.

Now look at the below-equilibrium $450 billion output (Table 13·1). Because households save only $15 billion of their $450 billion D!, consumption is $435 billion. Businesses want or intend to invest $20 billion, so aggregate demand is $455 billion. That is, sales exceed production by $5 billion. How can this be? The answer is that an unplanned or unintended decline in business inventories has occurred. More specifically, businesses have unintentionally *dis*-invested $5 billion in inventories. Note once again that *realized* investment is $15 billion ($20 intended

or planned *minus* $5 unintended or unplanned) and equal to *realized* saving of $15 billion, even though intended investment exceeds intended saving by $5 billion. This unintended decline in investment in inventories due to the excess of sales over production will induce businessmen to increase the NNP by expanding production.

To summarize: At all above-equilibrium levels of NNP (where intended saving exceeds intended investment), realized investment and realized saving are equal because of unintended increases in inventories which, by definition, are included as a part of actual or realized investment. Graphically (Figure 13·2) the unintended inventory increase is measured by the vertical distance by which the (intended) saving schedule lies above the (intended) investment schedule. At all below-equilibrium levels of NNP (where intended investment exceeds intended saving), realized investment will be equal to realized saving because of unintended decreases in inventories which must be subtracted from intended investment to determine actual investment. These unintended inventory declines are shown graphically as the vertical distance by which the (intended) investment schedule lies above the (intended) saving schedule.

These distinctions are important because they correctly suggest that it is the equality of intended investment and intended saving which determines the equilibrium level of NNP. We can think of the process by which equilibrium is achieved as follows:

1. A difference between intended saving and intended investment causes a difference between the production and spending plans of the economy as a whole.

2. This difference between aggregate production and spending plans results in unintended investment or disinvestment in inventories.

3. As long as unintended investment in inventories persists, businessmen will revise their production plans downward and thereby reduce the NNP. Conversely, as long as unintended disinvestment in inventories exists, firms will revise their production plans upward and increase the NNP. Both types of movements in NNP are toward equilibrium in that they tend to bring about the equality of intended saving and intended investment.

4. Only where intended saving and intended investment are equal will the level of NNP be stable or in equilibrium; that is, only where intended investment equals intended saving will there be no unintended investment or disinvestment in inventories to drive the NNP downward or upward.

CHANGES IN EQUILIBRIUM NNP AND THE MULTIPLIER

Thus far we have been concerned with explaining the equilibrium levels of total output and income. But we saw in Chapter 11 that actually the NNP of American capitalism is seldom stable; rather it is characterized by long-run growth punctuated by cyclical fluctuations. Let us turn to the questions of *why* and *how* the equilibrium level of NNP fluctuates.

The equilibrium level of NNP will change in response to changes in the investment schedule or the saving-consumption schedules. Because investment spending generally is less stable than the consumption-saving schedules, we shall assume that changes in the investment schedule occur. The impact of changes in investment can be readily envisioned through Figure 13·3*a* and *b*. If technological advance, population growth, or simply business optimism enhances profit expectations, investment spending by businesses will increase by, say, $5 billion. This is indicated in Figure 13·3*a* as an upward shift in the aggregate demand schedule from $(C + I_n)_0$ to $(C + I_n)_1$ and in Figure 13·3*b* as an upward shift in the investment schedule from I_{n0} to I_{n1}. In each of these portrayals the result is a rise in the equilibrium NNP from $470 to $490 billion.

Conversely, a $5 billion decline in investment stemming from such considerations as high acquisition and maintenance costs on capital, a high interest rate, a low rate of technological advance, or general business pessimism will shift the investment schedule downward from I_{n0} to I_{n2} in Figure 13·3*b* and the aggregate demand schedule from $(C + I_n)_0$ to

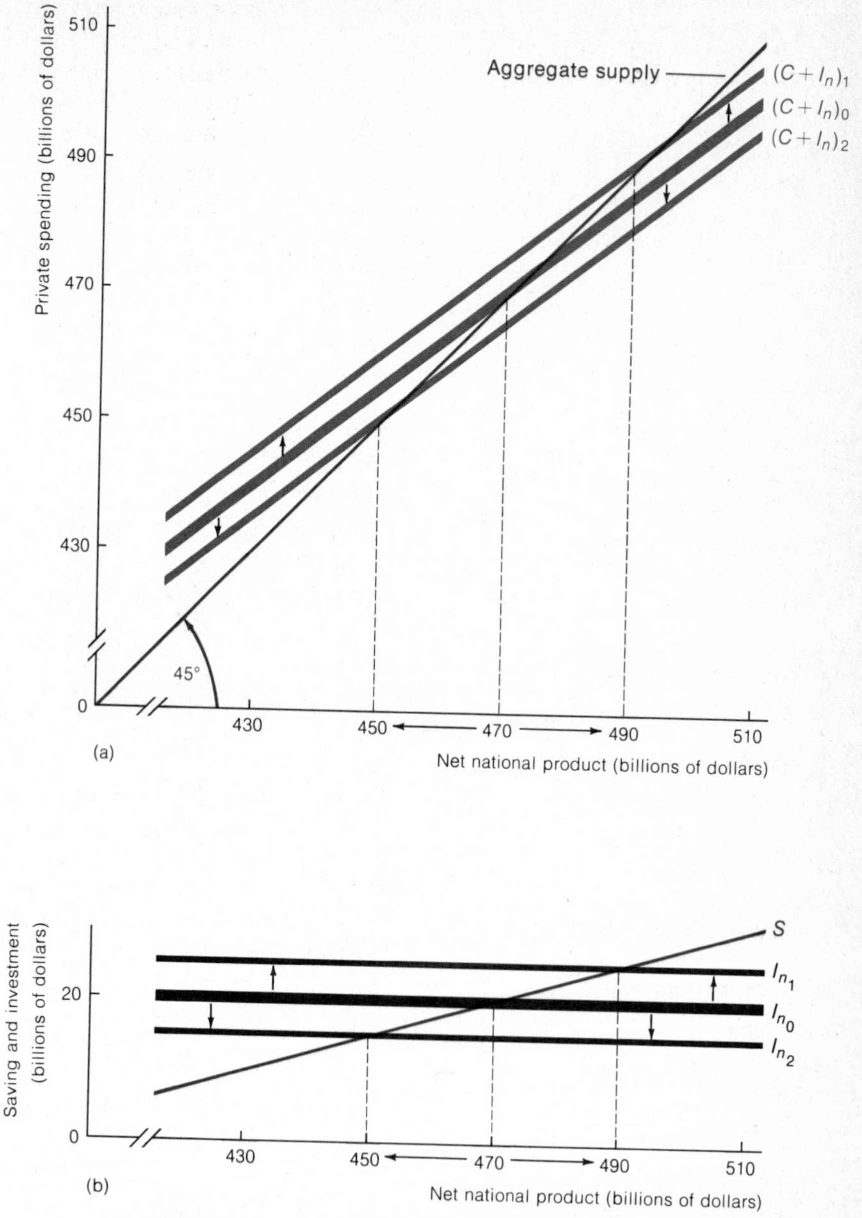

FIGURE 13 · 3 CHANGES IN THE EQUILIBRIUM NNP CAUSED BY SHIFTS IN (*a*) THE AGGREGATE DEMAND SCHEDULE AND (*b*) THE INVESTMENT SCHEDULE

An upshift in the aggregate demand schedule from, say, $(C + I_n)_0$ to $(C + I_n)_1$ will increase the equilibrium NNP. Conversely, a downshift in the aggregate demand schedule from, say, $(C + I_n)_0$ to $(C + I_n)_2$ will lower the equilibrium NNP. In the saving-investment figure an upshift schedule (I_{n_0} to I_{n_1}) will raise, and downshift (I_{n_0} to I_{n_2}) will lower, the equilibrium NNP.

$(C + I_n)_2$ in 13·3*a*. In each case these shifts cause the equilibrium NNP to fall from the original $470 billion level to $450 billion. The reader should verify these conclusions in terms of Table 13·1 by substituting $25 billion and then $15 billion for the $20 billion investment figure given in the table.

When changes in the consumption-saving schedules occur, they will have similar effects. If households want to consume more (save less) at each level of NNP, the aggregate demand schedule will shift upward and the saving schedule downward in Figure 13·3*a* and *b*, respectively. In either portrayal these shifts will mean an increase in the equilibrium NNP. If households want to consume less (save more) at each possible NNP, the resulting drop in the consumption schedule and the increase in the saving schedule will in turn reduce the equilibrium NNP.

The multiplier effect

You have undoubtedly detected a curious feature of the above examples: A $5 billion change in investment spending has given rise to a $20 billion change in the output-income level. This surprising result is called the *multiplier effect.* It is based upon two seemingly innocent facts. On the one hand, the economy is characterized by repetitive, continuous flows of expenditures and income wherein the dollars spent by Smith are received as income by Jones. On the other hand, any change in income will cause both consumption and saving to vary in the same direction as, and by a fraction of, the change in income.

It follows from these two facts that an initial change in the rate of spending will cause a chain reaction which, although of diminishing importance at each successive step, will cumulate to a multiple change in NNP. The multiplier effect is illustrated numerically in Table 13·2 for a $5 billion increase in investment spending. We assume that the MPC is three-fourths; the MPS is therefore one-fourth.

The initial increase in investment generates an equal amount of wage, rent, interest, and profit income for the simple reason that spending and receiving income are two sides of the same transaction. This $5 billion income increase causes consumption to rise by $3.75 billion and saving by $1.25 billion. The $3.75 billion which is spent is received by other households as income. They in turn consume three-fourths, or $2.81 billion, of this $3.75 billion and save one-fourth, or $0.94 billion. The $2.81 billion which is consumed flows to still other households as income. Though the spending and respending effects of the initial in-

TABLE 13·2 THE MULTIPLIER: A TABULAR ILLUSTRATION (*hypothetical data; in billions*)

	Change in income	Change in consumption (MPC = $\frac{3}{4}$)	Change in saving (MPS = $\frac{1}{4}$)
Assumed increase in investment	$ 5.00	$ 3.75	$1.25
Second round	3.75	2.81	0.94
Third round	2.81	2.11	0.70
Fourth round	2.11	1.58	0.53
Fifth round	1.58	1.19	0.39
All other rounds	4.75	3.56	1.19
Totals	$20.00	$15.00	$5.00

crease in investment diminish with each successive round of spending, the cumulative increase in the output-income level will be $20 billion if the process is carried through to the last dollar.

It is no coincidence that the multiplier effect ends at the point where exactly enough saving has been generated to offset the initial $5 billion increase in investment spending. It is only then that the disequilibrium created by the investment increase will be corrected. In this case NNP and total incomes must rise by $20 billion to create $5 billion in additional saving to match the $5 billion increase in investment spending. Income must increase by four times the initial excess of investment over saving, because households save one-fourth of any increase in their incomes. In this example the multiplier—the number of times the ultimate increase in income exceeds the initial increase in investment spending—is 4.

Characteristics of the multiplier Several noteworthy characteristics of the multiplier are not sufficiently emphasized by mere illustrations of its mechanics:

1. Remember that a change in any of the components of the aggregate demand schedule will give rise to a multiplier effect. In practice, economists usually associate the multiplier with changes in investment because of the relative instability of the investment schedule as compared with the consumption schedule. But keep in mind that a shift in the consumption schedule or, as we shall see shortly, a shift in the schedule of government spending will also prompt a similar chain reaction.

2. Keep in mind too that the multiplier works in both directions. That is, a small increase in spending can give rise to a multiple increase in NNP, or a small decrease in spending can be magnified into a much larger decrease in NNP by the multiplier. Note carefully the effects of the shift in $(C + I_n)_0$ to $(C + I_n)_1$ or $(C + I_n)_2$ and I_{n_0} to I_{n_1} or I_{n_2} in Figure 13·3*a* and *b*.

3. You may have sensed from Table 13·2 that a relationship of some sort must exist between the MPS and the size of the multiplier. There is such a relationship: the fraction of an increase in income which is saved—that is, the MPS—determines the cumulative respending effects of any initial change in I_n, G, or C, and therefore the multiplier. More specifically, *the size of the MPS and the size of the multiplier are inversely related.* The smaller the fraction of any change in income which is saved, the greater the respending at each round and the greater the multiplier. If the MPS is one-fourth, as in our example, the multiplier is 4. If the MPS were one-third, the multiplier would be 3. If the MPS were one-fifth, the multipler would be 5. Look again at Table 13·2 and Figure 13·3*b*. Initially the economy is in equilibrium at the $470 billion level of NNP. Now businessmen increase investment by $5 billion so that intended investment of $25 billion exceeds intended saving of $20 billion at the $470 billion level. That is, $470 billion is obviously no longer the equilibrium NNP. The question is: By how much must net national product or income rise to restore equilibrium? The answer is: By enough to generate $5 billion of additional saving to offset the $5 billion increase in investment. Because households save $1 out of every $4 of additional income they receive (MPS = ¼), NNP must obviously rise by $20 billion—four times the assumed increase in investment—to create the $5 billion of extra saving necessary to restore equilibrium. Hence, a multiplier of 4. If the MPS were one-third, NNP would only have to rise by $15 billion (three times the increase in investment) to restore equilibrium, and the multiplier therefore would be 3. But if the MPS were one-fifth, NNP would have to rise by $25 billion in order for an extra $5 billion of saving to be forthcoming and equilibrium to be restored, yielding a multiplier of 5.

We can summarize these and all other possibilities by simply saying that *the multiplier is equal to the reciprocal of the MPS.* The reciprocal of any number is the quotient you obtain by dividing 1 by that number. In short, we can say

$$\text{The multiplier} = \frac{1}{\text{MPS}}$$

This formula provides us with a shorthand method of determining the multiplier. All we need to know

is the MPS (or MPC) to calculate the size of the multiplier quickly.[2]

Significance of the multiplier The significance of the multiplier is almost self-evident. A relatively small change in the investment plans of businesses or the consumption-saving plans of households can trigger a much larger change in the equilibrium level of NNP. The multiplier magnifies the fluctuations in business activity initiated by changes in spending.

Note that the larger the MPC, the greater will be the multiplier. For example, if the MPC is $\frac{3}{4}$ and the multiplier is therefore 4, a $10 billion decline in investment will reduce the equilibrium NNP by $40 billion. But if the MPC is only $\frac{2}{3}$ and the multiplier is thereby 3, the same $10 billion drop in investment will cause the equilibrium NNP to fall by only $30 billion. We will find in discussing the so-called "built-in stabilizers" in Chapter 14 that one of the major goals of public policy is to structure a system of taxes and transfer payments which will reduce the MPC and diminish the size of the multiplier, thereby lessening the destabilizing effect of a given change in investment or consumption expenditures.

The complex multiplier The multiplier concept which we have just developed is called the *simple multiplier* by economists because it is based upon a very simple model of the economy—a model which includes only the leakage of saving. But in the real world the successive rounds of income and spending can be dampened by other leakages such as taxes and imports. That is, in addition to the leakage into saving, some portion of income at each round would be siphoned off as additional taxes, and another part would be used to purchase additional goods from abroad. When all these leakages—saving, taxes, and imports—are taken into account in a more realistic *complex multiplier,* the effect is to reduce the size of the multiplier. The Council of Economic Advisors has estimated the complex multiplier for the United States to be about 2.

Paradox of thrift

A curious paradox is suggested by the saving-investment approach to NNP determination and by our analysis of the multiplier. The paradox is that if society attempts to save more, it may end up actually saving the same amount, or even less. Figure 13·4 is relevant. Suppose I_n and S_1 are the current investment and saving schedules which determine a $470 billion equilibrium NNP. Now assume that households, perhaps anticipating a recession, attempt to save, say, $5 billion more at each income level in order to provide a nest egg against the expected bad times. This attempt to save more is reflected in an upward shift of the saving schedule from S_1 to S_2. But this very upshift creates an excess of planned saving over planned investment at the current $470 billion equilibrium output. And we know that the multiplier effect will cause this small increase in saving (decline in consumption) to be reflected in a much larger—$20 billion ($5 times 4) in this case—decline in equilibrium NNP.

There is a paradox here in several different senses. First, note that at the new $450 billion equilibrium NNP households are saving the same amount they did at the original $470 billion NNP. Society's attempt to save more has been frustrated by the multiple decline in the equilibrium NNP which that attempt itself caused. Second, this analysis suggests that thrift, which has always been held in high esteem in our economy, now can be something of a social vice. From the individual point of view a penny saved

[2]Since MPS + MPC = 1, it is also true that MPS = 1 − MPC. Substituting in the above formula, we say that

$$\text{The multiplier} = \frac{1}{1 - \text{MPC}}$$

Furthermore, the importance of footnote 7 in Chapter 12 now becomes clear. There we noted that the MPS measures the slope of the saving schedule. In terms of the savings-equals-investment approach this means that if the MPS is relatively large (say, one-half) and the slope of the saving schedule is therefore relatively steep (one-half), any given upward shift in investment spending will be subject to a relatively small multiplier. For example, a $5 billion increase in investment will entail a new point of intersection of the S and I_n schedules only $10 billion to the right of the original equilibrium NNP. The multiplier is only 2. But if the MPS is relatively small (say, one-sixth), the slope of the saving schedule will be relatively gentle. Therefore, a $5 billion upward shift in the investment schedule will provide a new intersection point some $30 billion to the right of the original equilibrium NNP. The multiplier is 6 in this case. The reader should verify these two examples by drawing appropriate saving and investment diagrams.

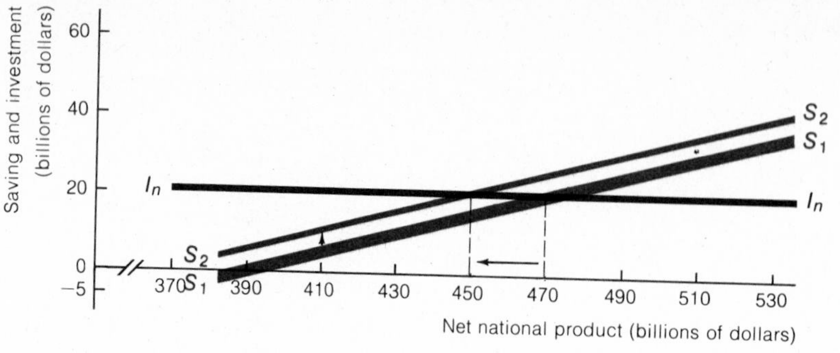

FIGURE 13·4 THE PARADOX OF THRIFT

Unless offset by an upshift in the investment schedule, any attempt by households to save more (S_1 to S_2) will be frustrated by a multiple decline in the equilibrium NNP.

may be a penny earned. But from the social point of view a penny saved is a penny not spent and therefore a decline in someone's income. The act of thrift may be virtuous from the individual's point of view but disastrous from the social point of view because of its undesirable effects upon total output and employment. Third, it is ironic, if not paradoxical, that households may be most strongly induced to save more (consume less) at the very time when increased saving is most inappropriate and economically undesirable, that is, when the economy seems to be backsliding into a recession. An individual fearing the loss of his job will hardly be inclined to go on a spending spree.

The reader will find it challenging and rewarding to pursue this analysis of the paradox of thrift and the multiplier by substituting an upsloping investment schedule for the simplified investment schedule we have employed. In the case of the paradox of thrift you should conclude that the attempt of households to save more will not simply be frustrated but will actually give rise to a decline in the amount actually saved. You should also find that a positively sloped investment schedule will increase the size of the multiplier and in effect make it a "supermultiplier."[3]

[3]*Hints:* (1) Substitute the investment schedule of columns 1 and 3 in Table 12·2 in column 5 of Table 13·1; (2) assume a $5 billion increase in saving; (3) compute (estimate) the new equilibrium point at which intended saving equals intended investment; (4) compare the original and the new amounts saved; and (5) calculate the size of the multiplier.

EQUILIBRIUM VERSUS FULL-EMPLOYMENT NNP

We now turn from the task of explaining to that of evaluating the equilibrium NNP.

Too much emphasis cannot be placed upon the fact that the $470 billion equilibrium NNP embodied in our analysis (Table 13·1 and Figures 13·1 and 13·2) may or may not entail full employment. Remember: The basic theme of Keynesian economics is that capitalism contains no mechanisms capable of automatically creating that particular level of aggregate demand which will induce businessmen to produce a full-employment noninflationary level of output. For example, if we assume the full-employment noninflationary output to be $490 billion, it would only be by chance that the aggregate demand schedule would be at the $(C + I_n)_0$ level in Figure 13·5 to intersect the aggregate supply schedule at this desired level of output. Aggregate demand might very well lie below this ideal location at, say, the $(C + I_n)_2$ level, or above the full-employment noninflationary output at, say, the $(C + I_n)_1$ level.

Deflationary gap

Suppose in Figure 13·5 that the aggregate demand schedule is at $(C + I_n)_2$, which, incidentally, happens to be the aggregate demand schedule developed and

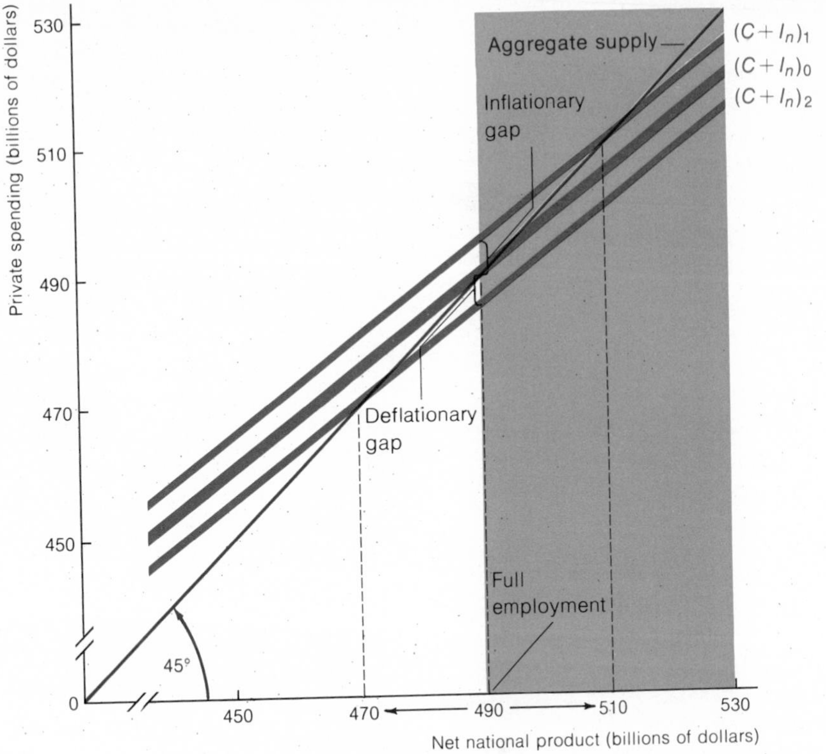

FIGURE 13·5 DEFLATIONARY AND INFLATIONARY GAPS

In a capitalistic system the equilibrium and full employment NNPs may not coincide. Deflationary and inflationary gaps refer to the deficiency or excess of total spending which may exist at the full-employment NNP. A deflationary gap will cause a multiple decline in the real NNP, whereas an inflationary gap will give rise to a multiple increase in the money NNP.

employed in this chapter. This schedule intersects aggregate supply to the left of the full-employment output, causing the economy's aggregate production to fall $20 billion short of its capacity production. In terms of Table 13·1 the economy is failing to employ 5 million of its 70 million available workers and, as a result, is sacrificing $20 billion worth of output. Looked at from a slightly different vantage point, we find that total spending is deficient by $5 billion (see Table 13·1) at the $490 billion level of NNP. This deficiency is called a *deflationary gap* for the simple reason that it has a deflationary, depressing, or contractionary impact upon the economy. This $5 billion deficiency of total spending, subject to a multiplier of 4, accounts for the $20 billion difference between the equilibrium and the full-employment NNP.

Inflationary gap

Now let us suppose that the aggregate demand schedule happens to be at $(C + I_n)_1$ in Figure 13·5, intersecting the aggregate supply schedule at some point to the right of the $490 billion full-employment output. In this case there exists $5 billion of excess spending at the full-employment output, which economists call an *inflationary gap.* Because $490 billion is the economy's full-employment or maximum output (as valued at current or existing prices), it is quite obvious that a *real* NNP of $510 billion, indicated by the intersection of $(C + I_n)_1$ and the aggregate supply schedule, is unobtainable. The effect of the excess spending—the inflationary gap—will be to pull up the prices on the economy's fixed physical volume of production. More specifically, the $5 billion inflationary gap, subject to a multiplier of 4, will cause *money* NNP to rise by $20 billion while *real* NNP remains unchanged. Businesses as a whole cannot respond to the $5 billion in excess spending by expanding their real outputs for the simple reason that all available resources are already employed; the economy is already operating at some point on its production possibilities curve. Putting the matter quite bluntly, NNP changes to the left of the full-employment output (the white area of Figure 13·5) are *real* changes; NNP changes to the right of full-employment output (the yellow area) are merely monetary or "paper" changes in NNP.[4]

[4]The alert reader will have detected a simplification or two in our deflationary-inflationary gap analysis. We have implicitly assumed that the price level is perfectly constant until full employment is reached; that is, up to the $490 billion NNP, increases in total spending would simply bring about proportionate increases in output and employment. Then, further increases in spending beyond the full-employment output are purely inflationary. Actually, we know that increases in total spending *near* the full-employment level will usually cause both the price level and the level of real NNP to increase. In the context of Figure 11·1 we are here assuming that the price-level line is -shaped rather than -shaped. The transition from the white to the yellow area is not so abrupt as in Figure 13·5, but is actually rather blurred. Similarly, full employment (or capacity production) itself is something of an elastic concept because a given number of workers can increase their hours of work by simply working overtime, or, as a matter of fact, persons who are not ordinarily in the labor force may be induced to offer their services when job opportunities are abundant. The general validity of our analysis is not impaired by ignoring these refinements.

The main objective of Chapter 14 is to understand how governmental fiscal (taxation and expenditure) policy might be used to close deflationary or inflationary gaps.

SUMMARY

1. The equilibrium level of NNP is that at which the aggregate quantity demanded and the aggregate quantity supplied are equal or, graphically, where the $C + I_n$ line intersects the 45-degree line. At any NNP greater than the equilibrium NNP, aggregate quantity supplied will exceed the aggregate quantity demanded, resulting in unsold goods, depressed profits, and eventual declines in output, employment, and income. At any below-equilibrium NNP the aggregate quantity demanded will exceed the aggregate quantity supplied, thereby resulting in substantial profits, declining inventories, and eventual increases in NNP.
2. An alternative, complementary approach determines the equilibrium NNP at the point where the amount households plan to save and the amount businesses plan to invest are equal. This is at the point where the saving and investment schedules intersect. Any excess of planned saving over planned investment will cause a shortage of total spending, forcing NNP to fall. Any excess of planned investment over planned saving will cause an excess of total spending, inducing NNP to rise. These changes in NNP will in both cases correct the assumed discrepancies in investment and saving plans.
3. Shifts in the saving-consumption schedules or in the investment schedule will cause the equilibrium output-income level to change by several times the amount of the initial change in spending. This phenomenon, which accompanies both increases and decreases in spending, is called the *multiplier effect.* The simple multiplier is equal to the reciprocal of the marginal propensity to save.
4. The *paradox of thrift* is that the attempt of society to save more may be frustrated by the multiple decline in the equilibrium NNP which the increased saving will cause.

5. The equilibrium level of NNP and the full-employment noninflationary NNP need not coincide. The amount by which aggregate demand falls short of the full-employment NNP is called the deflationary gap; this gap prompts a multiple decline in real NNP. The amount by which aggregate demand exceeds the full-employment NNP is the inflationary gap; it causes a multiple increase in money NNP.

QUESTIONS AND STUDY SUGGESTIONS

1. Explain graphically the determination of the equilibrium NNP by *a.* the aggregate demand–aggregate supply approach and *b.* the saving-equals-investment approach for the private sector of the economy. Why must these two approaches always yield the same equilibrium NNP?

2. Explain in detail the difference between planned saving and investment and realized saving and investment. Why is the distinction significant?

3. Critically evaluate: "It is socially desirable for households to attempt to increase their rate of saving whenever a recession begins. In this way households will be able to accumulate the financial resources to pay their way through bad times." Explain the paradox of thrift, indicating its significance.

4. "The fact that households may try to save more than businesses want to invest is of no consequence, because events will in time force households and businesses to save and invest at the same rates." Critically evaluate.

5. What is the multiplier effect? What relationship does the MPC bear to the size of the multiplier? The MPS? What will the multiplier be when the MPS is 0, 0.4, 0.6, and 1? When the MPC is 1, $\frac{8}{9}$, $\frac{2}{3}$, $\frac{1}{2}$, and 0? How much of a change in NNP will result if businesses increase their rate of investment by $8 billion and the MPC in the economy is $\frac{4}{5}$? If the MPC is $\frac{2}{3}$?

6. What effect will each of the changes designated in question 7 at the end of Chapter 12 have upon the equilibrium level of NNP? Explain your answers.

7. Assuming the level of investment is $16 billion and independent of the level of total output, complete the following table and determine the equilibrium level of output and income which the private sector of the economy would provide.

Possible levels of employment, millions	Aggregate supply (NNP = DI), billions	Consumption, billions	Saving, billions
40	$240	$244	$____
45	260	260	____
50	280	276	____
55	300	292	____
60	320	308	____
65	340	324	____
70	360	340	____
75	380	356	____
80	400	372	____

a. If this economy has a labor force of 70 million, will there exist an inflationary or deflationary gap? Explain the consequences of this gap.

b. Will an inflationary or deflationary gap exist if the available labor force is only 55 million? Trace the consequences.

c. What are the sizes of the MPC and the MPS?

d. Use the MPC and MPS concepts to explain the increase in the equilibrium NNP which will occur as the result of an increase in investment spending from $16 to $20 billion.

8. Using the consumption and saving data given in question 7, what will the equilibrium level of income be if investment is $2 billion at the $240 billion level of NNP and increases by $2 billion for every $20 billion increase in NNP? Assuming that businessmen decide to invest $4 billion more at each level of NNP, what will be the new equilibrium NNP? What is the size of the "supermultiplier"? Explain why it is larger than the multiplier derived in question 7.

9. Using the consumption and saving data given in question 7 and assuming the level of investment is $16 billion, what are the levels of intended saving and invest-

ment at the \$380 billion level of aggregate supply? What are the levels of realized saving and investment? What are intended saving and investment at the \$300 billion level of aggregate supply? What are the levels of realized saving and investment? Use the concept of unintended investment to explain adjustments toward equilibrium from both the \$380 and \$300 billion levels of aggregate supply.

10. *Advanced analysis:* Assume the consumption schedule for the economy is such that $C = 50 + 0.8Y$. Assume further that investment is autonomous or exogenous (indicated by I_o); that is, investment is independent of the level of income and in the amount $I = I_o = 30$. Recall also that in equilibrium the aggregate amount of output supplied (Y) is equal to the aggregate amount demanded ($C + I$), or $Y = C + I$.

a. Calculate the equilibrium level of income for this economy. Check your work by putting the consumption and investment schedules in tabular form and determining the equilibrium income.

b. What will happen to equilibrium Y if $I = I_o = 10$? What does this tell you about the size of the multiplier?

11. *Advanced analysis:* If $I = I_0 = 50$ and $C = 30 + 0.5Y$, what is the equilibrium level of income? If $I = 10 + 0.1Y$ and $C = 50 + 0.6Y$, what is the equilibrium level of income?

SELECTED REFERENCES

Economic Issues, 4th ed., reading 30.

Hansen, Alvin: *A Guide to Keynes* (New York: McGraw-Hill Book Company, 1953).

Lindauer, John: *Macroeconomics*, 2d ed. (New York: John Wiley & Sons, Inc., 1971), chaps. 1–4.

McKenna, Joseph P.: *Aggregate Economic Analysis*, 3d ed. (New York: Holt, Rinehart and Winston, Inc., 1969).

Peterson, Wallace C.: *Income, Employment, and Economic Growth*, rev. ed. (New York: W. W. Norton & Company, Inc., 1967), chaps. 5–9.

Ross, Myron H.: *Income: Analysis and Policy*, 2d ed. (New York: McGraw-Hill Book Company, 1969), chaps. 5–11.

Shapiro, Edward: *Macroeconomic Analysis*, 2d ed. (New York: Harcourt, Brace & World, Inc., 1970), chaps. 6–14.

14

THE ECONOMICS OF FISCAL POLICY

This chapter is a continuation of Chapters 12 and 13. Its fundamental purpose is to add the public sector to our analysis of the equilibrium NNP.

FISCAL POLICY

In particular we want to assess the impact of fiscal policy, that is, the manipulation of taxes and government spending for the expressed purpose of achieving the full-employment noninflationary level of NNP. But first we must pause for some preliminary considerations.

Rationale

The rationale underlying government spending and taxation decisions—particularly at the Federal level—differs in one crucial respect from the consumption-saving and investment decisions of the private sector of the economy. The consumption-saving decisions of households and the investment decisions of businesses are based upon what each group feels to be the course of action that will best further its own self-interest. Households divide their disposable incomes between consumption and saving in the manner most satisfying to them; businesses will invest only when they feel prospective profits to be lucrative enough to justify such spending. A basic notion of modern employment theory is that the sum of these individual decisions, motivated by self-interest, need not provide for the full-employment noninflationary level of NNP. Millions of individual consumption and investment decisions, based on private self-interest, need not necessarily provide for the realization of the social goal of full employment. Government, however, is an instrument of society as a whole, and within limits its spending and taxation decisions can be made to influence the equilibrium NNP in terms of the general welfare. Indeed, the task of fiscal policy is to manipulate government spending and taxation to close deflationary or inflationary gaps.

Employment Act of 1946

The notion that governmental fiscal actions can exert an important stabilizing influence upon the economy began to gain widespread acceptance during the Depression crisis of the 1930s. As previously noted, Keynesian employment theory played a major role in emphasizing the importance of remedial fiscal measures. But it was not until 1946, when the end of World War II recreated the specter of unemployment, that the Federal government formalized in law its area of responsibility in promoting economic stability. The Employment Act of 1946 proclaims:

> The Congress hereby declares that it is the continuing policy and responsibility of the Federal Government to use all practicable means consistent with its needs and obligations and other essential considerations of national policy, with assistance and cooperation of industry, agriculture, labor and State and local governments, to coordinate and utilize all its plans, functions, and resources for the purpose of creating and maintaining, in a manner calculated to foster and promote free competitive enterprise and the general welfare, conditions under which there will be afforded useful employment opportunities, including self-employment, for those able, willing, and seeking to work and to promote maximum employment, production, and purchasing power.

The Employment Act of 1946 is a landmark in American socioeconomic legislation in that it commits the Federal government to take positive action through monetary and fiscal policy to maintain economic stability.

The CEA

Responsibility for fulfilling the purposes of the act rests with the executive branch; the President must submit an annual economic report which describes the current state of the economy and makes appropriate policy recommendations. The Act also established a three-man Council of Economic Advisors (CEA) to assist and advise the President on economic matters and a Joint Economic Committee (JEC) of the Congress, which has investigated a wide range of economic problems of national interest. In its advisory capacity as "the President's intelligence arm in the eternal war against the business cycle," the CEA and its staff gather and analyze relevant economic data and use them to make forecasts; formulate programs and policies designed to fulfill the goals of the Employment Act; and "educate" the President, congressmen, and the general public on problems and policies relevant to the nation's economic health.[1]

DISCRETIONARY FISCAL POLICY

Let us first focus attention upon *discretionary* fiscal policy. Discretionary fiscal policy is the deliberate changing of taxes and government spending by the Congress for the purpose of offsetting cyclical fluctuations in output and employment and stimulating economic growth. To keep a potentially complex discussion as simple as possible, three simplifying assumptions are invoked. First, we continue to employ the simplified investment schedule in our analysis. Second, we shall suppose that the initial impact of government spending is such that it neither depresses nor stimulates private spending. That is, government spending will not cause any upward or downward shifts in the consumption and investment schedules. Third, it will be presumed that the government's net tax revenues[2] are derived entirely from personal taxes. The significance of this is that although DI will fall short of PI by the amount of government's tax revenues, NNP, NI, and PI will remain equal.

In Figure 14·1*a* and *b* we have repeated our equilibrium NNP models for the private sector (Figures 13·1 and 13·2). The intersection of private aggregate demand ($C + I_n$) and aggregate supply in Figure 14·1*a* indicates the equilibrium NNP, as does the

[1]Walter W. Heller's *New Dimensions of Political Economy* (New York: W. W. Norton & Company, Inc., 1967) provides an incisive explanation of the functions of CEA and an intriguing account of the Council's operation under Dr. Heller's Chairmanship during the 1961–1964 period. Arthur M. Okun's *The Political Economy of Prosperity* (New York: W. W. Norton & Company, Inc., 1970) is also highly recommended.

[2]By net taxes we mean total tax revenues less negative taxes in the form of transfer payments.

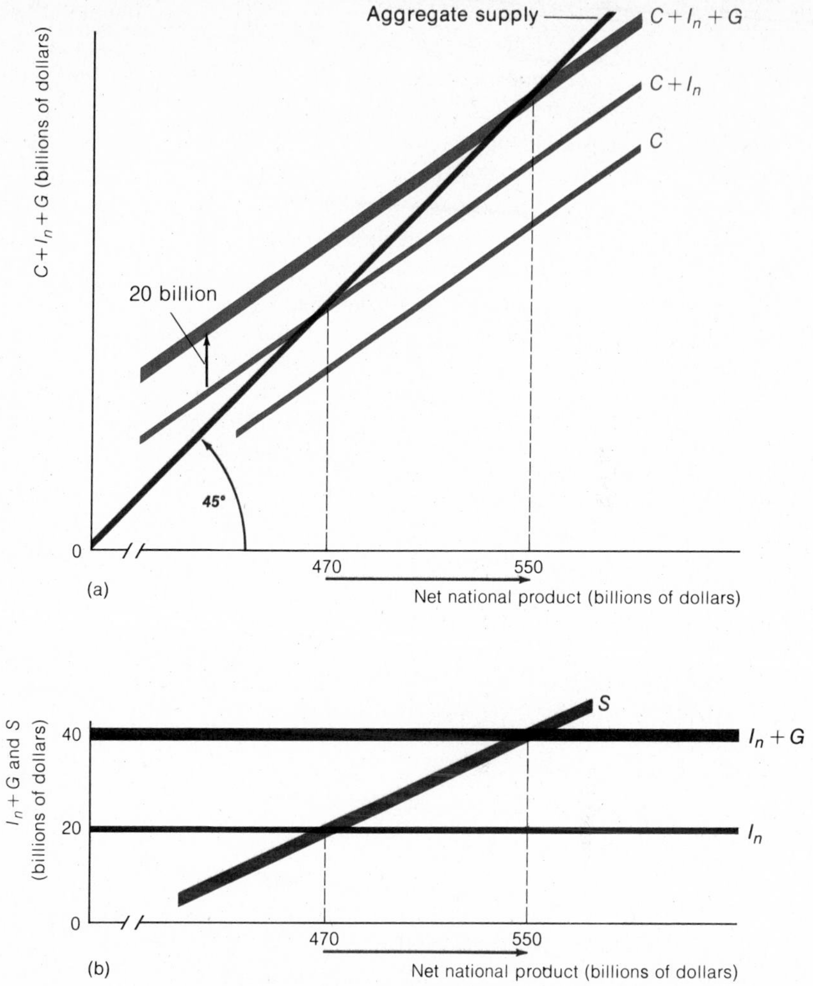

FIGURE 14·1 GOVERNMENT SPENDING AND THE EQUILIBRIUM NNP

(*a*) The aggregate demand–aggregate supply approach. The addition of government expenditures G to our analysis raises the aggregate demand ($C + I_n + G$) schedule and increases the equilibrium level of NNP as would an increase in C or I_n. Note that changes in government spending are subject to the multiplier effect. (*b*) $S = I_n$ approach. In terms of the saving-equals-investment approach, government spending supplements private investment spending ($I_n + G$), increasing the equilibrium NNP.

intersection of I_n and S in Figure 14·1*b*. You will recall from our gap analysis of Chapter 13 that the $470 billion equilibrium NNP is short of the assumed $490 billion full-employment noninflationary NNP.

In our discussion of the private sector of the economy we implicitly assumed that government purchases of goods and services (G) and tax revenues (T) were both zero. Now let us suppose that G and T both increase from zero to, say, $20 billion, and note the impact of each and then the combined impact of the two. As before, we pursue our analysis both graphically and tabularly.

Government spending and equilibrium NNP

Suppose that government decides to purchase $20 billion worth of goods and services regardless of what the level of NNP might be. By adding this amount of public spending G to the level of private spending, $C + I_n$, in Figure 14·1*a* we find that the total spending schedule (public plus private) has been increased to $C + I_n + G$. That is, the aggregate demand schedule now has a third component, which gives us a new and higher aggregate demand schedule. And this means a new and higher equilibrium level of NNP. In particular, the equilibrium level of NNP has increased from $470 to $550 billion. Increases in public spending, like increases in private spending, will boost the aggregate demand schedule in relation to the aggregate supply schedule and result in a higher equilibrium NNP. Note, too, that government spending is subject to the multiplier.

Figure 14·1*b* shows the same change in the equilibrium NNP in terms of the $S = I_n$ analysis. With G added to our discussion, the equilibrium level of NNP is now determined where the amount households plan to save is offset exactly by the amount which businesses plan to invest *plus* the amount government desires to spend on goods and services. That is, the equilibrium NNP is determined by the intersection of the S schedule and the $I_n + G$ schedule. Note that either approach indicates the same new equilibrium NNP.

What of the effect of a decline in government spending? Obviously, a decline in G will cause the aggregate demand schedule to fall or the $I_n + G$ schedule to fall. In either case the result is a multiple *decline* in the equilibrium NNP.

Taxation and equilibrium NNP

But government also collects tax revenues. How do tax collections affect the equilibrium level of NNP? Obviously, if government increases its tax revenues from zero to $20 billion, the immediate effect will be to lower DI by $20 billion. And, because DI is made up of consumer spending and saving, we can expect a decline in DI to lower both consumption and saving. But by how much will each decline? The MPC and the MPS hold the answer: The MPC tells us what fraction of a decline in DI will come at the expense of consumption, and the MPS indicates what fraction of a drop in DI will come at the expense of saving. Assuming that the MPC equals three-fourths and the MPS equals one-fourth, we can conclude that if government collects $20 billion in taxes at each possible level of NNP, the amount of consumption forthcoming at each level of NNP will drop by $15 billion (three-fourths of $20 billion), and the amount of saving at each level of NNP will fall by $5 billion (one-fourth of $20 billion).

The impact of a $20 billion increase in taxes is shown graphically in Figure 14·2*a* and *b*. In Figure 14·2*a* the $20 billion increase in taxes shows up as a $15 billion decline in the aggregate demand ($C + I_n + G$) schedule. Under our simplifying assumption that all taxes are personal income taxes, this decline in aggregate demand is solely the result of a decline in the consumption component of the aggregate demand schedule. The equilibrium NNP shifts from $550 billion to a $490 billion level as a result of this tax-caused drop in consumption.

The imposition of $20 billion in taxes has a twofold effect in Figure 14·2*b*. First, the taxes reduce DI by $20 billion and, with the MPS at one-fourth, cause saving to fall by $5 billion at each level of NNP. In Figure 14·2*b* this is shown as a shift from S_b (saving before taxes) to S_a (saving after taxes). Then the $20

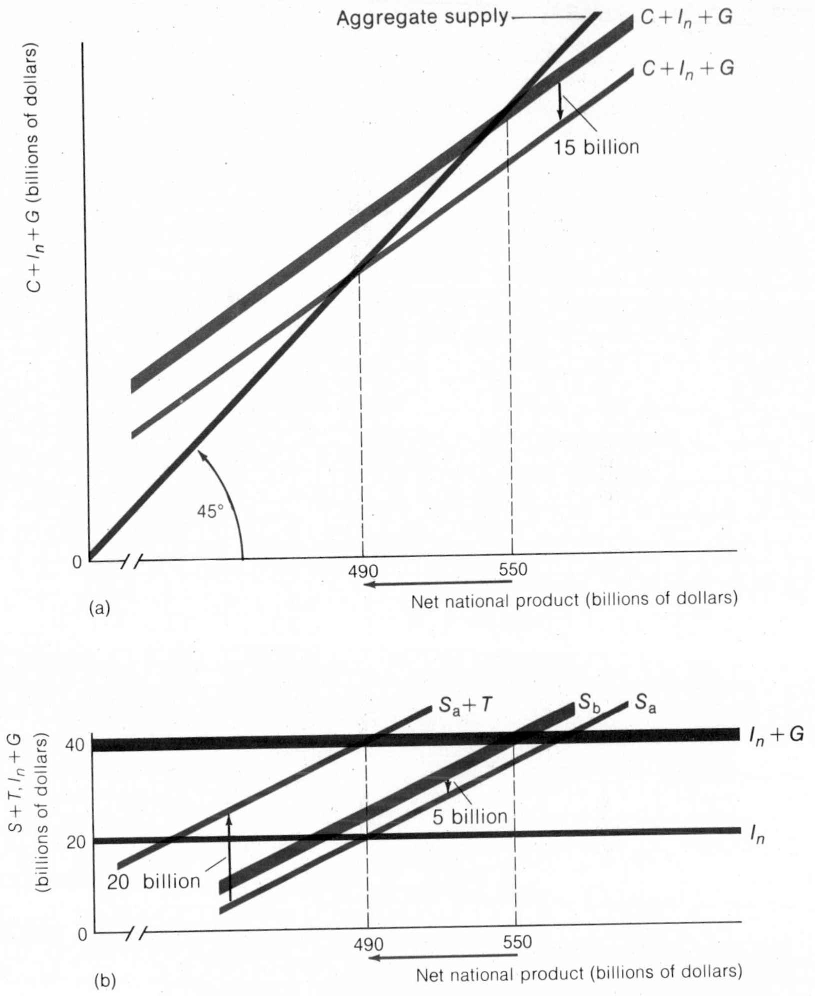

FIGURE 14 · 2 TAXES AND THE EQUILIBRIUM NNP

(*a*) The aggregate demand–aggregate supply approach. If the MPC is three-fourths, the imposition of \$20 billion of taxes will lower the consumption schedule by \$15 billion and thereby cause a decline in the equilibrium NNP. (*b*) The $S = I_n$ approach. Here taxes have a twofold effect. First, with an MPS of one-fourth, the imposition of taxes of \$20 billion will reduce disposable income by \$20 billion and saving by \$5 billion at each level of NNP. This is shown by the shift from S_b (saving before taxes) to S_a (saving after taxes). Second, the \$20 billion of taxes constitute an additional \$20 billion leakage at each NNP level, giving us $S_a + T$. By adding government, the equilibrium condition changes from $S = I_n$ to $S_a + T = I_n + G$.

billion in taxes as such appear as a $20 billion additional leakage at each NNP level which must be added to S_a, giving us $S_a + T$. Equilibrium now exists at the $490 billion NNP, where the total amount which households plan to save plus the amount of taxes government intends to collect are equal to the total amount businesses desire to invest plus the amount government plans to spend. The equilibrium condition now is $S_a + T = I_n + G$. Graphically, it is the intersection of the $S_a + T$ and the $I_n + G$ schedules which determines the equilibrium NNP.

A decline in existing taxes will cause the aggregate demand schedule to rise as a result of an upward shift in the consumption schedule or it will cause a decline in the $S_a + T$ schedule. The result in either case is a multiple *increase* in the equilibrium NNP.

Postscript: To simplify our discussion we are using a regressive tax system whereby the tax rate (T/NNP) falls as income rises. Most industrially advanced economies have proportional or progressive tax systems. The important modifications to which these latter two systems give rise will be noted shortly.

The budget impact

Table 14·1 shows the net impact of government spending and taxation upon the equilibrium NNP in terms of simple arithmetic data. This table is merely Table 13·1 adjusted to allow for $20 billion worth of tax revenues (column 3) and $20 billion of government spending (column 8) at each possible level of NNP. The immediate effect of taxes is shown in column 4: DI falls by $20 billion. Supposing the MPC and MPS are three-fourths and one-fourth, respectively, we find in columns 5 and 6 that the amounts of consumption and saving forthcoming at each level of NNP are $15 and $5 billion less, respectively, than the figures in Table 13·1.

Thus, for example, before the imposition of taxes, where NNP equaled DI, consumption was $420 billion and saving $10 billion at the $430 billion level of NNP (Table 13·1). After taxes are imposed, DI is $410 billion, obviously $20 billion short of the $430 billion NNP, with the result that consumption is only $405 billion and saving is $5 billion. It is in this manner that columns 4, 5, and 6 of Table 14·1 are determined. Column 7 carries over investment from Table 13·1, and column 8 adds government spending.

What is the equilibrium level of output now that taxation and government spending have been brought into the picture? The aggregate demand–aggregate supply, or $C + I_n + G =$ NNP, approach tells us to compare columns 2 and 9. It is apparent that the aggregate amounts demanded and supplied are equal only at the $490 billion NNP. At all higher levels businesses will attempt to produce in excess of what the economy, including both the private and public sectors, plans to spend. The resulting deficiency of total spending will force these higher levels of NNP downward back to the $490 billion level. Conversely, at all levels of NNP below the $490 billion level the economy will spend at a rate in excess of NNP, inducing businesses to expand NNP. We can conclude that $490 billion is the equilibrium NNP.

Our alternative approach must and does yield the same results. With the public sector added to the private sector, equilibrium will prevail where $S_a + T = I_n + G$. And this is at the $490 billion level. At all lower levels you should verify that investment and government spending will more than compensate for the saving and taxation leakages, causing $C + I_n + G$ to exceed NNP and thereby inducing the latter to rise. Conversely, at all levels of NNP above the $490 level, you should note that the saving and taxation leakages are not offset by investment and government spending, thus causing $C + I_n + G$ to fall short of NNP and forcing declines in NNP.

Balanced-budget multiplier

Note an important and curious thing about our tabular and graphic illustrations. *Equal increases in government spending and taxation increase the equilibrium NNP. That is, if* G *and* T *are both increased by* $X, *the equilibrium level of national output will rise by* $X. The $20 billion increase in G and T causes the equilibrium NNP to increase from $470 to $490 billion. The rationale for this so-called *balanced-budget multiplier* is revealed in our example. The $20 billion increase in personal taxes only reduces consumption

TABLE 14·1 DETERMINATION OF THE EQUILIBRIUM LEVELS OF EMPLOYMENT, OUTPUT, AND INCOME: PRIVATE AND PUBLIC SECTORS (*hypothetical data*)

(1) Possible levels of employment, millions	(2) Possible levels of aggregate supply (NNP = NI = PI), billions	(3) Taxes, billions	(4) Possible levels of disposable income, billions, or (2) − (3)	(5) Consumption, billions
40	$370	$20	$350	$360
45	390	20	370	375
50	410	20	390	390
55	430	20	410	405
60	450	20	430	420
65	470	20	450	435
70	490	20	470	450
75	510	20	490	465
80	530	20	510	480

by $15 billion, the extra $5 billion in tax revenues coming at the expense of saving. Thus the *net* effect is a $5 billion increase in total spending—the combination of a $20 billion increase in public spending and a $15 billion decline in private spending. Being subject to the multiplier, the $5 billion net increase in spending boosts NNP by $20 billion. Equal changes in *G* and *T* are expansionary. The reader should experiment to verify that the balanced-budget multiplier is valid regardless of the sizes of the marginal propensities to consume and save.

Fiscal policy over the cycle

In our illustration—thanks to the net expansionist effect of the balanced-budget multiplier—fiscal policy has moved the economy from the unemployment NNP of $470 billion to the full-employment noninflationary NNP of $490 billion. The net $5 billion increase in spending afforded by equal increases in government spending and taxation has closed the existing $5 billion deflationary gap.

More generally, a level of private spending which fails to provide the full-employment noninflationary NNP calls for an *expansionary* fiscal policy. An expansionist policy obviously entails (1) increased government spending, (2) lower taxes, or (3) a combination of the two. In other words, if the budget is balanced at the outset, fiscal policy should move in the direction of a government budget *deficit* during a recession or depression to close the existing deflationary gap. Conversely, a level of private spending which threatens to cause inflation, that is, a spiraling up of the money GNP, calls for a restrictive or *contractionary* fiscal policy. A contractionary policy is composed of (1) decreased government spending, (2) higher taxes, or (3) a combination of these two policies. Fiscal policy should move toward a *surplus* in the government's budget when the economy is faced with the problem of closing an inflationary gap.[3]

[3]Minor qualification: Because, as we have just noted, a balanced budget is actually expansionary, a relatively small budget surplus might be slightly expansionary rather than deflationary.

(6) Saving, billions, or (4) − (5)	(7) Investment, billions	(8) Government expenditures, billions	(9) Aggregate demand ($C + I_n + G$), billions, or (5) + (7) + (8)	(10) Tendency of employment, output, and income
$−10	$20	$20	$400	Increase
−5	20	20	415	Increase
0	20	20	430	Increase
5	20	20	445	Increase
10	20	20	460	Increase
15	20	20	475	Increase
20	20	20	490	Equilibrium
25	20	20	505	Decrease
30	20	20	520	Decrease

NONDISCRETIONARY FISCAL POLICY: BUILT-IN STABILIZERS

To some extent appropriate changes in tax receipts and government spending occur automatically over the business cycle. Such changes are labeled *nondiscretionary fiscal policy* because they arise from the kinds of taxes and disbursement programs built into our fiscal system and do not require congressional action. That is, the existing tax structure and existing spending programs are such that declines in the levels of output and national income automatically tend to create budget deficits, and increases in output and income automatically tend to cause budget surpluses. Let us examine the main automatic stabilizers.

Personal and corporate income taxes

Because both personal and corporate income taxes entail progressive tax rates, any rise in the national income will result in more than proportionate increases in government tax receipts, which puts the brakes on an economic expansion or boom. Conversely, as the national income falls, tax collections will fall more than proportionately, thereby cushioning a recession.

Transfers and subsidies

Certain government disbursements also change automatically in such a way as to diminish cyclical instability. During recession incomes do not decline as much as otherwise because unemployed workers receive unemployment compensation payments under our social security system. Relief payments flow to those who do not qualify for unemployment compensation or who have used up their benefits. During prosperity when unemployment is low, unemployment compensation and relief payments obviously will decline. Similarly, falling farm prices during recession cause the volume of price support subsidies to agriculture to increase; rising farm prices during the cyclical upswing cause these subsidies to diminish.

Recalling (footnote 2) that the term net taxes means tax revenues less "negative taxes" in the form of transfers and subsidies, we can simply say that built-in stability means that net taxes rise and fall with increases and decreases in the national income. From now on, we will use the term "taxes" to mean net taxes.

Consequences

The net effect of tax revenues moving directly with and transfer payments and farm subsidies varying inversely with national income is that changes in disposable income and consumption will be less than proportionate to the changes in national income (see Table 10·7). Automatic changes in tax receipts and transfer payments partially insulate disposable income, and therefore consumption, from changes in national income. Because a decline in national income causes tax collections to decline and transfer payments to rise, disposable income will decline by less than does national income. This means in turn that consumption declines by less than would otherwise be the case and therefore the cumulative downward movement is less than it otherwise would be. Similarly, because an increase in national income automatically causes tax receipts to rise and transfers to decline, disposable income will rise less than does national income. In turn this means that consumption will increase less than would otherwise be the case, cushioning the cumulative upward movement in national income. The reader can verify the operation of these automatic stabilizers by observing the course of personal and corporate income taxes (lines 11 and 14) and transfer payments (line 13) during the 1949, 1954, 1958, and 1970 recessions on the table inside the covers of this book. The important point is that an element of *built-in stability* is injected into our economy by these nondiscretionary changes in tax receipts and transfer payments. In technical terms, nondiscretionary fiscal policy reduces the size of the marginal propensity to consume and therefore the size of the multiplier effect, making the economy more stable.

BUILT-IN STABILITY AND THE TAX SYSTEM[4]

It is important to recognize that the existence and degree of built-in stability depend upon the kind of tax system the economy utilizes. Recalling that the MPC and the multiplier vary directly, we must first discover how the various tax systems will affect the MPC. Figure 14·3 is helpful in envisioning graphically the possible effects of the tax structure upon stability. Consumption schedule C is a pretax schedule, such as that shown by columns 2 and 3 in Table 13·1. The MPC is assumed to be $\frac{3}{4}$. Schedule C_1 shows the consumption schedule after we have imposed a *regressive tax system* such as that of Table 14·1. Here the same absolute amount of taxes is collected at each level of income, which means, of course, that the tax rate (T/NNP) varies inversely with income. In this case the "tax gap" between the pretax and the regressive tax schedule is a constant amount. If taxes are \$20 billion at each level of NNP as in Table 14·1, C_1 will lie \$15 billion below C at all levels of NNP. (The other \$5 billion of taxes is paid at the expense of saving.) The crucial point is that the MPC—the slope of the consumption schedule—is unchanged by the imposition of this regressive tax system.

How does a *proportional tax system* affect the MPC? A proportional tax system means a constant tax *rate* is applied to all levels of income so that the absolute amount taken in taxes rises with income. Graphically, this rising absolute volume of tax collections shows up as a widening tax gap between the pretax schedule C and C_2, the consumption schedule after the imposition of the proportional tax. Obviously C_2 has a smaller slope; in other words, the MPC has been reduced. Note that C_2 is a straight line, that is, the new MPC is the same at all NNP levels, but it is simply of a lesser value—say $\frac{1}{2}$ rather than $\frac{3}{4}$—than previously.

Finally consider a *progressive tax system,* wherein the tax rate (T/NNP) rises with income. Here we find

[4]The remaining sections of this chapter are optional and may be omitted without loss of continuity.

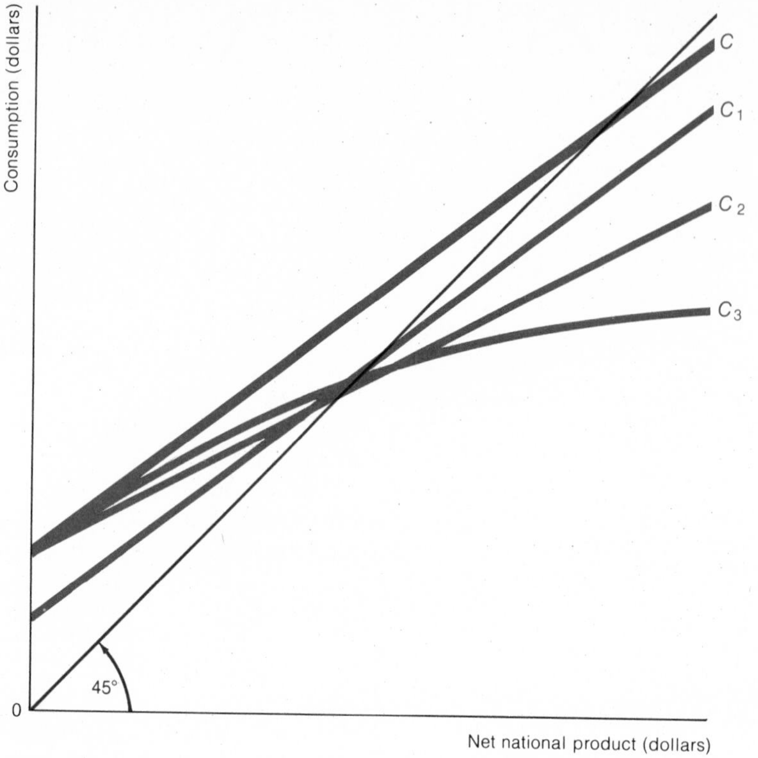

FIGURE 14·3 THE TAX SYSTEM AND THE CONSUMPTION SCHEDULE

A regressive tax system which collects the same amount of revenue at all levels of NNP will shift the consumption schedule downward (C to C_1), but will not alter the MPC (the schedule's slope). A proportional or progressive tax will shift the consumption schedule to C_2 or C_3, respectively, and lower the MPC.

that not only does the absolute amount paid in taxes rise with income, but so does the fraction or proportion paid in taxes. This means that the ''tax gap'' between C and C_3 (consumption with progressive taxes) widens at an increasing rate. That is, the fraction of each increase in income paid as taxes will grow as income expands. This in turn means that the fraction of each increase in income consumed must fall. That is, the MPC falls as NNP rises. This falling MPC is reflected in the diminishing slope of C_3 in Figure 14·3.[5]

[5]The reader can firm up his understanding of this discussion by working question 5 at the end of the chapter.

To recapitulate: A regressive tax system does not alter the MPC from its pretax level (C and C_1). A proportional tax system lowers the MPC, but the MPC does not change with the level of NNP (C and C_2). A progressive tax system lowers the MPC and also causes the MPC to fall as income rises (C and C_3). These consequences have great relevance for economic stability when we recall (Chapter 13) that *the MPC and the multiplier are directly related.* A smaller MPC means a smaller multiplier and therefore a lesser degree of instability in response to a given change in spending. For example, a given change in aggregate demand—say, a $10 billion downshift in the investment schedule—will lower NNP by $40

billion with our regressive system, because the relatively high MPC of $\frac{3}{4}$ yields a multiplier of 4. But with our proportional tax system the same $10 billion drop in investment will lower NNP by only $20, because the tax system has lowered the MPC to, say, $\frac{1}{2}$ and the multiplier to 2. A proportional tax system builds more stability into the economy. This comparison is made graphically in Figure 14·4, wherein AD_1 represents an aggregate demand schedule comprised of the regressive-tax consumption schedule (C_1) and levels of investment and government spending which are the same regardless of the NNP. The slope of AD_1 is relatively steep, reflecting the fact that the MPC is relatively large ($\frac{3}{4}$).[6] Hence, an assumed $10 billion decline in investment shifts aggregate demand from AD_1 to AD_1' and lowers NNP by $40 billion. In contrast AD_2 shows the same I_n and G figures added to consumption schedule C_2, which embodies a proportional tax system. Now we find that, because the MPC has been reduced from $\frac{3}{4}$ to, say, $\frac{1}{2}$ by the tax system, the same $10 billion drop in investment will shift aggregate demand from AD_2 to AD_2', but the

[6]Because G and I_n are assumed to be independent of the level of NNP, the G and I_n schedules are parallel to the horizontal axis (see I_n in Figure 12·5) and therefore have no slope. Hence, the slopes of C_1 and AD_1 are identical; both reflect the MPC of $\frac{3}{4}$.

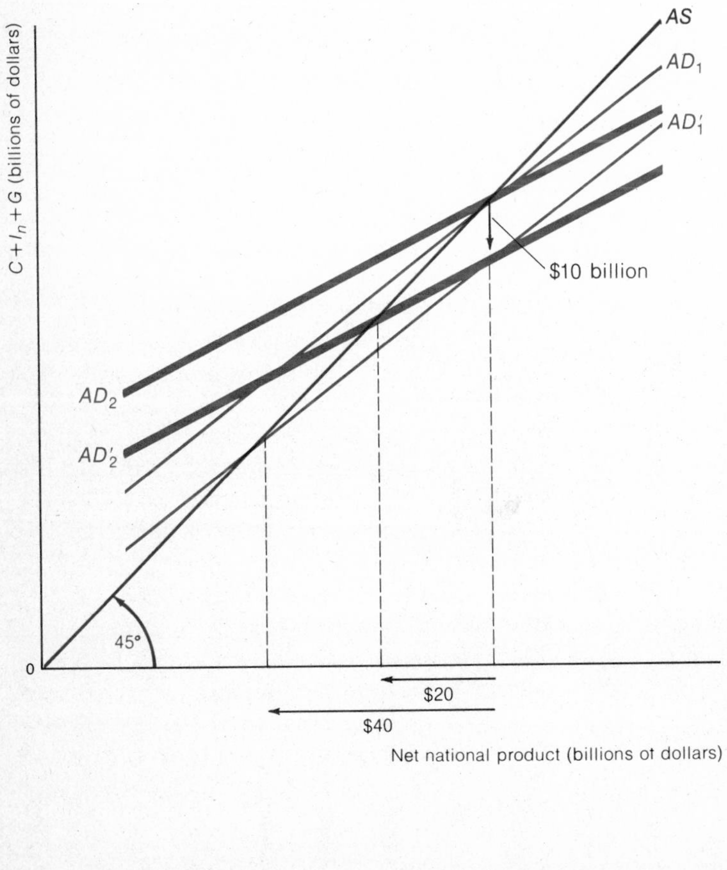

FIGURE 14·4 BUILT-IN STABILITY AND THE TAX SYSTEM

A proportional or progressive tax system will reduce the slope of the aggregate demand schedule from AD_1 to AD_2. As a result, the same given decline in spending of, say, $10 billion will cause a smaller decline in NNP with a proportional or progressive tax system (say $20 billion) than with no taxes or a regressive tax system (say $40 billion).

smaller multiplier will cause the NNP to decline by only $20 billion. The economy is obviously more stable (actually less unstable) with the proportional tax system. A progressive tax system could provide even greater stability by reducing the MPC even further.

Limitations

Although they have served the economy well, it must be emphasized that these automatic, or built-in, stabilizers are not sufficiently strong to offset any serious variations in the level of economic activity. Discretionary action—that is, changes in tax rates, tax structure, and expenditure programs—by Congress is required to alleviate inflation or recession of any appreciable magnitude. In particular, automatic stabilizers do not correct inflation or unemployment, but merely reduce their magnitude and severity. It is estimated that in the United States built-in stabilizers are currently strong enough to reduce fluctuations in national income by one-third or more. One recent study suggests that the built-in stabilizers during recent recessions prevented an average of 36 to 52 percent of the income declines which would have occurred in their absence. On the other hand, during recent expansions potential income increases were reduced by as much as 25 to 42 percent.[7]

DYNAMICS OF FISCAL POLICY

The difference between discretionary fiscal policy and the automatic stabilizers can be clarified, and the functioning of the latter more clearly envisioned, through Figure 14·5. The vertical axis simply shows the Federal budget surplus or deficit as a percentage of the GNP. The utilization rate, measured on the horizontal axis, is the ratio of actual GNP to potential or full-employment GNP. If we regard full employment as being achieved when 4 percent of the labor force is out of work (Chapter 11), then a 100 percent utilization rate means 4 percent unemployment, and lower utilization rates mean higher levels of unemployment.

The two lines on the graph are *budget lines* or fiscal program lines for years 1 and 2; these lines, incidentally, closely approximate the actual fiscal programs for 1962 and 1960 respectively.[8] A number of significant points can be made on the basis of this diagram.

1. The fact that the budget lines are upsloping to the right is a reflection of the built-in stability characteristic of our fiscal programs. Look for a moment at budget line 1. Each point on this line entails the same expenditure programs and the same progressive tax system. At a low level of output and employment—say a 92 percent utilization rate—net tax revenues will be low because income is low. The result is a deficit. But as the utilization rate and income rise, the progressive tax system will bring in more and more revenue. At the 95 percent utilization rate, the budget deficit disappears, and at higher levels of output and income, tax revenues expand above expenditures and a surplus appears. The deficits at low utilization rates are automatic and appropriately expansionary; the surpluses at high utilization rates are also automatic and appropriately restrain the economy as full employment is approached.

2. Discretionary fiscal policy—changing the level of expenditures or tax rates—will shift the whole budget line. A reduction in government expenditures and an increase in tax rates will cause the budget line to shift upward, as from line 1 to line 2 in Figure 14·5. With lower expenditures and higher tax rates, the surplus will be greater or the deficit will be smaller at any given utilization rate with line 2 than is the case with line 1. Budget line 1 embodies a more expansionary fiscal program than does line 2.

An easy way to measure the relative contractionary or expansionary impact of alternative fiscal programs is to compare the sizes of the surpluses which each would yield at full employment, or 100 percent utilization. The budget line which results in the smaller *full-employment surplus* is the more expansionary. In

[7]Peter Eilbott, "The Effectiveness of the Automatic Stabilizers," *American Economic Review*, June 1966, pp. 450–465.

[8]*Economic Report of the President, 1962,* pp. 78–81.

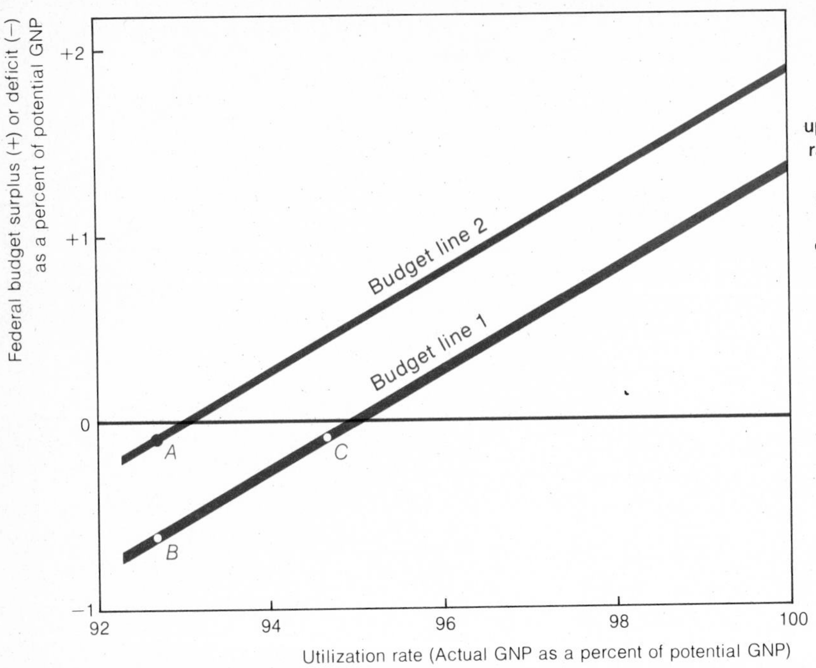

FIGURE 14·5 THE BUDGET AND THE LEVEL OF GNP

Fiscal programs characterized by built-in stability cause the budget line to be upsloping. This means that a high utilization rate will result in a budgetary surplus and a lower utilization rate will bring about a deficit. Discretionary fiscal policy shifts the entire budget line; line 1 reflects a more expansionary fiscal program than does line 2. (Adapted from *Economic Report of the President, 1962,* p. 79.)

Figure 14·5 the full-employment surplus for budget line 1 is about 1⅓ percent of the GNP; for line 2 it is almost 2 percent of the GNP.

To summarize, the automatic or built-in stabilizing effects of a given budget program are represented by movements along a given budget line and are caused by changes in the level of economic activity. Discretionary fiscal policy—changes in government expenditures and tax rates—entail an upward shift (less expansionary) or downward shift (more expansionary) of the entire budget line.

3. The upsloping budget line suggests another obvious, but very important, point: The actual deficit or surplus realized by the Federal government in a particular year depends not only upon its fiscal programs, but also upon the level of economic activity. That is, the location of the budget line *and* the utilization rate are both crucial determinants of the actual size of the deficit or surplus which is incurred in a particular year. A relatively expansionary fiscal program (line 1) can yield a substantial surplus, *if* it is accompanied by a high (for example, 99 percent) utilization rate. A more restrictive (less expansionary) program (line 2) may result in a deficit, *if* the utilization rate is low—at, say, 92 percent. The astute reader will note that, other things being equal, line 1 is indeed more conducive to a high utilization rate than is line 2!

1964 tax cut

This fact—that the actual surplus or deficit depends upon the fiscal program and the level of national income—was the basis for the paradoxical rationale which underlay the massive corporate and income tax cuts of 1964. President Kennedy took office in

1961 committed to the elimination of the above-normal unemployment and general sluggishness which characterized the economy in the late 1950s. Applying modern fiscal concepts, he knew that either a tax cut or an increase in government spending would stimulate the economy. He chose to cut taxes, and justified this action at a time when budget deficits were already being incurred by arguing:[9]

> It is a paradoxical truth that tax rates are too high today [1962] and tax revenues are too low and the soundest way to raise revenues in the long run is to cut [tax] rates now. . . . And the reason is that only full employment can balance the budget and tax reduction can pave the way to full employment. The purpose of cutting taxes now is not to incur a budget deficit, but to achieve the more prosperous, expanding economy which will bring a budget surplus.

In terms of Figure 14•5, the President was saying in effect that the economy was currently operating at point *A* on budget line 2. A deficit is incurred at this point because the fiscal program embodied in line 2 is not very expansionary; the utilization rate is low, and therefore tax collections are low. By cutting tax rates we can move to the more expansionary budget line 1. This will stimulate the economy via the multiplier, raise the utilization rate, and bring in more tax revenues. Hence, instead of the tax cut increasing the deficit by moving from point *A* to point *B*, the deficit will remain substantially unchanged or even diminish as a rising national income takes us from point *A* to some point like *C*.

The 1964 tax cut of almost $11 billion was a bold and dramatic application of modern fiscal policy for the specific purpose of stimulating the economy. Did it work? Although the inability to conduct controlled experiments makes it impossible to be absolutely conclusive, available evidence strongly suggests that the tax cut did indeed bring about the predicted expansion of the economy. The CEA has estimated that by early 1965 the tax cut was responsible for increases in consumption and investment spending totaling over $20 billion; by the end of 1965 these increases in private spending attributable to the tax cut had cumulated to an estimated $30 billion.[10] As a result, the unemployment rate fell and the "gap" between actual and potential GNP declined significantly in 1964 and 1965 (Figure 11•2). Similarly, as predicted, the economy's growth rate rose perceptibly. And finally, as our discussion of the tax cut rationale suggests, Federal tax collections increased substantially as a result of expanding corporate and personal income taxes.[11]

"Fiscal drag" and its cure

Modern fiscal policy clearly envisions the Federal budget as an instrument for achieving full employment, price stability, and a high level of economic growth. But Figure 14•5 suggests an ironic feature of a fiscal system characterized by built-in stability: An economy which operates consistently close to full employment (a 100 percent utilization rate) and which grows quite rapidly may find that over time a *given* budget program will exert a greater and greater contractionary effect upon the economy! We know that a budget line with built-in stability is upsloping; the deficits which occur with substantial unemployment give way to surpluses as full employment is approached. The surplus which is realized at a 100 percent utilization rate is called simply a *full-employment surplus.* Now we must recognize that, given a particular fiscal program or budget line, the absolute size of the full-employment surplus will rise over time, for the simple reason that ours is a growing economy and the full-employment (100 percent utilization rate) GNP will be larger and larger each successive year. For example, if GNP expands by 4 or 5 percent per year, tax revenues and, given government expenditures, the size of the full-employment surplus will grow by some $12 to $15 billion per year. Of course, this growth in the full-employment surplus is desirable if inflation is being incurred, that is, if the growth in GNP is monetary rather than real. But if there is little or no inflation and real GNP is growing by 4 or 5

[9]Speech before the Economics Club of New York, Dec. 14, 1962, printed in *Congressional Record,* Jan. 15, 1963.

[10]*Economic Report of the President, 1966,* p. 34.

[11]In Chapter 19 we will encounter the minority view of the "monetarists" who feel that there is no convincing evidence that the 1964 tax cut worked as described here.

percent each year, this automatic $12 or $15 billion expansion in the Federal budgetary surplus will have a contractionary impact upon the economy, tending to choke off economic expansion and precipitate unemployment. This possibility, which has been dubbed the *fiscal drag,* suggests that the very built-in stabilizers which cushion the economy during a recession may prove to be a mixed blessing, because during periods of substantial growth budget surpluses automatically appear and tend to inhibit the further expansion of real output.

Fortunately, there are obvious means by which the potentially undesirable consequences of a fiscal drag can be offset. In particular, the retarding effects of a fiscal drag can be avoided by simply not allowing the $12 to $15 billion potential annual growth in tax revenue to be realized. That is, the government can take steps over time to push the budget line downward so as to reduce the absolute size of the full-employment surplus. This can be achieved by (1) lowering tax rates, (2) increasing Federal expenditures, or (3) making Federal grants to the states and localities which they might use in coping with the expanding problems they face. This third option, you will recall, is the essence of the Heller Plan (Chapter 9).

SOME REFINEMENTS

The built-in stabilizers have undoubtedly played an important role in cushioning fluctuations in output, income, employment, and prices. Yet economists are in general agreement that the correction of significant business-cycle movements will require discretionary fiscal action by Congress.

A recession-ridden economy can be stimulated by cutting taxes and increasing government spending, that is, by incurring a budget deficit. Higher taxes and decreased government spending can be used to fight inflation; that is, inflations call for surpluses. In addition, the greater a deficit, the greater its expansionary effect. And the greater a surplus, the greater the contractionary impact of government. Now we must add one or two embellishments to these cursory statements of fiscal policy.

Financing deficits and disposing of surpluses

Given the size of a deficit, its expansionary effect upon the economy will depend upon the method by which it is financed. Similarly, given the size of a surplus, its deflationary impact will depend upon its disposition.

Financing deficits: borrowing versus creating new money One usually thinks of borrowing as the obvious means by which government can spend in excess of its receipts or income. That is, government can finance a deficit by selling bonds to the public—to households and to business firms.

Borrowing from individuals will reduce total spending to the degree that households use disposable income which would otherwise be consumed to buy government bonds. Similarly, a portion of the funds used by businesses to buy bonds might otherwise be spent on capital goods or paid out as dividend income which households then might consume. However, the purchase of government bonds is a voluntary act insofar as buyers are concerned. And it is not likely that households will greatly restrict their standard of living, or businesses their investment plans, in order to buy government bonds. The poor man simply will not be able or willing to purchase bonds, and the bond purchases of the rich man will be made mostly out of funds which otherwise would have been saved in some other form. The point is this: Borrowing from the public reduces the anti-depression impact of a government deficit to the extent that consumption and investment spending are reduced by the borrowing. But in all probability these declines in private spending will not be particularly great.

Government has a second basic means of financing a deficit. This method of finance is to *create new money.* In its simplest terms we can think of Congress authorizing the printing of the paper money needed to finance the deficit. By financing in this way, government can avoid the depressing effects upon consumption and investment which borrowing from the public may have. Printing and spending new money permit increased government spending which does

not entail direct reductions in private spending. For this reason it is a more expansionary method than borrowing in financing a deficit.

It is noteworthy that past experiences of the United States and of other nations have led the public to look upon financing of deficits by running the printing presses with profound distrust. We will discover in Chapter 17 that government can accomplish the same results by borrowing from (selling bonds to) central banks.

Disposing of a surplus: debt retirement versus an idle surplus Inflation calls for fiscal action by government which will result in a budget surplus. However, the anti-inflationary effect of this surplus depends upon what government does with it. Generally speaking, government can dispose of a surplus in one of two ways. Let us assess these options.

First, in view of the fact that the Federal government has an outstanding debt of some $389 billion, it is logical that government should use a surplus to retire outstanding debt. The anti-inflationary impact of a surplus, however, may be reduced somewhat by this. In retiring debt held by the general public, the government transfers its surplus tax revenues into the hands of households and businesses that *might* in turn spend these funds on consumer and capital goods. But this potential increase in private spending should not be exaggerated. In all probability a sizable portion of the surplus funds received by households and businesses as their bonds mature will be used to purchase private securities rather than goods and services. In brief, debt retirement will lessen the anti-inflationary impact of a surplus to the degree that holders of maturing bonds spend the surplus funds they receive. In all likelihood these increases in private spending will not be very large.

On the other hand, government can realize a greater anti-inflationary impact from its budgetary surplus by simply impounding the surplus funds, that is, by allowing them to stand idle. An impounded surplus means that the government is extracting and withholding purchasing power from the income-expenditure stream. If surplus tax revenues are not reinjected into the economy, there is no possibility of the surplus being spent. That is, there is no chance that the funds will create inflationary pressure to offset the deflationary impact of the surplus itself.

Types of expenditures and taxes

The expansionary impact of a deficit and the anti-inflationary significance of a surplus depend in part upon the types of taxes and expenditures employed.

Purchases versus transfers Generally speaking, there are two types of government disbursements: expenditures on goods and services and transfer payments. The former includes defense spending and what the man in the street terms "public works" projects—the building of dams, highways, parks, and public buildings. Transfer payments refer to unemployment compensation payments, subsidies to businesses, interest on the public debt, and the like.

Economists agree that government expenditures are subject to a larger multiplier effect and thus stimulate the NNP more than would transfer payments of the same amount. The reason for this can be seen by referring to Table 13·2, which describes the multiplier process. In the case of government expenditures the initial increase in spending of, say, $5 billion obviously gives rise to an increase in output (for example, the construction of highways, parks, and so forth) of $5 billion *and* will also induce another $15 billion increase in consumption. The total increase in output and real income is clearly $20 billion, indicating a multiplier of 4. But in the case of a $5 billion increase in transfer payments we must remember that, by definition, transfers themselves do *not* give rise to output. For example, if Congress increases social security payments to retired workers by $5 billion, the recipients obviously do not provide $5 billion worth of goods and services in return. However, the $5 billion received by these senior citizens will induce the $15 billion consumption chain reaction, as shown in Table 13·2. Thus the $5 billion transfer payment increases total output by only $15 billion, so the multiplier associated with the transfer payment is only 3.

Caution: The above conclusion that government

expenditures will tend to provide a greater stimulus to the economy than would the same volume of transfers assumes that government expenditures will be judicious, in the sense that they do not entail projects which will discourage and displace private investment.

The deflationary impacts of different taxes What about taxes? Because they tap potential purchasing power from the income-expenditures stream, all taxes tend to be deflationary. But, given the size of government's tax collections, some taxes seem to be more deflationary than others. Most economists feel that consumption taxes—excises and sales taxes—are more deflationary than are personal and corporate income taxes. In other words, regressive taxation is thought to depress private spending more than does progressive taxation. It must be added, however, that this conclusion is not universally accepted. Some authorities contend that although regressive taxation may dampen consumer spending more than does progressive taxation, heavy taxes on corporate income might entail considerable reduction in business investment. Hence, they conclude that corporate and personal income taxation cause a greater decline in consumption and investment combined than do sales and excise taxes.

SOME COMPLICATIONS

Unfortunately, there is a great deal of difference between fiscal policy on paper and fiscal policy in practice. It is therefore imperative that we examine some specific problems which may be encountered in enacting and applying appropriate fiscal policy.

Problems of timing

Several problems of timing may arise in connection with fiscal policy.

1. It is very difficult to predict accurately the future course of economic activity. Business forecasting is a very imperfect science. The result is that fiscal policy is typically put into effect only after recession or inflation is upon us. The inability to predict upswings and downswings injects a time lag between the economic illness and the fiscal medicine.

2. The expenditure aspect of fiscal policy is lacking in flexibility. Spending on public works—the construction of dams, interstate highways, and so forth —entails long planning periods and even longer periods of construction. Such spending is of questionable usefulness in offsetting short—for example, six- or eighteen-month—periods of recession.

3. The wheels of democratic government are often slow in turning. The $11 billion tax cut which became law in February of 1964 was first proposed by President Kennedy in late 1962. The 1968 surcharge on personal and corporate incomes was enacted approximately a year after it was requested by President Johnson. Indeed, Congress has on occasion consumed so much time in adjusting fiscal policy that the economic situation has taken a turnabout in the interim, thereby rendering the policy action completely inappropriate.

A frequent proposal is that Congress give the President limited authority to alter tax rates for purposes of countercyclical fiscal policy and thereby circumvent time-consuming congressional debate. Opponents argue that the proposal transfers an important function of the legislative branch to the executive branch of government and disturbs the "balance of power" between the two.

Political problems

Fiscal policy is created in the political arena. Will political considerations outweigh economic factors in the formation of fiscal policy? Given the general unpopularity of tax increases, can Congress be expected to increase tax rates quickly and sufficiently when severe inflation is encountered? Even if Congress quickly agrees upon needed tax increases, might its efforts founder on disagreement as to what specific types of taxes are to be raised? Can Congress reasonably be expected to reach agreement as to what specific types of expenditures should be trimmed (for example, highway construction, agricultural research, education) during inflation? More

generally put, is the public willing to accept, and the politician to enact, the fiscal cures which inflation and deflation require? There is no simple answer here. But at a minimum it must be noted that the democratic political processes simply do not lend themselves to the making of such decisions quickly and smoothly. "Ineffectual or undesirable changes, or more likely, fiscal inertia, may often result from the interaction of political considerations."[12]

The historical record with respect to fiscal action is mixed. Prior to the 1964 tax cut, Congress had been reluctant to employ tax changes for countercyclical purposes. And in general, the discretionary increases in government spending invoked during recessions have been tardy in timing and probably too modest in size. Furthermore, sudden and substantial changes in government military outlays have on balance exerted a *destabilizing* influence on the economy.[13] On the other hand, the increasing economic literacy of the general public and the business community—not to mention congressmen and Presidents—may have paved the way for more appropriate and more timely fiscal action in the future. The tax cut of 1964 gives us reason to be optimistic.

State and local finance

From the viewpoint of the economy as a whole it would be desirable for the fiscal policies of all levels of government—Federal, state, and local—to be of a countercyclical nature. Unfortunately, this is not the case. State and local finance often tend to reinforce, rather than alleviate, cyclical fluctuations. State and local governments do most of their spending for schools, libraries, and streets and highways during prosperity. As is true of households and private businesses, they cut expenditures and sometimes even retire debt during depression. The 1930s provide an excellent illustration of how declines in state and local expenditures partially negated increases in Federal spending designed to boost the economy from the Great Depression. In the 1930–1934 period total state and local expenditures declined steadily from $8.2 billion to $6.4 billion, thereby canceling a sizable portion of the $3.6 billion increase in Federal spending which occurred in the same period. At the other extreme, state and local governments have on occasion cut taxes during periods of inflationary pressure.

The reasons for the perverse nature of state and local finance are many: the weaker credit standings of state and local governments, the relative instability of state and local tax systems, statutory or constitutional limits on their debts, and a rather widespread belief in the alleged virtues of an annually balanced budget all contribute to the procyclical character of state and local finance.

Public debt

Countercyclical fiscal policy suggests the possibility of budget deficits. And, as a matter of fact, sizable and quite persistent deficits have given rise to a large public debt. In the next chapter we probe the causes and consequences of this debt.

SUMMARY

1. Government responsibility for achieving and maintaining full employment is set forth in the Employment Act of 1946. The Council of Economic Advisors (CEA) was established to advise the President on policies appropriate to fulfilling the goals of the act.

2. Increases in government spending expand, and decreases contract, the equilibrium NNP. Conversely, increases in taxes reduce, and decreases expand, the equilibrium NNP. Appropriate fiscal policy therefore calls for increases in government spending and decreases in taxes—that is, for a budget deficit—to correct for unemployment. Decreases in government spending and increases in taxes—that is, a budget surplus—is appropriate fiscal policy for correcting inflation.

3. The balanced-budget multiplier indicates that equal increases in government spending and taxation will increase the equilibrium NNP.

[12] Joint Economic Committee, *Staff Report on Employment, Growth, and Price Levels* (Washington, 1960), p. 209.
[13] Ibid., chap. 8.

4. Built-in stability refers to the fact that net taxes rise and fall with the level of business activity. Progressive or proportional tax systems lower the MPC and the multiplier, thereby lessening the change in NNP associated with a given change in spending.

5. A fiscal program which embodies built-in stabilizers is reflected in an upsloping budget line. The operation of the stabilizers is represented by movements along the budget line; these movements make it clear that the actual budget deficit or surplus incurred in a given year depends upon *a.* the fiscal program and *b.* the level of GNP. Discretionary fiscal policy shifts the budget line. The larger the full-employment surplus associated with a budget line, the less expansionary is the fiscal program upon which the line is based.

6. As GNP grows over time, the absolute size of the full-employment surplus associated with a given fiscal program will increase. Unless taxes are cut or government expenditures or grants to states and localities are increased, this growing surplus may become a "fiscal drag" upon the economy by contributing to unemployment and retarding the rate of growth.

7. Financing a government deficit through the creation of new money is more expansionary than financing the same deficit by borrowing. A surplus is more deflationary when impounded by government than it is when used to retire outstanding public debt.

8. The multiplier associated with an increase in government spending is greater than that associated with an increase in transfer payments. Similarly, sales and excise taxes are generally felt to be more deflationary than are personal and corporate income taxes.

9. The enactment and application of appropriate fiscal policy are subject to certain problems and questions. Some of the most important are these: *a.* Can the enactment and application of fiscal policy be better timed so as to maximize its effectiveness in heading off economic fluctuations? *b.* Can the economy rely upon Congress to enact appropriate fiscal policy? *c.* State and local finance generally work to intensify rather than alleviate the cycle.

QUESTIONS AND STUDY SUGGESTIONS

1. Explain graphically the determination of equilibrium NNP through both the aggregate demand–aggregate supply approach and the saving-equals-investment approach for the private sector. Now add government spending and taxation, showing the impact of each upon the equilibrium NNP.

2. Refer to the tabular data for question 7 at the end of Chapter 13. Now, assuming investment is $16 billion, incorporate government into the table by assuming that it plans to tax and spend $20 billion at each possible level of NNP. Assume all taxes are personal taxes and that government spending does not entail shifts in the consumption and investment schedules. Explain the changes in the equilibrium NNP which the addition of government entails.

3. What is the balanced-budget multiplier? Explain: "Equal increases in government spending and tax revenues of *n* dollars will increase the equilibrium NNP by *n* dollars." Does this hold true regardless of the size of the MPS?

4. Distinguish between discretionary fiscal policy and the built-in stabilizers. Explain how discretionary fiscal policy can be used to close inflationary and deflationary gaps.

5. Assume that in the absence of any taxes the consumption schedule for an economy is as follows:

NNP, billions	Consumption, billions
$100	$120
200	200
300	280
400	360
500	440
600	520
700	600

a. Graph this consumption schedule and note the size of the MPC.

b. Assume now a regressive tax system is imposed such

that the government collects $10 billion in taxes at all levels of NNP. Calculate the tax rate at each level of NNP. Graph the resulting consumption schedule and compare the MPC with that of the pretax consumption schedule.

c. Now suppose a proportional tax system with a 10 percent tax rate is imposed instead of the regressive system. Calculate the new consumption schedule, graph it, and note the MPC.

d. Finally, impose a progressive tax system such that the tax rate is zero percent when NNP is $100, 5 percent at $200, 10 percent at $300, 15 percent at $400, and so forth. Determine and graph the new consumption schedule, noting the effect of this tax system on the MPC.

e. Explain why the proportional and progressive tax systems contribute to greater economic stability, while the regressive system does not. Demonstrate graphically.

6. Use a budget line to explain the functioning of the built-in stabilizers. Show how ***a.*** a tax cut and ***b.*** a decrease in government spending would affect the budget line. Define the "full-employment surplus" and explain its significance.

7. Explain: "The actual deficit or surplus realized in a given year depends upon the budget line *and* the level of economic activity." Discuss the rationale underlying the 1964 tax cut. What is a "fiscal drag"? How might its effects be offset?

8. What is the best method of financing a government deficit during depression? What is the best means of disposing of a surplus during inflation? Explain your answers.

9. "If the economy needs $10 billion with which to finance the expansion and improvement of its highways, it should simply print up the needed money to finance the undertaking. In this way we'll get the roads, and no one will be hurt by having to pay higher taxes." Evaluate this suggestion, first under conditions of full employment, and second under depressed conditions.

10. Briefly state and evaluate the major problems encountered in enacting and applying fiscal policy. Which do you feel are the most significant?

11. Evaluate: "Rising prices cause real incomes to fall. In such circumstances all levels of government should cut taxes. This will permit the American people to maintain their standard of living."

12. *Advanced analysis.* We can add the public sector to the private economy model of question 10 at the end of Chapter 13 as follows. Assume $G = G_o = 28$ and $T = T_o = 30$. Because of the presence of taxes, the consumption schedule, $C = 50 + 0.8Y$, must be modified to read $C = 50 + 0.8(Y - T)$, where the term $(Y - T)$ is disposable (after-tax) income. Assuming all taxes are on personal income, investment remains $I = I_o = 30$. Using the equilibrium condition $Y = C + I + G$, determine the equilibrium level of income. Explain why the addition of the public budget with a slight surplus *increases* the equilibrium income. Now substitute $T = 0.2Y$ for $T = T_o = 30$, and solve again for the level of income.

SELECTED REFERENCES

Economic Issues, 4th ed., reading 23.

Economic Report of the President (Washington, published annually in January).

Heller, Walter W.: *New Dimensions of Political Economy* (New York: W. W. Norton & Company, Inc., 1967).

Sharp, Ansel M., and Bernard F. Sliger: *Public Finance,* rev. ed. (Austin, Tex.: Business Publications, Inc., 1970), chaps. 7–10.

Slesinger, Reuben E.: *National Economic Policy: The Presidential Reports* (Princeton, N.J.: D. Van Nostrand Company, Inc.,1968).

Thurow, Lester C. (ed.): *American Fiscal Policy* (Engelwood Cliffs, N.J.: Prentice-Hall, Inc., 1967).

Ulmer, Melville J.: *The Welfare State: U.S.A.* (Boston: Houghton Mifflin Company, 1969).

15

FISCAL POLICY AND THE PUBLIC DEBT

Fiscal policy is a cause of great concern to the populace because it suggests the sometime economic desirability of deficits. Deficits mean debt, and debt—particularly when measured in terms of hundreds of billions of dollars—is a most worrisome phenomenon. It is the basic purpose of this chapter to explore the causes and consequences of the public debt and, more particularly, to explode many of the fallacies associated with its existence. As a preliminary matter, we want to trace the evolution of several alternative budget policies and assess their capacities to stabilize the economy.

THREE BUDGET PHILOSOPHIES

A basic tenet of modern fiscal policy is that unbalanced budgets are helpful in stabilizing the economy. Surpluses—or, more accurately, greater surpluses or smaller deficits—are appropriate in tempering inflation. Deficits—or, again more accurately, larger deficits or smaller surpluses—are needed to cushion recessions. We can deepen our understanding of unbalanced budgets by exploring several alternative budget philosophies.

Generally speaking, there are three prevailing budget philosophies. The most conservative—not to say reactionary—policy is that which advocates an *annually* balanced budget. At the other extreme is *functional finance,* the most liberal view; it assigns a secondary priority to balancing the Federal budget annually or over any other time period. Standing between the two is the idea of a *cyclically* balanced budget, wherein the Federal budget is to be balanced over the course of the business cycle rather than annually.

Annually balanced budget

Until the Great Depression of the 1930s the annually balanced budget was generally accepted without question as a desirable goal of public finance. An

incorrect identification of private and public finance and widespread belief in the classical theory of employment both fostered this acceptance.

Upon examination, however, it becomes evident that an annually balanced budget largely rules out government fiscal activity as a countercyclical force. Worse yet, an annually balanced budget actually intensifies the business cycle. To illustrate, suppose that the economy encounters a siege of unemployment and falling incomes. As we have already noted, in such circumstances tax receipts will automatically decline. In seeking to balance its budget, government must either (1) increase tax rates, (2) reduce government expenditures, or (3) employ a combination of these two. It is obvious that all these policies are deflationary; each one further dampens rather than stimulates the level of aggregate demand.

Similarly, an annually balanced budget will intensify inflation. As money incomes rise during the course of inflation, tax collections will automatically increase. To avoid the impending surplus, government must either (1) cut tax rates, (2) increase government expenditures, or (3) adopt a combination of both. It is clear that all three of these policies will add to inflationary pressures.

The basic conclusion, then, is evident: *An annually balanced budget is not economically neutral; the pursuit of such a policy is procyclical, not countercyclical.*

Cyclically balanced budget

The Great Depression, general acceptance of Keynesian employment theory, and the recognition that public and private finance are not entirely comparable all contributed to the development of the idea of a cyclically balanced budget. This budget philosophy envisions government exerting a countercyclical influence and at the same time balancing its budget. In this case, however, the budget would not be balanced annually—after all, there is nothing sacred about twelve months as an accounting period—but rather over the course of the business cycle.

The rationale of this budget philosophy is simple, plausible, and appealing. To offset depression, government should lower taxes and increase spending, thereby purposely incurring a deficit. During the ensuing inflationary upswing, taxes would be raised and government spending slashed. The resulting surplus could then be used to retire the Federal debt incurred in financing the depression. In this way government fiscal operations would exert a positive countercyclical force, and the government could still balance its budget—not annually, but over a period of years.

A little reflection will reveal one big shortcoming of this budget philosophy which goes far to rob it of much of its luster: The upswing and downswing of the cycle may not be of equal magnitude and duration. Figure 11·3 makes this strikingly clear. In particular the very real possibility of persistent government deficits and a growing public debt arises. For example, should a long and severe depression be followed by a rather modest and brief prosperity, there would be little chance of obtaining surpluses in the good years sufficient to retire the deficits incurred in alleviating the bad years. Or the period of prosperity may be one wherein military considerations call for high levels of government spending, thereby ruling out the possibility of government's realizing a surplus. In brief, although the idea of a cyclically balanced budget looks fine on paper, there is some real question as to whether or not it is workable in practice.

Functional finance

Out of the problems associated with any application of the cyclically balanced budget has evolved the idea of functional finance. According to this budget philosophy, the question of a balanced budget—either annually or cyclically—is of secondary importance. The primary purpose of Federal finance is to provide for noninflationary full employment. If the attainment of this objective entails either persistent surpluses or a large and growing public debt, so be it. The problems involved in government deficits or surpluses are relatively minor compared with the extremely unsavory alternatives of prolonged depression or severe inflation. The Federal budget is first and foremost an instrument for achieving and maintaining a noninfla-

tionary full-employment level of output. Government should not hesitate to incur any deficits and surpluses required in achieving this goal. In response to those who express concern about the large Federal debt which the pursuit of functional finance might entail, proponents of this budget philosophy offer three arguments. First, they contend that the problems of a large Federal debt are not as burdensome as most people think. In particular, public debt does not involve the same problems as does private debt. Second, the government's ability to finance deficits is almost unlimited. The credit standing of the government is exceedingly good; hence, the government should have no difficulty in borrowing. Furthermore, if its credit standing should somehow deteriorate, the government has the power to create money for the financing of deficits by running the printing presses. Finally, recalling Figure 14·5, proponents of functional finance point out that, given a fiscal system characterized by built-in stability, the successful application of functional finance will in fact tend to bring about budgetary surpluses rather than deficits.

Over the years tremendous changes have occurred in our thinking concerning public finance. Worship of a small and annually balanced budget has given way to the notion that government expenditures and taxes should be manipulated so as to compensate for any substantial deficiency or excess of private spending in promoting full employment without inflation. Further, the budget should be balanced cyclically, or, if this is not feasible, not at all. In general the contention that government finance should be based upon "sound financial principles"—implicitly those principles which apply to private finance—has been largely supplanted by a recognition of the fact that public and private finance are so different as to be incomparable.

THE PUBLIC DEBT

Because modern fiscal policy stresses unbalanced budgets, its application will quite possibly lead to substantial growth in the public debt. Let us consider the public debt and the real and imaginary problems associated with its growth.

It has been said in reference to the public debt that "Never have so many understood so little about so much." To a very considerable degree this statement is true. The public debt is surrounded by awe, ignorance, and, in the extreme, outright fear. It is vital that we accurately comprehend the size, significance, and real problems associated with it. In doing so we must be particularly alert for false impressions and inappropriate analogies and comparisons.

Dimensions of debt

Growth of the public debt, as Table 15·1 indicates, has been substantial since 1930. *The primary cause of this expansion was the financing of World War II, rather than deficits incurred as a result of countercyclical fiscal policy.* In 1929, on the eve of the Great Depression, the public debt stood at $16.3 billion. At the end of the depressed thirties (1940) the debt had grown to $50.9 billion. The debt clearly expanded by a considerable amount as the result of deficits incurred in the 1930s. But this growth is dwarfed by the more than fivefold increase of the World War II era. Much of the postwar increase in the debt can be traced to the Korean and Vietnam wars and to recessions which have caused the national income and therefore tax revenues to be lower than planned (see Figure 14·5).

There is no denying it: The absolute size of the public debt is so large—$389.2 billion in 1970—as to be almost beyond comprehension. But we must not fear large numbers per se. Let us therefore put the size of the public debt in better perspective.

1. A bald statement of the absolute size of the debt glosses over the fact that the wealth and productive ability of our economy have also increased tremendously over the years. It is safe to say that a wealthy nation has greater ability to incur and carry a large public debt than does a poor nation. In other words, it seems more realistic to measure changes in the public debt *in relation to* changes in the economy's GNP. Column 5 in Table 15·1 presents such data. Note that instead of the almost eightfold increase in the debt between 1940 and 1970 shown in column 2, we now find that the debt has not grown at all!

TABLE 15·1 QUANTITATIVE SIGNIFICANCE OF THE PUBLIC DEBT: THE PUBLIC DEBT AND INTEREST PAYMENTS IN RELATION TO GNP, 1929–1970

(1) Year	(2) Public debt, billions	(3) Gross national product,* billions	(4) Interest payments, billions	(5) Public debt as percent of GNP, (2) ÷ (3)	(6) Interest payments as percent of GNP, (4) ÷ (3)	(7) Per capita public debt
1929	$ 16.3	$103.1	$ 0.7	16%	0.7%	$ 134
1940	50.9	99.7	1.1	51	1.1	382
1942	112.5	157.9	1.3	71	0.8	833
1946	259.5	208.5	4.2	124	2.0	1,827
1950	256.7	284.8	4.5	90	1.6	1,689
1954	278.8	364.8	5.0	76	1.4	1,404
1958	283.0	447.3	5.6	63	1.3	1,617
1960	290.4	503.7	7.1	58	1.4	1,604
1962	304.0	560.3	7.2	54	1.3	1,626
1964	318.7	632.4	8.3	50	1.3	1,651
1966	329.3	749.9	11.2	44	1.5	1,672
1968	358.0	865.0	13.7	41	1.6	1,779
1970	389.2	976.5	18.3	40	1.9	1,895

* In current dollars; 1970 data are preliminary.
Source: *Economic Report of the President* (Washington, 1971).

As a matter of fact, the *relative* size of the debt has *declined* very considerably since 1946. And this ratio of Federal debt to GNP, incidentally, is small when compared with similar ratios for other advanced nations. Note, too, in column 7 that the per capita size of the public debt is about the same as at the close of World War II.

2. As we shall see in a moment, many economists feel that the primary burden of the debt is the annual interest charge that accrues as a result of the debt. The absolute size of these interest payments is shown in column 4. Interest charges as a percentage of GNP are presented in column 6. In these latter terms the burden of the debt has increased by very small amounts over the last four decades, and currently is slightly less than the 1946 figure. The failure of this ratio to fall significantly in the last twenty years reflects the phenomenon of rising interest rates much more than a rising debt.

3. Although the size and growth of public debt are looked upon with awe and alarm, private debt has grown much faster. Private and public debt were of about equal size in 1947. But private debt has grown much faster and is now over three times as large—about $1,350 billion, compared with $389 billion—as the public debt. If one insists upon worrying about debt, you will do well to concern yourself with private rather than public indebtedness.

Let us turn now from the causes and size of the debt to the question of ownership. The basic point here is that the public debt is *internally* held; that is, it is held by American citizens and American

institutions. This, as we shall see shortly, is of considerable importance, because the problems posed by an *externally* held debt, that is, a public debt which is held by foreign individuals, foreign institutions, and foreign governments, are different from those of an internally held debt.

Public and private debt

But this brings us to another consideration: The debts of individuals and the public debt are not readily comparable. Public debt is basically a macroeconomic concept and private debt a microeconomic concept. The fallacy of composition reminds us that different principles may govern macro and micro concepts. More specifically, one must be very cautious in applying the principles and practices surrounding private debt to the public debt. Much misunderstanding of the significance and burden of the public debt stems from such a misguided application. Let us be more specific.

Characteristics of private debt The debts of private individuals are owed by one person to some other individual or organization. In incurring such debt, the individual obtains funds which expand his dollar claims over output and permit him to currently increase his standard of living. But individuals are mortal, and creditors will demand repayment of loans at some future date. This repayment obviously invokes a decline in the debtor's ability to obtain goods and services and a reduction in his standard of living.

Characteristics of public debt Public debt differs on all counts. First, the public debt is a debt which we—American citizens and institutions—owe to ourselves. Whereas a private debt is one between distinct economic units, a public debt is one held within a single economic unit. Strictly speaking, the public debt is owed by the United States government to bondholding citizens and institutions—banks, insurance companies, and businesses—within the United States. But should the government decide to retire this debt, how would the needed funds be obtained? By collecting taxes from American citizens and institutions. Hence, the public debt is one which we owe to one another. Were the public debt externally held, that is, held by foreigners, it would be like a private debt—a debt between distinct economic units—and this owe-it-to-ourselves characteristic would not be applicable.

Second, nations—not to mention large corporations—are quite immortal, and there is no compelling reason why their debt need be retired. Indeed, as Table 15·1 suggests, no serious attempt has been made in recent decades to reduce the public debt. As a relatively small portion of the total debt falls due each month or year, the government does not cut expenditures or boost taxes to provide funds for *retiring* the debt. (Indeed, we know that with depressed economic conditions this would be a most unwise fiscal policy.) Rather, the government sells new bonds and uses the proceeds to pay off holders of the maturing bonds. Debt *refunding* is a less troublesome task both economically and politically than is debt retirement.

Furthermore, the owe-it-to-ourselves character of the public debt tells us that even if the public debt were to be retired, there would be no direct loss of wealth for the economy as a whole. Retirement of the public debt would call for a gigantic transfer payment whereby American individuals and institutions would pay higher taxes and the government in turn would pay out those tax revenues to those same taxpaying individuals and institutions in the aggregate in redeeming the bonds which they hold. Although a redistribution of wealth would result from this gigantic financial transfer, it need not entail any immediate decline in the economy's aggregate wealth or standard of living. The repayment of an internally held public debt entails no leakage of purchasing power from the economy of the country as a whole.

There is a final significant distinction between individual and public debt. If you or I as individuals were to increase or reduce our indebtedness, the impact of so doing upon the economy would be negligible. But the Federal government is obviously so large relative to the economy that changes in its debt can and do have very substantial effects upon the economic health of society. Indeed, fiscal policy is predicated upon this fact.

Debt burdens and war finance

There are many gross misconceptions concerning the burden or disadvantages associated with the public debt. The crucial question is: What costs or disadvantages are imposed upon the economy when government expenditures are financed by borrowing rather than taxation?

The cost of an increase in the public debt depends upon the economic conditions under which it is incurred. If the public debt is increased during a period of substantial unemployment, the real cost of the debt is zero. Why? Because the expansionary effect of the deficit puts idle resources back to work, and the resulting increase in the national output is all a net gain. No alternative products are sacrificed, and therefore no real costs are involved in putting idle resources back to work by increasing the debt. We have noted in Table 15·1 that both the absolute size of the debt and the strength of the economy have grown historically. As a matter of fact, *some of the economy's healthiest periods of expansion and growth in real output have occurred at times when the public debt was increasing most rapidly.* It is no mystery why this is so: a budget deficit means a net injection of purchasing power into the economy by government, and this, of course, is expansionary.

Deficit spending during full employment is a different matter. In the first place, we know that such spending is completely inappropriate insofar as stabilization policy is concerned. Yet during the full-employment years of World War II, when the bulk of our present public debt was incurred, government found that it was neither politically nor economically feasible to finance the war on a pay-as-you-go basis through taxation. Borrowing was chosen as the best alternative to supplement taxes that were considered to be at the upper limit of the economy's tolerance. This spending pulled resources from the production of private goods to the production of armaments. The burden of deficit spending during full employment is that alternative private goods—in this case automobiles, refrigerators, vacuum cleaners, and a host of other consumer goods—were not produced.

These observations answer a frequently heard question: Does government borrowing as a method of finance permit society to pass a portion of the economic cost of a war to future generations? Certainly not if government borrows internally, that is, from people and institutions within the country. It is the wartime generation itself which must tighten its civilian standard of living in order to free scarce resources for the production of armaments. There is no way of sidestepping or postponing these costs. Putting the matter in specific terms, it was the population living during 1941–1946 which did without a multitude of consumer durables to permit the United States to arm itself and its allies.

In money, or financial, terms the waging of World War II increased the public debt by well over $200 billion. Is this not a financial burden for future generations to bear? For the economy as a whole, no. The making of interest and principal payments on the war-born portion of the public debt will constitute transfers of funds from future Americans as taxpayers to future Americans as bondholders. Such a financial transfer, as we have already seen, does not entail a direct decline in the total wealth of that future generation. The fact that each American baby born in 1972 may be, say, $1,900 or $2,000 in debt at the time he enters the world is not quite as disturbing as it sounds. Each member of the 1972 baby crop will also inherit, on the average, ownership of that same amount in government bonds. The higher taxes *paid* by our grandchildren in paying interest and principal on the war-incurred public debt will be *received* by that same group of grandchildren. In short, the real economic cost of a war must be shouldered at the time the war is being fought.

There is one notable exception: The emergency of wartime production may cause a nation's stock of capital to cease to grow or to dwindle as precious resources are taken from the production of capital goods and shifted to the production of war goods. As a result, future generations inherit a smaller stock of capital goods than would otherwise be the case. This occurred in the United States during World War II (see table on inside covers, line 2). But this shifting of costs is independent of how a war is financed. Whereas an internally held public debt is a debt

existing within an economic unit (a nation), an externally held public debt is a debt between distinct economic units (two nations). As a result, an externally held public debt has the characteristics of a private debt. Hence, a nation can ease the immediate economic burden of a war by obtaining loans from other nations and spending the proceeds on the goods and services of the lending nation. Imports thus received supplement the borrowing nation's standard of living and ease the wartime strain on its own resources. But the tables are turned when time for repayment of the loan rolls around, say, twenty years later. The borrowing nation must then make enough of its currency available to the lending nation to retire its matured bonds. The lending nation spends these funds in acquiring a portion of the borrowing nation's GNP. In other words, the generation living at the time the bonds fall due must tighten their belts to make goods and services available for repayment of a loan incurred some twenty years earlier. A portion of the real economic cost of a war has been shifted two decades into the future by increasing a nation's externally held public debt.

Real burden of the debt

But we must be careful not to whitewash the public debt. The existence of a large public debt does pose real and potential problems.

Incentives Table 15·1 makes evident the fact that the present public debt necessitates an annual interest payment of over $18 billion. With no increase in the size of the debt, this annual interest charge must be paid out of tax revenues. Taxes may tend to dampen incentives to bear risk, to innovate, to invest, and to work. In this indirect way the existence of a large debt can impair economic growth.

Income inequality In all probability the payment of interest and principal on the public debt contributes to income inequality. Common sense and available statistical evidence concerning the income status of savers suggest that most government bondholders are in the middle- and upper-income brackets. On the other hand, under the prevailing tax structure the revenue needed to pay interest and principle on the debt would come rather evenly from all income groups (see Table 9·6). In all probability the net result of interest or principal repayment is greater income inequality, held by many to be undesirable on equity grounds.

A word of caution: In weighing the possible impact of the public debt upon incentives and the personal distribution of income, two points should be kept in mind. First, the size of the annual interest charge on the debt is relatively small—about 1.9 percent of the GNP. Second, the relative size of this interest charge has been fairly stable for the last twenty-five years. Actually, it has declined slightly since 1946.

Debt, liquidity, and inflation The very existence of a large debt tends to be inflationary. This is so for at least two reasons:

1. Because they are highly liquid assets, the possession of government bonds makes consumers feel wealthier. This feeling of wealth leads to greater consumption out of their incomes. In short, the existence of a large public debt tends to shift the consumption schedule upward. If the economy is already at full employment, this shift will be inflationary.

2. Furthermore, government bonds can be converted into money easily and with little or no risk of loss. Government bonds, therefore, constitute a potential backlog of purchasing power which can add materially to inflationary fires. During periods of inflation it is very tempting for consumers to dig into this reserve of purchasing power in an attempt to beat rising prices. Such an attempt to beat inflation will cause more inflation. Something like this happened at the end of World War II; the inflation-causing buying spree of 1946–1947 was financed partly by the cashing in of bonds purchased during the war.

But the contention that a large public debt has an inflationary bias must be qualified. First, *changes* in the size of the public debt have a much greater impact upon employment, output, and the price level than does the *absolute size* of the existing debt. Thus a $5 billion increase in the debt can be expected to exert a much greater expansionary or inflationary effect on the economy than the mere presence of

an existing debt of, say, $389 billion. Furthermore, remember that deficit spending is inflationary only if it is inappropriate fiscal policy. Deficit spending under full-employment conditions is inflationary; but this is ill-advised fiscal policy. Deficit spending during recession is expansionary; it increases employment and output and is therefore well advised.

Wasteful government spending It is frequently argued that wasteful government expenditures are more likely to creep into the Federal budget when deficit financing is readily available. Politicians are motivated to screen expenditures more carefully when they are faced with the delicate problem of financing such programs out of tax increases. The fact that deficit financing gives the illusion of deferring the costs of government expenditures makes it easier for projects of dubious merit to find their way into the budget.

Debt management dilemma Every month several billion dollars worth of outstanding government bonds mature and must be refinanced. Decisions made in managing the public debt may have a significant impact upon the stability of the economy and may be at odds with countercyclical fiscal policy.

The basic dilemma is between the Treasury's desire for low interest costs, on the one hand, and economic stabilization, on the other. For example, because interest rates tend to fall during the downswing of the cycle, the Treasury can minimize its interest costs by selling long-term bonds during recession periods. But such sales are likely to intensify the recession by driving up interest rates and drawing scarce money capital away from potential private spenders. Similarly, in Chapter 18 we shall find that during inflation the Treasury's desire for low interest rates conflicts with the desire of the monetary authorities to raise interest rates for the purpose of limiting investment and consumer spending.

Advantages of a public debt

There is a brighter side to the public debt. The most significant point to keep in mind is that a *changing* public debt is, or at least should be, a reflection of sound fiscal management for stability. An expansionary fiscal policy designed to stimulate a slack economy will tend to increase the public debt; a contractional fiscal policy designed to cool an overheated, inflationary economy will be mirrored in a decline in the public debt. Furthermore, in at least three respects the very *existence* of a large debt can be desirable.

1. Because government bonds are highly liquid and virtually risk-free securities, they make an excellent purchase for small and conservative savers.
2. It should also be noted that although a large debt may pose inflationary problems in a full-employment economy, the same debt can cushion a cyclical downswing. That which is potentially undesirable in a full-employment economy may be very desirable in a less-than-full-employment economy. A large public debt may prove to be a kind of built-in stabilizer insofar as recessions are concerned.
3. Finally, Chapter 18 will reveal the important role which government bonds play in effectuating monetary policy. The sale and purchase of government bonds by the economy's central banks influence the money supply, the level of spending, and hence the level of economic activity.

DEBT AND STABILITY

In analyzing the details of the public debt and in discussing the real and imagined problems associated therewith, we must not lose sight of the fact that debt—both public and private—plays a positive role in a prosperous and growing economy. We know that as income expands so does saving; indeed, as NNP grows, total saving expands absolutely and as a percentage of NNP. Modern employment theory and fiscal policy tell us that if aggregate demand is to be sustained at the full-employment level, this expanding volume of saving or its equivalent must be obtained and spent by consumers, businesses, or government. The process by which saving is transferred to spenders is debt creation. Now, as a matter of fact, consumers and businesses do borrow and spend a great amount of saving. Private debt has increased spectacularly—much faster than public

debt—since World War II. But if households and businesses are not willing to borrow and thereby increase private debt sufficiently fast to absorb the growing volume of saving, then an increase in public debt must absorb the remainder or the economy will falter from full employment and fail to realize its growth potential.

SUMMARY

1. Historically, the concept of an annually balanced budget has given ground to that of the cyclically balanced budget and, more recently, to the idea of functional finance.

2. The public debt is now $389 billion, about 40 percent of the GNP. The main source of the debt was the financing of World War II.

3. Public debt has different characteristics from individual debt. Public debt **a.** is owed by Americans to Americans, *b.* need not be retired, and *c.* does not entail a reduced standard of living for the economy as a whole when payment of interest or principal is made.

4. The real cost of a war or of a depression cannot be shifted to future generations by increasing the internally held public debt.

5. A large public debt may *a.* impair incentives to innovate and invest, *b.* contribute to income inequality, *c.* add to inflationary pressures, *d.* be conducive to wasteful government spending, and *e.* entail knotty problems of debt management.

6. Debt creation transfers saving to spenders and thereby plays a positive function in maintaining a high level of output and of employment.

QUESTIONS AND STUDY SUGGESTIONS

1. Explain each of the following statements:

a. "No budget-balancing principle can be as important as maintaining full employment and preventing inflation."

b. "A national debt is like a debt of the left hand to the right hand."

c. "Find an individual who is steadily accumulating debt, and you have probably found one who is in trouble; find one who is paying off his debts, and you have probably found one in good economic health. But find a nation whose domestic debts are mounting, whose mortgages year by year are increasing, whose corporate debentures are proliferating, whose state and local and federal bond issues are growing, and chances are that you have found a nation whose rate of growth is high, whose economy is buoyant, whose savings are abundant, whose business is booming."[1]

2. Explain the three major budget philosophies. To which do you subscribe? Why? Why is an annually balanced budget not economically neutral?

3. How do private and public debts differ? How does an internally held public debt differ from an externally held public debt? What would be the effects of retiring an internally held public debt?

[1]Robert L. Heilbroner and Peter L. Bernstein, *A Primer on Government Spending,* 2d ed. (New York: Vintage Books, Random House, Inc., 1970), p. 45.

4. In what ways might the mere existence of a large public debt contribute to inflationary pressures? "Incurring a public debt is more inflationary than carrying an existing public debt." Do you agree?

5. Distinguish clearly between refunding and retiring public debt.

6. Explain: "As a society becomes wealthier, saving increases. If prosperity is to be sustained, the private and public sectors together must borrow and spend an amount sufficient to offset this saving. The expansion of debt is therefore a prerequisite of full employment."

SELECTED REFERENCES

Economic Issues, 4th ed., reading 25.

Bowen, William G., Richard G. Davis, and David H. Kopf: "The Public Debt: A Burden on Future Generations?" *American Economic Review,* September 1960, pp. 701–706.

Buchanan, James M.: *The Public Finances,* rev. ed. (Homewood, Ill,: Richard D. Irwin, Inc., 1965), chaps. 28–30.

Hamovitch, William (ed.): *The Federal Deficit* (Boston: D. C. Heath and Company, 1965).

Heilbroner, Robert L., and Peter L. Bernstein: *A Primer on Government Spending,* 2d ed. (New York: Vintage Books, Random House, Inc., 1970).

MONEY, MONETARY POLICY, AND ECONOMIC STABILITY

3

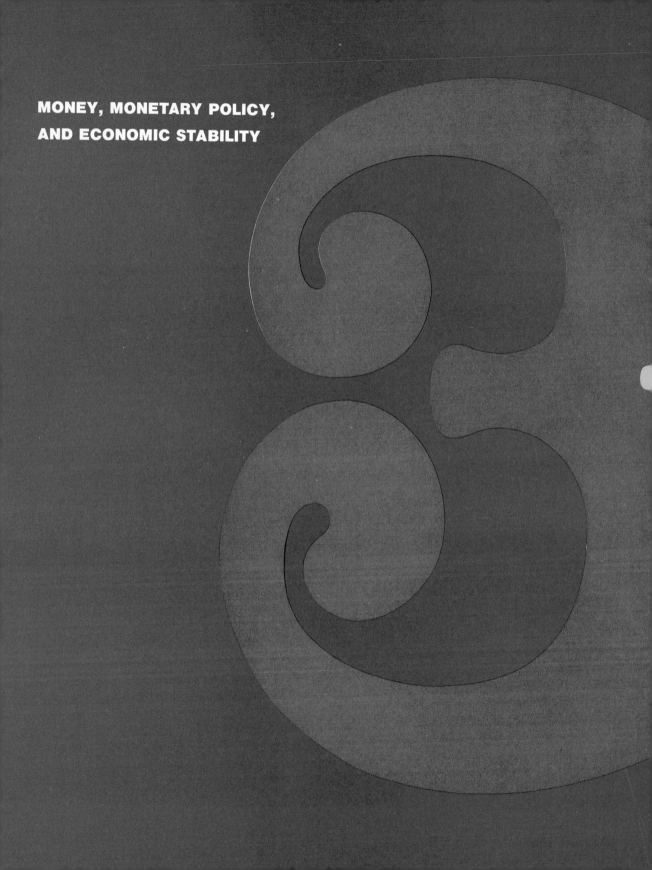

16

MONEY AND BANKING IN AMERICAN CAPITALISM

> Money—one of the truly great inventions of man—constitutes a most fascinating aspect of economic science.[1]

Money bewitches people. They fret for it, and they sweat for it. They devise most ingenious ways to get it, and most ingenuous ways to get rid of it. Money is the only commodity that is good for nothing but to be gotten rid of. It will not feed you, clothe you, shelter you, or amuse you unless you spend it or invest it. It imparts value only in parting. People will do almost anything for money, and money will do almost anything for people. Money is a captivating, circulating, masquerading puzzle.

Money is also one of the most crucial elements of economic science. It is much more than a passive component of the economic system—a mere tool for facilitating the economy's operation. When operating properly, the monetary system is the lifeblood of the circular flows of income and expenditure which typify all economies. A well-behaved money system is conducive to both full production and full employment. Conversely, a malfunctioning monetary system can make major contributions to severe fluctuations in the economy's levels of output, employment, and prices.

In this chapter we are concerned with the nature and functions of money and the basic institutions of the American banking system. Chaper 17 looks into the methods by which individual commercial banks and the banking system as a whole can vary the money supply. In Chapter 18 we discuss how the central banks of the economy attempt to regulate the supply of money so as to promote full employment and price level stability.

The specific objectives of the present chapter are fourfold. We begin with a review of the functions of money. Next we designate and assess the relative importance of the various types of money used in American capitalism. Third, we pose a query: What "backs" money in the United States? Finally, the institutional structure and the basic functions of the American banking system will be described.

[1] Federal Reserve Bank of Philadelphia, "Creeping Inflation," *Business Review,* August 1957, p. 3.

THE FUNCTIONS OF MONEY

What is money? Money is what money does. Anything that performs the functions of money is money. There are three functions of money:

1. First and foremost, money is a *medium of exchange;* that is, money is usable in buying and selling goods and services. As a medium of exchange, money allows society to escape the complications of barter and thereby to reap the benefits of geographic and human specialization (see Chapter 3).

2. Money is also a *standard of value.* Society finds it convenient to use the monetary unit as a yardstick for measuring the relative worth of heterogeneous goods and resources. This has obvious advantages. With a money system, we need not state the price of each product in terms of all other products for which it might possibly be exchanged; that is, we need not state the price of cows in terms of corn, cream, cigars, Chevrolets, cravats, and so forth. This use of money as a common denominator means that the price of each product need *only* be stated in terms of the monetary unit. By dramatically reducing the number of prices in the economy, this use of money permits transactors to readily compare the relative worth of various commodities and resources. Such comparisons facilitate rational decision making. Money is also used as a standard of value for transactions involving future payments. Debt obligations of all kinds are measured in terms of money.

3. Finally, money serves as a *store of value.* Because money is the most liquid of all assets, it is a very convenient form in which to store wealth. Though it does not yield monetary returns such as one gets by storing wealth in the form of real assets (property) or paper assets (stocks, bonds, and so forth), money does have the advantage of being immediately usable by a firm or a household in meeting any and all financial obligations.

MONEY IN AMERICAN CAPITALISM

Historically, such diverse items as whales' teeth, elephant tail bristles, circular stones, nails, slaves, cattle, beer, cigarettes, and pieces of metal have functioned as media of exchange. More recently, the debts of governments and of banks have been employed as money.

Insofar as the United States is concerned, the money supply is composed of only three items: (1) coins, (2) paper money, and (3) demand deposits, or checking accounts. The first two items are debts of government and governmental agencies; the third represents a debt of commercial banks. Table 16·1 shows the quantitative importance of each money item in both absolute and relative terms. Let's comment briefly on each of these components of the money supply.

Coins

Ranging from copper pennies to silver dollars, coins constitute the "small change" of our money supply. As Table 16·1 indicates, coins constitute a very small portion of our total money supply. Coins are essentially "convenience money" in that they permit us to make all kinds of very small purchases.

It is notable that all coins in circulation in the United States are token money. This simply means that the intrinsic value—that is, the value of the bullion contained in the coin itself—is less than the face value of the coin. This is purposely the case so as to avoid the melting down of token money for profitable sale as bullion. If a 50-cent piece contained, say, 75

TABLE 16·1 MONEY IN THE UNITED STATES, JANUARY 1971

Money	Billions of dollars	Percent of total
Coins	$ 6	3
Paper money	42	21
Demand deposits	155	76
Total	$203	100

Source: Federal Reserve Bulletin, February 1971.

cents' worth of silver bullion, it would be highly profitable to melt these coins for sale as bullion. Despite the illegality of such a procedure, 50-cent pieces would tend to disappear from circulation. This is one of the potential defects of commodity money: Its worth as a commodity may come to exceed its worth as money, causing it to cease functioning as a medium of exchange.

Paper money

Much more significant than coins, paper money constitutes about one-fifth of the economy's money supply. Virtually all this $42 billion of paper currency is in the form of *Federal Reserve Notes.* These notes are issued by the Federal Reserve Banks with the authorization of Congress. There are a few minor types of paper money still in existence, but most of them are being retired from use in the interest of a more uniform currency. These minor kinds of paper money are collectively called *Treasury currency* for the simple reason that, at one time or another, they were directly issued by the Treasury. The coin and paper money components of the money supply are frequently lumped together and simply labeled *currency.*

Demand deposits

The safety and convenience of using checks, or bank money, have made demand deposits the most important type of money in the United States. Despite the integrity of our postal employees, one would not think of stuffing, say $4,896.47 in an envelope and dropping it in a mailbox in paying a debt; but to write and mail a check for a large sum is commonplace. A check must be endorsed by the person cashing it; the drawer of the check subsequently receives the canceled check as an endorsed receipt attesting to the fulfillment of his obligation. Similarly, because the writing of a check requires endorsement by the drawer, the theft or loss of one's bankbook is not nearly so calamitous as would be the losing of an identical amount of currency. It is, furthermore, simply more convenient to write a check in many cases than it is to transport and count out a large sum of currency. For all these reasons checkbook money has come to be the dominant form of money in American capitalism. Even Table 16·1 belittles the significance of bank money; it is estimated that dollarwise, about 90 percent of all transactions are carried out by the use of checks.

It might seem strange that demand deposits or checking accounts are a part of the money supply. But the reason for their inclusion is clear: Checks, which are nothing more than a means for transferring the ownership of demand deposits, are generally acceptable as a medium of exchange. Furthermore, demand deposits can be immediately converted into paper money and coins on demand; demand deposits are for all practical purposes the equivalent of currency.

In short,

$$\text{Money} = \text{demand deposits} + \text{currency}$$

Currency is essentially government-created money, and demand deposits, we shall discover in Chapter 17, are bank-created money.

Near-monies and bank and Treasury holdings

Two qualifications of our definition of money must be noted.

1. The line between what we have defined as money and certain highly liquid assets called *near-monies* is a very fine one. Near-monies are certain financial assets which can be easily converted into money. The two most important near-monies are time deposits, or savings accounts, and United States government bonds. Households and businesses currently hold about $130 billion worth of government bonds and own in the neighborhood of $305 billion worth of savings deposits in commercial banks and mutual savings banks.

Some economists argue that our definition of money as demand deposits plus currency is too narrow and that at least time deposits should be added to it. They contend that savings accounts are an excellent store of value, superior to currency or demand deposits in that a saving account yields interest income. Fur-

thermore, in practice time deposits are quickly and cheaply convertible into demand deposits or currency. But we will exclude time deposits from the definition of money because they are not a medium of exchange. You cannot write checks on a savings account in making purchases or in paying debts. Much the same can be said of United States government bonds: most are highly marketable and can be readily converted into currency or demand deposits with little fear of loss. As a matter of fact, your Series E bonds can be converted into currency or demand deposits at commercial banks at a stipulated price upon demand. Yet, as such, government bonds are not a medium of exchange.

Near-monies are important to our discussion for three related reasons. First, the fact that people have such highly liquid assets available affects their consuming–saving habits. Generally speaking, the greater the amount of wealth people have in the form of near-monies, the greater is their willingness to spend out of their money incomes. Second, a sudden conversion of easily cashable near-monies into money adds significantly to the money supply and, if not offset, can pose serious problems during inflationary periods. Finally, the existence of near-monies points up the fact that the definition of money is somewhat arbitrary. In modern complex economies there is no clear-cut distinction between money and certain highly liquid assets.

A final point in anticipation of Chapter 18: The specific definition of money employed is important for purposes of monetary policy. For example, the money supply measured narrowly (currency plus demand deposits) might be quite constant while money broadly defined (currency plus demand deposits plus time deposits) might be increasing. Now, if the monetary authorities feel appropriate policy calls for an expanding supply of money, acceptance of our narrow definition would call for specific actions to increase currency and demand deposits. But acceptance of the broader definition would suggest that the desired expansion of the money supply is taking place and that no specific policy action is required.

2. The second qualification of our definition of money is of a somewhat technical nature. In the definition of the money supply, currency and demand deposits owned by government and by Federal Reserve or commercial banks are excluded. This exclusion is partly to avoid overstating the money supply and partly because money in the possession of households and businesses is more relevant to the level of spending in the economy.[2]

WHAT "BACKS" THE MONEY SUPPLY?

This is a slippery question; any reasonably complete answer is likely to be at odds with the preconceptions many of us hold with respect to money.

Money as debt

The first point to recognize is that the major components of the money supply—paper money and demand deposits—are simply debts, or promises to pay. Paper money is the debt of the Federal Reserve Banks.[3] Paper currency is merely the circulating IOUs of the government and the central banks. Demand deposits are simply the debts of commercial banks.

Furthermore, paper currency and demand deposits have no intrinsic value. A $5 bill is just a piece of paper, and a demand deposit is merely a bookkeeping entry. And coins, we already know, have an intrinsic value less than their face value. Nor will government redeem the paper money you hold for anything tangible such as gold. Insofar as our domestic money supply is concerned, the supplies of gold which the government has hidden away in as-

[2] A paper dollar in the hands of John Doe obviously constitutes just $1 of the money supply. But, if we were to count dollars held by banks as a part of the money supply, that same $1 would count for $2 when deposited in a commercial bank. It would count for a $1 demand deposit owned by Doe and also for $1 worth of currency resting in the bank's vault. This problem of double counting can be avoided by excluding currency resting in commercial banks (and currency redeposited in the Federal Reserve Banks or other commercial banks) in determining the total money supply. The exclusion of currency held by, and demand deposits owned by, government is somewhat more arbitrary. The major reason for this exclusion is that it permits us better to gauge the money supply and rate of spending which occurs in the private sector of the economy apart from spending initiated by government policy.

[3] Federal Reserve Notes in circulation are the debts or obligations of the Federal Reserve Banks, and all other forms of paper money (Treasury currency) are debts of the United States Treasury.

sorted holes in the ground are of little consequence. In effect, American capitalism has wisely chosen to "manage" its money supply in seeking to provide the amount of money needed for that particular volume of business activity which will foster full employment, price level stability, and a healthy rate of economic growth. Such management of the money supply is eminently more sensible than linking the money supply to gold or any other commodity whose supply might arbitrarily and capriciously change. After all, a substantial increase in the nation's gold stock as the result of mining or importation might increase the money supply far beyond that amount needed to transact a full-employment level of business activity and therefore might result in sharp inflation. Conversely, the loss of gold in settling international transactions (Chapters 43 and 44) could reduce the domestic money supply to the point where economic activity was choked off and unemployment and a retarded growth rate resulted. The important point is that paper money cannot be converted into gold but is only exchangeable for other pieces of paper money. For example, Federal Reserve Notes boldly proclaim that "the United States of America will pay to the bearer on demand" the number of dollars stated on the note. But what form will these dollars which the government promises to pay assume? They will be in the form of other paper currency, that is, other paper promises to pay! The government will swap one paper $5 bill for another bearing a different serial number. That is all you can get should you ask the government to redeem some of the paper money you hold. Similarly, demand deposit money cannot be exchanged for gold but only for paper money, which, as we have just seen, will not be redeemed by the government for anything tangible.

Value of money

Now don't get discouraged and tear up the $5 bill you have in your pocket. Actually, the fact that the government does not stand ready to hand you a lump of gold for every dollar you possess really is not as significant as it might first sound. *Paper money does have value, because you can exchange it for the goods and services you wish to obtain in order to satisfy your wants.* Although the government will not give you anything tangible for your $5 bill, businesses and households are willing to exchange goods, services, and resources for it. Suppose you swap a $10 bill for a sweater at a clothing store. Why does the merchant accept this piece of paper in exchange for one of his products? The answer is tricky: The merchant accepts paper money because he is confident that others will also be willing to accept it in exchange for goods and services. He knows that he can purchase the services of his clerks, acquire products from wholesalers, pay the rent on his store, and so forth. Each of us accepts paper money in exchange because he has confidence that it will be exchangeable for real goods and services when he chooses to spend it.

This confidence in the acceptability of paper money is partly a matter of law; currency has been designated as *legal tender* by government. This means that paper currency must be accepted in the payment of a debt or the creditor forfeits the privilege of charging interest and the right to sue the debtor for nonpayment. Put more bluntly, the acceptability of paper dollars is bolstered by the fact that government says these dollars are money. The paper money in our economy is basically *fiat money;* it is money because the government says it is, not because of redeemability in terms of some precious metal. The general acceptability of currency is also bolstered by the willingness of government to accept it in the payment of taxes and other obligations due the government.

Lest we be overimpressed by the power of government, it should be noted that the fact that paper currency is generally accepted in exchange is decidedly more important than government's legal tender decree in making these pieces of paper function as money. Indeed, the government has not decreed checks to be legal tender, but they nevertheless successfully perform the vast bulk of the economy's exchanges of goods, services, and resources.

But let us consider the value of money in more positive terms. The value of money, like the economic value of anything else, is essentially a supply and demand phenomenon. That is, money derives its

value from its scarcity relative to its usefulness. The usefulness of money, of course, lies in its unique capacity to be exchanged for goods and services, either now or in the future. The economy's demand for money thus depends upon its total dollar volume of transactions in any given time period plus the amount of money individuals and businesses want to hold for possible future transactions. Given a reasonably constant demand for money, the value or "purchasing power" of the monetary unit will be determined by the supply of money. Let us see why this is so.

Money and prices

The real value or purchasing power of money is simply the amount of goods and services a unit of money will buy. It is obvious, furthermore, that the amount a dollar will buy varies inversely with the price level; stated differently, a reciprocal relationship exists between the general price level and the value of the dollar. Figure 16·1 allows us to visualize this inverse relationship.[4] When the consumer price

[4]Figure 16·1 is called a "ratio" or "semi-log" chart, because equal vertical distances measure equal percentage changes rather than equal absolute changes.

FIGURE 16·1 THE PRICE LEVEL AND THE VALUE OF MONEY

A reciprocal or inverse relationship exists between the general price level and the purchasing power of the dollar.

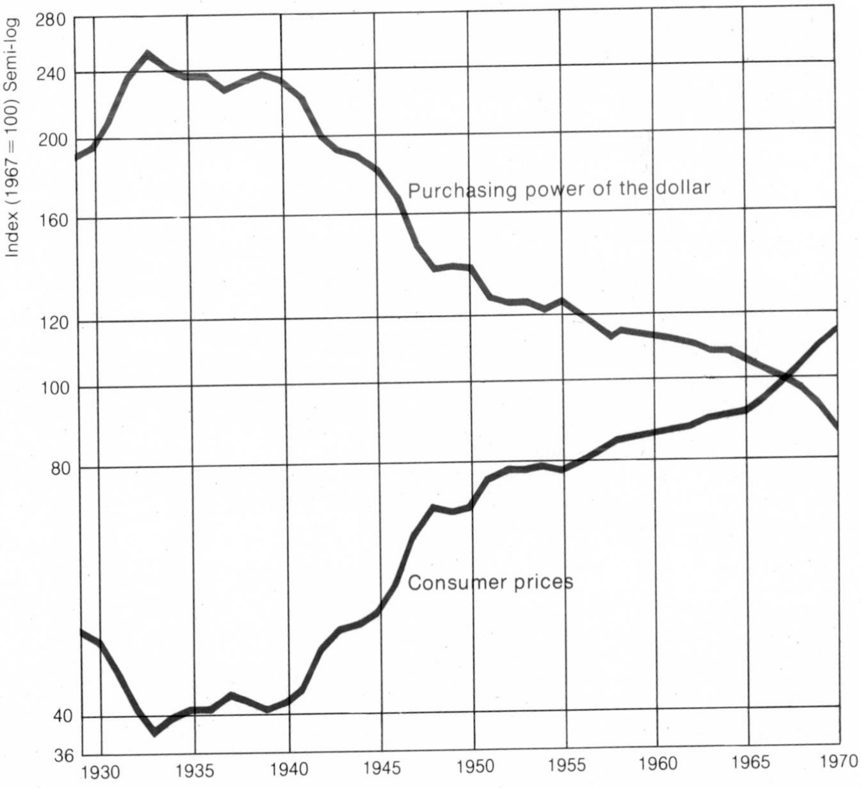

index or "cost-of-living" index goes up, the purchasing power of the dollar necessarily goes down, and vice versa. Higher prices lower the value of the dollar because it will now take more dollars to command a given amount of goods and services. Conversely, lower prices increase the purchasing power of the dollar because you will now need fewer dollars to obtain a given quantity of goods and services. If the price level doubles, the value of the dollar will decline by one-half, or 50 percent. If the price level falls by one-half or 50 percent, the purchasing power of the dollar will double.[5]

You have probably heard or read of situations wherein a nation's currency became worthless and unacceptable in exchange. Indeed, we noted several in Chapter 11. With few exceptions these were situations where government issued so many pieces of paper currency that the value of each of these units of money was almost totally undermined. The infamous post–World War I inflation in Germany is a most notable example. In December of 1919 there were about 50 billion marks in circulation. Exactly four years later this figure had expanded to 496,585,345,900 billion marks! The result? The German mark in 1923 was worth an infinitesimal fraction of its 1919 value.[6] Inflation, you will recall, is typically the consequence of society's spending beyond its capacity to produce. Other things being equal, increases in the money supply tend to increase total spending. Once full employment is reached and total output becomes virtually fixed, this added spending can only serve to make prices spiral up. The sweater which sold for $10 in our previous illustration may, after severe inflation, cost $100. This means that the dollar which was formerly worth one-tenth of a sweater is now worth just one-hundredth of a sweater. The dollar's value, or purchasing power, has obviously been reduced to 10 percent of its former value by inflation.

[5]The arithmetic of this relationship is slightly more complex than these examples suggest. If we let P equal the price level expressed as an index number and D equal the value of the dollar, then our reciprocal relationship is

$$D = \frac{1}{P}.$$

If P equals 1.00, then D obviously is 1.00. But if the price level rises to 1.20, then D will be .83⅓. Hence, a 20 percent *increase* in the price level will cause a 16⅔ percent *decline* in the value of the dollar.

[6]Frank G. Graham, *Exchange, Prices and Production in Hyper-inflation Germany, 1920–1923* (Princeton, N.J.: Princeton University Press, 1930), p. 13.

How might inflation and the accompanying decreases in the value of the dollar affect the acceptability of paper dollars as money? Households and businesses are willing to accept paper currency as a medium of exchange so long as they know it can in turn be spent by them without any noticeable loss in its purchasing power. But with spiraling inflation this is not the case. Runaway inflation, such as Germany faced in the early 1920s, may significantly depreciate the value of money between the time of its receipt and its expenditure. Money will be "hot" money. It is as if the government were constantly taxing away the purchasing power of dollars. Rapid depreciation of the value of the dollar may cause it to cease functioning as a medium of exchange. Businesses and households may refuse to accept paper money in exchange, because they do not want to bear the loss in its value which will occur while it is in their possession. (All this despite the fact that government says the paper currency is legal tender.) Without an acceptable medium of exchange, the economy will revert to inefficient barter.

Similarly, people are willing to use money as a store of value so long as there is no unreasonable deterioration in the value of those stored dollars because of inflation. And the economy can effectively employ the monetary unit as a standard of value only when its purchasing power is relatively stable. A yardstick of value which is subject to drastic shrinkage no longer permits buyers and sellers to establish clearly the terms of trade. When the value of the dollar is declining rapidly, sellers will not know what to charge and buyers will not know what to pay for the various goods and services.

Managing money

Now the overriding implication of this discussion of the value of money is this: The major "backing" of paper money is the public's confidence in the gov-

ernment's ability to keep the value of money reasonably stable. This entails (1) appropriate fiscal policy, as explained in Chapter 14, and (2) intelligent management or regulation of the money supply, as noted above. The acceptability of paper money depends in part upon sound management of the monetary system and in part upon the pursuit of appropriate fiscal measures by government. Businesses and households accept paper money in exchange for goods and services so long as they know it will command a roughly equivalent amount of goods and services when they in turn spend it. In our economy a blending of legislation, government policy, and social practice serves as a bulwark against any imprudent expansion of the money supply which might jeopardize money's value in exchange.

What we have said with respect to paper currency also applies to demand deposit money. In this case money is the debt of the commercial banks. If you have a checking account worth $100, this simply means that your commercial bank is indebted to you for that number of dollars. You can collect this debt in one of two ways. You can go to the bank and demand paper currency for your demand deposit; this simply amounts to changing the debts you hold from bank debts to government-issued debts. Or, and this is more likely, you can "collect" the debt which the bank owes you by transferring this claim by check to someone else. For example, if you buy a $100 suit from your clothier, you can pay for it by writing a check, which transfers the bank's indebtedness from you to your clothier. The bank now owes your clothier the $100 which it previously owed to you. Why does the clothier accept this transfer of indebtedness (the check) as a medium of exchange? Because he can convert it into currency on demand or can in turn transfer the debt to others in making purchases of his choice. Thus checks, as means of transferring bank debts, are acceptable as money because of the public's confidence in commercial banks' ability to honor these claims.

In turn, the ability of commercial banks to honor claims against them depends upon their not creating too many of these claims. We shall find in a moment that a decentralized system of private, profit-seeking banks does not contain sufficient safeguards against the creation of too much check money. Hence, the American banking system has a substantial amount of centralization and governmental control to guard against the imprudent creation of check money by commercial banks.

Let us now summarize the major points of this section:

1. In the United States and other advanced economies, all money is essentially the debts of government and commercial banks.
2. These debts efficiently perform the functions of money so long as their value, or purchasing power, is relatively stable.
3. The value of money is no longer rooted in carefully defined quantities of precious metals, but rather in the amount of goods and services money will purchase in the marketplace.
4. Government's responsibility in stabilizing the value of the monetary unit involves (1) the application of appropriate fiscal policies and (2) effective control over the supply of money.

INSTITUTIONAL FRAMEWORK OF THE AMERICAN BANKING SYSTEM

We have noted that the major component of the money supply, demand deposits, is created by commercial banks and that government-created money, coins and paper currency, typically comes into circulation through the commercial banks. It is essential, then, that we take a thorough look at the framework of the American banking system prior to a detailed analysis in Chapter 17 of how commercial banks create money.

Need for centralization

It became painfully apparent rather early in American history that, like it or not, centralization and public control were prerequisites of an efficient banking system. Congress became increasingly aware of this about the turn of the twentieth century. Decentralized banking fostered the inconvenience and confu-

sion of a heterogeneous currency, monetary mismanagement, and an inflexible supply of money. This latter problem was particularly acute. A dynamic and growing economy demands a flexible money supply—one which will respond to the economy's varying needs. The volume of trade expands and contracts unevenly and irregularly; hence, the supply of money must be elastic in meeting the needs of the economy. "Too much" money can precipitate dangerous inflationary problems; "too little" money can stunt the economy's growth by hindering the production and exchange of goods and services. The United States and innumerable foreign countries have learned through bitter experience that a decentralized banking system is not likely to provide that particular money supply which is most conducive to the welfare of the economy as a whole.

An unusually acute money panic in 1907 was the straw that broke Congress's back. A National Monetary Commission was established to study the monetary and banking problems of the economy and to outline a course of action for Congress. The end result was the Federal Reserve Act of 1913.

Structure of the Federal Reserve System

The banking system which has developed under the frequently amended Federal Reserve Act is sketched in Figure 16·2. It is important that we understand the nature and functions of the various segments which compose the banking system and the relationships which the parts bear to one another.

Board of Governors The kingpin of our money and banking system is the Board of Governors of the Federal Reserve System. The seven members of this Board are appointed by the President with the confirmation of the Senate. Terms are long—fourteen years—and staggered so that one member is replaced every two years. The intention is to provide the Board with continuity and experienced membership. The

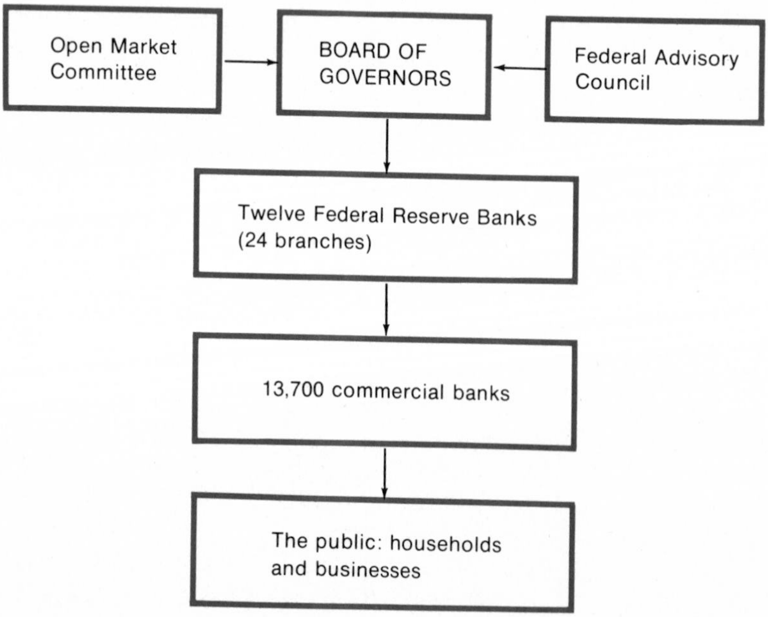

FIGURE 16·2 FRAMEWORK OF THE FEDERAL RESERVE SYSTEM AND ITS RELATIONSHIP TO THE PUBLIC

With the advice and counsel of the Open Market Committee and the Federal Advisory Council, the Board of Governors makes the basic policy decisions which regulate our money and banking systems. These decisions are made effective through the twelve Federal Reserve Banks.

Board is staffed by appointment rather than elections in an attempt to divorce monetary policy from partisan politics. An important argument for this philosophy of independence currently is that it is politically expedient for the administration in power to invoke expansionary fiscal policies and the monetary authorities can only offset the resulting inflation if it is independent of the administration.

The Board of Governors has the responsibility of exercising general supervision and control over the operation of the money and banking system of the nation. The Board's actions, which are to be in the public interest and designed to promote the general economic welfare, determine the basic policies which the commercial banking system is to follow. These basic policy decisions are made effective through the twelve Federal Reserve Banks and entail the use of two sets of control techniques which are at the disposal of the Board. *Quantitative credit controls,* consisting of (1) the reserve requirement, (2) open-market operations, and (3) the discount rate, are designed to negotiate those changes in the money supply which the Board deems most conducive to a stable and expanding economy. From time to time the Board invokes *selective* or *qualitative credit controls* to regulate the availability of certain specific types of credit—for example, consumer credit in the purchase of housing or durables, and credit in buying securities in the stock market. Much of Chapter 18 will be concerned with a discussion of these two types of credit controls and the manner in which they permit the Board of Governors to influence the activities of commercial banks.

Two important bodies assist the Board of Governors in determining basic banking policy. On the one hand, the Federal Open Market Committee, made up of the seven members of the Board plus five of the presidents of the Federal Reserve Banks, sets the System's policy with respect to the purchase and sale of government bonds in the open market. These open-market operations constitute the most significant technique by which the monetary authorities can affect the money supply. On the other hand, the Federal Advisory Council is composed of twelve prominent commercial bankers, one selected annually by each of the twelve Federal Reserve Banks. The Council meets periodically with the Board of Governors to voice its views on banking policy. However, as its name indicates, the Council is purely advisory; it has no policy-making powers.

The twelve Federal Reserve Banks The twelve Federal Reserve Banks have three major characteristics. They are (1) central banks, (2) quasi-public banks, and (3) bankers' banks.

1. Americans are blessed with a more or less inherent fear of centralization. As a result, the American banking system is less centralized than most of the other advanced economies of the world. As a matter of fact, the Federal Reserve Act was a compromise between exponents of centralization and advocates of decentralization. Hence, instead of creating a single central bank, the act divided the nation into twelve districts and provided for a Federal Reserve Bank to function as a central bank in each of these districts. Figure 16·3 shows these twelve Federal Reserve districts. Geographic considerations were also of significance in the creation of the twelve Federal Reserve Banks. It was felt that a single central bank would be unresponsive to the peculiar economic problems faced by the various regions of the economy. In any event, the net result is that the twelve Federal Reserve Banks make up the central banking system of the economy. It is through these central banks that the basic policy directives of the Board of Governors are made effective. The Federal Reserve Bank of New York City is by far the most important of these central banks. The development of modern communication and transportation facilities has undoubtedly lessened the geographic need for a system of regional banks.

2. The twelve Federal Reserve Banks are quasi-public banks. They reflect an interesting blend of private ownership and public control. The Federal Reserve Banks are owned by the member banks in their districts. Upon joining the Federal Reserve System, commercial banks are required to purchase shares of stock in the Federal Reserve Bank in their district. But the basic policies which the Federal Reserve Banks pursue are set by a public body—the

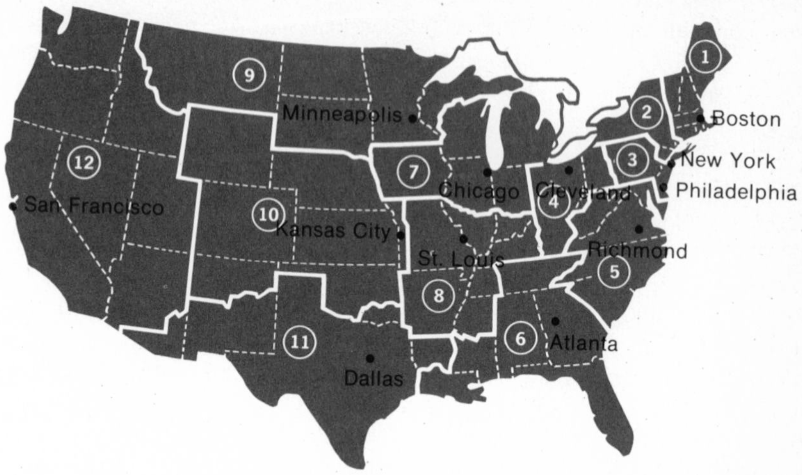

FIGURE 16·3 THE TWELVE FEDERAL RESERVE DISTRICTS

The Federal Reserve System divides the United States into twelve districts, each of which has one central bank and in some instances one or more branches of the central bank. Hawaii and Alaska are included in the twelfth district. (*Federal Reserve Bulletin.*)

Board of Governors. The central banks of American capitalism are privately owned but governmentally controlled.

The fact that the Federal Reserve Banks are essentially public institutions is vitally important to an understanding of their operation. In particular it must be emphasized that the Federal Reserve Banks are not motivated by profits as are private enterprises. The policies followed by the central bank are those which tend to promote the economic well-being of the economy as a whole. Hence, the activities of the Federal Reserve Banks will frequently be at odds with the profit motive.[7] Furthermore, the Federal Reserve Banks are not in competition with commercial banks. With rare exceptions, the Federal Reserve Banks do not deal with the public, but rather with the government and the commercial banks.

3. Finally, the Federal Reserve Banks are frequently called ''bankers' banks.'' This is a shorthand way of saying that the Federal Reserve Banks perform essentially the same functions for commercial banks as commercial banks perform for the public. Just as commercial banks accept the deposits of and make loans to the public, so the central banks accept the deposits of and make loans to commercial banks. But the Federal Reserve Banks have a third function which commercial banks no longer perform: the function of issuing currency. Congress has authorized the Federal Reserve Banks to put into circulation Federal Reserve Notes, which constitute the bulk of the economy's paper money supply.

[7] Though it is not their basic goal, the Federal Reserve Banks have actually operated profitably, largely as the result of Treasury debts held by them. A part of the profits has been used to pay 6 percent dividends to member banks on their holdings of stock; the bulk of the remaining profits has been turned over to the United States Treasury.

The commercial banks The workhorses of the American banking system are its 13,671 commercial banks. The majority of these are *state banks,* that is, private banks operating under state charters. But a good many have received their charters from the Federal government; that is, they are *national banks.* Roughly one-half of all existing commercial banks are members of the Federal Reserve System. The 4,637 national banks in our economy are required by law to join the Federal Reserve System; the remaining 9,034 state banks have the option of joining or declining to do so. As Figure 16·4 indicates, 1,166 of the state banks have chosen to join the Federal Reserve System.

These statistics, however, tend to underestimate grossly the significance of the Federal Reserve System. Virtually all the larger commercial banks are members of the System, nonmembers being the smaller "country banks" for the most part. Thus, about 80 percent of all deposits held by the commercial banking system rest in member banks. In addition, nonmember banks can participate on a limited basis in the functioning of the Federal Reserve System. For example, nonmember banks can avail themselves of the Federal Reserve System's program for the efficient collection of checks. Nonmember banks are not entirely disassociated from the Federal Reserve System or immune to its policy decisions.

Commercial banks, as already noted, have two basic functions. First, they hold the money deposits of businesses and households. Second, commercial banks make loans to the public and, in so doing, increase the economy's supply of money. Detailed analysis of these functions is the main objective of Chapter 17.

Although the present analysis will be concerned only with ordinary commercial banks, it is important to recognize that the commercial banking system is thoroughly supplemented by a diverse group of specialized banking and financial institutions. For example, savings banks and savings and loan associations accept the funds of relatively small savers as time deposits and make these funds available to investors by extending mortgage loans or by purchasing marketable securities. Investment banks, on the other hand, perform the task of marketing the newly issued

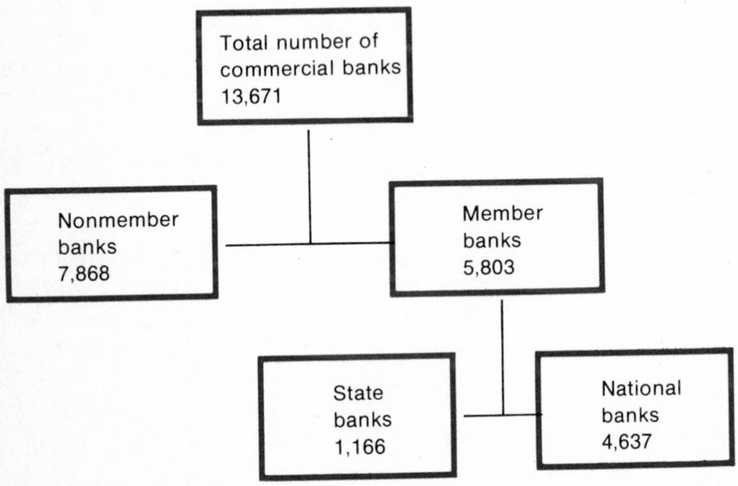

FIGURE 16·4 THE CLASSIFICATION OF COMMERCIAL BANKS, 1970

Less than half of all commercial banks are members of the Federal Reserve System. However, these member banks hold about 80 percent of all commercial bank deposits. (*Federal Reserve Bulletin.*)

bonds and stocks of corporations which desire funds for capital expansion. Insurance companies accept huge volumes of savings in the form of premiums on insurance policies and annuities and use these funds, wholly or in part, to buy a variety of private, corporate, and government securities. These banking and financial institutions are merely representative; the list is by no means exhaustive.

All banking and financial institutions, including commercial banks, have one point in common: They are all dealers in credit or debt. *These individual institutions lend the savings deposited with them or acquired by them, receiving credit instruments—bonds, stocks, mortgages, or promissory notes—in return.* Hence, these institutions play a significant role in the economy, functioning as *intermediaries between savers and investors.* But from the social point of view, you will recall, their operation falls short of perfection (Chapter 12). These banking and financial institutions do not provide for an exact and continuing balance of investment spending and the full-employment volume of saving. Why? Because savers and investors are essentially different groups that make their decisions in response to different motivations.

Commercial banks, accepting both time and demand deposits and using the proceeds wholly or in part to acquire income-earning securities, also function as intermediaries between savers and investors. But commercial banks perform an additional function which other banking and financial institutions do not. That function is *to create money by extending bank credit*—that is, *by making loans—to businesses and households.* Other financial institutions can only *transfer* money from savers to spenders. In doing so they do not affect the total supply of money available. Commercial banks, however, can *create* demand deposit money and make it available for use by potential spenders. Banks are by no means totally dependent upon the deposits of savers in making money available to spenders. Within limits, commercial banks can create the money that spenders desire. Generally speaking, it works this way: Banks accept the credit of borrowing individuals and businesses (their promissory notes) and give these borrowers bank credit (demand deposits) in return. By exchanging debts that are not money (promissory notes) for debts that are money (demand deposits), commercial banks perform the unique function of increasing the money supply. In retiring bank credit, commercial banks decrease the money supply. The mechanics of these transactions will be studied in some detail in the ensuing chapter. At this juncture, the basic point to recognize is this: *Because of their money-creating and money-destroying abilities, commercial banks are highly strategic institutions in our economy.* Commercial banks play a particularly vital role in affecting the volume of money and hence the levels of spending, output, employment, and prices. Therefore, our attention is centered upon the functioning of commercial banks as opposed to the more specialized banking and financial institutions mentioned above.

Functions of the Federal Reserve System[8]

The Federal Reserve System—in particular, the twelve Federal Reserve Banks and the Board of Governors—was established to achieve certain definite objectives. These goals largely stem from the defects inherent in the system of uncoordinated state and national banks which prevailed prior to the passage of the Federal Reserve Act.

Holding the deposits of member banks Federal Reserve Banks hold the deposits, or "reserves," of member banks. Private businesses and individuals find it convenient to establish checking accounts at commercial banks. These accounts are simply reserves of funds which the owner more or less regularly draws upon and occasionally replenishes. In the same manner member banks keep reserves—that is, money deposits—with the Federal Reserve Bank of their district. When in need of currency, the commercial banks can, within limits, draw upon these reserves. When in possession of surplus cash, commercial banks may deposit this extra currency in their

[8]For a more detailed look at the service functions of the Federal Reserve Banks, see Board of Governors of the Federal Reserve System, *The Federal Reserve System: Purposes and Functions*, 5th ed. (1963), chaps. 16 and 17.

reserves. Or, just as you may buy a bond or fulfill an obligation by drawing a check on your bank account, so may a commercial bank buy a government bond or honor some claim against itself by drawing down its reserves at the Federal Reserve Bank. Much of the daily work of the Federal Reserve Banks is concerned with increasing and decreasing the reserves of commercial banks as routine banking transactions occur.

Providing for the collection of checks As previously noted, a check is merely a written order which the drawer may use in making a purchase or paying a debt. A check is collected, or "cleared," when one or more banks negotiate a transfer of part of the drawer's checking account, or demand deposit, to the demand deposit of the recipient of the check. If Jones and Smith have checking accounts in the same commercial bank and Jones gives Smith a $10 check, Smith can collect this check by taking it to the commercial bank, where his account will be increased by $10 and Jones's reduced by $10. In many cases, however, the drawer and receiver of a check will be located in different towns or different states and therefore have their accounts in commercial banks far distant from one another. An important function of the Federal Reserve Banks is to provide facilities for the collection of checks where the banks of the drawer and receiver are geographically remote.

Though routine, this function is important, because the bulk of the exchange which occurs in our economy is transacted by the use of check money. A money system so heavily committed to the use of check money obviously needs some mechanism for the quick and cheap collection of checks, particularly if payer and payee are geographically remote from one another. A basic function of the Federal Reserve Banks is to fulfill this need. At present the maximum time for collecting a check through the Federal Reserve System is three days, and the service is performed free of charge to all member banks. The mechanics of check collecting and the effect it has upon the financial position of commercial banks will be outlined in detail in the next chapter.

Supplying the economy with paper currency It is also the responsibility of the Federal Reserve Banks to supply the economy with most of its paper currency. The bulk of the economy's paper money—Federal Reserve Notes—is issued directly by the central banks. As the fountainhead of the economy's paper money supply, the Federal Reserve Banks function as a reservoir of cash. When the economy needs more currency, the reservoir is opened and currency spills into the economy. When the economy has more currency than it desires to hold, the excess is channeled back into the reservoir. The commercial banks act as intermediaries between the public and the Federal Reserve Banks in each case. Specifically, it works something like this: During the Christmas buying rush, for example, the public wants more currency in circulation. To get this additional cash, individuals and businesses cash checks at the commercial banks. This lowers the amounts of currency resting in bank vaults. Commercial banks then turn to the bankers' banks and draw checks against their deposits (reserves) with the Federal Reserve Banks to replenish their vault cash. After the Christmas rush has subsided, less currency is needed. The public deposits this extra currency in their bank accounts. As a result, commercial banks find they have an overabundant stock of currency in their vaults. They deposit their surplus cash in the Federal Reserve Banks, thereby increasing their reserves.

Acting as fiscal agents for government The Federal Reserve Banks act as fiscal agents for the Federal government. As we have seen, government—the Federal government in particular—is an exceedingly big business. As such, it collects huge sums through taxation, spends equally astronomical amounts, and sells and redeems bonds. Naturally, the government wants to avail itself of banking facilities in carrying out these functions. The Federal Reserve Banks function as bankers for the Federal government. The bankers' banks hold a part of the Treasury's checking accounts, aid the government in collecting various tax revenues, and administer the sale and redemption of government bonds.

Supervising member banks The Federal Reserve Banks supervise the operations of member banks. A banking system stands or falls on the financial soundness of the individual commercial banks of which it is composed. Unsound banking practices can have widespread repercussions, to the point of threatening the financial structure of the entire economy. Since commercial banking is "vested with a public interest," it has been subject to government supervision.

The Federal Reserve has supervisory powers over all member commercial banks.[9] This supervision usually takes the form of periodic unannounced examinations of the commercial banks. Banks which do not conform to the standards set forth by the Federal Reserve authorities may be denied the privilege of borrowing from the Federal Reserve Banks, and in extreme cases the officers and directors of offending banks may be removed by the Board of Governors.

Regulating the supply of money Finally—and most important of all—the Federal Reserve System has ultimate responsibility for regulating the supply of money. The major task of the Federal Reserve authorities is to manage the money supply in accordance with the needs of the economy as a whole. In the dynamic and expanding economy of American capitalism, this task entails making that amount of money available which is consistent with high and steadily rising levels of output and employment and a relatively constant price level. It is through the previously mentioned quantitative and qualitative credit controls that the Federal Reserve authorities attempt to manipulate the supply of money in terms of short-run stability and long-run economic growth.

[9] The Federal Reserve is not alone in the task of supervision. The individual states supervise all banks which they charter. The Comptroller of the Currency supervises all national banks. Finally, the Federal Deposit Insurance Corporation has the power to supervise all banks whose deposits it insures. Hence, a member national bank which belongs to the FDIC will be subject to three supervisory agencies—the Federal Reserve, the Comptroller of the Currency, and the FDIC.

In addition to being the most vital objective of the Federal Reserve System, the regulation of the money supply differs from the other Federal Reserve functions in another significant respect: Whereas all the other functions are of a more or less routine or service nature, the goal of correctly managing the money supply entails the making of basic and unique policy decisions of a nonroutine character. Chapter 18 is concerned with Federal Reserve monetary policy and its effectiveness in achieving economic stability in a growing economy.

SUMMARY

1. Anything that functions as *a.* a medium of exchange, *b.* a standard of value, and *c.* a store of value is money.

2. In the United States money is defined as demand deposits plus currency (coins and paper money) in circulation. By far the most important component of the money supply is demand deposits. Demand deposits are money because they can be spent if checks are written against them. Currency and demand deposits owned by the Treasury or by commercial or central banks are not "in circulation."

3. Money, which is essentially the debts of government and commercial banks, has value because of the goods and services which it will command in the market. Maintenance of the purchasing power of money depends to a considerable degree upon the effectiveness with which government manages the money supply.

4. The American banking system is composed of *a.* the Board of Governors of the Federal Reserve System, *b.* the twelve Federal Reserve Banks, and *c.* some 13,700 commercial banks. The Board of Governors is the basic policy-making body for the entire banking system. The directives of the Board are made effective through the twelve Federal Reserve Banks, which are simultaneously *a.* central banks, *b.* quasi-public banks, and *c.* bankers' banks. The commercial banks of the economy perform the tasks of accepting money deposits and making loans.

In lending, commercial banks create demand deposits; these deposits are money. Commercial banks, then, are money-creating institutions.

5. The major functions of the Federal Reserve System are *a.* to hold the deposits or reserves of commercial banks, *b.* to provide facilities for the rapid collection of checks, *c.* to supply the economy's needs for paper currency, *d.* to act as fiscal agent for the Federal government, *e.* to supervise the operations of member banks, and *f.* to regulate the supply of money in terms of the best interests of the economy as a whole.

QUESTIONS AND STUDY SUGGESTIONS

1. What are the three basic functions of money? Describe how drastic inflation can undermine the ability of money to perform these functions.

2. What are the disadvantages of commodity money? What are the advantages of *a*. paper money and *b*. check money as compared with commodity money?

3. "Money is only a bit of paper or a bit of metal that gives its owner a lawful claim to so much bread or beer or diamonds or motorcars or what not. We cannot eat money, nor drink money, nor wear money. It is the goods that money can buy that are being divided up when money is divided up."[10] Evaluate and explain.

4. Fully evaluate and explain the following statements:

a. "The invention of money is one of the great achievements of the human race, for without it the enrichment that comes from broadening trade would have been impossible."

b. "Money is whatever society says it is."

c. "When prices of everything are going up, it is not because everything is worth more, but because the dollar is worth less."

d. "The difficult questions concerning paper [money] are . . . not about its economy, convenience or ready circulation but about the amount of the paper which can be wisely issued or created, and the possibilities of violent convulsions when it gets beyond bounds."[11]

5. What items constitute the money supply in American capitalism? What is the most important component of the money supply? What are near-monies? Of what significance are they? Why is the face value of a coin greater than its intrinsic value?

[10] George Bernard Shaw, *The Intelligent Woman's Guide to Socialism and Capitalism* (New York: Brentano's, Inc., 1928), p. 9. Used by permission of the Public Trustee and the Society of Authors.

[11] F. W. Taussig, *Principles of Economics*, 4th ed. (New York: The Macmillan Company, 1946), pp. 247–248.

6. "In most modern industrial economies of the world the debts of government and of commercial banks are used as money." Explain.

7. What "backs" the money supply in the United States? Be as specific as you are able.

8. What determines the value of money? Who is responsible for maintaining the value of money? Why is it important for the money supply to be elastic, that is, capable of increasing or decreasing in size? What is meant by *a.* "sound money" and *b.* a "52-cent dollar"?

9. What is the major responsibility of the Board of Governors? Discuss the major characteristics of the Federal Reserve Banks. Of what significance is the fact that the Federal Reserve Banks are quasi-public?

10. What are the two basic functions of commercial banks? How do commercial banks differ from other financial institutions?

11. State and briefly discuss the major functions of the Federal Reserve System.

SELECTED REFERENCES

Economic Issues, 4th ed., reading 27.

Board of Governors of the Federal Reserve System: *The Federal Reserve System: Purposes and Functions*, 5th ed. (1963), particularly chaps. 1 and 4.

Chandler, Lester V.: *The Economics of Money and Banking*, 5th ed. (New York: Harper & Row, Publishers, Incorporated, 1969), chaps. 1–5 and 9.

Cochran, John A.: *Money, Banking, and the Economy*, 2d ed. (New York: The Macmillan Company, 1971), chaps. 1–6.

Robertson, D. H.: *Money*, 6th ed. (New York: Pitman Publishing Corporation, 1948).

17

HOW BANKS CREATE MONEY

In Chapter 16 we saw that the Federal Reserve Banks are the primary source of the economy's paper money. However, we shall find in the present chapter that commercial banks are the fountainhead of the major component of the money system—demand deposits.

More specifically, in this chapter we want to explain and compare the money-creating abilities of

1. A single commercial bank which is part of a multibank system
2. A monopoly bank
3. The commercial banking system as a whole

It will be convenient for us to seek these objectives through the commercial bank's balance sheet. An understanding of the basic items which make up a bank's balance sheet and the manner in which various transactions change these items will provide us with a valuable analytical tool for grasping the workings of our monetary and banking systems.

THE BALANCE SHEET OF A COMMERCIAL BANK

What is a *balance sheet?* It is merely a statement of assets and claims which portrays or summarizes the financial position of a firm—in this case a commercial bank—at some specific point in time. Every balance sheet has one overriding virtue: By definition, it must balance. Why? Because each and every known *asset,* being something of economic value, will be claimed by someone. Can you think of an asset—something of monetary value—which no one claims? A balance sheet balances because assets equal claims. The claims shown on a balance sheet are divided into two groups: the claims of the owners of a firm against the firm's assets, called *net worth,* and the claims of nonowners, called *liabilities.* Thus, it can be said that a balance sheet balances because

Assets = liabilities + net worth

A balance-sheet approach to our study of the money-creating ability of commercial banks is invaluable in two specific respects: On the one hand, a bank's balance sheet provides us with a convenient point of reference from which we can introduce new terms and concepts in a more or less orderly manner. On the other hand, the use of balance sheets will allow us to quantify certain strategic concepts and relationships which would defy comprehension if discussed in verbal terms alone.

A SINGLE COMMERCIAL BANK IN A BANKING SYSTEM

Our immediate goal is an understanding of the money-creating potential of a single bank which is part of a multibank banking system. What accounts comprise a commercial bank's balance sheet? How does a single commercial bank create and destroy money? What factors govern the money-creating abilities of such a bank?

Formation of a commercial bank

The answers to these questions demand that we understand the ins and outs of a commercial bank's balance sheet and how certain rather elementary transactions affect that balance sheet. We start with the organization of a local commercial bank.

Transaction 1: The birth of a bank Let us start from scratch. Suppose some farsighted citizens of the metropolis of Wahoo, Nebraska, decide that their town is in need of a new commercial bank to provide all the banking services needed by that growing community. Assuming these enterprising individuals are able to secure a state charter for their bank, they then turn to the task of selling, say, $250,000 worth of capital stock to buyers, both in and out of the community. These financing efforts having met with success, the Merchants and Farmers Bank of Wahoo now exists—at least on paper. How does the Wahoo bank's balance statement appear at its birth?

The new proprietors of the bank have sold $250,000 worth of shares of stock in the bank—some to themselves, some to other people. As a result, the bank now has $250,000 in cash on hand and $250,000 worth of capital stock outstanding. Obviously the cash is an asset to the bank. The cash held by a bank is sometimes dubbed *vault cash* or *till money.* The outstanding shares of stock, however, constitute an equal amount of claims which the owners have against the bank's assets. That is, the shares of stock are obviously the net worth of the bank, though they are assets from the viewpoint of those who possess these shares. The bank's balance sheet would read:

BALANCE SHEET 1: WAHOO BANK

Assets		Liabilities and net worth	
Cash	$250,000	Capital stock	$250,000

Transaction 2: Becoming a going concern The newly established board of directors must now breathe life into their infant enterprise. They must get the newborn bank off the drawing board and make it a living reality. The first step will be to acquire property and equipment. Suppose the directors, confident of the success of their venture, purchase a building for $220,000 and some $20,000 worth of office equipment. This simple transaction merely changes the composition of the bank's assets. The bank now has $240,000 less in cash and $240,000 worth of new property assets. Using an asterisk to denote those accounts which are affected by each transaction, we find that the bank's balance sheet at the conclusion of transaction 2 appears as follows:

BALANCE SHEET 2: WAHOO BANK

Assets		Liabilities and net worth	
Cash*	$ 10,000	Capital stock	$250,000
Property*	240,000		

Note that the balance sheet still balances, as indeed it must.

Transaction 3: Accepting deposits We have already emphasized that commercial banks have two basic functions: to accept deposits of money and to make loans. Now that our bank is in operation, let us suppose that the citizens of Wahoo decide to deposit some \$100,000 in the Merchants and Farmers Bank. What happens to the bank's balance sheet?

The bank receives cash, which we have already noted is an asset to the bank. Suppose this money is placed in the bank in the form of demand deposits (checking accounts), rather than time deposits (savings accounts). These newly created demand deposits constitute claims which depositors have against the assets of the Wahoo bank. Thus the depositing of money in the bank creates a new liability account—demand deposits. The bank's balance sheet now looks like this:

BALANCE SHEET 3: WAHOO BANK

Assets		Liabilities and net worth	
Cash*	\$110,000	Capital stock	\$250,000
Property	240,000	Demand deposits*	100,000

You should note that, although there is no change in the total supply of money, a change in the composition of the economy's money supply has occurred as a result of transaction 3. Bank money, or demand deposits, have *increased* by \$100,000 and currency in circulation has *decreased* by \$100,000. Currency held by a bank, you will recall, is not considered to be a part of the economy's money supply.

It is obvious that a withdrawal of cash will reduce the bank's demand deposit liabilities and its holdings of cash by the amount of the withdrawal. This, too, changes the composition, but not the total supply, of money.

Transaction 4: Joining the Federal Reserve System Being a state bank, the Merchants and Farmers Bank of Wahoo will have the option of joining or not joining the Federal Reserve System. Suppose the directors of the bank decide in favor of joining. To accomplish this, the bank must meet a very specific requirement: It must keep a *legal reserve deposit* in the Federal Reserve Bank of its particular district.

This legal reserve deposit is *an amount of cash equal to a specified percentage of its own deposit liabilities which a member bank must keep on deposit with the Federal Reserve Bank in its district.* Since 1960 banks have been permitted to count vault cash as a part of reserves. As a matter of banking practice, however, the vast bulk of bank reserves are in the form of deposits in the Federal Reserve Banks. We shall simplify our discussion by supposing that our bank keeps its legal reserve *entirely* in the form of deposits in the Federal Reserve Bank of its district.

The "specified percentage" of its deposit liabilities which the commercial bank must deposit in the central bank is known as the *reserve ratio.* Why? Because that is exactly what it is—a ratio between the size of the deposits which the commercial bank must keep in the Federal Reserve Bank and the commercial bank's own outstanding deposit liabilities. This ratio is as follows:

$$\text{Reserve ratio} = \frac{\text{commercial bank's required deposit in Federal Reserve Bank}}{\text{commercial bank's demand-deposit liabilities}}$$

Hence, if the reserve ratio were 10 percent, our bank, having accepted \$100,000 in deposits from the public, would be obligated to keep \$10,000 as a deposit, or reserve, in the Federal Reserve Bank in Kansas City. If the ratio were 20 percent, \$20,000 would have to be deposited in the Federal Reserve Bank. If 50 percent, \$50,000, and so forth.

How is the exact size of the reserve ratio determined? Congress has the responsibility for setting the upper and lower limits within which the ratio may vary. These legal limits differ, depending upon the size and location of commercial banks, as Table 17·1 indicates. The Board of Governors can vary the ratio at its discretion within these limits.[1] To avoid a lot of messy computations, we shall suppose that the reserve ratio for all banks is 20 percent. This is a

[1]State nonmember banks are required by state laws to keep reserves. These reserves usually take the form of cash and deposits in other commercial banks. Though the reserve ratio varies considerably among the states, 15 percent is about the average.

TABLE 17·1 LEGAL RESERVE REQUIREMENTS OF MEMBER BANKS, 1971

Type of bank	Reserve ratio against demand deposits	
	Upper and lower legal limits, percent	Actual ratio, percent
Reserve city banks (member banks in large and medium-sized cities)	10–22	17
All other member banks (country or small town)	7–14	13

Source: Federal Reserve Bulletin, February 1971.

nice round figure and is reasonably close to reality. It is to be emphasized that reserve requirements are *fractional,* that is, less than 100 percent. This consideration will be vital in the ensuing analysis of the lending abilities of various possible banking systems.

The Wahoo bank will just be meeting the required 20 percent ratio between its deposit in the Federal Reserve Bank and its own deposit liabilities by depositing $20,000 in the Federal Reserve Bank. To distinguish this deposit from the public's deposits in commercial banks, we shall use the term *reserves* in referring to those funds which commercial banks deposit in the Federal Reserve Banks.

But let us suppose that the directors of the Wahoo bank anticipate that their holdings of the public's deposits will grow in the future. Hence, instead of sending the minimum amount, $20,000, they send an extra $90,000, making a total of $110,000. In so doing, the bank will avoid the inconvenience of sending additional reserves to the Federal Reserve Bank each time its own deposit liabilities increase by some small amount. And we shall see shortly that it is upon the basis of extra reserves that banks can lend and thereby earn interest income.[2]

[2] Actually, of course, the bank would not deposit all its cash in the Federal Reserve Bank. However, because (1) banks as a rule only hold vault cash in the amount of 1½ or 2 percent of their total assets and (2) vault cash can be counted as reserves, we shall find it expedient to assume that all the bank's cash is deposited in the Federal Reserve Bank and therefore constitutes the commercial bank's total reserves. The cumbersome process of adding two assets—"cash" and "deposits in the Federal Reserve Bank"—to determine "reserves" is thereby avoided.

At the completion of this transaction, the balance sheet of the Merchants and Farmers Bank will appear as follows:

BALANCE SHEET 4: WAHOO BANK

Assets		Liabilities and net worth	
Cash*	$ 0	Capital stock	$250,000
Property	240,000	Demand deposits	100,000
Reserves (deposits in the Federal Reserve Bank)*	110,000		

There are several points relevant to this transaction which must still be explained:

1. A note of terminology: The amount by which the bank's actual reserves exceed its required reserves is the bank's *excess* reserves. In this case,

Actual reserves	$110,000
Required reserves	−20,000
Excess reserves	$ 90,000

The only reliable way of computing excess reserves is to multiply the bank's demand deposit liabilities by the reserve ratio ($100,000 times 20 percent equals $20,000) to obtain required reserves, then to subtract this figure from the actual reserves listed on the asset side of the bank's balance sheet. To ensure an understanding of this process, the reader should com-

pute excess reserves for the bank's balance sheet as it stands at the end of transaction 4 on the assumption that the reserve ratio is (*a*) 10 percent, (*b*) 33⅓ percent, and (*c*) 50 percent.

Because the ability of a commercial bank to make loans depends upon the existence of excess reserves, this concept is of vital importance in grasping the money-creating ability of the banking system.

2. What is the rationale underlying the requirement that member banks deposit a reserve in the Federal Reserve Bank of their district? One might think that the basic purpose of reserves is to enhance the liquidity of a bank and thereby protect commercial bank depositors from losses; that is, it would seem that reserves constitute a ready source of funds from which commercial banks can meet large and unexpected withdrawals of cash by depositors. But this reasoning does not hold up under close scrutiny. Although historically reserves were looked upon as a source of liquidity and therefore protection for depositors, *legal,* or required, reserves cannot be used for the purpose of meeting unexpected cash withdrawals. If the banker's nightmare materialized—that is, if everyone having a demand deposit in his bank appeared on the same morning to demand his deposits in cash—the banker could not draw upon his required reserves to meet this "bank panic" without violating the legal reserve ratio and thereby incurring the wrath and penalties of the Federal Reserve authorities. In practice, legal reserves are not an available pool of liquid funds upon which commercial banks can rely in times of emergency.[3] As a matter of fact, even if legal reserves were accessible to commercial banks, they would not be sufficient to meet a serious "run" on a bank. Why? Because, as we shall soon discover, demand deposits may be three, four, or five times as large as a bank's required reserves.

It is not surprising that commercial bank depositors are protected by other means. As noted in Chapter 16, periodic bank examinations are an important device for promoting prudent commercial banking practices. Furthermore, the Federal Deposit Insurance Corporation was established in 1933 to insure the deposit liabilities of member banks and qualified nonmember banks that voluntarily become members of the FDIC. At the present time about 99 percent of all depositors have their deposits insured up to a maximum of $20,000 by the FDIC. FDIC members pay insurance premiums equal to one-twelfth of 1 percent of their total deposits, from which the FDIC has built up a substantial insurance fund.

If the purpose of reserves is not to provide for commercial bank liquidity, what is their function? *Control* is the basic answer. Legal reserves are a means by which the Board of Governors can influence the lending policies of commercial banks. The next chapter will explain in detail how the Board of Governors can invoke certain policies which either increase or decrease commercial bank reserves and thereby affect the ability of banks to grant credit. The object is to prevent banks from *over*extending or *under*extending bank credit. To the degree that these policies are successful in influencing the volume of commercial bank credit, the Board of Governors can help the economy avoid the business fluctuations which give rise to bank runs, bank failures, and collapse of the monetary system. It is in this indirect way—as a means of controlling commercial bank credit—that reserves protect depositors, not as a source of liquidity. As we shall see in a moment another function of reserves is to facilitate the collection or "clearing" of checks.

3. Let us pause to note a rather obvious accounting matter which transaction 4 entails. Specifically, *the reserve created in transaction 4 is an asset to the depositing commercial bank but a liability to the Federal Reserve Bank receiving it.* To the Wahoo bank the reserve is an asset. Why? Because it is a claim

[3]This amendment must be added: As depositors withdraw cash from a commercial bank, the bank's demand-deposit liabilities will obviously decline. This lowers the absolute amount of required reserves which the bank must keep, thereby freeing some of the bank's actual reserves for use in meeting cash withdrawals by depositors. To illustrate: Suppose a commercial bank has reserves of $20 and demand-deposit liabilities of $100. If the legal reserve ratio is 20 percent, all the bank's reserves are obviously required. Now, if depositors withdraw, say, $50 worth of their deposits as cash, the bank will only need $10 as required reserves to support the remaining $50 of demand-deposit liabilities. Thus $10 of the bank's actual reserves of $20 is no longer required. The bank can draw upon this $10 in helping to meet the cash withdrawals of its depositors.

which this commercial bank has against the assets of another institution—the Federal Reserve Bank. To the Federal Reserve Bank this reserve is a liability, that is, a claim which another institution—the Wahoo bank—has against it. Just as the demand deposit you get by depositing money in a commercial bank is an asset to you and a liability to your commercial bank, so the deposit or reserve which a commercial bank establishes by depositing money in a banker's bank is an asset to the commercial bank and a liability to the Federal Reserve Bank. An understanding of this relationship is necessary in pursuing transaction 5.

Transaction 5: A check is drawn against the bank Now let us tackle a very significant and somewhat more complicated transaction. Suppose that Clem Bradshaw, a Wahoo farmer who deposited a substantial portion of the $100,000 in demand deposits which the Wahoo bank received in transaction 3, purchases $50,000 worth of farm machinery from the Ajax Farm Implement Company of Beaver Crossing, Nebraska. Bradshaw very sensibly pays for this machinery by writing a $50,000 check, against his deposit in the Wahoo bank, in favor of the Ajax company. We want to determine (1) how this check is collected or cleared and (2) the effect that the collection of the check has upon the balance sheets of the banks involved in the transaction.

To accomplish this, we must consider the Wahoo bank, the Beaver Crossing bank, and the Federal Reserve Bank of Kansas City.[4] Let us suppose that both the commercial banks are members of the Federal Reserve System. And to keep our illustration as clear as possible, we shall deal only with the changes which occur in those specific accounts affected by this transaction.

Let us trace this transaction in three related steps, keying the steps by letters to Figure 17·1.

a. Mr. Bradshaw gives his $50,000 check, drawn against the Wahoo bank, to the Ajax company. The Ajax company in turn deposits the check in its account with the Beaver Crossing bank. The Beaver Crossing bank increases the Ajax company's demand deposit by $50,000 when it deposits the check. (The Ajax company is now paid off.) Bradshaw is elated over his new machinery, for which he has now paid.

b. But now the Beaver Crossing bank has Bradshaw's check in its possession. This check is simply a claim against the assets of the Wahoo bank. How will the Beaver Crossing bank collect this claim? By sending this check—along with checks drawn on other banks—to the Federal Reserve Bank of Kansas City. Here a clerk will clear, or collect, this check for the Beaver Crossing bank by increasing its reserve in the Federal Reserve Bank by $50,000 and by decreasing the Wahoo bank's reserve by a like amount. The check is collected simply by making bookkeeping notations to the effect that the Wahoo bank's claim against the Federal Reserve Bank has been reduced by $50,000 and the Beaver Crossing bank's claim increased accordingly. Note these changes on the balance sheets in Figure 17·1.[5]

c. Finally, the cleared check is sent back to the Wahoo bank, and for the first time the Wahoo bank discovers that one of its depositors has drawn a check for $50,000 against his demand deposit. Accordingly, the Wahoo bank reduces Mr. Bradshaw's demand deposit by $50,000 and recognizes that the collection of this check has entailed a $50,000 decline in its reserves at the Federal Reserve Bank. Note that the balance statements of all three banks will still balance. The Wahoo bank will have reduced both its assets and liabilities by $50,000. The Beaver Crossing bank will have $50,000 more in reserves and in demand deposits. The ownership of reserves

[4] Actually, the Omaha Branch of the Federal Reserve Bank of Kansas City would handle the process of collecting this check.

[5] Here is an interesting sidelight: The collection of Bradshaw's check by the Beaver Crossing bank through the Federal Reserve Bank involves the same type of procedure as the collection of a check between two individuals who have deposits in the same commercial bank. Suppose you and I both have checking accounts in the Wahoo bank. I owe you $10 and I pay this debt by check. You deposit the $10 check in the bank. Here a bank clerk collects the check for you by noting a "+$10" in your account and a "−$10" in my account. And that's that. The same thing happens at the Federal Reserve Bank of Kansas City when the Beaver Crossing bank clears a $50,000 check against the Wahoo bank. The banker's bank increases the Beaver Crossing bank's deposit in the Federal Reserve Bank—that is, its reserve—by $50,000 and lowers the Wahoo bank's reserve by the same amount. The check is then cleared.

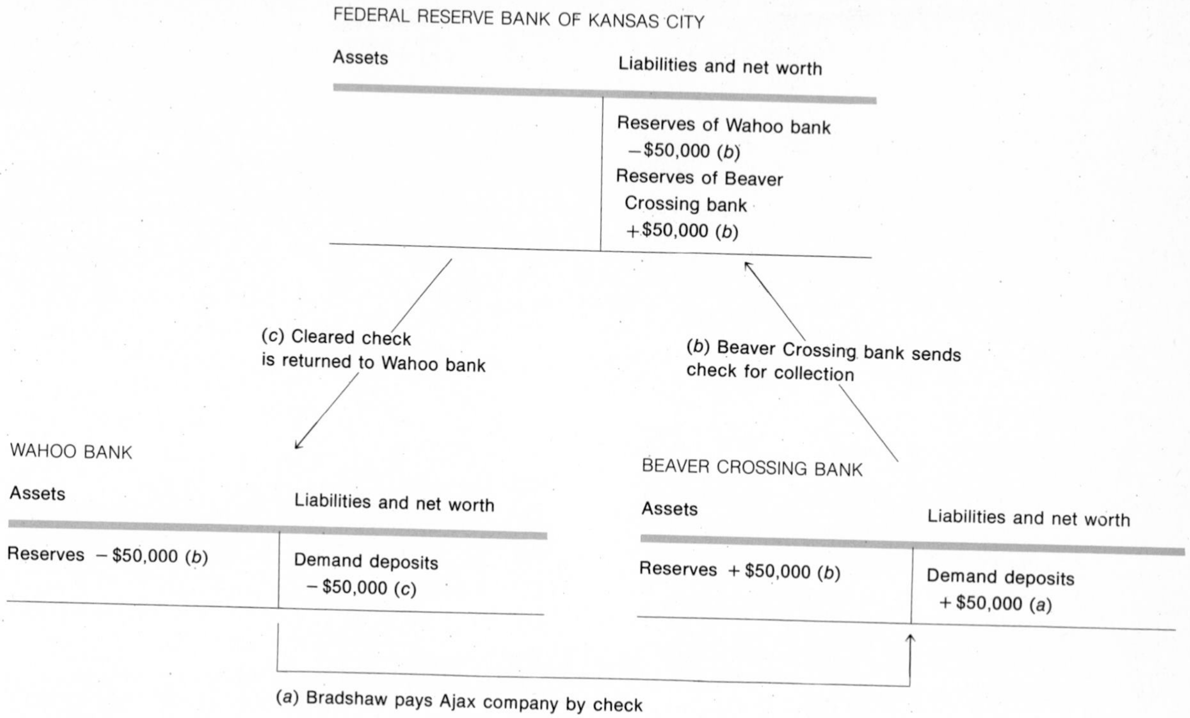

FIGURE 17·1 THE COLLECTION OF A CHECK THROUGH A FEDERAL RESERVE BANK

at the Federal Reserve Bank will have changed, but total reserves will stay the same.

The point we are making is this: *Whenever a check is drawn against a bank and deposited in another bank, the collection of that check will entail a loss of both reserves and deposits by the bank upon which the check is drawn.* Conversely, if a bank receives a check drawn on another bank, the bank receiving the check will, in the process of collecting it, have its reserves and deposits increased by the amount of the check. In our example, the Wahoo bank loses $50,000 in both reserves and deposits to the Beaver Crossing bank. But there is no loss of reserves or deposits for the banking system as a whole. What one bank loses another bank gains.

Bringing all the other assets and liabilities back into the picture, the Wahoo bank's balance sheet looks like this at the end of transaction 5:

BALANCE SHEET 5: WAHOO BANK

Assets		Liabilities and net worth	
Property	$240,000	Capital stock	$250,000
Reserves*	60,000	Demand deposits*	50,000

The reader should verify that with a 20 percent reserve requirement the bank's *excess* reserves now stand at $50,000.

This transaction indicates the manner in which commercial banks acquire the bulk of their reserves and deposits: from other banks through the check clearing process. While most of us in our personal dealings with banks think of demand deposits as being created by customer deposits of currency, and of reserves arising as the result of the bank's re-depositing some of this currency with the Federal Reserve Banks, this is not actually the case. Most bank deposits and reserves are received from other banks in the way the Beaver Crossing bank has acquired new reserves and deposits in the present transaction.

Transaction 5 is obviously reversible. If a check drawn against another bank is deposited in the Wahoo bank, the Wahoo bank will receive both reserves and deposits equal to the amount of the check as it is collected.

Let us designate here some of the salient conclusions from the first five transactions we have analyzed:

1. When a bank accepts deposits of cash, the composition of the money supply is changed, but the total supply of money is not altered.

2. Commercial banks which are members of the Federal Reserve System are required to keep legal reserve deposits, or simply "reserves," equal to a specified percentage of their own deposit liabilities on deposit with the Federal Reserve Bank of their district. The reserve ratio indicates the size of this "specified percentage." Reserves are a means by which the monetary authorities can control the lending policies of commercial banks. They do this by varying the percentage required as reserves.

3. The amount by which a bank's actual reserves exceed its required reserves is called "excess reserves."

4. Commercial bank reserves are an asset to the commercial bank but a liability to the Federal Reserve Bank holding them.

5. A bank which has a check drawn and collected against it will lose both reserves and deposits equal to the value of the check to the bank receiving the check.

Money-creating transactions of a commercial bank

The next two transactions are particularly crucial because they explain how a single commercial bank can literally create money by making loans to, and by purchasing government bonds from, individuals and businesses. Though these transactions are similar in many respects, we treat them separately.

Transaction 6: Granting a loan You will recall that in addition to accepting deposits, a basic function of commercial banks is the granting of loans to borrowers. What effect does commercial bank lending have upon the balance sheet of a commercial bank?

Suppose that the Grisley Meat Packing Company of Wahoo decides that the time is ripe to expand its facilities. Suppose, too, that the company needs exactly $50,000—which, by some unexplained coincidence, just happens to be equal to the Wahoo bank's excess reserves—to finance this project.

The company approaches the Wahoo bank and requests a loan for this amount. The Wahoo bank is acquainted with the Grisley company's fine reputation and financial soundness and is convinced of its ability to repay the loan. So the loan is granted. The president of the Grisley company hands a promissory note—a high-class IOU—to the Wahoo bank. The Grisley company, like all other modern firms, is interested in paying its obligations by check. Hence, instead of receiving a bushel basket full of cash from the bank, the Grisley company will simply get a $50,000 increase in its demand deposit in the Wahoo bank. From the Wahoo bank's standpoint it has purchased an interest-earning asset (the promissory note) and has created demand deposits to pay for this asset.

In short, the Grisley company has swapped an IOU for the right to draw an additional $50,000 worth of checks against its demand deposit in the Wahoo bank. Both parties are pleased with themselves. The Wahoo bank now possesses a new asset—an interest-bearing promissory note which it happily files under the general heading of "Loans." The Grisley

company, sporting a fattened demand deposit, is now in a position to expand its operations.

At the moment the loan is negotiated, the balance sheet of the Wahoo bank looks like this:

BALANCE SHEET 6a: WAHOO BANK (*when loan is negotiated*)

Assets		Liabilities and net worth	
Property	$240,000	Capital stock	$250,000
Reserves	60,000	Demand deposits*	100,000
Loans*	50,000		

All this looks innocent enough. But a closer examination of the Wahoo bank's balance statement will reveal a startling fact: *When a bank makes loans, it creates money.* The president of the Grisley company went to the bank with something which is not money—his IOU—and walked out with something that is money—a demand deposit.[6] When banks lend, they create demand deposits which are money. By extending credit the Wahoo bank has "monetized" an IOU. The Grisley company and the Wahoo bank have created and then swapped claims. The claim created by the Grisley company and given to the bank is not money; an individual's IOU is not generally acceptable as a medium of exchange. But the claim created by the bank and given to the Grisley company is money; checks drawn against a demand deposit are acceptable as a medium of exchange. It is through the extension of credit by commercial banks that the bulk of the money used in our economy is created.

But there are important forces which circumscribe the ability of a commercial bank to create demand deposits—that is, "bank money"—by lending. In the present case, the Wahoo bank can expect the newly created demand deposit of $50,000 to be a very active account. The Grisley company would not borrow $50,000 at, say, 7 or 8 percent for the sheer joy of knowing the funds were available if needed. Let us assume that the Grisley company awards a $50,000 contract to the Quickbuck Construction Company of Omaha. Quickbuck, true to its name, completes the expansion job and is rewarded with a check for $50,000 drawn by the Grisley company against its demand deposit in the Wahoo bank. The Quickbuck company, having its headquarters in Omaha, does not deposit this check back in the Wahoo bank but instead deposits it in the Fourth National Bank of Omaha. The Fourth National Bank now has a $50,000 claim against the Wahoo bank. This check is collected in the manner described in transaction 5. As a result, the Wahoo bank *loses* both reserves and deposits equal to the amount of the check; the Fourth National Bank *acquires* $50,000 of reserves and deposits. In short, assuming a check is drawn by the borrower for the entire amount of the loan ($50,000) and given to a firm which deposits it in another bank, the Wahoo bank's balance sheet will read as follows *after the check has been cleared against it:*

BALANCE SHEET 6b: WAHOO BANK (*after a check drawn on the loan has been collected*)

Assets		Liabilities and net worth	
Property	$240,000	Capital stock	$250,000
Reserves*	10,000	Demand deposits*	50,000
Loans	50,000		

You will note immediately that, after the check has been collected, the Wahoo bank is just barely meeting the legal reserve ratio of 20 percent. The bank has *no excess reserves.* This poses an interesting question: Could the Wahoo bank have safely lent an amount greater than $50,000—an amount greater than its excess reserves—and still have met the 20 percent reserve requirement if a check for the full amount of the loan cleared against it? The answer

[6]In transaction 3 demand deposits were created, but only by currency going out of circulation. Hence, there was a change in the composition of the money supply but no change in the total supply of money.

is "No."For example, suppose the Wahoo bank had loaned $55,000 to the Grisley company. Collection of the check against the Wahoo bank would have lowered its reserves to $5,000 (equal to $60,000 minus $55,000) and deposits would again stand at $50,000 (equal to $105,000 minus $55,000). The ratio of actual reserves to deposits would now be only $5,000/$50,000, or 10 percent. The Wahoo bank could thus not safely have lent $55,000. By experimenting with other figures in excess of $50,000, the reader will find that the maximum amount which the Wahoo bank could safely lend at the outset of transaction 6 is $50,000. This figure is identical with the amount of excess reserves which the bank had available at the time the loan was negotiated. We can conclude that *a single commercial bank in a multibank banking system can safely lend only dollar for dollar with its initial pre-loan excess reserves.* Why? Because when it lends, it faces the likelihood that checks for the entire amount of the loan may be drawn and cleared against the lending bank. A lending bank can anticipate the loss of reserves to other banks equal to the amount it lends.

There is a qualification to this discussion: When a bank makes a loan, some of the checks drawn by the borrower *may* be redeposited back in the lending bank. To the extent that this happens, the bank is able to lend an amount greater than its excess reserves. You might try this problem: Suppose a bank with $1,000 in excess reserves knows from past experience that for every loan it negotiates, checks drawn on that loan equal to one-tenth of the value of the loan will be redeposited in the bank. Thus, if the bank makes a $100 loan, the borrower promptly draws ten checks for $10 each. Nine of these wind up in other banks. The tenth is redeposited by its recipient in the lending bank. Knowing this in advance, what is the maximum amount this bank can safely lend on the basis of $1,000 of excess reserves?

Now that you are convinced that this credit-creating business can be complicated, let us accept our original conclusion that commercial banks can safely lend dollar for dollar with their excess reserves as being accurate enough for our purposes. It is a pretty good approximate statement of a single commercial bank's credit-creating potential.

If commercial banks create demand deposits—that is, money—when they make loans, it seems logical to inquire whether money is destroyed when the loans are repaid. The answer is "Yes." Using Balance Sheet 6b, let us see what happens when the Grisley company repays the $50,000 it borrowed.

To simplify, we shall (1) suppose that the loan is repaid not in installments but rather in one lump sum three years after the date of negotiation, and (2) ignore interest charges on the loan. Repayment may take two forms. Most likely the Grisley company will write a check for $50,000 against its demand deposit, which presumably has been fattened by extra profits resulting from the company's expanded operations. As a result the Wahoo bank's demand-deposit liabilities decline by $50,000; the Grisley company has given up $50,000 worth of its claim against the bank's assets. In turn the bank will surrender the Grisley company's IOU which it has been patiently holding these many months. The bank and the company have reswapped claims. But the claim given up by the Grisley company is money; the claim it is repurchasing—its IOU—is not. The supply of money has therefore been reduced by $50,000; that amount of demand deposits has been destroyed, unaccompanied by any increase in the money supply elsewhere in the economy. The Grisley company's IOU has been "demonetized." On the Wahoo bank's balance sheet, demand deposits and loans both fall by $50,000. You will note that the decline in demand deposits increases the bank's holdings of excess reserves; this provides the basis for new loans to be made.

The second repayment alternative open to the Grisley company is to repay by cash. It would be very unlikely that the company would want to bear the risk of accumulating such a large sum of money in its safe. But even if it did, the supply of money would still decline by $50,000 when cash repayment was made. In this case, the Grisley company would repurchase its IOU by handing over $50,000 in cash to the bank. This causes loans to fall on the bank's balance sheet by $50,000 and, obviously, cash to

increase by $50,000. Remember that we specifically excluded currency held by banks from the money supply on the ground that to include such cash would be double counting; it is apparent that this constitutes a $50,000 reduction in the supply of money. The Wahoo bank would probably use this additional cash either to enhance its reserves so as to permit new lending or to purchase securities.

Transaction 7: Buying government securities When a commercial bank buys government bonds[7] from individuals and business concerns, the effect is substantially the same as that of lending. New money is created. To illustrate, let us assume that the Wahoo bank's balance sheet initially stands as it did at the end of transaction 5. Now let us suppose that instead of borrowing all the needed $50,000 from the Wahoo bank, the Grisley company borrows just $25,000 and obtains an additional $25,000 by selling government bonds which it holds to the bank. The Wahoo bank pays for the Grisley company's IOU and the IOUs (bonds) of the government in the same way, by increasing the Grisley company's demand deposit. Demand-deposit liabilities increase by $50,000, and the bank's assets of securities and loans increase by $25,000 each. Immediately after negotiating the loan and bond purchase, the Wahoo bank's balance sheet will appear as follows:

BALANCE SHEET 7a: WAHOO BANK (*when loan is negotiated and bonds purchased*)

Assets		Liabilities and net worth	
Property	$240,000	Capital stock	$250,000
Reserves	60,000	Demand deposits*	100,000
Securities*	25,000		
Loans*	25,000		

The important point is that demand deposits, that is, the supply of money, have been increased by a total of $50,000, as in transaction 6. *Commercial bank bond purchases from the public increase the supply of money in the same way as does lending to the public.* The bank accepts government bonds—which are not money—and gives the Grisley company an increase in its demand deposits—which is money. The only real difference between selling a government bond to a commercial bank and negotiating a loan is that in the first case one gives the banker a claim against someone else (the United States Treasury), and in the second case a claim against one's own assets (one's IOU).

As in transaction 6, the effect of the Grisley company's drawing a $50,000 check in favor of the Quickbuck company will be for the Wahoo bank to lose reserves and demand deposits of $50,000 to the bank in which Quickbuck deposits the check. When the check is cleared against the Wahoo bank, the balance sheet will appear as follows:

BALANCE SHEET 7b: WAHOO BANK (*after collection of check*)

Assets		Liabilities and net worth	
Property	$240,000	Capital stock	$250,000
Reserves*	10,000	Demand deposits*	50,000
Securities	25,000		
Loans	25,000		

As you must now suspect, the selling of government bonds by a commercial bank will reduce the supply of money. If the Grisley company were to repurchase $25,000 worth of securities at some future date, it would in all probability pay by check. This, of course, reduces the quantity of demand deposits or bank money. If payment were made in cash, the quantity of currency in circulation would decline, thereby reducing the supply of money. The only difference between a commercial bank's selling a government bond and receiving payment on a loan is that in the former case the bank gives up a claim against the government, and in the latter a claim against a private borrower.

[7] Commercial banks are restrained by law in their purchase of private securities. It is felt that banks should be restricted to the performance of recognized banking functions and not permitted to become holding companies or speculative institutions.

The impact of buying and selling government bonds upon the commercial bank's balance sheet will be explored in greater detail in Chapter 18.

Profits and liquidity

The relative importance of the various asset items on a commercial bank's balance sheet is the result of the banker's pursuit of two conflicting goals. One goal is profits. Commercial banks, like any other business, are seeking profits. To this end the bank is desirous of holding loans and securities. These two items are the major earning assets of commercial banks. On the other hand, a commercial bank must seek safety. For a bank, safety lies in liquidity—specifically such liquid assets as cash and excess reserves. Banks must be on guard for depositors' transforming their demand deposits into cash. Similarly, the possibility exists that more checks will be cleared against a bank than are cleared in its favor, causing a net outflow of reserves. Bankers are thus seeking a proper balance between prudence and profits. The compromise that is achieved determines the relative size of earning assets as opposed to highly liquid assets.

A MONOPOLY BANK

We have just gauged the lending ability of a single commercial bank which is part of a multibank banking system. Our conclusion is that such a bank can only lend an amount equal to its excess reserves. This is so because a single bank faces the prospect of losing reserves equal to the demand deposits it creates by lending. The drawing of a check equal to the amount of a loan will whisk reserves and demand deposits off to the bank in which the check is deposited.

Let us now consider for a moment the lending, or money-creating, potential of a monopoly bank. Suppose that, instead of some fourteen thousand commercial banks in our economy, there existed just one huge commercial bank. This is admittedly unrealistic, but there is an important lesson to be learned from studying the lending ability of such a bank. Suppose that the balance sheet of this gigantic monopoly bank initially is as follows:

MONOPOLY BANK OF THE UNITED STATES
(*in billions*)

Assets		Liabilities and net worth	
Property	$ 5	Capital stock	$25
Reserves	5	Demand deposits	25
Securities	20		
Loans	20		

If the reserve ratio is 20 percent, we find that our monopoly bank is "loaned up." It is just barely meeting its reserve requirement and consequently has no excess reserves upon which to make loans. But suppose that some citizens decide to exchange $1 billion in cash for some government bonds which the monopoly bank is willing to sell. When the public buys these bonds from the monopoly bank, the bank's holdings of securities fall to $19 billion. The monopoly bank acquires in return $1 billion in cash. Assuming the bank has on hand sufficient cash to meet the day-to-day withdrawals of people cashing checks against their deposits, the bank adds the $1 billion to its reserves. Reserves will now stand at $6 billion. As a result of this transaction, it is obvious that the bank now has $1 billion in excess reserves. On the basis of this excess reserve, by how much can the monopoly bank increase the economy's supply of money by lending?

Careful consideration of the situation reveals that on the basis of this $1 billion in excess reserves, the monopoly bank can support an additional $5 billion in new loans. Why? *The monopoly bank with a 20 percent reserve ratio can lend $5 for every $1 of excess reserves, because it has no fear of losing reserves when it lends.* Indeed, by assumption, there are no other banks to which reserves can be lost! In lending $5 billion, the bank increases its outstanding loans from $20 to $25 billion, and its demand deposits will increase from $25 to $30 billion.

And remember: This $5 billion increase in demand deposits constitutes a $5 billion increase in the supply of money. Now what if the borrowers draw $5 billion worth of checks against these new deposits as they purchase various goods and services? Will the monopoly bank face the loss of reserves and deposits as did the single bank? No, because the recipients of these checks *must* deposit them back in the monopoly bank. Checks drawn against the demand deposits of the monopoly bank must come directly home to roost. These checks are cleared by simply transferring the ownership of demand deposits from the drawer of the check to the recipient of the check. But the total volumes of the monopoly bank's reserves and demand deposits are unchanged when checks are drawn and used to finance purchases and sales of goods and services. With a 20 percent reserve ratio the monopoly bank's $1 billion in excess reserves will permit a $5 billion expansion of loans from $25 to $30 billion. At the end of these transactions, the monopoly bank's balance sheet will stand as follows:

MONOPOLY BANK OF THE UNITED STATES
(*in billions*)

Assets		Liabilities and net worth	
Property	$ 5	Capital stock	$25
Reserves*	6	Demand deposits*	30
Securities*	19		
Loans*	25		

The astute reader will recognize that the ability of the monopoly bank to lend by a multiple—5, in this case—of its excess reserves is related to the size of the reserve ratio. Suppose for the moment that the monopoly bank's reserve ratio is just 10 percent and that at the outset its reserves are $2 billion and its outstanding demand deposits $20 billion. Again, the bank would be loaned up; it would have no excess reserves. Now the public buys $1 billion of securities and pays by cash. As before, the cash is added to reserves, giving the bank $1 billion in excess reserves. With a 10 percent reserve ratio, how much can the monopoly bank safely lend? The answer is clear: It can lend $10 billion, thereby increasing demand deposts by $10 billion. In this case, we find that with a 10 percent reserve ratio the monopoly bank can lend a multiple of 10 for every dollar's worth of excess reserves it acquires.

If you are suspicious that a generalization is lurking in these two examples, you are absolutely right. A 10 percent reserve ratio—that is, a ratio between reserves and demand deposits of 1:10—permits the monopoly bank to lend by a multiple of 10. A 20 percent reserve ratio—that is, a 1:5 ratio between reserves and deposits—allows the monopoly bank to create new money by a multiple of 5 for each dollar's worth of excess reserves. If the ratio were 33⅓ percent, the multiple would be 3. If 50 percent, it would be 2. If 100 percent, just 1. There is obviously an inverse relationship between the size of the reserve ratio and the multiple by which the monopoly bank can lend; the smaller the reserve ratio, the greater the multiple. More specifically, our generalization is this: *The multiple by which a monopoly bank can create new money by lending is the reciprocal of the reserve ratio.* The reciprocal of any number is the quotient you obtain by dividing that number into 1. Keep in mind, however, that the ability of the monopoly bank to lend anything at all is dependent upon the existence of excess reserves. No excess reserves, no lending—regardless of the size of the multiple.

Is this process of multiple credit creation reversible? Yes, it is. Suppose the monopoly bank has $4 billion in reserves and $25 billion in outstanding demand deposits. If the reserve ratio is 20 percent, the bank would be faced with a $1 billion deficiency in reserves. It would have to call in $5 billion in loans and extend no new credit to get its house back in order. The needed contraction in the supply of bank money is five times the deficiency of reserves.

In short, we can say that the monopoly bank can lend by a multiple of its excess reserves for two reasons. First, the monopoly bank, in sharp contrast to the single bank in the banking system, cannot lose reserves. When the recipients of new loans draw

checks to make purchases or pay debts, these checks must be redeposited back in the monopoly bank. The bank clears these checks by merely transferring claims against its assets—the payer's deposit is reduced and the payee's deposit increased by the amount of the check. The total volumes of demand deposits and reserves remain unchanged. Second, the monopoly bank's ability to lend by a multiple of its excess reserves hinges on the fact that the reserve ratio is fractional—that is, less than 100 percent. A 100 percent ratio would permit the monopoly bank to lend only dollar for dollar with its excess reserves.

THE COMMERCIAL BANKING SYSTEM AS A WHOLE

Thus far we have discovered that:

1. A single bank in a banking system can safely lend dollar for dollar with its excess reserves.
2. A monopoly bank, if one existed, could lend by a multiple of its excess reserves.

Now what of the lending ability of all commercial banks taken as a group? Jumping to our conclusions, we shall find that *the commercial banking system, as is true of a monopoly bank, can lend by a multiple of its excess reserves. This multiple lending is accomplished despite the fact that each bank in the system can only lend dollar for dollar with its excess reserves.* The immediate task is to uncover how these seemingly paradoxical conclusions come about.

To do this it is necessary that we keep our analysis as simple as possible. Therefore, we shall rely upon three simplifying assumptions. First, suppose that the reserve ratio for all commercial banks is 20 percent. Second, assume initially that all banks are exactly meeting this 20 percent reserve requirement. No excess reserves exist; all banks are "loaned up." Third, we shall suppose that if any bank becomes able to increase its loans as a result of acquiring excess reserves, an amount equal to these excess reserves will be loaned to one borrower, who will write a check for the entire amount of the loan and give it to someone else, who deposits the check in another bank. This messy assumption simply means that we are assuming the worst thing possible that can happen to any lending bank—a check for the entire amount of the loan is drawn and cleared against it and in favor of another bank.

The banking system's lending potential

To get the ball rolling, suppose that one of the twelve Federal Reserve Banks buys a $100 government bond in the open market from a private individual or business firm. The seller of the bond deposits the $100 check he receives in bank A and, having ample till money, bank A adds this $100 to its reserves. (We shall find in Chapter 18, incidentally, that such bond purchases by the central banks are a part of their deliberate policy to increase the excess reserves of commercial banks and ultimately the supply of money through bank lending.) Since we are recording only *changes* in the balance sheets of the various commercial banks, bank A's balance sheet now appears as follows (a_1):

BALANCE SHEET: COMMERCIAL BANK A

Assets		Liabilities and net worth	
Reserves	$+100 ($a_1$) − 80 ($a_3$)	Demand deposits	$+100 ($a_1$) + 80 ($a_2$) − 80 ($a_3$)
Loans	+ 80 (a_2)		

How much *excess reserves* does bank A now have? It has acquired $100 in new reserves, but in the process it has also acquired $100 in new demand deposits. This means that 20 percent of the new reserves must be earmarked as required reserves to offset the new deposits. In short, $20 of the new reserves will be required, freeing the remaining $80 as excess reserves. Remembering that a single commercial bank such as bank A can only lend an amount equal to its excess reserves, we conclude that bank A can safely lend a maximum of $80. When a loan for this amount is negotiated, bank A's loans

will increase by $80, and the borrower will get an $80 demand deposit. Let us add these figures to bank A's balance sheet (a_2).

But now we must invoke our third assumption: The borrower draws a check for $80—the entire amount of the loan—and gives it to someone who deposits it in another bank, bank B. As we saw in transaction 6, bank A *loses* both reserves and deposits equal to the amount of the loan (a_3). The net result of all the transactions is that bank A's reserves now stand at $20 (equal to $100 minus $80), loans at $80, and demand deposits at $100 (equal to $100 plus $80 minus $80). Note that when the dust has settled, bank A is just meeting the 20 percent reserve ratio.

Bank B *acquires* both the reserves and the deposits which bank A has lost. Bank B's balance sheet looks like this (b_1):

BALANCE SHEET: COMMERCIAL BANK B

Assets		Liabilities and net worth	
Reserves	$+80 ($b_1$) −64 ($b_3$)	Demand deposits	$+80 ($b_1$) +64 ($b_2$) −64 ($b_3$)
Loans	+64 (b_2)		

When the check is drawn and cleared, bank A *loses* $80 in reserves and deposits and bank B *gains* $80 in reserves and deposits. But 20 percent, or $16, of bank B's newly acquired reserves must be kept as required reserves against the new $80 in demand deposits. This means that bank B has $64 (equal to $80 minus $16) in excess reserves. It can therefore lend $64 ($b_2$). When the borrower draws a check for the entire amount and deposits it in bank C, the reserves and deposits of bank B both fall by the $64 ($b_3$). As a result of these transactions, bank B's reserves will now stand at $16 (equal to $80 minus $64), loans at $64, and demand deposits at $80 (equal to $80 plus $64 minus $64). Note that after all this has transpired, bank B is just meeting the 20 percent reserve requirement.

We are off and running again. Bank C has acquired the $64 in reserves and deposits lost by bank B. Its balance statement appears as follows (c_1):

BALANCE SHEET: COMMERCIAL BANK C

Assets		Liabilities and net worth	
Reserves	$+64.00 ($c_1$) −51.20 ($c_3$)	Demand deposits	$+64.00 ($c_1$) +51.20 ($c_2$) −51.20 ($c_3$)
Loans	+51.20 (c_2)		

Exactly 20 percent, or $12.80, of this new reserve will be required, the remaining $51.20 being excess reserves. Hence, bank C can safely lend a maximum of $51.20. Suppose it does ($c_2$). And suppose the borrower draws a check for the entire amount and gives it to someone who deposits it in another bank (c_3).

Bank D—the bank receiving the $51.20 in reserves and deposits—now notes these changes on its balance sheet (d_1):

BALANCE SHEET: COMMERCIAL BANK D

Assets		Liabilities and net worth	
Reserves	$+51.20 ($d_1$) −40.96 ($d_3$)	Demand deposits	$+51.20 ($d_1$) +40.96 ($d_2$) −40.96 ($d_3$)
Loans	+40.96 (d_2)		

It can now lend $40.96 ($d_2$). The borrower draws a check for the full amount and deposits it in another bank (d_3).

Now if we wanted to be particularly obnoxious, we could go ahead with this procedure by bringing banks E, F, G, H, . . . , N into the picture. We shall simply suggest that the student check through computations for banks E, F, and G, to ensure that he has the procedure firmly in mind.

TABLE 17·2 EXPANSION OF THE MONEY SUPPLY BY THE COMMERCIAL BANKING SYSTEM

Bank	(1) Acquired reserves and deposits	(2) Required reserves	(3) Excess reserves, or (1) − (2)	(4) Amount which the bank can lend, = (3)
Bank A	\$100.00 (a_1)	\$20.00	\$80.00	\$ 80.00 (a_2)
Bank B	80.00 (a_3, b_1)	16.00	64.00	64.00 (b_2)
Bank C	64.00 (b_3, c_1)	12.80	51.20	51.20 (c_2)
Bank D	51.20 (c_3, d_1)	10.24	40.96	40.96 (d_2)
Bank E	40.96	8.19	32.77	32.77
Bank F	32.77	6.55	26.22	26.22
Bank G	26.22	5.24	20.98	20.98
Bank H	20.98	4.20	16.78	16.78
Bank I	16.78	3.36	13.42	13.42
Bank J	13.42	2.68	10.74	10.74
Bank K	10.74	2.15	8.59	8.59
Bank L	8.59	1.72	6.87	6.87
Bank M	6.87	1.37	5.50	5.50
Bank N	5.50	1.10	4.40	4.40
Other banks	21.97	4.40	17.57	17.57
Total amount loaned				\$400.00

The nucleus of this analysis is summarized in Table 17·2. Data for banks E through N are supplied so you may check your computations. Our conclusion is a rather startling one: On the basis of the \$80 in excess reserves (acquired by the banking system when someone deposited the \$100 received from the sale of a government bond in bank A), the *commercial banking system* is able to lend \$400. Lo and behold, the banking system is able to lend by a multiple of 5 when the reserve ratio is 20 percent! Yet you will note that each single bank in the banking system is only lending an amount equal to its excess reserves. How do we explain these seemingly conflicting conclusions? Why is it that the *banking system* can lend by a multiple of its excess reserves, but *each individual bank* can only lend dollar for dollar with its excess reserves?

The answer lies in the fact that reserves lost by a single bank are not lost to the banking system as a whole. The reserves lost by bank A are acquired by bank B. Those lost by B are gained by C. C loses to D, D to E, E to F, and so forth. Hence, although reserves can be and are lost by *individual* banks in the banking system, there can be no loss of reserves for the banking *system* as a whole. Remember that the monopoly bank was able to lend by a multiple of its excess reserves because it could not lose reserves. For the same reason the banking system as a whole can lend by a multiple of its excess reserves. This contrast, incidentally, is a fine illustration of why it is imperative that we keep the fallacy of composition firmly in mind. Commercial banks *as a group* can create money by lending in a manner much different from that of the individual banks in that system.

The rationale involved in this bank money, or de-

posit, multiplier is not unlike that underlying the income multiplier discussed in Chapter 13. The income multiplier was based on the fact that the expenditures of one household are received as income by another; the deposit multiplier rests on the fact that the reserves and deposits lost by one bank are received by another bank. And, just as the size of the income multiplier is determined by the reciprocal of the MPS, that is, by the leakage into saving which occurs at each round of spending, so the deposit multiplier D is the reciprocal of the required reserve ratio R, that is, of the leakage into required reserves which occurs at each step in the lending process. In short,

$$D = \frac{1}{R}$$

In this formula D tells us the maximum number of new dollars of demand deposits which can be created for a *single dollar* of excess reserves, given the value of R. We can easily adjust the formula to show the maximum amount of new deposits which can be created for *any amount* of excess reserves E, by simply substituting E for 1 in the numerator, so that

$$D = \frac{E}{R}$$

Thus in our example of Table 17·2,

$$\$400 = \frac{\$80}{.20}$$

But keep in mind that, despite the similar rationale underlying the income and deposit multipliers, the former has to do with changes in income and the latter with changes in the supply of money.

The reader might experiment with these teasers in testing his understanding of multiple credit expansion by the banking system:

1. Rework the preceding analysis (at least three or four steps of it) on the assumption that the reserve ratio is 10 percent. What is the maximum amount of money the banking system could create upon acquiring $100 in new reserves and deposits? (No, the answer is not $800!)

2. Explain how a banking system which is "loaned up" and faced with a 20 percent reserve ratio might be forced to *reduce* its outstanding loans by $400 as a result of a Federal Reserve Bank's *selling* a $100 bond to a private individual or business.

Some modifications

Our discussion of credit expansion has been conducted in a somewhat rarefied atmosphere. There are certain complications which might modify the quantitative preciseness of our analysis.

Other leakages Aside from the leakage of required reserves at each step of the lending process, two other leakages of money from the commercial banks might occur, thereby dampening the money-creating potential of the banking system.

1. A borrower may request that a part of his loan be paid in cash. Or the recipient of a check drawn by a borrower may present it at his bank to be redeemed partially or wholly in currency rather than added to his account. Thus, if the person who borrowed the $80 from bank A in our illustration asked for and got $16 of it in cash and the remaining $64 as a demand deposit, bank B would only receive $64 in new reserves (of which only $51.20 would be excess) rather than $80 (of which $64 was excess). This decline in excess reserves reduces the lending potential of the banking system accordingly. As a matter of fact, if the first borrower had taken the entire $80 in cash, and this currency remained in circulation, the multiple expansion process would have stopped then and there. But the convenience and safety of demand deposits make this unlikely.

2. Our analysis of the commercial banking system's ability to expand the money supply by lending is based on the supposition that commercial banks are willing to meet precisely the legal reserve requirement. In practice bankers are more prudent than this and arrange to have a "safety margin" of excess reserves to avoid the embarrassment of falling below the legal reserve ratio in the event that an unusually large amount of checks is cleared against them. Therefore bank A, upon receiving $100 in new cash, might choose to add $25 rather than the legal minimum of $20 to its reserves, the extra $5 serving as

a buffer, or cushion, against adverse check clearings. The overall credit expansion potential of the banking system would obviously be reduced by such additions to a bank's excess reserves.

Willingness versus ability to lend It is only fair to emphasize that our illustration of the banking system's ability to create money rests upon the supposition that commercial banks are willing to exercise their abilities to create money by lending and that households and businesses are willing to borrow. In practice, this need not be the case. Bankers, you will recall, seek a proper balance between prudence and profits. When prosperity reigns, banks may expand credit to the maximum of their ability. Why not? Loans are interest-earning assets, and in good times there is little fear of borrowers defaulting. But if depression clouds appear on the economic horizon, bankers may hastily withdraw their invitations to borrow, seeking the safety of liquidity even if it involves the sacrifice of potential interest income. Bankers may fear the large-scale withdrawal of deposits by a panicky public and simultaneously doubt the ability of borrowers to repay. It is not too surprising that during some years of the Great Depression of the 1930s, banks had considerable excess reserves but lending was at a low ebb. Obviously, if the amount actually loaned by each commercial bank falls short of its excess reserves, the resulting multiple expansion of credit will be curtailed.

The fact that bankers may not expand the supply of money to their maximum ability is of more than passing interest. It may be a factor which contributes significantly to business fluctuations. By holding back on credit expansion as the economy begins to slip into a depression, commercial banks may further inhibit total spending and intensify that cyclical downswing. Indeed, we noted in Chapter 11 that a rapid shrinkage of the money supply contributed to the Great Depression of the 1930s. Conversely, by lending and thereby creating money to the maximum of their ability during prosperity, commercial banks may contribute to an excess of total spending and to the resulting inflationary pressures. In Chapter 18 the means by which the Board of Governors attempts to influence the lending policies of commercial banks, so that they will offset rather than enforce cyclical fluctuations, will be explored.

SUMMARY

1. Commercial banks create money—that is, demand deposits, or bank money—when they make loans. The creation of demand deposits by bank lending is the most important source of money in American capitalism.
2. The ability of a single commercial bank to create money by lending depends upon the size of its *excess* reserves. Generally speaking, a commercial bank can safely lend only an amount equal to the size of its excess reserves. It is thus limited because, in all likelihood, checks drawn by borrowers will be deposited in other banks, causing a loss of reserves and deposits to the lending bank equal to the amount which it has loaned.
3. A monopoly bank would be in a position to lend by a multiple of any excess reserves which it might acquire. This is so because ***a.*** a monopoly bank could not lose reserves as the result of checks drawn by borrowers, and ***b.*** the reserve ratio is assumed to be less than 100 percent. The multiple by which a monopoly bank could expand the money supply through lending is the reciprocal of the reserve ratio.
4. The commercial banking system as a whole can also lend by a multiple of its excess reserves. As is the case with the monopoly bank, the banking *system* cannot lose reserves, although individual banks can lose reserves to other banks in the system. The multiple by which the banking system can lend is, once again, the reciprocal of the reserve ratio. This multiple credit expansion process is reversible.

QUESTIONS AND STUDY SUGGESTIONS

1. Why must a balance sheet always balance? What are the major assets and claims on a commercial bank's balance sheet?

2. Why are commercial banks required to have reserves? Explain why reserves are assets to commercial banks but liabilities to the Federal Reserve Banks. What are excess reserves? How are they calculated? What is their significance?

3. "Whenever currency is deposited in a commercial bank, cash goes out of circulation and, as a result, the supply of money is reduced." Do you agree? Explain.

4. "When a check is drawn against bank A and deposited in another bank, bank A will lose reserves as the check is cleared. Yet the collection of checks entails no loss of reserves by the commercial banking system." Explain. Of what significance is this for the lending ability of the banking system?

5. "When a commercial bank makes loans, it creates money; when loans are retired, money is destroyed." Explain.

6. Explain why a single commercial bank can safely lend only an amount equal to its excess reserves but the commercial banking system can lend by a multiple of its excess reserves. Why is the multiple by which the banking system can lend equal to the reciprocal of its reserve ratio?

7. Assume that Jones deposits $500 in currency in the First National Bank. A half hour later Smith negotiates a loan for $750 at this bank. By how much and in what direction has the money supply changed? Explain.

8. Suppose the Continental Bank has the following simplified balance sheet. The reserve ratio is 20 percent.

Assets		(1)	(2)	Liabilities and net worth		(1)	(2)
Reserves	$22,000	____	____	Demand deposits	$100,000	____	____
Securities	38,000	____	____				
Loans	40,000	____	____				

a. What is the maximum amount of new loans which this bank can safely make? Show in column 1 how the bank's balance sheet will appear after the bank has loaned this additional amount.

b. By how much has the supply of money changed? Explain.

c. How will the bank's balance sheet appear after checks drawn for the entire amount of the new loans have been cleared against this bank? Show this new balance sheet in column 2.

d. Answer parts *a, b,* and *c* on the assumption that the reserve ratio is 15 percent.

9. Suppose the National Bank of Commerce has excess reserves of $8,000 and outstanding demand deposits of $150,000. If the reserve ratio is 20 percent, what is the size of the bank's actual reserves?

10. Suppose the Fourth National Bank has the following simplified balance sheet. The reserve ratio is 20 percent.

Assets		(1)	(2)	Liabilities and net worth		(1)	(2)
Reserves	$40,000	____	____	Demand deposits	$200,000	____	____
Securities	90,000	____	____				
Loans	70,000	____	____				

Assume that households and businesses deposit $5,000 worth of currency in this bank and that this currency is added to the bank's reserves.

a. In column 1 show how the bank's balance sheet would appear after this transaction. Has there been a change in the supply of money as a result of these deposits?

b. How much excess reserves does this bank now have? By how much can it safely expand its loans? In column 2 show the bank's balance sheet as it appears after those loans have been made.

c. To what extent, if at all, will this lending alter the supply of money? Explain.

11. Suppose the following is a simplified consolidated balance sheet for the commercial banking system. All figures are in billions. The reserve ratio is 20 percent.

Assets		(1)	Liabilities and net worth		(1)
Reserves	$40	____	Demand deposits	$186	____
Securities	56	____			
Loans	90	____			

a. How much excess reserves does the commercial banking system have? How much can the banking system lend? Show in column 1 how the consolidated balance sheet would look after this amount has been lent.

b. Answer question 11*a* on the assumption that the reserve ratio is 15 percent. Explain the resulting difference in the lending ability of the commercial banking system.

12. The Third National Bank has reserves of $20,000 and demand deposits of $100,000. The reserve ratio is 20 percent. Households deposit $5,000 in currency in the bank. This $5,000 is added by the bank to its reserves. How much excess reserves does the bank now have?

13. Suppose again that the Third National Bank has reserves of $20,000 and demand deposits of $100,000. The reserve ratio remains at 20 percent. The bank now sells $5,000 in securities to the Federal Reserve Bank in its district, receiving a $5,000 increase in reserves in return. How much excess reserves does the bank now have? Why does your answer differ (yes, it does!) from the answer to question 12?

14. What are "leakages"? How might they affect the money-creating potential of the banking system? Be specific.

SELECTED REFERENCES

Bernstein, Peter L.: *A Primer on Money, Banking, and Gold* (New York: Random House, Inc., 1965).

Chandler, Lester V.: *The Economics of Money and Banking,* 5th ed. (New York: Harper & Row, Publishers, Incorporated, 1969), chaps. 6 and 7.

Duesenberry, James S.: *Money and Credit: Impact and Control,* 2d ed. (Englewood Cliffs, N.J.: Prentice-Hall, Inc., 1967).

Klein, John J.: *Money and the Economy,* 2d ed. (New York: Harcourt, Brace & World, Inc., 1970), chaps. 5–8.

18

THE FEDERAL RESERVE BANKS AND MONETARY POLICY

In Chapter 17 our attention was focused upon the money-creating ability of individual banks and the commercial banking system. Our discussion ended on a disturbing note: Unregulated commercial banking might contribute to cyclical fluctuations in business activity. That is, commercial banks will find it profitable to expand the supply of money during inflationary prosperity and to restrict the money supply in seeking liquidity during depression. It is the task of this chapter to see how the monetary authorities of American capitalism attempt to reverse the procyclical tendencies of the commercial banking system through a variety of control techniques.

More specifically, the goals of the present chapter are these: First, the objectives of monetary policy, the roles of participating institutions, and the route by which monetary policy affects the operation of the economy are detailed. Next, the balance sheet of the Federal Reserve Banks is surveyed, because it is through these central banks that monetary policy is largely effectuated. Third, the quantitative and qualitative techniques of monetary control are analyzed in considerable detail. What are the major instruments of monetary control and how do they function? Fourth, a monetary approach to output and price level determination, based upon the so-called equation of exchange, is presented. Finally, monetary policy is evaluated as to its overall effectiveness in restraining fluctuations in economic activity.

OBJECTIVES OF MONETARY POLICY

Before analyzing the techniques through which monetary policy is effectuated, it is essential that we clearly understand the objectives of monetary policy and locate the institutions responsible for the formulation and implementation of that policy. Certain key points made in Chapter 16 merit reemphasis at the outset of our discussion. The Board of Governors of the Federal Reserve System has the responsibility of supervising and controlling the operation of our

monetary and banking systems. It is this Board which formulates the basic policies which the banking system follows. Because it is a public body, the decisions of the Board of Governors are made in the interests of the general economic welfare of society as a whole. The twelve Federal Reserve Banks—the central banks of American capitalism—implement the policy decisions of the Board. As quasi-public banks, the Federal Reserve banks are not guided by the profit motive, but rather pursue those measures which the Board of Governors recommends.

However, to say that the Board follows policies which "promote the general economic welfare" is not enough. We must pinpoint the goal of monetary policy. It will come as no great surprise that *the objective of monetary policy is to assist the economy in achieving a full-employment noninflationary level of total output.*

Cause-effect chain

But precisely how does monetary policy work toward this goal? The process is complicated, but essentially it boils down to this:

1. By invoking certain control techniques, the Board of Governors and the Federal Reserve Banks can influence the size of both actual and required reserves—and therefore the excess reserves—of commercial banks.

2. Because excess reserves are the basis upon which commercial banks can expand the money supply by lending, any manipulations of excess reserves through the control techniques of the Board of Governors will affect the supply of money, that is, the amounts which commercial banks will be able and willing to lend at various possible interest rates.

3. Given the demand for money, changes in the supply of money will affect the cost and availability of money. That is, changes in the supply of money will affect the interest rate and the amount of credit bankers are willing to make available to borrowers.

4. Changes in the cost and availability of bank credit will in turn have an impact upon the spending decisions of society, particularly upon investment decisions, and therefore upon the levels of output, employment, income, and prices.

The cause-effect chain between monetary policy and output and employment is summarized in the outline below.

Federal monetary policy influences commercial bank reserves

which

Influence the supply of money

which

Influences the interest rate (the cost) and the availability of bank credit

which

Influences investment spending, output, employment, and the price level

Let us examine the operation of monetary policy through a simple example. Suppose the economy is operating below the full-employment mark. Sidestepping troublesome complications and qualifications for the moment, we find that monetary policy would work something like this:

1. The Board of Governors would direct the Federal Reserve Banks to pursue certain policies designed to increase the (excess) reserves of commercial banks.

2. Finding themselves with abundant excess reserves, commercial banks are now in a position to make available a greater supply of money by granting bank credit. The banking *system* can expand the supply of money by a multiple of its excess reserves.

3. With an increase in the supply of money relative to the demand for it, interest rates will decline, and the quantity of bank credit (money) taken by borrowers will increase.

4. Low interest rates and the ready availability of bank credit will induce increases in spending. These increases in spending will be subject to the multiplier effect, driving the equilibrium NNP upward by a multiple of the increase in total spending.

The above comments detail the ideal operation of an "easy money" policy. A "tight money" policy follows the same route, but the procedure is to lower commercial bank reserves, reduce the supply of

money, raise the cost and lessen the availability of bank credit, and thereby curtail spending. Tight money should obviously be invoked when an excess of total spending is causing inflation in the economy.

Monetary policy and investment

Economists are in general agreement that the investment component of total spending is more likely to be affected by changes in the interest rate than is consumer spending. The interest rate does not seem to be a very crucial factor in determining how households divide their disposable income between consumption and saving. Indeed, it is not clear whether decreases in the interest rate will tend to increase or decrease the amount of consumption. On the one hand, a lower interest rate may induce some households, particularly those operating small businesses, to save less, because it is now cheap to finance by borrowing. On the other hand, we have noted that those who save to provide a given retirement income or to provide funds for the education of their children find that a lower interest rate will mean that a larger volume of saving will be required to earn the needed income. Then, too, the effect of higher interest rates on consumer installment buying is not great, because considerable increases or decreases in the interest rate have little impact on the size of each monthly payment; that is, the consumer is not impressed by the total interest charge but only by how much interest he must pay per month. Furthermore, any tendency for higher interest charges to diminish consumer installment buying can be largely canceled by extending the repayment period from, say, twenty-four to thirty-six months.

The impact of changing interest rates upon investment spending is greater because of the size and long-term nature of such purchases. Capital equipment, factory buildings, warehouses, and so forth are tremendously expensive purchases. In absolute terms the interest charges on funds borrowed for these purchases will be considerable. Similarly, the interest cost on a house purchased on a long-term contract will be very large: A ½ percent change in the interest rate could easily amount to hundreds or even thousands of dollars on the total cost of a home. It is important to note as well that changes in the interest rate may also affect investment spending by changing the relative attractiveness of capital equipment purchases and bond purchases. If the interest rate rises on bonds, then, given the profit expectations on capital good purchases, businesses will be more inclined to purchase securities than to buy capital equipment. Conversely, given profit expectations on investment spending, a fall in the interest rate makes capital purchases more attractive than bond ownership. In short, the impact of changing interest rates will be primarily upon investment spending and, through this channel, upon output, employment, and the level of prices.

So much for the objectives of monetary policy and the cause-effect chain which its application entails. We now seek an understanding of the techniques by which the Board of Governors can manipulate the size of commercial bank reserves.

CONSOLIDATED BALANCE SHEET OF THE FEDERAL RESERVE BANKS

Because monetary policy is implemented by the twelve Federal Reserve Banks, it is essential to consider the nature of the balance sheet of the Federal Reserve Banks. Some of the assets and liabilities found here are considerably different from those found on the balance sheet of a commercial bank. Table 18·1 is a consolidated balance sheet which shows all the pertinent assets and liabilities of the twelve Federal Reserve Banks as of January 27, 1971.

Assets

Cash This is the Federal Reserve Banks' holdings of Treasury currency. The Federal Reserve Banks may have received this cash as a result of Treasury or commercial bank deposits.

Gold certificates Gold certificates are simply warehouse receipts for the gold bullion held by the

TABLE 18·1 TWELVE FEDERAL RESERVE BANKS' CONSOLIDATED BALANCE SHEET, JANUARY 27, 1971 (*in billions*)

Assets		Liabilities and net worth	
Cash	$ 0.2	Reserves of member banks	$25.0
Gold certificates	10.5	Treasury deposits	1.2
Securities	61.9	Federal Reserve Notes (outstanding)	48.9
Loans to commercial banks	0.7	All other liabilities and net worth	10.7
All other assets	12.5	Total	$85.8
Total	$85.8		

Source: Federal Reserve Bulletin, February 1971.

Treasury. In settling international payments the United States Treasury may buy gold from foreign monetary authorities. The Treasury pays for such gold by drawing checks against its deposit in the Federal Reserve Banks. The clearing of these checks reduces Treasury deposits in the Federal Reserve Banks. To replenish these deposits the Treasury issues gold certificates—claims or warehouse receipts against the newly obtained gold—and deposits them in the Federal Reserve Banks. Treasury sales of gold to foreign monetary authorities have the opposite effect, reducing the Federal Reserve Banks' holdings of gold certificates.

Securities This refers to the government bonds which the Federal Reserve Banks are holding. Some of these bonds may have been purchased directly from the Treasury, but most are bought in the open market from commercial banks or the public. Although these bonds are an important source of income to the Federal Reserve Banks, they are not bought and sold primarily for income. Rather they are bought and sold primarily to influence the size of commercial bank reserves and therefore their ability to create money by lending.

Loans to commercial banks Commercial banks occasionally borrow from the Federal Reserve Banks. The IOUs which the commercial banks give to the bankers' banks in negotiating loans are listed as loans to commercial banks. From the Federal Reserve Banks' point of view, these IOUs are assets, that is, claims against the commercial banks that have borrowed from them. To the commercial banks, these IOUs are liabilities. In borrowing, the commercial banks obtain increases in their reserves in exchange for their IOUs.

Before shifting to the liability side of the Federal Reserve Banks' balance sheet, one note on terminology: "Securities" and "loans to commercial banks" are sometimes called "Reserve Bank credit." These two accounts represent credit which the bankers' banks have extended to (1) the government by buying government securities and (2) commercial banks by accepting their IOUs in return for increases in their reserves.

Liabilities

On the liability side we find three major items:

Reserves of member banks We are already familiar with this account. It is an asset from the viewpoint of the member banks but a liability to the Federal Reserve Banks.

Treasury deposits Just as businesses and private individuals find it convenient and desirable to pay their obligations by check, so does the United States Treasury. It keeps deposits in the various Federal Reserve Banks and draws checks on them in paying its obligations. To the Treasury such deposits are obviously assets; to the Federal Reserve Banks, liabilities. The Treasury creates and replenishes these deposits by depositing tax receipts, money borrowed from the public or the banks through the sale of bonds, and gold certificates.

Federal Reserve Notes Virtually all of our paper money supply is Federal Reserve Notes. These notes are issued by the Federal Reserve Banks. When in circulation, these pieces of paper money constitute circulating claims against the assets of the Federal Reserve Banks and are therefore treated by them as liabilities. Just as your own IOU is neither an asset nor a liability to you when it is in your own possession, so Federal Reserve Notes resting in the vaults of the various Federal Reserve Banks are neither an asset nor a liability. Only those notes in circulation are liabilities to the bankers' banks. These notes, which come into circulation through commercial banks, are not a part of the money supply until they are in the hands of the public.

MONETARY POLICY: QUANTITATIVE CONTROLS

With this cursory understanding of the Federal Reserve Banks' balance sheet, we are now in a position to explore how the Board of Governors of the Federal Reserve System can influence the money-creating abilities of the commercial banking system. What devices can be employed at the discretion of the Board of Governors to influence commercial bank reserves?

The general, or quantitative, controls of the monetary authorities are three in number: (1) changing the reserve ratio, (2) open-market operations, and (3) changing the discount rate. These controls are general, or quantitative, in that they seek to manipulate the total quantity of bank credit. Later we shall discuss selective, or qualitative, controls, which are aimed at influencing the volume of specific types of credit.

The reserve ratio

How can the Board of Governors influence the ability of commercial banks to lend through manipulation of the legal reserve ratio? A simple example will supply a clear answer to this query. Suppose a commercial bank's balance sheet is such that reserves are $5,000 and demand deposits $20,000. If the legal reserve ratio stands at 20 percent, the bank's *required* reserves are $4,000. Since *actual* reserves are $5,000, it is apparent that the *excess* reserves of this bank are $1,000. On the basis of this $1,000 of excess reserves we have seen that this single bank can lend $1,000, but the banking system as a whole could create a maximum of $5,000 in new bank money by lending (Table 18·2). Now, what if the Board of Governors raised the legal reserve ratio from 20 to 25 percent? Required reserves would jump from $4,000 to $5,000, shrinking excess reserves from $1,000 to zero. It is obvious that *raising the reserve ratio increases the amount of required reserves banks must keep. Either banks lose excess reserves, diminishing their ability to create money by lending, or else they find their reserves deficient and are forced to contract the money supply.* In the above case, excess reserves are transformed into required reserves, and the money-creating potential of our bank is reduced from $1,000 to zero.

What if the Board of Governors announced a forthcoming increase in the legal reserve requirement to 30 percent? The commercial bank would be faced with the embarrassing prospect of failing to meet this requirement. To protect itself against such an eventuality, the bank would be forced to lower its outstanding demand deposits and at the same time to increase its reserves. To reduce its demand deposits, the bank would be prone to let outstanding loans mature and be repaid without extending new credit. To increase reserves, the bank might sell some of its holdings of securities, adding the proceeds to its

TABLE 18·2 THE EFFECTS OF CHANGES IN THE RESERVE RATIO UPON THE LENDING ABILITY OF COMMERCIAL BANKS (*hypothetical data*)

(1) Legal reserve ratio, percent	(2) Demand deposits	(3) Actual reserves	(4) Required reserves	(5) Excess reserves, or (3) − (4)	(6) Money-creating potential of single bank, = (5)	(7) Money-creating potential of banking system
10	$20,000	$5,000	$2,000	$ 3,000	$ 3,000	$ 30,000
20	20,000	5,000	4,000	1,000	1,000	5,000
25	20,000	5,000	5,000	0	0	0
30	20,000	5,000	6,000	−1,000	−1,000	−3,333

reserves. Both courses of action will reduce the supply of money (see transactions 6 and 7, Chapter 17).

What would be the effect if the Board of Governors lowered the reserve ratio from the original 20 to 10 percent? In this case required reserves would decline from $4,000 to $2,000, and as a result excess reserves would jump from $1,000 to $3,000. We can conclude that *lowering the reserve ratio changes required reserves to excess reserves, thereby enhancing the ability of banks to create new money by lending.* Table 18·2 summarizes all the reserve ratio changes just discussed.

Table 18·2 reveals that a change in the reserve ratio actually affects the money-creating ability of the banking *system* in two ways. First, it affects the size of excess reserves. Second, it changes the multiple by which the banking system can lend. Thus, raising the reserve ratio from 10 to 20 percent reduces the money-creating potential of the banking system from $30,000 to $5,000.

Although changing the reserve ratio is a potentially powerful technique of monetary control, it is actually used quite infrequently. The Board of Governors controls the money supply primarily through open-market operations.

Open-market operations

The buying and selling of government bonds by the Federal Reserve Banks in the open market—that is, from or to commercial banks and the general public—also affect the excess reserves of commercial banks.

Buying securities Suppose the Board of Governors orders the Federal Reserve Banks to buy government bonds in the open market. From whom may these securities be purchased? In general, from commercial banks and the public. In either case the overall effect is basically the same—commercial bank reserves are increased.

Let us trace through the situation in which the Federal Reserve Banks buy government bonds *from commercial banks.* This transaction is a simple one.

a. The commercial banks give up a part of their holdings of securities to the bankers' banks.

b. The Federal Reserve Banks pay for these securities by increasing the reserves of the commercial banks by the amount of the purchase.

Just as the commercial bank may pay for a bond bought from a private individual by increasing the seller's demand deposit, so the bankers' bank may

pay for bonds bought from commercial banks by increasing the banks' reserves. In short, the consolidated balance sheets of the commercial banks and the Federal Reserve Banks will change as follows:

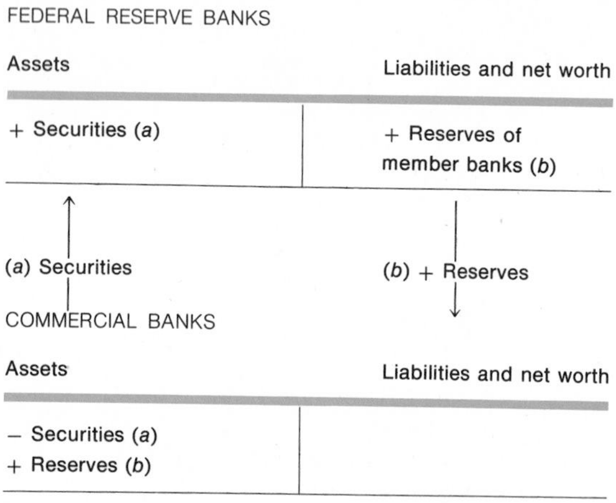

The most important aspect of this transaction is that, when Federal Reserve Banks purchase securities from commercial banks, the reserves—and therefore the lending ability—of the commercial banks are increased.

If the Federal Reserve Banks should purchase securities *from the general public,* the effect on commercial bank reserves would be substantially the same. Suppose that the Grisley Meat Packing Company possesses some negotiable government bonds which it sells in the open market to the Federal Reserve Banks. The transaction goes like this:

a. The Grisley company gives up securities to the Federal Reserve Banks and gets in payment a check drawn by the Federal Reserve Banks on themselves.

b. The Grisley company promptly deposits this check in its account with the Wahoo bank.

c. The Wahoo bank collects this check against the Federal Reserve Banks by sending it to the Federal Reserve Banks for collection. As a result the Wahoo bank receives an increase in its reserves.

Balance sheet changes are as follows:

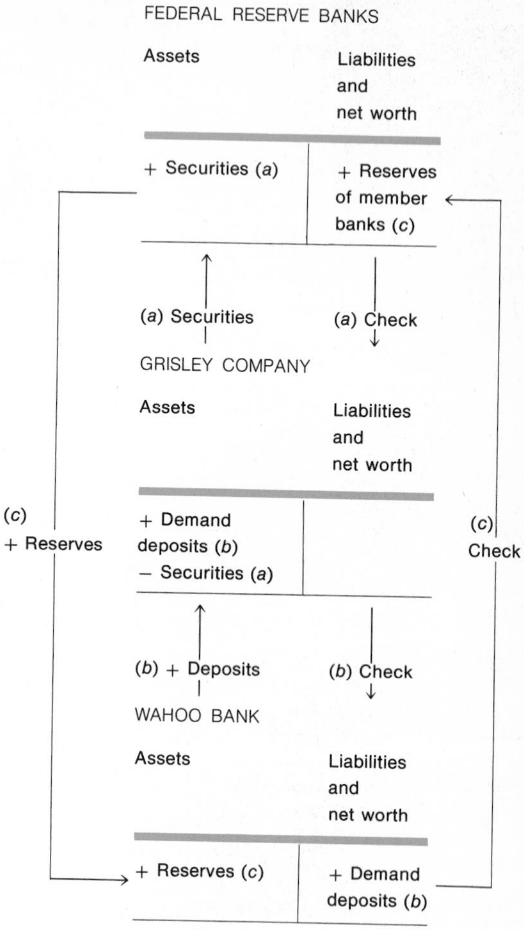

Two aspects of this transaction are noteworthy. First, as with Federal Reserve purchases of securities directly from commercial banks, the reserves and lending ability of the commercial banking system have been increased. Second, in this instance the supply of money is directly increased by the central banks' purchase of government bonds, aside from any expansion of the money supply which may occur as the result of the increase in commercial bank reserves.

You may detect a slight difference between the Federal Reserve Banks' purchases of securities from the commercial banking system and from the public. Assuming all commercial banks are "loaned up"

initially, Federal Reserve bond purchases from commercial banks will increase the actual reserves and excess reserves of the commercial banks by the entire amount of the bond purchases. Thus a $1,000 bond purchase from commercial banks would increase both the actual and excess reserves of the commercial banks by $1,000. On the other hand, Federal Reserve Bank purchases of bonds from the public increase actual reserves but also increase demand deposits. Thus a $1,000 bond purchase from the public would increase actual reserves of the "loaned up" banking system by $1,000; but with a 20 percent reserve ratio, the excess reserves of the banking system would only amount to $800. In the case of bond purchases from the public, it is *as if* the commercial banking system had already used one-fifth or 20 percent of its newly acquired reserves to support $1,000 worth of new demand deposit money.

However, in each transaction the basic conclusion is the same: *When the Federal Reserve Banks buy securities in the open market, commercial banks' reserves will be increased.*

Selling securities We should now be highly suspicious that Federal Reserve Bank sales of government bonds will reduce commercial bank reserves. Let us confirm these suspicions.

Suppose the Federal Reserve Banks sell securities in the open market to *commercial banks:*

a. The Federal Reserve Banks give up securities which the commercial banks obviously acquire.

b. The commercial banks pay for these securities by drawing checks against their deposits—that is, their reserves—in the Federal Reserve Banks. The Federal Reserve Banks collect these checks by reducing the commercial banks' reserves accordingly.

In short, the balance sheet changes appear as shown in the next column.

Note specifically the reduction in commercial bank reserves.

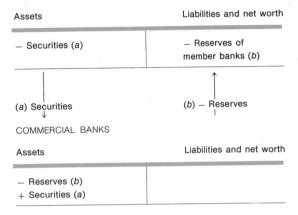

Should the Federal Reserve Banks sell securities *to the public,* the overall effect is substantially the same. Let us put the Grisley company on the buying end of government bonds which the Federal Reserve Banks are selling.

FEDERAL RESERVE BANKS

Assets	Liabilities and net worth
− Securities (*a*)	− Reserves of member banks (*b*)

(*a*) Securities ↓ (*b*) − Reserves ↑

COMMERCIAL BANKS

Assets	Liabilities and net worth
− Reserves (*b*) + Securities (*a*)	

a. The Federal Reserve Bank sells government bonds to the Grisley company, the latter paying for these securities by a check drawn on the Wahoo bank.

b. The Federal Reserve Banks clear this check against the Wahoo bank by reducing its reserves.

c. The Wahoo bank returns the Grisley company's check to it, reducing the company's demand deposit accordingly.

The balance sheets change as shown on page 315.

Note that Federal Reserve bond sales of $1,000 to the commercial banking system reduce the system's actual and excess reserves by $1,000. But a $1,000 bond sale to the public reduces excess reserves by $800 because demand deposit money is also reduced by $1,000 by the sale. In the case of bond sales to the public, it is *as if* the commercial banking system had reduced its outstanding demand deposits by $1,000 to cushion the decline in excess reserves to the extent of $200.

In each of the two variations of the Federal Reserve bond sale transaction, however, the basic conclusion is the same: *When the Federal Reserve Banks sell securities in the open market, commercial bank reserves are reduced.*

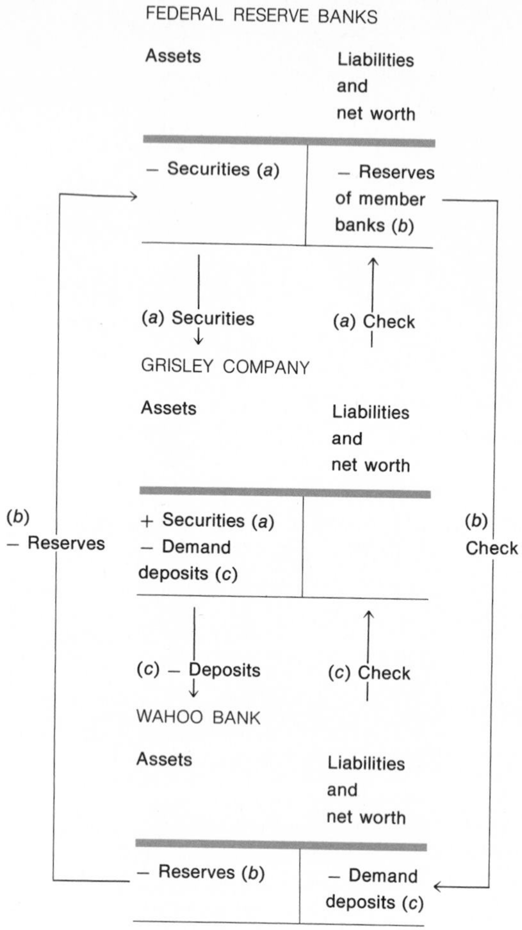

The discount rate

The Federal Reserve Banks perform essentially the same functions for commercial banks as the commercial banks perform for the public. One of these functions is the making of loans. Just as commercial banks extend credit to the public, so the bankers' banks may lend to the commercial banks.

When commercial banks borrow from Federal Reserve Banks, they may turn over to the bankers' banks either IOUs drawn against themselves or the promissory notes of businesses and individuals which they hold as security against loans granted to the public. Just as commercial banks charge interest on their loans, so do the Federal Reserve Banks charge interest on the loans they grant to commercial banks. This interest rate is called the *discount rate,* the interest on such loans being discounted at the time the loan is negotiated rather than collected at the time the loan is repaid.

Let us suppose commercial banks borrow from the Federal Reserve Banks by drawing IOUs against themselves. These IOUs, being claims against the commercial banks, are assets to the Federal Reserve Banks and appear on their balance sheet as "loans to commercial banks." To the commercial banks these IOUs are liabilities, appearing as "loans from the Federal Reserve Banks" on the commercial banks' balance sheets. In payment of the loan the Federal Reserve Banks will increase the reserves of the borrowing commercial banks. Since no required reserves need be kept against loans from the Federal Reserve Banks, *all* new reserves acquired by borrowing from the Federal Reserve Banks would be excess reserves. These changes are reflected in the balance sheets of the commercial banks and the bankers' banks as shown below:

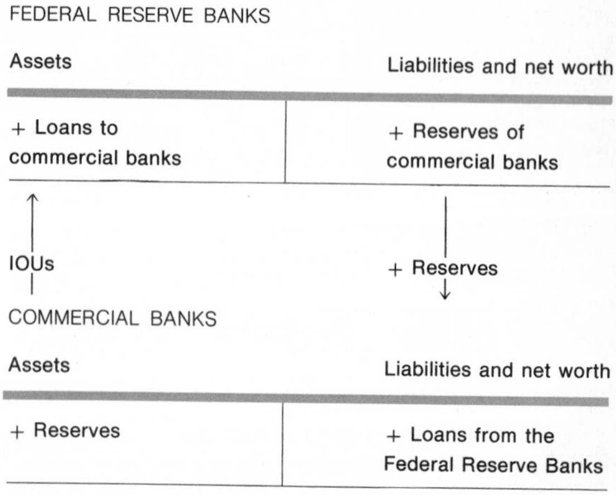

It is interesting to note that this transaction is analogous to a private person's borrowing from a commercial bank (see transaction 6, Chapter 17).

The important point, of course, is that *commercial bank borrowing from the Federal Reserve Banks increases the reserves of commercial banks, thereby enhancing their ability to extend credit to the public.*

The Board of Governors of the Federal Reserve System has the power to establish and manipulate the discount rate at which commercial banks can borrow from the Federal Reserve Banks. From the commercial banks' point of view, the discount rate obviously constitutes a cost entailed in acquiring reserves. Hence, a *decrease* in the discount rate encourages commercial banks to build up their reserves by borrowing. Although not obligated to do so, the Federal Reserve Banks usually stand ready to extend credit to borrowing banks that can offer acceptable collateral. But if the discount rate is high, this means that commercial banks that borrow must in turn boost the interest rate at which they lend to the public to make such transactions profitable. If a commercial bank has to pay 5 percent for the attainment of new reserves, it may have to charge 9 percent for loans made on these new reserves to the public in order to earn an acceptable profit. Such a high rate discourages the public from increasing the money supply by borrowing from the commercial banks. Conversely, a low discount rate permits commercial banks to acquire new reserves cheaply from the Federal Reserve Banks. This allows the commercial banks to lend profitably at relatively low interest rates to the public, thereby encouraging an expansion in the supply of money. Apart from these quantitative considerations, changes in the discount rate may well have significant psychological effects upon the credit policies of banks and the public. Changes in the discount rate are a very explicit means by which the Board of Governors can communicate the overall direction of monetary policy to banks and the public.

As evidenced by the consolidated balance sheet of the Federal Reserve Banks (Table 18·1), commercial banks borrow rather infrequently and modestly from the Federal Reserve Banks. For this reason the discount rate is a relatively weak instrument of monetary policy.

Reserve Bank credit

Early in this chapter we noted that the sum of loans to commercial banks and securities appearing on the Federal Reserve Banks' balance sheet constitutes Reserve Bank credit. Loans to commercial banks represent credit extended to the commercial banks, and the Federal Reserve Banks' holdings of securities indicate credit granted to the government.

Obviously, when the Federal Reserve Banks increase the volume of loans to commercial banks by lowering the discount rate and buy securities in the open market, Reserve Bank credit increases. An expansion of Reserve Bank credit increases the reserves of commercial banks and thereby enhances their ability to increase the supply of money by lending to the public. On the other hand, if the Federal Reserve Banks choose to decrease loans to commercial banks by boosting the discount rate and sell securities in the open market, Reserve Bank credit will decline. This decline in Reserve Bank credit destroys commercial bank reserves and limits further increases in the supply of money. It may even force a contraction in the money supply. In short, *there is a direct relationship between the volume of Reserve Bank credit and the size of commercial bank reserves.*

Easy money and tight money

Suppose the economy is faced with unemployment and deflation. The monetary authorities correctly decide that an increase in the supply of money is needed to stimulate the volume of spending in order to help absorb the idle resources. To induce an increase in the supply of money, the Board of Governors must see to it that the excess reserves of commercial banks are expanded. What specific policies will bring this about?

1. The reserve ratio should be reduced, automatically changing required reserves into excess reserves.
2. The Board of Governors should order the Federal Reserve Banks to buy securities in the open market.

This will build up the size of commercial bank reserves.

3. The discount rate should be lowered to induce commercial banks to add to their reserves by borrowing from the Federal Reserve Banks. The second and third policies can be combined by simply saying that Reserve Bank credit should be expanded.

For obvious reasons, this set of policy decisions is called an *easy money policy.* Its purpose is to make credit easily available, so as to increase the volumes of spending and employment.

Suppose, on the other hand, an excess of spending is pushing the economy into an inflationary spiral. The Board of Governors should attempt to reduce total spending by limiting or contracting the supply of money. The key to this goal lies in reducing the reserves of commercial banks. How is this done?

1. Increasing the reserve ratio will automatically strip commercial banks of excess reserves.

2. The Federal Reserve Banks should sell government bonds in the open market to tear down commercial bank reserves.

3. A boost in the discount rate will discourage commercial banks from building up their reserves by borrowing at the Federal Reserve Banks. These latter two policies constitute a reduction in Reserve Bank credit.

This group of directives is appropriately labeled a *tight money policy.* The objective is to tighten the supply of money in order to reduce spending and inflationary pressures.

MONETARY POLICY: QUALITATIVE CONTROLS

The major techniques of monetary control are (1) changing the reserve ratio, (2) changing the discount rate, and (3) open-market operations. These devices are quantitative controls; they are designed to control the quantity of bank credit generally available. But these instruments of monetary management are supplemented periodically by certain other less important credit controls in the form of (1) qualitative, or selective, credit controls and (2) moral suasion.

Selective credit controls

The monetary authorities have deemed it advisable to control certain specific types of credit.

1. Stock market credit In some instances the overall flow of money and credit in the economy has been fairly serene, and at the same time speculative stock market purchases threaten to precipitate economic difficulties. To thwart this possibility the Board of Governors has the authority to specify the *margin requirement,* or minimum percentage down payment which purchasers of stock must make. Thus a margin requirement of 65 percent means that only 35 percent of the purchase price of a security may be borrowed, the remaining 65 percent being paid "cash on the barrelhead." This rate will be raised when it is deemed desirable to restrict speculative stock purchases and lowered to revive a sluggish market.

2. Consumer and real-estate credit Congress occasionally has authorized the Board of Governors to invoke specific restraints on consumer credit. During World War II, money incomes were increasing at a time when the output of civilian goods was declining because of the drastic rechanneling of resources to the production of war goods. The result was sharp inflationary pressure in certain consumer goods industries. To dampen this pressure Congress gave the Board of Governors temporary authority to specify minimum down payments and maximum repayment periods on loans involving the purchase of real estate and a variety of consumer durables.

3. Interest rate ceilings: Regulation Q. Since the 1930s the Board of Governors has had the authority under Regulation Q to establish maximum or ceiling interest rates which commercial banks can pay on time deposits. Until the 1960s these ceiling rates were kept above market rates, and therefore Regulation Q was of no particular significance. However, in the early 1960s market rates of interest rose and with some frequency pressed above the ceiling set by Regulation Q. Hence, the ceiling interest rates of

Regulation Q became economically meaningful. But specifically what do they mean?

The clearest and perhaps most significant effect of commercial bank interest ceilings concerns the shifting of deposits between commercial banks and other financial institutions such as savings and loan associations and mutual savings banks. Now, unlike commercial banks, these latter financial institutions use most of their deposits to finance mortgage loans. Furthermore, economic activity in the construction industry is highly sensitive to changes in the availability of mortgage funds and in interest rates. That is, during a period of rising interest rates and scarcities of loanable funds, the effects upon the construction industry are adverse and severe.

Let us illustrate how Regulation Q might influence the allocation of deposits between commercial banks and savings and loan associations. Suppose an extended period of economic expansion becomes inflationary and the monetary authorities decide that it is appropriate to invoke a tight money, high interest rate policy. But the monetary authorities also want to avoid the disproportionately large contractionary effect which a tight money policy typically has upon the construction industry. What to do? Use Regulation Q. By holding to existing ceilings under Regulation Q, the tight money policy will cause the market rate of interest on time deposits to rise above the ceiling or maximum rates. At this point commercial banks are legally unable to raise further the interest rates paid to attract time deposits. But the savings and loan associations are not subject to Regulation Q, and hence, they can continue to raise the interest rates paid on deposits. These higher rates induce people to shift their funds from commercial banks to the savings and loan associations. In other words, the impact of effective Regulation Q ceilings is to make commercial banks less competitive, and savings and loan associations more competitive, for funds. Hence, although money is tight for the economy as a whole, this shifting of funds tends to cushion the construction industry from potential shortages of mortgage money. If the interest rate ceilings of Regulation Q were now raised by the monetary authorities, the commercial banks would raise the interest rates paid on their time deposits and attract funds from the savings and loan associations. The result would be shortages of mortgage funds and a contractionary effect on the construction industry. It is precisely because of its selective effect upon the construction industry that Regulation Q is generally regarded as a selective, rather than a general, credit control.

Moral suasion

The monetary authorities sometimes use the less tangible technique of moral suasion to influence the lending policies of commercial banks. Moral suasion simply means the employment by the monetary authorities of "friendly persuasion"—policy statements, public pronouncements, or outright appeals—warning that excessive expansion or contraction of bank credit might involve serious consequences for the banking system and the economy as a whole. Such pronouncements are not limited to bank credit in general; they may call for the curtailment of specific types of bank credit. For example, in attempting to relieve inflationary pressures during the Korean conflict in 1951, the public statements and publicity releases of the monetary authorities pleaded for the curtailment of bank lending not essential to the war effort and the general exercise of voluntary restraint by commercial bankers in creating money by lending. Private bankers' associations often aid the Federal monetary authorities in the application of moral suasion by echoing the pleas of the Board of Governors.

RELATIVE EFFECTIVENESS OF CONTROLS

It is generally agreed that the most important single credit control device is open-market operations—the reserve ratio, the discount rate, and selective controls being of less significance. The reasons for this are somewhat complex. As things now stand, actual reserve ratios are pushing the upper limits set by Congress (see Table 17·1). This means that the anti-inflationary influence of higher reserve ratios is definitely limited in terms of future effectiveness. The obvious suggestion is that Congress raise the upper limits on the reserve ratio to permit further boosts in the actual ratio when inflation threatens. But this

is more easily said than done. Further boosts in the actual reserve ratio would mean that commercial banks must keep more of their assets in reserves and therefore less as earning assets (loans and securities). This might work rather severe hardships on those banks whose profits are not particularly large.

The importance of the discount rate has not been particularly great in recent years, simply because commercial banks have not needed to borrow very extensively from the Federal Reserve Banks.

But why the great importance of open-market operations as such? A glance at the consolidated balance sheet for the Federal Reserve Banks (Table 18·1) reveals very large holdings of government bonds ($61.9 billion) the sales of which could easily reduce commercial bank reserves from $25.0 billion to zero! In short, the ability of the Federal Reserve Banks to affect commercial bank reserves through bond sales and purchases is potentially very great.

Note finally that the manipulation of commercial bank reserves through open-market operations is accomplished at the initiative of the Federal Reserve System. By way of contrast the discount rate, to be influential as a technique of monetary policy, depends on commercial bank initiative in borrowing from the Federal Reserve Banks.

MONEY, OUTPUT, AND PRICES: A SECOND APPROACH

The cause-and-effect chain outlined at the start of this chapter suggests how changes in the supply of money may affect the level of NNP and the price level through their effect upon aggregate demand or, alternatively stated, upon the saving-investment relationship. The possible impact of changes in the supply of money upon output, employment, and prices can be seen more directly through a second, complementary approach, which centers upon the equation of exchange.

Equation of exchange

The equation of exchange is essentially a restatement of a truism which we encountered earlier in our analysis of national income accounting (Chapter 10). Specifically, the total amount spent by buyers is equal to the total amount that is received by sellers. Buying and selling are two sides of the same transaction and the equation of exchange is merely a useful way of presenting this identity. According to this second approach, total spending or aggregate demand is equal to the supply of money M multiplied by V, the income of circuit velocity of money—that is, the number of times per year the average dollar is spent on final goods. Because MV is aggregate demand or total spending on all final goods in one year, it is obviously equal to the NNP. On the other hand, the total dollar amount received from the sale of any year's output can be thought of as Q, the physical volume of all goods produced, multiplied by P, the price level or, more specifically, the average price at which each unit of final goods is sold. In short, we may state the identity between the value of what is bought and what is sold as:

$$MV = PQ$$

Consider an extremely simple illustration. If the supply of money is $150 and each of these dollars on the average is spent 4 times a year, total expenditures will be $600. If the economy produced 200 units of only one commodity, the price level or price per unit would be $3. That is,

$$M \cdot V = P \cdot Q$$
$$\$150 \cdot 4 = \$3 \cdot 200$$

What lessons can be learned from the equation of exchange? More particularly for our purposes, what does the equation tell us about changes in the money supply and the other terms in the equation, specifically output and the price level? It is quite obvious, for example, that if the supply of money M increases *and the velocity of money V is constant,* the price level P *or* the quantity of goods Q *or* both P and Q must increase. The effects on P and Q will depend upon whether the economy is experiencing recession or full employment at the time M is increased. Recalling Figure 11·1, an increase in M will raise Q proportionately with virtually no change in P if substantial unemployment exists initially. As full employment is approached, P and Q may both rise some-

what as M is increased. At full employment Q becomes constant because the economy is producing its capacity or maximum output; hence, increases in M will be purely inflationary and will cause P to increase proportionately.

Whereas the expenditures approach to output and price level determination of Chapters 12 and 13 emphasizes the importance of saving and investment decisions, the above illustrations make it abundantly clear that the equation of exchange or monetary approach puts the spotlight upon the supply of money as the immediate determinant of output and the price level. And M, we know, is subject to manipulation by public policy decisions. If V is relatively constant and we have a recession, the monetary authorities should increase M by such an amount that Q will increase to the full-employment level. If V is quite stable and the economy is faced with serious inflation, the monetary authorities should restrict M in order to stabilize P, the price level.

Velocity and the demand for money

You will note in these examples that the effective functioning of monetary policy is dependent upon the constancy of the velocity of money. Changes in V can clearly complicate and decidedly "loosen" any relationship between changes in M, on the one hand, and desired changes in Q and P, on the other, which the equation of exchange might otherwise suggest. We must therefore explore more fully the determinants of V.

We know that by definition the velocity of money is the number of times per year that the representative or average dollar flows around the circular flow—that is, the number of times it is spent on final goods and received as income—each year. Furthermore, the velocity of money is intimately linked to the fact that both households and businesses demand money; rather than immediately spend all the income they receive, these decision makers will choose to hold a certain amount of money—a cash balance—on hand. Thus we can think of dollars being detained temporarily in both the household and business sectors as they make their way around the circular flow. The amount of time they are delayed in each sector obviously determines the velocity of money. For example, suppose every household and every business on the average held each dollar received for two months, or stated differently, each household and business wanted to hold a money balance equal to one-sixth of its annual income. This would mean that the average dollar would make one complete trip around the circular flow every four months or one-third of a year. V would therefore be 3. If the "resting time" of the average dollar in each sector is longer (or the fraction of their incomes which households and businesses want to hold as money balances is larger), it will complete the income-expenditure circuit fewer times each year. If households and businesses each held the average dollar three months—that is, held a money balance equal to one-fourth of its annual income—the typical dollar would be spent on final goods and received as income just twice each year, and V would be only 2. If the resting time of money in each sector were just one and a half months—that is, if households and businesses each wanted to hold money balances equal to one-eighth of their annual incomes—V would obviously be 4. *It is quite clear that the greater the demand for money, that is, the longer the "resting time of money" in the household and business sectors, the lower will be the velocity of money, and vice versa.*

The majority of economists—and "Keynesian economists" in particular—feel that V *cannot* be regarded as constant. Why might V increase or decrease? Or, stated differently, why might households and businesses want to hold money for shorter or longer periods, that is, hold smaller or larger money balances as a fraction of their annual incomes? The answer depends partly upon expectations. For example, if households and businesses feel optimistic about the economic future and therefore more certain about the regularity of their incomes and receipts, or if they feel that inflation is going to occur and thereby erode the value of the dollar, these decision makers will be inclined to hold smaller cash balances. Dollars will be detained for shorter periods in each sector, and V will obviously increase. The opposite circumstances—a poor economic outlook

and the expectation of deflation—will cause households and businesses to hold larger cash balances, and *V* will decline as a result.

A potentially more important cause of variations in velocity are changes in the rate of interest. This is a particularly crucial consideration because monetary policy—changes in *M*—is designed to alter interest rates. The majority of economists contend that the demand for money—the size of the money balances that households and businesses want to hold—will depend upon how costly it is to hold money. And, of course, the interest rate is the opportunity cost of holding money. It is cheap to hold money balances when the interest rate or opportunity cost is low; thus a low interest rate means households and businesses will tend to hold larger money balances and *V* will be small. Conversely, when the interest rate is high it will be costly to hold large money balances, and so *V* will tend to rise.

Now the crucial point is that changes in *V* are important because they may either reinforce or conflict with monetary policy. To illustrate: An easy money policy designed to increase *M* by some desired amount may result in too large an increase in aggregate demand if accompanied by an unanticipated increase in *V;* or the increase in *M* may result in too small an increase in aggregate demand—perhaps in no increase at all—if *V* should decline.

In the following chapter we will examine the position of the "monetarists" who argue in effect that *V* is indeed quite stable and that changes in *M* are therefore intimately tightly linked to the level of economic activity.

Velocity and the multiplier

One other point of interest is suggested by our discussion of *V*. The impact of the multiplier effect (Chapter 13) in any time period—say, a year—will depend upon *V*. For example, Table 13·2 demonstrates how a multiplier of 4 will cause a $5 billion increase in investment to boost the equilibrium NNP by $20 billion. But this increase will not occur instantaneously; it takes time for each of the "rounds" of spending and receiving income to occur. How much time? This obviously depends upon the velocity of money. Thus in Table 13·2 if we assume *V* is 3, the first three expenditure-income rounds will occur in a year, and the total increase in NNP realized in that year will be $11.56 (= $5.00 + $3.75 + $2.81) rather than $20 billion.

The two approaches

The saving-investment and equation-of-exchange approaches to analyzing the levels of output and prices are not necessarily incompatible with each other. Indeed, the saving-investment approach can be easily reinterpreted in terms of the equation of exchange. For example, assume businesses plan to invest more than households plan to save. Our expenditures model (Figure 13·3), based upon the imbalance of saving and investment, tells us this will mean an increase in the equilibrium NNP. But the equation of exchange suggests the same result. How can businesses invest more than households save? By borrowing from banks (which increases *M*) or by digging into their past accumulations or stocks of savings (which increases *V*). With *M* or *V* or both increasing, the level of aggregate demand (= *MV*) is obviously rising. The result is the same as what the saving-investment approach would suggest—a rising NNP. If the economy has substantial unemployment, the rise in NNP will be real; that is, *Q* will increase, and *P* will be virtually unchanged. If full employment already exists, the rise in NNP will be purely monetary; the increase in *MV* will leave *Q* unchanged and serve only to increase *P*. Conversely, if households plan to save more than businesses intend to invest, our expenditures approach will predict a decline in NNP (Figure 13·3). So, too, will the equation of exchange. If households use their saving to retire existing bank debts, *M* will obviously fall. If the saving is held as idle cash balances, *V* will fall. In either case *MV* or aggregate demand will decline, and so will *P* or *Q* or both *P* and *Q*.

The equation of exchange is clearly a useful way of organizing one's thinking about the forces which bear upon the levels of output and prices. In particular, by focusing attention upon the supply of money

and the desires of households and businesses to hold money, the equation of exchange stresses considerations which are underemphasized or suggested only indirectly and obliquely by the saving-investment approach. In a sense, each approach is incomplete without some understanding of the other. The saving-investment approach fails to stress the influence of a changing money supply upon the levels of output and prices. The monetary approach, on the other hand, does not bring to the fore the underlying changes in saving-investment decisions which cause variations in V.

EFFECTIVENESS OF MONETARY POLICY

How well does monetary policy work? Actually the effectiveness of monetary policy is subject to considerable debate.

Shortcomings of monetary policy

It must be recognized that monetary policy entails certain inherent limitations and encounters a number of real-world complications.

1. Cyclical asymmetry If pursued vigorously enough, tight money can actually destroy commercial bank reserves to the point where banks are *forced* to contract the volume of loans. As tight money eliminates excess reserves, banks will be forced to allow outstanding loans to mature without making offsetting loans to other borrowers. This means a contraction in the money supply. But an easy money policy suffers from a "You can lead a horse to water, but you can't make him drink" kind of problem. An easy money policy can do no more than see to it that commercial banks have the ability—that is, the excess reserves needed—to make loans. It cannot guarantee, however, that loans will actually be negotiated and the supply of money increased. If the public does not want to borrow, or commercial banks, seeking liquidity, are unwilling to lend, the easy money efforts of the Board of Governors will be to little avail. An easy money policy can do no more than create excess reserves upon which loans may or may not be made.[1] During the first few years of the Great Depression an easy money policy did little to expand the supply of money and stimulate investment. Commercial banks, fearful of becoming insolvent, built up substantial excess reserves in the late 1930s to ensure their liquidity rather than risk holding the less liquid assets of loans and securities.

2. Private offsets Within limits, monetary policy can be offset by the actions of banks and private businesses. To illustrate: Both commercial banks and businesses hold large quantities of "near-monies" in the form of government bonds. Hence, commercial banks can sell off some of their securities and add the proceeds to their reserves, thereby offsetting the efforts of a tight money policy to reduce bank reserves. Similarly, corporations can sell their bond holdings or convert savings accounts into demand deposits and use the proceeds for investment purposes or to extend credit to customers. Both these actions were taken during the 1955–1957 upswing, complicating the Board of Governors' efforts to tighten up on credit and spending. Conversely, the tendency of banks and businesses to purchase government bonds during recession collides with an easy money policy. Banks and corporations bought a substantial volume of government securities during the 1958 recession, canceling in part the easy money efforts of the monetary authorities.

3. Velocity and financial intermediaries A related point is that a tight money policy might be partially frustrated by increases, and an easy money policy by decreases, in the velocity of money. This possibility, you will recall, is clearly suggested by the equation of exchange. Indeed, empirical evidence bears out the fear that changes in V have been at odds with policy-instigated changes in M. During inflation, when M is restrained by policy, V tends to

[1] *Qualification:* Remember that Federal Reserve purchases of securities *from the public* directly increase the supply of money apart from any expansion of bank credit which commercial banks may make available on the basis of the reserves they acquire as the result of these bond purchases.

increase. Conversely, when policy measures are taken to increase *M* during a recession, *V* may very well fall!

But why might *V* behave this way? Two considerations are relevant. First, this tendency of changes in *V* to frustrate changes in *M* becomes quite clear if one recalls the determinants of *V*. During a boom period, economic optimism and expectations of rising prices make businesses and households less anxious to hold money, and so *V* rises. During recession, a pessimistic outlook and expected deflation increase the demand for money and cause *V* to fall. Secondly, our economy is characterized by a myriad of nonbank lending institutions in the form of savings and loan associations, personal finance companies, mutual savings banks, credit unions, and so forth. These institutions are called *financial intermediaries* because, although they do not create money as do commercial banks, they do gather or mobilize savings and make them available by lending to spenders. During economic expansion, for example, these institutions, prompted by rising interest rates, pursue more aggressively and more effectively the task of getting funds from savers into the hands of spenders. To the extent that they are successful, they increase *V* and offset the objectives of a tight money policy. Some economists feel that a more effective monetary policy depends upon making these financial intermediaries directly subject to control by the Board of Governors.

4. Conflict with Treasury goals The United States Treasury is the world's greatest, and most renowned, debtor. As such, it is naturally interested in low interest rates: An increase in interest rates of 1 percent on government bonds can cost the Treasury approximately $3 billion in interest payments each year. But we know that during periods of inflation the Board of Governors is obligated to undertake a tight money policy for the purpose of raising interest rates. Hence, a conflict arises during inflation between the Treasury's desire for low interest rates and the monetary authority's obligation to boost interest rates. During such periods these two agencies attempt to work out an acceptable compromise or "accord" which, as the case might be, could weaken the effectiveness of a tight money policy.

5. Cost-push inflation As is the case with fiscal policy, monetary policy is designed to control inflation by restraining excess total spending. That is, an anti-inflationary monetary policy is geared to alleviate or correct demand-pull inflation. It is not very relevant in getting at the causes of inflation which might lie on the cost or supply side of the market. As a matter of fact, given the downward inflexibility of resource and product prices, the vigorous use of a tight money policy in an inflationary situation where total demand is not excessive (and possibly is deficient) might increase unemployment and retard the growth rate (Chapter 22).

6. The investment impact As noted earlier in this chapter, it is generally agreed that tight money probably has little direct effect upon consumer spending. Some economists also doubt its ability to curtail investment. And for several reasons: First, the interest rate is only one of some half-dozen determinants of the level of investment spending, and it is far from the most significant. It is very possible that changes in the noninterest determinants of investment—for example, technological advance or favorable business expectations—will cause the level of investment spending to increase *despite* increases in the interest rate. Of particular importance is the fact that the rising product and stock prices which are part of inflation lead to business optimism and a strong incentive to invest at the very time this investment will be most inflationary. Second, large monopolistic firms—the very firms which do the bulk of the investing—are in a position to pass on any increase in interest costs to consumers in the form of higher product prices. Indeed, in many cases monopolistic firms are able to finance substantial portions of their investment programs internally and therefore will not be hindered by the unavailability of credit for investment purposes. However, tight money is likely to have a considerable impact upon smaller firms in competitive industries. This is another criticism of tight money: it discriminates against such firms.

Advantages of monetary policy

But one should *not* deduce from this discussion of limitations and complications that monetary policy is a weak and ineffectual technique for economic stabilization. Monetary policy *is* an important stabilization device which has proved its worth in helping to offset, for example, the recessions of 1949 and 1958 and to restrain inflation throughout a good portion of the 1950s and more recently in the late 1960s. Several specific points can be made on behalf of monetary policy.

1. **Speed and flexibility** In comparison with fiscal policy, monetary policy can be quickly altered. We have seen (Chapter 14) that the application of appropriate fiscal policy may be seriously delayed by congressional deliberations. In contrast the Open Market Committee of the Federal Reserve Board can literally buy or sell securities on a daily basis and thereby influence the money supply and interest rates.

2. **Political acceptability** Monetary policy is a more subtle and more politically conservative measure than is fiscal policy. Changes in government spending directly affect the allocation of resources, and, of course, tax changes can have extensive political ramifications. By contrast monetary policy works by a more circuitous, subtler route and therefore seems to be more politically palatable.

3. **Monetarism** In the next chapter we will examine in some detail the current debate over the relative effectiveness of monetary and fiscal policy. Let us merely note here that, although most economists view fiscal policy as a more powerful stabilization technique than monetary policy, there is a group of respected economists who feel that changes in the money supply is the key determinant of the level of economic activity.

SUMMARY

1. The goal of monetary policy is full employment without inflation. The route, or cause-effect chain, through which monetary policy functions is complex: *a.* Policy decisions affect commercial bank reserves; *b.* changes in reserves affect the supply of money; *c.* changes in the supply of money influence the

TABLE 18·3 A SUMMARY OF MONETARY POLICY

I. Problem: unemployment and deflation
II. Remedy: to induce an expansion in the supply of money, and therefore spending, by reducing the cost and increasing the availability of bank credit.
III. Techniques:
   A. General, quantitative controls: easy money policy
      1. Lower reserve ratio.
      2. Buy bonds in the open market.
      3. Lower discount rate.
   B. Selective, qualitative controls
      1. Lower margin requirements.
      2. Ease credit regulations on consumer durables and real estate.
      3. Use moral suasion to induce banks to lend.

I. Problem: inflation
II. Remedy: to induce a contraction in the supply of money, and therefore spending, by increasing the cost and reducing the availability of bank credit
III. Techniques:
   A. General, quantitative controls: tight money policy
      1. Raise reserve ratio.
      2. Sell bonds in the open market.
      3. Raise discount rate.
   B. Selective, qualitative controls
      1. Raise margin requirements.
      2. Tighten credit regulations on consumer durables and real estate.
      3. Use moral suasion to encourage banks to be more selective in lending.

interest rate and the availability of bank credit; and *d.* changes in the interest rate and availability of credit affect investment, the equilibrium NNP, and the price level.

2. For a consideration of monetary policy the most important assets of the Federal Reserve Banks are cash, gold certificates, securities, and loans to commercial banks. The basic liabilities are the reserves of member banks, Treasury deposits, and Federal Reserve Notes.

3. Table 18·3 draws together all the basic notions relevant to the application of tight and easy money policies. It therefore merits careful study.

4. The equation of exchange, $MV = PQ$, provides a convenient way of viewing the possible effects of changes in the supply and circuit velocity of money upon the level of economic activity or, more specifically, upon the levels of output and prices.

5. Monetary policy is subject to a number of limitations. *a.* The excess reserves which an easy money policy provides may not be used by banks to expand the supply of money. *b.* The converting of near-monies into money or reserves may partially offset monetary policy. *c.* Policy-instigated changes in the supply of money may be partially offset by changes in the velocity of money. *d.* The Treasury's desire for low interest rates conflicts with the higher rate of interest which tight money entails. *e.* A tight money policy is of questionable relevance in correcting cost-push inflation. *f.* The weight of the many noninterest determinants of investment, the ability of monopolistic firms to pass increases in interest costs on to consumers through price increases, and internal financing may all weaken the ability of tight money to curtail investment spending.

6. The advantages of monetary policy include its flexibility and political acceptability. Further, the monetarists feel that the supply of money is the single most important determinant of the level of national output.

QUESTIONS AND STUDY SUGGESTIONS

1. What is the basic objective of monetary policy? Describe the cause-effect chain through which monetary policy is made effective. Critics of monetary policy assert that this cause-effect chain contains too many "loose links." What do they mean?

2. Suppose you are a member of the Board of Governors of the Federal Reserve System. The economy is experiencing a sharp and prolonged inflationary trend. What changes in *a.* the reserve ratio, *b.* the discount rate, and *c.* open-market operations would you recommend? Explain in each case how the change you advocate would affect commercial bank reserves and influence the money supply. Explain how Regulation Q might be used in this situation to shield the construction industry from the effects of tight money.

3. Specify the impact of each of the following transactions upon commercial bank reserves:

a. The Federal Reserve Banks purchase securities from private businesses and consumers.

b. Commercial banks borrow from the Federal Reserve Banks.

c. The Board of Governors reduces the reserve ratio.

4. Evaluate the overall effectiveness of monetary policy. Why are open-market operations regarded as a more effective credit control technique than changes in the rediscount rate and the reserve ratio? Discuss the specific limitations of monetary policy.

5. On page 326 are simplified consolidated balance sheets for the commercial banking system and the twelve Federal Reserve Banks. In columns 1 through 3 indicate how the balance sheets would read after each of the three ensuing transactions is completed. Do not cumulate your answers; that is, analyze each transaction separately, starting in each case from the given figures. All accounts are in billions of dollars.

a. Suppose a decline in the discount rate prompts commercial banks to borrow an additional $1 billion from the Federal Reserve Banks. Show the new balance sheet figures in column 1.

CONSOLIDATED BALANCE SHEET:
ALL COMMERCIAL BANKS

		(1)	(2)	(3)
Assets:				
Reserves	$ 33			
Securities	60			
Loans	60			
Liabilities and net worth:				
Demand deposits	$150			
Loans from the Federal Reserve Banks	3			

CONSOLIDATED BALANCE SHEET:
TWELVE FEDERAL RESERVE BANKS

		(1)	(2)	(3)
Assets:				
Gold certificates	$20			
Securities	40			
Loans to commercial banks	3			
Liabilities and net worth:				
Reserves of commercial banks	$33			
Treasury deposits	3			
Federal Reserve Notes	27			

b. The Federal Reserve Banks sell $3 billion in securities to private business firms and consumers, who pay for the bonds with checks. Show the new balance sheet figures in column 2.

c. The Federal Reserve Banks buy $2 billion of securities from commercial banks. Show the new balance sheet figures in column 3.

d. Now review each of the above three transactions, asking yourself these three questions: (1) What change, if any, took place in the money supply as a direct and immediate result of each transaction? (2) What increase or decrease in commercial banks' reserves took place in each transaction? (3) Assuming a reserve ratio of 20 percent, what change in the money-creating potential of the commercial banking *system* occurred as a result of each transaction?

6. What is the significance of the equation of exchange? What conditions must prevail for an increase in the money supply to cause ***a.*** a rise in output and employment and *b.* an increase in the price level? What determines the velocity of money? Explain why a change in *M* might be accompanied by a change in *V* in the opposite direction.

SELECTED REFERENCES

Economic Issues, 4th ed., reading 26.

Board of Governors of the Federal Reserve System: *The Federal Reserve System: Purposes and Functions,* 5th ed. (1963), particularly chaps. 1 and 4.

Chandler, Lester V.: *The Economics of Money and Banking,* 5th ed. (New York: Harper & Row, Publishers, Incorporated, 1969, chaps. 21–26.

Ritter, Lawrence S., and William L. Silber: *Money* (New York: Basic Books, Inc., 1970).

Smith, Harlan M.: *Elementary Monetary Theory* (New York: Random House, Inc., 1968).

Williams, Harold R., and Henry W. Woudenberg (eds.): *Money, Banking, and Monetary Policy* (New York: Harper & Row, Publishers, Incorporated, 1970), parts 3 and 4.

Wrightsman, Dwayne: *An Introduction to Monetary Theory and Policy* (New York: The Free Press, 1971).

19

ECONOMIC STABILITY: THEORY AND POLICY

This chapter has three basic purposes. First, it is a recapitulation and synthesis of the theory of employment and the public policies designed to achieve economic stability. We want to see how the theory and policy aspects of macroeconomics discussed in the preceding nine chapters fit together. Second, we want to consider the current debate over "monetarism." Finally, we will summarize President Nixon's recent "New Economic Policy."

EMPLOYMENT THEORY

Figure 19·1 embodies the "big picture" we seek. The overriding virtue of this diagram is that it does remind us that the many concepts and relationships discussed in Parts 2 and 3 are something more than a series of unrelated principles and notions. On the contrary, we find that these concepts are related to one another and constitute a coherent and meaningful theory of what determines the level of resource use in a market economy. The coherence and relevance of this theory are reflected in its acceptance as a framework for the formulation of national economic policy.

Now let us review the substance of Figure 19·1. Reading from left to right, the key point, of course, is that the levels of output, employment, income, and prices are all directly related to the level of aggregate demand. The decisions of business firms to produce goods and therefore to employ resources depend upon the total amount of money spent on these goods. To discover what determines the level of aggregate spending, we must examine its three major components.[1]

Consumption

The absolute level of consumption spending depends upon the position of the consumption schedule and the level of net national product or disposable income. Although the determinants of the consumption

[1]We assume a closed economy, that is, net exports are zero.

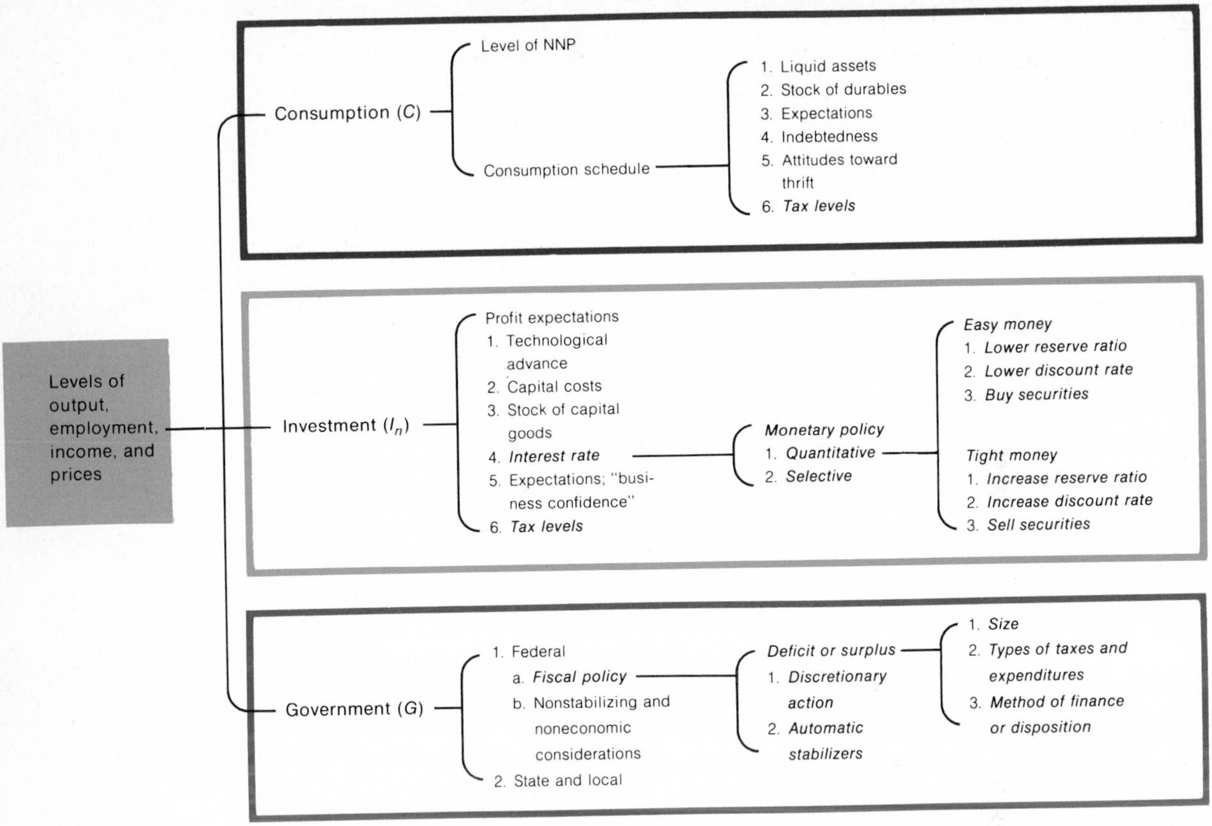

FIGURE 19·1 THE THEORY OF EMPLOYMENT AND STABILIZATION POLICIES

This figure integrates the various components of employment theory and stabilization policy. Note that determinants which constitute, or are strongly influenced by, public policy are shown in bold italics.

schedule are numerous, economists are convinced that the schedule is quite stable. Therefore, the absolute level of consumption spending usually can be thought of as changing in response to changes in NNP brought about by fluctuations in other components of aggregate demand.

Furthermore, the seemingly innocent fact that households will consume part and save part of any change in their incomes is actually of great significance, because the exact division of a change in income between consumption and saving determines the size of the multiplier. Specifically, the size of the multiplier effect and the marginal propensity to save are inversely related; the smaller the MPS, the greater will be the change in NNP due to a given change in aggregate demand.

Investment

Investment spending is a highly volatile component of aggregate demand and therefore likely to be a cause of fluctuations in the levels of output, employment, and prices. The instability of investment lies in its determinants: Business confidence is subject to frequent and substantial revision; technological progress occurs at an uneven rate; and the durability of capital goods makes their purchase postponable. Furthermore, business profits—an increasingly important source of funds for investment—are highly variable. It is reasonably correct to think of changes in investment as the main source of output and price-level instability in our economy and to regard changes in consumption largely as the result of moving from one equilibrium NNP to another along a quite stable consumption schedule.

Government spending

Government purchases of goods and services are the third major component of total spending. But this component differs from consumption and investment in that it is determined by public policy. Consumption and investment decisions are made in the self-interest of the household and business sectors, respectively. Government spending decisions, on the other hand, are made, at least in part, to fulfill society's interest in high levels of output and employment and a stable price level. With this motivational distinction in mind, let us examine the major components and characteristics of stabilization policy.

STABILIZATION POLICY

Government seeks to stabilize the economy primarily through (1) fiscal policy and (2) monetary policy.

Fiscal policy

Fiscal policy refers, of course, to changes in government spending and tax revenues which are designed to eliminate either an inflationary or a deflationary gap. Figure 19·1 makes the potential stabilizing role of government quite evident; government spending, as one of the three major components of aggregate demand, directly affects output, employment, and the price level. Tax policy, on the other hand, works through the other two major components of total spending; taxation is a determinant of both consumption and investment.[2] In particular, reductions in the personal income tax tend to shift the consumption schedule upward; tax increases tend to shift it downward. Corporation income tax cuts tend to improve profit expectations and stimulate investment; tax increases weaken profit expectations and reduce the willingness to invest.

Fiscal policy is both *discretionary* and *automatic*. The automatic or built-in stabilizers—the progressiveness of the Federal tax structure, unemployment compensation payments, subsidies to farmers—cause tax collections to vary directly, and government disbursements inversely, with the level of national income. Discretionary policy consists of the changing of spending levels and the manipulation of tax rates or the tax structure by Congress for the explicit purpose of achieving greater stability in the economy. The impact of discretionary fiscal policy depends upon (1) the size of the budgetary deficit or surplus, (2) the specific types of taxes and government expenditures invoked, and (3) the manner in which a deficit is financed and the method of disposing of a surplus (Figure 19·1).

Monetary policy

Although monetary policy may have some impact upon consumption, the primary effect is undoubtedly upon investment spending, where the interest rate is a determinant of some importance. Other things being equal, the pursuit of an easy money policy by the Board of Governors will reduce the interest rate and make bank credit (money) more readily available, thereby stimulating investment and the levels of output and employment. A tight money policy will have

[2]In our earlier tabular (Table 14·1) and graphic (Figure 14·2) models of the economy we made the simplifying assumption that all taxes were personal taxes.

the reverse effects and presumably will be invoked only when the level of aggregate demand is excessive and inflation is feared.

COMPLICATIONS AND PROBLEMS

As a summary view of employment theory and stabilization policy, Figure 19•1 is useful. But it does not reveal all. It does not make explicit the many problems of achieving the proper timing of fiscal policy or mention the fact that congressmen are often subject to economically irrational demands from pressure groups and individual voters (Chapter 14). Nor does it point out the cyclical asymmetry of monetary policy, or the complicating role of financial intermediaries and changes in the velocity of money (Chapter 18). But there are even further complications and problems associated with Figure 19•1 which we must consider.

Complexity of interrelationships

Cause-effect relationships are much more complicated and intermixed than Figure 19•1 suggests. In the first place, some of the relationships suggested by this figure may actually be quite loose. Recall, for example, that the relationship between a change in total spending, on the one hand, and the resulting changes in the levels of output, employment, and prices, on the other, depends itself upon the level of employment that currently exists in the economy (Figure 11•1). Second, we shall soon discover (Chapter 22) that structural unemployment and cost-push inflation complicate the relationship between aggregate demand and the levels of output, employment, and prices. Unemployment and inflation may have causes other than an inappropriate level of aggregate demand. Third, the various determinants of output and employment are actually interdependent. Examples: A reduction in personal income taxes may give rise to an increase in consumption and expand the levels of output and employment and, perhaps, the price level too. But in turn this expansion may well have a favorable effect upon "business confidence" and stimulate investment spending. Or an increase in the rate of technological progress might increase the demand for money capital on the part of investors and, unless offset by appropriate monetary policy, cause interest rates to rise. In brief, there are many behind-the-scenes interrelationships of an intricate and complicated character at work which Figure 19•1 fails to reveal. Stated differently, Figure 19•1 is a summary statement of a theory and cannot be expected to mirror the full bloom of reality.

Quantification and policy

We must also recognize that there exist important problems in quantifying the interrelationships of Figure 19•1 and therefore in formulating quantitatively precise stabilization policies. To illustrate: Suppose a deflationary gap exists. Let us say that the level of NNP is $30 billion below the full-employment noninflationary level. We know the general character of the monetary and fiscal policies needed to close the gap. What we do *not* know—or at least do not know with great accuracy—is the size of the deficit needed or the extent to which bank credit should be eased. We are not certain of the size of the multiplier effect, that is, of the magnitude of the chain reaction which an increase in government spending or a decline in taxes would precipitate. Nor are we certain of the size of the impacts which changes in government spending and tax collections might have upon the consumption or investment schedules. All of this is not to say that the policy implications of our theoretical framework cannot be made operational. It does suggest, however, that it is not realistic to expect stabilization policy to work perfectly so as to provide continuous full employment and absolute price stability. Economists are in general agreement that "fine tuning" of the economy through monetary and fiscal policy is not easily realized.

Noneconomic goals

There is another reason why we should not expect stabilization policy to function perfectly. Government spending and taxing decisions are not governed

solely by the goal of stabilization (Chapter 1). For example, war may necessitate increases in government military spending at a time when the economy is threatened with inflation. Or a political party's commitment to relieve certain social problems—to ameliorate the poverty problem or expand public school facilities—may call for changes in spending or the tax structure that destabilize the economy. Indeed, Figure 19·1 reminds us that the fiscal operations of state and local governments simply do not have an anticyclical orientation at all, but one concerned with the allocation of resources between private and public uses. In brief, budgetary policy is designed and altered not only with stability in mind, but also in response to international political-military factors, pressing domestic needs, and considerations of equity and social justice.

KEYNESIANISM VERSUS MONETARISM

Economists have vacillated over time in the importance they have attached to money as a basic determinant of the level of economic activity. At present there is a deep split among economists on the question of the importance of money and monetary policy as compared with fiscal policy. We contrast the Keynesian (majority) and the monetarist (minority) views.

The Keynesian position

The so-called Keynesian, or "new economics," conception of the determinants of output, employment, and the price level are those we have discussed in Parts 2 and 3; Figure 19·1 is essentially a summary of the Keynesian position. Both monetary and fiscal policy are held to be significant, but fiscal policy is viewed as the primary economic stabilizer. Monetary policy is of some importance in that by altering interest rates it can influence aggregate demand through the investment component and, perhaps to a lesser degree, through the consumption component. But, as Figure 19·1 suggests, monetary policy's cause-effect chain is lengthy and, because of the shortcomings of monetary policy discussed in Chapter 18, there is considerable uncertainty and therefore looseness at each link in the chain. Hence, in the Keynesian view the role of monetary policy is clearly secondary to that of fiscal policy. Keynesians *do* recognize that an expansionary fiscal policy, for example, will have a greater net impact upon output and employment if monetary policy is congenial. As already noted, a fiscal deficit financed by government and the economic expansion it induces will both increase the demand for money and tend to increase interest rates. Rising interest rates in turn will have an adverse effect upon investment, thereby partially offsetting and weakening the expansionary impact of the deficit. Monetary ease sufficient to offset this rise in the interest rates would have avoided any dilution of the deficit's expansionary impact. But to most Keynesians the potentially adverse monetary (interest-rate) effects of fiscal policy are not critical obstacles to the overall effectiveness of fiscal actions.

The monetarist position

In the past few years the theory and the policy prescriptions of the Keynesians have been challenged by a relatively small, but astute and persuasive, group of economists led by the University of Chicago's Milton Friedman. Professor Friedman's pioneering work in monetary economics has been crucial in reviving interest in the role of money as a determinant of the level of economic activity. But this interest has also been fostered by two other considerations. First, the tax cut of 1964 and the income tax surcharge of 1968 were only legislated after considerable time lags, making the quick-implementation feature of monetary policy look very desirable by comparison. Second, we saw in Chapter 18 that the potential effectiveness of monetary policy is greater in dealing with inflation than in coping with recession. The dominant economic problem during the latter half of the 1960s was in fact inflation, and, hence, monetary policy seemed to be an appropriate and quite powerful technique of control

As the label suggests, the monetarists feel that money and monetary policy are much more important

in determining the level of economic activity than the Keynesian framework suggests. To these economists money matters a great deal. The monetarists hold that changes in the money supply are the single most important factor in determining the levels of output, employment, and prices. They feel that the cause-effect chain between the supply of money and the level of economic activity is short, direct, and tight.

The demand for money The monetarists contend that the spotlight should be shifted from Keynes's aggregate demand and all its varied components and determinants to the demand for money. The basic tenet of the monetarists' theory is that a stable, predictable relationship exists between the amount of money which people—households and businesses—desire or want to hold and the level of national income. In other words, the monetarists argue that the demand for money—the amount of money which people want to hold expressed as a fraction or percentage of their annual incomes—is quite constant. Recalling our discussion of the equation of exchange and the velocity of money, the monetarist view holds that the velocity of money, *V*, is stable.

Let us suppose, for example, that the demand for money is stable at one-fifth, or 20 percent; that is, households and businesses together demand or want to hold an amount of money equal to one-fifth of the national income. So, if the national income is $400 billion, they will want money balances of $80 billion. If national income is $500 billion, people will want $100 billion of money balances; if $600 billion, they'll want $120 billion, and so forth.

Let us now assume that the level of national income is currently $500 billion and that people therefore want to hold $100 billion of money balances. Assume, too, that for the moment the actual money supply made available by the Federal Reserve System happens to be $100 billion, so that the actual supply of money and the amount which people want to hold are equal. This equality, as we shall make clear in a moment, means that the national income is in equilibrium. Suppose now that for some reason the monetary authorities increase the money supply to, say, $120 billion. This obviously means that the actual amount of money which households and businesses are holding will exceed the amount they want to hold by $20 billion. What will happen? According to the monetarists, people will spend away their excess money balances, and this will be expansionary. How expansionary? National income will rise until the desired 1 to 5 relationship between desired money balances and national income is reestablished. That is, when the spending of the excess money brings the national income up to the $600 billion level, then the stable 1 to 5 relationship between the money balances people want to hold and national income will be reestablished ($120/$600 billion). Given the supposition that people want to hold an amount of money equal to one-fifth of the national income, we will find that at this new, higher $600 billion income level none of the enlarged money supply will be excess. As national income expands from $500 to $600 billion, the amount of money that people desire to hold will grow from $100 to $120 billion, and so the demand for money will now equal the actual money supply, and the economy will be back in equilibrium at the higher $600 billion level.

Conversely, starting again with an assumed $500 billion national income and the assumption that people want money balances equal to one-fifth of national income, we know that an actual money supply of $100 billion will result in equilibrium. Why? Because the amount of money people want to hold and the actual supply of money are equal at $100 billion. Now what if the monetary authorities reduce the money supply to $80 billion? The economy will obviously have smaller money balances than it desires; to remedy the situation households and businesses will take steps to build up their money balances. How will they accomplish this? By reducing spending. The drop in spending will reduce the national income to the $400 billion level at which the desired 1 to 5 relationship between desired money balances and national income will be restored ($80/$400 billion) and a new, lower equilibrium level of national income realized.

This discussion of the monetarist view can be quite readily and simply restated in terms of the equation of exchange $MV = PQ$. In the alleged stability of the

demand for money as a fraction of national income the monetarists are saying that V is stable. Hence, any change in M will cause P and/or Q to change in the same direction as the change in the money supply.

Empirical evidence The monetarists bolster their position with empirical data. They argue that intensive empirical studies of the monetary history of the United States show a strong positive correlation between changes in the money supply and changes in the national output. According to the monetarists, changes in the money supply will *cause* changes in the level of economic activity; therefore, a change in the money supply will—after a somewhat variable time lag—cause a predictable change in the national income. Furthermore, the monetarists assert that the casual observation of specific economic episodes underscores the primary role of money as a determinant of economic activity. For example, the dramatic decline in the money supply in the early 1930s was of fundamental importance in determining the course and severity of the Great Depression. Similarly, according to the monetarists, the income tax surcharge of 1968 which was designed to restrain inflation was not effective for the simple reason that the money supply continued to expand at an excessive rate.

Fiscal ineffectiveness The monetarists also attack the Keynesian conception of how fiscal policy works. They feel that the state of the budget per se has no significant impact upon the level of economic activity; a fiscal deficit or surplus can affect the national income only to the extent that the method of financing changes the money supply. To illustrate: Suppose the Federal government tries to stimulate the economy by running a deficit, for example, by increasing spending without raising taxes. If government finances the deficit by borrowing from the public, the money supply will remain unchanged, and so will the levels of output, employment, and prices. While the checks received by the recipients of the increased government outlays will be deposited in commercial banks and become increases in the money supply, the households and businesses which buy the new government bonds will pay by check, and thus demand-deposit money will be reduced by the same amount. The latter cancels the former, and the money supply—and therefore the level of economic activity—will be unaffected. The monetarist view that fiscal policy will be ineffective unless accompanied by an appropriate increase in the money supply can also be envisioned from the demand-for-money vantage point. An increase in government spending will initially tend to drive the national income upward. But, assuming a stable relationship between the demand for money and national income, the existing supply of money will now be inadequate. People will want to hold larger money balances now that income is higher. To achieve these larger balances they cut back on their consumption and investment spending. These declines in private spending frustrate the potential expansionary effect of the increase in government spending, and the equilibrium level of national income remains unchanged. In short, the monetarists say, fiscal policy doesn't work.

On the other hand, if an increase in government spending is financed by the creation of new money—by borrowing from the central banks—an expansionary effect will occur. But the expansionary impact, argue the monetarists, results from the increase in the money supply which the method of finance has induced and not from the increase in government spending as such. On the basis of this kind of reasoning the monetarists would not regard the economic expansion which followed the 1964 tax cut (Chapter 14) as evidence of the effectiveness of Keynesian fiscal policy. Rather the tax cut coincided with an expansive monetary policy, and it was the latter which stimulated the economy.

The monetary rule While arguing that the money supply is the crucial determinant of economic activity, it is interesting that Professor Friedman and some other monetarists are strongly opposed to a discretionary monetary policy. Friedman contends, first of all, that the economy has a greater inherent tendency toward stability—a greater capacity to function and grow at full employment with relative price stability—than Keynesians recognize. More importantly, he

argues that historically the discretionary changes in the money supply made by the monetary authorities have in fact been a *destabilizing* influence in the economy. Examining the monetary history of the United States from the Civil War up to the establishment of the Federal Reserve System in 1914 and comparing this with the post-1914 record, Professor Friedman concludes that, even if the war and immediate postwar periods are ignored, the latter period was clearly more unstable. Much of this decline in economic stability in the post–Federal Reserve period is attributed to faulty decisions on the part of the monetary authorities; economic instability is more a product of monetary mismanagement than of any inherent destabilizers in the economy. This mismanagement stems both from difficulties in assessing and forecasting the economy's health and from the fact that there is a variable time lag between a change in the money supply and its effect upon the economy. Hence, it often happens that, when a policy of monetary ease is invoked during a recession, its impact is not felt until some six or twelve months later. During the interim, recession may have given way to inflation which is reinforced by the easy money policy. Similarly, a tight money policy intended to fight current inflation may become effective nine months from now, only to aggravate a recession! Thus, the monetarists allege that discretionary changes in the money supply can *cause* economic instability. Given these arguments, Friedman concludes that we will enjoy greater stability in the economy by stabilizing the growth of the money supply. Specifically, he advocates legislating the monetary rule that the money supply be expanded each year at the same annual rate as the potential growth of our real GNP; that is, the supply of money should be increased steadily at 3 to 5 percent per year.

The Keynesian rebuttal

Let us briefly assert several counterarguments made by Keynesians.

1. Keynesians feel that the monetarist view grossly understates the complexity of our economy. Changes in the money supply may, indeed, affect aggregate demand. But so may a host of nonmonetary considerations. For example, the investment expenditures of businessmen and consumer spending may both be altered by expectations—expectations of either inflation or recession. Both may adjust their spending as the result of, or in anticipation of, changes in tax rates. Strikes in important industries—such as the extended General Motors strike of late 1970—can depress aggregate demand. Such changes in aggregate demand are quite unrelated to changes in the money supply, but obviously affect the level of economic activity and the price level.

2. Keynesians also argue that the cause-effect relationship envisioned by the monetarists may in fact be reversed in some instances: changes in aggregate demand whose causes are unrelated to the supply of money may stimulate demands for additional money which the Federal Reserve System may accommodate by increasing the money supply!

3. The basic monetarist contention that V is highly stable is challenged by the Keynesians who argue that the demand for money, and therefore V, varies with changes in expectations and in the interest rate (Chapter 18). Thus the impact of a change in M upon aggregate demand, and therefore upon output, employment, and the price level, is neither "tight" nor certain. Available evidence does *not* indicate a constant, dependable relationship between the money supply and the level of aggregate expenditures.

4. Keynesians feel that, despite a somewhat spotty record, it would be foolish to replace discretionary monetary policy with a monetary rule. Arguing that the demand for money, and therefore V, is variable both cyclically and secularly, they contend that a constant annual increase in the money supply could contribute to substantial fluctuations in aggregate demand and promote economic instability. As one critic of the monetarist position has quipped, the trouble with the monetary rule is that it tells the policy maker: "Don't do something, just stand there."

The Keynesian-monetarist debate over theory and policy is one that we can expect to persist for some time. The controversy is a healthy one in that it is forcing economists and policy makers to reexamine in depth the policy-mix issue and at least to recognize

the need to coordinate monetary and fiscal policies.[3] But at the present time the Keynesian view is most widely accepted. The majority of economists seem to share the view of one prominent Keynesian who summarized his position by asserting: "Money, yes; monetarism, no."

STABILIZATION POLICY IN ACTION: THE NIXON PROGRAM

President Nixon's dramatic announcement of a "New Economic Policy" in mid-August 1971 constitutes an intriguing case study in stabilization policy, the outcome and implications of which remain to be determined. Recall from Chapter 11 that the sharp inflation of the 1966–1969 period became in 1970–1971 an "inflationary recession" or "stagflation"—an unhappy situation of simultaneous increases in the price level and unemployment. Anti-inflationary policies failed to counter the prevailing wage-price spiral of the late 1960s, but ironically did contribute to unemployment. This situation was complicated by the disquieting deterioration of our international trade position (Chapter 43). Largely because of domestic inflation, United States's exports were declining while its imports were rising. Stated differently, the net export (Chapter 10) component of total spending was diminishing to the end that unemployment tended to rise. In short, three serious and interrelated problems—unemployment, inflation, and a weakening international trade position—existed simultaneously. The basic dilemma confronting the administration was how to stimulate employment and economic growth without accelerating (and hopefully ameliorating) the rate of inflation. The President's response essentially was to cut taxes to stimulate employment and growth while imposing a temporary wage-price freeze in the hope of thwarting the inflationary expectations—the "inflationary psychosis"—that underlay the wage-price inflationary spiral.

[3] The student wishing to pursue the debate should consult Milton Friedman and Walter W. Heller, *Monetary vs. Fiscal Policy* (New York: W. W. Norton & Company, Inc., 1969).

Fiscal policy

The President's tax proposals to Congress were threefold. First, an investment tax credit of 10 percent was recommended for businesses on purchases of new machinery and equipment. That is, companies that buy domestically produced equipment or plants may subtract 10 percent of the cost from their tax bill during the following year; in ensuing years this tax credit will fall to 5 percent. The short-run intent here was to give a direct inducement to increasing the investment component of aggregate demand, thereby also increasing employment. The longer-run goal was to enhance the productivity and therefore the competitiveness of American producers in world markets. Second, the President proposed to rescind the existing 7 percent excise tax on automobiles with the understanding that manufacturers would cut auto prices accordingly, that is, by $150 or $200 per auto. The intended result is obviously a substantial stimulus to the automobile and ancillary industries. Finally, President Nixon recommended that the $50 per person increase in personal income tax exemptions scheduled to go into effect on January 1, 1973, be moved up one year so as to become effective on January 1, 1972. The resulting increase in disposable income would hopefully stimulate the consumption component of aggregate demand and create more employment. These tax cuts are on the order of $7 or $8 billion. However, their expansionary impact would be partially blunted by the President's promise to trim government spending by some $4.7 billion and to defer administration proposals on revenue sharing and welfare reform. Aside from these quantitative aspects, it was the administration's hope that the breadth and decisiveness of the overall economic program would have a stimulating effect upon consumer and business confidence and thereby boost private demand.

The wage-price freeze

Problem: What would prevent the increases in investment and consumption induced by the President's tax reductions from being translated into additional

inflation, rather than increases in employment and real output? Solution: A temporary 90-day freeze on wages, prices, and rents—clearly the most unconventional component of the Nixon policy package. Specifically, the President exercised the standby powers to institute a 180-day freeze on wages, prices, and rents given him in the Economic Stabilization Act of 1970. The President thus had the option of extending the freeze for another 90 days. Specifically, the President's executive order made it illegal to (1) increase wages or salaries, (2) charge more for a product than the highest price charged in the 30-day period prior to the freeze, and (3) raise the rents landlords charged tenants. The Office of Emergency Preparedness (OEP) was given the heavy responsibility of monitoring the freeze. However, in view of the OEP's small staff and the potential immensity of the enforcement task, it is clear that the success of the freeze was heavily dependent upon voluntary compliance and the reporting of violators by individual citizens. Violators faced prosecution by the Justice Department; injunctions and $5,000 fines could be imposed upon willful violators. Although dividends and interest rates were not included in the freeze, the President exerted "moral suasion" in urging businesses not to increase their dividend payments and banks not to raise interest rates.

Looking to the longer run for more permanent solutions to the problem of wage-price inflation, the President established a new Cost of Living Council. The council is comprised of the Secretaries of Agriculture, Commerce, Labor, Housing and Urban Development, and the Treasury in addition to the Budget Director, the chairman of the Council of Economic Advisors, the director of OEP, and the President's Special Consultant for Consumer Affairs. The Secretary of the Treasury is chairman of the council, and the chairman of the Board of Governors of the Federal Reserve System serves the council in an advisory capacity. It was the council's basic task to "develop and recommend to the President additional policies, mechanisms and procedures to maintain economic growth without inflationary increases in prices, rents, wages and salaries" after the expiration of the temporary wage-price-rent freeze.

International economic policy

Although details are deferred until Chapter 44, let us note in passing that these domestic measures were accompanied by two important changes in the United States's international economic policies. First, the President exercised authority under existing legislation in imposing an extra 10 percent tax or surcharge on all imports now subject to tariffs. The goal was to make foreign-produced goods more expensive relative to competing domestic goods, thereby diverting consumption and investment spending from foreign to domestically produced goods. In addition to stimulating domestic output and employment, it was hoped that this policy action would strengthen our international trade position. Secondly, the traditionally fixed relationship between the international value of the dollar and foreign monies was severed. The expectation was that the value of the dollar would fall relative to other currencies, making American goods more attractive to foreigners and foreign goods less attractive to Americans. Again, the intent was to stimulate domestic employment and production and restore balance in our world trade.

Evaluation

Given the complexity of these policy changes and the hazards of economic forecasting, the ultimate consequences of the New Economic Policy are difficult to predict. The initial reaction of both liberal and conservative economists was generally favorable; the program was regarded as a decisive and bold effort to deal with our most pressing economic problems on a broad front. Nevertheless, a number of legitimate questions and criticisms were posed.

1. The basic criticism of the international trade policies was that the 10 percent surcharge on dutiable imports might precipitate a "trade war," that is, our trading partners might retaliate with similar tariff increases, choking off free trade and sacrificing the gains from international specialization.

2. A major criticism of both the tax cuts and the wage-price freeze was that they are inequitable; they allegedly favor business at the expense of labor, the

consumer, and particularly the poor. The specific points are as follows: First, the lion's share of the direct benefits of the proposed tax cuts will accrue to business rather than the consumer. Second, many labor leaders were highly critical of the freeze because they felt that the major economic sacrifices fell upon labor. They noted that although wages and prices were legally frozen, dividends and interest rates were not. Also, they pointed out, productivity increases during the freeze would accrue entirely to the benefit of businesses; that is, the revenue from any increases in output due to a rising output per worker would not be shared by workers because their wages were frozen. Third, the deferring of important programs to improve our welfare system and provide financial aid through revenue sharing to the cities denied much-needed help to the poor (Chapters 37 and 38).

3. It was questionable whether a 90-day—or, if extended, a 180-day—wage-price pause would have the intended effect of ameliorating the inflationary psychosis underlying recent inflation. Would inflationary pressures merely be delayed? Or, indeed, would inflationary pressures be intensified in the post-freeze period as labor and business sought higher wages and prices more fervently in anticipation of future freezes?

"Phase two": an incomes policy

In fact, as the second, post-freeze phase of the New Economic Policy began to take shape in the fall of 1971, it was evident that economic policy would not quickly revert to the status quo; rather it was clear that an "incomes policy"—controls over wage, profit, and rental incomes—was to be added at least temporarily to our arsenal of stabilization weapons. Specifically, in early October of 1971 President Nixon proposed new mechanisms designed to stabilize wages and prices in the long run. The President created two new agencies to operate under the Cost of Living Council. First, a *Pay Board* was set up to establish wage guidelines consistent with reasonable price stability. Comprised of fifteen members—five each from management, labor, and the public at large—the Pay Board has the authority to review wage increases and to prohibit, reduce, or defer any proposed increases which it judges to be inflationary, that is, at odds with its guidelines. Second, the President also created a *Price Commission* comprised of seven public members. Its primary task is to establish specific standards for price and rent increases which are consistent with long-term price stability. The Cost of Living Council will supervise the overall operation of Phase Two and will determine general policy goals which guide the Pay Board and Price Commission. Thus the Council's primary goal for 1972 is to cut the rate of inflation to one-half the 1971 rate, that is, to about 2 or 3 percent.

It is anticipated that major industries such as automobiles, steel, and coal will be required to notify the Pay Board and the Price Commission of intended increases in wages or prices. These proposed increases might then be accepted, reduced, or rejected by the Board or Commission. A second and somewhat less strategic group of industries will be required to report actual changes in wages and prices and the Board and the Commission have the authority to rescind excessive increases. Finally, small businesses will not be obligated to report wage and price adjustments, but will be subject to spot checks to ensure that wage and price boosts have not exceeded the guidelines set forth by the Pay Board and the Price Commission.

It is an interesting conjecture as to whether macroeconomic policy has entered a new historic phase wherein the indirect and general tools of monetary and fiscal policy will be *permanently* supplemented by some form of specific and direct governmental control over the functioning of product and labor markets. Whether or not the New Economic Policy represents such an historic turning point in policy, we can be assured that the 1970s will be an intriguing period for economy watchers.

SUMMARY

1. The levels of output, income, employment, and prices are determined by the level of spending. Of the three major components of total spending, investment is relatively unstable as compared with con-

sumption. Government spending is policy-determined.

2. Stabilization policy consists of fiscal policy, which may be either discretionary or automatic, and monetary policy.

3. Although the various components of employment theory fit together in a coherent framework which is useful for policy formulation, it must be recognized that ***a.*** the cause-effect interrelationships between the components are complex, ***b.*** the interrelationships are difficult to quantify precisely, and ***c.*** noneconomic goals may interfere with the attainment of economic stability.

4. In the controversy over the relative importance of monetary and fiscal policy, the Keynesian position is essentially that implied in Figure 19·1. Fiscal policy is regarded as the primary economic stabilizer; monetary policy is of importance, but its contact with aggregate demand is indirect and subject to offsets and uncertainties in its operation.

5. The monetarist position is that, because the demand for money as a proportion of national income is stable, the supply of money is of strategic significance in determining the level of economic activity. In terms of $MV = PQ$, a stable demand for money makes V constant so that P and/or Q move in the same direction as M.

6. President Nixon's new stabilization program is based upon a variety of tax cuts, a temporary wage-price freeze, and policies to improve our world trade position.

QUESTIONS AND STUDY SUGGESTIONS

1. Summarize the theory of employment graphically, using the aggregate demand–aggregate supply approach. Show in detail how monetary and fiscal policies might affect the various components of aggregate demand.

2. Why is it unrealistic to expect fiscal and monetary policies to result in complete economic stability? What might be done to improve monetary and fiscal policies?

3. Design an antirecession stabilization policy, involving both fiscal and monetary policy, which is consistent with *a.* a relative decline in the public sector, *b.* greater income equality, and *c.* a high rate of economic growth.

4. Briefly summarize the monetarist view, indicating clearly the role of the demand for money. According to the monetarists, what happens when the supply of money exceeds the amount of money which households and businesses want to hold?

5. What rationale is used by the monetarists in discounting the effectiveness and significance of fiscal policy?

6. Explain and evaluate these statements in terms of the Keynesian-monetarist controversy:

a. "If the national goal is to raise income, it can be achieved only by raising the money supply."

b. "The size of a Federal budget deficit is not important. What is important is how the deficit is financed."

c. "There is no reason in the world why, in an equation like $MV = PQ$, the V should be thought to be independent of the rate of interest. There is every plausible reason for the velocity of circulation to be a systematic and increasing function of the rate of interest."

7. Discuss the primary components of President Nixon's new stabilization program, explaining the purpose of each component and its relationship to each of the other components. Do you feel the various criticisms of the program are valid? Explain.

SELECTED REFERENCES

Economic Issues, 4th ed., readings 22, 24, 28, and 29.

Anderson, Clay J.: "Fiscal-Monetary Policies: What Mix?" *Business Review* (Federal Reserve Bank of Philadelphia, January 1967), pp. 3–12.

Committee for Economic Development: *Further Weapons against Inflation: Measures to Supplement General Fiscal and Monetary Policies* (New York: CED, 1970).

Dillard, Dudley: *The Economics of John Maynard Keynes* (Englewood Cliffs, N.J.: Prentice-Hall, Inc., 1948), pp. 48–51.

Federal Reserve Bank of Boston, *Controlling Monetary Aggregates* (Boston, 1969).

Friedman, Milton, and Walter W. Heller: *Monetary vs. Fiscal Policy* (New York: W. W. Norton & Company, Inc., 1969).

Okun, Arthur M.: *The Political Economy of Prosperity* (New York: W. W. Norton & Company, Inc., 1970).

AMERICAN ECONOMIC GROWTH: ACHIEVEMENTS, PROBLEMS, AND POLICIES

20

THE SIMPLE ANALYTICS OF ECONOMIC GROWTH

In less than 200 years our economy has grown from an industrial infant to a vigorous productive giant. This long-run growth has not occurred at a steady pace. On the contrary, it has been punctuated by periods of instability—unemployment and inflation. Parts 2 and 3 of this book have dealt with the causes and cures of short-run economic instability. The business cycle, the theory of employment, and fiscal and monetary policy have been the focal points of our analysis.

The task of Part 4 is to take a searching look at economic growth. In Chapter 20 we are concerned primarily with the basic theory of economic growth. Chapter 21 focuses upon the growth record of American capitalism. Costs and problems associated with growth and relevant public policies are discussed in Chapter 22. Later in Chapter 45 we shall look at the problem of economic growth from the viewpoint of the underdeveloped countries.

GROWTH ECONOMICS

Modern employment theory—detailed along with stabilization policy in Parts 2 and 3—is of a static or short-run character. That is, it assumes the economy has fixed amounts of resources or inputs available and therefore is capable of producing some capacity or full-employment level of national output. The central question of modern employment theory is: How can output be increased by more fully utilizing *existing* productive capacity? The essence of Keynes's answer, of course, was that aggregate demand should be adjusted through fiscal and monetary measures to the full-employment noninflationary level of output at which actual NNP will equal capacity or potential NNP. In terms of Figure 19·1, modern employment theory *assumes* that at full employment the economy can produce some fixed aggregate output

and therefore concentrates on the forces which determine whether $C + I_n + G$ will be sufficient to induce the production of that capacity output.

We now turn to the economics of growth, which is concerned with this question: After full employment is reached and actual NNP equals capacity or full-employment NNP, how can the economy's output be further increased? Thus, while employment theory is couched in terms of a fixed-capacity or full-employment output (Figure 13·5), the economics of growth takes a long-run perspective and seeks to uncover the forces that alter the economy's capacity to produce over time. We might say that employment theory is mostly concerned with the adjustment of aggregate demand, while the emphasis in growth theory is upon changes in aggregate real output or supply.

Two definitions

"Economic growth" is a much-used and much-abused term. Indeed, it is a slippery concept. What is economic growth? Two related definitions of economic growth are commonly offered.

Definition one Economic growth may be defined in terms of the total physical output, or real income, of the economy. Or, to be more sophisticated about it, economic growth refers to increases in the economy's *real* gross national product, or *real* national income. An expanding real output means that the economy is growing. A stable or declining output means that the economy is static or declining. Note that this definition hinges upon *real* and not *money* output. The production of a larger amount of goods and services signifies growth; paying a larger number of dollars for a fixed or declining quantity does not.

Definition two A second and somewhat more refined definition links economic growth to real *per capita* output. This definition correctly recognizes that the standard of living of any economy is best measured in terms of real output per person. The actual standard of living could decline in an economy if the population increased at a faster rate than the volume of real output.

Which of these definitions is best? It depends upon the specific problem with which one is dealing. If one is concerned with the question of military potential, for example, total real output is the more appropriate measure of growth. On the other hand, per capita real income is superior for comparisons of living standards between regions or nations. Both definitions suffer from important limitations. The measures do not directly reflect, for example, changes in leisure and environmental quality. We know, too, that the good life involves political, spiritual, and cultural as well as material objectives. Nevertheless, our definitions of economic growth will be useful because (1) our immediate concern as students of economics is with material well-being, and (2) as a matter of fact, a free nation which is wealthy in material things is in a strategic position to realize, if it chooses, the environmental and nonmaterial aspects of the good life.

Importance of growth

Why be concerned with economic growth? Why should an economy grow? The answer to these questions is almost self-evident: The growth of total output relative to population means a higher standard of living. An expanding real output means greater material abundance and implies a more satisfactory answer to the economizing problem. Our questions can be answered from a slightly different perspective. *A growing economy is in a superior position to meet new needs and resolve socioeconomic problems both domestically and internationally.* A growing economy, by definition, enjoys an increment in its annual real output which it can use to satisfy existing needs more effectively or to undertake new projects. An expanding real wage or salary income makes new opportunities available to an individual and his family—a trip to Europe, a new stereo, a college education for the children, and so forth—without the sacrifice of other opportunities and enjoyments. Similarly, for the economy as a whole a growing annual output provides the wherewithal to fulfill new needs and undertake new endeavors. For example, in recent years the United States has been realizing increases in its real

GNP on the order of $30 to $35 billion per year. This extra output provides the means by which we have been able to undertake an ambitious program of space exploration, wage a costly and controversial war in Vietnam, inaugurate a domestic war on poverty, and make a modest beginning to ameliorate air and water pollution, without dramatically impairing domestic consumption and investment. In contrast, in a static economy—one wherein real GNP was constant year after year—the undertaking of any of these programs would obviously entail a cutback in some other areas of production. For a static economy, more military goods, a new space program, or more resources for antipoverty endeavors would mean less consumer goods and fewer capital goods than previously. *Growth lessens the burden of scarcity.* To a degree, a growing economy, unlike a static one, can have its cake and eat it too. By easing the burden of scarcity—by relaxing society's production constraints—economic growth allows a nation to realize existing economic goals more fully and to undertake new output-absorbing endeavors. In short, our capacity to assume the material burden of war, to explore space, to fight poverty, to provide schools and highways, and to raise the general standard of living are all intimately linked to economic growth. Caution: Growth eases, but certainly does not resolve, the economizing problem. Witness, for example, the obvious competition for the country's available economic resources between the Vietnam war and the war on poverty.

Arithmetic of growth

Laymen sometimes wonder why economists get so excited about seemingly minuscule changes in the rate of growth. Does it really matter very much whether our economy grows at 4 percent or 3 percent? It matters a great deal! For the United States, which has a current GNP of about $1,000 billion, the difference between a 3 and 4 percent growth rate is about $10 billion worth of output per year. For a very poor country, a 1 or 2 percent change in the growth rate may well mean the difference between starvation and merely going hungry.

Furthermore, when envisioned over a period of years, an apparently small difference in the rate of growth becomes exceedingly important owing to the "miracle" of compound interest. Example: Suppose Alphania and Betania have identical GNPs. But Alphania begins to grow at a 4 percent annual rate, while Betania grows at only 2 percent. Alphania would find that its GNP would double in only about eighteen years; Betania would take thirty-five years to accomplish the same feat. Example: For the United States with its near–$1,000 billion GNP, the difference between a 3 and a 4 percent annual rate of growth over a ten-year period amounts to some $136 billion of total output! The importance of the growth rate is undeniable.

INGREDIENTS OF GROWTH: A FIRST LOOK

What are the sources of economic growth? Basically, there are six strategic ingredients in the growth of any economy. Four of these factors relate to the physical ability of an economy to grow. They are (1) the quantity and quality of its natural resources, (2) the quantity and quality of its human resources, (3) the supply or stock of capital goods, and (4) technology. These four items may be termed the *supply factors* in economic growth. These are the physical agents of greater production. It is the availability of more and better resources, including the stock of technological knowledge, which permits an economy to produce a greater real output.

But the ability to grow and the actual realization of growth may be quite different things. Specifically, two additional considerations contribute to growth. First, there is a *demand factor* in growth. To realize its growing productive potential a nation must obviously provide for the full employment of its expanding supplies of resources. This requires a growing level of aggregate demand. Second, there is the *allocative factor* in growth. To achieve its productive potential a nation must provide not only for the full employment of its resources, but also for full production from them. The ability to expand production is not a sufficient condition for the expansion of total output; the

actual utilization of available resources and the allocation of those resources in such a way as to get the maximum amount of useful goods produced are also required.

These factors can be placed in proper perspective by recalling the production possibilities curve, reproduced in Figure 20·1. This is a best-performance curve in that it indicates the various *maximum* combinations of products the economy can produce, given the quantity and quality of its natural, human, and capital resources, and its stock of technological know-how. Obviously an improvement in any of the supply factors will push the production possibilities curve to the right, as indicated by the shift from *AB* to *CD* in Figure 20·1. Increases in the quantity or quality of resources and technological advances push the curve to the right. But the demand and allocative factors remind us that the economy need not realize its maximum productive potential; the curve may shift to the right and leave the economy behind at some level of operation *inside* the curve. In particular, an increase in the productive *potential* of the economy will not be realized if the economy fails to generate a level of aggregate demand sufficient to provide full employment, and fails to maintain the flexibility to adjust to those changes in the allocation of resources demanded by changes in the relative supplies of resources or technological knowledge. That is, to stay on the rightward-shifting production possibilities curve, the economy must avoid *un*employment (apparent unemployment) and *under*employment (disguised unemployment).

FIGURE 20·1 ECONOMIC GROWTH AND THE PRODUCTION POSSIBILITIES CURVE

Economic growth is indicated by an outward shift of the production possibilities curve, as from *AB* to *CD*. Increases in the quantity and quality of resources and technological advance permit this shift; full employment and allocative efficiency are essential to its realization.

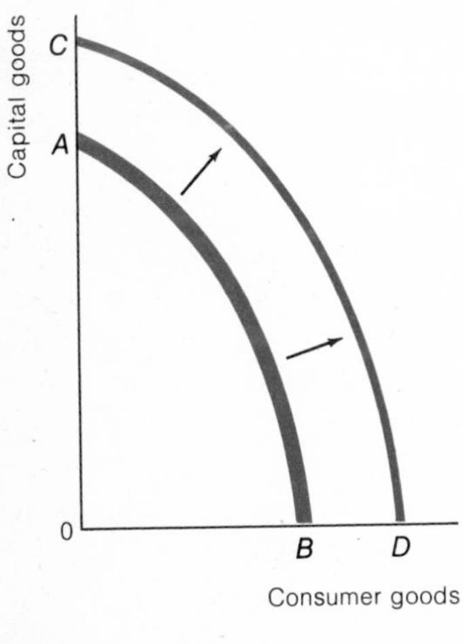

Example: The net increase in the labor force of the United States is about 1.8 million workers per year. As such this increases the productive capacity, or potential, of the economy. But the realization of the extra output these additional workers are capable of producing presumes an appropriate increase in aggregate money demand. Furthermore, achieving the maximum additional output from this increase in the labor force presumes that these new workers will be efficiently allocated within the economy; that is, additions to the labor force should be apportioned to those industries and firms wherein the value of their contribution to total output will be greatest.

It is notable that the supply and demand factors in growth are related. For example, unemployment tends to retard the rate of capital accumulation and may slow expenditures for research. And, conversely, a low rate of innovation and investment can be a basic cause of unemployment.

GROWTH: A MORE SOPHISTICATED VIEW

Recognizing that growth can be represented by a rightward shift of the production possibilities curve, we now come to a more sophisticated aspect of growth economics. *The degree to which total output can be expanded depends upon the proportion in which resource inputs are expanded.* Curve C_1R_1 in Figure 20·2*a* shows the production possibilities curve

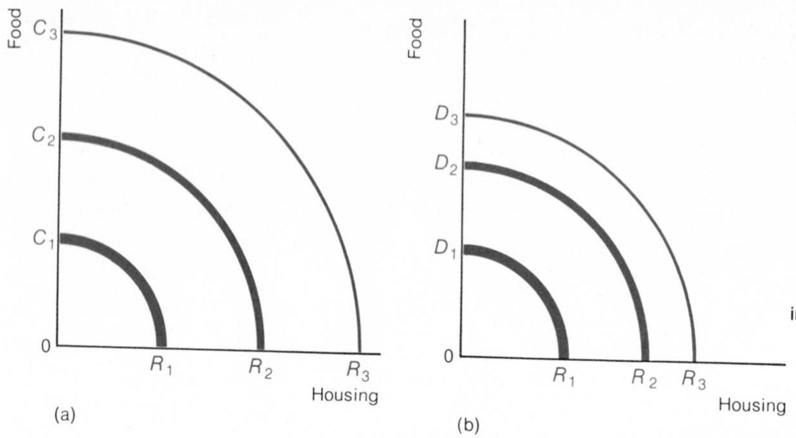

FIGURE 20·2 CONSTANT (*a*) AND DIMINISHING (*b*) RETURNS

If all inputs are increased proportionately, total output should increase proportionately. That is, if all inputs are doubled, then total output should double, as indicated by the shift of the production possibilities curve from C_1R_1 to C_2R_2 in (*a*). But if one or more resources are fixed, as is assumed in (*b*), then equal increases in another resource (say, labor) will result in smaller and smaller increases in total output. That is, diminishing returns will result because labor is now being combined with smaller amounts of other resources per worker.

for an economy which has available certain given quantities of human and property resources. Now assume that each of the resources of this economy is suddenly doubled. What will happen to total output? Common sense correctly deduces that a doubling of resource inputs would double output, as suggested by the shift of C_1R_1 to C_2R_2.[1] Note that $OC_1 = C_1C_2$ and $OR_1 = R_1R_2$. Furthermore, having doubled both the number of labor inputs and total output, it is clear that output per worker will be the same for both production possibilities curves. Increasing resource inputs by the same absolute amounts once again would shift the production possibilities curve to C_3R_3, where $R_2R_3 = R_1R_2 = OR_1$ and $C_2C_3 = C_1C_2 = OC_1$.

Law of diminishing returns

But an economy may find it extremely difficult to increase *all* its resources in a balanced or proportionate manner. Land, in particular, is a relatively fixed resource. Typically the mineral deposits and amount of arable land available to a nation can be increased only within narrow limits. What will happen to total output when inputs are increased *dis*proportionately, that is, property resources (land) are held constant and more labor is applied to them? The answer to this question has its roots in the famous *law of diminishing returns,*[2] which has applications both to the economy as a whole and to individual firms and industries (Chapters 26 and 31).

The concept of diminishing returns can best be understood by performing a simple mental experiment. Imagine an economy whose property resources (land and real capital) are absolutely fixed. In particular, visualize a primitive, underdeveloped economy whose stock of capital goods is negligible and whose supply of arable land is fixed. Assume, too, that technology—the stock of technological knowledge—is fixed; this means that the *quality* of capital and labor are both given. Assuming its population is growing, this simple agrarian society is concerned primarily with adding labor to a fixed amount of land and a few rudimentary farm tools to produce the food and fiber needed by its population. What happens to total output as equal increments—equal doses—of labor are added to a fixed amount of property (primarily land) resources? The law of diminishing returns in-

[1]We shall find later in Chapter 26 that, because of *economies of scale*, this may not be precisely true. But we can regard this statement as substantially correct.

[2]This law goes by other names: for example, the principle of diminishing marginal productivity and the law of variable proportions.

dicates that *as successive equal increments of one resource (labor, in this case) are added to a fixed resource (land and property), beyond some point the resulting increases in total output will diminish in size.* The *increase* in total product resulting from each successive dose of labor is called the *marginal physical product* or simply *marginal product.* Our law, then, says that as successive inputs of labor are added to a fixed amount of some other resource(s), the resulting marginal product will diminish beyond some point.

Qualification: Note we say "beyond some point." The initial increments or doses of labor may be subject to *increasing returns*—marginal product may rise for a time. The reason for this is that initially, with a very small labor force, property resources will be grossly underutilized. The fixed supplies of land and capital will be seriously undermanned. A very small amount of labor combined with a very large amount of land will result in relatively inefficient production. As equal increments or doses of labor are added to the fixed amount of land, the problem of underutilization is overcome and the resulting marginal product will increase for a time.

But this stage of increasing returns will inevitably reverse itself. As more and more labor is added to the fixed amount of property resources, a point will be reached where land and capital come to be overmanned or overutilized. That is, *each* worker will be equipped with smaller and smaller amounts of land and capital. In our simple agrarian society, more and more workers will be farming each acre of arable land and *each* worker will have fewer tools. Hence, successive equal doses of labor will result in smaller and smaller increases in total output. Diminishing returns have been encountered; the marginal product of successive doses of labor diminishes and may eventually become negative in the extreme!

The production possibilities curve and diminishing returns

Let us now interpret the law of diminishing returns within the framework of the production possibilities curve. While a proportionate increase in *all* inputs will cause total output to increase proportionately as suggested by Figure 20·2*a*, a disproportionate increase in inputs—increasing the labor force while holding property resources constant—will cause total output to increase less than proportionately to the increase in labor. As Figure 20·2*b* indicates, if the labor force is doubled and the inputs of property resources are held constant, total output will less than double. The production possibilities curve will move from D_1R_1 to only D_2R_2. Why? Because property resources will tend to be overmanned. Double the labor force again and the overutilization of property resources will become more severe. This means that total output will rise by a still smaller amount—from D_2R_2 to, say, D_3R_3. Note that $OR_1 > R_1R_2 > R_2R_3$ and $OD_1 > D_1D_2 > D_2D_3$.

Diminishing returns: arithmetic example

Table 20·1 presents a more conventional and somewhat more sophisticated illustration of the law of diminishing returns. It provides us with a reference point from which we can further explore the causes of, and the constraints upon, economic growth. Here we are adding equal increments or doses of labor to fixed amounts of land and capital. To simplify our exposition, total output (real GNP) consists of only one product—say, corn (food). Column 2 indicates the total output which will result from each level of labor input in column 1. Column 3, marginal physical product, shows us the change in total output associated with each additional unit of labor. Note that with no labor inputs, total output is zero; empty, untilled land will yield no output. The first two doses of labor reflect increasing returns, their MPs being 100 and 150 tons of food respectively. But then, beginning with the third increment of labor, marginal physical product—the increase in total output—diminishes continuously and actually becomes negative with the eighth dose of labor.

Figure 20·3*a* and *b* shows the law of diminishing returns in terms of total product and marginal product respectively. The MP curve simply reflects the increases in total product associated with each successive dose of labor. Geometrically, marginal physi-

TABLE 20·1 A MACROECONOMIC ILLUSTRATION OF DIMINISHING RETURNS (*hypothetical data*)

(1) Inputs of labor (millions of man-years)	(2) Total product, TP (millions of bushels of food)	(3) Marginal physical product, MP (millions of bushels of food)	(4) Average physical product, AP (bushels of food per man-year)
0	0		—
		100	
1	100		100
		150	
2	250		125
		125	
3	375		125
		101	
4	476		119
		74	
5	550		110
		50	
6	600		100
		30	
7	630		90
		−6	
8	624		78

cal product is the slope of the total product curve. Note that so long as MP is positive, TP is increasing. And when MP is zero, TP is at its peak. Finally, when MP becomes negative, TP is necessarily declining. Increasing returns are reflected in a rising marginal physical product curve; diminishing returns in a falling marginal physical product.

In our discussion we will find it particularly useful to note what the law of diminishing returns means for *average product* or output per input of labor. AP is calculated in column 4 of Table 20·1 simply by dividing TP by the number of inputs of labor, that is, by dividing column 2 by column 1. Note in both the table and Figure 20·3*b* that AP reflects the same general "rising-maximum-declining" relationship between variable inputs of labor and output with which the law of diminishing returns has already familiarized us.

Also note this technical point concerning the relationship between MP and AP: Where MP exceeds AP, the latter must rise. And wherever MP is less than AP, then AP must be declining. It follows that MP intersects AP where the latter is at a maximum. This relationship is a matter of mathematical necessity. You raise your average grade in a course only when your score on an additional (marginal) examination is greater than the average of all your past scores. If your grade on an additional exam is below your current average, your average will be pulled down.

Optimum population

Average physical product is a convenient and important indicator of growth because output per worker (AP) and real income per worker are essentially the same thing. That is, average physical product or output per worker is our second definition of economic growth. In Table 20·1 and Figure 20·3*a* and *b* we find that growth in terms of definition one continues through the seventh input of labor. But in terms of definition two—output per worker—growth reaches a maximum at some point between the second and third units of labor.

That particular population size at which real output or income per person is at a maximum is called the *optimum population* for society. The optimum population is that population which, given the economy's property resources and technology, will yield the

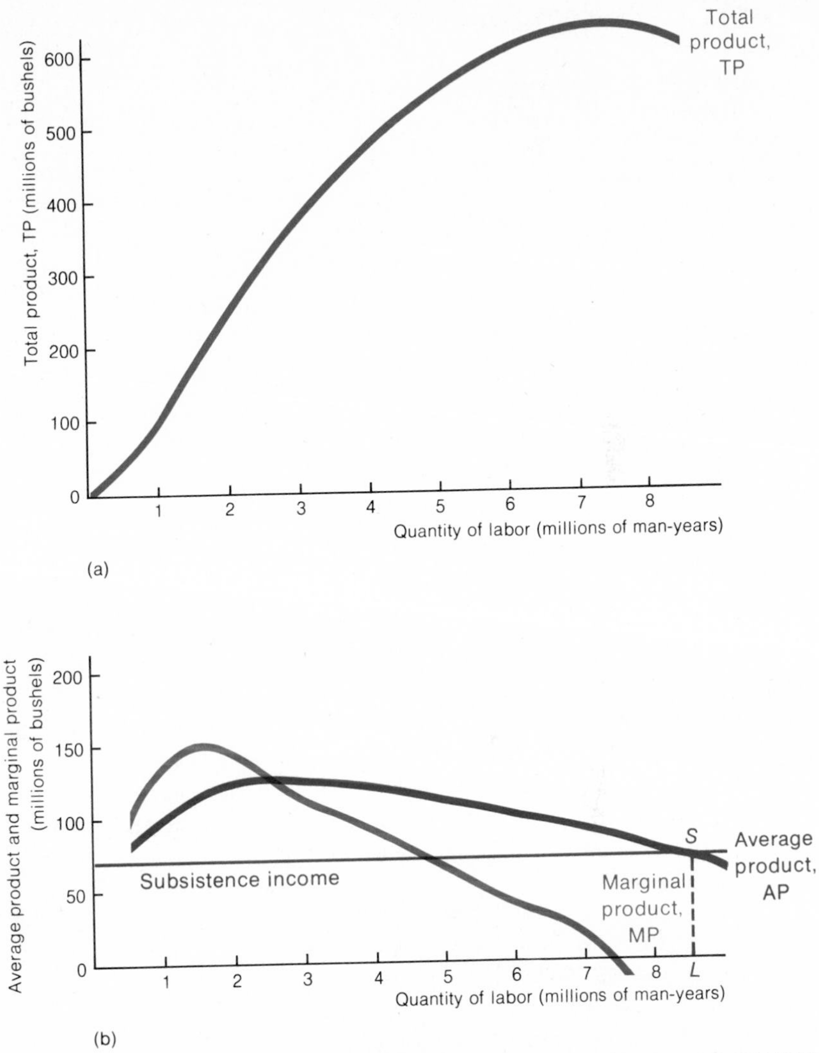

FIGURE 20·3 THE LAW OF DIMINISHING RETURNS

As a variable resource (labor) is added to fixed amounts of other resources (land and capital), the resulting total product will eventually increase by diminishing amounts, reach a maximum, and then decline as in (*a*). Marginal product in (*b*) reflects the changes in total product associated with each extra input of labor. Average product is simply output per worker. Note that marginal product intersects average product at the maximum average product.

greatest income per person. This concept reinforces an earlier point: Population growth may be a mixed blessing insofar as growth is concerned. An expansion of the population and labor force typically (but not always) increases real GNP, that is, contributes to growth in the sense of definition one. But in terms of definition two, population may be either too large or too small.

Malthus and misery

Diminishing returns correctly suggest that the relationship between the size of a country's population (labor force) and its property resources is highly relevant in determining both its total output and its output per person or standard of living. Indeed, this fact was perceived by the English economist Thomas R. Malthus at the close of the eighteenth century and enunciated in his famous *Essay on the Principle of Population* (1798). Malthus's explicit purpose was "to account for much of that poverty and misery observable among the lower classes of every nation," and his explanation of this misery was rooted firmly in the law of diminishing returns.

The essence of Malthus's thesis was quite simple: *The population of a nation tends to outrun its capacity to produce the food and fiber needed to sustain itself.* Population tends to increase at a constant geometric rate (2, 4, 8, 16, 32, 64, 128, 256, and so on). But the output of food, on the other hand, only increases *at best* at a constant arithmetic rate (1, 2, 3, 4, 5, 6, and so forth). Given these different rates of increase, population will in time inevitably press upon the food supply and the results will be subsistence living levels, misery, and, in the extreme, starvation. But why won't the food supply increase at a more rapid rate? Because of diminishing returns. As the growing population puts more and more laborers to work on a fixed amount of arable land, both marginal and then average product (Figure 20·3*b*) will diminish. Each worker is combined with less and less land, so his productivity declines.

We have just seen that a society's output per worker is its income per worker. A diminishing average product therefore means a falling standard of living. In short, the pressure of an expanding population and labor force upon fixed land resources invokes the law of diminishing returns. Total output increases less than proportionately to population, so the standard of living necessarily declines. The result was the widespread misery and poverty which Malthus readily observed. We might draw a subsistence level-of-living line in Figure 20·3*b* and summarize Malthus's position by saying that, given the reality of diminishing returns, persistent and substantial population growth (a rightward movement along the horizontal axis) will keep the level of living (vertical axis) perilously close to the bare subsistence level (point *S*). Only the gloomy team of disease, malnutrition, and famine will bring population growth to a halt at *OL*.

We are all well aware that mankind has been undergoing an extraordinary expansion of numbers. The magnitude of this unparalleled population explosion is portrayed vividly in Figure 20·4. The growth of population in just the last two centuries has been three times larger than the cumulated expansion of mankind during all the previous millennia of man's existence! Given this incredible growth of population and its projected continuance, *and* given the hard fact that only a finite amount of land exists on our planet, it is highly relevant to inquire as to the extent to which Malthus's gloomy forecast has come to pass. Is the Malthusian prediction being realized in any of today's nations?

Clearly the specter of Malthus stalks many of the so-called "underdeveloped" nations of the world. In India and China, for example, rapid population growth has been a basic factor in making malnutrition, famine, and disease a way of life—and of death. Indeed, most of the nations of Africa, South America, and Asia are finding it extremely difficult to raise their living standards, because rapid population growth means that year after year there are simply more mouths to feed and more bodies to clothe and shelter. While Egypt's Aswan Dam will make a substantial contribution to that nation's output of food, the growth in population which has occurred during the period of construction will have the effect of leaving per capita food production substantially unchanged!

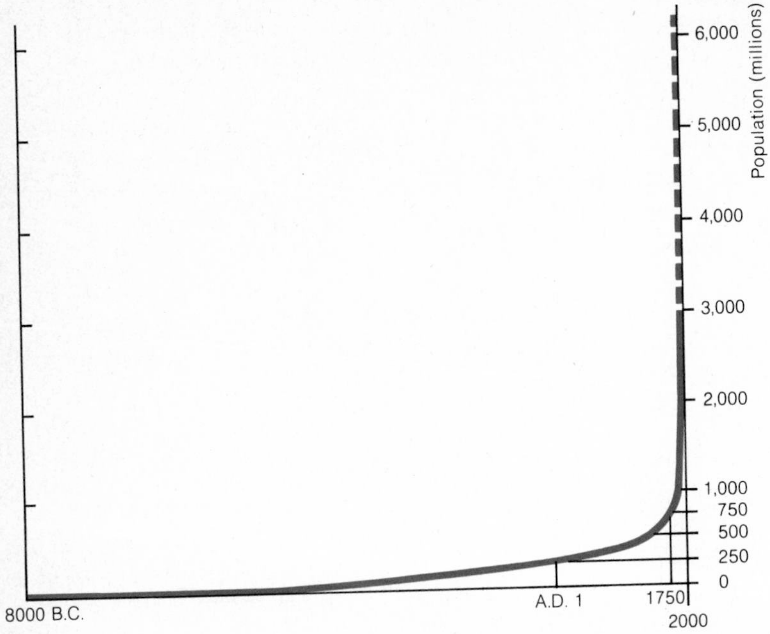

FIGURE 20·4 THE LONG-RUN TREND OF WORLD POPULATION GROWTH

A dramatic acceleration of world population growth has been experienced in modern times. (John D. Durand, "A Long-range View of World Population Growth," *The Annals,* January 1967, p. 3.)

Rising productivity and growth

In contrast, the "advanced" nations of the world—the United States, Canada, the countries of Western Europe, Australia, New Zealand, and Japan—enjoy high and rising standards of living despite considerable population growth. The question is: Why the differences? Why poverty in India and plenty in Indiana? The answer can be found by pursuing our discussion of diminishing returns. While Figure 20·3*a* and *b* implies the possibility of Malthusian misery, these same curves and, more specifically, *the assumptions upon which they are based,* suggest the possibility of growth and a rising standard of living.

Let us perform a second mental experiment similar to that underlying Figure 20·3*a* and *b.* Again we add a growing labor force to a constant conglomerate of property resources and technical knowledge, as before. But now let us assume that these property resources are fixed at a higher level both quantitatively and qualitatively.[3] Specifically, suppose each worker, instead of being equipped with a negligible amount of capital, is aided in his productive efforts with, say, $100 worth of machinery and equipment. Suppose, too, that technology is better than in our first experiment: for example, farmers now have discovered the contribution which contour plowing and crop rotation can make to output. And let us assume the labor force itself is qualitatively superior—physically and mentally—to that of our first experiment.

Would these changes—more capital, an improved technology, and a better labor force—revoke the law of diminishing returns? Although "revoke" is perhaps too strong a word, these factors can offset or forestall diminishing returns. We can envision what happens

[3]In Chapter 45 we shall find that less tangible "resources"—for example, attitudes and institutional arrangements—must often be changed if growth is to occur.

by looking at the curves in Figure 20·5. The average-product curve designated as AP_1 is taken from Figure 20·3*b* and merely repeats the results of our original experiment. AP_2 portrays the results of our second experiment. Note that this new curve still reflects the law of diminishing returns but is at a higher level, and the point at which average product begins to fall corresponds with a larger population or labor force. Why? Because each level of labor input is now equipped with more capital and better technological know-how, and the labor force itself is superior. For all these reasons any given number of workers will produce a larger total output, and hence a larger output per worker, than under the inferior conditions of our first experiment. A third experiment involving still more capital, a further advanced technology, and a labor force of even higher quality will again raise the average-product curve and locate its maximum point further to the right, as indicated by AP_3. Still further improvements in the quantity of capital, technology, and labor force would yield AP_4.

A bit of reflection reveals that, for any nation with a growing population and labor force, we can think of the course of its standard of living as the net result of two opposed forces. On the one hand, diminishing returns cause the application of successive inputs of labor to result eventually in smaller and smaller increases in total product, a declining average product, and a falling standard of living. On the other hand, we have the "forces of growth"—increases in the stock of capital, technological progress, and a qualitatively improved labor force—tending to offset diminishing returns by violating the very assumptions or conditions upon which the functioning of the law depends.

Now, and at the hazard of oversimplification, what has happened in the underdeveloped countries is that the forces of growth have been absent or, at best, present in only modest degrees, so that diminishing

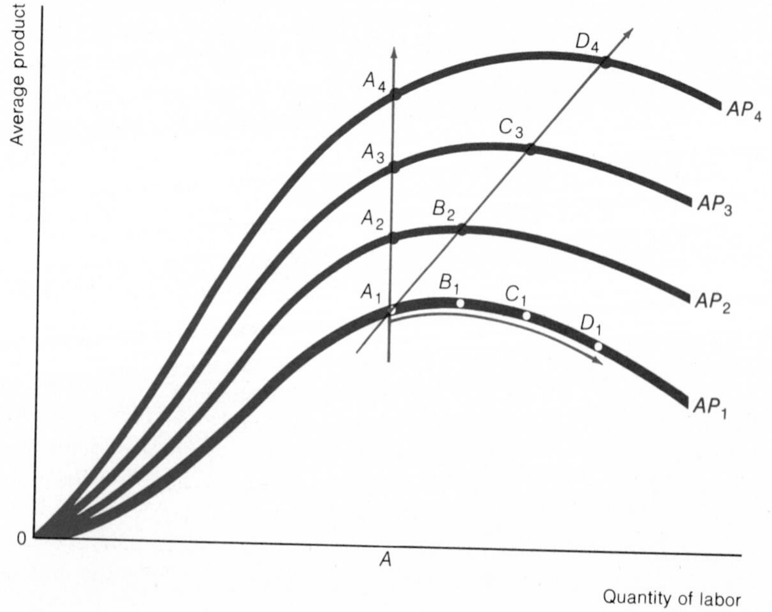

FIGURE 20·5 RISING PRODUCTIVITY AND ECONOMIC GROWTH

The "forces of growth"—increases in the stock of capital, technological progress, and improvements in the quality of labor—may offset diminishing returns by shifting the average-product curve upward. A growing economy with a constant population will follow the $A_1A_2A_3A_4$ path. A growing economy with an expanding population will achieve a higher output per worker along the $A_1B_2C_3D_4$ path. A nongrowing economy whose population is expanding will follow the $A_1B_1C_1D_1$ path on an unchanging average-product curve and will be subject to a declining output per worker.

returns have prevailed. And as Malthus envisioned, population has indeed tended to press upon the food supply, to the end that living standards have remained pitifully low (Table 45·1). In Figure 20·5 this case can be envisioned as the movement down a stable average-product curve, as from A_1 to B_1 to C_1 and so forth, on curve AP_1. As our diagram suggests, such an economy is literally going "over the hill."

At the other extreme, suppose population and the labor force are constant at, say, *OA* in Figure 20·5 and the forces of growth are strongly evident. These improvements in technology and the labor force and increases in the stock of capital would shift the average productivity curve upward and trace the path suggested by A_1, A_2, A_3, and A_4. In general the developed countries of the world have been experiencing growth in their populations and labor forces. But at the same time the forces of growth have been pushing their *AP* curves upward. Hence, the advanced nations have been following the kind of path suggested by A_1, B_2, C_3, and D_4. Diminishing returns have *tended* to be at work, but these nations, by adding to their stocks of capital and of knowledge and by improving the quality of their labor forces, have been able to more than offset diminishing returns and to achieve a higher and higher standard of living over time.

AGGREGATE DEMAND AND GROWTH

Up to this point our discussion has centered upon the supply side of economic growth, that is, upon those factors which determine the productive capacity of the economy. We now want to consider the demand side of economic growth.

The essence of the problem is that in an economy whose productive capacity is expanding, the full-employment noninflationary NNP will obviously be increasing over time. Therefore, the realization or achievement of that desired output is clearly dependent upon an expanding level of aggregate demand. We discovered in Chapter 13 that whether a private economy achieves full employment depends upon the interaction of its saving and investment plans. Businesses must be willing to invest an amount equal to the full-employment volume of saving if full employment is to be attained. In a static or stationary economy—that is, an economy whose permissive factors are such that its productive potential is fixed and unchanging—this is largely a matter of sustaining a constant level of investment year after year. But in a growing economy—one whose real national income is expanding—the problem is decidedly more complex. Why? Because in an expanding economy saving increases. Remember: Households save a larger proportion of a large income than they do of a small income. This obviously means that if the expanding productive capacity of a growing economy is to be realized, investment spending must increase by the same amount as the full-employment level of saving increases. Let us now consider the specifics of the demand side of growth in two slightly different ways.

1. Consider, first, the very simple model presented in Table 20·2. Suppose that the economy is initially (in year 1) at the full-employment noninflationary level of output. Assume this entails a $500 billion NNP and a $50 billion level of investment. Suppose, secondly, that the economy is capable of expanding its total real output by 4 percent per annum. And finally, let us assume as in Chapter 13 that the MPS is one-fourth. Column 2 of Table 20·2 indicates that a 4 percent rate of growth means the economy is capable of producing $520 billion in year 2 ($500 billion plus 4 percent of $500 billion). If businessmen attempt to utilize this increase in the economy's productive potential—that is, if businessmen produce the $520 billion NNP—will the economy spend enough to sustain this output? The answer hinges upon the rate of investment. The $20 billion increase in output and income will cause saving to increase by $5 billion (one-fourth of $20 billion). Investment spending must expand by a like amount in year 2 to compensate for this increase. Investment spending must expand from $50 to $55 billion for the growth potential of the economy to be realized in year 2. In year 3 the investment requirement is even greater. The economy is capable of producing an output of $540.8 billion. But the $20.8 billion increase in output and income

TABLE 20·2 INVESTMENT REQUIREMENTS IN A GROWING ECONOMY (*hypothetical data; in billions*)

(1) Year	(2) Full-employment NNP at 4 percent annual growth rate	(3) Annual increase in saving	(4) Investment required to achieve full-employment NNP
1	$500.0	—	$50.0
2	520.0	$5.0	55.0
3	540.8	5.2	60.2
4	562.4	5.4	65.6
	etc.	etc.	etc.

which occurs between years 2 and 3 gives rise to $5.2 billion in additional saving. This means that investment spending must rise from an annual rate of $55 billion in year 2 to $60.2 billion rate in year 3. And so it goes for succeeding years. The basic lesson of this simplified illustration is clear: *The maintenance of a given rate of growth requires a constantly expanding volume of investment spending.* Needless to say, to increase the rate of growth requires that investment increase even more rapidly.

2. A related and somewhat more sophisticated view of the demand side of growth focuses attention upon the growth-inducing role of investment. This approach can be presented graphically as an extension of the tools of Keynesian employment theory.[4]

Consider Figure 20·6, wherein we have drawn the now familiar consumption schedule and the aggregate supply (45-degree line) schedule. For simplicity's sake we ignore government and consider only the private sector. Assume initially—in year 1—that capacity production, that is, the full-employment noninflationary NNP as determined by the permissive factors, is ON_1 (say, $470 billion, as shown by the equilibrium position in Table 13·1). We know that the production of this output will bring forth consumption of C_1N_1 (say, $450 billion). Planned saving, which you will recall from Chapter 12 is the vertical distance between the consumption schedule and the 45-degree line, is S_1C_1 ($20 billion). Let us suppose that, happily, intended investment is the same amount, S_1C_1 or $20 billion, so saving equals net investment and initially the full-employment noninflationary output is being realized.

But now a new consideration comes to the fore. In our earlier analysis of output determination we looked only at the *income-creating* aspect of investment spending. That is, in Chapters 12 and 13 we were interested in investment only as a component of aggregate demand which helped to generate and sustain some level of NNP. Our discussion of capital formation in this chapter, however, tells us that net investment also has a *capacity-creating* aspect; net investment, by expanding the nation's stock of capital facilities, will enhance the economy's productive capacity. Simply stated, because net investment has occurred in year 1, the economy has the capacity to produce a still larger full-employment noninflationary NNP in year 2.

How much larger? This depends upon what economists call the *capital-output ratio,* that is, the relationship between net investment and the resulting increase in the productive or output capacity of the economy. Let us suppose this ratio is 2:1; every $2

[4]See William Fellner, *Trends and Cycles in Economic Activity* (New York: Holt, Rinehart and Winston, Inc., 1956), chap. 4.

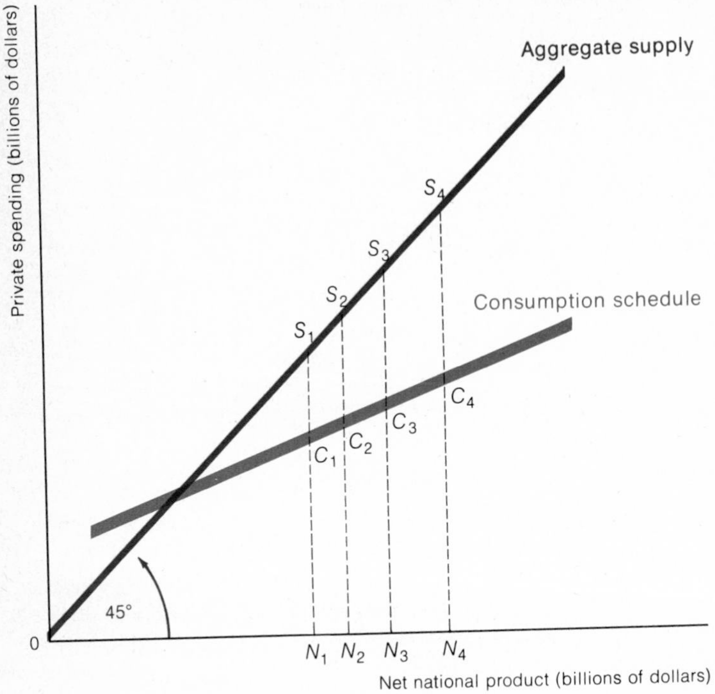

FIGURE 20·6 THE DEMAND SIDE OF ECONOMIC GROWTH

Achievement of the full-employment noninflationary NNP of N_1 in year 1 will require net investment equal to saving of S_1C_1. But this investment will raise the economy's productive capacity by N_1N_2. To achieve this higher level of production net investment must rise to S_2C_2. But this level of investment will increase capacity by N_2N_3, which, to be realized, calls for a still-higher investment level of S_3C_3, and so forth.

of net investment in year 1 makes the economy capable of producing $1 of additional output in year 2 and succeeding years. Specifically, $20 billion of net investment will increase the economy's productive capacity by $10 billion, from $470 to $480 billion. In Figure 20·6 the amount added to the full-employment noninflationary or capacity NNP as the result of year 1's net investment is N_1N_2. Note that because the capital-output ratio is 2:1, N_1N_2 equals $\frac{1}{2}S_1C_1$.

Will this new, higher NNP which the economy is capable of producing in year 2 be realized? It depends, as in year 1, on whether planned investment is equal to the new and higher level of planned saving S_2C_2 that occurs in year 2. Specifically, if we assume the marginal propensity to save is, say, one-fifth, S_2C_2 will be $22 billion in year 2. Planned investment must then be equal to S_2C_2 or $22 billion if year 2's expanded productive capacity is to be realized. But, once again, if planned investment is actually S_2C_2, the economy's productive potential will be larger by N_2N_3 ($= \frac{1}{2}S_2C_2$) in year 3. Specifically, with a capital-output ratio of 2:1 the economy will be capable of producing a $491 billion NNP in year 3. For this greater productive capacity to be realized, businesses must be prepared to invest at the higher S_3C_3 level in year 3 to absorb that same volume of saving. The same reasoning applies to years 4, 5, and so on. The basic conclusion is quite evident: *The maintenance of economic growth relies upon an expanding level of investment.*

What will happen if intended investment fails to equal intended saving at each of the successively higher levels of full-employment noninflationary NNP? The answer obviously is that the economy will be faced

with unemployment and underutilized productive facilities. Furthermore, the lower-than-desired rate of investment will cause the economy to grow less rapidly than depicted in Figure 20·6. If planned investment is persistently in excess of planned saving at the various full-employment levels of NNP, the economy will realize rapid growth accompanied by chronic inflation. Appropriate monetary and fiscal measures would be called for in either case. We shall have more to say about policies to achieve economic growth in Chapter 22.

ALLOCATIVE EFFICIENCY AND GROWTH

The forces of growth—both the supply factors and an appropriately expanding level of aggregate demand—will call for changes in the allocation of the economy's resources over time. If these changes in resource use do not occur with reasonable speed and completeness, the economy will fail to realize fully its capacity for growth.

On the supply side, if we were to disaggregate the economy's overall growth, we would find that the productive capacities of some industries and firms are expanding rapidly while those of others are growing slowly or perhaps even contracting. Such changes obviously imply appropriate adjustments in the allocation of resources. Where, for example, do expanding industries obtain the resources which their growth requires? In part, they may be obtained from current increases in our total supplies of resources. Thus an expanding industry may get a part of the additional labor it needs from new labor force entrants. It may obtain the remainder of its added labor from other, declining industries. In either event some mechanism is needed to guide new resources into their most productive uses or, as the case may be, to direct currently employed resources from low-productivity to high-productivity employments. In short, changes in technology (as reflected in either new productive techniques or new goods) and changes in the relative scarcities and, therefore, prices of resources which are germane to growth call for constant reallocations of human and property resources among alternative uses. As noted above, if these resource realignments do not occur with reasonable rapidity and completeness, the economy's capacity for growth may be underfulfilled.

The need for sustained allocative efficiency also has roots on the demand side. We already know that aggregate demand must expand appropriately if the full-capacity output of an expanding economy is to be realized. This generalization, however, conceals the fact that as total demand grows, its composition or structure will change. The demands for some goods will be highly sensitive to increases in income. For other goods demand might be quite insensitive to income growth. For example, the demands for potatoes, soap, and wheat grow very modestly as income expands, but the demands for steak, jewelry, and automobiles tend to increase sharply as income rises. In any event, extensive shifts in the allocation of resources will again be necessary.

We will have substantially more to say about the allocative aspect of economic growth in Chapters 21 and 22. In Chapter 21 we will attempt a general assessment of the efficiency with which the price system has negotiated required reallocations of resources in our economy. Then in Chapter 22 we will discuss some of the costs associated with these adjustments, for example, the problem of technological unemployment. At this point you might find it of interest to look ahead and attempt to explain the causes of the reallocations of labor evidenced in Figures 22·2 and 22·3.

SUMMARY

1. Economic growth may be defined either in terms of *a.* an expanding real national output (income) or *b.* an expanding per capita real output (income). Growth lessens the burden of scarcity and provides increases in the national output which can be used in the resolution of domestic and international socioeconomic problems.

2. The supply factors in economic growth are *a.* the quantity and quality of a nation's natural resources, *b.* the quantity and quality of its human resources, *c.* its stock of capital facilities, and *d.* its

technology. Two other factors—a sufficient level of aggregate demand and allocative efficiency—are essential if the economy is to realize its growth potential.

3. The principle of diminishing returns exercises a constraint upon growth where one or more resources are fixed in supply. This law tells us that with a given technology, the addition of successive units of one resource (labor) to fixed amounts of other resources (land and capital) will ultimately result in smaller and smaller increases in total output. That is, the increases in output will be less than proportionate to the increases in the inputs of the variable resource. This means that the average output or productivity per worker will ultimately diminish as more and more labor is added (Figure 20·3).

4. Thomas Malthus used the law of diminishing returns over a century and a half ago to explain the widespread poverty which then existed. In particular, Malthus argued that rapid population growth, coupled with diminishing returns in agricultural production, was tending to keep real income per capita at the subsistence level.

5. Technological progress, increases in the stock of capital, and improvements in the quality of labor have the effect of offsetting diminishing returns by increasing the productivity of labor (Figure 20·5).

6. An expanding productive potential will not be achieved unless aggregate demand expands at an appropriate rate. In particular, investment spending not only generates income and sustains output, but also adds to productive capacity. As capacity and the economy's full-employment noninflationary NNP rise, so does saving, and this means still more investment is needed to sustain this expanded output.

7. The realization of the growth potential of an economy presumes that appropriate reallocations of resources are achieved.

QUESTIONS AND STUDY SUGGESTIONS

1. Define economic growth. What difficulties are involved in measuring economic growth?

2. Why is economic growth important? Explain why the difference between a 3.5 percent and a 3.0 percent annual growth rate might be of great importance.

3. What are the major causes of economic growth? "There are both a demand and a supply side to economic growth." Explain. Illustrate the operation of both sets of factors in terms of the production possibilities curve.

4. State fully and precisely the law of diminishing returns. Use production possibilities curves to illustrate economic growth under conditions of constant and diminishing returns. Why are diminishing returns significant for a nation's economic growth?

5. Explain: "Rapid population growth may both contribute to, and detract from, a nation's economic progress." What is meant by an "optimum population"?

6. Use the following data to calculate marginal physical product and average physical product. Plot total, marginal, and average physical product and explain in detail the relationship between each pair of curves. What is the optimum population or labor force for this economy?

Inputs of labor	Total physical product	Marginal physical product	Average physical product
1	18		
2	33		
3	51		
4	65		
5	74		
6	80		
7	82		
8	81		

7. How did Malthus explain the extremely low levels of income which were so common in the eighteenth century?

To what extent, if any, is Malthus's explanation of poverty relevant today?

8. How can an economy with a rapidly growing population and labor force effectively offset diminishing returns?

9. Discuss the importance of the income-creating and the capacity-creating aspects of investment for economic growth. What is the importance of the capital-output ratio? Using a diagram similar to Figure 20·6, illustrate what differences an increase or decrease in ***a.*** the MPS and ***b.*** the capital-output ratio would make for the rate of growth and the volume of investment required to maintain the full-employment noninflationary NNP over time.

10. *Advanced analysis.* If the economy's capital-output ratio is 3:1 and the MPS is ½, at what annual rate must real NNP increase if full employment is to be maintained?

SELECTED REFERENCES

Economic Issues, 4th ed., readings 5, 6, and 34.

Fabricant, Solomon: *A Primer on Productivity* (New York: Random House, 1969).

Gill, Richard T.: *Economic Development: Past and Present,* 2d ed. (Englewood Cliffs, N.J.: Prentice-Hall, Inc., 1967), particularly chaps. 1–4.

Morris, Bruce R.: *Economic Growth and Development* (New York: Pitman Publishing Corporation, 1967).

Rostow, W. W.: *The Stages of Economic Growth* (New York: Cambridge University Press, 1960).

"World Population," *The Annals,* January 1967.

21

ECONOMIC GROWTH: THE AMERICAN EXPERIENCE

On December 15, 1970, the United States' money GNP broke the $1 *trillion* barrier! In celebration of the event President Nixon unveiled a new Gross National Product clock which ticks off the growth of the nation's output of goods and services at the rate of $2,000 per second. During the President's brief talk the clock ticked off some $5 million in output.[1]

The basic purpose of the present chapter is to summarize and explain the growth record of the United States. In doing this we will rely upon the analytical framework developed in Chapter 20. In general, we found six basic factors in growth: four supply factors—natural resources, human resources, the stock of capital, and technology—a demand factor—the necessity for fully employing or utilizing the supply factors—and an allocative factor.

In the present chapter we seek the answers to two questions. What level of economic growth has been achieved in American capitalism? How can this growth be explained in terms of the six growth factors?

GROWTH RECORD OF AMERICAN CAPITALISM

Table 21·1 gives us a rough idea of economic growth in the United States over the past six decades as viewed through our two definitions of growth. Column 2 summarizes the economy's growth as measured by increases in real GNP. It is to be emphasized that these figures have been adjusted for price differences and hence reflect changes in *real* output. Although not steady, the growth of real GNP has been quite remarkable. *The real GNP has increased sixfold in the last sixty years.* It is remarkable that the growth in the real GNP in the last ten years exceeded its total growth in the entire period between 1776 and 1940!

But our population has also grown significantly.

[1]The clock is a somewhat deceptive timepiece in that it measures changes in the *money* GNP. Ironically, on the afternoon of December 15 the President met with his economic advisors to map strategy for slowing inflation and accelerating the growth of real output.

TABLE 21·1 REAL GNP AND PER CAPITA GNP, 1909–1970

(1) Year	(2) GNP, billions of 1958 dollars	(3) Per capita GNP, 1958 dollars
1909	$117	$1,351
1915	125	1,238
1920	140	1,315
1925	179	1,549
1930	183	1,490
1935	169	1,331
1940	227	1,720
1945	355	2,538
1950	355	2,342
1955	438	2,650
1960	488	2,699
1965	614	3,158
1970	724	3,532

Source: Department of Commerce, *Long-term Economic Growth* (Washington, 1966), pp. 166–169, and Department of Commerce data.

Hence, using our second definition of growth, we find in column 3 that *per capita GNP is almost three times what it was some five decades earlier.* The growth portrayed in Table 21·1 is expected to continue. Government estimates indicate that in 1980 our real GNP will range from $1,155 to $1,165 billion, which means that real GNP per person will be in the neighborhood of $5,000![2]

What about our *rate* of growth? Recent statistical data (Table 21·2) suggest that the long-term growth rate of the United States's real GNP over the 1870–1964 period was about 3.6 percent per year, while the annual increase in real GNP per capita was 1.9 percent per year. However, as Table 21·2 clearly indicates, the growth rate achieved by a nation can vary substantially from one period of years to another. For example, short-term growth rates for the 1960–1967 period show that our real GNP has grown at 4.8 percent and real per capita GNP at 3.3 percent.

[2]U.S. Department of Labor, *Patterns of U.S. Economic Growth* (Washington, 1970), p. 3.

For at least two reasons these quantitative conclusions understate the economic growth which American capitalism has actually experienced. First, the figures of Tables 21·1 and 21·2 do not fully take into account improvements in product quality. Purely quantitative data do not provide an accurate comparison between an era of crystal sets and one of stereophonic phonographs. Second, the increases in real GNP and per capita GNP shown in Table 21·1 were accomplished despite very sizable increases in leisure. The seventy-hour work week is a thing of the distant past. The standard work week is now less than forty hours, with the more aggressive unions, much to the dismay of American housewives, whetting their appetites for a 36- or 32-hour, four-day workweek. On the other hand, GNP tends to overstate economic growth in that it does not adequately consider adverse effects upon the environment. We shall pursue this question in some detail in Chapter 22.

While impressive, the United States growth record has been somewhat less dramatic than those achieved by a number of other developed countries. As Table 21·2 indicates, in recent years Japan and a number of countries of Western Europe—not to mention the Soviet Union (Chapter 46)—have reached comparable or superior rates of growth. This kind of comparison has helped to stimulate considerable debate concerning the adequacy of our growth rate and our public policies designed to accelerate growth.

SUPPLY FACTORS

Now let us explain the growth record of American capitalism in terms of the six basic factors in economic growth. We look first to the supply factors.

Natural resources

Climate, soil, rainfall, mineral deposits, and sources of power are all important facets of any nation's natural resource base. These natural resource en-

TABLE 21 · 2 GROWTH OF REAL GNP AND REAL GNP PER CAPITA IN SELECTED COUNTRIES

	Growth rates of real GNP			
	1870–1964	1929–1964	1950–1964	1960–1967
United States	3.6%	3.0%	3.6%	4.8%
Japan	3.8	4.2	9.9	10.2
Germany	2.8	3.9	7.0	3.9
United Kingdom	1.9	2.2	3.0	3.0
France	1.7	1.9	4.8	5.1
Italy	2.0	2.9	5.8	5.4
Canada	3.5	3.6	4.3	5.3

	Growth rates of real GNP per capita			
	1870–1964	1929–1964	1950–1964	1960–1967
United States	1.9%	1.7%	1.8%	3.3%
Japan	—	—	8.7	9.1
Germany	1.7	2.8	5.9	2.8
United Kingdom	1.3	1.7	2.4	2.3
France	1.5	1.4	3.8	3.8
Italy	1.4	2.2	5.2	4.3
Canada	1.7	1.8	1.8	3.3

Source: Department of Commerce, *Long-term Economic Growth, 1860–1965* (Washington, 1966), p. 101; and *Statistical Abstract of the United States, 1970,* p. 314.

dowments constitute an obvious but fundamental factor in its capacity to expand, because, in contrast to the quantity and quality of labor and capital resources, the quantity and quality of a nation's natural resources are relatively fixed in supply. Note that we say "relatively" fixed: within limits, *available* natural resources can be increased in supply. True, given a nation's territorial limits, its mineral deposits of, for example, lead, copper, and zinc are present only in fixed amounts. The same holds true for petroleum and natural-gas deposits. Yet the discovery and appropriation of existing deposits can add significantly to available, or usable, supplies of these resources. Similarly, arable land, pasture land, and timberland which have been exploited can frequently be renewed by modern conservation practices. Irrigation and drainage can and have added significantly to the supply of arable land. And, as we shall soon discover, technological advancement has added significantly to available resource supplies.

For present purposes, the major question is this: Are the supplies of natural resources with which the United States is endowed sufficient to permit continued economic growth? There is no simple, unqualified answer to this question. But insofar as the majority of natural resources are concerned, the United States has been most generously endowed in terms of both quantity and quality. It is generally agreed

that, with the possible exception of Soviet Russia, the United States has a larger variety and greater quantities of resources than any other nation. Actually, we are not sure of the exact quantities available—as noted, exploration and discovery continue. We are aware that known reserves of most resources ensure us against severe scarcities in the immediate future—say, over the next three or four decades.

But we are less sanguine about the longer run. Projections of substantial population growth—estimates suggest we could *add* anywhere from 95 to 235 million to our population in the next half century—coupled with rising affluence suggest enormous demands upon our natural resources. These demands take two forms. First, the rising pressure of population may mean serious scarcities and rising resource costs. Even in recent years the production and consumption of certain metals—for example, lead, zinc, and copper—indicate the need for conservation in their use. One can speculate that natural resource bottlenecks may well become more common and more severe in the future than has heretofore been the case. Secondly, there are environmental and ecological aspects of the natural resource question. Rapid absolute growth of population coupled with a rising real income per capita raises serious and much-publicized questions about the capacity of our natural resources to absorb and recycle the resulting wastes. We will examine this aspect of the natural resources problem in Chapter 22 and again in Chapter 37.

Alleviating scarcities It is noteworthy that two alleviating factors have almost invariably come to the rescue when the United States has encountered serious shortages of specific raw materials.

1. Technological advance, in addition to being a basic determinant of economic growth in and of itself, has bailed American capitalism out of resource difficulties on many occasions. On the one hand, technological advance has led to greater economy in the *use* of scarce materials. For example, the development of electroplating as a substitute for the hot-dip method of manufacturing tin plate saves 60 percent of this scarce metal. Furthermore, technology has permitted greater efficiency in the *acquisition* of natural resources. Evidence?[3]

> Sixty years ago copper deposits of less than 3 percent metal content would have been considered poor; now the average grade is less than one percent. A few decades ago aluminum was so difficult to extract and so costly that it was scarcely used at all; now it ranks second only to steel in terms of metal volume. . . . The deepest oil well drilled in 1900 was about 3,000 feet; by 1950 the world's deepest well went down more than 20,000 feet—about four miles.

The development of new instruments in the fields of geology, geophysics, and geochemistry—for example, magnetometers, scintillometers, and electromagnetic surveyors—are undoubtedly of great long-run significance in the discovery of new sources of raw materials. Lastly, technological advances have developed *new materials* to replace resources in particularly scarce supply. The development of plastics and synthetic rubber to supplement strategic materials during World War II provides outstanding examples.

In brief, technological advance has played a key role (*a*) in achieving greater economy in the use of available supplies of resources, (*b*) in developing means for the economical recovery of known sources of raw materials, and (*c*) in the discovery of new substitute materials.

2. Foreign supplies of resources can be used to supplement domestic supplies. As a matter of fact, the United States has historically changed from a world supplier to an importer of raw materials. Despite dramatic increases in the domestic *production* of most basic raw materials, simultaneous and more than proportionate increases in the domestic *consumption* of these materials have caused our economy to become a net importer of raw materials. The important point is this: Foreign resources acquired through international trade can and have effectively combatted specific raw-material shortages.

Scarcities and the price system A final but highly important point: The price system can play a vital

[3] J. Frederic Dewhurst and Associates, *America's Needs and Resources: A New Survey* (New York: The Twentieth Century Fund, Inc., 1955), p. 757.

role in prompting the prudent use of our scarcest resources. For example, should a mineral resource, say, copper, come to be in particularly scarce supply in relation to the demand for it, its price will rise. This higher price has two related effects.

First, it signals manufacturers to "go easy" in the use of copper and to employ substitute materials in production where this is feasible. Stated differently, a high price for copper will tend to ration the available supply to those uses deemed most vital by society; only the manufacturers of products wanted most intensely by consumers will be able to pay the high price for copper and achieve a profit in the sale of their finished products. In addition, manufacturers who are dependent upon copper may be prompted by its high price to direct research activities toward the more efficient use of copper or toward finding suitable substitute materials. If successful, this will tend to take pressure off the price of copper from the demand side of the market.

Second, the high price of copper induces suppliers of copper to step up production to overcome the shortage. The high price may now make possible the mining of lower-grade ores, which was not economically feasible at a lower price. Similarly, the high price for copper may well induce technological advances in the mining and smelting of copper. Success in such ventures will tend to reduce the price of copper from the supply side of the market. The basic point is that the price mechanism simultaneously promotes conservation in the use of particularly scarce resources and may induce means for alleviating such severe shortages.[4]

Human resources

The productive capacity of a nation depends not only upon the size of its labor force but also upon its quality. The size of any nation's labor force is determined primarily by the overall size of its population. The quality of the labor force depends upon its personal health and vigor, its education and training, its morale, and its attitude toward work.

[4]See the President's Materials Policy Commission, *Resources for Freedom* (Washington, 1952), pp. 17–18.

Population and the labor force Let us first explore the *quantitative* aspect of human resources. An increase in the quantity of human resources will obviously enhance the economy's productive potential, permitting an outward shift of the production possibilities curve.

What long-run changes have occurred in the size of the United States population and labor force? Table 21·3 provides us with the overall picture. A quite high birth rate, a declining death rate, and—for a time—heavy immigration have teamed to provide the United States with substantial population growth through most of its history. The population quadrupled during the first half of the nineteenth century. It more than trebled during the last half, and has increased over $2\frac{1}{2}$-fold since 1900. There are nine times as many Americans today as there were in 1850. In 1970 the population exceeded the 205 million level and continues to grow.

Where will it all end? Demographers differ on this point. "Low" Census Bureau estimates envision a population of 266 million by the year 2000 and 299 million in 2020; "high" projections indicate 321 million by 2000 and 440 million by 2020. Even if fertility rates were to suddenly drop to the level required for

TABLE 21·3 POPULATION AND TOTAL LABOR FORCE, 1900–1970 (*in millions*)

Year	Population	Total labor force
1900	76	29
1910	92	37
1920	106	42
1930	123	49
1940	132	56
1950	152	65
1960	181	73
1970	205	86

Source: Bureau of the Census data.

an eventually stable population, population stability would not be realized until the year 2037 because of the high proportion of young people in the current population. And in 2037 the population of the United States would be 276 million as compared to 205 million in 1970. Thus significant future population growth is in the demographic cards. There is little prospect that future American economic growth will be retarded by an inadequate supply of labor; as we shall see in a moment, the problem may be substantially the reverse.

While it is correct to think of an increasing population and labor force as pushing the production possibilities curve to the right and tending to increase real GNP, we must keep in mind the impact of the law of diminishing returns. Specifically, beyond some point the mere addition of more labor to relatively fixed quantities of other inputs will result in smaller and smaller increases in real GNP. Although real GNP rises, inputs of labor may be increasing more rapidly and thereby cause real GNP per person (average product) to decline. Stated differently, the simple expansion of the population and labor force may simultaneously result in an expanding real GNP (growth in terms of definition one), and a constant or falling real GNP per capita (stagnation or decline in terms of definition two). Our *optimum population* concept (Chapter 20) is a convenient reminder that population expansion can be a mixed blessing insofar as economic growth is concerned. Up to a point, a growing population and labor force will be associated with a growing GNP per head; but beyond that point further labor force and population growth will cause output per person to diminish. Furthermore, environmental and "quality of life" considerations are also prompting economists and others to look more critically at the role of population expansion in economic growth.

Quality of the labor force Man for man, the American labor force is among the best in the world. The overall health, education, training, and versatility of the labor force all contribute to its high quality. One eminent scholar has concluded that if the age composition and state of health of the population of underdeveloped countries could be "Westernized," per capita incomes in these countries might rise 20 to 30 percent or more above existing levels.[5]

Statistics on educational attainment reflect improvement in the quality of the labor force in the United States. Figure 21·1 indicates that impressive gains have been made in educational attainment in recent years. Between 1952 and 1970 the percentage of workers aged eighteen or over who have finished high school rose from about 43 percent to about 65 percent. The percentage of the labor force who have completed four or more years of college increased from 8 to about 13 percent over the same period.

[5] J. J. Spengler, "The Population Obstacle to Economic Betterment," *American Economic Review, Proceedings,* May 1951, p. 344.

FIGURE 21 · 1 RECENT CHANGES IN THE EDUCATIONAL ATTAINMENT OF THE LABOR FORCE

The percentage of the labor force completing high school and college has been rising steadily in recent years, while the percentage who did not go to high school or complete elementary school has been falling. (*Manpower Report of the President.*)

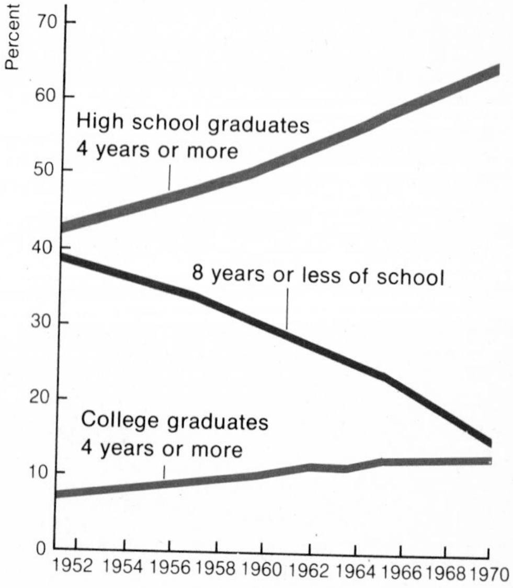

And, of course, these statistics conceal that the quality of education itself has been improving. Figure 21·2, which indicates occupational shifts since 1929, generally reflects an upgrading of the labor force. Note the relative decline in agriculture and the corresponding gains in private services and in government.

But we must not gloss over some less encouraging aspects of our educational system and policies as they relate to economic growth.

1. The quality and quantity of public school education is sometimes quite low, particularly in low-income urban areas and in rural areas. The results of screening manpower for military service during World War II were traumatic: of some 18 million young American males subject to military service, approximately 2 million were rejected because they were wholly or substantially illiterate![6]

2. A closely related fact is that educational opportunities are frequently denied minority groups. For

[6] Eli Ginzberg, *Manpower Agenda for America* (New York: McGraw-Hill Book Company, 1967), p. 12.

FIGURE 21 · 2 THE CHANGING OCCUPATIONAL STRUCTURE OF THE LABOR FORCE, 1929–1970

Long-term occupational shifts generally reflect an upgrading of the labor force. (*Economic Report of the President, 1970.*)

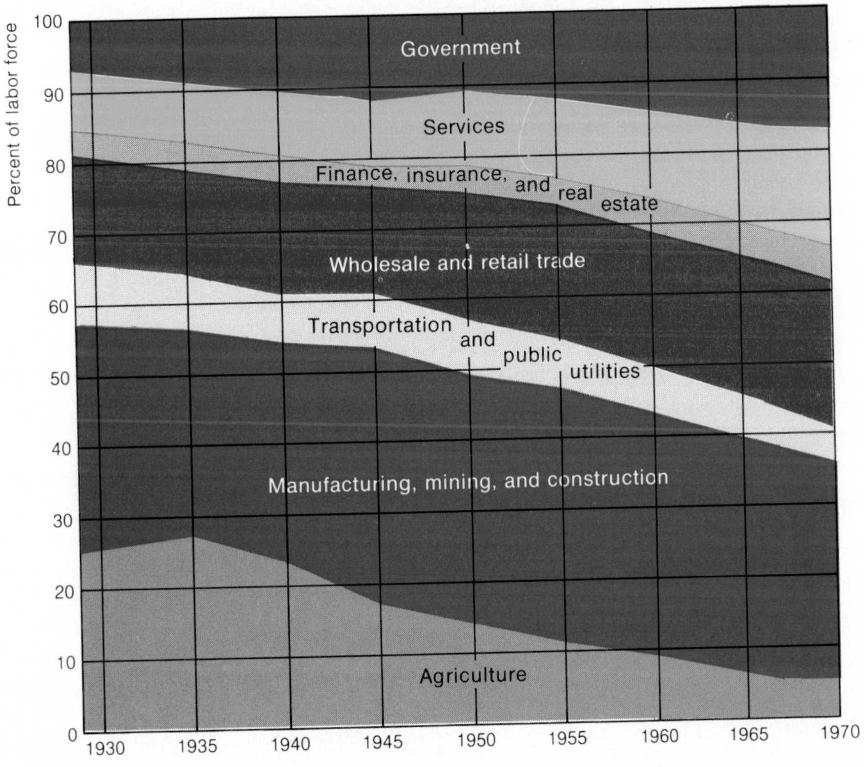

example, we have clearly underinvested in the education of Negroes as compared with whites (Chapter 38).

3. Apparently we do a rather poor job of recruiting our best brains for higher education. Again, the problem relates back to the unequal distribution of educational opportunities:[7]

> Of those high school seniors who are in the top one-fifth in terms of academic ability, 95 percent will ultimately go on to college if their parents are in the top socioeconomic quartile, but only half of the equally able students from the bottom socioeconomic quartile will attend college. Students from the top socioeconomic quartile are five times as likely to go to graduate school as comparably able students from the bottom socioeconomic quartile.

4. Our educational system is only beginning to undertake seriously programs of continuing education and retraining necessary to make the labor force more flexible and adaptable to changes in the occupational structure (Figure 21·2) which a dynamic economy imposes.

The same general picture presents itself with respect to health. Despite the overall physical well-being and vigor of the population and labor force and the dramatic long-term gains in health and life expectancy, the record since the 1950s is spotty. The number of years of healthy life that Americans can now look forward to has not increased significantly since the late 1950s. There are some fifteen other nations wherein life expectancy at birth is greater than in the United States. Our infant mortality rate has a similarly mediocre ranking. A combination of factors including environment, life styles, and serious inequalities in the distribution of medical care all help to blemish our health record.[8]

Technological advance

Technological advance and capital formation are closely related processes. Technological advance, the development and application of new products or new productive techniques, typically entails investment in new machinery and equipment. The idea that there is a more efficient way to catch a rabbit than running it down led to investment in the bow and arrow. Yet in some instances technological advance and capital accumulation are distinct. Example: Modern crop rotation practices and contour plowing are ideas which contribute greatly to output, although they do not necessarily entail the use of more capital equipment. In any event we shall find it rewarding to discuss technological advance and capital formation separately, recognizing that the two are usually birds of a feather. Going a step further, we should note that technological advance involves both *invention*—the discovery and development of a new product or technique of production—and *innovation*—the practical application of the method, or commercial production of the product, which invention has provided.

What has been the rate of technological advance in the United States? Casual observation suggests it has been both rapid and profound. Gas and diesel engines, conveyer belts, and assembly lines come to mind as obviously significant developments of the past. More recently, the lamp of technology has freed the automation jinni and with it the potential wonders of the electronic brain and the push-button factory. Television, supersonic jets, computers, and nuclear power—not to mention space travel—are technological achievements which were in the realm of fantasy a mere generation ago.

Research and invention But aside from such anecdotal evidence it is difficult to measure accurately scientific output and the rate of technological progress. There are available, however, rough measures of scientific inputs, that is, of the amount of human and property resources devoted to scientific-technological pursuits. One such measure is our stock of scientists and engineers and here we find remarkable growth:[9]

> Between 1950 and 1965 the number of scientists and engineers nearly doubled, reaching about a million and a half in the latter year. About a million were engineers, a half a

[7] Department of Health, Education, and Welfare, *Toward a Social Report* (Washington, 1969), p. xx.
[8] Ibid., chap. 1.

[9] Ibid., p. 72.

million scientists. This increase in the number of scientists and engineers was 4.5 times the rate of growth of the total labor force. The number of scientists and engineers getting doctorates has doubled in the last 10 years.

A second measure of technological inputs is total research and development expenditures for the economy as a whole. Table 21·4 summarizes this data for the post–World War II era. Note that there has been a dramatic increase in the level of R & D expenditures since the war. Moreover, these outlays have grown substantially as a percentage of the GNP. It is also significant that the public sector is the primary source of financial support for research and development activity in the United States.

These R & D statistics conceal one or two interesting and pertinent points which merit at least brief comment.

1. Although the lone-wolf inventor continues to make important contributions to technological progress, there has been substantial growth in group research in recent years. In growing numbers teams of scientists in large corporations, in universities, and in government agencies are assembled for the explicit purpose of developing new products, materials, or processes.

2. One may express satisfaction with the overall size of our research effort and yet be concerned about the allocation of our R & D outlays. For example, technological advance in agriculture, amply supported by Federal funds, has been very rapid. Indeed, agricultural productivity and output have increased much faster than has the demand for farm products; the result has been a relative decline in farm prices and incomes (Chapter 36). By way of contrast, technological progress in the construction industry and in railway transportation has been notoriously slow. Furthermore, a substantial portion of government's research outlays is related to the military and to space programs. While these expenditures may be justified on noneconomic grounds, one can question their carry-over value for civilian uses and their overall contribution to economic growth. Similarly, private R & D expenditures are often not for basic research but rather for applied research of a frequently trivial nature or for superficial product development. Of the estimated $27 billion spent for R & D in 1970, only about $4 billion was for basic research.[10]

[10] On this last point see Daniel Hamberg, "Invention in the Industrial Research Laboratory," *Journal of Political Economy*, April 1963, pp. 95–115.

TABLE 21·4 SOURCES OF FUNDS FOR RESEARCH AND DEVELOPMENT IN THE UNITED STATES, 1945–1970 (*in millions*)

Year	(1) Total expenditures, or (2) + (3) + (4)	(2) Federal government	(3) Industry	(4) Universities and nonprofit institutions	(5) Total research expenditures as a percent of GNP
1945	$ 1,520	$ 1,070	$ 430	$ 20	0.7
1950	2,870	1,610	1,180	80	1.0
1955	6,270	3,490	2,510	270	1.6
1960	13,710	8,720	4,510	480	2.7
1965	20,449	13,025	6,541	883	3.0
1970	27,250	15,000	10,895	1,355	2.8

Source: Statistical Abstract of the United States, 1970, p. 519. Data for 1970 are preliminary.

Innovation But the discovery of new technological knowledge is only half the battle. The commercial application of such discoveries in the production of goods is equally essential in achieving economic growth through technological advance. It is here that the size, vigor, and ability of the entrepreneurial class become all-important. Certainly other factors are vital: The costliness of financing the application of a technological improvement and its anticipated profitability undoubtedly play major roles in determining whether or not a new bit of technological know-how gets off the drawing board and is commercially applied. Yet in the long pull, the most fundamental determinant of the commercial application of new technological knowledge is the character of the entrepreneur. Insight, foresight, vision, courage, adventuresomeness, the desire to make good—call it what you may, the leadership and vigor of the entrepreneurial class play the key role in determining how much new technological know-how gets out of the research department and onto the assembly line. The overall social-cultural-political environment of our economy generally has been highly receptive to the introduction of new products and new methods of production.

Recent studies suggest that the amount of time which elapses between the discovery of a new scientific or technological idea and its commercial application has been declining. "The time elapsed between technical discovery and commercial recognition fell from about thirty years before the First World War to sixteen years between the wars, and to nine years after the Second World War. The additional time required to convert these technical discoveries to initial commercial application has decreased from about seven to about five years."[11] In short, new ideas and inventions are being translated into innovations at a more rapid rate.

Capital formation: investment

To a very considerable degree workers, regardless of their skills and training, are no better than the capital goods with which they are equipped. The indirect or roundabout production which capital goods afford is a basic means of enhancing productive efficiency. A nation's stock of capital goods is clearly a crucial factor in its growth potential. American capitalism has managed to accumulate a larger stock of real capital than has any other nation of the world. Surprisingly, we are not exactly sure how much capital our economy has managed to accumulate in its lifetime. The difficulties of taking such an inventory are great; in particular, the problem of defining what is meant by "capital goods" is a difficult one.

We do know that on the average the American worker is better equipped with capital goods in his productive efforts than is the worker of any other nation. The average American worker in manufacturing is equipped with approximately $30,000 worth of capital equipment. We also know that the growth in capital facilities has been very rapid in recent years. During the war-postwar decade of the 1940s, American capitalism "doubled the aggregate manufacturing capacity of 1939–40 which had taken nearly three centuries to develop and build."[12] A recent estimate for 1968 sets the value of America's stock of fixed business capital at $1.3 trillion![13]

In 1970 private businesses in the economy spent almost $103 billion on capital facilities—machinery, equipment, and nonresidential construction. This means that about 11 percent of the economy's GNP is currently devoted to maintaining and expanding the productive facilities of private industry. Were we to add the basic "social capital" constructed by government—highways, hydroelectric dams, harbor and waterway improvements, and so forth—another $30 billion would be added to this $103 billion figure. Residential construction would involve still another $30 billion.

SOURCES OF UNITED STATES GROWTH

Is it possible to assess the quantitative significance of the various supply factors in accounting for this country's past growth? Table 21·5 summarizes the

[11] Howard R. Bowen and Garth L. Mangum (eds.), *Automation and Economic Progress* (Englewood Cliffs, N.J.: Prentice-Hall, Inc., 1966), p. 9.

[12] Dewhurst, op. cit., p. 813.

[13] U.S. Department of Commerce, *Survey of Current Business*, February 1968, p. 20.

TABLE 21·5 THE SOURCES OF GROWTH IN U.S. REAL NATIONAL INCOME

Source	Percent of total growth 1909–1929	1929–1957
Increase in quantity of labor	39	27
Increase in quantity of capital	26	15
Improved education and training	13	27
Improved technology	12	20
All other	10	11
Total	100	100

Source: Edward Denison, *The Sources of Economic Growth in the United States* (New York: Committee for Economic Development, 1962).

findings of a recent pioneering study which provides such estimates. While these figures must be regarded as rough approximations, they do afford an interesting perspective on our growth record.

Note, first of all, that in the early 1909–1929 period some 65 percent of our increase in real GNP was due simply to increased inputs of labor and capital. And in the later 1929–1957 period 42 percent of the increase in real output was attributable to the same cause. In other words, increases in the *quantity* of resources explain a substantial share of the growth in real GNP which was realized in both periods. But what explains the remainder? The answer is that improvements in the *quality* or productivity of our resources have occurred, so that the output per unit of labor and capital has risen. More and better education and training for the labor force and improvements in the quality of capital through technological progress have increased the productivity of each unit of labor and capital. Comparing the two periods, we note that qualitative improvements—increases in the productivity of labor and capital—appear to be of growing importance in explaining our economic growth. Finally, the "all others" category in Table 21·5 refers primarily to the fact that a growing domestic market has permitted producers to achieve greater "mass-production economies."

INSTABILITY AND GROWTH

An expanding productive capacity as such does not guarantee growth in the real GNP. We know from Chapter 20 that aggregate demand must expand by an appropriate amount in order for an expanded productive capacity to be utilized. If the expansion of aggregate demand is too small, unemployment and underutilized capacity will result. If the expansion of aggregate demand is too large, inflation will result. Our study of employment theory and the business cycle revealed that historically the United States has experienced both unemployment and inflation. Emphasis here is upon unemployment because of the harmful repercussions which we will discover it has upon the supply factors in growth.

Figure 11·2 reminds us vividly of the extent to which the actual performance of our economy has fallen short of its potential output in recent years. The result? A wasteful GNP gap and a rate of growth substantially less than that which higher levels of aggregate demand would have brought about. For example, over the 1955–1958 period the annual growth rate was about 0.5 percent—a far cry from our long-run rate of 3 or 3½ percent—due to a deficient level of total spending. Looking back further into history, we find that the Great Depression of the 1930s was a serious blow to the United States's long-run growth record. Between 1929 and 1933 our real GNP (measured in 1958 prices) actually *declined* from \$204 to \$142 billion! In 1937 the real GNP was approximately at the same level as in 1929 (see line 20 on table inside front covers).

But this is only a part of the picture. Cyclical *unemployment* can have certain harmful "carryover" effects upon the growth rate in subsequent years of full employment through the adverse effects it may have upon the supply factors in growth. For example, unemployment depresses investment and capital accumulation; it may give rise to a decline in the work

week, which is frequently demanded by organized labor as a technique to more equitably apportion the burden of unemployment; the expansion of research budgets may be slowed by recession; union resistance to technological change may stiffen, and so forth. Though it is impossible to quantify the impact of these considerations upon the growth rate, they undoubtedly can be of considerable importance.

ALLOCATIVE EFFICIENCY AND UNITED STATES GROWTH

The social environment of an economy can be every bit as significant as its physical environment in influencing economic growth. The social environment of any society must meet two requirements to facilitate economic growth. First, it must encourage those changes in products, productive techniques, and capital facilities which are vital to economic growth. Second, it must provide a suitable mechanism for negotiating with reasonable efficiency the reallocation of resources which are appropriate to the development of new products, new productive techniques, and changes in resource supplies and the structure of demand.

The social environment

The overall social-cultural-political environment of the United States has been very conducive to economic growth. Several interrelated factors contribute to this favorable environment. First, as opposed to many other nations, there are virtually no social or moral taboos upon production and material progress. The free and individualistic nature of our economy has been generally conducive to the development of new products and new methods of production. Consumers are free and ordinarily willing to try new products. Indeed, American social philosophy has embraced the notion that material advance is an attainable and highly desirable economic goal. The inventor, the innovator, and the business executive are accorded high degrees of prestige and respect in American society. Second, Americans have traditionally possessed healthy attitudes toward work and risk taking; our society has benefited from a willing labor force and an ample supply of entrepreneurs. Third, our economy has been characterized by a stable political system wherein internal order, the right of property ownership, the legal status of enterprise, and the enforcement of contracts have been fostered. Though not subject to quantification, this bundle of characteristics has undoubtedly provided an excellent foundation for American economic growth. *Qualification:* We will see in Chapter 22 that an environment-conscious society is having second thoughts about economic growth and technological progress as top-priority goals.

The price system

Historical observation also suggests that the price system of American capitalism has performed reasonably well as a mechanism for negotiating the reallocations of resources which economic growth demands. New methods, new products, and changes in resource supplies and consumer demand all call for realignments of resources. And the price system, we have seen, provides the carrot of profits and the stick of losses to induce the expansion of innovating industries and to force the contraction of those industries whose products have been rendered obsolete or less desirable by these changes. The ebb and flow of economic progress shove old industries into oblivion and create whole new industries to replace the old. The demise of the steam locomotive industry and the more or less simultaneous rise of the diesel locomotive industry is one of innumerable examples. The tremendous stimulus which the automobile industry gave to the steel, rubber, and petroleum industries has already been cited. The deathblow which the automobile industry dealt the carriage makers is the other side of the picture.

Figure 21·2 provides a rough outline of some of the reallocations of labor which the price system has negotiated over a long period of years. Most obvious is the relative shift of labor from agricultural pursuits to other types of productive endeavor—particularly to trade, transportation, and white-collar work. Agriculture accounted for one-fourth of the economy's em-

ployment in 1929, but only about 5 percent in 1970. In contrast, professional and public service engaged about 15 percent of the economy's labor force in 1929; by 1970 this figure was about 33 percent. These are clearly significant shifts in the allocation of manpower.

Impediments to allocative efficiency

The rise of new prosperous industries and the decline of old unprosperous industries is an essential feature of economic progress and is clearly desirable from the viewpoint of society as a whole. However, specific businesses and resource suppliers caught in declining industries are adversely affected by economic growth; they face declining incomes and the prospect of painful and costly readjustments to other expanding lines of production. It is not surprising that adversely affected groups have sought to impede the reallocations of resources essential to economic growth. Illustrations are rather numerous.

Monopolies in both product and resource markets have retarded the reallocations of resources required for economic growth. Business monopolies may find it more profitable to suppress a newly discovered product or productive technique than to have their present capital facilities rendered obsolete before they have been fully depreciated. Furthermore, remember that the expansion of prosperous industries is a self-limiting process; as new firms enter growing industries, economic profits are competed away. Therefore, firms now established in these prosperous industries may contrive monopolistic restrictions upon the entry of new firms in an effort to preserve economic profits for themselves. Some labor unions have followed similar policies, resisting new work methods which threaten to cause unemployment by making workers more productive. To illustrate: Unions in the building trades have frequently resisted the use of spray guns, fearing that workers will paint themselves out of jobs. And some unions, following restrictive membership policies, such as limiting the number of apprentices or charging high initiation fees, have created an artificial obstacle to labor mobility and have therefore limited the reallocation of human resources demanded by economic growth. Example: A growing economy typically wants more and better housing and relatively less food. This calls for fewer farmers and more carpenters, that is, a rechanneling of labor from the farm to housing projects. But the restrictive membership practices of certain building trades unions have impeded this shift.[14]

Other groups adversely affected by economic growth have been unable to resist its effects by their own tactics. Many of these have exerted political pressure for assistance, and some have received it. For example, a variety of forces (which will be detailed in Chapter 36) have made agriculture a declining industry; that is, a smaller number of farmers can now produce more than enough food and fiber for the economy. This calls for a reallocation of resources from agriculture to relatively more productive uses in industry. However, public policy in the form of price supports and other subsidies have bolstered farmers' incomes and impeded the price system in reallocating farmers from agriculture to other industries where their productivity and incomes would be considerably higher. Similarly, the American watch industry has long been faced with the prospect of extinction because of the severe competition provided by foreign watches. But the American industry—manufacturers supported by the unions—has retarded this decline by seeking and getting a measure of relief from foreign competition through governmental enactment of higher tariffs (excise taxes) on imported watches. Later in Chapter 38 we will consider the harmful effects of resource immobilities based upon racial discrimination.

These artificial impediments to growth are enforced by certain inherent resource immobilities. Apart from union and business monopolies, resources are far from perfectly mobile. The obstacles to labor mobility,

[14] It should be emphasized that most unions have been receptive to technological advance, demanding only that (1) new machines and methods be introduced in an orderly way to facilitate the reabsorption of technologically unemployed workers and (2) the business community and society as a whole share in the costs of technological unemployment.

for example, are many and varied. Geographic immobility stems from the reluctance of workers to break existing social ties, move to a new community, meet new people, and take roots. Moreover, insofar as occupational mobility is concerned, it is no easy chore to abandon one's life work at, say, middle age and assume the responsibility, costs, and inconvenience of learning a new trade. Immobility is even more evident when it comes to property resources. To use an extreme example, a wheat combine is completely immobile in the sense that it has only one use; price system or no price system, a combine cannot be shifted to the manufacture of automobiles or plastic toys.

But over time, resource immobilities become less important. The sixty-year-old farmer who has worked the land since he was sixteen is not likely to obey the dictates of the price system to seek a factory job in the city. But his son, particularly if he goes to college, will probably not go back to the farm. Instead, he is likely to seek out employment in more profitable, expanding, and therefore higher-paying industries. Many a farmer's son is now in engineering college, and if he ever comes into contact with a John Deere tractor, it will probably be on a drafting board and not in a cornfield. Figure 21·2 makes it clear that decades may be involved in negotiating significant transfers in the employment of human resources. Furthermore, even durable capital wears out in time and may go unreplaced. A farm combine is useless in automobile manufacturing, but in time the combine may wear out and not be replaced. Money capital formerly flowing into farm equipment may now finance new and expanded capital facilities for the automobile industry. Hence, over the years the composition of the economy's stock of real capital changes; capital goods are in effect shifted among alternative uses.

SUMMARY

1. The real GNP of the United States has increased sixfold in the past sixty years; real GNP per capita has increased threefold in the past fifty years.

2. The long-term growth rate of real GNP for the United States has been 3 to 3½ percent, although in the past few years the figure has been over 4½ percent.

3. In general the economy of the United States is amply endowed with natural resources. Scarcities of specific resources have been largely overcome by technological advances which have permitted the more efficient use and acquisition of such resources and the development of new substitute materials. Furthermore, in some cases abundant foreign supplies have been tapped to relieve specific scarcities. Lastly, the price system automatically tends to conserve those resources which are most scarce.

4. Historically, the American population and labor force have grown quite rapidly. Legitimate questions can be raised, however, about the quality of education and about inequalities in educational opportunities for Americans.

5. Many economists are inclined to assign an increasingly important role to technological progress—research and innovation—in the growth process. The United States currently devotes about 3 percent of its GNP to research and development activity.

6. In relation to other nations, American workers are very well equipped with capital facilities. However, growth in our stock of capital goods has been irregular.

7. The real GNP of the United States has grown, not only because of increased inputs of labor and capital, but because of increases in output per input. Empirical evidence suggests that over time, increases in productivity have become more important, and increases in the quantity of resources less important, in accounting for American economic growth.

8. The American social-cultural-political environment has been conducive to economic growth. The price system has been a reasonably efficient mechanism for negotiating those resource reallocations which economic progress invariably entails. However, impediments to reallocations do exist, particularly in the form of product and resource market monopolies and the more or less inherent immobilities of both human and property resources.

QUESTIONS AND STUDY SUGGESTIONS

1. Briefly describe the growth record of the United States in this century. Compare the rates of growth in real GNP and real GNP per capita, explaining any differences. Specifically, what roles do leisure and improvements in product quality play in the growth process?

2. "The greatest conserver of scarce natural resources is the price mechanism." Explain. In what ways has technological advance alleviated acute resource shortages? Be specific.

3. What major occupational shifts have occurred in the allocation of labor resources? How are they to be explained?

4. To what extent have increases in our real GNP been the result of more capital and labor inputs? Of increasing productivity?

5. "Technological advance is bound to play a more important role in economic growth in the future than it has in the past." Do you agree? Explain and evaluate: "The American economy invests too much in machinery and not enough in people."

6. "If we want economic growth in a free society, we may have to accept a measure of instability." Evaluate. The noted philosopher Alfred North Whitehead once remarked that "the art of progress is to preserve order amid change and to preserve change amid order." What did he mean? Is this contention relevant for economic growth? What implications might this have for public policy? Explain.

7. Why is resource mobility essential to economic growth? "Resource immobilities are less in the long run than they are in the short run." Explain.

8. What role do social, cultural, political, and institutional forces play in economic growth? Be as specific as you can.

SELECTED REFERENCES

Economic Issues, 4th ed., readings 36 and 37.

Cochran, Thomas C., and Thomas B. Brewer (eds.): *Views of American Economic Growth,* vol. II, *The Industrial Era* (New York: McGraw-Hill Book Company, 1966).

Coleman, John R., (ed.): *The Changing American Economy* (New York: Basic Books, Inc., 1967).

Committee for Economic Development: *Economic Growth in the United States* (New York: CED, 1969).

Department of Labor: *Patterns of U.S. Economic Growth* (Washington, 1970).

Guttmann, Peter M. (ed.): *Economic Growth: An American Problem* (Englewood Cliffs, N.J.: Prentice-Hall, Inc., 1964).

Landsberg, Hans H.: *Natural Resources for U.S. Growth* (Baltimore: The Johns Hopkins Press, 1964).

Mansfield, Edwin: *Technological Change* (New York: W. W. Norton & Company, Inc., 1971).

GROWTH IN AMERICAN CAPITALISM: COSTS, PROBLEMS, AND POLICIES

Economic growth is not free for the asking. Growth entails not only benefits, but also costs. And growth may create, contribute to, or complicate a number of specific economic problems. It is the purpose of this chapter to examine some of these less pleasant facets of economic growth. First, the controversial question of whether growth should be a high-priority social goal is analyzed. Second, we explore the impact of automation upon the economy. A third and closely related aspect of our discussion deals with manpower problems and planning in a dynamic economy. Finally, we examine the contention that the causes and character of inflation may change as an expanding economy reaches an advanced stage of growth, and we study the implications of this eventuality for public policy.[1] All of this discussion is placed in the context of American capitalism. That is, we are addressing ourselves to the growth problems of an advanced economy rather than to those great obstacles faced by underdeveloped nations (Chapter 45).

[1] Another problem associated with a growing, increasingly affluent economy will be deferred until Chapter 41. This is the problem of social balance—the question of whether an expanding economy tends to produce too many private goods and not enough social goods.

THE GROWTH CONTROVERSY

We noted in Chapter 21 that over a long period of years the United States has realized an enviable growth record. Yet, interestingly enough, neither laymen nor economists were actively interested in economic growth until the late 1950s. While there was considerable concern with the maintenance of full employment and reasonable price stability, growth was more or less taken for granted. In the late 1950s two developments heightened our interest in growth. First, the American economy fell into a period of decided sluggishness; unemployment was disconcertingly high, and the GNP gap was large

(Figure 11 • 2). Secondly, Americans became aware of the fact that other nations were making rapid advances economically and technologically. The launching of Sputnik and an abundance of studies which revealed a high Soviet growth rate created the challenge of a growth race with the Soviet Union. The issue of economic growth became a matter of national concern and, indeed, was the major economic issue in the presidential campaign of 1962.

Although the dimensions of the growth debate have changed in recent years, the controversy itself persists. Let us now examine this controversy in an admittedly brief, unqualified form.

The case for growth

The case for economic growth—for a *rapid* rate of growth—seems both self-evident and compelling. The analytics and data of the previous two chapters imply several interrelated arguments for growth.

1. Most obviously, economic growth is the primary path to material abundance. Growth makes the unlimited wants–scarce resources dilemma less acute. It is through economic growth that any society realizes a higher standard of living.

2. Growth is also a palliative for domestic economic problems. For example, growth is an important means of alleviating poverty in our society. Growth will tend to raise the entire income distribution absolutely and will also enhance the ability and willingness of society to provide public assistance to low-income groups. More generally, only through rapid growth can we realize the annual increments of real output requisite to the simultaneous pursuit of potentially competing and mutually exclusive goals. Thus, without rapid growth the channeling of substantial resources into a program of space exploration involves a crude and direct conflict with, for example, the domestic war on poverty. With no growth and therefore a fixed income pie, a larger slice for space means a smaller slice for poverty problems. But with a rapidly growing income pie, larger slices can be accorded to space *and* to antipoverty programs.

3. American growth is also important from an international point of view. The reputation or image of our economy—indeed, of our entire society—as evaluated by underdeveloped nations is highly dependent upon our growth performance. Economic growth, rightly or wrongly, *is* widely accepted as an index of a nation's vitality, efficiency, and capacity for survival in the cold war. Growth rates *do* impress the uncommitted underdeveloped nations. More specifically, it is important that our growth rate compare favorably with that of the Soviet Union.

The case against growth

In recent years an increasing number of influential economists have become somewhat disenchanted with the goal of growth. While growth is admittedly of great importance to an underdeveloped country, they feel there are compelling reasons to question growth as a high-priority national objective in an already affluent society.

1. Adverse spillovers Current concern with environmental deterioration is an important component of the antigrowth position. The basic point here is that industrialization and growth result in serious problems of air, water, and land pollution. Furthermore, economic growth means industrial noise and stench, ugly cities, traffic jams, and many other of the disamenities of modern life. These adverse social or spillover costs are the consequence of the obvious fact that the production of the GNP changes the form of resources, but does not destroy them. Virtually all inputs in the productive process are eventually returned to the environment in some form of waste. For example, in the United States each person accounts for an estimated 2,000 pounds of solid wastes per year. The more rapid our growth and the higher our standard of living, the more waste there is for the environment to absorb—or attempt to absorb. An economic policy designed to maximize the GNP is allegedly a policy which maximizes resource depletion and environmental pollution.

Growth critics argue that society must come to grips with the fact that the production of more goods and

services simultaneously creates "bads" and "disservices." Indeed, in an already wealthy society further growth may simply mean the satisfaction of increasingly trivial wants at the cost of mounting threats to our ecological system. Ironically, our solution to these environmental problems has been to increase the output of goods and services designed to protect us from the adverse spillover effects of an already huge GNP. We foolishly seek more growth—more GNP—to defend ourselves from the social costs of an already gigantic GNP. Antigrowth economists feel that a more rational policy should be based upon the proposition that future growth should be purposely constrained. A few economists would recommend a policy of zero growth—of both population and GNP. Others simply argue that the GNP should be constrained by some socially acceptable standard of living which is significantly below the maximum attainable.

2. Problem resolution? Does economic growth promote the resolution of socioeconomic problems as its proponents claim? Antigrowth economists are highly skeptical. For example, the domestic problem of poverty—income inequality—is essentially a problem of distribution, not production. The United States, it is argued, has possessed for many years the productive capacity to provide all its citizens with a decent standard of living, but it has simply not been sufficiently charitable to do so. The requisites for solving the poverty problem are commitment and political courage, not further increases in output. In general, there is no compelling evidence that growth has been, or will be, a palliative for domestic problems.

Internationally it is doubtful that the size and rate of growth in our GNP are particularly crucial. It is not so much the size of the GNP, but rather its composition, which determines our military position vis-â-vis the Soviet Union. After all, the Soviet military posture is roughly the equivalent of ours, although their GNP is only about 50 percent of ours.[2] Nor is it clear that the future of the underdeveloped nations will be determined primarily by bald comparisons of U.S. and U.S.S.R. growth rates.[3]

> In short, there is little to show that the issues between us and the rest of the world will be governed predominantly by our economic successes, or that we can buy safe survival with an additional percent or two of economic growth.

3. Human obsolescence and insecurity Antigrowth economists also associate less tangible disadvantages and costs with rapid growth. Rapid growth—and in particular the changing technology which is the core of growth—poses new anxieties and new sources of insecurity for man. Both high-level and low-level manpower face the prospect of having their hard-earned skills and experience rendered obsolete by an onrushing technology.[4]

> Since change today is faster and more thorough than it was, say, a generation ago, and the generation hence will be faster yet, every one of us, manager, workman or scientist, lives closer to the brink of obsolescence. Each one of us that is adult and qualified feels menaced in some degree by the push of new developments which establish themselves only by discarding the methods and techniques and theories that he has learned to master.

4. Growth and human values Critics of growth also offer a group of related arguments which say, in effect, that while growth may permit us to "make a living," it does not provide us with "the good life." Indeed, the requisites of growth may preclude attainment of the good life. For example, growth focuses upon the quantitative relationship between inputs and outputs. Output satisfies wants. Therefore, any increase in output from a given quantity of inputs means growth and presumably an increase in human welfare. Antigrowth economists retort that one must also recognize that human welfare depends upon the character of the inputs. Must not the "loss of aesthetic and instinctual gratification suffered by ordinary

[2]Cynics point out that the GNP of the barbarians was undoubtedly much less than that of the Romans.

[3]Henry C. Wallich, *The Cost of Freedom* (New York: Harper & Row, Publishers, Incorporated, 1960), p. 158.

[4]E. J. Mishan, *Technology and Growth* (New York: Praeger Publishers, 1970), p. 115.

working men over two centuries of technological innovation that changed them from artisans and craftsmen into machine-minders and dial-readers" be entered on the liability side of the balance sheet of economic growth?

At a more philosophical level it is argued that a growth-oriented society confers a "sweat-and-strain, look-to-the-future" conception of life upon its members.[5]

Thus, the pure taste of the present eludes us. For in this world that we are intent on changing as rapidly as we can, the material advantages are to be reaped by those who look farthest ahead—those who treat the receding present as a jumping-off ground for the future. But this 'futurism,' this greed for the rewards of the future, this impatience to realize the shape of things to come, which inspires and fuels the present technological revolution, is just the phenomenon that hastens us through our brief lives and effectively cheats us of all sense of the spaciousness of time.

Or, as another critic has put it:[6]

Less than fifty years ago a person could reach the economic goals of his life when he married, bought and furnished a house, educated his children, and accumulated some savings for his old age. Today he is lured further and further away from rest and satisfaction by more and more new goods and gadgets; they keep him tied to the leash of work and acquisition until he is buried without ever having reached a moment of peace where he could look back to his work and say: It is good.

Now, admittedly, a part of our increasing affluence has been taken in the form of a declining workweek, and individuals therefore have more nonwork time available to them. But this doesn't mean they have more leisure. Some workers have responded to a shortened workweek by "moonlighting"—by taking a second job. Others are burdened with more work around the home because their wives have entered the labor force. Still others find their shortened workweek offset by increased commuting time. As a matter of fact, one can argued that with rising productivity, leisure has become more costly. Rising productivity means that output and real income per hour of work has risen. This in turn means that leisure is more costly. Because leisure is more expensive in terms of goods, fewer leisure activities are "worth the time." A growth-oriented society thus tends to become goods-rich and time-poor. People attempt to adjust to this imbalance by crowding more and more activities into a limited amount of nonwork time. The unfortunate result is a "harried leisure class."[7]

POLICIES TO ACCELERATE GROWTH

There is no doubt that the antigrowth arguments have tarnished the widely held view that growth is essentially an unmitigated good. Nevertheless, growth remains a high-priority economic goal. Let us therefore survey certain policies which are conducive to a high rate of growth. Our earlier discussion of the underlying forces of growth suggests a number of strategic policies for accelerating growth: (1) the achievement of continuous full employment, (2) a high level of investment, (3) greater emphasis upon research and development activity, and (4) increased spending on education.

Continuous full employment

Achieving and maintaining full employment is a basic factor in economic growth. Total demand must increase at a rate equal to the expansion of the economy's productive capacity, or potential growth will not be realized (Chapter 20). If total spending is not growing appropriately, all other efforts to raise total output will be frustrated.

The immediate impact of unemployment upon the growth rate is clear. For example, because of the 1957–1958 recession, the annual realized growth rate of the United States in the 1955–1958 period was about 0.5 percent, short of the $3\frac{1}{2}$ or 4 percent which the United States has achieved over a long span of years. It is notable, too, as analysis of the

[5] Ibid., p. 122.

[6] Walter A. Weisskopf, "Economic Growth and Human Well-being," *Quarterly Review of Economics and Business,* Summer 1964, p. 20.

[7] For an intriguing and readable discussion of this theme see Staffan Linder, *The Harried Leisure Class* (New York: Columbia University Press, 1970).

production possibilities curve reminds us, that to move from a position of unemployment to one of full employment entails no cost or sacrifice for society; we recall from the "GNP gap" concept (Chapter 11) that it is unemployment itself which imposes the cost of forgone production upon society.

A thorough grasp of the significance of full employment for economic growth requires the understanding of two additional points. On the one hand, the movement from less than full employment to full employment provides a one-shot stimulus to the economy's growth rate. Thus a movement from a 6 percent to a 3 percent unemployment rate will stimulate the GNP and the growth rate in the year this is achieved. But afterward, as full employment is maintained, there will occur no further windfall increases in output and the rate of growth in succeeding years.

On the other hand, recall from Chapter 21 that unemployment can have harmful "carryover" effects upon economic growth. Periods of unemployment motivate businessmen to cut back on capital formation and to reduce their R & D budgets. Unions may display greater resistance to technological change and may press for a shorter workweek to spread the burden of unemployment.

Investment: capital accumulation

The composition of GNP also has a significant bearing upon the rate of growth. In particular, the level of net investment affects the amount of capital with which workers are combined and therefore the productivity of labor. Output per worker will increase as workers are combined with more capital goods.

What steps can be taken to increase investment? More specifically, what mixture of monetary and fiscal measures can be invoked to alter the composition of GNP away from consumption and in favor of investment?

Assuming full employment initially, one way of doing the job would be to invoke an expansionary "easy" money policy and a contractionary fiscal policy. Recall from our discussion of monetary policy (Chapter 18) that an easy money policy (open-market bond purchases, a lowering of the discount rate, and the reduction of reserve requirements) has the effect of reducing interest rates. Recall, too, that the interest rate has its primary impact upon investment rather than consumption. In particular, a reduction in the interest rate—a decline in the cost of acquiring money capital—will stimulate investment. Thus an easy money (low interest rate) policy will lead to a faster rate of capital accumulation and help accelerate growth.

But in a full-employment economy, an increase in investment will be inflationary unless fiscal policy is used to curtail noninvestment spending by a compensating amount. Specifically, consumption expenditures can be restrained by raising personal income taxes, and Congress can act to trim government outlays.

You may sense that our fiscal policy prescription is quite crude and unsophisticated. We can actually utilize fiscal policy in a more effective, more active way to stimulate investment. In Chapter 12's discussion of the determinants of investment, we saw that corporate income taxes obviously affect the net expected profitability of investment spending. When corporate income taxes are reduced, some additional investment opportunities which were previously unprofitable now become profitable and are undertaken. Furthermore, since many firms are inclined to finance their investment internally, lower corporate income taxes mean that firms will now have greater after-tax profits with which to undertake additional investment. But if we couple lower corporate taxes with low interest rates to get an even greater stimulus to investment, personal income taxes must be raised and government expenditures reduced by even larger amounts to prevent this larger volume of investment from being inflationary. And this can pose problems.

Many kinds of public expenditures make important contributions to economic growth. Increased capital accumulation at the expense of education and research and development may *not* have a net accelerating effect upon the rate of growth. Similarly, public expenditures for streets and highways are an important form of social investment which also have an impact upon growth. To cut other kinds of governmental expenditures, for example, welfare and anti-

poverty programs, raises serious questions of social priorities. Which social goal—an equitable distribution of income or rapid growth—do we value most highly? There is still another problem posed by a low interest rate policy: In Chapter 43 we will find that, if interest rates are low in the United States relative to those in foreign countries, the higher returns abroad will cause money capital to flow out of the United States. Such capital outflows aggravate our balance of payments problem.

Growth and the research revolution

We emphasized in the previous chapter that research and its end result—technological advance—are widely recognized as a most significant ingredient in economic growth.[8]

> Fundamentally, economic growth means growth in a nation's underlying ideas and skills. The immediate generator of economic growth is investment . . . but . . . investment arises from new ideas, new developments in science and technology, from education, research, innovations—new products, new processes, new resources; all of these are the real seeds of long-term economic growth.

If we accept the basic role of research as a determinant of the growth rate, it is obvious that a major policy step in accelerating economic growth is to increase expenditures upon research and development activities. Fortunately, the absolute and relative levels of R & D spending have grown substantially in the post–World War II period (Table 21·4). A number of forces have been operating in this period to accelerate research spending—to foster a "research revolution": (1) Our World War II experience demonstrated the feasibility of organizing and carrying through to completion large-scale basic research projects and also created a backlog of technological information applicable to peacetime products; (2) research and development activity has generally proved to be highly profitable; (3) 1954 revisions of our tax laws make research expenditures deductible as a current expense; and (4) research spending tends to be cumulative; that is,[9]

> Research feeds upon itself: Discovery breeds discovery; innovation breeds innovation; and with each new discovery or innovation, the total body of scientific and technological knowledge increases.

To these considerations we must add the crucial role of the Federal government in financing research activity.

Education: investment in human capital

Productivity depends not only upon the quantity and technological quality of the real capital with which labor is combined, but also upon the quality of labor itself. That is, the productivity and growth potential of the economy can be enhanced through investment in human capital—by expenditures on the education, training, health, and mobility of the labor force. Indeed, we have already noted (Table 21·5) that improvements in the education and training of the labor force have become an increasingly important source of economic growth over time. The basic point is that the diversion of resources from current consumption to investment in human capital can contribute to growth in essentially the same way as does the diversion of resources from consumption to real capital. More specifically, the educational system must not only supply the high-level-manpower requisite to fruitful R & D spending, but also provide better-trained and more adaptable workers to meet the changing labor force requirements which accompany technological progress and economic growth (Figure 21·2).

Research, education, and spillover benefits

We know that government plays an active and significant role in the provision of R & D resources and education. Can this be justified on economic grounds? The case for public support of education and research rests primarily upon the argument that significant social or spillover benefits result from such spending.

Let us examine the area of basic scientific research. The first point to note is that basic research may entail benefits which go far beyond those realized by the sponsoring firm, that is, substantial benefits may

[8]Leonard S. Silk, *The Research Revolution* (New York: McGraw-Hill Book Company, 1960), p. 203.
[9]Ibid., pp. 162–163.

accrue to society as a whole. For example, provided the new knowledge is made freely available, the development of a new heat-resistant material might yield substantial benefits for, say, the electronics industry which sponsored the development, but also for a host of other industries ranging from automobiles and home appliances to our national space program. This means that, because it is geared to private benefit as measured by profitability, research activity of this type carried on by private firms will be deficient in amount. In other words, the demand for basic research facilities will understate the total benefits derivable from resulting discoveries. You will recall from Chapter 6 that the correction of such an underallocation calls for government subsidization.

Secondly, in some instances—for example, atomic energy, space exploration, oceanography, meteorology, preventive medicine, and so forth—the required scope of the research undertaking is simply beyond the means of private enterprise. That is, research in these areas is a social good. The price system would allocate few or no resources to such projects, despite their obvious real and potential significance. Finally, resources may also be underallocated to basic research activities because of the great uncertainty as to profitability and the potentially long payoff period on successful research, which may cause risk-avoiding and conservative firms to shun basic research in favor of more practical applied research undertakings.

Similar arguments can be made with respect to education. The private benefits or returns from education are clearly substantial. The lifetime earnings of a high school graduate are estimated to be over 40 percent greater than those of an elementary school graduate. And in turn, the lifetime earnings of a college graduate will be 70 percent higher than those of a high school graduate.[10] But society also realizes substantial benefits. Employers benefit from a literate and well-trained labor force. Taxpayers benefit because higher levels of education mean less unemployment, less crime and delinquency, less social unrest, and so forth. In other words, more education means smaller public expenditures for crime prevention and law enforcement and for unemployment and welfare payments. Most important, education is a primary contributor to economic growth (Table 21·5), and an expanding GNP is beneficial to the economy as a whole.[11]

THE GREAT AUTOMATION DEBATE

We have just noted that research and technological progress, on the one hand, and high levels of employment, on the other, are both important means of achieving a high rate of growth. But it has been argued recently that a dilemma exists with respect to these two forces of growth. In particular, a number of influential individuals and groups have held that a high rate of technological progress and full employment are mutually exclusive. They contend that rapid technological advance as reflected in *automation* is destroying jobs to the extent that substantial and persistent unemployment will soon pose a serious threat to the viability of our society. Let us state and critically evaluate this position.

The alarmist view

Those who are alarmed by the prospect of rapid technological advance causing a serious unemployment problem contend that recent technological advance in the form of *automation* or *cybernation* is of a profoundly different character from the technological progress we have experienced in the past. What is automation or cybernation?[12]

> The word is used to describe the multiplicity of electronic devices now used to control industrial processes—to monitor the quality of the product and adjust the machine to correct for deviations, to compute in advance the rate at which materials and parts of particular types should be fed into a complex assembly line, and to continue the process of taking over more and more of the repetitious processes

[10] See Seymour L. Wolfbein, *Employment, Unemployment, and Public Policy* (New York: Random House, Inc., 1965), p. 146.

[11] Burton A. Weisbrod, "Investing in Human Capital," *Journal of Human Resources,* Summer, 1966, pp. 5–21.

[12] Lee A. DuBridge, "Educational and Social Consequences," in John T. Dunlop (ed.), *Automation and Technological Change* (Englewood Cliffs, N.J.: Prentice-Hall, Inc., 1962), p. 29.

formerly done by hand—and performing them with a delicacy, precision, and speed that human hands could never match.

A number of individuals and groups, whom we shall (perhaps uncharitably) label "the alarmist view," hold that the emerging reality of the automated "push-button" factory will mean a massive and permanent displacement of workers.

> Let us remember that the automatic machine . . . is the precise economic equivalent of slave labor. Any labor which competes with slave labor must accept the economic conditions of slave labor. It is perfectly clear that this will produce an unemployment situation, in comparison with which. . . . the depression of the thirties will seem a pleasant joke.[13]

> A new era of production has begun. . . . The cybernation revolution has been brought about by the combination of the computer and the automated self-regulating machine. This results in a system of almost unlimited productive capacity which requires progressively less human labor. . . . potentially unlimited output can be achieved by systems of machines which will require little cooperation from human beings.[14]

Although there is some presumption that the job-destroying impact of automation will be centered on manual blue-collar occupations, it is also felt that white-collar workers and middle-management will be displaced in substantial numbers. If accurate, these are indeed alarming forecasts. If automation is a potential source of catastrophic unemployment and "unprecedented economic and social disorder," it might cause one to stop and ponder the very desirability of a rapid rate of technological progress as an economic goal.

A more realistic view

Fortunately, there is a great deal of evidence to suggest that the alarmist view has substantially distorted both the character and the potential impact of automation. Here is a summary of the kinds of arguments which have been used to counter the alarmist view.

First and in general, it is held that automation is basically a continuation of, rather than a radical departure from, the ongoing trend of technological advance. Automation is a gradual, evolutionary development in the historical course of technological progress. While productivity has been rising, it has been accelerating at a modest rate; the rate of productivity increase in recent years has been quite compatible with the long-run trend. Dramatic breakthroughs in the rate of productivity increase and peopleless plants are more fantasy than fact. It is interesting that productivity in manufacturing—where most of the alarmists would predict the more serious inroads on employment—has grown more slowly in recent years than the average rate for the entire economy.

Second and more specifically, the impact of automation upon employment has been grossly misunderstood and overstated. This misunderstanding arose because of the historical coincidence in the late 1950s of rising unemployment, on the one hand, and the development and expanding use of computers, on the other. While these two developments were occurring more or less simultaneously, their causes were in fact substantially independent. The rising unemployment rates of the late 1950s were caused primarily by a deficiency of aggregate demand, aggravated by quite rapid increases in the size of the labor force. If the predictions of the alarmists are correct and automation is spreading rapidly through our economy, then a growing body of displaced and unemployed workers should be evident. But this has simply not happened! On the contrary, unemployment rates, which rose to almost 7 percent in the late 1950s, gave way to full employment in the middle and late 1960s (Chapter 11). In short, the fact is that these gloomy predictions of mass technological unemployment have simply not borne fruit.

The impact of automation upon employment has been exaggerated for other reasons. First of all, there

[13] Norbert Wiener, *The Human Use of Human Beings* (Boston: Houghton Mifflin Company, 1950), p. 189.

[14] Ad Hoc Committee on the Triple Revolution, *The Triple Revolution* (Santa Barbara, Calif.: The Center for the Study of Democratic Institutions, 1964), p. 5. See also W. H. Ferry, "Caught on the Horn of Plenty" and Donald H. Michael, "Cybernation: The Silent Conquest" in Andrew Hacker (ed.), *The Corporation Take-over* (Garden City, N.Y.: Doubleday & Company, Inc., 1965).

is actually very little automation in existence. In the words of one writer,[15]

> Fifteen years after the concepts of "feedback" and "closed-loop control" became widespread, and ten years after computers started coming into common use, *no fully automated process exists for any major product in any industry in the United States.* Nor is any in the prospect in the immediate future. Furthermore, the extent and growth of several partially automated processes has been wildly exaggerated. . . .

The main reason for the modest inroads of automation is that most manipulative operations (for example, the guiding of a tool in an appropriate way by an automobile assembly-line worker) are in fact extremely difficult to automate. In addition, such important industries as agriculture, construction, and transportation are highly resistant to automation because of the large number of small, geographically dispersed firms and operations involved. This dispersion and the small size of individual operations also tend to make many service industries (merchandising, restaurants, repair shops, personal services, and so forth) immune to automation. And in fact, most manufacturing operations are organized on a customized "job shop" basis—the antithesis of the completely standardized, long-run production process which is conducive to automation. The inclination of the alarmists to impute the anticipated consequences of a few impressive cases of automation to the economy as a whole—to arrive at generalizations upon the basis of a very small number of special cases—yields a highly exaggerated impression of the past *and* potential unemployment effects of the "new technology."

This brings us to another point. There is an unfortunate tendency to confuse what is technologically or scientifically possible with that which is economically feasible. There are undoubtedly many areas of production in which it is now technologically possible to replace men with machines. But the actual combination of men and machines—of labor and capital—which businesses employ depends upon the very mundane consideration of production costs (Table 5·1). Many of the scientifically or technologically possible uses of automation entail the substitution of very complex and very expensive machines for relatively cheap labor. Unless the resulting increases in output are unusually dramatic, the substitution of expensive capital for cheap labor may well be at odds with the profit-seeking objective of the firm. The point is that technological inventions may substantially outdistance commercial feasibility; and to the extent that this occurs, the economic impact of technological progress is dampened.

[15] Charles E. Silberman, *The Myths of Automation* (New York: Harper & Row, Publishers, Incorporated, 1967), p. 2. Also see George Terborgh, *The Automation Hysteria* (New York: W. W. Norton & Company, Inc. 1966).

Resolving technological unemployment

Although the employment effects of technological advance have been exaggerated by the alarmists, it does not follow that automation poses no employment problems at all. *A changing technology can and does destroy particular jobs and displace particular groups of workers.* But this job displacement problem can be ameliorated by appropriate public policies. At the macro level, public policy must see to it that aggregate demand expands so that full employment is sustained—in other words, so that actual and potential NNP coincide. At the micro level, public policy must provide technologically displaced workers with the opportunities to obtain the education, skills, and mobility requisite for taking advantage of alternative employment opportunities.

Using highly simplified figures, let us first examine the problem of technological unemployment within the context of modern macroeconomics or employment theory. Suppose the economy currently has a labor force of 50 workers and the average productivity of each worker is \$10 worth of goods and services per year. This means that the economy's full-employment NNP is currently \$500. Then assume that the economy is realizing this full-employment NNP, as shown by the intersection of aggregate demand or $(C + I_n + G)_1$ and aggregate supply in Figure 22 · 1.

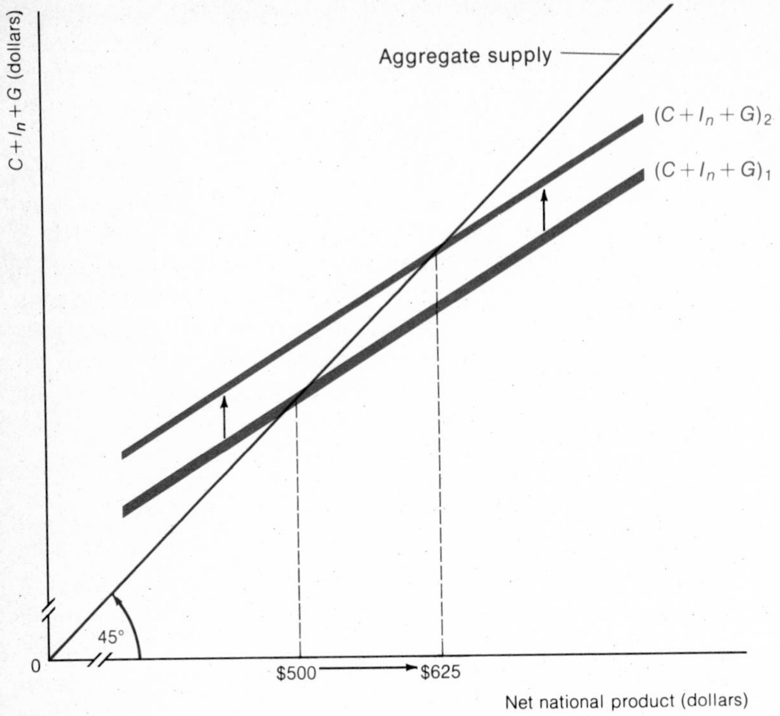

FIGURE 22·1 AUTOMATION AND FULL EMPLOYMENT

As automation increases the productivity of labor, the economy's potential or full-employment NNP increases from, say, \$500 to \$625. But to realize this expanded productivity capacity, aggregate demand must increase from $(C + I_n + G)_1$ to $(C + I_n + G)_2$. If aggregate demand remains at $(C + I_n + G)_1$, technological progress and rising productivity will be reflected in involuntary unemployment, a below-capacity NNP, and retarded growth.

Now suppose that productivity increases by, say, 25 percent as the result of technological progress or automation, so that each worker on the average can now produce \$12.50 worth of output per year. This means that the potential or full-employment NNP has increased from \$500 to \$625 (50 × \$12.50). But employment theory tells us that, if aggregate demand remains at $(C + I_n + G)_1$, actual output will remain at \$500. And because this level of output can be produced with only 40 workers (40 × \$12.50 = \$500), one-fifth of the labor force will now be unemployed. On the other hand, if aggregate demand can be shifted from $(C + I_n + G)_1$ to $(C + I_n + G)_2$ through some appropriate mixture of an expansionary fiscal policy and an easy money policy, then the economy can keep its labor force fully employed and enjoy the \$625 output which the productivity increase now makes it capable of producing. At the risk of oversimplification, we may say that automation can mean an unchanged output and substantial involuntary unemployment, on the one hand, or a significantly larger output and full employment, on the other. The outcome depends upon whether aggregate demand expands at a rate sufficient to maintain full employment. Fortunately, we have the knowledge and the policy tools to realize the latter outcome. Question: What complication would be posed by the assumption of a growing labor force?

MANPOWER PROBLEMS AND PLANNING

Our macroeconomic analysis of technological unemployment implicitly assumes that workers displaced by machines are readily transferable to other

jobs; we have supposed thus far that workers are interchangeable and highly mobile. We must now recognize that in a dynamic economy such factors as technological change, changes in the pattern of consumer demand, and shifts in the geographic location of industry all imply a problem of matching available manpower to the changing labor requirements of the economy. Economic growth entails significant shifts in the structure of employment opportunities; these shifts may make it quite difficult for displaced workers to be readily reabsorbed in new jobs.

From brawn to brains

Generally speaking, automation and related economic changes have brought about a decline in the demand for unskilled and semiskilled "blue-collar" workers and an increase in the demand for skilled, technical, and professional "white-collar" workers. Bluntly put, there has been a significant shift from brawn to brains in the structure of labor demand. Figures 22·2 and 22·3 are instructive in that they present an overview of the changes in job opportu-

FIGURE 22·2 EMPLOYMENT IN GOODS-PRODUCING INDUSTRIES AND IN SERVICE INDUSTRIES

In the last four decades employment has increased rather steadily in the service industries. The goods-producing industries, on the other hand, provide about the same number of jobs now as they did at the end of World War I. [Joint Economic Committee, *Staff Report on Employment, Growth and Price Levels* (Washington, 1959), p. 174, and U.S. Department of Labor data.]

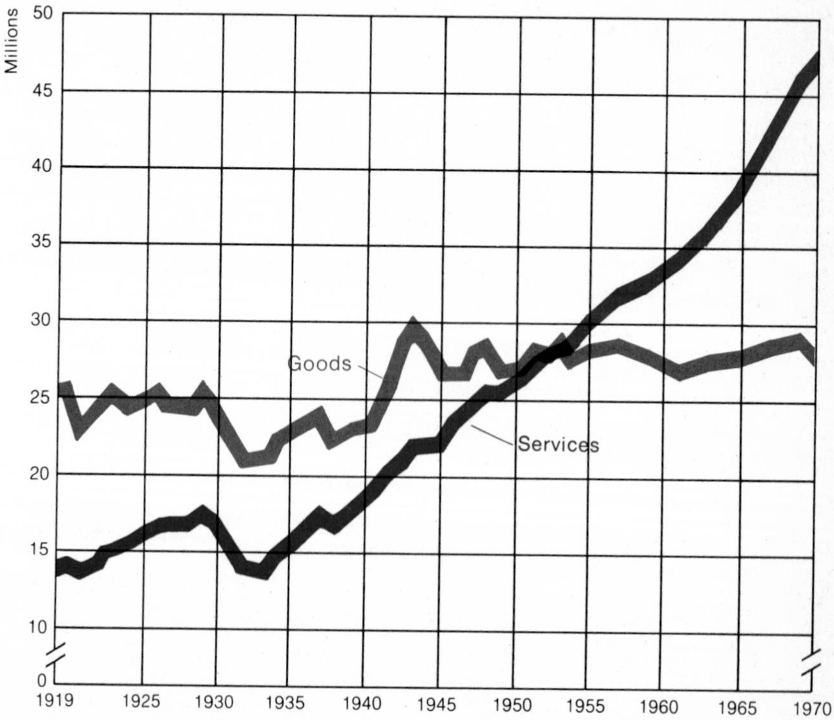

Occupational groups	Number of workers (thousands) 1950	1970	Percent change
Professional, technical and kindred workers	4,490	11,140	+148
Clerical and kindred workers	7,632	13,714	+80
Service workers	6,535	9,712	+49
Craftsmen, foremen and kindred workers	7,677	10,158	+32
Managers, officials and proprietors except farm	6,429	8,289	+29
Sales workers	3,822	4,854	+27
Operatives and kindred workers	12,146	13,909	+15
Laborers, except farm and mine	3,520	3,724	+5
Farmers and farm laborers	7,408	3,126	−58
Total	59,659	78,627	+32

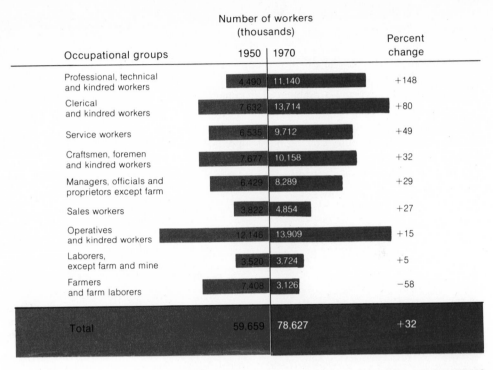

FIGURE 22·3 SHIFTS IN THE SIZE OF MAJOR OCCUPATIONAL GROUPS BETWEEN 1950 AND 1970

National requirements for higher skills have been increasing, while automation has been replacing workers in many of the less skilled occupations. The shifts toward higher proportions of professional, technical, and highly trained workers are expected to continue through the 1970s. (U.S. Department of Labor data.)

nities. Figure 22·2 indicates that employment in goods-producing industries is about the same as it was some fifty years ago; the service-producing industries are clearly the major source of new jobs in recent decades. Figure 22·3 provides a more detailed picture of this phenomenon. The main point is that the new growth industries—electronics, antibiotics, plastics, synthetic fibers—frequently demand skills and levels of educational attainment which workers who are discharged from declining industries—agriculture, the railroads, coal mining—may simply not possess. It may take more than a high level of aggregate demand to reduce the level of unemployment to desired levels.

Active manpower policies

Beginning in the late 1950s, the Federal government has pursued an "active" manpower policy which "embraces programs to stimulate more employment opportunities, to upgrade the skills and adaptability of our work force, and to link the two—jobs and

men—more effectively."[16] In practice, our manpower policy has followed several related lines.

1. Education and training The provision of education and training is the basic means by which displaced workers can avail themselves of new and more demanding employment opportunities. A multidimensioned effort has been made in this area. In the past decade the Federal government has dramatically increased its support of public education in an attempt to upgrade the quality of the labor force. The Manpower Development and Training Act (MDTA) of 1962 was a major piece of legislation which provides for both institutional and on-the-job training programs for unemployed and underemployed workers. Similarly, the Economic Opportunity Act of 1964 established the Job Corps, whose function is to provide basic education and vocational training for disadvantaged youth who might otherwise be unemployable.

2. Improving the labor market A second aspect of our manpower policy is concerned with improving the flow of information between unemployed workers and potential employers and to enhance the mobility of labor. In particular, a number of proposals have been made to modernize the U.S. Employment Service in order to increase its effectiveness in bringing job seekers and employers together. There is evidence that a better flow of job information is needed. Various pieces of Federal legislation have experimented with subsidies to help defray the moving costs of workers who are transferring from high-unemployment to more prosperous areas.

3. Regional rehabilitation The decline of important industries can result in economically distressed areas. The most dramatic instance is the sharp decline in employment opportunities in the Appalachia region due to shrinking employment in mining and agriculture. The Area Redevelopment Administration (ARA) was created in 1961 to help improve economic opportunities in areas of persistently high unemployment. ARA made loans to commercial and industrial enterprises in such areas, gave grants to towns and cities for the improvement of public facilities, offered technical assistance, and provided funds for the retraining of workers. Although Congress discontinued appropriations for the ARA in 1965, many of its functions have been taken over by MDTA.

4. Reducing social obstacles to employment Prejudice and discrimination have been an important roadblock in the matching of men and jobs; discrimination is a primary factor in explaining the fact that unemployment rates for Negroes are twice as high as those for whites. The Civil Rights Act of 1964 attempts to improve manpower utilization by removing discrimination because of race, religion, or ethnic background as an obstacle to employment or union membership (Chapter 38).

By their very nature these programs are not easily evaluated. Because they generally involve disadvantaged individuals with little education and often meager motivation for self-betterment, the expectation of sudden and spectacular success is perhaps unwarranted. On the other hand, there is small doubt that these manpower programs reflect a realistic appraisal of what must be done if America's employment and growth records are to be improved.[17]

GROWTH AND PREMATURE INFLATION

Having discussed the controversy over the adequacy of our growth rate and the automation debate, we now turn to a final growth-related problem. Can we simultaneously achieve a satisfactory rate of growth *and* price stability? Can we grow without inflation?

Traditionally, inflation has been regarded as the result of excess total demand. That is, the *demand-pull theory* of inflation states that once the economy is operating at the full-employment level and the total output therefore becomes fixed, an excess of total demand will necessarily have the effect of pulling up

[16] *Manpower Report of the President, 1965* (Washington), p. ix.

[17] The interested reader should consult Garth L. Mangum, *The Emergence of Manpower Policy* (New York: Holt, Rinehart and Winston, Inc., 1969).

the price level. Because the demand-pull theory assumes considerable flexibility of resource and product prices, changes in the composition or structure—but not the size—of total demand will leave the price level unchanged. In those sectors of the economy in which demand is increasing, prices will rise; but these increases will be offset by compensating price declines in those segments of the economy in which demand has fallen. On balance, then, a change in the structure of demand should change the *structure* of prices yet leave the overall price *level* constant.

Policies for dealing with demand-pull inflation are evident and familiar to us (Chapters 14 and 18). The policy goal is to eliminate the excess of total demand which is pulling the price level upward. Appropriate fiscal policy calls for tax increases and reductions in government spending, whereas monetary policy demands tight money.

The new inflation: two theories

The demand-pull theory of inflation is widely accepted by economists, and over the years it has provided a useful and accurate explanation of our inflationary experiences. At least, it did until the late 1950s. In the 1955–1958 period in particular, price-level–employment fluctuations occurred which were not readily explainable in terms of a simple demand-pull theory. During the 1957–1958 recession, for example, economists were embarrassed to find that employment and output were *declining,* while at the same time the general price level was *rising.* Between 1956 and 1958 the consumer price index rose by 5 points, while in the same period the index of industrial production fell by 6 points, and unemployment jumped from 4.2 to 6.8 percent of the labor force (see table on inside covers). Major industries, such as automobiles and steel, found themselves with excess capacity and partially employed labor forces; yet wages and prices continued to creep upward. The "inflationary recession" of 1969–1970 confirmed the possible coincidence of rising prices and rising unemployment. Furthermore, data indicate that during periods of recovery and expansion, inflation tends to occur before the economy reaches full employment (Figure 11·1). That is, prices and wages begin to climb substantially before aggregate demand becomes excessive. In short, premature inflation occurs.

These considerations prompted economists to restudy in detail the whole inflationary problem and have resulted in two possible explanations of the "new" inflation: the cost-push theory and the theory of structural inflation. Both of these new explanations are closely associated with institutional changes—particularly the development of strong labor unions and monopolistic businesses—which have accompanied the process of growth in our economy. Let us consider these new interpretations of inflation.

Cost-push inflation The cost-push theory explains inflation in the absence of full employment in this way: Unions have considerable control over wage rates; that is, they possess considerable market power. Indeed, they have so much market power that even with a moderate deficiency of total demand, some unemployment, and some excess industrial capacity, the stronger unions can demand and obtain wage increases. Large employers, faced now with increased costs but also in the possession of market power, push their increased wage costs and "something extra" on to consumers by raising the prices of their products. This theory is obviously based on the presumption that both unions and businesses typically possess some significant degree of market power and therefore can within limits manipulate wages and prices independent of overall conditions of total demand. Thus it is that we find cost-push inflation sometimes labeled "administered price" inflation or simply "seller's inflation."

Not surprisingly, management contends that wage increases initiate price increases, and therefore unions are obviously the villain, nudging wages and necessarily prices upward at a time when inflation otherwise would not occur. Labor counters by charging that big businesses' power to adjust or administer prices results in price increases which are neither initiated nor justified by increases in wage costs.

Structural inflation[18] A second, more recent explanation of the inflation-with-unemployment situation centers upon the effects of a change in the structure, though not the size, of total demand. Briefly stated, the rationale is based on the fact that for a number of reasons—a basic one of which is the market power of businesses and unions—prices and wages tend to be flexible upward but inflexible downward (Chapters 11 and 12). Now let us suppose that total demand is not excessive; as a matter of fact, let us assume that it is slightly deficient, resulting in, say, 5 percent unemployment. Now a rather sharp change in the structure or composition of this total demand occurs. This structural change in demand means that prices and wages will rise in those segments of the economy experiencing an expanding demand. However, because of their downward stickiness, wages and prices will not fall, or at least will not fall by much, in those sectors of the economy witnessing a declining demand. The result is a net increase in the price and wage levels; that is, inflation will occur. Remember: This inflation arises despite the fact that there is less than full employment and the economy is failing to realize its growth potential.

But this is not all. Secondary effects may intensify structural inflation by transmitting wage and price rises from the increasing-demand segments of the economy to other sectors where demand might be unchanged or even falling. Suppose, for example, that one of the industries most favorably affected by our assumed change in the structure of total demand is the steel industry. The result will be a tendency for steel prices and profits to rise. But now the big steel firms are a lucrative target for the United Steelworkers of America, which demands and receives wage increases. At this point the secondary, transmitting effects enter the picture. On the one hand, a host of industries using significant quantities of steel—including those unaffected and adversely affected by the change in the structure of total demand—find themselves faced with higher material costs. So they raise their prices to cover these cost boosts. And, as it happens, the wage increases which occur in the steel industry tend to create pressures for wage increases in related industries such as aluminum, copper, and other fabricated metal product industries—even though these industries may be among those faced with a constant or sagging product demand. Wage rates in these related industries are traditionally patterned after wages in steel. Hence, when steel wages go up, union leaders in these related industries will be under pressure to secure comparable increases for their constituents. And, of course, the fact that the cost of living is rising provides the basis for demanding these increases. As a matter of fact, if existing collective bargaining agreements in these related or, indeed, in other unrelated industries, contain "escalator clauses," wage rates will automatically go up as the consumer price index rises.

Oddly enough, employers in the related industries may feel obligated to grant wage increases because the severing of a traditional relationship between wages in the steel industry and the related industries may undermine worker morale and impair productivity in the latter. Firms in the related industries then recover these wage increases by raising product prices. The point is this: Through these several avenues, wage and price increases originating in those sectors of the economy which are prosperous because of the favorable change in the composition of demand spill over into other sectors of the economy where the change in the structure of demand has caused unemployment and excess productive capacity. In short, a sharp change in the composition of a given level of total demand may be inflationary in both favorably and unfavorably affected segments of the economy. This helps to explain the paradox of inflation with unemployment; changes in the composition of demand may cause the price level to rise even though total demand is deficient and unemployment is increasing.

It must be emphasized that these three theories—demand-pull, cost-push, and structural inflation—are

[18]See Charles L. Schultze, *Recent Inflation in the United States*, Study Paper No. 1 for the Joint Economic Committee (Washington, 1959) and also Professor Schultze's "Creeping Inflation: Causes and Consequences," *Business Horizons*, Summer 1960, pp. 65–77.

not unrelated or mutually exclusive. All three can operate simultaneously. For example, a rising level of total demand whose composition is significantly changing can cause both demand-pull and structural inflation simultaneously. And the exertion of market power may cause cost-push forces to accentuate this inflation, particularly in those industries where unions are strong and demand most favorably affected.

FIGURE 22·4 THE PHILLIPS CURVE

The Phillips curve portrays the problem of premature inflation. It indicates that full employment can be achieved only with inflation (point *S*) and, conversely, that price level stability means excess unemployment (point *U*). The purpose of the wage-price guideposts is to shift the curve to the right (the broken curve) to make the goals of full employment and price stability compatible (point *F*).

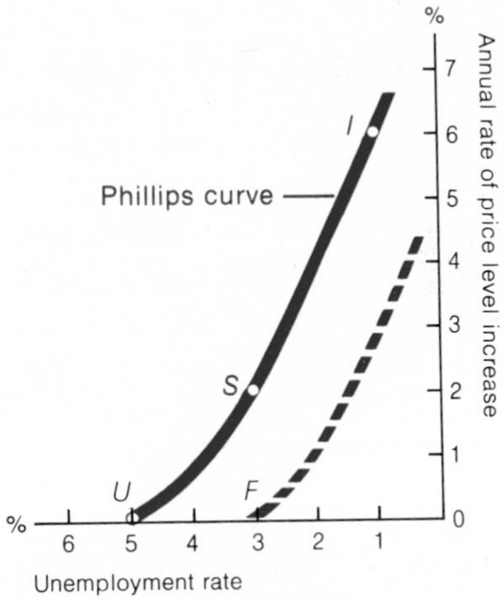

Public policy dilemma

To the extent that premature inflation—cost-push or structural—occurs in a growing economy, a serious public policy dilemma is posed. The expansionary fiscal policy and easy money policy which combine to boost aggregate demand, bring full employment, and stimulate growth, will simultaneously entail inflation. Conversely, a restrictive fiscal policy and tight money can be used to achieve price-level stability, but only at the cost of excess unemployment and a retarded growth rate. The nature of this policy dilemma—this trade-off between employment and price stability—is portrayed through the red *Phillips curve*[19] of Figure 22·4. This curve is essentially a restatement of Phase 2 of Figure 11·1. Each point on the Phillips curve reflects an "unemployment rate–price level increase" combination available to society; that is, it shows the amount of inflation associated with each particular rate of unemployment. Assuming that "full employment" means a 3 percent unemployment rate (Chapter 11), at point *U* we can realize price stability, but only at the cost of excess unemployment. At point *S* society can achieve full employment, but the price of full employment is some inflation—in this case, a 2 percent annual increase in the price level. Point *I* suggests a position of "overfull" employment accompanied by rapid inflation. Ideally, we would like to achieve full employment without inflation at point *F*. But given the red Phillips curve, this choice is simply not available to us.

In addition to choosing a point on a given Phillips curve through the manipulation of aggregate demand, policymakers are faced with a more basic question. Is there any way of shifting the Phillips curve to a more acceptable position—such as the broken curve in Figure 22·4—at which higher levels of employment and price stability are more compatible? Can we somehow achieve a better menu of choices so that we might come closer to point *F*? The location of the Phillips curve is determined basically by bottlenecks and by the structure and behavior of the institutions of the economy and, more specifically, by the fact that strong unions and large firms have sufficient market power to "administer" wages and prices in the absence of excessive aggregate demand.

[19]Named after the British economist A. W. Phillips, who developed this concept. See his "The Relationship between Unemployment and the Rate of Change in Money Wage Rates in the United Kingdom, 1862–1957," *Economica*, November 1958, pp. 283–299.

The wage-price guideposts and "voluntary" restraint The Kennedy and Johnson administrations

attempted to make wage and price decisions more responsive to the public's desire to increase the compatibility of high employment levels and price stability by setting forth "guideposts for noninflationary wage and price behavior." The basic guidepost is that, as a general rule, wage increases should be limited to the overall rate of increase in the nation's productivity.[20] The rationale of this guidepost is simply that if the average hourly output of workers increases by, say, 3 percent, employers can increase wages by 3 percent without experiencing any increase in labor costs per unit of output.[21] Because wage increases of this magnitude keep labor costs per unit of output constant, there is no cost-push pressure to increase product prices.

The approach followed by the Federal government has been basically one of using moral suasion, or what critics have labeled an "open-mouth" policy. The President, the Secretary of Labor, and other high public officials make appeals and admonitions to labor and business leaders, encouraging them to exercise self-restraint in reaching wage-price decisions.

There has been considerable debate as to the effectiveness of the guidelines. Critics hold that such "creeping admonitionism" is doomed to failure because it in effect asks businessmen and labor leaders to abandon their primary functions—to forgo the goals of higher wages and maximum profits. For this reason there is little expectation that voluntary cooperation will be forthcoming from labor and management. More fundamentally, the guideposts are seriously in conflict with freedom of action and choice. Furthermore, the incentive structure implied by the guidelines is perverse: those who ignore or evade the guideposts are rewarded with higher wages and greater profits, while those who comply forgo these economic gains. Too, where they are effective, the guideposts tend to interfere with the allocative or guiding function of the price system and thereby jeopardize allocative efficiency. Resource and product prices must respond freely and fully to changes in the level and composition of demand if resource allocation is to remain efficient over time; the wage-price guidelines tend to thwart these responses.

But there are reputable economists who see some value in the guidelines and offer important defenses. Although problems of measurement are great, the best available evidence suggests that the guideposts have made at least a modest contribution to wage-price stability. Nor is there any clear evidence to suggest that the guideposts have interfered in any substantial way with the allocative function of the price system. The guideposts, after all, are not aimed at the highly competitive markets where allocation tends to conform to the public interest, but to those labor and product markets where unions and businesses have considerable market power and the capacity to distort the allocation of resources to their own advantage. In any event one cannot consistently claim, on the one hand, that the guideposts are ineffective and, on the other, that they interfere with the allocation of resources. Finally, it is held that, despite various shortcomings, the guideposts are a more realistic and more palatable means of achieving a more acceptable employment–price level solution than the two alternatives to which we now turn.[22]

Reducing market power A second avenue for attacking the problem embraces the rationale that, if the market power of business and labor is the source of premature inflation, this market power must be reduced or eliminated. The effect will be to shift the Phillips curve to the right. Unions and businesses must be made to face such vigorous competition that they will be unable to increase wage rates ahead of productivity. But how? One recommendation is to apply our antitrust laws more vigorously to big busi-

[20] *Economic Report of the President, 1962* (Washington), pp. 185–190.

[21] Labor cost per unit of output (L) is equal to the wage rate (W) divided by the productivity of labor (P). That is, $L = W/P$. Thus if the wage rate is \$5 per hour and productivity or output per hour is 100 units, then labor cost per unit of product is obviously \$.05 (=\$5.00/100). If both W and P now increase by the same percent, L will be constant. For example, if productivity and wage rates both rise by 3 percent, then labor cost per unit of output will remain at \$.05 (=\$5.15/103).

[22] The essays by Milton Friedman, Robert Solow, Gardner Ackley, and John T. Dunlop in George P. Shultz and Robert Z. Aliber (eds.), *Guidelines: Informal Controls and the Market Place* (Chicago: The University of Chicago Press, 1966), contain pointed criticisms and defenses of the guidelines. John Sheehan's *The Wage-Price Guideposts* (Washington: The Brookings Institution, 1967) is also recommended.

ness, and possibly to unions too. Or another proposal is to prohibit unions from bargaining on a centralized, nationwide level, forcing each local union to bargain with its own immediate employer. This decentralization of union power and authority, it is hoped, will ameliorate cost-push inflation.

But serious questions can be raised about such proposals. Antitrust legislation, we shall discover (Chapter 35), has not been particularly successful in restricting the power of big business. Nor is it clear that antitrust can be applied to labor without virtually destroying unions and the institution of collective bargaining. Finally, there is little evidence to suggest that localized wage setting results in more socially acceptable wage rates than does centralized bargaining. Indeed, interlocal union rivalries, petty grievances, and less ability to realize the social consequences of its actions may all tend to make local bargaining more aggressive and potentially more inflationary than centralized bargaining.

Increased government participation and control Given President Nixon's temporary wage-price freeze of August 1971, it is not at all unrealistic to consider direct government control of wages and prices as a more-or-less permanent component of stabilization policy. A variety of techniques might be employed. For example, the Federal government might simply establish a "study group" to publicize wage and price changes in key industries. Or a fact-finding board might hold hearings on proposed wage and price increases, and possibly issue a report or recommendations based thereon. Others suggest that, because major wage agreements affect the price level, and therefore the public interest, the public interest should be represented by having public officials participate actively in key collective bargaining negotiations. Or the government may legislate the right to suspend or delay wage or price increases which are significantly in excess of productivity increases. Finally, government, at the extreme, might simply establish public control over wages and prices in crucial industries such as steel, where the inflationary potential of substantial wage and price increases is great. These wage-price controls would be reminiscent of those exercised by the government during World War II to contain the strong inflationary pressures then existing.

These various proposals clearly entail considerable gradations in the degree of government control and participation. In particular, government participation in wage negotiations, public authority to reject proposed wage-price increases, and direct wage-price controls embody far-reaching changes in our economic way of life. Hence, many economists feel these techniques to be of a "last resort" character, to be used only if less drastic means are ineffective and if the inflationary problem becomes severe. On the other hand, the problem of "stagflation"—stagnation in output and employment accompanied by substantial inflation—imposes great socioeconomic costs which perhaps can only be lessened by policies which embody greater constraints upon the goal of economic freedom.

Finally, a recent proposal attempts to thwart wage-push inflation effectively without resort to potentially authoritarian techniques. The suggestion is that a special *excess wage settlement tax* be imposed upon firms which grant inflationary wage increases, for example, increases in excess of 3 percent. The larger the wage increase in excess of 3 percent which the firm allows, the larger is the special surtax on its profits. The purpose of the tax is to stiffen the resistance of management to union wage demands and result in collective bargaining agreements more conducive to price stability. Proponents of the plan argue that it could be made effective without the need for a new and costly administrative bureaucracy; that it does not call for radical institutional surgery on either unions or businesses; that it is quite compatible with the market system; and, more importantly, that it would work.[23]

SUMMARY

1. Proponents of rapid growth point out that growth *a*. means a better solution to the wants-resources dilemma and a higher standard of living, *b*. alleviates

[23] For details, see Sidney Weintraub, "An Incomes Policy to Stop Inflation," *Lloyds Bank Review*, January 1971, pp. 1–12.

domestic economic problems, and *c*. illustrates the vitality and efficiency of our economy to the rest of the world. Critics *a*. cite adverse environmental effects, *b*. argue that domestic and international problems are essentially matters of distribution, not production, *c*. contend that growth is a major source of human obsolescence and insecurity, and *d*. argue that growth is frequently in conflict with certain human values.

2. Basic policies for accelerating United States growth include *a*. the maintenance of full employment, *b*. achievement of a high level of investment, *c*. increased spending on research, and *d*. expanded outlays on education. The fact that research and education entail substantial social revenues or are social goods underlies the argument that substantial public support in these areas is justified.

3. Although technological progress or automation eliminates specific kinds of jobs, it need not result in a growing problem of unemployment if appropriate public policies are invoked. At the macro level, aggregate demand must rise sufficiently to provide new job opportunities for the technologically unemployed. At the micro level, manpower policies in the areas of education and training, improving the labor market and labor mobility, regional rehabilitation, and discrimination are needed to match unemployed workers to jobs more effectively.

4. Although the demand-pull theory still provides the basic explanation of inflation, our unemployment-with-inflation experiences of the late 1950s and again in 1969–1970 have caused economists to talk of a "new inflation" explainable in terms of cost-push forces and changes in the structure of total demand. These new theories help explain premature inflation; that is, the price level tends to rise *before* full employment is achieved. The policy dilemma posed by premature inflation is embodied in the Phillips curve.

5. Government has tried to implement the basic wage-price guidepost—that wage increases should not exceed productivity increases—through the voluntary restraint of labor and management in determining wages and prices. Alternative means of implementing the guidepost so as to shift the Phillips curve to the right are *a*. reducing the market power of businesses and unions through antitrust action and the decentralization of collective bargaining; and *b*. increased government control of, or participation in, the wage- and price-setting processes.

QUESTIONS AND STUDY SUGGESTIONS

1. Identify the costs of economic growth. Which do you feel are the most significant? To what degree, if any, are these various costs avoidable? "Growth contributes to instability and insecurity, but also provides the means to provide for those adversely affected by instability and insecurity." Comment.

2. "Our prime national goal . . . should be to reach a zero growth rate as soon as possible. Zero growth in people, in GNP, and in our consumption of everything. That is the only hope of attaining a stable economy: that is, of halting deterioration of the environment on which our lives depend." Do you agree?

3. What programs and policies might be used if we sought to accelerate our rate of growth? Outline in detail the fiscal and monetary policies which might increase investment in a full-employment economy without causing inflation.

4. Is automation a major source of unemployment in our economy? Explain the importance of effective monetary and fiscal policies in an economy characterized by a rapid rate of technological progress. What is an "active manpower policy" and how does it relate to the problem of technological unemployment?

5. "The problem of reemploying the workers of the chronically depressed areas is, in a sense, an aspect of the law of increasing costs." Do you agree? Explain.

6. Contrast and evaluate the following two statements:

a. "Government measures to reverse or slow down such declines in employment in particular sectors of the economy

are not likely to be successful and are likely to be extremely costly. . . . We should beware of becoming involved in a . . . hopeless and . . . costly program for rescuing distressed areas."[24]

b. "It does not seem fair to deny progress to a society in order to protect a few. Nor does it seem fair for society to accept all the gain at the expense of a few. Therefore, it would seem that society should find some way of caring for those who lose out by progress."[25]

7. Briefly analyze and evaluate:

a. "Human capabilities do not stay abreast of physical capital, and they do become limiting factors in economic growth."

b. "We should consider creating government-sponsored productivity institutes to stimulate research for industries where increases in output appear particularly necessary."

c. "Under our present economic structure the social benefits of basic research are not adequately reflected in opportunities for private profit. Indeed, there is a basic contradiction between the conditions necessary for efficient basic research—few or no constraints on the direction of research with full and free dissemination of research results—and full appropriation of the gains from sponsoring basic research in a competitive economy."[26]

d. "The best way to stimulate growth is to fight inflation. This is so for several reasons. First, inflation will undermine incentives to save and therefore limit investment. Furthermore, only with price stability is healthy, maintainable growth possible. Finally, creeping inflation inevitably accelerates to a gallop and precipitates economic collapse."

8. Discuss and compare the assumptions and operations of *a.* demand-pull, *b.* cost-push, and *c.* structural inflation. What is meant by premature inflation? Draw a Phillips curve to illustrate and explain the policy dilemma posed by premature inflation. Outline a program to deal with inflation which occurs when 6 percent of the labor force is unemployed.

9. Explain the wage-price guidepost, indicating why wage increases which do not exceed productivity increases leave labor costs per unit of output unchanged. How successful has the guidepost been in controlling premature inflation?

10. Would you favor a special tax on firms which granted wage increases in excess of productivity increases?

[24] *Unemployment: Causes and Cures* (New York: National Association of Manufacturers, April 1961), pp. 8–9.

[25] Bruce R. Morris, *Problems of American Economic Growth* (Fair Lawn, N.J.: Oxford University Press, 1961), p. 219.

[26] Richard R. Nelson, "The Simple Economics of Basic Scientific Research," *Journal of Political Economy,* June 1959, p. 305.

SELECTED REFERENCES

Economic Issues, 4th ed., readings 31, 32, 33, 35, and 38.

Mangum, Garth L.: *The Emergence of Manpower Policy* (New York: Holt, Rinehart and Winston, Inc., 1969).

Manpower Report of the President (Washington, published annually).

Mishan, E. J.: *Technology and Growth* (New York: Praeger Publishers, 1970).

Sheehan, John: *The Wage-Price Guideposts* (Washington: The Brookings Institution, 1967).

Terborgh, George: *The Automation Hysteria* (New York: W. W. Norton & Company, Inc., 1966).

THE ECONOMICS OF THE FIRM AND RESOURCE ALLOCATION

5

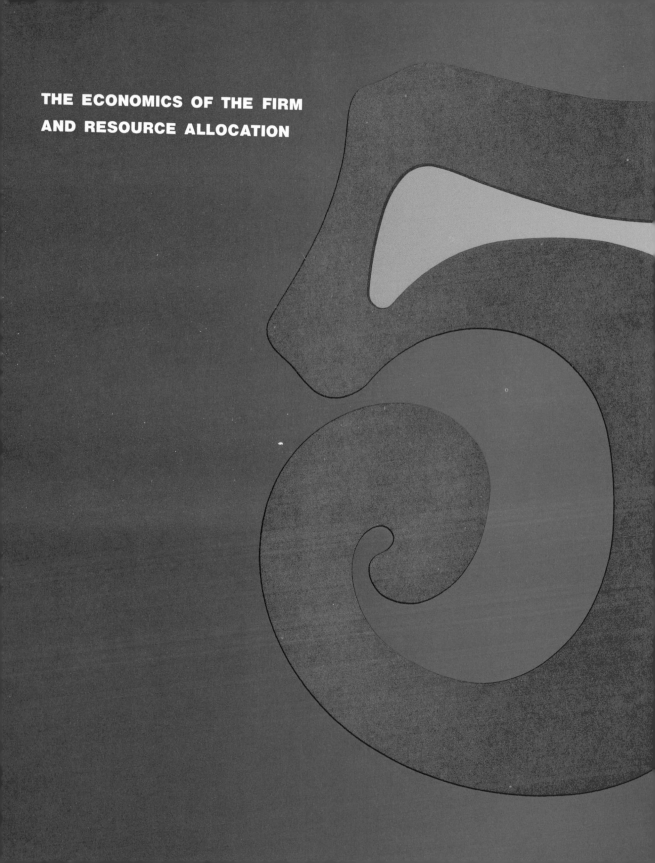

THE MARKET STRUCTURES OF AMERICAN CAPITALISM

Scarce resources and unlimited wants, you will recall, are the foundation of economic science. The efficient management of scarce resources is the social goal of all economic processes. Furthermore, there are two major facets to the problem of achieving efficient resource use. The first, which we have examined in Parts 2 and 3 and, to some degree, in Part 4 of this book, centers upon the full employment of available resources. The second aspect of the economizing problem—the one to which we now turn—has to do with allocating employed resources among alternative uses in the most efficient manner. Stated differently, Parts 2, 3, and 4 focused upon the last of the Five Fundamental Questions posed in Chapter 2: "Can the economy achieve the full employment of its available resources?" Part 5 deals with the first four questions: "Can the economy produce that output most desired by society?" "Will the production of that output be organized in the most efficient manner?" "Can the economy successfully distribute that output?" "Is the economy capable of maintaining efficiency in the use of its resources in the face of changes in the relative supplies of resources, changes in consumer tastes, and changes in technology?" All four of these questions obviously have an important bearing on the problem of achieving and maintaining an efficient allocation of available resources.

We are well aware that one of the major characteristics of capitalistic economies is their heavy reliance upon a price system as a means for allocating resources (Chapter 5). Our major topics of discussion, then, are prices and the price system. Specifically, our basic goal in the ensuing chapters is to acquire a comprehensive understanding of the operation and relative efficiency of the *price system* in allocating resources within the framework of American capitalism. As a means to achieving this primary goal, we also seek a thorough analysis of *individual prices* under a variety of contrasting market arrangements.

Using the product market as a point of reference,

the present chapter defines and describes the various market arrangements we propose to examine. In the subsequent chapters in Part 5 we review and apply our previous analysis of demand and supply, enhance our understanding of the demand side of the market, explore the production (supply) side of the market through a discussion of production costs—the major determinant of a firm's willingness to supply a given product—and examine in some detail the interaction of supply and demand under the various market arrangements described in the present chapter. Our attention will then shift to the functioning of prices in the resource market. Finally, the overall operation of the price system in American capitalism is examined.

FOUR BASIC MARKET MODELS

There is no such thing as an "average" or "typical" industry. Detailed examination of the business sector of American capitalism reveals an almost infinite number of different market situations; no two industries are alike. At one extreme we may find a single producer completely dominating a particular market. At the other we discover thousands upon thousands—yes, even millions—of firms, each of which supplies a minute fraction of total or market output. Between these extremes lies an almost unlimited variety of market arrangements, most of which shade into one another.

Obviously, any attempt to examine each specific industry would be an endless and impossible task. There are simply too many of them. Hence, we seek a more realistic objective—to define and discuss several basic market structures, or models. In so doing we shall acquaint ourselves with the *general* way in which price and output are determined in most of the market types which characterize American capitalism.

But the use of a few market models as typifying most of American industries calls for a word or two of caution. First, the market models to be considered are necessarily abstractions. They are merely first approximations and as such do not purport to present a complete picture of reality (see Chapter 1). In no case will the market models we are about to define provide a *detailed* explanation of the functioning of any specific firm. Yet they will do a reasonably good job of outlining the operation of many firms.

Furthermore, some firms and industries will not fall neatly within any of the market models we are about to outline; rather they will bear characteristics of two or more of these models. This means that the classification of a given firm or industry might entail an element of arbitrariness. This is the same type of problem which other scientists encounter. The botanist, for example, classifies all plants under three family groups—algae and fungi (thallophytes), moss plants (bryophytes), and vascular plants (tracheophytes). Yet many forms of plant life do not neatly fit into any one of these families but rather are borderline cases. So it is with the economist in classifying industries.

Finally, it is important to recognize at the outset that the economist's definitions of the basic market models do not coincide with those typically employed by businessmen and laymen. The definitions which follow are not of commonsense vintage. "Competition," for example, has a much more precise meaning to the economist than it does to the average businessman.

Economists envision four relatively distinct market situations. These are (1) pure competition, (2) pure monopoly, (3) monopolistic competition, and (4) oligopoly. The immediate task is to describe the major characteristics of each of these four market models. In doing so we shall use the seller's side of the product market as a point of reference. We shall see later that the same general models also are relevant for the buying side of the market.

Pure competition

A purely competitive market has several distinct characteristics which set it off from other market structures.

1. A main feature of a purely competitive market

is the presence of a large number of independently acting sellers, usually offering their products in a highly organized market.

2. Competitive firms are producing a standardized or virtually standardized product. Given price, the consumer is indifferent as to the seller from which he purchases. In a competitive market the products of firms B, C, D, E, and so forth are looked upon by the buyer as perfect substitutes for that of firm A.

3. In a purely competitive market *individual firms* exert no significant control over product price. This characteristic follows from the preceding two. Under pure competition each firm produces such a small fraction of total output that increasing or decreasing its output will have no perceptible influence upon total supply or, therefore, product price. To illustrate, assume there are 10,000 competing firms, each of which is currently producing 100 units of output. Total supply is obviously 1,000,000. Now suppose one of these 10,000 firms cuts its output to 50 units. Will this affect price? No. And the reason is clear: This restriction of output by a single firm has an almost imperceptible impact on total supply—specifically, the total quantity supplied declines from 1,000,000 to 999,950. This is obviously not enough of a change in total supply to affect product price noticeably. In short, the individual competitive producer cannot adjust market price; he can only adjust to it.

Stated differently, pricewise the individual competitive producer is at the mercy of the market; to him product price is a given datum over which he exerts no influence. He can get the same price per unit for a large output as he can for a small output. To ask a price higher than the going market price would be futile. Consumers will not buy anything from firm A at a price of $2.10 when his 9,999 competitors are selling an identical and therefore perfect substitute product at $2 per unit. Conversely, because firm A can sell as much as it chooses at $2 per unit, there is no reason for it to charge some lower price, say, $1.95. Indeed, to do so would shrink its profits.

Finally, a subtle but highly important point: Although the *individual* firm cannot influence product price by varying its output, all firms in a competitive industry taken *as a group* can cause market price to vary. Should all 10,000 firms cut their outputs from 100 to 50 units, the total quantity supplied will decline from 1,000,000 to 500,000 units. This is most certainly a very significant change and can be expected to boost product price considerably. In brief, the individual firm cannot significantly influence price, but all firms as a group can. Although product price to an individual competitive seller is fixed, that price is free to move up or down in accordance with changes in either *total* demand or *total* supply.

4. New firms are free to enter and existing firms are free to leave purely competitive industries. In particular, no significant obstacles—legal, technical, financial, or other—exist to prohibit new firms from coming into being and selling their outputs in competitive markets.

5. Because purely competitive firms are producing a standardized product, there is virtually no room for *nonprice competition,* that is, competition on the basis of differences in product quality, advertising, or sales promotion. By definition each firm in a competitive market is producing an identical product. Hence, no firm has a quality edge over its rivals. Advertising by individual firms will be to no avail, because each firm's product has no distinguishing features to be advertised or promoted. Buyers will know that the products of all firms in the industry have the same features. Advertising has virtually no chance of convincing them otherwise.

What about examples? Really precise examples of pure competition are few and far between. If we neglect the government's farm program, agriculture provides us with most of the good illustrations. Thus, we find, for example, that there are literally millions of farmers producing class I corn—a product which is obviously standardized or uniform. Class I corn is class I corn! Each firm supplies such a small fraction of the total that no single farmer has any control over the market price for class I corn. He accepts the market price which exists in the highly organized market as a datum over which he has no influence; the individual farmer can sell as much or as little as

he wants without affecting that price. He does not squander his financial resources on advertising or sales promotion. Farmer Jones knows that millions of other farmers are producing an identical product and that buyers are well aware of this. Hence, advertising would be futile, a sheer waste of time, effort, and money. The markets for wheat, cotton, barley, oats, the various types of livestock, and a good many other farm staples also fit rather well into the competitive mold we have outlined. While only a few industries approximate pure competition, the purely competitive market model provides a norm against which less competitive markets can be evaluated.

Pure monopoly

Now we turn to the other extreme of the spectrum. Pure monopoly provides us with the sharpest contrast to pure competition.

1. A pure, or absolute, monopolist is a one-firm industry. A single firm is the only producer of a given product or the sole supplier of a service; hence, the firm and the industry are synonymous.

2. It follows from this first characteristic that the monopolist's product is unique in the sense that there are no good, or close, substitutes available. From the buyer's point of view this means that he has no reasonable alternatives to which he can turn. He must buy the product from the monopolist or do without.

A question arises at this point: When are products "good" substitutes? There is no clear answer to this query. In a very broad sense all goods and services which compete for the consumer's dollar are substitutes. A down payment on a house may be a substitute for a new automobile. A two-week vacation may be a substitute for a television set. A pair of shoes may be a substitute for a new pair of slacks. A symphony concert may be a substitute for a fraternity dance. Yet in a more restricted sense of the term it is clear that some products and services simply do not have reasonably good substitutes. Candles and kerosene lamps are not good substitutes for electric lights. Other spices are poor substitutes for salt. Bus or train transportation may be a poor substitute for owning one's own automobile. To some, a symphony concert is no substitute at all for the Signa Phi Nothing formal.

In our discussion we shall employ the idea of substitution in the narrower sense of the term. Hence, we can agree that, as most consumers see it, there are no good substitutes for the water piped into our homes by the municipal waterworks or the electric power provided by the local power company. Digging a well or importing water from a neighboring community are not realistic substitutes for running water in one's home. And few would regard candles and kerosene lighting as acceptable substitutes for electric lights. In any event your television set will not run on kerosene. Up to World War II, manufacturers whose products entailed the need for a strong but lightweight metal had little choice but to purchase aluminum from Alcoa; no competing aluminum producers were in existence prior to the war.

3. We have emphasized that the individual firm operating under pure competition exercises no influence over product price. This is so because he contributes only a negligible portion of total supply. In vivid contrast, the pure monopolist exercises considerable control over price. And the reason is obvious: He is responsible for, and therefore controls, the total quantity supplied. By manipulating the amount supplied, he can cause product price to change. If it is to his advantage, we can expect him to use his power in this way.

4. If, by definition, a pure monopolist has no immediate competitors, there must be a reason for this lack of competition. And there is: The existence of monopoly depends upon the existence of barriers to entry. Be they economic, technological, legal, or other, certain obstacles must exist to keep new competitors from coming into the industry if monopoly is to persist. Entry is not easy under conditions of pure monopoly; on the contrary, it is blocked. More of this in Chapter 28.

5. Depending upon the type of product or service involved, monopolists may or may not engage in extensive advertising and sales promotion activity. Local public utilities see no point in large expenditures for advertising; any local citizen who wants

water, gas, and electric power and telephone service already knows from whom he must buy.

If pure monopolists do advertise, such advertising is likely to be of a public relations, or goodwill, character rather than highly competitive, as is the advertising associated with, say, cigarettes, soap flakes, and beer. Because they have no immediate rivals, monopolists, in trying to induce more people to buy their products, need not invoke the ours-is-better-than-theirs type of advertising which plagues radio, television, and otherwise scenic highways. Rather the monopolist's pitch is likely to be "We're really nice fellows and certainly wouldn't do anything to exploit other firms, our beloved employees, or, heaven forbid, consumers." Or the monopolist may be anxious for the public to recognize that at least 90 percent of the firm's stock is held by destitute widows and orphans. Or, finally, the monopolist may be content simply to point out the technological progress for which the firm has been responsible.

Because pure monopoly is admittedly an extreme market model, we once again find relatively few precise illustrations. Most local public utilities are pure monopolists for the municipalities which they serve. Thus consumers either purchase their water, electricity, gas, and telephone service from the local utility or do without. Much the same may hold true of railway service in rural areas. On a nationwide basis American Telephone and Telegraph approximates a pure monopoly. As we have said, Alcoa was a virtual monopolist in the production of most basic aluminum products until World War II; now it faces some competition from Reynolds and Kaiser. The United Shoe Machinery Company is the only manufacturer of certain equipment used in the production of shoes. IBM is the only source of certain calculating machines.

This is not to say that the pure monopolist will charge the highest price he can get for his product or service. Consumers may find it impossible to do without some amount of water and highly inconvenient to do without some quantity of electricity. But the amounts they purchase will vary inversely with price. If the prices of electricity and water were extremely high, the poor (but cheap) substitutes of kerosene lamps and digging a well would become relevant. And an extremely high price on office machines might induce firms to substitute bookkeepers for the machines.

Monopolistic competition

As its name indicates, monopolistic competition stands between the extremes of pure competition and pure monopoly. It embraces characteristics of both, but for the most part it stands closer to pure competition.

1. As is the case with pure competition, monopolistic competition entails a large number of sellers acting independently. This does not mean that there need be 1,000, 10,000, or 1,000,000 firms in the industry; 30, 40, or 100 firms of more or less equal size may prevail. The important point is that each firm produces a fairly small share of the total output.

2. In contrast to pure competition, wherein the product is standardized, *product differentiation* is a major characteristic of monopolistically competitive industries. Product differentiation entails not only physical differences in the products of various producers or sellers in the industry, but also differences in such factors as the location and "snob appeal" of the seller's store, the packaging of the product, the cordiality of the firm's salespeople, the effectiveness of its advertising, the availability of credit, the company's reputation for servicing or "making good on" defective products, and so forth. The net result is that, although all firms in such an industry are producing the same general type or class of product, the particular product of each firm will have certain distinguishing features which set it off to some extent from those of other firms in the industry. In other words, the products of monopolistically competitive firms are close, but not perfect, substitutes. Just as the presence of a relatively large number of firms makes for competition, product differentiation gives rise to a measure of monopoly power. Indeed, monopolistic competition is sometimes called "the case of differentiation and large numbers."

3. Monopolistically competitive producers have a limited amount of control over product price. The

control that exists depends essentially upon the degree of product differentiation and the number and proximity of competitors. The monopolistically competitive producer can raise his price modestly without having his sales fall to zero. Why? Because buyers recognize some differences between the products of various sellers. In the presence of product differentiation, consumers are likely to have definite preferences for the products of specific sellers, and relatively small price increases by one firm will not cause all buyers to seek out the close substitute products of rival firms in that industry. Generally, when the rivals of a monopolistically competitive firm are many in number and in close proximity, each firm's control over price will be less than would otherwise be the case.

4. Entry into monopolistically competitive industries is typically easy. Nevertheless, entry may be a bit more difficult under monopolistically competitive conditions than when pure competition prevails. This is so because of product differentiation. A new firm must not only obtain the capital necessary to go into business but must also win clients away from existing firms. Securing a share of the market might entail considerable research and product development costs by the new firm to ensure that its product will have features which distinguish it from products already on the market. Similarly, considerable advertising outlays may be necessary to inform consumers of the existence of a new brand and to convince a number of them that it will be to their advantage to switch to the new product. In short, greater financial obstacles may face the potential newcomer under monopolistic competition than under pure competition.

5. Because products are differentiated, monopolistically competitive industries are ordinarily characterized by vigorous competition in areas other than price. Economic rivalry, as we have seen, may be based not only on price, but also on product quality, advertising, and conditions or services associated with the sale of a product. Great emphasis is placed upon trademarks and brand names as means for convincing the consumer that the products of one's rivals are not as good substitutes for brand X as might first seem to be the case. Indeed, quality and advertising competition go hand in hand. Advertising proclaims and, if possible, magnifies real differences in product quality. While quality competition manipulates the firm's product, advertising and sales promotion attempt to manipulate the consumer.

A considerable number of industries approximate the conditions of monopolistic competition (see Table 29·1). At the manufacturing level the women's dress industry provides a good example; New York City and a few other large metropolitan areas are the locations of the large number of small manufacturers which constitute this industry. The shoe industry also has features which make it reasonably close to being monopolistically competitive. A good many types of retail trade, particularly in cities of any size, occur under conditions which approximate monopolistic competition. Most cities contain a fairly large number of grocery stores, cleaning establishments, clothing shops, gasoline stations, restaurants, barber shops, and so forth, all of which are providing differentiated products and services.

Oligopoly

The remaining market model—oligopoly—is less precisely defined by economists than are the three market structures just discussed. Two reasons go far to explain this lack of preciseness. On the one hand, oligopoly includes a wider range of market structures than do the other three market models; in effect it embraces all the remaining market situations which do not fit the rather clearly defined market models of pure competition, monopolistic competition, and pure monopoly. On the other hand, as we shall discover in a moment, oligopoly has certain characteristics which make it difficult to come up with hard and fast predictions about the behavior of oligopolistic industries.

1. The basic characteristic of oligopoly is "fewness." Oligopoly exists whenever a few firms dominate the market for a product. When we hear of the "Big Three," "Big Four," or "Big Six," we can be

relatively certain that the industry is oligopolistic. This does not mean, of course, that the Big Three or Four necessarily share the total market. The dominant few may control, say, 70 or 80 percent of a market, with a competitive fringe—a group of smaller firms—sharing the remainder.

When a few firms dominate a market, each of these firms will have a share of the market sufficiently large so that its actions and policies will have repercussions on the other firms. Because each firm supplies a large portion of the total industry output, actions taken by any one firm to improve its share of the market will directly and immediately affect its rivals. Hence, each firm must carefully weigh the expected reactions of its rivals when considering changes in product price, advertising outlays, product quality, and so forth. Such clear-cut *mutual interdependence* is peculiar to oligopoly. It is not present in pure competition or monopolistic competition because of the large numbers of firms involved. The pure monopolist has no need to worry about the reactions of rivals, because he has none. Indeed, it can be said that oligopoly exists whenever the number of sellers is so few that the actions of one will have obvious and significant repercussions on the others. The firms of an oligopolistic industry are all in the same boat. If one rocks the boat, the others will be affected and in all probability will know the identity of the responsible firm and can retaliate.

2. Oligopolists may be producing virtually standardized products or differentiated products. Speaking very generally, those oligopolistic industries which are producing raw materials or semifinished goods are typically offering virtually uniform products to buyers. For example, most metal products—steel, copper, zinc, lead, and aluminum—along with cement, rayon, explosives,industrial alcohol, and some building materials, are virtually uniform goods produced in markets in which a few large firms are dominant. On the other hand, oligopolistic industries producing finished consumer goods are typically offering differentiated products to buyers. Automobiles, tires, petroleum products, soap, cigarettes, fountain pens, breakfast foods, aircraft, farm implements, plus a host of electrical appliances—refrigerators, radios, electric razors, and so forth—are produced by oligopolistic industries wherein product differentiation is considerable.[1]

3. An individual oligopolistic firm's control over price tends to be closely circumscribed by the mutual interdependence which characterizes such markets. Specifically, if a given firm lowers price, it will initially gain sales at the expense of its several rivals. However, these adversely affected rivals will have little choice but to retaliate to recover their shrinking shares of the market; they will match or even undercut the given firm to preserve their market share. The result may be a price war and possibly losses for all firms. Conversely, if a given oligopolist increases his price, rival firms stand to gain sales and profits by adhering to their present prices. That is, a price-boosting oligopolist runs the risk of "pricing himself out of the market" to the benefit of his rivals. For both these reasons there is a strong tendency for firms in oligopolist markets not to alter their prices very frequently.

The potentially adverse effects of price warring or pricing oneself out of the market can be largely avoided by a group of oligopolistic firms through the establishment of some sort of collusive agreement by which all firms either increase or decrease their prices as a group. Under such a collusive arrangement the firms as a group can exert control over price in much the same way that a pure monopolist can.

4. Obstacles to entry are typically formidable in oligopolistic industries. The ownership of strategic patents or essential raw materials by existing firms may virtually prohibit the entry of new firms. Furthermore, the technology of heavy industry may demand that a new competitor be a large-scale producer from the outset, thus ruling out the possibility of a new firm's starting on a small-scale basis and in time expanding into a significant rival of existing firms. In addition, certain advantages of being established—that is, the mere fact that existing firms are producing

[1]Illustrations are from Joe S. Bain, *Pricing, Distribution, and Employment,* rev. ed. (New York: Holt, Rinehart and Winston, Inc., 1953), pp. 273–274, 333.

well-known, highly advertised products and selling them through long-established marketing outlets—may work against the successful entrance of new firms into the industry. Yet, in contrast to pure monopoly, entry is not usually blocked completely in oligopolistic industries. For example, the entry of Sylvania Electric into the electrical equipment industry after World War II presented a formidable rival for General Electric and Westinghouse. Entry into oligopolistic industries is very difficult, but by no means impossible.

5. Oligopolistic industries frequently channel considerable amounts of resources into advertising and other promotional activities. But the type and amount of advertising will depend upon whether or not the firms are producing standardized or differentiated products.

Advertising competition is likely to be strong among oligopolists who are producing differentiated products. For example, each major automobile producer or cigarette manufacturer will have a large budget for convincing the consumer that his particular product is in all ways superior to those of his rivals. Such advertising is likely to be of a highly competitive ours-is-better-than-theirs nature. On the other hand, public relations advertising is the bill of fare for oligopolists who are producing virtually standardized products. United States Steel does not try to convince the public that its sheet steel is superior to that produced by Republic, Bethlehem, or any of its other rivals. Skilled buyers who purchase the raw or fabricated steel products from these firms know that any differences are negligible. Hence, advertising in such industries is to keep the company in the public's eye, to convince the public that big business is an essential cog in the American economy, and so forth.

Quality competition may be intense under oligopoly, particularly so when product differentiation prevails. The research and design departments of many oligopolistic industries are becoming increasingly important over the years. Indeed, it is through research and rapid product development that the entry of potential rivals into the industry may be thwarted.

A good many American industries fall under the heading of oligopoly. As a matter of fact, most of those industries which come to mind when we think of big business are some form or another of oligopoly. In addition to the specific examples previously mentioned, Table 30•1 contains a list of industries which are oligopolistic.

Imperfect competition

We shall find it convenient from time to time to distinguish between the characteristics of a purely competitive market and those of all other basic market arrangements—pure monopoly, monopolistic competition, and oligopoly. To facilitate such comparisons we shall employ "imperfect competition" as a generic term to designate all those market structures which deviate from the purely competitive market model.

THE BUYER'S SIDE OF THE MARKET

The preceding definitions of the four basic market models are couched in terms of the seller's side of the market. The same variety of market arrangements can and does exist on the buying or demand side. Here, however, the classification is almost exclusively based on the number of buyers. For example, a very large number of purchasers obviously means pure competition on the buying side of the market. *Monopsony* describes the situation in which there is only one buyer. When a few buyers dominate a market, *oligopsony* exists. *Monopsonistic competition* designates the presence of a fairly large number of buyers.

With the selling and buying sides of the market placed together as in Figure 23•1, it is easy to recognize that an almost infinite number of seller-buyer relationships can exist. A few representative examples will help underscore this point. The public utilities field is usually characterized by pure monopoly on the selling side and pure competition on the buying side. The market for raw tobacco links a large number of purely competitive tobacco farmers on the selling side with a few large buyers—American, Liggett and Myers, Lorillard, and Reynolds—dominating the demand side. Where a strong union exists, specific labor markets often approximate *bilateral monopoly*—

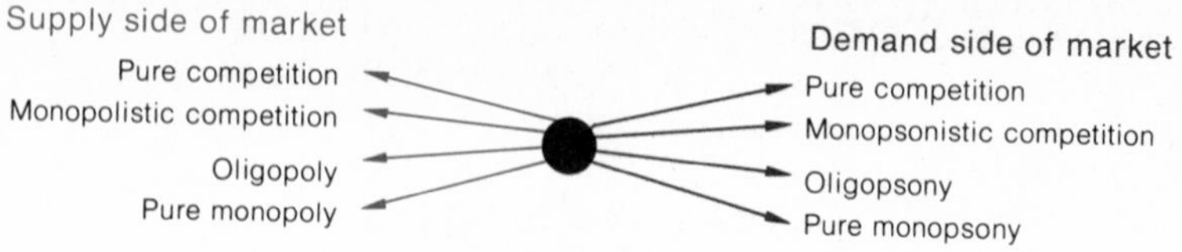

FIGURE 23 · 1 SOME BASIC MARKET RELATIONSHIPS

The four basic market models are pertinent to both the selling and buying sides of markets; this suggests the existence of a very large number of selling-buying relationships.

pure monopoly on one side and pure monopsony on the other. The local union is the "seller" of labor services, and the company is the single buyer. In the "original equipment" segment of the automobile tire market, we have oligopsonistic buyers—General Motors, Ford, and Chrysler—linked with oligopolistic sellers—Goodyear, Firestone, U.S. Rubber, and B. F. Goodrich. A similar arrangement exists in the market for tin plate—a few large steel companies are the sole producers, and two large tin-can manufacturers are the major buyers. And so it goes. When all the hybrid cases falling between the four basic market models are taken into account, it is clear that the number of possible market arrangements can be and actually is extremely large.

OTHER COMPETITIVE DIMENSIONS

It is important that we qualify and amend the foregoing definitions and explanations of the various market models in several ways.

Geographic factor

In practice the competitiveness of an industry or firm is a geographic phenomenon. That is, the degree of competition in a particular industry depends upon the size of the market. Although a given city may have seventy or eighty grocery stores, a particular supermarket in a suburban area may, for all practical purposes, be competing only with three other chain stores and one or two independent corner groceries. Similarly, commercial banking appears to be highly competitive at first glance—after all, there are some 13,700 banks in our economy providing essentially identical services. But to the farmer in Podunk Center, Iowa, borrowing from the Chase National Bank in New York City or the Bank of America in California is out of the question. In negotiating a loan Farmer Jones will look to the Podunk Center State Bank or possibly one or two of the larger banks in a nearby city. These comments correctly imply that improved transportation tends to strengthen competition; more efficient, lower-cost transportation and communication bring geographically remote producers into competition with one another.

In short, before hastily labeling an industry as "competitive" or "monopolistic," we must be very sure that we have properly delineated the geographic boundaries of the market. The number of firms alone is not a sufficient criterion by which to gauge the competitiveness of an industry; proximity is important, too.

Interindustry competition

It is important to recognize the significance of interindustry or interproduct competition. Although a few firms may be the only ones producing a specific product, they may face rather severe rivalry from other somewhat distinct products. Illustrations of such interproduct competition are numerous. The aluminum industry is a strong oligopoly with three firms—Alcoa, Reynolds, and Kaiser—dominating the market. Buyers who must use aluminum have no choice but to do business with one of these three industrial giants. However, in many cases other

materials—steel, copper, and even wood or plastics—are suitable substitutes for aluminum. Hence, steel competes with aluminum in the manufacturing of many automobile parts. Aluminum and copper hotly contest the market for transmission lines. Aluminum battles both steel and wood in the construction field. Pricewise, these comments add up to the fact that the control over price which the Big Three of the aluminum industry possess is subject to limitations dictated by the prices of distinct but nevertheless competing products. Another example: The Big Two of the tin-can industry—American Can and Continental Can—dominate over 80 percent of their market. From within the industry they face little serious competition. But from without they face the competition of glass, plastic, and paper containers.

Nonprice competition

This is a convenient juncture at which to restate a point emphasized earlier: Competition is something more than the willingness and ability to cut prices. Competition in other areas than price may be vigorous and important in an industry. Variations in product quality, advertising and promotional activities, and so forth are important elements of competition which may supplement or, in some cases, supplant price competition.

Technological advance

The previous explanations of the four basic market models tend to classify the various markets at some particular *point* in time. Hence, they neglect an important competitive force which only functions over a *period* of time. That competitive force is technological advance. The development of new products and new techniques of production can result in new competition for producers who previously enjoyed a considerable degree of monopoly power. Thus the leading proponent of the role of technological advance as a competitive force has argued that[2]

> In capitalist reality . . . it is . . . competition from the new commodity, the new technology, the new source of supply, the new type of organization (the largest-scale unit of control for instance)—competition which commands a decisive cost or quality advantage and which strikes not at the margins of the profits and the outputs of the existing firms but at their foundations and their very lives. This kind of competition is . . . so . . . important that it becomes a matter of comparative indifference whether competition in the ordinary sense functions more or less promptly; the powerful lever that in the long run expands output and brings down prices is in any case made of other stuff.
>
> . . . that competition of the kind we now have in mind acts not only when in being but also when it is merely an ever-present threat. It disciplines before it attacks. The businessman feels himself to be in a competitive situation even if he is alone in his field. . . . In many cases, though not in all, this will in the long run enforce behavior very similar to the perfectly competitive pattern.

An example or two may help to underscore this point. For over a decade a single firm enjoyed the position of a pure monopolist in the production of rayon. Its profits, enormous by any standard, were the results of the successful competition this innovation provided for other textiles. But more recently the development of acetates, nylon, acrilon, and other "miracle fibers" has in turn provided considerable competition for rayon.[3] In a similar manner the rapid development of the dehydrated and quick-frozen food industries during World War II has permitted an intensification of the competition which paper, fiber, and plastic containers provides for the Big Two of the tin-can industry.

DETERMINANTS OF MARKET STRUCTURE

Agriculture is an almost purely competitive industry. The clothing industry fits roughly into the mold of monopolistic competition. The steel and automobile industries are obviously oligopolistic. American Telephone and Telegraph nationally, and public utilities

[2]Joseph A. Schumpeter, *Capitalism, Socialism, and Democracy,* 3d ed. (New York: Harper & Row, Publishers, Incorporated, 1950), pp. 84–85.

[3]A. D. H. Kaplan, *Big Enterprise in a Competitive System,* rev. ed. (Washington: The Brookings Institution, 1964), p. 185.

locally, approximate pure monopolies. What forces explain the emergence of these different market structures? What factors have caused agriculture to remain highly competitive and the automobile industry, spiced in its infancy with seventy-odd producers, now to be a tight oligopoly dominated by the Big Three? Although there exists no short, easy answer to these questions, we can put our fingers on some of the more important forces which historically have played significant roles in determining the competitive structures of the various American industries. Generally speaking, such factors as (1) legislation and government policy, (2) the policies and practices of business firms, (3) technological considerations, and (4) institutions and characteristics inherent in the capitalistic ideology go far to explain the variety of market structures which characterizes American capitalism.

Legislation and government policy

Government has promoted both monopoly and competition. By issuing *exclusive franchises* to so-called natural monopolies (for example, public utilities), government has purposely created many pure monopolies in industries which might otherwise have attained some degree of competition. Federal government commissions—the Interstate Commerce Commission, Civil Aeronautics Board, and Federal Communications Commission—play the major role in determining the degree of competition in the land and air transportation, radio, and television industries. Similarly, *patent laws* have promoted monopoly by giving innovating firms the exclusive right to manufacture a product for extended periods of time. *High tariffs* and other artificial barriers to international trade have promoted and preserved monopoly power in many domestic industries. On the other hand, there is but little doubt that the liberal Homestead Act of 1862 provided a competitive base for American agriculture. *Antitrust legislation*—the Sherman and Clayton Acts—is explicitly designed to curb the abuses of monopoly power.

We find here seemingly inconsistent government policies; but this inconsistency can be at least partly explained. Although government has pursued a generally antimonopolistic social policy, it simultaneously seeks other social objectives. One of these goals is the promotion of technological advance—an aim which patent legislation tends to foster. And in the case of public utilities, competition has simply not functioned effectively; here government has condoned and promoted monopoly, but has then provided regulatory commissions designed to prevent the abuse of this government-sponsored monopoly power.

Business policies and practices

The practices and policies pursued by various firms and industries can also be critical in determining the structure of industry. In some industries mergers, consolidations, and the development of holding companies have pushed in the direction of oligopoly or monopoly. The evolution of the corporate form of business enterprise and collusive practices between legally independent firms have played a similar role. In other industries cutthroat competition has resulted in some firms driving others from existence, thereby lowering the number of competitors in the industry. In still other instances firms have acquired ownership or control over vital raw materials so as to eliminate present rivals and destroy the possibility of new firms coming into being. These practices and developments, however, have occurred unevenly among various industries, causing some to move in the direction of monopoly and others to remain quite highly competitive.

Technology

Technology has undoubtedly become an increasingly important determinant of industrial structure. In a good many industries technology has developed to the point where the existence of large industrial giants is necessary if efficient low-cost production is to be achieved. Technology has given rise to economies of mass production which only large

producers can realize. This means that, given consumer demand, efficient production necessitates the existence of a small number of large producers rather than a large number of small producers. It is thus that technological advance has "forced" the market structure of many "heavy" industries—for example, the automobile, steel, and aluminum industries—in the direction of oligopoly. Economists differ in evaluating the extent to which technological factors require bigness; we shall examine the conflicting views in greater detail in Chapter 35.

In some industries technological advance has worked toward the same end but in a somewhat different manner. Superior research on product development has permitted some firms to outgrow and often eliminate less progressive rivals. Furthermore, this tendency is frequently cumulative; by gaining a larger share of the market through its superior research, a firm realizes the financial rewards that facilitate a widening of the technological advantages which it possesses over its rivals.

Capitalistic institutions

We must be reminded that the institutions of American capitalism are permissive of the concentration of economic power and the development of oligopoly and monopoly. The relatively free, individualistic economic environment of the economy is a fertile ground for the most efficient, the most courageous, the most fortunate, or the most crafty producer to conquer his rivals in an effort to free himself from the regulatory powers of competition. Freedom of contract, private property, and inheritance rights have also contributed to the concentration of economic power. And, too, the business cycle has probably abetted the tendency toward monopoly. As one scholar puts it:[4]

> Weaklings may still fail, and disappear, especially in more difficult times. Good times make it easy to finance consolidations, and tempting for the strong company to expand and the weak to sell out. Thus, both adversity and prosperity work alike to reduce the number of firms in an industry.

[4] John K. Galbraith, *American Capitalism*, rev. ed. (Boston: Houghton Mifflin Company, 1956), p. 35.

SUMMARY

1. American industry is characterized by differing degrees of competition. The market models of ***a.*** pure competition, ***b.*** pure monopoly, ***c.*** monopolistic competition, and ***d.*** oligopoly are classifications into which most industries can be fitted with reasonable accuracy. These market models, however, are merely first approximations of reality.

2. Table 23·1 provides a convenient summary of the major characteristics of these four market models.

3. Similar market classifications, based essentially upon numbers, are applied to the buying, or demand, side of the market.

4. The economist's definitions of the four market models focus attention upon ***a.*** the number of firms, ***b.*** the degree of product differentiation, and ***c.*** the ease or difficulty encountered by new firms in entering the industry. However, certain other important factors which have a bearing upon the competitive nature of an industry must also be considered: ***a.*** In practice, any meaningful description of the market structure of an industry requires a proper definition of the geographic limits of the market. ***b.*** Interindustry or interproduct competition is a significant force in many markets which might otherwise appear to be lacking in competition. ***c.*** Nonprice competition may be an important supplement to price competition. ***d.*** Technological advance, working as a competitive force through time, often undermines existing industries characterized by strong monopolistic elements.

5. Legislation, government policies, research and technological development, industry practices, and a variety of other factors have all played significant roles in determining the present structure of American industry.

TABLE 23·1 CHARACTERISTICS OF THE FOUR BASIC MARKET MODELS

Characteristic	Market model			
	Pure competition	Monopolistic competition	Oligopoly	Pure monopoly
Number of firms	A very large number	Many	Few	One
Type of product	Standardized	Differentiated	Standardized or differentiated	Unique; no close substitutes
Control over price	None	Some, but within rather narrow limits	Circumscribed by mutual interdependence; considerable with collusion	Considerable
Conditions of entry	Very easy, no obstacles	Relatively easy	Significant obstacles present	Blocked
Nonprice competition	None	Considerable emphasis on advertising, brand names, trademarks, etc.	Typically a great deal, particularly with product differentiation	Mostly public relations advertising
Example	Agriculture	Retail trade, dresses, shoes	Steel, automobiles, farm implements, many household appliances	AT&T, local utilities

QUESTIONS AND STUDY SUGGESTIONS

1. Under which of the four market classifications discussed in the chapter do each of the following most accurately fit: *a.* a supermarket located in your home town; *b.* the steel industry; *c.* a Kansas wheat farm; *d.* the commercial bank in which you or your family has an account; *e.* the automobile industry. In each case justify your classification. In making your classifications, specify assumptions you have made about the geographic limits of the various markets.

2. "Purely competitive producers have no price policy, but monopolistically competitive, oligopolistic, and purely monopolistic firms do." Explain.

3. In 1950 Crawford H. Greenewalt, president of E. I. du Pont de Nemours & Company, made the following statements before a House committee which was studying the monopoly problem:

> The difference between three and one [firms] is very substantial. It is the difference between monopoly and no monopoly.

> Oligopoly . . . to me is meaningless, because there is either competition or there is not. If there is competition, the public interest is being served.

What differences, if any, can you detect between Mr. Greenewalt's definition of "competition" and the economist's definition of "pure competition"? Do you feel that all industries can be meaningfully categorized as competitive or not competitive? Explain your answers.

4. A single farmer is "at the mercy of the market" in that he must regard the market price for his products as being fixed. Yet agricultural prices are very flexible. Reconcile these two statements.

5. What is interindustry competition? How important is it in each of the following industries? In each case specify the competing products or industries.

a. Automobile
b. Railway
c. Cement
d. Steel
e. Coal
f. Glass container

6. What is nonprice competition? How prevalent do you think nonprice competition to be in the industries mentioned in questions 1 and 5?

7. Why doesn't a purely competitive producer advertise his product?

8. "Competition should be judged solely on the basis of the number of firms in the industry; the larger the number, the greater the competition." Critically evaluate.

9. What are some of the major forces which determine the market structure of industries? Drawing on your knowledge of American history, what is the relative significance of these forces in explaining the market structures of the following industries?

a. Automobile
b. Television
c. Tobacco
d. Steel
e. Petroleum
f. Agriculture
g. Chemical

Be as specific as you can in your answers.

10. "Technological advance has both encouraged and limited the development of monopoly." Do you agree? Explain.

SELECTED REFERENCES

Averitt, Robert T.: *The Dual Economy: The Dynamics of American Industry Structure* (New York: W. W. Norton & Company, Inc., 1968).

Dean, Joel: *Managerial Economics* (Englewood Cliffs, N.J.: Prentice-Hall, Inc., 1951), chap. 2.

Due, John F., and Robert W. Clower: *Intermediate Economic Analysis,* 5th ed. (Homewood, Ill.: Richard D. Irwin, Inc., 1966), chap. 3.

Fellner, William: *Modern Economic Analysis* (New York: McGraw-Hill Book Company, 1960), chap. 17.

Heilbroner, Robert L.: *The Making of Economic Society* (Englewood Cliffs, N.J.: Prentice-Hall, Inc., 1962), chap. 5

Weiss, Leonard W.: *Economics and American Industry* (New York: John Wiley & Sons, Inc., 1961), chap. 1.

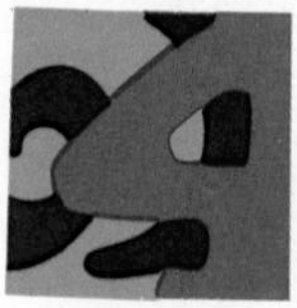

DEMAND, SUPPLY, AND ELASTICITY: SOME APPLICATIONS

In Chapter 4 we familiarized ourselves with the rudiments of demand and supply analysis. In the present chapter we seek a more sophisticated understanding of demand and supply. Specifically, the tasks of this chapter are threefold. First, a brief summary of the elements of demand and supply analysis is presented. Second, we shall consider the concept of elasticity as applied to both demand and supply. Third, some specific applications of demand and supply analysis are discussed.

DEMAND, SUPPLY, AND MARKET PRICE[1]

Demand and supply both refer to schedules. The demand schedule shows the relationship between various possible prices of a product and the quantities which consumers will purchase at each of these prices (columns 1 and 2, Table 24·1). The price–quantity-demanded relationship thus portrayed is an inverse one. Consumers typically buy less at a high price than at a low price. This commonsense relationship is called the *law of demand.* Graphically the demand curve is downsloping (*DD* in Figure 24·1).

The supply schedule embodies the relationship between possible product prices and the quantities which producers will supply at each of those prices (columns 2 and 3, Table 24·1). The relationship between price and quantity supplied is a direct one. The *law of supply* states that producers will find it profitable to devote more resources to the production of a good when its price is high than they will when it is low. When graphed, this direct relationship results in an upsloping supply curve (*SS* in Figure 24·1).

The intersection of demand and supply determines the market, or equilibrium, price and quantity. Both Table 24·1 and Figure 24·1 clearly show that the demand and supply data here assumed result in an equilibrium price of $3 and an equilibrium quantity

[1]This brief review is not a substitute for Chapter 4. The student is strongly urged to reread Chapter 4 at this point.

TABLE 24·1 THE DEMAND FOR, AND SUPPLY OF, CORN (*hypothetical data*)

(1) Total quantity demanded per week	(2) Price per bushel	(3) Total quantity supplied per week	(4) Surplus (+) or shortage (−) (arrow indicates effect on price)
2,000	$5	12,000	+10,000↓
4,000	4	10,000	+ 6,000↓
7,000	3	7,000	0
11,000	2	4,000	− 7,000↑
16,000	1	1,000	−15,000↑

of 7,000 units. Competition guarantees that any other price will be unstable. The shortages which accompany below-equilibrium prices will prompt competing buyers to bid up the price, as consumers want to avoid doing without the product. A rising price will (1) induce firms to allocate more resources to the production of this good and (2) ration some consumers out of the market. These adjustments are illustrated in Figure 24·1 by the arrows moving up the supply curve and up the demand curve respectively. The surpluses which result at any above-equilibrium price will induce competing sellers to shade their prices to work off these excess stocks. The falling price will (1) prompt firms to allocate fewer resources to this line of production and (2) ration some additional buyers into the market. These adjustments are shown by the arrows moving down the supply and demand curves respectively in Figure 24·1.

Changes in the determinants of either demand or supply can cause the demand and supply schedules (curves) to shift. Variations in consumer tastes, incomes, the prices of related goods, consumer expectations, and the number of buyers in the market all will account for shifts in demand. Changes in any of those factors which affect production costs will cause supply to shift. The relationship between a change in demand and the resulting changes in equilibrium price and quantity is a direct one. An inverse relationship exists between a change in supply and the ensuing change in price. However, the relationship between a change in supply and the ensuing change in quantity is direct.

ELASTICITY OF DEMAND

The law of demand tells us that consumers will respond to a price decline by buying more of a product. But the degree of responsiveness of consumers to a price change may vary considerably from product to product. Furthermore, we will find that consumer responsiveness typically varies substantially between different price ranges for the same product.

Economists measure how responsive, or sensitive, consumers are to a change in the price of a product by the concept of *elasticity.* The demand for some products is such that consumers are relatively responsive to price changes; price changes give rise to very considerable changes in the quantity purchased. The demand for such products is said to be *elastic.* For other products consumers are relatively unresponsive to price changes; that is, price changes result in modest changes in the amount purchased. In such cases demand is *inelastic.*

The elasticity formula

Economists measure the degree of elasticity or inelasticity by the *elasticity coefficient*, or E_d, in this formula:

$$E_d = \frac{\text{percentage change in quantity demanded}}{\text{percentage change in price}}$$

One calculates these *percentage* changes, of course, by dividing the change in price by the original price and the change in quantity demanded by the original quantity demanded. Thus we can restate our formula as

$$E_d = \frac{\text{change in quantity demanded}}{\text{original quantity demanded}} \div \frac{\text{change in price}}{\text{original price}}$$

But why use percentages rather than absolute amounts in measuring consumer responsiveness? The answer is that if we simply use absolute changes, our impression of buyer responsiveness will be arbitrarily affected by the choice of units. To illustrate: If the price of product X falls from \$3 to \$2 and consumers, as a result, increase their purchases from 60 to 100 pounds, we get the impression that consumers are quite sensitive to price changes and therefore that demand is elastic. After all, a price change of "one" has caused a change in the amount demanded of "forty." But by changing the monetary unit from dollars to pennies (why not?) we find a price change of "one hundred" causes a quantity change of "forty," giving the impression of inelasticity. The use of percentage changes avoids this problem. The given price decline is 33 percent whether measured

FIGURE 24·1 THE EQUILIBRIUM PRICE FOR CORN AS DETERMINED BY MARKET DEMAND AND MARKET SUPPLY

Equilibrium price and equilibrium quantity are determined by the intersection of demand *DD* and supply *SS*.

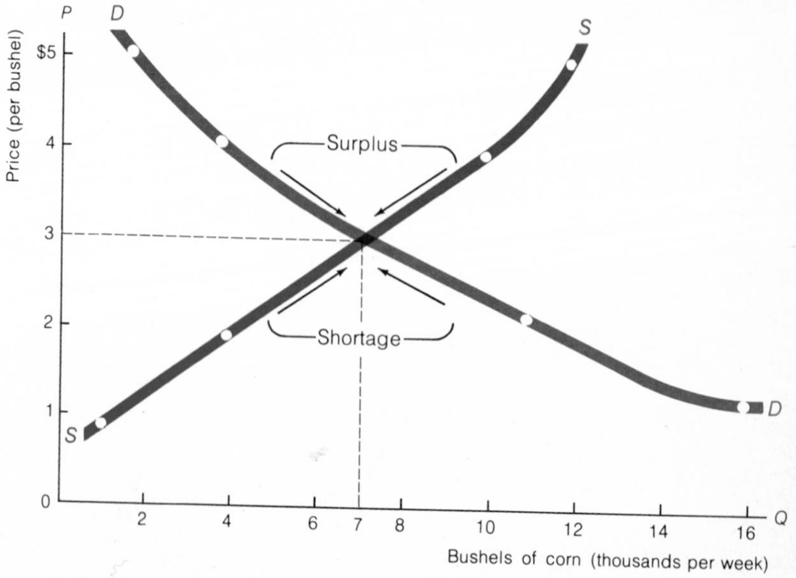

in terms of dollars ($1/$3) or pennies (100¢/300¢).[2]

Now let us interpret our formula. Demand is *elastic* if a given percentage change in price results in a larger percentage change in quantity demanded. Example: If a 2 percent decline in price results in a 4 percent increase in quantity demanded, demand is elastic. In all such cases, where demand is elastic, the elasticity coefficient will obviously be greater than 1. If a given percentage change in price is accompanied by a relatively smaller change in the quantity demanded, demand is *inelastic.* Illustration: If a 3 percent decline in price gives rise to a 1 percent increase in the amount demanded, demand is inelastic. It is apparent that the elasticity coefficient will always be less than 1 when demand is inelastic. The borderline case which separates elastic and inelastic demands occurs where a percentage change in price and the accompanying percentage change in quantity demanded chance to be equal. For example, a 1 percent drop in price causes a 1 percent increase in the amount sold. This special case is termed *unit elasticity,* because the elasticity coefficient is exactly 1, or unity.

It must be emphasized that when economists say demand is "inelastic," they do not mean consumers are completely unresponsive to a price change. The term *perfectly inelastic* demand designates the extreme situation wherein a change in price results in no change whatsoever in the quantity demanded. Approximate example: An acute diabetic's demand for insulin. A demand curve parallel to the vertical axis—such as D_1 in Figure 24·2—shows this situation graphically. Conversely, when economists say demand is "elastic," they do not mean that consumers are completely responsive to a price change. In the extreme situation, wherein there is some small price reduction which would cause buyers to increase their purchases from zero to all they could obtain, we say that demand is *perfectly elastic.* A perfectly elastic demand curve is a line parallel to the horizontal axis; D_2 in Figure 24·2 is illustrative. We shall find later in this chapter that such a demand curve applies to a firm which is selling in a perfectly competitive market.

FIGURE 24·2 PERFECTLY INELASTIC AND ELASTIC DEMAND

A perfectly inelastic demand curve, D_1, graphs as a line parallel to the vertical axis; a perfectly elastic demand curve, D_2, is drawn parallel to the horizontal axis.

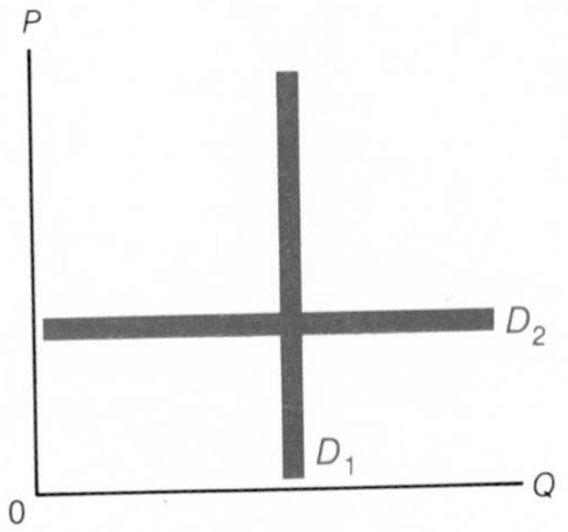

Refinement: midpoints formula

An annoying problem arises in applying the elasticity formula. To illustrate: In calculating the elasticity coefficient for corn for the $5–$4 price range in Table 24·2, should we use the $5–2,000-bushel price-quantity combination or the $4–4,000-bushel combination as a point of reference in calculating the percentage changes in price and quantity which the elasticity formula requires? Our choice will influence the outcome. Using the $5–2,000-bushel reference point, we find that the percentage decrease in price is 20 percent and the percentage increase in quantity is 100 percent. Substituting in the formula, the elas-

[2] The careful reader will note that the elasticity coefficient of demand will always be negative. This is so for the obvious reason that the demand curve is downsloping; that is, price and quantity are inversely related. Economists are generally inclined to ignore the minus sign (as we do here) in order to avoid an ambiguity which might otherwise arise. It can be confusing to say that an elasticity coefficient of −4 is greater than one of −2; this possible confusion can be avoided if we simply say a coefficient of 4 indicates greater elasticity than one of 2. This difficulty does not arise with supply because price and quantity are directly related.

TABLE 24·2 ELASTICITY OF DEMAND AS MEASURED BY THE TOTAL-RECEIPTS TEST AND THE ELASTICITY COEFFICIENT (*hypothetical data*)

(1) Total quantity demanded per week	(2) Price per bushel	(3) Total revenue (expenditures)	(4) Total-revenue test	(5) Elasticity coefficient E_d (approximate)
2,000	$5	$10,000		
			Elastic	$\frac{2,000}{6,000/2} \div \frac{1}{9/2} = 3.00$
4,000	4	16,000		
			Elastic	$\frac{3,000}{11,000/2} \div \frac{1}{7/2} = 1.91$
7,000	3	21,000		
			Elastic	$\frac{4,000}{18,000/2} \div \frac{1}{5/2} = 1.11$
11,000	2	22,000		
			Inelastic	$\frac{5,000}{27,000/2} \div \frac{1}{3/2} = 0.56$
16,000	1	16,000		

ticity coefficient is 100/20 or 5. But using the $4–4,000-bushel reference point, we find that the percentage increase in price is 25 percent and the percentage decline in quantity is 50 percent. The elasticity coefficient is therefore 50/25, or 2, in this case. Although the formula indicates that demand is elastic in both cases, the two solutions involve a considerable difference in the degree of elasticity. In other instances—experiment, for example, with the $3–$2 price range—the formula may indicate a slightly elastic demand for one price-quantity combination and slight inelasticity of demand for the other.

Economists have reached a workable compromise to this problem by using the averages of the two prices and the two quantities under consideration for reference points. In the $5–$4 price range case, the price reference is $4.50 and the quantity reference 3,000 bushels. The percentage change in price is now about 22 percent and the percentage change in quantity about 67 percent, giving us an elasticity coefficient of 3. Instead of gauging elasticity at either one of the extremes of this price-quantity range, this solution estimates elasticity at the midpoint of the $5–$4 price range. More positively stated, we can refine our earlier statement of the elasticity formula to read

$$E_d = \frac{\text{change in quantity}}{\text{sum of quantities}/2} \div \frac{\text{change in price}}{\text{sum of prices}/2}$$

Substituting data for the $5–$4 price range, we get

$$E_d = \frac{2,000}{6,000/2} \div \frac{1}{9/2} = 3.00$$

In column 5 of Table 24·2 we have calculated the elasticity coefficients for the demand data of Table 24·1, using the midpoints formula. The reader should verify each of these calculations.

The total-revenue test

Perhaps the easiest way to gauge whether demand is elastic or inelastic is to note what happens to total revenue or receipts—total expenditures from the buyer's viewpoint—when product price changes.

1. If demand is *elastic,* a decline in price will result in an increase in total revenue. Why? Because even though a lesser price is being received per unit, enough additional units are now being sold to more than make up for the lower price. This is illustrated in Figure 24·3*a* for the \$5–\$4 price range of our demand curve from Table 24·1. Total revenue, of course, is price times quantity. Hence, the area shown by the rectangle OP_1AQ_1 is total revenue (\$10,000) when price is P_1 (\$5) and quantity demanded is Q_1 (2,000 bushels). Now when price declines to P_2 (\$4), causing the quantity demanded to increase to Q_2 (4,000 bushels), total revenue changes to OP_2BQ_2 (\$16,000), which is obviously larger than OP_1AQ_1. It is larger because the *loss* in revenue due to the lower price per unit (area P_2P_1AC) is *less* than the *gain* in revenue due to the larger sales (area Q_1CBQ_2) which accompanies the lower price. This reasoning is reversible: If demand is elastic, a price increase will reduce total revenue. Why? Because the *gain* in total revenue caused by the higher unit price (area P_2P_1AC) is less than the *loss* in revenue associated with the accompanying fall in sales (Q_1CBQ_2).

2. If demand is *inelastic,* a price decline will cause total revenue to fall. The modest increase in sales which occurs will be insufficient to offset the decline in revenue per unit, and the net result is that total revenue declines. This situation exists for the \$2–\$1 price range of our demand curve, as shown in Figure 24 · 3*b*. Initially total revenue is OP_4FQ_4 (\$22,000) when price is P_4 (\$2) and quantity demanded is Q_4 (11,000 bushels). If we reduce price to P_5 (\$1), quantity demanded will increase to Q_5 (16,000 bushels). Total revenue will change to OP_5GQ_5 (\$16,000), which is obviously less than OP_4FQ_4. It is smaller because the loss in revenue due to the lower unit price (area P_5P_4FH) is larger than the *gain* in revenue due to the accompanying increase in sales (area Q_4HGQ_5). Again our analysis is reversible: If demand is inelastic, a price increase will increase total revenue.

3. In the special case of unit elasticity, an increase or decrease in price will leave total revenue un-

FIGURE 24 · 3 ELASTICITY AND TOTAL REVENUE

If demand is elastic, as in the \$5–\$4 price range in (*a*), a change in price will cause total revenue to change in the opposite direction. Conversely, if demand is inelastic, as in the \$2–\$1 price range in (*b*), price and total revenue will move in the same direction.

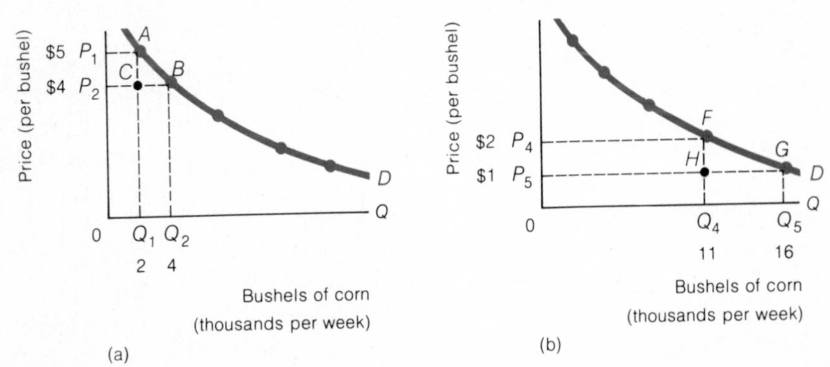

changed. The loss in revenue due to a lower unit price will be exactly offset by the gain in revenue brought about by the accompanying increase in sales. Conversely, the gain in revenue due to a higher unit price will be exactly offset by the loss in revenue associated with the accompanying decline in the amount demanded.

Columns 3 and 4 of Table 24·2 apply the total-revenue test to the entire demand curve for corn.

Characteristics

The alert reader may have detected two subtle but notable characteristics of elasticity from our applications of the elasticity formula and the total-revenue tests. First, as Table 24·2 indicates, elasticity typically varies over the different price ranges of the same demand schedule or curve. In the case of the demand curve for corn, demand is considerably more elastic at higher prices than at low prices. Crudely stated, this correctly suggests that as the price of a product falls, sales will increase to the saturation point, at which consumers are virtually "filled up" on the product. When this is the case, further price cuts will not induce buyers to take much more. Conversely, when prices are already relatively high, further price increases will induce buyers to seek out substitute products or do without, causing relatively sharp declines in sales. There is a tendency for most demand curves to be elastic at high prices and inelastic at low prices.

In the second place, the graphic appearance of a demand curve is *not* a sound basis upon which to judge its elasticity. For example, in Figure 24·2 we find that because the demand curve has a steeper slope at relatively higher prices and a flatter slope at relatively lower prices, one is tempted to associate an inelastic demand with high prices and an elastic demand with low prices. But this is dangerous reasoning. Have we not just discovered that the elasticity formula and the total-revenue test indicate that the reverse is true? The catch lies in the fact that the flatness or steepness of a demand curve is based upon absolute changes in price and quantity, while elasticity has to do with relative changes in price and quantity. The fact that slope and elasticity are quite different can also be made quite clear by calculating elasticity for various price-quantity combinations on a straight-line (constant slope) demand curve. Question 15 at the end of this chapter is relevant.

Determinants of elasticity of demand

What makes the demand for any specific product elastic or inelastic? Generally speaking, the elasticity of demand for any product is greater (1) the larger the number of good substitutes available, (2) the larger the item as a part of one's total budget, and (3) the more the product is regarded as a luxury item and therefore dispensable. A couple of illustrations will help.

The demand for salt tends to be highly inelastic on all three counts. There are simply no good substitutes for salt to which consumers can turn if its price rises from, say, 15 cents to 20 cents per pound. Furthermore, a household's expenditures on salt are such a small fraction of a family's weekly or monthly budget that the total impact of this price increase is negligible for all practical purposes. And, finally, the product is a necessity; unsalted cooking leaves much to be desired. On the other hand, the demand for a brand X stereophonic phonograph may be relatively elastic. There are many good substitutes available in the form of competing brands of stereo, not to mention FM radios. The price of the item is large in relation to one's budget, so a given percentage change in price will have a significant impact dollarwise upon that budget. And to many families a stereo phonograph is something of a luxury and therefore an expendable item in their budget.

Other factors also influence elasticity. Consumers are creatures of habit. It is only over a period of time that they alter their customary expenditure patterns in response to given price changes. Demand therefore tends to be more elastic in the long run than in the short run. Furthermore, the durability of some

products has a bearing upon the elasticity of the demand for them. Few consumers actually face the choice of doing without a refrigerator or automobile. The question is rather one of repairing your old refrigerator or car or buying new ones. Repairing older durable goods is frequently a very good substitute for buying a new model. Durability therefore tends to make demand more elastic than would otherwise be the case.

In Chapter 31 we shall discover that a somewhat different group of factors determines the elasticity of demand for resources.

Some practical applications

The concept of elasticity of demand is something more than a theoretical notion designed to confuse unwary students. It is a notion of great practical significance. Some examples will make this evident.

In the late 1950s the United Automobile Workers contended that automobile manufacturers should raise wages and simultaneously cut automobile prices. Arguing that the elasticity of demand for automobiles was about 4, the UAW concluded that a price cut would help check inflation, boost the total receipts of manufacturers, and preserve or even increase the profits of producers. A spokesman for the Ford Motor Company, however, claimed that available studies suggest an elasticity of demand for automobiles in the 0.5–1.5 range. He held that price cuts would therefore shrink profits or result in losses for manufacturers. In this case, the elasticity of demand for automobiles was a strategic factor in labor-management relations and wage bargaining.[3]

Another example: Studies indicate that the demand for most farm products is highly inelastic. As a result, increases in the output of farm products due to a good growing season or productivity increases depress both the prices of farm products and the total receipts (incomes) of farmers. For farmers the inelastic nature of the demand for their products means that a bumper crop may be a mixed blessing. For policy makers it means that higher farm incomes depend upon the restriction of farm output.

Finally, the impact of automation, that is, of rapid technological advance, upon the level of employment depends in part upon the elasticity of demand for the product being manufactured. Suppose a firm installs new laborsaving machinery, resulting in the technological unemployment of, say, 500 workers. Suppose too that a part of the cost reduction resulting from this technological advance is passed on to consumers in the form of reduced product prices. Now the effect of this price reduction upon the firm's sales and therefore the quantity of labor it needs will obviously depend upon the elasticity of product demand. An elastic demand might increase sales to the extent that some, all, or even more than the 500 displaced workers are reabsorbed by the firm. An inelastic demand will mean that few, if any, of the displaced workers will be reemployed, because the increase in the volume of the firm's business will be small.

These examples could be multiplied; we will examine the important question of tax incidence through use of the elasticity concept in a moment. But the main point is clear. Elasticity of demand is vitally important to businessmen, farmers, labor, and government policy makers.

Elasticity of supply

The concept of price elasticity can also be applied to supply. If producers are responsive to price changes, supply is elastic. If they are relatively insensitive to price changes, supply is inelastic.

The elasticity formula is pertinent in determining the degree of elasticity or inelasticity of supply. The only obvious alteration is the substitution of percentage change in quantity supplied for percentage change in quantity demanded.

The main determinant of the elasticity of supply is the amount of *time* which a producer has to respond to a given change in product price. Generally speaking, we can expect a greater output response—and therefore greater elasticity of supply—the longer the amount of time a producer has to adjust to a given price change. Why? Because a producer's response

[3] See the statement by Theodore Yntema, vice president of finance, Ford Motor Company, before the Subcommittee on Antitrust and Monopoly of the Committee on the Judiciary, United States Senate, Feb. 4–5, 1958.

to an increase in the price of product X depends upon his ability to shift resources from the production of other products[4] to the production of X. And the shifting of resources takes time: the greater the time, the greater the resource "shiftability." Hence, the greater will be the output response and the elasticity of supply.

In analyzing the impact of time upon the elasticity of supply economists find it useful to distinguish between the immediate market period, the short run, and the long run.

1. The market period The immediate market period is so short a period of time that producers cannot respond to a change in demand and price. Example: Suppose a small truck farmer brings his entire season's output of tomatoes—one truckload—to market. His supply curve will be perfectly inelastic; he will sell the truckload whether the price is high or low. Why? Because he cannot offer more tomatoes than his one truckload if the price of tomatoes should be higher than he had anticipated. Even though he might like to offer more, tomatoes simply cannot be produced overnight. It will take him another full growing season to respond to a higher-than-expected price by producing more than one truckload. Similarly, because his product is perishable, he cannot withhold it from the market. If the price is lower than he had anticipated, he will still sell the entire truckload. Costs of production, incidentally, will not be important in making this decision. Even though the price of tomatoes may fall far short of his production costs, he will nevertheless sell out to avoid a total loss through spoilage. In a very short period of time, then, our farmer's supply of tomatoes is fixed; he can offer one truckload no matter how high the price. The perishability of his product forces him to sell all no matter how low the price.

Figure 24·4*a* illustrates the truck farmer's perfectly inelastic supply curve in the market period. Note that he and other truck farmers are unable to respond to an assumed increase in demand; they do not have time to increase the amount supplied. The price increase from P_o to P_m simply rations a fixed supply to buyers, but elicits no increase in output.

[4]The prices of which we assume to remain constant.

FIGURE 24·4 TIME AND THE ELASTICITY OF SUPPLY

The greater the amount of time producers have to adjust to a change in demand, the greater will be their output response. In the immediate market period (*a*) there is insufficient time to change output, and so supply is perfectly inelastic. In the short run (*b*) plant capacity is fixed, but output can be altered by changing the intensity of its use; supply is therefore more elastic. In the long run (*c*) all desired adjustments—including changes in plant capacity—can be made, and supply becomes still more elastic.

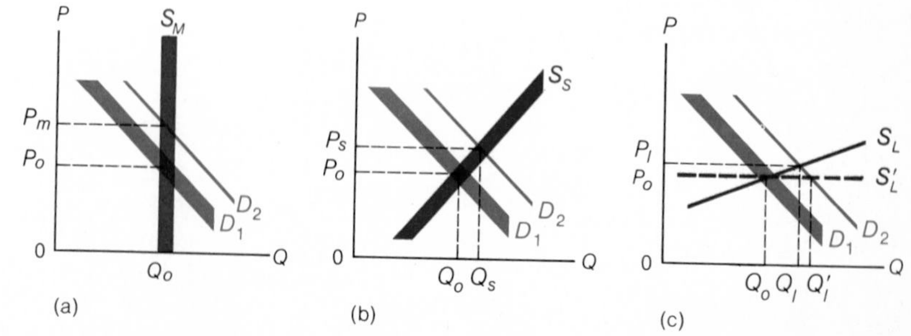

2. The short run In the short run, the plant capacity of individual producers and of the industry is presumed to be fixed. But firms do have time to use their plants more or less intensively. Thus in the short run our truck farmer's plant, which we shall consider as his land and farm machinery, is presumed fixed. But he does have time in the short run to cultivate tomatoes more intensively by applying more labor and more fertilizer and pesticides to his crop. The result is a greater output response to the presumed increase in demand; this greater output response is reflected in a more elastic supply of tomatoes as shown by S_S in Figure 24·4*b*. Note that the increase in demand is met by a larger quantity adjustment (Q_o to Q_s) and a smaller price adjustment (P_o to P_s) than in the market period; price is therefore lower than in the market period.

3. The long run The long run is a time period sufficiently long so that firms can make all desired resource adjustments; individual firms can expand (or contract) their plant capacities, and new firms can enter (or existing firms can leave) the industry. In the "tomato industry" our individual truck farmer is able to acquire additional land and buy more machinery and equipment. Furthermore, more farmers may be attracted to tomato production by the increased demand and higher price. These adjustments mean an even greater supply response, that is, an even more elastic supply curve S_L. The result, shown in Figure 24·4*c*, is a small price effect (P_o to P_l) and a large output effect (Q_o to Q_l) in response to the assumed increase in demand.

The solid supply curve in Figure 24·4*c* entails a new long-run equilibrium price P_l which is somewhat higher than the original price, P_o, in Figure 24·4*a*. Why higher? The presumption is that the expansion of the tomato industry has caused the prices of some relevant resources to rise. The increased demand for fertilizer and farm equipment has pushed their prices up somewhat; the expanded demand for land has increased its value. In short, it is common and realistic to expect the expansion of an industry to result in "increasing costs." Hence, while P_o was sufficient for profitable production in Figure 24·4*a*, a higher price, P_l, is required for profitable production in the enlarged industry. If the tomato industry hired very small or negligible portions of relevant resources, then its increased demand for these inputs would leave their prices unchanged. In this "constant-cost" case the long-run supply curve would be perfectly elastic, as shown by the dashed curve in Figure 24·4*c*. The new price would be equal to the original price, P_o, in Figure 24·4*a*. We shall discuss these cases more fully in Chapter 27.

A final point: You may have noted that no mention has been made of a total-revenue test for elasticity of supply. Indeed, there is none. Supply shows a direct relationship between price and the amount supplied; that is, the supply curve is upsloping. Thus, regardless of the degree of elasticity or inelasticity, price and total receipts will always move together.

APPLICATIONS OF SUPPLY AND DEMAND ANALYSIS

Supply and demand analysis and the elasticity concept will be applied repeatedly in the remainder of this book. Let us strengthen our understanding of these analytical tools and their significance by examining three important applications: (1) legal prices, (2) the incidence of sales taxes, and (3) demand from the viewpoint of the individual firm.

Legal prices

For the most part the price system functions effectively in rationing goods and services and in allocating resources. But at certain times, under certain circumstances, and in certain sectors of the economy, the market fails to perform as well as society feels it might. Specifically, the prices of certain products and resources may be judged by society as being "too high" or "too low." Acting through government, society may attempt to bring a "proper" adjustment in such prices. Let us examine in turn the cases in which prices are felt to be unduly high and unjustly low and, in the process, explore some of the complications entailed in correcting these errant prices.

Price ceilings and shortages With few exceptions, ceiling prices in the United States have been a wartime phenomenon. Direct controls on wages and prices were used extensively during World War II and to a lesser extent during the Korean conflict. Government expenditures for war goods invariably cause the general level of product prices to rise. On the other hand, government spending has varying effects upon the money incomes of households. Generally speaking, workers who are supplying human and property resources essential to the war effort will find their money incomes booming. Those who are offering nonessential resources may experience modest increases or, conceivably, decreases in their money incomes. The net effect of these distortions in money incomes in the midst of product price inflation is obviously an arbitrary redistribution of real incomes. Those essential-resource suppliers whose money incomes race ahead of the level of product prices realize sharply increasing real incomes. Those offering nonessential resources find that the price level spurts ahead of their money incomes to the end that their real incomes are curtailed. Government imposition of ceiling prices is a means of alleviating this arbitrary redistribution of real income so that the real economic cost of the war will be more equitably distributed among the citizenry.

More recently, a few economists have recommended direct wage and price controls as a means of making the goals of full employment and price stability more compatible; that is, they have recommended direct controls as a device for resolving the Phillips curve dilemma (Figure 22·4).

Let us examine the effect of a ceiling price upon a specific product—say, butter. Suppose that the war severely disrupts agriculture in allied countries, obliging the United States to provide large amounts of foodstuffs for foreign peoples and their armies. This obviously increases the demand for American butter in relation to its supply. The resulting market price, let us assume, is $1.20 per pound. The government then imposes a legal price of, say, 90 cents per pound. What will be the effects of this price ceiling? The rationing ability of the market mechanism will be rendered ineffective. Although the equilibrium price ($1.20) would bring quantity demanded and quantity supplied into balance, the imposition of the ceiling price will prompt producers to cut back on the rate of production and will induce consumers to step up their rate of purchase. The net result will be a persistent shortage of the product.[5]

Figure 24·5 illustrates graphically the effect of a ceiling price. Let *SS* and *DD* be the supply and demand curves for butter. The equilibrium price and quantity will be *P* and *Q*, respectively. If government now makes it illegal to sell butter at any price above the ceiling price of P_c the quantity forthcoming onto the market will be only Q_s despite the fact that consumers would purchase Q_d at the ceiling price. The shortage is measured by the excess of Q_d over Q_s.

But ceiling prices pose problems for government. First, effective ceiling prices invite the development of black markets. Such illegal markets, wherein sales

[5] When a shortage exists in a free market, competition among buyers will bid up price. This induces a greater output and simultaneously rations some buyers out of the market, thereby bringing quantity demanded and quantity supplied into equality at the equilibrium price. But with an effective ceiling price, it is of course illegal to bid price up to the equilibrium point.

FIGURE 24 · 5 CEILING PRICES RESULT IN PERSISTENT SHORTAGES

Because the imposition of a price ceiling such as P_c results in a persistent product shortage as indicated by the distance Q_sQ_d, government must undertake the job of rationing the product in order to achieve an equitable distribution.

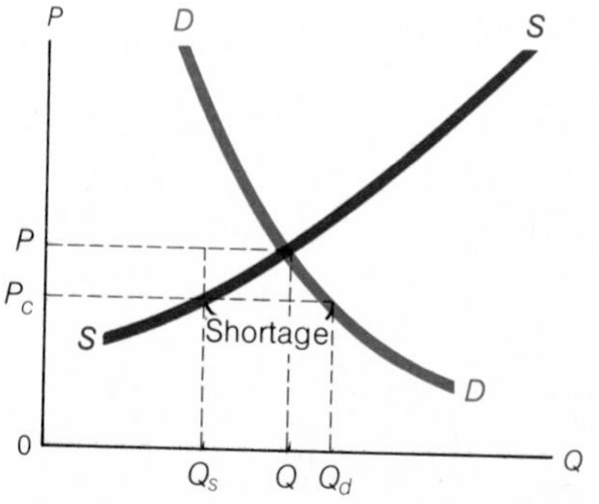

take place at prices above the ceiling price, can be exceedingly difficult to detect and eliminate. Second, government must undertake the job of rationing butter to consumers. Should government take no formal step to ensure a fair distribution of butter, it would probably be sold on a first-come–first-served basis. But such unregulated shortages may result in some consumers doing without any butter while others—those who are first in line or who manage to cultivate a friendship with the corner grocer—get as much as or more than they want. An unregulated shortage may foster the very problem the ceiling price was designed to solve—the inequitable distribution of a product. To avoid a catch-as-catch-can distribution of the product, government must undertake the task of fairly distributing it to consumers. This is done by issuing ration coupons to consumers on an equitable basis.

Price supports and surpluses While the imposition of price ceilings in the United States has been a wartime proposition, this has not been the case with price supports. Price supports have generally been invoked when society has felt that the free functioning of the market system has failed to provide an equitable distribution of income. Minimum-wage legislation and the supporting of agricultural prices are the two most widely discussed examples of government price supports. Let us examine price supports as applied to a specific farm commodity.

Suppose the going market price for corn is $1 per bushel, and as a result of this price, farmers realize extremely low incomes. Government decides to lend a helping hand by establishing a legal supported price of, say, $1.50 per bushel.

What will be the effects? At any price above the equilibrium price, quantity supplied will obviously exceed quantity demanded; there will be a persistent surplus of the product. Farmers will be willing to produce and offer for sale more than private buyers are willing to purchase at the supported price. The size of this surplus will vary directly with the elasticity of demand and supply. The greater the elasticity of demand and supply, the greater the resulting surplus. As is the case with a ceiling price, the rationing ability of the free market obviously has been disrupted by the imposition of a legal price.

Figure 24·6 provides us with a graphic illustration of the effect of a supported price. Let *SS* and *DD* be the supply and demand curves for corn. Equilibrium price and quantity are obviously *P* and *Q*, respectively. If government imposes a supported price of P_s, farmers will be willing to produce Q_s, but private buyers will only take Q_d off the market at that price. The surplus entailed is measured by the excess of Q_s over Q_d.

Government inherits the task of coping with the surplus which a supported price entails. There are two general approaches open to government. First, it might invoke certain programs to restrict supply (for example, acreage allotments) or to increase demand (for example, research on new uses for agricultural products) in order to reduce the difference between the equilibrium price and the supported price and thereby the size of the resulting surplus. If these efforts are not wholly successful, then, secondly, government must simply purchase the surplus output (thereby subsidizing farmers)

FIGURE 24·6 SUPPORTED PRICES RESULT IN PERSISTENT SURPLUSES

A price support such as P_s gives rise to a persistent product surplus as indicated by the distance Q_dQ_s. Government must either purchase these surpluses or take measures to eliminate them by restricting product supply.

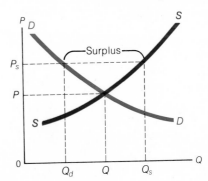

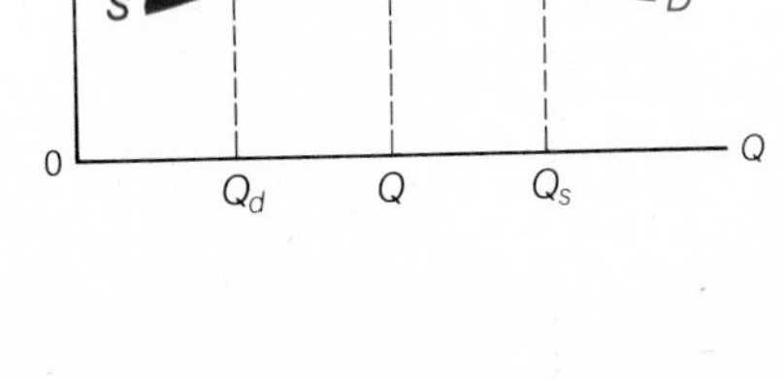

and store or otherwise dispose of it. We shall have more to say about agricultural surpluses in Chapter 36.

Government imposes price ceilings or price supports when hyperinflation or unusually depressed prices are working undue economic hardships on some buyers or sellers and are resulting in arbitrary windfall gains to others. But ceiling and supported prices rob the free-market forces of supply and demand of their ability to bring the supply decisions of producers and the demand decisions of buyers into accord with one another. Freely determined prices automatically ration products to buyers; legal prices do not. Therefore, government must accept the administrative problem of rationing which stems from price ceilings and the problem of buying or eliminating surpluses which price supports entail. Legal prices simply do not work unless accompanied by programs to control consumption or production.

Although legal prices involve knotty problems for government by upsetting the rationing ability of the market mechanism, one must be careful not to prejudge ceilings or supports as undesirable. Remember: Legal prices are designed to correct alleged inequities which free-market prices entail.

Tax incidence

The concepts of supply and demand *and* the notion of elasticity are useful in determining who pays a sales or excise tax. Relying once again upon the market situation shown in Table 24·1, let us suppose government levies a specific sales tax of $1 per bushel on corn. Who actually pays this tax—producers or consumers? In technical terms (Chapter 9), what is the *incidence* of this tax?

The initial effect of the tax is upon supply. Specifically, the tax can be viewed as an addition to the supply price of the product; therefore, the tax shifts the supply curve upward by the amount of the tax. For example, while producers were willing to offer 12,000 bushels of untaxed corn per week at $5 per bushel, they must now receive $6 per bushel—$5 plus the $1 tax—for each taxed bushel. Producers must get $1 more for each quantity supplied in order to receive the same price per unit as they were getting before the tax. In Table 24·1, 12,000 units will now be offered at $6; 10,000 at $5; 7,000 at $4, and so forth. Every quantity supplied entails a price which is higher by the amount of the tax. This tax-caused upshift in the supply curve is shown in Figure 24·5, where S is the untaxed supply curve and S_t is the "after-tax" supply curve.

Careful comparison of after-tax supply with demand indicates that the new equilibrium price is approximately $3.50, in contrast to the before-tax price of $3.00. Thus in this particular case, one-half of the tax is paid by consumers and the other half by producers. Consumers obviously pay 50 cents more per unit and, after remitting the $1 tax per unit to government, producers receive $2.50, or 50 cents less per unit. In this instance consumers and producers share the burden of the tax equally; producers shift half the tax forward to consumers in the form of a higher price and bear the other half themselves. But if the elasticities of demand and supply were different from those shown in Figure 24·7, the incidence of the tax

FIGURE 24·7 THE INCIDENCE OF A SALES TAX

The imposition of a sales tax of a specified amount, say $1 per unit, shifts the supply curve upward by the amount of the tax. This results in a higher price ($3.50) to the consumer and a lower after-tax price ($2.50) to the producer. In this particular case the burden of the tax is shared equally by consumers and producers.

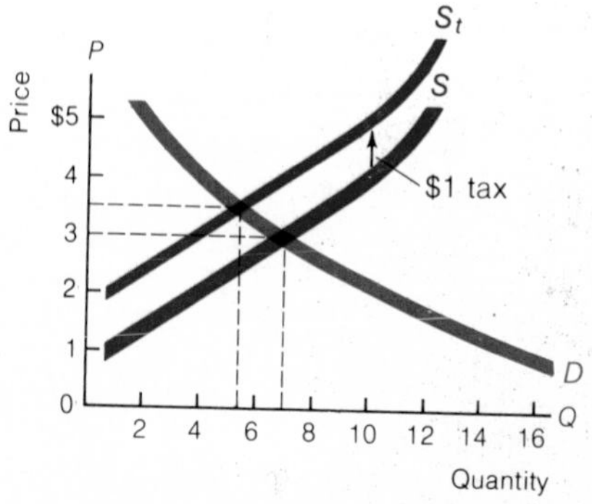

would also be different. Two generalizations are relevant.

1. *Given supply, the more inelastic the demand for the product, the larger the portion of the tax shifted forward to consumers.* The reader should sketch graphically the polar case wherein demand is completely inelastic, in order to demonstrate that the tax will be shifted forward in its entirety to consumers and output will be unchanged. Figure 24·8*a* contrasts the more likely cases where demand might be relatively elastic (D_e) or relatively inelastic (D_i). In the elastic demand case, a small portion of the tax (P_oP_e) is shifted forward, and most of the tax is borne by producers. In the inelastic demand case, most of the tax (P_oP_i) is shifted to consumers, and only a small amount is paid by producers. Note, too, that the reduction in equilibrium quantity is greater the more elastic the demand.

2. *Given demand, the more inelastic the supply, the larger the portion of the tax borne by producers.* Figure 24·8*b* explains this generalization. S_e is a relatively elastic and S_i is a relatively inelastic supply curve. S_{et} and S_{it} show these two curves after the imposition of an identical sales or excise tax. With the inelastic supply, we find that price rises by only P_oP_i; but if supply is elastic, price will rise by the larger amount P_oP_e. Quantity also declines less with an inelastic supply than it does with an elastic supply.

There are numerous additional implications which can be derived from this kind of analysis. The reader is urged to pursue some of these. For example, recalling that subsidies are negative taxes, what generalizations can you derive which relate the incidence of the benefits from a per unit subsidy to the elasticity of demand? The elasticity of supply? Also, you might demonstrate graphically how excise taxes

FIGURE 24·8 ELASTICITY AND THE INCIDENCE OF A SALES TAX

In (*a*) we find that if demand is elastic (D_e), price will rise modestly (P_o to P_e) when a sales or excise tax is imposed; hence the producer bears most of the tax burden. But if demand is inelastic (D_i), price will increase substantially (P_o to P_i) and most of the tax will be shifted to consumers. Part (*b*) demonstrates that a sales or excise tax of a given amount will fall primarily upon producers when supply is inelastic (S_i), but largely upon buyers when supply is elastic (S_e).

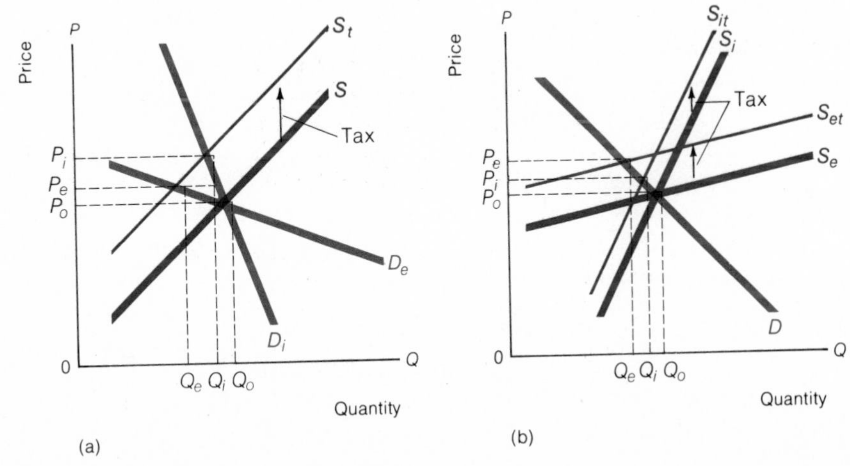

and subsidies can be used to adjust output and therefore improve the allocation of resources when substantial spillover costs and benefits are present in the production or consumption of certain goods (Chapter 6). Finally, you might compare the amount of tax revenue a given sales or excise tax will yield when demand is elastic with its yield when demand is inelastic. The point to be stressed is that the tools of supply and demand and elasticity are of great significance in analyzing the full implications of taxes and subsidies.

Demand from the individual firm's viewpoint

The concepts of demand and supply are also of vital importance from the seller's point of view. Whereas demand indicates price and amount purchased from the consumer's standpoint, it simultaneously reflects revenue per unit and sales from the seller's standpoint. We first seek to examine the demand or average-revenue curve of an individual competitive producer.

Demand to a purely competitive seller You will recall (Chapter 23) that a purely competitive market entails a very large number of producers selling a standardized product. Because he offers a negligible fraction of total supply, the individual competitive seller exerts no influence whatever on market price. Price is set by the market, and the individual firm can sell as much or as little as it chooses at that price. Stated differently, the demand schedule is perfectly elastic to the individual competitive firm.

But let us digress here for a moment to voice a word of caution. We are not saying that the *market* demand curve is perfectly elastic in a competitive market. Indeed, it is not, but rather it is typically a downsloping curve as shown in Figure 24·9*b*. As a matter of fact, the total-demand curves for most agricultural products are quite *in*elastic, even though agriculture is the most competitive industry in our economy. We are saying that the demand schedule faced by the *individual firm* in a purely competitive industry is perfectly elastic. The distinction comes about in this way. For the industry—that is, for all firms producing a particular product—a larger volume of sales can be realized only by accepting a lower product price. All firms, acting independently but simultaneously, can and do affect total supply and therefore market price. But not so for the individual firm. If a single producer increases or decreases his output, the outputs of all other competing firms being constant, the effect on total supply and market price is negligible.

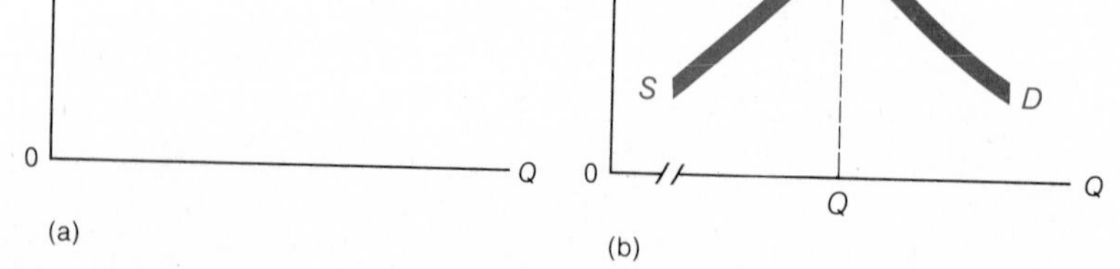

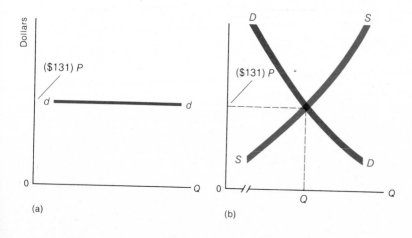

FIGURE 24·9 THE INDIVIDUAL COMPETITIVE FIRM'S DEMAND CURVE (*a*) AND DEMAND TO A COMPETITIVE INDUSTRY (*b*)

Industry demand is downsloping, such as *DD* in (*b*); that is, firms as a group must accept a lower price in order to sell a greater output. However, the product price which is determined by market demand and supply is given to the individual firm, making his demand curve *dd* perfectly elastic at that price, as shown in (*a*).

TABLE 24·3 THE DEMAND AND REVENUE SCHEDULES FOR AN INDIVIDUAL PURELY COMPETITIVE FIRM (*hypothetical data*)

Firm's demand or average-revenue schedule		Revenue data	
(1) Product price (average revenue)	(2) Quantity demanded (sold)	(3) Total revenue	(4) Marginal revenue
$131	0	$ 0	
			$131
131	1	131	
			131
131	2	262	
			131
131	3	393	
			131
131	4	524	
			131
131	5	655	
			131
131	6	786	
			131
131	7	917	
			131
131	8	1,048	
			131
131	9	1,179	
			131
131	10	1,310	

The single firm's sales schedule is therefore perfectly elastic, as shown in Figure 24·9*a*. This is an instance in which the fallacy of composition is worth remembering. What is true for the group of firms (a downsloping, less than perfectly elastic demand curve), is *not* true for the individual firm (a perfectly elastic demand curve).

Columns 1 and 2 of Table 24·3 show a perfectly elastic demand curve where market price is assumed to be $131. Note that the firm cannot obtain a higher price by restricting output; nor need it lower price in order to increase its volume of sales.

Average, total, and marginal revenue to a purely competitive seller A moment's reflection reveals that this demand schedule is simultaneously a revenue schedule. What appears in column 1 as price per unit to the purchaser is obviously revenue per unit, or *average revenue,* to the seller. To say that a buyer must pay a price of $131 per unit is to say that the revenue per unit, or average revenue, received by the seller is $131. Price and average revenue are the same thing looked at from different points of view.

Total revenue for each level of sales can obviously be determined by multiplying price by the corresponding quantity which the firm can sell. Multiply column 1 by column 2, and the result is column 3. In this case total receipts increase by a constant amount, $131, for each additional unit of sales. Each unit sold adds exactly its price to total revenue.

Whenever a firm is pondering a change in its output,

it will be concerned with how its revenue will change as a result of that change in output. What will be the additional revenue from selling another unit of output? *Marginal revenue* is the addition to total revenue, that is, the extra revenue, which results from the sale of one more unit of output. In other words, in Table 24·3 marginal revenue is simply the rate of change in total revenue. In column 3 we note that total revenue is obviously zero when zero units are being sold. The first unit of output sold increases total revenue from zero to $131. Marginal revenue—the increase in total revenue resulting from the sale of the first unit of output—is therefore $131. The second unit sold increases total revenue from $131 to $262, so marginal revenue is again $131. Indeed, you will note in column 4 that marginal revenue is a constant figure of $131. Why? Because total revenue increases at a constant rate with every extra unit sold. Under purely competitive conditions product price is constant to the individual firm; added units therefore can be sold without lowering product price. This means that each additional unit of sales adds exactly its price—$131 in this case—to total revenue. And marginal revenue is this rate of increase in total revenue. Marginal revenue is constant under pure competition, because additional units can be sold at a constant price.

The competitive firm's demand curve and total-and marginal-revenue curves are shown graphically in Figure 24·10. The demand or average-revenue curve is perfectly elastic. The marginal-revenue curve coincides with the demand curve because the market is a purely competitive one and, as a result, product price is constant to the single firm. Each extra unit of sales increases total revenue by $131. Total revenue is a straight line up to the right. Its slope is

FIGURE 24·10 DEMAND, MARGINAL REVENUE, AND TOTAL REVENUE OF A PURELY COMPETITIVE FIRM

Because it can sell additional units of output at a constant price, the marginal-revenue curve (MR) of a purely competitive firm coincides with its perfectly elastic demand curve (*D*). The firm's total-revenue curve (TR) is a straight upsloping line.

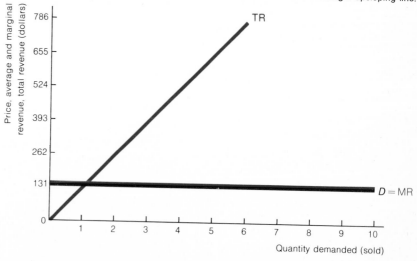

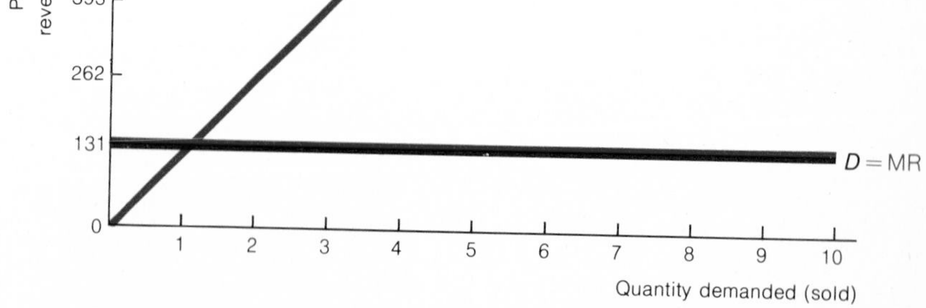

constant—that is, it is a straight line—because marginal revenue is constant.

In order to test his grasp of these new concepts, the reader should pause at this point and explain both tabularly and graphically what happens to average, total, and marginal revenue if price is, say, increased to $151 or lowered to $81.

Let us now consider the nature of the demand and revenue schedules faced by imperfectly competitive producers, that is, firms which are pure monopolies, monopolistically competitive, or oligopolistic.

Demand to an imperfectly competitive seller Though they differ in details, the demand schedules facing imperfectly competitive firms have one basic point in common: They are downsloping. The demand curve of a pure monopolist, a monopolistically competitive producer, and an oligopolist may differ considerably in elasticity; yet all are less than perfectly elastic and therefore downsloping.

Why? An imperfectly competitive producer sells a significant percentage of the industry's total output. Therefore any decision one firm makes to increase or reduce its output will have a noticeable effect on total supply and consequently market price. This is most obvious in the case of the pure monopolist, where the firm and the industry are synonymous. Here the firm's output and market output are identical.

Specifically, when an imperfectly competitive producer attempts to sell more, market supply increases in relation to market demand, and price falls. As a result, the demand schedule faced by the individual firm is downsloping, that is, less than perfectly elastic. The firm must accept a lower price to achieve a larger volume of sales. Columns 1 and 2 of Table 24·4

TABLE 24·4 THE DEMAND AND REVENUE SCHEDULES FOR AN INDIVIDUAL IMPERFECTLY COMPETITIVE FIRM (*hypothetical data*)

Firm's demand or average-revenue schedule		Revenue data	
(1) Product price (average revenue)	(2) Quantity demanded (sold)	(3) Total revenue	(4) Marginal revenue
$172	0	$ 0	
			$162
162	1	162	
			142 (152 – 10)
152	2	304	
			122 (142 – 20)
142	3	426	
			102 (132 – 30)
132	4	528	
			82 (122 – 40)
122	5	610	
			62 etc.
112	6	672	
			42
102	7	714	
			22
92	8	736	
			2
82	9	738	
			–18
72	10	720	

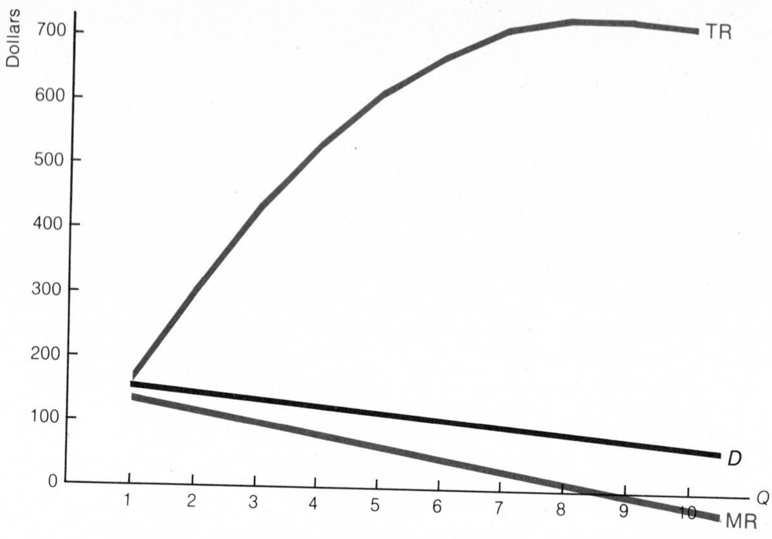

FIGURE 24·11 DEMAND, MARGINAL REVENUE, AND TOTAL REVENUE OF AN IMPERFECTLY COMPETITIVE FIRM

Because it must lower price to increase its sales, the marginal-revenue curve (MR) of an imperfectly competitive firm lies below its downsloping demand curve (*D*). Total revenue (TR) increases at a decreasing rate, reaches a maximum, and then declines.

portray this situation. We assume in this particular instance that the firm must accept a $10 price cut in order for it to sell each succeeding unit of output.

Average, total, and marginal revenue to an imperfectly competitive seller As with the purely competitive firm, price and average revenue are identical to the imperfectly competitive producer. Total revenue is again the product of price and the corresponding volume of sales. Note, however, that the rate of increase in total revenue is not constant, as it was under purely competitive conditions. As a matter of fact, total revenue reaches a maximum of $738 with the ninth unit sold and declines thereafter.

Under pure competition, each successive unit sold adds the same amount—its price—to total revenue. Marginal revenue is constant under competition because price is constant to the individual firm. But with imperfect competition, price declines as sales increase. Hence, we should expect marginal revenue to decline. It does, and as a glance at columns 1 and 4 reveals, it falls *faster* than does price. Why? The catch is this: *When an imperfectly competitive firm cuts price to increase its volume of sales, this lower price will apply not only to the extra unit sold but also to all other units of sales.* For example, when our imperfectly competitive firm is selling 1 unit at $162, total revenue is obviously $162. To increase its sales to 2 units, price must be cut by $10 to $152. This new price applies not only to the extra (second) unit of sales but also to the first unit, which could have been sold at $162. In short, the second unit adds $152 (its price) less $10 (the price cut which the firm must take on the first unit), or $142, to total revenue. Similarly, to sell 3 units the firm must lower price from $152 to $142. The resulting marginal revenue will be just $122—the $142 addition to total revenue which the third unit of sales provides less $10 price cuts on the first 2 units of output. These calculations are shown in the marginal-revenue column in Table 24·4. Note that with the tenth unit of sales, marginal revenue becomes negative. Why?

Graphically the data of Table 24·4 appear as in Figure 24·11. The points of contrast with Figure 24·10 are clear. The demand or average-revenue curve is, of course, downsloping. Total revenue increases, but at an ever-declining rate. In time total revenue reaches a maximum and then actually de-

clines. Aside from the first unit of sales, marginal revenue lies below the demand curve. The reason? Marginal revenue is derived from total revenue and therefore reflects price declines not only on the extra unit sold but also on all prior units of output which otherwise could have been sold at a higher price.

SUMMARY

1. The present chapter extends the rudiments of demand and supply analysis developed in Chapter 4. The summarizing statements pertinent to that chapter should be reviewed at this point.

2. Elasticity of demand measures the responsiveness of consumers to price changes. If consumers are sensitive to price changes, demand is elastic. If consumers are unresponsive to price changes, demand is inelastic.

3. The price elasticity formula measures the degree of elasticity or inelasticity of demand. The formula is

$$E_d = \frac{\text{percentage change in quantity demanded}}{\text{percentage change in price}}$$

The averages of the prices and quantities under consideration are used as reference points in determining the percentage changes in price and quantity. If E_d is greater than 1, demand is elastic. If E_d is less than 1, demand is inelastic. Unit elasticity is the special case in which E_d equals 1.

4. Price elasticity of demand can be determined by observing the effect of a price change upon total receipts from the sale of the product. If price and total receipts move in opposite directions, demand is elastic. If price and total receipts move in the same direction, demand is inelastic.

5. The number of available substitutes, the size of an item in one's budget, whether the product is a luxury or necessity, the time period involved, and the durability of a product are all considerations which influence elasticity of demand.

6. Elasticity varies at different price ranges on a demand curve. Furthermore, it is not safe to judge elasticity by the steepness or flatness of a demand curve on a graph.

7. The elasticity concept is also applicable to supply. Elasticity of supply depends upon the shiftability of resources between alternative employments. This shiftability in turn varies with the amount of time producers have to adjust to a given price change.

8. Legal prices upset the rationing function of free-market prices. Effective price ceilings result in persistent product shortages, and if an equitable distribution of the product is sought, government will have to ration the product to consumers. Price supports give rise to product surpluses; government must purchase these surplus products or take what measures are possible to eliminate them by imposing restrictions on production or by increasing demand.

9. Sales and excise taxes affect supply and therefore equilibrium price and quantity. The more inelastic the demand for a product, the greater is the portion of the tax which is shifted to consumers. The greater the inelasticity of supply, the larger the portion of the tax borne by sellers.

10. The demand or average-revenue curve faced by a purely competitive seller is perfectly elastic. In contrast, the demand curve facing an imperfectly competitive seller is downsloping, that is, less than perfectly elastic.

11. Under pure competition product price is constant to the individual seller; therefore each extra unit of output adds exactly the same amount (its price) to total revenue. In other words, marginal revenue is constant and equal to price. Graphically, the marginal-revenue curve coincides with the firm's perfectly elastic demand curve. Total revenue is a straight upsloping line.

12. The imperfectly competitive seller must lower price to sell more, and this lower price will apply to all prior units of sales. As a result, marginal revenue is less than price. Graphically, the firm's marginal-revenue curve lies below its demand curve. Total revenue increases at a declining rate, reaches a maximum, and finally declines.

QUESTIONS AND STUDY SUGGESTIONS

1. Answer questions 1, 2, and 11 at the end of Chapter 4.

2. In many oligopolistic industries, for example, the petroleum industry, producers justify their reluctance to lower prices by arguing that the demand for their products is inelastic. Explain.

3. How will the following changes in price affect total receipts (expenditures)—that is, will total receipts *increase, decline*, or *remain unchanged?*

a. Price falls and demand is inelastic.
b. Price rises and demand is elastic.
c. Price rises and supply is elastic.
d. Price rises and supply is inelastic.
e. Price rises and demand is inelastic.
f. Price falls and demand is elastic.
g. Price falls and demand is of unit elasticity.

4. Determine the elasticity of demand and supply for the following demand and supply schedules. Use the total-revenue test to check the answers given by the E_d formula.

E_s	Quantity supplied	Product price	Quantity demanded	Total revenue	E_d
	28,000	$10	10,000	$____	
____					____
	22,500	9	13,000	____	
____					____
	17,000	8	17,000	____	
____					____
	15,500	7	22,000	____	
____					____
	11,000	6	25,000	____	

5. What are the major determinants of elasticity of demand? Use these determinants in judging whether the demand for the following products is elastic or inelastic.

a. Oranges
b. Cigarettes
c. Automobiles
d. Gasoline
e. Butter
f. Salt
g. Winston cigarettes
h. Football games
i. Diamond bracelets
j. This textbook

6. Why is it difficult to judge elasticity of demand or supply by simply observing the appearance of a demand or supply curve on a graph?

7. Why is it necessary for ceiling prices to be accompanied by government rationing? And for price supports to be accompanied by surplus-purchasing or output-restricting or demand-increasing programs? Show graphically why price ceilings entail shortages and price supports result in surpluses. What effect, if any, does the elasticity of demand and supply have upon the size of these shortages and surpluses? Explain.

8. New York City has had rent controls since 1941. What effect do you think this has had upon the demand for housing? Upon the construction of new housing?

9. How would you expect the elasticity of supply of product X to differ as between a situation of full employment in industry X, on the one hand, and considerable unemployment in the industry, on the other? Explain.

10. "If the demand for farm products is highly inelastic, a bumper crop may reduce farm incomes." Evaluate and illustrate graphically.

11. What is the incidence of *a.* a sales tax and *b.* a subsidy, when demand is highly inelastic? Elastic? What effect does the elasticity of supply have upon the incidence of a sales tax? A subsidy?

12. Suppose you are chairman of a state commission charged with the responsibility of establishing a program to raise new revenue through the use of excise taxes. Would elasticity of demand be important to you in determining those products upon which excises should be levied? Explain.

13. Use the following demand schedule to determine total and marginal revenue for each possible level of sales.

Product price	Quantity demanded	Total revenue	Marginal revenue
$2	1	$____	
			$____
2	2	____	
			____
2	3	____	
			____
2	4	____	
			____
2	5	____	
			____
2	6	____	

a. What can you conclude about the structure of the industry in which this firm is operating? Explain.

b. Graph the demand, total-revenue, and marginal-revenue curves for this firm.

c. Why do the demand and marginal-revenue curves coincide?

d. "Marginal revenue is the rate of change in total revenue." Do you agree? Explain verbally and graphically, using the above data.

14. Now determine total and marginal revenue for each level of sales for this set of data:

Product price	Quantity demanded	Total revenue	Marginal revenue
$7	0	$____	
			$____
6	1	____	
			____
5	2	____	
			____
4	3	____	
			____
3	4	____	
			____
2	5	____	
			____
1	6	____	

a. What can you conclude about the structure of the industry in which this firm is operating? Explain.

b. Graph the demand, total-revenue, and marginal-revenue curves for this firm.

c. Why does the marginal-revenue curve lie below the demand curve?

15. *Advanced analysis.* The price-quantity data of question 14 constitute a straight-line demand curve. Use either the elasticity coefficient or the total-revenue test to determine the elasticity of demand for each possible price change. What can you conclude about the relationship between the slope of a curve and its elasticity? Use your answer to 14*b* to derive a generalization concerning the relationship between marginal revenue and elasticity of demand.

16. *Advanced analysis.* Explain the error in the following argument: "For the past four years the prices of automobiles have been rising and each year people have purchased more autos. Price and quantity are directly related and the economists' law of demand is obviously incorrect."

SELECTED REFERENCES

Economic Issues, 4th ed., readings 42 and 43.

Allen, Clark Lee: *The Framework of Price Theory* (Belmont, Calif.: Wadsworth Publishing Company, Inc., 1967), chaps. 2–4.

Boulding, Kenneth E.: *Economic Analysis: Microeconomics,* 4th ed. (New York: Harper & Row, Publishers, Incorporated, 1966), chaps. 7–12.

Brennan, Michael J.: *Theory of Economic Statics,* 2d ed. (Englewood Cliffs, N.J.: Prentice-Hall, Inc., 1970), chaps. 4–8.

Rogers, Augustus J., III: *Choice: An Introduction to Economics* (Englewood Cliffs, N.J.: Prentice-Hall, Inc., 1971), chaps. 2–3.

Watson, Donald S.: *Price Theory in Action,* 2d ed. (Boston: Houghton Mifflin Company, 1969), part 1.

Watson, Donald S.: *Price Theory and Its Uses,* 2d ed. (Boston: Houghton Mifflin Company, 1968), chap. 3.

25

FURTHER TOPICS IN THE THEORY OF CONSUMER DEMAND[1]

In Chapter 24 we extended our understanding of demand and supply by introducing the concept of price elasticity and by discussing some specific applications of demand and supply analysis. The present chapter is devoted to further consideration of the demand side of the market. In Chapter 26 we shall discuss production costs, which, we shall discover, are the major determinant of supply. The goal of Chapters 27 to 30 is to use our understanding of demand and supply in analyzing pricing and output decisions under the various market structures which were outlined in Chapter 23.

Now for a more detailed look at the two main objectives of the present chapter. First, we seek a more sophisticated explanation of the law of demand. Second, we want to understand how consumers allocate their money incomes among various goods and services. Why does a consumer buy some specific bundle of goods rather than any one of a number of other collections of goods which are available to him?

[1]To the instructor: This is an optional chapter which may be omitted without impairing the continuity and meaning of ensuing chapters.

TWO EXPLANATIONS OF THE LAW OF DEMAND

Thus far we have accepted the law of demand as a commonsense notion. We have simply appealed to observation in claiming an inverse relationship between price and quantity demanded. A high price usually does discourage consumers from buying; a low price typically does encourage them to buy. Now let us explore two complementary explanations of the downsloping nature of the demand curve which will back up our everyday observations.[2]

Income and substitution effects

One explanation of the law of demand says in essence that as the price of a product declines, consumers will be both *able* and *willing* to buy more of it.

[2]A third explanation, based upon *indifference curves,* is in some respects more precise and more sophisticated than the two we now discuss. The interested reader should refer to Richard H. Leftwich, *The Price System and Resource Allocation,* 4th ed. (Hinsdale, Ill.: The Dryden Press, Inc., 1970), chap. 4, or John F. Due and Robert W. Clower, *Intermediate Economic Analysis,* 5th ed. (Homewood, Ill.: Richard D. Irwin, Inc., 1966), chap. 5.

As the price of steak declines, you are obviously able to buy more of it with your money income. With a constant money income of, say, $10 per week you can purchase 10 pounds of steak at a price of $1 per pound. But if the price of steak falls to 50 cents per pound and you buy 10 pounds of steak, $5 per week is freed for buying more of this and other commodities. A decline in the price of steak increases the real income of the consumer. This is called the *income effect.*

But being able to buy more steak at a lower price is not a complete explanation of why you actually do buy more. As the price of steak falls—the prices of other products being unchanged—steak will become more attractive to the buyer. At 50 cents per pound it is a "better buy" than at $1 per pound. Consequently, the lower price will induce the consumer to substitute steak for some of the now less attractive items in his budget. Steak may well be substituted for pork, mutton, veal, and a variety of other foods. A lower price increases the relative attractiveness of a product and makes the consumer willing to buy more of it. This is known as the *substitution effect.*

The income and substitution effects combine to make a consumer able and willing to buy more of a specific good at a low price than at a high price.

Law of diminishing marginal utility

A second explanation centers upon the notion that, although consumer wants in general may be insatiable, wants for specific commodities can be fulfilled. In a given span of time, wherein the tastes of buyers are unchanged, consumers can get as much of specific goods and services as they want. The more of a specific product a consumer obtains, the less anxious he is to get more units of the same product. This can be most readily seen for durable goods. A consumer's want for an automobile, when he has none, may be very strong; his desire for a second car is much less intense; for a third or fourth, very weak. Even the wealthiest of families rarely have more than a half-dozen cars, despite the fact that their incomes would allow them to purchase and maintain a whole fleet of them.

Economists put forth the idea that specific consumer wants can be fulfilled with succeeding units of a commodity in the *law of diminishing marginal utility.* Let us dissect this law to see exactly what it means. A product has utility if it has the power to satisfy a want. Utility is want-satisfying power. Two characteristics of this concept must be emphasized: First, "utility" and "usefulness" are by no means synonymous. Diamond rings and paintings by Picasso may be useless in the functional sense of the term yet be of tremendous utility to senior coeds and art connoisseurs, respectively. Second—and implied in the first point—utility is a subjective notion. The utility of a specific product will vary widely from person to person. A nip of Old Tennisshoes will yield tremendous utility to the Skid Row alcoholic, but zero or negative utility to the local WCTU president.

By marginal utility we simply mean the extra utility, or satisfaction, which a consumer gets from one additional unit of a specific product. In any relatively short period of time, wherein the consumer's tastes can be assumed not to change, the marginal utility derived from successive units of a given product will decline.[3] Why? Because a consumer will eventually become saturated, or "filled up," with that particular product. The fact that marginal utility will decline as the consumer acquires additional units of a specific product is known as the *law of diminishing marginal utility.*

We have noted that utility is a subjective concept. As a result it is not susceptible to precise quantitative measurement. But for purposes of illustration, let us assume that we can measure satisfaction with units we shall call "utils." This mythical unit of satisfaction is merely a convenient pedagogical device which will allow us to quantify our thinking about consumer behavior. Thus in Table 25·1 we can illustrate the relationship between the quantity obtained of a prod-

[3]For a time the marginal utility of successive units of a product may increase. A third cigarette may yield a larger amount of extra satisfaction than the first or second. But beyond some point, we can expect the marginal utility of added units to decline.

TABLE 25·1 THE LAW OF DIMINISHING MARGINAL UTILITY AS APPLIED TO PRODUCT A (*hypothetical data*)

Unit of product A	Marginal utility, utils	Total utility, utils
First	10	10
Second	8	18
Third	7	25
Fourth	6	31
Fifth	5	36
Sixth	4	40
Seventh	3	43

uct—say, product A—and the accompanying extra utility derived from each successive unit. Here we assume that the law of diminishing marginal utility sets in with the first unit of A obtained. Each successive unit yields less and less extra utility than the previous one as the consumer's want for A comes closer and closer to fulfillment. Total utility can obviously be found for any number of units of A by cumulating the marginal-utility figures as indicated in Table 25·1. The third unit of A has a marginal utility of 7 utils; 3 units of A yield a total utility of 25 utils (10 + 8 + 7).

Now how does the law of diminishing marginal utility explain why the demand curve for a specific product is downsloping? If successive units of a good yield smaller and smaller amounts of marginal, or extra, utility, the consumer will buy additional units of a product only if its price falls. The consumer for whom these utility data are relevant may buy, say, 2 units of A at a price of $1. But owing to diminishing marginal utility from additional units of A, he will choose not to buy more at this price, because giving up money really means giving up other goods, that is, alternative ways of getting utility. Therefore, it is "not worth it" unless the price (sacrifice of other goods) declines. From the seller's viewpoint, diminishing marginal utility forces the producer to lower the price in order to induce buyers to take a larger quantity of the product.

THEORY OF CONSUMER BEHAVIOR

In addition to providing a basis for explaining the law of demand, the idea of diminishing marginal utility also plays a key role in explaining how a consumer should allocate his money income among the many goods and services which are available for him to buy.

Consumer choice and budget restraint

We can picture the situation of the typical consumer as being something like this:

1. The average consumer is a fairly rational fellow. He attempts to dispose of his money income in such a way as to derive the greatest amount of satisfaction, or utility, from it. This is not to say he is always able to achieve the maximum amount of utility from his money income; for example, inadequate knowledge of the goods available to him and the force of habit work against achieving the utility-maximizing pattern of expenditures. But we may safely assume that the typical consumer wants to get the most for his money.
2. We may suppose, too, that the average consumer has rather clear-cut preferences for various goods and services available in the market. Buyers have a pretty good idea of how much marginal utility they will get from successive units of the various products which they might choose to purchase.
3. The consumer's money income is limited in amount. Because he supplies limited amounts of human and property resources to businesses, the money income he receives will be limited. Whether the consumer finds himself at the top or bottom of the income pyramid, his income will be a finite amount. With a few exceptions—perhaps Howard Hughes and King Faisal—all consumers are subject to a *budget restraint.*
4. The goods and services available to consumers

have price tags on them. Why? Because they are scarce in relation to the demand for them, or, stated differently, their production entails the use of scarce and therefore valuable resources. In the ensuing examples we shall suppose that product prices are not affected by the amounts of specific goods which the individual consumer buys; pure competition exists on the buying or demand side of the market.

Obviously, if a consumer has a limited number of dollars in his pocket and the products he wants have price tags on them, he will only be able to purchase a limited amount of goods. The consumer cannot buy everything he might want when each purchase exhausts a portion of his limited money income. It is precisely this obvious point which brings the economic fact of scarcity home to the individual consumer.[4]

> In making his choices, our typical consumer is in the same position as the Western prospector . . . who is restocking for his next trip into the back country and who is forced by the nature of the terrain to restrict his luggage to whatever he can carry on the back of one burro. If he takes a great deal of one item, say baked beans, he must necessarily take much less of something else, say bacon. His job is to find that collection of products which, in view of the limitations imposed on the total, will best suit his needs and tastes.

In short, the consumer must make compromises; he must do some picking and choosing among alternative goods to obtain with his limited money resources the collection most satisfying to him.

Utility-maximizing rule

The question then boils down to this: Of all the collections of goods and services which a consumer can obtain within the limits of his budget, which specific collection will yield him the greatest utility or satisfaction? Bluntly put, the rule to be followed in maximizing his satisfactions is that *the consumer should allocate his money income so that the last dollar spent on each product purchased yields the same amount of extra utility.* We shall call this the *utility-maximizing rule.* When the consumer is ''balancing his margins'' in accordance with this rule, there will be no incentive for him to alter his expenditure pattern. He will be in equilibrium, and, barring a change in his tastes, his income, or the prices of the various goods, he will be worse off—his total utility will decline—by any alteration in the collection of goods he is purchasing.

Now a detailed illustration will help explain the validity of the rule. For simplicity's sake we limit our discussion to just two products. Keep in mind that the analysis can readily be extended to any number of goods. Suppose that consumer Brooks is trying to decide which combination of two products—A and B—he should purchase with his limited weekly income of $10. Obviously, Brooks's preferences for these two products and their prices will be basic data determining the combination of A and B which will maximize his satisfactions. Table 25·2 summarizes Brooks's preferences for products A and B. Column 2a shows the amount of extra or marginal utility Brooks will derive from each successive unit of A. Column 3a reflects Brooks's preferences for product B. In each case the relationship between the number of units of the product obtained and the corresponding marginal utility reflects the law of diminishing marginal utility. Diminishing marginal utility is assumed to set in with the first unit of each product purchased.

But before we can apply the utility-maximizing rule to these data, we must put the marginal-utility information of columns 2a and 3a on a per-dollar-spent basis. Why? Because a consumer's choices will be influenced not only by the extra utility which successive units of, say, product A will yield, but also by how many dollars (and therefore how many units of alternative good B) he must give up to obtain those added units of A. First example: Brooks may clearly prefer to own a Cadillac rather than a Ford; he may be twice as happy with a Cadillac than with a Ford. Yet he may buy a Ford because a Cadillac costs three or four times as much as a Ford. Brooks may feel that *per dollar spent,* a Ford is a better buy. The

[4] E. T. Weiler, *The Economic System* (New York: The Macmillan Company, 1952), p. 89.

TABLE 25·2 THE UTILITY-MAXIMIZING COMBINATION OF PRODUCTS A AND B OBTAINABLE WITH AN INCOME OF $10* (*hypothetical data*)

(1)	(2) Product A: price = $1		(3) Product B: price = $2	
Unit of product	(a) Marginal utility, utils	(b) Marginal utility per dollar (MU/price)	(a) Marginal utility, utils	(b) Marginal utility per dollar (MU/price)
First	10	10	24	12
Second	8	8	20	10
Third	7	7	18	9
Fourth	6	6	16	8
Fifth	5	5	12	6
Sixth	4	4	6	3
Seventh	3	3	4	2

*It is assumed in this table that the amount of marginal utility received from additional units of each of the two products is independent of the quantity of the other product. For example, the marginal-utility schedule for product A is independent of the amount of B obtained by the consumer.

point is this: To make the amounts of extra utility derived from differently priced goods comparable, marginal utility must be put on a per-dollar-spent basis. This is done in columns 2b and 3b. These figures are obtained simply by dividing the marginal-utility data of columns 2a and 3a by the assumed prices of A and B—$1 and $2, respectively.

Now we have Brooks's preferences—on unit and per dollar bases—and the price tags of A and B before us. Brooks stands patiently with $10 to spend on A and B. In what order should he allocate his dollars on units of A and B to achieve the highest degree of utility within the limits imposed by his money income? And what specific combination of A and B will he have obtained at the time that he exhausts his $10?

Concentrating on columns 2b and 3b of Table 25·2, we find that Brooks should first spend $2 on the first unit of B. Why? Because its marginal utility per dollar of 12 utils is higher than A's. But now Brooks finds himself indifferent about whether he should buy a second unit of B or the first unit of A. Suppose he buys both of them: Brooks now has 1 unit of A and 2 of B. Note that with this combination of goods the last dollar spent on each yields the same amount of extra utility. Does this combination of A and B therefore represent the maximum amount of utility which Brooks can obtain? The answer is "No." This collection of goods only costs $5 [(1 × $1) + (2 × $2)]; Brooks has $5 of income remaining, which he can spend to achieve a still higher level of total utility.

Examining columns 2b and 3b again, we find that Brooks should spend the next $2 on a third unit of B. But now with 1 unit of A and 3 of B we find he is again indifferent to a second unit of A and a fourth unit of B. Let us again assume Brooks purchases one more unit of each. Marginal utility per dollar is now the same for the last dollar spent on each prod-

uct, and Brooks's money income of \$10 is exhausted [(2 × \$1) + (4 × \$2)]. *The utility-maximizing combination of goods attainable by Brooks is 2 units of A and 4 of B.*[5]

It is to be emphasized that there are other combinations of A and B which are obtainable with \$10. But none of these will yield a level of total utility as high as do 2 units of A and 4 of B. For example, 4 units of A and 3 of B can be obtained for \$10. However, this combination violates the utility-maximizing rule; total utility here is only 93 utils, clearly inferior to the 96 utils yielded by 2 of A and 4 of B. Furthermore, there are other combinations of A and B (such as 4 of A and 5 of B *or* 1 of A and 2 of B) wherein the marginal utility of the last dollar spent is the same for both A and B. But such combinations are either unobtainable with Brooks's limited money income (as 4 of A and 5 of B) or fail to exhaust his money income (as 1 of A and 2 of B) and therefore do not yield him the maximum utility attainable.

An algebraic restatement

We are now in a position to restate the utility-maximizing rule in simple algebraic terms. Our rule simply says that a consumer will maximize his satisfaction when he allocates his money income in such a way that the last dollar spent on product A, the last on product B, and so forth, yield equal amounts of additional, or marginal, utility. Now the marginal utility per dollar spent on A is indicated by MU of product A/price of A (column 2b of Table 25·2) and the marginal utility per dollar spent on B by MU of product B/price of B (column 3b of Table 25·2). Our utility-maximizing rule merely requires that these ratios be equal. That is,

$$\frac{\text{MU of product A}}{\text{price of A}} = \frac{\text{MU of product B}}{\text{price of B}}$$

and, of course, the consumer must exhaust his available income. Our tabular illustration has shown us that the combination of 2 units of A and 4 of B fulfills these conditions in that

$$\frac{8}{1} = \frac{16}{2}$$

and the consumer's \$10 income is spent.

If the equation is not fulfilled, there will be some reallocation of the consumer's expenditures between A and B, from the low to the high marginal-utility-per-dollar product, which will increase the consumer's total utility. For example, the consumer may spend his \$10 on 4 of A and 3 of B. But here we find that

$$\frac{\text{MU of A: 6 utils}}{\text{price of A: \$1}} < \frac{\text{MU of B: 18 utils}}{\text{price of B: \$2}}$$

The last dollar spent on A provides only 6 utils of satisfaction, and the last dollar spent on B provides 9. On a per dollar basis, units of B provide more extra satisfaction than units of A. The consumer will obviously increase his total satisfaction by purchasing more of B and less of A. As dollars are reallocated from A to B, the marginal utility from additional units of B will decline as the result of moving down the diminishing marginal-utility schedule for B, and the marginal utility of A will rise as the consumer moves up the diminishing marginal-utility schedule for A. At some new combination of A and B—specifically, 2 of A and 4 of B—the equality of the two ratios and therefore consumer equilibrium will be achieved. As we already know, the net gain in utility is 3 utils (96 − 93).

Now there are admittedly a number of criticisms of this theory of consumer behavior. Most obviously, we have no "utilometer" by which the consumer's preferences can be set down precisely as in Table 25·2. Nor is it easy to incorporate large, indivisible products such as houses, automobiles, pianos, and a college education in our analysis. Nevertheless, there is little doubt that the theory accurately describes the basic rationale underlying consumer behavior. In a general way the theory does explain how consumers behave. Albeit in a loose fashion, consumers do seek to maximize their satisfaction. And though the process may be crude, consumers do make marginal com-

[5] To simplify, we assume in this example that Brooks spends his entire income; he neither borrows nor saves. Saving can be treated as a utility-yielding commodity and incorporated in our analysis and is to be treated thus in question 4 at the end of the chapter.

parisons in allocating their limited incomes. In formulating its budget, a family must choose between, say, a food freezer, a television set, and building a recreation room in the basement. And the college student must weigh the relative satisfaction to be derived from spending $10 on a Saturday-night date as opposed to a new pair of shoes or a couple of shirts. Despite its limitations, the utility-maximizing rule is a meaningful general statement of how consumers behave.

MARGINAL UTILITY AND THE DEMAND CURVE

It is a quite simple step from the utility-maximizing rule to the construction of an individual's downsloping demand curve. Recall from Chapters 4 and 24 that the basic determinants of an individual's demand curve for a specific product are (1) his preferences or tastes, (2) his money income, and (3) the prices of other goods. Now the utility data of Table 25·2 reflect our consumer's preferences. Let us continue to suppose that his money income is given at $10. And, concentrating upon the construction of a simple demand curve for product B, let us assume that the price of A—representing "other goods"—is given at $1. We should now be able to derive a simple demand schedule for B by considering alternative prices at which B might be sold and determining the corresponding quantity our consumer will choose to purchase. Of course, we have already determined one such price-quantity combination in explaining the utility-maximizing rule: Given tastes, income, and the prices of other goods, the rational consumer will purchase 4 units of B at a price of $2. Now assume the price of B falls to $1. This means that the marginal-utility-per-dollar data of column 3b will double, because the price of B has been halved; the new data for column 3b is in fact identical to that shown in column 3a. The purchase of 2 units of A and 4 of B is no longer an equilibrium combination. By applying the same reasoning used to develop the utility-maximizing rule, we now find Brooks's utility-maximizing position entails 4 units of A and 6 of B.

TABLE 25·3 THE DEMAND SCHEDULE FOR PRODUCT B

Price per unit of B	Quantity demanded
$2	4
1	6

That is, we can sketch Brooks's demand curve for B as in Table 25·3. This, of course, confirms the downsloping demand curve of earlier chapters.

SUMMARY

1. The law of demand can be explained on the basis of the income and substitution effects or the law of diminishing marginal utility.
2. The income effect says that a decline in the price of a product will enable the consumer to buy more of it with his fixed money income. The substitution effect points out that a lower price will make a product relatively more attractive and therefore increase the consumer's willingness to substitute it for other products.
3. The law of diminishing marginal utility states that beyond some point, additional units of a specific commodity will yield ever-declining amounts of extra satisfaction to a consumer. It follows that a lower price will be needed to induce the consumer to increase his purchases of such a product.
4. We may assume that the typical consumer is rational and acts on the basis of rather well-defined preferences; consumers act sensibly and know roughly the satisfaction they will derive from successive units of various products available to them. Because his income is limited and goods have prices on them, the consumer cannot purchase all the goods and services he might like to have. He should therefore select that attainable combination of goods which will maximize his utility or satisfaction.
5. The consumer's utility will be maximized when he is allocating his income so that the last dollar spent

on each product purchased yields the same amount of extra satisfaction. Algebraically, the utility-maximizing rule is fulfilled when

$$\frac{\text{MU of product A}}{\text{price of A}} = \frac{\text{MU of product B}}{\text{price of B}}$$

and the consumer's income is spent. Though subject to limitations, this rule is a meaningful guide in explaining consumer behavior.

6. The utility-maximizing rule and the downsloping demand curve are logically consistent.

QUESTIONS AND STUDY SUGGESTIONS

1. Explain the law of demand through the income and substitution effects, using a price increase as a point of departure for your discussion.

2. Explain the law of diminishing marginal utility. Explain the law of demand in terms of diminishing marginal utility.

3. Mrs. Peterson buys loaves of bread and quarts of milk each week at prices of 20 cents and 30 cents, respectively. At present she is buying these two products in amounts such that the marginal utilities from the last units purchased of the two products are 40 and 70 utils, respectively. Is Mrs. Peterson currently buying the best, that is, the utility-maximizing, combination of bread and milk? If not, in what manner should she reallocate her expenditures between the two goods?

4. Columns 1 through 4 of the following table show the marginal utility, measured in terms of utils, which Mr. Black would get by purchasing various amounts of products A, B, C, and D. Column 5 shows the marginal utility Black gets from saving. Assume that the prices of A, B, C, and D are \$24, \$4, \$6, and \$18, respectively, and that Black has a money income of \$106.

Column 1		Column 2		Column 3		Column 4		Column 5	
Units of A	MU	Units of B	MU	Units of C	MU	Units of D	MU	No. of dollars saved	MU
1	36	1	15	1	24	1	72	1	5
2	30	2	12	2	15	2	54	2	4
3	24	3	8	3	12	3	45	3	3
4	18	4	7	4	9	4	36	4	2
5	13	5	5	5	7	5	27	5	1
6	7	6	4	6	5	6	18	6	½
7	4	7	3½	7	2	7	15	7	¼
8	2	8	3	8	1	8	12	8	⅛

a. What quantities of A, B, C, and D will Black purchase in maximizing his satisfactions?

b. How many dollars will Black choose to save?

c. Check your answers by substituting in the algebraic statement of the utility-maximizing rule.

5. "Nothing is more useful than water: but it will purchase scarce any thing; scarce any thing can be had in exchange for it. A diamond, on the contrary, has scarce any value in use; but a very great quantity of other goods may frequently be had in exchange for it."[6] Explain.

6. "In the long run it may be irrational to purchase goods on the basis of habit; but in the short run habitual buying may prove to be a very sensible means of allocating income." Do you agree? Explain.

7. *Advanced analysis.* Let $MU_a = z = 10 - x$ and $MU_b = z = 21 - 2y$, where z is marginal utility measured in utils, x is the amount spent on product A, and y is the amount spent on product B. Assume the consumer has \$10 to spend on A and B; that is, $x + y = 10$. How is this \$10 best allocated between A and B? How much utility will the marginal dollar yield?

SELECTED REFERENCES

Economic Issues, 4th ed., reading 39.

Braff, Allan J.: *Microeconomic Analysis* (New York: John Wiley & Sons, Inc., 1969), chap. 3.

Ferguson, C. E., and S. Charles Maurice: *Economic Analysis* (Homewood, Ill.: Richard D. Irwin, Inc., 1970), chaps. 3 and 4.

Leftwich, Richard H.: *The Price System and Resource Allocation,* 4th ed. (Hinsdale, Ill.: The Dryden Press, Inc., 1970), chaps. 4 and 5.

Mansfield, Edwin: *Microeconomics: Theory and Applications* (New York: W. W. Norton & Company, Inc., 1970), chaps. 2 and 3.

[6] Adam Smith, *The Wealth of Nations* (New York: Modern Library, Inc., originally published in 1776), p. 28.

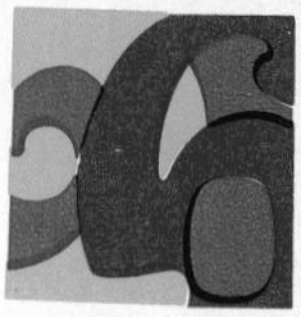

THE COSTS OF PRODUCTION

Product prices are determined by the interaction of the forces of demand and supply. Preceding chapters have focused our attention upon the factors underlying demand. The basic factor underlying the ability and willingness of firms to supply a product in the market is the cost of production. The production of any good requires the use of economic resources which, because of their relative scarcity, bear price tags. The amount of any product which a firm is willing to supply in the market depends upon the prices, or costs, of the resources essential to its production, on the one hand, and the price which the product will bring in the market, on the other. The present chapter is concerned with the general nature of production costs. Product prices are introduced in the following several chapters, and the supply decisions of producers are then explained.

ECONOMIC COSTS

The economist's notion of costs goes back to the basic fact that resources are scarce and have alternative uses. Thus, to use a bundle of resources in the production of some particular good means that certain alternative products have been forgone. *Costs in economics have to do with missed opportunities or forgone alternatives.* This conception of costs is clearly embodied in the production possibilities curve of Chapter 2. Note, for example, that at point *C* in Table 2·1 the cost of producing 100,000 more units of bread is the 3,000 units of drill presses which must be forgone. This notion of cost is called the *opportunity* or *alternative cost doctrine.* The steel that is used for armaments is simply not available for the manufacture of new automobiles or apartment buildings. And if an assembly-line worker is capable of producing automobiles or washing machines, then the cost to society in employing this worker in an automobile plant is the contribution he would otherwise have made in producing washing machines. The cost to you in reading this chapter is the alternative uses of your time which you must forgo.

Explicit and implicit costs

Let us now consider costs from the viewpoint of an individual firm. Given the notion of opportunity or alternative costs, we can say that *economic costs are those payments a firm must make, or incomes*

it must yield, to resource suppliers in order to attract these resources away from alternative lines of production. These payments or incomes may be either *explicit* or *implicit.* The monetary payments—that is, cash outlays, which a firm makes to those "outsiders" who supply labor services, materials, fuel, transportation services, power, and so forth—are called *explicit costs.* But in addition a firm may use certain resources which the firm itself owns. Our notion of opportunity costs tells us that regardless of whether a resource is owned or hired by an enterprise, there is a cost involved in using that resource in a specific employment. The costs of such self-owned, self-employed resources are nonexpenditure or *implicit costs.* To the firm those implicit costs are the money payments which the self-employed resources could have earned in their best alternative employments. For example, suppose Brooks operates a corner grocery as a sole proprietor. He owns his store building and supplies all his own labor and money capital. Though his enterprise has no explicit rental or wage costs, implicit rents and wages are incurred. By using his own building for a grocery, Brooks sacrifices the $200 monthly rental income which he could otherwise have earned by renting it to someone else. Similarly, by using his money capital and labor in his own enterprise, Brooks sacrifices the interest and wage incomes which he otherwise could have earned by supplying these resources in their best alternative employments. And, finally, by running his own enterprise, Brooks forgoes the earnings he could realize by supplying his entrepreneurial efforts in someone else's firm.

Normal profits as a cost

The minimum payment required to keep Brooks's entrepreneurial talents engaged in this enterprise is sometimes called a *normal profit.* As is true of implicit rent or implicit wages, this normal return for the performing of entrepreneurial functions is an implicit cost. If this minimum, or normal, return is not realized, the entrepreneur will withdraw his efforts from this line of production and reallocate them to some alternative line of production. Or the individual may cease being an entrepreneur in favor of becoming a laborer.

In short, the economist includes as costs all payments—explicit and implicit, the latter including a normal profit—required to retain resources in a given line of production.

Economic, or pure, profits

Our discussion of economic costs correctly suggests that economists and accountants use the term "profits" differently. By "profits" the accountant generally means total receipts less explicit costs. But to the economist "profits" means total receipts less *all* costs (explicit and implicit, the latter including a normal return to the entrepreneur). Therefore, when an economist says that a firm is just covering its costs, he means that all explicit and implicit costs are being met and that the entrepreneur is therefore receiving a return just large enough to retain his talents in his present line of production. If a firm's total receipts exceed all its economic costs, any residual accrues to the entrepreneur. This residual is called an *economic, or pure, profit.* It is not a cost, because by definition it is a return in excess of the normal profit required to retain the entrepreneur in this particular line of production. In Chapter 33 we shall find that economic profits are associated with risk bearing and monopoly power.

Short run and long run

The costs which a firm or industry incurs in producing any given output will depend upon the types of adjustment it is able to make in the amounts of the various resources it employs. The quantities employed of many resources—labor, raw materials, fuel, power, and so forth—can be varied easily and quickly. But the amounts of other resources demand more time for adjustment. For example, the capacity of a manufacturing plant, that is, the size of the factory building and the amount of machinery and equipment therein, can only be varied over a considerable period of time. In some heavy industries it may take several years to alter plant capacity.

These differences in the time necessary to vary the quantities of the various resources used in the productive process make it essential to distinguish between the short run and the long run. The *short run* refers to a period of time too short to permit an enterprise to alter its plant capacity yet long enough to permit a change in the level at which the fixed plant is utilized. The firm's plant capacity is fixed in the short run, but output can be varied by applying larger or smaller amounts of manpower, materials, and so forth, to that plant. Existing plant capacity can be used more or less intensively in the short run.

From the viewpoint of existing firms, the *long run* refers to a period of time long enough to allow these firms to change the quantities of *all* resources employed, including plant capacity. From the viewpoint of an industry, the long run also encompasses enough time for existing firms to dissolve and leave the industry and for new firms to be created and enter the industry. While the short run is a "fixed-plant" time period, the long run is a "variable-plant" time period.

Some examples will make clear the distinction between the short run and the long run. If a General Motors plant were to hire an extra 100 workers or to add an entire shift of workers, these would be short-run adjustments. If the same GM plant were to add a new wing to its building and install more equipment, this would be a long-run adjustment. Studebaker's abandonment of its South Bend, Indiana plant in 1964 was a long-run adjustment.

It is important to note that the short run and the long run are conceptual rather than specific calendar time periods. In light manufacturing industries, changes in plant capacity may be negotiated almost overnight. A small firm making men's clothing can increase its plant capacity in a few days or less simply by ordering and installing a couple of new cutting tables and several extra sewing machines. But heavy industry is a different story. It may take Ford or General Motors several years to construct a new assembly plant and to install elaborate assembly-line equipment.

We turn now to the task of analyzing production costs in the short-run, or fixed-plant, period. Following this we consider costs in the long-run, or variable-plant, period.

PRODUCTION COSTS IN THE SHORT RUN

A firm's costs of producing any output will depend not only upon the prices of needed resources, but also upon technology—the quantity of resources it takes to produce that output. It is the latter, technological aspect of costs with which we are concerned for the moment. In the short run a firm can change its output by adding variable resources to a fixed plant. Question: How does output change as more and more variable resources are added to the firm's fixed resources?

Law of diminishing returns

The answer is provided in general terms by the *law of diminishing returns.* (You will recall that we applied this famous law in aggregative terms in Chapter 20). This engineering law states that *as successive units of a variable resource (say, labor) are added to a fixed resource (capital), beyond some point the extra, or marginal, product attributable to each additional unit of the variable resource will decline.* Stated somewhat differently, if additional workers are applied to a given amount of capital equipment, as is the case in the short run, eventually output will rise less than in proportion to the increase in the number of workers employed. A couple of examples will illustrate this law.

Suppose a farmer has a fixed amount of land—say, 80 acres—in which he has planted corn. Assuming the farmer does not cultivate his cornfields at all, his yield will be, say, 40 bushels per acre. If he cultivates the land once, output may rise to 50 bushels per acre. A second cultivation may increase output to 57 bushels per acre, a third to 61, and a fourth to, say, 63. But further cultivations will add little or nothing to total output. Successive cultivations add less and less to the land's yield. If this were not the case, the world's needs for corn could be fulfilled by extremely

TABLE 26·1 THE LAW OF DIMINISHING RETURNS (*hypothetical data*)

(1) Inputs of the variable resource (labor)	(2) Total product	(3) Extra, or marginal, product
0	0	
		5
1	5	
		8
2	13	
		5
3	18	
		4
4	22	
		3
5	25	
		2
6	27	

intense cultivation of this single 80-acre plot of land. Indeed, if diminishing returns did not occur, the world could be fed out of a flowerpot.

The law of diminishing returns also holds true in nonagricultural industries. Assume a small planing mill is manufacturing unupholstered furniture. The mill has a given amount of equipment in the form of lathes, planers, saws, sanders, and so forth. If this firm hired just one or two workers, total output and production per man would be very low. These workers would have a number of different jobs to perform, and the advantages of specialization would be lost. Time would also be lost in switching from one job operation to another, and the machines would stand idle much of the time. In short, the plant would be undermanned, and production therefore would be inefficient. These difficulties would disappear as more workers were added. Equipment would be more fully utilized, and workers could now specialize on a single job. Thus as more workers are added to the initially undermanned plant, the extra or marginal product of each will tend to rise as a result of more efficient production. But this cannot go on indefinitely. As still more workers are added, problems of overcrowding will arise. Workers must wait in line to use the machinery, so now *workers* are underutilized. The extra, or marginal, product of additional workers declines because the plant is overmanned. There is too much labor in proportion to the fixed amount of capital goods. In the extreme case, the continuous addition of labor to the plant would use up all standing room, and production would be brought to a standstill!

Table 26·1 illustrates the law of diminishing returns numerically. In this instance diminishing marginal product is incurred with the hire of the third worker. Total product is found by simply accumulating the extra, or marginal, product attributable to each successive worker. Total product will increase so long as marginal product is positive.

Fixed, variable, and total costs

The production data described by the law of diminishing returns must be coupled with resource prices to determine the total and per unit costs of producing various outputs. We have already emphasized that in the short run some resources—those associated

with the firm's plant—are fixed. Others are variable. This correctly suggests that in the short run, costs can be classified as either fixed or variable.

Fixed costs are those costs which in total do not vary with changes in output. Fixed costs are associated with the very existence of a firm's plant and therefore must be paid even if the firm's rate of output is zero. Such costs as interest on a firm's bonded indebtedness, rental payments, a portion of depreciation on equipment and buildings, insurance premiums, and the salaries of top management and key personnel are generally fixed costs. In column 2 of Table 26·2 we have assumed that the firm's fixed costs are $100. Note that this fixed-cost figure prevails at all levels of output, including zero.

Variable costs are those costs which increase with the level of output. Variable costs include payments for labor, materials, fuel, power, transportation services, and similar variable resources. In column 3 of Table 26·2 we find that the total of variable costs changes with output; but note that the increases in variable costs associated with each one-unit increase in output are not constant. As production begins, variable costs will for a time increase by a decreasing amount; this is true through the fourth unit of output. Beyond the fourth unit, however, variable costs increase for each successive unit of output. The explanation of this behavior of variable costs lies in the law of diminishing returns. Because of increasing marginal product, smaller and smaller increases in

TABLE 26·2 TOTAL- AND AVERAGE-COST SCHEDULES FOR AN INDIVIDUAL FIRM IN THE SHORT RUN (*hypothetical data*)

Total-cost data, per week				Average-cost data, per week			
(1) Total product	(2) Total fixed cost	(3) Total variable cost	(4) Total cost	(5) Average fixed cost, or (2) ÷ (1)	(6) Average variable cost, or (3) ÷ (1)	(7) Average total cost, or (4) ÷ (1)	(8) Marginal cost, or Δ(4)
0	$100	$ 0	$ 100				
1	100	90	190	$100.00	$90.00	$190.00	$ 90
2	100	170	270	50.00	85.00	135.00	80
3	100	240	340	33.33	80.00	113.33	70
4	100	300	400	25.00	75.00	100.00	60
5	100	370	470	20.00	74.00	94.00	70
6	100	450	550	16.67	75.00	91.67	80
7	100	540	640	14.29	77.14	91.43	90
8	100	650	750	12.50	81.23	93.73	110
9	100	780	880	11.11	86.67	97.78	130
10	100	930	1,030	10.00	93.00	103.00	150

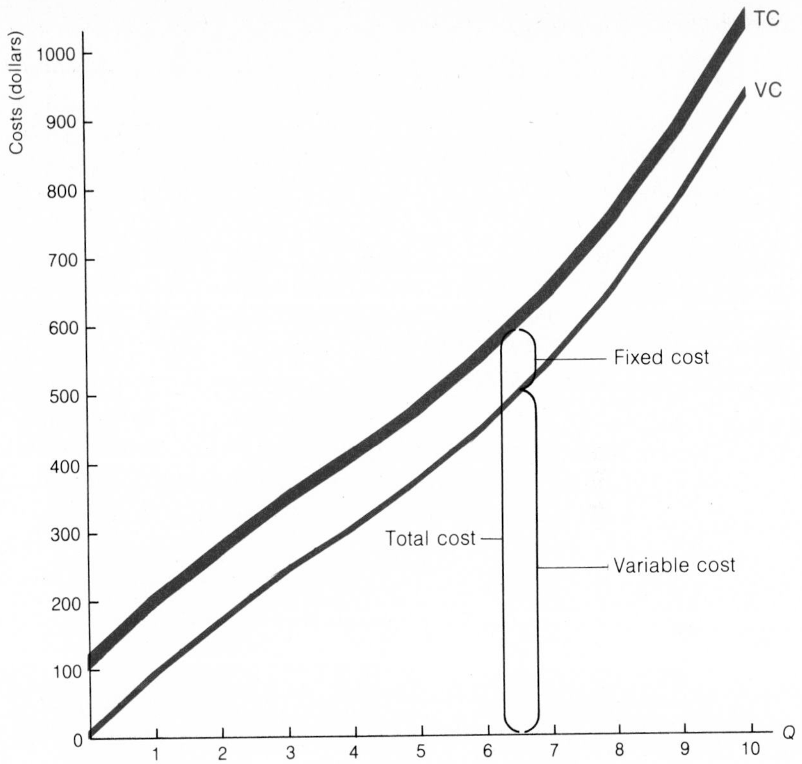

FIGURE 26·1 TOTAL COST IS THE SUM OF FIXED AND VARIABLE COSTS

Variable costs (VC) vary with output. Fixed costs are independent of the level of output. The total cost (TC) of any output is the (vertical) sum of the fixed and variable costs of that output.

the amounts of variable resources will be needed for a time to get successive units of output produced. This means that total variable costs will increase by decreasing amounts. But when marginal product begins to decline as diminishing returns are encountered, it will be necessary to use larger and larger additional amounts of variable resources to produce each successive unit of output. Total variable costs will therefore increase by increasing amounts.

Total cost is self-defining: it is the *sum of fixed and variable costs at each level of output.* It is shown in column 4 of Table 26·2. At zero units of output, total cost is equal to the firm's fixed costs. Then for each unit of production—1 through 10—total cost varies at the same rate as does variable cost.

Figure 26·1 shows graphically the fixed-, variable-, and total-cost data of Table 26·2. Note that total variable cost is measured from the horizontal axis and total fixed cost is added vertically to total variable cost in locating the total-cost curve.

The distinction between fixed and variable costs is of no little significance to the businessman. Variable costs are those costs which the businessman can control or alter in the short run by changing his level

of production. On the other hand, fixed costs are clearly beyond the businessman's control; such costs are incurred and must be paid regardless of output level.

Per unit, or average, costs

Producers are certainly interested in their total costs, but they are equally concerned with their per unit, or average, costs. In particular, average-cost data are more usable for making comparisons with product price, which is always stated on a per unit basis. Average fixed cost, average variable cost, and average total cost are shown in columns 5 to 7 of Table 26·2. It is important that we know how these unit-cost figures are derived and how they vary as output changes.

Average fixed cost (AFC) is found by dividing total fixed costs by the corresponding output. AFC declines as output increases. Whereas total fixed costs are, by definition, independent of output, AFC will decline as output increases. As output increases, a given total fixed cost of $100 is obviously being spread over a larger and larger output. When output is just 1 unit, total fixed costs and AFC are equal—$100. But at 2 units of output, total fixed costs of $100 become $50 worth of fixed costs per unit; then $33.33, as $100 is spread over 3 units; $25, when spread over 4 units; and so forth. This is what businessmen commonly refer to as ''spreading the overhead.'' We find in Figure 26·2 that AFC graphs as a continually declining figure as total output is increased.

Average variable cost (AVC) is found by dividing

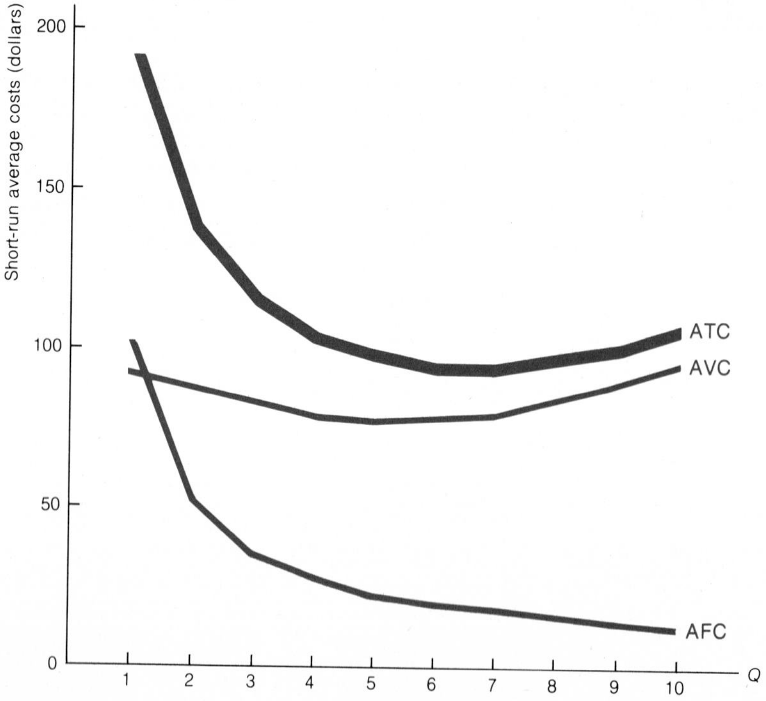

FIGURE 26·2 THE AVERAGE-COST CURVES

Average total cost (ATC) is the vertical sum of average variable cost (AVC) and average fixed cost (AFC). AFC necessarily falls as a given amount of fixed costs is apportioned over a larger and larger output. AVC initially falls because of increasing physical returns but then rises because of diminishing physical returns.

total variable cost by the corresponding output. AVC declines initially, reaches a minimum, and then increases again. Graphically, this provides us with a U-shaped or saucer-shaped AVC curve, as is shown in Figure 26·2.

Because total variable cost reflects the law of diminishing returns, so must the AVC figures, which are derived from total variable cost. Because of increasing returns it takes fewer and fewer additional variable resources to produce each of the first 4 units of output. As a result, variable cost per unit will decline. AVC hits a minimum with the fifth unit of output, and beyond this point AVC rises as diminishing returns necessitate the use of more and more variable resources to produce each additional unit of output. In more direct terms, at low levels of output production will be relatively inefficient and costly, because the firm's fixed plant is undermanned. Not enough variable resources are being combined with the firm's plant; production is inefficient, and per unit variable costs are therefore relatively high. As output expands, however, greater specialization and a more complete utilization of the firm's capital equipment will make for more efficient production. As a result, variable cost per unit of output will decline. As more and more variable resources are added, some point will eventually be reached where diminishing returns are incurred. The firm's capital equipment will now be overmanned, and the resulting overcrowding and overutilization of machinery impair efficiency. This means that AVC will increase.

Average total cost (ATC) can be found by dividing total cost by total output or, more simply, by adding AFC and AVC for each of the ten levels of output. These data are shown in column 7 of Table 26·2. Graphically, ATC is found by adding vertically the AFC and AVC curves, as in Figure 26·2. Thus the vertical distance between the ATC and AVC curves reflects AFC at any output.

Marginal cost

There remains one final and very crucial cost concept—marginal cost. *Marginal cost* (MC) *is the extra, or additional, cost of producing one more unit of output.* MC can be determined for each additional unit of output simply by noting the change in total cost which that unit's production entails. In Table 26·2 we find that production of the first unit of output increases total cost from $100 to $190. Therefore, the additional, or marginal, cost of that first unit is $90. The marginal cost of the second unit is $80 ($270 – $190); the MC of the third is $70 ($340 – $270); and so forth. MC for each of the ten units of output is shown in column 8 of Table 26·2. MC can also be calculated from the total-variable-cost column. Why? Because the only difference between total cost and total variable cost is the constant amount of fixed costs. Hence, the change in total cost and change in total variable cost associated with each additional unit of output is the same.

Marginal cost is a strategic concept, because it designates those costs over which the firm has the most direct control. More specifically, MC indicates those costs which are incurred in the production of the last unit of output and, simultaneously, the cost which can be "saved" by reducing total output by the last unit. Average-cost figures do *not* provide this information. For example, suppose the firm is undecided as to whether it should produce 3 or 4 units of output. At 4 units of output Table 26·2 indicates that ATC is $100. But the firm does not increase its total costs by $100 by producing, nor does it "save" $100 by not producing, the fourth unit. Rather the change in costs involved here is only $60, as the MC column of Table 26·2 clearly reveals. A firm's decisions as to what output to produce are marginal decisions, that is, decisions to produce a few more or a few less units. Marginal cost reveals the change in costs which one more unit or one less unit of output entails. When coupled with marginal revenue, which we found in Chapter 24 indicates the change in revenue from one more or one less unit of output, marginal cost allows a firm to determine whether it is profitable to expand or contract its level of production. The analysis in the next four chapters centers upon these marginal calculations.

Marginal cost is shown graphically in Figure 26·3. Note that marginal cost declines sharply, reaches a minimum, and then rises rather sharply. This mirrors

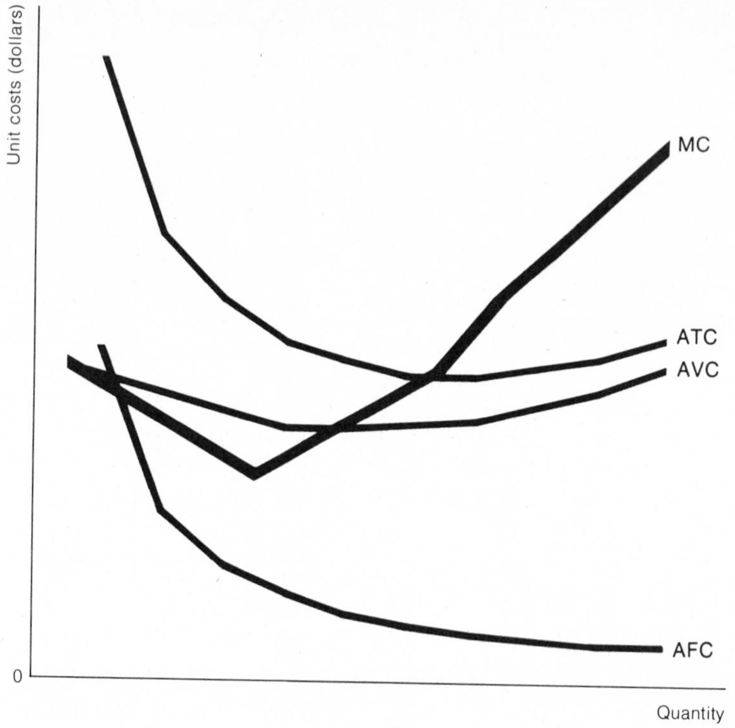

FIGURE 26·3 THE RELATIONSHIP OF MARGINAL COST TO AVERAGE TOTAL COST AND AVERAGE VARIABLE COST

Marginal cost (MC) cuts both ATC and AVC at their minimum points. This is so because whenever the extra or marginal amount added to total cost (or variable cost) is less than the average of that cost, the average will necessarily fall. Conversely, whenever the marginal amount added to total (or variable) cost is greater than the average of total cost, the average must rise.

the fact that variable cost, and therefore total cost, increases first by decreasing amounts and then by increasing amounts (see Figure 26·1 and columns 3 and 4 of Table 26·2).

The shape of the marginal-cost curve is a reflection of, and the consequence of, the law of diminishing returns. The relationship between marginal product and marginal cost can be readily grasped by looking back to Table 26·1. If each successive unit of a variable resource (labor) is hired at a constant price, the marginal cost of each extra unit of output will *fall* so long as the marginal product of each additional work is *rising*. This is so because marginal cost is simply the price or cost of an extra worker divided by his marginal product. Hence, in Table 26·1 suppose each worker can be hired at a cost of $10. Because the first worker's marginal product is 5 and the hire of this worker increases the firm's costs by $10, the marginal cost of each of these 5 extra units of output will be $2 ($10 ÷ 5). The second worker also increases costs by $10, but his marginal product is 8, so that the marginal cost of each of these 8 extra units of output is $1.25 ($10 ÷ 8). In general, so long as marginal product is rising, marginal cost will be falling. But as diminishing returns set in—in this case, with the third worker—marginal cost will begin to rise. Thus for the third worker, marginal cost is again $2 ($10 ÷ 5); $2.50 for the fourth worker; $3.33 for the fifth; and $5 for the sixth. The relationship between marginal product and marginal cost is evident: Given the price (cost) of the variable resource, increasing returns will be reflected in a

declining marginal cost and diminishing returns in a rising marginal cost.

Furthermore, it is notable that marginal cost cuts both AVC and ATC at their minimum points. This marginal-average relationship is a matter of mathematical necessity, which a commonsense illustration can make readily apparent. Suppose a baseball pitcher has allowed his opponents an average of 3 runs per game in the first three games he has pitched. Now whether his average falls or rises as a result of pitching a fourth (marginal) game will depend upon whether the additional runs he allows in that extra game are fewer or more than his current 3-run average. If he allows fewer than 3 runs—for example, 1—in the fourth game, his total runs will rise from 9 to 10, and his average will fall from 3 to $2\frac{1}{2}$ (10 ÷ 4). Conversely, if he allows more than 3 runs—say, 7—in the fourth game, his total will rise from 9 to 16 and his average from 3 to 4 (16 ÷ 4). So it is with costs. When the amount added to total cost (marginal cost) is less than the average of total cost, ATC will fall. Conversely, when marginal cost exceeds ATC, ATC will rise. This means in Figure 26·3 that so long as MC lies below ATC, the latter will fall, and where MC is above ATC, ATC will rise. Therefore at the point of intersection where MC equals ATC, ATC has just ceased to fall but has not yet begun to rise. This, by definition, is the minimum point on the ATC curve. Because MC can be defined as the addition either to total cost or to total variable cost resulting from one more unit of output, this same rationale explains why MC also cuts AVC at the latter's minimum point. No such relationship exists for MC and average fixed cost, because the two are simply not related; marginal cost embodies only those costs which change with output, and fixed costs by definition are independent of output.

Let us now turn to the relationship between output and unit costs when all inputs are variable.

PRODUCTION COSTS IN THE LONG RUN

In the long run all desired resource adjustments can be negotiated by an industry and the individual firms which it comprises. The firm can alter its plant capacity; it can build a larger plant or revert to a smaller plant than that assumed in Table 26·2. The industry can also change its plant size; the long run is an amount of time sufficient for new firms to enter or old firms to leave an industry. The impact of the entry and exodus of firms from an industry will be discussed in the next chapter; here we are concerned only with changes in plant capacity made by a single firm. And in considering these adjustments, we couch our analysis in terms of ATC, making no distinction between fixed and variable costs for the obvious reason that all resources and therefore all costs are variable in the long run.

Suppose a single-plant manufacturing enterprise starts out on a small scale and then, as the result of successful operations, expands to successively larger plant sizes. What will happen to average total costs as this growth occurs? The answer is this: For a time successively larger plants will bring lower average total costs. However, eventually the building of a still larger plant will cause ATC to rise.

Figure 26·4 illustrates this situation for five possible plant sizes. ATC-1 is the average-total-cost curve for the smallest of the five plants, and ATC-5 for the largest. The relationship of the five plant sizes to one another is clearly that stated above. Constructing a larger plant will entail lower per unit costs through plant size 3. But beyond this point a larger plant will mean a higher level of average total costs.

The dotted lines perpendicular to the output axis are crucial. They indicate those points at which the firm should change plant size in order to realize the lowest attainable per unit costs of production. To illustrate in terms of Figure 26·4: For all outputs up to 20 units, the lowest per unit costs are attainable with plant size 1. However, if the firm's volume of sales expands to some level greater than 20 but less than 30 units, it can achieve lower per unit costs by constructing a larger plant—plant size 2. For any output between 30 and 50 units, plant size 3 will yield the lowest per unit costs. For the 50–60-unit range of output, plant size 4 must be built to achieve the lowest unit costs. Lowest per unit costs for any output in excess of 60 units demand the construction of the still larger plant of size 5.

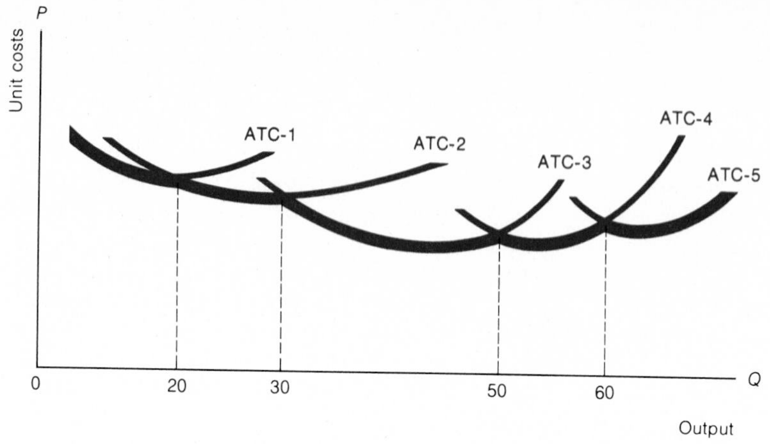

FIGURE 26·4 THE LONG-RUN AVERAGE-COST CURVE: FIVE POSSIBLE PLANT SIZES

The long-run average-cost curve is made up of segments of the short-run cost curves (ATC-1, ATC-2, etc.) of the various-sized plants from which the firm might choose. Each point on the bumpy planning curve shows the least unit cost attainable for any output when the firm has had time to make all desired changes in its plant size.

Tracing these adjustments, we can conclude that the long-run ATC curve for the enterprise will comprise segments of the short-run ATC curves for the various plant sizes which can be constructed. *The long-run ATC curve shows the least per unit cost at which any output can be produced after the firm has had time to make all appropriate adjustments in its plant size.* In Figure 26·4 the heavy, bumpy curve is the firm's long-run ATC curve or, as it is often called, the firm's planning curve. In most lines of production the choice of plant sizes is much wider than that assumed in our illustration. In fact, in many industries the number of possible plant sizes is virtually unlimited. This means that in time, very small changes in the volume of output (sales) will prompt appropriate changes in the size of the plant. Graphically this means that the planning curve will be smooth rather than bumpy. Figure 26·5 is illustrative.

Economies and diseconomies of scale

We have patiently accepted the contention that for a time a larger and larger plant size will entail lower unit costs but that beyond some point successively larger plants will mean higher average total costs. Now we must explain this point. Exactly why is the long-run ATC curve U-shaped? It must be emphasized, first of all, that the law of diminishing returns is not applicable here, because it presumes that one resource is fixed in supply and, as we have seen, the long run assumes that all resources are variable. What then is our explanation? The U-shaped long-run average-cost curve is explainable in terms of what economists call "economies and diseconomies" of large-scale production.

Economies of large scale Economies of scale or, more commonly, economies of mass production, explain the downsloping part of the long-run ATC curve. As the size of a plant increases, a number of considerations will for a time give rise to lower average costs of production.

1. Increased specialization in the use of labor is feasible as a plant increases in size The hire of more workers means that jobs can be divided and subdivided. Instead of performing five or six distinct operations in the productive process, each worker may now have just one task to perform. Workers can be used full time on those particular operations at which they have special skills. In a small plant a

skilled machinist may spend half his time performing unskilled tasks. This makes for high production costs. Further, the dividing of work operations which large scale allows will give workers the opportunity to become very proficient at the specific tasks assigned them. The Jack-of-all-trades who is burdened with five or six jobs will not be likely to become very efficient in any of them. When allowed to concentrate on one task, the same worker may become highly efficient. Finally, greater specialization tends to eliminate the loss of time which accompanies the shifting of workers from one job to another.

2. ***Large-scale production also permits better utilization of, and greater specialization in, management*** A foreman capable of handling fifteen or twenty men will be underutilized in a small plant hiring only eight or ten men. The production staff can be doubled with no increase in administrative costs. In addition, small firms will not be able to use management specialists to best advantage. In a small plant a sales specialist may be forced to divide his time between several executive functions—for example, sales, personnel, and finance. A larger scale of operations will mean that the sales expert can devote full time to supervising sales while appropriate specialists are added to perform other managerial functions. Greater efficiency and lower unit costs are the net result.

3. ***Small firms are often not able to utilize the most efficient productive equipment*** In many lines of production the most efficient machinery is available only in very large and extremely expensive units. Furthermore, effective utilization of this equipment demands a high volume of production. This means only large-scale producers are able to afford and operate efficiently the best available equipment. To illustrate: In the automobile industry the most efficient fabrication method entails the use of extremely elaborate assembly-line equipment. The efficient use of this equipment demands an annual output of thousands of automobiles. Only very large-scale producers can afford to purchase and use

FIGURE 26 · 5 THE LONG–RUN AVERAGE–COST CURVE: UNLIMITED NUMBER OF PLANT SIZES

If the number of possible plant sizes is very large, the long-run average-cost curve approximates a smooth curve. Economies and diseconomies of scale cause the curve to be U-shaped.

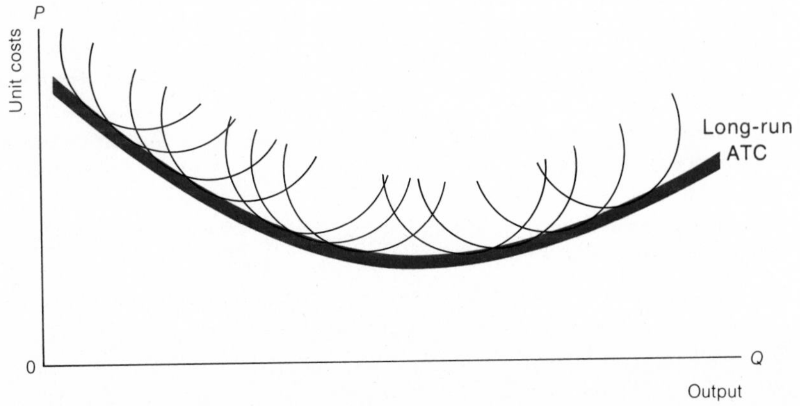

this equipment efficiently. The small-scale producer is between the devil and the deep blue sea. To fabricate automobiles with the use of other equipment is inefficient and therefore more costly per unit. The alternative of purchasing the most efficient equipment and underutilizing it with a small level of output is equally inefficient and costly.

4. The large-scale producer is in a better position to utilize by-products than is a small firm The large meat-packing plant makes glue, fertilizer, pharmaceuticals, and a host of other products from animal remnants which would be discarded by smaller producers.

All these technological considerations—greater specialization in the use of labor and management, the ability to use the most efficient equipment, and the effective utilization of by-products—will contribute to lower unit costs for the smaller producer who is able to expand his scale of operations.

Diseconomies of large scale But in time the expansion of a firm may give rise to diseconomies and therefore higher per unit costs.

The main factor causing diseconomies of scale has to do with certain managerial problems which typically arise as a firm becomes a large-scale producer. In a small plant a single key executive may render all the basic decisions relative to his plant's operation. Because of the firm's smallness he is close to the production line. He can therefore comprehend the various aspects of the firm's operations and digest the information fed to him by his subordinates, to the end that efficient decision making is possible.

This neat picture changes, however, as a firm grows. The management echelons between the executive suite and the assembly line become many; top management is far removed from the actual production operations of the plant. It becomes impossible for one man to assemble, understand, and digest all the information essential to rational decision making in a large-scale enterprise. Authority must be delegated to innumberable vice-presidents, second vice-presidents, and so forth. This expansion in the depth and width of management entails problems of coordination and bureaucratic red tape which can eventually impair the efficiency of a firm and lead to higher costs.

Significance of economies and diseconomies of scale Economies and diseconomies of scale are something more than a plausible pipedream of economic theorists. Indeed, in most American manufacturing industries economies of scale have been of great significance. Firms which have been able to expand their scale of operations to realize the economies of mass production have survived and flourished. Those unable to achieve this expansion have found themselves in the unenviable position of high-cost producers, doomed to a marginal existence or ultimate insolvency.

Diseconomies of scale, when encountered, can be equally significant. The organizational structure of General Motors, for example, is designed to avoid managerial diseconomies which its gigantic size would otherwise entail. This industrial colossus has subdivided itself into some thirty-six operating subdivisions, each of which is basically autonomous and in some cases—for example, its five automobile-producing divisions (Chevrolet, Buick, Oldsmobile, Pontiac, and Cadillac)—competing. A degree of decentralization has been sought which will allow full realization of the economies of mass production yet help to avoid diseconomies of scale.[1] Another example: Some economists feel that over the years U.S. Steel has declined in relative importance in the steel industry because of diseconomies of scale. One authority has described U.S. Steel as[2]

> . . . a big sprawling inert giant, whose production operations were improperly coordinated; suffering from a lack of a long-run planning agency; relying on an antiquated system of cost accounting: with an inadequate knowledge of the costs or of the relative profitability of the many thousands of items it sold; with production and cost standards generally below those considered everyday practice in other industries; with inadequate knowledge of its domestic markets and

[1]See Leonard W. Weiss, *Economics and American Industry* (New York: John Wiley & Sons, Inc., 1961), pp. 347–350.

[2]Statement by George Stocking, cited in Walter Adams (ed.), *The Structure of American Industry*, 3d ed. (New York: The Macmillan Company, 1961), p. 180.

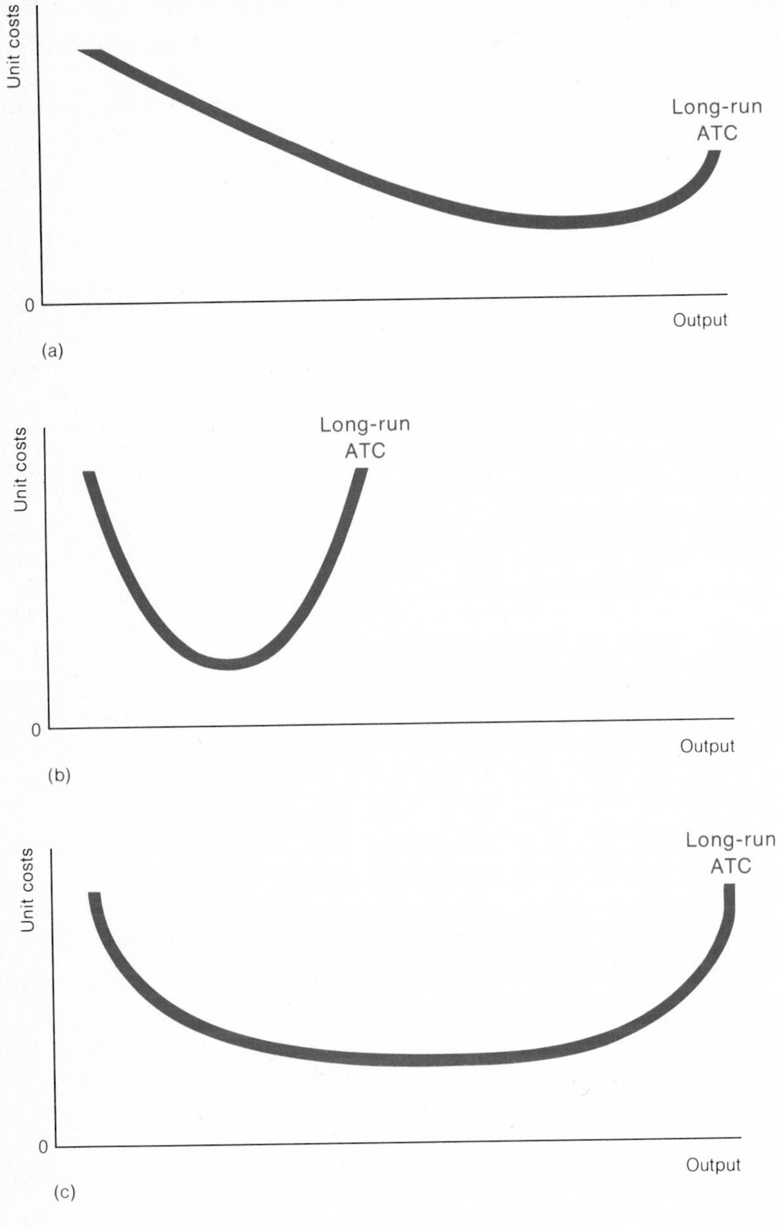

FIGURE 26·6 VARIOUS POSSIBLE LONG-RUN AVERAGE-COST CURVES

(*a*) When economies of scale are many and diseconomies remote, the ATC will fall over a wide range of production. (*b*) If economies of scale are few and diseconomies are quickly incurred, minimum unit costs will be encountered at a relatively low output. (*c*) Where economies of scale are rather rapidly exhausted and diseconomies not encountered until a considerably large scale of output has been achieved, long-run average costs will be relatively constant over a wide range of output.

no clear appreciation of its opportunities in foreign markets; with less efficient production facilities than its rivals had; slow in introducing new processes and new products.

These comments correctly imply that economies and diseconomies of scale are a fundamental determinant of the structure of any industry. Where economies of scale are many and diseconomies are remote, the long-run ATC curve will decline over a long range of output, as in Figure 26·6*a*. Such is the case in the automobile, aluminum, steel, and a host of other heavy industries. This means that, given consumer demand, efficient production will be achieved only with a small number of large producers. On the other hand, where economies of scale are few and diseconomies quickly encountered, minimum unit costs will be achieved at a modest level of production. The long-run ATC curve for such a situation is shown in Figure 26·6*b*. In such industries a given level of consumer demand will support a large number of relatively small producers. Many of the retail trades and some types of farming fall into this category. So do certain types of light manufacturing, for example, the baking, clothing, and shoe industries. Fairly small firms are as efficient as, or more efficient than, large-scale producers in such industries.

In some industries we find a mixture of large and small producers operating with roughly the same degree of efficiency—the meat-packing, furniture, and some aspects of the household-appliance industries are representative. In such industries the long-run ATC curve may be such that there exists a wide range of output between the point at which available economies of scale are exhausted and the point at which diseconomies of scale are encountered. Or, alternatively, economies and diseconomies of scale may be largely self-canceling over an extended range of output. Figure 26·6*c* illustrates the situation in which average costs are relatively constant over a wide range of output.

Caution: We are not implying here that long-run unit costs are the only determinant of the structure of industry. Indeed, it was stressed in Chapter 23 that the major determinants of the competitiveness of industry are several and varied. We are saying that there is considerable evidence that cost considerations are one important force in determining the number and size of firms in a particular industry.

SUMMARY

1. Economic costs include all payments which must be received by resource owners in order to assure their continued supply in a particular line of production. This definition includes explicit costs which flow to resource suppliers who are separate from a given enterprise and also implicit costs which are the remuneration of self-owned and self-employed resources. One of the implicit cost payments is a normal profit to the entrepreneur for the functions he performs.
2. In the short run a firm's plant capacity is fixed. The firm can use its plant more or less intensively by adding or subtracting units of variable resources, but the firm does not have sufficient time to alter its plant size.
3. The law of diminishing returns describes what happens to output as a fixed plant is used more intensively. The law states that, as successive units of a variable resource such as labor are added to a fixed plant, beyond some point the resulting marginal product associated with each additional worker will decline.
4. Because some resources are variable and others fixed, costs can be classified as variable or fixed in the short run. Fixed costs are those which are independent of the level of output. Variable costs are those which vary with output. The total cost of any output is the sum of fixed and variable costs at that output.
5. Average fixed, average variable, and average total costs are simply fixed, variable, and total cost per unit of output. Average fixed costs decline continuously as output increases, because a fixed sum is being apportioned over a larger and larger number of units of production. Average variable costs are U-shaped, reflecting the law of diminishing returns. Average total cost is the sum of average fixed and average variable cost; it too is U-shaped.

6. Marginal cost is the extra, or additional, cost of producing one more unit of output. Graphically, marginal cost cuts ATC and AVC at their minimum points.

7. The long run is a period of time sufficiently long for a firm to vary the amounts of all resources used, including plant size. Hence, in the long run all costs are variable. The long-run ATC, or planning, curve is composed of segments of the short-run ATC curves, which represent the various plant sizes a firm is able to construct in the long run.

8. The long-run ATC curve is generally U-shaped. Economies of scale are first encountered as a small firm expands. A number of considerations—greater specialization in the use of labor and management, the ability to use the most efficient equipment, and the more complete utilization of by-products—contribute to these economies of scale. Diseconomies of scale stem from the managerial complexities which accompany large-scale production.

9. The relative importance of economies and diseconomies of scale in an industry is often a major determinant of the structure of that industry. Generally speaking, where economies of scale extend to large levels of output, an industry tends to comprise a small number of large-scale producers. When economies of scale are exhausted at relatively low levels of output, there tends to be a large number of small firms in an industry.

QUESTIONS AND STUDY SUGGESTIONS

1. How do economists define costs? Distinguish between explicit and implicit costs, giving examples of each. What are the explicit and implicit costs of going to college? What are "normal profits"? Why does the economist classify normal profits as a cost? What are "economic profits"? Are economic profits a cost of production?

2. Distinguish between the short run and the long run. Which of the following are short-run and which are long-run adjustments? *a.* General Motors builds a new assembly plant; *b.* Acme Steel Corporation hires 200 more workers; *c.* a farmer increases the amount of fertilizer used on his corn crop; and *d.* an Alcoa plant adds a third shift of workers.

3. State and explain the law of diminishing returns. What bearing does this law have upon short-run costs? Be specific.

4. Distinguish between fixed and variable costs. Why can this distinction be made in the short run? Classify the following as fixed or variable costs: advertising expenditures, fuel, interest on company-issued bonds, shipping charges, payments for raw materials, real estate taxes, executive salaries, insurance premiums, wage payments, depreciation and obsolescence charges, sales taxes, and rental payments on leased office machinery. "There are no fixed costs in the long run; all costs are variable." Explain.

5. Assume a firm has fixed costs of $60 and variable costs as indicated on page 455. Complete the table on page 455. When finished, check your calculations by referring to question 4 at the end of Chapter 27.

a. Graph fixed cost, variable cost, and total cost. Explain how the law of diminishing returns influences the shapes of the variable-cost and total-cost curves.

b. Graph AFC, AVC, ATC, and MC. Explain the derivation and shape of each of these four curves and the relationships which they bear to one another. Specifically, explain in nontechnical terms why MC cuts both AVC and ATC at their minimum points.

6. What are economies and diseconomies of scale? How do they affect the shape of a firm's long-run ATC curve? What bearing may the exact shape of this curve have upon the structure of an industry?

7. "When marginal product is rising, marginal cost is falling. And when marginal product is diminishing, marginal cost is rising." Illustrate and explain graphically and through a numerical example.

Total product	Total fixed cost	Total variable cost	Total cost	Average fixed cost	Average variable cost	Average total cost	Marginal cost
0	$____	$ 0	$____	$____	$____	$____	
							$____
1	____	45	____	____	____	____	
							____
2	____	85	____	____	____	____	
							____
3	____	120	____	____	____	____	
							____
4	____	150	____	____	____	____	
							____
5	____	185	____	____	____	____	
							____
6	____	225	____	____	____	____	
							____
7	____	270	____	____	____	____	
							____
8	____	325	____	____	____	____	
							____
9	____	390	____	____	____	____	
							____
10	____	465	____	____	____	____	

SELECTED REFERENCES

Economic Issues, 4th ed., reading 41.

Bain, Joe S.: *Industrial Organization,* 2d ed. (New York: John Wiley & Sons, Inc., 1968), pp. 166–180.

Haynes, Warren W.: *Managerial Economics: Analysis and Cases,* rev. ed. (Austin, Tex.: Business Publications, Inc., 1969), chaps. 5 & 6.

Robinson, E. A. G.: *The Structure of Competitive Industry* (Chicago: The University of Chicago Press, 1958).

Stigler, George J.: *The Theory of Price,* 3d ed. (New York: The Macmillan Company, 1966), chaps. 6–8.

Watson, Donald S. (ed.): *Price Theory in Action,* 2d ed. (Boston: Houghton Mifflin Company, 1969), part 3.

PRICE AND OUTPUT DETERMINATION: PURE COMPETITION

We now have at our disposal the basic tools of analysis needed to understand how product price and output are determined. These analytical tools are applicable to all four basic market models—pure competition, pure monopoly, monopolistic competition, and oligopoly. In this chapter we focus attention upon price and output determination in a purely competitive industry.

CONCEPT AND OCCURRENCE OF PURE COMPETITION

Pure competition, you will recall, presupposes that certain specific conditions are fulfilled.

1. A purely competitive industry is composed of a large number of independent sellers.
2. The firms offer a standardized product. This feature rules out nonprice competition, that is, advertising, sales promotion, and so forth.
3. No individual firm supplies enough of the product to influence its market price noticeably.
4. In a competitive industry no artificial obstacles prevent new firms from entering or old firms from leaving the industry. Firms and the resources they employ are shiftable, or mobile.

The third characteristic is particularly important. The individual competitive firm has nothing to say about determining market price. Because it supplies a negligible portion of total output, the competitive firm cannot significantly influence the market price which the forces of total demand and supply have established. The competitive firm does not have a price policy, that is, the ability to adjust price. Rather the firm can merely *adjust to* the market price, which it must regard as a given datum determined by the market.

Pure competition is rare in practice. This does not mean, however, that an analysis of how competitive markets work is a useless and irrelevant exercise in logic. In the first place, there are a few industries which more closely approximate the competitive model than they do any other market structure. For

example, much can be learned about American agriculture by understanding the functioning of competitive markets. Secondly, pure competition provides the simplest context in which to apply the revenue and cost concepts developed in previous chapters. Pure competition is a simple and meaningful starting point for any discussion of price and output determination. Finally, in the concluding section of this chapter we shall discover that the operation of a purely competitive economy provides us with a standard, or norm, against which the efficiency of the real-world economy can be compared and evaluated. Though pure competition is a relatively rare market structure in our economy, it is one of considerable analytical and some practical importance.

Our analysis of pure competition centers upon three major objectives. First, we seek an understanding of how a competitive producer adjusts to market price in the short run. Next, the nature of long-run adjustments in a competitive industry is explored. Finally, we seek to evaluate the efficiency of competitive industries from the standpoint of society as a whole.

PROFIT MAXIMIZATION IN THE SHORT RUN

In the short run the competitive firm has a fixed plant and is attempting to maximize its profits or, as the case may be, minimize its losses by adjusting its output through changes in the amounts of variable resources (materials, labor, and so forth) it employs. The economic profits it seeks are obviously the difference between total revenue and total costs. Indeed, this points out the direction of our analysis. The revenue data of Chapter 25 and the cost data of Chapter 26 must be brought together in order that the profit-maximizing output for the firm can be determined.

There are two complementary approaches to determining the level of output at which a competitive firm will realize maximum profits or minimum losses. The first involves a comparison of total revenue and total costs; the second, a comparison of marginal revenue and marginal cost. Both approaches, incidentally, can be applied not only to a purely competitive firm but also to firms operating in any of the other three basic market structures. To ensure an understanding of output determination under pure competition, we shall invoke both approaches, emphasizing the marginal approach. Furthermore, both hypothetical data and graphic analysis will be employed to bolster our understanding of the two approaches.

Total-receipts–total-cost approach

Given the market price of its product, the competitive producer is faced with three related questions: (1) Should I produce? (2) If so, what amount? (3) What profit (or loss) will be realized?

At first glance the answer to question 1 seems obvious: "You should produce if it is profitable to do so." But the situation is a bit more complex than this. In the short run a part of the firm's total costs is variable costs, and the remainder is fixed costs. The latter will have to be paid "out of pocket" even when the firm is closed down. In the short run a firm takes a loss equal to its fixed costs when it is producing zero units of output. This means that, although there may be no level of output at which the firm can realize a profit, the firm might still produce, provided that in so doing it can realize a loss less than the fixed-cost loss it will face in closing down. In other words, the correct answer to the "Should I produce?" question is this: *The firm should produce in the short run if it can realize an economic profit or a loss which is less than its fixed costs.*

Assuming the firm *will* produce, the second question becomes relevant: "How much should be produced?" The answer here is fairly obvious: *In the short run the firm should produce that output at which it maximizes profits or minimizes losses.*

Now let us examine three cases which will demonstrate the validity of these two generalizations and answer our third query by indicating how profits and losses can be readily calculated. In the first case the firm will maximize its profits by producing. In the second case it will minimize its losses by producing. In the third case the firm will minimize its losses by closing down. Our plan of attack is to assume given short-run cost data for all three cases and to explore

the firm's production decisions when faced with three different product prices.

Profit-maximizing case In all three cases we employ cost data with which we are already familiar. Columns 3 through 5 of Table 27·1 merely repeat the fixed-, variable-, and total-cost data which were developed in Table 26·2. Assuming that market price is $131, we can derive total revenue for each level of output by simply multiplying output times price, as we did in Table 24·3. These data are presented in column 2. Then in column 6 the profit or loss which will be encountered at each output is found by subtracting total cost from total revenue. Now we have all the data needed to answer the three questions.

Should the firm produce? Yes, because it can realize a profit by doing so. How much? Nine units, because column 6 tells us that this is the output at which profits will be at a maximum. The size of that profit? $299.

Figure 27·1*a* compares total revenue and total cost graphically. Total revenue is a straight line, because under pure competition each additional unit adds the same amount—its price—to total revenue (Chapter 24). Total costs increase with output; more production requires more resources. But the rate of increase in total costs varies with the relative efficiency of the firm. For a time the rate of increase in total cost is less and less as the firm utilizes its fixed resources more efficiently. Then, after a time, total cost begins to increase by ever-increasing amounts because of the inefficiencies which accompany overutilization of the firm's plant. A *break-even point* occurs at about 2 units of output. And, if our data were extended beyond 10 units of output, another such point would be incurred where total cost would catch up with total revenue, as is shown in Figure 27·1*a*. Any output within these break-even points will entail an economic profit. The maximum profit is obviously achieved where the vertical difference between total revenue and total cost is greatest. For our data this is at 9 units of output.

Loss-minimizing case Assuming no change in costs, the firm may not be able to realize economic profits if the market yields a price considerably below

TABLE 27·1 THE PROFIT-MAXIMIZING OUTPUT FOR A PURELY COMPETITIVE FIRM: TOTAL-REVENUE—TOTAL-COST APPROACH (PRICE = $131) (*hypothetical data*)

(1) Total product	(2) Total revenue	(3) Total fixed cost	(4) Total variable cost	(5) Total cost	(6) Profit (+) or loss (−), = (2) − (5)
0	$ 0	$100	$ 0	$ 100	$−100
1	131	100	90	190	− 59
2	262	100	170	270	− 8
3	393	100	240	340	+ 53
4	524	100	300	400	+124
5	655	100	370	470	+185
6	786	100	450	550	+236
7	917	100	540	640	+277
8	1,048	100	650	750	+298
9	1,179	100	780	880	+299
10	1,310	100	930	1,030	+280

$131. To illustrate: Suppose the market price is $81. As column 6 of Table 27·2 indicates, at this price all levels of output will entail losses. But the firm will not close down. Why? Because by producing, the firm can realize a loss considerably less than the fixed-cost loss it would incur by closing down. Specifically, the firm will minimize its losses by producing 6 units of output. The resulting $64 loss is clearly preferable to the $100 loss which closing down would involve. Stated differently, by producing 6 units the firm earns a total revenue of $486, sufficient to pay all the firm's variable cost ($450) and also a substantial portion—$36 worth—of the firm's fixed costs. There are, you will note, several other outputs which entail a loss less than the firm's $100 fixed costs; but at 6 units of output the loss is minimized.

Close-down case Assume finally that the market price is a mere $71. Given short-run costs, column 9 of Table 27·2 clearly indicates that at all levels of output losses will exceed the $100 fixed-cost loss the firm will incur by closing down. Obviously, then, the firm will minimize its losses by closing down, that is, by producing zero units of output.

Figure 27·1*b* demonstrates the loss-minimizing and close-down cases graphically. In the loss-minimizing case, the total-revenue line TR (P = $81) exceeds total variable cost by the maximum amount at 6 units of output. Here total revenue is $486, and the firm recovers all of its $450 of variable costs and also $36 worth of its fixed costs. The firm's minimum loss is $64, clearly superior to the $100 fixed-cost loss involved in closing down. In the close-down case, the total-revenue line TR (P = $71) lies below the total-variable-cost curve at all points; there is no output at which variable costs can be recovered. Therefore, by producing the firm would incur losses in excess of its fixed costs. The firm's best choice is to close down and pay its $100 fixed-cost loss out of pocket.

Marginal-revenue–marginal-cost approach

An alternative means for determining the amounts which a competitive firm will be willing to offer in the market at each possible price is for the firm to determine and compare the amounts that each additional unit of output will add to total revenue, on the one hand, and to total cost, on the other. That is, the

TABLE 27·2 THE LOSS-MINIMIZING OUTPUTS FOR A PURELY COMPETITIVE FIRM: TOTAL-REVENUE—TOTAL-COST APPROACH (PRICES = $81 AND $71) (*hypothetical data*)

Product price = $81						Product price = $71		
(1) Total product	(2) Total revenue	(3) Total fixed cost	(4) Total variable cost	(5) Total cost	(6) Profit (+) or loss (−), = (2) − (5)	(7) Total revenue	(8) Total cost	(9) Profit (+) or loss (−), = (7) − (8)
0	$ 0	$100	$ 0	$ 100	$−100	$ 0	$ 100	$−100
1	81	100	90	190	−109	71	190	−119
2	162	100	170	270	−108	142	270	−128
3	243	100	240	340	− 97	213	340	−127
4	324	100	300	400	− 76	284	400	−116
5	405	100	370	470	− 65	355	470	−115
6	486	100	450	550	− 64	426	550	−124
7	567	100	540	640	− 73	497	640	−143
8	648	100	650	750	−102	568	750	−182
9	729	100	780	880	−151	639	880	−241
10	810	100	930	1,030	−220	710	1,030	−320

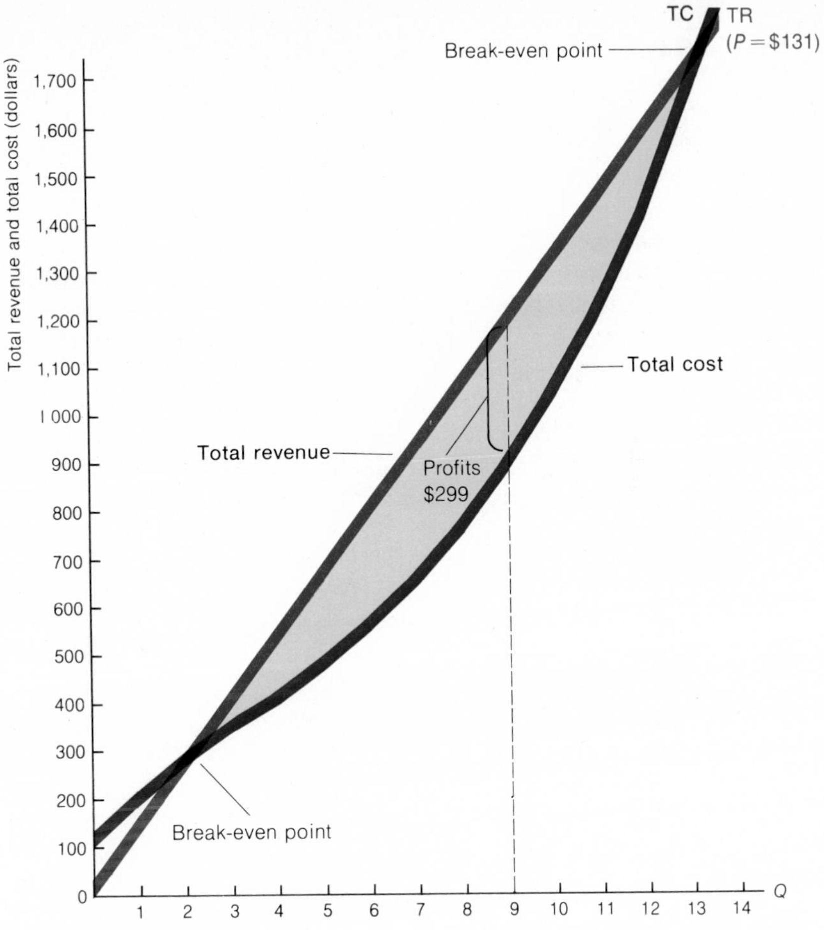

(a)

firm should compare the *marginal revenue* (MR) and the *marginal cost* (MC) of each successive unit of output. Any unit whose marginal revenue exceeds its marginal cost should obviously be produced. Why? Because on each such unit, the firm is gaining more in revenue from its sale than it adds to costs in getting that unit produced. The unit of output is adding to profits or, as the case may be, subtracting from losses. Similarly, if the marginal cost of a unit of output exceeds its marginal revenue, the firm should avoid producing that unit. It will add more to costs than to revenue; such a unit will not ''pay its way.''

In the initial stages of production, where output is relatively low, marginal revenue will usually (but not always) exceed marginal cost. It is therefore profitable to produce through this range of output. But at later stages of production, where output is relatively high, rising marginal costs will cause the reverse to be true. Marginal cost will exceed marginal revenue. Production of units of output falling in this

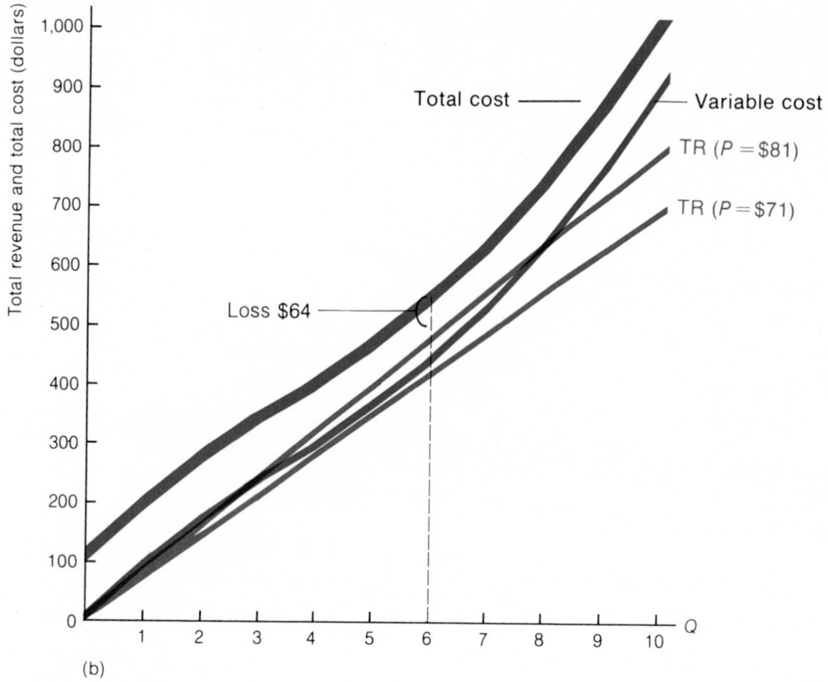

FIGURE 27 · 1 THE PROFIT-MAXIMIZING (*a*), LOSS-MINIMIZING, AND CLOSE-DOWN CASES (*b*), AS SHOWN BY THE TOTAL-REVENUE–TOTAL-COST APPROACH

A firm's profits are maximized in (*a*) at that output at which total revenue exceeds total cost by the maximum amount. A firm will minimize its losses in (*b*) by producing at that output at which total cost exceeds total revenue by the smallest amount. However, if there is no output at which total revenue exceeds variable costs, the firm will minimize losses in the short run by closing down.

range is obviously to be avoided in the interest of maximizing profits. Separating these two production ranges will be a unique point at which marginal revenue equals marginal cost. This point is the key to the output determining rule: *The firm will maximize profits or minimize losses by producing at that point where marginal revenue equals marginal cost.* For convenience we shall call this profit-maximizing guide the MR = MC rule. For most sets of MR and MC data, there will be no nonfractional level of output at which MR and MC are precisely equal. In such instances the firm should produce the last complete unit of output whose MR exceeds its MC.

Two features of this MR = MC rule merit comment. First, a qualification: The rule presumes that the firm will choose to produce rather than close down. Shortly we shall note that marginal revenue must be equal to or exceed average variable cost, or the firm will find it preferable to close down rather than produce the MR = MC output.

Second, it is to be emphasized that the MR = MC rule is an accurate guide to profit maximization for all firms, be they purely competitive, monopolistic, monopolistically competitive, or oligopolistic. The rule's application is not limited to the special case of pure competition. At the same time it is noteworthy that the MR = MC rule can be conveniently restated in a slightly different form when being applied to a purely competitive firm. You will recall that product price is determined by the broad market forces of supply and demand, and although the competitive firm can sell as much or as little as it chooses at that price, the firm cannot manipulate the price itself. In technical terms the demand, or sales, schedule faced by a competitive seller is perfectly elastic at the going market price. The result is that product price and marginal revenue are equal; that is, each extra unit sold adds precisely its price to total revenue (Chapter 24). Thus under pure competition—and *only* under pure competition—we may substitute price for marginal revenue in the rule, so that it reads as follows: *To maximize profits or minimize losses the competitive firm should produce at that point where price equals marginal cost* (*P* = MC). This *P* = MC rule is simply a special case of the MR = MC rule.

Now let us apply the MR = MC or, if you prefer, MR (*P*) = MC rule, using the same three prices employed in our total-revenue–total-cost approach to profit maximization.

Profit-maximizing case Table 27·3 reproduces the unit- and marginal-cost data derived in Table 26·2. It is, of course, the marginal-cost data of column 5 in Table 27·3 which we wish to compare with price (equal to marginal revenue) for each unit of output. Suppose first that market price, and therefore marginal revenue, is $131, as shown in column 6. What is the profit-maximizing output? It is readily seen that

TABLE 27·3 THE PROFIT-MAXIMIZING OUTPUT FOR A PURELY COMPETITIVE FIRM: MARGINAL-REVENUE-EQUALS-MARGINAL-COST APPROACH (PRICE = $131) (*hypothetical data*)

(1) Total product	(2) Average fixed cost	(3) Average variable cost	(4) Average total cost	(5) Marginal cost	(6) Price = marginal revenue
0					
1	$100.00	$90.00	$190.00	$ 90	$131
2	50.00	85.00	135.00	80	131
3	33.33	80.00	113.33	70	131
4	25.00	75.00	100.00	60	131
5	20.00	74.00	94.00	70	131
6	16.67	75.00	91.67	80	131
7	14.29	77.14	91.43	90	131
8	12.50	81.23	93.73	110	131
9	11.11	86.67	97.78	130	131
10	10.00	93.00	103.00	150	131

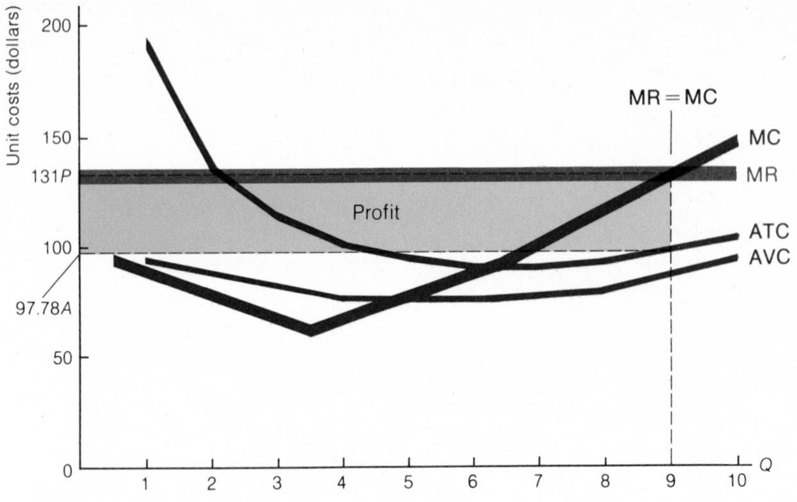

FIGURE 27·2 THE SHORT-RUN PROFIT-MAXIMIZING POSITION OF A PURELY COMPETITIVE FIRM

The P = MC output allows the competitive producer to maximize profits or minimize losses. In this case price exceeds average total cost at the P = MC output of 9 units. Economic profits per unit of AP are realized; total economic profits are indicated by the yellow rectangle.

each and every unit of output up to and including the ninth adds more to total revenue than to total cost. That is, price, or marginal revenue, exceeds marginal cost on all of the first 9 units of output. Each of these units therefore adds to the firm's profits and should obviously be produced. The tenth unit, however, will not be produced, because it would add more to costs ($150) than to revenue ($131.)

The level of economic profits realized by the firm can be readily calculated from the unit-cost data. Multiplying price ($131) times output (9), we find total revenue to be $1,179. Total cost of about[1] $880 is found by multiplying average total cost ($97.78) by output (9). The difference of $299 is economic profits. An alternative means of calculating economic profits is to determine profit *per unit* by subtracting average total cost ($97.78) from product price ($131) and multiplying the difference (per unit profits of $33.22) by the level of output (9). The skeptical reader should calculate profits at outputs other than those indicated to be most profitable by the MR (P) = MC rule to verify that they entail either losses or profits less than $299.

Figure 27·2 makes the comparison of price and marginal cost graphically. Here per unit economic profit is indicated by the distance AP. When multiplied by the profit-maximizing output, the resulting total economic profit is shown by the yellow rectangular area.

It should be noted that the firm is seeking to maximize its *total* profits, not its *per unit* profits. Per unit profits are largest at 7 units of output, where price exceeds average total cost by $39.57 ($131 minus $91.43). But by producing only 7 units, the firm would be forgoing the production of additional units of output which would clearly contribute to total profits. The firm is happy to accept lower per unit profits if the resulting extra units of sales more than compensate for the lower per unit profits.

Loss-minimizing case Now let us apply the same reasoning on the assumption that market price is $81

[1] In most instances the unit-cost data are rounded figures. Therefore, economic profits calculated from them will typically vary by a few cents from the profits determined in the total-revenue–total-cost approach. We here ignore the few-cents differentials and make our answers consistent with the results of the total-revenue–total-cost approach.

rather than $131. Should the firm produce? If so, how much? And what will the resulting profits or losses be? The answers, respectively, are "Yes," "Six units," and "A loss of $64."

Column 6 of Table 27·4 shows the new price (equal to marginal revenue) alongside the same unit- and marginal-cost data presented in Table 27·3. Comparing columns 5 and 6, we find that the first unit of output adds $90 to total cost but only $81 to total revenue. One might be inclined to conclude: "Don't produce—close down!" But this would be hasty. Remember that in the very early stages of production marginal physical product is low, making marginal cost unusually high. The price–marginal-cost relationship might improve with increased production. And it does. On the next 5 units—2 through 6—price exceeds marginal cost. Each of these 5 units adds more to revenue than to cost, more than compensating for the "loss" taken on the first unit. Beyond 6 units, however, MC exceeds MR (*P*). The firm should therefore produce at 6 units. In general, the profit-seeking producer should always compare marginal revenue (or price under pure competition) with the rising portion of his marginal-cost schedule or curve.

Will production be profitable? No, it will not. At 6 units of output, average total costs of $91.67 exceed price of $81 by $10.67 per unit. Multiply by the 6 units of output, and the firm's total loss is about $64. Then why produce? Because this loss is less than the firm's $100 worth of fixed costs—the $100 loss the firm would incur in the short run by closing down. Looked at differently, the firm receives enough revenue per unit ($81) to cover its variable costs of $75

TABLE 27·4 THE LOSS-MINIMIZING OUTPUTS FOR A PURELY COMPETITIVE FIRM: MARGINAL-REVENUE-EQUALS-MARGINAL-COST APPROACH (PRICES = $81 AND $71) (*hypothetical data*)

(1) Total product	(2) Average fixed cost	(3) Average variable cost	(4) Average total cost	(5) Marginal cost	(6) $81 price = marginal revenue	(7) $71 price = marginal revenue
0						
				$ 90	$81	$71
1	$100.00	$90.00	$190.00			
				80	81	71
2	50.00	85.00	135.00			
				70	81	71
3	33.33	80.00	113.33			
				60	81	71
4	25.00	75.00	100.00			
				70	81	71
5	20.00	74.00	94.00			
				80	81	71
6	16.67	75.00	91.67			
				90	81	71
7	14.29	77.14	91.43			
				110	81	71
8	12.50	81.23	93.73			
				130	81	71
9	11.11	86.67	97.78			
				150	81	71
10	10.00	93.00	103.00			

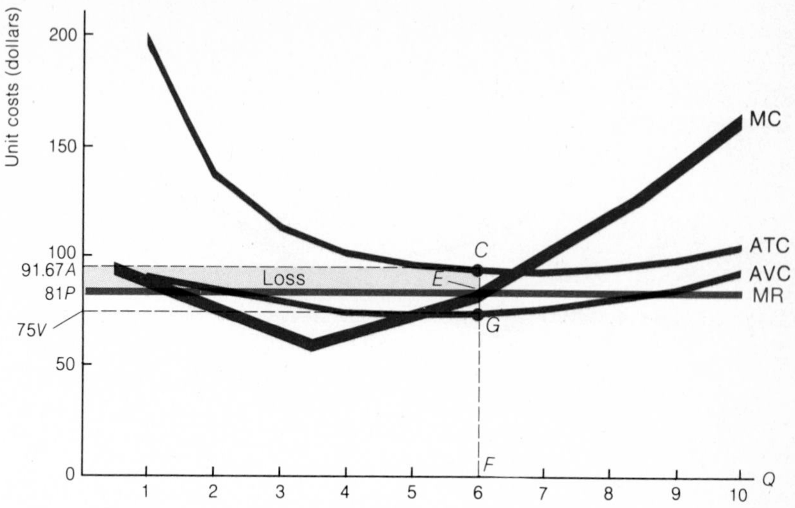

FIGURE 27·3 THE SHORT-RUN LOSS-MINIMIZING POSITION OF A PURELY COMPETITIVE FIRM

If price exceeds the minimum AVC but is less than ATC, the $P = \text{MC}$ output of 6 units will permit the firm to minimize its losses. In this instance losses are *AP* per unit; total losses are shown by the area *APEC*.

and also provide $6 per unit, or a total of $36, to apply against the payment of fixed costs. Therefore, the firm's loss is only $64 ($100 minus $36), rather than $100.

This case is shown graphically in Figure 27·3. Whenever price exceeds the minimum average variable cost but falls short of average total cost, the firm can pay a part of, but not all, its fixed costs by producing. In this instance total variable costs are shown by the area *OVGF*. Total revenue, however, is *OPEF*, greater than total variable costs by *VPEG*. This excess of revenue over variable costs can be applied against total fixed costs, represented by area *VACG*.

Close-down case Suppose now that the market yields a price of only $71. In this case it will pay the firm to close down, to produce nothing. Why? Because there is no output at which the firm can cover its average variable costs, much less its average total cost. In other words, the smallest loss it can realize by producing is greater than the $100 worth of fixed costs it will lose by closing down. The smart thing is obviously to close down. This can be verified by comparing columns 3 and 7 of Table 27·4 and can be readily visualized in Figure 27·4. Price comes closest to covering average variable costs at the MR (P) = MC output of 5 units. But even here, price or revenue per unit would fall short of average variable cost by $3 ($74 minus $71). By producing at the MR (P) = MC output the firm would lose its $100 worth of fixed costs *plus* $15 ($3 on each of the five units) worth of variable costs, for a total loss of $115. This clearly compares unfavorably with the $100 fixed-

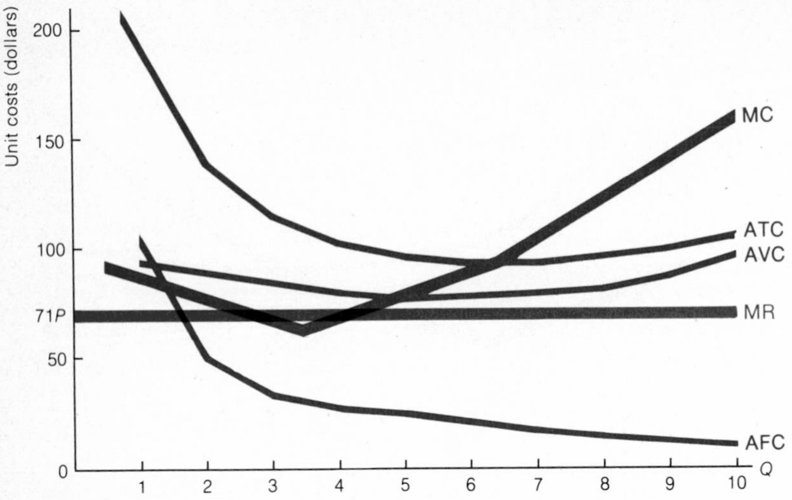

FIGURE 27·4 THE SHORT-RUN CLOSE-DOWN POSITION OF A PURELY COMPETITIVE FIRM

If price falls short of minimum AVC, the competitive firm will minimize its losses in the short run by closing down. There is no level of output at which the firm can produce and realize a loss smaller than its fixed costs.

cost loss the firm would incur by choosing to close down. In short, it will obviously pay the firm to close down rather than operate at a $71 price or, for that matter, at any price less than $74.

The close-down case obligates us to modify our MR (*P*) = MC rule for profit maximization or loss minimization. A *competitive firm will maximize profits or minimize losses in the short run by producing at that output at which MR* (P) = *MC, provided that price exceeds the minimum average-variable-cost figure.*

Marginal cost and the short-run supply curve Now the astute reader will recognize that we have simply selected three different prices and asked how much the profit-seeking competitive firm, faced with certain costs, would choose to offer or supply in the market at each of these prices. This information—price and corresponding quantity supplied—obviously constitutes the supply schedule for the competitive firm. Table 27·5 summarizes the supply schedule data for the three prices we have chosen—$131, $81, and $71. The reader is urged to apply the MR (*P*) = MC rule (as modified by the close-down case) to verify the quantity-supplied data for the $151, $111, $91, and $61 prices and calculate the corresponding profits or losses. The supply schedule is obviously

TABLE 27·5 THE SUPPLY SCHEDULE OF A COMPETITIVE FIRM CONFRONTED WITH THE COST DATA OF TABLE 27·3 (*hypothetical data*)

Price	Quantity supplied	Maximum profit (+) or minimum loss (−)
$151	10	$
131	9	+299
111	8	
91	7	
81	6	− 64
71	0	−100
61	0	

upsloping. In this instance price must be $74 (equal to minimum average variable cost) or greater before any output is supplied. The profit-seeking firm is induced to offer more of the product as higher and higher prices are equated with the marginal cost of larger and larger outputs in the cost table.

Figure 27·5 generalizes upon our application of the MR (P) = MC rule. Here we have drawn the appropriate cost curves. Then from the vertical axis we have extended a series of marginal-revenue lines from some of the various possible prices which the market might set for the firm. The crucial prices are P_2 and P_4. Our close-down case reminds us that at any price *below* P_2—that price equal to the minimum average variable cost—the firm should close down and supply nothing. Actually, by producing Q_2 units of output at a price of P_2, the firm will just cover its variable costs, and its losses will be equal to its fixed costs. The firm therefore would be indifferent as between closing down and producing Q_2 units of output. But at any price below P_2, such as P_1, the firm will close down and supply zero units of output. P_4 is strategic because it is the price at which the firm will just break even by producing Q_4 units of

FIGURE 27·5 MARGINAL COST AND THE COMPETITIVE FIRM'S SHORT–RUN SUPPLY CURVE

Application of the P = MC rule, as modified by the close-down case, reveals that the segment of the firm's MC curve which lies above AVC is its short-run supply curve. At any price between P_2 and P_4, such as P_3, losses will be minimized by producing the P = MC output. At any price above P_4, such as P_5 or P_6, profits will be maximized at the P = MC output.

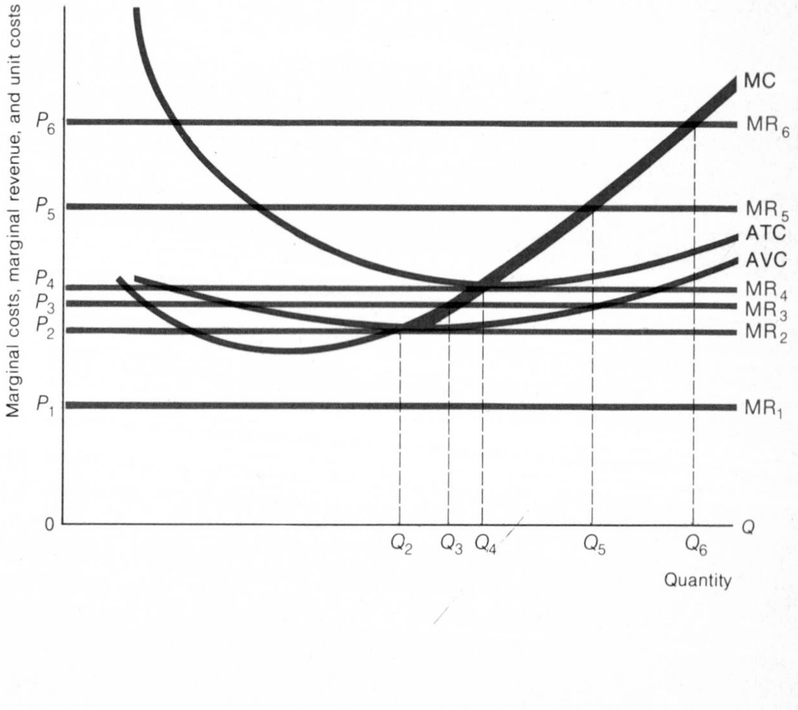

output, as indicated by the MR (*P*) = MC rule. Here total revenue will just cover total costs (including a normal profit). At P_3 the firm supplies Q_3 units of output and in so doing minimizes its losses. At any other price between P_2 and P_4 the firm will minimize its losses by producing to the point where MR (*P*) = MC. At any price above P_4 the firm will maximize its economic profits by producing to the point where MR (*P*) = MC. Thus at P_5 and P_6 the firm will realize the greatest profits by supplying Q_5 and Q_6 units of output.

Now the basic point is this: Each of the various MR (*P*) = MC intersection points shown in Figure 27•5 indicates a possible product price and the corresponding quantity which the profit-seeking firm would supply at that price. These points, by definition, constitute the supply curve of the competitive firm. Because nothing would be produced at any price below the minimum average variable cost, we can conclude that *the portion of the firm's marginal-cost curve which lies above its average-variable-cost curve is its short-run supply curve.* The heavy segment of the marginal-cost curve is the short-run supply curve in Figure 27•5. This is the link between production costs and supply in the short run.

Short-run competitive pricing

Let us now pause to summarize the main points we have made concerning short-run competitive pricing. Table 27•6 provides a convenient check sheet on the total-revenue–total-cost and MR = MC approaches to determining the competitive firm's profit-maximizing output. This table warrants careful study by the reader. In the MR = MC approach it is noteworthy that in deciding whether or not to produce, it is the comparison of price with minimum average variable cost which is all-important. Then, in determining the profit-maximizing or loss-minimizing amount to produce, it is the comparison—or better yet, the equality—of MR (*P*) and MC which is crucial. Finally, in determining the actual profit or loss associated with the MR (*P*) = MC output, price and average total cost must be contrasted. A final basic conclusion implied in Table 27•6 is that the segment of the short-run marginal-cost curve which lies above the average-variable-cost curve is the competitive firm's short-run supply curve. This conclusion stems from the application of the MR (*P*) = MC rule and the necessary modification suggested by the close-down case.

TABLE 27•6 SUMMARY OF COMPETITIVE OUTPUT DETERMINATION IN THE SHORT RUN

	Total-revenue–total-cost approach	Marginal-revenue–marginal-cost approach
Should the firm produce?	Yes, if TR exceeds TC or if TC exceeds TR by some amount less than total fixed costs.	Yes, if price is equal to, or greater than, minimum average variable cost.
What quantity should be produced to maximize profits?	Produce where the excess of TR over TC is a maximum or where excess of TC over TR is a minimum (and less than total fixed costs).	Produce where MR or price equals MC.
Will production result in an economic profit?	Yes, if TR exceeds TC. No, if TC exceeds TR.	Yes, if price exceeds average total cost. No, if average total cost exceeds price.

TABLE 27·7 FIRM AND MARKET SUPPLY AND MARKET DEMAND (*hypothetical data*)

(1) Quantity supplied, single firm	(2) Total quantity supplied, 1,000 firms	(3) Product price	(4) Total quantity demanded
10	10,000	$151	4,000
9	9,000	131	6,000
8	8,000	111	8,000
7	7,000	91	9,000
6	6,000	81	11,000
0	0	71	13,000
0	0	61	16,000

Firm and industry: equilibrium price

Now one final wrap-up step remains. Having developed the competitive firm's short-run supply curve through the application of the MR (*P*) = MC rule, we must determine which of the various price possibilities will actually be the equilibrium price. Recalling Chapter 4, we know that in a purely competitive market, equilibrium price is determined by *total,* or market, supply and total demand. To derive total supply we know that the sales schedules or curves of the individual competitive sellers must be summed. Thus in Table 27·7, columns 1 and 3 repeat the individual competitive firm's supply schedule just derived in Table 27·5. Let us now conveniently assume that there are a total of 1,000 competitive firms in this industry, each having the same total and unit costs as the single firm we have been discussing. This allows us to calculate the total- or market-supply schedule (columns 2 and 3) by multiplying the quantity-supplied figures of the single firm (column 1) by 1,000.

Now in order to determine equilibrium price and output, this total-supply data must be compared with total-demand data. For purposes of illustration, let us assume total-demand data are as shown in columns 3 and 4 of Table 27·7. Comparing the total quantity supplied and total quantity demanded at the seven possible prices, we readily determine that the equilibrium price is $111 and that equilibrium quantity is 8,000 units for the industry and 8 units for each of the 1,000 identical firms.

Will these conditions of market supply and demand make this a prosperous or unprosperous industry? Multiplying product price ($111) by output (8), we find the total revenue of each firm to be $888. Total cost is $750, found by multiplying average total cost of $93.73 by 8, or simply by looking at column 5 of Table 27·1. The $138 difference is the economic profit of each firm. Another way of calculating economic profits is to determine *per unit* profit by subtracting average total cost ($93.73) from product price ($111) and multiplying the difference (per unit profits of $17.27) by the firm's equilibrium level of output (8). For the industry, total economic profit is obviously $138,000. This, then, is a prosperous industry.

Figure 27·6*a* and *b* shows this analysis graphically. The individual supply curves of each of the 1,000 identical firms—one of which is shown as *ss* in Figure 26·6*a*—are summed horizontally to get the total-supply curve *SS* of Figure 27·6*b*. Given total demand

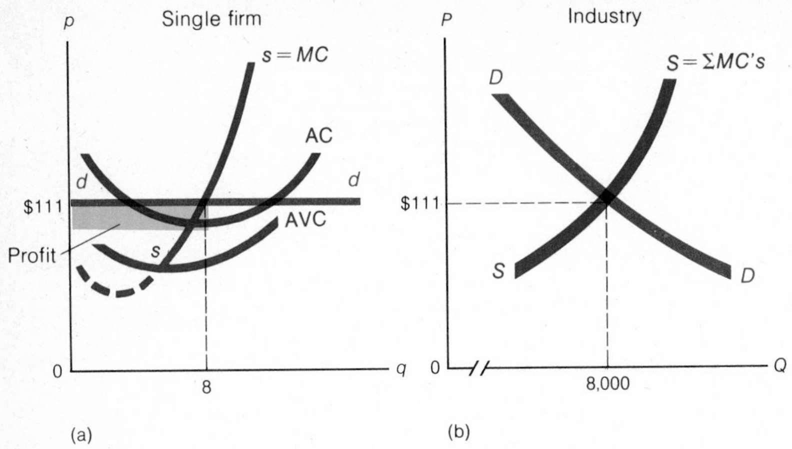

FIGURE 27·6 SHORT-RUN COMPETITIVE EQUILIBRIUM FOR A REPRESENTATIVE FIRM (*a*) AND THE INDUSTRY (*b*)

The horizontal sum of the 1,000 firms' supply curves (*ss*) determines the industry supply curve (*SS*). Given industry demand (*DD*), the short-run equilibrium price and output for the industry are $111 and 8,000 units. Taking the equilibrium price as given datum, the representative firm establishes its profit-maximizing output at 8 units and, in this case, realizes the economic profit shown by the yellow area.

DD, equilibrium price is found to be $111, and equilibrium quantity for the industry is 8,000 units. This equilibrium price is given and unalterable to the individual firm; that is, the typical firm's demand curve is perfectly elastic at the equilibrium price, as indicated by *dd*. Because price is given and constant to the individual firm, the marginal-revenue curve coincides with the demand curve. Price obviously exceeds average total cost at the firm's equilibrium MR (*P*) = MC output, resulting in a situation of economic profits similar to that already portrayed in Figure 27·2.

Assuming that no changes in costs or market demand occur, these diagrams reveal a genuine short-run equilibrium situation. There are no shortages or surpluses in the market to cause price or total quantity to change. Nor can any of the firms making up the industry improve themselves profitwise by altering their output. Note, too, that higher unit and marginal costs, on the one hand, or a weaker market demand situation, on the other, could have posed a loss situation similar to Figure 27·3. The student is urged to sketch in Figure 27·6*a* and *b* how higher costs and a less favorable demand could cause a short-run equilibrium situation entailing losses.

Figure 27·6*a* and *b* brings out a final notable point. We have emphasized that product price is a given datum to the *individual* competitive firm. But at the same time the supply plans of all competitive producers *as a group* are a basic determinant of product price. If we recall the fallacy of composition, we find there is no inconsistency here. Though each firm, supplying a negligible fraction of total supply, cannot affect price, the sum of the supply curves of all the many firms in the industry constitutes the industry supply curve, and this curve does have an important bearing upon price. In short, under competition, equilibrium price is a given datum to the individual firm and simultaneously is the result of the production (supply) decisions of all firms taken as a group.

PROFIT MAXIMIZATION IN THE LONG RUN

The long run permits firms to make certain adjustments which time does not allow in the short run. In the short run there is a given number of firms in an industry, each of which has a fixed, unalterable plant. True, firms may close down in the sense that they produce zero units of output in the short run;

but they do not have sufficient time to liquidate their assets and go out of business. By contrast, in the long run firms already in an industry have sufficient time either to expand or to contract their plant capacities, and, more important, the number of firms in the industry may either increase or decrease as new firms enter or old firms leave. We want to discover how these long-run adjustments modify our conclusions concerning short-run output and price determination.

It will facilitate our analysis greatly to make certain simplifying assumptions, none of which will impair the general validity of our conclusions.

1. We shall suppose that the only long-run adjustment is the entry and exodus of firms. Furthermore, for simplicity's sake we ignore the short-run adjustment already analyzed, in order to grasp more clearly the nature of long-run competitive adjustments.

2. It will also be assumed that all firms in the industry have identical cost curves. This allows us to talk in terms of an "average," or "representative," firm with the knowledge that all other firms in the industry are similarly affected by any long-run adjustments which occur.

3. We assume for the moment that the industry under discussion is a constant-cost industry. This means simply that the entry and exodus of firms will not affect resource prices or, therefore, the locations of the unit-cost schedules of the individual firms.

Now our goal is to describe long-run competitive adjustments both verbally and through simple graphic analysis. It will be well to state in advance the basic conclusion we seek to explain: *After all long-run adjustments are completed, that is, when long-run equilibrium is achieved, product price will be exactly equal to, and production will occur at, each firm's point of minimum average total cost.* This conclusion follows from two basic facts: (1) firms seek profits and shun losses, and (2) under competition firms are free to enter and leave industries. If price exceeds average total costs, the resulting economic profits will attract new firms to the industry. But this expansion of the industry will increase product supply until price is brought back down into equality with average total cost. Conversely, if price is less than average total cost, the resulting losses will cause firms to leave the industry. As they leave, total product supply will decline, bringing price back up into equality with average total cost.

Our conclusion can best be demonstrated and its significance evaluated by assuming that the average or representative firm in a purely competitive industry is initially in long-run equilibrium. This is shown in Figure 27·7*a*, where price and minimum average total cost are equal at $50. Economic profits here are zero; hence, the industry is in equilibrium or "at rest," because there is no tendency for firms to enter or leave the industry. As we know, the going market price is determined by total, or industry, demand and supply, as shown by D_1D_1 and S_1S_1 in Figure 27·7*b*. (The market supply schedule, incidentally, is a short-run schedule; the industry's long-run supply schedule will be developed in our discussion.) By examining the quantity axes of the two graphs, we note that if all firms are identical, there must be 1,000 firms in the industry, each producing 100 units, to achieve the industry's equilibrium output of 100,000 units.

Entry of firms eliminates profits

Now our model is set up. Let us upset the serenity of this long-run equilibrium situation and trace the subsequent adjustments. Suppose that a change in consumer tastes increases product demand from D_1D_1 to D_2D_2. This favorable shift in demand obviously makes production profitable; the new price of $60 exceeds average total cost. *These economic profits will lure new firms into the industry.* Some of the entrants will be newly created firms; others will shift from less prosperous industries. But as the firms enter, the market supply of the product will increase, causing product price to gravitate downward from $60 toward the original $50 level. Assuming, as we are, that the entry of new firms has no effect upon costs, economic profits will persist, and entry will therefore continue until short-run market supply has increased to S_2S_2. At this point price is again equal to minimum average total cost at $50. The economic profits caused by the boost in demand have been competed away to zero, and as a result the previous

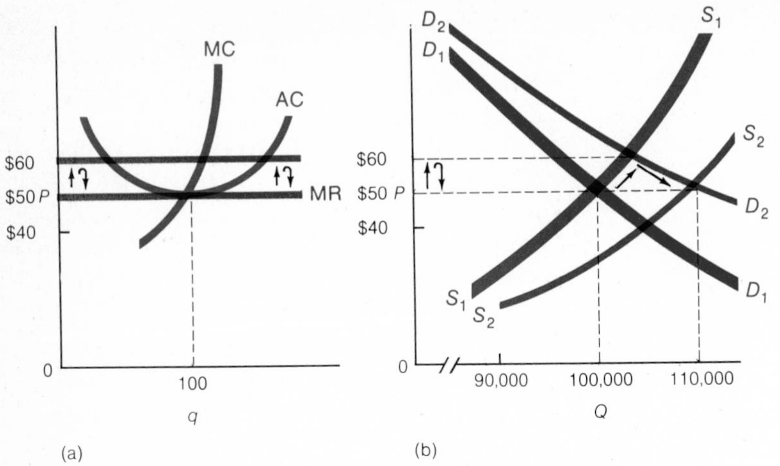

FIGURE 27·7 TEMPORARY PROFITS AND THE REESTABLISHMENT OF LONG-RUN EQUILIBRIUM IN A REPRESENTATIVE FIRM (*a*) AND THE INDUSTRY (*b*)

A favorable shift in demand (D_1D_1 to D_2D_2) will upset the original equilibrium and cause economic profits. But profits will cause new firms to enter the industry, increasing supply (S_1S_1 to S_2S_2) and lowering product price until economic profits are once again zero.

incentive for more firms to enter the industry has disappeared. Long-run equilibrium has been restored at this point.

Figure 27·7 tells us that upon the reestablishment of long-run equilibrium, industry output is 110,000 units and that each firm in the now expanded industry is producing 100 units. We can therefore conclude that the industry is now composed of 1,100 firms; that is, 100 new firms have entered the industry.

Exodus of firms eliminates losses

To strengthen our understanding of long-run competitive equilibrium, let us throw our analysis into reverse. In Figure 27·8*a* and *b* the heavy lines show once again the initial long-run equilibrium situation used as a point of departure in our previous analysis of how the entry of firms eliminates profits.

Now let us suppose that consumer demand falls from D_1D_1 to D_3D_3. This forces price down to $40, making production unprofitable. In time these losses will force firms to leave the industry. As capital equipment wears out and contractual obligations expire, some firms will simply toss in the sponge. As this exodus of firms proceeds, however, industry supply will decrease, moving from S_1S_1 toward S_3S_3. And as this occurs, price will begin to rise from $40 back toward $50. Assuming costs are unchanged by the exodus of firms, losses will force firms to leave the industry until supply has declined to S_3S_3, at which point price is again exactly $50, barely consistent with minimum average total cost. The exodus of firms continues until losses are eliminated and long-run equilibrium is again restored.

The reader will note from Figure 27·8*a* and *b* that total quantity supplied is now 90,000 units and each firm is producing 100 units. This obviously means that the industry is now populated by only 900 firms rather than the original 1,000. Losses have forced 100 firms out of business.

Our prestated conclusion has now been verified. Competition, as reflected in the entry and exodus of firms, forces price into equality with the minimum long-run average total cost of production, and each firm produces at the point of minimum long-run average total cost. We should now ask: What is the nature

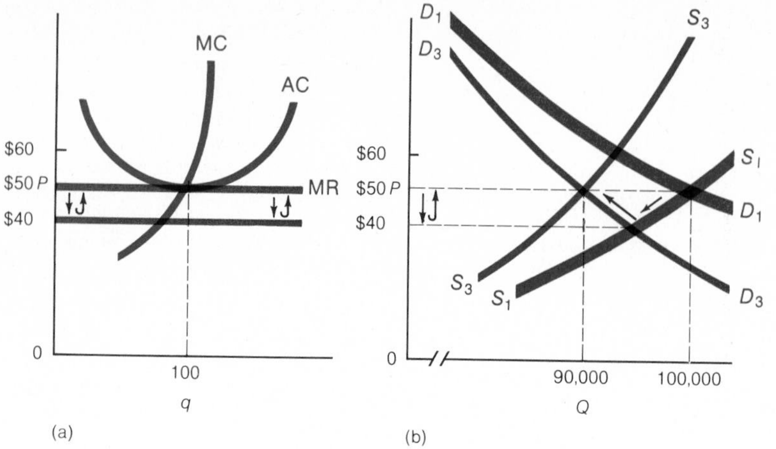

FIGURE 27·8 TEMPORARY LOSSES AND THE REESTABLISHMENT OF LONG-RUN EQUILIBRIUM IN A REPRESENTATIVE FIRM (*a*) AND THE INDUSTRY (*b*)

An unfavorable shift in demand (D_1D_1 to D_3D_3) will upset the original equilibrium and cause losses. But losses will cause firms to leave the industry, decreasing supply (S_1S_1 to S_3S_3) and increasing product price until all losses have disappeared.

of the long-run supply curve which evolves from this analysis of the expansion or contraction of a competitive industry?

Long-run supply for a constant-cost industry

Even though our discussion is concerned with the long run, we have noted that the market supply curves of Figures 27·7*b* and 27·8*b* are short-run curves. However, our analysis itself permits us to sketch the nature of the long-run supply curve for this competitive industry. The crucial factor in determining the shape of the industry's long-run supply curve is the effect, if any, which changes in the number of firms in the industry will have upon the costs of the individual firms in the industry.

In the forgoing analysis of long-run competitive equilibrium we assumed the industry under discussion was a *constant-cost industry*. By definition, this means that the expansion of the industry through the entry of new firms will have no effect upon resource prices or, therefore, upon production costs. Graphically, the entry of new firms does not change the position of the long-run average-cost curves of the individual firms in the industry. When will this be the case? For the most part, when the industry's demand for resources is small in relation to the total demand for those resources. And this is most likely to be the situation when the industry is employing unspecialized resources which are being demanded by many other industries. In short, when the particular industry's demand for resources is a negligible component of the total demand, the industry can expand without significantly affecting resource prices and costs.

What will be the nature of the long-run supply curve for a constant-cost industry? The answer is contained in our previous discussion of the long-run adjustments toward equilibrium which profits or losses will initiate. Here we assumed that the entry or exodus of firms would not affect costs. The result was that the entry or exodus of firms would alter industry output but always bring product price back to the original $50 level, where it is just consistent with the unchanging minimum average total cost of production. Specifically, we discovered that the industry would supply 90,000, 100,000, or 110,000 units of

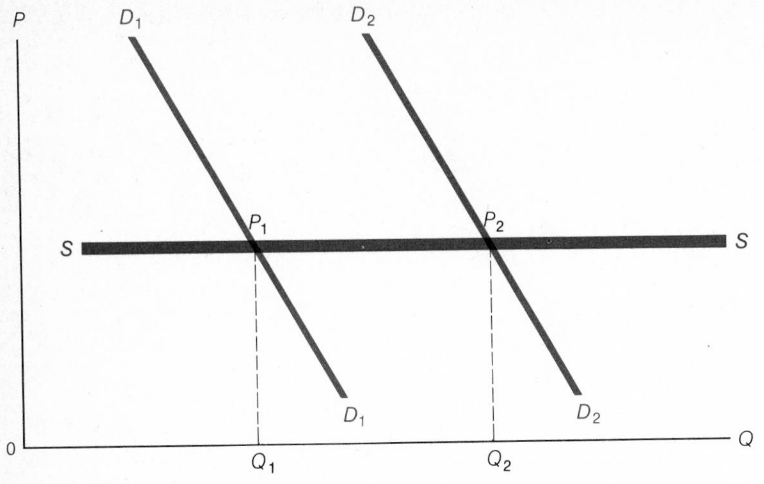

FIGURE 27·9 THE LONG-RUN SUPPLY CURVE FOR A CONSTANT-COST INDUSTRY IS PERFECTLY ELASTIC

Because the entry of new firms does not affect resource prices or, therefore, unit costs, an increase in demand (D_1D_1 to D_2D_2) will cause an expansion in industry output (Q_1 to Q_2) but no alteration in price ($Q_1P_1 = Q_2P_2$). This means that the long-run industry supply curve (*SS*) will be perfectly elastic.

output, all at a price of $50 per unit. In technical terms the long-run supply curve of a constant-cost industry is perfectly elastic.

This is demonstated graphically in Figure 27·9. Suppose that product demand for the industry is originally at D_1D_1, industry output is Q_1, and product price is Q_1P_1. This situation, let us suppose, is one of long-run equilibrium. Now assume that demand increases to D_2D_2, upsetting this equilibrium. The resulting economic profits will attract new firms. Because this is a constant-cost industry, entry will continue and industry output will expand until price is driven back down to the unchanged minimum average-total-cost level. This will be at price Q_2P_2 and output Q_2. The long-run industry supply curve *SS*, which connects these equilibrium points, is obviously perfectly elastic.

Long-run supply for an increasing-cost industry

But constant-cost industries are a special case. In most instances the entry of new firms will affect resource prices and therefore unit costs for the individual firms in the industry. When an industry is using a relatively large portion of some resource whose total supply is not readily increased, the entry of new firms will increase resource demand in relation to supply and boost resource prices. This is particularly so in industries which are using highly specialized resources whose initial supply is not readily augmented. The result of higher resource prices will be higher long-run average costs for firms in the industry. These higher costs, it should be noted, take the form of an upward shift in the long-run average-cost curve for the representative firm.

The net result is that when an increase in product demand causes economic profits and attracts new firms to the industry, a two-way squeeze on profits will occur to eliminate those profits. On the one hand, the entry of new firms will increase market supply and lower product price, and, on the other, the entire average-total-cost curve of the representative firm will shift upward. This means that the equilibrium price will now be higher than it was originally. The industry will only produce a larger output at a higher price. Why? Because expansion of the industry has increased average total costs, and in the long run

product price must cover these costs. A greater industry output will be forthcoming at a higher price, or, more technically, the industry supply curve for an increasing-cost industry will be upsloping. Instead of getting either 90,000, 100,000, or 110,000 units at the same price of $50, in an increasing-cost industry 90,000 units might be forthcoming at $50; 100,00 at $55; and 110,000 at $60. The higher price is required to induce more production because costs increase as the industry expands.

This can be seen graphically in Figure 27·10. Original market demand, industry output, and price are D_1D_1, Q_1, and Q_1P_1, respectively. An increase in demand to D_2D_2 will upset this equilibrium and give rise to economic profits. As new firms enter, (1) industry supply will increase, driving price down, and (2) resource prices will rise, causing the average total costs of production to rise. Because of these average-total-cost increases, the new long-run equilibrium price will be established at some level above the original price, such as Q_2P_2.

Which situation—constant or increasing costs—is characteristic of American industry? It is hard to say. Agriculture and extractive industries such as mining and lumbering are increasing-cost industries, because each utilizes a very large portion of some basic resource—farmland, mineral deposits, and timberland. Expansion will significantly affect the demand for these resources and result in higher costs. It is almost impossible to generalize with respect to manufacturing industries. In their early stages of development such industries may well be relatively constant-cost industries.[2] But as continued expansion increases the importance of these industries in resource markets, they may in time become increasing-cost industries.

[2]Under certain very special circumstances an industry may be for a time a *decreasing-cost industry*. For example, as more mines are established in a given locality, each firm's costs in pumping out water seepage may decline. With more mines pumping, the seepage into each is less, and pumping costs are therefore reduced. Furthermore, with only a few mines in an area, industry output might be so small that only relatively primitive and therefore costly transportation facilities are available. But as the number of firms and industry output expand, a railroad might build a spur into the area and thereby significantly reduce transportation costs. Under such special conditions a firm's long-run supply curve may shift *downward*. We will have more to say about this kind of cost economy in Chapter 37.

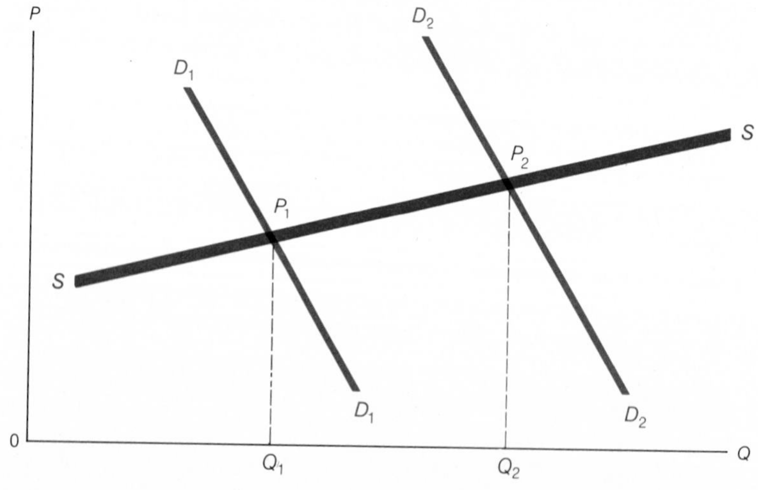

FIGURE 27·10 THE LONG-RUN SUPPLY CURVE FOR AN INCREASING-COST INDUSTRY IS UPSLOPING

In an increasing-cost industry the entry of new firms in response to an increase in demand (D_1D_1 to D_2D_2) will bid up resource prices and thereby increase unit costs. As a result, an increased industry output (Q_1 to Q_2) will be forthcoming only at a higher price (Q_2P_2 is greater than Q_1P_1). The long-run industry supply curve (*SS*) is therefore upsloping.

AN EVALUATION OF COMPETITIVE PRICING

Whether a purely competitive industry is one of constant or increasing costs, the final long-run equilibrium position for each firm will have the same basic characteristics. As in Figure 27·11, price (and marginal revenue) will settle at the level where it is equal to minimum average cost. However, we discovered in Chapter 26 that the marginal-cost curve intersects, and is therefore equal to, average cost at the point of minimum average cost. In the long-run equilibrium position, "everything is equal." MR (P) = AC = MC. This triple equality is of more than geometric interest. It tells us that, although a competitive firm may realize economic profits or losses in the short run, it will barely break even by producing in accordance with the MR (P) = MC rule in the long run. Furthermore, this triple equality suggests certain conclusions concerning the efficiency of a purely competitive economy which are of great social significance. It is to an evaluation of competitive pricing from society's point of view that we now turn.

You will recall that the overview of the price system in Chapter 5 yielded some general conclusions with respect to the efficiency of any economy characterized by a competitive price system. Equipped now with a better understanding of costs and of price-output determination under competition, we are in a position to sharpen our understanding of the efficiency of a competitive price economy. Specifically, we want to see how our analysis of long-run competitive equilibrium implies certain highly desirable features of a competitive price system.

FIGURE 27 · 11 FOR THE COMPETITIVE FIRM IN LONG-RUN EQUILIBRIUM, P = AC = MC

The equality of price and minimum average cost indicates that the firm is using the most efficient known technology and is charging the lowest price P and producing the greatest output Q consistent with its costs. The equality of price and marginal cost indicates that resources are being allocated in accordance with consumer preferences.

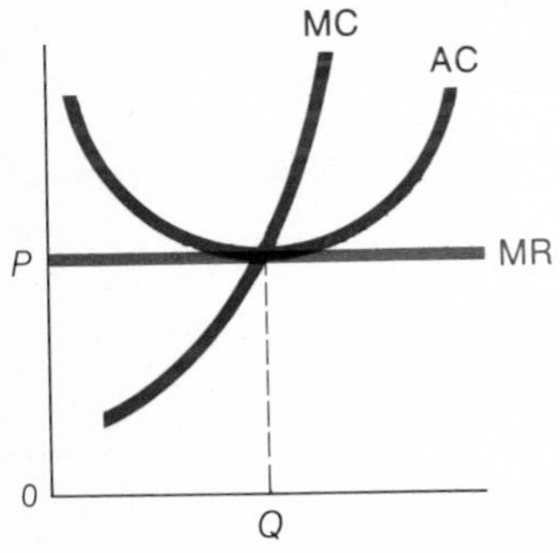

Efficient allocation of resources

Most economists argue that, subject to certain limitations and exceptions, a purely competitive economy will lead to the most efficient, or "ideal," allocation of resources. That is, *a competitive price economy will tend to allocate the fixed supplies of resources available to society in such a way as to maximize the satisfactions of consumers.* Actually, there are two related points which underlie this conclusion. First, it is argued that under pure competition firms will be forced to produce those goods which consumers want the most. Second, competition forces firms to use the most efficient methods in the production of these goods. To facilitate our discussion we shall examine the second point first.

1. P = AC We have just noted that in the long run, competition forces firms to produce at the point of minimum average total cost of production and to charge that price which is just consistent with these costs. This is obviously a most desirable situation from the consumer's point of view. It means that firms must use the best available (least-cost) technology or they will simply not survive. And, too, it means that consumers benefit from the highest volume of production and the lowest product price which are possible under the cost conditions which currently prevail. Furthermore, the costs involved in each instance are only those costs essential in producing a product. Because products are standardized in

competitive industries, there will be no selling or promotional costs which must be added to production costs in determining product price.

2. *P* = MC But the competitive production of *any* collection of goods does not necessarily make for an efficient allocation of resources. Production must not only be technologically efficient, but it must also entail the "right goods," that is, the goods that consumers want the most. The competitive price system will see to it that resources are allocated so as to result in a total output whose composition best fits the preferences of consumers.

Let us see precisely how this comes about. We must first grasp the social meaning of competitive product and resource prices. The money price of any product—product X—is society's measure, or index, of the relative worth of that product at the margin. Similarly, the marginal cost of producing X measures the value, or relative worth, of the other goods that the resources used in the production of an extra unit of X could otherwise have produced. In short, product price measures the benefit, or satisfaction, which society gets from additional units of X, and the marginal cost of an additional unit of X measures the sacrifice, or cost to society, of other goods in using resources to produce more of X. Now, under competition the production of each product will occur up to that precise point at which price is equal to marginal cost (Figure 27·11). The profit-seeking competitor will only realize the maximum possible profit by equating price and marginal cost. To produce short of the MR (*P*) = MC point will mean less than maximum profits to the individual firm and an *under*allocation of resources to this product from society's standpoint. The fact that price exceeds marginal cost indicates that society values additional units of X more highly than the alternative products which the appropriate resources could otherwise produce.

For similar reasons, the production of X should not go beyond the output at which price equals marginal cost. To do so would entail less than maximum profits for producers and an *over*allocation of resources to X from the standpoint of society. To produce X at some point at which marginal cost exceeds price means that resources are being used in the production of X at the sacrifice of alternative goods which society values more highly than the added units of X. In brief, *under pure competition producers will be forced to produce each commodity up to that precise point at which price and marginal cost are equated. This means that resources are efficiently allocated under competition.* Each good is produced to the point at which the value of the last unit is equal to the value of the alternative goods sacrificed by its production. To alter the production of X would necessarily reduce consumer satisfactions. To produce X beyond the *P* = MC point would result in the sacrifice of alternative goods whose value to society exceeds that of the extra units of X. To produce X short of the *P* = MC point would involve the sacrifice of units of X which society values more than the alternative goods resources can produce.

A further attribute of the competitive price system is its ability to negotiate appropriate adjustments in resource use as changes occur in basic data of the economy. In a competitive economy any changes in consumer tastes, resource supplies, or technology will automatically set in motion appropriate realignments of resources. For example, an increase in consumer demand for product X will increase its price. Disequilibrium will occur, in that at its present output the price of X will now exceed its marginal cost. This will create economic profits in industry X and stimulate its expansion. Its profitability will permit the industry to bid resources away from less pressing uses. Expansion in this industry will end only when the price of X is again equal to its marginal cost, that is, when the value of the last unit produced is once again equal to the value of the alternative goods society forgoes in getting that last unit of X produced. Similarly, changes in the supplies of particular resources or in the techniques pertinent to various industries will upset existing price–marginal-cost equalities by either raising or lowering marginal cost. These inequalities will cause businessmen in either pursuing profits or shunning losses to reallocate resources until price once again equals marginal cost in each line of production. In so doing, they correct any inefficiencies in the allocation of resources which

changing economic data may temporarily impose upon the economy.

A final appealing feature of a purely competitive economy is that the highly efficient allocation of resources which it fosters comes about because businesses and resource suppliers freely seek to further their own self-interests. That is, the "invisible hand" (Chapter 5) is at work in a competitive market system. In a competitive economy, businessmen employ resources until the extra, or marginal, costs of production equal the price of the product. This not only maximizes the profits of the individual producers but simultaneously results in a pattern of resource allocation which maximizes the satisfactions of consumers. The competitive price system organizes the private interests of producers along lines which are fully in accord with the interests of society as a whole.

Shortcomings of the competitive price system

Despite these several virtues, economists acknowledge certain limitations of the price system which may impair its ability to allocate resources efficiently. Some of these criticisms have been previously noted in Chapter 5.

1. The competitive price system does not accurately reflect the needs of consumers There are two major facets of this criticism. On the one hand, the price system registers and responds only to those wants which can be expressed by individuals in the market. The competitive price system therefore ignores certain important social goods and services—for example, education, highways, and national defense—which consumers need and want. On the other hand, it is also argued that the market demand for various goods does not reflect the needs of consumers very accurately, because income is unequally distributed in a competitive price economy. This uneven distribution of "dollar votes" will lead to the production of trifles for the rich and deny the most basic needs of the very poor. The price system allocates resources in accordance with a given unequal distribution of income. Some economists argue that the needs of society might be better served by altering the distribution of income which pure competition provides. More will be said on this point in Chapter 34.

2. The competitive price system does not accurately measure costs and benefits where spillover costs and benefits are significant Competition forces each producer to assume only those costs which he must pay. This correctly implies that in some lines of production there are significant costs which producers can and do avoid. These avoided costs accrue to society and are aptly called *spillover* or *social costs.* Firms may avoid the cost of properly disposing of waste materials or of buying smoke- and dust-abatement equipment. The result is significant spillover costs in the form of polluted rivers, smog, and a generally debased community. Similarly, unbridled competition may cause profit-seeking firms to brutally exploit farmland, timberland, and mineral deposits through the use of the cheapest production methods. The cost to society is the permanent loss of irreproducible natural resources. On the other hand, you will recall from Chapter 6 that the consumption of certain goods and services such as chest x-rays and polio shots yields widespread satisfactions, or benefits, to society as a whole. These satisfactions are called *social* or *spillover benefits.*

Now the significance of spillover costs and benefits for present purposes is this: The profit-seeking activities of producers will bring about an allocation of resources which is efficient from society's point of view only if marginal cost embodies *all* the costs which production entails and product price accurately reflects *all* the benefits which society gets from a good's production (see Figure 6·1). Only in this case will competitive production at the MR (P) = MC point balance the total sacrifices and satisfactions of society and result in an efficient allocation of resources. To the extent that price and marginal cost are not accurate indexes of sacrifices and satisfactions—in other words, to the extent that spillover costs and benefits exist—production at the MR (P) = MC point will not signify an efficient allocation of resources.

3. The competitive price system may not always

entail the use of the most efficient productive techniques or the development of improved techniques There are both a static or "right now" aspect and a dynamic or "over time" aspect of this general criticism. The static aspect argues that in certain lines of production, existing technology may be such that a firm must be a large-scale producer in order to realize the lowest unit costs of production. Given consumer demand, this suggests that a relatively small number of efficient, large-scale producers is needed if production is to be carried on efficiently. In other words, existing mass production economies might be lost if such an industry were populated by the large number of small-scale producers which pure competition requires. This point was discussed in some detail in Chapter 26.

The dynamic aspect of this criticism concerns the willingness and ability of purely competitive firms to undertake technological advance. The progressiveness of pure competition is debated by economists. For present purposes we simply call attention to the fact that some authorities feel that a purely competitive economy would not foster a very rapid rate of technological progress. They argue, first, that the incentive for technological advance may be weak under pure competition, because the profit rewards accruing to an innovating firm as the result of a cost-reducing technological improvement will be quickly competed away by rival firms who readily adopt the new technique. Second, the small size of the typical competitive firm raises serious questions as to whether or not such producers could finance substantial programs of organized research. We will return to this controversy in Chapter 30.

4. ***The competitive price system may not provide for a sufficient range of consumer choice or for the development of new products*** This criticism, like the previous one, has both a static and a dynamic aspect. Pure competition, it is contended, entails product standardization, whereas other market structures—for example, monopolistic competition and, frequently, oligopoly—entail a wide range of types, styles, and quality gradations of any product. This product differentiation widens the consumer's range of free choice and simultaneously allows his preferences to be more completely fulfilled. Similarly, critics of pure competition point out that, just as pure competition is not likely to be progressive with respect to the development of new productive techniques, neither is this market structure conducive to the improvement of existing products or the creation of completely new ones.

The question of the progressiveness of the various market structures in terms of both productive techniques and product development will be a recurring one in the following three chapters.

SUMMARY

1. A purely competitive industry comprises a large number of independent firms producing a standardized product. Pure competition assumes that firms and resources are mobile as between different industries. No single firm can influence market price in a competitive industry; price therefore equals marginal revenue.

2. Short-run profit maximization by a competitive firm can be analyzed by a comparison of total revenue and total cost or through marginal analysis. A firm will maximize profits by producing that output at which total revenue exceeds total cost by the greatest amount. Losses will be minimized by producing where the excess of total cost over total revenue is at a minimum and less than total fixed costs.

3. Provided price exceeds minimum average variable cost, a competitive firm will maximize profits or minimize losses by producing at that output at which price or marginal revenue is equal to marginal cost. If price is less than average variable cost, the firm will minimize its losses by closing down. If price is greater than average variable cost but less than average total cost, the firm will minimize its losses by producing the $P = \text{MC}$ output. If price exceeds average total cost, the $P = \text{MC}$ output will provide maximum economic profits for the firm.

4. Applying the MR $(P) = \text{MC}$ rule at various possi-

ble market prices leads to the conclusion that the segment of the firm's short-run marginal cost curve which lies above average variable cost is its short-run supply curve.

5. In the long run, competitive price will tend to equal the minimum average cost of production. This is so because economic profits will cause firms to enter a competitive industry until those profits have been competed away. Conversely, losses will force the exodus of firms from the industry until product price once again barely covers unit costs.

6. The long-run supply curve of a constant-cost industry is perfectly elastic. However, for an increasing-cost industry the long-run supply curve is up-sloping.

7. In a purely competitive economy the profit-seeking activities of producers will result in an allocation of resources which maximizes the satisfactions of consumers. The long-run equality of price and minimum average cost indicates that competitive firms will use the most efficient known technology and charge the lowest price consistent with their production costs. The equality of price and marginal cost indicates that resources will be allocated in accordance with consumer tastes. The competitive price system will reallocate resources in response to a change in consumer tastes, technology, or resource supplies so as to maintain allocative efficiency over time.

8. Economists recognize four possible deterrents to allocative efficiency in a competitive economy. *a.* Income inequality and the unresponsiveness of the price system to social wants suggest that the competitive price economy does not accurately reflect the needs of consumers. *b.* In allocating resources, the price system does not allow for spillover costs and benefits. *c.* A purely competitive industry may preclude the use of the best known productive techniques and foster a slow rate of technological advance. *d.* A competitive system provides neither a wide range of product choice nor an environment conducive to the development of new products.

QUESTIONS AND STUDY SUGGESTIONS

1. Strictly speaking, pure competition never has existed and probably never will. Then why study it?

2. Why is the equality of marginal revenue and marginal cost essential for profit maximization in all market structures? Explain why price can be substituted for marginal revenue in the MR = MC rule when an industry is purely competitive.

3. Explain: "A competitive producer must look to average variable cost in determining whether or not to produce in the short run, to marginal cost in deciding upon the best volume of production, and to average total cost to calculate his profits or losses." Explain why a firm might produce at a loss in the short run rather than close down.

4. Assume the following unit-cost data for a purely competitive producer:

Total product	Average fixed cost	Average variable cost	Average total cost	Marginal cost
0				
1	$60.00	$45.00	$105.00	$45
2	30.00	42.50	72.50	40
3	20.00	40.00	60.00	35
4	15.00	37.50	52.50	30
5	12.00	37.00	49.00	35
6	10.00	37.50	47.50	40
7	8.57	38.57	47.14	45
8	7.50	40.63	48.13	55
9	6.67	43.33	50.00	65
10	6.00	46.50	52.50	75

a. At a product price of $32, will this firm produce in the short run? Why, or why not? If it does produce, what will be the profit-maximizing or loss-minimizing output? Explain.

Specify the amount of economic profit or loss per unit of output.

b. Answer the questions of 4*a* on the assumption that product price is $41.

c. Answer the questions of 4*a* on the assumption that product price is $56.

d. Complete the following short-run supply schedule for the same firm, and indicate the profit or loss incurred at each output (columns 1 to 3).

(1) Price	(2) Quantity supplied, single firm	(3) Profit (+) or loss (−)	(4) Quantity supplied, 1,500 firms
$26	______	$______	______
32	______	______	______
38	______	______	______
41	______	______	______
46	______	______	______
56	______	______	______
66	______	______	______

e. Explain: "That segment of a competitive firm's marginal-cost curve which lies above its average-variable-cost curve constitutes the short-run supply curve for the firm." Illustrate graphically.

f. Now assume there are 1,500 identical firms in this competitive industry; that is, there are 1,500 firms, each of which has the same cost data as shown above. Calculate the industry supply schedule (column 4).

g. Suppose the market demand data for the product are as follows:

Price	Total quantity demanded
$26	17,000
32	15,000
38	13,500
41	12,000
46	10,500
56	9,500
66	8,000

What will equilibrium price be? What will equilibrium output be for the industry? For each firm? What will profit or loss be per unit? Per firm?

5. Using diagrams for both the industry and a representative firm, illustrate competitive long-run equilibrium. Employing these diagrams, show how **a.** an increase and **b.** a decrease in market demand will upset this long-run equilibrium. Trace graphically and describe verbally the adjustment processes by which long-run equilibrium is restored. Assume the industry is one of constant costs.

6. Distinguish carefully between a constant-cost and an increasing-cost industry. Answer question 5 on the assumption that the industry is one of increasing costs. Compare the long-run supply curves of a constant-cost and an increasing-cost industry.

7. Suppose a decrease in demand occurs in a competitive increasing-cost industry. Contrast the product price and industry output which exist after all long-run adjustments are completed with those which originally prevailed.

8. In long-run equilibrium, $P = AC = MC$. Of what significance for the allocation of resources is the equality of P and AC? The equality of P and MC?

9. Explain why some economists feel that an unequal distribution of income might impair the efficiency with which a competitive price system allocates resources. What other criticisms can be made of a purely competitive economy?

SELECTED REFERENCES

Economic Issues, 4th ed., readings 40, 54, and 55.

Hibdon, James E.: *Price and Welfare Theory* (New York: McGraw-Hill Book Company, 1969), chap. 8.

Leftwich, Richard H.: *The Price System and Resource Allocation,* 4th ed. (Hinsdale, Ill.: The Dryden Press, Inc., 1970), chap. 9.

Mansfield, Edwin: *Microeconomics: Theory and Applications* (New York: W. W. Norton & Company, Inc., 1970), chap. 8.

Stigler, George J.: *The Theory of Price,* rev. ed. (New York: The Macmillan Company, 1952), chap. 10.

Stonier, Alfred W., and Douglas C. Hague: *A Textbook of Economic Theory,* 3d ed. (New York: Longmans, Green & Co., Inc., 1964), chaps. 6 and 7.

PRICE AND OUTPUT DETERMINATION: PURE MONOPOLY

Let us now jump to the opposite end of the industry spectrum and examine the characteristics, the bases, the price-output behavior, and the social desirability of pure monopoly.

CONCEPT AND OCCURRENCE OF PURE MONOPOLY

Pure or absolute monopoly exists when a single firm is the sole producer of a product for which there are no close substitutes. By the absence of close substitutes we mean that there are no other firms producing the same product or products varying only in very minor ways from that of the monopolist. Thus there is no close substitute for the electricity or water supplied by local utilities. And, if there existed only one manufacturer of automobiles, consumers would have no reasonably good alternative to buying from the monopolistic producer. Of course, as mentioned earlier, there may be competition in the broad sense that a food freezer or color television set is a "substitute" for a down payment on an automobile. But these products are clearly distinct from automobiles and do not fulfill the customer's need for convenient local transportation. The important point is that the monopolist is the only supplier of a certain product for which there are no close substitutes available. Defined in this way, pure monopoly is a rare phenomenon.

Yet a brief analysis of pure monopoly is important for two related reasons. First, some industries are reasonable approximations of pure monopoly. The behavior of firms with 80, 70, or even 60 percent of a market can often be explained with considerable accuracy through the pure monopoly market model. For all practical purposes the dominant firm *is* the industry in such instances. Second, a study of pure monopoly provides us with valuable insights concerning the more realistic market structures of monopolistic competition and oligopoly, which will be discussed in Chapters 29 and 30. These two market situations combine in differing degrees the characteristics of pure competition and pure monopoly.

BARRIERS TO ENTRY

It was noted in Chapter 23 that the absence of competitors which characterizes pure monopoly is largely explainable in terms of barriers to entry, that is, considerations which prohibit additional firms from entering an industry. These barriers are also pertinent in explaining the existence of oligopoly and monopolistic competition between the market extremes of pure competition and pure monopoly. In the case of pure monopoly, entry barriers are sufficiently great to block completely all potential competition. Somewhat less formidable barriers permit the existence of oligopoly, that is, a market dominated by a few firms. Still weaker barriers permit the fairly large number of firms which characterize monopolistic competition. The virtual absence of entry barriers helps explain the very large number of competing firms which is the basis of pure competition. The important point is this: Barriers to entry are pertinent not only to the extreme case of pure monopoly but also to the "partial monopolies" which are so characteristic of American capitalism.

What forms do these entry barriers assume?

Economies of scale

Modern technology is such in many industries that efficient, low-cost production can be achieved only if producers are extremely large both absolutely and in relation to the market. Where economies of scale are very significant, a firm's average-cost schedule will decline over a wide range of output (Figure 26·6*a*). Given market demand, the achieving of low unit costs and therefore low unit prices for consumers depends upon the existence of a small number of firms or, in the extreme case, only one firm. The automobile, aluminum, and steel industries are a few of many heavy industries which reflect such conditions. If three firms currently enjoy all available economies of scale and each has roughly one-third of a market, it is easy to see why new competitors may find it extremely difficult to enter this industry. On the one hand, new firms entering the market as small-scale producers will have little or no chance to survive and expand. Why? Because as small-scale entrants they will be unable to realize the cost economies enjoyed by the existing "Big Three" and therefore will be unable to realize the profits necessary for survival and growth. New competitors in the steel and automobile industries will not come about as the result of the successful operation and expansion of small "backyard" producers. They simply will not be efficient enough to survive. The other option is to start out big, that is, to enter the industry as a large-scale producer. In practice, this is virtually impossible. It is extremely unlikely that a new and untried enterprise will be able to secure the money capital needed to obtain capital facilities comparable to those accumulated by any of the Big Three in the automobile industry. The financial obstacles in the way of starting big are so great in many cases as to be prohibitive.

Public utilities: natural monopolies

In a few industries economies of scale are particularly pronounced, and at the same time competition is impractical, inconvenient, or simply unworkable. Such industries are called *natural monopolies,* and most of the so-called public utilities—the electric and gas companies, bus and railway firms, and water and communication facilities—can be so classified. These industries are generally given exclusive franchises by government. But in return for this sole right to supply electricity, water, or bus service in a given geographic area, government reserves the right to regulate the operations of such monopolies to prevent abuses of the monopoly power it has granted.

Let us examine some illustrations. It would be exceedingly wasteful for a community to have a number of firms supplying water or electricity. Technology is such in these industries that heavy fixed costs on generators, pumping and purification equipment, water mains, and transmission lines are required. This is aggravated by the fact that capital equipment must be sufficient to meet the peak demands which occur on hot summer days when lawns are being watered and air conditioners turned on. These heavy fixed costs mean that unit costs of production decline with

the number of cubic feet of water or kilowatt hours of electricity supplied by each firm. The presence of a number of water and electricity suppliers would divide the total market and reduce the sales of each competitor. Each firm would be pushed back up its declining average-cost curve. Firms would underutilize their fixed plants, with the result that unit cost and therefore electricity and water rates would necessarily be high. In addition, competition might prove to be highly inconvenient. For example, the presence of a half-dozen telephone companies in a municipality would entail the inconvenience of having six telephones and six telephone books—not to mention six telephone bills—to ensure communications with all other residents in the same town.

Because firms are eager to spread their fixed costs and thereby achieve lower unit costs, cutthroat price competition tends to break out when a number of firms exist in these public utilities industries. The result may be losses, the bankruptcy of weaker rivals, and the eventual merger of the survivors. The evolving pure monopoly may be anxious to recoup past losses and to profit fully from its new position of market dominance by charging exorbitant prices for its goods.

To spare society from such disadvantageous results, government will usually grant an exclusive franchise to a single firm to supply water, natural gas, electricity, telephone service, or train or bus transportation. In return government reserves the right to designate the monopolist's geographic area of operation and the prices which it may charge. The result is a regulated or government-sponsored monopoly—monopoly designed to achieve low unit costs but regulated to guarantee that consumers will benefit from these cost economies. We shall examine some of the problems associated with regulation later in this chapter.

Ownership of essential raw materials

The institution of private property can be used by a monopoly as a means of achieving an effective obstacle to potential rivals. A firm owning or controlling a raw material which is essential in production can obviously prohibit the creation of rival firms. There are several classic examples. The Aluminum Company of America retained its monopoly position in the aluminum industry for many years by virtue of its control of all basic sources of bauxite, the major ore used in aluminum fabrication. The International Nickel Company of Canada controls approximately 90 percent of the world's known nickel reserves. Most of the world's diamond mines are owned by the De Beers Company of South Africa.

Patents and research

By granting an inventor the exclusive right to control a product for some seventeen years, American patent laws are aimed at protecting an inventor from having his product or process usurped by rival enterprises which have not shared in the time, effort, and money outlays which have gone into its development. By the same token, of course, patents may provide the inventor with a monopoly position for the life of the patent. Patent control figures prominently in the growth of many modern-day industrial giants—National Cash Register, General Motors, General Electric, Du Pont, to name a few. The United Shoe Machinery Company provides a notable example of how patent control can be abused to achieve monopoly power. In this case United Shoe became the exclusive supplier of certain essential shoemaking machines through patent control. It extended its monopoly power to other types of shoemaking machinery by requiring all lessees of its patented machines to sign a "tying agreement" in which shoe manufacturers agreed also to lease all other shoemaking machinery from United Shoe. This allowed United Shoe to monopolize the market until partially effective antitrust action was taken by the government in 1955.

Research, of course, underlies the development of patentable products. Firms which gain a measure of monopoly power by their own research or by purchasing the patents of others are in a strategic position to consolidate and strengthen their market position. The profits provided by one important patent can be used to finance the research required to develop new patentable products. Monopoly power achieved through patents may well be cumulative.

Unfair competition

A firm's rivals may be eliminated and the entry of new competitors blocked by aggressive, cutthroat tactics. Familiar techniques entail product disparagement, pressure on resource suppliers and banks to withhold materials and credit, the hiring away of strategic personnel, and aggressive price cutting designed to bankrupt competitors. Though many of these facets of unfair competition are now illegal or fringe upon illegality, they are of more than historical interest. For example, although Federal legislation prohibits price cutting intended to reduce competition, how is one to distinguish in practice between legitimate price competition based upon cost advantages and price competition designed to bankrupt rivals?

Economies of being established

A bit of reflection will reveal that for a variety of reasons an established, going concern has numerous advantages over new, embryonic rivals. There are good reasons why existing firms should survive and prosper, whereas new firms have every reason to founder and fail. Established firms which have proved themselves by their continued existence and prosperity will have relatively easy access to the capital market, on favorable terms. This advantage is not unrelated to the fact that an established concern will tend to have a relatively efficient administrative framework staffed by competent and experienced personnel. The firm's longevity will have allowed it to eliminate inappropriate policies and to have screened the dolts from its administrative ranks. It must be added that going concerns will also be in a position to expand their size and market share by internal financing.

The new concern may have great difficulties in securing needed money capital. Its personnel and policies are untried and untested; it is an industrial question mark. If funds are available to newcomers, the added risks of investing in a new concern are likely to make the terms unattractive to the firm.

In addition, an established firm will be likely to have a widely known and highly advertised product, which it sells through well-established marketing channels to long-standing customers. A new firm faces serious financial obstacles in developing and advertising a product, in establishing marketing outlets, and in building up a clientele.

Two implications

Our discussion of barriers to entry suggests two noteworthy points. First, barriers to entry are rarely complete; indeed, this is simply another way of stating our earlier point that pure monopoly is rare. Although, as we have seen, research and technological advance may strengthen the market position of a firm, technology may also undermine existing monopoly power. Existing patent advantages may be circumvented by the development of new and distinct, yet substitutable, products. New sources of strategic raw materials may be found. It is probably not an overstatement to say that monopoly in the sense of a one-firm industry only persists over time with the sanction or aid of government.

Second, it is implied in our discussion that monopolies may be desirable or undesirable from the standpoint of economic efficiency. The public utilities and economies-of-scale arguments suggest that market demand and technology may be such that efficient low-cost production presupposes the existence of monopoly. On the other hand, our comments upon materials ownership, patents, and unfair competition as sources of monopoly imply more undesirable connotations of business monopoly.

With these points in mind let us analyze the price-output behavior of a pure monopolist. Important insights with respect to the social desirability of monopoly will be revealed.

PRICE AND OUTPUT DETERMINATION

Let us assume a pure monopolist who through, say, patent and materials control is able to block the entry of new firms to the market. Suppose, too, that the monopolist is unregulated; he is unhampered by the

existence or the prospect of a regulatory commission. In short, we have a monopolist who is ideally situated to exploit his market fully. The pure monopolist will determine his profit-maximizing output on the basis of his cost and demand data.

Monopoly demand

The crucial difference between a pure monopolist and a purely competitive seller lies on the demand side of the market. We recall from Chapter 27 that the purely competitive seller faces a perfectly elastic demand schedule at the market price determined by industry supply and demand. The competitive firm can sell as much or as little as it wants at the going market price. It follows that each additional unit sold will add a constant amount—its price—to the firm's total revenue. In other words, for the competitive seller marginal revenue is constant and equal to product price. But the competitive seller can do nothing about market price; he has no price policy. For better or worse, he must accept the market-determined price.

The monopolist's demand curve is much different. Because the pure monopolist *is* the industry, his demand, or sales, curve is the industry demand curve. And the industry demand curve is not perfectly elastic but rather is downsloping.[1] This is illustrated by columns 1 and 2 of Table 28·1.

There are two implications of a downsloping demand curve which must be understood. In the first place, a downsloping demand curve means that a pure monopoly can increase its sales only by charging a lower unit price for its product. *Furthermore, the fact that the monopolist must lower price to boost sales causes marginal revenue to be less than price (average revenue) for every level of output except the first.* The reason? Price cuts will apply not only to the extra output sold but also to all other units of output which otherwise could have been sold at a higher price. Each additional unit sold will add to total revenue its price less the sum of the price cuts which must be taken on all prior units of output.[2] The marginal revenue of the second unit of output in Table 28·1 is $142 rather than its $152 price, because a $10 price cut must be taken on the first unit to increase sales from 1 to 2 units. It is this rationale which explains why the marginal-revenue data of column 4 of Table 28·1 fall short of product price in column 2 for all levels of output save the first.

The second implication of a downsloping demand curve is this: In all imperfectly competitive markets in which such demand curves are relevant—that is, purely monopolistic, oligopolistic, and monopolistically competitive markets—firms have a price policy. By virtue of their ability to influence total supply, the output decisions of such firms necessarily affect product price. This is most evident, of course, in the present case of pure monopoly, where one firm controls total output. Faced with a downsloping demand curve, wherein each output is associated with some unique price, the monopolist unavoidably determines price in deciding what volume of output to produce. The monopolist simultaneously chooses both price and output. In columns 1 and 2 of Table 28·1 we find that the monopolist can sell only an output of one unit at a price of $162, only an output of two units at a price of $152, and so forth.[3]

But all this is not to imply that the monopolist is "free" of market forces in establishing price and output or that the consumer is somehow completely at the monopolist's mercy. In particular, the monopolist's downsloping demand curve means that high

[1]Beware of this pitfall: Because the individual competitive firm's demand curve is perfectly elastic, it does not follow that the monopolist's demand curve will be perfectly *in*elastic. Remember: Even though the individual competitor regards his demand as perfectly elastic, the demand curve for a competitive *industry* is downsloping. The pure monopolist's demand curve is downsloping, but not perfectly inelastic, because here the firm *is* the industry. As with competitive-industry demand, the degree of elasticity or inelasticity which characterizes the pure monopolist's demand curve depends upon those elasticity-determining factors discussed in Chapter 24.

[2]At this point it may be helpful to reread the discussion of the mechanics of this process in Chapter 24.

[3]The notion of a supply curve does not apply in a purely monopolistic (or any other imperfectly competitive) market because of the ability of the seller to control product price. A supply curve shows the amounts producers will offer at various *given* prices which may confront them in the market. But prices are not "given" to the pure monopolist; he does not respond to a fixed price, but rather sets the price himself.

TABLE 28·1 REVENUE AND COST DATA OF A PURE MONOPOLIST *(hypothetical data)*

Revenue data				Cost data			
(1) Quantity of output	(2) Price (average revenue)	(3) Total revenue	(4) Marginal revenue	(5) Average total cost	(6) Total cost	(7) Marginal cost	(8) Profit (+) or Loss (−)
0	$172	$ 0			$ 100		$−100
1	162	162	$162	$190.00	190	$ 90	− 28
2	152	304	142	135.00	270	80	+ 34
3	142	426	122	113.33	340	70	+ 86
4	132	528	102	100.00	400	60	+128
5	122	610	82	94.00	470	70	+140
6	112	672	62	91.67	550	80	+122
7	102	714	42	91.43	640	90	+ 74
8	92	736	22	93.73	750	110	− 14
9	82	738	2	97.78	880	130	−142
10	72	720	−18	103.00	1,030	150	−310

prices are associated with low volumes of sales and, conversely, low prices with larger outputs. The monopolist cannot raise price without losing sales or gain sales without charging a lower price. The question which now arises is this: What specific price-quantity combination on his demand curve will the pure monopolist choose? This depends not only upon demand and marginal-revenue data but also upon costs.

Cost data

On the cost side of the picture we shall assume that, although the firm is a monopolist in the product market, it hires resources competitively and employs the same technology as our competitive firm in the preceding chapter. This permits us to use the cost data developed in Chapter 26 and applied in Chapter 27, thereby facilitating a comparison of the price-output decisions of a pure monopoly with those of a pure competitor. Columns 5 through 7 of Table 28·1 merely restate the pertinent cost concepts of Table 26·2.

Equating marginal revenue and marginal cost

A profit-seeking monopolist will employ the same rationale as a profit-seeking firm in a competitive industry. He will produce each successive unit of output so long as it adds more to his total revenue than it does to his total costs. In technical language, the firm will produce up to that output at which marginal revenue equals marginal cost.

A comparison of columns 4 and 7 in Table 28·1

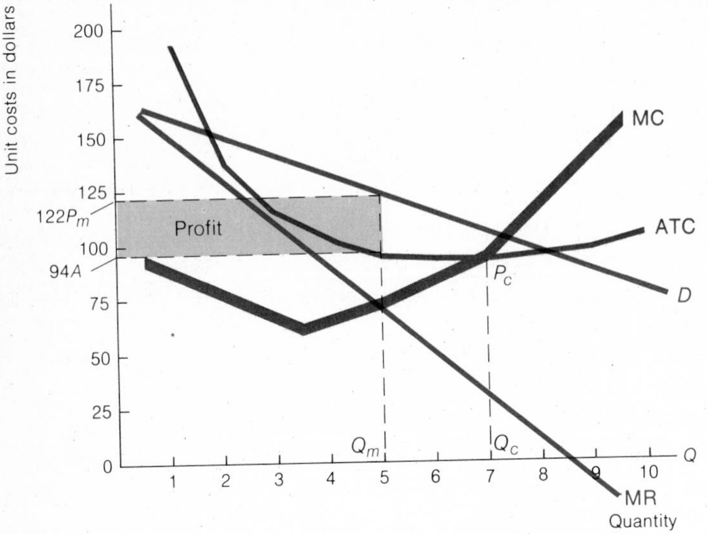

FIGURE 28 · 1 THE PROFIT-MAXIMIZING POSITION OF A PURE MONOPOLIST

The pure monopolist maximizes profits by producing the MR = MC output. In this instance profit is AP_m per unit, total profits are measured by the yellow rectangle.

indicates that the profit-maximizing output is 5 units; the fifth unit is the last unit of output whose marginal revenue exceeds its marginal cost. What price will the monopolist charge? His downsloping demand curve of columns 1 and 2 in Table 28 · 1 shows him that there is only one price at which 5 units can be sold: $122.

This same analysis is presented graphically in Figure 28·1, where the demand, marginal-revenue, average-total-cost, and marginal-cost data of Table 28·1 have been drawn. A comparison of marginal revenue and marginal cost again indicates that the profit-maximizing output is 5 units or, more generally, Q_m. The unique price at which Q_m can be sold is found by extending a perpendicular up from the profit-maximizing point on the output axis and then at right angles from the point at which it hits the demand curve to the vertical axis. The indicated price is P_m. By charging a price higher than P_m, the monopolist must move up his demand curve, and this means that his sales will fall short of the profit-maximizing level Q_m. If the monopolist charges less it would involve a volume of sales in excess of the profit-maximizing output.

Columns 2 and 5 of Table 28·1 indicate that, at 5 units of output, product price of $122 exceeds average total cost of $94. Economic profits are therefore $28 per unit; total economic profits are then $140 (or 5 times $28). In Figure 28·1 per unit profit is indicated by the distance AP_m, and total economic profits—the yellow area—are found by multiplying this unit profit by the profit-maximizing output Q_m.

The same profit-maximizing combination of output and price can also be determined by comparing the total revenue and total costs incurred at each possible level of production. The reader should employ columns 3 and 6 of Table 28·1 to verify all the conclusions we have reached through the use of marginal-revenue–marginal-cost analysis. Similarly, an accurate graphing of total revenue and total cost against output will also show the greatest differential (the maximum profit) at 5 units of output.

Misconceptions concerning monopoly pricing

Our analysis explodes some popular fallacies concerning the behavior of monopolies.

1. Because a monopolist can manipulate output and price, it is often alleged that a monopolist "will charge the highest price he can get." This is clearly a misguided assertion. There are many prices above P_m in Figure 28·1, but the monopolist shuns them for the simple reason that they entail a smaller than maximum profit. Total profits are the difference between total revenue and total costs, and each of these two determinants of profits depends upon the quantity sold as much as upon the price and unit cost.

2. The monopolist seeks maximum *total* profits, not maximum *unit* profits. In Figure 28·1 a careful comparison of the distance between average cost and price at various possible outputs indicates that per unit profits are greater at a point slightly to the left of the profit-maximizing output Q_m. This is more readily seen in Table 28·1, where unit profits are $32 at 4 units of output as compared with $28 at the profit-maximizing output of 5 units. In this instance the monopolist is accepting a lower-than-maximum per unit profit for the simple reason that the additional sales more than compensate for the lower unit profits. A profit-seeking monopolist would obviously rather sell 5 units at a profit of $28 per unit than sell 4 units at a profit of $32 per unit.

3. It must also be emphasized that pure monopoly does not guarantee economic profits. True, the likelihood of economic profits is greater for a pure monopolist than for a purely competitive producer. In the long run the latter is doomed by the free and easy entry of new firms to a normal profit; barriers to entry permit the monopolist to perpetuate economic profits in the long run. Of course, like the pure competitor, the monopolist cannot persistently operate at a loss. The monopolist must realize a normal profit or better in the long run or will simply not survive. However, if the demand and cost situation faced by the monopolist is less favorable than that shown in Figure 28·1, the monopolist may realize short-run losses. Despite his dominance in the market, the monopolist shown in Figure 28·2 realizes a loss in the short run by virtue of a weak demand and high costs.

Possible restraints upon profit maximization

The comments just made indicate that certain restraints are imposed upon the monopolist by the market. Cost and demand considerations set restrictions upon the monopolist's price-output behavior. Actually, certain other forces may cause the monopolist to exercise restraint; these forces may cause him purposely to charge a lower price and produce a greater output than is consistent with maximum profits. Two of these restraints merit further comment.

In the first place, the monopolist does not have anonymity; the identity of monopolistic sellers is typically well known. It follows that the monopolist who fully exploits his market position may find himself the target of public criticism. After all, in Figure 28·1 there are many prices less than P_m which will entail outputs greater than Q_m and still yield substantial economic profits to the monopolist. If criticism is widespread and persistent, it can lead to a loss of goodwill or, worse yet from the firm's viewpoint, some form of governmental intervention—antitrust action, rate regulation, government stimulation of new competitors, or, at the extreme, nationalization of the firm. Thus, from a very long-run standpoint it may be sensible for the monopolist to avoid unfavorable comment with respect to its market behavior, even at the sacrifice of some profits.

Secondly, the monopoly may deliberately limit its profits so as not to attract new competitors. A highly profitable monopoly may cause potential rivals to double their efforts to overcome the monopolist's barriers. And remember: Barriers to entry are rarely insurmountable over time. Full exploitation of a monopolist's position in the short run may destroy that monopolistic position in the long pull.

The importance of these "voluntary" restraints is subject to heated debate. It would be a mistake to

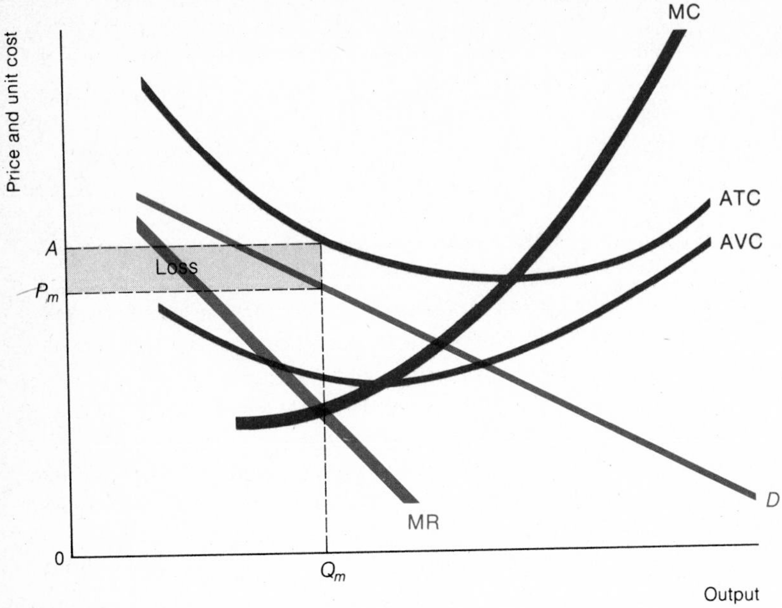

FIGURE 28 · 2 THE LOSS–MINIMIZING POSITION OF A PURE MONOPOLIST

If demand *D* is weak and costs AC are high, the pure monopolist may be unable to make a profit. He will minimize his losses in the short run by producing at that output where MR = MC. Loss per unit is AP_m, and total losses are indicated by the gray rectangle.

say that they undermine our profit-maximizing analysis; at best they probably cause minor deviations from the most profitable price-output combination.

ECONOMIC EFFECTS

Let us now evaluate pure monopoly from the standpoint of society as a whole. Our emphasis will be upon (1) price, output, and resource allocation, (2) the distribution of income, and (3) economic progress, that is, technological advance. To sharpen our analysis we ignore any possible restraints upon the monopolist's policies and presume that the monopolist seeks the maximum profit that his cost-revenue situation permits.

Price, output, and resource allocation

In Chapter 27 we concluded that pure competition would result in a highly efficient, or "ideal," allocation of resources. In the long run the free entry and exodus of firms would force firms to operate at the optimum rate of output where unit costs of production were at a minimum. Product price would be at the lowest level consistent with average total costs. To illustrate: In Figure 28·1 the competitive firm would sell Q_c units of output at a price of Q_cP_c. Furthermore, long-run competitive equilibrium would also entail an efficient allocation of resources, in that production would occur up to that point at which price (the measure of a product's value to society) equals marginal cost (the measure of the alternative products forgone by society in the production of any given commodity).

Figure 28·1 indicates that, given the same costs, a purely monopolistic firm will give much less desirable results. As we have already discovered, the pure monopolist will maximize his profits by producing an output of Q_m and charging a price of P_m. It can be readily seen that the monopolist will find it profitable to sell a smaller output and to charge a higher price

than would a competitive producer.[4] Furthermore, it is clear that, at Q_m units of output, product price is considerably greater than marginal cost. This means that society values additional units of this monopolized product more highly than it does the alternative products which resources could otherwise produce. In other words, the monopolist's profit-maximizing output results in a misallocation of resources; the monopolist finds it profitable to restrict output and therefore employ fewer resources than are justified from society's standpoint.

[4] In Figure 28·1 the price-quantity comparison of monopoly and pure competition is from the vantage point of the single purely competitive *firm* of Figure 27·6*a*. An equally illuminating approach is to start with the purely competitive *industry* of Figure 27·6*b*, which is reproduced below. Recall that the competitive industry's supply curve

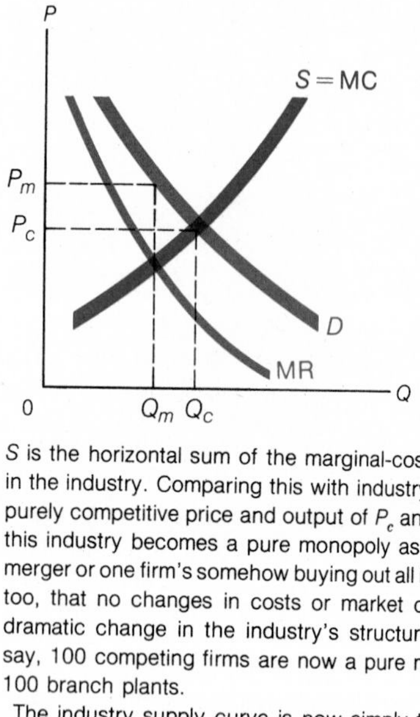

S is the horizontal sum of the marginal-cost curves of all the firms in the industry. Comparing this with industry demand *D*, we get the purely competitive price and output of P_c and Q_c. Now suppose that this industry becomes a pure monopoly as a result of a wholesale merger or one firm's somehow buying out all its competitors. Assume, too, that no changes in costs or market demand result from this dramatic change in the industry's structure. What were formerly, say, 100 competing firms are now a pure monopolist consisting of 100 branch plants.

The industry supply curve is now simply the marginal-cost curve of the monopolist, the summation of the MC curves of its many branch plants. The important change, however, is on the market-demand side. From the viewpoint of each individual competitive firm, demand was perfectly elastic, and marginal revenue was therefore equal to price. Each firm equated MC to MR (and therefore to *P*) in maximizing profits (Chapter 27). But industry demand and individual demand are the same to the pure monopolist; the firm *is* the industry, and thus the monopolist correctly envisions a downsloping demand curve *D*. This means that marginal revenue MR will be less than price; graphically the MR curve lies below the demand curve. In choosing the profit-maximizing MC = MR position, the monopolist selects an output Q_m which is smaller, and a price P_m which is greater, than would be the case if the industry was organized competitively.

Given identical costs, a purely monopolistic firm will find it profitable to charge a higher price, produce a smaller output, and foster an allocation of economic resources inferior to that of a purely competitive firm. These contrasting consequences are rooted in the barriers to entry which characterize monopoly.

There is one basic exception to these conclusions: The assumption that the unit costs available to the purely competitive and the purely monopolistic firm are the same does not always hold in practice. Given production techniques and therefore production costs, consumer demand may simply not be sufficient to support a large number of competing firms, each producing at an output which permits it to realize all known economies of scale. In such instances a firm must be large in relation to the market—that is, it must be monopolistic—to produce efficiently (at low unit cost). Our previous discussion of economies of scale as a barrier to entry and the desirability of establishing public utilities in certain fields is based primarily upon such cost considerations (see Chapter 26).

How important is this exception? Most economists feel that it applies for the most part only to public utilities and is therefore not significant enough to undermine our general conclusions concerning the restrictive nature of monopoly. The best available evidence (see footnote 3 in Chapter 8) suggests that the giant corporations which populate many manufacturing industries now have more monopoly power than can be justified on the grounds that these firms are merely availing themselves to existing economies of scale.

Income distribution

Business monopoly probably contributes to inequality in the distribution of income in our society. By virtue of their market power, monopolists charge a higher price than would a purely competitive firm with the same costs; monopolists are in effect able to levy a "private tax" upon consumers and thereby to realize substantial economic profits. These monopolistic profits, it should be noted, are not widely distributed for the simple reason that corporate stock ownership is largely concentrated in the hands of upper income

groups. The owners of monopolistic enterprises thereby tend to be enriched at the expense of the rest of society.

Assuming monopoly does contribute to income inequality, is this necessarily undesirable? There is no agreement here, and no scientifically correct answer will ever be found because any view entails a value judgment with respect to what one feels the distribution of income ought to be. Nevertheless, there is a rather widespread feeling in our society that the extreme degrees of income inequality to which pure monopoly frequently contributes are undesirable (see Chapter 38).

Technological advance

We have already qualified our condemnation of pure monopoly by noting that in a few instances *existing* mass-production economies may be lost if an industry comprises a large number of small, competing firms. There is also a dynamic aspect to this line of reasoning. To be specific, will competition or monopoly foster the more rapid improvement of products and productive techniques over time? This is fertile ground for honest differences of opinion.

Competitive firms certainly have the incentive—indeed, a market mandate—to employ the most efficient *known* productive techniques. We have seen that their very survival depends upon being efficient. But at the same time, competition tends to deprive firms of economic profit—an important means and a major incentive to develop *new* products and *new* improved productive techniques. The profits of technological advance will be short-lived to the innovating competitor. An innovating firm in a competitive industry will find that its many rivals will soon duplicate or imitate any technological advance it may achieve; rivals will share the rewards but not the costs of successful technological research.

In contrast, we have seen that a monopolist may persistently realize substantial economic profits. Hence, the pure monopolist will have greater financial resources for technological advance than will competitive firms. But what about the monopolist's incentives for technological advance? Here the picture is clouded.

There is one imposing argument which suggests that the monopolist's incentives to develop new products and new techniques will be weak: the absence of competitors means that there is no automatic stimulus to technological advance in a monopolized market. Because of its sheltered market position, the pure monopolist can afford to be inefficient and lethargic. The keen rivalry of a competitive market penalizes the inefficient; an inefficient monopolist does not face this penalty for the simple reason that he has no rivals. The monopolist has every reason to become satisfied with the status quo, to become complacent. It might well pay the monopolist to withhold or "file" technological improvements in both product and productive techniques in order to exploit existing capital equipment fully. New and improved products and techniques, it is argued, may be suppressed by monopolists to avoid any losses caused by the sudden obsolescence of existing machinery and equipment. And, even when improved techniques are belatedly introduced by monopolists, the accompanying cost reductions will accrue to the monopolist as increases in profits and only partially, if at all, to consumers in the form of lower prices and an increased output. Proponents of this view point out that in a number of industries which approximate pure monopoly—for example, steel and aluminum—the interest in research has been minimal. Such advances as have been realized have come largely from outside the industry or from the smaller firms which make up the "competitive fringe" of the industry.

Basically there are three offsetting arguments:

1. Any gross failure to achieve some minimum level of technological advance will induce public criticism and, in time, government control.

2. Technological advance is a means of lowering unit costs and thereby expanding profits. As our analysis of Figure 28·1 implies, lower costs will give rise to a profit-maximizing position which involves a larger output and a lower price than previously. Furthermore, any expansion of profits will not be of a transitory nature; barriers to entry protect the monopolist from profit encroachment by rivals.

3. Research and technological advance may be one of the monopolist's barriers to entry; hence, the monopolist must persist and succeed in the area of

technological advance or eventually fall prey to new competitors.

Which view is more accurate? Frankly, economists are not sure. Most economists do not envision pure monopoly as a particularly progressive market structure. At the same time they acknowledge that agriculture, the industry which most nearly fits the competitive model, has only on rare occasions provided itself with innovations in product and method. Government research and the oligopolistic firms which produce farm equipment have provided this competitive industry with most of its improvements in products and techniques. As we shall see in Chapter 30, some respected economists seem to feel that oligopolistic industries, wherein firms are large enough to have the ability to finance research and at the same time are compelled to engage in such research because of the presence of a moderate number of rivals, may be more conducive to technological advance than any other market structure.

Now what can be offered by way of a summarizing generalization as to the economic efficiency of pure monopoly? Simply this: In a static economy, wherein economies of scale are equally accessible to purely competitive and monopolist firms, pure competition will be superior to pure monopoly in that pure competition forces use of the best-known technology and allocates resources in accordance with the wants of society. On the other hand, when economies of scale available to the monopolist are not attainable by small competitive producers, or in a dynamic context in which changes in the rate of technological advance must be considered, the inefficiencies of pure monopoly are not so evident.

REGULATED MONOPOLY

Most purely monopolistic industries are "natural monopolies" and therefore subject to social regulation. In particular, the prices or rates which public utilities—railroads, telephone companies, natural gas and electricity suppliers—can charge are determined by a Federal, state, or local regulatory commission or board. Can such regulation improve the social acceptability of monopoly?

Socially optimum price

Figure 28·3 is informative. We know that P_m and Q_m are the profit-maximizing price and output which the unregulated monopolist would choose. Because price exceeds average total cost, the monopolist enjoys a substantial economic profit which is likely to contribute to income inequality. Furthermore, price exceeds marginal cost, which indicates an underallocation of resources to this product or service.

Now if the objective of our regulatory commission is to achieve an efficient allocation of resources, it should obviously establish a legal (ceiling) price for the monopolist that is equal to marginal cost. Remembering that each point on the market demand curve designates a price-quantity combination, and noting that marginal cost cuts the demand curve only at point *R*, it is quite obvious that P_r is the only price which is equal to marginal cost. The imposition of this maximum or ceiling price causes the monopolist's effective demand curve to become P_rRD; the demand curve becomes perfectly elastic, and therefore P_r = MR out to point *R*, where the regulated price ceases to be effective. The important point is that, given the legal price P_r, the monopolist will maximize profits by producing Q_r units of output, because it is at this output that MR (P_r) = MC. By making it illegal to charge more than P_r per unit, the regulatory agency has eliminated the monopolist's incentive to restrict output in order to benefit from a higher price. In short, by imposing the legal price P_r and letting the monopolist choose his profit-maximizing output, the allocative results of pure competition can be simulated. Production takes place where P_r = MC, and this equality indicates an efficient allocation of resources to this product or service.

"Fair-return" price

But the socially optimum price P_r is likely to pose a problem of losses for the regulated firm. The price which equals marginal cost is likely to be so low that average total costs are not covered. The inevitable result is losses. The reason for this lies in the basic character of public utilities. Because they are re-

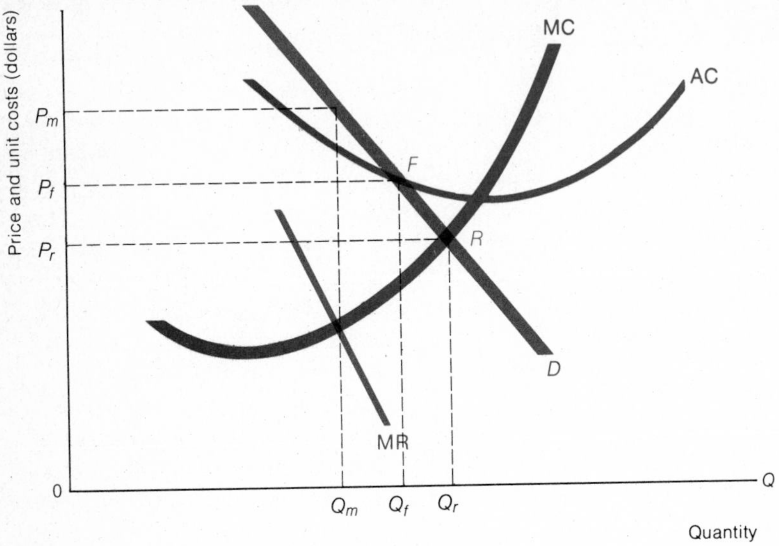

FIGURE 28·3 REGULATED MONOPOLY

Price regulation can improve the social consequences of a natural monopoly. The socially optimum price P_r will result in an efficient allocation of resources but is likely to entail losses and therefore call for permanent public subsidies. The "fair return" price P_f will allow the monopolist to break even, but will not fully correct the underallocation of resources.

quired to meet "peak" demands (both daily and seasonally) for their product or service, they tend to have substantial excess productive capacity when demand is relatively "normal." This high level of investment in capital facilities means that unit costs of production are likely to decline over a wide range of output. In technical terms, the market demand curve in Figure 28·3 cuts marginal cost at a point to the left of the marginal-cost–average-total-cost intersection, so the socially optimum price is necessarily below AC. Therefore, to enforce a socially optimum price upon the regulated monopolist would mean short-run losses, and in the long run, bankruptcy for the utility.

What to do? In practice, regulatory commissions have tended to back away somewhat from the objective of allocative efficiency and marginal-cost pricing. Most regulatory agencies in the United States are concerned with establishing a "fair-return" price. This is so in no small measure because, as the courts have envisioned it, an unembellished socially optimum price would lead to losses and eventual bankruptcy and thereby deprive the monopoly's owners of their private property without "due process of law." Indeed, the Supreme Court has held that the regulatory agencies must permit a "fair return" to owners.

Remembering that total costs include a normal or "fair" profit, the "fair" or "fair-return" price in Figure 28·3 would obviously be P_f. Because the demand curve cuts average cost only at point *F*, it is clear that P_f is the only price which permits a fair return. The corresponding output at regulated price P_f will be Q_f.

Dilemma of regulation

A comparison of the results of the socially optimum price and the "fair-return" price suggests a policy dilemma. When price is set to achieve the most efficient allocation of resources ($P = MC$), the regulated utility is likely to suffer losses. Survival of the firm would presumably depend upon permanent public subsidies out of tax revenues. On the other

hand, although a fair price allows the monopolist to cover costs, it only partially resolves the underallocation of resources which the unregulated monopoly would foster. That is, the fair-return price would only increase output from Q_m to Q_f, whereas the socially optimum output is Q_r. Despite this knotty problem, the basic point is that regulation can improve upon the results of monopoly from the social point of view. Price regulation can simultaneously reduce price, increase output, and reduce the economic profits of monopolies.[5]

SUMMARY

1. A pure monopolist is the sole producer of a commodity for which there are no close substitutes.

2. Barriers to entry, in the form of **a.** economies of scale, **b.** natural monopolies, **c.** the ownership or control of essential raw materials, **d.** patent ownership and research, **e.** unfair competition, and **f.** economies of being established, help explain the existence of pure monopoly and other imperfectly competitive market structures. Barriers to entry which are very formidable in the short run may prove to be surmountable in the long run.

3. The pure monopolist's market situation differs from that of a competitive firm in that the monopolist's demand curve is downsloping, causing the marginal-revenue curve to lie below the demand curve. Like the competitive seller, the pure monopolist will maximize profits by equating marginal revenue and marginal cost. Barriers to entry may permit a monopolist to acquire economic profits even in the long run. It is noteworthy, however, that **a.** the monopolist does not charge "the highest price he can get"; **b.** the maximum total profit sought by the monopolist rarely coincides with maximum unit profits; and **c.** high costs and a weak demand may prevent the monopolist from realizing any profit at all.

4. Given the same costs, the pure monopolist will find it more profitable to restrict output and charge a higher price than would a competitive seller. This restriction of output causes resources to be misallocated, as is evidenced by the fact that price exceeds marginal cost in monopolized markets.

5. Monopoly tends to increase income inequality.

6. Economists disagree as to how conducive pure monopoly is to technological advance. Some feel that pure monopoly is more progressive than pure competition because its ability to acquire economic profits provides for the financing of technological research. Others, however, argue that the absence of rival firms and the monopolist's desire to exploit fully his existing capital facilities weaken the monopolist's incentive to innovate.

7. Price regulation can be invoked to eliminate wholly or partially the tendency of monopolists to underallocate resources and to earn economic profits.

[5] The interested reader should consult Clark Lee Allen, James M. Buchanan, and Marshall R. Colberg, *Prices, Income, and Public Policy,* 2d ed. (New York: McGraw-Hill Book Company, 1959), chap. 30, from which the present discussion has benefited.

QUESTIONS AND STUDY SUGGESTIONS

1. "No firm is completely sheltered from rivals; all firms in fact compete for the dollars of consumers. Pure monopoly, therefore, simply does not exist." Do you agree? Explain.

2. Discuss the major barriers to entry. In particular, what are "the economies of being established"? Explain how each barrier can foster monopoly or oligopoly. Which barriers, if any, do you feel give rise to monopoly that is socially justifiable?

3. Critically evaluate and explain:

a. "Because they can control product price, monopolists are always assured of profitable production by simply charging the highest price consumers will pay."

b. "The pure monopolist seeks that output which will yield the greatest per unit profit."

c. "An excess of price over marginal cost is the market's way of signaling the need for more production of a product."

d. "The more profitable a firm, the greater its monopoly power."

e. "The monopolist has a price policy; the competitive producer does not."

f. "With respect to resource allocation the interests of the seller and of society coincide in a purely competitive market but conflict in a monopolized market."

g. "In a sense the monopolist makes a profit for not producing; the monopolist produces profits more than he does goods."

4. Carefully evaluate the following widely held viewpoint. Can you offer any arguments to the contrary?[6]

> Competition is congenial to material progress. It keeps the door open to new blood and new ideas. It communicates to all producers the improvements made by any one of them. Monopoly, as such, is not conducive to progress. The large firm may engage in research and invent new products, materials, methods and machines. But when it possesses a monopoly, it will be reluctant to make use of these inventions if they would compel it to scrap existing equipment or if it believes that their ultimate profitability is in doubt. The monopolist may introduce innovations and cut costs, but instead of moving goods by reducing prices he is prone to spend large sums on alternative methods of promoting sales. His refusal to cut prices deprives the community of any gain.

5. Suppose a pure monopolist is faced with the demand schedule shown in the next column and the same cost data as the competitive producer discussed in question 4 at the end of Chapter 27. Calculate marginal revenue and determine the profit-maximizing price and output for this monopolist. Verify your answer graphically.

6. Explain verbally and graphically how price (rate) regulation may improve the performance of monopolies. What is the "dilemma of regulation"?

7. How does the demand curve faced by a purely monopolistic seller differ from that confronting a purely competitive firm? Why does it differ? Of what significance is the difference? Why is the pure monopolist's demand curve not perfectly inelastic?

8. Assume a pure monopolist and a purely competitive firm have the same unit costs. Contrast the two with respect to *a.* price, *b.* output, *c.* profits, *d.* allocation of resources, and *e.* impact upon the distribution of income. Since both monopolists and competitive firms follow the MC = MR rule in maximizing profits, how do you account for the different results?

[6]Clair Wilcox, *Public Policies toward Business* (Homewood, Ill.: Richard D. Irwin, Inc., 1955), p. 12.

Price	Quantity demanded	Marginal revenue
$100	1	
		$____
83	2	
		____
71	3	
		____
63	4	
		____
55	5	
		____
48	6	
		____
42	7	
		____
37	8	
		____
33	9	
		____
29	10	

9. What considerations might restrain a monopolist from maximizing profits? In practice, how important do you feel these restraints might be?

SELECTED REFERENCES

Economic Issues, 4th ed., readings 48, 49, and 50.

Adams, Walter (ed.): *The Structure of American Industry,* 4th ed. (New York: The Macmillan Company, 1971), chap. 11.

Ferguson, C. E., and S. Charles Maurice: *Economic Analysis* (Homewood, Ill.: Richard D. Irwin, Inc., 1970), chap. 8.

MacAvoy, Paul W. (ed.): *The Crisis of the Regulatory Commissions* (New York: W. W. Norton & Company, Inc., 1970).

Robinson, E. A. G.: *Monopoly* (London: Nesbit and Company, 1941).

Schumpeter, Joseph A.: *Capitalism, Socialism, and Democracy,* 3d ed. (New York: Harper & Row, Publishers, Incorporated, 1950), chaps. 7 and 8.

Watson, Donald S. (ed.): *Price Theory in Action,* 2d ed. (Boston: Houghton Mifflin Company, 1969), parts 5 and 8.

Weiss, Leonard W.: *Case Studies in American Industry,* 2d ed. (New York: John Wiley & Sons, Inc., 1971), chap. 3.

PRICE AND OUTPUT DETERMINATION: MONOPOLISTIC COMPETITION

Pure competition and pure monopoly are the exception, not the rule, in American capitalism. Most market structures fall somewhere between these two extremes. In Chapter 30 we shall discuss oligopoly, a market structure which stands close to pure monopoly. In the present chapter we are concerned with monopolistic competition. Monopolistic competition correctly suggests a blending of monopoly and competition; more specifically, monopolistic competition involves a very considerable amount of competition with a small dose of monopoly power intermixed.

Our basic objectives in this chapter are:

1. To define and discuss the nature and prevalence of monopolistic competition.

2. To analyze and evaluate the price-output behavior of monopolistically competitive firms.

3. To explain and assess the role of nonprice competition, that is, competition based upon product quality and advertising, in monopolistically competitive industries.

CONCEPT AND OCCURRENCE OF MONOPOLISTIC COMPETITION

First of all, let us recall, and also expand upon, the definition of monopolistic competition.

Monopolistic competition refers to that market situation in which a relatively large number of small producers or suppliers are offering similar but not identical products. The contrasts between this and pure competition are important. Monopolistic competition does not require the presence of hundreds or thousands of firms but only a fairly large number—say 25, 35, 60, or 70.

Several important characteristics of monopolistic competition follow from the presence of relatively large numbers. In the first place, each firm has a relatively small percentage of the total market, so each has a very limited amount of control over market price. Then too, the presence of a relatively large number of firms also ensures that collusion—

concerted action by the firms to restrict output and rig price—is all but impossible. Finally, with a large number of firms in the industry, there is no feeling of mutual interdependence between them; that is, each firm determines its policies without considering the possible reactions of rival firms. And this is a very reasonable way to act in a market in which one's rivals are very numerous. After all, the 10 or 15 percent increase in sales which firm X may realize by cutting price will be spread so thinly over its 20, 40, or 60 rivals that for all practical purposes the impact upon their sales will be imperceptible. Rivals' reactions can be ignored, because the impact of one firm's actions upon each of its many rivals is so small that these rivals will have no reason to react.

Also in contrast to pure competition, monopolistic competition has the fundamental feature of *product differentiation.* Purely competitive firms produce a standardized product; monopolistically competitive producers turn out variations of a given product. Many firms produce toothpaste, but the product of each differs from its rivals in one or more respects. Indeed, it must be emphasized that product differentiation has more dimensions than are immediately apparent. "Real," or physical, differences involving functional features, materials, design, and workmanship are obviously important aspects of product differentiation. But "imaginary" differences created through advertising, packaging, and the use of trademarks and brand names can be equally significant. Finally, the conditions of sale make for differentiation; the location of a store, the courteousness of its clerks, the firm's reputation for servicing its products, and the availability of credit are all facets of product differentiation.

The significance of product differentiation is basically twofold. On the one hand, despite the presence of a relatively large number of firms, monopolistically competitive producers have limited amounts of control over the prices of their products because of differentiation. Consumers have preferences for the products of specific sellers and *within limits* will pay a higher price to satisfy those preferences. Sellers and buyers are no longer linked at random, as in a purely competitive market. On the other hand, the fact that products are differentiated adds a new and complicating factor to our analysis: *nonprice competition.* Because products are differentiated, it can be supposed that products can be varied over time and that the differentiating features of each firm's product will be susceptible to advertising and other forms of sales promotion. In a monopolistically competitive market economic rivalry centers not only upon price but also upon product variation and product promotion.

Entry into monopolistically competitive industries tends to be relatively easy. The fact that monopolistically competitive producers are typically small-sized firms, both absolutely and relatively, suggests that economies of scale and capital requirements are few. On the other hand, as compared with pure competition, there may be some added financial barriers posed by the need for deriving a product different from one's rivals and the obligation to advertise that product. Existing firms may hold patents on their products and copyrights on their brand names and trademarks, enhancing the difficulty and cost of successfully imitating them.

In short, monopolistic competition refers to industries that comprise a relatively large number of firms, operating noncollusively, in the production of differentiated products. Nonprice competition accompanies price competition. Ease of entry makes for competition by new firms in the long run.

It is difficult to find clear-cut illustrations of monopolistically competitive industries. Many industries which approximate monopolistic competitions also embody one or more characteristics of oligopoly. Table 29·1 contains a group of manufacturing industries which approximate monopolistic competition. Retail stores in larger cities and metropolitan areas are generally monopolistically competitive; grocery stores, gasoline stations, barber shops, dry cleaners, clothing stores, and so forth, operate under conditions similar to those we have described.

PRICE AND OUTPUT DETERMINATION

Let us now analyze the price-output behavior of a monopolistically competitive firm. To facilitate this task we assume initially that the firms in the industry are producing *given* products and are engaging in

TABLE 29·1 PERCENTAGE OF OUTPUT* PRODUCED BY FIRMS IN SELECTED LOW-CONCENTRATION MANUFACTURING INDUSTRIES

Industry	Four largest firms	Eight largest firms	Twenty largest firms
Plywood	23%	31%	42%
Costume jewelry	17	25	39
Men's and boys' suits and coats	14	23	38
Metal house furniture	13	20	34
Upholstered furniture	13	18	28
Paperboard boxes	12	19	30
Wood furniture	11	16	25
Millinery	9	14	22
Women's suits, coats, and skirts	8	11	17
Dresses	6	9	14
Concrete block and brick	5	7	12

*As measured by value of shipments. Data are for 1963.
Source: Senate Subcommittee on Antitrust and Monopoly, *Concentration Ratios in Manufacturing Industry, 1963* (Washington, 1966), part 1, table 2.

a *given* amount of promotional activity. Later we shall note how product variation and advertising modify our discussion.

The firm's demand curve

Our explanation is couched in terms of Figure 29·1*a*. The basic feature of this diagram, which sets it off from our analyses of pure competition and pure monopoly, is the elasticity of the firm's individual demand, or sales, curve. The demand curve faced by a monopolistically competitive seller is highly, but not perfectly, elastic. It is much more elastic than the demand curve of the pure monopolist, because the monopolistically competitive seller is faced with a relatively large number of rivals producing close-substitute goods. The pure monopolist, of course, has no rivals at all. Yet, for two reasons, the monopolistically competitive seller's sales curve is not perfectly elastic as is the purely competitive producer's:

1. The monopolistically competitive firm has a smaller number of rivals.
2. The products of these rivals are close but not perfect substitutes.

Generally speaking, the precise degree of elasticity embodied in the monopolistically competitive firm's demand curve will depend upon the exact number of rivals and the degree of product differentiation. The larger the number of rivals and the weaker the product differentiation, the greater will be the elasticity of each seller's demand curve, that is, the closer the situation will be to pure competition.

The short run: profits or losses

The firm will maximize its profits or minimize its losses in the short run by producing that output designated by the intersection of marginal cost and marginal revenue, for reasons with which we are now familiar. The representative firm of Figure 29·1*a* produces an output *Q*, charges a price *P*, and is fortunate enough to realize a total profit of the size indicated in yellow. But a less favorable cost and demand situation may exist, putting the monopolistically competitive firm in

FIGURE 29·1 MONOPOLISTICALLY COMPETITIVE FIRMS TEND TO REALIZE A NORMAL PROFIT IN THE LONG RUN

The economic profits shown in (*a*) will induce new firms to enter, causing the profits to be competed away. The losses indicated in (*b*) will cause an exodus of firms until normal profits are restored. Thus in (*c*), where price just covers unit costs at the MR = MC output, the firm's long-run equilibrium position is portrayed.

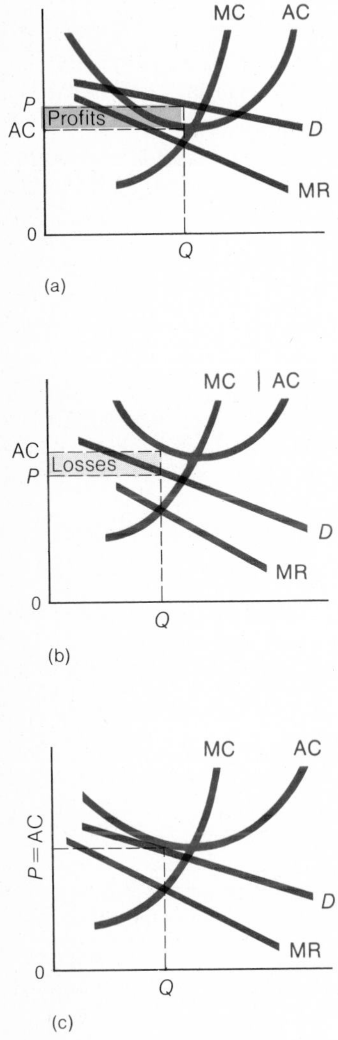

the position of realizing losses in the short run. This is illustrated by the gray area in Figure 29·1*b*. In the short run the monopolistically competitive firm may either realize an economic profit or be faced with losses.

The long run: break-even

In the long run, however, the tendency is for monopolistically competitive firms to earn a normal profit, that is, to break even. In the short-run profits case, Figure 29·1*a,* we can expect the economic profits to attract new rivals, because entry is relatively easy. As new firms enter, the demand curve faced by the typical firm will fall (shift to the left) and become more elastic. Why? Because each firm has a smaller share of the total demand and now faces a larger number of close-substitute products. This in turn tends to cause the disappearance of economic profits. When the demand curve is tangent to the average-cost curve at the profit-maximizing output, as shown in Figure 29·1*c,* the firm is just breaking even. Output *Q* is the equilibrium output for the firm; as Figure 29·1*c* clearly indicates, any deviation from that output will entail average costs which exceed product price and, therefore, losses for the firm. Furthermore, economic profits have been competed away, and there is no incentive for additional firms to enter. In the short-run losses case, Figure 29·1*b,* we can expect an exodus of firms to occur in the long run. Faced with fewer substitute products and blessed with an expanded share of total demand, surviving firms will find that their losses disappear and gradually give way to approximately normal profits.[1]

Note that we have been very careful in designating our long-run analysis as a statement of a tendency. The representative firm in a monopolistically competitive market *tends* to break even in the long run. There are certain complicating factors which prevent us from being more dogmatic. First, some firms may achieve a measure of product differentiation which cannot be duplicated by rivals even over a long span

[1]For simplicity's sake we assume constant costs; shifts in the cost curves as firms enter or leave would complicate our discussion, but would not alter the conclusions.

of time. A given gasoline station may have the only available location at the busiest intersection in town. Or a firm may hold a patent which gives it a slight and more or less permanent advantage over imitators. Such firms may realize a sliver of economic profits even in the long run. Second, remember that entry is not completely unrestricted. Because of product differentiation, there are likely to be greater financial barriers to entry than otherwise would be the case. This again suggests that some economic profits may persist even in the long run. A third consideration may work in the opposite direction, causing losses—below-normal profits—to persist in the long run. The proprietor of a corner delicatessen persistently accepts a return less than he could earn elsewhere, because his business is a way of life to him. The suburban barber ekes out a meager existence, because cutting hair is "all he wants to do." With all things considered, however, the long-run profitless equilibrium of Figure 29·1*c* is probably a reasonable portrayal of reality.

WASTES OF MONOPOLISTIC COMPETITION

Recalling our evaluation of competitive pricing in Chapter 27, we know that economic efficiency requires the triple equality of price, marginal cost, and average cost. The equality of price and marginal cost is necessary for a correct allocation of resources to the product. The equality of price with minimum average total cost suggests the use of the most efficient (least-cost) technology; this equality means that consumers will enjoy the largest volume of product and the lowest price which prevailing cost conditions will allow.

An examination of Figure 29·1*c* suggests that the monopolistic element in monopolistic competition causes a modest underallocation of resources to goods produced under this market structure. Price exceeds marginal cost in long-run equilibrium, thereby indicating that society values additional units of this commodity more than the alternative products which the needed resources can otherwise produce.

Furthermore, in contrast to purely competitive firms, as suggested in Figure 29·1*c*, monopolistically competitive firms produce somewhat short of the most efficient (least unit cost) output. Production entails higher unit costs than the minimum attainable. This in turn means a somewhat higher price than would result under pure competition. Consumers do *not* benefit from the largest output and lowest price which cost conditions permit. Indeed, monopolistically competitive firms must charge a higher than competitive price in the long run in order to manage a normal profit. Looked at differently, if each firm were able to produce at the most efficient output, a smaller number of firms could produce the same total output, and the product could be sold to consumers at a lower price. Monopolistically competitive industries tend to be overcrowded with firms, each of which is underutilized, that is, operating short of optimum capacity. This is typified by many types of retail establishments, for example, the highway intersection adorned with four gleaming gasoline stations all operating far short of capacity. Underutilized plants, consumers penalized through higher than competitive prices for this underutilization, and producers just making a normal return in the long run—these are the so-called "wastes" of monopolistic competition.

But we must not be hypercritical of monopolistic competition. Some economists argue that in many monopolistically competitive industries the price and output results are not drastically different from those of pure competition. The highly elastic nature of each firm's demand curve guarantees that the results are nearly competitive. Furthermore, it must be kept in mind that any deviations from the purely competitive output and price may be offset by the fact that with monopolistic competition the consumer now can choose from a variety of products; he is not faced with a homogeneous commodity.

NONPRICE COMPETITION

For reasons cited above, we can conclude that the situation portrayed in Figure 29·1*c* may not be particularly beneficial to society. It can also be surmised that it is not very satisfying to the monopolistically

competitive producer who barely captures a normal profit for his efforts. We can therefore expect monopolistically competitive producers to take steps to improve upon the long-run equilibrium position. But how can this be accomplished? The answer lies in product differentiation. Each firm has a product which is currently distinguishable in some more or less tangible way from those of his rivals. The product is presumably subject to further variation, that is, to product development. Then, too, the emphasis of real product differences and the creation of imaginary differences may be achieved through advertising and related sales promotion. In short, the profit-realizing producer of Figure 29·1*a* is loath to stand by and watch new competitors encroach upon his profits by duplicating or imitating his product, copying his advertising, and matching his services to consumers. Rather, he will attempt to sustain these profits and "stay ahead" of competitors through further product development and by enhancing the quantity and quality of advertising. In this way he might prevent the long-run tendency of Figure 29·1*c* from becoming a reality. True, product development and advertising will add to the firm's costs. But they can also be expected to increase the demand for his product. If demand increases by more than enough to compensate for development and promotional costs, the firm will have improved its profit position. As Figure 29·1*c* suggests, the firm may have little or no prospect of increasing profits by price cutting. So why not practice nonprice competition?

Product differentiation and product development

The likelihood that easy entry will promote product variety and product improvement is possibly a redeeming feature of monopolistic competition which may offset, wholly or in part, the "wastes" associated with this market structure. There are really two somewhat distinct considerations here: (1) product differentiation at a point in time and (2) product improvement over a period of time.

1. Product differentiation means that at any point in time the consumer will be offered a wide range of types, styles, brands, and quality gradations of any given product. As compared with the situation under pure competition, this correctly suggests possible advantages to the consumer. His range of free choice is widened, and variations and shadings of consumer tastes are more fully met by producers. But skeptics warn that product differentiation is not an unmixed blessing. Product proliferation may reach the point where the consumer becomes confused and rational choice is highly unlikely. Variety may add spice to the consumer's life, but only up to a point. Worse yet, some observers fear that the consumer, faced with a myriad of similar products, may rely upon such a dubious expedient as judging product quality by price; that is, the consumer may irrationally assume that price is necessarily an index of product quality.

2. Product competition is an important avenue of technological innovation and product betterment over a period of time. Such product development may be cumulative in two different senses. (*a*) A successful product improvement by one firm obligates rivals to imitate or, if they can, improve upon this firm's temporary market advantage or suffer the penalty of losses. (*b*) Profits realized from a successful product improvement can be used to finance further improvements. Again, however, there are notable criticisms of the product development which may occur under monopolistic competition. Critics point out that many product alterations are more apparent than real, consisting of frivolous and superficial changes in the product which do not improve its durability, efficiency, or usefulness. A more exotic container, bright packaging, or "shuffling the chrome" are frequently the focal points for product development. It is argued, too, that particularly in the cases of durable and semidurable consumer goods, development seems to follow a pattern of "planned obsolescence," wherein firms improve their product only by that amount necessary to make the average consumer dissatisfied with last year's model.

Do the advantages of product differentiation, properly discounted, outweigh the "wastes" of monopolistic competition? It is difficult to say, short of examining specific cases; and even then concrete conclusions are difficult to come by. For example,

a recent study of the (oligopolistic) automobile industry attempts to measure the cost of model changes in recent years.[2] Specifically, this question was posed: What has been the aggregate annual cost of the increases in automobile size, increases in horsepower, increased gasoline consumption caused by the "horsepower race," "power" accessories, and the cost of factory retooling required by such model changes? The investigators concluded that "the estimated costs of model changes since 1949 . . . run about 5 billion dollars per year over the 1956–60 period." Thus, although there is no question that the automobile today is a better product than it was in 1949, it is nevertheless quite legitimate to inquire: Is it *that much* better?

Advertising

A monopolistically competitive producer may gain at least a temporary edge on his rivals by manipulating his product. He may achieve the same result by manipulating the consumer through advertising and sales promotion. While product differentiation adapts the product to consumer demand, advertising adapts consumer demand to the product. In practice these two aspects of nonprice competition may be difficult to disentangle. Does a new and colorful method of packaging a product constitute a change in the product, or is it a means of advertising and promotion?

Though we might tentatively agree that product development is a desirable feature of monopolistic competition, the advertising which accompanies it is more difficult to evaluate. The social desirability of extensive advertising expenditures is a very controversial and clouded topic. A basic reason for this is the fact that some advertising is *informative,* that is, accurately descriptive of the qualities and prices of products, while other advertising is *competitive,* consisting of unsubstantiated ours-is-better-than-theirs exhortation. Local newspaper advertising is informative, for example, a grocery store's listing of prices and special buys. The beer and soap advertisements that the television industry funnels into American living rooms are generally competitive.

This controversy is not an unimportant one. Currently advertising and promotional expenditures in American capitalism are now about $20 billion per year. This is equal to two-thirds the nation's annual outlay on primary and secondary public education. Hence, if advertising is generally wasteful, any potential virtues of monopolistically competitive markets are thereby dimmed, and the need for corrective public policies is indicated.

Extreme arguments are prevalent. Some economists are prone to write off all advertising as sheer economic waste. Others—the admen themselves—manage to associate all that is just and good in American society with advertising. An accurate picture lies in the middle ground. Let us survey the basic claims for and the charges against advertising.

The case for advertising Some of the arguments in favor of advertising follow:

1. Advertising allegedly provides the information which assists consumers in making rational choices. In a dynamic, complex economy there is an acute need for the consumer to be closely acquainted with new firms, new products, and improvements in existing products. Advertising is the medium which disperses such information.

2. Advertising supports national communications. Radio, television, magazines, and newspapers are supported wholly or in part through advertising.

3. It has been argued more recently that advertising is a stimulant to product development. Successful advertising is frequently based upon unique and advantageous features of a firm's product. Hence, a firm is obligated to improve its product to provide "sales points" for competing successfully in the advertising sphere.

4. Through successful advertising a firm can expand its production and thereby realize greater economies of scale. As shown in Figure 29·2, by shifting the firm's demand curve to the right through advertising, production will expand from, say, Q_1 to

[2] F. M. Fisher, Z. Griliches, and C. Kaysen, "The Costs of Automobile Model Changes since 1949," *Journal of Political Economy,* October 1962, pp. 433–451.

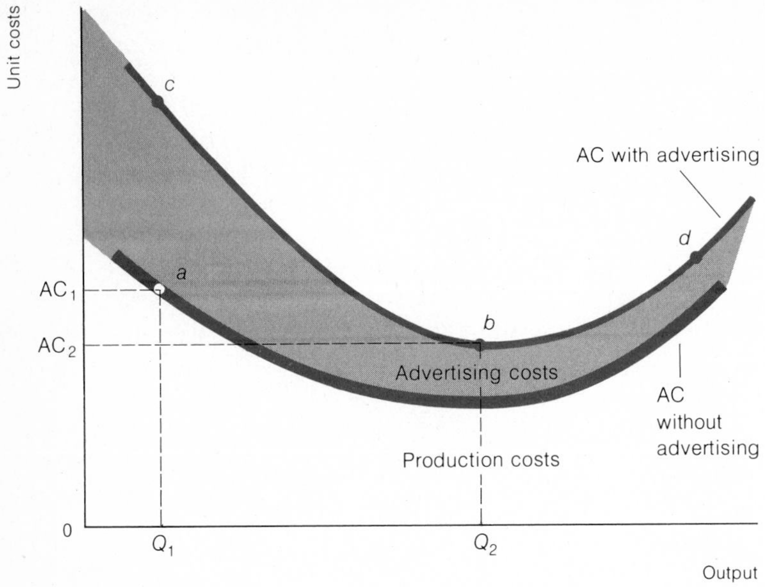

FIGURE 29 · 2 THE POSSIBLE EFFECTS OF ADVERTISING UPON A FIRM'S OUTPUT AND AVERAGE COSTS

Proponents of advertising contend that resulting economies of scale will expand the firm's production from, say *a* to *b* and lower unit costs as economies of scale are realized. Some critics argue that advertising is more likely to increase costs and leave output largely unchanged, as is suggested by the movement from *a* to *c*. Others point out that expansion realized through advertising may force diseconomies of scale upon the firm, as the movement from *a* to *d* indicates.

Q_2. Despite the fact that advertising outlays will shift the firm's average-cost curve upward, unit costs will nevertheless decline from, say, AC_1 to AC_2. Greater productive efficiency resulting from economies of scale more than offsets the increase in unit costs due to advertising. Consumers will therefore get the product at a lower price with advertising than they would in its absence.

5. It is also contended that advertising promotes full employment by inducing high levels of consumer spending. This is particularly crucial, it is argued, in a wealthy society such as that of American capitalism, where much of total production takes the form of luxury or semiluxury goods which fulfill no basic wants. One need not advertise to sell food to a hungry man, but advertising and sales promotion are essential in persuading families that they need a second car, color television, or an automatic dishwasher. Stability in an opulent society calls for want-creating activities—in particular, advertising—or high levels of production and employment will not be sustainable.

The case against advertising Some of the arguments on the other side of the picture allegedly "debunk" the claims for advertising; others raise new points.

1. Critics of advertising point out that the basic objective of advertising is to persuade, not to inform. Competitive advertising is based upon misleading and extravagant claims which serve to confuse and frequently insult the intelligence of the consumer, not enlighten him. Little of real value in the rendering of rational choices can be garnered from the soap and beer advertising which crowds our television screens and adds bulk to our slick magazines. Indeed, advertising may well persuade consumers in some cases to pay high prices for much-acclaimed but inferior products, forgoing better but unadvertised products selling at lower prices. The Pure Food and Drug and Federal Trade Commission Acts, which are aimed at protecting consumers from product misrepresentation and misleading advertising, testify to past and present abuses by modern-day hucksters.

2. Advertising expenditures as such are relatively unproductive; they add little or nothing to the well-being of society. Advertising diverts human and property resources from other more pressing areas. For example, lumber which is sorely needed in the production of low- and medium-priced housing is squandered on the construction of unsightly billboards. In short, advertising gives rise to a gross misallocation of resources.

In recent years the general criticism that advertising promotes a misallocation of resources has assumed a special form: advertising allegedly contributes to *social imbalance.* That is, advertising, in conjunction with a number of other factors, has given rise to the overproduction of private goods relative to public or social goods. It is argued that advertising is peculiar to, and an integral part of, the production and sale of private goods. Gigantic advertising campaigns extoll the merits of electric can openers, self-propelled lawnmowers, and eight-speaker stereophonic phonographs. But no similar force proclaims the virtues of social goods and services; similar persuasion does not exist to whet the consumer's appetite for better schools, improved streets and highways, increased expenditures for medical research, and so forth. The net result, it is contended, is a misallocation of resources; resources are overallocated to private goods and underallocated to public goods. Private goods are superabundant; the quantity and quality of social goods are remarkably deficient. The problem of social imbalance will be pursued at length in Chapter 41.

3. Significant social costs are entailed by advertising. Billboards blot out roadside scenery and generally debase the countryside. Sound trucks disrupt suburban serenity. Of potentially greater importance are the effects which advertising's support of national communications may have upon the accuracy and quality of those communications. Will a newspaper present an unprejudiced report of the labor dispute in which its major advertiser is involved? Will a television newscast conveniently ignore the fact that antitrust action has been initiated against its sponsor? Will a firm which distributes its product nationally permit the television playhouse it sponsors to present an honest and frank portrayal of America's racial problems? In more general terms, it is charged that competitive advertising offends the common sense and tries the patience of society. The fact that water consumption rises enormously during television commercials adds some credulity to this latter contention.

4. Critics of advertising are very dubious of the argument that advertising permits firms to expand, to achieve lower unit costs, and to offer their products at lower prices to consumers. There are several reasons for this doubt. First, it is contended that much advertising tends to be self-canceling. The million-dollar advertising campaign of one cigarette manufacturer is largely offset by equally expensive campaigns waged by its rivals. Few additional people smoke cigarettes. Each firm has about the same portion of the market as it had originally. And the cost, and therefore the price, of cigarettes is higher. In Figure 29·2 self-canceling advertising may move the firm from point *a* to point *c,* not from *a* to *b.* Second, if advertising can cause a firm to realize economies of scale through growth, can it not also cause a firm to encounter diseconomies? Might not advertising shift the firm's level of output from point *a* to point *d* in Figure 29·2? Third, are there not more desirable and less costly alternative means by which a firm might expand output and achieve economies of scale? Would not product development or research on production methods permit a firm to achieve economies of scale and at the same time avoid the upshift in its average-cost schedule which advertising entails? Finally, even if a firm achieves lower unit costs through advertising, will the consumer benefit through proportionate price reductions? This point is particularly pertinent in view of the fact that the expansion of those firms whose advertising is most successful implies that less successful advertisers will fall by the wayside, causing the industry to move away from monopolistic competition and in the direction of oligopoly, wherein firms have greater control over product price.

5. Most economists are reluctant to accept advertising as an important determinant of the levels of output and employment. There has been little evi-

dence of economic stagnation in the post–World War II years that would seem remediable by advertising and promotional outlays. Furthermore, the most volatile aspect of aggregate demand is not so much highly advertised consumer goods as it is little-advertised investment goods. The consensus seems to be that advertising probably affects the composition more than it does the volume of spending. And those economists who do accept the contention that advertising now has an impact upon consumer spending suggest that at some future time its effect on the level of spending may diminish to zero.[3]

> On some not distant day, the voice of each individual seller may well be lost in the collective roar of all together. Like injunctions to virtue and warnings of socialism, advertising will beat helplessly on ears that have been conditioned by previous assault to utter immunity. . . . It will be worth no one's while to speak, for since all speak none can hear.

At this point an economy whose level of spending is supported by effective advertising will be plagued by serious instability. If consumer wants and consumer spending are contrived through advertising, the future failure of that contrivance could materially contribute to recession and unemployment. The argument has also been made that advertising expenditures are procyclical, that is, they fluctuate *with* total spending, intensifying unemployment during bad times and adding to inflationary pressures during prosperous times.

6. There is evidence that in some industries advertising has become such a large part of the cost of doing business that it constitutes an important financial barrier to entry. This is generally recognized to be the case in the tobacco industry, where producers as a group may spend considerably in excess of $350 million per year on advertising and related promotional activities. The three major auto manufacturers—GM, Ford, and Chrysler—currently spend over $500 million for advertising per year.

Empirical evidence The economic implications of advertising have been probed through a number of recent empirical studies. Unfortunately, such studies are subject to serious problems with respect to both the acquisition and analysis of relevant data; hence conclusions are necessarily tentative. Nevertheless, empirical research suggests that perhaps the microeconomic effects of advertising are *not* as adverse as economists have traditionally presumed. In particular, a substantial portion of total advertising is of an informative type and therefore is a basic means by which consumers are informed of prices and terms of sale. Furthermore, advertising does not seem to be a mechanism by which competition is necessarily reduced; on the contrary, advertising is frequently a means by which new firms gain entrance to an industry.[4]

[3]John K. Galbraith, *The Affluent Society* (Boston: Houghton Mifflin Company, 1958), p. 202.

Monopolistic competition and economic analysis

Our discussion of nonprice competition correctly infers that the equilibrium situation of a monopolistically competitive firm is actually much more complex than the previous graphic analysis indicates. Figure 29·1*a, b,* and *c assumes* a given product and a given level of advertising expenditures. But, alas, these we now know are not given in practice. The monopolistically competitive firm must actually juggle three variable considerations—price, product, and promotion—in seeking maximum profits. What specific variety of product, selling at what price, and supplemented by what level of promotional activity, will result in the greatest level of profits attainable? This complex situation is not readily expressed in a simple, meaningful economic model. At best we can note that each possible combination of price, product, and promotion poses a different demand and cost (production plus promotion) situation for the firm, some one of which will allow him maximum profits. In practice, this optimum combination cannot be readily forecast but must be sought by the process of trial

[4]The pioneering work of Richard G. Telser is recommended to the ambitious student. See his "Advertising and Competition," *Journal of Political Economy,* December, 1964, pp. 537–562. Jules Backman's *Advertising and Competition* (New York: New York University Press, 1967) is an interesting and useful summary of recent empirical studies of advertising.

and error. And even here, certain limitations may be imposed by the actions of rivals. A firm may not risk the elimination of advertising expenditures for fear its share of the market will decline sharply, to the benefit of its rivals who do advertise. Similarly, patents held by rivals will rule out certain desirable product variations.

SUMMARY

1. The distinguishing features of monopolistic competition are: *a.* There is a large enough number of firms so that each has little control over price, mutual interdependence is absent, and collusion is virtually impossible; *b.* products are characterized by real and imaginary differences and by varying conditions surrounding their sale; and *c.* entry to the industry is relatively easy. Many aspects of retailing, and some industries wherein economies of scale are few, approximate monopolistic competition.

2. Monopolistically competitive firms may earn economic profits or incur losses in the short run. The easy entry and exodus of firms gives rise to a long-run tendency for them to earn a normal profit.

3. The long-run equilibrium position of the monopolistically competitive producer is less socially desirable than that of a purely competitive firm. Under monopolistic competition price exceeds marginal cost, suggesting an underallocation of resources to the product, and price exceeds minimum average total cost, indicating that consumers do not get the product at the lowest price which cost conditions would allow. However, because the firm's demand curve is highly elastic, these "wastes" of monopolistic competition should not be overemphasized.

4. Product differentiation provides a means by which monopolistically competitive firms can offset the long-run tendency for economic profits to approximate zero. Through product development and advertising outlays, a firm may strive to increase the demand for its product more than nonprice competition increases its costs.

5. Although subject to certain dangers and problems, product differentiation affords the consumer a greater variety of products at any point in time and improved products over time. Whether these features fully compensate for the wastes of monopolistic competition is a moot question.

6. There is sharp disagreement as to the economic benefits of advertising. Proponents justify advertising on the grounds that it *a.* aids consumers in exercising rational choices, *b.* supports national communications, *c.* speeds product development, *d.* permits firms to realize economies of scale, and *e.* encourages spending and a high level of employment. Critics assert that advertising *a.* confuses rather than informs, *b.* misallocates resources away from more urgent employments (particularly from the production of social goods), *c.* involves a variety of social costs, *d.* results in higher, not lower, costs and prices, *e.* is not a strategic determinant of spending and employment, and *f.* often constitutes a significant financial barrier to entry.

7. In practice the monopolistic competitor seeks largely through trial and error that specific combination of price, product, and promotion which will maximize his profits.

QUESTIONS AND STUDY SUGGESTIONS

1. How does monopolistic competition differ from pure competition? From pure monopoly? Explain fully what product differentiation entails.

2. Compare the elasticity of the monopolistically competitive producer's demand curve with that of *a.* a pure competitor and *b.* a pure monopolist. Assuming identical long-run costs, compare graphically the prices and output which would result under pure competition and monopolistic competition. "Monopolistically competitive industries are characterized by too many firms, each of which produces too little." Explain.

3. "Monopolistic competition is monopoly up to the point at which consumers become willing to buy close substitute products and competitive beyond that point." Explain.

4. What is nonprice competition? "Competition in quality and in service may be quite as effective in giving the buyer more for his money as is price competition." Do you agree? Explain why monopolistically competitive firms frequently prefer nonprice to price competition.

5. Critically evaluate and explain:
a. "In monopolistically competitive industries economic profits are competed away in the long run; hence, there is no valid reason to criticize the performance and efficiency of such industries."
b. "Monopolistic competition is merely a way station on the road to oligopoly."
c. "In the long run monopolistic competition leads to a monopolistic price but not to monopolistic profits."

6. Do you agree or disagree with the following statements? Why?
a. "The amount of advertising which a firm does is likely to vary inversely with the real differences in its product."
b. "If each firm's advertising expenditures merely tend to cancel the effects of its rivals' advertising, it is clearly irrational for these firms to maintain large advertising budgets."

7. Carefully evaluate the two views expressed in the following statements:
a. "It happens every day. Advertising builds mass demand. Production goes up—costs come down. More people can buy—more jobs are created. These are the ingredients of economic growth. Each stimulates the next in a cycle of productivity and plenty which constantly creates a better life for you."
b. "Advertising constitutes 'inverted education'—a costly effort to induce people to buy without sufficient thought and deliberation and therefore to buy things they don't need. Furthermore, advertising intensifies economic instability because advertising outlays vary directly with the level of consumer spending. Indeed, by contributing to inflation during prosperous periods, advertising may foster political pressures for the curtailment of government spending on much-needed social goods and services, thereby promoting a misallocation of resources."
Which view do you feel is the more accurate? Justify your position.

SELECTED REFERENCES

Economic Issues, 4th ed., reading 44.

Adams, Walter (ed.): *The Structure of American Industry,* 4th ed. (New York: The Macmillan Company, 1971), chap. 2.

Backman, Jules: *Advertising and Competition* (New York: New York University Press, 1967).

Bain, Joe S.: *Industrial Organization,* 2d ed. (New York: John Wiley & Sons, Inc., 1968), chaps. 7 and 8.

Leftwich, Richard H.: *The Price System and Resource Allocation,* 4th ed. (Hinsdale, Ill.: The Dryden Press, Inc., 1970), chap. 12.

Watson, Donald S. (ed.): *Price Theory in Action,* 2d ed. (Boston: Houghton Mifflin Company, 1969), part 6.

Weiss, Leonard W.: *Case Studies in American Industry,* rev. ed. (New York: John Wiley & Sons, Inc., 1971), chap. 5.

30

PRICE AND OUTPUT DETERMINATION: OLIGOPOLY

In many of the manufacturing, mining, wholesaling, and retailing industries of American capitalism a few firms are dominant. Such industries are called *oligopolies.* It is with these industries that the present chapter is concerned. Specifically, we have four objectives. We seek first to define oligopoly, assess its occurrence, and note the reasons for its existence. The second and major goal is to survey the possible courses of price-output behavior which oligopolistic industries might follow. Third, the role of nonprice competition, that is, competition on the basis of product development and advertising, in oligopolistic industries is discussed. Finally, some comments with respect to the economic efficiency and social desirability of oligopoly are offered.

CONCEPT AND OCCURRENCE OF OLIGOPOLY

What are the basic characteristics of oligopoly? How frequently is it encountered in American capitalism? Why has this industry structure developed?

Fewness

The outstanding feature of oligopoly is "fewness." When a relatively small number of firms dominates the market for a good or service, the industry is oligopolistic. But what specifically is meant by "a few" firms? This is necessarily vague, because the market model of oligopoly covers a great deal of ground, ranging from pure monopoly, on the one hand, to monopolistic competition, on the other. Thus oligopoly encompasses the tin-can industry, in which two firms virtually dominate an entire national market, and the situation in which, say, fifteen or twenty gasoline stations may enjoy roughly equal shares of the petroleum products market in a medium-sized town. Table 30·1 lists a number of industries in which fewness is present in varying degrees. This table correctly suggests that the market structure of oligopoly is very common in American capitalism. At the local level many aspects of the retail trades are characterized by oligopoly.

TABLE 30·1 PERCENTAGE OF OUTPUT* PRODUCED BY FIRMS IN SELECTED HIGH-CONCENTRATION MANUFACTURING INDUSTRIES

Industry	Percent of industry output produced by first four firms
Primary aluminum	100
Passenger cars	99
Locomotives and parts	97
Steam engines and turbines	93
Sewing machines	93
Electric lamps (bulbs)	92
Telephone and telegraph equipment	92
Gypsum products	84
Synthetic fibers	82
Cigarettes	80
Typewriters	76
Tin cans and tinware	74
Soap and detergents	72
Tires and inner tubes	70
Phonograph records	69
Distilled liquor	58

* As measured by value of shipments. Data are for 1963.
Source: Senate Subcommittee on Antitrust and Monopoly, *Concentration Ratios in Manufacturing Industry, 1963* (Washington, 1966), part I, table 2.

Oligopolies may be *homogeneous* or *differentiated;* that is, the firms in an oligopolistic industry may produce standardized or differentiated products. Many industrial products—steel, zinc, copper, aluminum, lead, cement, industrial alcohol, and so forth—are virtually standardized products in the physical sense and are produced under oligopolistic conditions. Of course, even here slight physical differences may exist, and the service, credit, and speed of delivery may differ between sellers, making for a measure of differentiation. But for most practical purposes these are standardized products. On the other hand, many consumer goods industries—automobiles, tires, typewriters, petroleum products, soap, cigarettes, fountain pens, and a host of electrical appliances—are differentiated oligopolies.

Underlying causes

Why do industries composed of a few firms exist? Specific reasons are manifold, but two related factors—economies of scale and the advantages of merger—are perhaps of greatest importance.

Economies of scale We discovered in Chapter 26 that, where economies of scale are substantial (see Figure 26·6*a*), reasonably efficient production will be possible only with a small number of producers; in other words, efficiency requires that the productive capacity of each firm be large relative to the total market. Indeed, it is an unstable situation for an industry to have a large number of high-cost firms each of which is failing to realize existing economies of scale. In Figure 26·4, for example, a firm currently operating with the small and inefficient plant size indicated by ATC-1 will recognize that this short-run position is unsatisfactory; it can realize substantially lower unit costs and a larger profit by expanding its plant to ATC-2. The same can be said for the move to ATC-3. However, given a reasonably stable market demand, all the large number of firms with small (ATC-1) plant sizes cannot now survive. The profitable expansion to larger plant sizes by some will necessarily come at the expense of rival producers. In short, the realization of economies of scale by some firms implies that the number of rival producers is simultaneously being reduced through failure or merger.

Historically, what has happened in many industries is that technological progress has made more and more economies of scale attainable over time. Thus many industries started out with a primitive technology, few economies of scale, and a relatively large number of competitors. But then as technology improved and economies of scale became increasingly pronounced, the less alert or less aggressive firms

fell by the wayside and a few producers emerged. For example, estimates suggest that as many as seventy to eighty firms populated the automobile industry in its infancy. Over the years, the development of mass-production techniques reduced the field through failure and combination. Now the Big Three—General Motors, Ford, and Chrysler—have over 90 percent of the automobile market.

But why, you may ask, aren't new firms created to enter the automobile industry? The answer, of course, is that to achieve the low unit costs essential to survival, any new entrants must necessarily start out as large producers. This may require hundreds of millions of dollars worth of investment in machinery and equipment alone. Economies of scale can prove a formidable barrier to entry. Hence, economies of scale not only explain the evolution of oligopoly in many industries, but also explain why such industries are not likely to become more competitive.

We must note that the development or persistence of some oligopolies can be traced at least in part to other entry barriers. In the electronics, chemical, and aluminum industries, the ownership of patents and the control of strategic raw materials have been important. And perhaps prodigious advertising outlays may provide an added financial barrier to entry, as some economists argue has been the case in the cigarette industry. But in general, economies of scale are the dominant barrier in most oligopolies.

The urge to merge The second factor in explaining oligopoly or fewness is merger. The motivation for merger has diverse roots. Of immediate relevance is the fact that the combining of two or more formerly competing firms by merger may increase their market share substantially and enable the new and larger production unit to achieve greater economies of scale. Another significant motive underlying the "urge to merge" is the market power which may accompany merger. A firm that is larger both absolutely and relative to the market may have greater ability to control the market for, and the price of, its product than does a smaller, more competitive producer. Furthermore, the large size which merger entails may give the firm the advantage of being a "big buyer" and permit it to demand and obtain lower prices (costs) from input suppliers than previously.

Mutual interdependence

Regardless of the means by which oligopoly evolves, it is clear that rivalry between a small number of firms interjects a new and complicating factor into our discussion: *mutual interdependence.* Imagine three firms, A, B, and C, each of which has about one-third of the market for a particular product. If A cuts price, its share of the market will increase. But B and C will be directly, immediately, and adversely affected by A's price cutting. Hence, we can expect some *reaction* on the part of B and C to A's behavior: B and C may match A's price cut or even undercut A, thereby precipitating a price war. This correctly suggests that no firm in an oligopolistic industry will dare to alter its price policies without attempting to calculate the most likely reactions of its rivals. To be sure, cost and demand data are important to the oligopolist in establishing price, but to these we must add the reaction of rivals—a highly uncertain factor. The situation faced by oligopolistic producers resembles that of participants in games of strategy such as poker, bridge, or chess. There is no means of knowing beforehand the best way of playing your cards, because this depends upon the way other participants play theirs! Each player must pattern his actions according to the actions and expected reactions of his rivals.

It is to be emphasized that the mutual interdependence resulting from fewness, and the consequent need for a firm to weigh the possible reactions of rivals in altering its price policy, are unique features of oligopoly. The large number of rivals which characterizes pure competition and monopolistic competition and the absence of rivals which is the earmark of pure monopoly rule out mutual interdependence in these market structures. Indeed, a good, workable definition of oligopoly is this: Oligopoly exists when the number of firms in an industry is so small that each must consider the reactions of rivals in formulating its price policy.

ANALYTICAL COMPLEXITIES

The theories of competitive, monopolistic, and monopolistically competitive markets as presented in prior chapters are quite standard and widely accepted segments of microeconomics. But economic analysis offers no standard portrait of oligopoly. In general, there are two major reasons why it is difficult to use formal economic analysis in explaining the price behavior of oligopolies.

1. The previously noted fact that oligopoly encompasses many specific market situations works against the development of a single, generalized explanation or model of how an oligopoly determines price and output. Pure competition, monopolistic competition, and pure monopoly all refer to rather clear-cut market arrangements; oligopoly does not. It includes the situation in which two or three firms dominate an entire market as well as the situation in which twelve or fifteen firms compete. It includes both product differentiation and standardization. It encompasses the cases in which firms are acting in collusion and those in which they are not. It embodies the situations in which barriers to entry are very strong and those in which they are not quite so strong. In short, the many breeds, or strains, of oligopoly preclude the development of any simple market model which provides a general explanation of oligopolistic behavior.

2. The element of mutual interdependence which fewness adds to the analysis is a most significant complication. To be specific, the inability of a firm to predict with certainty the reactions of its rivals makes it virtually impossible to estimate the demand and marginal-revenue data faced by an oligopolist. And without such data, firms cannot determine their profit-maximizing price and output even in theory, as we shall presently make clear.

Despite these analytical difficulties, two interrelated characteristics of oligopolistic pricing stand out. On the one hand, oligopolistic prices tend to be inflexible, or "sticky." Prices change less frequently in oligopoly than they do under pure competition, monopolistic competition, and in some instances, pure monopoly. Figure 11·4 provides some interesting data on this point. On the other hand, when oligopolistic prices do change, firms are likely to change their prices together; that is, oligopolistic price behavior suggests the presence of incentives to act in concert or collusively in setting and changing prices.

PRICE-OUTPUT BEHAVIOR

Let us now examine two oligopolistic market models—noncollusive oligopoly and collusive oligopoly—in an effort to shed some light upon these two pricing characteristics.

Noncollusive oligopoly and price rigidity

Again imagine an oligopolistic industry comprised of just three firms, A, B, and C, each having about one-third of the total market for a differentiated product. Assume the firms are "independent" in the sense that they do not engage in collusive practices in setting prices. Suppose, too, that the going price for firm A's product is *QP* and its current sales are *Q*, as shown in Figure 30·1. Now the question is "What does the firm's demand, or sales, curve look like?" We have just noted that mutual interdependence, and the uncertainty of rivals' reactions which interdependence entails, make this question difficult to answer. The location and shape of an oligopolist's demand curve depends upon how the firm's rivals will react to a price change introduced by A. There are two plausible assumptions about the reactions of A's rivals with which we might experiment.

One possibility is that firms B and C will exactly match any price change initiated by A. In this case A's demand and marginal-revenue curves will look something like D_1D_1 and MR_1MR_1 in Figure 30·1. If A cuts price, its sales will increase very modestly, because its two rivals will follow suit and thereby prevent A from gaining any price advantage over them. The small increase in sales which A (and its two rivals) will realize is at the expense of other industries; A will gain no sales from B and C. If A raises the going price, its sales will fall only modestly. Why? Because B and C match its price increase, so A does not price itself out of the market. The industry

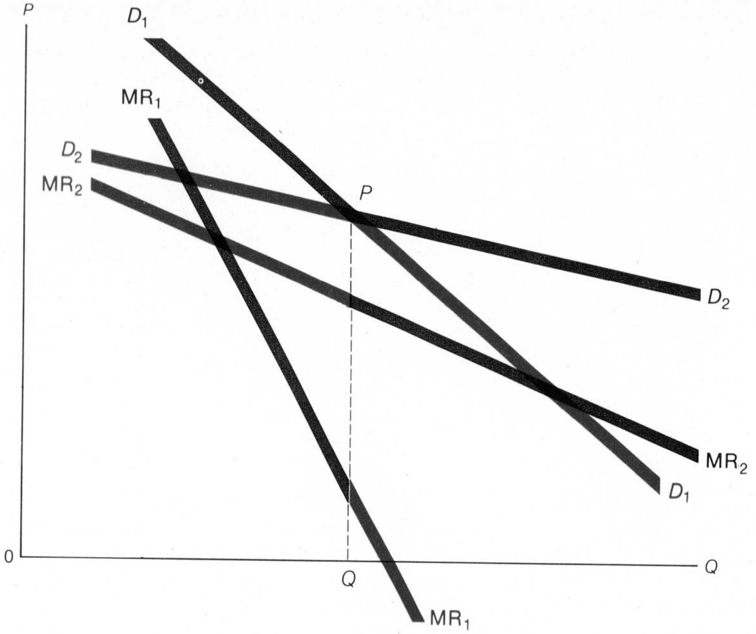

FIGURE 30·1 THE KINKED DEMAND CURVE

The nature of a noncollusive oligopolist's demand and marginal-revenue curves will depend upon whether his rivals will match (D_1D_1 and MR_1MR_1) or ignore (D_2D_2 and MR_2MR_2) any price changes which he may initiate from the current price *QP*. In all likelihood an oligopolist's rivals will ignore a price increase but follow a price cut. This causes the oligopolist's demand curve to be kinked (red D_2PD_1) and his marginal revenue curve to have a vertical break, or gap (red MR_2MR_1).

now loses some sales to other industries, but A loses no customers to B and C.

The other obvious possibility is that firms B and C will simply ignore any price change invoked by A. In this case the demand and marginal-revenue curves faced by A will resemble D_2D_2 and MR_2MR_2 in Figure 30·1. The demand curve in this case is considerably more elastic than under the assumption that B and C will match A's price changes. The reasons are clear. If A lowers its price and its rivals do not, A will gain sales sharply at the expense of its two rivals because it will obviously be underselling them. Conversely, if A raises price and its rivals do not, A will be pricing itself out of the market and will lose many customers to B and C, which are now underselling it. Because of product differentiation, however, A's sales do not fall to zero when it raises price; some of A's customers will pay the higher price because they have strong preferences for A's product.

Now, which is the most logical assumption for A to make as to how its rivals will react to any price change it might initiate? The answer is "some of each"! Common sense and observation of oligopolistic industries suggest that price declines will be matched as a firm's competitors act to prevent the price cutter from taking their customers, but that price increases will be ignored, because rivals of the price-increasing firm stand to gain the business lost by the price booster. In other words, the red-colored D_2P segment of the "rivals ignore" demand curve seems relevant for price increases, and the red-colored PD_1 segment of the "rivals follow" demand curve is more realistic for price cuts. It is logical, or at least a good guess, that an oligopolist's demand curve is "kinked" on the order of the red D_2PD_1. The curve is highly elastic above the going price, but much less elastic or even inelastic below the current price. Note also that if it is correct to

suppose that rivals will follow a price cut but ignore an increase, the marginal-revenue curve of the oligopolist will also have an odd shape. It, too, will be made up of two segments—the red part of the marginal-revenue curve appropriate to D_1D_1 and the red chunk of the marginal-revenue curve appropriate to D_2D_2. Because of the sharp differences in elasticity of demand above and below the going price, there occurs a gap, or what we can treat as a vertical segment, in the marginal-revenue curve. In Figure 30·1 the marginal-revenue curve is shown by the two red lines connected by the dotted vertical segment, or gap.

This analysis is important in that it goes far to explain why price changes are infrequent in noncollusive oligopolistic industries. On the one hand, the kinked demand schedule gives each oligopolist good reason to believe that any change in price will be for the worse. A firm's customers will desert it in quantity if it raises price. If it lowers price, its sales at best will increase very modestly. Even if a price cut increases its total revenue somewhat, the oligopolist's costs may well increase by a more than offsetting amount. Should the red PD_1 segment of its sales schedule be inelastic in that E_d is less than 1, the firm's profits will surely fall. A price decrease will lower the firm's total receipts, and the production of a somewhat larger output will increase total costs. Worse yet, a price cut by A may be *more than* met by B and C. That is, A's initial price cut may precipitate a price war; so the amount sold by A may actually decline as its rival firms charge still lower prices. These are all good reasons on the demand side of the picture why noncollusive oligopolies might seek "the quiet life" and follow live-and-let-live and don't-upset-the-applecart price policies. More specifically, if the resulting profits are satisfactory to the several firms at the existing price, it may seem prudent to them not to alter that price.

A second reason for price inflexibility under noncollusive oligopoly works from the cost side of the picture. The broken marginal-revenue curve which accompanies the kinked demand curve suggests that within limits, substantial cost changes will have no effect upon output and price. To be specific, any shift in marginal cost between MC_1 and MC_2 as shown in Figure 30·2 will result in no change in price or output, because the oligopolist fears a price war, on the one hand, and fears that he may price himself out of the market, on the other.

All this is not to say that the prices of noncollusive oligopolists are completely inflexible, but rather that they are likely to change only when significant and mutually applicable cost changes occur. For example, price adjustments may await substantial wage or tax increases which collective bargaining or government imposes uniformly upon the firms. Knowing its rivals are also afflicted with these cost increases, each firm boosts price with considerable certainty that each and every rival will follow suit. The practice of linking price increases to wage or tax hikes has the further advantage of shielding oligopolies from public criticism. To many the price increase—even if in excess of cost increases—will clearly seem the fault of irresponsible unions and the insatiable appetite of government for tax revenues.

Collusion: joint-profit maximization

The kinked-demand situation just described may be decidedly unappealing to oligopolists. It is surrounded by an air of uncertainty. Although there may be a strong disposition toward price stability, the possibility always does exist that a firm may shade its price to expand its share of the market and thereby precipitate disastrous rounds of price cutting. This is particularly likely if firms have excess capacity because of, say, a general business recession; under these circumstances a firm can lower unit costs by increasing its market share. Then, too, the possibility is always present that new firms may surmount barriers to entry and initiate aggressive price cutting to gain a foothold in the market. In addition, the tendency toward rigid prices may adversely affect profits if general inflationary pressures increase costs.

The kinked-demand analysis is also a source of uneasiness to economists because it contains a crucial shortcoming. The analysis simply does not explain how the going price gets to be at *PQ* (Figure 30·1) in the first place. Rather, it merely helps to

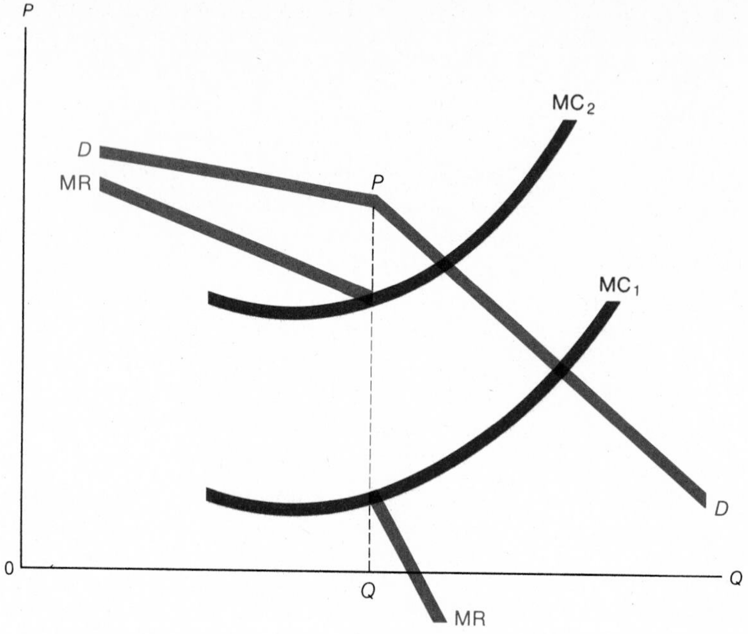

FIGURE 30·2 COST CHANGES AND PRICE STABILITY UNDER OLIGOPOLY

The kinked demand curve *DPD* and the accompanying broken marginal-revenue curve MRMR help explain the price inflexibility which characterizes oligopoly. Because any shift in marginal costs between MC_1 and MC_2 will cut the vertical (dashed) segment of the marginal-revenue curve, no change in either price *QP* or output *Q* will occur.

explain why oligopolists may be reluctant to deviate from an existing price which yields them a "satisfactory" or "reasonable" profit. The kinked demand curve explains price inflexibility but not price itself.

In short, oligopolistic firms frequently behave collusively to avoid the uncertainties of noncollusive oligopoly. Economists are interested in collusive oligopoly in that it provides a more satisfactory explanation of price and output.

Where will price and output be established under collusive oligopoly? To answer this question we must construct a highly simplified situation. Assume once again there are three firms—A, B, and C—producing homogeneous products. Each firm has identical cost curves. Each firm's demand curve is indeterminate unless we know how its rivals will react to any price change. Therefore, let us suppose each firm assumes that its two rivals will match either a price cut or a price increase. In other words, each firm's demand curve is of the D_1D_1 type in Figure 30·1. Assume further that the demand curve for each firm is identical. Given identical cost and identical demand and marginal-revenue data, we can say that Figure 30·3 represents the position of each of our three oligopolistic firms.

What price-output combination should each firm choose? If firm A was a pure monopolist, the answer would be clear enough: Establish output at *Q*, where marginal revenue equals marginal cost, charge the corresponding price *PQ*, and enjoy the maximum profit attainable. However, firm A *does* have two rivals selling identical products, and if A's assumption that his rivals will match his price[1] proves to be incorrect, the consequences could be disastrous for A. Specifically, if B and C actually charge prices below *PQ*, then firm A's demand curve will shift quite sharply

[1]Recall that this is the assumption upon which A's demand curve in Figure 30·3 is based.

FIGURE 30 · 3 COLLUSION AND THE TENDENCY TOWARD JOINT-PROFIT MAXIMIZATION

If oligopolistic firms are faced with identical or highly similar demand and cost conditions, they will tend to behave collusively and maximize joint profits. The price and output results are essentially the same as those of pure (unregulated) monopoly; each oligopolist charges price *QP* and produces output *Q*.

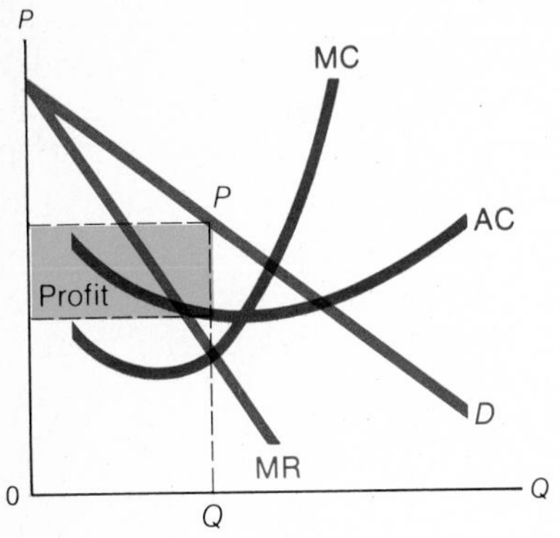

to the left as its potential customers turn to its rivals who are now selling the same product at a lower price. Of course, A can retaliate by cutting its price too; but this will have the effect of moving all three firms down their demand curves, lowering their profits, and perhaps even driving them to some point where average cost exceeds price. So the question becomes "Will B and C want to charge a price below *PQ*?" Under the assumptions we have made, and recognizing that A will have little choice except to match any price they may set below *PQ*, the answer is "No." Faced with the same demand and cost circumstances, B and C will find it in their interest to produce *Q* and charge *PQ*. This is a curious situation; each firm finds it most profitable to charge the same price *PQ*, but only if its rivals will actually do so! How can the three firms realize the *PQ*-price and *Q*-quantity solution in which each is keenly interested? How can this be made a reality so that all three can avoid the less profitable outcomes associated with either higher or lower prices? The answer is obvious: The firms will all be motivated to collude—to "get together and talk it over"—and agree to charge the same price *PQ*. As a result, each firm will realize the maximum profit. And for society, the result is likely to be about the same as if the industry were a pure monopoly composed of three identical plants (Chapter 28).

Obstacles to collusion

But we must keep in mind that this discussion of collusive oligopoly and the resulting maximization of joint profits is based upon a number of simplifying assumptions. Release of these assumptions and the introduction of certain legal realities create obstacles to collusion and make the outcome of collusive oligopoly no more than a *tendency* to maximize joint profits. In practice, price collusion may be difficult to achieve and to maintain over time.

Legal obstacles: antitrust Blatant price fixing as described in our collusive-oligopoly model is at odds with existing antitrust legislation (Chapter 35). For example, *cartels*—formal arrangements embodying written or explicit verbal agreements among producers to regulate price or output or to divide markets geographically—are illegal in the United States. This, however, does not mean that collusion is absent, but rather that it takes more informal, more subtle forms. To illustrate, *gentlemen's agreements* are undoubtedly widespread in our economy. Such agreements arise when competing oligopolists reach a verbal agreement on product price, market shares almost invariably being left to the ingenuity of each seller as reflected in nonprice competition. Gentlemen's agreements arise at trade conventions, on the golf course, or at cocktail parties, not in a lawyer's office. Although they too collide with the antitrust laws, their *sub rosa* and intangible character makes them more difficult to detect and prosecute successfully.

Price leadership is a still less formal means by which oligopolists can coordinate their price behavior and avoid the uncertainties of noncollusive action. In this

case, one firm—usually the largest in the industry—initiates price changes, and all other firms more or less automatically follow that price change. In some cases—for example, the oil and cigarette industries—the identity of the price leader may vary over time, whereas in other industries—the steel industry—a single firm may persistently enjoy the position of price leader. The importance of price leadership is evidenced in the fact that such industries as farm machinery, anthracite coal, cement, copper, gasoline, newsprint, tin cans, lead, sulfur, rayon, fertilizer, glass containers, and nonferrous metals are practicing or have in the recent past practiced price leadership. Because price leadership is an informal, tacit agreement involving no written or spoken commitments, it is generally accepted as a legal technique by the courts in interpreting the antitrust laws.

Despite the existence of these less formal techniques of collusion, antitrust legislation is still a formidable obstacle and persistent threat to collusive oligopoly.

Number of firms Other things being equal, the smaller the number of firms, the easier it is to achieve price collusion. Agreement on price by three or four producers who control an entire market is much more readily accomplished than it is in the situation where ten firms each have roughly 10 percent of the market, or where the Big Three have, say, 70 percent of the market, while a "competitive fringe" of eight or ten smaller firms do battle for the remainder. Furthermore, some of the smaller firms may aspire to become one of the Big Four and may feel that aggressive pricing below the profit-maximizing level is a means of achieving this goal. The resulting price competition may force the dominant firms to charge prices below that which would maximize joint profits. Or smaller firms may feel that they must compensate for the absence of nationwide advertising by charging a price below that of the Big Three.

Differentiation Our model of collusive oligopoly assumed identical cost and demand curves for each firm. This is unrealistic. Where products are differentiated, we would certainly expect considerable differences in cost and demand data. Indeed, even with highly standardized products, we would expect that firms might have somewhat different market shares and would operate with differing degrees of productive efficiency. Thus it is likely that even homogeneous oligopolists would have somewhat different demand and cost curves. In either event, differences in costs and demand will mean that the profit-maximizing price for each firm will differ; there will be no single price which is readily acceptable to all. Price collusion therefore depends upon the ability to achieve compromises and concessions—to arrive at a degree of "understanding" which in practice is not readily attainable. For example, the MR = MC positions of firms A, B, and C may call for them to charge $12, $11, and $10 respectively, but this price cluster or range may be unsatisfactory to one or more of the firms. Firm A may feel that differences in product quality justify only a $1.50 rather than a $2 price differential between his product and that of firm C. In short, cost and demand differences make it difficult for oligopolists to agree on a single price or a "proper" cluster of prices; these differentials are therefore an obstacle to collusion.

Price breaks Legal obstacles, fairly "large" numbers of firms, and product differentiation are obstacles to collusive pricing. In addition, even when an oligopolistic industry has achieved a deeply entrenched practice of price collusion—for example, through price leadership—this collusion may break down periodically. Two related reasons for such price breaks are the occurrence of a business recession and the temptation of firms to engage in secret price cutting.

Recession is an enemy of collusion, because slumping markets cause average costs to rise. In technical terms, as the oligopolists' demand and marginal-revenue curves shift to the left (Figure 30·4), each firm moves back to a higher point on its average-cost curve. The firms find they have substantial excess productive capacity, sales are down, unit costs are up, and profits are being squeezed. Under such conditions businesses may feel they are in a better position to avoid serious profit reductions

FIGURE 30·4 SECRET PRICE CONCESSIONS UNDER OLIGOPOLY

Secret price concessions can add to an oligopolist's profits. In this case the sale of Q_1Q_2 extra units of output at a price of Q_2P_2 can add the amount TSP_2U to the profits earned by selling to other customers at the higher price P_1. If other customers or rival firms learn of the price concessions, however, the existing price collusion may break down and profits may decline.

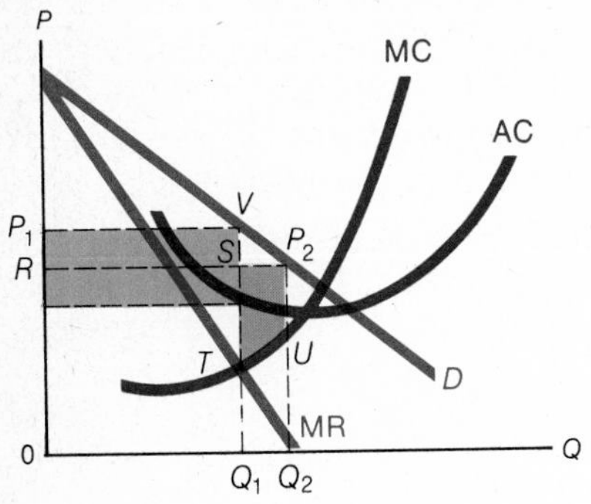

by price cutting in the hope of gaining sales at the expense of rivals.

There is also a more or less persistent temptation for collusive oligopolists to engage in clandestine price cutting, that is, to make secret price concessions in order to get a little additional business. This temptation to cheat upon one's price-fixing partners stems from the simple fact that such action can be profitable, *provided* the firm can keep such price concessions secret from (1) rival firms and (2) other customers who are paying a higher price.

Figure 30·4 is instructive. Here our collusive oligopolist is maximizing profits by selling an output of Q_1 at a quoted or list price of P_1. Now, the firm's downsloping demand curve indicates there are other customers who would buy additional output at a price below P_1 $(= Q_1V)$. For example, buyers would take an additional Q_1Q_2 units at price P_2Q_2. Are these extra sales profitable to the firm? Yes they are, because they add $Q_1SP_2Q_2$ to the firm's total revenue while the firm incurs additional costs of only Q_1TUQ_2 (the area under the marginal-cost curve between Q_1 and Q_2) in producing them. The resulting addition to the firm's profits is the area TSP_2U. In general, so long as the secret price exceeds the firm's marginal cost, the additional secret-price sales will be profitable.[2]

But the profitability and very possibility of secret price concessions disappear if either of the aforementioned provisions is violated. If price concessions become an "open secret," other customers will balk at paying P_1 and insist upon paying only Q_2P_2. That is, the firm will be forced to take a price cut on all prior (Q_1) sales. This will trim off a substantial portion (RP_1VS) of the profits derived from sales to these customers. Such a loss in profits, as Figure 30·4 indicates, can more than offset the possible profits from secret price concessions. Stated differently, if all buyers become aware of price concessions by a firm, the firm's ability to practice price discrimination among its customers will vanish. As a result, the firm may simply end by producing beyond the profit-maximizing output and charging a price (Q_2P_2) *to all customers* which is below the profit-maximizing level.

Similarly, buyers receiving price concessions from one oligopolist may use this concession as a wedge to getting even larger price concessions from the firm's rivals. The attempt of buyers to play sellers against one another may precipitate price warring among these firms. In short, although it is potentially profitable, the use of secret price concessions is a threat to the maintenance of collusive oligopoly over time.[3]

[2] Technical note: Contrary to first-glance impressions, this discussion does not violate the MR = MC profit-maximizing rule. This is an instance of price discrimination where through secrecy, the buyers of Q_1 *and* Q_1Q_2 are in effect divided into two separate markets. Sales of output to the first group occur up to the profit-maximizing point; added sales to the second group (in the "second market") occur because marginal revenue (P_2Q_2) exceeds the marginal cost of each of these units.

[3] For a fascinating case study of collusive pricing, read Clarence C. Walton and Frederick W. Cleveland, Jr., *Corporations on Trial: The Electric Cases* (Belmont, Calif.: Wadsworth Publishing Company, Inc., 1964).

OLIGOPOLY AND GAMES[4]

We have already noted that the mutual interdependence which characterizes oligopoly makes it necessary that each firm consider the possible reactions (countermoves) of rivals to any action (move) it initiates. This means that oligopolists face a situation similar to that of participants in such games of strategy as poker or chess. Economists have developed a *theory of games*[5] which is very useful in analyzing possible game strategies. In particular, many of the salient behavioral characteristics of oligopoly can be grasped through a simple game-theory illustration.

The profits-payoff table

Table 30·2 is a *price-profits* or *profits-payoff* table. Let us examine the assumptions upon which it has been constructed and the nature of the data in it. The table assumes that a two-firm oligopoly or *duopoly* exists. We assume that products are differentiated and that the amount of sales and promotional activity is fixed. The figures along the top of the table show three possible prices that oligopolistic firm B might charge for its product; the figures down the left side indicate various prices rival firm A might charge. The entries in the body of the table show the resulting profit payoffs to A and B for each possible combination of prices they might charge. Firm A's profit payoff is shown in the lower left (blue) portion and B's profit is in the upper right (red) portion of each box or cell. For example, if B charges $8 and A charges $9, we find in cell VI that B will receive a profit of $23 (thousand) and A a profit of $19. Note that even if the firms selected the same price, their profits would differ. This is so because we are assuming differentiated oligopoly, and therefore A and B have different cost and demand data.

Reading across any row, we can see the profits for the two firms as a *given* price for A is compared with all the possible prices B might charge. Thus in row (1) we find that, if firm A charges $10, its profits will be $24, $19, or $15 respectively, depending upon whether B reacts with a price of $10, $9, or $8. Similarly, by reading down any column, we can determine the profit payoffs for the two firms as we compare a *given* price for B against the various prices A might charge. For example, reading down column (3) we see that, if B charges $8, its profits will be $28, $23, or $18, depending upon whether A charges $10, $9, or $8.

Although the data in Table 30·2 are hypothetical, the profit figures are by no means arbitrarily chosen. We would expect that if one firm (say, A) committed itself to a given price—for example, $10—and did not vary from it, the rival firm (B) generally could increase

TABLE 30·2 A PROFITS-PAYOFF TABLE FOR A TWO-FIRM OLIGOPOLY (*hypothetical data; profit data in thousands of dollars*)

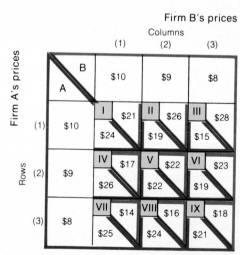

Firm A's prices (Rows)	B / A	Firm B's prices (Columns) (1) $10	(2) $9	(3) $8
(1)	$10	I $21 $24	II $26 $19	III $28 $15
(2)	$9	IV $17 $26	V $22 $22	VI $23 $19
(3)	$8	VII $14 $25	VIII $16 $24	IX $18 $21

[4] This is an optional section which instructors may choose to omit without impairing the continuity of the discussion. Game theory is applied to the problem of disarmament in Chapter 40.

[5] The interested reader should consult two informative and delightful books on the subject: John D. Williams, *The Compleat Strategyst*, rev. ed. (New York: McGraw-Hill Book Company, 1965), and John McDonald, *Strategy in Poker, Business and War* (New York: W. W. Norton & Company, Inc., 1950).

profits by lowering the price of its product. That is, if A sticks to $10, B can make a profit of $21 by also charging $10, but can increase this profit to $26 and $28 by cutting price to $9 and $8 respectively.[6]

Interdependence of behavior

In examining Table 30·2 we have seen once again that fewness means mutual interdependence. The best (profit-maximizing) price for firm B to charge depends upon firm A's reaction or response to B's price—that is, upon the price A charges. Example: If B initially chooses $10 as its price, A will maximize profit at $26 if its "price strategy" is $9 (cell IV). But with A charging $9, it will pay B to drop price to $8 (cell VI). However, with B now charging $8, A finds that it will maximize profits by dropping price from $9 to $8 (cell IX). Another example: If A sets its price at $10, B will maximize profits at $28 with a price strategy of $8 (cell III). But if B is charging $8, A will no longer want to keep price at $10; with B charging $8, A will find it most profitable to charge $8 also (cell IX). It is clear that the profit-maximizing price for each firm depends upon the price reaction or price strategy of its rival.

Price rigidity

Our kinked-demand analysis was useful in explaining the price rigidity which is characteristic of oligopoly. The profits-payoff table provides a complementary explanation of this phenomenon.

Price rigidity stems from the expectation of each firm that it will generally be profitable for its rival to ignore a price increase but to follow a price cut. To illustrate: Suppose A and B are both charging $9 and each is realizing profits of $22 (cell V). On the assumption that A will ignore (not follow) a price increase, B will foresee its own profits falling from $22 to $17 if B raises price to $10 (cell V to cell IV). And indeed, our table makes it quite clear why A should want to ignore B's price increase. When B goes to $10 and A stays at $9, A's profits rise from $22 to $26; if A were to follow B and raise price to $10, its profits would only rise from $22 to $24 (cell I). In any event, a price increase by B which A does not follow will cause B's profits to fall. Hence, B will not be anxious to raise price.

What about a price cut by B? Again suppose both firms are initially charging $9. Now, if A continues to charge $9, B could increase profits from $22 to $23 (cell V to cell VI) by lowering its price to $8. But A will not want to charge $9 when B has cut price to $8. Why? Because moving from cell V to cell VI cuts A's profits from $22 to $19. Firm A can reduce this profit decline to $21 by also cutting price to $8, thereby moving the two firms to cell IX. When we compare the $9-$9 situation (cell V) with the $8-$8 situation (cell IX), it is obvious that both firms have experienced reduced profits by cutting prices. Hence, neither firm will be anxious to cut prices.

The important point is that B's profits will fall if (1) B raises price and A does not follow *or* (2) B cuts price and A cuts price too. Furthermore, we have seen that there are profit incentives for A to ignore B's price increase and to follow B's price cut! We may conclude that, if the two oligopolists are currently charging a mutually satisfactory ("reasonably profitable") price, both may be fearful of altering that price. Hence the price rigidity which characterizes many oligopolistic industries over time.

Collusion and merger

As our previous analysis has demonstrated, another characteristic of oligopoly is that collusive pricing may be mutually profitable. Adam Smith perceptively remarked almost 200 years ago, "People of the same trade seldom meet together, even for merriment and

[6] This need not always be the case. If, for example, B sticks to $10, A can increase its profit from $24 to $26 by lowering its own price from $10 to $9. But a further price cut to $8 lowers A's profit to $25. Why might this happen? The answer is that lower prices mean a larger output, and this expanding output in time will lead to rising unit costs. Also, recall from Chapter 24 that demand tends to become less elastic at lower prices, which means that further price cuts cause total revenue to expand by smaller and smaller amounts. These two factors—rising costs and increasingly modest growth of total revenue—may make it disadvantageous to sell at a price too far below one's rival. Stated differently, price cutting by one firm may bring it to some cost-revenue position beyond which marginal cost exceeds marginal revenue.

diversion, but the conversation ends in a conspiracy against the public, or in some contrivance to raise prices.'' The profits-payoff table yields some insights as to why collusive action is tempting under oligopoly.

Assume that through noncollusive action, firms A and B have both settled upon a price of $8. This price may well have been reached as a result of earlier competitive price cutting. Both firms realize that higher prices would be mutually beneficial. That is, A could increase its profits from $21 to $22 and B its profits from $18 to $22 *if* both would raise their prices to $9 (cell IX to cell V). But note that if A raises price to $9 and B stays at $8, B's profits will rise to $23 while A's profits fall to $19 (cell IX to cell VI). Firm A, therefore, may be understandably reluctant to raise price from $8 to $9 without assurance that B will also raise price from $8 to $9. Firm B is confronted with the same situation: If B goes to $9 and A stays at $8, A's profit will jump from $21 to $24 (cell IX to cell VIII). This new $24 profit is obviously superior to the $22 A would realize by also raising price to $9 (cell IX to cell V). So there is a dilemma: Both firms will realize a greater profit if both charge $9 instead of $8. Yet each is afraid to initiate such a price increase independently of its rival, because each knows there is a profit incentive for the rival *not* to match a price increase. How can A and B both make certain that if either raises price to $9, the other will do the same? The answer, of course, is for them not to act independently, but to engage in collusion by which both firms commit themselves to raise price from $8 to $9. To act noncollusively is to remain at $8-$8 (cell IX) and realize profits inferior to those associated with the $9-$9 situation (cell V) attainable through some form of collusive price fixing.

Now you may ask: Having agreed collusively to increase price from $8 to $9, why don't both firms take the next step and raise their prices to $10? The problem here is that it does not pay firm B to move from $9-$9 position (cell V) to the $10-$10 position (cell I). Specifically, this move would reduce B's profits from $22 to $21, although it would increase A's from $22 to $24. This conflict of interest could be resolved by forming a trust to coordinate formally the price decisions of the two firms or, alternatively, by negotiating a merger of the two firms. The trust or single firm that evolved from the merger would find it most profitable to have both plants (formerly independent firms) charge $10 (cell I), because the total or joint profits here would be greater at $45 ($24 + $21) than at a price of $9 (cell V), where profits are $44 ($22 + $22).

BASIC ROLE OF NONPRICE COMPETITION

We have noted that, for several reasons, oligopolists have a notable aversion to price competition. This aversion may lead to some more or less informal type of collusion on price. In the United States, however, price collusion is usually accompanied by nonprice competition. It is typically through nonprice competition that each firm's share of the total market is determined. This emphasis upon nonprice competition has its roots in two basic facts.

1. Price cuts can be quickly and easily met by a firm's rivals. Because of this the possibility of significantly increasing one's share of the market through price competition is small; rivals will promptly cancel any potential gain in sales by matching price cuts. And, of course, the risk is always present that price competition will precipitate disastrous price warring. More positively stated, oligopolists seem to feel that more permanent advantages can be gained over rivals through nonprice competition, because product variations, improvements in productive techniques, and successful advertising gimmicks cannot be duplicated so quickly and so completely as can price reductions. And there is less likelihood of nonprice competition's forcing all firms to the wall profitwise in the manner of unbridled price competition. Nonprice competition is less likely to get out of hand. It might be added that many oligopolistic producers of consumer goods apparently are of the opinion that consumers are more product- and advertising-conscious than they are price-conscious.

2. There is a more obvious reason for the tremendous emphasis which oligopolists put upon nonprice competition: Manufacturing oligopolists are typically blessed with substantial financial resources with

which to support advertising and product development. Hence, although nonprice competition is a basic characteristic of both monopolistically competitive and oligopolistic industries, the latter are in a financial position to indulge more fully.

We need not restate the pros and cons of advertising. The arguments stated in Chapter 29 with respect to advertising under monopolistic competition are pertinent when applied to oligopoly. However, the implications of the rather prodigious outlays which manufacturing oligopolies sometimes make for technological research on both product quality and productive techniques are a matter of major concern.

OLIGOPOLY AND ECONOMIC EFFICIENCY

The troublesomeness of evaluating the economic efficiency of oligopoly is matched only by the importance of such an evaluation. The root difficulty is that of deciding whether it is more realistic to look at the probable effects of oligopoly in a short-run (static) or in a long-run (dynamic) environment.

Restrictive oligopoly

The more or less traditional view holds that, because oligopoly is close to pure monopoly in structure, we should expect it to operate in a similar way. Being characterized by barriers to entry, oligopoly can be expected, according to this view, to result in a restriction of output short of the point of lowest unit costs and a corresponding market price which yields substantial, if not maximum, economic profits. These points usually rest upon an analysis similar to that shown in Figure 30·5*a*. Facing a *given* demand and a *given* cost situation, the oligopolist will find that it pays him to be restrictive. As indicated in Figure 30·5*a,* higher unit costs will soon arise if output is expanded far beyond Q_1, and the lowering of price which such an expansion requires courts the disaster of a price war. Other things being equal, the price and output results under such an oligopoly would be clearly inferior to those of pure competition. Furthermore, we saw earlier that the results of collusive oligopoly may approximate those of pure monopoly. As a matter of fact, one may even argue that oligopoly is actually less desirable than pure monopoly for the simple reason that pure monopoly in the United States is almost invariably subject to government regulation to mitigate abuses of such market power. Informal collusion among oligopolists may yield price and output results similar to pure monopoly, yet at the same time maintain the outward appearance of several independent and "competing" firms.

FIGURE 30·5 RESTRICTIVE OLIGOPOLY AND PROGRESSIVE OLIGOPOLY

Restrictive oligopoly (*a*): Faced with given demand and marginal-revenue data (such as DP_1D and MRMR) and given cost data (such as AC and MC), the oligopolist will maximize profits by restricting output to Q_1 and charging price Q_1P_1. In expanding output beyond Q_1, the oligopolist must accept considerable price reductions and run the risk of starting a price war. Furthermore, by expanding the output, the producer may soon encounter rising average costs AC.

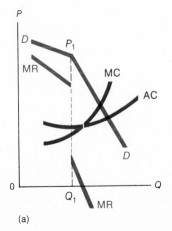

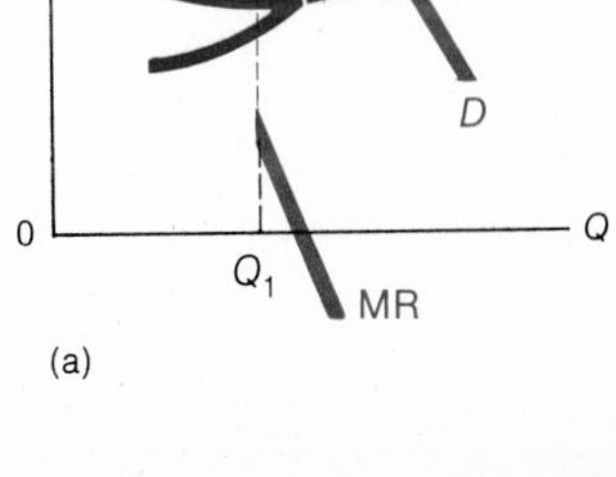

(a)

At the level of macroeconomics, we have previously noted that cost-push and structural inflation are based upon the existence of market power. Therefore, oligopoly may also be criticized as a potential source of inflationary pressure.

Progressive oligopoly

The above view of oligopoly seems at odds with the historical facts surrounding the operation of many oligopolistic manufacturing industries such as the automobile, farm equipment, electronics, home appliance, and steel industries. These industries have been characterized by falling product prices, improvements in product quality, and expanding levels of output and employment over a period of years. But caution is required here. The basic issue is whether this progress would have been even greater had these industries been organized on a purely competitive basis. And, lacking the ability to conduct controlled laboratory experiments, the economist cannot offer a clear-cut answer. It is evident, however, that there has been significant progress in some oligopolistic industries, and the possibility does exist that in the long run some oligopolistic industries may well have fostered product improvement, lower unit costs, lower prices, and a greater output than the same industry would have provided if organized competitively. Graphically, the restrictive situation portrayed in Figure 30·5*a* may give way over time to the progressive situation reflected in Figure 30·5*b*, wherein demand and output have been substantially increased and unit cost and price reduced as compared with Figure 30·5*a*.[7]

Technological progress: the argument Generally speaking, the reasons for this possible progressiveness lie in the fact that many oligopolistic industries focus their competitive energies upon technological competition as reflected in both the development of productive techniques and improvement of product quality. The betterment of productive techniques will have the effect of expanding the range of constant or, better yet, declining unit costs. Advances in product quality, accompanied by advertising and related want-creating activities, will shift the firm's demand curve to the right. As indicated in Figure 30·5*b*, product price is very likely to decline with declines in unit costs.

At present there is a rather widely held presumption that modern oligopolies have both greater means and a stronger inclination for technological advance than

[7]This comparison of restrictive and progressive oligopoly and the graphic presentation of Figure 30·5 are based upon Henry Grayson, *Price Theory in a Changing Economy* (New York: The Macmillan Company, 1965).

Progressive oligopoly (*b*): In fact some oligopolists have been progressive, achieving lower average costs AC and marginal costs MC through technological advance. Similarly, demand DP_2D and marginal revenue MRMR have been pushed far to the right as a result of product development and want-creating activities. As compared to the restrictive oligopoly of (*a*), the net result of progressive oligopoly has frequently been a larger output (Q_2 as compared with Q_1) and a lower price (Q_2P_2 as compared with Q_1P_1).

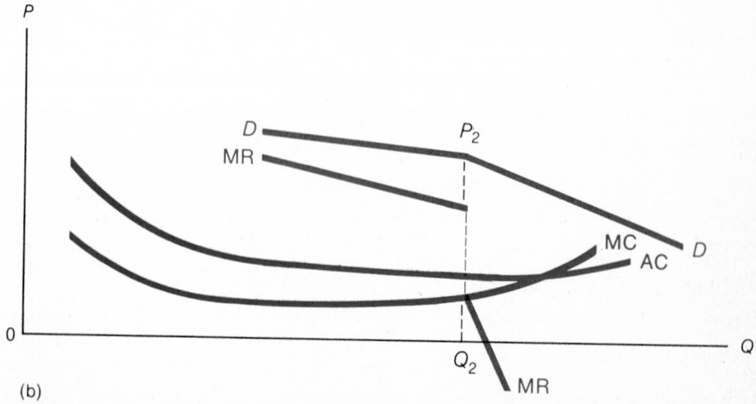

does any other market structure. Let us summarize the arguments underlying this presumption and then test them against such statistical data as are available.

First, oligopolies typically possess the *means*—substantial profits—with which to undertake the incredibly expensive task of modern research. Technological progress, it is contended, is no longer in the domain of the backyard Edison or the basement Whitney. Rather, it is the result of highly organized and cooperative efforts of a variety of scientists and engineers housed in the elaborate research departments of such giant oligopolies as du Pont and General Electric. Purely and monopolistically competitive firms, being smaller and less prosperous, are decidedly less progressive.

Second, oligopolistic producers have a host of good *incentives* for accelerating technological advance:

1. Given their disposition to avoid price competition, technological, or cost, competition provides an obvious alternative means for enlarging total profits through an expanded product demand and lower unit costs. Like advertising and product development, the discovery of more efficient productive techniques is less certainly and less quickly matched by one's rivals than is a price cut.

2. Technological superiority is a basic means by which an oligopolist can ensure survival in the event that a price war should somehow plague the quiet life of the industry.

3. In contrast to an unrivaled pure monopolist, the presence of several strong rivals puts the oligopolist under considerable pressure to seek maximum productive efficiency. Failure to do so may mean that his several competitiors will in time drive him out of business. The pure monopolist, being devoid of rivals, is under no competitive spur to technical progress. But the oligopolist, having a few rivals, clearly is in an environment of technological competition.

4. The existence of barriers to entry gives the progressive oligopolist some assurance that he will actually realize the profit rewards to which his research expenditures may give rise. This is in contrast to a monopolistically competitive market, wherein the rewards of a new productive technique will be shared by many competitors who will quickly copy or imitate a progressive firm without bearing any of the research and development costs. And the presence of a large number of rivals will hasten price reductions to consumers, based upon the cost reductions stemming from the advance. The presence of fewer rivals and the proclivity of oligopolists not to cut price enhance the possibility of the innovating oligopolist's realizing greater profit rewards from his technical progress. This is an important point in an economy such as American capitalism, wherein the basic drive wheel is profits.

Technological progress: the evidence[8] Such data as are available do considerable damage to the image of the oligopolistic industry as a mainspring of research and development activity. Available statistics suggest that the research laboratories of giant corporate oligopolies are *not* the fountainhead of technological advance. A recent study[9] of 61 important inventions made since 1900 indicates that over half were the work of independent inventors, quite disassociated from the industrial research laboratories of corporate enterprise. Such substantial advances as air conditioning, power steering, cellophane, the jet engine, insulin, the helicopter, and the catalytic cracking of petroleum have this individualistic heritage. Other equally important advances have been provided by small- and medium-sized firms. According to this study, about two-thirds—40 out of 61—of the basic inventions of this century have been fathered by independent inventors or the research activities of relatively small firms. Other studies—for example, analyses of patent statistics—reinforce the conclusion that a large proportion of basic technological advances originates outside the laboratories of giant oligopolies.

This, of course, is the overall picture and does not

[8] This section draws heavily upon Daniel Hamberg, "Size of Firm, Monopoly, and Economic Growth," in *Employment, Growth, and Price Levels, Hearings of the Joint Economic Committee, Part 7* (Washington, 1959), pp. 2337–2352, and "Invention in the Industrial Research Laboratory," *Journal of Political Economy,* April 1963, pp. 95–115.

[9] John Jewkes, David Sawers, and Richard Stillerman, *The Sources of Invention* (New York: St Martin's Press, Inc., 1958).

in any way repudiate the fact that in a number of oligopolistic industries—for example, the aircraft, chemical, petroleum, and electrical equipment industries—research activity has been pursued vigorously, fruitfully, and on an expanding scale. But even here we must amend at least two important qualifications. In the first place, there are a number of other oligopolistic industries wherein it is generally agreed that the interest in research and development activity has been modest at best; the steel, cigarette, and aluminum industries are cases in point. Secondly, a very substantial portion of the research carried on by oligopolistic industries is actually financed with public funds. For example, about 90 percent of the research performed in the aircraft-missile industry is government sponsored, almost 60 percent in the electrical equipment industry, 71 percent in the communications industry, and so forth. Despite the increased interest of businesses, the Federal government remains the most important source of funds for research and development activity.

Countervailing power

There is a second consideration which brightens somewhat the traditional dim view of oligopoly. John K. Galbraith of Harvard has developed the notion that many oligopolies (and monopolies) tend to induce the development of oligopolies (and monopolies) on the opposite side of the market.[10] That is, the existence of a monopolistic (or oligopolistic) seller tends to stimulate the growth of a monopsonistic (or oligopsonistic) buyer, and vice versa. More specifically, there is a tendency for "countervailing power" to evolve on the opposite side of those markets in which strong positions of "original power" have already developed. The development of countervailing power is not a matter of chance. It stems, on the one hand, from the desire of resource suppliers or customers to protect themselves from any abuses of the original-power position and, on the other hand, from the desire to share in the profits of the original-power position. Stated differently, for both defensive and offensive reasons, countervailing power is self-generating. Oligopoly begets oligopoly on the opposite side of the market. Oligopoly, in effect, generates its own antidote.

The significance of countervailing power is implicit in the concept itself. Countervailing power, or "across-the-market" competition, can be an important competitive force in those very markets in which "same-side-of-the-market" rivalry is weak. Oligopolistic sellers may be restrained by a few large buyers. The Big Four of the tire industry face the Big Three of the automobile industry; chain grocery stores and mail order houses buy in quantity from oligopolistic food processors and manufacturers. Oligopsonistic buyers may be faced with a small number of sellers. Labor unions face gigantic employers; agricultural marketing cooperatives sell to large food processors. Now, to the degree that these opposed positions of market power are successful in checking or restraining the power of one another, the successful operation of a market system characterized by oligopoly will be furthered. Buyer and seller may cancel the power and negate the potential market abuses of one another. The monopolistic seller who seeks a high monopolistic price is faced with a monopsonistic buyer who obviously is interested in a low monopsonistic price. That is, each seeks to use his market power to raise or depress price to his own advantage. The market power of each may be largely self-canceling, and the resulting compromise price close to the competitive level. Furthermore, given the compromise price, the monopolist will have no incentive to restrict his output and sales as he would be obligated to do in establishing a monopolistic price. Thus the net result of monopoly on both sides of the market may be a price and output closer to those of pure competition than if monopoly existed on only one side of the market. This is true of oligopoly as well. Countervailing power is an important regulatory force in American capitalism and makes the economy more competitive than any discussion limited to same-side-of-the-market competition would lead one to conclude.[11]

[10] John Kenneth Galbraith, *American Capitalism*, rev. ed. (Boston: Houghton Mifflin Company, 1956), particularly chap. 9.

[11] The reader should consult the "bilateral monopoly model" of Chapter 32 for the theoretical details of countervailing power as it might apply to the labor market.

Countervailing power, however, is not devoid of shortcomings and criticisms. One shortcoming is that it is not universally present. In the automobile industry, for example, dealers are highly dependent upon manufacturers and thus in a poor position to bargain for lower automobile prices which may benefit both themselves and consumers. In other cases—for example, the petroleum industry—manufacturers are integrated vertically down to the consumer, thus excluding the possibility of countervailing power. Because the residential construction industry is composed of thousands of small and unorganized contractors, no countervailing power is exerted against oligopolistic suppliers of building materials.

Even where countervailing power is firmly established, it does not function with equal effectiveness under all economic conditions. In particular, during periods of inflation countervailing power does not operate effectively as a competitive force, because with excess demand buyers are no longer able to restrain sellers. When a resource buyer enjoys a seller's market for his product, he is not apt to offer stiff resistance to the demands of resource suppliers. This is best exemplified in the labor market, where unions as "sellers" of labor are in a most strategic position in bargaining with employers during inflation. Management does not want to risk a work stoppage when consumer demand is burgeoning. Why resist? Increases in wage costs (and more) can be readily passed on to the consumer through price increases with no loss of sales, and profits thereby can be maintained or even expanded. The results of this situation are anything but socially desirable.

Finally, it has been pointed out that the two power positions may both benefit at the expense of the rest of the economy by combining their forces rather than by offsetting one another. Across-the-market rivals may find mutual advantages in collusive action or outright merger rather than in expanding their energies in negating the market power of one another.

Oligopoly: tentative appraisal

Having surveyed these two viewpoints, what, if anything, can we conclude about the economic efficiency of oligopolistic industries? Not much more than this: Assuming *given* long-run costs of production, an oligopolistic industry will produce less, provide fewer jobs, and charge a higher product price than would the same industry organized competitively. But to the extent that oligopoly results in lower unit costs and improvements in product quality, this conclusion must be altered in a manner less condemnatory of oligopoly. That is, *if* large oligopolistic producers are in a better position than competitive firms to realize existing (known) economies of scale, or *if* they are more able and willing to develop improved productive techniques and better products, then oligopoly *may* be more desirable socially than competition. However, despite plausible arguments as to why oligopoly may be progressive, such empirical evidence as is available suggests that giant oligopolistic corporations are not the basic source of technological advance in our society. Furthermore, there are many known instances (see footnote 3) in which oligopolists, unbridled by countervailing power, have sorely abused their market power, to the detriment of society as a whole. Indeed, the picture is a mixed one. The examination of specific cases will reveal both restrictive and progressive oligopolies. This tentative conclusion is worth venturing: Oligopolistic industries may be much more palatable over time, that is, in the long run, than they seem to be at a particular point in time.

SUMMARY

1. Oligopolistic industries are characterized by few firms, each of which has a significant fraction of the market. Firms thus situated are mutually interdependent; the behavior of any one firm directly affects and is affected by the actions of rivals. Products may be virtually uniform or significantly differentiated. Underlying reasons for the evolution of oligopoly are economies of scale and the advantages of merger.

2. The wide variety of oligopolistic markets and the uncertainty which stems from mutual interdependence limit the applicability of formal economic analysis to oligopolistic markets. The factual record indicates, however, that ***a.*** oligopolistic prices tend to

be inflexible or "sticky" and *b.* the price changes which do occur are "orderly" and thereby imply some form of collusion.

3. Noncollusive oligopolists in effect face a kinked demand curve. This curve and the accompanying marginal-revenue curve help explain the price rigidity which characterizes such markets; they do not, however, explain the level of price.

4. The uncertainties inherent in noncollusive pricing are conducive to collusion. There is a tendency for collusive oligopolists to maximize joint profits—that is, to behave in a way similar to a pure monopolist. However, antitrust legislation, the presence of a "large" number of firms, and differences in cost and demand curves serve as impediments to collusion. Furthermore, collusive price arrangements are difficult to maintain during recessions. Though potentially profitable, secret price concessions can lead to the breakdown of price collusion.

5. Insights into the character and behavior of oligopolistic industries—mutual interdependence, price rigidity, the tendency toward collusion—can be gained through the examination of a profits-payoff table.

6. Market shares in oligopolistic industries are usually determined on the basis of nonprice competition. Oligopolists emphasize nonprice competition because *a.* advertising and product variations are less easy for rivals to match and *b.* oligopolists frequently have ample financial resources to finance nonprice competition.

7. There is no clear-cut conclusion as to the social desirability of oligopoly; oligopoly may be either restrictive or progressive. Where oligopoly is restrictive, abuses of its market power may sometimes be curbed by countervailing power.

QUESTIONS AND STUDY SUGGESTIONS

1. What features distinguish oligopoly from monopolistic competition? Be specific.

2. "Fewness of rivals means mutual interdependence, and mutual interdependence means uncertainty as to how those few rivals will react to a price change by any one firm." Explain. Of what significance is this for determining demand and marginal revenue? Other things being equal, would you expect mutual interdependence to vary directly or inversely with the degree of product differentiation? Explain.

3. What are the basic characteristics of oligopolistic prices? How are these characteristics best explained?

4. What assumptions concerning a rival's responses to price changes underlie the kinked demand curve? Why is there a gap in the marginal-revenue curve? How does the kinked demand curve help explain oligopolistic price rigidity?

5. Why is there a tendency for price collusion to occur in oligopolistic industries? Assess the economic desirability of collusive pricing. Explain: "If each firm knows that the price of each of its few rivals depends on its own price, how can the prices be determined?"

6. What is price leadership? Explain its operation.

7. Explain the general character of the data in the following profits-payoff table for oligopolists C and D. All profit figures are in thousands.

D's price ↓ / C's price →	$40	$35	$30
$40	$54 / $60	$59 / $55	$57 / $49
$35	$50 / $69	$55 / $58	$56 / $50
$30	$40 / $70	$49 / $60	$51 / $52

a. Use the table to explain the mutual interdependence which characterizes oligopolistic industries.

b. Assuming both firms are initially charging $35 and there

is no collusion, explain why each firm may be hesitant to alter its price.

c. Assuming both firms are charging $30 initially, explain why the firms might find collusive pricing to be mutually advantageous. Why might the firms find it difficult to raise their prices up to $40?

8. "Oligopolistic industries have both the means and the inclination for technological progress." Do you agree? Explain.

9. Under what conditions will oligopoly be economically efficient? Economically inefficient? Which set of conditions do you feel better describes oligopoly in American capitalism? Justify your answer.

10. What is countervailing power? How does it differ from ordinary competition? Why is it self-generating? What are its limitations?

SELECTED REFERENCES

Economic Issues, 4th ed., readings 45, 46, and 47.

Adams, Walter (ed.): *The Structure of American Industry,* 4th ed. (New York: The Macmillan Company, 1971), chaps. 3, 5, and 7–9.

Bain, Joe S.: *Industrial Organization,* 2d ed. (New York: John Wiley & Sons, Inc., 1968), chap. 9.

Colberg, Marshall R., Dascomb R. Forbush, and Gilbert R. Whitaker, Jr.: *Business Economics: Principles and Cases,* 4th ed. (Homewood, Ill.: Richard D. Irwin, Inc., 1970), chap. 12.

Galbraith, John K.: *American Capitalism,* rev. ed. (Boston: Houghton Mifflin Company, 1956), chaps. 7 and 9.

Mansfield, Edwin: *Microeconomics: Theory and Applications* (New York: W. W. Norton & Company, Inc., 1970), chap. 11.

Papandreou, Andreas G., and John T. Wheeler: *Competition and Its Regulation* (Englewood Cliffs, N.J.: Prentice-Hall, Inc., 1954), chap. 8.

Weiss, Leonard W.: *Economics and American Industry* (New York: John Wiley & Sons, Inc., 1961), chaps. 7 and 8.

31

PRODUCTION AND THE DEMAND FOR ECONOMIC RESOURCES

The preceding four chapters have been concerned with the pricing and output of goods and services under a variety of product market structures. In producing any commodity, a firm must hire productive resources which, directly or indirectly, are owned and supplied by households. It is appropriate that we now turn from the pricing and production of goods to the pricing and employment of resources needed in accomplishing production. In terms of our circular flow diagram of the economy (Chapter 3), we now shift our attention from the bottom loop of the diagram, where firms supply and households demand products, to the top loop, where households supply and businesses demand resources. It is in part this reversal of roles which makes necessary a separate discussion of resource pricing.

SIGNIFICANCE OF RESOURCE PRICING

The importance of studying resource pricing is almost self-evident. The most basic fact about resource prices is that they constitute a major determinant of money incomes. The expenditures which businesses make in acquiring economic resources flow as wage, rent, interest, and profit incomes to those households which in turn supply the human and property resources at their disposal. Here we are concerned with explaining the resource prices which play such a crucial role in determining the distribution of income.

Another important aspect of resource pricing is that, just as product prices ration finished goods and services to consumers, so resource prices allocate scarce resources among various industries and firms. An understanding of the manner in which resource prices negotiate the allocation of resources is particularly significant in view of the fact that in a dynamic economy such as American capitalism, the efficient allocation of resources over time calls for continuing shifts in resources among alternative uses.

A very special aspect of the resource allocation problem faces the individual firm. To the firm, resource prices are costs, and to realize maximum profits a firm must produce the profit-maximizing output with the most efficient (least costly) combina-

tion of resources. Given technology, it is resource prices which play the major role in determining how much land, labor, capital, and entrepreneurial ability are to be combined in the productive process.

Finally, aside from these objective facets of resource pricing, there are a myriad of ethical questions and public policy issues surrounding the resource market. In particular, the amoral nature of resource prices results in considerable inequality in the personal distribution of income. Too, the age-old question of the sizes of the income shares going to specific groups is still very much alive. What is the proper distribution of the national income between profits and wages? What shares should go to farmers, factory workers, white-collar employees? Indeed, the pursuit of these questions leads into a consideration of the alternative economic ideologies. Much of Part 6 of this book is concerned with endeavors—both public and private—to alter the distribution of income. Chapter 38 is concerned specifically with the ethics of income distribution.

COMPLEXITIES OF RESOURCE PRICING

Economists are in substantial agreement as to the basic principles of resource pricing. Yet there exists considerable disagreement and sometimes an element of confusion as to the variations in these general principles which must be made as they are applied to specific resources and particular markets. While economists are in general agreement that the pricing and employment of economic resources, or factors of production, are a supply and demand phenomenon, they also recognize that in particular markets, resource supply and demand may assume strange and often complex dimensions. This is further complicated by the fact that the operation of supply and demand forces may be muted or even largely supplanted by the policies and practices of government, business firms, or labor unions, not to mention a host of other institutional considerations.

Our major objective in this chapter is a limited one: to explain the basic factors which underlie the demand for economic resources. We shall couch our discussion in terms of labor, recognizing that the principles outlined in our discussion are also generally applicable to land, capital, and entrepreneurial ability. In Chapter 32 we shall combine our understanding of resource demand with a discussion of labor supply in analyzing wage rates. Then in Chapter 33 we shall emphasize the supply side of the market for property resources.

MARGINAL PRODUCTIVITY THEORY OF RESOURCE DEMAND

The simplest approach to resource demand is that which assumes a firm is hiring a single resource in a competitive market and in turn is selling its product in a competitive market. The simplicity of this situation lies in the fact that under competition the firm can dispose of as little or as much output as it chooses at the going market price. The firm is selling such a negligible fraction of total output that it exerts no influence whatever on product price. Similarly, in the resource market, competition means that the firm is hiring such a small fraction of the total supply of the resource that its price is unaffected by the quantity the firm purchases.

Resource demand as a derived demand

Having specified these simplified conditions, the most crucial point to note is that the demand for resources is a *derived* demand, that is, derived from the finished goods and services which resources help produce. Resources do not directly satisfy consumer wants, but do so indirectly by producing goods and services. No one wants to consume an acre of land, an International Harvester tractor, or the labor services of a farmer, but households do want to consume the various food and fiber products which these resources help produce.

Marginal revenue product (MRP)

The derived nature of resource demand correctly implies that the strength of the demand for any resource will depend upon (1) the capability of the

resource in producing a good and (2) the value of the good it is producing. In other words, the demand for a resource depends upon its productivity and the market price of the commodity it is producing. A resource which is highly productive in turning out a commodity highly valued by society will be in great demand. On the other hand, demand will be very weak for a relatively unproductive resource which is only capable of producing some good not in great demand by households. There will be no demand for a resource which is phenomenally efficient in the production of something which no one will want to purchase!

The roles of productivity and product value in determining resource demand can be brought into sharper focus through Table 31·1. Here it is assumed that a firm is adding one variable resource—labor—to its fixed plant. Columns 1 through 3 remind us that the law of diminishing returns will be applicable in this situation, causing the marginal physical product (MPP) of labor to fall beyond some point. For simplicity's sake it is here assumed that diminishing marginal physical product sets in with the first worker hired. But we have already emphasized that the derived demand for a resource depends not only upon the productivity of that resource but also upon the price of the commodity it produces. Column 4 adds this information. Note that product price is constant at $1 because we are supposing a competitive product market. Multiplying column 2 by column 4, we get the total-revenue data of column 5. From these total-revenue data we can readily compute *marginal revenue product (MRP)—the increase in total revenue resulting from the use of each additional variable input (labor, in this case)*. This is indicated in column 6.

Rule for employing resources

The MRP schedule—columns 1 and 6—is crucial in that it constitutes the firm's demand schedule for labor. To explain why this is so we must first discuss the rule which guides a profit-seeking firm in hiring any resource. To maximize profits, a firm should hire additional units of any given resource so long as each successive unit adds more to the firm's total revenue

TABLE 31·1 THE DEMAND FOR A RESOURCE: PURE COMPETITION IN THE SALE OF THE PRODUCT *(hypothetical data)*

(1) Units of resource	(2) Total product	(3) Marginal physical product (MPP), or Δ(2)	(4) Product price	(5) Total revenue, or (2) × (4)	(6) Marginal revenue product (MRP), or Δ(5)
1	15	15	$1	$15	$15
2	27	12	1	27	12
3	36	9	1	36	9
4	42	6	1	42	6
5	45	3	1	45	3
6	46	1	1	46	1

than it does to its total costs. Economists have special terms which designate what each additional unit of a resource adds to total cost and what it adds to total revenue. We have just noted that MRP measures how much each successive worker adds to total revenue. The amount which each additional unit of a resource adds to the firm's total (resource) cost is called *marginal resource cost (MRC)*. Thus we can restate our rule for hiring resources as follows: *It will be profitable for a firm to hire additional units of a resource up to the point at which that resource's MRP is equal to its MRC.* If the number of workers a firm is currently hiring is such that the MRP of the last worker exceeds his MRC, the firm can clearly profit by hiring more workers. But if the number being hired is such that the MRC of the last worker exceeds his MRP, the firm is hiring workers who are not "paying their way," and it can thereby increase its profits by laying off some workers. The reader will recognize that this MRP = MRC rule is very similar to the MR = MC rule employed throughout our discussion of product pricing. The rationale of the two rules is the same, but the point of reference is now inputs of resources, not outputs of product.

MRP is a demand schedule

Just as product price and marginal revenue are equal in a purely competitive product market, so resource price and marginal resource cost are equal when a firm is hiring a resource competitively. In a purely competitive labor market the wage rate is set by the total, or market, supply of, and the market demand for, labor. Because it hires such a small fraction of the total supply of labor, a single firm cannot influence this wage rate. This means that total resource cost increases by exactly the amount of the going wage rate for each additional worker hired; the wage rate and MRC are equal. It follows that so long as it is hiring labor competitively, *the firm will hire workers to the point at which their wage rate (or MRC) is equal to their MRP.*

Accordingly, employing the data in column 6 of Table 31·1, we find that if the wage rate is $14.95, the firm will hire only one worker. This is so because

TABLE 31·2 THE DEMAND FOR A RESOURCE: IMPERFECT COMPETITION IN THE SALE OF THE PRODUCT (*hypothetical data*)

(1) Units of resource	(2) Total product	(3) Marginal physical product (MPP), or Δ(2)	(4) Product price	(5) Total revenue, or (2) × (4)	(6) Marginal revenue product (MRP), or Δ(5)
		15			$19.50
1	15		$1.30	$19.50	
		12			12.90
2	27		1.20	32.40	
		9			7.20
3	36		1.10	39.60	
		6			4.50
4	42		1.05	44.10	
		3			0.90
5	45		1.00	45.00	
		1			−1.30
6	46		0.95	43.70	

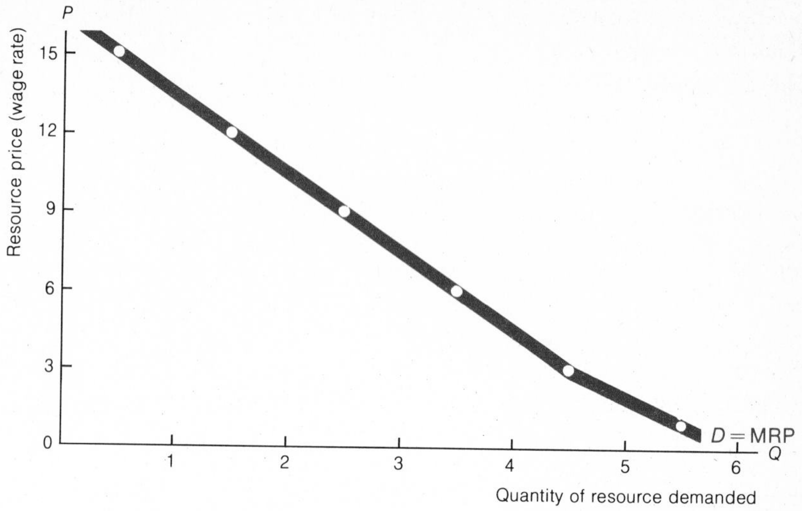

FIGURE 31 · 1 THE PURELY COMPETITIVE SELLER'S DEMAND FOR A RESOURCE

The MRP curve is the resource demand curve. The location of the curve depends upon the marginal productivity of the resource and the price of the product. Under pure competition product price is constant; therefore, it is solely because of diminishing marginal productivity that the resource demand curve is downsloping.

the first worker adds $15 to total revenue and slightly less—$14.95—to total costs. For each successive worker, however, we find that his MRC exceeds his MRP, indicating that it will not be profitable to hire him. If the wage rate is $11.95, we apply the same reasoning and discover that it will pay the firm to hire both the first and second workers. Similarly, if the wage rate is $8.95, three will be hired. If $5.95, four. If $2.95, then five. And so forth. It is evident that *the MRP schedule constitutes the firm's demand for labor, because each point on this schedule (curve) indicates the number of workers which the firm would hire at each possible wage rate which might exist.* This is shown graphically in Figure 31·1.

Resource demand under imperfect competition

Our analysis of labor demand becomes slightly more complex when we assume that the firm is selling its product in an imperfectly competitive market. Pure monopoly, oligopoly, and monopolistic competition in the product market all mean that the firm's product demand curve is downsloping; that is, the firm must accept a lower price in order to increase its sales. Table 31·2 takes this into account. The productivity data of Table 31·1 are retained, but it is now assumed in column 4 that product price must be lowered in order to sell the marginal product of each successive worker. The MRP of the competitive seller falls for one reason: marginal physical product diminishes. But the MRP of the imperfectly competitive seller falls for two reasons: marginal product diminishes, and product price falls as output increases.

It must be emphasized that the lower price which accompanies every increase in output applies in each case not only to the marginal product of each successive worker but also to all prior units which otherwise could have been sold at a higher price. To

illustrate: The second worker's marginal product is 12 units. These 12 units can be sold for $1.20 each or, as a group, for $14.40. But this is not the MRP of the second worker. Why? Because in order to sell these 12 units the firm must take a 10-cent price cut on the 15 units produced by the first worker—units which could have been sold for $1.30 each. Thus the MRP of the second worker is only $12.90 [$14.40 − (15 × 10 cents)]. Similarly, the third worker's MRP is $7.20. Although the 9 units he produces are worth $1.10 each in the market, the third worker does not add $9.90 to the firm's total revenue when account is taken of the 10-cent price cut which must be taken on the 27 units produced by the first two workers. In this case the third worker's MRP is only $7.20 [$9.90 − (27 × 10 cents)]. And so it is for the other figures in column 6.

The net result is obvious: The MRP curve—the resource demand curve—of the imperfectly competitive producer tends to be less elastic than that of a purely competitive producer. At a wage rate or MRC of $11.95 both the purely competitive and the imperfectly competitive seller will hire two workers. But at $8.95 the competitive firm will hire three and the imperfectly competitive firm only two. And at $5.95 the purely competitive firm will take four and the imperfect competitor only three. This difference in elasticity can be readily visualized by graphing the

FIGURE 31 · 2

THE IMPERFECTLY COMPETITIVE SELLER'S DEMAND FOR A RESOURCE

An imperfectly competitive seller's resource demand curve slopes downward because marginal product diminishes and product price falls as output increases.

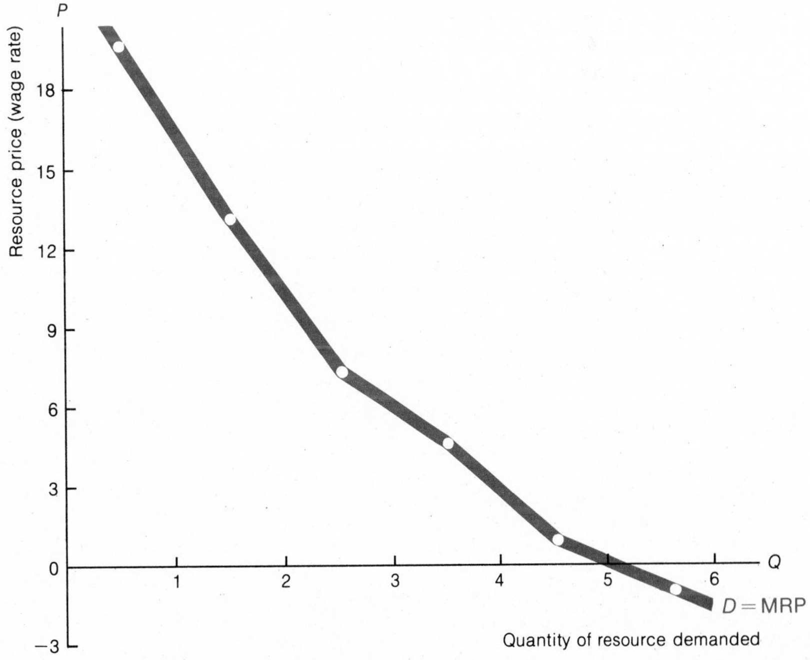

MRP data of Table 31·2 as in Figure 31·2 and comparing them with Figure 31·1. It is not surprising that the imperfectly competitive producer is less responsive to wage cuts in terms of workers employed than is the purely competitive producer. The relative reluctance of the imperfect competitor to employ more resources and thereby produce more output when resource prices fall is merely the resource market reflection of the imperfect competitor's tendency to restrict output in the product market. Other things being equal, the imperfectly competitive seller will produce less of a product than would a purely competitive seller. In producing this smaller output, he will demand fewer resources.

But one qualification is pertinent. We noted in Chapters 28 and 30 that in some instances the market structures of oligopoly and pure monopoly might be progressive rather than restrictive. That is, they might give rise to a higher level of production, more employment, and lower prices in the long run than would a purely competitive market arrangement. This seems more likely in the case of oligopoly. The resource demand curve for progressive oligopoly and monopoly would not be so restricted.

Market demand for a resource

Can we now derive a market demand curve for a resource? Yes, we can. You will recall that the total, or market, demand curve for a product is developed by summing the demand curves of all individual buyers in the market. Similarly, the market demand curve for a particular resource can be derived in essentially the same fashion, that is, by summing the individual demand or MRP curves for all firms hiring that resource.[1]

[1]The matter is actually not quite this simple. The resource demand, or MRP, curve *for each firm* is drawn on the assumption that product price is constant. However, if a lowering of resource price causes *all firms* in the industry to hire more of the resource and thereby expand total output, we can expect product price to decline. The result is that the resource market demand curve will not be quite identical with the sum of the individual firms' demand curves for that resource. The whole will not equal the sum of the parts. We shall ignore this complication in our discussion and accept the approximation in the text. If interested, consult Neil W. Chamberlain and Donald E. Cullen, *The Labor Sector,* 2d ed. (New York: McGraw-Hill Book Company, 1971), pp. 360–361.

CHANGES IN RESOURCE DEMAND

What will alter the demand for a resource, that is, shift the demand curve? The very derivation of resource demand immediately suggests two related factors—the resource's productivity and the market price of the product it is producing. And our previous analysis of changes in product demand (Chapter 4) indicates another factor—changes in the prices of other resources.

1. Because resource demand is a derived demand, it is obvious that any change in the demand for the product will affect product price and therefore the MRP of the resource. An increase in the demand for automobiles will increase automobile prices and therefore cause the demand for the services of automobile workers to shift to the right; a decline in the demand for automobiles will reduce automobile prices and thereby shift the demand for automobile workers to the left.

2. Changes in productivity will also cause resource demand to shift. The productivity of any resource can be altered in several ways. (*a*) The marginal productivity data for, say, labor will depend upon the quantities of other resources with which it is combined. The greater the amount of capital and land resources with which labor is combined, the greater will be the marginal productivity and the demand for labor. (*b*) Technological improvements will have the same effect. The better the quality of the capital, the greater the productivity of labor. A worker equipped with a power shovel is very much more productive than the same worker armed with a spade. (*c*) Improvements in the quality of the variable resource itself—labor—will increase the marginal productivity and therefore the demand for labor.

All these considerations, incidentally, are important in explaining why the average level of (real) wages is higher in the United States than in foreign nations. American workers are generally healthier and better trained than those of foreign nations, and in most industries they work with a larger and more efficient stock of capital goods and more abundant natural resources than do the workers of most foreign na-

tions. This spells a strong demand for labor. On the supply side of the market, labor is *relatively* scarce as compared with most foreign nations. A strong demand and a relatively scarce supply result in high wage rates. This will be discussed further in Chapter 32.

3. Just as changes in the prices of other products will change the demand for a specific commodity, so changes in the prices of other resources can be expected to alter the demand for a particular resource. And just as the effect of a change in the price of product X upon the demand for product Y depends upon whether X and Y are substitute or complementary goods, so the effect of a change in the price of resource A upon the demand for resource B will depend upon their substitutability or their complementariness.

Within limits, resources are typically substitutes for one another. A drop in the price of machinery may prompt a firm to substitute machinery for labor; this is the obvious adjustment to make if the firm seeks to produce any given output in the least costly fashion. At given wage rates, less labor will now be employed. The demand for labor will have fallen. But this *substitution effect* may be offset wholly or in part by an accompanying *output effect.* Because the price of machinery has fallen, the cost of producing various outputs will also have declined. And with lower costs, the firm will produce and sell a larger output. This greater output will tend to increase the demand for all resources, including labor. The net effect of a decline in the price of machinery upon the demand for labor will depend upon the sizes of these two opposed effects. If the substitution effect outweighs the output effect, the demand for labor will decline. If the reverse holds true, the demand for labor will increase.

When resources are complementary or jointly demanded, the situation is a bit more clear cut. In some situations the nature of the productive process allows little or no room for substituting resources; resources are combined in fixed proportions. Suppose, for example, that a small manufacturer of metal products uses punch presses as its basic piece of capital equipment. Each press is designed to be operated by one worker; the machine is not automated—it won't run itself—and a second or third worker would be wholly redundant. Now assume that a significant technological advance in the production of these presses substantially reduces their cost. Other things being unchanged, this reduction in the price of capital goods will induce our manufacturer to use more presses. However, because labor and capital are required in fixed proportions—one man for one machine—there will be no substitution of capital for labor. On the contrary, the purchase of more machines will increase the firm's demand for punch-press operators. The output effect will bolster this increase in labor demand. To the extent that the firm's metal products are reduced in price because of the drop in the cost of the presses, its volume of sales and therefore its demand for labor will increase.

ELASTICITY OF RESOURCE DEMAND

The considerations just discussed are responsible for shifts in the location of resource demand curves. Such changes in demand are to be carefully distinguished from a change in the quantity of a resource demanded. The latter, you will recall, does not entail a shift in the resource demand curve but rather a movement from one point to another on a stable resource demand curve, because of a change in the price of the specific resource under consideration. To illustrate: An increase in the wage rate from \$5.95 to \$8.95 will reduce the quantity of labor demanded from four to three workers, as can be readily seen in Table 31·1 and Figure 31·1.

This raises a question: What determines the sensitivity of producers to changes in resource prices? Or, more technically, what determines the elasticity of resource demand? Several long-standing generalizations provide some important insights in answering this question.

1. A purely technical consideration is of importance to us—the rate at which the marginal physical product of the variable resource declines. If the marginal product of labor declines slowly as it is added to a fixed amount of capital, the MRP, or demand curve

for labor, will decline slowly and tend to be highly elastic. A small decline in the price of such a resource will give rise to a relatively large increase in the amount demanded. Conversely, if the marginal productivity of labor declines sharply, the MRP, or labor demand curve, will decline rapidly. This means that a relatively large decline in the wage rate will be accompanied by a very modest increase in the amount of labor hired; resource demand will be inelastic.

2. The degree to which resources are substitutable for one another is a highly important determinant of elasticity. The larger the number of good substitute resources available, the greater will be the elasticity of demand for a particular resource. If a furniture manufacturer finds that some five or six different types of wood are equally satisfactory in making coffee tables, a rise in the price of any one type of wood may cause a very sharp drop in the amount demanded as the producer readily substitutes other woods. At the other extreme, it may be impossible to substitute: bauxite is absolutely essential in the production of aluminum ingots. This means that the demand for it tends to be very inelastic.

3. The elasticity of demand for any resource will depend upon the elasticity of demand for the product which it helps produce. The greater the elasticity of product demand, the greater the elasticity of resource demand. The derived nature of resource demand would lead us to expect this relationship. A small rise in the price of a product with great elasticity of demand will give rise to a sharp drop in output and therefore a relatively large decline in the amounts of the various resources demanded. Indeed, our comparisons of resource demand when output is being sold competitively (Table 31·1 and Figure 31·1), on the one hand, and under imperfectly competitive conditions (Table 31·2 and Figure 31·2), on the other, have already suggested that, other things being the same, the greater the elasticity of product demand, the greater the elasticity of resource demand.

4. Finally, the larger the portion of production costs accounted for by a resource, the greater will be the elasticity of demand for that resource. The rationale here is rather evident. If labor costs account for, say, three-fourths of the total cost of a product, a given increase in wage rates will alter total cost by a relatively large amount, resulting in a significant increase in product price. Given the elasticity of product demand, this substantial price increase will cause a relatively large decline in sales and a sharp decline in the amount of labor demanded. But if labor cost is only 5 or 10 percent of total cost, the same given increase in wage rates will have little effect upon total cost and product price. Given the same elasticity of product demand, a small decline in sales and therefore in the amount of labor demanded will result.

A FIRM'S DEMAND FOR SEVERAL RESOURCES

We know that the production of any commodity will involve the use of several inputs. It is, therefore, important to generalize our discussion of the demand for a single resource to the demand for a number of resources. While our analysis will proceed on the basis of two resources, it can readily be extended to any number one chooses to consider.

The profit-maximizing combination of resources

The generalization of our discussion of resource demand to several resources is quite easily accomplished. Assume a firm is hiring two resources, capital and labor, in purely competitive markets. This means that the price of capital and the price of labor are given to the firm and will not change with the amount purchased. Now we have seen that in determining the profit-maximizing amount of any single resource—say, labor—to hire, the firm must ask itself: How much will an extra worker add to total costs? And how does this compare with what he will add to total revenue? Or, more formally, what is the resource price (wage rate) of an extra worker as compared with his marginal revenue product? We know that so long as an extra worker's MRP exceeds his wage rate, it remains profitable to add more workers. But if the firm is employing some quantity of labor such that the wage

rate exceeds the MRP, it has hired too large a labor force and can increase profits by terminating the employment of all workers who add more to costs than they do to revenue. The profit-maximizing quantity of labor to employ is that quantity at which the wage rate or price of labor (P_L) equals the marginal revenue product of labor (MRP_L) or, more simply, $P_L = \text{MRP}_L$.

Now, the same rationale applies to any other resource—for example, capital. Capital will also be employed in the profit-maximizing amount when its price equals its marginal revenue product, or $P_C = \text{MRP}_C$. Thus in general we can say that, when hiring resources in competitive markets, a firm will realize the profit-maximizing combination of resources when each input is employed up to the point at which its price equals its marginal revenue product:

$$P_L = \text{MRP}_L$$
$$P_C = \text{MRP}_C$$

This rule is sometimes alternatively expressed as

$$\frac{\text{MRP}_L}{P_L} = \frac{\text{MRP}_C}{P_C} = 1 \qquad (1)$$

Note two things. First, in equation (1) it is not sufficient that the MRPs of the two resources be *proportionate to* their prices; the MRPs must be *equal to* their prices and therefore equal to 1. For example, if $\text{MRP}_L = \$15$, $P_L = \$5$, $\text{MRP}_C = \$9$, and $P_C = \$3$, the firm would be underemploying both capital and labor even though the ratios of MRP to resource price were identical for both resources. That is, the firm could expand its profits by hiring additional amounts of both capital and labor until it had moved down their downsloping MRP curves to the point at which MRP_L was equal to \$5 and MRP_C was \$3.

Secondly, the problem faced by the producer is much like that confronting the consumer. You will recall from Chapter 25 that the consumer seeks the particular combination of goods which will yield the maximum utility for his money income. In achieving the utility-maximizing collection of goods, the consumer considers both his preferences as reflected in diminishing marginal-utility data and the prices of the various products. The producer is in a similar boat. He obviously wants to maximize his profits, just as the consumer seeks to maximize his utility. In pursuing this combination of resources, the producer must consider both the productivity of the resource as reflected in diminishing marginal-physical-productivity data and the prices (costs) of the various resources. A firm may well find it profitable to employ very small amounts of an extremely productive resource if its price is high. Conversely, it may be sensible to hire large amounts of a relatively unproductive resource if its price is sufficiently low.

The least-cost combination of resources

Determination of the profit-maximizing combination of several inputs obviously implies repeated comparisons of total revenue and total costs to ascertain that output at which the difference between the two is maximized. Given product price, the maximization of this difference—the maximization of profits—will pinpoint some unique output (Figure 27·1*a*). But of course, product price might change and thereby cause some alternative output to become the profit-maximizing level of production (Figure 27·5). In short, depending upon the level of product price, any one of a large number of possible outputs may be the profit-maximizing or loss-minimizing output. However, these various possible outputs can only be a profit-maximizing level of production if each is produced in the least costly way. In other words, a necessary condition for profit maximization is the production of any relevant output with the minimum attainable cost outlay for resources. *Indeed, all the cost curves developed in Chapter 26 and applied in the ensuing product market chapters implicitly assume that each possible level of output is being produced with the least costly combination of inputs.* If this were not the case, then presumably there would exist lower attainable positions for the cost curves (Figure 27·2, for example), and consequently there would be some other (larger) output than that designated at which greater profits could be realized.

When is a firm producing any given output with the least costly combination of resources? The answer

is: When the last dollar spent on each resource entails the same marginal physical product. That is, *the cost of any output is minimized when the marginal physical product per dollar's worth of each resource used is the same.* If we are thinking in terms of just two resources, labor and capital, the cost-minimizing position occurs where

$$\frac{\text{MPP of labor}}{\text{price of labor}} = \frac{\text{MPP of capital}}{\text{price of capital}} \tag{2}$$

It is not difficult to see why the fulfillment of this condition means least-cost production. Suppose, for example, that the prices of capital and labor are both $1 per unit, but that capital and labor are currently being employed in such amounts that the marginal physical product of labor is 9 and the marginal physical product of capital is 5. Our equation immediately tells us that this is clearly not the least costly combination of resources: MPP_L/P_L is 9/1 and MPP_C/P_C is 5/1. If the firm spends a dollar less on capital and shifts that dollar to labor, it will lose the 5 units of output produced by the marginal dollar's worth of capital, but will gain the 9 units of output from the employment of an extra dollar's worth of labor. *Net* output will increase by 4 (=9 − 5) units for the same total cost. Note that this shifting of dollars from capital to labor will push the firm down its MPP curve for labor and back up its MPP curve for capital, moving the firm toward a position of equilibrium wherein equation (2) is fulfilled. At this point the MPP of both labor and capital might be, for example, 7.

Whenever the same total cost results in a greater total output, it means that cost per unit—and therefore the total cost of any given level of output—is being reduced. Stated somewhat differently, to be able to produce a *larger* output with a *given* total-cost outlay is the same thing as being able to produce a *given* total output, it means that cost per unit—and therehave seen, the cost of producing any given output can be reduced so long as $\text{MPP}_C/P_C \neq \text{MPP}_L/P_L$. But when dollars have been shifted among capital and labor to the point at which equation (2) holds, then there are no further changes in the amounts of capital and labor employed which will reduce costs more. The least-cost combination of capital and labor is being realized for that output. Question 7 at the end of this chapter stresses the distinction between the profit-maximizing and the least-cost combination of resources.

A final point in anticipation of Chapter 32: When a firm is hiring resources under imperfectly competitive conditions, its decision to hire more inputs will affect resource prices. Specifically, if a firm is large relative to a resource market, it will have to increase the current resource price to attract more inputs. And this higher price must be paid not only to the extra inputs employed, but also to all units of the resource already in the employment of the firm. This means that marginal resource cost (MRC)—the cost of an extra input—is actually greater than resource price. The fact that MRC exceeds resource price when resources are hired or purchased under imperfectly competitive conditions calls for appropriate adjustments in equations (1) and (2). Specifically, in making marginal decisions to determine the profit-maximizing and least-cost combination of resources, the firm must substitute MRC for resource price in the denominators of our two equations. That is, with imperfect competition in the hiring of both labor and capital, equation (1) becomes

$$\frac{\text{MRP}_L}{\text{MRC}_L} = \frac{\text{MRP}_C}{\text{MRC}_C} = 1 \tag{1'}$$

and equation (2) is restated as

$$\frac{\text{MPP}_L}{\text{MRC}_L} = \frac{\text{MPP}_C}{\text{MRC}_C} \tag{2'}$$

As a matter of fact, equations (1) and (2) can be regarded as special cases of (1′) and (2′) wherein firms happen to be hiring under purely competitive conditions and resource price is therefore equal to, and can be substituted for, marginal resource cost.

SUMMARY

1. Resource prices are a major determinant of money incomes, and simultaneously perform the function of rationing resources to various industries and firms.

2. Though economists agree that resource pricing is a supply and demand phenomenon, they frequently

disagree as to the exact characteristics of, and the operation of, supply and demand in particular resource markets.

3. The fact that the demand for any resource is derived from the product it helps produce correctly suggests that the demand for a resource will depend upon its productivity and the market value of the good it is producing.

4. The marginal-revenue-product schedule of any resource is the demand schedule for that resource. This follows from an application of the rule that a firm operating under competitive conditions will find it most profitable to hire a resource up to the point at which the price of the resource equals its marginal revenue product.

5. The demand curve for a resource is downsloping, because the marginal physical product of additional inputs of any resource declines in accordance with the law of diminishing returns. When a firm is selling in an imperfectly competitive market, the resource demand curve will fall, too, because product price must be reduced in order to permit the firm to sell a larger output.

6. The market demand for a resource can be derived by summing the demand curves of all firms hiring that resource.

7. The demand for a resource will change, that is, a resource demand curve will shift, as the result of *a.* a change in the demand for, and therefore the price of, the product the resource is producing, *b.* changes in the productivity of the resource due either to increases in the quantity or improvements in the quality of the resources with which a given resource is being combined, or improvements in the quality of the given resource itself, and *c.* changes in the prices of other resources.

8. A decline in the price of resource A will typically give rise to a substitution effect; that is, resource A will tend to be substituted for resources B and C. But these declines in the demand for resources B and C may be partially, wholly, or more than offset by an output effect; that is, the decrease in cost which the decline in the price of resource A entails will increase output and tend to increase the demand for resources B and C. When resources are not substitutes but are complementary, a decline in the price of resource A will increase the demand for complementary resource B.

9. The elasticity of resource demand depends upon *a.* the rate at which the marginal physical product of the resource declines, *b.* the number of good substitute resources available, *c.* the elasticity of demand for the product, and *d.* the portion of total production costs attributable to the resource.

10. A firm will employ the profit-maximizing combination of resources when the price of each resource is equal to its marginal *revenue* product or, algebraically, when

$$\frac{\text{MRP of labor}}{\text{price of labor}} = \frac{\text{MRP of capital}}{\text{price of capital}} = 1$$

11. Any level of output will be produced with the least costly combination of resources when the marginal *physical* product per dollar's worth of each input is the same, that is, when

$$\frac{\text{MPP of labor}}{\text{price of labor}} = \frac{\text{MPP of capital}}{\text{price of capital}}$$

12. Imperfect competition in hiring labor and capital is accounted for by substituting the marginal resource cost of labor and capital for their prices in the profit-maximizing and least-cost equations.

QUESTIONS AND STUDY SUGGESTIONS

1. Explain or define the following terms: *a.* marginal physical product, *b.* marginal revenue product, *c.* marginal resource cost, *d.* output effect, and *e.* substitution effect.

2. Complete the labor demand table on page 541 for a firm which is hiring labor competitively and selling its product in a competitive market.

a. How many workers will the firm hire if the going wage rate is $27.95? $19.95? Explain why the firm will not hire

Units of labor	Total product	Marginal physical product	Product price	Total revenue	Marginal revenue product
1	17	______	$2	$______	$______
2	31	______	2	______	______
3	43	______	2	______	______
4	53	______	2	______	______
5	60	______	2	______	______
6	65		2	______	

a larger or smaller number of workers at each of these wage rates.

b. Show in schedule form and graphically the labor demand curve of this firm.

c. Now redetermine the firm's demand curve for labor on the assumption that it is selling in an imperfectly competitive market and that, although it can sell 17 units at $2.20 per unit, it must lower product price by 5 cents in order to sell the marginal physical product of each successive worker. Compare this demand curve with that derived in question 2*b*. Explain any differences.

3. What is the significance of resource pricing? Explain in detail how the factors determining resource demand differ from those underlying product demand. Explain the meaning and significance of the notion that the demand for a resource is a *derived* demand. Why do resource demand curves slope downward?

4. Distinguish between a change in resource demand and a change in the quantity of a resource demanded. What specific factors might give rise to a change in resource demand? A change in the quantity of a resource demanded?

5. Using the substitution and output effects, explain how a decline in the price of resource A *might* cause an increase in the demand for substitute resource B.

6. What factors determine the elasticity of resource demand? What effect will each of the following have upon the elasticity or the location of the demand for resource C, which is being used in the production of commodity X? Where there is any uncertainty as to the outcome, specify the causes of that uncertainty.

a. An increase in the demand for product X.

b. An increase in the price of substitute factor D.

c. An increase in the number of resources which are substitutable for C in producing X.

d. A technological improvement in the capital equipment with which resource C is combined.

e. A decline in the price of complementary resource E.

f. A decline in the elasticity of demand for product X due to a decline in the competitiveness of the product market.

7. Suppose the productivity of labor and capital is as shown below. The output of these resources sells in a purely competitive market for $1 per unit. Both labor and capital are hired under purely competitive conditions at $1 and $3 respectively.

Units of capital	MPP of capital	Units of labor	MPP of labor
1	24	1	11
2	21	2	9
3	18	3	8
4	15	4	7
5	9	5	6
6	6	6	4
7	3	7	1
8	1	8	½

a. What is the least-cost combination of labor and capital to employ in producing 80 units of output? Explain.

b. What is the profit-maximizing combination of labor and capital for the firm to employ? Explain.

c. When the firm is employing the profit-maximizing combination of labor and capital as determined in 7*b*, is this combination also the least costly way of producing the profit-maximizing output? Explain.

SELECTED REFERENCES

Chamberlain, Neil W., and Donald E. Cullen: *The Labor Sector*, 2d ed. (New York: McGraw-Hill Book Company, 1971), chaps. 17 and 18.

Heneman, Herbert G., Jr., and Dale Yoder: *Labor Economics*, 2d ed. (Cincinnati: South-Western Publishing Company, 1965), chaps. 5 and 21.

Hyde, Francis E., et al.: *A New Prospect of Economics* (Liverpool: Liverpool University Press, 1958), chap. 7.

Leftwich, Richard H.: *The Price System and Resource Allocation*, 4th ed. (Hinsdale, Ill.: The Dryden Press, Inc., 1970), chaps. 13 and 14.

Mansfield, Edwin: *Microeconomics: Theory and Applications* (New York: W. W. Norton & Company, Inc., 1970), chaps. 12 and 13.

39

THE PRICING AND EMPLOYMENT OF RESOURCES: WAGE DETERMINATION

Armed with some understanding of the strategic factors underlying resource demand, we must now combine this information with the supply situations which characterize the markets for labor, land, capital, and entrepreneurial ability to see how wages, rents, interest, and profits are determined. For two reasons we discuss wage rates prior to other resource prices.

1. The marginal productivity theory of resource demand is probably more applicable to an explanation of wage rates than it is to the pricing of other resources.

2. To most households the wage rate is the most important price in the economy; it is the sole or basic source of income. At least two-thirds of the national income is in the form of wages and salaries.

Our basic objectives in discussing wage determination are as follows:

1. To understand the forces underlying the general level of wage rates in the United States.

2. To see how wage rates are determined in particular labor markets and therefore to discuss several representative labor market models.

3. To discuss the economic effects of the minimum wage.

4. To assess the impact of unions upon the structure and level of wages.

5. To explain wage differentials.

6. To introduce and briefly discuss the concept of investment in human capital.

Throughout this chapter we shall rely upon the marginal productivity theory of Chapter 31 as an explanation of labor demand.

MEANING OF WAGES

Wages, or wage rates, are the price paid for the use of labor. Economists often employ the term "labor" broadly to apply to the payments received by (1) workers in the narrow sense of the term, that is, blue- and white-collar workers of infinite variety, (2) pro-

fessional people—physicians, lawyers, dentists, teachers, and so forth, and (3) small businessmen—barbers, plumbers, television repairmen, and a host of retailers—for the labor services they provide in operating their own businesses. This broad definition of labor, incidentally, encompasses individuals who would be considered as profit receivers in national income accounting. Hence, under this definition, wages would clearly amount to more than two-thirds of the national income.

Though in practice wages may take the form of bonuses, royalties, commissions, and monthly salaries, we shall use the term "wages" to mean wage rates per unit of time—per hour, per day, and so forth. This designation has the advantage of reminding us that the wage rate is a price paid for the use of units of labor service. It also permits us to distinguish clearly between "wages" and "earnings," the latter depending upon wage rates and the number of hours or weeks of labor service supplied in the market. It is important, too, to make a distinction between money wages and real wages. *Money wages* are simply the amount of money received per hour, per day, per week, and so forth. *Real wages,* on the other hand, are the quantity of goods and services which one can obtain with his money wages; real wages are the "purchasing power" of money wages. Obviously one's real wages depend upon his money wages and the prices of the goods and services he buys. Note that money wages and real wages need not move together. For example, money wages may rise and real wages simultaneously decline if product prices rise more rapidly than do money wages. Unless otherwise indicated, our discussion will be couched in terms of real wage rates by making the simple assumption that the level of product prices is constant.

GENERAL LEVEL OF WAGES

Wages tend to differ among nations, among regions, among various occupations, and among individuals. Wage rates are vastly higher in the United States than in China or India; wage rates are generally higher in the North and East of the United States than in the South; plumbers are paid more than cotton pickers; physician Abrams may earn three times as much as physician Bennett for the same number of hours of work.

Our approach will involve moving from the general to the specific. In this section we are concerned with explaining why the general level of wages is higher in the United States than in foreign nations. This explanation will be largely applicable to regional wage differences within nations. In the following section we seek to explain wages in terms of markets for specific types of labor. In both these discussions a supply and demand approach will offer the most fruitful results.

The general level of wages, like the general level of prices, is a composite concept encompassing a wide range of different specific wage rates. This admittedly vague concept is a useful point of departure in making and explaining international and interregional wage comparisons. Statistical data indicate that the general level of real wages in the United States is higher than that of any other nation. The simplest explanation of this fact is that in the United States the demand for labor has been great in relation to the supply.

Let us look behind these forces of demand and supply. We know that the demand for labor—or any other resource—depends upon its productivity. The greater the productivity of labor, the greater the demand for it. And, given the total supply of labor, the stronger the demand, the greater the level of real wages. The demand for American labor has been high because American labor is highly productive. But why the high productivity? The reasons are several:

1. American workers are used in conjunction with large amounts of capital equipment. For example, the average American worker in manufacturing is assisted by over $30,000 worth of machinery and equipment.

2. Natural resources are very abundant in relation to the size of the labor force. The United States is richly endowed with arable land, basic mineral resources, and ample sources of industrial power.

3. The level of technological advance is generally higher in the United States than in foreign nations. American workers in most industries not only use more capital equipment but better (that is, technologically superior) equipment than do foreign workers. Similarly, work methods are steadily being improved through detailed scientific study and research.

4. The health, vigor, education and training, work attitudes, and adaptability of American workers to the discipline of factory production are generally superior to those of the labor of other nations. This means that, even with the same quantity and quality of natural and capital resources, American workers typically would be somewhat more efficient than their foreign brethren.

5. Less tangible yet important items underlying the high productivity of American labor are (*a*) the effi-

FIGURE 32·1 OUTPUT PER HOUR AND REAL AVERAGE HOURLY EARNINGS

Over a long period of years there has been a close relationship between real hourly wages and output per man hour. (*Economic Report of the President, 1964*, p. 89, and Department of Labor data.)

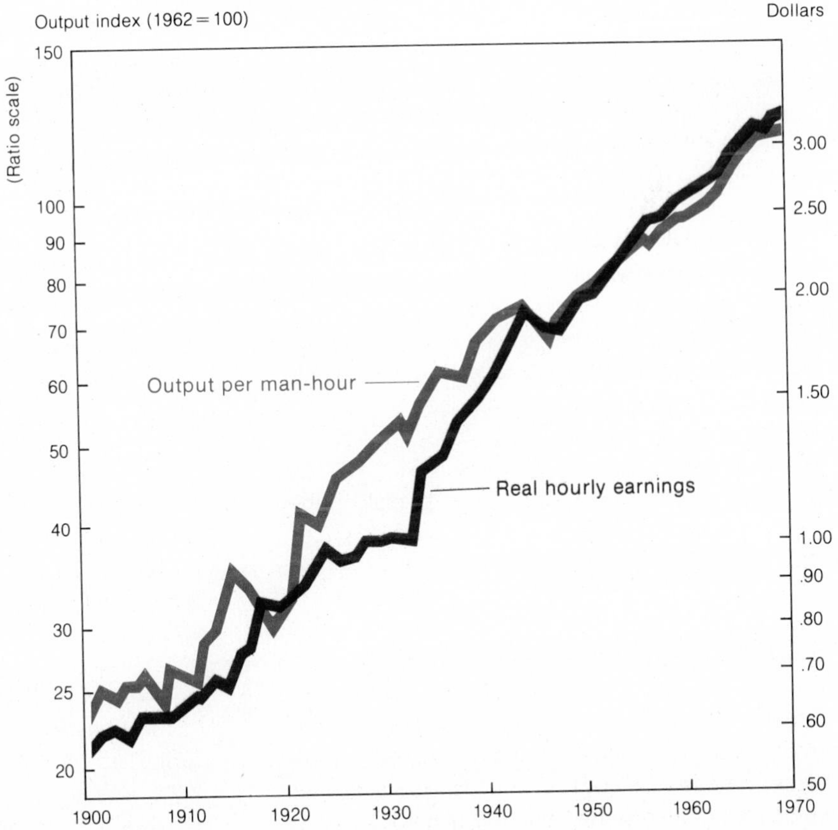

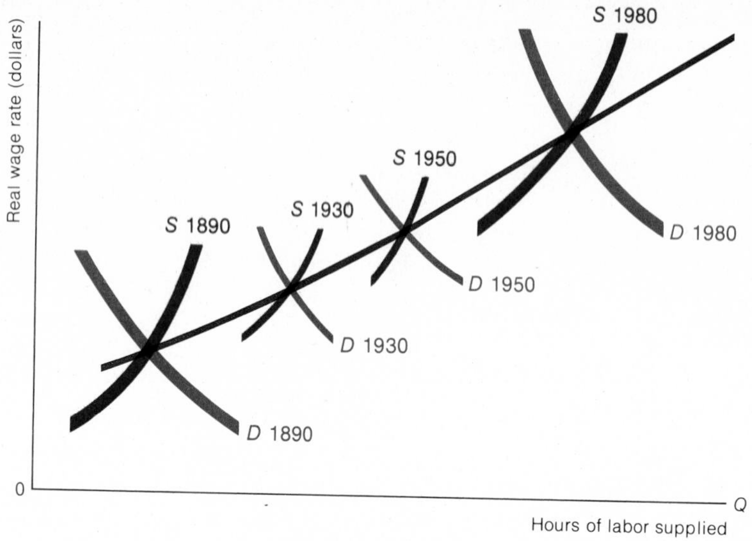

FIGURE 32·2 THE SECULAR TREND OF REAL WAGES IN THE UNITED STATES

The productivity of American labor has increased substantially in the long run, causing the demand for labor to increase in relation to the supply. The result has been increases in real wages.

ciency and flexibility of American management, (*b*) a business, social, and political environment which puts great emphasis upon production and productivity, and (*c*) the vast size of the domestic market, which provides the opportunity for firms to realize mass-production economies.

The reader will recognize that the aforementioned factors are merely a restatement of the cornerstones of economic growth (Chapter 20). It is also notable that the productivity of labor depends to a very great degree upon considerations other than the quality of labor itself. Specifically, a worker's productivity is determined largely by the quantity and quality of the property resources at his disposal.

The dependence of real hourly wages upon the level of productivity is indicated in Figure 32·1. Note the relatively close relationship in the long run between real hourly wages and output per man-hour in nonfarm private industries. When one recalls that real income and real output are two ways of viewing the same thing, it is no surprise that income per worker can only increase at about the same rate as output per worker.

But simple supply and demand analysis suggests that, even if the demand for labor is strong in the United States, increases in the supply of labor will cause the general level of wages to decline over time. It is certainly true that the American population and the labor force have grown significantly over the decades. However, these increases in the supply of labor have been more than offset by increases in the demand for labor stemming from the productivity-increasing factors discussed above. The result has been a long-run, or secular, increase in wage rates, as suggested by Figure 32·2.

WAGES IN PARTICULAR LABOR MARKETS

We now turn from the general level of wages to the wage structure, that is, to the system of specific wage rates which the general level of wages comprises.

The question now is this: What determines the wage rate received by some specific type of worker? Demand and supply analysis again provides the most revealing approach. Our analysis covers some half-dozen basic market models.

Competitive model

Let us suppose that there are many—say, 200—firms demanding a particular type of semiskilled or skilled labor.[1] The total, or market, demand for this labor can be determined by summing the labor demand curves (the MRP curves) of the individual firms, as suggested in Figure 32·3*a* and *b*. On the supply side of the picture we assume there is no union; workers compete freely for available jobs. The supply curve for a particular type of labor will be upsloping, reflecting the fact that, in the absence of unemployment, hiring firms as a group will be forced to pay higher wage rates to obtain more workers. Why? Because the firms must bid these workers away from other industries and other localities. Within limits, workers have alternative job opportunities; that is, they may work in other industries in the same locality, or they may work in their present occupations in different cities or states. In a full-employment economy the group of firms in this particular labor market must pay higher and higher wage rates to attract this type of labor away from these alternative job opportunities.

The equilibrium wage rate and the equilibrium level of employment for this type of labor are obviously determined by the intersection of the labor demand and labor supply curves. In Figure 32·3*b* the equilib-

[1] These firms need not be in the same industry; industries are defined in terms of the products they produce and not the resources they employ. Thus firms producing unupholstered furniture, window and door frames, and cabinets will all demand carpenters.

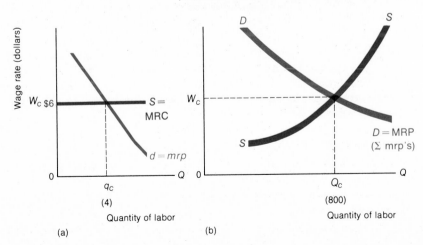

FIGURE 32·3 THE SUPPLY OF, AND THE DEMAND FOR, LABOR TO A SINGLE COMPETITIVE FIRM (*a*) AND IN A COMPETITIVE MARKET (*b*)

In a competitive labor market the equilibrium rate W_c and number of workers employed Q_c are determined by supply *SS* and demand *DD*, as shown in (*b*). Because this wage rate is given to the individual firm hiring in the market, its labor supply curve, *S* = MRC, is perfectly elastic, as in (*a*). The firm finds it most profitable to hire workers up to the MRP = MRC point.

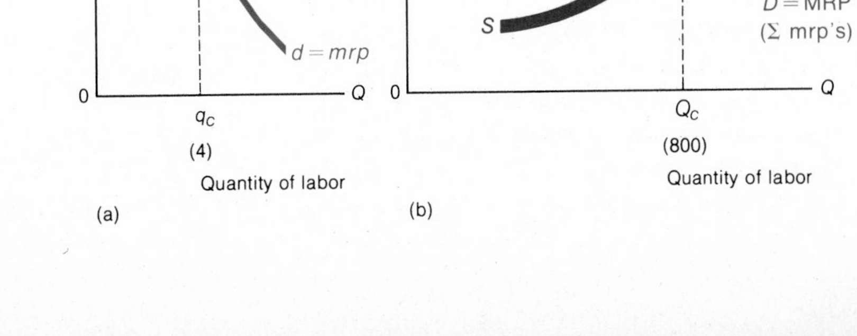

TABLE 32·1 THE SUPPLY OF LABOR: PURE COMPETITION IN THE HIRE OF LABOR (*hypothetical data*)

(1) Units of labor	(2) Wage rate	(3) Total labor cost (wage bill)	(4) Marginal resource (labor) cost
1	$6	$ 6	$6
2	6	12	6
3	6	18	6
4	6	24	6
5	6	30	6
6	6	36	6

rium wage rate is W_c ($6), and the number of workers hired is Q_c (800). To the individual firm the wage rate W_c is given. Each of the many hiring firms employs such a small fraction of the total available supply of this type of labor that none can influence the wage rate. Technically, the supply of labor is perfectly elastic to the individual firm, as shown by *S* in Figure 32·3*a*. Each individual firm will find it profitable to hire workers up to the point at which the going wage rate is equal to labor's MRP. This is merely an application of the MRP = MRC rule developed in Chapter 31. (Indeed, the demand curve in Figure 32·3*a* is based upon Table 31·1.) As Table 32·1 indicates, if the resource price is given to the individual firm, the marginal cost of that resource (MRC) will be constant and equal to resource price. In this case the wage rate and hence the marginal cost of labor are constant to the individual firm. Each additional worker hired adds precisely his wage rate to the firm's total resource cost. The firm then will maximize its profits by hiring workers to the point at which their wage rate, and therefore marginal resource cost, equals their marginal revenue product. In Figure 32·3*a* the "typical" firm will hire q_c (4) workers.

Monopsony model

But in many labor markets workers are not hired competitively. Rather, employers are *monopsonists;* that is, they have some monopolistic buying power. In some instances the monopsonistic power of employers is virtually complete in the sense that there is only one major employer in a labor market. For example, the economies of some towns and cities depend almost entirely upon one major firm. A silver mining concern may be the basic source of employment in a remote Colorado town. A New England textile mill, a Wisconsin paper mill, or a farm-belt food processor may provide a large proportion of the employment in its locality. In other cases *oligopsony* may prevail; three or four firms may each hire a large portion of the supply of labor in a particular market. Our study of oligopoly correctly suggests that there is a strong tendency for oligopsonists to act in concert—much like a monopsonist—in hiring labor.

The important point is this: When a firm hires a considerable portion of the total available supply of a particular type of labor, its decision to employ more or fewer workers will affect the wage rate paid to

that labor. Specifically, if a firm is large in relation to the labor market, it will have to pay a higher wage rate in order to obtain more labor. For simplicity's sake let us suppose there is only one employer of a particular type of labor in a specified geographic area. Obviously, the labor supply curve to that firm and the total supply curve for the labor market are identical. This supply curve, for reasons already made clear, is upsloping, indicating that the firm must pay a higher wage rate to attract more workers. This is shown by *SS* in Figure 32·4. The supply curve is in effect the average-cost-of-labor curve from the firm's point of view; each point on it indicates the wage rate (cost) per worker which must be paid to attract the corresponding number of workers.

But the higher wages involved in attracting additional workers will also have to be paid to all workers currently employed at lower wage rates. If not, labor morale will surely deteriorate, and the employer will be plagued with serious problems of labor unrest because of the wage-rate differentials existing for the same job. Costwise the payment of a uniform wage to all workers will mean that the cost of an extra worker—the marginal resource (labor) cost (MRC) —will exceed the wage rate by the amount necessary to bring the wage rate of all workers cur-

FIGURE 32·4 THE WAGE RATE AND LEVEL OF EMPLOYMENT IN A MONOPSONISTIC LABOR MARKET

In a monopsonistic labor market the employer's marginal resource (labor) cost curve (MRC) lies above the labor supply curve (*S*). Equating MRC with labor demand MRP at point *b*, the monopsonist will hire Q_m workers (as compared with Q_c under competition) and pay the wage rate W_m (as compared with the competitive wage W_c).

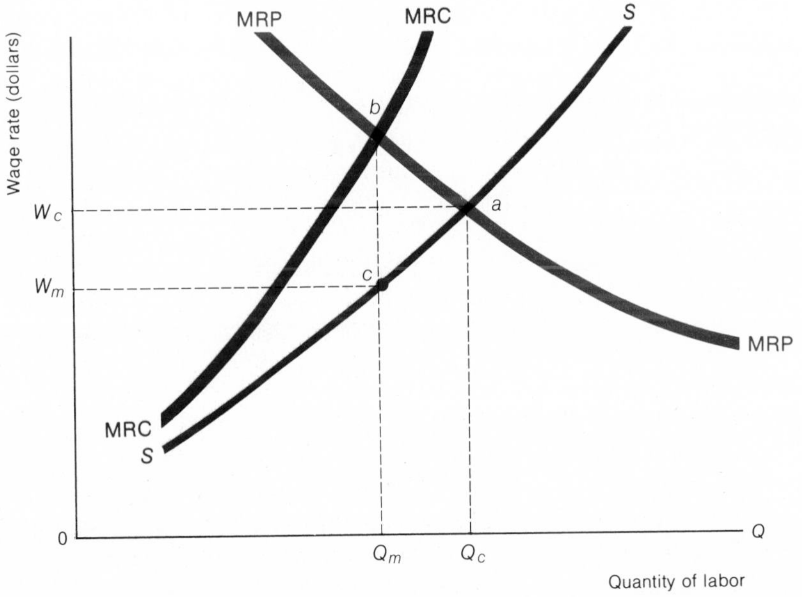

TABLE 32·2 THE SUPPLY OF LABOR: MONOPSONY IN THE HIRE OF LABOR
(hypothetical data)

(1) Units of labor	(2) Wage rate	(3) Total labor cost (wage bill)	(4) Marginal resource (labor) cost
1	$ 6	$ 6	$ 6
2	7	14	8
3	8	24	10
4	9	36	12
5	10	50	14
6	11	66	16

rently employed up to the new wage level. Table 32·2 illustrates this point. One worker can be hired at a wage rate of $6. But the hire of a second worker forces the firm to pay a higher wage rate of $7. Marginal resource (labor) cost is $8—the $7 paid the second worker plus a $1 raise for the first worker. Similarly, the marginal labor cost of the third worker is $10—the $8 which must be paid to attract him from alternative employments plus $1 raises for the first two workers. The important point is that to the monopsonist, marginal resource (labor) cost will exceed the wage rate. Graphically, the MRC curve (columns 1 and 4 in Table 32·2) will lie above the average cost, or supply, curve of labor (columns 1 and 2 in Table 32·2). This is shown graphically in Figure 32·4. How much labor will the firm hire, and what wage rate will it pay? To maximize profits the firm will equate marginal resource (labor) cost with the MRP. The number of workers hired by the monopsonist is indicated by Q_m, and the wage rate paid, W_m, is indicated by the corresponding point on the resource supply, or average-cost-of-labor, curve. It is particularly important to contrast these results with those which a competitive labor market would have yielded. With competition in the hire of labor, the level of employment would have been greater (Q_c), and the wage rate would have been higher (W_c). It simply does not pay the monopsonist to hire workers up to the point at which the wage rate and labor's MRP are equal. Other things being equal, he maximizes his profits by hiring a smaller number of workers and thereby paying a less than competitive wage rate. In the process society gets a smaller output,[2] and workers get a wage rate less by *bc* than their marginal revenue product. Just as a monopolistic seller finds it profitable to restrict product output to realize an above-competitive price for his goods, so the monopsonistic employer of resources finds it profitable to restrict employment so as to depress wage rates and therefore costs, that is, to realize below-competitive wage rates.

Will a monopsonistic employer also be a monopo-

[2] This is analogous to the monopolist's restricting output as he sets product price and output on the basis of marginal revenue, not product demand. In this instance resource price is set on the basis of marginal labor (resource) cost, not resource supply.

listic seller in the product market? Not necessarily. The New England textile mill may be a monopsonistic employer, yet face severe domestic and foreign competition in selling its product. In other cases—for example, the automobile and steel industries—firms have both monopsonistic and monopolistic (oligopolistic) power. How does the presence of monopoly or oligopoly power affect our analysis of a monopsonistic labor market? The answer is: through the labor demand curve. If the monopsonistic employer is also a restrictive monopoly or oligopoly, we can expect the resource demand curve of Figure 32·4 to be depressed. The result will be a wage rate even lower than W_m and a volume of employment less than Q_m. On the other hand, a progressive monopoly or oligopoly may entail a resource demand curve to the right of that shown in Figure 32·4, with the result that the wage rate and level of employment will exceed W_m and Q_m. In short, monopoly (oligopoly) power will depress or increase labor demand, depending upon whether the monopoly is restrictive or progressive.

Some union models

Thus far we have been content to assume that workers are actively competing in the sale of their labor services. In a good many markets, workers sell their labor services collectively through unions. To envision the economic impact of unions in the simplest context, let us suppose a union is formed in an otherwise competitive labor market. That is, a union is now bargaining with a relatively large number of employers. Later we shall consider the case where the union faces a large single employer.

Unions seek many goals. The basic objective, however, is to raise wage rates. The union can pursue this objective in several different ways.

Increasing the demand for labor From the union's point of view, the most desirable technique for raising wage rates is to increase the demand for labor. As shown in Figure 32·5, an increase in the demand for labor will result in both higher wage rates and a larger number of jobs. The relative sizes of these increases will depend upon the elasticity of labor supply. Classic examples are the International Ladies' Garment Workers Union and the Amalgamated Clothing Workers Union, both of which have positively assisted clothing firms to increase their productivity. The New York locals of the ILGWU have even assisted employers in financing advertising campaigns to bolster the demand for their products. And it is no accident that some unions have vigorously supported their employers in seeking to maintain protective tariffs designed to exclude competing foreign products. The American Watch Workers Union is a case in point. Some unions have sought to expand the demand for labor by forcing make-work, or "featherbedding," rules upon employers. Prior to recent court rulings, the Railway Brotherhoods forced railroads to hire train crews of a certain minimum size; diesel engines had to have a fireman even though there was no fire.

But the opportunity for unions to increase the demand for labor is limited. The main reason is obvious: As noted in our earlier discussion of the general level of wages, the basic forces underlying the productivity and therefore the demand for labor are largely outside the control of labor unions. The quantity and quality of the capital equipment with which labor is combined are the basic determinants of labor productivity in most firms, and this is a matter over which unions typically have little or no control. It should be noted, too, that in many of the instances in which unions have pleaded for tariff protection and have practiced featherbedding, the situation has been that of a union's attempting to forestall anticipated declines in the demand for labor rather than actually increasing the existing demand for a particular type of labor. This comment seems pertinent to the watchmakers and the Railway Brotherhoods, both of which find themselves in the unfortunate position of being employed in declining industries or faced with job-destroying technological advances. In view of these considerations it is not surprising that union efforts to increase wage rates have concentrated upon the supply side of the market.

Exclusive or craft unionism Unions may boost wage rates by reducing the supply of labor, that is,

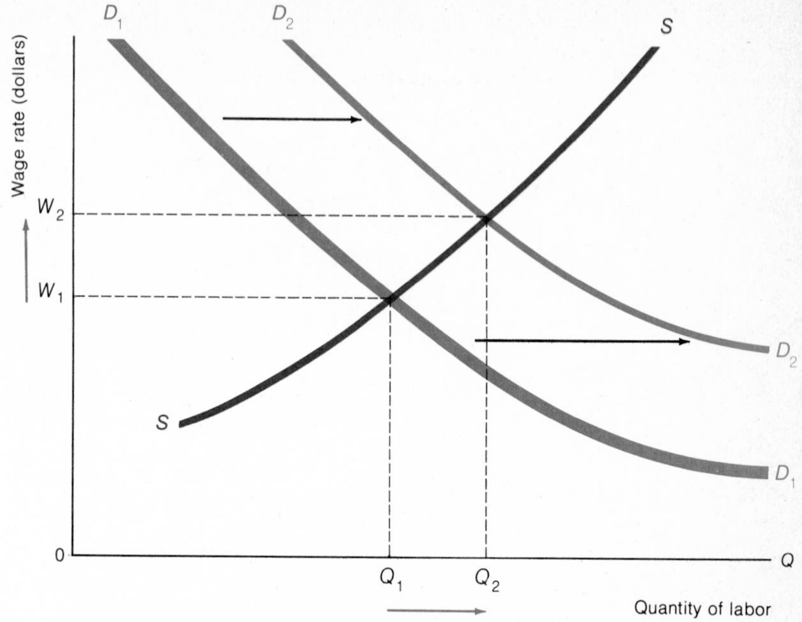

FIGURE 32·5 UNIONS AND THE DEMAND FOR LABOR

When unions can increase the demand for labor (D_1D_1 to D_2D_2), higher wage rates (W_1 to W_2) and a larger number of jobs (Q_1 to Q_2) can be realized.

by shifting the supply curve of a particular type of labor to the left. Historically, the labor movement has favored policies designed to restrict the supply of labor to the economy as a whole in order to bolster the general level of wages. Labor unions have supported legislation which has (1) restricted immigration, (2) reduced child labor, (3) encouraged compulsory retirement, (4) enforced a shorter workweek, and so forth.

More relevant for present purposes is the fact that specific types of workers have adopted through unions a host of techniques designed to restrict their numbers. This has been especially true of *craft unions*—that is, unions which comprise workers of a given skill, such as carpenters, bricklayers, plumbers, and printers. These unions have in many instances forced employers to agree to hire only union workers, thereby giving the union virtually complete control of the supply of labor. Then, by following restrictive membership policies—long apprenticeships, exorbitant initiation fees, the limitation or flat prohibition of new members—the union causes an artificial restriction of the labor supply. As indicated in Figure 32·6, this results in higher wage rates. For obvious reasons this approach to achieving wage increases might be called "exclusive" unionism. Higher wages are the result of excluding workers from the union and therefore from the supply of labor.

Inclusive or industrial unionism Most unions, however, do not attempt to limit their membership. On the contrary, they seek to organize all available

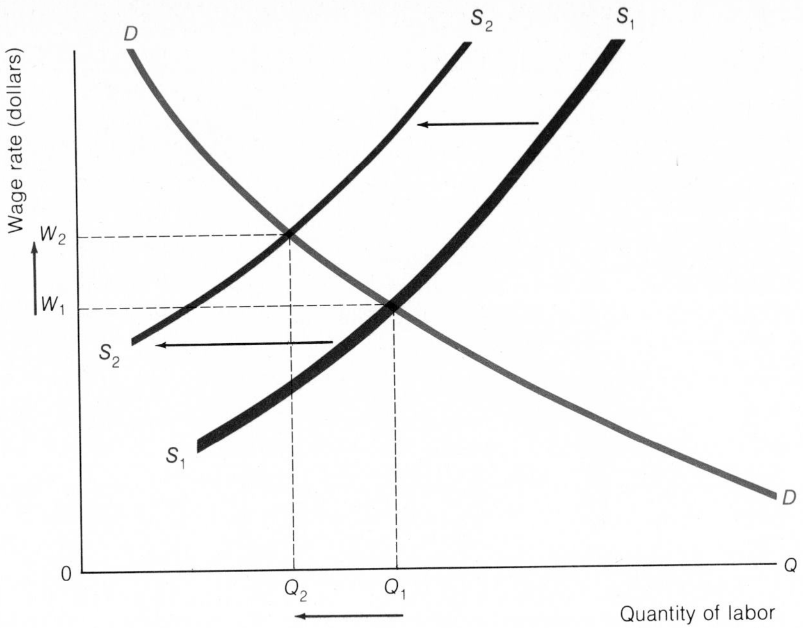

FIGURE 32·6 EXCLUSIVE OR CRAFT UNIONISM

By reducing the supply of labor (S_1S_1 to S_2S_2) through the use of restrictive membership policies, exclusive unions achieve higher wage rates (W_1 to W_2). However, the restriction of labor supply also reduces the number of workers employed (Q_1 to Q_2).

or potential workers. This is characteristic of the so-called *industrial unions*—unions such as the automobile workers and steelworkers which include all unskilled, semiskilled, and even skilled workers in a given industry. A union can afford to be exclusive when its members are skilled craftsmen for whom substitute workers are not readily available in quantity. But a union that comprises largely unskilled and semiskilled workers will undermine its own existence by limiting its membership and thereby causing numerous highly substitutable nonunion workers to be readily available for employment.

If an industrial union is successful in including virtually all workers in its membership, firms will be under great pressure to come to terms at the wage rate demanded by the union. Why? Because the union can obviously deprive the firm of its entire labor supply.

Inclusive unionism is illustrated graphically in Figure 32·7. Initially the competitive equilibrium wage rate is W_c, and the level of employment is Q_c. Now an industrial union is formed, and it imposes a higher, above-equilibrium wage rate of, say, W_u. The imposition of this wage rate changes the supply curve of

labor to the firms from the preunion *SS* curve to the postunion $W_u aS$ curve shown by the heavy blue line.[3] No workers will be forthcoming at a wage rate less than that demanded by the union. If the employers decide it is better to pay this higher wage rate than to suffer a strike, they will cut back on employment from Q_c to Q_u. In other words, the above-equilibrium wage rate will cause some unemployment of union workers in this particular labor market.

Needless to say, this unemployment effect constitutes an important restraining influence upon the union in formulating its wage demands. A union cannot expect to maintain solidarity within its ranks if it seeks a wage rate so high that the result will be joblessness for 20, 30, or 40 percent of its members. The elasticity of labor demand is the basic consideration in determining the amount of unem-

[3] Technically, the imposition of the wage rate W_u makes the labor supply curve perfectly elastic over the $W_u a$ range in Figure 32·7. If employers hire any number of workers within this range, the union-imposed wage rate is effective and must be paid, or the union will supply no labor at all—the employers will be faced with a strike. If the employers want a number of workers in excess of $W_u a$ (which they never will when the union sets an above-equilibrium wage rate), they will have to bid up wages above the union's minimum.

FIGURE 32 · 7 INCLUSIVE OR INDUSTRIAL UNIONISM

By organizing virtually all available workers and thereby controlling the supply of labor, inclusive industrial unions may impose a wage rate, such as W_u, which is above the competitive wage rate W_c. The effect is to change the labor supply curve from *SS* to $W_u aS$. At the W_u wage rate employers will cut employment from Q_c to Q_u.

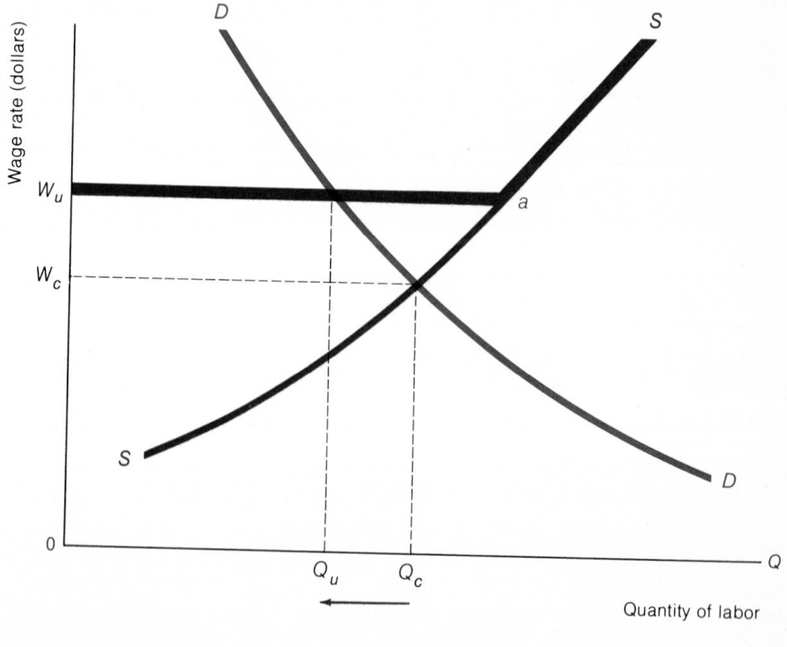

ployment which will accompany a wage hike: the more inelastic the demand for labor, the smaller will be the resulting unemployment. You will recall from Chapter 31 that the determinants of the elasticity of labor demand include the elasticity of demand for the product, the portion of total costs for which wages account, and the substitutability of other resources for labor. It is notable that substitutability and hence elasticity vary directly with time. That is, over a short period of time—say a few weeks or months—a firm may hire about the same number of workers after a pay hike as it did before. But then, as the months pass, employers have sufficient time to substitute labor-saving capital equipment for workers. The practical significance of this is that, as substitution occurs, workers will be *gradually* unemployed and typically will drift into other jobs and other geographic areas. And with the absence of job opportunities, new workers entering the labor force will be discouraged from entering this line of work. For these reasons the unemployment restraint upon union wage demands may be less pressing than it first appears to be.

Even though industrial unions encourage rather than restrict membership, there is clearly a restrictive aspect to this analysis. But in contrast to the practices of exclusive unionism, the restriction of employment here is made not by directly influencing labor supply, but by enforcing an above-equilibrium wage rate and allowing the market to restrict the number of jobs available.

The United Mine Workers provide an excellent illustration of how an industrial union can achieve substantial wage increases, but only at the cost of a reduction in the number of jobs the industry has to offer. The UMW has clearly done an outstanding job of raising wage rates for miners. In December 1970, the average weekly earnings of bituminous coal workers were $195.64, as compared with $138.05 for all manufacturing industries. However, employment in December 1970 stood at only 146,000 in bituminous coal as compared with a peak figure of almost 705,000 in 1923 and 400,000 in 1945. There is little doubt that UMW wage pressure has been a major cause of this decline in the number of jobs. Labor costs constitute about 70 percent of total costs in bituminous coal production. Hence, union-imposed wage increases have increased the total cost of coal sharply in relation to those of oil and gas, causing a sharp drop in coal output and in the number of jobs the industry can offer. Simultaneously, the increased cost of labor has accelerated the substitution of machinery for labor, causing further diminutions in the number of miners employed. The UMW has explicitly taken the position that the fattening of pay envelopes which it has brought about more than compensates for the sacrifice of jobs that these high wages have entailed.[4]

Bilateral monopoly model

Now let us suppose that a union is formed in a labor market which is not competitive but monopsonistic. Let us assume further that the union is a strong industrial union. In other words, let us combine the monopsony model with the inclusive unionism model. The result is a case of *bilateral monopoly.* The union is a monopolistic "seller" of labor in that it can exert an influence over wage rates; it faces a monopsonistic employer (or combination of oligopsonistic employers) of labor who can also affect wages. Is this an extreme or special case? Not at all. In such important industries as steel, automobiles, meatpacking, and farm machinery, "big labor"—one huge industrial union—bargains with "big business"—a few huge industrial giants.

This situation can be shown graphically as in Figure 32·8, which merely superimposes Figure 32·7 upon 32·4. The monopsonistic employer will seek the wage rate W_m and the union presumably will press for some above-equilibrium wage rate such as W_u. Which of these two outcomes will result? We cannot say with any certainty. The outcome is logically indeterminate in the sense that economic theory does not explain what the resulting wage rate will be. We

[4]See Gordon F. Bloom and Herbert R. Northrup, *Economics of Labor Relations*, 5th ed. (Homewood, Ill.: Richard D. Irwin, Inc., 1965), pp. 469–472.

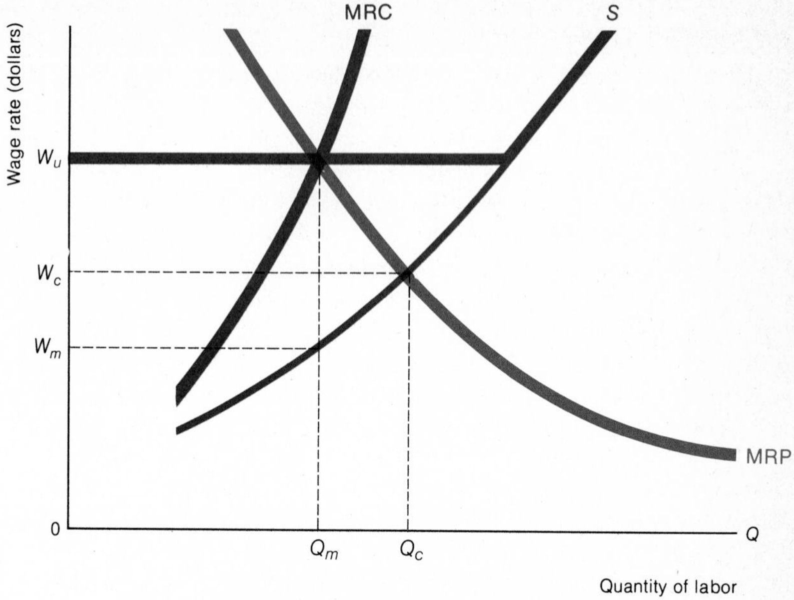

FIGURE 32·8 BILATERAL MONOPOLY IN THE LABOR MARKET

When a monopsonistic employer seeks the wate rate W_m and the inclusive union he faces seeks an above-equilibrium wage rate such as W_u, the actual outcome is logically indeterminate.

should expect the resulting wage to lie somewhere between W_m and W_u. Beyond that, about all we can say is that the party with the most bargaining power and the most effective bargaining strategy will be able to get his opponent to agree to a wage close to that which he seeks.[5]

These comments suggest another important feature of the bilateral monopoly model. The kind of labor market we are here describing may be an important manifestation of countervailing power. If either the union or management prevailed in this market—that is, if the actual wage rate were determined at W_u or W_m—employment would be restricted to Q_m, which is obviously below the competitive level. But now let us suppose the countervailing power of the union roughly offsets the original monopsony power of management and a bargained wage rate of about W_c, which is the competitive wage, is agreed upon. Once management agrees to this wage rate, its incentive to restrict employment disappears; no longer can the employer depress wage rates by restricting employment. Thus management equates the bargained wage rate W_c (= MRC) with MRP and finds it most profitable to hire Q_c workers. In short, with monopoly on both sides of the labor market, it may be possible that the resulting wage rate and level of employment will be closer to competitive levels than if monopoly existed on only one side of the market.

[5] Economists are now actively developing a number of bargaining theories. The ambitious reader should consult Carl M. Stevens, *Strategy and Collective Bargaining Negotiation* (New York: McGraw-Hill Book Company, 1963).

The minimum-wage controversy

Since the passage of the Fair Labor Standards Act in 1938, the United States has had a Federal minimum wage. The analysis of the effects of union wage-fixing raises the much-debated question of the efficacy of this minimum-wage legislation as an antipoverty device.

Critics of the minimum wage, reasoning in terms of Figure 32·7, contend that the imposition of effective (above-equilibrium) minimum wages will simply push employers back up their MRP or labor demand curves because it is now profitable to hire fewer workers. The higher wage costs may even force some firms out of business. The result is that many of the poor, low-wage workers whom the minimum wage was designed to help will now find themselves out of work. Is it not obvious, critics contend, that a worker who is unemployed at a minimum wage of $1.60 per hour is clearly worse off than if he were employed at the market wage rate of, say, $1.20 per hour? Some discharged workers may drift off into other labor markets and find employment, but in so doing they increase the supply of labor in these markets and tend to depress wage rates therein.

Advocates of the minimum wage allege that critics have analyzed the impact of the minimum wage in an unrealistic context. Figure 32·7, advocates claim, presumes a competitive and static market. The imposition of a minimum wage in a monopsonistic labor market (Figure 32·8) suggests that the minimum wage can increase wage rates without causing unemployment; indeed, higher minimum wages may even result in more jobs by eliminating the monopsonistic employer's motive to restrict employment. Furthermore, the imposition of an effective minimum wage may increase labor productivity, shifting the labor demand curve to the right and offsetting any unemployment effects which the minimum wage might otherwise induce. But how might a minimum wage increase productivity? First, a minimum wage may have a *shock effect* upon employers. That is, firms using low-wage workers may tend to be inefficient in the use of labor; the higher wage rates imposed by the minimum wage will presumably force these firms to use labor more efficiently, and so the productivity of labor rises. Second, it is argued that higher wages will tend to increase the incomes and therefore the health, vigor, and motivation of workers, making them more productive.

Which view is correct? It is hard to say, because empirical studies of the effects of increases in the minimum wage run into the problems of distinguishing the effects of the minimum wage per se from the effects of other developments—growth, inflation, recession—occurring in the economy. On balance, however, the evidence seems to suggest that periodic increases in the minimum wage are followed by employment declines in affected industries. The other side of the coin, of course, is that those who remain employed receive higher incomes and tend to escape poverty. The overall antipoverty effect of the minimum wage may thus be a mixed, ambivalent one. Those who lose their jobs are plunged deeper into poverty; those who remain employed tend to escape poverty.[6]

Do unions raise wages?

Our union models (Figures 32·5, 32·6, and 32·7) all imply that unions have the capacity to raise wage rates. Has this in fact been the case? Has unionization caused wage rates to be higher than otherwise? On the face of it this might seem to be a naïve question, the answer to which must be an unqualified "Yes." Don't we persistently read of specific unions successfully bargaining for substantial wage gains? And is it not also true that the average wage of organized workers is 10 to 15 percent higher than for unorganized workers?

Yet one may have second thoughts. For example, we know that the long-run trend of real wages in the United States has been upward (Figure 32·2). So the real question is not simply whether unions successfully bargain for wage increases, but rather whether these increases are larger, smaller, or about the same

[6] See Lloyd G. Reynolds, *Labor Economics and Labor Relations*, 5th ed. (Englewood Cliffs, N.J.: Prentice-Hall, Inc., 1970), pp. 273–275, for an excellent summary of recent empirical work on the minimum wage.

as those which the subtle, undramatic workings of the market would have brought about. Although the UAW now negotiates wage increases in the automobile industry, we must keep in mind that wages rose in the industry long before it was organized in 1938–1941 and undoubtedly would have risen substantially in the past several decades had the industry remained unorganized. Furthermore, there is the simple historical fact that unions have been most successful in organizing the more prosperous industries. Many of the now-unionized high-wage industries were also high-wage industries *before* they were organized. Again the automobile industry is a good illustration. Thus one may legitimately ask if the fact that unionized industries pay higher wages than unorganized industries is the result of unionization or, alternatively, if unions are getting credit for wage increases attributable to favorable market forces.

As with the minimum wage, empirical studies which attempt to compare union and nonunion wages encounter severe conceptual obstacles, and their conclusions are invariably questionable. For example, if it is found that unionized carpenters get $4.00 per hour in city X while unorganized carpenters earn only $3.00 per hour in city Y, can we say with certainty that the differential is attributable to unionization or to some other variable? Perhaps city X is a dynamic, growing economic area, while city Y is in a depressed area where wage rates are generally low. Given such difficulties, it is not too surprising that labor economists offer a tentative two-part response to the question "Do unions raise wages?" The first portion of the response compares union with nonunion wages; the second is concerned with the impact of unions upon the wage level of all workers.

1. *Unions have raised wages modestly in organized industries. Specifically, through unions organized workers have probably achieved wage rates 10 to 15 percent higher than would otherwise be the case.*[7] Although this is not an insignificant accomplishment, the advantage is not so large as to imply that the formation of unions and the determination of wages through collective bargaining somehow permit labor to break free of market restraints and to establish wage rates largely at their discretion. In particular, higher wages tend to mean fewer jobs, and this inverse relationship between wages and employment acts as an important constraint upon the wage-raising activities of labor unions.

2. *On the other hand, unions have probably had little or no perceptible impact upon the average level of real wages received by labor—both organized and unorganized—taken as a whole.*

At first glance these two conclusions might seem inconsistent. But they need not be if the wage gains of organized workers are at the expense of unorganized workers. Imagine an economy divided into two sectors which are identical except that one is unionized and the other is not. Now, consistent with generalization 1 above, suppose the organized sector realizes a 10 percent money-wage increase. Assuming constant productivity, unit production costs and the price level will rise by 10 percent in the organized sector and, given constant prices in the unorganized sector, the overall price level will rise by 5 percent. This will obviously mean that real wages have risen by 5 percent in the organized sector, because money wages have gone up 10 percent, and the price level by only 5 percent. But it also means a *fall* in real wages in the unorganized sector, where money-wage rates have assumedly remained constant while the price level has gone up by 5 percent. This tendency for higher union wages to result in lower nonunion wages may be reinforced by shifts in labor supply. Higher wages in the organized sector will tend to reduce employment therein; these unemployed workers may then seek jobs in the unorganized sector. This increase in the supply of labor will tend to depress the money and real wages of workers in the unorganized sector. In short, higher real wage rates for organized workers may well be at the expense of unorganized workers with the result that the average level of real wages for labor as a whole is unaltered. Stated differently, the tight relationship between productivity and the average level of real wages shown in Figure 32·1 correctly suggests that unions have little power to raise real wage rates for labor as a whole. But Figure 32·1 is an average

[7] Albert Rees, *The Economics of Trade Unions* (Chicago: The University of Chicago Press, 1962), p. 79.

relationship and is therefore compatible with certain groups of (union) workers getting higher relative wages if other (nonunion) workers are simultaneously getting lower real wages.

WAGE DIFFERENTIALS

We have discussed the general level of wages and the role of supply and demand in a series of specific labor market situations. Yet the wage differences which persist between different occupations and different individuals in the same occupations still have not been explained. Why does a corporate executive or a movie star receive $200,000 per year while garbage collectors and retail clerks get a paltry $2,000 per year? Table 32·3 indicates the substantial wage differentials which exist among certain common occupational groups. Our problem is to explain these differences.

Once again the forces of supply and demand provide a general answer. If the supply of a particular type of labor is very great in relation to the demand for it, the resulting wage rate will be low. But if demand is great and the supply very small, wages will be very high. Though it is a good starting point, this supply and demand explanation is not particularly revealing. We want to know *why* supply and demand conditions differ in various labor markets. To do this we must probe those factors which lie behind the supply and demand of particular types of labor.

If (1) all workers were homogeneous, (2) all jobs were equally attractive to workers, and (3) labor markets were perfectly competitive, all workers would receive precisely the same wage rate. As such, this is not a particularly startling statement. It merely suggests that, in an economy having one type of labor and in effect one type of job, competition will result in a single wage rate for all workers. The statement is important in that it suggests the reasons why wage rates do differ in practice. (1) Workers are not homogeneous. They differ in capacities and in training and, as a result, fall into noncompeting occupational groups. (2) Jobs vary in attractiveness; the nonmonetary aspects of various jobs are not the same. (3) Labor markets are typically characterized by imperfections.

TABLE 32·3 AVERAGE HOURLY AND WEEKLY EARNINGS IN SELECTED INDUSTRIES, DECEMBER 1970

Industry	Average hourly gross earnings	Average weekly gross earnings
Contract construction	$5.43	$203.63
Bituminous coal	4.76	195.64
Motor vehicles	4.51	183.11
Printing and publishing	4.05	153.50
Chemicals	3.80	157.32
Fabricated metals	3.67	149.37
Food products	3.27	133.42
Retail trade	2.47	83.73
Apparel and finished textiles	2.44	85.89
Laundries and dry cleaning	2.24	79.97
Hotels and motels	2.06	69.42

Source: Department of Labor, *Earnings and Employment*, February 1971.

Noncompeting groups

Workers are not homogeneous; they differ tremendously in their mental and physical capacities and in their education and training. Hence, at any point in time the labor force can be thought of as falling into a number of *noncompeting groups,* each of which may be composed of several or possibly just one occupation for which the members of this group qualify. For example, a relatively small number of workers have the ability—the capacity and the training—to be brain surgeons, concert violinists, and research chemists. Few people have the inherent capacity to enter these occupations, and even fewer have the financial means of acquiring the necessary training. The result is obviously that the supplies of these particular types of labor are very small in relation to the demand for them and the resulting wages and salaries are high. These and similar groups do not compete with each other or with other skilled or semiskilled workers. The violinist does not compete with the surgeon, nor does the garbage collector or retail clerk compete with either the violinist or the surgeon.

This is not to say that each of the thousands of specific occupations in the United States constitutes a noncompeting group of workers or that workers fall into isolated occupational compartments. A number of unskilled or semiskilled occupations may well fall into one noncompeting group. For example, gasoline station attendants, farmhands, and unskilled construction workers may all fall into the same group, because each is capable of doing the others' jobs. Yet none of the workers in this group currently offers severe competition for printers or electricians, who find themselves in other, more exclusive groups.

It should be noted, too, that the lack of competition between noncompeting groups of workers is actually a matter of degree. *Within limits* unskilled construction workers can be substituted for printers and electricians. Furthermore, this substitutability will be greater over a period of time than it is in the short run; over time workers may move from one noncompeting group to another as they are able to develop their native capacities through education and training. The assembly-line worker who has an IQ of 130 may become an accountant or lawyer by going to night school. But here another obstacle arises: education is a costly business. Our ambitious but low-income laborer does not have the same opportunity of entering the higher-paid occupational groups as do the offspring of the lawyers and accountants who are already in those groups. And, needless to say, differences in inherent capacities provide an even more permanent obstacle to occupational mobility. In short, both native capacity and the opportunity to train oneself are unequally distributed, causing the wage differentials of noncompeting groups to persist.

The concept of noncompeting groups is a flexible one; it can be applied to various subgroups and even to specific individuals in a given group. Some especially skilled surgeons are able to command wages considerably in excess of their run-of-the-mill colleagues who perform the same operations. Wilt Chamberlain, Lew Alcindor, and a few others demand and get salaries many times that of the average professional basketball player. Why? Because in each instance their colleagues are only imperfect substitutes.

Equalizing differences

Now if a group of workers in a particular noncompeting group is equally capable of performing several different jobs, one might expect that the wage rate would be identical for each of these jobs. But this is not the case. A group of high school graduates may be equally capable of becoming bank clerks or unskilled construction workers. But these jobs pay different wages. In virtually all localities construction laborers receive better wages than do beginning bank clerks.

These differences can be explained on the basis of the *nonmonetary aspects* of the two jobs. The construction job involves dirty hands, a sore back, the hazard of accidents, and irregular employment, both seasonally and cyclically. The banking job entails a white shirt, pleasant air-conditioned surroundings, and little fear of injury or layoff. Other things being equal, it is easy to see why workers will prefer picking

up a deposit slip rather than a shovel. The result is that construction contractors must pay higher wages than banks to compensate for the unattractive nonmonetary aspects of construction jobs. These wage differentials are sometimes called *equalizing differences,* because they must be paid to compensate for the nonmonetary differences in various jobs.

Market imperfections

The notion of noncompeting groups helps explain wage differentials between different jobs for which limited numbers of workers are qualified. Equalizing differences aid in understanding wage differentials on different jobs for which workers in the same noncompeting group are equally qualified. Market imperfections in the form of various immobilities help explain wage differences paid on identical jobs.

1. **Geographic immobilities** Workers take root geographically. They are reluctant to leave friends, relatives, and associates, to force their children to change schools, to sell their houses, and to incur the costs and inconveniences of adjusting to a new job and a new community. Geographical mobility is likely to be particularly low for older workers who have seniority rights and substantial claims to pension payments upon retirement. Then, too, workers who may be willing to move may simply be ignorant of job opportunities and wage rates in other geographic areas. As Adam Smith noted almost two centuries ago, "a man is of all sorts of luggage the most difficult to be transported." The reluctance or inability of workers to move obviously causes geographic wage differentials for the same occupation to persist.

2. **Artificial institutional immobilities** Geographic immobilities may be reinforced by artificial restrictions on mobility which are imposed by institutions. In particular, we have already noted that craft unions find it to their advantage to restrict their membership. After all, if carpenters and bricklayers become plentiful, the wages they can command will decline. Thus the low-paid nonunion carpenter of Brush, Colorado, may be willing to move to Chicago in the pursuit of higher wages. But his chances of successfully doing so are slim. He will be unable to get a union card; and no card, no job. The professions impose similar artificial restraints. For example, at most universities individuals lacking advanced degrees are simply not considered for employment as teachers. Quite apart from one's competence as a teacher and command of the subject matter, a "union card"—an M.A. or Ph.D.—is the first requisite for employment.

3. **Sociological immobilities** Finally, we must acknowledge sociological immobilities. Despite recent regulatory legislation to the contrary, women workers frequently receive less pay than men working at the same job. The consequence of racial and ethnic discrimination is that Negroes, Mexicans, Jews, and other minority groups are often forced to accept lower wages on given jobs than fellow workers receive.

A final point: It is more than likely that all three considerations—noncompeting groups, equalizing differences, and market imperfections—will play a role in the explanation of actual wage differentials. For example, the differential between the wages of a physician and a construction worker is largely explainable on the basis of noncompeting groups. Physicians fall into a noncompeting group where, because of mental and financial requisites to entry, the supply of labor is small in relation to demand, and wages are therefore high. In construction work, where mental and financial prerequisites are much less significant, the supply of labor is great in relation to demand and wages low as compared with those of physicians. However, were it not for the unpleasantness of the construction worker's job and the fact that his craft union pursues restrictive membership policies, the differential would probably be even greater than it is.

INVESTMENT IN HUMAN CAPITAL

We have just seen that the concept of noncompeting groups is a very important part of the explanation of wage differentials. Let us probe more carefully the

question of why these noncompeting groups exist. Although inherent mental and physical differences are undoubtedly important, noncompeting groups—and therefore wage differentials—exist to a large extent because of differing amounts of investment in human capital. Generally speaking, investments in human capital are of three kinds. Common to all is the fact that each contributes to the productivity and therefore the market value of the future flows of labor services that an individual can provide. First, expenditures on *education*—including general and specific education, formal and informal education, on-the-job training, and so forth—is the most obvious and perhaps most important kind of investment in human capital. Education contributes to a labor force which is more skilled and more productive. Second, expenditures on *health* are also significant. Better health—the consequence of expenditures on preventive medicine and medical care, improved diets, and better housing—gives rise to greater vigor, longevity, and higher productivity among workers. Finally, expenditures on *mobility* which shift workers from relatively low to relatively high productivity uses are a less obvious form of investment in human capital. Like education, the geographic movement of workers may raise the value of their labor services. In short, each employable person has embodied within himself a future flow of labor services. The productivity and therefore the market value of his labor services (his wages) are determined to a great degree by the amount which the individual, his family, and society have chosen to invest in his education and training, his health, and his location.

Now it may seem odd or even repugnant to analyze investment in manpower in the same way one would explore the decision to buy a machine. But in fact the two decisions are very similar. The purchase of a machine (real capital) will give rise to a flow of additional net revenues over the estimated years of life of the machine. Potential investors can discount this lifetime flow of earnings, compare their present value with the cost of the machine, and determine a rate of return on the investment. By contrasting this rate of return with the expected rates on alternative investments, a firm can rationally decide whether the purchase of this machine is profitable and, if so, whether it is the most profitable purchase of real capital it might make. Similarly, one might subject the decision to invest in, say, a four-year college education to the same analysis. Figure 32·9 makes it clear that the families of those with larger investments in education achieve higher incomes initially and throughout their work careers than do those who have made smaller educational investments. The economic return from investment in a college education can therefore be regarded as the additional lifetime earnings which the college graduate will earn as compared with the earnings of a high school graduate. The present value of this difference in lifetime earnings can be determined, compared with the cost of the education, and the rate of return on the investment in the college education can be calculated. This rate will be useful to the individual in determining whether investment in additional educa-

FIGURE 32·9 EDUCATION LEVELS AND FAMILY INCOME

Investment in education yields a return in the form of an income differential enjoyed both initially and throughout one's worklife. (U.S. Bureau of the Census).

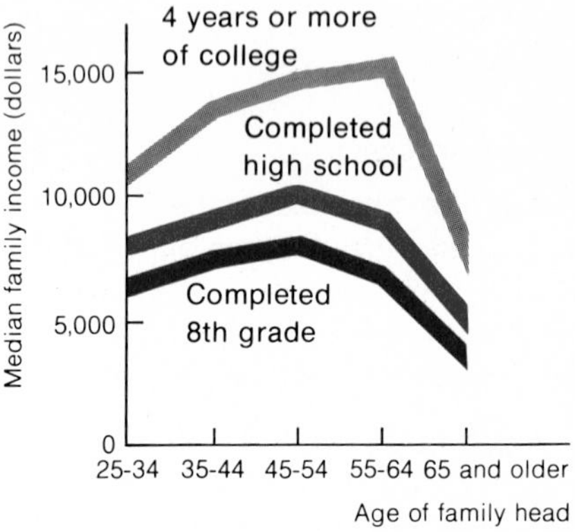

tion is economically justifiable. It will be helpful to society in determining the proper balance between investment in men and investment in machinery.[8]

The notion of investment in human capital has considerable explanatory value. We have emphasized that different individuals and groups in our society have been accorded differing amounts of investment in their education, health, and mobility; the consequence of this is the existence and persistence of noncompeting groups and wage differentials. Furthermore, the lower earnings of Negroes and other minority groups in the United States are in part a reflection of past discrimination in investment in human capital; on the average less has been invested in the education and training of blacks than of whites (see Table 38·3). Much the same can be said of women. Women, their parents, and society at large have taken the view that most women will spend only a portion of their adult lives in the labor market and therefore have felt it less important to invest in their training and education. These decisions are reflected in lower earnings for women.[9] The fact that wages in the South have been persistently lower than in the rest of the country is partly the result of different levels of spending on education. The concept of human capital is also a part of the explanation of the rising level of real wages which the United States has enjoyed historically (Figure 32·2). If our economy had the same natural resources and real capital we now possess, but a completely uneducated and untrained labor force or even a labor force with the educational and skill levels of, say, 1929, our GNP and real wage levels would obviously be much lower than is now the case. Recall (Table 21·5) that improved education and training are of increasing importance in explaining the economic growth which our economy has enjoyed.

[8]For a discussion of the many problems in estimating the returns from investment in human capital see the articles by Theodore W. Schultz, Harry G. Shaffer, and William G. Bowen in M. Blaug (ed.), *Economics of Education 1* (Baltimore: Penguin Books, 1968).

[9]This, of course, is not to deny that other forms of discrimination on the basis of race and sex are important in explaining wage differences between whites and blacks, on the one hand, and men and women, on the other.

SUMMARY

1. Wages are the price paid per unit of time for the services of labor.

2. The general level of wages in the United States is higher than in foreign nations because the demand for labor is great in relation to the supply. The strong demand for American labor is based upon its high productivity, which in turn depends upon the quantity and quality of the capital equipment and natural resources used by labor, the quality of the labor force itself, the efficiency of management, a favorable sociopolitical environment, and the vast size of the domestic market. Over time these factors have caused the demand for labor to increase in relation to the supply, accounting for the long-run rise of real wages in the United States.

3. The determination of specific wage rates depends upon the structure of the particular labor market. In a competitive market the equilibrium wage rate and level of employment will be determined by the intersection of labor supply and demand.

4. Under monopsony, however, the marginal-resource-cost curve will lie above the resource supply curve, because the monopsonist must bid up wage rates in hiring extra workers and pay that higher wage to *all* workers. The monopsonist will hire fewer workers than he will under competitive conditions in order to achieve less than competitive wage rates (costs) and thereby greater profits.

5. A union may raise competitive wage rates by ***a.*** increasing the derived demand for labor, ***b.*** restricting the supply of labor through exclusive unionism, and ***c.*** directly enforcing an above-equilibrium wage rate through inclusive unionism.

6. In many important industries the labor market takes the form of bilateral monopoly; that is, a strong union "sells" labor to a monopsonistic employer. Although the outcome of this labor market model is logically indeterminate, it might entail an important manifestation of the concept of countervailing power.

7. Economists disagree about the desirability of the

minimum wage as an antipoverty mechanism. While it causes unemployment for some low-income workers, it raises the incomes of others who retain their jobs.

8. Unionized workers have probably realized wage rates 10 to 15 percent higher than would otherwise have been the case; but there is little evidence to suggest that unions have been able to raise the average level of real wages for labor as a whole.

9. Wage differentials are largely explainable in terms of ***a.*** noncompeting groups, that is, differences in the capacities and training of different groups of workers, ***b.*** equalizing differences, that is, wage differences which must be paid to offset nonmonetary differences in jobs, and ***c.*** market imperfections in the form of geographic, artificial, and sociological immobilities.

10. Investment in human capital takes the form of expenditures on education and training, health, and location. The concept of human capital is useful in explaining ***a.*** wage differentials based upon occupation, race, sex, and geography and ***b.*** the long-run rise in the average level of real wages.

QUESTIONS AND STUDY SUGGESTIONS

1. Explain why the general level of wages is higher in the United States than in foreign nations. What is the most important single factor underlying the long-run increase in the average real wage rates in the United States? What, if anything, does this suggest concerning the ability of unions to raise real wages?

2. *a.* Describe wage determination in a labor market in which workers are unorganized and many firms are actively competing for the services of labor. Show this situation graphically, using W_1 to indicate the equilibrium wage rate and Q_1 to show the number of workers hired by the firms as a group.

b. Suppose now that the formerly competing firms form an employers' association which hires labor as a monopsonist would. Describe verbally the impact upon wage rates and employment. Adjust the graph drawn for question 2*a*, showing the monopsonistic wage rate and employment level as W_2 and Q_2, respectively.

3. Describe the techniques which unions might employ to raise wages. Evaluate the desirability of each from the viewpoint of ***a.*** the union and ***b.*** society as a whole. Explain: "Craft unionism directly restricts the supply of labor; industrial unionism relies upon the market to restrict the number of jobs."

4. Assume a monopsonistic employer is paying a wage rate of W_m and hiring Q_m workers, as is indicated in Figure 32·8. Now suppose that an industrial union is formed and that the union forces the employer to accept a wage rate of W_c. Explain verbally and graphically why in this instance the higher wage rate will be accompanied by an *increase* in the number of workers hired.

5. Complete the following labor supply table for a firm hiring labor competitively.

Units of labor	Wage rate	Total labor cost (wage bill)	Marginal resource (labor) cost
1	$14	$____	$____
2	14	____	____
3	14	____	____
4	14	____	____
5	14	____	____
6	14	____	

a. Show graphically the labor supply and marginal resource (labor) cost curves for this firm. Explain the relationships of these curves to one another.

b. Compare these data with the labor demand data of question 2 in Chapter 31. What will the equilibrium wage rate and level of employment be? Explain.

c. Now redetermine this firm's supply schedule for labor on the assumption that it is a monopsonist and that, although it can hire the first worker for $14, it must increase the wage rate by $1 to attract each successive worker. Show the new labor supply and marginal labor cost curves graphically and

explain their relationships to one another. Compare these new data with those of question 2 for Chapter 31. What will be the equilibrium wage rate and the level of employment? Why does this differ from your answer to question 5*b*?

6. A critic of the minimum wage has contended that "The effects of minimum wage legislation are precisely the opposite of those predicted by those who support them. Government can legislate a minimum wage, but cannot force employers to hire unprofitable workers. In fact, minimum wages cause unemployment among low-wage workers who can least afford to give up their small incomes." Do you agree? What bearing does the elasticity of labor demand have upon this assessment? What factors might possibly offset the unemployment effects of a minimum wage?

7. Explain: "Although unions have altered the wage structure, they have not been successful in raising the average real wage of the American labor force."

8. What are the basic considerations which help explain the wage differentials between particular labor markets?

9. Evaluate and explain these two statements:

a. "Wage differentials can be explained in terms of two factors: first, vertical immobilities, that is, obstacles to the movement of workers from one occupational level to another, and, second, horizontal immobilities, that is, factors which prevent workers from being perfectly mobile geographically."

b. "If all workers were of equal capacity and training, all jobs were equally attractive to workers, and labor markets were free of imperfections, all workers would receive the same wage rate."

10. What is meant by investment in human capital? Use this concept to explain ***a.*** wage differentials and ***b.*** the long-run rise in real wage rates in the United States.

SELECTED REFERENCES

Economic Issues, 4th ed., readings 51 and 52.

Bloom, Gordon F., and Herbert R. Northrup: *Economics of Labor Relations,* 6th ed. (Homewood, Ill.: Richard D. Irwin, Inc., 1969), chaps. 8–15.

Galenson, Walter: *A Primer on Employment and Wages,* 2d ed. (New York: Random House, Inc., 1970).

McConnell, Campbell R. (ed.): *Perspectives on Wage Determination* (New York: McGraw-Hill Book Company, 1970), parts 2, 4, and 5.

Reynolds, Lloyd G.: *Labor Economics and Labor Relations,* 5th ed. (Englewood Cliffs, N.J.: Prentice-Hall, Inc., 1970), chaps. 1–9, 23, and 24.

Thurow, Lester: *Investment in Human Capital* (Belmont, Calif.: Wadsworth Publishing Company, 1970).

33

THE PRICING AND EMPLOYMENT OF RESOURCES: RENT, INTEREST, AND PROFITS

The discussion of wages in Chapter 32 is rather lengthy. In contrast the discussions of the income shares—rent, interest, and profits—found in the present chapter are relatively brief. There are two reasons for this difference in emphasis.

1. Wage incomes are clearly the major component of the national income. Statistics tell us that about 70 percent of the national income is in the form of wage and salary incomes, the remainder accruing as rent, interest, and profit incomes. And because economists define wages more broadly and interest, rent, and profits more narrowly than do national income accountants, labor's share is understated in national income figures, and the size of the other three shares is overstated.

2. The economic theories of rent, interest, and profit are very unsettled; there are honest differences among authorities as to definitions, explanations, and implications where nonwage incomes are concerned. For these two reasons we shall concentrate upon the basic features of rent, interest, and profit determination and forgo the many controversial points and the often ambiguous details which are encountered in more advanced discussions of these income shares.

ECONOMIC RENT

To most people the term "rent" means the seemingly exorbitant sum one must pay for a two-bedroom apartment or a dormitory room. To the businessman "rent" is a payment made for the use of a factory building, machinery, or warehouse facilities. Closer examination finds these commonsense definitions of rent to be confusing and ambiguous. Dormitory room rent, for example, includes interest on the money capital the university has borrowed from the government or private individuals in financing the dormitory's construction, wages for custodial and maid service, utility payments, and so forth. Economists therefore use the term "rent" in a narrower but less ambiguous sense: *Economic rent is the price paid*

for the use of land and other natural resources which are completely fixed in total supply. It is the unique supply conditions of land and other natural resources—their fixed supply—which makes rental payments distinguishable from wage, interest, and profit payments.

Let us examine this feature and some of its implications through simple supply and demand analysis. To avoid complications, assume, first, that all land is of the same grade or quality—in other words, that each available acre of land is equally productive. Suppose, too, that all land has just one use, being capable of producing just one product—say, corn. And assume that land is being rented in a competitive market—that many corn farmers are demanding and many landowners offering land in the market.

In Figure 33·1, *SS* indicates the supply of arable farmland available in the economy as a whole and D_2 the demand of farmers for the use of that land. As with all economic resources, demand is a derived demand. It is downsloping because of the law of diminishing returns and the fact that, for farmers as a group, product price must be diminished to sell additional units of output.

FIGURE 33·1 THE DETERMINATION OF LAND RENT

Because the supply of land and other natural resources is perfectly inelastic (*SS*), demand is the sole active determinant of land rent. An increase (D_2 to D_1) or decrease (D_2 to D_3) in demand will cause considerable changes in rent (R_2 to R_1 and R_2 to R_3). If demand is very small (D_4) relative to supply, land will be a "free good."

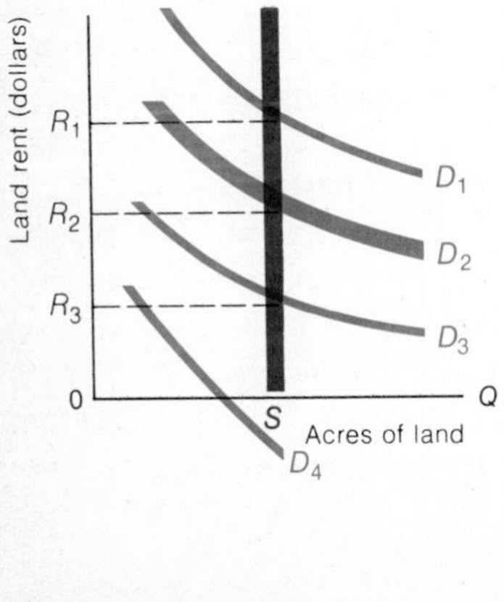

The unique feature of our analysis is on the supply side: for all practical purposes the supply of land is perfectly inelastic, as reflected in *SS*. Land has no production cost; it is a "free and nonreproducible gift of nature." The economy has so much land, and that's that. It is true, of course, that within limits existing land can be made more usable by clearing, drainage, and irrigation. But these programs constitute capital improvements and not changes in the amount of land as such. Furthermore, such variations in the usability of land are a very small fraction of the total amount of land in existence and therefore do not undermine the basic argument that land and other resources are in virtually fixed supply.

The fixed nature of the supply of land means that demand is the only active determinant of land rent; supply is passive. And what determines the demand for land? Those factors discussed in Chapter 31—the price of the product grown on the land, the productivity of land (which depends in part upon the quantity and quality of the resources with which land is combined), and the prices of those other resources which are combined with land. If in Figure 33·1 the demand for land should increase from D_2 to D_1 or decline from D_2 to D_3, land rent would change from R_2 to R_1 or R_3, but the amount of land supplied would remain unchanged at *OS*. In technical terms there is a large price effect and no quantity effect when the demand for land changes. If the demand for land is only D_4, land rent will be zero; that is, land will be a "free good," because it is not scarce enough in relation to the demand for it to command a price. This situation was approximated in the free-land era of American history. Changes in economic rent will have no impact upon the amount of land available; the supply of land is simply not augmentable.

Land rent is a surplus

The perfect inelasticity of the supply of land must be contrasted with the relative elasticity of such property resources as apartment buildings, machin-

ery, and warehouses. These resources are not fixed in total supply. A higher price will give entrepreneurs the incentive to construct and offer larger quantities of these property resources. Conversely, a decline in their prices will induce suppliers to allow existing facilities to depreciate and not be replaced. The same general reasoning applies to the total supply of labor. Within limits, a higher average level of wages will induce more workers to enter the labor force, and lower wages will cause them to drop out of the labor force. In other words, the supplies of nonland resources are upsloping, or, stated differently, the prices paid to such resources perform an *incentive function.* A high price provides an incentive to offer more; a low price, to offer less.

Not so with land. Rent serves no incentive function, because the total supply of land is fixed. If rent is $10,000, $500, $1, or $0 per acre, the same amount of land will be available to society to make a contribution to production. Rent, in other words, could be eliminated without affecting the productive efficiency of the economy. For this reason economists consider rent to be a *surplus,* that is, a payment which is not necessary to ensure that land will be available to the economy as a whole.

A single tax on land?

If land is a free gift of nature, costs nothing to produce, and would be available even in the absence of rental payments, why should rent be paid to those who by historical accident or inheritance happen to be landowners? Socialists have long argued that all land rents are unearned incomes. Therefore, they argue, land should be nationalized—owned by the state—so that any payments for its use can be utilized by the state in furthering the well-being of the entire population rather than a landowning minority. In the United States criticism of rental payments has taken the form of a *single-tax movement* which gained considerable support in the late 1800s. Spearheaded by Henry George's provocative book, *Progress and Poverty* (1879), this reform movement centered upon the notion that economic rent might be taxed away completely without impairing the available supply of land or therefore the productive potential of the economy as a whole.

George observed that, as population grew and the geographic frontier closed, landowners came to enjoy larger and larger rents from their landholdings. These increments in rent were simply the result of a growing demand for a resource whose supply was perfectly inelastic; some landlords were receiving fabulously high incomes, not through rendering any productive effort, but simply as the result of holding advantageously located land. Henry George took the position that these increases in land rent belonged to the economy as a whole; he held that land rents should be taxed away and spent for public uses.

To illustrate: If the relevant supply and demand conditions for land are as shown by SS and D_2 in Figure 33·1, land rent will be OR_2 per acre. Suppose government imposes a tax equal to, say, half of the rent per acre. That is, a tax of R_2R_3 per acre is levied where $R_2R_3 = \frac{1}{2}OR_2$. Now, you will recall from Chapter 24 the generalization that the more inelastic the supply of a product (or resource), the larger will be the portion of a tax borne by the producer (or resource owner). In the case of land, the supply is completely inelastic, so all the tax must be borne by the landowner; it is impossible to shift any part of the tax to renters. Of course, the landowner could withdraw his land from production, but this would simply mean no rental income for him at all!

As George saw it, the fact that the tax burden remained on the landowner was perfectly justifiable; land rent, after all, was unearned income. Population growth and the closing of the geographic frontier were conferring windfall rental income upon landowners, and government was fully justified in taxing away such rental income. Indeed, George held that there was no reason to tax away only 50 percent of the landowner's unearned rental income. Why not take 70 or 90 or 99 percent? In seeking popular support for his ideas on land taxation, Henry George proposed that taxes on rental income be the only tax levied by government.

Criticisms Critics of the single tax on land make these points: First, current levels of government

spending are such that a land tax alone would clearly not bring in enough revenue; it cannot be considered realistically as a *single* tax. Second, as noted earlier, in practice most income payments combine elements of interest, rent, wages, and profits. Land is typically improved in some manner by productive effort, and economic rent cannot be readily disentangled from payments for capital improvements. As a practical matter, it would be very difficult to determine how much of any given income payment is actually rent. Third, the question of unearned income goes beyond land and land ownership. One can readily argue that many individuals and groups other than landowners benefit from the receipt of "unearned" income associated with the overall advance of the economy. For example, consider the capital gains income received by an individual who, some fifteen or twenty years ago, chanced to purchase (or inherit) stock in a firm which has experienced rapid growth (say, IBM or Xerox). How is this income different from the rental income of the landowner?

Renewed interest On the other hand, there is a renewed interest in land taxation on the part of urban economists, city planners, and public officials. Many of them contend that a strong case can be made on grounds of both equity and efficiency for a heavy tax on land values.

1. With respect to *equity* they argue, like Henry George, that much of the value of urban land results from population growth, community development, and, very significantly, public decisions to invest in roads, schools, and water, gas, and sewer utilities. Furthermore, zoning changes made by public bodies can sharply increase the value of affected land overnight. This result is that landowners, who are typically high-income people initially, realize large "unearned increments" of income with little or no expenditure of effort or money. Because the value of urban land is largely determined by public decision and public investment, it is held that the community should recapture the resulting increases in land value through taxation and use these revenues for public purposes.

2. The *efficiency* argument is that a tax on land value has a neutral effect upon the allocation or use of land; unlike most other taxes a tax on land value does not contribute to the malallocation of resources. For example, glancing back at Figures 24•5 and 24•6, we find that sales and excise taxes have the effect of increasing prices and reducing output. Assuming allocative efficiency initially, the allocation of resources to affected products would obviously be less efficient as a result of the tax. Assume now that Figure 24•5 shows the demand for and supply of labor in a competitive market. The imposition of an income tax of a certain amount per worker per day would have the effect of reducing the supply of labor, distorting the workers' preferred balance between work and leisure away from the optimum. The tax would cause workers to offer less productive effort and to take more leisure. In comparison, the complete inelasticity of the supply of land means that a tax on land rent has no effect on price or output and therefore does not alter resource allocation. "The most profitable use of the [land] site before the tax is imposed continues to be the most profitable use."[1] This outcome is in contrast to property taxes on buildings—the major alternative revenue source for cities—wherein there is an adverse incentive effect; that is, taxes on buildings lower their return to investors and discourage their construction. We will find in Chapter 37 that high property taxes on buildings have been an important factor in the physical deterioration of the central city of many major metropolitan areas. Hence, more and more urban economists favor greater use of taxes on land and less use of property taxes on buildings.

Productivity differences and alternative uses

Our analysis thus far has proceeded upon the assumption that all units of land are of the same grade. In practice, this simply is not so. Different acres vary greatly in productivity. These productivity differences stem primarily from differences in soil fertility and such climatic factors as rainfall and temperature. It is these factors which explain why Iowa soil is excellently suited to corn production, the plains of

[1]Dick Netzer, *Economics and Urban Problems* (New York: Basic Books, Inc., 1970), p. 197.

eastern Colorado are much less so, and desert wasteland of New Mexico is incapable of corn production. These differences in productivity will be reflected in resource demand. Competitive bidding by farmers will establish a high rent for the very productive Iowa land. The less productive Colorado land will command a much lower rent, and the New Mexico land no rent at all. Location may be equally important in explaining differences in land rent. Other things being equal, renters will pay more for a unit of land which is strategically located with respect to materials, labor, and customers than for a unit of land whose location is remote from these markets. Witness the extremely high land rents in large metropolitan areas.

The rent differentials to which quality differences in land would give rise can be easily seen by looking at Figure 33·1 from a slightly different point of view. Suppose, as before, that only one agricultural product, say corn, can be produced on four grades of land, *each* of which is available in the fixed amount *OS.* When combined with identical amounts of capital, labor, and other cooperating resources, the productivity—or, more specifically, the marginal revenue productivity—of each grade of land is reflected in demand curves D_1, D_2, D_3, and D_4. Grade 1 land is the most productive, as reflected in D_1, whereas grade 4 is the least productive, as is shown by D_4. The resulting rents for grades 1, 2, and 3 land will obviously be R_1, R_2, and R_3, respectively, the rent differentials mirroring the differences in the productivity of the three grades of land. Grade 4 land is so poor in quality that it would simply not pay farmers to bring it fully into production; it would be a "free" and only partially used resource.

We have also supposed thus far that land has only one use. Actually, we know that land usually has a number of alternative uses. An acre of Iowa farmland may be useful in raising not only corn, but also wheat, oats, milo, and cattle, or it may be useful as a site for a house or factory. What is the importance of this obvious point? It indicates that, although land is a free gift of nature and has no production cost from the viewpoint of society as a whole, the rental payments of individual producers are *costs.* The total supply of land will be available to society even if no rent at all is paid for its use, but, from the standpoint of individual firms and industries, land has alternative uses, and therefore payments must be made by specific firms and industries to attract that land from those other uses. Such payments by definition are costs. Once again the fallacy of composition has entered our discussion. From the standpoint of society there is no alternative but for land to be used by society. Therefore to society, rents are a surplus, not a cost. But because land has alternative uses, the rental payments of corn farmers or any other individual user are a cost; such payments are required to attract land from alternative uses.

INTEREST

Interest is the price paid for the use of money or, better yet, for the use of loanable funds. Three related aspects of this income payment are immediately notable:

1. Because it is paid in kind, interest is typically stated as a percentage of the amount of money being borrowed rather than as an absolute amount. It is less clumsy to say that one is paying 5 percent interest than to proclaim that interest is "$50 per year per $1,000." Furthermore, stating interest as a percentage facilitates the comparison of interest paid on loans of much different absolute amounts. By expressing interest as a percentage we can immediately compare an interest payment of, say, $144 per year per $2,880 and one of $600 per year per $12,000. In this case both interest payments are 5 percent—a fact not at all obvious from the absolute figures. Recall (Chapter 7) that the Truth in Lending Act calls for the uniform statement of interest costs so that borrowers will understand the interest rate they are paying.

2. Money is not an economic resource. As such, money is not productive; it is incapable of producing goods and services. However, businessmen "buy" the use of money, because money can be used to acquire capital goods—factory buildings, machinery, warehouses, and so forth. And these facilities clearly

do make a contribution to production. Thus in hiring the use of money capital, businessmen are ultimately buying the use of real capital goods. As a matter of fact, it is the expected marginal revenue productivity of capital goods which sets an upper limit upon the rate of interest businessmen will pay to obtain the funds needed for the purchase of those capital goods.

3. Though economists find it convenient to talk as if there existed a single interest rate, it must be recognized that there are actually many different rates of interest. The Federal government currently borrows at 5 to 6 percent on its long-term securities. Corporate bonds may pay 6 to 7 percent. FHA mortgage loans may entail interest rates of 7½ to 8 percent. Bank loans to consumers for automobile or refrigerator purchases may run 10 or 15 percent. Those whose credit standing forces them to borrow from consumer finance companies may pay extremely high rates—24 or 36 percent is not uncommon.

Why the differences?

1. The varying degrees of *risk* on loans are important. The greater the chance the borrower will not repay the loan, the more interest the lender will charge to compensate for this risk.

2. The *length* of a loan also affects the interest rate. Other things being equal, long-term loans usually command higher rates of interest than do short-term loans, because the long-term lender suffers the inconvenience and possible financial sacrifice of forgoing alternative uses for his money for a greater period of time.

3. Given two loans of equal length and risk, the interest rate will be higher on the smaller of the two loans. This happens because the *administrative costs* of a large and a small loan are about the same absolutely.

4. *Market imperfections* are also important in explaining some interest rate differentials. The small-town bank which monopolizes the local money market may charge high interest rates on loans to consumers because households find it inconvenient to "shop around" at banks in somewhat distant cities. The large corporation, on the other hand, is able to survey a number of rival investment houses in disposing of a new bond issue and thereby to secure the lowest obtainable rate.

To circumvent the difficulties involved in discussing the whole structure of interest rates, economists talk of "the" interest rate or the "pure" rate of interest. This pure rate is best approximated by the interest paid on long-term, virtually riskless bonds such as the long-term bonds of the United States government or of American Telephone and Telegraph. This interest payment can be thought of as being made solely for the use of money over an extended time period, because the risk factor and administrative costs are negligible and the interest on such securities is not distorted by market imperfections. The pure interest rate is currently about 6 percent.

If the interest rate can be defined as the price paid for the use of loanable funds, it is clear that to understand the determination of the rate of interest we must understand the factors which underlie the demand for, and the supply of, loanable funds.

Demand for loanable funds

Who borrows money? For what purposes? Generally speaking, businesses, households, and government are the primary demanders of loanable funds.

The great bulk of loanable funds is borrowed by *businesses* for use in the purchase of more and better capital goods. Businesses seek the use of capital goods (Chapter 3) because "roundabout production" through the use of tools and equipment increases productivity. Hence, we can draw a marginal-revenue-product curve—a capital demand curve—for the various specific types of capital goods. Like other resource demand curves, this MRP curve will diminish because of the law of diminishing returns. However, this resource demand curve is more complex than other resource demand curves, because capital goods are durable. A lathe or drill press may have a life of ten or fifteen years. Therefore, businessmen must assess as best they can the uncertainties of the future and estimate the return above acquisition, maintenance, and operating costs which the purchase of additional units of capital will probably yield.

This net *expected* return can be expressed as a percentage of the cost of the capital goods and compared with the rate of interest.

Now we found in Chapter 31 that under competition, it is profitable for a firm to purchase any resource up to the point at which the price of that resource equals its marginal revenue product. In this instance the marginal revenue productivity of a capital good is measured by the expected net return on the capital good expressed as a percentage of its cost. The price of the loanable funds required to purchase the capital good is obviously the interest rate. Hence, it will pay businessmen to demand loanable funds up to the point at which the expected net rate of return on the capital good equals the rate of interest.

Households also demand loanable funds when they wish to make purchases in excess of their current incomes and cash resources. The long-run relative increase in the production of durable goods which has taken place in our economy has encouraged the growth of consumer credit. Automobiles, refrigerators, and television sets are typically purchased on credit.

Governments—Federal, state, and local—are also major borrowers. Although this borrowing is at its zenith during wartime, governments are rather persistently borrowing against future tax revenues to finance highways, education, welfare programs, and so forth (Chapter 9). The Federal government is almost continuously in the money market as it refinances and expands the public debt.

The demand for loanable funds is clearly downsloping. Businessmen will find it profitable to purchase large amounts of capital goods when the price of loanable funds declines. Similarly, lower interest rates may encourage some increase in consumer and governmental borrowing.

Potential supply of loanable funds

There are three basic sources of loanable funds.

1. The current saving and the past savings accumulated by households are one potential source of loanable funds. In any reasonably prosperous year, households as a group will consume less than their disposable incomes, the difference being personal saving. These funds may be augmented by decreases in the liquid savings which households now hold as idle hoards; these accumulations may be drawn down and offered in the money market.

2. The current saving and accumulated savings of businesses are a major source of loanable funds. In each prosperous year, businesses save very substantial amounts in the form of depreciation charges and undistributed corporate profits. And, as with households, current business saving may be supplemented by declines in the cash hoards or bank balances of businesses. These business sources of loanable funds are often demanded for investment purposes by the firms themselves and therefore do not enter the market for loanable funds.

3. A potential source of loanable funds is newly created money, that is, money created by commercial bank lending.

Actual supply of loanable funds

We have been careful to designate the current saving and past savings of households and businesses and commercial bank lending as the *potential* supply of loanable funds. The reason is that households, businesses, and banks may not actually be willing to make these funds available to borrowers. Money, remember, is a store of value. Households and businesses may not want to offer either their current saving or any of their accumulated savings to borrowers. On the contrary, they may choose to add a portion of their current saving to their accumulated savings balances.

Having made choices as to how to divide their incomes and receipts between spending and saving, households and businesses must then decide the specific form in which to hold their savings. The basic choice is between money in the form of either idle cash or bank accounts, on the one hand, and securities of some sort, on the other. Idle cash and bank accounts are highly liquid assets; securities acquired from borrowers are somewhat less liquid. That part of savings (current or accumulated) which households and businesses want to hold as securities flows

into the money market as the supply of loanable funds. That part which households and businesses want to hold as cash obviously does not. This division depends upon the *liquidity preferences* of households and businesses. More specifically, there are three main reasons why households and businesses prefer to hold cash rather than securities:

1. There is a *transaction motive* for holding money rather than securities. Households and businesses both need a stock of cash on hand to make ordinary day-to-day purchases. Households, for example, receive a sizable chunk of income every two weeks or every month. Disbursements, on the other hand, occur more or less evenly over time. This means that households have an average money balance of some size bridging the gap between paydays. And it is simply more convenient to have one's assets in their most liquid form, that is, as idle cash balances or bank accounts, than in the form of securities. Furthermore, there are costs—brokerage fees—in transferring cash into securities and back again.

2. There is a *precautionary motive* for holding money. Households and businesses may hold cash balances to meet any rainy-day contingencies which might arise. Particularly relevant are those risks which one cannot protect himself against by purchasing insurance policies—prolonged illness, unemployment, unfavorable shifts in consumer demand, and so forth.

3. There is a *speculative motive* for holding money. At any point in time there is a certain rate of interest which households and businesses as potential suppliers of loanable funds consider to be about "normal." If the rate of interest is currently low, that is, "below normal," households and businesses may withhold a part of their savings which would otherwise flow into the money market as a part of the supply of loanable funds. They hold more money and less securities than they normally would. Why? Because they expect that the current below-normal interest rate will probably rise in the future. Hence, households and businesses refrain from supplying their current loanable funds in anticipation of a higher interest return in the future. Conversely, if the current interest rate is unusually high, that is, "above normal," households and businesses will choose to hold less money and more securities to take advantage of high current interest rates as opposed to the lower normal rate expected to prevail again in the future.

The supply of loanable funds is clearly upsloping. Though the interest rate probably does not exert a very strong influence upon the amount households and businesses save, higher and higher interest rates will induce households and businesses to be less liquid. At relatively high interest rates, households and firms will prefer to hold their assets in the form of interest-bearing securities rather than as non-interest-bearing checking accounts and idle cash balances. There is little clear-cut evidence as to how sensitive or insensitive the supply of loanable funds is to changes in the interest rate.

The interaction of the upsloping supply-of-loanable-funds curve and the downsloping demand-for-loanable-funds curve determines the equilibrium rate of interest.

Interest rate: an administered price

Though we have concluded that the interest rate is determined by the demand for, and the supply of, loanable funds, few would argue that the interest rate is genuinely a free-market price. The interest rate is actually an administered price—a price which is profoundly and purposely influenced by government. Government's influence is apparent on both the demand and the supply sides of the picture. As previously noted, government is an important borrower. Fiscal policies appropriate to recession and depression call for Federal deficits. During wartime, government assumes the dominant role on the demand side of the market for loanable funds. Finally, the Treasury is constantly refunding portions of the public debt as outstanding government bonds mature. On the supply side, the Federal Reserve authorities influence the supply of loanable funds and therefore the interest rate through the application of tight and easy money policies (Chapter 18).

The reasons why government is interested in administering the interest rate are apparent upon examination of the ways in which the interest rate may influence the operation of the economy. Specifically,

the interest rate affects both the *level* and the *composition* of investment goods production.

Interest, capital accumulation, and employment The interest rate affects the level of investment and therefore the level of employment in the economy. Other things being equal, a lowering of the interest rate will induce businessmen to increase their purchases of investment goods. This stimulates total spending and the volume of employment. Conversely, other things being equal, an increase in the interest rate will cause businessmen to cut their expenditures for capital goods, thereby causing total spending and employment to fall.

This is not to say, however, that adjustments in the interest rate brought about by changes in either the private or public components of the demand for, and supply of, loanable funds will be sufficient to alter investment spending to the level required for achieving full employment. Recall that the interest rate is only one of many forces which have a bearing upon the investment plans of businesses. The rate of technological advance, population growth, the acquisition and operating costs of capital goods, government tax and expenditure policies, the stocks of capital goods on hand, anticipated market conditions, and business confidence are all important determinants of investment. Changes in any or all of these factors may easily offset any alterations in the interest rate which government may initiate in seeking to influence investment spending and employment. Stated differently, frequent and significant fluctuations in all those factors which affect the expected marginal revenue productivity of capital goods are considerably more important than changes in the interest rate in determining the actual level of investment spending. We must conclude that there is nothing inherent in the market for loanable funds or, more specifically, the interest rate—even as influenced by government—which gives rise to the level of investment required for achieving full employment.

Interest and the allocation of capital Prices, you will recall, are rationing devices. The interest rate, being the price of loanable funds, is no exception. The interest rate performs the function of allocating money capital and therefore real capital to various firms and investment projects. It rations the available supply of loanable funds to those investment projects whose rate of return or expected profitability is sufficiently high to warrant payment of the going interest rate. If the expected marginal revenue productivity of additional real capital in industry X is 10 percent and the required loanable funds can be secured at an interest rate of 6 percent, industry X will be in a position, profitwise, to borrow and expand its capital facilities. On the other hand, if the marginal productivity of additional capital in industry Y is expected to be only 3 percent, it will be unprofitable for this industry to accumulate more capital goods. In short, the interest rate allocates money, and ultimately real capital, to those industries in which it will be most productive and therefore most profitable. Such an allocation of capital goods is obviously in the interest of society as a whole.

But the interest rate does not perform perfectly the task of rationing capital to its most productive uses. Large oligopolistic borrowers are in a better position than competitive borrowers to pass interest costs on to consumers by virtue of their ability to manipulate their prices. And, too, the sheer size and prestige of large industrial concerns might allow them to obtain money capital on favorable terms, whereas the market for loanable funds screens out less well-known firms whose profit expectations might actually be superior.

BUSINESS PROFITS AND ECONOMIC PROFITS

As is the case with rent, economists find it advantageous to define profits more narrowly than do businessmen or accountants. To most businessmen "profit" is what remains of a firm's total revenue after it has paid other individuals and firms for materials, capital, and labor supplied to the firm. To the economist this conception is too broad and therefore ambiguous. The difficulty, as the economist sees it, is that this view of profits takes into account only *explicit*

costs, that is, payments made by the firm to outsiders. It therefore ignores *implicit* costs, that is, payments to similar resources which are owned and self-employed by a firm. In other words, the businessman's concept of profits fails to allow for implicit wage, rent, and interest costs. *Economic,* or *pure, profits* are what remain after all opportunity costs—both explicit and implicit wage, rent, and interests costs and a normal profit—have been subtracted from a firm's total revenue (Chapter 26). Economic profits may be either positive or negative (losses).

An example may sharpen these comments. As the economist sees it, a farmer who owns his land and equipment and provides all his own labor is grossly overstating his economic profits if he merely subtracts his payments to outsiders for seed, insecticides, fertilizer, gasoline, and so forth, from his total receipts. Actually, much or possibly all of what remains are the implicit rent, interest, and wage costs which the farmer forgoes in deciding to self-employ the resources he owns rather than make them available in alternative employments. Interest on the capital or wages for the labor contributed by the farmer himself are no more profits than are the payments which would be made if outsiders had supplied these resources. In short, the businessman's definition and the economist's definition of profits are compatible only if the businessman includes both explicit and implicit costs in determining total costs. Economic profits are a residual—the total revenue remaining after *all* costs are paid.

Economic profits and the entrepreneur

Speaking very generally, the economist views profits as the return to a very special type of human resource—entrepreneurial ability. A part of this return, you will recall, is called a *normal profit.* This is the minimum return or payment necessary to retain the entrepreneur in some specific line of production. By definition, this normal profit payment is a cost (Chapter 26). However, we know that a firm's total revenue may exceed its total costs (explicit, implicit, and inclusive of a normal profit). This extra or excess revenue above all costs is an *economic,* or *pure, profit.* This residual—which is not a cost because it is in excess of the normal profit required to retain the entrepreneur in the industry—accrues to the entrepreneur. The entrepreneur, in other words, is the residual claimant.

Economists offer several theories to explain why this residual of economic profit might occur. As we will see in a moment, these explanations relate to:

1. The risks which the entrepreneur necessarily bears as he functions in a dynamic and therefore uncertain environment or as he undertakes innovational activity.
2. The possibility of attaining monopoly power.

Sources of economic profit

Our understanding of economic profits and the entrepreneur's functions can be both deepened and widened by describing an artificial economic environment within which pure profits would be zero. Then, by noting real-world deviations from this environment, we can lay bare the sources of economic profit.

In a purely competitive, static economy pure profits would be zero. By a static economy we mean one in which all the basic data—resource supplies, technological knowledge, and consumer tastes—are constant and unchanging. A static economy is a changeless one in which all the determinants of cost and supply data, on the one hand, and demand and revenue data, on the other, are constant. Given the static nature of these data, the economic future is perfectly foreseeable; economic uncertainty is nonexistent. The outcome of price and production policies is accurately predictable. Furthermore, the static nature of such a society precludes any type of innovational change. Under pure competition any pure profits (positive or negative) which might have existed initially in various industries will disappear with the entry or exodus of firms in the long run. All costs—both explicit and implicit—will therefore be precisely covered in the long run, leaving no residual in the form of pure profits.

The notion of zero economic profits in a static, competitive economy enhances our understanding of

profits by suggesting that the presence of profits is linked to the dynamic nature of real-world capitalism and the accompanying uncertainty. Furthermore, it indicates that economic profits may arise from a source apart from the directing, innovating, risk-bearing functions of the entrepreneur. And that source is the presence of some degree of monopoly power.

Uncertainty, risk, and profits In a dynamic economy the future is always uncertain. This means that the businessman necessarily assumes risks. Profits can be thought of in part as a reward for assuming these risks.

In linking pure profits with uncertainty and risk bearing, it is important to distinguish between risks which are insurable and those which are not. Some types of risks—for example, fires, floods, theft, and accidents to employees—are measurable in the sense that actuaries can estimate their occurrence with considerable accuracy. As a result, these risks are typically insurable. Firms can avoid, or at least provide for, these risks by incurring a small known cost in the form of an insurance premium. It is the bearing of uninsurable risks, then, which is a potential source of economic profits.

What are such uninsurable risks? Basically, they are uncontrollable and unpredictable changes in demand (revenue) and supply (cost) conditions facing the firm. Some of these uninsurable risks stem from unpredictable changes in the general economic environment or, more specifically, from the business cycle. Prosperity brings substantial windfall profits to most firms, whereas depression means widespread losses. But in addition, changes are constantly taking place in the structure of the economy. Even in a full-employment noninflationary economy, changes are always occurring in consumer tastes, resource supplies, and so forth. These changes continually alter the revenue and cost data faced by individual firms and industries, leading to changes in the structure of the business population as favorably affected industries expand and adversely affected industries contract. Changes in government policies are pertinent at both levels. Appropriate fiscal and monetary policies of government may reverse a recession, whereas a tariff may significantly alter the demand and revenue data of the protected industry.

The point is this: Profits and losses can be associated with the assumption of uninsurable risks stemming from both cyclical and structural changes in the economy.

Uncertainty, innovations, and profits The uncertainties just discussed are external to the firm; they are beyond the control of the individual firm or industry. One other extremely important dynamic feature of capitalism—innovation—occurs at the initiative of the entrepreneur. Business firms deliberately introduce new methods of production and distribution to affect their costs favorably and new products to influence their revenue favorably. The entrepreneur purposely undertakes to upset his existing cost and revenue data in a way he hopes will be profitable to him.

But once again uncertainty enters the picture. Despite exhaustive market surveys, entrepreneurs do not know in advance whether consumers actually want more horsepower in their automobiles, clothing made of paper, color television sets, three-dimensional movies, and ball-point pens. Nor do they know certainly whether a new machine will actually provide the cost economies predicted for it while it is still in the blueprint stage. Innovations purposely undertaken by entrepreneurs entail uncertainty, just as do those changes in the economic environment over which an individual enterprise has no control. In a sense, then, innovation as a source of profits is merely a special case of risk bearing.

Under competition and in the absence of patent laws, innovational profits will be temporary. Rival firms will imitate successful (profitable) innovations, thereby competing away all economic profits. Nevertheless, innovational profits may always exist in a progressive economy as new successful innovations replace those older innovations whose associated profits have been competed away.

Monopoly profits Thus far we have emphasized that profits are related to the uncertainties and un-

insurable risks surrounding dynamic events which enterprises are exposed to or initiate themselves. The existence of monopoly in some form or another is a final source of economic profits. As explained previously, because of his ability to restrict entry, a monopolist may persistently enjoy economic profits, provided demand is strong relative to cost (Figure 28·1). This profit stems from the monopolist's ability to restrict output and influence product price to his own advantage.

There are both a causal relationship and a notable distinction between uncertainty, on the one hand, and monopoly, on the other, as sources of profits. The causal relationship involves the fact that an entrepreneur can reduce uncertainty, or at least manipulate its effects, by achieving monopoly power. The competitive firm is unalterably exposed to the vagaries of the market; the monopolist, however, can control the market to a degree and thereby offset or minimize potentially adverse effects of uncertainty. Furthermore, innovation is an important source of monopoly power; the short-run uncertainty associated with the introduction of new techniques or new products may be borne for the purpose of achieving a measure of monopoly power.

The notable distinction between profits stemming from uncertainty and from monopoly has to do with the social desirability of the two sources of profits. Bearing the risks inherent in a dynamic and uncertain economic environment and the undertaking of innovations are socially desirable functions. The social desirability of monopoly profits, on the other hand, is subject to a very great doubt. Monopoly profits typically are founded upon output restriction, above-competitive prices, and a contrived misallocation of resources.

Functions of profits

Profit is the prime mover, or energizer, of the capitalistic economy. As such, profits influence both the level of resource utilization and the allocation of resources among alternative uses. It is profits—or better, the *expectation* of profits—which induce firms to innovate. And innovation stimulates investment, total output, and employment. Innovation is a fundamental aspect of the process of economic growth, and it is the pursuit of profit which underlies most innovation. We know from our previous analysis of the determination of national income that profit expectations are highly volatile, with the result that investment, employment, and the rate of growth have been unstable. Profits have functioned imperfectly as a spur to innovation and investment.

Profits perform more effectively the task of allocating resources among alternative lines of production. Businessmen seek profits and shun losses. The occurrence of economic profits is a signal that society wants that particular industry to expand. Indeed, profit rewards are more than an inducement for an industry to expand; they also are the financial means by which firms in such industries can add to their productive capacities. Losses, on the other hand, signal society's desire for the afflicted industries to contract; losses penalize businesses which fail to adjust their productive efforts to those goods and services most preferred by consumers. This is not to say that profits and losses result in an allocation of resources which is now and forever attuned to consumer preferences. In particular, the presence of monopoly in both product and resource markets impedes the shiftability of firms and resources, as also do the various geographic, artificial, and sociological immobilities discussed in Chapter 32.

SUMMARY

1. Economic rent is the price paid for the use of land and other natural resources whose total supplies are fixed.

2. Rent is a surplus in the sense that land would be available to the economy as a whole even in the absence of all rental payments. The notion of land rent as a surplus gave rise to the single-tax movement of the late 1800s. Currently many urban economists and planners advocate a tax on land value on both equity and efficiency grounds.

3. Differences in land rent are explainable in terms of differences in productivity due to the fertility and climatic features of land and in its location.

4. Land rent is a surplus rather than a cost to the

economy as a whole; however, because land has alternative uses from the standpoint of individual firms and industries, rental payments of firms and industries are correctly regarded as costs.

5. Interest is the price paid for the use of loanable funds. Specific interest rates vary because of differences in the degree of risk loans entail, the length of loans, the relative size of administrative costs associated with lending, and market imperfections.

6. Businesses, households, and government are the principal demanders of loanable funds. The current and past savings of businesses and households and commercial bank credit are the major potential sources of loanable funds. However, the actual supply of loanable funds may differ from the potential supply because of changes in the liquidity preference of households, businesses, and banks. The intersection of the supply of loanable funds and the demand for them determines the equilibrium interest rate.

7. Because of the borrowing activities of the Treasury and the Board of Governors' control over the loan-creating activities of commercial banks, the price of loanable funds is largely administered by government.

8. The interest rate influences the level of capital accumulation and helps ration capital goods to specific firms.

9. Economic, or pure, profits are the difference between a firm's total revenue and its total costs, the latter defined to include implicit costs and a normal profit.

10. Profits accrue to entrepreneurs for assuming the uninsurable risks associated with the organizing and directing of economic resources and innovating. Profits also result from monopoly power.

11. Profit expectations influence innovating and investment activities and therefore the level of employment. The basic function of profits and losses, however, is to induce that allocation of resources which is in general accord with the tastes of consumers.

QUESTIONS AND STUDY SUGGESTIONS

1. Define economic rent. How does the economist's usage of the term "rent" differ from everyday usage? "Though rent need not be paid by society to make land available, rental payments are very useful in guiding land into the most productive uses." Explain.

2. Explain why economic rent is a surplus to the economy as a whole but a cost of production from the standpoint of individual firms and industries. Explain: "Rent performs no 'incentive function' in the economy." What arguments can be made for and against a heavy tax on land?

3. How is interest defined? What considerations account for the fact that interest rates differ greatly on various types of loans? Use these considerations to explain the relative size of the interest rates charged on the following: ***a.*** a long-term \$1,000 government bond; ***b.*** a \$20 pawnshop loan; ***c.*** an FHA mortgage loan on a \$27,000 house; ***d.*** a \$2,500 commercial bank loan to finance the purchase of an automobile; and ***e.*** a \$100 loan from a personal finance company.

4. If money capital, as such, is not an economic resource, why is interest paid and received for its use? Answer from the standpoint of both borrower and lender, and from the borrower's standpoint distinguish between business and consumer borrowing.

5. What are the three sources of the demand for loanable funds? What are the three potential sources of the supply of loanable funds? Explain liquidity preference in terms of its underlying motives. Use this concept to explain the difference between saving and the supply of loanable funds.

6. What are the major economic functions of the interest rate? Of economic profits? How might the fact that more and more businesses are financing their investment activities internally affect the efficiency with which the interest rate performs its functions?

7. How do the concepts of business profits and economic profits differ? Why are economic profits smaller than business profits?

8. What are the three basic sources of economic profits?

Classify each of the following in accordance with these sources: *a.* The profits acquired by a firm from developing and patenting a ball-point pen containing a permanent ink cartridge; *b.* the profit of a restaurant which results from construction of the interstate highway past its door; *c.* the profit received by a firm benefiting from an unanticipated change in consumer tastes.

9. Distinguish between insurable and uninsurable risks. Why is this distinction significant for the theory of profits? Carefully evaluate: "All economic profits can be traced to either uncertainty or the desire to avoid it."

10. Explain the absence of economic profit in a purely competitive static economy. Realizing that the major function of profits is to allocate resources in accordance with consumer preferences, evaluate the allocation of resources in such an economy.

SELECTED REFERENCES

Economic Issues, 4th ed., reading 53.

Due, John F., and Robert W. Clower: *Intermediate Economic Analysis,* 5th ed. (Homewood, Ill.: Richard D. Irwin, Inc., 1966), chaps. 14–17.

Hansen, Alvin: *A Guide to Keynes* (New York: McGraw-Hill Book Company, 1953), chaps. 6 and 7.

Meyers, Albert L.: *Elements of Modern Economics,* 4th ed. (Englewood Cliffs, N.J.: Prentice-Hall, Inc., 1956), chaps. 14–16.

Stonier, Alfred W., and Douglas C. Hague: *A Textbook of Economic Theory,* 3d ed. (New York: Longmans, Green & Co., Inc., 1964), chaps. 13–15.

34

GENERAL EQUILIBRIUM: THE PRICE SYSTEM AND ITS OPERATION[1]

It is the basic purpose of this chapter to draw together the discussion of product and resource markets which has been the dominant theme of Part 5. We have analyzed the various categories of individual product and resource markets in some detail. Our present goal is to reemphasize that the many diverse markets of our economy are interwoven into a highly complex *price system.* This price system is responsible for the production of about four-fifths or more of our national product and therefore for the allocation of a comparable proportion of available resources. It is imperative that we grasp how this price system works.

PARTIAL AND GENERAL EQUILIBRIUM

Thus far our discussion of prices has been compartmentalized; we have examined representative product and resource prices one at a time, in isolation, and apart from any detailed interrelationships each may bear to the other. In the jargon of the economist, we have been concerned with *partial equilbrium analysis*—a study of equilibrium prices and outputs in the many specific markets which are the component *parts* of the price system.

But the economy is not merely a myriad of isolated and unrelated markets. On the contrary, it is an interlocking network of prices wherein changes in one market are likely to elicit numerous and significant changes in other markets. Hence, our vantage point now shifts from individual markets and prices in isolation to an analysis of the price system as a whole. In technical language, our discussion now shifts to *general equilibrium analysis*—an overall big-picture view of the interrelationships between all the various prices (parts) which make up the price *system.*

We will attempt to grasp the interrelatedness of various industries and markets through a series of three general equilibrium illustrations. We begin with a verbal model of the automobile industry wherein

[1] As a prologue to the present chapter, it might be helpful for the reader to scan Chapter 5 and the concluding section of Chapter 27, which evaluates competitive pricing.

the many possible repercussions of a change in demand are traced. Next we turn to a hypothetical model of two industries which makes explicit use of the formal analytical tools of microeconomics. Then we will embark upon an important digression which summarizes the implications of the functioning of a purely competitive price system for allocative efficiency and recalls some real-world complications. A third and final model views the interdependence of the various sectors of the economy through what is called input-output analysis. The chapter closes with a discussion of the relevance of general equilibrium analysis for economic understanding.

MARKET INTERRELATIONSHIPS: AUTOMOBILES[2]

Suppose initially that general equilibrium exists—in other words, that all product and resource markets are "at rest." Now assume there occurs an increase in the demand for automobiles. What will be the effects?

The immediate impact is obviously an increase in automobile prices. As automobile manufacturers react by increasing production, an increase will occur in the derived demands for, and therefore the prices of, all those resources used in the production of automobiles. These interrelationships between product and resource prices are not new to us; they were a key point in our analysis of resource demand (Chapter 31). In any event, the prospect of higher earnings in the automobile industry will attract resources to it. Industries losing labor to the automobile industry may find it necessary to pay higher wages to counteract this loss, and these higher wage costs imply declining profits for the affected industries. Furthermore, if the shift of labor to the automobile industry involves a geographic relocation of workers and their families, we can expect repercussions upon a number of other industries. For example, the residential construction industry—and therefore cement, lumber, and glass suppliers in the area—will experience an increase in the demand for their products. Too, the demand for the services of various skilled and semiskilled construction workers will increase, imposing additional changes on the other labor markets. A similar analysis would apply to nonlabor resources. An increase in the demand for automobiles will increase the demand for steel, and we know that the list of firms and industries using substantial amounts of steel reads like a *Who's Who* of American industry. In brief, innumerable other industries using the same types of land, labor, and capital as the automobile industry will find that their costs have increased. This will give rise to increases in the prices and declines in the sales of the products produced by these industries.

But we must not conclude that the effects of an increase in the demand for automobiles emanate solely from the resource market. An increase in the price of automobiles will affect the demand for, and prices of, other goods. The demand for, and prices of, such products as gasoline, motor oil, and tires will increase in response to the initial increase in the demand for automobiles. The demand for, and prices of, the services provided by bus lines, interurban railways, and taxis will tend to decline. And these changes in the prices of goods and services will be communicated back into the resource markets relevant to all these industries.

This is still not all: An equally subtle series of price alterations will emanate in the resource market from the initial price increases of resources used by the automobile industry. To illustrate: If the increase in the automobile industry's derived demand for steel significantly increases the price of steel, automobile manufacturers may substitute aluminum where possible for engine and body parts. All other industries using steel may make similar substitutions. As the prices of resources change, all industries and firms employing these resources will tend to shuffle the quantities of the various resources used to reachieve the least costly combination of resources (Chapter 31). This will affect the demand for, and prices of, these resources.

Noteworthy, too, is the fact that all the changes in

[2]This illustration follows the excellent example discussed in Francis E. Hyde et al., *A New Prospect of Economics* (Liverpool: Liverpool University Press, 1958), chap. 9.

resource prices which we have sketched will affect the personal distribution of income. In our example, automobile workers will find themselves moving into higher income brackets as the result of the initial increase in the demand for automobiles. They may well react by demanding more superior, or normal, goods such as butter and steak and less of such inferior goods as oleomargarine and potatoes. Indeed, they may even decide to buy still more automobiles, prompting a whole new series of price interactions such as we have already outlined.

The reader will readily note many loose ends in our discussion. If one had the patience and inclination, these price interrelationships could be pursued almost indefinitely. But our discussion is sufficiently detailed to emphasize our major point. Individual prices are interrelated in a number of both evident and subtle ways. Any initial disturbance such as a change in demand, a change in technology, or a change in resource supply will set off a highly complex economic chain reaction.

GENERAL EQUILIBRIUM: A TWO-INDUSTRY MODEL

Let us now consider a hypothetical illustration which explicitly embodies the formal tools of economic analysis. In Figure 34•1, which is merely a somewhat sophisticated version of Figure 3•4, the discussion focuses upon two product markets, X and Y. And although each industry would actually employ a number of different inputs, it will facilitate our analysis to concentrate only upon the labor market relevant to each industry. It is assumed that industry X uses type A labor and Y uses type B labor.

Behind the curves

A word or two is in order to remind us of the concepts which underlie the demand and supply curves of both product and resource markets. The product demand curves are downsloping because of *diminishing marginal utility* (Chapter 25). Successive units of a given product yield less and less additional satisfaction or utility to buyers, so that consumers will purchase more of that product only if its price falls. The upsloping product supply curves are based upon the concept of *increasing marginal costs* (Chapter 26). Because extra units of output are more costly, firms must receive a higher price before it will be profitable for them to produce this extra output. The downsloping labor demand curves are based upon the law of diminishing returns or *diminishing marginal physical productivity* (Chapter 31). Beyond some point, the addition of labor or any other variable resource to fixed resources will result in smaller and smaller increases in total output. And as we recall these concepts from earlier chapters, do not overlook the obvious link between the upsloping product supply curve and the downsloping resource demand curve. It is the diminishing marginal productivity of the resource which *causes* marginal costs to increase as output is increased. If each successive unit of labor (hired at a constant wage cost) adds less and less to output, then the cost of *each* successive unit of output must be more and more. Finally, the upsloping labor supply curves reflect the *work-leisure preferences* of individuals. A firm or industry must pay higher and higher wage rates to obtain larger amounts of labor service.

We assume long-run equilibrium initially, so that P_{x_1} and w_{a_1} are the equilibrium product price and wage rate for industry X, and P_{y_1} and w_{b_1} represent the equilibrium price and wage for industry Y. Firms are making normal profits, and there is no reason for either industry to expand or contract. The two labor markets are similarly "at rest"; there is no incentive for workers to move out of or into either market.

Suppose now that something happens to upset this equilibrium. What will be the character of the resulting adjustments? Specifically, let us say that a change occurs in consumer preferences or tastes so that consumer demand for X increases and consumer demand for Y simultaneously decreases.

Short-run adjustments

What short-run adjustments will occur in response to these changes in consumer demand? First of all, production, which was normally profitable in industry

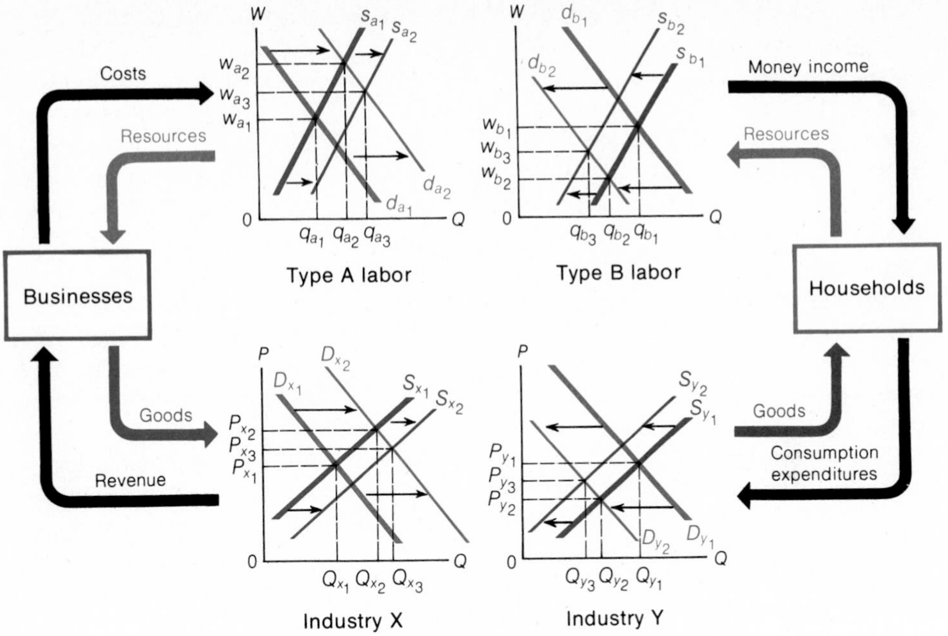

FIGURE 34·1 GENERAL EQUILIBRIUM AND THE INTERACTION OF PRODUCT AND RESOURCE MARKETS

These diagrams show the short-run and long-run adjustments resulting from an assumed increase in the demand for product X and assumed decline in the demand for product Y. Emphasis here is upon product and resource market interactions, and the diagrams therefore conceal many of the less obvious repercussions. For example, the given changes in demand for X and Y will affect the demands for substitute and complementary goods and alter the distribution of income.

X before demand rose from D_{x1} to D_{x2}, now results in economic profits. Firms in industry X, faced with the new higher price of P_{x2}, find it profitable to move to some point further up and to the right on their marginal-cost curves (Figure 27·5). Collectively these marginal-cost curves are the supply curve S_{x1} for the industry. Thus in Figure 34·1 existing firms find it profitable to expand output as a group from Q_{x1} to Q_{x2}.

But to expand output, the firms in industry X must acquire more resources, such as type A labor. Remembering that the demand for resources is a *derived demand,* it is no surprise that the expansion of output by firms in X will increase the demand for labor from d_{a1} to, say, d_{a2}. Workers in this labor market are willing to offer more of their services, perhaps by working longer hours or more days per week, moving up s_{a1} in response to the higher wage rate w_{a2}.

An opposite set of short-run adjustments will be experienced in industry Y. Product demand falls to, say, D_{y2}, causing price to fall from P_{y1} to P_{y2}. At this lower price individual firms incur losses. These firms will react by moving down and to the left on their

marginal-cost curves as they seek their loss-minimizing positions. The decline in demand for product Y is reflected back in the resource market. In particular, the demand for type B labor falls from d_{b_1} to d_{b_2}, causing the equilibrium wage rate to decline to w_{b_2}.

Long-run adjustments

But we have only traced the first round of market adjustments. At the conclusion of these short-run adjustments, the production of X still yields an economic profit, while losses persist in industry Y. This means that, given sufficient time, new firms will enter industry X, while firms will fall into bankruptcy and fail in industry Y. That is, the presumed changes in consumer demand have made X a prosperous, expanding industry and Y an unprosperous, declining industry.

As new firms enter X, the industry supply curve will shift to the right from S_{x1} to, say, S_{x2}. This increase in supply tends to bring price back down to, say, P_{x3}. Equilibrium output of X has further increased to Q_{x3}. If P_{x3} and Q_{x3} represent a new long-run equilibiium, as we presume is the case, we can note in passing that industry X must be an increasing-cost industry. Why? Because the new long-run equilibrium entails a higher price than the initial equilibrium price P_{x1} (Figure 27·10). If this was a constant-cost industry, the new price would be the same as the old price. It is to be emphasized that in the new equilibrium position consumers are getting a larger output of X—which is, of course, precisely what they wanted. In other words, these adjustments are a manifestation of *consumer sovereignty.*

Losses in industry Y force firms to leave the industry. As they do, industry supply will decline from S_{y1} to, say, S_{y2}. This raises price somewhat from P_{y2} to P_{y3}. If we assume industry Y is also an increasing-cost industry, contraction of the industry will lower unit costs. Thus in the new long-run equilibrium position at P_{y3} price will be lower than originally, production will be normally profitable once again, and industry size will be stabilized.

These long-run adjustments have counterparts in the resource markets. The supply curve for type B labor, s_{b_1}, is drawn on the assumption that other wage rates—for example, the wage rate received by type A labor—are given. The same holds true for the type A labor supply curve, s_{a_1}. But our short-run changes in the demand for labor have increased the wage rate for type A labor and reduced the wage rate for type B labor. The stage is set for type B labor to shift from industry Y, where job opportunities and wage rates have been declining, to industry X, where employment has been expanding and wage rates increasing. Thus we would expect the supply of type A labor to increase from s_{a_1} to, say, s_{a_2} and the supply of type B labor to fall from s_{b_1} to, say, s_{b_2}. As a result, wage rates for type A labor fall somewhat from w_{a_2} to w_{a_3}. And for type B labor, wage rates tend to go back up from w_{b_2} to, say, w_{b_3}.

But note several related points about these labor market adjustments. First, we are assuming that type B labor can become qualified as type A labor without too much difficulty and retraining. We know from Chapter 22 that occupational shifts may actually be complicated and costly to achieve. A second and closely related point is that supply shifts might take a substantial period of time. As suggested, type B workers may in fact require additional education, job retraining, and geographic relocation before becoming type A workers. Finally, because of various immobilities (Chapter 32), we would not expect the supply curve shifts to be sufficiently great to restore the wage rates of the original equilibrium. The new equilibrium wage rate will be w_{a_3} (higher than w_{a_1}) for type A labor and w_{b_3} (lower than w_{b_1}) for type B labor. Indeed, these long-run wage adjustments are consistent with, and a factor in, the increasing-cost character of industries X and Y.

Further adjustments

But this is only the beginning of the repercussions which stem from our original change in the structure of consumer demand. There are innumerable more subtle adjustments which we might take into account.

Other industries Consider now a third industry—call it industry Z. Will the initial increase in the price of X have any impact upon industry Z? It might! Recall

that one of the determinants of the demand for Z is the prices of related goods, and X just might be "related" to Z. But any shift in the demand for Z which stems from the increase in the price of X depends on precisely how products X and Z are related. Recall (Chapter 4) that any two products might be *substitutes* (butter and oleo), *complements* (gas and oil), or substantially *independent* (raisins and wristwatches). If X and Z are independent, then a rise in the price of X will have no significant effect on the demand for Z. But if X and Z are substitutes, the rise in the price of X will increase the demand for Z. Therefore, a series of adjustments will be precipitated in the product and resource markets for Z similar to those just sketched for X. And if X and Z are complements, the higher price for X will lower the demand for Z. This would precipitate adjustments in Z like those already traced for industry Y.

Other resources The initial changes in the demands for type A and type B labor may have an impact upon other resource markets. Suppose that technology in industry X is such that labor and capital must be used in virtually fixed proportions, for example, one machine is needed for every two workers. This means that the expansion in the employment of type A labor will stimulate the demand for relevant kinds of capital goods.

Income distribution It is also quite evident that our short-run and long-run adjustments will alter the distribution of income. Workers and entrepreneurs associated with industry X will receive higher incomes; those in industry Y, lower incomes. It is realistic to assume some differences in tastes which will be transformed into further changes in the structure of consumer demand. These new changes in demand will trigger new rounds of short-run and long-run adjustments.

We could go on, but the basic point is clear. The adjustments stemming from our initial changes in demand are much more complex and go far beyond the simple supply and demand shifts portrayed in Figure 34·1.

ECONOMIC WELFARE AND THE PRICE SYSTEM

Now that we have some appreciation of the mechanics of the price system and the many complex market interrelationships it implies, we must inquire once again as to the efficiency of the system. How effectively does the price system function?

Although there is no unequivocal answer to this question, we can certainly say some things on behalf of a competitive price system. The fundamental argument for it is that *its operation is conducive to an efficient allocation of resources.* More precisely, *given the distribution of income among consumers, purely competitive product and resource markets tend to give rise to the production of that collection of goods and services which maximizes the satisfactions of consumers.* Earlier discussion, particularly in Chapters 5 and 27, provided the analytical grounding for this claim of allocative efficiency. The following three technical points simply suggest that the price system provides economically desirable answers to the questions: What should the economy produce? How should that output be produced? And for whom should it be produced?

1. Self-interest drives purely competitive firms to produce that output at which price equals marginal cost. Remember that the price of a product reflects its value or worth to society, while marginal cost measures the value of the resources needed in its production. This means that additional units of any product are produced as long as they are valued by society more highly than are the alternative products which the needed resources could otherwise have produced. In other words, the "right" or most desirable output of each commodity—and therefore the best mixture of goods and services—gets produced.

2. Pure competition also results in the production of each good at minimum average cost (Figure 27·11). In terms of the resource market, competition forces producers to employ the least costly combination of resources or, more specifically, that combination wherein the last dollar spent on each resource

entails the same marginal physical product (Chapter 31).[3]

3. Not only does competition cause the right collection of goods and services to be produced and production to be at least cost, but free choice by consumers in competitive markets will result in the distribution of this output so as to maximize consumer satisfactions. *Given their incomes and their tastes,* each consumer will purchase that collection of goods and services which is most satisfying to him. Technically speaking, he will buy various products in such amounts that the last dollar spent on each item yields equal amounts of extra satisfaction or marginal utility.[4]

And finally, remember that these desirable consequences follow from the free decisions of participants made in their own self-interest. Businessmen are motivated in their decision making to maximize profits; resource suppliers to increase their incomes; consumers to maximize their satisfactions. Quite miraculously, the overall outcome of these freely rendered decisions, once coordinated and synchronized by the price system, is in the public interest. Scarce resources are apparently used with maximum efficiency.

THE REAL WORLD AND IMPERFECT COMPETITION

Having discussed the adjustments of a purely competitive price system in moving toward long-run equilibrium and the consequences of these adjustments for allocative efficiency, we must now understand that the competitive price system is clearly a rough approximation of reality. The competitive model is essentially a simplified way of envisioning the operation of a market economy; it does not purport to be a description of reality.

One basic way in which the real world differs from our model is that in actuality most product and resource markets are imperfectly competitive; they deviate in varying degrees from the purely competitive model. As a result, resources may well be allocated less efficiently than under pure competition. Imperfectly competitive producers find it in their private interest as profit seekers to produce short of the price-equals-marginal-cost output, and an underallocation of resources to the production of this good occurs. The private interest of the firm is now somewhat at odds with society's interest in allocative efficiency. Similarly, monopsony (Figure 32·4) or monopoly (Figure 32·7) can cause prices in the resource market to vary from the competitive level and impair allocative efficiency.

Imperfect competition also means that adjustments of the type described in our general equilibrium models will be more sluggish and less complete. This is not to say the price system won't make generally appropriate adjustments. It will. But under imperfect competition, these adjustments will be only rough approximations of those described, for example, in our two-industry model. In general, most economists are willing to conclude that with imperfect competition, resource allocation is less efficient and the price system less responsive to changes in tastes, technology, or resource availability than if pure competition prevailed.

But even this cautious conclusion must be modified. The possibility of more rapid technological progress and the alleged advantages stemming from greater product variety under imperfectly competitive conditions must be regarded as potential offsets to diminished allocative efficiency. And as we shall see later (Chapter 35), estimates of the "cost" of monopoly in our economy as reflected in forgone GNP due to allocative inefficiency suggest that the impact of monopoly can easily be overdrawn. Finally, despite

[3] If any two resources—labor and capital—are being employed, then costs will be minimized when they are used in such amounts that

$$\frac{\text{MPP of labor}}{\text{price of labor}} = \frac{\text{MPP of capital}}{\text{price of capital}}$$

[4] If the consumer is buying just two products, X and Y, he will maximize his utility by purchasing them in such quantities that

$$\frac{\text{MU of product X}}{\text{price of X}} = \frac{\text{MU of product Y}}{\text{price of Y}}$$

the many possible imperfections of the competitive price system, it is rather ironic and extremely interesting to find various centrally planned economies—including the Soviet Union—experimenting with the free-price system on a widening scale as they seek to enhance allocative efficiency within their existing economies.

OUTPUT, INCOME, AND ETHICS

Even if the purely competitive model of the price system was an accurate portrayal of the real world, we would nevertheless be justified in questioning its capacity to allocate resources efficiently. This is so for at least two reasons.

Allocative activities of government

In the first place, we know that the production of certain products may entail benefits and costs which are external to the demand and supply curves of the market. If substantial *spillover benefits* are involved in the production or consumption of some good or service (for example, education), the market will understate the demand for such goods, and resources will be underallocated to their production. Conversely, if the production or consumption of some good entails significant *spillover costs* (for example, air pollution), the market supply curve will understate costs, and resources will be overallocated to that commodity's production. The imposition of special excise taxes along the lines suggested in Chapter 24 is one of several ways of correcting for this overallocation of resources which accompanies spillover costs. The reader should employ simple supply and demand analysis to convince himself that special public subsidies can be useful in correcting the underallocation of resources which characterizes the production of goods whose spillover benefits are substantial. Furthermore, the price system would ignore or grossly neglect the production of such *social goods* as national defense, streets and highways, flood control, courthouses, and so forth.

Government and distributive justice

A most perplexing question—to which economists as social scientists do not know the answer—now looms before us. The question is this: What is the "best" or optimal distribution of income?

Let us back up a moment and reexamine our claim that, aside from social goods and instances of substantial spillover benefits and costs, a competitive price system will negotiate that allocation of resources which maximizes consumer satisfaction. This claim is predicated upon a "given" or "assumed" distribution of income. Money income is presumably distributed among consumers in a certain way, and on the basis of their incomes each consumer makes his wants effective in the various markets by his expenditures for different goods. This is what we rather quaintly termed "dollar voting" in Chapter 5. In any event these consumer decisions, based upon money income, are reflected in the product demand curves of our general equilibrium models. Given the structure of demand which results from this distribution of income, we have seen that it is a primary virtue of the price system that it brings about the allocation of resources and resulting product-mix which best fulfills the wants of consumers.

This is all well and good. But now an awkward question arises. *If* we were now to suppose, or bring about, a *different* distribution of money income so as to get a *different* structure of consumer demand, would not the competitive price system negotiate a new allocation of resources and a new product-mix which would result in the maximum satisfaction of this new pattern of consumer demand? The answer is: Yes, this is exactly what the price system would do! This answer leads inevitably to a further question: Which of these two allocations of resources—the one which is "most efficient" for the first income distribution or the one which is "most efficient" for the second income distribution—is truly optimal or best?

Economists have been unable to provide a satisfactory answer because they cannot measure and compare the ability of various individuals to derive satisfaction or utility from money income. If every individual were precisely identical in his capacity to

TABLE 34·1 A SIMPLIFIED INPUT-OUTPUT TABLE (*hypothetical data*)

Producing sectors	Consuming or using sectors					
	(1) Metal	(2) Machinery	(3) Fuel	(4) Agriculture	(5) Households (labor)	(6) Total output
(1) Metal	10	65	10	5	10	100
(2) Machinery	40	25	35	75	25	200
(3) Fuel	15	5	5	5	20	50
(4) Agriculture	15	10	50	50	525	650
(5) Labor (households)	100	200	100	550	50	1,000

enjoy income, economists would say that income should be distributed equally and that the allocation of resources which was most efficient in response to *that* distribution of income would result in the greatest possible level of consumer satisfaction. But people differ by virtue of their inherited physical and mental characteristics, not to mention their education, training, environment, experiences, and so forth. And we cannot meaningfully gauge the extent to which they are different; the capacity to derive satisfaction or utility is a highly subjective, psychological thing, elusive of measurement. So how can we determine whether some distribution of income, other than the existing one, is superior or inferior? In short, the whole question of what is the optimum distribution of income remains an ethical one. We will return to this question of distributive justice in Chapter 38 and discuss in some detail the ways in which government has altered the distribution of income from that which the unmodified price system would have provided. Indeed, all the chapters of Part 6 bear upon the question of income distribution.

GENERAL EQUILIBRIUM: INPUT-OUTPUT ANALYSIS

The relatively simple general equilibrium models thus far explored contain important insights into the operation and social implications of the price system. They also serve the major purpose of emphasizing the interrelatedness of the many decision makers who comprise the economy. Further appreciation of the intricate interrelationships between the various sectors or industries of the economy can be gained through an input-output table. Table 34·1 is a very simplified hypothetical input-output table for an economy.[5] Listed down the left side of the table are the five producing sectors (industries) of the economy. Column 6 shows the total output associated with each of the five sectors; the metal sector produces 100 units, the machine sector 200 units, and so forth. These same five sectors are also the consuming sectors of the economy and are shown in this capacity across the top of the table. Looking across each of the horizontal rows of figures, we can see how the total output of each sector is disposed of, or consumed, among the five sectors. For example, of the 200 units of output of the machinery sector, 40 units go to the metal sector, 25 to the machinery sector itself (because it takes machines to produce machines!), and 35, 75, and 25 units go to the fuel, agriculture, and household sectors, respectively, thereby exhausting the units produced.

[5] Wassily W. Leontieff is largely responsible for input-output analysis. See his simplified discussion of "Input-output Economics," *Scientific American*, October 1951, pp. 15–21. Table 34·1 and portions of the accompanying discussion are from Francis M. Boddy, "Soviet Economic Growth," in Robert T. Holt and John E. Turner (eds.), *Soviet Union: Paradox and Change* (New York: Holt, Rinehart and Winston, Inc., 1962), pp. 77–79, with permission of the publisher.

Following through on this disposition-of-output procedure for all five sectors, we find that each vertical column must and does show the units of output of each producing sector which are consumed as inputs by the five sectors. For example, we find in column 2 that to produce 200 units of machinery, an input of 65 units of metal, 25 of machinery, 5 of fuel, 10 of agricultural products, and 200 of labor is required. In this way the table vividly reveals the highly interdependent character of the various sectors or industries. Any given industry or sector employs the outputs of other sectors—and indeed, some of its own output—as its inputs! And the outputs of that given sector are similarly the inputs of the other sectors. To cite a real-world example: While outputs of steel are inputs in the production of railroad cars, these railroad cars are, in turn, used to transport both steel and the various inputs—coke, pig iron, and so forth—which are necessary to its production.

The interdependence of the economy's sectors or industries can be further demonstrated by tracing the repercussions of an assumed change in the output of some commodity. Consider, for example, the repercussions of a 20-unit (10 percent) increase in machinery production. This means that a 10 percent increase in the production of all the outputs which are used as inputs in the production of machinery is required.[6] These inputs, as we know, are listed in column 2 of the table. Applying the 10 percent figure, we find that 6.5 additional units (outputs) of metal, 0.5 unit of fuel, 1 unit of agricultural products, 20 units of labor, and 2.5 units of machinery will be needed to produce another 20 units of machinery. But this is just the beginning: obviously, a myriad of further adjustments are also required. Because each sector which supplies inputs to the machinery sector must expand its output, these supplying sectors in turn will require more inputs from other sectors. Example: The additional 6.5 units of metal needed as inputs to produce the extra 20 units of machinery will in turn call for an appropriate—6.5 percent, in this case—increase in the production of all the inputs shown in column 1 to be needed in producing metal. The same reasoning, of course, is applicable to the fuel, agriculture, and labor sectors. That is, the 0.5-unit increase in fuel production required in producing the extra 20 units of machinery will call for an appropriate (1 percent) increase in the production of all the inputs listed in column 3, and similarly for the agricultural and labor sectors. Example: We noted earlier that the production of 20 more units of machinery output requires as inputs the production of 2.5 units of machinery. This 2.5-unit increase will require "second-round" increases (of 1.25 percent in this case) in the inputs of all the resources shown in column 2 in the same general fashion as did the initial 20-unit increase in machinery output. The reader will clearly recognize that the chain reaction is by no means at an end. All the repercussions cited in these examples call for still further adjustments similar to those already described. The crucial point, of course, is that, because of the high degree of interrelatedness between the sectors of the economy, a change in the figure in any one "cell" or "box" of the input-output table will precipitate an almost endless series of adjustments in other figures. In our illustration, the expansion of production in one sector has nearly innumerable repercussions which reach into virtually every nook and cranny of the economy.

[6]We invoke here one of the simplifying assumptions underlying the input-output table, namely, that production occurs under conditions of constant returns to scale (see Chapter 26).

GENERAL EQUILIBRIUM AND ECONOMIC UNDERSTANDING

In what respects, if any, is a knowledge of general equilibrium analysis important? Is an understanding of the interrelationships of prices or sectors useful? Up to a point, at least, an understanding of these interrelationships is an indispensable tool in evaluating the overall operation of the economy, in understanding specific economic problems, and in formulating policies. A failure to recognize price and sector interrelationships is an important source of misunderstanding and faulty reasoning about major economic problems. Furthermore, input-output analysis lends itself to an abundance of practical applications.

Some examples will clarify these points. One might

expect that the effect of a general or widespread wage cut is to reduce the costs of specific firms. And, other things being equal, lower costs will cause a firm to lower prices, increase production, and hire more workers. But general equilibrium analysis suggests that this seemingly obvious conclusion is of doubtful validity. Lower wages mean lower incomes, which are communicated into the product market as general declines in the demand for, and prices of, products. These price declines are then projected back into the resource market once again as declines in resource demand. And these declines in resource demand will mean unemployment. The immediate impact of wage cuts (more employment) which partial equilibrium analysis suggests may be swallowed up by the secondary effects (less employment), which are discernible only by an understanding of general equilibrium analysis.

Another example: Many people favor protective tariffs levied on, say, Japanese or German toys, because the immediate and obvious effect is to increase the price of foreign toys and therefore increase the demand for American-made toys. The result is that output and employment rise in the American toy industry. But this ignores the fact that incomes in Japan and Germany will decline as a result of their inability to sell toys in the United States. And with smaller incomes they will be less able to buy from American industries exporting machine tools, chemicals, grains, and so forth. The obvious increase in employment in the protected industry may well be offset, wholly or in part, by the indirect, subtle declines in employment in American export industries. As a matter of fact, apart from any decline in domestic employment stemming from tariff-induced declines in exports, general equilibrium analysis reminds us that the extra resources which are shifted into the expanding toy industry must come from other industries. That is, in a full-employment economy the tariff-inspired expansion of the toy industry will entail a contraction in the production of other goods.

A final illustration: It would not be legitimate to consider the impact of a general sales tax upon the production of one industry in isolation, thereby ignoring its simultaneous effects upon related products. In analyzing the effects of the imposition of a sales tax upon the butter industry one must not ignore the fact that oleomargarine will also be subject to the same tax.

While our interest in input-output analysis has centered upon the pedagogical goal of emphasizing that "everything depends upon everything else" in the economy, it should be noted that input-output analysis has resulted in empirical measurement of the various interactions between sectors of the economy, and these measurements have proved of considerable value as an instrument of economic forecasting and prediction. Assume for the moment a much more detailed input-output table containing 50 or even 500 individual sectors with each box filled with accurate empirical data. Now, for example, if the government should decide to undertake the production of fifty new supersonic bombers, the impact of this decision upon affected sectors could be quite accurately predicted; we can forecast quantitatively "what it will take" in terms of the outputs of all the many affected industries to fulfill this goal. Input-output analysis also has great relevance for the underdeveloped nations, virtually all of which seek growth through some form of planning (Chapter 45), and for more advanced centrally planned systems such as the Soviet Union (Chapter 46). By revealing the quantitative interrelationships between various sectors of the economy, input-output analysis allows the planners to determine how realistic—how feasible—planned production targets actually are. By tracing the repercussions of, say, a planned increase in steel production of 10 percent, the Central Planning Board of the U.S.S.R. can determine what outputs of coal, iron ore, transportation, manpower, relevant capital equipment, and all other inputs used in the production of steel will be needed to fulfill this target. In this way potential bottlenecks to the realization of this goal (or others) may be uncovered; for example, transportation problems may be uncovered, or it may be found that the additional plant capacity required conflicts severely with the planned production of housing or the planned expansion of the chemicals industry. Appropriate adjustments may therefore be made in the production targets for steel or other

products to make the plan more realistic and more consistent with the constraints imposed by technology and overall scarcities of economic resources.

General equilibrium analysis provides a broader perspective for analyzing the effects of given economic disturbances or policies than does partial equilibrium analysis. Partial equilibrium analysis shows merely "the big splash" of an initial disturbance; general equilibrium analysis traces the waves and ripples emanating from the big splash. In some instances the waves and ripples are relatively unimportant; in others they may prove to be a tidal wave which completely changes conclusions one would draw from the big splash viewed in isolation. As we noted in Chapter 1, a basic task of the economist is that of ascertaining which waves and ripples are important to the analysis of a given question and which can be safely ignored. In any event, a grasp of the general equilibrium point of view is essential in understanding and evaluating our economy.

SUMMARY

1. General equilibrium analysis is concerned with the operation of the entire price system and the interrelationships between different markets and prices. These interrelationships are important in that they might modify or negate the immediate effects of economic disturbances or policies which partial equilibrium analysis reveals.

2. A purely competitive price system would tend to allocate resources so as to provide the maximum satisfaction of consumer wants.

3. The fact that imperfect competition generally exists in both product and resource markets detracts from the price system's capacity to allocate resources efficiently and makes it less responsive to changes in tastes, technology, resource supplies, and so forth.

4. Efficient resource allocation would depend on an active role for government even if the price system were purely competitive. The price system would underproduce goods which entail substantial spillover benefits and overproduce those which embody substantial spillover costs. Also, the price system would tend to ignore the production of social goods.

5. Because of the inability to measure and compare the capacity of various individuals to derive satisfaction from income, economists are unable to determine what is the optimum distribution of income.

6. The input-output table provides a kind of general equilibrium analysis which reveals the overall fabric of the economy by focusing upon the interdependencies that exist between the various sectors or industries which it comprises. Input-output analysis has many practical applications to economic forecasting and planning.

QUESTIONS AND STUDY SUGGESTIONS

1. Compare partial and general equilibrium analysis. In what respect is each useful?

2. Trace through the price system the economic effect of: *a.* The development of a man-made fiber which never wears out, fades, or stains; *b.* a permanent increase in the demand for leather; *c.* a sharp decline in the size of the labor force; *d.* the development of a new production technique which cuts the cost of color television by 50 percent; *e.* the imposition of a 20 percent excise tax on shoes.

3. Explain the following statements:

a. "Allocative efficiency does not mean distributive justice."

b. "There is an 'efficient' or 'optimal' allocation of resources for every conceivable distribution of money income."

4. What is an input-output table? Using Table 34·1, trace some of the repercussions of a 5-unit (10 percent) increase in fuel production. What insights might input-output analysis provide as to the operation of a capitalistic system? How might input-output analysis be used as a "mechanism of coordination" in a centrally planned system?

SELECTED REFERENCES

Economic Issues, 4th ed., readings 56 and 57.

Bowen, Howard R.: *Toward Social Economy* (New York: Holt, Rinehart and Winston, Inc., 1948), particularly chaps. 15 and 16.

Brennan, Michael J.: *Theory of Economic Statics,* 2d ed. (Englewood Cliffs, N.J.: Prentice-Hall, Inc., 1970), chap. 25.

Köhler, Heinz: *Welfare and Planning* (New York: John Wiley & Sons, Inc., 1966), particularly chaps. 1–5.

Lange, Oskar, and Fred M. Taylor: *On the Economic Theory of Socialism* (Minneapolis: University of Minnesota Press, 1938).

Miernyk, William H.: *The Elements of Input-Output Analysis* (New York: Random House, Inc., 1965).

Phelps-Brown, E. H.: *The Framework of the Pricing System* (London: Chapman & Hall, Ltd., 1936).

Ryan, W. J. L.: *Price Theory* (New York: St. Martin's Press, Inc., 1958), chap. 8.

Stigler, George J.: *The Theory of Price,* rev. ed. (New York: The Macmillan Company, 1952), chap. 16.

6

CURRENT DOMESTIC ECONOMIC PROBLEMS

35

THE MONOPOLY PROBLEM: THE SOCIAL CONTROL OF INDUSTRY

Previous chapters have made these two contrasting points:

1. Many important American industries are characterized by considerable monopoly power. Some of these industries were shown in Table 30·1.

2. It was noted in Chapter 6 that one of the basic economic functions of government is to preserve competition as a key mechanism of control in the economy.

It is the overall objective of the present chapter to describe and evaluate governmental policies toward business monopolies. More specifically, the objectives of this chapter are threefold:

1. To examine the case for, and then the case against, business monopolies

2. To understand and appraise government policies toward business monopolies

3. To explore several possible future public policy alternatives.

BIG BUSINESS AND MONOPOLY

Before considering the pros and cons of business monopoly, we must pause to define our terminology. In Chapters 23 and 28 we developed and applied a very strict definition of monopoly. A *pure,* or *absolute,* monopoly, we said, is a one-firm industry—a situation in which a unique product is produced entirely by one firm, entry to the industry being blocked by certain insurmountable barriers. When a single firm controls an entire market, pure monopoly exists.

In the present chapter we shall find it convenient to use the term "monopoly" in a broader, generic sense. *Monopoly exists whenever a small number of firms controls all or a large portion of the output of a major industry.* This definition, which comes closer to the way the man in the street understands monop-

oly, includes a large number of industries which we have heretofore designated under the category of oligopoly.

What is the difference between monopoly (as we have just defined it) and big business? The term "big business" may be defined either in terms of a firm's share of the total market for its product or in terms of some absolute measure such as the volume of its assets, sales, or profits, the number of workers employed, or the number of stockholders. A firm can obviously be large *in relation to* the size of the total market but small in an *absolute* sense. The Weeping Water General Store may almost completely dominate the local market for a good many products, yet be exceedingly small by any meaningful absolute standard. Conversely, a firm might be very large in the absolute sense but small in relation to the total market. For example, American Motors is large by most absolute standards one can employ. In 1970 its net sales revenue was $1,089,787,000 and some 23,769 employees were on its payroll. Yet American Motors sells only about 5 percent of all automobiles in the United States. Insofar as the automobile industry is concerned, American Motors is a small producer. However, *in a good many instances, absolute and relative bigness go hand in hand.* A firm which is large in absolute terms very frequently controls a significant portion of the market for its product. Thus, although "big business" and "monopoly" are not necessarily synonymous, they frequently do go together. The present chapter is concerned with the type of situation in which absolute and relative bigness are both present. In using the term "business monopoly" in this chapter, we refer to those industries in which firms are large in absolute terms and in relation to the total market. Examples are the electrical equipment industry, where General Electric and Westinghouse, large by any absolute standard, dominate the market; the automobile industry, where General Motors, Ford, and Chrysler are similarly situated; the chemical industry, dominated by du Pont, Union Carbide, and Allied Chemical; the aluminum industry, where three industrial giants—Alcoa, Reynolds, and Kaiser—reign supreme; and the cigarette industry, where the four giant firms of Reynolds, Liggett and Myers, American Tobacco, and Lorillard currently command the lion's share of this large market.[1]

MONOPOLY: GOOD OR EVIL?

It is not at all clear whether business monopolies are on balance advantageous or disadvantageous to the functioning of American capitalism. Note these two statements—one bitterly opposed to monopoly in any form or context and the other viewing business monopoly as an integral part of modern American capitalism:

> Monopoly power must be abused. It has no use save abuse. . . . There must be an outright dismantling of our gigantic corporations and persistent prosecution of producers who organize, by whatever methods, for price maintenance or output limitation.
>
> . . . Legislation must prohibit, and administration effectively prevent, the acquisition by any private firm, or group of firms, of substantial monopoly power.[2]

> In our economy big business undertakes the major role of coordinating individual efforts and resources into collective achievement. This is a function that must be undertaken under modern technology, whether by private enterprise or by the state. In the United States it has been possible so to mix dispersion with centralization that the major job can be left to private competition, under government regulation. Big business has not merely been kept effectively subject to a competitive system; on the whole it has also made an essential contribution to its scope, vitality, and effectiveness.[3]

These are not propaganda blasts sponsored by antimonopoly and promonopoly pressure groups. Rather they are the well-considered arguments of respected scholars. These two assertions accurately show that there is ample room for serious disagree-

[1]See George J. Stigler, "The Case against Bigness in Business," *Fortune,* May 1952, p. 123.

[2]Henry C. Simons, *Economic Policy for a Free Society* (Chicago: The University of Chicago Press, 1948), pp. 129, 158.

[3]A. D. H. Kaplan, *Big Enterprise in a Competitive System* (Washington: The Brookings Institution, 1954), p. 248.

ment as to the desirability of business monopolies in American capitalism. Almost endless debate on this issue has precipitated a series of rather well-defined arguments on both sides. Our immediate goal is to outline these divergent and contradictory views.

THE CASE FOR MONOPOLY

Business monopoly is not without substantial defenses. A series of plausible arguments with which we are only partially familiar have been evolved to explain and justify the existence of the giant business enterprises which currently dominate various markets.

"Workable competition"

It is alleged, first of all, that, although the stringent conditions of pure competition as set forth in Chapter 27 are rarely if ever met, the presence of *workable competition* effectively regulates the operations of big businesses. It is argued that there exist certain types of competition, more subtle than the mere presence of a large number of rival producers, which in fact make so-called monopolistic industries "workably competitive." This contention suggests that any judgment of the competitiveness of an industry which rests solely on the number of existing producers is incomplete and misleading, because it overlooks other important dimensions of competition.

What are some of these more subtle dimensions of competition?

1. Pervasive competition All products are in competition for the dollars of consumers. A down payment on a house is often a good substitute for a new automobile. A new dress and accessories are sometimes in strong competition with a new vacuum cleaner for the housewife's dollars. Refrigerators compete with washing machines, television sets, and air conditioners.

2. Interproduct competition The contention that competition is pervasive shades into the notion of interproduct competition. Although only a small number of firms may produce certain specific products, these apparent monopolists may in fact face severe competition from firms producing distinct but highly substitutable products. The fact that only three firms are responsible for the nation's output of aluminum belies the competition which aluminum faces in specific markets from steel, copper, wood, plastics, and a variety of other products. These first two aspects of workable competition both suggest that the demand for the products of a monopolistic industry may be considerably more elastic than the small number of firms in that specific industry would seem to imply.

3. Innovative competition Technological advance operates over time so as to circumscribe and undermine existing monopoly positions. Innovation, in particular the development of new products, is a force which persistently destroys the market power of individual firms, making monopoly power a precarious and transitory phenomenon.

4. Countervailing power Competition in the form of countervailing power must not be ignored (Chapter 30). An original position of monopoly power tends to induce the growth of monopoly power on the opposite side of the market. This across-the-market competition provides effective checks, or restraints, on both the original and the countervailing power position. Countervailing power effectively prevents abuses of monopoly power in those very markets in which traditional same-side-of-the-market competition is weak.

5. Potential competition It is argued that *potential* competition and the fear of censure can regulate the behavior of monopolists almost as effectively as does the actual presence of a large number of rivals. The possibility that new rival firms will be formed or that other industrial giants will branch out works against the monopolist's exploiting his market power. The fear of public censure, the embarrassment of an antitrust suit, or the possibility of government regula-

tion may also contribute to the monopolist's disinclination to exert his monopoly power.

Economists who emphasize the importance of workable competition feel that firms and industries should be judged not on the basis of their market structure but rather in terms of their performance. Such characteristics as the number of firms in the industry and the importance of barriers to entry should be supplanted by criteria of performance—price, efficiency of production, and rate of technological advance—in gauging the social desirability of an industry or specific firm. Defenders of business monopoly contend that many industries which fall short of the large-numbers no-barriers criteria nevertheless perform very well, efficiently producing a quality product at a low price.

Technological determinism: a new industrial state?

The second major defense of monopoly centers upon technology as an aspect of efficient industry performance. Two related arguments are made.

Mass-production economies Existing mass-production economies can be realized only by big businesses. Where existing technology is highly advanced, only large producers—firms which are large both absolutely and in relation to the market—can realize low unit costs and therefore sell to consumers at relatively low prices. In short, the traditional antimonopoly contention that monopoly means less output, higher prices, and an inefficient allocation of resources assumes that cost economies would be equally available to firms whether the industry's structure was highly competitive or quite monopolistic. In fact this may not be the case; economies of scale may only be accessible if competition is absent.

Technological advance: Galbraith's thesis The idea that monopolistic industries—in particular, three- and four-firm oligopolies—are conducive to a high rate of technological progress is not new. But John Kenneth Galbraith has revitalized and forcefully pursued this notion and its potential consequences in his recent writings. He has argued that oligopolistic firms have both the financial resources and the incentives to undertake technological research.[4]

> The modern industry of a few large firms [is] an excellent instrument for inducing technical change. It is admirably equipped for financing technical development. Its organization provides strong incentives for undertaking development and for putting it into use. . . . In the modern industry shared by a few large firms, size and the rewards accruing to market power combine to insure that resources for research and technical development will be available. The power that enables the firm to have some influence on prices insures that the resulting gains will not be passed on to the public by imitators (who have stood none of the costs of development) before the outlay for development can be recouped. In this way market power protects the incentive to technical development.

Galbraith has extended this theme in his well-known book, *The New Industrial State*.[5] He argues that "technological imperatives" have brought the corporate giant to a dominant role in the American economy. Production requires not only huge quantities of capital, but also a highly sophisticated technology, and this means that firms must be large to be efficient. Furthermore, the successful functioning of giant enterprises presumes detailed planning, not only of new innovations and productive processes, but also of the manipulation of consumer demand. According to Galbraith, the "technostructure"—the technicians and professional managers of the corporation—carry out these planning and decision-making functions.

A primary goal of the modern "mature" corporation is security and stability—the avoidance of risk. In seeking security the giant corporation attempts to insulate itself from the vagaries of free markets. Thus the corporation integrates vertically; that is, it creates, controls, or merges with materials suppliers. It engages in the internal financing of capital expansion to eliminate its dependence upon the capital market.

[4] John Kenneth Galbraith, *American Capitalism*, rev. ed. (Boston: Houghton Mifflin Company, 1956), pp. 86–88.

[5] John Kenneth Galbraith, *The New Industrial State* (Boston: Houghton Mifflin Company, 1967). This book is highly recommended reading; the terse summary presented here does not do justice to Professor Galbraith's arguments.

On the demand side the corporation controls its customers through advertising and techniques of salesmanship, thereby supplanting "consumer sovereignty" with "producer sovereignty." In these ways the corporation dominates both suppliers and consumers, thereby signalling the demise of the free-market system as traditionally conceived. Furthermore, the corporate giant, by virtue of its size and crucial role in production, has achieved autonomy from government control. In fact, Galbraith feels that big business and government are in the process of establishing a tacit alliance to manage the economy. On the one hand, government plans and undertakes various functions—the stabilization of aggregate demand, the financing of research and development, the provision of highly educated manpower—which the technostructure and the corporate giants require for security and growth. On the other hand, the industrial giants assume responsibility for the planning of much of society's production. Galbraith feels that these trends are a "part of the broad sweep of economic development"; technological advance makes these developments necessary and immutable if productive efficiency is to be realized.

Other defenses: stability and responsibility

Although the primary defenses of monopoly cluster around the arguments of workable competition and technological determinism, two other points merit brief mention.

Macro stability Business monopolies exert a stabilizing influence upon the economy because of both their investment policies and their pricing policies. Concerning investment policies, it is argued that the absolute and relative size of business monopolies permits them to gear their investment spending to long-run business prospects rather than to the short-term cyclical upswings and downswings which are so influential in determining the investment outlays of smaller, competitive firms. Thus it has been argued that a part of the stability achieved in the 1950s and 1960s arose from the fact that the long-term investment programs of large monopolies were continued despite short-term changes in inventory investment and consumer spending. A more debatable assertion is that the ability of business monopolies to resist price reductions during recession (coupled with the propensity of unions to resist wage cuts) helps thwart the development of a cumulative wage-price deflationary spiral and the accompanying declines in output and employment.

Social responsibility A few economists and most business groups suggest that business leaders are blessed with a strong sense of social responsibility which will mitigate, if not eliminate entirely, abuses of monopoly power. Although industry leaders command tremendous economic power, we are assured that they have the social maturity not to wield this power in a manner detrimental to the public interest. The public-be-damned attitude of business monopolies in earlier decades is allegedly a thing of the past.[6]

THE CASE AGAINST MONOPOLY

The essence of the case against monopoly was stated in Chapter 28. Let us summarize and extend those arguments.

Inefficiency and inequality

Monopolists find it possible and profitable to restrict output and charge higher prices than would competitive producers. Furthermore, the monopolist's profit-maximizing output entails a misallocation of economic resources. It is through his ability to block or retard the entry of new firms and resources into an industry that the monopolist can realize economic profits in the long run. These profits are an indication that consumers want more resources allocated to the production of the monopolized commodity. More technically, monopolists maximize profits by producing an output at which price (society's measure of product X's relative worth) exceeds marginal cost

[6]The interested student will find Paul T. Heyne, *Private Keepers of the Public Interest* (New York: McGraw-Hill Book Company, 1968), to be challenging reading.

(society's measure of the worth of the alternative products which the resources used in producing an extra unit of X could otherwise have produced). Finally, the persistent economic profits which monopolists can realize contribute to inequality in the distribution of income.

Obstacle to progress?

Antimonopoly economists have attacked (1) the notion that only giant corporations can realize the economies of large-scale production and (2) Galbraith's argument that monopoly is essential to technological progress. In so doing they make a variety of interrelated arguments.

1. Empirical studies suggest that in the vast majority of manufacturing industries fewness is not essential to the realization of economies of scale. In most industries firms need only realize a small percentage of the total market to achieve low-cost production; monopoly is not a prerequisite of productive efficiency.[7]

2. The basic unit for technological efficiency is not the firm, but the individual plant. Thus one can correctly argue that productive efficiency calls for, say, a large-scale, integrated steel-manufacturing plant. But it is not inconsistent to argue that there is no technological justification for the existence of U.S. Steel, which is essentially a giant business corporation composed of a number of geographically distinct plants. Similarly, it is contended, for example, that the Chevrolet, Pontiac, Oldsmobile, Buick, and Cadillac divisions of General Motors are for operating purposes independent producers. How then can their legal unification be justified on the basis of mass-production economies? Furthermore, there are no efficiency grounds for the existence of huge conglomerate corporations engaged in the production of such widely divergent products as frozen foods, shoes, cosmetics, and office equipment. In short, many existing monopolies have attained a size and structure far beyond that necessary for the realization of existing economies of scale.

[7]The classic study is Joe S. Bain, *Barriers to New Competition* (Cambridge, Mass.: Harvard University Press, 1956).

3. Nor does technological progress depend upon the existence of huge corporations with substantial monopoly power. The evidence—one might review the closing pages of Chapter 30—does not support the view that large size and market power correlate closely with technological progress. Indeed, the sheltered position of the monopolist is conducive to inefficiency and lethargy; there is no competitive spur to productive efficiency. Furthermore, monopolists are inclined to resist or suppress technological advances which may cause the sudden obsolescence of their existing machinery and equipment.

Critics of Galbraith's technological determinism offer contrary case studies. For example, the American steel industry, dominated by a few industrial giants, should neatly fit Galbraith's portrayal of large firms as efficient planners for technological progress. But, critics contend, the steel industry is in fact sorely at odds with Galbraith's model.[8]

> The U.S. steel industry, which ranks among the largest, most basic, and most concentrated of American industries, certainly part of the industrial state that Professor Galbraith speaks of, affords a dramatic case in point. It spends only 0.7 percent of its revenues on research and, in technological progressiveness, the giants which dominate this industry lag behind their smaller domestic rivals as well as their smaller foreign competitors. Thus, the basic oxygen furnace—considered the "only major breakthrough at the ingot level since before the turn of the century" was invented in 1950 by a miniscule Austrian *firm* which was less than one-third the size of a single *plant* of the United States Steel Corp. The innovation was introduced in the United States in 1954 by McLouth Steel which at the time had about 1 percent of domestic steel capacity—to be followed some 10 years later by the steel giants: United States Steel in December 1963, Bethlehem in 1964, and Republic in 1965. . . .
>
> Only after they were subjected to actual and threatened competition from domestic and foreign steelmakers in the 1960's did the steel giants decide to accommodate themselves to the oxygen revolution. Thus, it was the cold wind of competition, and not the catatonia induced by industrial concentration, which proved conducive to innovation and technological progress.

[8]Testimony of Walter Adams at *Hearing before a Subcommittee of the Select Committee on Small Business* (Washington, June 29, 1967).

Instability

Monopoly is held by its critics to be an obstacle to the achievement of economic stability, that is, full employment with reasonable price stability. Two somewhat distinct assertions underlie this point. On the one hand, it was noted in Chapter 18 that business monopolies are in a position of relative immunity insofar as an anti-inflationary (tight) money policy is concerned. Indeed, the ability of monopolists to manipulate prices may cause a tight money policy to contribute indirectly to inflation as monopolists pass interest rate increases on to consumers through product price increases. On the other hand, we saw in Chapter 22 that business monopolies, in conjunction with labor monopolies, can cause cost-push inflation in the absence of full employment through the exertion of their market power. Business monopolies are allegedly active agents in an inflationary process which is not directly remedied by the demand-restricting efforts of a tight money policy or a fiscal surplus. In fact, instead of remedying inflation, such policies may simply have the effect of throttling economic growth.

Political dangers

Finally, business monopoly may pose serious political dangers. The growth of monopoly, it is argued, must result in one of two possible outcomes: Monopoly may come to exert undue influence upon government and therefore the formation of public policy, or government will be forced to regulate monopoly. In other words, government must control monopoly or be controlled by it. In either instance the result will be a basic alteration in the structure of our economy or the free political institutions which now characterize it.

Empirical evidence

The diverse arguments and counterarguments just outlined are reflected in empirical studies of the overall impact of monopoly (imperfect competition) upon the economy. In general, these studies reach two basic conclusions. First, the distinction which economists make between "competitive" and "monopolistic" industries is a valid one. In particular, evidence suggests that monopolistic industries do realize larger profits than competitive ones and do cause a misallocation of resources. Second, monopoly profits are not so much greater than those under competition as economic theory might lead us to believe; nor is the malallocation of resources caused by monopoly nearly so severe as some economists maintain.

One of the most recent estimates suggests that the dollar-value loss of output due to monopoly is on the order of 6 percent of the GNP, leading the investigator to conclude that the "inefficiency burden of monopoly does not appear to be overwhelming. But it is also not so slight that it can be ignored."[9] Postscript: Empirical research on the economic effects of monopoly is plagued by severe limitations, and conclusions must be regarded as rough estimates or best guesses.

PUBLIC POLICY TOWARD MONOPOLY

In view of the sharp conflict of opinion over the relative merits of business monopoly, it is not surprising to find that government policy toward business monopolies has been something less than clear-cut and consistent. As reflected in major pieces of legislation, the Federal government's stated policy objective is the maintenance of competition. Yet the government has passed legislation and at times pursued policies which have furthered the development of monopoly power. As one scholar has aptly phrased it,[10]

> Governments, apparently, have never been able to make up their minds as to which they dislike more, competition or monopoly. . . . Whether government activities, on the basis of the presently existing body of law, are on balance more favorable to monopoly or competition is controversial.

Government, in short, has both restrained business monopoly and promoted it.

[9] F. M. Scherer, *Industrial Market Structure and Economic Performance* (Chicago: Rand McNally & Company, 1970), p. 408.
[10] Fritz Machlup, *The Political Economy of Monopoly* (Baltimore: Johns Hopkins Press, 1952), p. 182.

Legislation and policies restricting monopoly

Historically, American capitalism, steeped in the philosophy of free, competitive markets, has been a fertile ground for the development of a suspicious and fearful public attitude toward business monopolies. Though relatively dormant for many decades, this fundamental distrust of monopoly came into full bloom in the decades following the Civil War. The widening of local markets into national markets as transportation facilities improved, the ever-increasing mechanization of production, and the increasingly widespread adoption of the corporate form of business enterprise were important forces giving rise to the development of "trusts"—that is, business monopolies—in the 1870s and 1880s. Trusts developed in the petroleum, meat-packing, sugar, lead, coal, whisky, and tobacco industries, among others, during this era. Not only were questionable tactics employed in monopolizing the various industries, but the resulting market power was almost invariably exerted to the detriment of all who did business with these monopolies. Farmers and small businessmen, being particularly vulnerable to the growth and tactics of the giant corporate monopolies, were among the first to censure their development. Consumers and labor unions were not far behind in voicing their disapproval of monopoly power.

Given the development of certain industries wherein market forces no longer provided adequate control to ensure socially tolerable behavior, two man-made techniques of control have been adopted as substitutes for, or supplements to, the market. First, in those few markets where economic realities are such as to preclude the effective functioning of the market—that is, where there tends to be a "natural monopoly"—we have established public *regulatory agencies* to control economic behavior. Second, in most other markets wherein economic and technological conditions have not made monopoly essential, social control has taken the form of antimonopoly or *antitrust legislation* designed to inhibit or prevent the growth of monopoly. Let us examine these two forms of social control in the order stated.

The regulation of natural monopolies

In certain industries a single firm can supply an entire market at lower per unit cost than could a number of competing firms. Competition, in short, is uneconomic. Two alternatives present themselves as means of ensuring socially acceptable behavior on the part of a "natural monopoly" or "public utility." One is nationalization and the other, chosen by the United States, is to provide for public regulation. We now have public regulatory commissions in such fields as transportation, communications, electric power, and radio and television.

To illustrate: the first of our several regulatory laws, the Interstate Commerce Act of 1887, was based on the supposition that competition was unworkable in the railroad industry. Certain industry characteristics ruled out the possibility of effective competition:

1. Relatively large fixed costs entailed the necessity of large-scale operations by each firm in order to achieve efficient, low-cost service.

2. The existence of several firms in this industry would entail the wasteful duplication of very costly capital facilities.

3. The service supplied—transportation—was essential to many firms and individuals.

And, as a matter of fact, "competition" had not worked well in this industry. Price competition aimed at the fuller realization of economies of scale often degenerated into cutthroat competition and losses for all participants. The results would be either the elimination of the weaker competitors and the evolution of monopoly or the establishment of a collusive price agreement of some sort by which the competitors sought to improve their lot. If monopoly resulted, the exploitation of that power through discriminatory pricing—that is, charging what the traffic would bear—was likely. If a collusive price resulted, the industry would then operate in much the same manner as a pure monopoly, at least until another round of price warring was precipitated.

In view of such circumstances the Interstate Commerce Act was passed by Congress to make railroads

regulated monopolies. Although their management and actual operation remained in private hands, an Interstate Commerce Commission was established to regulate the rates and monitor the services of the railroads.

The intent of this "natural monopoly" legislation is to regulate such industries effectively and for the benefit of the public, to the end that consumers might be assured quality service at reasonable rates. The rationale is this: If competition is inappropriate, *regulated* monopolies should be established to avoid possible abuses of uncontrolled monopoly power (Chapter 28). In particular, regulation should guarantee that consumers benefit from the economies of scale—that is, the lower per unit costs—which their natural-monopoly position allows public utilities to achieve. Few would quarrel with this reasoning.

But as the following discussion indicates, there is considerable disagreement about the effectiveness of the regulatory commissions in controlling the various natural monopolies.[11]

> The American experience with regulation, despite notable achievements, has had its disappointing aspects. Regulation has too often resulted in protection of the *status quo.* Entry is often blocked, prices are kept from falling, and the industry becomes inflexible and insensitive to new techniques and opportunities for progress. Competition can sometimes develop outside the jurisdiction of a regulatory agency and make inroads on the regulated companies, threatening their profitability or even survival. In such cases, pressure is usually exerted to extend the regulatory umbrella to guard against this outside competition, so that the problems of regulation multiply and detract from the original purpose of preventing overpricing and unwanted side effects.

Antitrust legislation

A number of antitrust laws have been passed to foster or enhance competition in those industries wherein technological and economic conditions do not make monopoly inevitable. The rationale underlying these laws contrasts sharply with that underlying the regulatory commissions. The basis of antitrust is[12]

> the assumption that by controlling or modifying certain aspects of industrial structure and competitive conduct, the public can avoid government intervention in the economically and politically hazardous thicket of specifying industrial performance. . . . [Antitrust] does not tell businessmen what and how much to produce or at what price to sell their products. Rather, the antitrust approach is directed at maintaining sufficient competition in the market place so that market forces will "compel" desirable economic performance.

The Sherman Act of 1890 Acute public resentment of the trusts which developed in the 1870s and 1880s culminated in the passage of the Sherman Antitrust Act in 1890. This cornerstone of antitrust legislation is surprisingly brief and, at first glance, directly to the point. The core of the act is embodied in two major provisions:

In Section 1:

> Every contract, combination in the form of a trust or otherwise, or conspiracy, in restraint of trade or commerce among the several states, or with foreign nations is hereby declared to be illegal. . . .

In Section 2:

> Every person who shall monopolize, or attempt to monopolize, or combine or conspire with any person or persons, to monopolize any part of the trade or commerce among the several states, or with foreign nations, shall be deemed guilty of a misdemeanor. . . .

The act had the effect of making monopoly and "restraints of trade" criminal offenses against the Federal government. Either the government or parties injured by business monopolies could file suits under the Sherman Act. Firms found in violation of the act could be ordered dissolved by the courts, or injunctions could be issued to prohibit practices deemed unlawful under the act. Fines and imprisonment were also possible results of successful prosecution. Further, parties injured by illegal combinations and

[11] *Economic Report of the President* (Washington, 1970), p. 107. The reader who is interested in the problems of regulation will do well to consult Paul W. MacAvoy (ed.), *The Crisis of the Regulatory Commissions* (New York: W. W. Norton & Company, Inc., 1970).

[12] Williard F. Mueller, *A Primer on Monopoly and Competition* (New York: Random House, Inc., 1970), p. 132.

conspiracies could sue for triple the amount of damages done them. The Sherman Act seemed to provide a sound foundation for positive government action against business monopolies.

A study of key antitrust cases indicates that at times the Sherman Act has been applied with great verve and effectiveness, whereas at other times it has lain dormant. Two considerations go far to explain this inconsistency:

1. The Federal government has varied considerably in its willingness to apply the act. Administrations "friendly" toward big business have sometimes emasculated the act by the simple process of ignoring it or by cutting the budget appropriations of enforcement agencies.

2. The courts have run hot and cold in interpreting the Sherman Act and its various amendments. At times the courts have applied the Sherman Act with vigor, adhering closely to the spirit and objectives of the law. In other cases, the courts have interpreted the act in such ways as to render it all but completely innocuous.

These varying interpretations of the act by the courts undoubtedly arose in good measure from its loose and general wording. Not too many years after the passage of the Sherman Act it was quite evident that a more explicit statement of the government's antitrust sentiments was in order.

The Clayton Act and the Federal Trade Commission Act, 1914 This needed elaboration of the Sherman Act took the form of the 1914 Clayton Antitrust Act. The following sections of the Clayton Act were designed to strengthen and make explicit the intent of the Sherman Act:

Section 2 outlaws price discrimination between purchasers when such discrimination is not justified on the basis of cost differences.

Section 3 forbids exclusive, or "tying," contracts, whereby a producer would sell a product only on the condition that the buyer acquire other products from the same seller and not from competitors.

Section 7 prohibits the acquisition of stocks of competing corporations when the effect is to lessen competition.

Section 8 prohibits the formation of interlocking directorates in large corporations where the effect will be to reduce competition.

Actually there was little in the Clayton Act which had not already been stated by implication in the Sherman Act. The Clayton Act merely attempted to sharpen and make clear the general provisions of the Sherman Act. Furthermore, the Clayton Act attempted to outlaw the techniques by which monopoly might develop and, in this sense, was a preventive measure. The Sherman Act, by contrast, was aimed at the punishment of existing monopolies.

The Federal Trade Commission Act was also passed in 1914. It too was based on the belief that preventive rather than more punitive measures were needed to sustain competition. Specifically, the act was designed to prevent competition from assuming certain aggressive forms which would tend to undermine competition and bring about the development of monopoly power. The act created the Federal Trade Commission, a permanent five-man board, and charged it with the power to investigate unfair competitive practices on its own initiative or at the request of injured firms. The Commission could hold public hearings on such complaints and, if necessary, issue cease-and-desist orders where "unfair methods of competition in commerce" were discovered.

The antitrust potential of the FTC has been limited by subsequent court rulings which have restricted the investigatory powers of the Commission and made it clear that the courts, not the FTC, have the final authority in interpreting the meaning of the antitrust laws. Then in 1938 the Wheeler-Lea Act amended the Federal Trade Commission Act by prohibiting "unfair or deceptive acts or practices in commerce." As a result, a primary task of the FTC now is the prohibition of false and misleading advertising and the misrepresentation of products.

More recent antitrust legislation More recent antitrust legislation has taken the form of amendments designed to plug loopholes in—and thereby strengthen—the Clayton Act.

The *Robinson-Patman Act* of 1936 amended Section 2—the price discrimination section—of the Clay-

ton Act. This section, you will recall, attempted to eliminate the practice by which producers charged different prices to different buyers, where the objective was to drive competing producers from business. The various trusts frequently employed such cutthroat tactics—charging extremely low prices in markets in which small competitors persisted but higher prices in markets where competition had already been eliminated—as a method of improving and strengthening their monopoly positions. The Robinson-Patman Act, or "Chain Store Law," had a different background. It was aimed at the growing number of chain stores which, so argued independent retailers, were obtaining large and unjustified price discounts from wholesalers because of their strong bargaining positions as large buyers. By passing some of these cost savings on to consumers in the form of price reductions, the chains allegedly were driving their independent competitors to the wall. The Robinson-Patman Act outlaws quantity discounts to large buyers when such discounts are not justified on the basis of actual cost economies arising from mass buying. And, in turn, the act prohibits retailers from selling "at unreasonably low prices" when the purpose is to eliminate competitors. Many economists feel that the effect of the act has been not so much to deter the growth of monopoly but rather to stifle price competition, particularly at the retail level, and therefore to sustain inefficient retailers who would otherwise succumb to more vigorous competition.

Finally, the *Celler Antimerger Act* of 1950 amended Section 7 of the Clayton Act, the section which prohibits one firm from acquiring the *stock* of competitors when the effect is to reduce competition. This provision had been weakened by court decisions and had been dodged by firms who merged with competitors by acquiring their *assets* rather than their stock. The Celler Act attempted to tighten the stock acquisition ban and also prohibited the acquisition of the assets of competitors when the effect was to lessen competition.

Effectiveness of antitrust Reasonable men can, and do, disagree about the relevance and effectiveness of antitrust. At one extreme Galbraith's view is that the antitrust laws are a charade. He contends that, in fact, the giant corporation which already has vast market power is substantially immune from antitrust prosecution. But if substantially smaller firms in the same industry attempt to merge so as to compete more effectively with the dominant giant, they will run afoul of antitrust. Furthermore, by giving the public the illusion that the market remains a viable form of social control, the antitrust laws protect the largest corporations from the alternative of public regulation.

On the other hand, many economists are of the opinion that the antitrust laws have worked reasonably well and that stronger antitrust laws coupled with more vigorous and more discriminating enforcement would do much to make our economy even more competitive. It is felt in some quarters that faulty judicial interpretations, legal loopholes, and indifferent Federal administrations have at times undermined and considerably weakened antitrust policy. Most importantly, there is rather widespread agreement that many of the government's most notable legal victories in applying the antitrust laws have proved to be economic defeats. That is, the guilty firms have agreed to cease-and-desist orders or have been subject to minor penalties rather than forced to dissolve. Indeed, even when dissolution has occurred, the economic benefits have been dubious: When it comes to price and output policies, a tight three- or four-firm oligopoly is likely to behave much as the absolute monopoly which once comprised it.

On the positive side, it must be recognized that there currently exists widespread interest in antitrust. Examples: The Senate Subcommittee on Antitrust and Monopoly has conducted detailed investigations of administered prices in the automobile, steel, and drug industries; the Department of Justice indicted the nation's principal electrical equipment producers in late 1960 for conspiracy in violation of the Sherman Act; and, finally, economists have reasserted their long-standing interest in the monopoly problem as the cost-push and structural theories of inflation have emphasized market power as a cause of rising prices.

The conglomerates: a special problem Existing antitrust laws, properly enforced, are quite adequate

to cope with horizontal and vertical mergers (Chapter 8). But the vast majority of the mergers of the last decade were conglomerate mergers; that is, a company in one industry takes over companies in unrelated industries. To illustrate:[13]

> The International Telegraph & Telephone Company (ITT) is a huge international conglomerate operating over 150 affiliated companies in fifty-seven countries; it is the fourth largest private industrial employer in the world. Most of its present size can be traced to the hundreds of mergers it has made during the years. During 1961–1968 it acquired at least 120 businesses with combined assets of nearly $2 billion. Perhaps more than any other corporation, ITT has acquired companies that are themselves large and leaders in their fields. For example, it has acquired Avis, the second largest car rental corporation; Sheraton Corporation, the largest hotel chain; Continental Baking Company, the country's largest bakery products manufacturer; and Educational Services, one of the leading suppliers of educational exhibit materials. During the first nine months of 1969, ITT's board of directors approved the consumation of thirty-three more acquisitions. Three of these were industry leaders with combined assets of about $2.2 billion: Grinnel Corporation, the nation's leading maker of automatic fire protection equipment, Canteen Corporation, one of the largest vending machine companies, and Hartford Fire Insurance Company, a leader in several lines of insurance.

On the surface conglomerate mergers would seem less detrimental to the public interest than would, for example, a horizontal merger of firms which directly compete in the same market. But conglomerates do pose serious problems. First, as the ITT illustration indicates, conglomerates are obviously a means for achieving great concentrations of wealth and economic power. Such concentration poses dangers not only for the market system, but also for the nation's political and social systems. Second, this amassed wealth can be used to weaken or destroy competitors in the conglomerates' various product markets. That is, the profits derived from markets wherein a conglomerate's monopoly power is currently great can be used to subsidize and promote its power in other markets which are currently quite competitive. Third, by their very nature conglomerates are in a position to use *reciprocal selling* as an anticompetitive device. Since its operations span many different markets, the conglomerate may be in the unique position to say to potential customers "I'll buy from you if you'll buy from me," which puts them at an obvious advantage over competing nonconglomerate firms which can only plead to customers "Please buy from me." Finally, it is notable that the growth of the conglomerates is not based upon technological imperatives; indeed, there is "persuasive evidence that many jerry-built conglomerates are less efficient then were the individual companies they absorbed."[14]

Although the Justice Department has challenged a few of the conglomerate mergers in the courts, new antitrust legislation may be necessary if the conglomerate merger movement is to be effectively curtailed.

Legislation and policies promoting monopoly

Let us now consider briefly the other side of the picture. Government has directly and indirectly promoted the growth of monopoly in several different ways.

Industry exemptions to the antitrust laws Over the years government has enacted certain laws which have either exempted certain specific industries or, alternatively, have excluded certain trade practices from antitrust prosecution. In doing so, the government has tended indirectly to foster the growth of monopoly power.

In 1918 the Webb-Pomerene Act exempted American exporters from the antitrust laws by permitting them to form export trade associations. Although the act was intended to put American exporters in a stronger competitive position with international cartels, the effect has probably been to reduce competition in both international and domestic markets.

We have already noted too that the Robinson-Patman Act of 1936 had the effect of dampening price competition at the retail level. The Miller-Tydings Act of 1937, amending the Sherman Act, moved in the direction of eliminating this competition. This

[13] Ibid., pp. 80–81.

[14] Ibid., p. 155.

so-called fair-trade law exempts from antitrust laws *resale price maintenance contracts* for branded and trademarked goods when such contracts are permitted by state legislation. Price maintenance contracts allow manufacturers to set the retail prices of their products by signing contracts to this effect with retailers. The Miller-Tydings Act has operated so that these agreements have applied not only to retailers who actually enter into such contracts but also to all other "nonsigner" retailers in the state. This means that if one retailer signs a price maintenance contract, the agreement is binding on *all* other retailers in the state. The net effect has been to restrict price competition on branded products at the retail level; a monopolistic practice—price fixing—has been injected by legislation into an otherwise highly competitive segment of the economy.

It should be noted, too, that labor unions and agricultural cooperatives have been exempt, subject to limitations, from the antitrust laws. We shall see in the next chapter that Federal legislation and policy have attempted to provide some measure of monopolistic power for agriculture, feeling that this would help alleviate the farm problem. Similarly, in a subsequent chapter we shall discover that since 1930, Federal legislation on balance has generally promoted the growth of strong labor unions. This federally sponsored growth has resulted, according to some authorities, in the development of union monopolies. This will later be discussed further.

Patent laws Technological research is a costly and risky procedure. American patent laws—the first of which was passed in 1790—are aimed at providing sufficient monetary incentive for innovators by granting them exclusive rights to produce and sell a new product or machine for a period of seventeen years. Patent grants have the effect of protecting the innovator from competitors who would otherwise quickly imitate his product and share in the profits, though not the cost and effort, of his research. Few contest the desirability of this particular aspect of our patent laws, particularly when it is recalled that innovation can weaken and undermine existing positions of monopoly power.

However, patents are a mixed blessing. The granting of a patent frequently amounts to the granting of monopoly power in the production of the patented item. Many economists feel that the length of patent protection—seventeen years—is much too long. Such an extended period of protection from competitors is likely to allow the innovator to entrench himself firmly in a monopoly position to the extent that he is able to block successfully any potential competition after his patent expires. This is particularly true if the innovating firm extends its patent rights longer than seventeen years by patenting improved models of the original innovation. By this and similar procedures innovating firms have often been able to extend their exclusive jurisdiction over a product for three or four decades!

When patents are licensed to competitors, the innovating firm has the right to specify the prices which these competitors may charge for the product, the markets in which they may sell, and even the amounts which they may produce. The result is that the innovator faces no genuine competition. The worst abuses of patent rights occur when one firm accumulates by research or purchase a large number of related patents or, alternatively, several firms in an industry "pool" the patents which they own and exclude potential rivals from their use. In such situations patents can constitute a very formidable barrier to entry and thereby create and perpetuate monopoly power.

And finally, a patent monopoly is an excellent basis for a tying agreement and the subsequent extension of monopoly power. The classic case is that of the United Shoe Machinery Corporation, which leased the machinery over which it has exclusive patents only on the condition that shoe manufacturers would purchase all their other machinery from United. This practice stripped United's competitors of their customers and firmly entrenched United as the dominant firm in the industry.

The importance of patent laws in the growth of business monopoly must not be underestimated. Such well-known firms as du Pont, General Electric, American Telephone and Telegraph, Eastman Kodak, Alcoa, and innumerable other industrial giants

have attained various measures of monopoly power in part through their ownership of certain patent rights.[15]

Protective tariffs Although we must postpone any detailed discussion of tariffs until a later chapter, it is most relevant at this point to recognize that tariffs and similar trade barriers have the effect of shielding American producers from foreign competition. Protective tariffs are in effect discriminatory taxes against the goods of foreign firms. These taxes make it difficult and often impossible for foreign producers to compete in domestic markets with American firms. The result? A less competitive domestic market and an environment frequently conducive to the growth of domestic business monopolies.

FUTURE POLICY ALTERNATIVES

Now let us look ahead. What is the most desirable path for public policy to follow in the future? There are three general positions and a host of hybrid views on this important question. There are those who are satisfied with the structure and performance of American industry and therefore generally content with the status quo or even in favor of some relaxation of antitrust enforcement. There are those who feel that American capitalism has no choice but to move in the direction of increased governmental regulation and/or ownership of monopolized industries. There are those who believe that it is both desirable and possible to make American industry more competitive.[16] The serious consequences of any choice between these sharply contrasting policy alternatives demand that we weigh each rather carefully.

Maintaining the status quo

Those who advocate maintaining the status quo are convinced that the presence of business monopolies and the degree of concentration of economic power which now exists are not only essential but also desirable. Supporting arguments are generally those made earlier in this chapter as the case for business monopoly.

Competition of all products for the dollars of consumers, interproduct competition, nonprice competition, countervailing power, potential competition and the fear of government regulation, and technological advance all render "workably competitive" industries which appear at first glance to be monopolistic. Then, too, it is contended that business leaders have attained levels of maturity and social responsibility far beyond those attained by their predecessors. Business leaders are trustees of economic power and can be expected not to abuse that trust.

But the most significant and the most frequently heard claim for preservation of the status quo is the doctrine of *technological determinism.* The current advanced stage of technological development, it is argued, makes it imperative that big businesses prevail. Business monopolies are necessary if the economy is to realize the productive efficiencies which modern technology now makes available. Furthermore, bigness is essential to continued large-scale expenditures on research and development and, therefore, to a future high rate of technological progress. A return to competition, in the sense of a large number of small producers, would be to forgo economies of scale and a rapid rate of technological advance. Any restoration of large-numbers competition is a step in the direction of economic *in*efficiency and the misuse of scare resources.

Toward public regulation and ownership

There are many observers who are less satisfied with the current structure of American industry. Public regulation or even public ownership and operation are envisioned as inevitable consequences of the need to control private monopoly power.

This position rests on three points:

1. Modern technology, it is assumed, is such that business monopoly is here to stay if we are to achieve and maintain productive efficiency.

2. The arguments underlying the status quo position

[15] For a sophisticated and detailed discussion of this topic see Scherer, *op. cit.*, chap. 16.

[16] The present discussion follows the general pattern outlined in Walter Adams (ed.), *The Structure of American Industry,* 4th ed. (New York: The Macmillan Company, 1971), chap. 13.

are discounted by those who view public regulation as the only course for future public policy. It is naïve to assume that monopolists will exercise self-restraint in using the economic power at their disposal. Workable competition is more a myth than a reality; it does not function as an effective regulatory device. Further, countervailing power is subject to many exceptions, and in many instances it functions in a very imperfect manner.

3. Present antitrust laws are deemed too weak to curb abuses of monopoly power, and if strengthened and vigorously enforced, antitrust laws would entail the loss of the productive efficiences which modern technology now provides.

It is concluded that the only real alternative is the social control of business monopolies through government regulation. Only in this way can business monopoly be operated in the public interest.

Restoring vigorous competition

A final alternative seeks the restoration of "effective" competition in what now are monopolistic industries. The objective sought is not the establishment of *pure* competition; this is recognized as unrealistic and in some instances economically undesirable. Rather the goal is the establishment of markets wherein (1) the number of producers is sufficiently large so that no individual firms possess considerable market power, (2) collusion is absent, and (3) the entry to markets is relatively unrestricted.

Proponents of this policy alternative contend that the goal of effective competition is realistic, attainable, and highly desirable. They argue that the status quo is intolerable. Monopoly power exists, workable competition and countervailing power to the contrary, and it is being sorely abused. No effective market or moral forces exist to protect consumers from business monopolies. Hence, the restoration of competion to such industries is highly desirable.

In the second place, it is felt that in most industries the growth of big-business monopolies has far exceeded that necessary for the attainment of all the economies of scale which modern technology allows. A considerable degree of competition can be reestablished in many now-monopolized markets with little or no impairment of productive efficiency or the rate of technological progress.

And, it is argued, past experience indicates that public regulation of monopoly has generally failed to function in the public interest. Public monopolies can abuse their power in the same way as can private monopolies.

Through what techniques is competition to be restored? On the one hand, antitrust laws should be strengthened and vigorously applied. A rear-guard defensive application of antitrust legislation to retard the rate of monopoly growth is wholly inadequate. The restoration of effective competition calls for positive action designed to *increase* the degree of competition in industries in which monopoly power is considerable. And, too, it is imperative that all exceptions to the antitrust laws be eliminated. Similarly, legislation and policies which now promote the growth of monopoly—for example, patent laws and protective tariffs—must be either eliminated or modified.

SUMMARY

1. The role of business monopolies in American capitalism is a highly controversial one. The defense of business monopoly is built around the following points: *a.* "Workable competition" prevails in many industries in which large-numbers competition is absent, *b.* the realization of mass-production economies often necessitates the presence of business monopolies, *c.* monopoly provides both the means and incentives for rapid technological advance, *d.* the investment and price policies of monopolies tend to stabilize the economy, and *e.* business monopolies are socially responsible.

2. The case against business monopoly centers upon the contentions that business monopoly *a.* results in high prices and output restriction, *b.* contributes to the misallocation of resources, *c.* promotes income inequality, *d.* retards the rate of technological advance, *e.* is an obstacle to the achievement of economic stability, and *f.* poses a threat to political democracy.

3. Government has attempted to exert social control

over monopoly by ***a.*** establishing regulatory commissions in markets where technological and economic considerations are conducive to natural monopoly and ***b.*** applying antitrust laws to markets wherein monopoly is not a prerequisite of economic efficiency.

4. The cornerstone of antitrust policy consists of the Sherman Act of 1890 and the Clayton Act of 1914. The Sherman Act specifies that "Every contract, combination . . . or conspiracy in the restraint of interstate trade . . . is . . . illegal" and that any person who monopolizes or attempts to monopolize interstate trade is guilty of a misdemeanor. The general wording of the act, however, has resulted in a variety of court interpretations, many of which have served to limit the effectiveness of the act.

5. The Clayton Act was designed to bolster and make more explicit the provisions of the Sherman Act. To this end the Clayton Act declared that price discrimination, tying contracts, intercorporate stockholdings, and interlocking directorates are illegal when the effect of their use is the lessening of competition.

6. The Federal Trade Commission Act of 1914 created the Federal Trade Commission to investigate antitrust violations and to prevent the use of "unfair methods of competition." Empowered to issue cease-and-desist orders, the Commission now serves as a watchdog agency for the false and deceptive representation of products.

7. Though designed to sustain competition between retail distributors, the Robinson-Patman Act of 1936 has stifled retail price competition by prohibiting chain stores from ***a.*** acquiring "unjustified" discounts in buying from wholesalers and ***b.*** selling to consumers at "unreasonably" low prices.

8. The Celler Antimerger Act of 1950 prohibits one firm from acquiring the assets of another firm where the result is a lessening of competition.

9. Government, however, has also done much to promote both directly and indirectly the concentration of economic power and the growth of monopoly. Industrial exceptions to antitrust laws include ***a.*** the exclusion of exporters by the Webb-Pomerene Act of 1918, ***b.*** partial exclusion of retailers by the Robinson-Patman Act (1936) and the Miller-Tydings Act (1937), and ***c.*** the exemption of unions and agricultural cooperatives. Patent laws and protective tariffs also constitute bases for the development of business monopoly.

10. Possible future policies for dealing with business monopolies include ***a.*** maintenance of the status quo, ***b.*** increasing public regulation and ownership of industry, and ***c.*** the restoration of effective competition.

QUESTIONS AND STUDY SUGGESTIONS

1. "All big firms are monopolistic, but not all monopolistic firms are big." Appraise critically.

2. Suppose you are president of one of the Big Three automobile producers. Discuss critically the case against business monopoly.

3. Now suppose you are a spokesman for a farm organization and are attempting to convince a congressional committee that the presence of business monopolies is a significant factor contributing to the farm problem. Critically evaluate the case for business monopoly.

4. Distinguish between "pure," "workable," and "effective" competition.

5. Discuss the evolution and the social desirability of the giant corporation as envisioned in Galbraith's *The New Industrial State.*

6. Briefly identify each of the following acts, specifying the manner in which each has restrained or contributed to the development of business monopoly:

a. Webb-Pomerene Act, 1918
b. Sherman Act, 1890
c. Interstate Commerce Act, 1887
d. Federal Trade Commission Act, 1914

e. Robinson-Patman Act, 1936
f. Miller-Tydings Act, 1937
g. Clayton Act, 1914
h. Celler Antimerger Act, 1950

7. What stake do you, as a consumer, have in the application of antitrust legislation? Do you feel that antitrust legislation should be applied to labor unions? Explain.

8. Which of the three policies outlined at the end of this chapter do you feel is the most desirable? What criticisms can be made of each of the three positions? Be as specific as you can.

9. Define the concept of countervailing power. Explain its operation. How does countervailing power differ from competition as we defined it in Chapter 27? What implication, if any, does countervailing power have for the application of antitrust policy?

10. Explain the meaning and significance of each of the following:
a. Resale price maintenance contracts
b. Interlocking directorates
c. Tying agreements
d. Cease-and-desist orders

11. What proposals can you make to strengthen the antitrust laws in their application to business monopolies? Be specific. Explain how conglomerates might tend to diminish competition.

12. "The social desirability of any given business enterprise should be judged not on the basis of the structure of the industry in which it finds itself, but rather on the basis of the market performance of that firm." Analyze critically.

13. A much-discussed policy alternative in dealing with the business monopoly problem suggests that ***a.*** government should establish and maintain "effectively competitive conditions in all industries where competition can function as a regulative agency" and ***b.*** government should gradually assume the "ownership and operation in the case of all industries where competition cannot be made to function effectively as an agency of control."[17] Evaluate these suggestions as to their social desirability and political feasibility. What practical problems do you think might be encountered in the application of these recommendations?

SELECTED REFERENCES

Economic Issues, 4th ed., readings 58, 59, 60, and 61.

Adams, Walter (ed.): *The Structure of American Industry,* 4th ed. (New York: The Macmillan Company, 1971), particularly chap. 13.

Adams, Walter, and Horace M. Gray: *Monopoly in America* (New York: The Macmillan Company, 1955).

Bain, Joe S.: *Industrial Organization,* 2d ed. (New York: John Wiley & Sons, Inc., 1968).

Galbraith, John Kenneth: *The New Industrial State* (Boston: Houghton Mifflin Company, 1967).

Leonard, William N.: *Business Size, Market Power, and Public Policy* (New York: Thomas Y. Crowell Company, 1969).

Mansfield, Edwin (ed.): *Monopoly Power and Economic Performance,* 2d ed. (New York: W. W. Norton & Company, Inc., 1968).

Mueller, Willard F.: *A Primer on Monopoly and Competition* (New York: Random House, Inc., 1970).

Scherer, F. M.: *Industrial Market Structure and Economic Performance* (Chicago: Rand McNally & Company, 1970).

Shepherd, William G.: *Market Power and Economic Welfare* (New York: Random House, Inc., 1970).

[17] Simons, op. cit., p. 57.

36

RURAL ECONOMICS: THE FARM PROBLEM

American agriculture is a paradox: ''Agriculture is one of the most progressive segments of the American economy. Productivity has grown faster there than in any other major economic sector. U.S. agricultural abundance is the envy of the world. Yet incomes of most farm families continue to fall short of those earned in other occupations. And agricultural employment is steadily declining.''[1]

The major objectives of this chapter are:

1. To describe and assess the severity of the farm problem
2. To outline the causes of the farm problem
3. To describe government policy toward American agriculture
4. To evaluate critically the effectiveness of public policy
5. To outline several future policy options

[1] *Economic Report of the President, 1966* (Washington), p. 131.

HISTORY OF THE FARM PROBLEM

The two decades prior to World War I were exceedingly prosperous ones for agriculture; indeed, this period has been dubbed ''the golden age of American agriculture.'' The demand for farm products, farm prices, and farm incomes all rose. World War I intensified these good times. Foreign demand for the output of American farmers skyrocketed during, and immediately following, the war. Foreign countries, diverting resources from agriculture to war goods production, turned to American agriculture for food and fiber. High prices and an almost insatiable demand were the happy lot of American farmers.

These highly favorable conditions were not to last. A sharp postwar depression in 1920 was a sudden and severe shock to agriculture. In particular, the large volume of mortgage indebtedness incurred

during the previous years of prosperity proved a heavy burden. The economy as a whole quickly recovered from this downturn, however, and by 1921 the booming twenties were upon us. But agriculture failed to share in this prosperity to the extent that other segments of the economy did.

The reasons for this were several. European agriculture not only recovered from the war but also began to expand rapidly under the impetus of new technological advances. Hence, foreign demand for American farm goods began to level off and decline. American foreign trade policies also contributed to this deterioration in foreign demand. High tariffs on goods imported to the United States helped undermine foreign demand for American farm products. To the extent that foreigners could not sell to us because of trade restrictions, they were unable to earn the funds they needed to buy from American producers. Furthermore, the domestic demand for farm products simply did not rise very much in the twenties. American stomachs were full, and as a result income increases were used to buy automobiles, refrigerators, and a host of new products of industry. Finally, on the supply side of the picture technological advances boosted farm output markedly. The net result of a lagging, inelastic demand and a sharply increasing supply of farm products was low farm prices and incomes.

The Great Depression of the 1930s was a particularly acute blow to American agriculture. The highly competitive nature of agriculture makes it especially vulnerable to bad times. Unlike sellers who possess a modicum of monopoly power, farmers are unable to influence their prices. They are "price takers" at the mercy of the market. Therefore, when market demand declines as it did during the Depression, farm prices and farm incomes fall sharply. Ironically, farmers buy in markets which are basically noncompetitive. Hence, while their incomes fell by very large amounts, the prices of farmers' purchases declined very modestly. As Figure 36·1 indicates, farmers in the 1920s and 1930s found themselves in a harsh price-cost squeeze.

World War II provided welcome but temporary relief for the farmer. Both domestic and foreign demand for agricultural products boomed during the war, and prosperity returned to agriculture. Except for the 1948–1949 slump, the middle and late forties were peak years for American farmers. Then in the 1950s a slow but certain relapse became evident, and agriculture was once again encountering difficulty. As farm prices faltered and declined, other prices inched upward. The farmer again found himself in the unenviable position of paying more and more for what he bought and getting less and less for what he sold (Figure 36·1).

FARM INCOMES AND RURAL POVERTY

The relative deterioration of the economic position of the farmer can be readily seen through income statistics. Indeed, low incomes are the most obvious symptom of the farm problem. Table 36·1 provides us with a comparison of per capita farm and nonfarm incomes since the mid-thirties. Note that farm income has been persistently lower than nonfarm income over the entire period and that the differential has been large. Per capita farm income is currently about 78 percent of per capita nonfarm income. About 20 percent of the farm population is living below the poverty income level.

But income statistics, of course, do not tell the whole story. The commentary of the National Advisory Commission on Rural Poverty is revealing:[2]

> Rural poverty is so widespread, and so acute, as to be a national disgrace. . . . Hunger, even among children, does exist among the rural poor. . . . [In the rural South] Negro children [are] not getting enough food to sustain life, and so disease ridden to be beyond cure. Malnutrition is even more widespread. . . . Disease and premature death are startlingly high among the rural poor. . . . medical and dental care is conspicuously absent. Unemployment and underemployment are major problems in rural America. . . . The rural poor have gone, and now go, to poor schools. . . . Most rural poor live in atrocious houses. . . . Most of the rural South is one vast poverty area. . . .

Furthermore, in comparison with the urban poor, the rural poor are badly organized and relatively ineffec-

[2] National Advisory Commission on Rural Poverty, *The People Left Behind* (Washington, 1967), pp. ix–x.

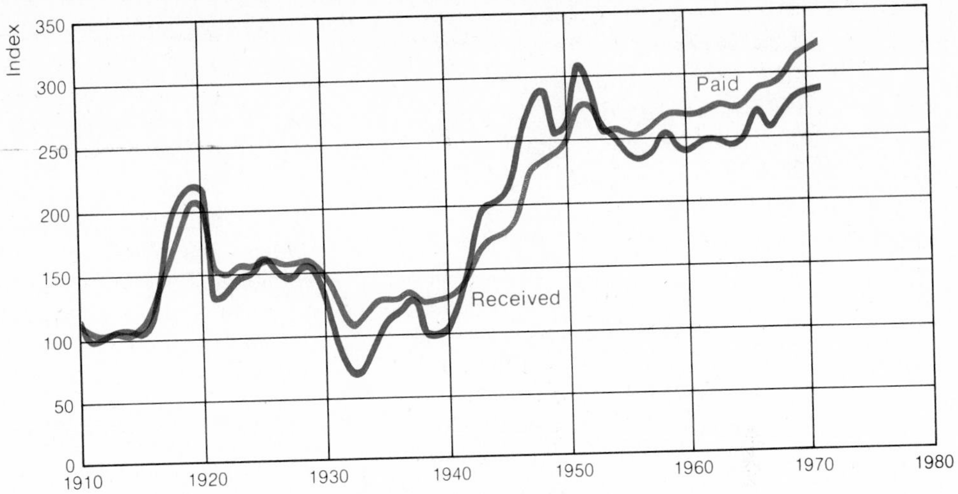

FIGURE 36·1 PRICES PAID AND RECEIVED BY FARMERS, 1910–1970

Throughout the twenties and thirties and again since the mid-fifties, the prices received by farmers have lagged behind the prices paid by them. (U.S. Department of Agriculture, *Agriculture Outlook Charts.*)

tive in the political arena; hence, the rural poor have been bypassed by many recent antipoverty programs. We will note later that government subsidy programs to agriculture also do little to help the poor farmer.

On the other hand, do not jump to the false conclusion that all farmers are poor. The data of Table 36·1 are average figures and tend to conceal the fact that some farmers are well off by any relevant standard.

Table 36·2 gives us a rough idea of the degree of income disparity *within* agriculture. These figures show that in 1969, 7 percent of the farms in the United States accounted for 48 percent of total farm output. At the other extreme, cumulating the figures for the bottom two economic classes makes it clear that 51 percent of all farms sold less than $5,000 worth of farm products in 1969 and that the output of these farms was a mere 8 percent of the total amount of farm products sold in that year. Note further that the 36 percent of our farms which market $10,000 or more each year produce 85 percent of all marketed farm products. The remaining 64 percent account for only 15 percent of marketed output. It is in this latter group that extremely low incomes—the main symptom of the difficulties which plague American agriculture—are predominant.

In addition to wide income disparities within agriculture, the data of Table 36·2 suggest a second point about which more will be said later: A substantial amount of human and property resources could leave agriculture without causing a very significant decline in total farm output.

CAUSES OF THE FARM PROBLEM

It is a bit misleading to talk of "the" farm problem. Actually, the changes which have occurred in farm incomes suggest the presence of both a long-run

TABLE 36·1 PER CAPITA DISPOSABLE INCOME OF FARM AND NONFARM PEOPLE, SELECTED YEARS, 1934–1970

Year	Farm people	Nonfarm people
1934	$ 163	$ 496
1937	283	637
1940	246	675
1942	477	979
1944	625	1,156
1946	743	1,222
1948	900	1,369
1950	841	1,464
1952	961	1,610
1954	915	1,670
1956	925	1,844
1958	1,119	1,904
1960	1,165	2,008
1962	1,309	2,121
1964	1,405	2,318
1967	1,692	2,796
1970	2,633	3,368

Source: U.S. Department of Agriculture, *Farm Income Situation.*

problem and a short-run problem. The long-run problem concerns those forces which have caused farm prices and incomes to decline over a period of years. The short-run problem has to do with the extreme year-to-year instability of farm incomes.

The long-run problem

Complex problems can rarely be stated accurately in brief terms. This is certainly true of the long-run problem which plagues American agriculture. Nevertheless a workable picture of the problem can be portrayed through the economic tools of demand and supply. In these terms, we may say that the causes of the long-run farm problem are embodied in

1. The *price inelasticity* of the demand for agricultural products
2. The *shifts* which have occurred over time in the demand and supply curves for farm products
3. The relative *immobility* of agricultural resources

The inelastic demand for agricultural products In most developed societies, the price elasticity of demand for agricultural products is low. For farm products in the aggregate the elasticity coefficient is estimated to be from .20 to .25.[3] These figures suggest that the prices of agricultural products would have to fall by 40 to 50 percent in order for consumers to increase their purchases by a mere 10 percent. Consumers apparently put a low value on additional agricultural output as compared with alternative goods. Why is this so? You will recall that the basic determinant of elasticity of demand is substitutability. That is, when the price of a product falls, the consumer will tend to substitute *that* product for other products the prices of which presumably have not fallen. But in wealthy societies this "substitution effect" (Chapter 25) is very modest. People simply do not switch from three to six or eight meals each

[3] Dale E. Hathaway, *Problems of Progress in the Agricultural Economy* (Chicago: Scott, Foresman and Company, 1964), p. 10. This short book is an incisive and highly readable survey of the farm problem.

TABLE 36·2 DISTRIBUTION OF COMMERCIAL FARMS BY ECONOMIC CLASS, 1969

Value of farm products sold	Percent of total farms	Percent of total output
$40,000 or more	7	48
$20,000–$39,999	12	21
$10,000–$19,999	17	16
$5,000–$9,999	13	7
$2,500–$4,999	10	3
Less than $2,500	41	5
Total	100	100

Source: U.S. Department of Agriculture data.

day in response to declines in the relative prices of agricultural products. An individual's capacity to substitute food for other products is subject to very real biological constraints. The inelasticity of agricultural demand can also be explained in terms of diminishing marginal utility. In a wealthy society the population by and large is well fed and well clothed, that is, relatively saturated with the food and fiber of agriculture. Therefore, additional agricultural output entails rapidly diminishing marginal utility. Thus it takes very large price cuts to induce small increases in consumption. Curve *D* in Figure 36·3 portrays an inelastic demand.

Technological advance and rapid increases in agricultural supply An inelastic demand for farm products is, in and of itself, innocent enough. It is the accompanying fact that the supply of agricultural products has increased in relation to the demand for them that has spelled declining farm incomes.

On the supply side of the picture a rapid rate of technological advance, particularly since World War I, has caused significant increases in the supply of agricultural products. This technological progress has many roots: the virtually complete electrification and mechanization of farms, improved techniques of land management and soil conservation, irrigation, the development of hybrid crops, the availability of improved fertilizers and insecticides, improvements in the breeding and care of livestock, and so forth.

How meaningful have these technological advances actually been? Very! The simplest index is the increasing number of people which a single farmer's output will support. Table 36·3 pictures the long-run trend. In 1820 each farm worker produced enough feed and fiber to support four persons. By 1970 each farmer produced enough to support forty-six! There can be no question but that productivity in agriculture has risen significantly. Since World War II productivity in agriculture has advanced at a rate which is *twice* as fast as that of the nonfarm economy.

Two additional important points must amend this discussion of the increasing productivity in American farming:

1. Most recent technological advances have not been initiated by farmers but are rather the result of government-sponsored programs of research and education and the work of farm machinery producers. Land-grant colleges, experiment stations, county agents of the Agricultural Extension Service, the inexhaustible supply of educational pamphlets issuing from the U.S. Department of Agriculture, and the research staffs of John Deere and International Harvester are the sources of technological advance in American agriculture.

2. Technological advance has not occurred evenly throughout agriculture. Many farmers—particularly those resting on the bottom rung of the income ladder—are undermechanized, uninformed, and inefficient.

TABLE 36·3 PERSONS SUPPORTED BY PRODUCTION OF ONE FARM WORKER, SELECTED YEARS, 1820–1970

Year	Persons supported per farm worker
1820	4
1870	5
1900	7
1910	7
1920	9
1930	10
1940	11
1950	15
1954	19
1957	24
1961	28
1964	33
1968	43
1970	46

Source: U.S. Department of Agriculture, *Agricultural Outlook Chartbook, 1971.*

Lagging demand for agricultural products Increases in the demand for agricultural commodities have failed to keep pace with technologically inspired

increases in their supply. Why? The answer lies in the two major determinants of agricultural demand—incomes and population.

In underdeveloped countries consumers must devote the bulk of their meager incomes to the products of agriculture—food and clothing—to sustain themselves. But as income expands beyond the subsistence level and the problem of hunger eventually gives way to one of obesity, consumers will increase their outlays on food and clothing at ever-declining rates. Once a consumer's stomach is filled, his thoughts turn to the amenities of life, which industry, not agriculture, provides. Economic growth in the United States has boosted average per capita income far beyond the level of bare subsistence. As a result, *increases in the incomes of American consumers lead to less than proportionate increases in expenditures on farm products.* In brief, the demand for farm products is *income-inelastic.* Recent estimates indicate that a 10 percent increase in real per capita disposable income entails at the most an increase in the consumption of farm products of only 2 percent.[4]

Population is a somewhat different proposition. Despite the fact that, after a minimum income level is reached, each individual consumer's intake of food and fiber will become relatively fixed, more consumers will mean an increase in the demand for farm products. And it has. But population increases, added to the relatively small increase in the purchase of farm products which occurs as incomes rise, have simply not been great enough to match the concomitant increases in farm output.

When coupled with the inelastic demand for agricultural products, these shifts in supply and demand have resulted in declining farm incomes. This is illustrated in Figure 36·2, where a large increase in supply is shown against a very modest increase in demand. Because of the inelastic demand for farm products, these shifts have resulted in a sharp decline in farm prices accompanied by relatively small increases in sales. This means that farm incomes decline. Diagrammatically, income before the increase

[4] Joint Economic Committee, *Staff Report on Employment, Growth, and Price Levels* (Washington, 1960), p. 190.

FIGURE 36·2 A GRAPHIC SUMMARY OF THE LONG-RUN FARM PROBLEM

In the long run, increases in the demand for agricultural products (D to D_1) have not kept pace with the increases in supply (S to S_1) which technological advances have permitted. Coupled with the fact that agricultural demand is inelastic, these shifts have tended to depress farm prices (as from P to P_1) and incomes (as from $OPAQ$ to OP_1BQ_1).

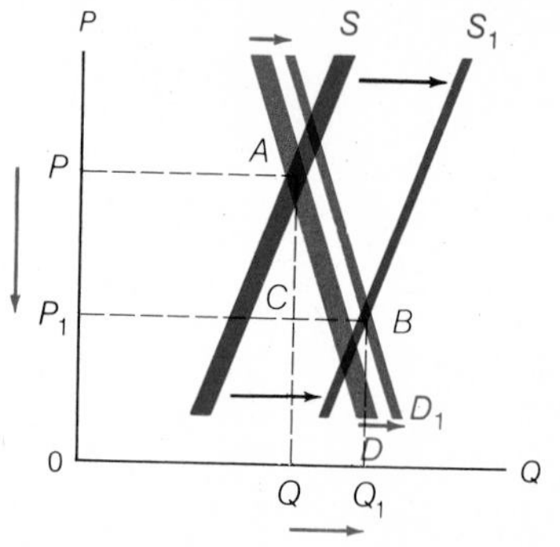

in supply occurs (measured by rectangle $OPAQ$) will exceed farm income after supply increases (OP_1BQ_1). The income "loss" of P_1PAC is not fully offset by the income "gain" of $QCBQ_1$. In summary, *given an inelastic demand for farm products, an increase in the supply of farm products relative to the demand for them has created persistent tendencies for farm incomes to fall.* This is not to say that farm incomes have fallen absolutely, but rather that farm incomes have clearly lagged behind the nonfarm sector of the economy (Table 36 · 1).

All this is not to say that farm prices and incomes are always declining. Figure 36·1 indicates that farm prices rose sharply during the 1940s and early 1950s, but the abnormal demand for farm products which accompanied World War II, European reconstruction, and the Korean conflict largely explain these increases. The price declines which farmers faced in the prosperous twenties and middle fifties are indicative of the persistent tendency of farm prices to fall.

Immobility of resources Our previous discussion of the workings of the price system (Chapter 34) would certainly suggest an obvious and automatic solution to the long-run problem faced by agriculture. In a price-directed economy one would expect declining farm prices and incomes to signal an exodus of resources from agriculture. Prices and incomes which are low in relation to the rest of the economy would seemingly prompt farmers to leave their farms in favor of more lucrative occupations. The adjustments of a competitive industry as outlined in Chapters 5 and 27 indicate that this exodus of farmers would reduce industry supply in relation to demand, thereby boosting farm prices and incomes. This reallocation of resources away from agriculture and toward industry, one can assume, would bring farm incomes into closer accord with those of the rest of the economy.

But, despite its competitiveness, agriculture has not behaved in quite the fashion economic analysis suggests. It is quite easy to understand why falling farm prices and incomes have not caused capital and land to move rapidly out of agriculture. These resources, after all, are highly specialized, and their value in alternative uses is very low. Except for the minute portion of total farmland which borders on metropolitan areas, farmland has no real alternative uses. Similarly, dairy barns, silos, and chicken coops are also physically fixed and have virtually no value in alternative employments. Although farm machinery is physically mobile, we must also recognize that combines and corn pickers are highly specialized and have no alternative uses.

It is extremely significant that farmers themselves have also become *relatively* fixed resources in agriculture. Now it is true that over the years many farmers have left agriculture for industry. Indeed, as Table 36·4 clearly indicates, there has been a remarkable outmigration of labor from agriculture. But ironically, this great outmigration has been insufficient to solve the farm problem. The net outmigration of human resources away from agriculture has not been large enough to alleviate the low-income crisis in American agriculture. *High birth rates and a relatively slow rate of outmigration of farmers have resulted in too many people trying to make a living in an industry which will not support them at an income level comparable with that of the rest of the economy.* Statistics underscore this point. In 1910 the farm population was about 35 percent of the total population and received about 19 percent of the national income; by 1970 the farm population had declined to less than 5 percent of the total, but farm income was about 3 percent of national income. It is a fact that agriculture's share of the national income has fallen roughly in proportion to the farm population, and this has caused low per capita incomes to persist in the agricultural segment of the economy.

In a broad sense, the relative slowness of the reallocation of farmers from agriculture to industry is the crux of the farm problem. Ironically enough, in an industry long associated with the word "surplus," we find that the biggest and most fundamental farm surplus of all is the number of farmers. Indeed, the farm problem can be correctly envisioned as a problem of resource misallocation. It is the fact that too

TABLE 36·4 THE DECLINING FARM POPULATION, SELECTED YEARS, 1910–1970

Year	Farm population, millions	Percentage of the total population
1910	32.1	35
1920	31.9	30
1930	30.5	25
1935	32.2	25
1940	30.5	23
1945	24.4	18
1950	23.0	15
1954	19.0	12
1958	17.1	10
1962	14.3	8
1964	13.0	7
1967	11.0	6
1970	9.7	5

Source: Statistical Abstract of the United States, 1962, p. 613, and *Economic Report of the President, 1971,* p. 293.

many farmers are sharing agriculture's shrinking slice of the national income pie that makes income per farmer small. Later in the chapter this point will be discussed further.

If the relative immobility of the farm population is a major dimension of the farm problem, it is certainly legitimate to inquire why farmers have been relatively slow in moving out of agriculture. There is no simple answer. Economic considerations certainly play a role. Of greatest importance is the fact that in a less than full-employment economy the farmer has little or no alternative but to stay on the farm. Why move to the city when industry has no jobs to offer? Indeed, many urban ghettos are heavily populated by unskilled and poorly educated people who have migrated from rural areas and are now unemployed or living on welfare. As the President's Commission on Rural Poverty put it: "The senseless piling up of refugees from rural America in our central cities provides no solution to the problems of rural areas or of the cities." And the costs of moving and retraining oneself for industrial employment may be significant, especially if the move occurs at a time when the farmer's financial plight is particularly acute. Similarly, the high fixed costs associated with farming work against any hasty decision to quit farming. Noneconomic and institutional factors are also significant: Any suggested movement from the farm to a metropolitan area, and the assembly-line environment it implies, strikes fear into the hearts of many farm families.

Then, too, the Negro sharecropper of the South is restricted by his color from many of the more desirable jobs available in urban areas; minority groups are all too often the last hired and the first fired by industry. In other cases restrictive membership practices by unions are pertinent. Or the mere lack of information about the availability of urban employment may be the vital factor.

The short-run problem

The fact that farm incomes lag behind the rest of the economy is evidence of the long-run agricultural problem. Substantial year-to-year fluctuations in farm incomes reflect a short-run problem. This short-run instability can be traced back to the inelastic demand for agricultural products. This inelastic demand contributes to the instability of farm prices and incomes in two different ways.

Fluctuations in output On the production side of the picture, the inelastic demand for farm products causes small changes in agricultural production to be magnified into relatively larger changes in farm prices and incomes. To understand this point we must first note that farmers possess only limited control over their production. Floods, droughts, insect damage, and similar disasters can mean short crops. Conversely, an excellent growing season may mean bumper crops. Weather factors are beyond the control of farmers, yet they exert an important influence upon production. Furthermore, the highly competitive nature of agriculture makes it virtually impossible for farmers to form a huge combination to control their production. Agriculture is a highly competitive industry, made up of millions of widely scattered and independent producers. If all should by chance plant an unusually large or abnormally small portion of their land, extra large or small outputs would result even if the growing season were normal.

Now, putting the instability of farm production together with an inelastic demand for farm products, we can readily discover why farm prices and incomes are highly unstable. Figure 36·3 is pertinent. Even if we assume that the market demand for agriculture products is stable at *D*, the inelastic nature of demand will magnify small changes in output into relatively large changes in farm prices and income. For example, assume that a "normal" crop of Q_n results in a "normal" price of P_n and a "normal" farm income of OP_nNQ_n. But a bumper crop or a short crop will cause large deviations from these normal prices and incomes; these results stem from the inelasticity of demand for farm products.

If an unusually good growing season occurs, the resulting bumper crop of Q_b will cause farm incomes to *fall* from OP_nNQ_n to OP_bBQ_b. Why? Because when demand is inelastic, an increase in the quantity sold will be accompanied by a more than proportionate

FIGURE 36 · 3 THE EFFECT OF OUTPUT CHANGES ON FARM PRICES AND INCOMES

Because of the inelasticity of demand for farm products, a relatively small change in output (Q_n to Q_s or Q_b) will cause relatively large changes in farm prices (P_n to P_s or P_b) and incomes (OP_nNQ_n to OP_sSQ_s or OP_bBQ_b).

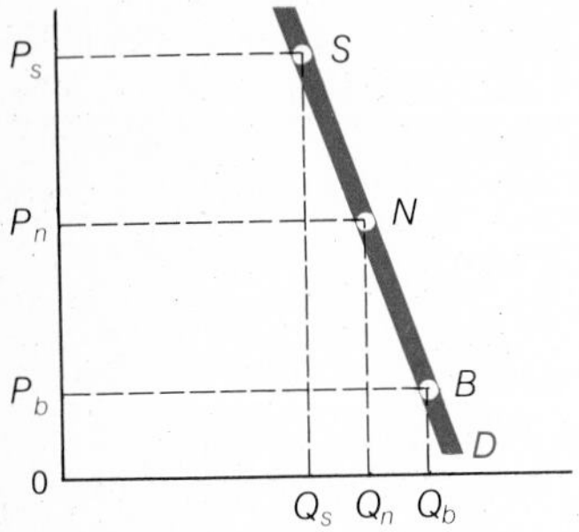

decline in price. The net result is that total receipts, that is, total farm income, will decline. Similarly, for farmers as a group a short crop caused by, say, drought may boost farm incomes. A short crop of Q_s will raise total farm income from OP_nNQ_n to OP_sSQ_s. Why? Because a decline in output will cause a more than proportionate increase in price when demand is inelastic. Ironically, for farmers as a group a short crop may be a blessing and a bumper crop a hardship. Our conclusion is this: Given a stable market demand for farm products, the inelasticity of that demand will turn relatively small changes in output into relatively larger changes in farm prices and incomes.

Fluctuations in demand The other aspect of the short-run instability of farm incomes has to do with shifts in the demand curve for agricultural products. Let us suppose that somehow agricultural output is stabilized at the "normal" level of Q_n in Figure 36·4. Now, because of the inelasticity of the demand for farm products, short-run fluctuations in the demand for farm products will cause markedly different prices and incomes to be associated with this level of production that we assume to be constant. That is, a slight drop in demand from D_1D_1 to D_2D_2 will cause farm incomes to fall from OP_1aQ_n to OP_2bQ_n. A relatively small decline in demand gives farmers a drastically reduced money reward for the same amount of production. Conversely, a slight increase in demand will bring an equally sharp increase in farm incomes for the same volume of output. These large price-income changes are linked to the fact that demand is inelastic. This can be grasped by observing the much smaller price-income changes which accompany an equal shift in demand from the more elastic demand curve D_3D_3.[5] If demand drops from D_3D_3 to D_4D_4, price will fall very modestly from P_1

[5] Though they may not appear so graphically, these two shifts in demand are equal in the sense that in each instance buyers want to purchase the same amount less at each possible price.

FIGURE 36 · 4 THE EFFECT OF DEMAND CHANGES ON FARM PRICES AND INCOMES

Because of the highly inelastic demand for agricultural products, a small shift in demand (D_1D_1 to D_2D_2) will cause drastically different levels of farm prices (P_1 to P_2) and farm incomes (OP_1aQ_n to OP_2bQ_n) to be associated with a given level of production Q_n. Note that equal changes in a more elastic demand curve (D_3D_3 to D_4D_4) will be accompanied by much smaller price (P_1 to P_4) and income (OP_1aQ_n to OP_4cQ_n) alterations.

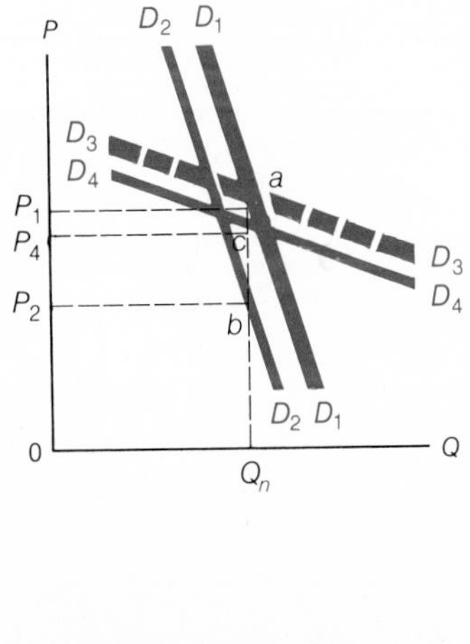

to P_4 and income will only fall from OP_1aQ_n to OP_4cQ_n.

It is tempting to argue that the sharp declines in farm prices which accompany a decrease in demand will cause many farmers to close down in the short run, thereby reducing total output and alleviating these price-income declines. But farm production is relatively insensitive to price changes, because the farmer's fixed costs are high as compared with his variable costs. Interest, rental, tax, and mortgage payments on buildings and equipment are the major costs faced by the farmer. These are clearly fixed charges. Furthermore, the labor supply of the farmer and his family can also be regarded as a fixed cost. So long as he stays on his farm, the farmer cannot reduce his costs by firing himself! This means that his variable costs are the small amounts of hired help he may employ, plus expenditures for seed, fertilizer, and fuel. As a result of this high volume of fixed costs, the farmer is almost invariably better off by working his land than he is by sitting idle and attempting to pay his fixed costs out of pocket. The other factors, noted previously, which contribute to the relative immobility of farmers are also pertinent. In particular, if a decline in the demand for farm output is part of an overall recession, there will be no real incentive for farmers to stop production in order to seek nonexistent jobs in industry. As a matter of fact, a migration in the opposite direction—from the city to the farm—often accompanies a full-scale depression. Note in Table 36·4 the absolute *increase* in the farm population which occurred between 1930 and 1935. Note, too, in Figure 11·4 that between 1929 and 1933 farm prices fell by 63 percent and farm output by a mere 6 percent.

A restatement

Let us pause at this point to bring our knowledge of the causes of the long- and short-run farm problems into sharper focus. The long-run problem is the result of the unhappy combination of four factors.

1. The demand for agricultural commodities is inelastic.
2. Rapid technological advance has given rise to significant increases in the supply of farm products.
3. The demand for agricultural commodities has increased very modestly. This consideration, combined with factors 1 and 2, has resulted in falling farm prices and incomes.
4. The relatively fixed nature of agricultural resources—land, capital, and farmers themselves—has caused low prices and incomes to persist; resources have not been reallocated from agriculture rapidly enough to offset the tendency for agricultural prices and incomes to decline.

In the short run the extreme sensitiveness of farm prices and incomes is based upon the inelastic demand for agricultural products which transforms small changes in farm output and demand into much larger changes in farm prices and incomes.

Agriculture and growth

An alternative explanation correctly puts emphasis upon resource misallocation as the core of the long-run farm problem and couches the problem in terms of a growing economy. Of necessity primitive or underdeveloped countries have essentially agrarian economies. The total population of such a nation must devote its efforts to agricultural endeavors to provide enough food and fiber to sustain itself. But as technological advance increases productivity per farmer, the economy can maintain or even increase its consumption of food and clothing and simultaneously transfer a portion of its population into nonagricultural pursuits. This is the path which any expanding, progressive economy follows. Indeed, the shift of resources from agricultural to industrial pursuits is the earmark of a growing economy. The experience of the United States is illustrative. About 90 percent of our population was devoted to agriculture in the eighteenth century. At present about 5 percent of the population is in farming, the remaining 95 percent being free to produce refrigerators, furniture, automobiles, and the thousand and one other goods and services which make up a high standard of living. But in American capitalism, the actual shift of resources to nonagricultural employments has not kept pace with the rate of reallocation which rapid

technological advance permits. The economy has thereby failed to realize the increases in nonfarm output which technological progress in farming has made available. In short, we need *less* than 5 percent of our population in agriculture.

PUBLIC POLICY TOWARD AGRICULTURE

Historically, many arguments have been used in seeking and rationalizing public aid to agriculture. It has been contended, for example, that farming, and particularly the family farm, is a fundamental American institution and should be nurtured as "a way of life." Furthermore, farmers are subject to certain extraordinary hazards—floods, droughts, and invasion by hordes of insects—to which other industries are not exposed. It has been held, too, that agriculture is a major cog in the American economy and therefore prosperity for farmers is a prerequisite for prosperity in the economy as a whole.

There are two additional arguments for special aid to agriculture which are of greater substance and merit more detailed consideration.

Costs-of-progress argument While agriculture has made great contributions to the nation's economic growth, it has had to bear a disproportionately large share of the costs associated with this progress. The high degree of progressiveness of American agriculture has resulted in substantial and widespread benefits to the economy as a whole. The population has been able to get more and better food and fiber from agriculture in exchange for a smaller portion of its money income. Furthermore, over the years agriculture has been a major source of labor for industry (Table 36·4).[6]

Farm families have for years produced children well in excess of the numbers needed to replace retiring members of the farm labor force. This, together with the absolute decline in the number of people on farms, means that a very substantial portion of our present productive nonfarm labor force was raised on a farm, educated in schools heavily dependent upon farm taxes, and migrated to the cities after finishing school.

On the other hand, the peculiar combination of economic circumstances already discussed—an inelastic demand for farm products, rapid technological progress, the slow growth of demand, and the relatively fixed nature of agricultural resources—has caused farm people to bear a large share of the costs of agricultural progress in the form of incomes substantially below those of nonfarm income receivers.

[6]Hathaway, op. cit., p. 5.

Market-power argument A second argument focuses upon the question of market power. Agriculture is a highly competitive industry, comprised of hundreds of thousands of small geographically dispersed producers. As a result, farmers have no control over the prices at which they must sell their products. Nonagricultural industries, on the other hand, have varying degrees of market power and, within limits, the capacity to adjust their prices. In particular, most of the firms from which farmers buy machinery, fertilizer, gasoline, and so forth, have some capacity to control their prices. Given the farmer's unenviable market position in comparison with the nonfarm sectors, it is not surprising that he gets a disproportionately small share of the national income. It is argued on the basis of this rationale that a special farm program to help agriculture is justified as a means of compensating for the weak market position of farmers. Stated differently, agriculture is the last stronghold of pure competition in an otherwise imperfectly competitive economy; it warrants public aid to offset the disadvantageous terms of trade which result.

The farm program

On the basis of these arguments and the disproportionately large voice which farmers have historically had in Congress, a detailed farm program has been established. Let us review the major elements of this program.

"The farm program" actually refers to a whole series of more or less related government programs con-

cerning (1) farm prices, incomes, and output, (2) soil conservation, (3) agricultural research, (4) farm credit, (5) crop insurance, and so forth. However, for the last thirty or thirty-five years the typical American farmer and the average politician have both viewed the farm problem as essentially a price-income problem. Low farm prices and the depressed farm incomes resulting therefrom are held to be the cause of the farmer's plight. As a consequence, the American farm program has become "price-centered." The major aim of agricultural policy is to raise farm incomes by raising the prices of farm products.

The enactment of the Agricultural Adjustment Act in 1933—at the depth of the Great Depression—set the pattern for American agricultural policy. This act established a framework for farm policy which has persisted down to the present time.

The concept of parity

Established in the Agricultural Adjustment Act of 1933 as the major objective of American farm policy, the concept of parity has acquired a degree of holiness over the last forty years. It is something of a symbol to American agriculture.

The simple rationale of the parity concept can be readily envisioned in both real and money terms. In real terms, parity simply says that year after year for a given output of farm products, a farmer should be able to acquire a given total amount of goods and services. A given real output should always result in the same real income. "If a man could take a bushel of corn to town in 1912 and sell it and buy himself a shirt, he should be able to take a bushel of corn to town today and buy a shirt."

In money terms the parity concept alleges that it is only fair that a certain relationship be maintained between (1) the prices which farmers *receive* for the products they sell and (2) the prices which they must *pay* for the goods and services they purchase. The money income which a farmer receives from a given volume of output should have the same purchasing power over the years. This implies that if the prices of the goods farmers purchase increase, the prices which farmers receive for their products should be increased accordingly.

Let us examine the simplest possible example to lay bare the parity principle and the manner in which parity prices are determined. Table 36·5 is relevant. Suppose a farmer produces 50 bushels of wheat in both year 1 and year 2. If the *market price* for wheat is $2 per bushel in year 1, the farmer's money income will obviously be $100. Suppose now that the farmer spends this money income entirely on one product—say, dress suits. If suits are selling at $25 each in year 1, the farmer will be able to buy four of them. Using year 1 as our point of reference, or *base year*, the parity concept says that for the same output—50 bushels of wheat—the farmer should be able to acquire the same real income—four suits—in succeeding years as he did in the base year.

TABLE 36·5 PARITY PRICING: A SIMPLE CASE (BASE: YEAR 1)
(*hypothetical data*)

Year	Bushels of wheat	Price per bushel	Money income	Price per suit	Real income, suits
1	50	$2	$100	$25	4
2	50	4	200	50	4
3	50			65	

What if in year 2 the farmer finds that the price of suits has doubled because of inflation and now stands at $50 per suit? This means that 50 bushels of wheat selling at $2 per bushel will only provide the farmer with enough income to buy two suits. Assuming the market price for wheat remains at $2, the farmer's real income has been halved, because the prices of the goods he buys have doubled. Obviously, the concept of parity applied to year 2 would entail a $4 *parity price* for wheat. The price of the given quantity of wheat must be doubled for the farmer to maintain his real income in the face of a doubling in his cost of living. The reader can complete Table 36·5 by determining the parity price for wheat in year 3.

Now an important word on the mechanics of calculating parity price. Note that it is the ratio of the price of suits in the current year (year 2) to the price of suits in the base year (year 1) that determines the multiple by which the price of wheat should be changed—increased in this case—to achieve parity. In our simple example, this ratio is $50/$25, or 2. Thus, multiplying the $2 base-period price of wheat by 2, we get the parity price of $4. In other words, the formula for determining the parity price for wheat in this example is

$$\text{Base-period price of wheat} \times \frac{\text{current price of suits}}{\text{base-year price of suits}} = \text{parity price of wheat}$$

Substituting the figures from our illustration, we get

$$\$2 \times \frac{\$50}{\$25} = \$4$$

In practice, of course, farmers purchase a wide variety of products and services. As a result, we must use an *index* of prices paid instead of focusing exclusively on the price of suits. The formula for determining parity thus becomes

$$\text{Base-period price of wheat} \times \frac{\text{current-prices-paid index}}{\text{prices-paid index in base year}} = \text{parity price of wheat}$$

Let us illustrate with actual data for wheat. In the 1910–1914 base period used in determining parity prices, the average price for wheat was 88.4 cents per bushel. The 1970 index of prices paid by farmers was about 313. In the 1910–1914 base period this index was, of course, 100 percent. In effect, the prices paid by farmers had increased 3.13 times between the base period and 1970. Therefore, wheat farmers must receive 3.13 times as much per bushel of wheat in 1970 as they did in 1910–1914 to achieve 100 percent parity. Substituting in the above formula, it is discovered that the parity price of wheat in 1970 was $2.77:

$$88.4 \text{ cents} \times \frac{313}{100} = \$2.77$$

In many instances government has supported prices at something less than 100 percent of parity. Legislation might give the Secretary of Agriculture the authority to establish the price of, say, wheat or corn at some level within, say, 70 to 90 percent of parity.

Three points are vital to a complete appreciation of the parity concept:

1. Despite the seemingly "scientific" manipulations involved in establishing parity prices, parity is actually an ethical concept. Parity is a notion concerning what the economic position of farmers *should,* or *ought to,* be.

2. A bit of reflection will make clear that, in any application of the parity concept, the choice of the base year, or base period, is all-important. If the base period were one wherein the farmer's economic position was good (prices received were relatively high and prices paid relatively low), a strict application of parity would guarantee farmers that the favorable situation would be perpetuated. Conversely, if the choice were a base period where farmers were squeezed between getting low prices and paying high prices, the application of parity would simply sustain the farmer's misery. In view of the strong political voice of agriculture, it is not surprising to find that a prosperous farm era—the 1910–1914 so-called "golden age" of American agriculture—is the actual base period for determining parity.[7]

[7] Recent modifications have adjusted some parity prices from the 1910–1914 base so as to allow for more recent price trends.

3. Also, it is notable that price parity is not income parity. For example, if price parity is rigidly maintained over a period of time wherein farm productivity is increasing significantly, price parity will mean rising rather than parity incomes for farmers.

FIGURE 36·5 EFFECTIVE PRICE SUPPORTS RESULT IN FARM SURPLUSES

Application of the parity concept obligates government to support farm prices at above-equilibrium levels. These supported prices result in persistent surpluses of farm products.

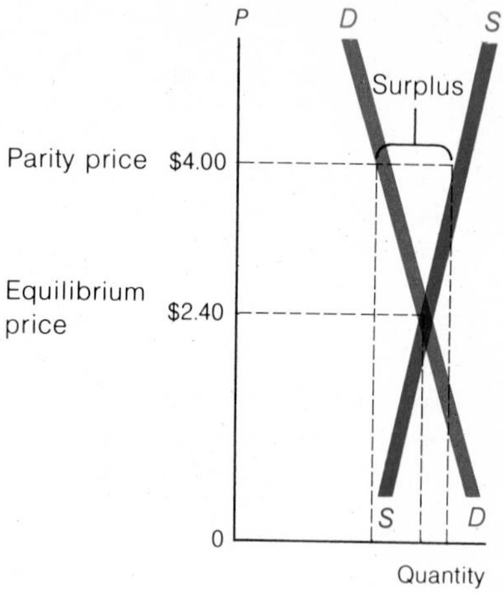

Price supports

The practical importance of the notion of parity prices lies in the fact that it is the focal point for government price-support programs designed to bolster farm incomes. Indeed, it is the concept of parity which provides the rationale and justification for government price supports on farm products. The fact that in the long run the actual market prices received by farmers have not kept abreast of prices paid by them means that to achieve parity or some percentage thereof, the government is likely to be required to establish above-equilibrium prices on farm products. The 1920–1941 and post-1953 periods in Figure 36·1 reflect the tendency of prices received to fall behind prices paid, as, indeed, does our hypothetical illustration in Table 36·5. Government must take action to boost prices received above the level established by the market to prevent the real-income position of the farmer from deteriorating. In short, government must support farm prices.

Effective price supports invariably result in product surpluses. Let us illustrate, using the data from Table 36·5. In this simple example the parity price for wheat in year 2 is $4 per bushel. Suppose that the market forces of supply and demand establish an equilibrium price of only $2.40 per bushel, as shown in Figure 36·5. Assuming the farmer's costs and productivity have not changed sufficiently to offset this below-parity market price, the farmer's income from the sale of a bushel of wheat will fail to keep his real income at the level of year 1. If 100 percent of parity is the objective of public policy, it is up to government to establish a legal, or supported, price of $4 per bushel for wheat in year 2. But it is all too evident from Figure 36·5 that private buyers will not be willing to consume the quantity of wheat forthcoming at this supported price. There will be a market imbalance; specifically, a *surplus* of wheat will result at the supported price of $4. The competitive price mechanism will no longer perform the rationing function of automatically equating quantity demanded and quantity supplied when a higher than equilibrium legal price is imposed.

What happens to the surplus, that is, the quantity of wheat which private buyers will not take at the $4 price? It is the government's headache. To make the above-equilibrium supported price effective, government must buy what private purchasers will not.

Farm surpluses are undesirable on several counts. First and foremost, the very existence of these surpluses indicates a misallocation of the economy's resources. Government-held surpluses reflect the fact that the economy is devoting large amounts of resources to the production of commodities which, *at existing supported prices,* are simply not wanted by consumers. And, of course, surpluses are politically embarrassing. They are impeccable evidence

that neither political party has made substantial progress in resolving the basic resource imbalance which lies at the heart of America's farm troubles. Furthermore, the storing of surplus products is a costly proposition which has added to the cost of the farm program and ultimately to the consumer's tax bill. Storage costs on surpluses have run as high as $1 billion per year when accumulated stocks were particularly large.

Coping with surpluses

By what means might government cope with the surplus farm output which accompanies effective price supports? An elementary knowledge of the tools of supply and demand suggests that programs designed to reduce market supply or increase market demand would help bring the market price up to the desired supported price, thereby reducing or eliminating farm surpluses (Figure 36·5).

Restricting supply On the supply side, public policy has long been aimed at restricting farm output. Of primary significance is the *acreage allotment program* which accompanies the application of price supports. In return for the privilege of getting price supports on their crops, farmers must agree to limit the number of acres planted. Attempting to bring quantity supplied and quantity demanded into balance, the Department of Agriculture estimates the amount of each product which private buyers will take at the supported price. This amount is then translated into the number of acres of planting which will produce this amount. The total acreage figure is apportioned among states, counties, and ultimately individual farmers. Similarly, under the *soil bank* program the Department of Agriculture was authorized to get farmland entirely out of production by "renting" land from farmers. Such idle land was to be planted in cover crops or in timber, not in cash crops.

Have these supply-restricting programs been successful? It is difficult to give an unqualified answer. Certainly they have not eliminated surplus farm production. The basic reason lies in the fact that acreage reduction invariably results in less than proportionate declines in production. Why? Farmers retire their worst land and keep the best in production. Those acres which are used are cultivated more intensively. The use of better seed, more and better fertilizer and insecticides, and more manpower will enhance output per acre. And, of course, the fortuitous occurrence of a good growing season will mean large per acre outputs. For these and other reasons the supply of farm products may actually *increase,* although acreage is reduced. To illustrate: In 1953 some 78.9 million acres of wheat were planted, and the resulting total output was about 1.2 billion bushels. Approximately 54.9 million acres of wheat were planted in 1960, and output was 1.4 billion bushels. A 30 percent *reduction* in wheat acreage was accompanied by a 17 percent *increase* in output! On the other hand, without these output controls there is no doubt that accumulated farm surpluses and their associated costs would have been much greater than has actually been the case.

Bolstering demand Government has followed a number of paths in seeking to augment the demand for agricultural products.

1. Both government and private industry have spent considerable sums for research to uncover new uses for agricultural commodities. Overall, the results have been modest. Most agricultural economists agree that in all probability such research activity will result in only slight increases in demand.

2. A variety of programs has been invoked to augment the domestic consumption of farm products. For example, the *food stamp program* is designed to distribute surplus farm products to low-income families. *School lunch programs* and the distribution of surpluses to welfare and charitable institutions have also had the effect of enhancing the domestic demand for farm output.

3. Partly as the result of a changing world market and partly as the result of governmental policy, the export demand for American farm products has been increasing. These increases have been instrumental in reducing vast accumulations of farm surpluses in recent years.

A number of forces underlie the rising world demand

for agricultural products. First, rising per capita incomes in Western Europe and Japan have increased the ability of these countries to purchase more and better food. Secondly, the socialist countries in their zeal for industrial development have tended to neglect their agricultural sectors and, as a result, have found it necessary to buy agricultural products in world markets. Russian purchases of United States wheat are a case in point. Third, many of the less developed nations are plagued by rapidly expanding populations, on the one hand, and severe obstacles to the expansion of their domestic agricultural production, on the other. Such nations, spurred by periodic crop failures, have necessarily turned to world markets for food.

One would think it a relatively simple matter for the United States to sell, or otherwise provide, a portion of its surplus farm output to the underdeveloped nations. Actually, there has been a serious problem of translating the food shortages and needs of underdeveloped countries into an effective demand for American farm products. The underdeveloped nations simply do not have the dollars to buy the foodstuffs they need at world prices. Our government's Food for Peace program under *Public Law 480* has attempted to meet this problem by accepting local currencies rather than dollars for our farm output. Because these local currencies are of limited use to the United States, there is admittedly a large element of subsidy in the program, and it is essentially a foreign aid measure. Yet it has been an important means for disposing of large quantities of surplus American farm output. Critics, however, hold that recipient nations are becoming increasingly dependent upon American foodstuffs and are delaying economically and politically painful measures necessary to the strengthening of their domestic agricultural sectors.

Surplus sizes

Although programs to increase the demand for, and curtail the supply of, farm products have undoubtedly been a restraining influence upon farm surpluses, surplus stocks grew to substantial proportions in the late 1950s and the 1960s. In 1948 the government had only $294 *million* tied up in surplus farm products. By 1954 this figure had jumped to $5.8 *billion.* In the late fifties and early sixties surpluses varied from $6.3 to $7.7 billion. In 1966 and 1967—thanks largely to Public Law 480 and domestic population growth—surplus stocks declined, amounting to $3.4 billion in 1967. Since 1967 surplus stocks of farm products have remained at reasonable levels. Given the high rate of productivity increases in agriculture, it is perhaps a significant accomplishment that efforts to reduce supply and increase demand were successful in curtailing the growth of farm surpluses.

EVALUATING THE FARM PROGRAM

How successful has public policy been in resolving the long-run farm problem? Although it is difficult to offer an unequivocal answer to this question, economists are generally critical of American farm policy. Let us note some of the major criticisms.

Symptoms and causes

First and foremost, the farm program has failed to get at the causes of the farm problem. Public policy toward agriculture is designed to treat symptoms and not causes. The root *cause* of the farm problem is a misallocation of resources between agriculture and the rest of the economy. Simply put, the problem is one of too many farmers. The effect or symptom of this misallocation of resources is low farm incomes. *For the most part, public policy in agriculture has been oriented toward supporting farm prices and incomes rather than alleviating the resource allocation problem, which is the fundamental cause of these sagging farm incomes.*

Some critics go further and argue that price-income supports have encouraged people to stay in agriculture who otherwise would have migrated to some nonfarm occupation. That is, the price-income orientation of the farm program has deterred the very reallocation of resources which is necessary to resolve the long-run farm problem. On the other hand,

one can argue that the extra income provided by price supports may have enabled farmers to provide more education for their children, thereby preparing them for better and higher-paying nonfarm jobs.

Misguided subsidies

A second criticism is this: The price-income support schemes which have been the focal point of our farm program tend to benefit most those farmers who least need government assistance. Assuming the goal of our farm program is the bolstering of low farm incomes, it follows that any program of government aid should be aimed at farmers at the bottom of the farm income distribution. It is the small-output, low-income farmer of Table 36·2 who desperately needs income subsidies. But such farmers get very little help from price supports. Why? Because the small farmer simply does not produce and sell enough in the market. The 64 percent of American farmers who produce only 15 percent of the total marketed output cannot gain much from any income subsidy based upon the quantity produced. It is the large farmers—the 36 percent who supply 85 percent of the marketed farm output—who reap the benefits of price supports. Individual subsidy checks running into hundreds of thousands of dollars are not easy to justify. If public policy must be designed to supplement farm incomes, a strong case can certainly be made for making those benefits vary inversely with one's position in the income distribution. An income-support program should be geared to *people,* not *commodities.*

Controversy surrounding huge subsidies resulted in the inclusion of a $55,000 maximum payment *per crop* for any single recipient in the Agriculture Act of 1970. This limit is proving to be quite ineffective in curtailing large subsidies. For example, a farmer who produces three major crops can collect $165,000 per year. By legally signing a portion of his farm to, say, his wife, the farmer's family can double its direct government subsidy to $330,000. On the other hand, the enactment of a subsidy limit does establish an important principle and more restrictive ceilings may be enacted in the near future.

The other side of the picture here is that our price-support programs are also output-restricting programs. Remember that to receive price supports a farmer must agree to restrict his supply. If only small (low-income) farmers were eligible for price supports, then little or no restricting of farm output would have occurred and our farm surplus problems would have been much more acute.

Policy conflicts

A final criticism is that there are certain embarrassingly evident inconsistencies within the farm program and between the farm program and other public policies. In particular, at the same time that government is making attempts to cut back on agricultural production, other government policies are aimed at boosting farm output. Specifically, acreage allotment, soil conservation, and land retirement programs work at cross purposes with government-sponsored research designed to increase farm output and Federal irrigation-reclamation programs tailored to increase the supply of arable land. There clearly exists a real dilemma here in public policy. As we have seen, in the long run technological advance in agriculture is a basic permissive force in economic growth. Furthermore, projected growth of world population (Figure 20·4) suggests that we press ahead with the development of both our land resources and our agricultural technology. Yet in the short run, given the lagging exodus of human resources from agriculture and government's commitment to a price-centered farm program, it is desirable to restrict farm production to avoid the problems and costs associated with ever-expanding surpluses.

POLICY DILEMMAS AND OPTIONS[8]

It is easy to be critical of American farm policy; indeed, such criticism has become something of a national pastime among economists. It is much more

[8]This section draws upon Willard W. Cochrane, *The City Man's Guide to the Farm Problem* (New York: McGraw-Hill Book Company, 1966), chap. 8.

demanding to offer positive solutions that are both economically workable and politically acceptable. The difficulty is that programs designed to correct the fundamental economic problem of excess productive capacity in agriculture are likely either to have highly adverse effects upon farm incomes or to collide severely with the freedom of farmers to produce. With this in mind let us briefly survey three policy options.

The free-market solution

One frequently mentioned option would be for government to simply abandon price supports and output-restriction programs. Given the characteristics of markets for farm products (Figure 36·2), this solution would result in sharply falling farm prices and depressed farm incomes. Estimates suggest that over a three-to-five-year period farm prices would decline by at least 20 to 25 percent and that total net farm income would fall by a minimum of 50 percent! Such extremely adverse consequences to price and income would undoubtedly drive existing resources from agriculture and restrict the entry of new resources. But this is obviously a harsh and inhumane approach. It is true that after a period of years the outmigration of agricultural resources, coupled with a modestly expanding domestic and foreign demand, would bring about a readjustment of supply and demand so that farm prices and incomes would probably rise. Such long-term speculation, however, is tenuous and far from certain. Furthermore, the simple political fact is that "the overwhelming majority of farmers want nothing to do with a free market."[9]

The production-controls solution

A second solution is for government to put sufficiently severe production controls on farmers so that supply is restricted relative to demand, and "fair" prices and incomes result. The goal here is "the establishment of effective manmade controls over the use of productive resources, where the controls have the sanction of law and are enforceable through the police powers of the state."[10] Techniques for implementation are similar to those already described in connection with the acreage-allotment program. The total quantity which will be demanded at the desired "fair" price is estimated. The output is apportioned among farmers as production quotas, probably on the basis of each farmer's past production of the commodity. But to avoid the problems associated with the acreage-allotment program, the production quota assigned each farmer would take the form of a marketing quota stated in terms of quantity of output (for example, bushels of wheat) rather than inputs of land. If farmers approve the program by referendum, it becomes law and is put into effect. Although this approach can clearly prevent the production of surplus output by forcing the restriction of inputs, its major shortcoming is that it obviously puts great restrictions upon the economic freedom of farmers. There are therefore serious doubts about the political acceptability of such a program.

The optimum R & D solution

Another recent and novel proposal suggests that the rate of technological progress in agriculture might be restrained as a means of alleviating the problem of excess capacity in farming. The argument is that in the past twenty or thirty years the agricultural resource-mix has changed dramatically. "Research and development resources added to the agricultural complex have produced the new technologies—the new and improved production practices and the capital goods—which have been substituted for both land and labor, thereby forcing those resources out of farming and increasing the total farm output."[11] Granted that past applications of R & D have been tremendously successful, we must now recognize that a continuation of this rate of progress will foster the problem of excess capacity—particularly in terms of land and human resources—in agriculture. Is there not some optimum rate of technological progress,

[9] Ibid., p. 132.

[10] Ibid., p. 137.

[11] Ibid., p. 130.

slightly slower than the current rate, which would bring the rate of increase in agricultural supply into better balance with the rate of increase in demand so that higher farm prices and incomes and smaller amounts of redundant labor and land can be realized in American agriculture?

A POSITIVE PROGRAM FOR AGRICULTURE

It is a reasonable guess that the majority of economists favor a return to free, or at least freer, markets in agriculture. But it is recognized that this return must be gradual if the extreme income consequences of the free-market solution are to be avoided. Let us then consider a more eclectic policy proposal than the three just outlined.

The Committee for Economic Development[12] has proposed an "adaptive" farm program which features a *gradual* return to free markets. The CED's proposal is inspired by the contention that the current farm program has been grossly unsuccessful in achieving the objective of stabilizing and supporting the incomes of farmers. The government, it is pointed out, has spent more than $50 billion over the last twenty-five years on programs of direct and indirect assistance to American agriculture, but farm incomes continue to decline, and agricultural surpluses continue to accumulate. If anything, the present farm program has perpetuated the misallocation of resources which is the core of agricultural difficulties. The positive program suggested by the CED centers around the following five points:

Return to free markets

Free markets should ultimately be restored in agriculture by the *gradual* elimination of price and income supports. The economic position of farmers should be bettered by means which are consistent with free markets. The key to success in achieving this goal is to bring agricultural supply (ultimately the number of farmers) and demand into balance at prices which yield reasonable incomes for the farm population.

Adaptive approach

The implementation of a return to free markets is not to be achieved as the result of a sudden and complete withdrawal of all public aid to agriculture but rather through an *adaptive approach* to the farm problem.[13]

> The adaptive approach calls for action by government working with the free market, not against it. It seeks to achieve the results of the free market more quickly and easily, rather than to keep those results from occurring. The adaptive approach works by permitting full production, rather than by limiting production. And government adaptive programs applied to particular industries can ordinarily be temporary, whereas protectionist government actions generate the need for their own indefinite continuance.

An adaptive program for agriculture is designed to accelerate the movement of human and property resources out of agriculture to the end that resulting farm prices would yield per family farm incomes comparable to those of nonfarm families. The adaptive or adjustment program for agriculture proposed by the CED entails policies designed to (1) attract excess resources out of agriculture and (2) cushion the effects of such adjustments upon those adversely affected.

Human exodus

The exodus of human resources from agriculture is to be accelerated through substantial improvements in the labor market. This is to be accomplished in two general ways. First, statistics make clear that farm youth get less education and therefore less preparation for alternative nonfarm employment than do nonfarm youth. And, ironically, about 45 percent of the nation's vocational education funds are for training in agriculture and therefore tend to retard

[12]The CED is a "non-profit, non-partisan, and non-political" organization of businessmen and scholars. The brevity of the present discussion does not do justice to the CED's program. The interested student is urged to read *An Adaptive Program for Agriculture* (New York: CED, 1962) and *Toward a Realistic Farm Program* (New York: CED, 1957).

[13]*An Adaptive Program for Agriculture,* p. 12.

the outflow of human resources from farming. The CED recommends programs designed to upgrade the overall quality of rural education and a revamping of vocational education to provide the training and skills needed to obtain employment in expanding (nonfarm) industries.

Second, the exodus of human resources from agriculture should be stimulated by increasing the mobility of farm labor through (1) providing better information to rural people about the availability, requirements, and rewards from off-farm employment, and (2) subsidizing both the retraining and moving costs of farm workers who seek nonfarm jobs. It is explicitly recognized by the CED that the success of an accelerated exodus of labor from agriculture depends heavily upon the maintenance of a high level of employment in the economy as a whole.

The movement of labor from agriculture envisioned by the CED is quite massive: about 2 million workers—roughly one-third of the agricultural labor force—over a five-year period.

Establishing adjustment prices

Supported farm prices fail to signal farmers as to how much output and what composition of output are wanted by society. Therefore, the present structure of price supports should be abandoned through a price adjustment program and replaced by "adjustment prices." The adjustment price for any commodity is

1. "A price at which the total output of the commodity can be sold to domestic consumers or in commercial export markets without government subsidy"

2. A price at which resources efficiently employed in agriculture, after a period of maximum freedom to move out, could earn incomes equivalent to those earned in the nonfarm economy."[14]

It is important to note that these adjustment prices are envisioned to be *below* the current level of supported prices but *above* the free competitive market prices which would result if all existing government farm programs were immediately terminated. The adjustment prices are below supported prices because government would no longer supplement private demand by buying the surpluses needed to keep prices at supported levels and because present restrictions on farm output would be removed. On the other hand, adjustment prices would be above present free-market prices because during a five-year adjustment or transitional period, substantial amounts of agricultural resources—labor, as described earlier, and land, as will be discussed in a moment—would have left agriculture. In other words, given agricultural demand, the withdrawal of resources from agriculture will reduce supply relative to what it would have been in the absence of these reallocations, and the resulting market prices will be higher.

Land retirement

Two temporary land retirement programs are recommended to cushion the adverse effects on farm incomes during the adjustment period when labor resources are leaving agriculture at an accelerated rate. A cropland adjustment program is recommended for the Western Plains and Mountain region to convert some 20 million acres of land from crops back to grassland. This conversion would be induced by temporary subsidies to cooperating farms. But then the downward drift of crop prices during the adjustment period would presumably cause farmers to continue using the land for grazing rather than crops. A temporary soil bank would also be employed to cut back on grain production. Land would be retired on a "whole farm" basis because first, it retires both labor and capital from agriculture, and second, this approach avoids a fundamental difficulty in current acreage allotment programs: Farmers cultivate their remaining land more intensely and thereby produce a larger output per cultivated acre.

As the CED sees it, the net result of its adaptive program would substantially correct the overallocation of resources to agriculture which now exists. The free-market prices which would prevail at the end of the five-year period of adjustment would involve *lower* average prices but *higher* average incomes per

[14] Ibid., pp. 40–41.

farmer because of the substantial decrease in the number of farmers. The CED acknowledges that its program would not immediately reduce government agricultural expenditures. But, it is contended, because its program gets at the cause of the farm problem, costs would be substantially reduced over time. In particular, the elimination of our price-support, surplus-storage programs would entail very significant declines in government outlays.

Regardless of whether one accepts or rejects the CED's proposals as a workable solution to our farm troubles, this much is reasonably certain: In the immediate years ahead we can expect our present farm policies to come under intense scrutiny. Existing farm programs have become very costly, and it is increasingly evident that they have accomplished remarkably little in resolving the causes of our farm problem. Furthermore, as the farm population has declined in numbers, so has its political power diminished. Sweeping changes in our agricultural policies seem possible in the not too distant future.

SUMMARY

1. The core of the long-run farm problem is a misallocation of resources between agriculture and the rest of the economy. Rapid technological advance coupled with a highly inelastic and relatively constant demand for agricultural output has caused low farm incomes. Because of the relatively fixed nature of both property and human resources, the price system has failed to correct the farm problem by reallocating sufficient amounts of resources out of agriculture.

2. In the short run the highly inelastic nature of agricultural demand translates small changes in output and small shifts in demand into large fluctuations in prices and incomes.

3. The two basic arguments for public assistance to agriculture are *a.* farmers have borne a disproportionately large share of the costs of economic progress in agriculture and *b.* farmers have little market power as compared with other sectors of the economy.

4. The farm program is price-centered and based upon the concept of parity. Parity is the notion that a given real output should always result in the same real income. Parity price can be determined by the following formula:

$$\text{Base-year price} \times \frac{\text{current-prices-paid index}}{\text{prices-paid index in base year}} = \text{parity price}$$

5. The application of price supports, based upon the parity concept, gives rise to surplus agricultural output. The government has pursued a variety of programs to reduce the supply of, and increase the demand for, agricultural products in order to limit the size of these surpluses.

6. Basic shortcomings of the current farm program are several. Foremost is the fact that the program treats symptoms rather than causes; public policy is designed to boost farm incomes rather than to speed the reallocation of resources away from agriculture. More specific criticisms concern *a.* the inverse relationship between the size of income subsidies and need, and *b.* certain inconsistencies which exist between short-run and long-run aspects of farm policy.

7. Possible policy options to resolve the problem of excess capacity in agriculture include a return to free markets, strict governmental controls over agricultural output, and a relaxation of the application of R & D resources to agriculture.

8. The CED has offered a thought-provoking adaptive program for agriculture. It envisions the return to free markets over a five-year adjustment period. During this time the exodus of labor from agriculture is to be accelerated through the general improvement of rural education and the subsidization of retraining and moving costs. Land retirement programs are proposed to cut back on grain production. The goal is to achieve higher farm incomes with lower free-market prices through the substantial outmigration of resources (particularly labor) from agriculture.

QUESTIONS AND STUDY SUGGESTIONS

1. Explain how each of the following contributes to the farm problem: **a.** the inelasticity of the demand for farm products, *b.* rapid technological progress in farming, *c.* the modest long-run growth in the demand for farm commodities, *d.* the competitiveness of agriculture, and **e.** the relative fixity or immobility of agricultural resources.

2. What relationship, if any, can you detect between the fact that the farmer's fixed costs of production are large and the fact that the supply of most agricultural products is generally inelastic? Be specific in your answer.

3. "The supply and demand for agricultural products are such that small changes in agricultural supply will result in drastic changes in prices. However, large changes in farm prices have modest effects on agricultural output." Carefully evaluate. *Hint:* A brief review of the distinction between *supply* and *quantity supplied* may be of assistance.

4. "The long-run demand for farm products depends more upon future growth in the size of our population than it does upon the growth which occurs in average family or per capita incomes." Do you agree? Explain. Of what relevance is Public Law 480 for the farm problem?

5. "The whole process of economic growth is one of making agriculture less fundamental in the economic system. The fewer people the nation needs to employ in the production of food and fiber, the better off it is—and the better off farm people are."[15] Evaluate this statement.

6. The key to efficient resource allocation is the shifting of resources from low-productivity to high-productivity uses. Given the high and expanding physical productivity of agricultural resources, explain why many economists want to get resources out of farming in the interest of greater allocative efficiency.

7. "Industry complains of the higher taxes it must pay to finance subsidies to agriculture. Yet the fact that the trend of agricultural prices has been downward while industrial prices have been moving upward suggests that on balance agriculture is actually subsidizing industry." Explain and evaluate.

[15] Lauren Soth, *Farm Trouble* (Princeton, N.J.: Princeton University Press, 1957), p. 40.

8. "Because consumers as a whole must ultimately pay the total incomes received by farmers, it makes no real difference whether this income is paid through free farm markets or through supported prices supplemented by subsidies financed out of tax revenues." Analyze this statement very carefully.

9. Suppose you are the president of a local chapter of one of the major farm organizations. You are directed by the chapter's membership to formulate policy statements for the chapter which cover the following topics: **a.** antitrust policy, *b.* monetary policy, **c.** fiscal policy, and ***d.*** tariff policy. Briefly outline the policy statements which will best serve the interests of farmers. What is the rationale underlying each statement? Do you see any conflicts or inconsistencies in your policy statements?

10. Explain and evaluate the following statements:

a. "Price supports intensify rather than resolve the farm problem."

b. "The best farm program is the Employment Act of 1946."

c. "The trouble with parity prices in agriculture is that they strip the price mechanism of its ability to allocate resources."

11. The CED concludes that in American agriculture, "Lower average prices can be made consistent with higher average income." Explain the assumptions which underlie this conclusion.

12. Reconcile these two statements: "The farm problem is one of overproduction." "Despite the tremendous productive capacity of American agriculture, plenty of Americans are going hungry." What assumptions about the price system are implied in your answer?

13. The price of wheat was 88.4 cents per bushel in the 1910–1914 base period. Assume in 1971 the prices-paid index is 321. If the government decided to support the price of wheat at 90 percent of the parity in 1971, what would the supported price be?

SELECTED REFERENCES

Economic Issues, 4th ed., readings 62, 63, and 64.

Cochrane, Willard W.: *The City Man's Guide to the Farm Problem* (New York: McGraw-Hill Book Company, 1966).

Hathaway, Dale E.: *Problems of Progress in the Agricultural Economy* (Chicago: Scott, Foresman and Company, 1964).

Heady, Earl O.: *A Primer on Food, Agriculture, and Public Policy* (New York: Random House, Inc., 1967).

National Advisory Commission on Rural Poverty: *The People Left Behind* (Washington, 1967).

Owen, Wyn F. (ed.): *American Agriculture: The Changing Structure* (Lexington, Mass.: D. C. Heath and Company, 1969).

Ruttan, Vernon W., Arley D. Waldo, and James P. Houck (eds.): *Agricultural Policy in an Affluent Society* (New York: W. W. Norton & Company, Inc., 1969).

37

URBAN ECONOMICS: THE PROBLEMS OF THE CITIES

America's cities are a curious paradox. They are the depositories of great wealth and the source of abundant incomes; they are the nucleus of economic activity and opportunity. Yet these same cities simultaneously embody blighted neighborhoods, faltering school systems, an acutely deteriorating physical environment, and a growing sense of social unrest and alienation.[1]

> Fly over Manhattan or Nob Hill or the Chicago Loop and the breathtaking skyline will excite your pride with the very grandeur of the American achievement. These towering symbols give dramatic character to the core of our giant cities. But their shadows cannot hide the disgrace at their feet.
>
> There we find the decayed and decaying center cities, traffic-clogged, smoke-polluted, crime-ridden, recreationally barren. It is there we find the segregated slum with its crumbling tenement house, waiting to crush the hope of the Negro and displaced farmer who has pursued his dream into the city. There too we find the suburbs ringing the cities in their rapid, undisciplined growth with ugly, congested webs of ticky-tacky houses and macadam-burst shopping centers. . . .
>
> How have we built, or let build, this somewhat lacking, somehow defective, maculate home for man?

This chapter will explore a number of the paradoxes and problems posed by the dominant role of the city in American life. First, what is the rationale for the evolution of cities? Why have cities developed and grown? A second and closely related objective is to explain the more recent phenomenon of suburban growth. What economic considerations underlie urban sprawl? Next we will consider a number of problems which have been spawned by the dynamics of urban growth. These include transportation problems, environmental pollution, and central-city poverty. Finally, we will consider some possible solutions

[1] Terry Sanford, "The States and the Cities: The Unfinished Agenda," in Brian J. L. Berry and Jack Meltzer (eds.), *Goals for Urban America* (Englewood Cliffs, N.J.: Prentice-Hall, Inc., 1967), pp. 52–53.

to the problems of the cities. As a prelude to these questions and issues, we must first determine the extent to which the United States is urbanized.

AN URBAN NATION

Today the United States is clearly an urban nation. But, as Table 37·1 indicates, this has not always been so. Musty records reveal that in 1790 some 95 percent of our population lived in rural areas, mostly on farms. But by 1920 a majority of the population had become urban. Currently almost three-fourths of our population is located in urban areas. Furthermore, although the larger and smaller cities have been experiencing about the same *rate* of growth, the *absolute* increases in population have been greater in the larger cities. Future projections suggest that virtually all the 100 million population growth anticipated by the year 2000 will accrue to urban areas! We are, indeed, a nation of city dwellers and apparently becoming more so.

WHY CITIES DEVELOP

There are substantial economic reasons why cities have evolved and grown. Let us look at these reasons—the economic rationale for cities—in both general and specific terms.

In general: where to produce?

To say the least, the production and distribution of goods do not occur at some mythical point having no length and breadth. The decision about where certain kinds of businesses should locate is as important as the decision to produce, say, more television sets and fewer radios. The very important question of business location was hidden in Chapter 5's discussion of the Five Fundamental Questions. In fact, the question of organizing production—*how* to produce?—implies the problem of location, or *where* to produce. Our analysis of the firm (particularly in Chapter 26) implicitly assumed that all production

TABLE 37·1 URBAN POPULATION GROWTH IN THE UNITED STATES (in millions)

Year	Urban population	Rural population	Urban as a percent of total population
1790	.2	3.7	5
1810	.5	6.7	7
1830	1.1	11.7	9
1850	3.5	19.6	15
1870	9.9	28.7	25
1890	22.1	40.8	35
1910	42.0	50.0	46
1930	69.0	53.8	56
1950	96.5	54.2	64
1970	149.8	53.9	73
1980	197.0	53.0	79

Source: Bureau of the Census. "Urban areas" are defined by the Census Bureau as cities and other incorporated places which have 2,500 or more inhabitants.

took place at some fixed geographic point. In effect we supposed that the market for inputs was located at the firm's back door, and the market for outputs at its front door. This is obviously unrealistic; transportation or transfer costs are involved both in getting raw materials and other inputs to the plant and in getting the finished product to buyers.

Stated differently, one of the important costs in organizing resources for production is the cost of overcoming geographic space, that is, the amounts of time and resources necessary for transportation and communication. If producers locate close to those from whom they purchase inputs and to those to whom they sell their outputs, then transportation and communication costs will obviously be reduced. Crudely put, there are economic advantages accruing to firms which agglomerate, that is, locate in proximity to one another and to their markets. These spatial advantages are fundamental to the economic rationale of urban growth.

In particular: economies of agglomeration

But let us back up and explain the economic reasons for the evolution of cities in more detail. In the first place, the necessary condition for the development of cities is the capacity of a nation's agriculture to produce surplus food and fiber. The rapidly expanding productivity of American agriculture, detailed in Chapter 36, has freed the vast majority of our population from farming so that this labor might turn to the production of nonagricultural goods and services. Because man is a social animal and because specialized industrial production demands large numbers of workers, it was only natural that labor released from an increasingly efficient agriculture would cluster in villages, towns, and cities.

Although an increasingly efficient agricultural sector has "pushed" labor out of farming, it has been *economies of agglomeration* which have "pulled" population and industry to the villages, towns, and cities. What specifically are agglomeration economies? Generally speaking, agglomeration economies refer to the "cheapening" of production or marketing which results from the fact that firms locate relatively close to one another. The economies which result from such agglomeration are of several interrelated and admittedly overlapping types.

Internal economies of scale Perhaps the simplest basis for spatial concentration is the economies of large-scale production. Recall that where economies of scale are substantial, reasonably efficient production will be possible only with a small number of producers relative to the total market. This suggests that one large producer can serve a number of market areas more cheaply than can a number of small, decentralized producers. Cities have large populations and therefore large potential markets which give producers the opportunity to move down their long-run average cost curves and achieve low unit costs (Figure 26·6*a*).

Locational (transport) economies The location of business enterprise is strongly influenced by the availability of transportation facilities. Transport costs will obviously be higher for a firm if required inputs and markets for outputs are not readily accessible. Hence, at any given time the locational choice of a firm will be strongly influenced by the existing transportation network. It is no accident that our major cities historically have grown around low-cost natural or man-made transportation nodes, that is, along seaboards (New York, San Francisco), on major rivers (St. Louis), or around railroad terminals (Chicago).

Perhaps less obvious as an incentive to agglomeration is the matter of "industrial linkages." Technological progress has caused the chain of goods production and assembly to become longer and more complex. The outputs of a growing number of firms and industries constitute the inputs of still other firms and industries. This growing specialization in production means that industrially linked firms can realize substantial economies in transportation and communication by locating in proximity. It is not difficult to see why the attraction of industry and therefore of population to the cities tends to be a self-perpetuating process. For obvious reasons, the location of an automobile assembly plant in a given city may

induce tire and glass producers, for example, to locate plants in the same area. In turn the existence of the glass and tire plants may induce still another automobile manufacturer to establish an assembly plant in the area. And so it goes.

Urban economies: specialization and infrastructure The foregoing discussion of internal economies of scale and locational economies is not sufficient to explain fully the phenomenon of urban growth. Nor does it explain why the larger cities have grown at the expense of the smaller cities. A more complete explanation involves *external economies of specialization* and the *infrastructure* of urban areas.

The economies of scale discussed earlier were labeled "internal economies of scale" because their realization depends solely upon the decisions and fortunes of individual firms. In other words, technology confronts the firm with a *given* average cost curve which declines over a very substantial range, such as in Figure 26·6*a*, and it is entirely up to the firm to achieve the high levels of production prerequisite to low unit costs. Now we must consider scale economies of a different type. Specifically, there may exist certain economies which cause the average cost curves of firms to shift downward. These downward shifts of the average cost curves of individual firms depend upon the expansion of the entire *industry* or group of firms, not of the single *firm.* Therefore, such economies are *external economies of scale,* for their realization lies beyond, or is external to, the actions and decisions of any single firm.

Specifically, as a number of firms agglomerate, they may *as a group* be able to realize lower input prices and therefore lower cost curves than if they were not geographically concentrated. That is, as firms agglomerate, it tends to become profitable for specialized firms to perform certain functions for the industry on a larger scale—and therefore more cheaply—than can each firm internally. For example, prior to agglomeration a manufacturer may be forced to repair its own machinery or conduct its own technological or marketing research. But as the number of firms in an industry, or even in different industries, concentrate in an area, the volume of repair or research business of the firms as a group becomes sufficient to support a firm specializing in these functions. The agglomerated firms can realize lower input prices—and lower unit costs—by "farming out" these functions to specialists rather than undertaking the tasks themselves.

This growing specialization obviously leads to an increased interdependence among various types of manufacturing and service establishments. Thus, the location of the individual establishments which are highly interdependent is, in a sense, determined simultaneously. Broadly speaking, producers of final goods must have easy access both to the intermediate goods and services needed as inputs and to the markets for their final product. Similarly, the suppliers of intermediate goods and services must have easy access to markets sufficient in scale to realize internal economies of large-scale production. It follows that the solution for both groups is the same—to cluster in cities that alone can provide both inputs and markets in sufficient scale and variety to meet their total needs. Thus, it is not difficult to see why the attraction of industry and therefore of population to the cities tends to be a self-perpetuating process.

Another illustration: The geographic concentration of a large number of firms requiring, say, unskilled and semiskilled labor may attract large pools of these kinds of labor to the area. The result? Lower wage rates for labor inputs and therefore lower average costs for the firms.

The *infrastructure* of an urban area is a source of economies or cost advantages not entirely unlike external economies of scale. Specifically, a city provides its firms with important services and facilities upon which producers rely and which would be costly for each firm to provide in the small amounts it alone needs. This infrastructure comprises such obvious things as ample water, electrical power, waste treatment facilities, transportation facilities, educational research and engineering facilities, financial and banking institutions, management and public relations consultants, and so forth.

A rich and varied infrastructure may be the strongest agglomerative force explaining the continuing and

persistent growth of our largest urban areas. For instance, one of the conclusions of a 1960 study of the New York metropolitan area pertained to the importance of the area's infrastructure in attracting new enterprises. The study noted that even though the New York metropolitan area has lost nearly every industry it has ever had—flour mills, foundries, meat-packing plants, textile mills, and tanneries—the area continues to grow and earn above-average income. The report noted that New York's ability to grow and earn above-average income can be attributed to its rich infrastructure which attracts new enterprises that require highly specialized and sophisticated services.

Amenities Related, noneconomic inducements for urban location are certain amenities—the theater, museums, art galleries, symphony orchestras, universities, highly specialized medical facilities, jet transportation, nightclubs, professional athletics, and so on—which are important attractions to many people, including those among management and the professions. In fact, many of the refinements of modern living are urban based; conversely, small towns are widely regarded as "dull."

Deglomerative forces

The advantages of agglomeration cannot be reaped indefinitely. Beyond some critical and difficult-to-specify point, continued city growth and geographic concentration of industry will tend to create counterforces which give rise to higher production costs. That is, continued efforts to realize the economies of agglomeration may create certain offsetting diseconomies, or what might be termed *deglomerative forces.* Certain costs associated with geographic concentration are internal to, and therefore must be borne by, the producers themselves. For example, a growing concentration of industry in a given geographic area will mean higher land values and rents. (Figure 33·1 reminds us that a rising demand for a perfectly inelastic supply of centrally located sites will have a large price effect.) In turn, rising land values will make it increasingly costly for new firms to locate in an area or for existing firms to expand facilities. Furthermore, the intensified demand for labor which accompanies industrial agglomeration may be reflected in increased bargaining power for workers and rising wage costs.

Other costs which accompany industrial agglomeration may be shifted by individual producers to society as a whole, that is, to other firms and to the population at large. These spillover costs in the form of air and water pollution or traffic congestion and noise contribute to the general debasement of the area and make it a less attractive place for firms and people to locate. The pollution problem merits separate discussion later in this chapter.

Have deglomerative forces become sufficiently important in recent years so that they offset some of the advantages of agglomeration? Recent changes in urbanization patterns seem to indicate that this is the case. The growth of suburbia and the decentralization of central business districts are consistent with the notion that deglomerative forces are at work. Note, however, that the simple fact of urban growth will result in urban spread—the fanning out of people and businesses from the central city.

THE FLIGHT TO THE SUBURBS: URBAN SPRAWL

This brief introduction to the economies and diseconomies of agglomeration helps explain the paradox stated at the outset of this chapter. The cities are centers of great wealth and income. They are centers of economic activity and for many people a magnet of economic opportunity. But the very growth and maturation of the city spawns spillover costs, not to mention the inevitable social tensions which characterize areas of high population density. These latter features of the cities obviously tend to make urban life less attractive. Hence, actual or potential urban residents—both businesses and households—ask themselves this question: How can the advantages and opportunities of the metropolitan area be realized without also incurring the disadvantages? How can one tap the economic activity of the city and realize a higher income *and* at the same time enjoy fresh air, space, privacy, and tranquillity?

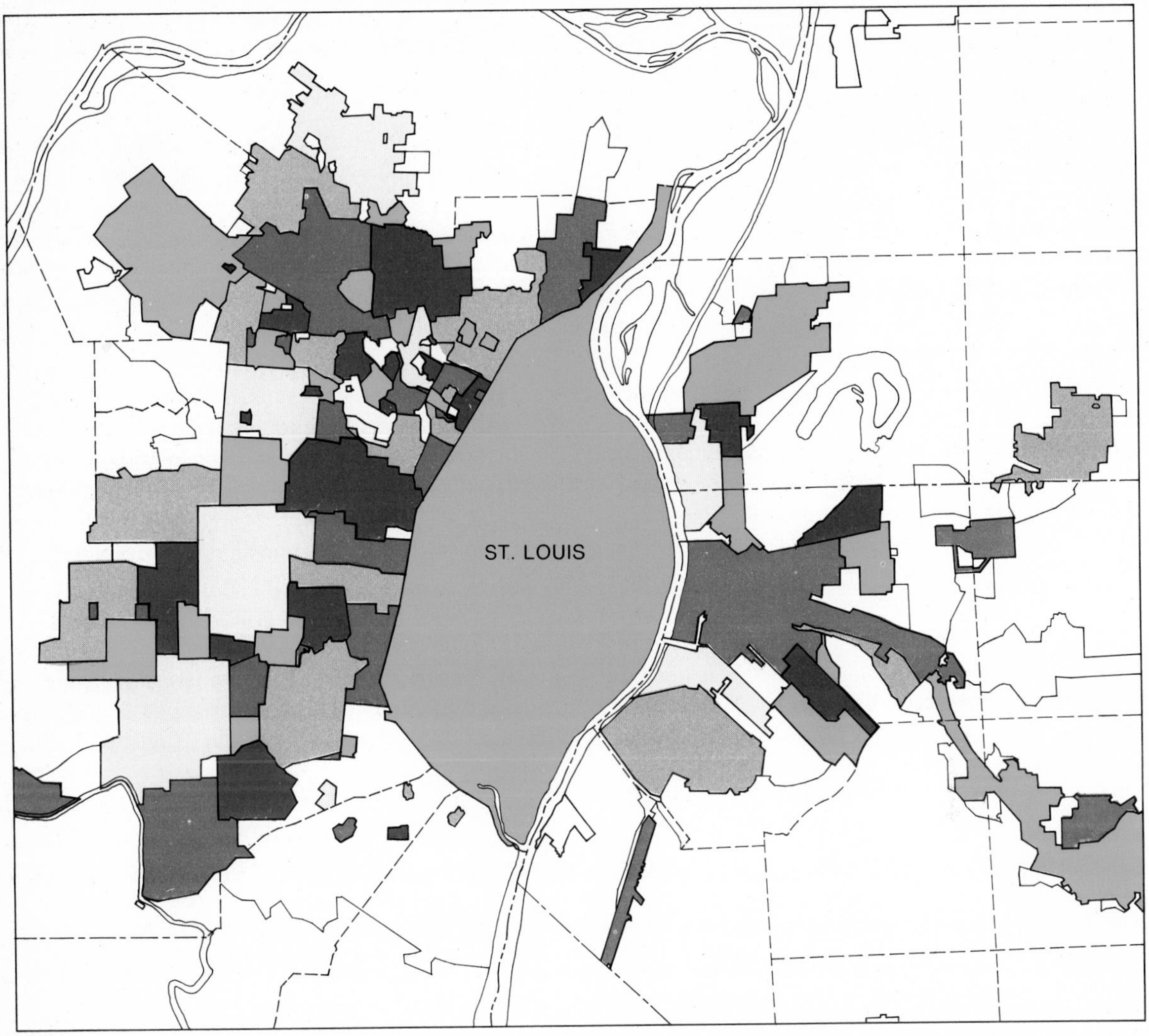

FIGURE 37·1 POLITICAL FRAGMENTATION: THE CASE OF ST. LOUIS

The dynamics of urban expansion has given rise to the growth of numerous politically distinct subdivisions around the central city. The 474 units of local government which comprise the St. Louis metropolitan area are quite typical of this political balkanization. (Advisory Commission on Intergovernmental Relations, *Urban America and the Federal System,* Washington, 1969, p. 85).

Millions of more affluent Americans have answered: Move to the suburbs! It is significant that the percentage of our population living in the central city has actually been declining since the turn of the century; virtually all of our metropolitan population growth has been in the suburbs. Many factors have contributed to rapid suburban growth. Rising postwar incomes, abetted by governmentally guaranteed mortgage credit, have made suburban living accessible to more and more families. Automobile ownership, as a convenient means of commuting, has been an important permissive factor.

Suburban growth has resulted not merely in the relocation of people, but also in the movement of businesses. The reasons for this are complex and diverse.[2] In the first place, it is easy to see why many of the retail and personal service industries—groceries, hardware and furniture stores, laundries and cleaners, barber and beauty shops—have moved to the suburbs. Such establishments must be close to people; in particular, to people who have money! But many manufacturing firms have also fled the central city. We have already hit upon a couple of reasons for such shifts. Rising land costs make plant expansion very costly in the central city. And spillover costs make downtown locations less attractive. Firms which are large enough to have their own truck transportation encounter costly problems of traffic congestion, loading and parking, and so forth. In addition, technological changes have encouraged many manufacturers to migrate to the suburbs. The rapid development of truck transportation has freed many firms from the need to locate near downtown railroad terminals and harbor facilities. Perhaps more important is the fact that modern production technology has put greater emphasis upon highly integrated, continuous processes which presume an extensive one-story plant layout. Space for the utilization of this technology simply is not available—or only available at prohibitive cost—in the central city.

Now this is not to suggest that *all* major businesses have fled to the suburbs. Certain kinds of businesses have remained—and prospered—in the central cities:[3]

> These are the highly specialized areas of finance, business services, and central office administration, whose inputs are skill or knowledge or information, whose outputs are not goods but service or advice or decisions. It is these establishments—banks and law offices, advertising agencies and central administrative offices, consulting firms and government agencies—which are filling more and more of the central cities of most urban areas, and are becoming the primary function of . . . the city's central business district.

Overall, however, the trend has been to the suburbs.

Political fragmentation

This dramatic flight to the suburbs has been accompanied by the political balkanization of our large cities. That is, the central cities have become encircled with a large number of new suburbs, each of which is a separate political entity. Figure 37·1 shows the case of St. Louis. The St. Louis urban area is served by 474 local governments which are almost equally divided between Illinois and Missouri. These 474 governmental units include over 100 separate municipalities. St. Louis is hardly an exceptional case. There are over 1,400 separate units of government in the New York City metropolitan area and almost 1,000 in the San Francisco Bay area.

Economic imbalance

Political fragmentation is the source of many urban problems. But it is particularly troublesome because the central city and the suburban municipalities are highly unequal in terms of wealth and income. The process of urban decentralization or suburban growth has brought about a highly unequal distribution of wealth and incomes geographically. The more prosperous people and many of the newer and more profitable industries have fled the central city in favor of the suburbs. By and large the poor people and many of the less profitable industries have been left behind in the central city.

[2] The following discussion is based upon Benjamin Chinitz (ed.), *City and Suburb* (Englewood Cliffs, N.J.: Prentice-Hall, Inc., 1964), pp. 23–27.

[3] Ibid., p. 26.

This dramatic process of change in the structure of metropolitan areas has been self-reinforcing and cumulative. The migration of both the wealthier people and businesses to new political entities in the suburbs seriously erodes the property tax base of the central cities.[4] New plants and new housing are built in the suburban ring, not in the central cities. To maintain public services property tax *rates* must be increased in the central city. But these rising rates simply provide further incentive for both households and businesses to flee to the suburbs.

Furthermore, the poor, predominantly black families who by virtue of their poverty and discrimination are left behind in the central cities are "high cost" citizens. An unusually high percentage are on welfare. Children are numerous, and education costs are high. High population densities—Harlem has 67,000 people per square mile—mean that the costs of governing, of collecting garbage, of maintaining law and order are high.

All of this is complicated and given further impetus by the fact that central-city decay, or urban blight, tends to be a cumulative process:[5]

> The older structures concentrated near the city center lose their economic usefulness as the functions of the downtown areas change. Extensive conversion, rehabilitation, and reconstruction are needed. If a few buildings need to be replaced or renovated in an otherwise prosperous area, the market provides private developers and builders with sufficient incentives to undertake the work. However, when a pattern of decay permeates a large area, the dilapidation of neighboring buildings reduces the profitability of improving a particular property. A large area must then be improved as a single unit, and the cost and difficulties of acquiring and redeveloping a large tract of central city land are likely to deter private investors from the undertaking.

To summarize: The basic consequence of the dynamics of urban growth and the accompanying political fragmentation has been "to forge a white, middle- and high-income noose around the increasingly black and poor inner city. . . . " The losers in the flight to politically splintered suburbs have been the central cities, saddled with an inadequate and shrinking tax base and the burgeoning expenditure demands "incident to the governing, educating, and 'welfaring' of an increasing proportion of relatively poor [and usually] black families."[6] The winners, on the other hand, have been the more wealthy white suburban localities wherein income and wealth have been sufficient to underwrite viable public services with relatively modest tax efforts.

The dynamics of urban growth and the crazy quilt of political entities which has accompanied this growth have spawned a host of acute and interrelated problems. Let us now briefly survey some of these problems and sketch possible avenues for their resolution. Although the problems of the cities are manifold and not subject to simple classification, we will concentrate on three main problem areas: urban transportation, the ghettos and central-city poverty, and pollution.

THE URBAN TRANSPORTATION PROBLEM

We have seen that one fundamental characteristic of urban growth is the direct relationship one finds between distance from the central city and income and wealth. Generally speaking, those living furthest from "downtown" are the professional, technical, and white-collar workers. A large proportion of these higher-income people work downtown; that is, they are employed in the banking and financial firms, the legal and consulting firms, and the advertising agencies which have remained in the central city. On the other hand, we have seen that many kinds of manufacturing, wholesale, retail, and personal service industries—industries which require blue-collar and less skilled workers—have moved to suburbia. The result is a significant locational mismatch of jobs and labor force between suburbs and central city. This mismatch creates the need for an effective transportation system to negotiate the required cross-hauling of the population.

[4]Recall from Table 9·3 that property taxes are the main source of revenue for local units of government.

[5]*Economic Report of the President, 1965,* pp. 149–150.

[6]Advisory Commission on Intergovernmental Relations, *Urban America and the Federal System* (Washington, 1969), pp. 2, 8.

But the need for efficient transportation is even more pervasive. Accessibility is the sine qua non of effective participation in urban life. Most of the cultural and social advantages of city life can only be efficiently realized through a viable transportation system. Museums, art galleries, and concert halls are indivisible, or "lumpy," social goods; since they cannot be divided and taken home by consumers, the consumer must go to them. Similarly, comparative shopping in the city presumes adequate transportation.

Given the convenience of private automobile travel, most suburbanites have chosen this form of transportation. Furthermore, large Federal subsidies to highway construction have created a substantial financial bias in favor of the automobile. But, ironically, dramatic increases in metropolitan automobile use and highway construction—Los Angeles is the classic case—have not solved the transportation problem. Indeed, the expanded use of auto transportation has given rise to increasingly acute problems of traffic congestion, not to mention the automobile's substantial contribution to air pollution. The response to traffic congestion, of course, has been to construct more highways. But the additional highways permit the growth of still more distant suburbs and elicit more traffic. Alas, more highways beget more autos. So mammoth highway construction programs have been accompanied by more—not less—traffic congestion and parking problems. We have witnessed a vicious cycle of more autos, more highways which induce more autos, and the construction of still more highways.

The other side of the coin has been the general deterioration of the mass-transit systems of the cities. The vast geographic dispersion of population throughout the suburbs has made it difficult for mass-transit systems to realize the heavy trunk-line operations requisite to their prosperity or survival. Again, we encounter a cumulative process. As patronage declines, unit costs rise and commuter fares must be increased, on the one hand, and the quality of both equipment and service deteriorates, on the other. So more people choose to drive their cars to work, and the process repeats itself.

Unfortunately, not all people can afford the automobile–mass-transit choice. The poor and less skilled of the central city must rely upon mass transit. Shrinkage and service deterioration of the transit system, accompanied by the shift of blue-collar jobs to the suburbs, simply leaves many of the central-city residents isolated from the economic opportunities of the metropolitan area.

IMPROVING URBAN TRANSPORTATION

In considering possible solutions, it is both convenient and meaningful to consider "the" urban transport problem in two parts: the short-run problem and the long-run problem.

The short run: user charges and peak pricing

First, there is a short-run problem: Given existing transportation facilities and technology, how can this transportation "plant" be used most efficiently? What is the best way of utilizing *existing* freeway-street-parking and mass-transit facilities? In our earlier discussion of the transportation problem we noted that governmental subsidies were heavily biased in favor of automobile transportation. Specifically, urban freeway and street construction is heavily subsidized by Federal grants; financing also comes from state gasoline tax revenues. Now a number of urban economists feel that a system of *user charges* on drivers would be very useful in achieving a better balance in the use of mass transit and auto transportation and, in particular, in alleviating the problem of traffic congestion. Advocates of user charges contend that the city's streets and highways are overused and congested because drivers do not bear the full cost of driving; they are in fact subsidized by society (taxpayers) at large. More specifically, it is argued that automobile drivers should be confronted "as near as possible in time and place to the act of making the decision to drive" with a price—a user charge—which covers the full cost of driving. By "full cost" is meant not only the cost of

highway construction and repair but also the cost of traffic control devices and traffic police and even automobile pollution costs. Price, after all, is a rationing device or disciplining mechanism, and traffic congestion is a symptom of quantity demanded in excess of quantity supplied at the going price. "Surely, we would have traffic jams in the aisles of food stores and 'shortages' of food if we tried to administer free food stores supported by general taxation. The food shortages would be analogous to the shortages of street space per automobile (traffic jams) and the shortages of parking places that characterize our underpriced and tax-supported urban transportation industry."[7]

What specifically will be the effects of a system of user charges on drivers? First, some will be rationed out of the "driving market"; that is, they will use the public transportation system or, if they have the option, will make fewer trips downtown. This response, of course, has the desired effect of relieving traffic congestion. Second, those who continue to drive will contribute more funds for the expansion and improvement of highway and parking facilities.

Recognizing that the morning and evening rush hours are the focal point of the urban transportation problem, many advocates of user charges also contend that the pricing of both auto and mass-transit facilities should vary to users according to the time of day. That is, *peak pricing* should be used. Specifically, charges should be higher during the peak or rush hours and lower during off-peak hours. The purpose, of course, is to "ration out" travelers whose need to travel during rush hours is less pressing or less necessary. For example, shoppers might be induced by a system of peak prices to alter the timing of their trips to and from downtown so that they do not coincide with the travel times of commuting workers.

Those who favor user charges admit that significant problems of application exist. For example, how does one calculate the costs of air pollution, noise, and delay and the opportunity cost of the land used in freeway and street construction in determining the full cost of an automobile trip to the downtown area? Then, too, there is the difficult problem of assessing and collecting user charges from drivers; can tolls be collected without creating toll station bottlenecks? Or is it possible to "include highly sophisticated electronic sensing devices mounted on cars and in the streets, which could result in computer-written monthly bills to motorists . . . , charging them more for the use of congested routes in crowded hours"?[8]

The long run: mass transit

This brings us to the long-run aspect of the urban transportation problem: What should be the character of future public investments in urban transportation facilities? For a variety of reasons there has been a revival of interest in the revitalization and development of public mass-transit systems—commuter railroads, subways, buses, monorails, and so forth. First, given projections of suburban population growth and the consequent possibility that the volume of urban automobile traffic may double in the next twenty years, many city planners and public officials feel that effective alternatives to auto transportation are imperative. This is particularly so in view of the previously noted point that increased investment in streets and freeways seems to induce a high volume of traffic, rather than relieve congestion. Secondly, interest in public mass transit has been stimulated by the recognition that past transportation subsidies have favored the automobile and that there is now a need to achieve a better balance between auto and mass transit. Finally, it is felt that an expanded and improved mass-transit system can yield substantial social benefits in terms of (1) a viable and revitalized central city with an expanding property tax base, (2) greater accessibility to suburban jobs for the central-city poor, and (3) avoidance of an increasingly acute pollution problem which an expansion of automobile transportation is likely to entail.

The Urban Mass Transit Acts of 1964 and 1966 have been in response to this interest in mass transit, providing Federal funds for the revitalization and

[7]Wilbur R. Thompson, *A Preface to Urban Economics* (Baltimore: The Johns Hopkins Press, 1965), pp. 340–341.

[8]Dick Netzer, *Economics and Urban Problems* (New York: Basic Books, Inc., Publishers, 1970), p. 158.

technological improvement of public transportation systems. It should be emphasized, however, that the solution—if there is one—to the urban transportation problem will not entail an either-or choice; some workable combination of automobile and public mass transit will be essential to a viable transportation system.

THE POLLUTION PROBLEM: THE EFFLUENT SOCIETY?

Cities do not have a monopoly on the pollution problem. Yet the high population densities and high levels of industrial concentration which are the earmarks of urban life make pollution problems most acute in the cities.

Dimensions of the problem

The seriousness of water, air, and solid-waste pollution has been well-documented in the popular press and needs only brief review here. We know that rivers and lakes have been turned into municipal and industrial sewers. Not only has Lake Erie become a national cesspool, but the Cuyahoga River which feeds into it has become so permeated with sludge and oil that it has been labeled a fire hazard! Leaks from offshore wells have plagued the Southern California and Gulf coasts. The drainage of DDT into streams and lakes has imperiled our fish and bird populations. Almost half of our population drinks water of dubious quality. A growing body of evidence links air pollution to lung cancer, emphysema, pneumonia, and other respiratory diseases. The toxics in New York City's air make a day's walking and breathing the equivalent of smoking two packages of cigarettes.[9] Cynics tell us that one wakes up in Los Angeles to the sound of birds coughing. Each American accounts for some 2,000 pounds of solid wastes—including, for example, 250 tin cans per person—each year.

Possible longer-run consequences of environmental pollution are even more disturbing. Competent scientists suggest that if current trends in automobile use continue, large densely populated areas of our country may become uninhabitable, the source of certain suffocation. Some scientists contend that in time air pollution could cause the slight rise in temperature sufficient to melt the polar ice caps and flood coastal areas with sea water.

Causes: materials balance approach

The roots of the pollution problem can best be envisioned through the *materials balance approach,* which is simply the notion that the weight of the inputs (fuels, raw materials, water, and so forth) used in the economy's production processes will ultimately result in a roughly equivalent residual of wastes. For example, each year[10]

> The economy . . . takes in about . . . [a] billion tons of minerals and food and forest products. Consumers use these goods in the form they receive them, or further transform them (e.g., by eating), but must sooner or later dispose of the end product, whether it be empty tin cans, "throw away" bottles, worn-out refrigerators, plastic toys or human excreta.

Fortunately, the ecological system—Nature, if you are over thirty—has the self-regenerating capacity which allows it, within limits, to absorb or recycle such wastes. But the problem is that the volume of such residuals has outrun this absorptive capacity; Nature is no longer a free good. Why has this happened? Why do we have a pollution problem? Causes are manifold, but perhaps four are paramount.

First, there is the simple matter of population growth. An ecological system which may accommodate 50 or 100 million people may break down under the

[9] In a penetrating satire on New York City ("fume city") Dick Schaap made this observation in *New York Magazine* (April 15, 1968):

> Beyond its natural loveliness, pollution serves the city of New York in so many ways. It helps keep the City from becoming overpopulated; it insures that only the fittest survive and the rest move to the suburbs. It helps keep the City from becoming overgrown with foliage; it kills roses and tulips and other harmful weeds. It provides employment for window washers and car-washers and eager little shoe-shine boys. And it saves money: it provides all the joys of cigarette smoking without any of the expenses.

[10] Department of Health, Education, and Welfare, *Toward a Social Report* (Washington, 1969), p. 28.

pressures of 200 or 300 million. As noted, the fact that the absorptive capacity of our natural environment is an increasingly scarce resource is most evident in urban areas where the concentration of population and economic activity is so great.

Secondly, per capita incomes have been rising. Industrial production, for example, has been growing at $4\frac{1}{2}$ percent per year, which means that industrial output will increase tenfold by the year 2020.[11] The materials balance approach reminds us that, barring significant changes in technology or the composition of output, the total weight of wastes generated will also increase tenfold. Paradoxically, the affluent society helps to spawn the effluent society. A rising GNP (gross national product) means a rising GNG (gross national garbage). Thus a high standard of living permits Americans to own some 100 million automobiles. But autos are a primary source of air pollution and, concomitantly, give rise to the hard problem of disposing of some 7 or 8 million junked autos each year. Furthermore, the fact that more leisure has been a component of our rising standard of living has increased public awareness of the pollution problem. When you have time to spend on a beach or at a lake you become concerned that the water is unfit for swimming or that the fish have been killed by thermal or chemical pollution.

Technological change is a third contributor to pollution. For example, the expanded use of pesticides, herbicides, and insecticides has proved to be a deadly enemy of our fish and bird populations. The addition of lead to gasolines poses a serious threat to human health. The development and widespread use of "throw-away" containers made of virtually indestructable aluminum or plastic add substantially to the solid-waste crisis. Detergent soap products have been highly resistant to sanitary treatment and recycling.

A fourth and crucial factor concerns economic incentives. Specifically, businesses find their private production costs will be less by polluting. In technical terms pollution is a problem in spillover costs (Chapters 6 and 27). Profit-seeking manufacturers choose the least-cost combination of inputs and will find it advantageous to bear only unavoidable costs. If they can dump waste chemicals into rivers and lakes rather than pay for expensive treatment and proper disposal, businesses will be inclined to do so. If manufacturers can discharge smoke and the hot water used to cool machinery rather than purchase expensive abatement and cooling facilities, they will tend to do so. The result is air and water pollution—both chemical and thermal—and, in the economist's jargon, the shifting of certain costs to the community at large as spillover costs. Enjoying lower "internal" costs than if he had not polluted the environment, the producer can sell his product more cheaply, expand his production, and realize larger profits. The supply curve of a polluting firm or industry lies too far to the right because it omits the cost which society bears in the form of a debased environment. The result is an overallocation of resources to the polluter's commodity.

But it is neither just nor accurate to lay the entire blame for pollution at the door of industry. Given the fact that an important function of government is to correct the misallocation of resources which accompany spillover costs (Chapter 6), it is ironic that most major cities are heavy contributors to the pollution problem. Municipal power plants are frequently major contributors to air pollution; many cities discharge untreated or inadequately treated sewage into rivers or lakes because it is cheap and convenient to do so. Similarly, individuals seek to avoid the costs of proper refuse pickup and disposal by burning their garbage. We also find it convenient to use throw-away containers rather than recycling "return" containers. And note in particular that a well-intentioned firm which wants to operate in a socially responsible way with respect to pollution finds itself in an awkward position. If an individual firm "internalizes" all of its external or spillover costs by installing, say, water-treatment and smoke-abatement equipment, the firm will find itself at a cost disadvantage in comparison to its polluting competitors. The socially responsible firm will have higher costs and will be forced to raise its price. The "reward" for the pollution-conscious firm is a declining market for its product, diminished

[11] Ibid., p. 28.

profits, and, in the extreme, the prospect of bankruptcy. This correctly suggests that effective action to combat pollution must be undertaken collectively through government.

Antipollution policies

Environmental pollution is a problem in spillover or external costs.[12] Therefore, the task of antipollution policy is to devise ways of "internalizing" the external costs of pollution. The objective is to make the polluter pay *all* the costs associated with his activities. In terms of Figure 6·1*b* we want to eliminate the discrepancy between private and total costs by shifting *SS* to, or at least toward, S_tS_t.

1. Direct controls through legislated standards One obvious approach is for governmental units to pass legislation which prohibits or regulates pollution. Legislation may establish minimum standards for air and water which polluters must observe or face legal sanctions. The legislation of pollution standards will presumably force polluters to install water-treatment and air-filter equipment and thereby force them to bear costs which would otherwise be shifted to society. A much-publicized illustration of this approach is Federal legislation requiring automobile manufacturers to meet exhaust-emission standards. In particular, recent amendments to the Clean Air Act of 1967 specify that cars of the 1975 model year must reduce carbon monoxide and hydrocarbon emissions by 90 percent from 1970 levels. On a broader front the Environmental Protection Agency was established by Congress in 1969 to develop quality standards for air and water in cooperation with state and local governments.

2. Special taxes: emission fees A second approach is to levy special charges or taxes—emission or effluent fees—on polluters. That is, a special tax or fee should be assessed per ton of pollutant discharged into the air or water. Ideally, fees would be set so that spillover costs would be exactly covered and each producer's cost curve would reflect *all* production costs.

For example, suppose a chemical plant is polluting a river. The resulting external costs are manifold: Other manufacturers and municipalities located downstream must pay to purify the water prior to use; businesses based upon fishing or recreational uses of the river will be injured; individuals will suffer the loss of recreational uses; the river may become a health hazard; and so forth. Now if a special tax or emission fee covering these spillover costs is imposed upon the chemical plant, these external costs will become internalized to the plant. The chemical firm must recalculate its cost alternatives. On the one hand, it can purchase pollution-abatement equipment and thereby reduce or eliminate the payment of emission fees. Or it can continue to pollute and pay the required fees. In this second case, government can use the revenue from the emission fees to cleanse the downstream water or to compensate injured parties. A system of water pollution fees has been used effectively in Germany's Ruhr River basin for some time.

3. A market for pollution rights One of the most novel policy suggestions is to create a market for pollution rights.[13] The rationale for this proposal is that the air, rivers, lakes, oceans, and public lands such as parks and streets are all primary objects for pollution because the *rights* to use these resources are either held "in common" by society or are unspecified by law. As a result, no specific private individual or institution has any incentive to restrict the use or maintain the purity or quality of these resources because he does not have the right to realize a monetary return from doing so. One maintains the property he owns—you paint and repair your home periodically—because he will capture the value of these improvements at the time of resale. But no economic incentive exists to maintain our air and water resources because they are not privately

[12] Rereading the section entitled "Spillovers or externalities" in Chapter 6 may be useful at this point.

[13] J. H. Dales, *Pollution, Property and Prices* (Toronto: University of Toronto Press, 1968).

owned. As long as the "rights" to air, water, and certain land resources are commonly held and these resources made freely available, there will be no incentive to maintain them or restrict their use. Hence, these natural resources are "overconsumed" and thereby polluted.

The proposal is therefore made that an appropriate pollution-control agency should determine the amount of pollutants which can be discharged into the water or air of a given region each year and still maintain the quality of the water or air at some acceptable standard. For example, the agency may determine that 500 tons of raw sewage may be discharged into Metropolitan Lake and be "recycled" by Nature. Hence, 500 sewage pollution rights, each entitling the owner to dump 1 ton of raw sewage into the lake in the given year, are made available for sale each year. The resulting supply of pollution rights is perfectly inelastic, as shown in Figure 37·2. The demand for pollution rights will take the same downsloping form as will the demand for any other input. At high prices polluters will either stop polluting or will pollute less by acquiring pollution-abatement equipment. Thus a market price for pollution rights will be determined at which an environment-preserving quantity of pollution rights will be rationed to polluters. Note that without this market 750 tons of sewage would be discharged into the lake and it would be "overconsumed," or polluted, in the amount of 250 tons. And over time, as human and business populations expand, demand will increase as from D_{1972} to D_{1982}. *Without* a market for pollution rights, pollution would occur in 1982 in the amount of 500 tons beyond that which can be assimilated by Nature. *With* the market for pollution rights price will now simply rise to $200 and the amount of discharged sewage will remain at 500 tons—the amount which the lake can recycle.

This proposal has a number of advantages. Potential polluters are confronted with an explicit monetary incentive not to pollute. Conservation groups can fight pollution by buying up and withholding pollution rights, thereby reducing actual pollution below governmentally determined standards. As the demand for pollution rights increases over time, the growing revenue from the sale of the given quantity of pollution rights could be devoted to environmental improvement. Similarly, over time the rising price of pollution rights should stimulate the search for improved techniques to control pollution.

FIGURE 37·2 THE MARKET FOR POLLUTION RIGHTS

Pollution can be controlled by having a public body determine the amount of pollution which the atmosphere or a body of water can safely recycle and sell these limited rights to polluters. The effect is to make the environment a scarce resource with a positive price. Economic and population growth will increase the demand for pollution rights over time, but the consequence will be an increase in the price of pollution rights rather than more pollution.

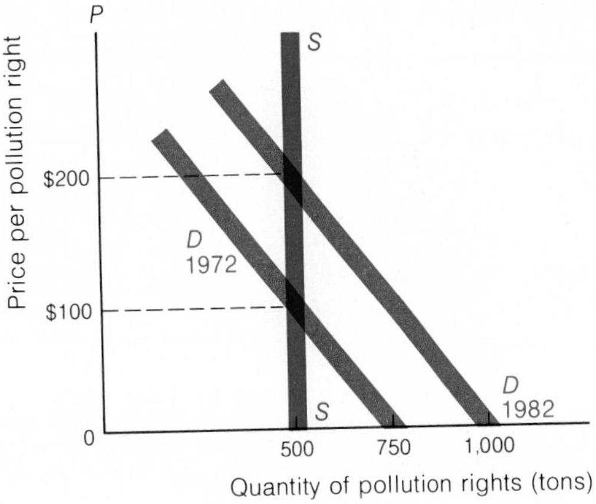

Problems The problems involved in establishing and administering these antipollution proposals are both numerous and substantial. First, pollution standards are difficult to establish because of incomplete and disputed technological and biological information. We simply do not know with certainty the effects—the economic and human costs—of certain pollutants. Witness the continuing dispute over the use of DDT. This lack of information is important because it is not economically rational to prohibit or

flatly eliminate pollution, but rather to use benefit-cost analysis (Chapter 6) to determine the optimum extent to which antipollution programs should be pursued. This entails the very difficult problem of calculating the marginal benefits and marginal costs of such programs. Secondly, the administration and enforcement of legislated controls or standards can be both difficult and costly. Finally, governmental units—the very institutions we would expect to create and enforce antipollution policies—are themselves major polluters![14]

THE GHETTOS: APARTHEID AMERICAN STYLE[15]

A combination of complex, interrelated forces have given rise to central-city ghettos, populated disproportionately by Negroes and other minority groups. The poverty and debased conditions of life which are pervasive in the ghettos are well known. The oldest, most deteriorated, and most crowded housing is in the central-city ghetto. In general, schools are grossly inadequate, and, as a result, ghetto students fall further behind nonghetto students with each level of school completed. Mortality rates are high, the result of inadequate nutrition, high incidence of disease, drug use, inadequate medical care, deplorable levels of sanitation, and so forth. Social disintegration is acute, and crime rates are high. And, perhaps most importantly, ghetto income levels are abysmally low; nearly 40 percent of central-city blacks live in poverty.

What combination of circumstances accounts for the ghettos? Most importantly, the whole process of urban decentralization is very much involved. Historically, the better educated, better trained, more prosperous whites have moved in large numbers from the central city to the suburbs, leaving behind obsolete housing in decaying neighborhoods. Their places have been taken by poorly educated, unskilled, low-income Negroes migrating largely from the rural South. Secondly, the dynamics of urban growth have shifted relevant job opportunities away from the central cities. "The activities which have been the traditional points of labor force entry for the urban unskilled—manufacturing, wholesale and retail trade, construction—are precisely those that have been suburbanizing most rapidly, making entry for the central-city poor difficult indeed."[16] And this movement of jobs to the suburbs is particularly adverse because of the previously noted deterioration of the public transportation system; it is both difficult and costly for central-city residents—most of whom do not own cars—to get to the suburbs for jobs.

But from a long-run viewpoint, racial discrimination is perhaps the most important force underlying the black ghettos. The Kerner Commission put the matter quite bluntly in asserting that past and present policies of discrimination have divided the nation into two societies, "one largely Negro and poor, located in the central cities; the other, predominantly white and affluent, located in the suburbs and outlying areas."[17] Discrimination has taken many forms: Blacks have been denied adequate education; they have been denied entry to certain occupations; they have been paid lower wages than whites on given jobs (see Table 38·3).

Given the complexity of the problems of the ghettos, our discussion of remedies will necessarily be brief and incomplete. To facilitate matters we will treat the human (poverty) and the physical (housing) aspects of the ghetto problem separately; in fact the two aspects of the problem are obviously very closely interrelated.

The human aspect: alleviating ghetto poverty

How can the poverty which is endemic to the black ghetto be alleviated? The causes and characteristics of the ghettos imply possible solutions.

[14] If you are inclined to pursue the economics of pollution, you will find Thomas D. Crocker and A. J. Rogers, III, *Environmental Economics* (Hinsdale, Ill.: The Dryden Press, Inc., 1971), to be entertaining reading.

[15] The organization and content of this section follows Dick Netzer, *Economics and Urban Problems* (New York: Basic Books, Inc., Publishers, 1970), chaps. 3 and 4. Netzer's book, which is both readable and perceptive, is recommended reading.

[16] Ibid., p. 29.

[17] *Report of the National Advisory Commission on Civil Disorders* (New York: Bantam Books, 1968), p. 22.

1. More and better jobs Unemployment among central-city blacks is notoriously high and a major cause of poverty. The unemployment rate for blacks is generally twice that for whites. Black teenagers face a chronic depression; their unemployment rates are typically 20 to 25 percent! Given the present education and qualifications of the ghetto labor force, how can the unemployment situation be improved?

Two complementary approaches present themselves: bring ghetto residents to existing jobs in the suburbs *and* bring new jobs to the ghettos. Consider the first approach. Mobility in terms of residence is extremely difficult for ghetto dwellers. On the one hand, the incomes of most central-city blacks are so low that they simply cannot afford to move to the suburbs. On the other hand, those who can afford suburban housing are confronted with severe problems of discrimination. Real estate agencies and landlords have used a variety of crude and subtle techniques for prohibiting or restricting these moves. Many suburban areas have purposely zoned for large minimum lot sizes and have enacted strict building and housing codes which push up housing prices to prohibit any influx of lower-income (black) families from the central city. A recent government report has summarized the situation in this way: "The different income levels of whites and Negroes contribute to the segregated pattern in housing. But race is a far better predictor of where a person will live than is income—or any other attribute."[18]

Another means of making suburban employment opportunities more accessible to the ghetto labor force is to provide improved transportation facilities. We have already discussed the urban transportation problem and noted that the renewed interest in mass transit is partially motivated by the ghetto-worker's need for greater accessibility to suburban jobs.

The second approach is to create new job opportunities in the ghettos. *Black capitalism* is a generic term which refers to the creation of new businesses, owned and operated by Negroes, in ghetto areas. A variety of proposals—a few of which have become operational—have been made in support of black capitalism. These proposals advocate governmentally sponsored programs to provide liberal credit, tax incentives and subsidies, managerial assistance and training, and so forth, to present or potential black entrepreneurs. Related proposals urge subsidies to major corporations which are willing to build plants in the ghettos and to train black workers to man them. The fundamental criticisms of black capitalism are twofold. First, the concept is flatly at odds with the strong economic forces which underlie the decentralization of economic activity in urban areas. Secondly, the types of industries which will be attracted to the ghetto are likely to be low-wage industries which largely provide "dead end" jobs.

[18]Department of Health, Education, and Welfare, *Toward a Social Report,* p. 37.

2. Income maintenance But a large fraction—perhaps as much as one-half—of the ghetto poor will not be helped by improved employment opportunities. The aged, the disabled, and the mothers of dependent children can only be assisted effectively by some sort of income maintenance program. The deficiencies of our present welfare programs and new proposals for a comprehensive income maintenance program will be discussed in Chapter 38.

3. Improved education and training Many of the ghetto blacks who are fully employed nevertheless live in poverty. The reason? They have not had access to sufficient education and training to qualify for jobs which pay higher wages. Again, programs designed to provide basic general education and specific vocational skills for the "working poor" will be examined in Chapter 38.

The physical aspect: housing and urban renewal

The urban ghetto is not only a visible and potentially explosive concentration of poverty. It is also characterized by extensive deterioration of the physical environment; much of the housing and many commercial buildings are substandard and dilapidated. Given the fact that all levels of government have long and varied histories of involvement in the housing industry, the persistence of urban blight may come

as something of a surprise. Consider some of the better known public efforts to stimulate construction.

1. For many years government—working through such agencies as the Federal Housing Administration (FHA) and the Veterans' Administration (VA)—has attempted in a variety of ways to reduce the cost and increase the availability of mortgage funds to finance housing purchases.

2. Since the late 1930s the Federal government has heavily subsidized the efforts of state and local governments to provide low-rent public housing for the poor.

3. Urban renewal programs—again, subsidized with Federal funds—have attempted to reverse the spread of urban blight by rebuilding central-city areas.

4. The National Housing Act of 1949 set forth the goal of "a decent home and a suitable living environment for every American family." The Housing Act of 1968 translated this goal into a projection of 26 million new and rehabilitated housing units in the 1968–1978 decade.

Despite these programs and well-intentioned goals, there is general agreement that efforts to provide adequate housing for all of America's population have been inadequate and unsuccessful. The housing problem remains particularly acute for low-income families. Why have we failed? Why do we seem to be losing the battle against urban blight? The reasons are varied.

1. Program inadequacies In many instances our housing programs have been inappropriate or inadequate to the task. Mortgage subsidies, for example, have been most helpful to middle- and high-income groups in obtaining good housing. But low-income people have generally not been able to enjoy the low FHA and VA interest rates (nor the tax deductibility of mortgage interest payments) because they simply have not been able to qualify for such loans. Lofty statements of goals to the contrary, some housing programs have foundered for the lack of adequate financing. Public housing and rent subsidy programs have undoubtedly helped some low-income families, but the poorest families cannot even afford the subsidized rental payments.

Ironically, on balance urban renewal programs have *reduced* the supply of housing available to low-income families. Some urban renewal efforts have not been primarily concerned with housing, but rather the strategy has been to shore up the vitality of the central city by replacing slum neighborhoods with new office buildings to house both public services and private enterprises. This helps explain the paradox that many ghetto dwellers are opposed to urban renewal! Witness the slogan: "Urban renewal is Negro removal." Furthermore, some families have been uprooted several times by public housing projects which have in fact increased the supply of housing available to middle-income families, but reduced it for low-income families.

But the relative ineffectiveness of government involvement in the physical restoration of the cities goes beyond the inadequacies of particular programs. Two other important considerations merit comment.

2. Problems of the construction industry The residential construction industry has been technologically unprogressive and hampered by the inability of thousands of small contractors to realize economies of scale. Furthermore, construction is cyclically vulnerable, being highly sensitive to changes in interest rates and the availability of mortgage funds (Chapter 18). Building codes frequently perpetuate the use of traditional materials and archaic working methods; the very abundance and diversity of these codes impede standardization in construction methods. Strong craft unions which control the supply of labor, coupled with material scarcities, have contributed significantly to high and rapidly rising construction costs. The high cost of urban housing has been aggravated by soaring land values and zoning regulations which specify large-sized lots.

Government is not unaware of these difficulties. In 1969 the Department of Housing and Urban Development inaugurated "Operation Breakthrough," a major effort to modernize the residential construction industry. HUD's objective is to sponsor an extensive research and development program to "break through" the archaic cut-and-fit methods of the in-

dustry and provide a foundation for mass-produced, low-cost housing. The program also seeks to modernize and standardize building codes which now perpetuate the status quo in construction methods and to bring about revisions of zoning laws which now impede volume production of moderate- and low-income housing. Currently twenty-two prototype builders are constructing some 2,000 innovative, mass-produced homes for testing and demonstration. It is clearly too early, however, to judge the success of these endeavors.

3. Discrimination Discrimination in housing has been a basic consideration in restricting Negroes to the decaying ghettos of the central cities. It is true that the incomes of many central-city blacks are so low that they cannot afford to move to the suburbs. But some could and would if housing were available to them.

One need simply recall the simple tools of supply and demand to grasp the impact of discrimination upon housing prices and rents. The immediate effect is to make available a disproportionately small supply of housing to blacks. This restricted supply means higher housing prices and rents. One result is that blacks are forced to use a very high proportion of their income for housing. But even so, the housing is likely to be of inferior quality. High rents induce ghetto families to "double up" on available housing. Landlords respond on the supply side by subdividing apartments. And, needless to say, a captive market provides little incentive for owners to repair or improve their property. The overall consequence is typically high rents for crowded and dilapidated housing.

SOLVING URBAN PROBLEMS: INSTITUTIONAL AND FINANCIAL PREREQUISITES

We have outlined the overall character of certain problems of the cities and have indicated specific remedies. We must now recognize that there exist certain institutional and financial prerequisites to these solutions. An obvious prerequisite to all proposed solutions is sufficient financial resources. This is not to say that urban problems will automatically disappear if we simply "throw money at them." Our knowledge of appropriate techniques and strategies for dealing effectively with the problems of the cities is embryonic and deficient. Nevertheless, adequately financed programs are essential. Furthermore, certain institutional changes may be required, not only to obtain adequate financing, but also to provide an effective and efficient decision-making environment.

Political consolidation

Most urbanologists agree that one of the basic prerequisites to resolving urban problems is political consolidation. In particular, the design of efficient and equitable solutions to the problems of the cities depends in good measure on overcoming the political fragmentation which now exists in most cities.

Urban areas are in fact highly integrated and highly interdependent economic units. Most urban problems—transportation; discrimination in housing, employment, and education; pollution; land use—are clearly area-wide in character. The individual, fragmented political units of the cities simply do not have effective jurisdiction over these problems; in our large cities the local units of government have been losing the capacity to govern effectively. The realization of efficient and equitable—as opposed to politically feasible—solutions to urban problems depends upon coordinated, area-wide action, that is, upon political consolidation.

Efficiency Looked at from the economist's point of view, political consolidation can stimulate more efficient decision making in dealing with urban problems for several reasons. First, small political subdivisions will frequently be unable to realize economies of scale in providing certain public facilities such as water and sewage systems. Levels of output will be low and these facilities will operate at points high on their unit cost curves (Figure 26·6*a*). A second and closely related point is that in such endeavors as police and fire protection, street construction, and

public transit, political fragmentation results in the loss of certain qualitative advantages which would stem from the planning and coordination of these public services at the metropolitan level. "The case for bigness in public services probably rests more on quality than on cost; an area-wide police force is better coordinated for traffic control and hot pursuit, and big enough to afford scientific crime detection facilities and specialists in juvenile and race problems."[19] Similarly, although the actual unit cost (per mile) of producing streets may be roughly the same whether provided by many small, independent municipalities or by a large metropolitan government, there are obvious advantages in having an overall plan to coordinate a given volume of street construction in the interest of maximum effectiveness.

A third reason why most urban economists favor political consolidation is that, because of the small geographic size of existing urban political units, many of the benefits associated with the provision of needed public facilities in such areas as, say, education, recreation, and environmental improvement will accrue to individuals and businesses residing in other political units. For example, a small urban political unit which builds an excellent school system, provides for the treatment of sewage and industrial wastes, and constructs ample recreational facilities will be providing benefits which in part spill over its political boundaries, that is, are external to it in that they are realized by the residents of other political units. Many of the graduates of its school system will take jobs in other areas. And those living in other political subdivisions will use its parks and playgrounds and benefit from its antipollution activities. The crucial point is that, when spillover benefits are large, a good or service will tend to be underproduced (Figure 6·1*c*). More specifically, the voters in each small, political entity will not be anxious to tax themselves heavily to provide services and facilities whose benefits accrue in significant amounts to others.

Equity The case for political consolidation also rests on grounds of equity. Political fragmentation has created serious fiscal disparities within the urban areas. Resources and needs have become separated in the political jungle of the cities:[20]

> Most of America's wealth and most of America's domestic problems reside in the metropolitan areas. Why, then, cannot this vast wealth be applied through vigorous social measures to meet the growing problems? Because the resources exist in one set of jurisdictions within the metropolitan areas and the problems in another. . . . This disparity between needs and resources is the disparity between the central city and its suburbs.

Political consolidation would obviously have the desirable effect of putting resources and needs within the same political jurisdiction.

Avenues of consolidation Political consolidation can be achieved in a variety of ways: the annexation of surrounding suburban areas by the city, the consolidation of city and county governments, the establishment of special regional authorities to deal with such particular problems as transportation or pollution.

But it would be unrealistic to expect that consolidation will be easily and quickly achieved. The "haves" of the wealthier suburbs have shown little inclination to assume the moral and financial responsibility for the glaring problems of the "have nots" in the central city. Nor can we expect the officials of local governmental units to be anxious to give up their power and functions. More positively, one can make counterarguments in favor of the present fragmented system. First, small local government is likely to be more conducive to personal political participation and more responsive to the needs and aspirations of its constituents than is a metropolitan-wide government. Second, "bureaucracy"—diseconomies of scale in public administration—may tend to offset assumed cost economies in the provision and coordination of public goods and services by a consolidated urban government. Finally, some would argue that small local governments contribute to the heterogeneity of urban living areas in that they pro-

[19] Thompson, op. cit., pp. 267–268.

[20] Advisory Commission on Intergovernmental Relations, *Urban America and the Federal System,* p. 1.

vide a variety of choices with respect to levels of local taxes and amounts and quality of public services among which residents may choose. Thus, although most urbanologists endorse political consolidation, the case is not as clear-cut as one might at first suppose.

The larger fiscal problem

The equity argument for political consolidation focuses upon the problem of residential segregation by income and the urban fiscal dilemma it creates: public service needs are divorced from the tax base. Although political consolidation will put resources and needs within the same political jurisdiction, a larger fiscal question remains. Even with political consolidation it is questionable that the tax resources of the urban areas will be sufficient to meet the obligations and problems which confront the cities.[21]

There are a number of proposed solutions to the revenue crisis faced by local governments: (1) Federal revenue sharing, (2) the shifting of certain fiscal burdens to the Federal government, and (3) the restructuring of the property tax.

Federal revenue sharing We are already familiar with the first proposal (Chapters 9 and 14) and its underlying rationale. The Federal government has great tax-raising ability but limited responsibilities for public spending on civilian goods and services. Local governments, on the other hand, are largely responsible for spending on civilian public needs, but are obstructed by the severe revenue-raising limitations associated with their heavy dependence upon property taxation. The Heller Plan, you will recall, argues that the fiscal disparity between the Federal government, on the one hand, and state and local governments, on the other, can be corrected by unconditional grants from the former to the latter. The prospect of such revenue sharing is clearly upon the political horizon. But critics feel that such grants may merely supplant, rather than supplement, local spending as local politicians use the grants to cut or forestall increases in local taxes.

[21]This discussion generally follows the recommendations of the Advisory Commission on Intergovernmental Relations, ibid.

Shifting financial responsibility Another recommendation designed to ease the fiscal crunch at the local level is to have the Federal or state governments assume the financial responsibility for meeting certain urban problems and obligations. In Chapter 38 we will discuss the suggestion that the Federal government establish and finance an income maintenance program to relieve poverty, thereby reducing the heavy welfare costs now borne by city governments. Similarly, the shifting of all local costs of elementary and secondary education to the Federal government would not only relieve the fiscal crisis of the cities, but might also help to ensure greater equality of educational opportunity.

Overhauling the property tax Like sin, everyone deplores the property tax. It is regressive because low-income people spend a larger proportion of their incomes for housing than do high-income people. It is difficult and costly to administer. Equitable assessment of property is difficult. Furthermore, we have seen that rising property tax rates have been a part of the self-reinforcing process by which wealthy people and prosperous businesses have fled to the suburbs. Yet the property tax is clearly the main source of revenue for local governments (Table 9·3) and is likely to remain so. It is therefore relevant to ask: Is it possible to restructure and revitalize the property tax so as to provide more revenue, on the one hand, and to reduce its harmful economic effects, on the other?

The basic proposal here is to shift the property tax emphasis from buildings to land. We noted in Chapter 33 the reasons for a renewed interest in land-value taxation. The equity argument is that much of the value of urban land reflects public decisions with respect to zoning and the provision of roads, schools, and utilities. Most of the dramatic increases in urban land values are windfall gains in the sense that they are not the consequence of the efforts or expenditures of landowners. It would seem fair for society to tax away much of the increase in land value which

society's decisions and expenditures have provided. The efficiency argument is that a tax on land has a neutral effect upon the use or allocation of land; a land-value tax does not contribute to a malallocation of land.

In the cities the present arrangement of relatively high property taxes on buildings and relatively low taxes on land tends to have perverse effects upon incentives. Specifically, heavy taxes on buildings harm the incentives of builders and property owners to construct new buildings and improve existing ones. This fact helps to explain central-city decay and blight. The light taxes on land mean that landowners find the tax costs involved in holding vacant land to be relatively small, and so they are encouraged to withhold land from productive uses in order to speculate on increases in its value. Such action—or inaction—prevents growth of the property tax base and contributes to the fiscal problems of the cities. But higher taxes on land values are advocated for reasons that go beyond the raising of additional revenue for city government:[22]

> There is poetic justice in heavy land value taxation: at present land is typically taxed at rates, relative to market value, that are less than half those applied to buildings. We now, perversely, favor the speculator who impedes development and discourage the investor in new and better buildings.

Postscript: The greater use of user charges which was recommended in connection with both the urban traffic and pollution problems would also be helpful in providing additional local revenue.

New cities

Some observers—dismayed at our apparent inability to cope with specific urban problems, dubious about the prospects for political consolidation and fiscal relief for the cities, and alarmed at the prospect of 100 million new city dwellers within the next thirty years—argue for the development of entirely new cities. These new cities might be satellites within the socioeconomic orbit of existing metropolitan areas or they might be new independent cities which are self-contained and distant from existing urban areas. In either event the prospect of "starting from scratch" and thereby avoiding the costly task of reversing the historical trends of urban dynamics and the associated problems is appealing. High central-city land values would be circumvented, as would the burden of prevailing building-code and zoning regulations. And there would be a number of more positive advantages.[23]

> Designing and building a new community from the ground up provides a unique opportunity to plan for orderly growth with the most desirable location, timing, and sequence. It is possible to relate the new community development to areawide, regional, and national urban development plans and objectives. The continuous planning process required permits adjustments between the actual rate of growth of a new community and job opportunities within or near the community and the need for public facilities, transportation, public services, and commercial and retail establishments. Public investments can be related both to a projected and an actual rate of growth and anticipated need and capacity can be incorporated into current construction, thereby avoiding the necessity for later costly replacement or upgrading.
>
> Planning and design in a new community can be on a large enough scale to incorporate features which are difficult to obtain on a piecemeal design basis. For example, an improved relationship between work and residential locations can be established through balanced development and distribution of economic activity. Greater ease of internal movement can be planned by separating types of motor vehicle traffic and in turn isolating them from pedestrians. Moreover, the size and location of commercial and public buildings and other facilities can be more easily related to traffic patterns in order to minimize congestion.
>
> The large-scale planning required for a new community can also produce an improved esthetic environment and provide amenities not otherwise available.

Despite the potential attractiveness of the new cities approach, it has been subjected to thoughtful criticism. Is the new cities concept merely a copout, a means of running away from the problems which our cities now face? The vast bulk of our population will continue to live in existing cities. Is it real-

[22] Netzer, op. cit., pp. 198–199.

[23] Advisory Commission on Intergovernmental Relations, *Urban and Rural America: Policies for Future Growth,* pp. 99–100.

istic to expect that model cities can make significant contributions to the problems confronting these people? Furthermore, existing cities have evolved and grown for compelling economic reasons. Can we expect contrived model cities—constructed to get away from the problems of existing cities—to have a viable economic base?[24]

SUMMARY

1. The United States is an urban nation and is becoming increasingly so.
2. The economies of agglomeration are significant in explaining the growth of cities. Similarly, deglomerative forces account for the shift of population and economic activity from the central city to the suburbs. Political fragmentation and pronounced economic imbalances have accompanied urban sprawl.
3. The short-run urban transportation problem is concerned with the most efficient use of existing transportation facilities. Although administrative problems are substantial, user charges and peak-pricing are advocated by many economists. The long-run problem is concerned with the character of future investment in transportation facilities. For a variety of reasons, city planners and public officials tend to favor expanded and improved mass-transit systems.

[24]See for example, William Alonso, "The Mirage of New Towns," *The Public Interest*, Spring 1970, pp. 3–17.

4. Pollution is a problem of spillover or external costs. Most proposed solutions—legislated controls and standards, emission fees, and markets for pollution rights—seek to internalize these spillover costs to offending firms.
5. The central-city ghettos are heavily populated by blacks and other minorities who, because of low incomes and discrimination, cannot escape to suburban areas. Enlarged job opportunities, income maintenance programs, and improved education and training are obvious ways of reducing ghetto poverty. Urban renewal and public housing programs have met with limited success in revitalizing the central-city areas and generally have done little to increase the supply of low-income housing.
6. Because of the area-wide character of urban problems and the unequal distribution of income and wealth between central city and suburbs, political consolidation would be very helpful in resolving many of the problems of the cities.
7. Even if political consolidation is realized, fiscal assistance in such forms as Federal revenue sharing and the shifting of fiscal responsibility for certain specific urban problems and obligations to the Federal government may be necessary. The cities may reduce the harmful effects of property taxation and simultaneously obtain more revenue by shifting the relative burden of the property tax away from buildings and toward land.
8. Some observers argue that many advantages may be realized by planning and building entirely new cities to accommodate future population growth.

QUESTIONS AND STUDY SUGGESTIONS

1. Explain: "To agglomerate is to economize." What specifically are the economies of agglomeration? Distinguish between internal and external economies of scale. What is the urban infrastructure?

2. What socioeconomic forces underlie urban sprawl? Explain in detail why the process of urban sprawl has been to the economic and fiscal disadvantage of the central city. Of what significance is the fact that suburbs are typically separate political entities? What arguments can be made in favor of political consolidation?

3. "If cities are too large to be efficient or are poorly organized, the problem can be traced in large part to a failure to charge people for all the costs they impose or to reward them fully for the benefits of their action." Explain. Do you agree with this assertion?

4. What is the nature of the urban transportation problem?

Comment: "Although improved transportation has been a necessary condition for decentralization and urban sprawl, this decentralization has also created acute transportation problems."

5. What are the main causes of environmental pollution? Comment: "Clean air and water have become increasingly scarce and valuable resources precisely because they have been treated in the past as if they were free and unlimited in supply." What methods might be used to internalize spillover costs?

6. What is the role of racial discrimination in explaining the poverty of central cities? Analyze the economics of the ghetto housing market. Comment: "Urban blight—the cumulative deterioration of entire neighborhoods or areas—occurs because individual owners have little or no economic incentive to improve their property."

7. "We can go far to solve the central-city housing crisis by simply changing tax policy. First, tax unused land at higher rates than land with buildings on it. Second, tax new and improved housing at low rates and dilapidated and old housing at high rates." Do you think these policies will have the indicated results? Explain.

8. "Increases in the value of land in cities are the consequence of public decisions about zoning and investment in public utilities and facilities, not the result of individual efforts by owners. Therefore, the city should recapture the unearned incomes from rising land values by taxation and use these revenues for public purposes." Do you agree?

9. Analyze the fiscal problems of the cities. What solutions do you recommend? What are "user charges"? "The purpose of user charges is to confront decision-makers with the social or spillover costs of their decisions and in so doing cause them to alter their decisions." Explain and illustrate this statement in terms of the urban transportation and pollution problems.

SELECTED REFERENCES

Economic Issues, 4th ed., readings 65, 66, 67, 68, and 69.

Chinitz, Benjamin (ed.): *City and Suburb* (Englewood Cliffs, N.J.: Prentice-Hall, Inc., 1964).

Durr, Fred: *The Urban Economy* (Scranton: Intext Educational Publishers, 1971).

Haddad, William F., and G. Douglas Pugh (eds.): *Black Economic Development* (Englewood Cliffs, N.J.: Prentice-Hall, Inc., 1969).

Hoover, Edgar M.: *An Introduction to Regional Economics* (New York: Alfred A. Knopf, Inc., 1971).

Netzer, Dick: *Economics and Urban Problems* (New York: Basic Books, Inc., Publishers, 1970).

Perloff, Harvey S., and Lowden Wingo, Jr. (eds.): *Issues in Urban Economics* (Baltimore: The Johns Hopkins Press, 1968).

Thompson, Wilbur R.: *A Preface to Urban Economics* (Baltimore: The Johns Hopkins Press, 1965).

38

THE ECONOMICS OF INEQUALITY AND POVERTY

The President's Commission on Income Maintenance Programs recently summarized its investigation of poverty in the United States with these poignant statements:[1]

> We have found severe poverty and its effects throughout the Nation and among all ethnic groups. This poverty is not only relative to rising American living standards, but is often stark and absolute. There are too many Americans with inadequate shelter, inadequate clothing, absolute hunger, and unhealthy living conditions. Millions of persons in our society do not have a sufficient share of America's affluence to live decently. They eke out a bare existence under deplorable conditions.

Our basic task in this chapter is to examine the dismal economics of poverty: Who are the poor? What are their numbers? Why does poverty persist amidst general abundance? Can the poverty problem be resolved and, if so, by what means?

[1] *Poverty Amid Plenty: The American Paradox* (Washington, November 1969), p. 2.

INCOME INEQUALITY

The first step in approaching the poverty problem is to analyze carefully available factual data on income inequality. Average income in the United States is the highest of any nation in the world; the median income for all families was $9,433 in 1969. But now we must envision how it is distributed around the average. Table 38·1 tells the story: *Income inequality in the United States is considerable.* At the low end of the scale we find that 9 percent of all families received about 2 percent of total personal income. A mere 6 percent of the total income went to the 20 percent of the families receiving an annual income of less than $5,000 per year in 1969. At the top of the income pyramid we find that 19 percent of the families received incomes of $15,000 or more per year; this group got about 39 percent of total personal income. These figures clearly point to considerable income inequality.

TABLE 38 · 1 THE DISTRIBUTION OF PERSONAL INCOME BY FAMILIES, 1969

(1) Personal income class	(2) Percent of all families in this class	(3) Percent of total personal income received by families in this class	(4) Percent of all families in this class and all lower classes	(5) Percent of income received by this class and all lower classes
Under $3,000	9	2	9	2
$3,000–$4,999	11	4	20	6
$5,000–$6,999	12	7	32	13
$7,000–$9,999	22	17	54	30
$10,000–$14,999	27	31	81	61
$15,000–$24,999	15	27	96	88
$25,000 and over	4	12	100	100
	100	100		

Source: Bureau of the Census, *Income in 1969 of Families and Persons in the United States,* Current Population Reports, Series P-60, No. 75, December 1970, Table 2.

Causes of income inequality

The price system is an impersonal mechanism. It has no conscience, and it does not cater to any set of ethical standards concerning what is an "equitable," or "just," distribution of income. As a matter of fact, the basically individualistic environment of the capitalist economy is more than permissive of a high degree of income inequality. Some of the more specific factors contributing to income inequality include:

1. Native abilities Nature has been very arbitrary in apportioning mental, physical, and aesthetic talents. Some individuals have had the good fortune to inherit the exceptional mental qualities essential to entering the relatively high-paying fields of medicine, dentistry, and law. Others, rated as "dull normals" or "mentally retarded," are assigned to the most menial and low-paying occupations or are incapable of earning income at all. Some are blessed with the physical capacity and coordination to become highly paid professional athletes. The clumsy and frail must settle for much less. Some have the aesthetic qualities prerequisite to becoming great artists or musicians. Others are simply not blessed with such talents. In brief, native talents put some individuals in a position to make contributions to total output which command very high incomes. Others are in much less fortunate circumstances.

2. Training, education, and opportunities to advance Despite high-sounding claims to the contrary, opportunities to develop latent talents and to acquire new abilities are not equally available to all. Discrimination on the basis of race, religion, ethnic background, and sex blocks many paths of self-betterment. Similarly, the inability to finance extended periods of training and the virtual closing of certain occupational doors by unions or professional associations are equally effective obstacles. Thus, even if everyone were blessed with identical physical and mental talents, income inequality would still result because of the fact that opportunities to develop and employ those talents are not equally available.

3. Property ownership The ownership of property resources, and hence the receipt of property incomes, is very unequal. The vast majority of households own little or no property resources, while the remaining few supply very great quantities of machinery, real estate, farmland, and so forth. Basically, property incomes account for the position of those households at the very pinnacle of the income pyramid. The right of inheritance and the fact that "wealth begets wealth" reinforce the role played by unequal ownership of property resources in determining income inequality.

4. Ability to exert market power Ability to "rig the market" on one's own behalf is undoubtedly a major factor in accounting for income inequality. Certain unions and professional groups have adopted policies which limit the supplies of their productive services, thereby boosting the incomes of those "on the inside." Exorbitant initiation fees, prolonged apprenticeship periods, flat refusal to accept new members, or the setting of unrealistic standards of performance are well-known and frequently employed tactics for manipulating the market on the behalf of a particular group. Legislation which provides for occupational licensure for barbers, beauticians, accountants, taxi drivers, and so forth can also be a basis for exerting market power on behalf of the licensed group. The same holds true in the product market: profit receivers in particular stand to benefit when their firm develops some degree of monopoly power.

5. Unequal distribution of misfortune Many households are at the base of the income pyramid as a result of economic misfortune. A host of economic hazards in such forms as prolonged illness, serious accident, death of the family breadwinner, and unemployment may plunge a family into relative poverty. The burden of such misfortunes is borne very unevenly by the population and hence contributes to the degree of income inequality.

6. Miscellaneous factors There are obviously other important forces which play a part in explaining income inequality. Luck, chance, and "being in the right place at the right time" have all caused individuals to stumble into fortunes. Discovering oil on a run-down farm, meeting the right press agent, or making a favorable impression on the boss's daughter has accounted for many high incomes. Nor can personal contacts and political influence be discounted as means of attaining the higher income brackets.

Trends in income inequality

We know from Chapter 21 that economic growth has brought increases in incomes: *Absolutely* the entire distribution of income has been moving upward over time. Changes in the *relative* distribution of income are quite another thing. Incomes can move up absolutely, and the degree of inequality may or may not be affected. Table 38·2 is instructive on this point. Here we divide the total number of income receivers into five numerically equal groups, or *quintiles,* and show the percentage of total personal income received by each.

These data suggest that a significant reduction in income inequality occurred between 1929 and 1944. Note in Table 38·2 the declining percentage of personal income going to the top quintile and the increasing percentage received by the other four quintiles during this period. Many of the forces at work during World War II undoubtedly contributed to this decline in inequality. War-born prosperity eliminated the many low incomes caused by the severe unemployment of the 1930s, brought a reduction of wage and salary differentials, boosted depressed farm incomes through sharp increases in farm prices, temporarily diminished discrimination in employment, was accompanied by a decline in property incomes as a share of the national income, and so forth.

The data for 1944, 1955, and 1969 suggest that in the postwar period the trend toward a more equal relative distribution of income has been decidedly less pronounced. The forces making for greater equality during the war ceased to be of great import after the war.

TABLE 38·2 PERCENTAGE OF TOTAL PERSONAL INCOME RECEIVED BY EACH ONE-FIFTH, AND BY THE TOP 5 PERCENT, OF FAMILIES, SELECTED YEARS

Quintile	1929	1935–1936	1944	1955	1969
Lowest } Second }	12.5				
Lowest		4.1	4.9	4.8	5.0
Second		9.2	10.9	12.2	11.8
Third	13.8	14.1	16.2	17.7	17.0
Fourth	19.3	20.9	22.2	23.7	23.1
Highest	54.4	51.7	45.8	41.6	43.0
Total	100.0	100.0	100.0	100.0	100.0
Top 5 percent	30.0	26.5	20.7	16.8	17.2

Source: Bureau of the Census data. Details may not add up to totals because of rounding.

The case against income inequality

The desirability of income inequality is anything but a new subject for debate. Indeed, the long-standing nature of the controversy has resulted in the development of a more or less standardized set of arguments that condemn and an equally traditional group of contentions that defend income inequality.

Four points constitute the case against inequality in the distribution of income:

1. Maximizing satisfactions It is alleged that income inequality is a large obstacle in maximizing consumer satisfaction. The underlying reasoning is this: Money income is subject to the principle of diminishing marginal utility. In any time period income receivers spend the first dollars received on those products which they value most, that is, on products whose marginal utility is high. As their most pressing wants become satisfied, consumers will spend additional dollars of income on increasingly frivolous, lower-marginal-utility items. Suppose, for example, that $20,000 worth of annual income is unequally distributed between Brooks and Anderson—the former getting $16,000 and the latter $4,000. As a result, the last, or marginal, dollars spent by Brooks will yield him relatively small increments of satisfaction or utility. Why? Because these dollars will be spent in satisfying less urgent needs; that is, they will be spent on frivolous products or on extra units of items already possessed in abundance. In either event the marginal utility of these dollars will be relatively low.

But, alas, $4,000-a-year Anderson is in a much different situation. His annual pittance is such that his marginal dollars are spent on very basic, high-marginal-utility products. He is able to buy such small quantities of most products that the marginal utility of added units is still relatively high. It is concluded that any transfer of money income from high-income Brooks to low-income Anderson will increase the satisfactions or utility of the latter by more than it will decrease those of the former. The result is a net increase in *total* consumer satisfaction. Greater income equality has moved the economy closer to the goal of maximizing aggregate satisfaction. In a somewhat altered form this argument contends that income inequality causes economic resources to be misallocated. Inequality results in inefficient resource use by drawing resources into the production of frivolous, unimportant products at the expense of more essential products that low-income groups desire but are unable to afford.

This is a very persuasive argument. But there is a major loophole: The argument assumes that Brooks

and Anderson have equal capacities to enjoy income. In fact, however, *interpersonal comparisons* of the subjective concept of utility cannot be scientifically made. Although the above argument against inequality rests on the supposition that Brooks and Anderson are equally capable of enjoying income, that is unlikely. The chances are at least fifty-fifty[2] that Brooks has a greater capacity to derive satisfaction from spending money income than does Anderson. Were this actually the case, an *unequal* distribution of income would be required to achieve maximum consumer satisfaction. So, although this argument for greater income equality cannot be disproved, it also cannot be proved valid. The ability to derive satisfaction from the expenditure of money income eludes quantitative measurement (Chapter 34).

2. Productivity It is also argued that excessive income inequality impairs productivity. In the first instance, laborers who find themselves at the base of the income pyramid may not be able to obtain that minimum of food and shelter needed to maintain their physical and mental vigor, not to mention the effects which poverty may have upon their morale. And, ironically enough, inequality may impair the productivity of those at the pinnacle of the pyramid. Leveling off the income peak might induce the "idle rich" and the "I retired at thirty-five" segment of the economy's human resources back into harness. That is, it is held that less income inequality might stimulate incentives to produce and invest.

3. Opportunity Income inequality means unequal opportunities for training and education. The sons of the poor have a decided handicap in getting the education required for entering many occupations. To overstate the situation, an individual must be an M.D. in order to finance a medical education for his son. The implications for resource allocation are clear: the unequal distribution of opportunities fostered by income inequality distorts the allocation of resources. Efficiency demands that human resources should be allocated in terms of ability and productivity, not by accident of birth.

4. Political inequality Another pillar in the case against inequality links income inequality to political and social inequality. In politics, money talks. Theoretically, of course, the rich man and the poor man have equal voices in politics; that is, each has one vote. In practice, it is no secret that the rich man, by virtue of his wealth, is in a position to influence many other votes. How? By financing the campaigns of "right-minded" politicians, by "recommending" candidates to subordinates, by using his resources to support lobbyists, and so forth. A similar set of arguments can be offered to support the view that there is a direct relationship between wealth and social inequality.

The case for income inequality

Three long-standing arguments anchor the defense of income inequality.

1. Capital formation Income inequality gives rise to sizable amounts of private savings, which, when invested, provide the capital goods which are the core of economic growth. Indeed, it is primarily as a result of this expanding stock of capital which the savings of the wealthy finance that the productivity and standard of living of the entire economy are bettered. The savings of the very wealthy, it is argued, provide the means for improving the lot of the very poor.

But proponents of greater income equality are quick to point out a major loophole in this capital formation argument: The alleged relationship between inequality and capital formation is not at all clear. Norway, for example, has moved far in the direction of income equality; yet in the post–World War II era it achieved a high rate of capital formation. In contrast, low rates of capital formation persist in those Middle Eastern nations in which income inequality is particularly great.

[2] They may be better than fifty-fifty. It is plausible to argue that the ability to enjoy income varies directly with the size of one's income. A high income provides (and presupposes!) the education prerequisite to the intelligent allocation of money income and the greater enjoyment of the goods and services thereby obtained.

2. Incentive effects Income inequality is also defended on the grounds that it furnishes the incentives to work, produce, and innovate which are the driving forces of any economy. Monetary gain—the opportunity to better oneself financially—is alleged necessary to induce workers and entrepreneurs to rise above mediocrity. Income inequality is essential if risky ventures are to be undertaken and workers are to perform effectively and faithfully over time. An unequal distribution of income is a necessary and desirable consequence of the price system in allocating resources in terms of their productivity.

Skeptics feel that this justification of income inequality has been overdrawn. They question, in particular, whether there is any firm relationship between income and productivity. Business executives, enthralled by their work and anxious to be heralded as "top men" in their field, may put out the same effort at $30,000 per year as they will at $100,000. Nor is it clear that the unskilled assembly-line worker will be more productive after his union negotiates a $300 increase in his annual income than before.

3. The "good life" Defenders of inequality also claim that high-income consumers have played a crucial role in the development of new products. The rich, it is said, support new industries in their high-cost, high-price infancies. This support allows low-cost mass production to evolve, bringing the products within the financial means of the masses of consumers. Stated differently, in the face of a drastic leveling of incomes, "The production of all first-quality goods would cease. The skill they demand would be lost and the taste they shape would be coarsened." A closely related and more general point is that the sociocultural fiber and viability of any society are directly related to, and dependent upon, income inequality. In short, it is alleged that the highly egalitarian society promises to be intellectually uncreative, culturally unappealing, technologically unprogressive, and socially unrewarding.[3]

Other points bolster the case for inequality. A most pragmatic point is this: Because of the relatively small number of people at the top of the income pyramid and the extremely large number at the base, a redistribution of income from rich to poor would only raise the income of the latter by minute amounts. And it is invariably argued that the philanthropic actions of the very wealthy devote resources to cultural and educational pursuits and to humanitarian activities—a reallocation of resources which greater income equality would not foster.

Thus go the cases for and against income inequality. Each of us must weigh the relative merits of the two positions and judge for himself which is superior.

A final comment must be appended to this discussion. Few would advocate complete equality or very extreme inequality in the distribution of income. The real problem is to find the optimum degree of income inequality. That is, we seek the particular distribution of income which will allow us to realize substantially the desirable aspects of income inequality without encountering to a serious degree the problems and disadvantages which accompany extreme income inequality.

THE DISMAL ECONOMICS OF POVERTY

With this background information on income inequality in mind, let us now turn to the poverty problem. How extensive is poverty in the United States? What are the characteristics of the poor? And what is the best strategy in a war on poverty?

Who are the poor?

Poverty does not lend itself to precise definition. But as a broad generalization, we might say that a family lives in poverty when its basic needs exceed its available means of satisfying them. A family's needs have many determinants: its size, its health, the ages of its members, and so forth. Its means include currently earned income, transfer payments, past savings, property owned, and so on. The definitions of poverty accepted by concerned government agencies are based on family size. Hence, in 1969 an un-

[3] Bertrand de Jouvenel, *The Ethics of Redistribution* (New York: Cambridge University Press, 1952), pp. 41, 46, 54.

attached individual receiving less than $1,800 per year is living in poverty. For a family of four the poverty line is $3,700. For a family of six, about $6,000. Applying these definitions to income data for the United States, it is found that *over 10 percent of the nation lives in poverty.*

Who are these 24 million or so souls who live in poverty? Unfortunately for purposes of public policy, the poor are heterogeneous; they can be found in all geographic regions, they are whites and nonwhites, they include large numbers of both rural and urban people, they are both old and young. Yet, despite this pervasiveness, some useful—though overlapping—guidelines serve to identify the greatest concentrations of poverty.

1. Poverty is common to the aged; about one-fourth of all people over sixty-five live in poverty.

2. Poverty is very common in agriculture—particularly in the South—where the tenant farmer, the small marginal farmer, and farm laborers are afflicted. About one-fourth of all rural people are poor.[4] One-half of all poor families live in the South.

3. The largest single group of poor people consists of children under eighteen. Two-fifths of the total poor are children.

4. Families headed by women—because, for example, of separation, divorce, or death of the husband—are very apt to be poor. Almost one-third of all poor people live in households headed by a woman. The main causes of this concentration of poverty are limited job opportunities and the need to stay at home to care for small children.

5. Health deficiencies—both physical and mental—are highly correlated with low incomes.

6. A very high percentage of the families of the unemployed and the partially employed are living in poverty.

7. Quite remarkably, about one-third of the poor live in families in which the head of the family works throughout the year. The "working poor" are relatively abundant because of the lack of education and training. That is, they possess neither the education nor the skills to hold a decent-paying position. Examples: the 11 million workers in retail stores earned an average of $80 per week in early 1971. Workers employed in laundry and dry-cleaning plants also received only $80 per week. Hotel and motel workers averaged the appalling sum of $69 per week.

[4]See the President's National Advisory Commission on Rural Poverty, *The People Left Behind* (Washington, 1967).

Economic status of nonwhites[5]

One important addition must be made to our list of guidelines for identifying the poor: The incidence of poverty is much greater—over three times as great—among nonwhites than it is among whites. Approximately 36 percent of all Negro families in the South and about 20 percent of those in the North fall within the poverty zone! As can be seen in Table 38·3, the difference in the comparative economic positions of whites and nonwhites is striking. The average (median) income of nonwhite families is only 63 percent that of white families.

This huge discrepancy has its roots in a number of forms of discrimination, some of which are reflected in Table 38·3. First, for the past fifteen or twenty years the unemployment rate for nonwhites has been double that of whites. Discrimination often causes Negroes to be the last hired and the first fired. Second, discrimination has barred Negroes and other nonwhites from the better-paying positions. Negro executives and salesmen, not to mention electricians, bricklayers, and plumbers, are few and far between. Many craft unions have effectively barred Negroes from membership and hence from employment. Third, discrimination has also taken the form of less investment in human resources for Negroes than for whites. The smaller amount (Table 38·3) and inferior quality of the education received by Negroes have had the obvious effect of denying them the opportunity to increase their productivity and qualify for better jobs. Indeed, one of the ironic developments of recent

[5]Readers who wish to pursue this topic in depth will do well to consult William K. Tabb, *The Political Economy of the Black Ghetto* (New York: W. W. Norton & Company, Inc., 1970); Carolyn Shaw Bell, *The Economics of the Ghetto* (New York: Pegasus, 1970); and William L. Henderson and Larry C. Ledebur, *Economic Disparity: Problems and Strategies for Black America* (New York: The Free Press, 1970).

TABLE 38·3 SELECTED MEASURES OF DISCRIMINATION AND INEQUALITY OF OPPORTUNITY, 1970

Selected measure	Whites	Negroes and other races
*Income**		
Median income of families	$9,794	$6,191
Percent of households in poverty	8	27
Percent of families with incomes of $7,000 or more	71	42
Education		
Percent of labor force 18 years and over completing 4 years of high school or more		
Males	65	43
Females	72	53
Percent of labor force 18 years and over completing 4 years of college or more	14	7
Employment (percent of total civilian employment)		
White-collar occupations	51	30
Craftsmen-foremen occupations	14	8
Unemployment rate (percent of civilian labor force)		
Adult males	4.0	7.3
Adult females	5.4	9.3
Teenagers†	15.7	27.8

* Income data are for 1969.
† Males, sixteen and seventeen years old.
Source: *Manpower Report of the President.*

years is that the rapid mechanization of agriculture in the South has caused a substantial migration of America's least-trained and least-educated Negroes to Northern cities at a time when trends in manufacturing are severely restricting the employment opportunities for unskilled and semiskilled workers (Figure 22·3).

In reality, the Negro's relative economic status is even worse than Table 38·3 suggests. A number of recent studies have demonstrated that the Negro generally gets less for his dollar than does the white consumer. In particular, the supply of housing available to Negroes is sharply restricted, forcing them to pay higher rents for poorer housing than do whites. Ironically, urban renewal has typically resulted in a net reduction in the supply of housing for low-income Negroes. In addition to housing, the limited consumer, banking and credit, insurance, and legal facilities found in urban ghettos have the effect of limiting supply, causing Negroes to pay higher prices for these goods and services than do whites.

Our discussion of antipoverty programs in the fol-

lowing section will describe several measures designed to eliminate the wide disparity in the economic status of white and nonwhite citizens. At this juncture it is important to note that the economic cost of discrimination is high. The Council of Economic Advisors[6] has recently estimated that if economic and social policies were successful in lowering the Negro unemployment rate to the level of the white rate, and if education and training opportunities were made available to the Negro labor force so that the average productivity of Negro labor became equal to that of white workers, the total output of the economy would rise by about 4 percent. For 1970 the economic cost of racial discrimination would be on the order of $40 billion!

The "invisible" poor

These facts and figures on the extent and character of poverty may be a bit difficult to accept. After all, ours is presumably the affluent society. How does one square the depressing statistics on poverty which permeate both government and private reports with everyday observations of abundance? The answer lies in good measure in the fact that much American poverty is hidden; it is largely invisible. First of all, poverty is increasingly isolated in the hearts of large cities, because the middle and upper classes have migrated away from them to suburbia. Poverty persists in the slums and ghettos not readily visible from the freeway or subway. Secondly, much poverty embraces the aged and infirm, who rarely venture from their meager rented rooms. Thirdly, rural poverty and the chronically depressed areas of Appalachia and Kentucky are also off the beaten path. Fourthly, and quite ironically, "America has the best dressed poverty the world has ever known." The relative cheapness of clothing means that the poor can be reasonably well dressed and therefore *look* prosperous, although they are inadequately housed, fed, and doctored. Finally, and perhaps most important,[7]

> The poor are politically invisible. . . . [They] do not, by far and large, belong to unions, to fraternal organizations, or to political parties. They are without lobbies of their own; they put forward no legislative program. As a group they are atomized. They have no face; they have no voice.

Indeed, the American poor have been labeled "the world's least revolutionary proletariate."

Vicious circle of poverty

Having noted the incidence of poverty and described its "invisible" nature, we must now emphasize an additional characteristic of poverty—the fact that it tends to be self-perpetuating.[8]

> Poverty breeds poverty. A poor individual or family has a high probability of staying poor. Low incomes carry with them high risks of illness; limitations on mobility; limited access to education, information, and training. Poor parents cannot give their children the opportunities for better health and education needed to improve their lot. Lack of motivation, hope, and incentive is a more subtle but no less powerful barrier than lack of financial means. Thus the cruel legacy of poverty is passed from parents to children.

SOCIAL WELFARE PROGRAMS

The fact that poverty persists in the world's most affluent nation is surprising. But poverty's persistence is even more surprising when we recognize that we have a welfare state—a variety of social welfare programs—which attempts to treat poverty in a number of ways. For example, the social security system, legislated in 1935 and put into operation in 1937, is an accepted feature of our society. It is essentially a social insurance program for the retired and unemployed.

Old age, survivors, disability, and health insurance OASDHI is essentially a gigantic program of compulsory saving. The program is financed by compulsory payroll taxes (premiums) levied upon both employers and employees. Currently these taxes are each 5.2 percent upon the first $7,800 of annual

[6] *Economic Report of the President, 1966* (Washington), p. 110.
[7] Michael Harrington, *The Other America* (Baltimore: Penguin Books, Inc., 1962), p. 14. This admirable and disturbing little book is required reading for anyone seriously interested in the poverty problem.

[8] *Economic Report of the President, 1964* (Washington), pp. 69–70.

income. Legislative provisions have been made which will increase the tax on both employer and employee to 5.9 percent by 1987. The self-employed now pay a tax of 7.5 percent, a figure which will rise to 7.9 percent by 1987. Benefit payments are made to those reaching the retirement age of sixty-five; when the worker dies, benefits accrue to his survivors. Widows can retire and collect old age benefits at age sixty-two. Special provisions provide benefits for disabled workers. Currently over 90 percent of all employed persons in the United States are covered by OASDHI.

The actual size of benefit payments varies according to the amount the worker has contributed to the program, the number of dependents, and so forth. At the end of 1970 some 26 million people were receiving OASDHI checks averaging about $110 per month. Benefit payments redistribute income to some degree; small contributors get relatively more in comparison with their contributions than do large contributors. On the other hand, benefit payments are not based upon the recipient's need; a participant's contribution gives him the right to benefits whether or not he would be otherwise financially secure.

Medicare is the newest feature of the OASDHI program. Compared with the rest of the population, older people tend to be ill more frequently and for longer periods of time. Because many old people have very modest incomes and the costs of hospitalization and medical care have been rising rapidly, it has become increasingly difficult for the aged to afford adequate medical treatment. Against this background Congress passed the "medicare" program in 1965. This new program provides, first, for compulsory hospitalization insurance covering up to ninety days for each "spell of illness." The beneficiary pays only the first $52 for each period of hospitalization. The cost of the program comes out of OASDHI taxes already described. Secondly, medicare provides a low-cost ($4 per month to the beneficiary) voluntary insurance program which helps pay doctor fees.

Unemployment insurance The Social Security Act does not provide for a federally operated program of *unemployment insurance.* But it does offer an incentive for the states to establish and operate such programs,[9] and all fifty states now have them. Though they are the same in principle, the programs of the various states differ considerably with respect to details.

The programs are financed by taxes on employers; these taxes probably average about 1½ percent of covered payrolls. Any insured worker who finds himself unemployed can, after a short waiting period (usually a week), become eligible for benefit payments. The size of the payments and the number of weeks they may be received vary considerably from state to state. In late 1970 some 2 million workers were receiving benefits; the average check was about $52 per week. Of course, the number of people receiving benefits at any time will vary with the overall health of the economy. Currently over 50 million people are covered by unemployment compensation. It is to be recalled that unemployment compensation benefits are one of the important built-in stabilizers of American capitalism.

Public Assistance Needy persons who do not qualify for OASDHI or unemployment compensation are assisted by a variety of special *public assistance* programs. These programs—for the needy aged and blind, the permanently and totally disabled, and dependent children—are administered by the state governments and financed out of state tax revenues and Federal grants-in-aid. In late 1970 almost 14 million persons were receiving benefits under the various assistance programs. In addition, all the states have passed legislation providing for workmen's compensation. These programs assure medical expenses and partial wages to workers who are victims of industrial accidents.

Paradox of the welfare state

Now there can be no doubt that the social security system—not to mention local relief, public housing, minimum-wage legislation, agricultural subsidies, and private transfers through charities, pensions, supple-

[9]The incentive: Congress levied a tax on employers, returning the tax collections only to those states willing to set up an unemployment insurance program.

mentary unemployment benefits, and so forth—provides important means of alleviating poverty. Indeed, transfer payments account for almost half of the income of poor families. Poverty would be more prevalent and more severe were it not for such programs.

But there are grave shortcomings in our welfare system. With considerable justification, a salient criticism of our existing welfare programs is that *they frequently tend to be of least benefit to those who need economic assistance the most.* The roots of our present welfare system, after all, go back to the Great Depression of the 1930s; the system was designed to protect the nation's workers against the economic hazards of temporary unemployment and retirement. It is now in many ways an outdated system. The basic problem is no longer that of temporary poverty resulting from mass unemployment, but rather one of assisting the chronically poor in a generally prosperous and expanding economy. More specifically, important gaps and deficiencies exist in our welfare programs with the result that many needy persons do not benefit. *It is estimated that about one-half of all those families and individuals now classified as poor receive no transfer payments at all.* Why is our welfare system so defective? Here are some of the basic reasons:

1. There are vast gaps in worker coverage under the state-administered unemployment compensation programs. Many workers do not qualify for benefits; benefits are only about one-third of average weekly incomes; and the benefits of the long-term unemployed simply expire.

2. There exist no Federal programs to assist the working poor. This is a crucial shortcoming because, you will recall, one-third of all poor people are in families headed by an employed person. The absence of a program to assist the working poor "not only creates economic disincentives and encourages family breakup; it also is socially divisive because it is possible for incomes of some aid recipients to exceed the incomes of low earners."[10]

3. There are a number of much-publicized deficiencies and inequities involved in our public assistance programs. For example, the disparities in the benefits provided by these state-run programs are vast. In many states public assistance is simply not sufficient to bring recipients above the poverty level. And, in addition to the working poor, the employable but unemployed poor are excluded from benefits. Furthermore:[11]

> Many of those who might be eligible for existing assistance programs—the aged, blind, disabled, dependent children and spouses—do not qualify for benefits because of the variety of Federal, State, and local nonfinancial eligibility requirements. Program features and regulations often seem designed to restrict benefits through the imposition of residence requirements, tests of 'moral worthiness,' mandatory acceptance of social services, overly stringent asset tests, income limits set below the poverty line, and the like. . . .
>
> Some persons decline to participate in welfare and food programs because of demeaning administrative techniques. Many people never are eligible for some programs because the States, counties, or cities in which they live have not elected to participate in the programs. . . .
>
> Those who do meet all of the requirements for eligibility receive income support that is generally inadequate.

4. Ironically, a number of government-sponsored programs which could be expected to benefit the poor in fact largely benefit middle- and high-income groups. Examples: It has been charged that public housing projects have benefited middle-income groups more than the poor and that the main beneficiaries of the farm program are wealthy corporate farms rather than the small or tenant farmer.

These kinds of shortcomings have caused Michael Harrington to lament that the "fundamental paradox of the welfare state" is that "it is not built for the desperate, but for those who are already capable of helping themselves. . . . The poor get less out of the welfare state than any group in America."[12]

Two philosophies

Given the persistence of poverty and the inadequacies of our traditional welfare system, it is legitimate and relevant to raise this question: Is the prob-

[10] *Poverty Amid Plenty,* p. 5.

[11] Ibid., p. 6.

[12] Harrington, op. cit., p. 172.

lem of poverty primarily a matter for government or individual action? A fundamental philosophical disagreement exists on this point.

Personal shortcomings? One view holds that most of the poor are ultimately responsible for their circumstances. They have forfeited or frittered away their educational opportunities. They lack salable skills and won't enroll in retraining programs. They live in now-depressed areas and, instilled with a "homing instinct," refuse to move. They have large families and are too shortsighted to use contraceptives. They have been spendthrifts in the days of youth and high earning power and now, in their old age, are unable to supplement their social security benefits or relief payments. Some are poor because they are slothful or lazy. The Bohemians, the hippies, and the skid-row alcoholic have willfully, and perhaps even joyously, chosen poverty as a way of life. In short, poverty is largely a matter of personal inadequacies, "attitudes of shiftlessness," shortsightedness, and, in some instances, preference. Poverty is therefore deserved and should be dealt with, if at all, through private charity and philanthropy.

Social victims? The virtually diametrically opposed position is that poverty is essentially the result of self-perpetuating cultural and social deficiencies which are beyond the capacities of individuals to remedy through self-help. The very characteristics of poverty suggest that poor families are by and large the victims of society and their environment. Some are the victims of rapid technological change. Others can't find employment because of racial discrimination or because society has provided them with inadequate education and training. And certainly the millions of children who live in poverty can hardly be held responsible for their plight. Can those suffering from physical or mental infirmities be held responsible for these tragedies? In brief, for the most part poverty is the social by-product of a complex, highly interdependent, dynamic economy; therefore, responsibility for alleviating this poverty rests primarily upon society as opposed to the individuals so afflicted.

The evidence The evidence resulting from this debate is not conclusive, and, of course, one can cite anecdotal support for both views. But a detailed analysis of the welfare rolls suggests that the vast majority of those receiving assistance are not self-supporting for legitimate cause.[13]

> It is evident that as prosperity has opened up new job opportunities, enabling people who are employable to cross the subsistence threshold, those left behind are the less-fortunate who are unable to fend for themselves because of circumstance, whether it be age, sickness or other incapacitation, lack of training, responsibility for young children, or whatever disability stands in the way of earning a decent living. . . .
>
> The outstanding fact emerging from [Bureau of Labor Statistics] studies is that most of the poor in the working age brackets, who might reasonably be expected to be in the labor force, in fact were in the labor force and a large proportion were employed.

ANTIPOVERTY PROGRAMS

In any event, the view that the poor are victims of misfortune rather than shiftless malingerers is more widely accepted in our society. What specific forms, then, might public policy assume in dealing with the poverty problem? The fact that the roots of poverty are manifold suggests that the strategy of an attack on poverty must operate on many fronts. Let us concentrate our discussion on two complementary areas: enlarging economic opportunities and income maintenance.

Expanding economic opportunities

Perhaps the most general measure for alleviating poverty is to achieve a prosperous and rapidly expanding economy. Job opportunities for the unemployed, the partially employed, and those employed in extremely low-paying positions will obviously improve in such an environment.

But in recent years a number of important programs have been inaugurated for the specific purpose of

[13] Committee for Economic Development, *Improving the Public Welfare System* (New York: CED, 1970), pp. 35–36, 43.

increasing economic opportunities for low-income groups. Let us briefly mention some of these. The Manpower Development and Training Act (MDTA) of 1962 provides substantial Federal subsidies for the training or retraining of unemployed workers throughout the nation. The purpose of the Job Corps is to place disadvantaged youths in a new environment in residential centers and to provide them with additional basic education and vocational training. The Neighborhood Youth Corps provides jobs for young people from low-income families, provided they remain in school. The new Work Incentive Program (WIN) is designed to provide job training and employment for people who are now on the welfare rolls. The Job Opportunities in the Business Sector (JOBS) program makes public subsidies to businesses that are willing to provide on-the-job training for the disadvantaged. An estimated 2 million people were involved in these and other manpower development programs in 1971; expenditures on these programs amounted to about $2.5 billion.[14]

Last, but certainly not least, the Civil Rights Act of 1964 merits comment. The act outlaws discrimination in hiring, firing, conditions of work, apprenticeship, or training. While one may debate the ability to "legislate away" prejudice, there is no question that this act is an important step in enlarging the economic opportunities of nonwhites.

Income maintenance: the negative income tax

Having noted the deficiencies of our present welfare system, one might argue that we should attack poverty by expanding, modernizing, and generally strengthening that system.

But some observers—economists, sociologists, social workers, civil rights workers—are convinced that the prospects for substantial improvement of the social security system in the immediate future are not good. In particular, the most inadequate and inequitable facets of the present system are public assistance and unemployment compensation. Because these programs are state-controlled, it would be difficult—perhaps impossible—to improve them to the extent needed to eliminate poverty. States which have limited resources and relatively low incomes are not likely to enact "adequate" public assistance programs. Hence, these observers recommend the establishment of a Federal *guaranteed income* for all citizens as an effective means of eliminating poverty.

The rationale for income maintenance—for a guaranteed income—goes something like this: Most of the poor are unwilling victims of personal misfortune or adverse economic changes over which they have no control. Existing welfare programs demonstrate that there already exists a broad consensus and an implied commitment by government to provide a minimum income for all families. However, the present mosaic of programs is unduly complex, very costly to administer, and inadequate to the task of eliminating poverty. What is needed is a single guaranteed-income program structured so as to eliminate the inequities and inadequacies of existing welfare programs. Proponents hold that a guaranteed income can be readily integrated with, and efficiently administered through, the existing Federal income tax system by making provisions for a *negative income tax*.

Table 38·4 presents a hypothetical illustration of how a negative income tax might be employed to implement an income maintenance program. Assume we are considering a family of four and that society agrees that a minimum income of $4,000 is desirable for a family of this size. Now families with earned incomes of less than $4,000 can be assisted by applying a negative income tax. That is, the Federal income tax might be structured so that, while a family pays taxes to the government for income earned in excess of $4,000, the government will make negative tax (subsidy) payments to the family on the amount by which its earned income falls short of $4,000. In Table 38·4 the negative tax rate is assumed to be 50 percent. This means, for example, that if the family's earned income is zero and its "income deficit" is therefore $4,000, the family will be entitled to a subsidy or negative tax payment equal to 50 percent of its income deficit, or $2,000. Similarly, a

[14]The annual *Manpower Report of the President* is a useful and up-to-date source of information on the characteristics and purposes of the various manpower development programs.

TABLE 38·4 NEGATIVE INCOME TAX: PLAN ONE *(hypothetical data)*

(1) Minimum income	(2) Earned income	(3) Income deficit	(4) Income subsidy	(5) = (2) + (4) Total income
$4,000	$ 0	$4,000	$2,000	$2,000
4,000	1,000	3,000	1,500	2,500
4,000	2,000	2,000	1,000	3,000
4,000	3,000	1,000	500	3,500
4,000	4,000	0	0	4,000

family which earns $1,000 will get a subsidy equal to 50 percent of its $3,000 income deficit, or $1,500. Adding this subsidy to the family's $1,000 earned income will provide a total income of $2,500. When the family's earned income reaches the $4,000 minimum level—that is, when its income deficit is zero—it ceases to receive subsidies.

Now, ideally, an income maintenance program of this general type should accomplish three objectives. First, it obviously should guarantee some minimum income for all poor people. Secondly, it should preserve incentives to work; that is, the program should not encourage people to drop out of the labor force in order to "go on welfare." Finally, the program should be efficient in that it should eliminate or ameliorate poverty to some stipulated extent at a minimum cost. In particular, the program should not subsidize people who are not poor. Unfortunately, as Table 38·4 implies, these three objectives conflict with one another, and compromises or trade-offs are necessary.

The negative tax program of Table 38·4 is specifically designed to sustain incentives to work. That is, the negative tax rate is 50 percent so that the family's subsidy only falls by one-half of any increase in its earned income. Thus when earned income rises by $1,000, the family's subsidy only falls by $500. A family always gets a larger total income by earning more income.

But the catch is that this particular negative tax program does *not* bring the poor family up to the $4,000 minimum income level. Any family whose earned income falls below $4,000 will get an income subsidy insufficient to bring total income to $4,000. What to do? One obvious alternative is to alter the income subsidies so as to bring every family's total income to the $4,000 level. Specifically, change the subsidies of column 4 to read: $4,000, $3,000, $2,000, $1,000, and $0. This, of course, would raise the cost of the program substantially. And, more importantly, it would tend to undermine work incentives. In effect, the tax rate *on earned income* now becomes 100 percent because the family will lose $1 of subsidy for every additional $1 it earns. Why work harder and longer to increase your income by $500 when the government will respond by reducing your negative income tax subsidy by the same amount? Indeed, any family earning less than $4,000 would be tempted to withdraw its breadwinners from the labor force and simply enjoy a $4,000 subsidy. Why work for $4,000 a year, receive no subsidy, and realize a total income of $4,000 when you can decide not to work and realize the same total income?

The question then is this: How do we adjust our program to get all incomes up to the $4,000 minimum level and still maintain work incentives? The answer: Apply the negative income tax to higher income levels. For example, substitute $8,000 for $4,000 in

TABLE 38·5 NEGATIVE INCOME TAX: PLAN TWO (*hypothetical data*)

(1) Minimum income	(2) Earned income	(3) Income deficit	(4) Income subsidy	(5) = (2) + (4) Total income
$8,000	$ 0	$8,000	$4,000	$4,000
8,000	1,000	7,000	3,500	4,500
8,000	2,000	6,000	3,000	5,000
8,000	3,000	5,000	2,500	5,500
8,000	4,000	4,000	2,000	6,000

column 1 of Table 38·4 and apply the 50 percent negative tax rate to the resulting higher deficits. Table 38·5 demonstrates how this would work. We find that all total incomes are now at the $4,000 minimum or above, remedying the basic shortcoming of Table 38·4. Furthermore, work incentives are provided for as in Table 38·4: for every $1,000 increase in earned income the income subsidy falls by only $500. The rub, of course, is that many people—in fact, every family with some earned income—will be subsidized to the extent that their total incomes will exceed the minimum level of $4,000. By extending Table 38·5 you will find that families whose earned incomes are $4,000 to $8,000—people who are *not* poor—will receive substantial income subsidies. Hence, this particular program will be costly and inefficient in the sense that people above the $4,000 poverty level are subsidized.

To summarize: Negative income tax proposals which are structured to maintain work incentives either fail to bring incomes to desired minimum levels or provide subsidies for families that are not poor. Proposals which bring incomes to the poverty level without subsidizing families whose incomes are above the poverty level tend to impair work incentives.

Critics of income maintenance proposals not only cite the dilemma just noted but also contend that such proposals do not get at the root causes of poverty; rather, they treat only its low-income symptoms. Instead of perpetuating the causes of low incomes through income guarantees, we should vigorously pursue programs directed at the causes of poverty—at reducing unemployment, eliminating discriminatory barriers to employment, providing high-quality education to the children of the poor, and so forth.

"Workfare": the Nixon plan

Citing the many shortcomings of our present welfare system and the apprehension that a guaranteed annual income would unduly undermine the incentive to work, President Nixon proposed in the fall of 1969 a new antipoverty program designed to replace the state-administered public assistance programs. In brief outline his "workfare" program is structured as follows:

1. A federally financed Family Assistance Plan (FAP) would provide $500 per year for the first two members of a family, plus $300 for each additional member. Hence, a family of four with no other income would receive $1,600; a family of six, $2,200; and so forth.

2. In addition the Federal Food Stamp Program would be expanded so that our family of four with no earned income would receive about $850 in food

stamps for a potential income of \$2,450 (= \$1,600 + \$850).

3. Payments under FAP are structured in an attempt to maintain incentives to work. Specifically, a family can earn \$720 per year without losing any FAP payments. Hence, our family of four can enjoy a cash income of \$2,320 (=\$1,600 + \$720) per year. Cash benefits from FAP fall by 50 percent of any earned income in excess of \$720. Thus if the family's earnings were \$1,720—\$1,000 in excess of the \$720 exemption—its total money income would be \$2,820, comprised of earned income of \$1,720 and FAP payments of \$1,100 (=\$1.600 – \$500).

4. A basic feature of the Nixon proposal is its emphasis upon work. Excepting mothers with children under six, all applicants for FAP benefits would be required to register with state employment agencies for training or suitable employment. Day care would be provided for mothers with dependent children so that these mothers could enter the work force or a vocational training program.

The workfare proposal has much to commend it. Although the term and concept are repudiated, the proposal does establish a modified guaranteed annual income and thereby would plug many of the gaps and inequities in our present welfare system. In particular, the gross interstate inequities of our present public assistance programs would be corrected. If enacted, the proposal would in fact provide for income levels well above those now provided by welfare payments in many states. Furthermore, the working poor would be eligible for benefits. And, in the President's words, his proposal "removes the present incentive not to work, and substitutes an incentive to work. It removes the present incentive for families to break apart and substitutes an incentive to stay together." The basic criticism of the proposal is that the embodied figures are too low; if the program were adopted, most beneficiaries would not in fact be raised above the government's own poverty thresholds.

A final point: Men of good will can agree that poverty in America clearly exists as a problem of substantial magnitude. They may also disagree as to which specific remedies are best and as to how massive and extensive the assault on poverty should be. The kinds of proposals just outlined will entail heavy costs.[15] But to do nothing at all—which, after all, is a "policy" of sorts—also imposes heavy costs upon society.

SUMMARY

1. The distribution of personal income in American capitalism reflects considerable inequality. Though income inequality lessened quite significantly between 1929 and the end of World War II, little change has occurred in the postwar period.

2. Four arguments constitute the case against income inequality. Income inequality ***a.*** impedes the maximization of consumer satisfaction; ***b.*** impairs productivity; ***c.*** limits the occupational opportunities of the poor; and ***d.*** fosters noneconomic inequalities.

3. Income inequality is defended as follows: ***a.*** income inequality is conducive to a high rate of saving, a rapid rate of capital accumulation, and therefore rapid economic growth; ***b.*** income inequality is essential as an incentive to work and invest; and ***c.*** income inequality is essential to a viable, progressive society.

4. Current statistics suggest that about 10 percent of the nation lives in poverty. Although the poor are a heterogeneous group, poverty is concentrated among the poorly educated, the aged, farmers, and families headed by women. The incomes of blacks and other races are very substantially below those of whites as the result of various forms of racial discrimination. There is evidence to indicate that poverty tends to be self-regenerating.

5. Most existing social welfare programs exclude, or provide for at very minimal levels, those families and individuals whose incomes are lowest.

6. Current efforts and proposals to alleviate poverty focus upon the expansion of economic opportunities for the poor and various income maintenance plans.

[15] Economists are inclined to remind each other that there is no such thing as a "free lunch."

QUESTIONS AND STUDY SUGGESTIONS

1. What are the major causes of income inequality? Outline and critically evaluate the arguments for and against income inequality. Which position do you favor? Why?

2. Are the issues of "equity" and "equality" in the distribution of income synonymous? To what degree, if any, is income inequality equitable?

3. Explain: "To endow everyone with equal income will certainly make for very unequal enjoyment and satisfaction."

4. "Poverty [in America] is not an economic malady so much as it is a social disgrace." Interpret and explain. Do you agree?

5. Who are the poor? Explain and comment: "We have socialism for the rich and free enterprise for the poor."

6. Compare and account for differences in the economic status of whites and Negroes.

7. A prominent economist has argued:[16]

> It is a striking historical fact that the development of capitalism has been accompanied by a major reduction in the extent to which particular religious, racial, or social groups have operated under special handicaps in respect of their economic activities; have, as the saying goes, been discriminated against. . . . there is an economic incentive in a free market to separate economic efficiency from other characteristics of the individual.

Do you agree with this view? Justify your position.

8. Comment on the following statement.[17]

> Education is the principal route to a high status occupation, but it is not obvious whether, on balance, it promotes social mobility. . . . In part . . . education is a "transmission belt," whereby initial advantages stemming from the family are maintained for the fortunate, whereas initial disadvantages are perpetuated for the unfortunate. On the other hand, education allows some able people to rise to a higher relative position in the society.

Do you believe on balance that the distribution of education and training in our society alleviates, or contributes to, income inequality? Explain.

9. "Under the welfare system we have clung to the notion that employment and receipt of assistance must be mutually exclusive. This view is untenable in a world in which employable persons may have earnings below assistance standards." Do you agree?

10. Outline the main characteristics of a comprehensive "war on poverty." Explain and evaluate: "The impact of a carefully conceived war on poverty will not be an increase in costs but rather a redistribution and more rational budgeting of costs which are now being met in a haphazard and inequitable way."

11. What is the guaranteed-income proposal? Discuss the case for and against the guaranteed income as a means of eliminating poverty. "The dilemma of the negative income tax is that you cannot bring families up to the poverty level on the one hand, and simultaneously preserve work incentives and minimize program costs on the other." Explain in detail.

12. Explain and evaluate: "Some freedoms may be more important in the long run than freedom from want on the part of every individual."

13. Should a nation's income be distributed to its members in accordance to their contributions to the production of that total income or in accordance to the members' needs? Do you think society's response to this question will depend upon its level of affluence? Explain.

SELECTED REFERENCES

Economic Issues, 4th ed., readings 70, 71, 72, and 73.

Ferman, Louis A., Joyce L. Kornbluh, and Alan Haber (eds.): *Poverty in America,* rev. ed. (Ann Arbor: The University of Michigan Press, 1968).

[16] Milton Friedman, *Capitalism and Freedom* (Chicago: University of Chicago Press, 1962), pp. 108–109.

[17] Department of Health, Education, and Welfare, *Toward a Social Report* (Washington, 1969), p. 19.

Harrington, Michael: *The Other America* (Baltimore: Penguin Books, Inc., 1962).

Kershaw, Joseph A.: *Government against Poverty* (Chicago: Markham Publishing Company, 1970).

Levitan, Sar A.: *Programs in Aid of the Poor for the 1970s* (Baltimore: The Johns Hopkins Press, 1969).

Will, Robert E., and Harold G. Vatter (eds.): *Poverty in Affluence,* 2d ed. (New York: Harcourt, Brace & World, Inc., 1970).

Wilcox, Clair: *Toward Social Welfare* (Homewood, Ill.: Richard D. Irwin, Inc., 1969).

39

LABOR UNIONS AND COLLECTIVE BARGAINING

About 20 million workers—about 28 percent of the nonagricultural labor force—now belong to labor unions. Bare statistics, however, understate the importance of unions. The wage rates, hours, and working conditions of nonunionized firms and industries are influenced by those determined in organized industries. Unions are clearly permanent and powerful institutions of American capitalism.

In this chapter we seek, first, an understanding of the historical background and the present status of labor unions. Attainment of this objective necessarily involves a discussion of government policy toward organized labor, because labor legislation and union growth are intimately related. A friendly government and prolabor legislation cause unions to flourish and grow; an indifferent government and unfavorable legislation can result in stagnation and decay of the labor movement. Second, we want to analyze labor-management relations. Here our discussion will center upon the process of collective bargaining. Finally, we must examine carefully different views as to the economic impact of unions upon the operation of American capitalism—what effect do they have on economic stability and efficient resource allocation?

BRIEF HISTORY OF AMERICAN UNIONISM

The history of the labor movement in America is long, colorful, and flavored with violence.

In terms of national labor policy the American labor movement has gone through three phases: repression (1790 to 1930), encouragement (1930 to 1947), and intervention (1947 to date). Though the dates are somewhat arbitrary, these three phases serve as an excellent guide for our discussion.[1]

[1] The following are highly recommended: U.S. Department of Labor, *Brief History of the American Labor Movement* (1964); Foster Rhea Dulles, *Labor in America*, 3d ed. (New York: Thomas Y. Crowell Company, 1960); and Joseph G. Rayback, *A History of American Labor* (New York: The Free Press, 1966).

Repression phase: 1790 to 1930

Labor unions have existed in the United States for some 175 years. The shoemakers, carpenters, printers, and other skilled craftsmen formed unions of some permanence in the early 1790s. As Figure 39·1 indicates, despite this early start, union growth was relatively slow and sporadic until the 1930s. Two considerations go far to account for this meager progress: (1) the hostility of the courts toward labor unions and (2) the extreme reluctance of American businessmen to recognize and bargain with unions.

Unions and the courts It was not until the 1930s that legislation spelled out the Federal government's policy toward labor unions. In the absence of a national labor policy it was up to the courts to decide upon specific union-management conflicts. And, much to the dismay of organized labor, the courts were generally hostile toward unions. This court hostility had two sources.

1. Most judges had propertied-class backgrounds.
2. The courts are inherently conservative institutions charged with the responsibility of protecting *established* rights. Unions, throughout the 1800s and the early decades of the 1900s, were in the unenviable position of seeking rights for labor at the expense of the *existing* rights of management.

The hostility of the courts was first given vent in the *criminal conspiracy doctrine.* This doctrine, "imported" by the American courts from English common law at the turn of the nineteenth century, was unbelievably narrow by modern standards. The doctrine flatly concluded that combinations of workmen

FIGURE 39·1 THE GROWTH OF UNION MEMBERSHIP

Most of the growth in organized labor has occurred since 1935. (U.S. Bureau of the Census and Bureau of Labor Statistics.)

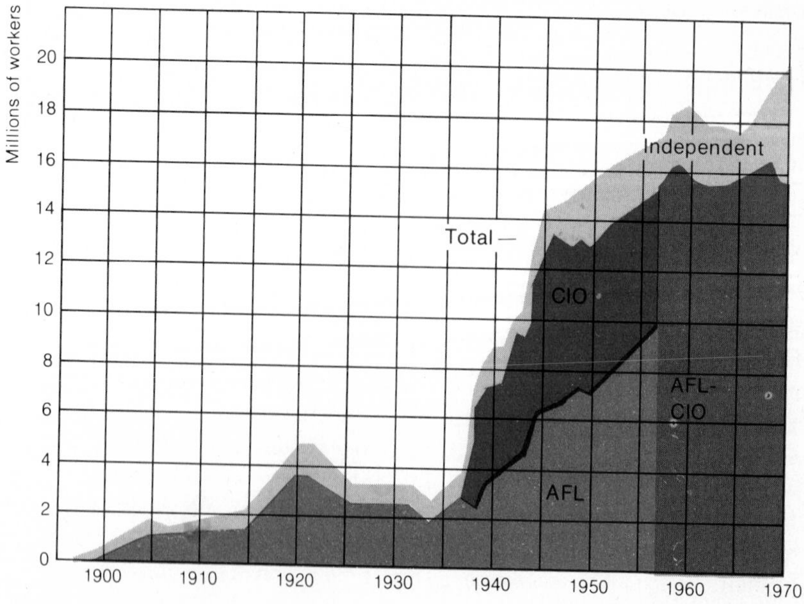

to raise wages were criminal conspiracies and hence illegal. Though weakened by subsequent court rulings in the 1840s, the shadow of the conspiracy doctrine hung heavy over organized labor throughout most of the 1800s. Although unions, as such, were later recognized by the courts as legal organizations, the techniques employed by unions to enforce their demands—strikes, picketing, and boycotting—were generally held to be illegal. And in the latter part of the 1800s the courts employed both antitrust laws and injunctions in such a way as to impede the labor movement significantly.

Although Congress passed the Sherman Act of 1890 for the express purpose of thwarting the growth of business monopolies, the courts interpreted the loose wording of the act to include labor unions as conspiracies in restraint of trade and frequently so applied the act.

A simpler and equally effective antiunion device was the *injunction.* An injunction, or restraining order, is a court order directing that some act not be carried out, on the grounds that irreparable damage will be done to those affected by the action. The attitude of the courts toward unions was such that it was extremely simple for employers to obtain injunctions from the courts, prohibiting unions from enforcing their demands by striking, picketing, and boycotting. Stripped of these weapons, unions were relatively powerless to obtain the status and rights they sought.

In brief, the courts employed the criminal conspiracy doctrine, the Sherman Act, and injunctions, to the end that union growth was greatly retarded during the 1790–1930 period.

Antiunion techniques of management American businessmen did not rely entirely upon the courts in their attempt to impede the growth of unions. The business community, hostile to unions from their inception, developed a group of antiunion techniques to undermine unions. A startlingly simple antiunion technique was that of ferreting out and firing prounion workers. Too, the average employer felt it his Christian duty to inform fellow employers that the discharged workers were "troublemakers" and "labor agitators" and not fit to be hired. This combination of *discriminatory discharge* and *blacklisting* made it extremely risky for workers even to think in terms of organizing a union. One's present and future employment opportunities were at stake.

Another potent weapon in management's struggle to keep unions down was the *lockout,* management's counterpart of the strike. By closing up shop for a few weeks, employers were frequently able to bring their employees to terms and to destroy any notions they might have about organizing a union. In some cases this might prove a bit costly to the employer in the short run. In other cases, when business was slack, the lockout was a good means of killing two birds with one stone—working off excess inventories and undermining worker attempts to organize. Remember: Workers of the late 1800s and early 1900s were not blessed with savings accounts or multimillion-dollar strike funds to draw upon in such emergencies.

Where workers were determined to organize, pitched battles often ensued. Rocks, clubs, shotguns, and an occasional stick of dynamite were the shadowy ancestors of collective bargaining. Some of the darkest pages of American labor history concern the violent clashes between workers and company-hired *strikebreakers.* The Homestead strike of 1892, the Pullman strike of 1894, and the Ludlow Massacre of 1914 are cases in point. Less dramatic skirmishes erupt down to the present time.

But management tactics were often more subtle than a cracked skull. The *yellow-dog contract* was one of the more ingenious antiunion devices fostered by management. In such contracts workers agreed to remain nonunion as a condition of employment. Workers often had little choice but to sign such contracts—no contract, no job. Violation of a yellow-dog contract exposed a worker to a lawsuit by his employer, the result of which might be a court-imposed fine or even imprisonment.

As a last resort, an employer might shower his work force with such amenities as group insurance and pension programs, stock ownership and profit-sharing schemes, and even company magazines to convince them that employers would look after the interests of the workers as effectively as would unions

established by "outsiders." The next step beyond such *paternalism* was employee representation schemes or *company unions,* that is, employer-dominated "dummy" unions which it was hoped would discourage the establishment of genuine unions. Paternalism and company unions were decidedly effective in retarding union growth as late as the 1920s.[2]

Evolution of business unionism The growth which occurred in the labor movement during the 1800s not only was modest, but it also embodied a variety of union philosophies. The mid-1800s were in effect a laboratory wherein American labor experimented with alternative forms of unionism—Marxism, utopianism, reformism, and a host of other isms. But such unions usually foundered in the span of a few short years because of the internal conflict between the workers' interest in short-run practical goals (higher wages and shorter hours) and the long-run utopian goals (producer cooperatives, creation of a labor party, and so forth) of the union leaders.

Then in 1886, a new labor organization—the American Federation of Labor—which was to dominate the labor movement for the next fifty years was formed. Under the leadership of Samuel Gompers, labor charted a conservative course which has been very influential down to the present date.[3] Appropriately honored as "the father of the American labor movement," Gompers preached three fundamental ideas: (1) practical business unionism, (2) political neutrality for labor, and (3) the autonomy of each trade or craft.

Gompers was firmly convinced that "safe and sane" business unionism was the only course for American labor to follow. In 1903 he declared[4]

> I want to tell you, Socialists, that I have studied your philosophy; read your works on economics . . . studied your standard works. . . . I have heard your orators and watched the work of your movement the world over. I have kept close watch upon your doctrines for thirty years; have been closely associated with many of you, and know how you think and what you propose. I know, too, what you have up your sleeve. And I want to say that I am entirely at variance with your philosophy. I declare it to you, I am not only at variance with your doctrines, but with your philosophy. Economically, you are unsound; socially, you are wrong; industrially, you are an impossibility.

Gompers flatly rejected long-run idealistic schemes entailing the overthrow of the capitalistic system. He spurned intellectuals and theorizers and emphasized that unions should be concerned with practical short-run economic objectives—higher pay, shorter hours, and improved working conditions. In the words of one scholar, Gompers felt that "you must offer the American working man bread and butter in the here and now instead of pie in the sky in the sweet by and by."[5]

In addition to espousing "bread and butter" unionism, Gompers had strong opinions on labor's role in politics and the basis upon which workers should be organized. Insofar as politics was concerned, Gompers was convinced that government should keep its nose out of labor-management relations and collective bargaining. Although he recognized that governmental interference on behalf of labor might be a boon to union growth, Gompers was equally certain that antiunion government policies could stifle the progress of the entire labor movement. In pursuing the idea of political neutrality, Gompers cautioned organized labor not to align itself with any political party. Preoccupation with long-run political

[2]During a prolonged strike in the bituminous coal industry in 1902, a spokesman for the mine operators, George F. Baer, issued the classic statement of business paternalism: "The rights and interests of the laboring man will be protected and cared for—not by the labor agitators, but by the Christian men to whom God in His infinite wisdom has given the control of the property interests of this country."

[3]This is not to say that all unions have followed conservative paths since Gompers first espoused the virtues of business unionism. The Industrial Workers of the World, founded in 1905, advocated a decidedly revolutionary brand of left-wing unionism. And in the late thirties and early forties Communists infiltrated a number of CIO unions. In 1949 and 1950 the CIO expelled eleven affiliated unions whose leaderships had come to be dominated by Communists.

[4]From the *Proceedings* of the 1903 AFL convention, reprinted in George P. Shultz and John R. Coleman, *Labor Problems: Cases and Readings,* 2d ed. (New York: McGraw-Hill Book Company, 1959), pp. 16–17.

[5]Charles C. Killingsworth, "Organized Labor in a Free Enterprise Economy," in Walter Adams (ed.), *The Structure of American Industry,* 3d ed. (New York: The Macmillan Company, 1961), p. 570.

goals, he argued, merely causes labor to lose sight of the short-run economic objectives it ought to seek. Gompers admonished organized labor to follow one simple principle in the political arena: rewarding labor's friends and punishing its enemies at the polls without regard to political affiliation.

Finally, Gompers was firmly convinced that "autonomy of the trade," that is, unions organized on the basis of specific crafts, was the only permanent foundation for the labor movement. Unions composed of many different crafts lack the cohesiveness, he argued, that is essential to strong, hard-hitting, business unionism. These craft unions should then be affiliated in a national federation. "One union to each trade, affiliated for one labor movement."

This philosophy—conservative business unionism, political "neutrality," and the craft principle of union organization—was destined to dominate the AFL and the entire labor movement for the next half century. Indeed, the AFL, operating under Gompers's leadership, met with considerable success—at least for a time. AFL membership hit a high-water mark of about 4 million members by the end of World War I. Then a combination of circumstances arose in the 1920s which forced the AFL into an eclipse (see Figure 39·1). One factor was a strong antiunion drive by employers. Spearheaded by the National Association of Manufacturers, businesses waged a last-ditch effort to stem the rising tide of organized labor. Then, too, many firms introduced employee representation plans, company unions, and a host of paternalistic schemes to convince workers that employers were better prepared to look out for their employees' interests than were labor leaders. Finally, the AFL clung tenaciously to the craft principle of union organization, thereby ignoring the ever-increasing number of unskilled workers employed by the rapidly expanding mass-production industries—the automobile and steel industries in particular.

Encouragement phase: 1930 to 1947

Two significant events occurred in the 1930s which revived the labor movement and inaugurated a period of rapid growth. Most importantly, the attitude of the Federal government toward unions changed from one of indifference, not to say hostility, to one of encouragement. Also, a major structural change in the labor movement accompanied the founding of the Committee (later the Congress) of Industrial Organizations in 1936. Both events, coupled with the wartime prosperity of the 1940s, greatly swelled the ranks of organized labor.

Prolabor legislation of the 1930s Against the background of the depressed thirties, the Federal government enacted two decidedly prolabor acts. In part the passage of these acts reflects the strong opposition of organized labor to the previously described weapons employed by the courts and by management to suppress unions. In part they reflect a Democratic administration replacing a Republican administration. In part they echo the widely held opinion that strong unions, by achieving higher wages through collective bargaining, would increase total spending and help alleviate the Great Depression.

The *Norris–La Guardia Act* of 1932 did much to clear the path for union growth by outlawing two of the more effective antiunion weapons. Specifically, the act

1. Made it decidedly more difficult for employers to obtain injunctions against unions
2. Declared that yellow-dog contracts were unenforceable

Three years later, in 1935, the Federal government took more positive steps to encourage union growth. The *Wagner Act* (officially the National Labor Relations Act) guaranteed the "twin rights" of labor: the right of self-organization and the right to bargain collectively with employers. The act listed a number of "unfair labor practices" on the part of management. Specifically it

1. Forbade employers from interfering with the right of workers to form unions
2. Outlawed company unions
3. Prohibited antiunion discrimination by employers in hiring, firing, and promoting
4. Outlawed discrimination against any worker who files charges or gives testimony under the act

5. Obligated employers to bargain in good faith with a union duly established by their employees

The Wagner Act was clearly "labor's Magna Charta."

A National Labor Relations Board was established by the act and charged with the authority to investigate unfair labor practices occurring under the act, to issue cease-and-desist orders in the event of violations, and to conduct worker elections in deciding which specific union the workers wanted to represent them.

The Wagner Act was tailored to accelerate union growth. It was extremely successful in achieving this goal. The protective umbrella provided to unions by this act in conjunction with the Norris–La Guardia Act played a major role in causing the ranks of organized labor to mushroom from about 4 million in 1935 to 15 million in 1947.

Industrial unionism We have already noted that one of the causes of stagnation in the AFL during the 1920s was its unwillingness to organize the growing masses of unskilled assembly-line workers. Though the majority of AFL leaders chose to ignore the unskilled workers, a vocal minority under the leadership of John L. Lewis contended that craft unionism would be completely ineffective as a means of organizing the hundreds of thousands of workers in the growing mass-production industries. According to Lewis and his followers, the basis for organization should be shifted from *craft unionism* to *industrial unionism,* that is, away from unions which only encompass a specific type of skilled workers to unions which include all workers—both skilled and unskilled—in a given industry or group of related industries. This conflict came to a head, and in 1936 Lewis and his sympathizers withdrew their unions (and were simultaneously expelled) from the AFL.

The withdrawing unions established themselves as the Congress of Industrial Organizations. The CIO met with startling success in organizing the automobile and steel industries. So great was this success that the AFL also moved in the direction of organizing on an industrial basis. By 1940 total union membership approximated 9 million workers.

Intervention phase: 1947 to date

In recent years there has been a decided increase in government regulation of, and intervention in, labor-management relations. It is important to understand the background of this governmental interference.

The prolabor legislation of the 1930s, the birth of industrial unionism, and the booming prosperity of the war years brought rapid union growth (see Figure 39·1). As unions gathered strength—both numerical and financial—it became increasingly evident that labor unions could no longer be regarded as the weak sister or underdog in their negotiations with management. Just as the growing power of business monopolies brought a clamor for public control in the 1870s and 1880s, the upsurge of union power in the 1930s and 1940s brought a similar outcry for regulation. This pressure for union control came to a head in the postwar years.

Many people felt that the wartime strike record of American labor left much to be desired. Despite no-strike pledges, work stoppages reached a new high at the height of the war effort in 1944. Equally harmful to the favorable climate of public opinion which labor enjoyed in the 1930s was the series of nationwide strikes which broke out during the reconversion period in such basic industries as steel, coal, meat-packing, and railway transportation. The man in the street felt that these strikes not only slowed the reconversion process but also inaugurated the severe wage-price inflationary spiral which was to plague the immediate postwar years (see Chapter 11). Many businessmen, needless to say, were happy to fan the flames of public resentment. By the mid-forties the prolabor climate of the prior decade had done a virtual turnabout.

Taft-Hartley Act of 1947 This growing public hostility toward unions was crystallized in the Taft-Hartley Act (officially the Labor-Management Relations Act) in 1947. A very detailed piece of legislation, this act mirrors the increasing complexity of labor-management relations. Generally its specific provisions fall under four headings: (1) provisions which designate

and outlaw certain "unfair union practices"; (2) provisions which regulate the internal administration of unions; (3) provisions which specify collective bargaining procedures and regulate the actual contents of bargaining agreements; and (4) provisions for the handling of strikes imperiling the health and safety of the nation.

1. You will recall that the Wagner Act outlined a number of "unfair labor practices" on the part of management. A new and crucial feature of the Taft-Hartley Act was that it introduced a number of "unfair labor practices" on the part of unions. These unfair practices, which constitute some of the most controversial sections of the act, are as follows: (*a*) Unions are prohibited from coercing employees to become union members. (*b*) *Jurisdictional strikes* (disputes between unions over the question of which has the authority to perform a specific job) are forbidden, as are *secondary boycotts* (refusing to buy or handle products produced by another union or group of workers) and certain *sympathy strikes* (strikes designed to assist some other union in gaining employer recognition or some other objective). (*c*) Unions are prohibited from charging excessive or discriminatory initiation fees or dues. (*d*) *Featherbedding,* a mild form of extortion wherein the union or its members receive payment for work not actually performed, is specifically outlawed. (*e*) Unions cannot refuse to bargain in good faith with management.

2. Taft-Hartley also imposes significant controls on the internal processes of labor unions: (*a*) Unions are obligated to make detailed financial reports to the National Labor Relations Board and to make such information available to its members. (*b*) Unions are prohibited from making political contributions in elections, primaries, or conventions which involve Federal offices. (*c*) Originally, union officials were required to sign non-Communist affidavits.

3. Other Taft-Hartley provisions are designed to control the actual collective bargaining process and the contents of the work agreement resulting therefrom: (*a*) The *closed shop* (which requires that a firm hire only workers who are already union members) is specifically outlawed for workers engaged in interstate commerce; that is, a closed-shop arrangement cannot be written into a collective bargaining agreement. (*b*) The *checkoff* (whereby union dues are deducted from the workers' pay checks by the employer and turned over to the union in a lump sum) cannot be written into a bargaining agreement unless authorized in writing by individual workers. (*c*) Collective bargaining agreements must provide that, where they exist, welfare and pension funds are kept separate from other union funds and jointly administered by the union and management. (*d*) Bargaining agreements must contain termination or *reopening clauses* whereby both labor and management must give the other party 60 days' notice of the intent to modify or terminate the existing work agreement.

4. Finally, the Taft-Hartley Act outlines a procedure for avoiding major strikes which might disrupt the entire economy and thereby imperil the health or safety of the nation. According to this procedure, the President may obtain an injunction to delay such strikes for an 80-day "cooling-off" period. Within this period the involved workers are polled by the NLRB as to the acceptability of the last offer of the employer. If the last offer is rejected, the union can then strike. The government's only recourse—one of questionable legality—is seizure of the industry.

The Taft-Hartley Act is difficult to evaluate.[6] It has been a subject of heated debate since its enactment. Unions have condemned Taft-Hartley as a "slave labor act," claiming that it has undermined the status of unions and imperiled many of organized labor's basic weapons. Most employers feel that the act is merely a step in the right direction—a long-overdue attempt to restore a better balance of power between labor and management.

This much is agreed upon: The Taft-Hartley Act represented a marked shift in public policy. This shift is essentially one from "government-sponsored" collective bargaining to "government-regulated" collective bargaining. The underlying philosophy of the Wagner Act was that a balance of bargaining power between labor and management should be established. This balance would be conducive to

[6]See "The Taft-Hartley Act after Ten Years: A Symposium," *Industrial and Labor Relations Review,* April 1958.

effective collective bargaining free of government intervention. The Taft-Hartley Act, however, envisioned a need for detailed and continuous government control of collective bargaining to assure labor-management relations which are not unduly injurious to the welfare of the general public. Most objective observers feel that this shift in public policy toward labor was a necessary one. Disagreement persists, however, with respect to the form these controls should take and the manner in which they should be applied.

Landrum-Griffin Act of 1959 Government regulation of the internal processes of unions was extended by passage of the Landrum-Griffin Act (officially the Labor-Management Reporting and Disclosure Act) in the fall of 1959. This act places regulations upon union elections and union finances and guarantees certain rights of union members. Specifically, the act regulates union elections by requiring regularly scheduled elections of officers and the use of secret ballots; restrictions are placed upon ex-convicts and Communists in holding union offices. Furthermore, union officials are now held strictly accountable for union funds and property. Officers handling union funds must be bonded, the embezzlement of union funds is made a Federal offense, and close restrictions are placed upon a union's loans to its officers and members. The act is also aimed at preventing autocratic union leaders from infringing upon certain rights of their constituents. The individual worker's rights to attend and participate in union meetings, to vote in union proceedings, and to nominate officers are guaranteed. The act permits a worker to sue his union if it denies him these rights. Under the act the Secretary of Labor is given broad powers in investigating violations of the act.

Labor unity

In 1955 unity was formally reestablished in the American labor movement with the merger of the AFL and CIO. Many forces were significant in closing the breach which had existed between the two for almost two decades:

1. The AFL's increased willingness to accept and practice industrial unionism lessened the original structural differences between the AFL and the CIO.
2. The political and legislative setbacks which labor has encountered since the prolabor era of the 1930s convinced labor leaders that unity in the labor movement is a necessary first step toward bolstering the political influence of organized labor.
3. Failure to achieve the desired rate of growth in the ranks of organized labor in the post–World War II years made evident to organized labor that a concerted, unified effort is needed to organize currently nonunion firms and industries.
4. Then, too, considerable turnover in top leadership in both the AFL and CIO pushed into the background certain personality conflicts which had proved to be a significant obstacle to reunification of the labor movement at an earlier date.

The postmerger era: stagnation

The achievement of labor unity seemed to set the stage for vigorous growth of the labor movement. In fact, the period since the AFL-CIO merger has *not* been characterized by a resurgence of organized labor. Union membership was virtually static between 1955 and 1965. Labor economists talk of an "organizational plateau" and "stagnation" in the labor movement. A number of factors, both within the labor movement and external to it, have made union growth difficult.

Internal obstacles In the first place, the AFL-CIO merger did not really resolve the issue of craft versus industrial unionism. Given the fact that blue-collar jobs have been shrinking, both industrial and craft unions have been anxious to establish their rights to jobs. The persistent internal squabbles which have resulted over job jurisdiction have diverted energies from expansion of the labor movement.

A second and more subtle consideration is apathy within the labor movement itself. While union members of the 1930s fought to establish their unions, workers currently accept membership as a convenient businesslike arrangement. The member pays his

dues and receives certain kinds of security and representation in return. Except in times of crisis there is little activism and ideological zeal among union members.

Finally, leadership rivalries continue to exist. For example, persistent differences between George Meany and Walter Reuther caused the latter to disaffiliate his 1.5 million member United Auto Workers in May of 1968, creating a significant new threat to a unified labor movement.

External obstacles Nor have external forces been conducive to rapid union growth.

First, the traditional organizational base of unions has not expanded significantly. In fact, the previously noted (Chapter 22) shift in the composition of the labor force from blue- to white-collar employment has probably reduced the potential membership base of organized labor. Despite some inroads, organized labor has not as yet found an effective formula for bringing large numbers of white-collar workers into the fold. Remaining unorganized blue-collar workers are in smaller plants, in agriculture, in service industries, and in the South—all of which are "hard-to-organize" jobs and areas.

Secondly, legislative reversals—namely, the shift of public policy from encouragement to intervention—pose a more hostile legal environment for organized labor.

Lastly, organized labor seems to have suffered from a deteriorating public image. Some liberal observers contend that labor's traditional progressive stance has given way to conservativism, complacency, and bureaucracy. The "hawkish" position of many union leaders and "hardhats" regarding Vietnam and membership policies which foster racial discrimination are also relevant. Furthermore, the growing number of public sector strikes, involving schoolteachers, garbage collectors, and municipal transit workers, has entailed more direct adverse effects upon the public than is usually the case with private sector strikes. Hence, such strikes have contributed to public impatience and dissatisfaction with unions.

But despite these internal and external impediments to union growth, it would be precipitate to regard the labor movement as a diminishing force in the economy. Unions have been making some new gains in organizing groups previously outside organized labor, for example, government employees and public school teachers. And more important, it is incorrect to equate the power of labor unions only with their membership. The actions of a relatively small union—for example, the Air Line Pilots Association—can have a great impact upon its own industry and the economy as a whole.

At present the AFL-CIO boasts almost 16 million members. Independent unions, of which the Teamsters, the United Auto Workers, and the United Mine Workers are the major ones, add another $4\frac{1}{2}$ million members. Hence, the ranks of organized labor now embody over 20 million workers, or slightly more than one-fourth of the nonfarm labor force.

COLLECTIVE BARGAINING

As a result of the rapid growth of unions in recent decades, collective bargaining has become a way of life in labor-management relations. It is estimated that over 150,000 collective bargaining agreements are now in force in the United States.

The bargaining process

To the outsider, collective bargaining is a dramatic once-a-year clash between labor and management. Chief participants are a John L. Lewis–type character with baggy suit, bushy eyebrows, and calloused hands, and on the other side of the table a Daddy Warbucks with diamond stickpin and formal attire. Furthermore, one gets the impression from the newspapers that labor and management settle their differences only with strikes, picketing, and not infrequent acts of violence.

These impressions are largely inaccurate. Collective bargaining is a somewhat less colorful process than most people believe. In negotiating important contracts, the union is represented by top local and national officials, duly supplemented with lawyers and research economists. Management representatives

include top policy-making executives, plant managers, personnel and labor relations specialists, lawyers, and staff economists. The union usually takes the initiative, outlining its demands. These take the form of specific adjustments in the current work agreement. The merits and demerits of these demands are then debated. Typically a compromise solution is reached and written into a new work agreement. Strikes, picketing, and violence are clearly the exception and not the rule. In recent years it has generally held true that less than one-fifth of 1 percent of all working time has been lost each year as a result of work stoppages resulting from labor-management disputes! *Labor and management display a marked capacity for compromise and agreement.* We must keep in mind that strikes and labor-management violence are newsworthy, while the peaceful renewal of a work agreement hardly rates a page-5 column.

The work agreement

Collective bargaining agreements assume a variety of forms. Some agreements are amazingly brief, covering two or three typewritten pages; others are highly detailed, involving two hundred or more pages of fine print. Some agreements involve only a local union and a single plant; others set wages, hours, and working conditions for entire industries. There is no such thing as an "average" or "typical" collective bargaining agreement. Nevertheless, the following skeleton agreement, based on an actual contract, provides a fairly accurate notion of the scope and content of collective bargaining.

CONTRACT AND AGREEMENT

Sample agreement

Article I. Intent, union status, management prerogatives *Section 1* This agreement entered into June 30, 1972, between the Deep South Manufacturing Company, hereinafter referred to as the "Employer," and the International Brotherhood of Boilermakers, Iron Shipbuilders, and Helpers of America, Local No. 167, hereinafter referred to as the "Union." It is the intent and purpose of the parties hereto that this Agreement will promote and improve industrial relations between the Employer and the Union.

Section 2 The Employer recognizes the Union as the sole and exclusive bargaining agency for the purpose of determining rates of pay, hours of employment, and all other conditions of employment for all the Employer's production and maintenance employees. It is understood and agreed that the Union shall designate a representative who is duly authorized and will be consulted in all matters pertaining to the application of this work agreement.

Section 3 There shall be in each unit no less than one (1), nor more than two (2), Shop Stewards, these Stewards to be appointed by the Union. A unit shall be defined as any part of the Company Organization that provides for a foreman. Shop Stewards may leave their work during their regular working hours, without loss of pay, for the purpose of adjusting grievances.

Section 4 The Employer shall have the sole right of determining plant layout, the means of manufacturing and distributing products, the scheduling of production operations, and the setting of work shifts.

Section 5 Upon receipt of a written authorization by an employee the Employer shall deduct from the first pay each month and remit to the local Union such sum as the employee shall specify in said authorization.

Article II. Wages, hours of work, holidays *Section 1* The minimum wage rates per hour shall be as follows:

Layout men	$2.85
Welders	2.40
Tackers	2.40
Painters	2.30
Riveting machine operators	2.08
Truck drivers	2.00
Helpers	1.87

When employees are transferred to a new job, their rate of pay shall not be changed for a period of fifteen

(15) working days. If they are retained on the new job after this probationary period, the job rate called for by this agreement shall then be paid to them. If such job change involves a pay raise, the new rate shall be retroactive to the date the job was assigned.

Section 2 Wage rates shall be adjusted every three (3) months in accordance with changes in the U.S. Department of Labor's Index of Consumer Prices. For each one (1) point change upward in the Index, there shall be a one (1) cent per hour raise in wages. For each one (1) point downward change in the Index, there shall be a one (1) cent per hour decrease in wages. Wages in no case shall fall by more than five (5) cents per hour in any three-month period.

Section 3 All employees shall receive a two (2) percent longevity increase in hourly wages for each year of service. This two (2) percent shall be based on the previous year's hourly base rates.

Section 4 Forty (40) hours shall constitute the workweek, from Monday to Friday, inclusive. The established schedule of hours shall be from 8 A.M. to 12 noon and from 12:30 noon to 4:30 P.M.

Section 5 Time and one-half shall be paid for work performed in excess of eight hours in one day and for hours worked on Saturday. Double time shall be paid for hours worked on Sunday.

Section 6 When the following legal holidays—New Year's Day, Memorial Day, Fourth of July, Labor Day, Thanksgiving Day, and Christmas Day—occur or are celebrated during the employee's workweek, he shall receive said holidays off duty with his regular straight-time pay, provided that he shall have been in the employ of the Employer at least thirty (30) calendar days. If said holiday falls on Saturday, it shall be celebrated on Friday, and if it falls on Sunday, celebration shall be on Monday. In the event an employee is required to work on one of the above-named holidays, he shall receive double time for such time worked in addition to his regular holiday pay. However, if any employee shall refuse to work on a holiday if he is requested by the Employer, he shall forfeit his holiday pay, but only if he refuses for other than a legitimate reason.

Section 7 All overtime work shall be divided among the workers according to seniority.

Section 8 All employees within the bargaining unit of the Union who shall have been in the service of the company one year and less than three years shall receive a paid vacation of five (5) days; those who have been in the service of the company three (3) years or more shall receive a paid vacation of ten (10) days.

Article III. Seniority and job opportunities *Section 1* Seniority is defined as the principle that if, because of lack of work, the employer deems it advisable to reduce his work force, the last man hired shall be the first man laid off, and, in rehiring, the last man laid off shall be the first man rehired, until the list of former employees is exhausted.

Section 2 Seniority shall be the determining factor regarding layoff and reemployment, transfers, demotions, promotions, or other job changes where the necessary skill and ability are present to perform the work required.

Section 3 Seniority shall be lost for the following reasons: (*a*) voluntary quitting; (*b*) discharge for cause; (*c*) layoff for twelve (12) months; (*d*) if laid-off employee is notified by the Employer by registered mail sent to his last known address to return and fails to do so within five (5) days of mailing the letter, unless a reasonable excuse shall be established.

Section 4 A seniority list shall be maintained and kept up to date by the Employer and shall be available to the Union at all times.

Article IV. Grievance procedure *Section 1* In the event a grievance arises between an employee or group of employees and the Employer, such grievance shall be handled as follows:

Section 2 The employee or employees having a grievance shall report the same in a signed statement to the Shop Steward, who will in turn take up the grievance with the Foreman verbally. The Foreman will attempt to make a satisfactory settlement and will advise the Steward of his decision.

Section 3 If the Steward and employee are not satisfied with the decision of the Foreman, the Steward shall then submit the grievance to the Plant Superintendent verbally. The Superintendent shall

make his decision within ten (10) days of the time the grievance is submitted to him. If the Steward or employee is not satisfied with the decision of the Superintendent, the Steward shall report the grievance to the Union's President, who shall submit the grievance to the management within ten (10) days and endeavor to reach an agreement.

Section 4 If no agreement is reached within ten (10) days, the grievance shall be submitted to an impartial arbitrator. The arbitrator shall be jointly selected by the Employer and the Union. The arbitrator shall be required to hand down a decision within thirty (30) days. This decision shall be binding, so long as it does not change the terms of this Agreement in any way.

Article V. Termination *Section 1* This Agreement shall remain in full force and effect until June 30, 1973, and thereafter from year to year unless, within the ten (10) day period immediately preceding the sixty (60) days prior to the day of expiration, notice is given in writing to the other party indicating a desire to change the agreement.

Section 2 Anything in this Agreement found to be contrary to any state or national law shall be automatically voided.

. . . .

International Brotherhood of Boilermakers,
Iron Shipbuilders, and Helpers of America,
Local 167
Deep South Manufacturing Company

Basic contract areas

This contract is representative in that it covers four basic areas: (1) the degree of recognition and status accorded the union and the prerogatives of management (Article I); (2) wages and hours (Article II); (3) seniority and job opportunities (Article III); and (4) a procedure for settling grievances (Article IV).

Union status Unions enjoy differing degrees of recognition from management. Listed in order of the union's preference are (1) the closed shop, (2) the union shop, and (3) the open shop.

Prior to being outlawed by the Taft-Hartley Act, the *closed shop* afforded the greatest security to a union. Under a closed shop a worker must be a union member before the employer can hire him. A *union shop,* on the other hand, permits the employer to hire nonunion workers but provides that these workers must join the union in a specified period—say, thirty days—or relinquish their jobs. Since it is not specified to the contrary, we may assume in our sample contract that an *open shop* exists (Article I, Section 2). Management may apparently hire union or nonunion workers. Those who are nonunion are not obligated to join the union; they may continue on their jobs indefinitely as nonunion workers. In this contract, the union is the bargaining agent for *all* the firm's production and maintenance workers. In other cases the union may bargain only for union members. In some instances union or open-shop status will be supplemented with *preferential hiring.* Management agrees to hire union members so long as they are available; then it can hire nonunion workers. Finally, we must also mention the *nonunion shop.* Here no union exists, and the employer makes a conscious effort to hire those workers who are least inclined to form or join a union.

One of the most controversial aspects of union status has grown out of the (in)famous section 14(b) of the Taft-Hartley Act. Section 14(b) makes the union shop a legal form of union status *unless* prohibited by state legislation. Some nineteen states now have so-called *right-to-work laws* which make compulsory union membership, and therefore the union shop, illegal.

Proponents of these laws (mainly employers) hold that an individual should be free to refrain from joining any organization without being denied access to a job. No worker, as a condition of employment, should be forced to join and support financially an organization whose principles he may hold to be unacceptable or which he feels is corrupt. Opponents (mainly organized labor) counter that employer support of right-to-work laws is motivated more by the desire to undermine unions than by an urge to protect

the freedom of workers. Furthermore, the union shop is held to be a desirable means of eliminating "free riders"—nonunion workers who benefit from, but do not financially support, the union. Finally, opponents of the right-to-work laws argue that an open-shop union, which must constantly strive to secure its position and gain wider worker support, is frequently forced to make unreasonable demands as a means of obtaining this support; a union whose existence is secure through a union shop can approach collective bargaining more reasonably and responsibly.

No easy resolution of the right-to-work controversy is apparent. Chances are that it will remain a prominent bone of contention in labor-management relations for some time to come.

The other side of the union-status coin is the issue of managerial prerogatives. Many businessmen fear that in time the expansion of the scope of collective bargaining may reach the point where certain fundamental management decisions will become matters to be decided jointly by management and labor. It is felt by businessmen that such an eventuality will "tie the hands" of management to the extent that efficient business operation may be jeopardized. For this reason at the insistence of management an increasing number of work agreements contain clauses which outline certain decisions which are to be made solely by management. These *managerial prerogatives* usually cover such matters as the size and location of plants, products to be manufactured, types of equipment and materials used in production, and the scheduling of production (Article I, Section 4). Frequently the hiring, transfer, discipline, discharge, and promotion of workers are decisions made solely by management but are subject to the general principle of seniority and to challenge by the union through the grievance procedure.

Wages and hours The focal point of any bargaining agreement is wages and hours. Our skeleton agreement is representative of most contracts in that basic hourly pay rates, length of workweek, overtime rates, holidays, and vacations are all specified (Article II).

Both labor and management tend to be highly pragmatic in wage bargaining. The standards, or "talking points," most frequently invoked by labor in demanding (and by management in resisting) wage boosts are (1) "what others are getting," (2) productivity, (3) ability to pay, and (4) cost of living. If a given firm has basic rates below those of comparable firms, the union is likely to stress that wages should be increased to bring them into line with what workers employed by other firms are getting. Similarly, if the firm has had a banner year, the union is likely to demand high wages on the grounds that the company has ample ability to grant such increments. In recent years unions have achieved considerable success in tying wages to the cost of living. It is estimated that work agreements covering about $2\frac{1}{2}$ million workers embody some kind of "escalator clause." This is true of our sample agreement (Article II, Section 2). And many contracts link wage rates to productivity; wages automatically increase in terms of an estimated "improvement factor."

Three points should be mentioned in connection with these wage criteria. In the first place, they are clearly two-edged propositions. For example, the cost-of-living criterion is only invoked by the union when prices are hurrying upward; unions conveniently ignore this criterion when prices are stable or declining. Similarly, the union only considers the ability-to-pay argument to be of importance when profits are large. Management is equally inconsistent in the evaluation it places on the various wage-bargaining standards.

It must be emphasized, too, that these wage criteria are considerably less objective than might first appear. Most people might agree that it is only fair that wage rates be adjusted for increases in productivity and the cost of living. But then arises the difficult question "By how much?" What wage boost should accompany, say, a 2-point increase in the Consumer Price Index? Similarly, not only are productivity increases difficult to gauge, but, once gauged, how does one determine how much of the increase should accrue to labor and how much to capital?

Another noteworthy point: Wage changes—either increases or declines—based on these criteria are not necessarily desirable on either economic or equity grounds. Many economists fear, for example, that

the widespread use of the cost-of-living criterion will cause a wage-price inflationary bias to be built into our economy. In like manner, indiscriminate application of the what-others-are-getting standard may push a relatively inefficient firm out of business, causing considerable hardship for its workers.

Seniority and the control of job opportunities The uncertainty of employment in a capitalistic economy, coupled with the fear of antiunion discrimination on the part of employers, has made workers and their unions decidedly "job-conscious." The explicit and detailed provisions covering job opportunities which most work agreements contain reflect this concern. The importance of seniority as the guiding principle in controlling job opportunities is apparent from Article III of our work agreement. It should be noted, however, that in many cases seniority is not rigidly applied. Strategic workers, or "key" personnel, will often be exempt from seniority regulations. And unions are typically willing to recognize that, particularly where promotion is concerned, ability must take precedence over seniority (Article III, Section 2).

Grievance procedure It has been quipped that a collective bargaining agreement is to labor relations what the wedding ceremony is to domestic relations—only the beginning. Despite formal agreements, it is the "living together" that counts. It is unthinkable that even the most detailed and comprehensive work agreement can anticipate all the issues and problems which might occur during its life. What if Local 167 members show up for work on a Monday morning to find that for some reason—say, a mechanical failure—the plant is closed down? Should they be given "show-up" pay amounting to, say, two or four hours' pay? This event is not covered in the contract and would therefore be a problem which might be ironed out through the grievance machinery. Then, too, there may be some disagreement in interpreting points covered in the work agreement. For example, the abbreviated work agreement upon which our discussion is centered poses some possible questions of interpretation which may make it necessary to invoke the grievance procedure. What is a "legitimate reason" for refusing to work on a holiday (Article II, Section 6)? Exactly how is "necessary skill and ability" to be defined in specific cases (Article III, Section 3)? What is meant by "discharge for cause" (Article III, Section 4)?

As a result, virtually all agreements contain a more or less explicit procedure for the handling of disputes which arise during the life of an agreement. In our sample agreement a very complete four-step procedure is clearly outlined. In this instance the grievance machinery culminates in arbitration, that is, a neutral third party is designated to render a decision by which both labor and management must abide.

Three implications

Three points implicit in our discussion of collective bargaining merit emphasis:

1. Collective bargaining is concerned not only with wage rates but also with the security and status of workers and of the union itself. Man does not live by bread alone. Workers seek protection from arbitrary actions by management; they seek a voice in determining the conditions under which they must work; they seek a means of voicing their grievances; they seek the status and dignity which accompany membership in economically powerful institutions. These objectives are fulfilled wholly or in part by membership in unions.

2. Also worthy of emphasis is the fact that collective bargaining is a continuous process. True, the *negotiation* of an agreement is an important and often dramatic point of departure. But this is followed by the equally important and continuing tasks of *administering* and *interpreting* (through the grievance procedure) the agreement. Collective bargaining is much more involved than a once-a-year clash of labor and management.

3. Finally, labor-management relations occur in a dynamic climate. Technological advance, business fluctuations, population changes, changes in the legislative framework, and changes in the character of business and unions themselves constitute some of the obvious dynamic aspects of the environment in which bargaining occurs. Changes such as these

virtually preclude the reaching of final, once-and-for-all solutions to labor-management problems. At best collective bargaining provides short-run, temporary adjustments to labor-management conflicts—adjustments which the changing economic milieu is likely to render obsolete in a relatively short span of time. In view of this observation the previously cited paucity of work stoppages due to labor-management disputes is all the more remarkable.

ECONOMIC IMPLICATIONS OF LABOR UNIONS

We must now look beyond the day-to-day dealings of a specific union and a specific firm and assume a broader perspective. What is the impact of strong unions upon the operation of American capitalism? More specifically, what implications do unions have for *full production*—that is, the efficient allocation of resources—and *full employment*—that is, economic stability and growth?

Widely divergent opinions exist on this question. To achieve the clearest picture of this controversy, let us sketch the extreme views on the question of the role of unions in modern capitalism.

The case against unions

Some economists and many businessmen take a decidedly dim view of labor unions. They envision unions as uncontrollable, socially irresponsible monopolies whose operation is inimical to efficient resource allocation and economic stability.

Character of unions The antiunion view holds that, by either restricting the supply of labor (exclusive unionism) or imposing above-equilibrium wage rates (inclusive unionism), unions impair the operation of the price mechanism in labor markets. Unions are monopolies, it is argued, in that they rig the labor market to their own advantage and to the detriment of the rest of the economy. By achieving above-equilibrium wage rates, unions restrict employment either directly (exclusive unionism) or indirectly (inclusive unionism). Workers deprived of job opportunities by these union tactics drift into nonunionized labor markets, causing wage rates there to fall.

Unions and resource allocation By thus distorting the wage structure, it is contended, unions alter the allocation of resources away from the ideal pattern which competitive labor markets would foster. We learned in a previous chapter that under competition the wage rates paid to labor would tend to equal labor's marginal revenue productivity. Now, assuming labor markets are competitive, labor will tend to move from low-wage, low-productivity jobs to high-wage, high-productivity jobs. Labor mobility, of course, is not perfect even under pure competition; but the tendency for this shifting to occur exists, and at least in the long run it would work with reasonable efficiency. The movement of labor from low- to high-productivity jobs which competition fosters is all to the good. Such shifting entails an expansion of total output; that is, it makes for an efficient allocation of labor resources.

The antiunion view contends that both exclusive and inclusive unionism impede the movement of labor from low- to high-marginal-productivity employments and therefore interfere with the efficient allocation of labor. By making a particular type of labor scarce in relation to the demand for it, exclusive unions move back up the MRP, or labor demand, curve and in so doing achieve above-competitive wages (see Figure 32·6). These high wages are sustained by restrictive membership policies which block the reallocation of workers into this occupation from other low-wage, low-productivity employments. Inclusive unionism accomplishes the same end indirectly by imposing above-equilibrium wage rates and allowing the market to restrict the number of jobs (see Figure 32·7). In this case the reallocation of workers from low-wage, low-productivity jobs to high-wage, high-productivity jobs is impeded not by the inability to get a union card but rather by the unwillingness of employers to take on more workers at the union-imposed wage rates. The basic conclusion is that by rigging wage rates, unions distort the allocation of labor away from the most efficient pattern.

But this is only half the story. The growth of union monopolies may induce the further development of business monopolies. This is particularly true where union power forces business firms to band together in employer associations for purposes of collective bargaining. It is only a short step from here to industry cartelization. Furthermore, union monopolies are not to be viewed as counterpoises to business monopoly; rather they are "ominously complementary" to industrial concentration. In short, "each tends to foster and to strengthen the other, fighting together to maximize joint exactions from the public while also fighting each other over division of the spoils." [7] By rigging resource prices and by contributing to the growth of business monopoly, unions contribute to an inefficient allocation of labor resources.

Unions and economic stability The antiunion position envisions unions as having highly undesirable implications for economic stability. It is contended that there exist no effective internal or external restraints upon the monopoly power of unions. It is naïve, according to the antiunion view, to argue that labor unions will not use their power; unions and their leaders are not socially responsible. Similarly, there are no external restraints sufficient to contain strong unions. In particular, business firms have neither the ability nor the desire to resist the demands of aggressive union monopolies. And, if the experience of the last three decades is meaningful, government has done more to promote than to curb the monopoly power of unions.

This unrestrained union power is allegedly a major cause of unemployment and inflation. The attainment of high wages, it is argued, will restrict the demand for labor, thereby causing unemployment and a slowing down of the growth rate. Marginal firms, finding it impossible to operate profitably in the face of above-competitive wage rates, will cease production and dismiss their labor forces. In addition, aggressive union wage policies can be expected to affect business profit expectations adversely. As a result the levels of investment spending, aggregate demand, and employment will be reduced.

On the other hand, if the economy manages to achieve full employment despite irresponsible union wage policies, unions will then cause inflationary pressure to arise. For example, suppose that government activates the monetary and fiscal tools at its disposal so as to sustain a full-employment level of spending. Blessed with a high level of aggregate demand, businessmen will find it a relatively simple matter to pass wage boosts on to consumers through price increases. But this rise in the cost of living will prompt unions to demand and receive another round of wage hikes. The wage-price spiral will then be on its way, causing a cumulative inflation problem for the economy (Figure 22·4).

Government policy toward unions Those who embrace the antiunion position conclude that either unemployment or inflation will eventually prove inimical to capitalism; either is held to be a sufficient cause for the demise of the free enterprise system. A variety of policy recommendations have been offered to deal with the threat posed by union monopolies. There are those who feel that the only real remedy is the outright destruction of unions. Unions simply cannot be allowed to endure. Others call for increased governmental regulation of collective bargaining. It is felt that the Taft-Hartley Act is a step in the right direction but that it fails to go far enough in regulating unions. It might be helpful, it is suggested, to subject unions once again to the antitrust laws. Or three-party bargaining involving labor, management, and the public as represented by government officials may be necessary to avoid the disruptive economic effects of strong unions. Still others envision the need for wage-price controls by government if economic stability is to be maintained (Chapter 19).

The case for unions

The antiunion view just outlined is hardly a happy one. However, there exists an equally important school of thought which paints a cautiously optimistic picture of unions as being compatible with economic

[7] Henry C. Simons, *Economic Policy for a Free Society* (Chicago: The University of Chicago Press, 1948), p. 35.

efficiency, stability, and growth. Let us sketch this prounion position.

Character of unions The prounion view holds that, although unions have a degree of monopoly power, there are effective internal and external restraints which guard against the abuse of that power. Internal restraints are several. It is argued that the larger unions in particular represent their constituents not only as wage earners but also as consumers and savers; hence, unions are obligated to concern themselves with the effects which their wage demands might have upon job opportunities and the cost of living. And, as collective bargaining tends to become more mature, labor leaders are acquiring a greater sense of social responsibility. In addition to these internal restraints on union power, there exist significant external restraints. Because of the extreme reluctance of unions to accept wage cuts, it is felt that in periods of both high and low aggregate demand employers can and do exhibit considerable resistance to union wage demands. It must be remembered, too, that, while a businessman stands to lose only a small fraction of his market as the result of a price increase, a union risks a work stoppage and the loss of income for *all* its members when it demands a wage increase. Unions may actually be subject to greater restraints in the resource market than are business monopolies in the product market.

Unions and resource allocation The prounion position holds that the antiunion view rests on the faulty assumption that labor markets would be highly competitive in the absence of unions. It is contended that this is simply not the case; labor markets would be imperfect ones even in the absence of unions. In particular, large business firms would exert considerable monopsonistic power in hiring workers (Figure 32·4).

More positively, the prounion view argues that the monopoly power of unions operates so as to offset or neutralize the monopsonistic power of large employers. Because the strongest unions have generally developed in the most highly monopolized industries, unions are felt to be a primary manifestation of countervailing power. By counterbalancing the economic power of business monopolies, unions contribute to a more efficient allocation of labor resources. In short, the presence of union monopoly power on the seller's side of the labor market may serve to cancel the monopsonistic power of large employers on the buyer's side. The result is a near-competitive wage rate accompanied by an allocation of labor resembling that which would have existed if competition had prevailed in the labor market. In terms of wage rates and resource allocation, monopoly power on both sides of the labor market is allegedly superior to the presence of such power only on the buying side (see Figure 32·8).

Unions and economic stability The prounion view alleges that it is flatly incorrect to make unions the scapegoat for unemployment and inflation. As previously explained, unions cannot and do not seek higher wages in a manner oblivious to employment and price implications. Both internal and external forces limit the exertion of economic power by unions. The wage-price spiral is a descriptive characteristic of inflation which would exist in modern capitalism with or without unions and collective bargaining. Stated differently, it is the myriad of forces which determine the level of aggregate demand, and not simply the existence of labor unions, which govern the amount of unemployment or inflation the economy experiences. Strong unions are compatible with economic stability and growth; collective bargaining is not inherently inflationary, nor is it a significant cause of unemployment. More positively, the role of unions in American capitalism may be such as to make them an integral force in the complex of balances and counterbalances which permits the relatively smooth functioning of our economy despite its many market imperfections.

Government policy toward unions The prounion school of thought concludes that government policy should be generally aimed at the goal of encouraging the growth of unions where they constitute positions of countervailing power. Furthermore, increasing maturity is envisioned in labor-management relations.

As a result, less control over collective bargaining will be needed in the future.

Although each of the two views just sketched can be applied with little or no modification to specific unions, both represent the extremes. Hence, neither is acceptable as a general explanation of the economic impact of unions. Their value lies in the fact that the contrast they provide serves as an important point of reference for policy makers and an informed citizenry.

SUMMARY

1. The growth of labor unions was slow and irregular until the 1930s. The repression of unions by the courts and by management was an important factor in accounting for this retarded growth. The courts employed the conspiracy doctrine, injunctions, and the antitrust laws against unions. Management invoked such varied antiunion techniques as discriminatory discharge, blacklisting, lockouts, strikebreakers, yellow-dog contracts, paternalism, and company unions in slowing the development of unions.

2. The AFL dominated the American labor movement from 1886 until the CIO was formed in 1936. Its philosophy was essentially that of Samuel Gompers—business unionism, political neutrality, and craft unionism.

3. Union growth was rapid in the 1930s and 1940s. The shift toward industrial unionism triggered by the formation of the CIO in 1936 was a significant factor in this growth. Equally important were the wartime prosperity of the 1940s and the prolabor legislation passed by the Federal government in the 1930s.

4. The Norris–La Guardia Act of 1932 rendered yellow-dog contracts unenforceable and sharply limited the use of injunctions in labor disputes.

5. The Wagner Act of 1935—"labor's Magna Charta"—guaranteed labor the rights to organize and to bargain collectively with management. The act prohibited certain "unfair labor practices" on the part of management, thereby paving the way for unions to organize, unimpeded by management.

6. The Taft-Hartley Act of 1947 brought about a shift from government-sponsored to government-regulated collective bargaining. The act ***a.*** specifically outlaws certain "unfair practices" of unions; ***b.*** regulates certain internal operations of unions; ***c.*** controls the content of collective bargaining agreements; and ***d.*** outlines a procedure for handling "national health and welfare" strikes.

7. The Landrum-Griffin Act of 1959 was designed to regulate the internal processes of unions—in particular the handling of union finances and the union's relationships with its members.

8. At the present time about 20 million workers are union members; this constitutes slightly more than one-fourth of the nonfarm labor force. A number of economists feel that, for a variety of reasons, future growth in the labor movement will be modest.

9. Labor and management "live together" under the terms of collective bargaining agreements. These work agreements cover four major topics: ***a.*** union status and managerial prerogatives; ***b.*** wages and hours; ***c.*** seniority and job control; and ***d.*** a grievance procedure. Experience indicates that both labor and management are very willing to compromise and reach agreement short of work stoppages.

10. There is considerable disagreement about the economic impact of strong unions. The antiunion view holds that unions are potent labor market monopolies. Exertion of their monopoly power allegedly contributes to a misallocation of resources and causes instability in the levels of employment and prices. The destruction of unions, increased public regulation of unions, three-part bargaining, and wage-price controls are possible public policy alternatives that have been suggested by various writers who embrace the antiunion position.

11. The prounion view contends that unions are socially responsible organizations which can be expected to temper their wage demands if unemployment or inflation looms as a probable consequence. The monopoly power which unions exert allegedly serves to counterbalance the monopsonistic power of large employers. The result is that labor allocation and wage rates are likely to be closer to the competitive situation than would be the case in the absence of unions. Collective bargaining is not a basic cause

of instability; rather instability stems from all those factors which influence the components of aggregate demand. The prounion view envisions increasing maturity in collective bargaining and a decline in the need for government controls over labor-management relations.

QUESTIONS AND STUDY SUGGESTIONS

1. Identify the following terms:
a. Injunction
b. Lockout
c. Featherbedding
d. Criminal conspiracy doctrine
e. Sympathy strike
f. Jurisdictional strikes
g. Blacklisting
h. Checkoff
i. Company unions
j. Secondary boycott
k. Discriminatory discharge
l. Yellow-dog contract

2. Distinguish clearly between craft and industrial unionism. Which is generally associated with the AFL? The CIO?

3. Distinguish between a closed shop, a union shop, an open shop, and a nonunion shop.

4. Summarize the controversy surrounding the so-called "right-to-work" laws.

5. "There are legislative, executive, and judicial aspects to collective bargaining." Explain.

6. What are the major provisions of the Norris–La Guardia Act? The Wagner Act? How do you account for the passage of these prolabor acts? What are the functions of the National Labor Relations Board? Briefly indicate the nature of the Landrum-Griffin Act.

7. "In the 1930s public opinion was prolabor, but by the mid-1940s the public was of an antilabor disposition." Account for this turnabout.

8. What are the major provisions of the Taft-Hartley Act? If you had the power to revise this act, what changes would you make? In what ways has the Taft-Hartley Act directly or indirectly affected the sample work agreement studied in this chapter? Be specific.

9. It has been said that the Taft-Hartley Act was passed to achieve three major goals: ***a.*** to reestablish an equality of bargaining power between labor and management to maintain industrial peace; ***b.*** to protect "neutrals," that is, third parties who are not directly concerned with a given labor-management dispute; ***c.*** to protect the rights of individual workers in their relations with unions. Review the Taft-Hartley provisions as outlined in this chapter, and relate each to these three major goals.

10. Suppose you are the president of a newly established local union which is about to bargain with an employer for the first time. Make a list of those points which you would want to be covered explicitly in the work agreement.

11. Suppose you are a union president bargaining for higher wages. Assuming the economic climate which exists at this moment, what wage criteria would you use in backing your demands? Explain.

12. Briefly contrast the antiunion and prounion views of organized labor. To what degree does the antiunion view depend upon an affirmative answer to the question "Do unions raise wages?" Which of the two views do you feel is the more accurate? Outline a compromise position less extreme than either the antiunion or the prounion view sketched in this chapter.

SELECTED REFERENCES

Economic Issues, 4th ed., readings 74 and 75.

Bloom, Gordon F., and Herbert R. Northrup: *Economics of Labor Relations,* 6th ed. (Homewood, Ill.: Richard D. Irwin, Inc., 1969).

Cohen, Sanford: *Labor in the United States,* 3d ed. (Columbus, Ohio: Charles E. Merrill Publishing Company, 1970).

Morgan, Chester A.: *Labor Economics,* 3d ed. (Austin, Tex.: Business Publication, Inc., 1970).

Williams, C. Glyn: *Labor Economics* (New York: John Wiley & Sons, Inc., 1970).

Wortman, Max S., Jr.: *Critical Issues in Labor* (New York: The Macmillan Company, 1969).

THE ECONOMICS OF THE WAR INDUSTRY

Stimulated by public debate over Vietnam, the defense sector of our economy has come under careful scrutiny in the past decade. The present chapter is a brief assessment of the economic impact of the war industry or "military-industrial complex."

But a caveat is immediately in order: There are many questions of a political-ideological, technological, and moral character—not to mention issues of integrity and honor—associated with our military posture. The economist has no particular expertise in these areas. That is, the size and character of our military posture cannot be prescribed on economic grounds alone. Nevertheless, economists can shed light upon some basic questions. Are we making too many or not enough resources available to the military? Are these resources being used efficiently in the acquisitions of weapons systems and other military goods? Is conscription an economically efficient means of acquiring military manpower? Does the existence of the defense sector pose any special problems for the achievement of economic stability? Perhaps the most difficult problem for the economist in examining the war industry is that in applying benefit-cost analysis (Chapter 6) great difficulties arise in measuring accurately the spillover benefits of defense. Economists speak with some certainty about the cost or burden of our defense posture; they speak with considerably less certainty about the necessity or desirability of that cost.

SIZE OF THE WAR INDUSTRY

It is essential at the outset to grasp an overall understanding of the aggregate size of America's military spending. In 1970 our military expenditures—primarily purchases by the Department of Defense (DOD)—were over $80 billion. This figure was about 41 percent of the total Federal budget for that year and slightly less than 10 percent of the GNP (Figure 40·1). Measured in terms of manpower, defense spending provides jobs for about 10 percent

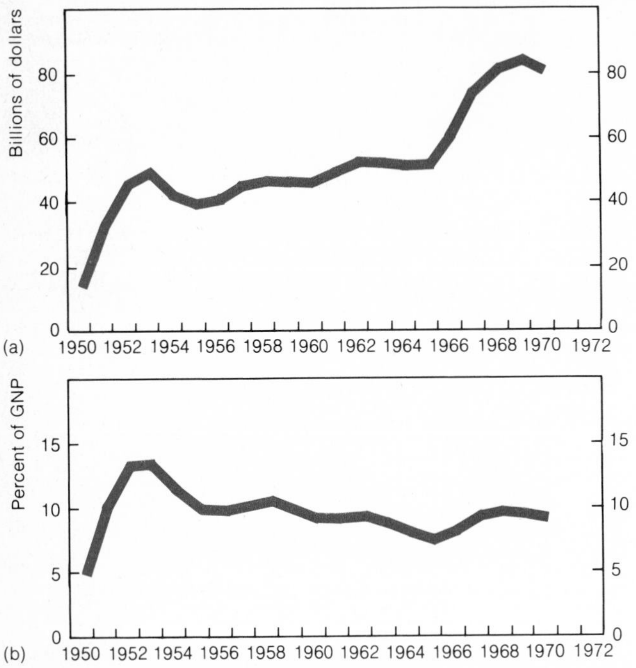

FIGURE 40·1 FEDERAL PURCHASES FOR NATIONAL DEFENSE

Expenditures by the Department of Defense were approximately $80 billion in 1970; this amounted to almost 10 percent of the GNP. (Department of Commerce and Council of Economic Advisors. Data are in current dollars.)

of the labor force. Cumulative data indicate that since 1946 the United States has expended in excess of $1 trillion for national security.

Except for World War I, defense spending in the half-century prior to World War II was less than 1 percent of national output. Two important factors contributed to this low level of spending. First, before the development of nuclear weapons and technologically advanced delivery systems, the United States was sheltered by geographic distance. Secondly, past wars were ''GNP wars'' in the sense that time was available to shift resources from civilian to war goods production. These interrelated considerations are now substantially changed. The existence of ICBMs and nuclear-armed submarines has virtually eliminated the protection afforded by distance. Furthermore, the amount and technological superiority of our immediately available military hardware will likely determine the ''winner'' of a third world war, if indeed such a designation is meaningful.

One can argue that Figure 40·1 understates the size and importance of the war industry. In the first place, at least a portion of the budgets of certain other governmental agencies, for example, NASA and the Atomic Energy Commission, has important military aspects, and therefore these amounts should be added to our total military-defense budget. Secondly, in our later discussion of the draft we will find that a part of the cost of military manpower procurement falls upon the draftee as a hidden ''implicit tax.'' If the military was forced to pay a market-determined wage to get manpower, as would be the case with a volunteer army, this implicit tax would disappear, and the military budget would increase by at least

$5 billion per year.[1] Finally, DOD purchases exclude such war-related expenditures as various veterans' benefits and interest on the public debt. The latter, you will recall (Chapter 15), is largely the consequence of financing World War II. These two items are of considerable magnitude—$9 and $18 billion respectively in 1970—and would add substantially to our measure of the war industry's aggregate size. It should be emphasized, however, that interest on the public debt and veterans' pensions are nonexhaustive transfer payments as opposed to exhaustive government purchases (Chapter 9). However, the higher taxes necessary to finance these transfers presumably have adverse effects in terms of incentives to work and invest and, in this sense, involve a cost.[2]

Aggregate data on the level of military spending conceal other important ramifications of the war industry. For example, it is significant that purchases of military goods and facilities entail the expansion of government's direct role as a consumer of output. In contrast to transfer payments, which shift income among various groups within the private sector, rising military spending means that government is directly absorbing a portion of GNP which could otherwise have been available for private uses. Much of the increase in military spending seems to have come at the expense of consumption; since 1929 military spending has risen from 1 to almost 10 percent of GNP, and during the same period consumption has fallen from 73 to 63 percent. In the public sector military spending dominates the Federal budget, accounting for four-fifths of all expenditures for goods and services.

Secondly, it is of considerable significance that a relatively small number of quite large corporations are the recipients of the majority of defense contracts; military outlays contribute to the concentration of economic power in industry. But a word of caution is in order here: While DOD contract recipients are large, they are *not* typically such corporate giants as General Motors, U.S. Steel, or AT&T.

Thirdly, military spending is also subject to very considerable geographic concentration. Some ten states receive about two-thirds of all military contracts; three of these—California, New York, and Texas—receive about one-third. This obviously implies that disarmament might necessitate serious economic readjustments for particular industries and particular areas of the country.

Finally, a sizable portion of the nation's R & D activities are oriented toward defense and space. Defense-space related R & D expenditures were 43 percent of the estimated $27 billion R & D spending in 1970. And about 40 percent of the nation's scientists and engineers are absorbed in R & D activities financed by the military.

ECONOMIC COSTS

Waiving the possibility of understatement, do the military expenditure data of Figure 40·1 accurately represent the burden of our military posture? Does our national security cost us about one-tenth of our national output?

The answer depends upon one's assumption concerning opportunity costs, that is, the alternative outputs society forgoes by allocating a tenth of its resources to the military. It can be argued that it is a gross overstatement to say that the military costs us a tenth of the GNP; it can be argued in the extreme that the cost of our military preparation is zero! The rationale for this view is that massive defense spending is the prerequisite of a high level of aggregate demand and therefore of full employment. After all, large military outlays have gone hand-in-hand with a generally prosperous economy for some thirty years. Indeed, was it not the upsurge in military

[1] *Economic Report of the President, 1969,* p. 206.

[2] It has been estimated that the ultimate cost of a war, including such nonexhaustive outlays as veterans' benefits and interest on war debt, may exceed the immediate costs of a war by a factor of three! For example, the total immediate costs of military operations in Vietnam totaled about $110 billion by the end of 1970; the addition of long-term costs in the form of veterans' benefits and interest on war loans results in an estimated total cost of $352 billion. Statement of James L. Clayton in Subcommittee on Economy in Government, *The Military Budget and National Economic Priorities, Part 1* (Washington, 1969), pp. 143–150.

spending occasioned by World War II which pulled our society out of the Great Depression of the 1930s? In brief, one can assume that resources devoted to defense would otherwise be idle and unemployed. Hence, our military posture in effect is "free" in the sense that society is not forgoing alternative civilian goods.

The difficulty with this line of reasoning is that it is based upon a highly pessimistic view of the economy's vitality and the efficacy of monetary and fiscal policy. In fact, the economy adjusted remarkably well to the massive decline in military outlays at the conclusion of World War II (Chapter 11). The sharp cutback in military spending after the Korean conflict probably contributed somewhat to the recession of 1953–1954, but the recession was short and mild and could have been ameliorated with more appropriate stabilization policies. Indeed, the appropriate use of monetary and fiscal policy—for example, easy money and tax cuts—provide the means of compensating for any decline in defense spending. Many would argue that a reduction in government spending on military goods can and should be replaced by increased government spending on the civilian economy—education, welfare, health, urban renewal, antipollution programs, and so forth (see footnote 16). In short, most economists would argue that defense spending is not the *sine qua non* of a prosperous economy and that our military posture clearly does come at the cost of forgone civilian output.

Foreign experience seems to bolster the view that military spending is not a prerequisite of full employment and therefore that military outlays are a burden. The capitalist nations of Western Europe have enjoyed full employment for the past twenty years with defense budgets much smaller—both absolutely and relatively—than those of the United States. Indeed, casual observation suggests a negative correlation between military expenditures as a percentage of GNP and an economy's growth rate. West Germany, France, and the Scandinavian countries immediately come to mind (Table 21·2). But Japan is perhaps the outstanding example; it has had virtually no military establishment since World War II and has been the world's outstanding performer in terms of economic growth. One can readily argue that Japan's remarkable technological progress in such fields as electronics, shipbuilding, and watchmaking is a reflection of the fact that virtually all of Japan's scientific and technical personnel have been available for civilian production. In fact, in the post–World War II period the United States has been partially defending Western European allies and Japan. That is, a portion of America's military resources have been transferred to these nations, permitting them to devote more of their domestic resources than they otherwise could to the development of their economies. This point is a key issue in discussions to reduce United States military spending and, as we shall discover in Chapter 44, in resolving our balance of payments problems.

These two views can be readily restated in terms of the production possibilities curve shown in Figure 40·2. The view that our military posture imposes no real cost on the civilian economy presumes that without defense spending the economy would be at a position of unemployment such as *A*. Defense

FIGURE 40·2 THE WAR INDUSTRY AND THE PRODUCTION POSSIBILITIES CURVE

The cost of an increase in military spending will be the sacrifice of civilian output in a full employment economy (*C* to *B*). But in an economy characterized by unemployment and excess productive capacity, more war goods can be produced at no cost in terms of civilian goods and services (*A* to *B*).

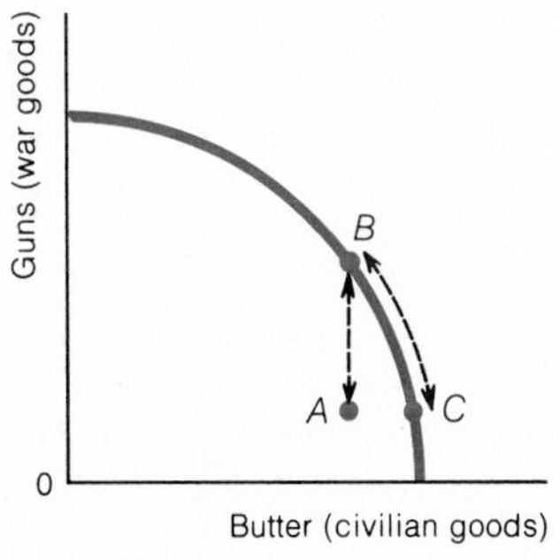

outlays move the economy from *A* to *B,* and the economy has gained *AB* in guns with no sacrifice of butter. The second view holds that the economy can enjoy full employment and be on the production possibilities curve at, say, *C* without a high level of military spending. Therefore, more military goods necessarily means a shift from *C* to *B,* and the cost is obviously less butter. Turning the issue around, if the economy is at full employment at *B* and "peace breaks out," we want to move from *B* to *C* if the civilian economy is to benefit from the release of resources by the military. But if stabilization policies fail to compensate for the decline in military spending, the economy will lapse from *B* to *A,* and society will have squandered a potential "peace dividend" on unemployment and idle resources.

But Figure 40·2 presumes that the issue of military versus civilian spending is a simple either-or proposition. Is there really a strict dichotomy between spending for military and civilian goods? If certain kinds of military outlays entail significant and beneficial spillover effects for the civilian economy, then it is an overstatement to contend that, say, $80 billion of military spending imposes a burden of $80 billion upon a fully employed civilian economy. There is in fact some spillover or fallout from military outlays which benefit the civilian economy: rockets designed for military uses can be used to launch civilian weather and communication satellites; many civilian airline pilots and electronics personnel received their early training in the military; military research gives rise to new materials, new products, and new production techniques which are relevant to the civilian economy, and so forth. But careful estimates suggest that in the aggregate these beneficial spillover effects are quite modest, amounting to perhaps no more than 10 or 15 percent of total military spending.

ALLOCATIVE ASPECTS

Let us shift our attention now from the aggregate size and cost of the military to its organizational and institutional characteristics. This is a necessary prelude to a discussion of the military establishment's microeconomic efficiency.

The military establishment and the firm

It is informative to contrast the military establishment—in particular, the Department of Defense—with a private firm.[3] A most obvious difference is the fact that the military establishment derives its revenue from the Federal government's budget, not from the sale of products in the market. But it must be noted that, like the private firm, the military establishment has a sales problem; that is, it is selling a "psychological product" called national security:

> The salesmen consist of the officers who work with the legislators and legislative committees which command the appropriations. There are also public relations officers who work with the general public who pay the taxes. The almost unfailing appearance of some kind of external threat in the news stories before the appropriations . . . are to be passed is a phenomenon strongly related to some things which go on in Madison Avenue.[4]

A second difference is that the military establishment is a nonprofit organization. But, once again, this does not preclude the possibility that the operation of the military establishment may entail considerable waste and the misuse of resources. One can argue that the military establishment is a kind of monopolist—the sole supplier of national security—and much like a private, profit-seeking monopolist it can obtain a total revenue larger than is essential to provide a given output or level of national security. This will be the focal point for our discussion of military procurement.

A third point of contrast between a private firm and the military establishment is that the demand for the latter's product is based upon the existence of another, potentially hostile military establishment in some other country. Looked at on a worldwide basis, the war industry produces its own demand. The existence of a military establishment in the United States can only be justified by the existence of a military establishment in the Soviet Union, Communist

[3] This discussion is based upon Kenneth E. Boulding, "The World War Industry as an Economic Problem," in Emile Benoit and Kenneth E. Boulding (eds.), *Disarmament and the Economy* (New York: Harper & Row, Publishers, Incorporated, 1963).

[4] Ibid., p. 8. It is perhaps relevant to note that the Pentagon's public relations budget exceeded $40 million in 1970.

China, and so forth. This is a point of no little import for our later discussion of the disarmament problem.

Finally, the military establishment and the private firm differ dramatically in the labor market. Private firms compete in the free market and obtain workers on a voluntary basis. The military relies upon the conscription of labor. In this respect the military is "an organization which lies somewhere on the continuum between the slave plantation and the free enterprise."[5] Again this is an important distinction which will merit further examination.

War goods procurement

With these distinctions in mind, let us now explore the operation of the military establishment in the product market. The Department of Defense does not actually produce military hardware, but it contracts with private firms to design and produce armaments systems. Has this process of arms procurement by the military been efficient? There is considerable evidence to suggest that it has not.

Ideally, taxpayers might hope for a bilateral monopoly confrontation (Figure 32•8) between the military and such giant corporate suppliers as General Dynamics, Lockheed, McDonnell Douglas, and General Electric wherein the military acts as a monopsonist and seeks below-competitive prices, and the corporations act as monopolists by seeking above-competitive prices. And, hopefully, the outcome might approximate the ideal countervailing power solution wherein actual price and output roughly approximate competitive results. But the relationships are more involved than the countervailing power model suggests, and the outcome is less socially desirable.

First, it is charged by some observers that a tacit "understanding" exists between the military and its weapons suppliers. It has been argued by Galbraith and others that the two have common interests—an expanding defense budget—and that in fact the suppliers come perilously close to being a part of the military bureaucracy.

> There is the fiction that the specialized arms contractor is separate from the services. The one is in the public sector. The other is private enterprise. . . . [But] the dividing line between the services and their specialized suppliers exists increasingly in the imagination. Where a corporation does all or nearly all of its business with the Department of Defense; uses much plant owned by the Government; gets its working capital in the form of progress payments from the Government; does not need to worry about competitors for it is the sole source of supply; accepts extensive guidance from the Pentagon on its management; is subject to detailed rules as to its accounting; and is extensively staffed by former service personnel, only the remarkable flexibility of the English language allows us to call it private enterprise. Yet this is not an exceptional case, but a common one. General Dynamics, Lockheed, North American-Rockwell and such are public extensions of the bureaucracy. Yet the myth that they are private allows a good deal of freedom in pressing the case for weapons, encouraging unions and politicians to do so, supporting organizations such as the Air Force Association which do so, allowing executives to press the case and otherwise protecting the military power. We have an amiable arrangement by which the defense firms, though part of the public bureaucracy, are largely exempt from its political and other constraints.[6]

"Pentagon capitalism"

An even harsher critic of the military establishment contends that we have moved significantly and ominously beyond the "military-industrial complex" about which President Eisenhower warned us in his now-famous farewell address in 1961. General Eisenhower had in mind a rather loose and informal group of high military officers, defense-oriented firms, and certain members of the Congress and executive branch of government who were bound together by a common "ideology" favorable to the maintenance and expansion of American military power. Seymour Melman has contended that during the Kennedy administration the military-industrial complex was in effect reorganized on the basis of the principles of corporate management into a "state-management" system. Under the new state-management the Pentagon is the central management office, and producers of military goods in effect have become

[5]Ibid., p. 7.

[6]Statement by John Kenneth Galbraith before the Subcommittee on Economy in Government, *The Military Budget and National Economic Priorities, Part 1* (Washington, 1969), pp. 5–6.

subsidiary enterprises of the Pentagon. That is, the buyer-seller market relationship which formerly existed between the Pentagon and military contractors and provided at least a measure of independence between the two was altered into state-management of the war industry because of the great dependence of the firms upon military contracts and the fact that elaborate military procurement procedures and practices resulted in deep penetration of the managerial decision making of military suppliers by the Pentagon. In Melman's words:

> An industrial management has been installed in the federal government, under the Secretary of Defense, to control the nation's largest network of industrial enterprises. With the characteristic managerial propensity for extending its power . . . the new state-management combines peak economic, political, and military decision-making. Hitherto, this combination of powers in the same hands has been a feature of statist societies—communist, fascist, and others—where individual rights cannot constrain central rule.[7]

According to Melman, the primary motivation of this new state-management is the maintenance and extension of its decision-making power; that is, like other large industrial managements, it is inclined to measure its own success by the volume of goods produced, the number of employees under its control, the volume of its investments, and so forth. Melman contends that this new military state-management system, which dwarfs such corporate giants as General Motors and AT&T, and its motivation to expand have resulted in decisions which are irrational on both military and economic grounds. Examples: The United States has developed an incredible overkill capacity whereby "we can now deliver more than six tons of TNT for each person on our planet;"[8] the continuation and expansion of an extremely costly war in Vietnam without discernible political-ideological or economic benefits; the Pentagon's position that the United States' balance of payments deficit should be alleviated, not by cutting military expenditures abroad, but by expanding international arms sales; the preference for universal military training or, at least, the military draft as a method of military procurement. All these decisions and positions, according to Melman, can only be deemed "rational" when viewed against the state-management's objective of maintaining and extending its control and size.

We will evaluate the Galbraith-Melman views later in our discussion. At this point let us consider in more detail the operation of DOD in both the product and labor markets.

The costs of military procurement

Recent congressional studies claim that literally billions of dollars have been wasted each year in the process of military procurement. For example, major weapons systems have frequently resulted in final costs two or three times as great as initial cost estimates. Consider two much-publicized illustrations. The original cost estimates of the F-111 airplane order was $4.9 billion in 1963. By 1968 a cost overrun of $9.7 billion had spiralled the cost of the original order to $14.6 billion, or $8.6 million per plane! Air Force cost estimates of $3.4 billion for 120 C-5A jet transports in 1965 had grown to $5.3 billion in 1968—a cost overrun of almost $2 billion.[9]

Why has this happened? The answer might lie in Galbraith's charge that DOD and its suppliers have a mutual interest in an expanding military budget. Or Melman may be correct in contending that the expansion of the military's managerial power and authority has taken precedent over "economizing" in resource use as a fundamental goal. Or the explanation may be the more mundane one that the practices and procedures of armaments procurement are simply faulty and wasteful and therefore have resulted in "a vast subsidy to the defense industry, particularly the larger contractors."[10] Or, as we will note later, cost overruns may be a more-or-less inevitable consequence of the technological complexity and experimental character of most new weapons systems.

[7]Seymour Melman, *Pentagon Capitalism* (New York: McGraw-Hill Book Company, 1970), p. 1.
[8]Ibid., p. 17.

[9]Ibid., pp. 21, 64, and Subcommittee on Economy in Government, *The Economics of Military Procurement* (Washington, 1969), p. 19.
[10]*The Economics of Military Procurement*, p. 4.

It does seem clear that a basic problem in military procurement is the inability of the military to enforce effective cost controls upon suppliers. For example, most contracts are not awarded on the basis of competitive bidding, but rather by direct negotiation with a single supplier. Some experts believe that the absence of competitive bidding by rival suppliers causes procurement costs to be 25 to 50 percent higher than would otherwise be the case. Furthermore, suppliers employ the "buy-in, get well later" method for obtaining defense contracts; that is, a contractor bids "a lower price, higher performance, and earlier delivery than his rivals, knowing Pentagon officials will accept increased costs, less than promised performance, and late delivery."[11] It is also a common occurrence that the development of complex military equipment will necessitate changes in design and production after a contract is awarded. For example, the Minuteman missile program embodied the issuance of thousands of "change orders." The Department of Defense has not required suppliers to keep detailed accounting records of how these change orders—frequently referred to as "contract nourishment" by suppliers—affect costs and therefore contract price. The point is that contractors can readily use change orders as a means for disproportionately inflating costs, contract prices, and their profits. Furthermore, the Pentagon makes "progress payments" which reimburse contractors for as much as 90 percent of their incurred costs; these payments mean that the government is extending interest-free credit to suppliers in advance of product delivery. The government also follows an extremely liberal patent policy in dealing with contractors. Contractors are allowed to obtain exclusive patent rights without charge on inventions developed in carrying out government contracts. "The contractor, in other words, obtains a monopoly which he can exploit for his own private gain in the commercial market for inventions paid for by public moneys."[12] Given the fact that most government contracts are awarded to giant corporations, this "fringe benefit" undoubtedly tends to increase the concentration of economic power.

[11]Ibid., p. 5.
[12]Ibid., p. 7.

The military in the labor market[13]

The use of conscription, or the "draft," as a means of acquiring much of its manpower puts the military at extreme odds with the traditional capitalist concept of free or voluntary occupational choice. Many economists take the position that a volunteer army would be a much superior alternative. But before examining the case for a volunteer army, let us summarize the basic characteristics of the draft.

Under the current conscription system most military manpower is obtained by nonmarket means. Young men reaching eighteen years of age must register with the Selective Service System and are liable for military conscription for one year. The manpower needs of the military, however, have been substantially less than the number of potentially eligible young people available. Thus a kind of rationing problem has existed: From the relatively large number potentially eligible for military service, who should actually serve? This rationing problem has been resolved through an elaborate system of exemptions, deferments, and rejections which has functioned with dubious equity. The system has recently been modified to embody a lottery method of selection. In any event, many economists feel that a volunteer army would be a substantial improvement upon the present system.

Case for a volunteer army

Advocates of a volunteer army rest their case upon a number of points.

1. A volunteer army will result in a more equitable distribution of military manpower costs Under

[13]The present discussion draws heavily upon James C. Miller, III (ed.), *Why the Draft?* (Baltimore: Penguin Books, 1968) and *Report of the President's Commission on an All Volunteer Armed Force* (Washington, 1970). Miller's book, incidentally, is an excellent illustration of the effective application of economic analysis to a specific socioeconomic problem.

conscription a small minority of Americans—those eligible young people who are draftees or "reluctant volunteers"—bear a large and discriminatory implicit tax. That is, they shoulder a disproportionately large and inequitable share of the cost of national defense. The discriminatory tax borne by the draftee is comprised of two parts. First, there is the difference between a draftee's pay (say $2,500 per year) and the income (say $4,500 per year) he might have earned in his best available civilian employment. But this $2,000 differential is based upon the assumption that the draftee would be indifferent between military and civilian employment if the pay rates were the same. In fact, we can presume that draftees and reluctant volunteers have some occupational preference for civilian employments; that is, the military might not simply have to pay $4,500—an amount equal to that obtainable in civilian employment—but perhaps an additional $500 as an "equalizing difference" (Chapter 32). Thus the total implicit tax is roughly equal to the difference between what the draftee is paid and the wage necessary to induce him to volunteer for military service. In our example that tax is $2,500 (=$5,000 − $2,500). Actual estimates suggest that this tax is high, for example, 40 to 50 percent of civilian income. Stated more positively, with a volunteer army manpower would be acquired by paying a market price (income) which would be substantially higher than that now paid to draftees. Taxpayers would have to pay higher taxes to finance the higher price for military labor, but this distribution of military manpower costs is much more equitable than a high and discriminatory implicit tax on the very small percentage of our total population who are draftees and reluctant volunteers.

But one may raise this question: Even if the voluntary army results in greater equity in sharing the cost burden of national defense, won't the total cost of military manpower be substantially increased?

2. The real cost of a volunteer army would be less than a conscripted army of the same size There is no question but that a volunteer army would entail higher budgetary or *money* costs than would a conscripted army of the same size. This is the case because the hidden implicit tax on draftees is shifted to taxpayers and therefore made explicit. But there are good reasons why a volunteer army would entail a smaller *real* cost than conscription. That is, a volunteer army of a given size could be expected to provide greater defensive capability or effectiveness than a conscripted army of the same size.[14] What real cost savings or increases in efficiency might be achieved through a volunteer army?

First, it is argued that the very high turnover rate for draftees (over 90 percent) could be reduced by substituting a volunteer army. This would reduce training costs, on the one hand, and result in a more experienced, more professional, and therefore more effective military force, on the other. Similarly, the morale and "productivity" of military personnel who are serving as the result of free choice would be higher than those of men who are coerced to serve.

It is also hoped that a higher monetary price for military manpower—one which more accurately reflects real costs—will give rise to more efficient decision making in the use of that manpower. Under a conscripted army the low budgetary cost of manpower is conducive to the use of too much labor and not enough capital in both combat and noncombat undertakings (Chapter 31). Furthermore, it is argued that at a higher level the increased budgetary costs of military manpower will cause voters and the Congress to examine military budgets more critically and to force the elimination of wasteful uses of military labor. Finally, it is held that a volunteer army would have beneficial allocative effects in the civilian economy. Employees could hire the best qualified workers rather than those least likely to be drafted. Young people would be less inclined to make irrational decisions with respect to occupational choice, education, and marriage as means of acquiring a draft deferment or exemption.

3. The volunteer army is more consistent with individual freedom of choice than is conscription A fundamental tenet of the capitalistic system is that

[14] Or, alternatively stated, a given level of military manpower effectiveness could be attained with a smaller volunteer army.

laborers should have freedom of occupational choice. Conscription is a system of "involuntary servitude" and is fundamentally inconsistent with free occupational choice. In a more positive sense a volunteer army would necessarily entail higher wages and better working conditions than the draft in order to attract an armed force of a given size. Therefore, a volunteer army would provide a new and improved occupational alternative to young people, thereby extending their range of free occupational choices.

Some objections

There are objections to the volunteer army, a few of which merit comment.[15]

1. In the first place, it is argued that a volunteer army "will cost too much." We know the answer to this point: The monetary or budgetary costs will indeed rise as the result of removing the heavy implicit tax on draftees and making this cost explicit. But as we have seen, the real cost—the sacrifice of real output by the civilian economy for a given level of military manpower effectiveness—will fall.

2. A second criticism is that the volunteer army will give us a powerful, professional military elite—an army of mercenaries—which in accordance with Melman's fears will constitute a growing threat to democratic processes and political freedom. The answer to this criticism is that the military's officers, and particularly the senior officers, are professionals, or "mercenaries," under the present system so this problem exists now. It must be admitted, however, that the problem implied here might be aggravated by a volunteer army. The possible development of a professional army whose corps of junior officers, noncommissioned officers, and enlisted men feel a primary allegiance to their senior officers and not to the nation is a disquieting prospect.

3. Other critics contend that the volunteer army will result in racial imbalance in the armed forces. Would we have a predominantly black army? The answer is that many underprivileged blacks with little education and training now find the military a relatively attractive option and enlist. But as civilian alternatives for blacks hopefully improve, the military may become less attractive to them. And as military wages and working conditions are improved by the volunteer army, blacks may find themselves competing against whites who have had the advantage of more and better education and training. Thus the proportion of blacks in the military will not necessarily rise.

4. Finally, advocates of the volunteer army admit that in the unlikely event of a nonnuclear world war, military manpower needs are not likely to be filled on a volunteer basis; therefore, under such circumstances the volunteer army will have to be supplemented by conscription.

[15]For a more extended discussion the reader should consult Miller, op. cit.

AGGREGATIVE ASPECTS

We have examined the size of the war industry, the costs associated with its existence, and some of the microeconomic aspects of the military establishment's operations in both the product and labor markets. Let us now turn to the implications of the war industry for aggregate economic stability.

Defense spending and stability

Perhaps the main characteristic of military spending by government is the fact that its underlying motivation and rationale is noneconomic. Government military outlays alter in response to international political and military events, rather than in terms of the goal of domestic economic stability. It is not surprising then that changes in military spending have been an important source of economic instability in the post–World War II period. Since World War II, defense spending has tended to fluctuate more than consumption, investment, or the expenditures of state and local governments.

From a long-term, historical standpoint war has been closely linked with inflation. Figure 40·3 is instructive. Consumer prices rose on the order of 15 and 13 percent per year respectively during the Civil War and World War I. Inflation was less dramatic—about 5 or 6 percent per year—during World War II. But this more

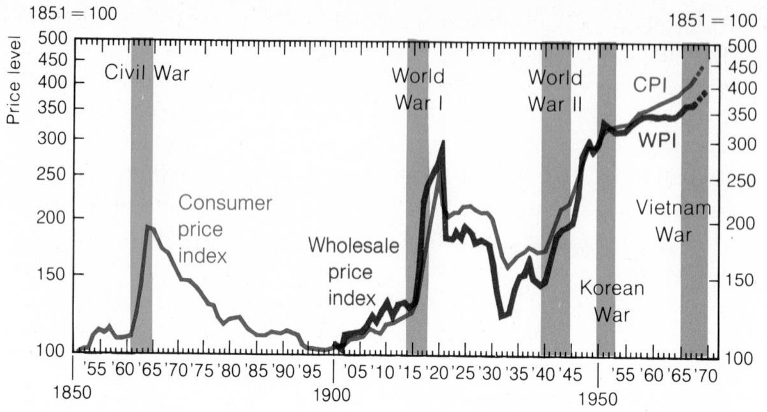

FIGURE 40·3 WAR AND INFLATION

Historically war—and, more specifically, high levels of spending on armaments—has been a cause of inflation in the United States. (First National City Bank of New York, *Monthly Economic Letter*, December 1969, p. 140.)

modest price rise was the result of our entering the war with substantial unemployment and excess productive capacity and the fact that inflationary pressures were suppressed with direct wage and price controls during the war. These controls largely shifted inflationary pressures into the immediate postwar period (Figure 40·3). The Korean War was much less resource demanding, but nevertheless gave rise to a sharp, but short, upsurge in prices. Finally, our recent inflation is traceable to the escalation of the Vietnam War in mid-1965.

Why does this close tie exist between war and inflation? A partial answer is to the effect that "War always fills the purse faster than the pantry." That is, during war, civilian output is curtailed or at least its growth is retarded. But the prosperity to which military spending contributes pumps a rising flow of money income into the civilian economy. The result is a classic case of demand-pull inflation in the civilian sector. However, this explanation is incomplete; we must add the supposition that government is unwilling or regards it inadvisable to levy sufficiently high taxes to match the flows of civilian demand and civilian goods output to the end that the prices of civilian goods and services remain stable. That is, sharp tax increases and a restrictive monetary policy could restrain consumption and investment in the civilian sector and prevent inflation. But government may simply lack the political will to take these steps, or, as was the case during World War II, it might be held that taxes would have to be so high to prevent inflation that work and investment incentives would be undermined. As a result, government may choose to finance a part of its military outlays by borrowing (Chapter 15). If it borrows extensively from the central and commercial banks, debt financing will expand the supply of money and tend to be particularly inflationary (Chapter 14). In any event, war does tend to spawn inflation.

Disarmament: if peace breaks out

What will happen if peace breaks out? The answer is that society can realize a potential "peace dividend" in the form of expanded civilian output. But the achievement of a peace dividend requires appropriate management of the national economy and careful advanced planning to cope with demobilization.

Fiscal-monetary policies We know in general the kinds of macroeconomic policies which would be

appropriate in offsetting a significant cutback in government military spending: (1) reduce net taxes—that is, reduce taxes and increase transfer payments, (2) increase government nondefense expenditures, and (3) move toward an easier money policy. The obvious purpose of all these measures is to bolster the nondefense components of aggregate demand so as to compensate for the cuts in military outlays.

Our experience with disarmament at the conclusion of World War II suggests that reconversion to civilian production can be achieved quite smoothly and without encountering significant unemployment (see table inside covers for 1945–1947, lines 1–5 and 25). Although military outlays fell from about $74 billion in 1945 to just $15 billion in 1946 and $9 billion in 1947, unemployment did not rise above 4 percent in the 1946–1948 period. On the other hand, disarmament took place under conditions which favored a smooth transition to peacetime production. A large portion of the war was financed by government borrowing rather than taxation; hence, consumers and businesses emerged from the war with large stocks of liquid assets or near-monies. Furthermore, the private sector had experienced an extended period of product shortages, the result of the war itself and the preceding Great Depression. Households and businesses converted near-monies into money at the war's end and indulged in a spending spree. Thus consumption and investment rose sharply at the conclusion of hostilities, compensating for most of the decline in military spending. Similarly, spending on civilian social goods and services by state and local governments increased quite spectacularly. Export demand also rose sharply as the devastated countries of Europe looked to America to provide the goods needed for economic recovery. National economic policy was also favorable: tax rates were reduced, and monetary policy made ample credit available at low interest rates. But the point is that we should perhaps be quite cautious in generalizing upon our World War II disarmament experience to conclude that disarmament can be achieved without adverse economic effects. Indeed, although unemployment was avoided after the war, we have noted that inflation was significant in the immediate postwar period.

Several other points about disarmament are in order. First, the task of maintaining full employment so as to realize a substantial peace dividend through disarmament depends upon the size and rapidity of the declines in military spending. Large and sudden cuts in military outlays will obviously be the most difficult to cope with. Second, in determining which policy-mix to use during disarmament we should keep the balanced budget multiplier in mind; a reduction in net taxes has a smaller expansionary impact than does an increase in nondefense government spending of the same amount (Chapter 14). Third, it is clear that the policy-mix chosen will determine the general form in which a peace dividend is taken. For example, cutting taxes is a decision to take the peace dividend in the form of additional private consumption and investment goods. Increased transfer payments imply the bolstering of social insurance and welfare payments or the inauguration of an income maintenance program (Chapter 38). Increased nonmilitary spending by government suggests new or expanded programs in such areas as urban development, pollution abatement, health and education, and crime prevention. The various forms which a peace dividend might take imply a final point: Advanced planning and general agreement on priorities for a peace dividend are crucial "so that wrangling will not paralyze action when the need arises."[16]

Structural problems The efficient adjustment to demobilization entails not only the maintenance of aggregate demand, but also the minimization of structural or allocational problems. In particular, disarmament means substantial changes in the structure of aggregate demand. While the market system tends automatically to negotiate the shift of resources from defense to civilian uses, we know that the market system works slowly and imperfectly. We also know

[16] Roger E. Bolton, *Defense and Disarmament* (Englewood Cliffs, N.J.: Prentice-Hall, Inc., 1966), p. 38. *Economic Report of the President, 1969,* pp. 185–211, contains an interesting "demobilization scenario" based upon the presumed end of hostilities in Vietnam.

that certain industries and regions are very heavily dependent upon military contracts. For example, firms and regions which are very heavily committed to the production of aircraft, missiles, munitions, and electronics equipment for the military might well be hard hit by disarmament. Areas such as Seattle, Boston, Wichita, Los Angeles, and San Diego, wherein military-aerospace work is the dominant source of employment, are obviously vulnerable to serious economic repercussions.

Government might want to alleviate the pains of reconversion to peacetime production in very adversely affected industries by granting temporary tax relief or other subsidies during the period of transition. Also note that the sharp alteration in the composition of aggregate demand implied by disarmament is fertile ground for structural inflation (Chapter 22). Prices may rise in those civilian industries experiencing an increase in aggregate demand, but not fall by offsetting amounts in defense-oriented industries; the net result could be a rising price level.

IN DEFENSE OF DEFENSE

The indictment of the military is a broad-ranging one. It ranges from inefficiencies in the procurement of weapons and manpower to the institutional-political threats implicit in "Pentagon capitalism." It maintains that the military has drained away resources acutely needed for the resolution of pressing domestic problems in the areas of poverty, urban renewal, pollution abatement, and so forth (Chapter 37). It is charged that the absorption of massive amounts of scientific talent in weaponry development and the space program has left many American industries—textiles, building and construction, food processing—in technological backwaters and has made our institutions of higher learning instruments of foreign policy rather than of basic research. This same diversion of resources has allegedly stifled product development in the civilian sector and acted as a drag upon our growth rate. We have overreacted to the threat of communism, it is argued, by developing an irrational "overkill" posture at enormous and needless cost. Indeed, in the nuclear age security is simply unattainable at any price. It is most doubtful, critics of the military contend, that spiraling military spending has brought us security internationally; furthermore, the diversion of resources to the military has contributed to domestic insecurity through the neglect of pressing socioeconomic problems at home.

Some rebuttals

These are obviously serious criticisms of the military, and therefore they deserve careful and critical review. Caught up in the divisive and emotional debate over the war in Vietnam, it is quite possible that war critics have been overzealous in laying the blame for the nation's socioeconomic ills at the door of the military. What can be said in defense of the war industry? Let us first consider rebuttals to some of the specific criticisms of the war industry; then we will consider a more basic positive point.

1. Guns and butter? Has the war industry drained the economic cupboard of resources to the extent claimed by critics? One can argue to the contrary, starting with the basic point that in a growing economy we can simultaneously have more guns *and* more butter. In fact, despite high levels of military spending, many important domestic programs have been initiated and accelerated during the past decade. For example, antipollution programs have expanded significantly, as have antipoverty efforts.

Furthermore, it may be a gross overstatement to contend that the employment of large amounts of high-level scientific manpower by the military-industrial complex has been a primary cause of technological deficiencies in the private economy. It must be recognized that our weapons expenditures affect not only the demand side of the labor market, but also the supply side. By providing fellowships, research grants, and training programs, the defense effort has *directly* increased the supplies of scientists, engineers, and technicians. And by providing a very favorable labor market, the war industry has *indirectly*

increased the supply of high-level scientific and technical manpower by inducing young people to enter these occupations. One can argue that the military-industrial complex has been a vital force in upgrading the quality of our labor force—an accomplishment which may yield substantial long-run social benefits. Finally, although certain industries have remained in the "technological backwaters," this may be more the result of the lethargy and indifference of those industries rather than scarcities of scientific talent.

2. Technological and organizational spillovers There is no question that the war industry has absorbed large amounts of scientific and technical resources which otherwise might have been available for civilian uses. But it must also be recognized that expenditures on defense and space have resulted in important technological "spillovers" for the civilian economy. The existence or commercial feasibility of nuclear power, transport aircraft, and high-speed computers is related to military R & D. Similarly, military research was highly instrumental in the development of silicon transistors, improved anti-motion-sickness drugs, and new flameproofing for fabrics.[17] The space effort has resulted in significant developments in the fields of communication, weather control, and navigation which can have important economic repercussions in both the short and long run. More generally, profound advances in the sciences and technology have been a consequence of generous military budgets.

Finally, complex weaponry and space programs have demonstrated both the ability and methods for organizing massive amounts of human and property resources in the resolution of complex, large-scale problems. These abilities and techniques may prove to be highly relevant in resolving domestic socio-economic problems.

3. Is war inherently inflationary? While there seems to be a positive correlation between wartime spending and rising prices (Figure 40·3), is it entirely accurate to say flatly that "military spending is inflationary"? Or is it perhaps fairer to say that "inflation has accompanied wartime spending because government has failed to invoke counterbalancing monetary and fiscal policies"? For example, inflation during and following World War II was quite severe; but during the Korean War inflation was modest. While much of the differential undoubtedly resulted from differences in the magnitudes of the conflicts, one can argue that the methods of finance were also of significance. During World War II heavy reliance was placed on deficit financing in contrast to the emphasis upon tax financing during the Korean War. These choices contributed to the differing severity of inflation (Chapter 14). Similarly, while it is correct to say that rising military expenditures in Vietnam was an important factor in the inflation of the 1960s (Chapter 11), it is equally correct to argue that more restrictive fiscal and monetary measures could have thwarted this price level instability.

4. Cost overruns: wasteful or inevitable? Perhaps the much-publicized question of cost overruns in military procurement deserves more dispassionate treatment than it has received in public hearings and in the press.

At the outset it is important to note that cost overruns are neither new nor peculiar to the military. Two examples: construction of the interstate highway system and the Rayburn addition to the House Office Building both entailed very substantial cost overruns.

> An office building is not a very complicated structure in comparison with modern military aircraft and guided missiles. . . . Yet we all know of office building after office building for commercial account in which substantial cost overruns were experienced. The same is true in the history of innumerable people who contracted for a house. They wind up paying substantially more than they originally bargained for in the building of their home . . . let us not be carried away by the current list of horrible [cost overrun] examples in the military and assume that this is the product of some evil conspiracy between the government and manufacturers of military goods.[18]

[17] Charles J. Hitch and Roland N. McKean, *The Economics of Defense in the Nuclear Age* (New York: Atheneum, 1967), p. 83.

[18] David Novick, "A Balanced View of Cost Overruns," *Business Horizons*, April 1970, p. 72.

Government committees and journalists who are critical of apparent waste in the military have equally unkind comments to make concerning public programs in such civilian areas as urban renewal, highway construction, Medicare, aid to education, and aviation—not to mention the foreign aid program.

Secondly, the alleged wastes and inefficiencies associated with military procurement may in fact be inevitable consequences of the transactions and products involved. A genuine market system does not and cannot exist for modern weapons, and it is therefore misleading to judge efficiency by conventional market standards or measures. The military, after all, is not purchasing mules and muskets, but highly complex and technologically advanced weapons systems, many of which are often only in the "idea stage" when contracts are let. Furthermore, the financial costs for requisite R & D and investment in productive capacity far exceed the resources of even the largest corporations. And the uncertainty over whether technical specifications desired by the military can in fact be realized may be highly doubtful. Private firms simply cannot undertake such financial risks and uncertainties on their own initiative. Hence, it should not be too surprising that the close interrelationship between buyer and seller and all that goes with it—contracts by negotiation, cost-plus-fixed-fee contracts, progress payments, government provision of real capital—are characteristic of modern weapons production. It is also inevitable that certain kinds of desired military hardware will prove not to be technologically feasible or, alternatively, that the equipment will be rendered technologically obsolete before it is fully developed. Stated differently, when working at the frontiers of technology, we should not be too surprised when a project such as the F-111 turns sour.

It is also important to recognize that technical performance is a much more compelling criterion in weapons acquisition than it is with most civilian goods. In a field noted for rapid technological progress and high rates of obsolescence, it makes little sense to stress cost minimization at the risk of technically inferior weaponry. While rivalry on price may be relatively weak in the weapons acquisition process, DOD can argue with some plausibility that supplier rivalry on the basis of scientific-technical capability is both strong and fundamental.

Survival and growth

But a more positive case can be made for the military: The basic prerequisite of economic development is peace. If we are to survive and to realize the socioeconomic fruits of our scientific and technological progress, major military conflict must be avoided. Ironically, "the very fearsomeness of the threat [of thermonuclear] war is an invitation to a calculating, ruthless power to remove it by force if any happy circumstance presents itself—as, for example, the temporary impotence or vulnerability of the opposing strategic air force; or his own temporary invulnerability resulting from, say, a break-through in air defense technology."[19] In short, given Communist ideological objectives and agreement by Western experts that the Soviet Union "would not hesitate to use force or the threat of force to gain advantage over the West,"[20] the United States has little choice but to make a substantial resource commitment to war goods in order to achieve a position of "mutual deterrence," or what Winston Churchill more pointedly termed a "balance of terror." Former Secretary of Defense Robert McNamara carried the point further, arguing that national security is "inherently priceless" and cannot be measured in terms of dollars: "Our children will hardly admire us for our frugality [in defense spending] if it is achieved at a price they will have to pay in blood and suffering."

THE NATIONAL PRIORITIES DEBATE

The expanding role of the military, on the one hand, and the growing acuteness and increasing awareness of domestic socioeconomic problems, on the other,

[19]Hitch and McKean, op. cit., p. 12.

[20]Subcommittee on Economy in Government, *The Military Budget and National Economic Priorities,* p. 8.

have set the stage for profound national debate concerning the character and objectives of our society. The war in Vietnam has been instrumental in bringing this debate to a head.

Two major schools of political thought have become locked in a contest for the mind and soul of America. One school draws much of its strength from the revolution of military technology, the other from the revolution of rising expectations. One school tends to regard communism as a centrally directed conspiracy that threatens our survival as a free people. The other school believes that communism is breaking up into independent national movements, and sees the main threat to free institutions in the deterioration of our cities and the sickness of our society. One school seeks overwhelming military power to deter fresh Communist adventures, and is willing to risk war in order to prevent the geographic expansion of communism. The other school seeks wider social justice and better economic conditions for Negroes and others who have not participated fully in the advance of prosperity, and holds that the force of moral example can contribute more to our national security than additional bombs or missiles.[21]

The focal point of this debate has been the Federal budget and, in particular, its division between military and civilian uses. In a very real sense the debate is concerned with the establishing of national priorities. Charles L. Schultze, former Director of the Bureau of the Budget, has put the matter this way: "The benefits and costs of proposed military programs cannot be viewed in isolation. They must be related to and measured against those other national priorities which, in the context of limited resources, their adoption must necessarily sacrifice." To this end Schultze proposed the establishment of an "appropriate committee," staffed in part with senators and congressmen chiefly concerned with domestic issues, to achieve a more careful assessment of national priorities as the result of rational and responsible debate which evaluates military and domestic needs directly against one another.[22]

[21]Arthur F. Burns, in Jacob K. Javits, Charles C. Hitch, and Arthur F. Burns, *The Defense Sector and the American Economy* (New York: New York University Press, 1968), pp. 85–86.
[22]Subcommittee on Economy in Government, *The Military Budget and National Economic Priorities,* pp. 45, 56–57.

ADDENDUM: THE DISARMAMENT PROBLEM

Our discussion of the war industry would be incomplete without a brief look at the disarmament problem. If military preparedness is very costly and demobilization problems are manageable, it follows that the potential economic payoff or peace dividend resulting from world disarmament would be large. Why, then, have we not disarmed? This is an extraordinarily complex question, the answer to which is obviously multidisciplinary. But economics—and, in particular, game theory (Chapter 30)—can portray the dilemma of disarmament; that is, economics can illustrate why such a seemingly rational policy is so difficult to realize.

Disarmament and game theory[23]

In the simple model of Table 40·1 we assume the United States and the Soviet Union have just two possible strategies; they may either "arm" or "disarm." The cells in the table show the payoffs from each possible combination of strategies. In reality the payoffs will be multidimensioned, involving not only economic well-being, but security, political prominence, prestige, and so forth. But let us envision the

[23]Our discussion again follows Boulding, op. cit.

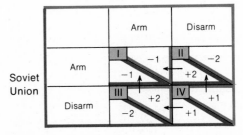

TABLE 40·1

		United States: Arm	United States: Disarm
Soviet Union	Arm	I: −1 / −1	II: −2 / +2
	Disarm	III: +2 / −2	IV: +1 / +1

numerical values as purely economic payoffs. If both nations decide to arm, the payoffs for both will be −1 (cell I). These negative payoffs reflect the diversion of economic resources from civilian uses that increase human welfare to uses that are potentially destructive. If both disarm (cell IV), the payoffs to each will be +1; that is, resources will be released from the war industry to civilian uses. In short, the total payoff is −2 equally distributed between the United States and the Soviet Union, if both arm. If both disarm, the total payoff is +2, again equally divided. But cells II and III complicate the problem. If one nation, say the Soviet Union, arms and the United States is disarmed, then (cell II) the Soviet Union has a payoff of +2, at the expense of the United States. We might suppose that the Soviet Union employs its military dominance to obtain favorable terms of trade with the United States or to otherwise exploit our economy. Cell III shows the opposite situation wherein an armed United States extracts a payoff of +2 from the Soviet Union. Note that total payoffs in cells II and III are zero.

The arrows of Table 40·1 are crucial in that they indicate the dynamics or direction of movement of the disarmament dilemma. Assume both nations are initially disarmed and enjoying payoffs of +1 each. Now it will apparently pay the Soviet Union to arm, thereby moving to cell II and a +2 payoff. But the move from cell IV to II changes the United States' payoff from +1 to −2. The United States can reduce the size of this (negative) payoff to −1 by also arming, moving the two nations to cell I. The same procedure would move the two nations from cell IV to I if the United States attempted to move the outcome from cell IV to cell III by arming. The point is that if either nation moves from a position of mutual disarmament (cell IV), the two nations will end up mutually armed (cell I) and in so doing be worse off.

Longsightedness and third parties

The problem obviously is this: If to both nations mutual disarmament is economically preferable to mutual armament, then how can mutual disarmament be realized? There are two basic possibilities. First, the behavior which causes either nation to move from the initial position of mutual disarmament (cell IV) is shortsighted in that hoped-for gains at an "arm-disarm" position (cell II or III) will be temporary, because the other nation will always react by also arming (cell I). A solution therefore is to instill "longsightedness" in the two parties, that is, "to change the behavior of the parties to conflict themselves, so that they come to take long views and learn to be realistic about the ultimate consequences of their behavior."[24] Specifically, each nation must recognize that the benefits of unilateral arming will be transitory and that its adversary will soon react in such a way as to make it worse off.

A second means of realizing mutual disarmament is to have a third party act as a kind of police force to penalize shortsighted behavior. That is, if the United Nations, for example, were able to impose a penalty of, say, 1½ upon any country that arms, the payoffs of Table 40·1 would obviously be altered so that it would be uneconomical for either party to arm.

While longsightedness—achieved either through moral education and altered behavior or a third party's efforts in altering payoffs—is an eminently sensible course of action in our barebones disarmament model, we must be aware of many real-world obstacles to mutual disarmament. Aside from the obvious prerequisite of mutual trust and appropriate inspection mechanisms, complete disarmament might substantially redistribute power among nations; in particular, the power and influence of the large, economically advanced nations might diminish relative to those of small, less-developed countries. Furthermore, if Melman's concept of "Pentagon capitalism" is reasonably valid, there will be great pressures against disarmament coming from the military who, of course, would be great losers in terms of status and prestige.

SUMMARY

1. Department of Defense expenditures indicate that the military absorbs about 10 percent of the GNP and 10 percent of the nation's manpower. For a

[24] Kenneth E. Boulding, *The Meaning of the Twentieth Century* (New York: Harper & Row, Publishers, Incorporated, 1964), p. 93.

variety of reasons these figures may understate the economic significance of the war industry. On the assumption that full employment can be realized without a large defense establishment, military outlays are a rough measure of the economic burden or real cost of our military posture.

2. The military establishment has encountered severe criticism in recent years as the result of allegedly wasteful practices in the acquisition of weapons systems; in addition some critics express serious alarm concerning the institutional and political overtones associated with the evolution of the "military-industrial complex" or "Pentagon capitalism." Critics also cite the destabilizing effects of military spending.

3. Many economists feel that the conscription of military manpower should be replaced by a volunteer army. They contend that the volunteer army has a number of advantages: *a,* it results in a more equitable distribution of military manpower costs; *b.* it lowers the real cost of achieving a given level of military manpower effectiveness; and *c.* it is consistent with free occupational choice.

4. Defenses of the war industry include the following: *a.* given Communist objectives, a high level of United States military preparedness is essential to peace and, hence, to continued economic development; *b.* military expenditures have resulted in technological advances of great importance to the civilian economy; and *c.* given the size and technological complexities of modern weapons systems, market tests of efficiency in weapons procurement are not relevant.

5. Disarmament implies a potential "peace dividend" as resources are reallocated from military to civilian uses. Full realization of this dividend presumes that demobilization will be unimpeded by unemployment or serious allocative bottlenecks. The basic character of the disarmament dilemma can be envisioned through a simple game-theory model (Table 40·1).

QUESTIONS AND STUDY SUGGESTIONS

1. What is the aggregate size of Department of Defense spending in the United States? How might this figure *a.* understate or *b.* overstate the cost of our military posture?

2. Explain and evaluate:

a. "The United States is an affluent society and therefore does not have to choose between guns and butter."

b. "The largest money costs of a war come after the fighting stops."

3. Compare the objectives and characteristics of the military establishment with those of a private firm. Why are any differences important? Explain why the procurement of weapons systems by the Department of Defense frequently entails large cost overruns.

4. How does the concept of "Pentagon capitalism" differ from the notion of a "military-industrial complex?"

5. What are the economic arguments for an all-volunteer army? Explain: "A volunteer army will result in higher budgetary costs, but lower real costs, for a given level of military manpower effectiveness."

6. Comment upon or critically evaluate each of the following statements:

a. "A great virtue of the volunteer army is that the difficult problems of determining deferments, exemptions and in particular conscientious objector status under the present draft are all automatically resolved."

b. "The trouble with a volunteer army is that it results in a professional army of mercenaries and the likelihood of a military *coup* or civilian control *by* the military is greatly enhanced."

c. "Decisions concerning who might die in defense of our country are too fundamental to be decided by the market."

7. Comment: "Federal spending will continue to be a major source of instability so long as it consists predominantly of military outlays."

8. Explain: "If taken literally, the questions, 'What can we afford for defense?' and 'What are our needs?' are the wrong ones to ask in deciding upon the size of the defense effort. The right question is, 'How much is needed for defense more than it is needed for other purposes?'"

9. Construct a simple game-theory model to portray the dilemma of disarmament.

SELECTED REFERENCES

Economic Issues, 4th ed., readings 76, 77, and 78.

Benoit, Emile, and Kenneth E. Boulding (eds.): *Disarmament and the Economy* (New York: Harper & Row, Publishers, Incorporated, 1963).

Bolton, Roger E. (ed.): *Defense and Disarmament* (Englewood Cliffs, N.J.: Prentice-Hall, Inc., 1966).

Clayton, James L. (ed.): *The Economic Impact of the Cold War* (New York: Harcourt, Brace & World, Inc., 1970).

Hitch, Charles J., and Roland N. McKean: *The Economics of Defense in the Nuclear Age* (New York: Atheneum, 1967).

Mansfield, Edwin (ed.): *Defense, Science, and Public Policy* (New York: W. W. Norton & Company, Inc., 1968).

Melman, Seymour: *Pentagon Capitalism* (New York: McGraw-Hill Book Company, 1970).

Melman, Seymour (ed.): *The War Economy of the United States* (New York: St. Martin's Press, 1971).

Subcommittee on Economy in Government: *The Military Budget and National Economic Priorities, Parts 1–3* (Washington, 1969).

31

THE SOCIAL IMBALANCE CONTROVERSY

The issues we have explored in Part 6—the monopoly and farm problems, the urban crisis, labor-management relations, income inequality, poverty, and the war industry—have all been policy-oriented. That is, they have been concerned with the question of what should be the proper role of government in dealing with particular problems. In the present chapter we raise this question in a more general form: In what proportions should resources be allocated by the private sector (the market system) and the public sector (the budgetary processes of taxing and spending)? This is the question of achieving *social balance,* that is, an optimum division or allocation of resources between the private and public sectors of the economy.

The primary purposes of this chapter are to

1. Present the arguments of those economists who feel a serious social imbalance exists in the composition of our total output
2. Outline a number of criticisms of, and counter-arguments to, the social imbalance position
3. Note briefly various policy means of alleviating social imbalance should it exist now or in the future

THE NATURE OF SOCIAL IMBALANCE

A number of well-known economists[1] currently argue that the evolution of the United States from a nation of relative poverty to one of relative abundance has created a distortion in the composition of the economy's total output. It is asserted that the increasing affluence of American capitalism has been accompanied by a lack of social balance. That is, an inefficient allocation of resources between private goods and services, on the one hand, and social goods and services, on the other, has arisen. Television sets, automobiles, and a profligacy of gadgetry are produced in abundance while education, police and fire protection, streets and highways, and a myriad of basic community services are slighted. In short, it is contended that the development of our economy has fostered the poverty-amidst-plenty problem in a new guise. Private goods abound, but

[1] See, in particular, the works of John Kenneth Galbraith and Francis M. Bator listed at the end of this chapter.

social goods are remarkably deficient. The most eloquent critic of this social imbalance summarizes the problem thus:[2]

> The line which divides our area of wealth from our area of poverty is roughly that which divides privately produced and marketed goods and services from publicly rendered services. Our wealth in the first is not only in startling contrast with the meagerness of the latter, but our wealth in privately produced goods is, to a marked degree, the cause of crisis in the supply of public services. For we have failed to see the importance, indeed the urgent need, of maintaining a balance between the two. . . . The family which takes its mauve and cerise, air-conditioned, power-steered, and power-braked automobile out for a tour passes through cities that are badly paved, made hideous by litter, blighted buildings, billboards, and posts for wires that should long since have been put underground. . . . They picnic on exquisitely packaged food from a portable icebox by a polluted stream and go on to spend the night at a park which is a menace to public health and morals. Just before dozing off on an air mattress, beneath a nylon tent, amid the stench of decaying refuse, they may reflect vaguely on the curious unevenness of their blessings. Is this, indeed, the American genius?

It must be acknowledged at the outset that the question as to whether social imbalance actually exists is ultimately an ethical one; that is, it is a question of what the proper or optimum balance of private and social goods *ought* to be. As a practical matter, it is impossible to compare scientifically the marginal utility of an extra dollar spent on an electric can opener or power mower with that of a marginal dollar of expenditures on education or space research. But admitting that the point of precise social balance is difficult to specify does not detract from the importance of the idea of social imbalance itself. And a group of influential economists has argued that the *direction* of America's social imbalance problem is quite evident. Simple observation—evidence of the eye—is said to be abundant: overcrowded and ill-equipped schools, a paucity of parks and recreation areas, overcrowded streets and inadequate highways, underpaid and undermanned police forces, and so on. Simple statistical comparisons may also be invoked as evidence. In 1970 United States consumers spent $36 billion on recreation as compared with the $17 billion which all state and local governments spent on highways. Approximately $20 billion was spent on advertising, over $10 billion on tobacco products, and almost $28 billion on automobile purchases, as opposed to total (public and private) spending of $27 billion for research and development.[3]

Can one present more comprehensive statistical information on the question of social imbalance? This is one of many instances wherein the choice of statistics and their manipulation can support about any conclusion desired. It is perhaps most relevant to compare government purchases of nondefense goods and services with the size of the nondefense GNP over a period of years, thereby envisioning what share of the "civilian" GNP has been in the form of social goods and services.[4] This comparison reveals that government's nondefense spending as a percentage of the civilian GNP rose quite sharply from 7.5 percent in 1929 to 13.5 percent in 1939. But the increase has been very modest since 1939; government's nondefense spending was slightly less than 16 percent of the civilian GNP in 1970.

SOCIAL IMBALANCE AS AN ECONOMIC PROBLEM

Those who embrace the social imbalance thesis argue that it constitutes a first-rank economic problem because it embodies a misallocation of resources, constitutes a threat to economic stability and full employment, and has critical implications for the economy's rate of economic growth.

[2]John Kenneth Galbraith, *The Affluent Society* (Boston: Houghton Mifflin Company, 1958), pp. 251 and 253. This chapter has drawn heavily upon chaps. 18, 19, and 22 of Professor Galbraith's brilliant but disturbing book.

[3]Data from U.S. Department of Commerce, *Survey of Current Business*, August, 1971.

[4]See Francis M. Bator, *The Question of Government Spending* (New York: Harper & Row, Publishers, Incorporated, 1960), pp. 21–22, and National Planning Association, *National Investment for Economic Growth* (Washington, 1957).

The allocation of resources

As already noted, social imbalance suggests a misallocation of economic resources and, therefore, a failure of the economic system to maximize the satisfactions of society. More specifically, private goods, because of their very superabundance, are now relatively low-priority (low-marginal-utility) goods; for the economy as a whole the production of additional private goods is not a matter of very high urgency. In contrast, the paucity of social goods makes them relatively high-priority (high-marginal-utility) goods; the production of more social goods *is* a matter of relatively high urgency. It is argued, in brief, that given an initial position of social imbalance—too much private and not enough public goods—a reallocation of resources in favor of the latter is a rechanneling of resources away from low- toward high-marginal-utility employments. This obviously accomplishes an increase in the total satisfaction (utility) of society.

Economic stability

Social imbalance is also a crucial economic problem because of the contribution it might make to economic instability and unemployment. Professor Galbraith has emphasized that a sustained demand for private consumer goods has become highly dependent upon want-creating activities (advertising) and the willingness and ability of consumers to increase their indebtedness. Now, if a point is reached at which the myriad of claims and counterclaims of advertisers renders consumers immune to the claims of all, or if any of the innumerable uncertainties which characterize our economy should interrupt the expansion of consumer credit, consumption spending would decline and unemployment would result. The reduction or amelioration of social imbalance would lessen the possibility of these difficulties arising.[5]

> Since public wants are not contrived, they are not subject to a failure of contrivance. Since they are not sold on the installment plan, they are not subject to curtailment by any of the factors which make people unwilling or unable to incur debt. Thus the better the social balance the more immune the economy to fluctuations in private demand.

To these contentions can be added the fact that social balance might contribute to stability for the simple reason that the production of public goods is not motivated by profit considerations.

Economic growth

The final reason for the great significance of social imbalance as an economic problem may well be the most crucial of all. The manner in which a nation chooses to divide its *current* output between public and private goods may well have a bearing upon the size of that economy's *future* output (Chapter 2). More specifically, the present relationship between private and social goods may be an important determinant of the nation's economic growth potential. This is so because many basic social goods—for example, education, basic scientific research, and preventive medicine—are important factors contributing to the process of economic growth. Thus a current public–private goods choice which puts heavy emphasis upon such private consumer goods as automobiles, television sets, and air conditioners and therefore slights the aforementioned social goods is tending to reduce the economy's potential rate of growth in so doing. Bluntly put, a nation which becomes overly obese with consumer goods may, by that very act, undermine its future economic health.

ALLEGED CAUSES OF SOCIAL IMBALANCE

How has this alleged paucity of social goods developed amidst an affluence of private goods? It would seem that mixed capitalism embodies the mechanisms necessary for obtaining a reasonably good balance between private and public output. Consumers govern the production of private goods by the dollar votes they register in the marketplace. Through political means—the process of political voting—consumers in effect select the amount of

[5]Galbraith, op. cit., p. 279.

social goods they desire. Isn't the considered judgment of the majority of citizens in a democracy transformed through dollar and political voting into a rational choice as to how total output is to be divided among private and social goods? How, then, can social imbalance arise?

Economists who envision a social imbalance in current GNP argue that the matter is not as simple as that just described. True, mechanisms exist in mixed capitalism by which the citizenry can render a private–social goods decision. But it is argued that in practice certain historical, attitudinal, and politico-economic forces bear upon this decision so as to cause the production of social goods to fall seriously out of balance with the production of private goods.

What are these distorting forces? In examining the alleged causes of social imbalance, we are in effect asking, "What happens to the amounts of social goods and services demanded and supplied in an expanding economy?"[6] If the amount of social goods demanded seems to increase ahead of the amount supplied, a "disequilibrium" in the form of social imbalance will result. Let us first consider the demand for social goods; then we shall turn to supply considerations.

DEMAND FOR SOCIAL GOODS: WAGNER'S LAW

The forces underlying the growing demand for social goods and services are well known: hot and cold wars, population growth, industrialization and the subsequent urbanization and socioeconomic complexity which it entails, and so forth. Also, of course, as real incomes rise, the demand for both private and social goods can be expected to increase. There are plausible reasons to argue that as real per capita incomes rise, the pattern of consumer wants may alter in favor of relatively more social goods and relatively fewer private goods. This alleged alteration of wants in the growing economy is named *Wagner's Law* for the nineteenth-century German economist Adolph Wagner, who first emphasized this phenomenon.

[6]This is loose terminology, because there is no market for social goods and services in the sense in which there is a market for private goods and services.

The rationale underlying Wagner's Law is relatively simple. The poor society, dominated by agriculture, must consume its entire real income in the form of such basic private goods as food, shelter, and clothing. After these basic wants have been largely fulfilled, the growing wealth of society permits it to turn its attention more and more to the satisfaction of somewhat less urgent but nevertheless important "new needs." Many of these new wants entail social goods—for example, education, streets and highways, police and fire protection. Economic growth is characterized by increasing industrialization and urbanization. This creates a demand for sanitation and sewerage facilities, a water supply, extensive police and fire protection, and similar social goods which in a poorer and simpler agrarian society would be provided by each family for itself or simply not provided at all. Similarly, the industrialization and urbanization which characterize an expanding economy lead to increasing interdependence and greater socioeconomic complexity. Government's regulatory role may therefore be expected to expand markedly. Further, the increased leisure which is typically a component of economic growth can be expected to enhance the demand for both educational and recreational facilities. And, too, the poor society spends little or nothing on national defense for the simple reason that it has little wealth to protect from external aggression; opulence changes this and makes armament expenditures an important social good. All these considerations may give rise to a tendency for the demand for social goods to increase, not only absolutely, but also relative to the demand for private goods.

SUPPLY OF SOCIAL GOODS

Economists who view social imbalance as an acute issue feel there are a number of considerations which prevent the supply of social goods from keeping pace with the growing demand for them.

The mechanisms and mores of capitalism

The very nature of the capitalistic ideology and the attitudes of large numbers of Americans concerning the public sector of the economy have fostered obstacles to an expanding volume of social goods production. As Galbraith has lamented: "Alcohol, comic books, and mouth wash all bask under the superior reputation of the market. Schools, judges, and municipal swimming pools lie under the evil reputation of bad kings." A number of related points are involved here.

The burden of proof The ideology of pure capitalism embraces the concepts of consumer sovereignty, free competitive markets, and a highly restricted economic role for government. This simple portrayal of capitalism provides that virtually all resources are channeled into the production of private goods and services. Furthermore, as the economy evolves and becomes more affluent, the capitalistic ideology obviously furnishes both the philosophical basis and the mechanism—consumer sovereignty and the price system—to ensure ever-increasing amounts of private goods. No such philosophy or mechanism exists to provide automatically for the additional social goods which a growing and more opulent nation may require. Indeed, to supply additional social goods, government must somehow take positive steps to divert resources from private to public uses. In practice, government must convince the citizenry—government must "prove"—that particular social goods are needed and are clearly to be preferred to the private goods at whose expense their production must come in a full-employment economy. An individual need not justify his purchase of a new car, an automatic dishwasher, or a color television set to his community or to the nation. Yet the burden of proof is on government to justify increases in expenditures on highways, educational facilities, urban renewal, or expanded police and fire protection.

The freedom issue In fulfilling its role as a provider of social goods, government is typically viewed as an intruder upon the private sector of the economy and therefore as a threat to individual freedoms. Tax payments which are needed to finance social goods are compulsory—as, indeed, is the consumption of certain social goods and services, such as education. And at any point in time the provision of more social goods in a full-employment economy necessarily entails a restriction of private goods production. Implicit in these observations is the frequently voiced contention that governmental provision of social goods necessarily impinges upon individual liberties. There is little doubt that this view of government as a freedom-limiting agency is partially a public reaction to the upsurges of governmental activity during the Great Depression and World War II.

Attitudes The attitude of much of the business community, large parts of the citizenry, and some political leaders envisions private goods as sacrosanct while public goods are held to be wasteful, of secondary significance, or at best a necessary evil. "The public, as a general rule . . . gets less production in return for a dollar spent by government than from a dollar spent by private enterprise."[7] The closely related notion that "economy in government" is synonymous with minimal public expenditures is still accepted in some quarters (Chapter 6); believers are apparently oblivious of the fact that "economy" is concerned with the employment and efficient allocation of resources.

Compensatory fiscal policy Ironically, the assumption of modern fiscal policy that public expenditure should accommodate itself to changes in the level of private spending has probably fostered such thinking indirectly and inadvertently by implying that public spending is unnecessary so long as the private sector is able to provide full employment. The notion that public expenditures should be of a compensatory character is an obstacle to a careful evaluation of the composition of total output between private and public goods.

[7] National Association of Manufacturers, *The American Individual Enterprise System* (New York: McGraw-Hill Book Company, 1946), p. 952.

Political realities

Because they are overweighted with the representatives of sparsely populated rural areas, the Federal legislature and many state legislatures are relatively insensitive to the acute social goods needs of the heavily populated metropolitan areas. Although recent Supreme Court decisions may provide the necessary corrective, "we do not [now] have majority rule in many of our State legislatures," with the result that rapidly expanding urban areas are denied even the traditional types of community services.[8] The dire social needs of the Negro have been clearly underrepresented, particularly in the Southern states. At the level of local government, we have noted (Chapter 37) heavy dependence upon property taxes works against the expansion of social goods production.

Character of social goods

The inherent characteristics of public goods, as opposed to private goods, also tend to impede their production (Chapter 6). Private goods are sold on the basis of this-for-that transactions in the marketplace. The consumer knows precisely how much he pays for a private good and the benefits he receives from such a purchase are immediate and certain; private goods entail a close link between costs and benefits. Not so with social goods and services. Here benefits are both more remote and less certain than in the case of private goods, and, with minor exceptions, the production of social goods is divorced from specific tax revenues (costs). The production of social goods is undertaken by the government and financed through taxes levied on the community or society as a whole. These differences in the characteristics of social goods and private goods tend to restrict the output of social goods in at least two ways.

Remoteness The remoteness and uncertainty of the benefits derived from social goods prejudice the consumer (voter) against their production. In the realm of goods and services, individuals prefer the immediate and certain benefits of automobiles, television sets, and automatic dishwashers to the remote benefits of public education, municipal libraries, streets and highways, a boost in the budget of the local park department, or the highly uncertain benefits of aid to underdeveloped countries, space research, and a continuing arms race. In general, in any expression of choice between public and private goods which the electorate may render, public goods find themselves at a decided psychological disadvantage because of the remoteness and uncertainty of their benefits.

Unfortunately, there appear to be no alleviating factors or correctives in the picture. As a matter of fact, as the economy matures and becomes more affluent and complex, the benefits of additional social goods may well become increasingly remote and uncertain, further threatening their production. That is, the benefits of the highways, sanitation programs, and public schools provided by the government of a semideveloped economy are less remote and less uncertain than are the benefits of the foreign aid and space research programs undertaken by the governments of those nations which are most highly advanced economically.

It is tempting to argue that if the tax payments which finance social goods were as vague to the citizenry as are their benefits, this would constitute a compensating factor by stimulating the flow of social goods. This is not felt to be the case, however. Relatively few taxes are really hidden taxes.[9] Income and property taxes entail explicit and often detailed consideration by the taxpayer, assuring his awareness of the cost of social goods to him. In contrast, the greatly expanded use of consumer credit in the post–World War II era has undoubtedly made the total cost of private durable consumer goods less immediate and less explicit to buyers, thereby increasing consumer preferences for private as opposed to social goods. In short, the remoteness and uncertainty of the benefits associated with the production

[8] Alvin H. Hansen, *Economic Issues of the 1960's* (New York: McGraw-Hill Book Company, 1961), pp. 111–112.

[9] Sales taxes, which are usually thought of as "hidden," constitute only about 15 percent of total governmental revenues.

of social goods coupled with the immediacy of their tax costs tend to prejudice the production of social goods.

Nonselectivity Another characteristic of social goods or, more precisely, of the public sector, allegedly impedes the achievement of social balance. In the private sector of the economy each individual consumer exercises a great deal of selectivity in his purchases. He considers the marginal utility of various commodities relative to their prices and, subject to his budget restraint, achieves consumer equilibrium by freely selecting those goods and services which yield the greatest marginal utility per dollar and rejecting those yielding less (Chapter 25).

However, the individual's economic dealings with government are on a nonselective basis. The consumer cannot select and therefore contribute financially only to those programs in the public sector's budget which he favors, thereby rejecting and withholding tax payments for programs he disfavors. Thus, assuming realistically that the policy mix of the government is so complex that it will not precisely match the social goods preferences of any specific consumer, it follows that there will invariably be a number of social goods and services which he is compelled to help finance, but of which he does not approve. The practical conclusion is that each voter feels the public budget is too high relative to the benefits he derives from it; that is, each taxpayer feels that a cut in government spending is warranted. Government, therefore, is persistently faced with significant pressure to reduce the flow of social goods and services.

Tax obstacles

It is also asserted that a number of tax problems contribute to social imbalance.

Tax levels Over a period of time the existing level of taxation tends to become acceptable—to become "proper"—to large numbers of households and business for the simple reason that they have had time to adjust to it. As a result, it becomes politically feasible to maintain existing levels of taxation, while at the same time it becomes extremely dangerous politically to raise tax levels. As the existing tax level acquires a measure of sanctity with the passage of time, it becomes exceedingly difficult—short of an obvious and acute military or domestic crisis—to raise the tax level in order to finance an increased flow of social goods production. No doubt the fact that added tax costs are not linked to specific social goods programs and their benefits contributes to this difficulty. Such thinking with respect to the tax level has been more or less formalized by a number of proposals seeking to limit the level of taxes and expenditures to a fixed proportion of the national income. For present purposes the important point is that allegiance to existing tax levels works against the expansion of social goods production.

Allocating tax burdens Even where voters are in general agreement as to the desirability of having more of particular social goods and are willing to accept a higher tax level to finance them, the problem of allocating the tax costs of these goods may still impede their production. For example, a majority of the voters of a community may be convinced of the need for street improvements and repairs, but they may be deadlocked with respect to what taxes should be used to finance these repairs. Should a special tax (for example, a wheel tax) be assessed on automobile and truck owners? Or should property taxes be raised? Or should a city sales tax be used? At the national level the citizenry might be convinced of the need to hasten the development of domestic natural resources or to rebuild many of our urban areas. Again, these projects might be blocked by disagreement as to how the tax cost should be distributed. Most liberals are likely to favor progressive (for example, individual and corporate income) taxes, whereas conservatives plump for regressive (for example, sales and excise) taxes. Inability to reach agreement on the distribution of tax costs may cause the community and the nation to forgo sorely needed social goods and services.

Tax competition A special tax obstacle to the increased production of social goods exists at the state level. States compete for industry on the basis of low rates or preferential tax structures—for example, a tax structure which omits the income tax. "States compete in niggardliness. . . . The result inevitably is that community services are starved." [10]

Advertising and emulation

Advertising and sales promotion activities, which are an integral part of the production and sale of private goods, are almost entirely absent with respect to social goods. For example, while gigantic advertising campaigns by automobile manufacturers operate to convince consumers of the virtues of being a two-car family, no similar persuasion extols to the citizenry the need for more and better roads on which to operate the ever-expanding mass of automobiles. While advertising stresses the merits of stereophonic phonographs, no similar persuasion suggests that better education may be a prerequisite to appreciating the fine recorded music playable thereon. The public sector, under persistent pressure to reduce expenditures, is prohibited from use of the exhortative techniques which characterize the private sector. The result is a tendency for private to expand ahead of social goods.

Like advertising, emulation also favors greater production of private goods. Families witness the new gadgetry of their neighbors—a second car, an automatic dishwasher, a food freezer, a backyard swimming pool—and feel compelled to "keep pace" by also acquiring these amenities. Emulative inducements work very weakly, if at all, between towns and between states in stimulating the output of social goods and services.

Inflation

The contribution of persistent inflation to the relative shrinkage and deterioration of public goods and services is twofold.

[10] Hansen, op. cit., pp. 112–113.

Labor diversion Inflation causes product and resource prices to rise in a very uneven and irregular fashion. While the incomes of most profit receivers (stockholders and proprietors) and many wage earners rise rapidly and significantly, the wages and salaries of public employees typically rise belatedly and by considerably less than the general level of prices. That is, inflation tends to reduce the real incomes of many government employees. This seems to be particularly true of the employees of state and local governments, where pay scales are highly formalized and quite insensitive to the overall economic environment. Thus, as a practical matter, it is particularly difficult for governmental agencies to match the increasingly lucrative salaries offered by private industries, which, in the mainstream of inflation, are generally in a good position to raise their prices and revenues in pace with or ahead of the general level of prices. In brief, inflation tends to divert human resources from public services to private industry. Through this diversion, inflation discriminates in favor of private goods at the expense of public goods.

Constraining government spending Inflation may contribute to social imbalance in another way. By producing inflationary pressure, a burgeoning private sector tends to create strong political pressures to retrench on government spending as an anti-inflationary technique. The dogma of price level stability is invoked to hold down government expenditures. Given the previously noted disposition to hold taxes at present levels and the questionable effectiveness of a tight money policy, the obvious and politically least offensive means of ameliorating inflation is to restrain government purchases of social goods and services. Thus it is that, when the rate of production of private goods is very high and inflation occurs, the pressure may be greatest for the output of social goods to be constrained. The congressman who, under these circumstances, advocates greater social balance finds himself in the embarrassing position of a "friend of inflation," no matter how crucial the need for the social goods he seeks.

SOME COUNTERARGUMENTS

There are those who seriously question that social imbalance exists or, at least, that it is a pressing problem; and even if it were to assume acute dimensions, it is argued that the suggested remedies may be both ineffective and very costly.[11]

Does social imbalance really exist?

Critics of the social imbalance thesis have raised a number of points in questioning whether or not social imbalance actually exists.

Affluence and the average consumer Overinfatuation with the notion of an affluent society and the conception of extravagant and frivolous consumer spending do not square very well with the fact that the median family income in the United States is currently $9,400, not to mention the fact that about one-tenth of the nation lives in poverty. The vast majority of consumers are *not* in a position to overindulge in unessential goods and trivia. It is inaccurate and misleading to classify any substantial portion of consumer spending as being devoted to low-priority goods or sheer gadgetry. Furthermore, because total spending for consumer durables is only about 15 percent of personal consumption, one must be cautious in exaggerating the emphasis our society puts upon such goods as color television sets, heavily chromed automobiles, and electric can openers.

Growing expenditures on "the new needs" The rates of increase in spending on the allegedly neglected "new needs" of the social imbalance position—for example, education, research, health and welfare services, and so forth—have been very substantial and, in general, have exceeded the rate of growth in the GNP. Although some social needs—for example, urban renewal and the economic revitalization of depressed areas—have admittedly been neglected, overall many of the "new needs" of the social imbalance position have clearly not been ignored by our society at all; on the contrary, they have been accorded substantial attention.

[11]The counterarguments of this section stem primarily from the writings of Henry C. Wallich cited at the end of this chapter.

Forces accelerating social goods production Though the aforementioned obstacles which allegedly impede the expansion of social goods production infer the existence of social imbalance, there are important counterbiases which facilitate the growth of social goods output at the expense of private goods.

1. The apparent unrelatedness of taxation and public spending decisions has admittedly caused the citizenry to view taxes only in the negative sense, that is, as a cost which entails no observable benefits. However, this same unrelatedness has encouraged the public attitude that government spending is costless, that is, the benefits of social goods and services are relatively free. It is argued that the latter attitude has encouraged public goods production more than the former has inhibited it.

2. Assuming that taxing and public spending decisions are related by the citizenry, it is admittedly true that some citizens rebel at paying taxes whose benefits to them as individuals are uncertain. By the same token, others are very willing to vote for expenditures from which they expect to benefit, although they have not contributed. Indeed, our progressive Federal income tax structure means that most of the taxpayers who are in the lower income brackets obtain many social goods at bargain prices; hence, there is every reason for them as a political majority to be inclined to favor and vote for the expansion of social goods.

3. Finally, political reality is such that vocal and active minorities constantly press for and achieve increased public expenditures.

The conclusion, then, is that, considering both the obstacles which inhibit *and* the forces which accelerate social goods production, it is difficult to determine whether, on balance, the public sector is expanding too slowly or too rapidly.

Public spending: a corrective?

Assuming social imbalance actually exists, will the advocated increases in public spending resolve this imbalance? It is argued that for at least two related reasons this need not be the case. First, the com-

plexity of the problem is such that it is misleading to pose it simply as a "public-versus-private expenditure" issue. To suggest that more public and less private spending will resolve social imbalance invokes the implicit assumption that the reallocation of resources from private to public uses will necessarily entail less "unwise" private expenditure and more "wise" public spending, given the value schema of those who insist social imbalance now exists. Is it not possible that reductions in private spending may come more at the expense of adequate housing, medical care, education, and cultural pursuits rather than at the expense of television sets, automobiles, and transistor radios? Might not a disproportionate share of any increase in public expenditures on, say, education be for gymnasiums and stadiums as opposed to laboratories and classrooms? There is no reason to suppose that public spending is inherently "wise" (on high-priority goods) and more conducive to growth, whereas private spending is "unwise" (on low-priority goods) and not conducive to rapid growth. As one critic has put it: "I do not see why transferring expenditures to a government no wiser than the voters who elect it . . . would solve the problem. It would probably replace private folly with official silliness."[12]

Secondly, it is not at all evident that the "new needs" of society are social goods and therefore clearly fall within the public sector. That is, education, research, providing for old age, health services, and so forth lie in the twilight zone between the public and private sectors of the economy. For example, about one-third of the nation's total research expenditures originates in private industry, and the remaining two-thirds in government. And a very substantial portion of total expenditures on education, particularly higher education, is private. Expenditures on health services are predominantly private.

For both these reasons it is allegedly a misleading oversimplification to say that our major scarcities of specific goods and services can be corrected by merely expanding the public sector at the expense of the private sector of the economy.

[12] Ernest van den Haag, "Private and Public Expenditures: A Reappraisal," *Modern Age*, Spring, 1962, p. 148.

The cost of social balance

Even if social imbalance is really an acute problem, certain very substantial costs may be involved in its resolution—costs which may well be prohibitive.

1. In the first place, the provision of tax-financed public services is a crude and inefficient way of meeting consumer needs. This is so because, in contrast to the market, there is no neat this-for-that adjustment of benefits and costs. This poor adjustment means that the taxpayer is likely to get more or less of some public service than he desires. Furthermore, the apparently "free" character of social goods and services provides no incentive for the taxpayer to economize in their use.

2. Short of a military emergency, the balance of interest in our society works against any marked shifts in the composition of public spending. This "balance of interests" effect causes components of the government budget to increase and decrease, not selectively, but rather on an across-the-board basis. Politicians, it is contended, have a low propensity for setting priorities on various social goods and services. If not all public expenditures are conducive to the elimination of social imbalance, the consequence is that increased spending on "desirable" public programs entails a heavy political surcharge in the form of increased spending on other "less desirable" programs. This means that the overall cost of those public programs which are essential in rectifying a condition of social imbalance may be inordinately high. In effect, the dollar of public spending is typically subject to a discount; it only buys, say, 75 or 80 cents' worth of needed, high-priority social goods and services.

3. Of greatest significance is the argument that the expansion of the public sector advocated as a corrective for social imbalance may come at the very high cost of freedom. The cumulative effect of expanding a number of particular government programs could be a serious threat to freedom, despite the fact that each individual program may be of merit. In drawing a line between the public and the private sectors, it must be recognized that not only economics, but also freedom, is involved. "The centralized

economy puts a strain upon democracy and freedom; the free economy does not." As a practical guide, Professor Wallich suggests that because the expansion of government impinges upon freedom and causes[13]

> the cumulative discouragement of private and local initiative . . . , it would have to be shown that the people could do something only very imperfectly, and the government very substantially better, before the government should step in.

CORRECTIVES FOR SOCIAL IMBALANCE

It is not the purpose of this chapter to argue that social imbalance does or does not exist in our economy, but rather to pose the controversy for the reader's understanding and evaluation. Nevertheless, it is interesting to examine what might be done to remedy social imbalance if it now exists or arises in the future as a significant economic problem. Several events and policies would be helpful in redressing social imbalance.

Disarmament

Potentially the happiest solution to the problem of social imbalance would be an end to the war in Vietnam and an effective disarmament agreement. These events would set the stage for a rechanneling of government military spending to such nonmilitary social goods and services as research, education, urban renewal, and so forth. This transfer of government expenditures from defense to nondefense categories has the virtue of imposing no direct constraints upon private goods output; a crude, direct clash between private and public wants is happily avoided. In fact, in the absence of the huge backlog of consumer and business demand and the condition of overemployment which facilitated reconversion after World War II, increased spending on public goods might be imperative in sustaining full employment.

But there is no guarantee that events would unfold in this way. Disarmament might generate tremendous public pressures for tax cuts; tax rates which are acceptable during hot or cold wars might prove highly objectionable when peace breaks out. Our post–World War II experience suggests that it might be naïve to expect any easy or automatic transfer of resources from armaments production to the production of "civilian" social goods and services.

Growth as a palliative

It must also be noted that the extent to which the provision of more social goods collides with the production of private goods depends upon the rate of growth achieved by the economy. The correcting of social imbalance in a static economy—that is, an economy whose GNP is unchanging—obviously implies a painful retrenchment in consumer goods production both absolutely and relatively. However, rapid growth means sizable annual increments in real output (Chapter 20), and a division of this increment which favors social goods can clearly alleviate social imbalance and simultaneously provide for modest increases in total consumption. Moreover, it is of no little significance that such a distribution of the increment might contribute to an acceleration of the growth rate.

Again, this solution is not devoid of problems. Even with a favorable annual growth rate, the correcting of fairly acute social imbalance may require an absolute decline in private consumption. Then, too, the growth process itself may intensify certain aspects of a social imbalance problem. Has it not been noted earlier that the industrialization, urbanization, and environmental problems which characterize economic growth are basic factors underlying the increasing demand for social goods and services?

The budget solution

Aside from the opportunities which disarmament and rapid growth afford for the relatively painless correction of a social imbalance problem, the obvious and more painful option which remains is that of increasing taxes and government spending.

Interestingly enough, some economists who feel

[13]Henry C. Wallich, *The Cost of Freedom* (New York: Harper & Row, Publishers, Incorporated, 1960), pp. 57 and 71.

social imbalance exists have strongly endorsed the greater use of sales taxation as a means of attacking social imbalance.[14] Because they are shifted to consumers, sales taxes raise the prices of consumer goods. The result is that a given total amount of consumer spending commands less private goods and automatically provides more government revenues to reabsorb the released resources through larger purchases of social goods. As private production expands, public revenues and therefore public goods increase on a pro rata basis. Furthermore, given the present high level of marginal income tax rates and the fact that sales taxes are effectuated through the price mechanism, the financing of increased public expenditures by sales rather than income taxation is less likely to blunt incentives. Finally, to the degree that sales taxes are hidden in prices and paid in relatively small amounts spread more or less evenly over a period of time, the cost of the social goods financed thereby is neither very explicit nor very immediate to the taxpayer. To the extent that this remoteness or vagueness of tax costs offsets the remoteness of social goods benefits, the cause of social balance may be furthered.

SUMMARY

1. Economists differ about whether economic growth and the affluence it has brought to our economy have created a social imbalance problem, that is, an overallocation of resources to private goods and an underallocation to social goods. In addition to having an obvious and direct bearing upon the problem of efficiently allocating resources, the social imbalance issue also has implications for economic stability and economic growth.

2. Those who feel that a social imbalance problem now exists argue that the amount of social goods and services demanded has increased ahead of the amount supplied. On the one hand, Wagner's Law asserts that as an economy becomes increasingly wealthy, the demand for social goods and services increases both absolutely and relative to the demand for private goods. On the other hand, there exist in our society a number of obstacles which inhibit social goods production. *a.* The ideological framework of capitalism and the attitudes fostered thereby are not conducive to an expansion of social goods production. *b.* The growing urban population whose social goods needs are most acute is allegedly underrepresented politically. *c.* The remoteness and uncertainty of the benefits from social goods put them at a psychological disadvantage compared with private goods. *d.* A number of tax problems make it difficult to finance social goods production. *e.* Advertising and emulation are forces which tend to pull resources toward private goods production and away from social goods production. *f.* Inflation draws resources from the public to the private sector and simultaneously creates political pressures to cut government spending because private spending is high.

3. Equally respected economists take the opposite position, and in so doing offer a number of counterarguments. *a.* Statistical evidence and a careful consideration of both those forces which retard and those which accelerate social goods production do not bear out the contention that social imbalance exists; they may even suggest that, in general, society's "new needs" are receiving ample attention. *b.* Increased public spending may not correct social imbalance because, first, this falsely assumes that all private goods are low-priority goods and all social goods are high-priority goods, and, second, it is not correct to suppose that all the "new needs" of society entail public, as opposed to private, goods. *c.* The economic and political costs of correcting a social imbalance problem might be more substantial than the problem itself: The nonmarket and "free" character of social goods means that they might

[14] Galbraith notes that the personal and corporate income taxes which provide over 60 percent of Federal tax revenues are progressive and thus admirable agents of social balance. That is, an increase in the national income will result in more than proportionate increases in tax revenues for Federal use. At the same time, he emphasizes that (1) about half of Federal revenues are committed to defense expenditures and (2) social imbalance is more crucial at state and local levels. Galbraith rejects property taxes as a means to social balance because, in contrast to the sales tax, the property tax base is relatively insensitive to changes in the overall level of economic activity. This means that property tax rates must be raised to finance additional social goods, resulting in a conflict with the aforementioned resistance to increases in tax rates. Galbraith, op. cit., pp. 311–315; Hansen, op. cit., pp. 104–110.

easily be overproduced; the tendency of public spending to increase "across the board" rather than selectively imposes a heavy surcharge on the production of high-urgency social goods; and, finally, a substantial increase in the production of social goods may seriously impair individual freedoms.

4. If social imbalance exists now or is encountered in the years ahead, the end of the Vietnam war, disarmament, and the achievement of rapid economic growth are potential means of redressing this imbalance. The most direct approach is simply to increase the public budget.

QUESTIONS AND STUDY SUGGESTIONS

1. What is social imbalance? Why is it an economic problem? Why is social imbalance more likely to arise in a wealthy, growing economy than in a poor, static economy?

2. What is Wagner's Law? Do you think this law is valid? Explain how *a.* the character of social goods, *b.* advertising, and *c.* inflation might contribute to a social imbalance problem.

3. Explain why one might argue that an increase in government spending may not resolve a social imbalance problem.

4. What are the possible economic and political costs of correcting social imbalance? How important do you estimate these costs to be? In your opinion are these costs prohibitive?

5. Carefully evaluate the following statement:[15]

> The root cause of our difficulty lies not in our income or our growth potential but in certain American habits of mind, carried over from earlier phases of our history, and in the workings of the political process, as they affect the allocation of resources. This interplay of intellectual conception and conventional politics conspires to make it difficult for Americans to increase the scale of public outlays except at moments of acute crises. Here lies a danger to the national interest as well as a threat to the quality of American society.

6. Why is the greater use of sales taxes, as opposed to income or property taxes, recommended as a corrective for social imbalance? Why might disarmament and rapid economic growth help correct a social imbalance?

[15] W. W. Rostow, "Summary and Policy Implications," in Joint Economic Committee, *Comparisons of the United States and Soviet Economies* (Washington, 1960), p. 601.

SELECTED REFERENCES

Economic Issues, 4th ed., readings 79 and 80.

Bator, Francis M.: *The Question of Government Spending* (New York: Harper & Row, Publishers, Incorporated, 1960).

Downs, Anthony: "Why the Government Budget Is Too Small in a Democracy," *World Politics,* July, 1960, pp. 541–563.

Galbraith, John Kenneth: *The Affluent Society* (Boston: Houghton Mifflin Company, 1958), particularly chaps. 18, 19, and 22.

Hayek, F. A.: "The *Non Sequitur* of the 'Dependence Effect'," *Southern Economic Journal,* April, 1961, pp. 346–348.

Wallich, Henry C.: *The Cost of Freedom* (New York: Harper & Row, Publishers, Incorporated, 1960), particularly chap. 5.

INTERNATIONAL ECONOMICS AND THE WORLD ECONOMY

7

42

INTERNATIONAL TRADE AND THE ECONOMICS OF FREE TRADE

Thus far our analysis of American capitalism has been based upon the assumption that it is a "closed," or isolated, economy. This obviously is not true. Our economy is linked to other nations of the world through a complex network of international trade and financial relationships. It is the purpose of this and the following two chapters to describe and analyze these relationships and to assess both the advantages and the problems associated with them.

The goals of the present chapter are modest in number, but of fundamental importance. First, we will look briefly at the volume and unique characteristics of international trade. Next, we want to explain the basis for international trade and to assess its economic impact. Our third objective is to set forth and evaluate the cases for free trade and protectionism.

IMPORTANCE AND UNIQUENESS OF WORLD TRADE

Is the volume of world trade sufficiently great or are its characteristics so unique as to merit special consideration? Table 42·1 provides us with a rough index of the importance of world trade for a number of representative countries. Many nations which have restricted resource bases and limited domestic markets simply cannot produce with reasonable efficiency all the goods they want to consume. For such countries exports may run from 30 to 35 percent or more of their GNP. Other countries—the United States and the Soviet Union, for example—have rich and highly diversified resource bases and vast internal markets and are therefore less dependent upon world trade.

But even in the case of the United States, where exports and imports are a small proportion of total output, international trade can be extremely important.

1. In this country, 4 percent of the GNP is a very large figure in absolute terms. In 1970, for example, American exports of goods and services totaled about $63 billion, and imports were about $59 billion. Though there are nations which derive 30 to 35 percent or more of their national incomes from international trade, *the absolute volume of American imports and exports exceeds that of any other nation.*

TABLE 42·1 EXPORTS AS A PERCENTAGE OF GROSS NATIONAL PRODUCT FOR SELECTED COUNTRIES

Country	Percent
The Netherlands	33
Canada	19
West Germany	15
Great Britain	15
Italy	14
France	10
Japan	9
United States	4

Source: United Nations, *Monthly Bulletin of Statistics.* Data are for 1968.

2. Despite the versatility of American capitalism, we are almost entirely dependent upon other countries for our supplies of specific commodities. Bananas, coffee, spices, tea, raw silk, nickel, tin, natural rubber, and diamonds are cases in point. Similarly, a host of American industries are highly dependent upon foreign markets. Almost all segments of agriculture rely heavily upon foreign markets—rice, wheat, cotton, and tobacco exports vary from one-fourth to more than one-half of total output. The chemical, automobile, machine tool, and textile industries are only a few of many American industries which sell significant portions of their output in international markets. Table 42·2 shows the major commodity exports and imports of the United States.

3. Changes in net exports, that is, in the difference between the value of a nation's exports and imports, have multiple effects upon the level of national income in roughly the same fashion as do fluctuations in the various types of domestic spending. A small change in the volume of American imports and exports can have magnified repercussions upon the domestic level of income, employment, and prices.

With these points in mind we need not belabor the significance of international trade for such nations as the Netherlands, Japan, Australia, and Great Britain, whose volumes of international trade constitute substantial fractions of their national incomes.

Aside from essentially quantitative considerations, world trade has certain unique characteristics which make it essential that we devote special attention to it.

1. Though the difference is a matter of degree, the mobility of resources is considerably less between nations than it is within nations. American workers, for example, are free to move from Iowa to California or from Maine to Texas. Of course, there are sociological limits on this mobility, but otherwise there are no serious obstacles. If a worker wants to move, he can do so. Crossing international boundaries is a different story. Immigration laws, not to mention language and cultural barriers, put severe restrictions upon the migration of labor between nations. Different tax laws, different governmental regulations, different business practices, and a host of other institutional barriers limit the migration of real capital over international boundaries.

International trade is a substitute for the international mobility of resources. If human and property resources do not move readily between nations, the movement of goods and services can provide an effective substitute.

2. Each nation uses a different currency. This poses complications (Chapter 43). For example, in buying a British automobile you must first buy British pounds sterling (£) and then spend these pounds on the Hillman or MG of your choice.

3. As we will note shortly, international trade is subject to political interferences and controls which differ markedly in degree and kind from those applying to domestic trade.

THE ECONOMIC BASIS FOR TRADE

But why do nations trade? What is the basis for trade between nations? Stated most generally, the answer is that international trade is a means by which nations can specialize, increase the productivity of their resources, and thereby realize a larger total output than otherwise. As we saw in Chapter 3, specialization

TABLE 42 · 2 PRINCIPAL COMMODITY EXPORTS AND IMPORTS OF THE UNITED STATES, 1970 *(in millions)*

Exports	Amount	Percent of total	Imports	Amount	Percent of total
Machinery	$11,372	27	Automobiles and parts	$ 5,067	13
Automobiles, tractors, etc.	6,549	15	Petroleum and products	2,770	7
Chemicals	3,826	9	Electrical machinery	2,272	6
Grains, cereals, etc.	2,588	6	Iron and steel products	2,032	5
Iron and steel manufactures	1,270	3	Nonferrous ores and metals	1,653	4
Nonferrous metals	893	2	Coffee and cocoa	1,360	3
All other exports	16,104	38	Textiles	1,135	3
Total	$42,602	100	All other imports	23,674	59
			Total	$39,963	100

Source: U.S. Department of Commerce, *Survey of Current Business,* March 1971, pp. S-22 and 23.

according to comparative advantage results in more output from a given volume of resources than does nonspecialized production. Interpersonal and interregional specialization and trade involve a more efficient use of economic resources. The advantages of specialization transcend international boundaries. Sovereign nations, like individuals and regions of a nation, can gain by specializing in those products which they can produce with greatest relative efficiency and trading for those goods they cannot produce efficiently.

While the above rationale for world trade is quite correct, it in a sense begs the question. A more sophisticated answer to the question "Why do nations trade?" hinges upon two points. First, the distribution of economic resources—natural, human, and man-made—among the nations of the world is quite uneven; nations are substantially different in their endowments of economic resources. Second, the efficient production of various goods requires different technologies or combinations of resources.

The character and interaction of those two points can be readily illustrated. Japan, for example, has a large and quite well-educated labor force; skilled labor is abundant and therefore cheap. Hence Japan can produce efficiently (at low cost) a variety of goods whose production requires much skilled labor: cameras, transistor radios, and tape recorders are some examples of such *labor-intensive* commodities. In contrast, Australia has vast amounts of land in comparison with its human and capital resources and hence can cheaply produce such *land-intensive* commodities as wheat, wool, and meat. Brazil possesses the soil, tropical climate, rainfall, and ample supplies of unskilled labor requisite to the efficient low-cost production of coffee. The United States possesses the iron ore, coal, large amounts of capital equipment, and a labor force of considerable skill and competence requisite to the production of steel. Similarly, the United States and other industrially advanced nations are in a strategic position to produce cheaply a variety of *capital-intensive* goods, for example, automobiles, machinery, and chemicals.

It is important to emphasize that the economic efficiency with which nations can produce various goods can and does change over time. Both the distribution

of resources and technology can change so as to alter the relative efficiency with which goods can be produced by various countries. For example, in the last forty to fifty years the Soviet Union has substantially upgraded the quality of its labor force and has greatly expanded its stock of capital. Hence, while Russia was primarily an exporter of agricultural products and raw materials a half century ago, it now exports large quantities of manufactured goods. Similarly, the new technologies which gave rise to man-made fibers and synthetic rubber drastically altered the resource-mix needed to produce these goods and thereby changed the relative efficiency of nations in manufacturing them. In short, as national economies evolve, the size and quality of their labor forces may change, the volume and composition of their capital stocks may shift, new technologies will develop, and even the quantity and quality of land and natural resources may be altered (Chapter 20). As these changes occur, the relative efficiency with which a nation can produce various goods will also change.

INTERNATIONAL SPECIALIZATION AND COMPARATIVE ADVANTAGE

Let us now recall the concept of comparative advantage from Chapter 3 and employ it in analyzing the basis for international specialization and trade in a more sophisticated manner.[1] We employ a simplified trade model to reveal most clearly the basic principles involved.

Two isolated nations

Suppose the world economy is composed of just two nations, say, the United States and Brazil. Assume further that each is capable of producing both steel and coffee, but at differing levels of economic efficiency. To be specific, let us suppose that the United States and Brazilian domestic production possibilities curves for coffee and steel are as shown in Figure 42·1*a* and *b*. Two characteristics of these production possibilities curves must be stressed.

1. We have purposely drawn the "curves" as straight lines, in contrast to the concave-from-the-origin type of production possibilities boundaries introduced in Chapter 2. That is, we have in effect replaced the law of increasing costs with the assumption of constant costs. This simplification will greatly facilitate our discussion. With increasing costs, the comparative costs of the two nations in producing coffee and steel would obviously vary with the amounts produced, and comparative advantages might even change. The assumption of constant costs permits us to complete our entire analysis without having to shift to different comparative-cost ratios with every variation in output. The constant-cost assumption will not seriously impair the validity of our analysis and conclusions. We shall note later in our discussion the effect of the more realistic assumption of increasing costs.

2. The production possibilities lines of the United States and Brazil are obviously different. As suggested in the preceding section concerning the basis for international trade, land is presumably abundant and capital is relatively scarce in Brazil. This biases Brazil's production possibilities line toward the production of land-intensive products such as coffee. Conversely, the presumed abundance of capital and other relevant resources (ore, coal, and so forth) biases the United States's production possibilities line toward the production of steel, a capital-intensive good. Stated another way, the resource endowments of the two nations differ and therefore their production possibilities differ.

We note in Figure 42·1*a* that under full-employment conditions the United States can increase its output of steel 1 ton by reducing its coffee output 1 ton. That is to say, in the United States the domestic exchange ratio or *cost ratio* for the two products is 1 ton of steel for 1 ton of coffee, or simply $1S = 1C$. The United States, in effect, can "exchange" a ton of steel for a ton of coffee domestically by shifting resources from steel to coffee. Our constant-cost assumption means that this exchange or cost ratio prevails for all possible shifts on the United States's

[1] The reader might want to review pages 43 to 46 at this point.

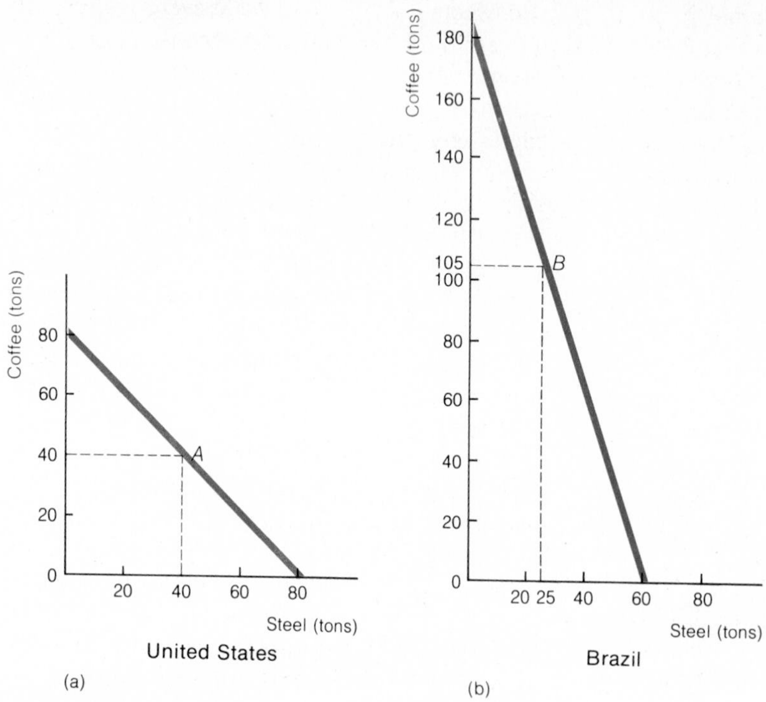

FIGURE 42·1 PRODUCTION POSSIBILITIES FOR THE UNITED STATES AND BRAZIL

The two production possibilities lines show the amounts of coffee and steel the United States (*a*) and Brazil (*b*) can produce domestically. The production possibilities for both countries are straight lines because we are assuming constant costs. The different cost ratios—$1S = 1C$ for the United States and $1S = 3C$ for Brazil—are reflected in the different slopes of the two lines.

production possibilities curve. We will assume that point *A* on the production possibilities line is regarded in the United States as the optimum product-mix. The choice of this combination of 40 tons of coffee and 40 tons of steel is presumably rendered through the price system, as described in Chapter 4.

Brazil's production possibilities line reveals a different exchange or cost ratio. In Brazil the domestic cost ratio for the two goods is 1 ton of steel for 3 tons of coffee, or $1S = 3C$. Suppose that the optimum product-mix in Brazil is indicated by point *B* in Figure 42·1*b* and entails 105 tons of coffee and 25 tons of steel.

It is essential to note that, measuring its price or cost in terms of steel, coffee is expensive in the United States; it takes a whole ton of steel to get 1 ton of coffee. By comparison, coffee is cheap in Brazil; a ton of steel is worth 3 tons of coffee there. Similarly, measured in terms of coffee, steel is expensive in Brazil; it costs 3 tons of coffee to get a single ton of steel. But steel is comparatively cheap in the United States; a single ton of coffee will exchange for a ton of steel.

Two nations with specialization and trade

The fact that the cost ratios for steel and coffee differ in the two countries is the basis for mutually beneficial specialization and trade. Specifically, we know that the United States has a comparative (cost) advantage in steel; that is, it must give up less coffee (1 ton) to get a ton of steel domestically than is the case in Brazil. Conversely, Brazil has a comparative (cost) advantage in coffee. As compared with the United States, where it costs a full ton of steel to get a ton

of coffee, it costs only $\frac{1}{3}$ ton of steel to get a ton of coffee in Brazil. The important point is that *if the United States and Brazil specialize according to comparative advantage and begin to trade with one another, combinations of steel and coffee become available to both nations which are superior to those attainable domestically.* This comes about because trade establishes a new exchange ratio between steel and coffee whereby the United States can obtain *more than* 1 ton of coffee for 1 ton of steel and Brazil can obtain 1 ton of steel for *less than 3* tons of coffee!

The terms of trade

How is this new exchange ratio determined? We know that the United States can get 1 ton of coffee at a price or cost of 1 ton of steel domestically, but by trading with Brazil the United States can get up to 3 tons of coffee for each ton of steel. Thus the United States will obviously gain by specializing in steel and exporting steel in exchange for Brazilian coffee. Similarly, Brazil can get a higher price in terms of steel in the United States for its coffee than it can domestically. So Brazil exports coffee to the United States in exchange for our steel. But we know that because $1S = 1C$ in the United States, the United States must get *more than* 1 ton of coffee for each ton of steel exported or it will simply not pay the United States to export steel in exchange for Brazilian coffee. That is, the United States must get a better price (more coffee) for its steel in the world market than it can get domestically, or else trade will not be advantageous. Similarly, because $1S = 3C$ in Brazil, we know that Brazil must be able to get 1 ton of steel by exporting some amount *less than* 3 tons of coffee. Brazil must be able to pay a lower price for steel in the world market than it must pay domestically, or it will not wish to engage in international trade. Thus we can be certain that the international exchange ratio or *terms of trade* must lie somewhere between

$1S = 1C$

and

$1S = 3C$

But where will the actual world exchange ratio fall between the $1S = 1C$ limit (established by cost conditions in the United States) and the $1S = 3C$ limit (determined by cost conditions in Brazil)? This question is very important, because the exchange ratio determines how the gains from international specialization and trade are divided among the two nations. Obviously, the United States will prefer a rate close to $1S = 3C$, say, $1S = 2\frac{1}{2}C$. Americans want to get a great deal of coffee for each ton of steel they export. Similarly, Brazil desires a rate approximating $1S = 1C$, say, $1S = 1\frac{1}{2}C$. Brazil wants to export as little coffee as possible for each ton of steel it receives in exchange.

The actual exchange ratio that will materialize between the two limits depends upon world supply and demand conditions for the two products. If the overall world demand for coffee is weak relative to its supply and the demand for steel is strong relative to its supply, the price of coffee will be low and that of steel high. The exchange ratio will settle near the $1S = 3C$ figure preferred by the United States. Under the opposite world supply and demand conditions, the ratio will settle near the $1S = 1C$ level most favorable to Brazil.

The gains from trade

Let us arbitrarily suppose that the international exchange ratio or terms of trade are actually $1S = 2C$. The possibility of trading on these terms permits each nation to supplement its domestic production possibilities line with a *trading possibilities line.* This can be seen in Figure 42·2*a* and *b*. Just as a production possibilities line shows the options that a full-employment economy has in obtaining one product by shifting resources from the production of another, so a trading possibilities line shows the options that a nation has by specializing in one product and trading (exporting) its speciality to obtain the other product. The trading possibilities lines in Figure 42·2 are drawn on the assumption that both nations specialize in accordance with comparative advantage and therefore that the United States specializes completely in steel (point S in Figure 42·2*a*) and Brazil

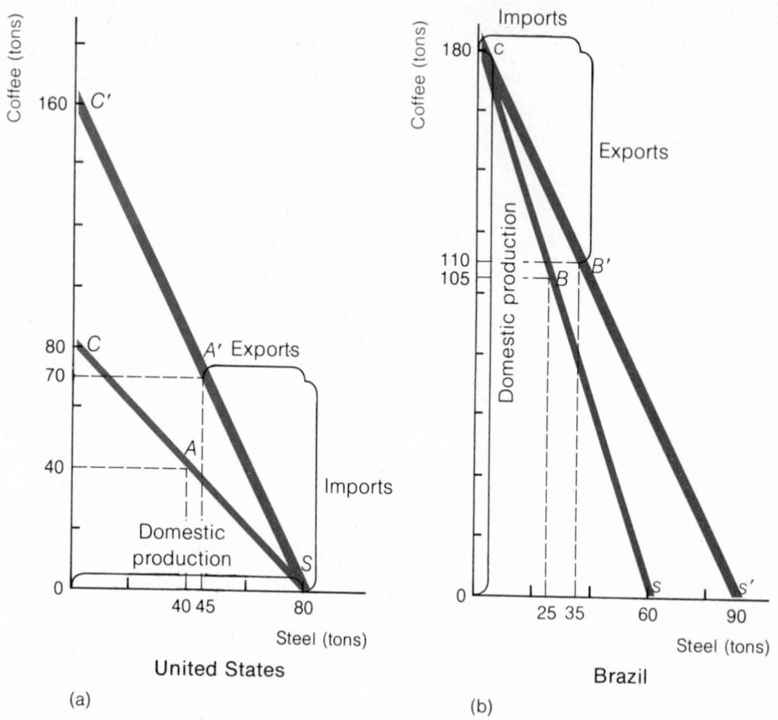

FIGURE 42·2 TRADING POSSIBILITIES LINES AND THE GAINS FROM TRADE

As a result of international specialization and trade, the United States and Brazil can both realize levels of output superior to those attainable on their domestic production possibilities curves. For example, the United States in (*a*) can move from point *A* on its domestic production possibilities line to point *A′* on its trading possibilities line; similarly, Brazil in (*b*) can move from *B* to *B′*.

completely in coffee (point *c* in Figure 42·2*b*). Now, instead of being constrained by its domestic production possibilities line and having to give up 1 ton of steel for every ton of coffee it wants as it moves up its domestic production possibilities line from point *S*, the United States, through trade with Brazil, can get 2 tons of coffee for every ton of steel it exports to Brazil as it moves up the trading line *SC′*. Similarly, we can think of Brazil as starting at point *c*, and instead of having to move down its domestic production possibilities line and thereby having to give up 3 tons of coffee for each ton of steel it wants, it can now export just 2 tons of coffee for each ton of steel it wants by moving down its *cs′* trading possibilities line.

The crucial fact to note is that by specializing according to comparative advantage and trading for those goods produced with the least relative efficiency domestically, both the United States and Brazil can realize combinations of steel and coffee which lie beyond their production possibilities boundaries. *Specialization according to comparative advantage results in a more efficient allocation of world resources, and larger outputs of both steel and coffee are therefore available to the United States and Brazil.* To be more specific, suppose that at the $1S = 2C$ terms of trade, the United States exports 35 tons of steel to Brazil and Brazil in return exports 70 tons of coffee to the United States. How do the new quantities of steel and coffee available to the two nations compare with the optimum product-mixes that existed before specialization and trade? Point *A* in

TABLE 42·3 INTERNATIONAL SPECIALIZATION ACCORDING TO COMPARATIVE ADVANTAGE AND THE GAINS FROM TRADE (*hypothetical data; in tons*)

Country	Outputs before specialization	Outputs after specialization	Amounts exported (−) and imported (+)	Outputs available after trade	Gains from specialization and trade
United States	40 steel 40 coffee	80 steel 0 coffee	−35 steel +70 coffee	45 steel 70 coffee	5 steel 30 coffee
Brazil	25 steel 105 coffee	0 steel 180 coffee	+35 steel −70 coffee	35 steel 110 coffee	10 steel 5 coffee

Figure 42·2*a* reminds us that the United States chose 40 tons of steel and 40 tons of coffee originally. Now by producing 80 tons of steel and no coffee, and by trading 35 tons of steel for 70 tons of coffee, the United States can enjoy 45 tons of steel and 70 tons of coffee. This new, superior combination of steel and coffee is shown by point *A′* in Figure 42·2*a*. Compared with the nontrading figures of 40 tons of steel and 40 tons of coffee, the United States's gains from trade are 5 tons of steel and 30 tons of coffee. Similarly, we assumed Brazil's optimum product-mix was 105 tons of coffee and 25 tons of steel (point *B*) before specialization and trade. Now by specializing in coffee, and thereby producing 180 tons of coffee and no steel, Brazil can realize a combination of 110 tons of coffee and 35 tons of steel by exporting 70 tons of its coffee in exchange for 35 tons of American steel. This new position is shown by point *B′* in Figure 42·2*b*. Brazil's gains from trade are 5 tons of coffee and 10 tons of steel. As a result of specialization and trade, both countries have more of both products.

The fact that points *A′* and *B′* are positions superior to *A* and *B* is extremely important. You will recall from Chapters 2 and 20 that the only ways a given nation can penetrate its production possibilities boundary are (1) to expand the quantity and improve the quality of its resources or (2) to realize technological progress. We have now discovered a third means—international trade—by which a nation can circumvent the output constraint imposed by its production possibilities curve. The effects of international specialization and trade are tantamount to having more and better resources or discovering improved production techniques.

Table 42·3 summarizes our discussion of comparative advantage and stresses the gains to both nations from specialization and trade. It merits careful consideration by the reader.

Increasing costs

In formulating a straightforward statement of the principles underlying international trade, we have invoked a number of simplifying assumptions. Our discussion was purposely limited to two products and two nations in order to minimize verbiage; multination and multiproduct examples yield similar conclusions. The assumption of constant costs, on the other hand, is a more substantive simplification. Let us therefore pause to consider the significance of increasing costs (concave-from-the-origin production possibility curves) for our analysis.

Suppose, as in our previous constant-cost illustration, that the United States and Brazil are at positions on their production possibilities curves where

their cost ratios are initially $1S = 1C$ and $1S = 3C$ respectively. As before, comparative advantage indicates that the United States should specialize in steel and Brazil in coffee. But now, as the United States begins to expand its steel production, its $1S = 1C$ cost ratio will rise; that is, it will have to sacrifice *more than* 1 ton of coffee to get 1 additional ton of steel. Resources are no longer perfectly shiftable between alternative uses, as the constant-cost assumption implied. Resources less and less suitable to steel production must be allocated to the American steel industry in expanding steel output, and this means increasing costs—that is, the sacrifice of larger and larger amounts of coffee for each additional ton of steel. Similarly, Brazil, starting from its $1S = 3C$ cost ratio position, expands coffee production. But as it does, it will find that its $1S = 3C$ cost ratio begins to fall. Sacrificing a ton of steel will free resources which are only capable of producing something *less than* 3 tons of coffee, because these transferred resources are less suitable to coffee production.

Hence, as the American cost ratio rises from $1S = 1C$ and Brazil's falls from $1S = 3C$, a point may be reached at which the cost ratios are equal in the two nations, for example, at $1S = 2C$. At this point the underlying basis for further specialization and trade—differing cost ratios—has obviously disappeared, and further specialization is uneconomic. And most important, this point of equal cost ratios may be realized where the United States is still producing *some* coffee along with its steel and Brazil is producing *some* steel along with its coffee. *The primary effect of increasing costs is to make specialization less than complete.*

ECONOMIC IMPACT OF WORLD TRADE

What are the major economic effects of international specialization and trade?

Resource allocation and output

We are familiar with the impact of specialization and trade upon resource allocation and output. International specialization causes each country to shift resources away from that product in which it has a comparative disadvantage and toward that product in which it has a comparative advantage. In our example, the United States shifts resources from coffee to steel and Brazil reallocates its resources from steel to coffee. Under the assumption of constant costs, specialization—and hence the reallocation of resources—would be complete. But as we have just seen, under the more realistic assumption of increasing costs, the reallocation of resources is partial and specialization less than complete. These reallocations of resources in accordance with comparative advantage give rise to the production of a larger world output from fixed amounts of resources. Once again, specialization and trade between nations on the basis of comparative advantage entail the more efficient use of world resources.

Product prices

International specialization and trade bring about the redirection of demand so that product prices in the trading countries move toward equality. Recall that prior to trade, steel was relatively cheap in the United States and relatively expensive in Brazil. With trade, Brazilians redirected their demand for steel from their domestic steel to American steel. The consequence was that the total demand (domestic plus foreign) for American steel rose, pulling up the price of American steel. Or, looking at the matter from the other vantage point, as American exports of steel augmented domestic supplies in Brazil, the price of steel in Brazil fell. Take your choice: either approach implies an equalization of the price of steel in the two countries as the result of trade. That is, a single world market and therefore a single world price for steel will result.[2] Recall that in real terms the price of 1 ton of steel before trade was 1 ton of coffee in the United States and 3 tons of coffee in Brazil. With trade, the price of a ton of steel became 2 tons of coffee in both countries.

The same rationale applies to coffee which, before trade, was relatively expensive in the United States

[2] We are simplifying here in that we ignore transportation costs, tariffs, and market imperfections.

and relatively cheap in Brazil. With trade, the demand for Brazilian coffee was augmented by a redirected American demand, and the price of coffee in Brazil therefore went up. Or we can think of Brazilian coffee flowing into the United States, increasing our domestic supply and therefore lowering the price in America. In either event, the price of coffee will tend to be equal in the two countries as the result of trade. In our example, after specialization and trade the world price of coffee became $\frac{1}{2}$ ton of steel for both countries.

Resource prices

Specialization and trade will also *tend* to equalize resource prices in the two countries. Recall that capital is relatively abundant in the United States and land relatively scarce, while in Brazil land is relatively abundant and capital relatively scarce. These conditions are mirrored in resource prices: the price of capital is relatively low in the United States, while the price of land is relatively high. The opposite is true in Brazil: the price of capital is relatively high and that of land relatively low.

Now international trade obviously permits both the United States and Brazil to specialize in that good whose production demands the relatively abundant resource. That is, trade allows the United States to increase its output of steel, a capital-intensive good. Brazil produces more coffee, a land-intensive good. The stimulus for this redirection of production is a redirection of demand. Through trade, the United States's domestic demand for steel is now supplemented by the foreign (Brazilian) demand for American steel. This increased demand for American steel is reflected in the resource market as an increase in the demand for capital. Hence, the price of capital in the United States rises. Conversely, as a result of opening up trade with Brazil, American demand for coffee is redirected from domestic to Brazilian coffee. In the American resource market this is reflected in a decline in the demand for land, and the price of land therefore falls.

The opposite tendencies are at work in Brazil. Through trade Brazil's domestic demand for coffee is now supplemented by foreign (American) demand. In the Brazilian resource market the demand for land will increase and its price will rise. Trade also causes Brazil's domestic demand for steel to be redirected toward American steel; hence the demand for and price of capital will tend to fall in Brazil.

Note carefully what is happening here: In both countries the prices of abundant, relatively cheap resources (capital in the United States and land in Brazil) tend to rise, while the prices of the scarce, relatively expensive resources (land in the United States and capital in Brazil) tend to fall. In short, international trade shifts demand from the scarce and toward the abundant resource in both countries, *tending* to equalize resource prices in the two countries.

Two final points merit emphasis. First, we noted earlier that international trade is a substitute for the international mobility of resources. The meaning of this assertion should now be evident. If capital resources, for example, could move freely between the United States and Brazil, capital would actually flow from the United States (where its price is initially low) to Brazil (where its price is initially high), and this would obviously increase the price of capital in the United States and lower it in Brazil. This would continue until the price of capital was equal in the two countries. While capital has not moved between the two countries, free trade has brought about similar changes in capital prices. The redirecting of Brazil's steel demand from its domestic producers to the United States has increased the price of capital in the United States and simultaneously reduced the price of capital in Brazil. In this sense, trade is a substitute for resource mobility.

Secondly, our discussion of the impact of trade upon commodity and resource prices rests on a number of simplifying assumptions. We have assumed that there are no transportation costs or barriers to trade—for example, tariffs and quotas. Further, both economies are presumably at full employment, and domestic product and resource markets are highly competitive. To the extent that these conditions are not realized, the weaker will be the tendency for product and resource prices to move toward equality.

FREE TRADE VERSUS PROTECTIONISM

The issue of protectionism versus free trade has long been a subject of academic and political debate. Let us first examine the character of tariffs and quotas, the primary means of protectionism.[3] Then we will survey the basic cases for and against free trade.

Protective tariffs and import quotas

Tariffs are simply excise taxes on imported goods; they may be imposed for purposes of revenue or protection. *Revenue tariffs* are usually applied to products which are not produced domestically, for example, tin, coffee, and bananas in the case of the United States. Rates on revenue tariffs are typically modest. *Protective tariffs,* on the other hand, are designed to shield domestic producers from foreign competition. Although protective tariffs are usually not high enough to prohibit the importation of foreign goods, they obviously put foreign producers at a competitive disadvantage in selling in domestic markets.

Import quotas specify the maximum amounts of specific commodities which may be imported in any period of time. Frequently import quotas are more effective in retarding international commerce than are tariffs. A given product might be imported in relatively large quantities despite high tariffs; low import quotas, on the other hand, completely prohibit imports once the quotas are filled. We will emphasize protective tariffs in the following discussion of protectionism.

The imposition of protective tariffs and import quotas is rooted in several motivations.

1. While nations as a whole gain from free international trade, particular industries and groups of resource suppliers can be hurt. In our earlier example, specialization and trade adversely affected the American coffee industry and the Brazilian steel industry. It is easy to see why such groups may seek to preserve or improve their economic positions by persuading the government to impose tariffs or quotas to protect them from the adverse effects of free trade. Such groups have sometimes been highly vocal and politically powerful.

2. During depressions or recessions, nations have sometimes attempted to stimulate their domestic economies by controlling or manipulating their world trade. In particular, recall (Chapter 10) that exports stimulate income and employment at home while imports have the opposite effect. Illustration: One goal of President Nixon's 10 percent import surcharge (Chapter 19) in 1971 was to reduce imports relative to exports, that is, to increase net exports and stimulate domestic income and employment.

3. Post–World War II international tensions have prompted nations to use tariffs and quotas to protect domestic producers of materials and goods essential to mobilization and war.

4. In Chapter 45 we will find that underdeveloped nations have sometimes turned to tariffs and quotas in attempting to industrialize and diversify their economies.

The case for free trade

The compelling logic of the case for free trade is hardly new. Indeed, in 1776 Adam Smith got to the heart of the matter by asserting:[4]

> It is the maxim of every prudent master of a family, never to attempt to make at home what it will cost him more to make than to buy. The taylor does not attempt to make his own shoes, but buys them of the shoemaker. The shoemaker does not attempt to make his own clothes but employs a taylor. The farmer attempts to make neither the one nor the other, but employs those different artificers. All of them find it for their interest to employ their whole industry in a way in which they have some advantage over their neighbors, and to purchase with a part of its produce, or what is the same thing, with the price of a part of it, whatever else they have occasion for.

In modern jargon, the case for free trade comes down to this one potent argument. *Through free trade*

[3] There are many other obstacles to free international trade. The interested reader might consult Committee for Economic Development, *Nontariff Distortions of Trade* (New York: CED, 1969).

[4] Adam Smith, *The Wealth of Nations* (New York: Modern Library, Inc., 1937), p. 424.

based upon the principle of comparative advantage, the world economy can achieve a more efficient allocation of resources and a higher level of material well-being. The resource mixes and technological knowledge of each country are different. Therefore, each nation can produce particular commodities at different real costs. Each nation should produce goods for which its costs are low relative to those of other nations and exchange these specialities for products for which its costs are high relative to those of other nations. If each nation does this, the world can fully realize the advantages of geographic and human specialization. That is, the world—and each free-trading nation—can realize a larger real income from the given supplies of resources available to it. Protection—barriers to free trade—lessens or eliminates the gains from specialization. If nations cannot freely trade, they must shift resources from efficient (low-cost) to inefficient (high-cost) uses in order to satisfy their diverse wants.

A collateral benefit of free trade also should be noted: Unimpeded international trade deters the establishment of domestic business monopolies. As opposed to free trade, protection from foreign competition creates a domestic economic environment more conducive to the development of monopoly and the host of restrictive practices associated therewith.

It is a fair statement to say that the vast majority of economists embrace the case for free trade as an economically valid position. However, economists do, as we shall note shortly, acknowledge the relevance of short-run and politically motivated exceptions to the case for free trade.

The case for protection

Though large in number, the arguments for protection vary greatly in quality. The first two arguments are of some validity under certain conditions and within certain limits. The remaining arguments vary from subtle half-truths to outright fallacies.

1. Infant-industry argument The infant-industry argument contends that protective tariffs are needed for the purpose of allowing new domestic industries to establish themselves. Temporarily shielding young domestic firms from the severe competition afforded by more mature and therefore currently more efficient foreign firms will give the infant industries a chance to develop and become efficient producers. This argument for protection rests upon an alleged exception to the case for free trade. The exception is that all industries have not had and, in the presence of mature foreign competition, will never have the chance to make long-run adjustments in the direction of larger scale and greater efficiency in production. The provision of tariff protection for infant industries will therefore correct a current misallocation of world resources now perpetuated by historically different levels of economic development between domestic and foreign industries.

Though the infant-industry argument has logical validity, these qualifying points must be noted. (*a*) This argument is not particularly pertinent to industrially advanced nations such as the United States. (*b*) In the underdeveloped nations it is very difficult to determine which industries are the infants capable of achieving economic maturity and therefore deserving of protection. (*c*) Unlike old soldiers, protective tariffs rarely fade away but rather tend to persist and increase even after industrial maturity has been realized. (*d*) Most economists feel that, if infant industries are to be subsidized, there are better means than tariffs for doing it. Outright subsidies, or "bounties," for example, have the advantage of making explicit what industries are being aided and to what degree.

2. Military self-sufficiency argument The argument here is that protective tariffs are needed to strengthen industries producing strategic goods and materials essential for defense or war. Unlike the infant-industry argument, the present argument is of a political-military nature. It very plausibly contends that in an uncertain world political-military objectives (self-sufficiency) must take precedence over economic goals (efficiency in the allocation of world resources). Unfortunately, there is no objective criterion for weighing the relative worth of the increase in national security, on the one hand, and the de-

crease in productive efficiency, on the other, which accompany the reallocation of resources toward strategic industries when such tariffs are imposed. The economist can only call the politician's attention to the fact that certain economic costs are involved when tariffs are levied to enhance military self-sufficiency.

This argument is also open to abuses. Virtually every industry can directly or indirectly claim a contribution to national security. Can you name an industry which did not contribute in some small way to the execution of World War II? Aside from abuses, are there not means superior to tariffs which will provide for needed strength in strategic industries? When achieved through tariffs, self-insufficiency gives rise to costs in the form of higher domestic prices on the output of the shielded industry. Hence, the cost of enhanced military security is apportioned arbitrarily among those consumers who buy the industry's product. Virtually all economists agree that a subsidy to strategic industries, financed out of general tax revenues, would entail a more equitable distribution of these costs.

Apart from the infant-industry and military self-sufficiency arguments, the case for restricted trade is very weak. Yet we must outline the remaining contentions in order to explore their shortcomings.

3. Increase domestic employment This argument for tariffs becomes increasingly fashionable as an economy encounters a recession. The core of the argument has already been noted: A trade surplus—that is, an excess of exports over imports—stimulates the domestic economy. By reducing imports, protective tariffs and import quotas will give rise to such a surplus, which will bolster domestic employment.

The shortcomings of this argument are several and serious. First, although the immediate effect of an export surplus is to bolster domestic employment, it is obvious that all nations cannot simultaneously succeed in this endeavor. The exports of one nation must be the imports of another. To the extent that one country is able to stimulate its economy through an excess of exports over imports, some other economy's unemployment problem is worsened by the resulting excess of imports over exports. It is no wonder that tariff boosts and the imposition of import quotas for the purposes of achieving domestic full employment are termed "beggar my neighbor" policies.

In the second place, nations adversely affected by tariffs and quotas are likely to retaliate, causing a competitive raising of trade barriers which will choke off trade to the end that all nations are worse off. It is not surprising that the Hawley-Smoot Tariff Act of 1930, which imposed the highest tariffs ever enacted in the United States, backfired miserably. Rather than stimulate the American economy, this tariff act only induced a series of retaliatory restrictions by adversely affected nations. This caused a further contraction of international trade and tended to lower the income and employment levels of all nations. More recently, the imposition in 1971 of the 10 percent surcharge on foreign imports to stimulate American employment and alleviate our balance of payments difficulties poses the threat of retaliatory measures by our major trading partners and precipitation of a "trade war."

Lastly, in the long run an excess of exports over imports is doomed to failure as a device for stimulating domestic employment. Remember: It is through American imports that foreign nations earn dollars with which to purchase American exports. In the long run a nation must import in order to export. Hence, the long-run impact of tariffs is not to increase domestic employment but at best to reallocate workers away from export industries and toward protected domestic industries. This shift implies a less efficient allocation of resources, that is, an increase in disguised unemployment. Tariffs shift resources away from those industries in which production is so efficient as to provide a comparative advantage. There is little doubt that intelligent, well-timed monetary and fiscal policies are far superior to tariff and quota adjustments as anticyclical techniques.

4. Diversification for stability Closely related to the increase-domestic-employment argument for tariff protection is the diversification-for-stability argument.

The point here is that highly specialized economies—for example, Brazil's coffee economy or Cuba's sugar economy—are dependent upon international markets for their incomes. Wars, cyclical fluctuations, and adverse changes in the structure of industry will force large and frequently painful readjustments upon such economies. It is therefore alleged that tariff and quota protection is needed in such nations to induce greater diversification and consequently less dependence upon foreign markets. This will help insulate the domestic economy from wars and depressions abroad and from random fluctuations in world supply and demand for one particular commodity, thereby providing greater domestic stability.

There is undoubtedly some truth in this argument. There are also serious qualifications and shortcomings. (*a*) The argument has little or no relevance to the United States and other advanced economies. (*b*) The economic costs of diversification may be great; one-crop economies are likely to be highly inefficient in manufacturing.

5. Protect domestic living standards Proponents of tariff protection frequently argue that tariffs are essential to *protect high wages and the high standard of living* now enjoyed in American capitalism. Cheap foreign labor, it is contended, will cause cheap foreign goods to flow into the United States. As a result, the prices of American goods and ultimately wage rates and the level of living will be driven down by this competition.

This appeal is tempting but fallacious. The argument falsely presumes that low foreign wages will automatically mean low prices on foreign goods and high domestic wages mean high prices on domestic goods. This is not necessarily the case. Indeed, the argument conveniently ignores the fact that wage rates and per unit production costs are related through productivity. Hourly wage rates may be high and unit costs and product price low, if productivity is high. And what determines the productivity of labor? Basically the quality of labor and the quality and quantity of the capital with which it is equipped. As compared with most other nations, American labor is high in quality and is extremely well equipped. The consequence is that high wages in the United States usually are accompanied by low unit costs and low product prices. As we have already discovered (Chapter 32), wages are high in the United States for the simple reason that productivity is high!

These comments, of course, do not rule out the fact that in the production of certain articles, higher American productivity is more than offset by the low money wages paid foreign workers. This is particularly likely to be the case where production of a commodity requires much hand labor and little capital equipment, for example, Swiss watches or Japanese toys. Is protection warranted under these circumstances? Certainly not on economic grounds. These nations will simply have a comparative advantage in these lines of production. Limiting American imports of such goods by imposing tariffs will also curtail American exports. The result is that American workers will be released from efficient, high-productivity export industries and absorbed in relatively inefficient, low-productivity industries which can only survive under an umbrella of protective tariffs. This reallocation will lower, not increase, real wages domestically and impair the domestic standard of living.

Though the arguments for protection are many and varied, they fail to overshadow the case for free trade: Unimpeded international trade permits greater specialization and a more efficient allocation of world resources. Under proper conditions, the infant-industry argument stands as a valid exception, justifiable on economic grounds. And on political-military grounds, the self-sufficiency argument can be used to validate protection. Both arguments, however, are susceptible to severe abuses, and both neglect alternative means of fostering industrial development and military self-sufficiency. Most other arguments are semiemotional appeals in the form of half-truths and outright fallacies. These arguments only note the immediate and direct consequences of protective tariffs. They ignore the simple truth that in the long run a nation must import in order to export.

We shall return later to the question of protec-

tionism. In Chapter 43 we will examine the use of tariffs and quotas as a means of correcting a balance of payments deficit. The historical course of American and world tariff policy will be summarized later in Chapter 44.

SUMMARY

1. International trade is important, quantitatively and otherwise, to most nations. World trade is vital to the United States in several respects. *a.* The absolute volumes of American imports and exports exceed those of any other single nation. *b.* The United States is completely dependent upon trade for certain commodities and materials which cannot be obtained domestically. *c.* Changes in the volume of net exports can have magnified effects upon the domestic levels of output and income.

2. International and domestic trade differ in that *a.* resources are less mobile internationally than domestically; *b.* each nation uses a different currency; and *c.* international trade is subject to more political controls.

3. World trade is ultimately based upon two considerations: the uneven distribution of economic resources among nations, and the fact that the efficient production of various goods requires particular techniques or combinations of resources.

4. Mutually advantageous specialization and trade is possible between any two nations so long as the cost ratios for any two products differ. By specializing according to comparative advantage, nations can realize larger real incomes with fixed amounts of resources. The terms of trade determine how this increase in world output is shared by the trading nations. Increasing costs impose limits upon the gains from specialization and trade.

5. In addition to reallocating resources toward those products in which a nation has a comparative advantage, international specialization creates tendencies for both product and resource prices in trading countries to move toward equality.

6. Artificial trade barriers usually take the forms of protective tariffs and import quotas. The basic argument for free trade is that it fosters a more efficient allocation of resources and a higher standard of living for the world as a whole. When applicable, the strongest arguments for protection are the infant-industry and military self-sufficiency arguments. Most of the other arguments for protection are half-truths, emotional appeals, or fallacies which typically emphasize the immediate effects of trade barriers while ignoring long-run consequences.

QUESTIONS AND STUDY SUGGESTIONS

1. In what ways are domestic and foreign trade similar? In what ways do they differ?

2. Answer question 7 at the end of Chapter 3.

3. Assume that by using all its resources to produce X, nation A can produce 80 units of X; by devoting all its resources to Y, it can produce 40 Y. Comparable figures for nation B are 30 X and 30 Y. Assuming constant costs, in which product should each nation specialize? Why? Indicate the limits of the terms of trade. Explain the effects of trade upon resource and product prices in the two nations.

4. "The United States is the world's most efficient producer of primary steel. Yet other nations of the world produce and export steel." Explain. "The United States can produce product X more efficiently than can Great Britain. Yet we import X from Great Britain." Explain.

5. Analyze the following statement carefully and completely:[5]

> In the international division of labor it is not *absolute* advantage that counts; a country's resources may be more productive in all branches of industry than those

[5] Jan Pen, *A Primer on International Trade* (New York: Random House, Inc., 1967), p. 17.

of another country, and yet trade might be profitable for both countries, provided that they concentrate their efforts on the products in which they have a *comparative* advantage. *It is the productivity* [*cost*] *ratios within a country that should differ from the productivity ratios in the partner country.* Commerce is profitable between countries that are unequal, at least in economic structure. *Levels of productivity are tremendously important to the real income of a country, but they do not indicate the possibilities of international trade.*

6. Explain the existence of artificial barriers to international trade.

7. Carefully evaluate the following statements:

a. "Protective tariffs limit both the imports and the exports of the nation levying tariffs."

b. "The extensive application of protective tariffs destroys the ability of the international price system to allocate resources efficiently."

c. "Apparent unemployment can often be reduced through tariff protection, but by the same token disguised unemployment typically increases."

d. "American imports and exports since World War II are higher than they have ever been. This indicates that tariffs are not restricting the volume of trade."

8. "The most valid arguments for tariff protection are also the most easily abused." What are these arguments? Why are they susceptible to abuse?

9. Suppose the existing American tariffs on Swiss watches were abolished. What would be the short-run economic effects upon the American and Swiss watch industries? Upon total American exports to and imports from Switzerland? What would be the long-run effects of this abolishment upon ***a.*** the volume of employment, ***b.*** the allocation of resources, and ***c.*** the standard of living in the two nations?

10. Carefully evaluate the use of artificial trade barriers such as tariffs and import quotas as a means of achieving and maintaining full employment.

SELECTED REFERENCES

Economic Issues, 4th ed., readings 81, 82, and 83.

Ellsworth, Paul T.: *The International Economy,* 4th ed. (New York: The Macmillan Company, 1969), chaps. 1–15.

Kenen, Peter B.: *International Economics,* 2d ed. (Englewood Cliffs, N.J.: Prentice-Hall, Inc., 1967), particularly chaps. 1, 2, and 4.

Kindleberger, Charles P.: *International Economics,* 4th ed. (Homewood, Ill.: Richard D. Irwin, Inc., 1968), chaps. 1–4.

Pen, Jan: *A Primer on International Trade* (New York: Random House, Inc., 1967).

Snider, Delbert A.: *Introduction to International Economics,* 5th ed. (Homewood, Ill.: Richard D. Irwin, Inc., 1971), chaps. 1–9.

THE BALANCE OF PAYMENTS AND EXCHANGE RATES

Chapter 42 was concerned with the underlying basis for international trade. Our discussion centered upon the law of comparative advantage and the fact that free trade would maximize the potential gains from international specialization. The present chapter builds upon Chapter 42 and has these objectives: (1) to introduce explicitly the monetary or financial aspects of international trade, (2) to define, analyze, and interpret the international balance of payments, and (3) to explain the various mechanisms for correcting a balance of payments disequilibrium.

FINANCING INTERNATIONAL TRADE

Although the particular techniques of financing international transactions are rather detailed, their general nature can be readily grasped. The basic feature which distinguishes international from domestic payments is the obvious fact that two different national currencies are involved. Thus, for instance, when American firms export goods to British firms, the American exporter will want to be paid in dollars. But the British importers have pounds sterling. The problem then is to exchange pounds for dollars to permit the American export transaction to occur.

American export transaction

Suppose our American exporter agrees to sell $30,000 worth of machinery to a British manufacturer. Assume that the *rate of exchange*—that is, the rate or price at which pounds can be exchanged for, or converted into, dollars, and vice versa—is $3 for £1. This means that the British importer must pay £10,000 to the American exporter. Let us summarize what occurs in terms of simple bank balance sheets (Figure 43·1) such as those employed in Part 3.

a. To pay for the American machinery, the British buyer goes to his London bank and draws a check on his demand deposit for £10,000.

b. The British firm then sends this £10,000 check

FINANCING A U.S. EXPORT TRANSACTION

LONDON BANK

Assets	Liabilities and net worth
	Demand deposit of British importer −£10,000(*a*)
	Deposit of New York bank +£10,000(*c*)

NEW YORK BANK

Assets	Liabilities and net worth
Deposit in London bank +£10,000(*c*) ($30,000)	Demand deposit of American exporter +$30,000(*b*)

FIGURE 43·1

to the American exporter. But the rub is that the American exporter must pay his employees and materials suppliers, as well as his taxes, in dollars, not pounds. So the exporter sells the £10,000 check or draft on the London bank to some large American bank, probably located in New York City, which is a dealer in foreign exchange. The American firm is given a $30,000 demand deposit in the New York bank in exchange for the £10,000 check.

c. And what does the New York bank do with the £10,000? It in turn deposits it in a correspondent London bank for future sale. To simplify, we assume this correspondent bank is the same bank from which the British firm obtained the £10,000 draft.

Note these salient points. First, American exports create a foreign demand for dollars, and the satisfaction of this demand increases the supply of foreign monies—pounds, in this case—held by American banks and available to American buyers. Second, the financing of an American export (British import) reduces the supply of money (demand deposits) in Britain and increases the supply of money in the United States by the amount of the purchase.

American import transaction

But a question persists: Why would the New York bank be willing to give up dollars for pounds sterling? As just indicated, the New York bank is a dealer in foreign exchange; it is in the business of buying—for a fee—and, conversely, in selling—also for a fee—pounds for dollars. Having just explained that the New York bank would buy pounds with dollars in connection with an American export transaction, we shall now examine how it would sell pounds for dollars in helping to finance an American import (British export) transaction. Specifically, suppose that an American retail concern wants to import £10,000 worth of woolens from a British mill. Again we rely on simple commercial bank balance sheets to summarize our discussion (Figure 43·2).

a. Because the British importer must pay his own obligations in pounds rather than dollars, the American importer must somehow exchange dollars for pounds. He can obviously do this by going to the New York bank and purchasing £10,000 for $30,000—perhaps he purchases the very same £10,000 which the New York bank acquired in the previous American export transaction. This reduces the American importer's demand deposit in the New York bank by $30,000 and, of course, the New York bank gives up its £10,000 deposit in the London bank.

b. The American importer sends his newly purchased check for £10,000 to the British firm, which deposits it in the London bank.

Note that American imports create a domestic demand for foreign monies (pounds sterling, in this

FINANCING A U.S. IMPORT TRANSACTION

LONDON BANK

Assets	Liabilities and net worth
	Demand deposit of British exporter +£10,000(*b*)
	Deposit of New York bank −£10,000(*a*)

NEW YORK BANK

Assets	Liabilities and net worth
Deposit in London bank −£10,000(*a*) ($30,000)	Demand deposit of American importer −$30,000(*a*)

FIGURE 43·2

case) and that the fulfillment of this demand reduces the supplies of foreign monies held by American banks. Similarly, an American import transaction increases the supply of money in Britain and reduces the supply of money in the United States.

By putting these two transactions together, a further point comes into focus. American exports make available, or "earn," a supply of foreign monies for American banks, and American imports create a demand for these monies. That is, in a broad sense, *any nation's exports finance or "pay for" its imports.* Exports provide the foreign currencies needed to pay for imports. From Britain's point of view, we note that its exports of woolens earn a supply of dollars, which are then used to meet the demand for dollars associated with its imports of machinery.

THE INTERNATIONAL BALANCE OF PAYMENTS

The generalization that exports finance imports is only a first approximation, because the economic relationships between nations involve much more than the exporting and importing of goods and services. The spectrum of international transactions is reflected in a nation's balance of payments. Specifically, nations of the world systematically record and summarize *all* the transactions which take place between their residents (including individuals, businesses, and governmental units) and the residents of all other foreign nations and present them in an annual accounting statement called the *international balance of payments.* Despite its name, this statement is more like a business firm's profit and loss statement than a balance sheet. Like a profit and loss statement, a nation's balance of payments records its sales to, and purchases from, all other nations, and it accounts for any differences between its sales (receipts) and its purchases (expenditures). A simplified balance of payments for the United States in 1970 is presented in Table 43·1. Let us analyze this accounting statement to see what it reveals about American international trade and finance. Specifically, what does it tell us about our position in world trade and finance?

Exports and imports of goods and services

The most obvious and perhaps most basic segment of the balance of payments involves the export and import of goods and services. As items 1 and 2 indicate, exports and imports are broadly defined. There is no question about the inclusion of items 1*a* and *b* as a part of American exports. As with domestic trade, international trade involves the exchange of both goods and services. The United States exports not only machinery, automobiles, and farm products, but also sells transportation services, insurance, and

TABLE 43·1 THE UNITED STATES BALANCE OF PAYMENTS, 1970 (*in billions*)

(1) United States exports		$+63.0
(*a*) Goods	$+43.5	
(*b*) Services	+9.8	
(*c*) Income from United States investments abroad	+9.8	
(2) United States imports		−59.3
(*a*) Goods	$−44.7	
(*b*) Services	−9.5	
(*c*) Income from foreign investments in United States	−5.1	
(3) Net balance due United States on exports and imports		$ +3.7
(4) Net remittances		−1.4
(5) Net government transactions: grants, loans, etc.		−3.2
(6) Net capital movements		−4.7
(*a*) United States capital outflow	$ −8.6	
(*b*) Foreign capital inflow to United States	+3.9	
(7) Balance due United States (+) or rest of world (−)		$ −5.6
(8) Financing (balancing) transactions		
(*a*) Decrease in United States holdings of gold and foreign currencies		+3.3
(*b*) Increase in liquid dollar balances held by foreigners		+2.3
		$ 0.0

Source: Federal Reserve Bulletin, April 1971. Details may not add to totals because of rounding.

brokerage services to residents of foreign nations. Note, however, that one of the very special services which foreigners get from the United States consists of the services of American money capital which has been invested abroad. As item 1*c* indicates, the dividend and interest income received from the use of American capital which has been invested in foreign nations is a payment for the American "export" of the services of this capital. United States imports, item 2, obviously include three analogous items. Americans import goods and services, including the services of foreign money capital which has been invested in the United States.

A comparison of items 1 and 2 reveals that United States exports of $63.0 billion exceeded United States imports of $59.3 billion by about $3.7 billion in 1970. Economists call the difference between a nation's total exports and its total imports the *balance of trade.* If a nation's exports exceed its imports, as is the case here, a nation is said to have a balance of trade *surplus.* On the other hand, if a country's imports exceed its exports, it is incurring a trade *deficit.* Note that, because United States exports are the rest of the world's imports and United States imports are the rest of the world's exports, an American trade surplus of $3.7 billion obviously appears as a trade deficit to the rest of the world in its trade with the United States.

In Table 43·1 we have designated American exports with plus signs and American imports with minus signs. You will recall from our earlier discussion of foreign exchange that American exports entail payments of dollars from foreign buyers to the United States. These transactions, which involve dollar "inpayments" to the United States, have been marked plus. Conversely, American imports require that Americans make dollars available to foreigners. Such transactions, which involve dollar "outpay-

ments'' from the United States, have been marked minus. Thus the fact that the balance-due figure is a *plus* \$3.7 billion indicates the United States incurred a trade surplus, and as a result net inpayments of that amount are due the United States from the rest of the world (item 3).

Remittances

A second component of the United States's balance of payments involves remittances—item 4 in Table 43·1. These are private gifts or grants: for example, immigrants' remittances sent to their families in the ''old country'' and pensions going to American citizens who are now living abroad. Note that net remittances to the rest of the world amounted to some \$1.4 billion during 1970.

Government transactions

The first four items in the balance of payments are concerned with transactions involving private parties.[1] Government is also engaged in a variety of international transactions. In particular, item 5 reflects the fact that the United States government makes substantial loans and grants to many nations, largely for purposes of economic development.

These government transactions entailed dollar outpayments of \$3.2 billion in 1970. That is, American government transactions were a source of that much purchasing power to foreign nations. The United States government was, in effect, ''importing'' claims against foreign nations in the case of loans and good will or, as it has been facetiously put, ''thank-you notes'' in the case of grants.

Net capital movements

Americans—both individuals and businesses—may choose to make investments in, and extend loans to, other nations. For example, American corporations may purchase or construct plants or outlets in foreign countries. Or Americans may buy the securities—stocks and bonds—of foreign firms. Or American individuals or firms may make dollar deposits in foreign banks.

All such transactions involve capital outflows in monetary or real form. That is, just like American imports of goods, most of these American investing and lending transactions provide foreigners with American dollars. Indeed, it is quite appropriate to think of American investors and lenders as importing securities—claims of ownership to foreign assets, claims against foreign borrowers, and passbook claims against foreign banks. As item 6*a* indicates, American capital flows going abroad amounted to \$8.6 billion in 1970.[2]

Of course, foreigners can and do engage in similar capital transactions. They may purchase real assets in the United States, buy American stocks and bonds, make deposits in United States banks, and so forth. In these instances, the United States is in effect exporting securities and claims and, as with merchandise or service exports, getting inflows or inpayments of dollars in return. In 1970 capital inflows to the United States were \$3.9 billion, as shown by item 6*b*.

It is appropriate to ask: Why did the United States experience a *net* capital outflow of \$4.7 billion in 1970? Why don't Americans make all their investments in, and loans to, American firms rather than foreign firms? The answer is that Americans invest and lend abroad when they expect the rates of return from these foreign loans and investments to be greater than they can realize domestically. Given the rapid pace of economic expansion experienced by the countries of Western Europe and by Japan (Table 21·2), Americans have simply found it profitable to channel a large volume of loans and investments overseas.

[1] Exception: Military sales by the United States government (\$1.5 billion in 1970) are included in item 1*a*, and government purchases of military goods (\$4.8 billion in 1970) are included in item 2*a* in Table 43·1.

[2] The gathering of data for the balance of payments statement is a most imperfect process. If you look at the official balance of payments statement, you will find an intriguing item called ''errors and omissions,'' which in 1970 amounted to \$1.3 billion. There are indications that the bulk of this item is unrecorded capital outflows, primarily deposits of dollars in foreign banks by Americans traveling abroad. Therefore, the United States capital outflow of \$8.6 billion, item 6*a* in Table 43·1, includes the ''errors and omissions'' item.

Let us now summarize our discussion to this point. Taking items 1 through 6 into account, we find that in 1970 the United States's net exports were positive; that is, we enjoyed a trade surplus and, as a result, foreigners "owed" us $3.7 billion. But as the consequence of American remittances abroad, United States government grants and loans, and private net capital outflows from this country, foreign nations actually obtained $9.3 billion, more than enough to cover *our* trade surplus (*their* trade deficit). Stated differently, as the result of trade and financial transactions, foreigners obtained $5.6 billion more in 1970 than they needed.

Financing transactions: gold and international reserves

The $5.6 billion shown as item 7 measures the United States's *balance of payments deficit* for 1970. This deficit, which we shall define in more detail shortly, means that the United States provided more dollars to the world as a result of its imports, remittances, grants, and net public and private capital outflows, than it earned back through its exports. That is, our exports were not sufficiently large to finance the sum of our imports, public and private grants and remittances, and public and private capital outflows.

What must the United States do to settle up the $5.6 billion difference? Under the existing rules and procedures of the present international monetary system (Chapter 44), the United States's $5.6 billion payments deficit can be financed in essentially two ways. First, the United States may sell off a part of its gold stock or a portion of some widely accepted foreign monies (for example, British pounds) which it may have on hand.[3] That is, gold and certain other widely accepted "convertible currencies" function internationally as money; their general acceptance internationally as a medium of exchange makes them international money or international monetary reserves. Item 8*a* in Table 43·1 suggests that in 1970 the United States relied on this option to a significant degree in settling its payments deficit. As Figure 43·3 indicates, the United States has been forced to sell a large portion of the huge gold stock it held at the end of World War II in settling the persistent and large payments deficits it incurred in the 1950s and 1960s. Our gold stock, which was almost $25 billion in 1949, had fallen to less than $11 billion by the spring of 1971.

A second way in which the United States payments deficit can be handled is simply for foreign countries to hold a part or all of the surplus dollars which reflect the deficit. These dollar balances represent claims against the future output of the United States economy. Hence, in holding larger dollar balances foreign countries are in effect granting us credit; they are saying to us: "We'll settle up later." Furthermore, until August 1971 the United States was committed to convert the dollar balances of foreign governments and their central banks into gold on demand at $35 per ounce.

Question: Why might foreign nations want to hold dollars rather than take gold? For two reasons. First, dollar deposits in banks yield interest income; stocks of gold do not. Second, until rescinded in 1971, the United States's commitment to sell gold at $35 per ounce made dollars "as good as gold."

Items 8*a* and 8*b* in Table 43·1 tell us that the United States settled its 1970 payments deficit partly by reducing its holdings of gold and foreign currencies and partly by having foreign nations hold larger dollar balances.

A peculiar deficit

Deficits usually occur when a nation has a *trade deficit,* that is, when its imports exceed its exports, and it does not receive sufficient inflows of remittances or public and private loans and grants to cover this trade deficit. It must then draw upon its international monetary reserves to finance the deficit.

Our analysis of Table 43·1 makes it clear that the balance of payments deficits which the United States has been encountering for a number of years are rather untypical. This country has typically enjoyed *trade surpluses,* that is, exports have exceeded im-

[3] In Chapter 44 we will find that a nation with a payments deficit can borrow gold and foreign currencies, within rather strict limits, from the International Monetary Fund (IMF).

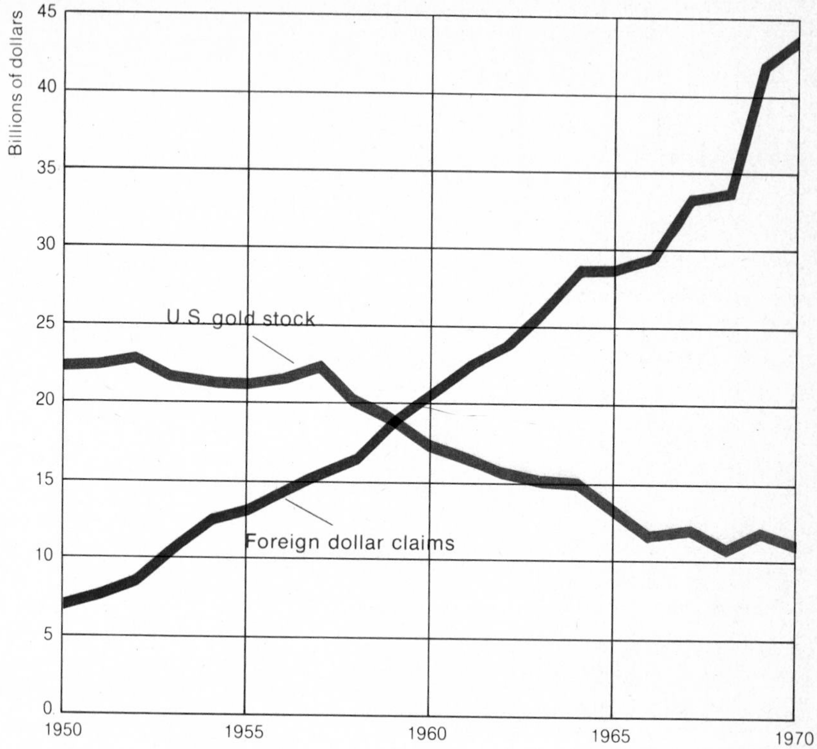

FIGURE 43·3 THE U.S. GOLD STOCK AND FOREIGN DOLLAR CLAIMS SINCE 1950

Chronic balance of payments deficits over almost two decades have drained off much of the United States's gold reserves and have resulted in large foreign holdings of dollar claims. (*Federal Reserve Bulletin.*)

ports. The problem has been that net outflows of remittances and private capital, plus substantial public foreign aid disbursements, have exceeded the trade surplus. Hence despite a trade surplus, the United States has been losing gold and has been faced with growing accumulations of foreign-held dollars. We will examine the historical causes of the United States deficit problem, along with a number of potential remedies, in Chapter 44.

INTERNATIONAL DISEQUILIBRIUM

The meaning of international disequilibrium or, in the present instance, the meaning of a payments deficit, merits further discussion. The balance of payments statement must always balance, for the simple reason that every transaction must be settled, or accounted for, in one way or another. But the fact that this accounting statement balances is of little economic

significance. The really important aspect of the balance of payments is the means by which that balance is achieved.

An analogy

Consider a crude analogy comparing two families. Family 1's earnings or income substantially exceeds its expenditures on goods and services. It uses its unconsumed income to buy stocks and bonds (make loans), to buy real assets such as real estate (make investments), perhaps to make some grants, and to add to its monetary reserves. We would agree that all is well with family 1; it is in good financial shape. Moreover, this family is in equilibrium, in the sense that it can indefinitely maintain this position.

Family 2 is in a different situation. Its expenditures exceed the sum of its earnings plus any loans or grants it might be fortunate enough to receive. Family 2 is in financial difficulty; it is "living beyond its income" and must draw upon its monetary reserves or must borrow to finance the shortfall of its receipts relative to its expenditures. Note that in an accounting sense, inpayments and outpayments are in balance for both families; each family's "balance of payments" with the rest of the economy is in balance. Yet family 2 is clearly in a nonmaintainable or disequilibrium position. Its monetary reserves are presumably limited, and so is its credit; and it therefore cannot continue indefinitely to spend in excess of its receipts. Family 2 is obliged to get its financial house in order.

Autonomous and accommodating transactions

The same general kind of comparison can be applied to nations. Once again, the important consideration is not the fact that the balance of payments balances, but what kinds of transactions occur in achieving that balance. To pursue this point, we must distinguish between autonomous transactions, on the one hand, and accommodating or compensating transactions, on the other.

Autonomous transactions are independent of the balance of payments in the sense that they arise from, or are caused by, factors lying outside the balance of payments statement itself. Five of the items discussed in Table 43·1 (items 1, 2, 4, 5, and 6) are generally considered to be autonomous: exports, imports, remittances, public transactions, and net capital movements. Thus Americans buy goods and services from, and sell goods and services to, foreign nations because of differences in comparative costs. Remittances and government grants and loans are based upon humanitarian, political, or military considerations. Capital movements occur on the expectation that the income earned abroad on investments and loans will exceed the income which is anticipated domestically.

Accommodating transactions occur in order to account or compensate for differences between the inpayments and outpayments which arise from a nation's autonomous transactions. Accommodating transactions can be thought of as balancing transactions, that is, transactions which take place to accommodate or finance payment imbalances associated with the autonomous transactions. Illustration: Suppose a nation's autonomous transactions are such that its exports are \$10 billion and its imports are \$15 billion; it receives remittances of \$1 billion and public grants and loans of another \$1 billion; finally, it receives net capital inflows of \$1 billion. The outpayments associated with these autonomous transactions are \$15 billion, and the inpayments or receipts are only \$13 (\$10 + \$1 + \$1 + \$1) billion. The country has a \$2 billion *dis*equilibrium or, more specifically, a \$2 billion deficit, in its balance of payments. The nation must undertake \$2 billion worth of financing or accommodating transactions to account for the difference between autonomous outpayments and inpayments. These financing transactions will involve sales from its gold stock, reductions in its balances of foreign monies, or increases in the balances of its currency held by other nations.

We can therefore say that the occurrence of accommodating or financing transactions is evidence of a balance of payments disequilibrium. In Table 43·1 items 8*a* and 8*b* are accommodating transactions and are evidence of the United States payments deficit. They indicate that the United States is not

"paying its way" internationally. And although the United States has been realizing deficits for a period of years, these accommodating transactions cannot be maintained indefinitely. We have already seen that the United States has used a substantial portion of its gold stock in financing its payments deficits. We will discover in the next chapter that its trading partners are becoming increasingly reluctant to hold larger dollar balances.

RESTORING INTERNATIONAL EQUILIBRIUM

Because it is a nonmaintainable situation, some adjustments must ultimately occur to correct a balance of payments disequilibrium. The basic problem is to bring autonomous inpayments or receipts into balance or equality with autonomous outpayments. Let us assume for simplicity's sake that a nation's imports exceed its exports and that all other autonomous transactions are zero (in other words, remittances, government transactions, and net capital flows are zero). In this simple framework the disequilibrium can be corrected by reducing imports, increasing exports, or both. There are essentially three means by which the country can return to equilibrium: (1) it can allow exchange rates to fluctuate freely, (2) it can permit adjustments in domestic levels of output, employment, and prices to occur, or (3) it can invoke governmental controls over international trade and finance.

Freely fluctuating exchange rates

When foreign currencies can be freely bought and sold, the rate of exchange between any two currencies will be determined by the forces of supply and demand. Let us examine the rate, or price, at which American dollars might be exchanged for British pounds sterling. As indicated in Figure 43·4, the demand for pounds will be downsloping, and the supply of pounds will be upsloping. Why? The down-

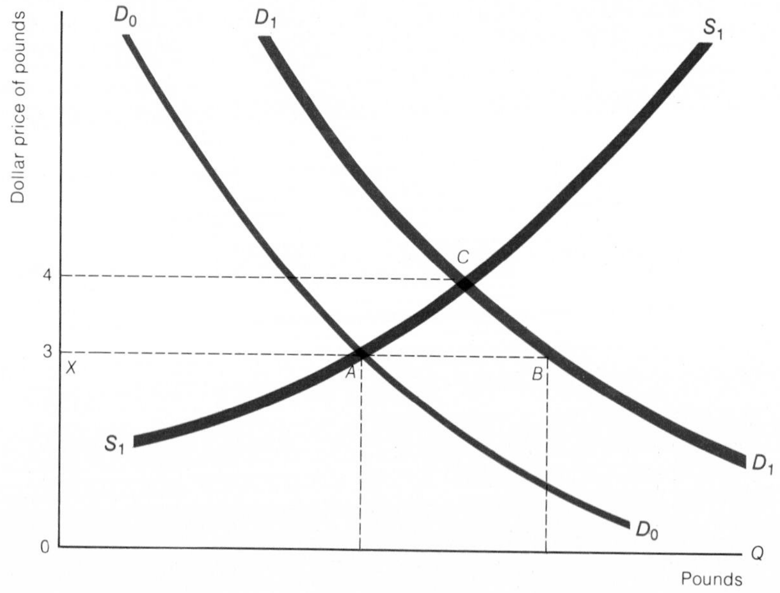

FIGURE 43·4 ADJUSTMENTS UNDER FLEXIBLE EXCHANGE RATES, THE GOLD STANDARD, AND EXCHANGE CONTROLS

Under flexible rates an American trade deficit at the \$3-for-£1 rate would be corrected by an increase in the rate to \$4 for £1. Under the gold standard the deficit would cause changes in domestic prices and incomes, which would shift the demand for (D_1D_1) and the supply of (S_1S_1) pounds into equilibrium at the \$3-for-£1 rate. Under exchange controls the government would ration the available supply of pounds *XA* among persons demanding the quantity *XB*.

sloping demand for pounds shown by D_0D_0 reflects the fact that, if pounds become less expensive to Americans, British goods will become cheaper to Americans. This causes Americans to demand larger quantities of British goods and therefore larger amounts of pounds with which to buy those goods. The supply of pounds is upsloping, as S_1S_1, because, as the dollar price of pounds rises (that is, the pound price of dollars falls), the British will be inclined to purchase more American goods. The reason, of course, is that at higher and higher dollar prices for pounds, the British can obviously get more American dollars and therefore more American goods per pound. In other words, American goods become cheaper to the British, inducing the British to buy more of these goods. Such purchases, we have seen, will make larger and larger quantities of pounds available to Americans.

The intersection of the supply and demand for pounds will determine the dollar price of pounds. Suppose that the equilibrium rate of exchange is $3 to £1. At this rate American-British trade is in balance; American imports from Great Britain create a demand for the precise quantity of pounds which American exports to Great Britain make available.

The adjustment process Now let us assume that American tastes change so that they begin to import more British goods. Americans want more Hillman automobiles, more Scotch whisky, and more Harris tweeds. This increase in imports causes an American trade deficit, and if it is not offset by long-term private loans, investments, and unilateral transfers from Britain, an American balance of payments deficit results. The immediate impact of the increase in American imports from Britain is an increase in the American demand for pounds, as indicated by the shift from D_0D_0 to D_1D_1 in Figure 43·4. Because of this shift, a shortage of pounds equal to *AB* now appears at the existing $3-for-£1 exchange rate. Since this is a free competitive market, the shortage will change the exchange rate (the dollar price of pounds) from $3 for £1 to, say, $4 for £1. This obviously means that the value of the dollar has *depreciated*—that is to say, the dollar is worth less—in international trade.

But at this point we must recognize that the exchange rate is a very special price. Why? Because the exchange rate is the link between *all* domestic (United States) prices and *all* foreign (British) prices. A change in the exchange rate therefore alters the prices of all British goods to Americans and all American goods to potential British buyers. Specifically, this particular change in the exchange rate will alter the relative attractiveness of American imports and exports in such a way as to restore equilibrium in the balance of payments of the United States. From the American point of view, as the dollar price of pounds changes from $3 to $4, the Hillman automobile priced at £500, which formerly cost an American $1,500, now costs $2,000. Other British goods will also be more expensive to Americans. Hence, American imports of British goods will tend to decline. Graphically, this is shown as a move from point *B* toward point *C* in Figure 43·4.

Conversely, from Britain's standpoint the exchange rate, that is, the pound price of dollars, has fallen (from £.33 to £.25 for $1). The international value of the pound has *appreciated.* The British previously got only $3 for £1; now they get $4 for £1. American goods are therefore cheaper to the British, and as a result American exports to Great Britain tend to rise. In Figure 43·4 this is indicated by the move from point *A* toward point *C*. The two adjustments described—a decrease in American imports from Great Britain and an increase in American exports to Great Britain—are precisely those needed to correct the American balance of payments deficit. (The reader should reason through the operation of freely fluctuating exchange rates in correcting an initial American balance of payments surplus in its trade with Great Britain). In short, the free fluctuation of exchange rates in response to shifts in the supply of, and demand for, foreign monies tends to restore international equilibrium automatically.

Disadvantages Though freely fluctuating exchange rates automatically correct a balance of payments disequilibrium, they may entail several serious problems:

1. The risks associated with flexible exchange rates are likely to discourage the flow of trade. To illustrate:

Suppose an American automobile dealer contracts to purchase ten Hillman cars for £5,000. At the current exchange rate of, say, $3 for £1, the American importer expects to pay $15,000 for these automobiles. But if in the two- or three-month shipping period the rate of exchange shifts to $4 for £1, the £5,000 payment contracted by the American importer will now amount to $20,000. Obviously, this unheralded increase in the dollar price of pounds may easily turn the American importer's anticipated profits into substantial losses. Aware at the outset of the possibility of an adverse change in the exchange rate, the American importer may simply not be willing to assume the risks involved. He therefore confines his operations to domestic automobiles, with the result that international trade does not occur in this item. Note, too, that contracting for payment in terms of dollars rather than pounds does not solve the risk problem, but merely shifts the risk to the British exporter.

2. A nation's terms of trade will tend to be worsened by a decline in the international value of its currency. For example, an increase in the dollar price of pounds will mean that the United States must export a larger volume of goods and services to finance a given level of imports from Britain.

3. Freely fluctuating exchange rates may also have some destabilizing effects upon the domestic economy as wide fluctuations stimulate and then depress those industries producing internationally traded goods. Furthermore, if the American economy is operating at full employment and the international value of its currency depreciates as in our illustration, the subsequent rise in American exports and decline in imports will tend to increase net exports and cause domestic price inflation. Conversely, appreciation of the dollar could lower exports and increase imports, tending to cause unemployment.

Changing price and income levels

As the preceding paragraphs explained, allowing the international value of the dollar to depreciate—that is, letting the dollar price of pounds rise—is one way to correct a payments deficit. Example: A ton of American steel may sell for $15 domestically. This ton of American steel will obviously cost a British buyer £5 if the exchange rate is $3 for £1, but only £3.75 when $4 exchange for £1. Depreciation of the value of the dollar as reflected in a shift in the exchange rate from $3 equals £1 to $4 equals £1 will stimulate American exports and help correct a United States payments deficit.

But domestic deflation can have an effect equivalent to that of exchange rate depreciation. *Given the $3 equals £1 exchange rate,* a decline in the domestic price of American steel from $15 to $11.25 per ton will have the same stimulating effect on steel exports, for at this exchange rate it will take only £3.75 to buy a ton of American steel! Obviously, inflation in Britain would also tend to correct a payments disequilibrium by making British goods less attractive to American importers.

If domestic price level changes—deflation in the United States and inflation in Britain—are a possible cure for an American payments deficit, how are these price level adjustments to be brought about? In the first place, the payments deficit itself would automatically tend to cause them. Recall from Figure 43·2 that American imports decrease the supply of money in the United States and increase the money supply in Britain. This obviously means that the net effect of a United States payments deficit—an excess of imports over exports, in our simple case—will be to reduce the money supply in the United States. And this reduction, we know from Chapter 18, tends to be deflationary. Conversely, the balance of payments surplus incurred by Britain will increase her supply of money and tend to cause inflation. In the second place, appropriate monetary and fiscal policies might be necessary in the two countries to ensure that the price level changes are sufficiently great to correct the payments disequilibrium. In particular, the United States might need to invoke a tight money policy and a contractionary fiscal policy to bring about the degree of deflation needed to eliminate its payments deficit.

Equilibrium: At what price? The main advantage of this means of correcting a balance of payments

disequilibrium is that it sidesteps the disadvantages associated with freely fluctuating exchange rates. Because exchange rates are held constant, the risks and uncertainties which accompany fluctuating rates and tend to discourage international trade are avoided, as is the prospect of worsening terms of trade.

But a moment's reflection will reveal formidable objections to stable exchange rates accompanied by domestic price level adjustments.

1. We know (Chapter 11) that changing price levels mean arbitrary changes in the distribution of real income. If these are severe, inflation and deflation can seriously disrupt normal economic activity.

2. More important, however, is the fact that the changes in the money supply which international disequilibrium entails will affect not only the price level, but also the levels of national output and employment. Recalling (Chapter 18) the equation of exchange, *MV* equals *PQ,* we see that a decline in *M* (the money supply) will tend to cause both *P* (the price level) and *Q* (real output and, implicitly, the level of employment) to decline. As a matter of fact, we know that prices are quite sticky or inflexible in a downward direction, so the brunt of any decline in aggregate demand (*MV*) will probably fall on output and employment rather than on the price level. Most economists take the position that such distasteful domestic adjustments are far too high a price to pay for a balance of payments equilibrium. In our example, the "price" of exchange rate stability for the United States is falling price, output, and employment levels—in other words, a recession! Achieving a balance of payments equilibrium and realizing domestic stability are both important national economic objectives; but to sacrifice the latter for the former is to let the tail wag the dog.

Digression: The gold standard It is interesting to note that for a half century prior to World War I, and again for a brief period in the 1920s, most of the major trading nations accepted and participated in an international monetary system whose operation was characterized by exchange rate stability and therefore domestic adjustment of price and output levels as a basic means of achieving balance of payments equilibrium. This system was the international gold standard.

A nation is on the gold standard when it fulfills two conditions:

1. It must define its monetary unit in terms of a certain quantity of gold and stand ready to convert gold into paper money and paper money into gold at the rate stipulated in its definition of the monetary unit.

2. It must allow gold to be freely exported and imported.

If each nation defines its monetary unit in terms of gold, the different currencies will have a fixed relationship to one another. For example, suppose the United States defines a dollar as being worth, say, 25 grains of gold and Britain defines its pound sterling as being worth 75 grains of gold. This means that a British pound is worth 75/25 dollars or, simply, £1 equals $3.

Now, if we momentarily ignore the costs of packing, insuring, and shipping gold between countries, under the gold standard the rate of exchange would not vary from this $3-for-£1 rate. And the reason is clear: No one in the United States would pay more than $3 for £1, because he could always buy 75 grains of gold for $3 in the United States, ship it to Britain, and sell it for £1. Nor would an Englishman pay more than £1 for $3. Why should he, when he could buy 75 grains of gold in England for £1, send it to the United States, and sell it for $3?

Of course, in practice the costs of packing, insuring, and shipping gold must be taken into account. But these costs would only amount to a few cents per 75 grains of gold. For example, if these costs were 3 cents for 75 grains of gold, Americans wanting pounds would pay up to $3.03 for a pound rather than buy and export 75 grains of gold to get that pound. Why? Because it would cost them $3 for the 75 grains of gold plus 3 cents to send it to England to be exchanged for £1. This $3.03 exchange rate, above which gold would begin to flow out of the United States, is called the *gold export point.* Conversely, the exchange rate would fall to $2.97 before gold would flow into the United States. Englishmen

wanting dollars would accept as little as $2.97 in exchange for £1, because from the $3 which they could get by buying 75 grains of gold in England and reselling it in the United States, 3 cents must be subtracted to pay shipping and related costs. This $2.97 exchange rate, below which gold would flow into the United States, is called the *gold import point.* Our basic conclusion is that under the gold standard the flow of gold between nations would result in exchange rates which for all practical purposes are fixed.

But these gold flows would do more than stabilize exchange rates. They would also cause internal adjustments within the domestic economies which would tend to restore equilibrium in the balance of payments.

Suppose, once again, that the United States incurs a balance of payments deficit by importing more from Great Britain than it exports to her. The immediate result is that the dollar price of pounds will move up to the $3.03 gold export point and, if at this exchange rate the quantity of pounds demanded still exceeds the quantity supplied, gold will flow from the United States to Great Britain to settle the deficit. But as gold leaves the United States, bank reserves and the amount of money in circulation will decline, credit availability will be lessened, and interest rates may rise. Other things being unchanged, this is conducive to a decline in aggregate demand and therefore in national income and the price level in the United States. The opposite occurs in Great Britain; the inflow of gold expands bank reserves and the money supply, causing aggregate demand, national income, and the price level to rise, and exerting downward pressure on interest rates. Declining American prices and rising British prices will encourage American exports to, and discourage American imports from, Great Britain, thereby tending to correct the initial American payments deficit. Income changes will work toward the same end. As their incomes fall, Americans import fewer British goods. As their incomes rise, the British buy more American exports.

Gold standard adjustments can be envisioned in terms of Figure 43·4. You will recall that under a system of freely fluctuating exchange rates an American payments deficit would be corrected by a rise in the exchange rate from, say, $3 to $4. In the case of the gold standard, gold flows between the two nations hold the exchange rate approximately at the $3 level. But gold flows result in changes in the price, income, and employment levels of the nations receiving and losing gold. These domestic adjustments shift the demand for and supply of foreign exchange so as to achieve equilibrium at the fixed $3-for-£1 exchange rate. Specifically, given the initial American payments deficit and the resulting American pound shortage of *AB* at the $3 exchange rate, gold will flow from the United States to Great Britain. The contractionary impact in the United States will tend to lower the American demand for pounds, and the expansionary impact in Great Britain will tend to increase the available supply of pounds. These shifts continue until equilibrium is restored at the $3-for-£1 gold standard rate. Graphically, this means the D_1D_1 curve of Figure 43·4 will shift to the left, and the S_1S_1 curve to the right, providing a new intersection (equilibrium) point somewhere on the broken black line between points *A* and *B*.

The gold standard entails obvious advantages:

1. The stable exchange rates which it fosters reduce the riskiness and thereby stimulate the volume of international trade.

2. The gold standard automatically corrects balance of payments disequilibria. International equilibrium under the gold standard does not require the action of governmental bodies; inevitable gold flows adjust trade deficits or surpluses to the end that a balance of payments disequilibrium will be resolved.

The basic drawback of the gold standard is apparent from our discussion of the adjustment processes it entails. Nations on the gold standard must accept domestic adjustments in such distasteful forms as deflation, unemployment, and falling incomes, on the one hand, or inflation, on the other.

Public controls

By allowing the forces of supply and demand in the foreign exchange market to alter the exchange rate or by permitting internal employment, output, and

price level adjustments to occur in response to a balance of payments disequilibrium, the government is assuming a passive role. Government is permitting "market forces" to work themselves out in ameliorating or correcting a balance of payments deficit or surplus. A third option is for government to adopt specific policies—to take positive action—to correct, say, a payments deficit by interfering with the functioning of market forces. In general, there are two variants of this method of adjustment to consider: (1) government control of the rate of exchange and the exchange market, and (2) control of the flow of international trade itself. Both attempt to correct a balance of payments disequilibrium by suppressing or altering the functioning of market forces.

Foreign exchange controls To see how exchange controls work, let us suppose the United States government has fixed the legal dollar price of pounds at \$3 to £1, as in Figure 43·4. Now assume as before that American imports increase, resulting in an American trade deficit. The main symptom of this deficit is an American foreign exchange shortage of *AB* in Figure 43·4. Under exchange controls, the government handles this problem by requiring that all foreign exchange obtained by American exporters and other recipients be sold to it. Then, in turn, the government allocates or rations this short supply of pounds (*XA*) among the various American importers and other users, who demand the quantity *XB*. In this way government can restrict American imports to the amount of foreign exchange earned by American exports. In effect, *government rationing of foreign exchange "forces" a balance of payments equilibrium by restricting imports to the value of exports.* The rationing process necessarily involves government discrimination between different importers, typically denying foreign exchange for the importation of luxury, or nonessential, goods in order to make the short supply available for necessary, or essential, goods.

But there are many objections to exchange controls. They obviously impinge upon freedom of consumer choice; American buyers may be forced to forgo Scotch and settle for bourbon. American importing firms will obviously be hurt by exchange controls. The government will be faced with an enforcement problem; the market forces of supply and demand indicate that there are American importers who want foreign exchange badly enough to pay more than the \$3 equals £1 official rate, and this sets the stage for extralegal or "black market" foreign exchange dealings. Furthermore, exchange controls do not completely free nations from internal price and income adjustments. Specifically, the restriction of imports in the control nation leads to domestic scarcities of certain goods and materials ordinarily imported. The prices of these products and resources therefore tend to rise. This is reinforced by the fact that the restricting of imports to the value of exports will increase national income in the control economy: expenditures formerly made on imported goods are now reallocated to domestically produced goods.

On the other hand, deflation tends to occur in other nations, for the exchange controls tend to curtail their export markets, and the production of goods normally exported begins to depress their domestic markets. Furthermore, the loss of export markets which the imposition of exchange controls forces upon foreign nations will cause the incomes of those nations to decline. The decline in the net exports of these nations will have a contractionary impact upon their economies.

We will discover in Chapter 44 that nations participating in the postwar international monetary system have gone to considerable lengths to keep their exchange rates stable. In particular, governments have manipulated the supply of, and demand for, their own currencies to keep their exchange rate from rising or falling. Occasionally, however, a nation will be faced with persistent balance of payments deficits or substantial domestic unemployment and will attempt to alleviate these problems by *devaluating*[4] its currency, that is, by purposely making its currency

[4]The term *depreciation* is used to describe a decline in the international value of a currency under a system of freely fluctuating (market-determined) exchange rates; *devaluation* refers to the cheapening of a currency as the result of a governmental redefinition of the value of a country's currency relative to gold or other currencies.

cheap relative to the currencies of other nations. For example, in November of 1967 Great Britain, faced with persistent and substantial payments deficits, devalued the pound, changing its dollar price from $2.80 to $2.40. The purpose of this dramatic devaluation was to make British goods cheaper for the rest of the world and to make foreign goods more expensive for the British, thereby increasing British exports and lowering imports to the end that its payments deficit would be relieved.

During the Great Depression, most nations devaluated their currencies in the hope of alleviating domestic unemployment. They reasoned that the increase in exports and decline in imports which devaluation would bring would stimulate domestic production and employment. However, most nations found that the resulting stimuli to their domestic economies were short-lived, as other nations embraced the same rationale and in turn devaluated their currencies. In Chapter 44 we will discuss President Nixon's 1971 "floating" of the dollar—a de facto devaluation—for the purpose of simultaneously correcting the United States's balance of payments deficit and boosting domestic employment.

Trade controls The government of a nation faced with a payments deficit can also undertake to manipulate imports and exports through the use of tariffs, quotas, subsidies, and the like. In correcting a payments deficit the problem obviously is to reduce imports and increase exports. On the one hand, imports can be reduced by imposing tariffs or import quotas (Chapter 42). Special taxes on foreign lending and investing by Americans have a similar effect in that such taxes tend to reduce United States capital outflows or, looked at differently, to cut our imports of foreign securities. Similarly, special taxes or outright limits might be imposed upon the expenditures of American tourists. On the other hand, the United States government might subsidize certain American exports (for example, farm products) to make them more competitive in world markets and thereby increase the volume of their sales.

The fundamental problem with these trade controls, and also with exchange controls, is that they reduce the volume of world trade and distort its composition or pattern away from that which is economically desirable. That is, exchange and trade controls can only be imposed at the sacrifice of some portion of the economic gains or benefits attainable from a free flow of world trade based upon the principle of comparative advantage. These effects should not be underestimated; remember that the imposition of exchange or trade controls can elicit retaliatory responses from other nations whose balance of payments is adversely affected.

SUMMARY

1. American exports create a foreign demand for dollars and make a supply of foreign exchange available to Americans. Conversely, American imports simultaneously create a demand for foreign exchange and make a supply of dollars available to foreigners. Generally speaking, a nation's exports earn the foreign currencies needed to pay for its imports.

2. The balance of payments is an annual accounting statement of all a nation's international trade and financial transactions. A nation's balance of trade is the difference between its exports and its imports. An excess of exports over imports is a trade surplus; an excess of imports over exports is a trade deficit.

3. In 1970 the United States realized a trade surplus of $3.7 billion. But remittances from the United States, government loans and grants, and net capital movements from the United States totaled $9.3 billion, resulting in a balance of payments deficit of $5.6 billion. This deficit was peculiar, but typical for the United States in the post–World War II period, in that it occurred despite a trade surplus.

4. In general, a balance of payments disequilibrium occurs when the inpayments and outpayments resulting from a nation's autonomous transactions do not balance. This imbalance necessitates accommodating or financing transactions. In the case of a deficit, financing transactions involve gold sales, reductions in the nation's holdings of foreign monies,

and increases in the amount of its liquid liabilities to nonresidents—mostly foreign central and commercial banks.

5. A balance of payments disequilibrium can be corrected by means of *a.* freely fluctuating exchange rates, *b.* changes in domestic levels of output and prices, and *c.* government controls over international trade and finance.

6. Freely fluctuating exchange rates restore international equilibrium primarily by affecting the relative attractiveness of internationally traded goods.

7. Given stable exchange rates, a nation can correct a payments deficit by undertaking contractionary policies domestically. Historically, the gold standard provided exchange rate stability. But under this system gold flows between nations precipitated sometimes painful changes in price, income, and employment levels in bringing about international equilibrium.

8. Through exchange controls, government can force imports into equality with exports by rationing foreign exchange. Similarly, trade controls—tariffs, import quotas, export subsidies, and so forth—can be used to alleviate or correct a payments disequilibrium.

QUESTIONS AND STUDY SUGGESTIONS

1. Explain how an American automobile importer might finance a shipment of Renaults from France.

2. Explain: "American exports earn supplies of foreign monies which Americans can use to finance imports."

3. What is the rate of exchange? "A rise in the dollar price of pesos necessarily means a fall in the peso price of dollars." Do you agree?

4. "Exports pay for imports. Yet in 1970 the rest of the world imported about $3.7 billion more worth of goods and services from the United States than were exported to the United States." Resolve the apparent inconsistency of these two statements.

5. Define and compare *a.* the balance of payments and the balance of trade and *b.* a balance of trade deficit and a balance of payments deficit. Explain how a nation can incur a balance of trade deficit or surplus and yet achieve equilibrium in its balance of payments. Use the distinction between autonomous and accommodating transactions to explain the notion of international disequilibrium.

6. Explain in detail the adjustments which must occur to resolve a balance of payments surplus under *a.* the gold standard, *b.* flexible exchange rates, and *c.* exchange controls. Now trace the adjustments entailed by a payments deficit. Evaluate the virtues and shortcomings of *a.* the gold standard and *b.* flexible exchange rates.

7. "The operation of the international gold standard undermines domestic full-employment policies, and, conversely, the active pursuit of full employment domestically is inimical to the operation of the gold standard." Explain and evaluate this statement.

8. Critically evaluate: "Exchange rate depreciation reduces the price of a country's goods to foreigners. Domestic deflation does the same thing. Therefore, a nation should be indifferent as to which of these two forces operates to correct a balance of payments deficit."

SELECTED REFERENCES

Economic Issues, 4th ed., reading 85.

Ellsworth, Paul T: *The International Economy,* 4th ed. (New York: The Macmillan Company, 1969), chaps. 18–24.

Ingram, James C.: *International Economic Problems,* 2d ed. (New York: John Wiley & Sons, Inc., 1970).

Kenen, Peter B.: *International Economics,* 2d ed. (Englewood Cliffs, N.J.: Prentice-Hall, Inc., 1967).

Snider, Delbert A.: *International Monetary Relations* (New York: Random House, Inc., 1966), particularly chaps. 1–4.

INTERNATIONAL TRADE AND FINANCE: PROBLEMS AND POLICIES

With the elements of international trade and finance in mind we are now in a position to explore international economic problems and the economic policies which have sometimes alleviated and sometimes contributed to these problems. As necessary background, we begin by explaining how depression, war, and political tensions caused world trade to disintegrate in the 1929–1946 period. After considering post-World War II economic reconstruction, we will concentrate upon those current problems and developments which are most crucial to a viable world economy. First, the problem of reducing artificial trade barriers will be explored. Next, the nature of the United States balance of payments problem, its causes, and possible cures, will be examined. And finally, we must consider the fundamental and highly complex question of reforming and restructuring the international monetary system. The acute problems which are associated with the underdeveloped nations will be reserved for Chapter 45.

DISINTEGRATION AND RECONSTRUCTION OF WORLD TRADE

During most of the nineteenth century a harmonious network of international trade and finance linked the nations of the world. Some nations—particularly those of northwestern Europe—quickly grasped the new techniques of the Industrial Revolution, while others remained almost completely unaffected. These differences formed the basis for a highly complementary pattern of trade wherein underdeveloped nations exported raw materials to the manufacturing nations. The latter in turn came to depend upon the expanding markets of the semideveloped and underdeveloped nations in selling their manufactured goods. This trade pattern was accompanied by relatively large flows of private long-term capital from the manufacturing to the raw materials nations. These flows increased the production of raw materials and simultaneously strengthened overseas markets in the raw

materials nations. Furthermore, laissez faire was the dominant ideology during this golden age of international trade. Governmental interference with the composition and volume of trade was at a minimum. Each nation accepted any and all internal adjustments which inevitable changes in the structure and terms of trade demanded. The international gold standard—characterized you will recall (Chapter 43) by gold movements and highly stable rates of exchange—worked automatically and effectively during much of this period to resolve balance of payments disequilibria. The world of the last half of the nineteenth century was a closely knit economic unit wherein the volume of trade was large and generally in accord with the principle of comparative advantage. Events of the twentieth century—the Great Depression, World War II, and the cold war—brought changes that have resulted in the demise of this golden age of international trade.

World trade in the thirties

The Great Depression of the 1930s severely disrupted the volume and composition of international trade. Nations heavily dependent upon foreign trade found that the Depression caused their overseas markets to collapse, preventing them from earning the foreign monies needed to finance the importation of essential goods. Nations which imported more than they exported witnessed the disappearance of the long-term capital flows which financed this difference as the Depression undermined profit expectations. Furthermore, drastic and uneven changes in the price levels of the various nations rendered existing exchange rates unrealistic and raised serious questions about the terms of trade. It is easy to see why many nations faced severe balance of payments difficulties during the thirties.

In addition to upsetting the international flow of goods and capital and posing exchange rate problems, the Great Depression prompted a myriad of trade controls. Serious domestic unemployment almost invariably gives rise to trade barriers designed to create more employment domestically. An obvious means of bolstering domestic employment and production is to increase exports and cut imports. Success in this endeavor expands net exports, which through the multiplier effect promises a magnified expansionary effect upon the domestic economy. In seeking this trade surplus, the nations of the world imposed high tariff barriers, created import quotas and export subsidies, established government controls upon foreign exchange, and devaluated their currencies. (Note, for example, in Table 44·2 the high American tariffs imposed in the early 1930s.) Unfortunately, because the exports of one nation are the imports of another, all nations could not succeed in stimulating their domestic economies by exporting more than they imported. But most tried. And the trade barriers which accompanied the attempts further distorted and choked off the declining flow of international trade.

World War II: disruption of trade

Following on the heels of the Great Depression, World War II completed the disintegration of world trade. The impact of war upon international trade is manifold:

1. Most obviously, the pattern of trade is altered so that it is in accord with military objectives rather than comparative advantage. At the outset of World War II the European belligerents sought to mobilize as many resources as possible—both domestic and foreign—for war goods production. On the one hand, this meant cutting exports, that is, shifting resources from export goods to war goods production. On the other hand, it meant increasing imports to supplement the productive capacity of the domestic economy. The resulting excess of imports over exports posed an obvious balance of payments problem: How could the warring nations, when restricting exports, obtain enough foreign exchange to expand greatly their volume of imports?

2. War almost invariably means inflationary pressures (Chapter 40), and, like depression, inflation affects different nations in differing degrees. Some encounter creeping inflation, and others are afflicted with the galloping variety. Those nations which experience the greatest amount of inflation find that at

existing exchange rates their goods are less attractive to foreign buyers and, unhappily, domestic consumers are attracted to foreign goods. Down go that nation's exports and up go its imports. This again contributes to a balance of payments deficit and a shortage of foreign monies.

3. World War II had dramatically different effects upon the productive capacities of nations. The capital facilities of some—particularly Great Britain, France, and Germany—were seriously reduced as the result of physical destruction through invasion, bombings, and the inability to replace depreciated capital during the wartime emergency. Those nations whose capital facilities are seriously impaired by war will want to achieve an excess of imports over exports to supplement domestic productive capacity in the postwar reconstruction period. But how is this trade deficit to be financed?

For example, Great Britain was the unwilling victim of all these war-born difficulties during the 1940s. The war itself called for persistent trade deficits. Inflationary pressures, though admirably contained, were strong, complicating domestic and international postwar adjustments. Finally, Great Britain faced the gigantic task of restoring its productive capacity at the cessation of hostilities. All these considerations meant long-term balance of payments deficits and posed in this instance the specific problem of a *dollar shortage.*

The cold war

The Great Depression and World War II destroyed the harmonious trade structure of earlier decades. The cold war of the postwar period has proved a hostile environment in which to rebuild world trade.

The World War II victors are ideologically divided. The cessation of hostilities brought forth no common ideological basis upon which world trade could be reconstructed. On the contrary, the end of the war merely ushered in the cold war and brought to the fore the ideological cleavages of the Communist bloc and the Western nations. The flow of trade between Communist nations and the West was sharply curtailed and has remained seriously distorted as political and military considerations have taken precedence over economic factors in determining the volume and composition of such trade.

Furthermore, as a result of the Great Depression of the 1930s, the governments of most nations now explicitly accept responsibility to maintain domestic full employment and reasonable price stability. The pursuit of domestic stability can and frequently does collide with the goal of rebuilding international trade and finance.

Finally, fired by a rising spirit of nationalism, the underdeveloped nations now seek to reduce their economic dependence upon the industrially advanced nations and to improve their domestic living standards. Industrialization and diversification of their domestic economies are held by these nations to be the best means of accomplishing these ends. Tariffs, import quotas, and similar impediments to the flow of international trade have been techniques by which industrialization and diversification have been sought.

Postwar trade problems

In short, at the close of World War II world trade was in a shambles. Old trade patterns were almost completely destroyed, the productive capacity of Europe was very low, the price levels of the various nations had changed in a disjointed fashion as a result of the war, and the Depression had imposed a myriad of restrictions upon the flow of trade. The problem of rebuilding the world economy in the postwar period was clearly a formidable one.

Postwar programs and institutions concerned with the immediate reconstruction of world trade sought to resolve several interrelated problems.

1. The most immediate problem was to achieve economic recovery in war-devastated Europe.

2. The artificial barriers to trade which accompanied and contributed to the disintegration of world trade had to be dismantled in order for trade to expand.

3. It was essential that an international monetary system capable of providing relatively stable exchange rates and sufficient supplies of foreign exchange be established.

Rebuilding the European economy

The most pressing postwar problem in the reconstruction of world trade was that of rebuilding the economy of Europe. The victorious and the conquered both paid heavily in terms of forgone consumption and tremendous physical destruction of their industries. The major economic problem of the postwar period was all too clear: to rebuild European economies and facilitate their transition to peacetime production. Europe was destitute; it needed crucial goods and services but had little to sell in financing their importation. American capitalism, on the other hand, emerged from the holocaust more vigorous and with a greater productive capacity than when it had entered. Thus the solution for reconstruction was almost as evident as the immediate problem: American economic aid to the needy nations. The fact that the United States had contributed some $37 billion to its allies through Lend-Lease during the war was indicative of the postwar role it was to play.

American postwar aid to foreign nations has assumed several different forms and has been extended with a number of different objectives in mind. Table 44·1 indicates that in the 1946–1969 period some $121 billion worth of aid in the form of military grants, economic grants, and loans has been extended by the United States. The bulk of this aid has been received by Western Europe. In the immediate postwar years foreign aid was aimed at reconstructing the war-torn economies of Europe. Later, however, aid was designed to provide the military and economic strength needed by foreign nations to resist the spread of communism. Though specific aid programs are difficult to classify in terms of these varying objectives, our present discussion will focus upon immediate postwar aid for the economic revival of Europe and more recent programs of military assistance. In Chapter 45 we shall survey those aid programs whose primary objective is the economic development of underdeveloped nations.

Immediate postwar aid The immediate, basic needs of postwar Europe were met through the United Nations Relief and Rehabilitation Administration (UNRRA). The aid extended by UNRRA amounted to almost $4 billion, centering for the most part upon the provision of food, clothing, and medical services.

TABLE 44·1 UNITED STATES POSTWAR FOREIGN AID, 1946–1969 (*in millions*)

Net United States military grants and loans		$38,798
Europe	$16,613	
Near East and South Asia	7,090	
Africa	294	
Far East and Pacific	13,617	
Latin America	1,184	
Net United States economic grants and loans		$81,968
Europe	$25,718	
Near East and South Asia	20,544	
Africa	3,533	
Far East and Pacific	18,685	
Latin America	8,414	
Through international organizations	5,074	
Net total military and economic aid		$120,766

Source: Tax Foundation, *Facts and Figures on Government Finance, 1971.*

About three-fourths of the total cost of this program was met through the contributions of the United States. Though successful in furnishing temporary relief, UNRRA did not provide in any significant way for the economic recovery of Europe.

Other American aid programs, however, supplemented UNRRA.

1. The United States distributed over $3.2 billion in emergency relief aid through the armed forces located in occupied countries.

2. Loans were made to specific foreign nations, the most notable of these being a $3.75 billion loan made by the United States Treasury to Great Britain in 1946 to help ease the acute dollar shortage then faced by the British.

3. Piecemeal grants of aid were made in 1947 to specific nations threatened by economic and political disorder. Austria, France, Italy, Greece, and Turkey were among the recipients of these grants.

All told, the United States extended some $16.8 billion in foreign aid between the end of World War II and early 1948. This aid was almost evenly divided between outright grants and loans.

The Marshall Plan (ERP) Though substantial, it became increasingly clear that this immediate postwar aid was simply not sufficient to cope with the economic and political crises of the postwar era. On the economic front, European recovery was lagging. American inflation in the late 1940s made serious inroads on the purchasing power of American loans and grants. Trade between European nations was stifled by serious balance of payments problems. Drought, crop failures, and material and fuel shortages added to these economic woes. It was more apparent than ever that a freer and an expanding volume of international trade depended upon European recovery. On the international political front, Soviet Russia was becoming increasingly aggressive in seeking the worldwide spread of communism. And the Russians found a potentially fertile ground for this advance in the destitute and hungry peoples of Europe. On the domestic political front, there was a growing desire to abandon piecemeal aid programs designed to meet each individual economic and political crisis in favor of a comprehensive and coordinated aid program designed to restore the economic health and the political stability of Europe once and for all.

Out of this background the United States established in 1948 the European Recovery Program (ERP), called the "Marshall Plan" for its progenitor, Secretary of State George Marshall. The fundamental objective was to restore the productive capacity of European industry and agriculture. Related objectives were domestic political stability, the establishment of sound monetary and fiscal systems in the reviving nations of Europe, and the overcoming of the serious balance of payments problems which hampered trade between the nations of Europe in particular and the world in general. In the less than four years of its existence the Marshall Plan channeled well over $10 billion in American aid to Europe, most of which was in the form of outright grants.

Although comprehensive aid programs such as the Marshall Plan elude precise evaluation, most experts agree that ERP was highly successful both economically and politically. In 1951 the average level of industrial production in all participating nations was 55 percent above the 1947 level. Though far from completely successful in resolving balance of payments difficulties, considerable progress was made in this area. A very rough indicator of the political success of ERP lies in the fact that after 1948 no European nations succumbed to communism. The political ties of the United States and Western Europe were strengthened immeasurably by the Marshall Plan.

Mutual Security programs Aid to Europe did not end with the expiration of the Marshall Plan in 1951. ERP in effect has been superseded by the Mutual Security Agency, which continues through a variety of specific programs to provide military, economic, and technical assistance to both European and non-European nations.

By the early 1950s European economic recovery was accomplished. Since that time American aid has been substantially redirected toward the underdeveloped areas of the world—the Near East, Africa,

Asia, and Latin America. From the outbreak of World War II to the present, the United States has extended some $158 billion worth of foreign aid, including our wartime Lend-Lease program.

LIBERALIZING WORLD TRADE

Clearly one of the necessary, though not sufficient, conditions for the reconstruction and expansion of world trade was the reduction or elimination of artificial barriers to trade. This problem has been attacked in two ways in the postwar period: (1) through the reciprocal negotiation of tariff reductions and the elimination of tariffs by trading nations, and (2) through economic integration.

Early United States tariff policies

Since the enactment of the first American tariff in 1789 and up to 1934, the long-run trend was in the direction of higher tariffs on American imports. This trend, however, encompasses periods of tariff boosting and tariff cutting—the Republicans usually doing the boosting and the Democrats the cutting. Intense foreign competition after World War I and during the Great Depression led to significant tariff increases in the 1920s and 1930s. The Hawley-Smoot Tariff Act of 1930 embodied the highest tariffs ever imposed by the United States.

In view of Chapter 42's discussion of the case for free trade, this trend toward higher tariffs may be a bit surprising. If tariffs are economically undesirable, why has Congress been so willing to employ them? The answer lies in the political realities of tariff making. Those interest groups who stand to benefit from protection have done an effective job of lobbying for tariffs. And in a sense the pressure for protection is cumulative. With some tariff protection, domestic producers increase their economic strength. This means they have greater financial resources to plead for more protection—and also more to lose if they fail in their efforts to sustain it. Most consumers, ignorant of all the economic implications of tariffs, are impressed by not only the vigor but also the plausibility ("Cut imports and prevent domestic unemployment") and the patriotic ring ("Buy American!") of the protectionists. Alleged tariff benefits seem immediate and clear-cut to the public. The adverse effects cited by economists seem ever so obscure and widely dispersed over the economy. Then, too, the public is likely to trip on the fallacy of composition: "If a protective tariff on Swiss watches will preserve profits and employment in the American watch industry, how can it be detrimental to the economy as a whole?" Those relatively few individuals who do recognize that the benefits gained by protected industries come at the expense of the general welfare are incapable of financing lobbyists to offset the protectionists. When political logrolling is added in—"You back tariffs for industry X in my state and I'll do the same for industry Y in your state"—the sum is protective tariffs and import quotas.

Reciprocal Trade Agreements Act

In the last thirty-five years the trend toward higher tariffs has been reversed. This turnabout in American tariff policy was inaugurated with the Reciprocal Trade Agreements Act of 1934.

Specifically aimed at tariff reduction, the act had two main features:

1. It authorized the President to negotiate agreements with foreign nations which would reduce American tariffs up to 50 percent of the existing rates. Tariff reductions were to hinge upon the willingness of other nations to reciprocate by lowering tariffs on American exports.
2. By incorporating "most-favored-nation" clauses in these agreements, the resulting tariff reductions not only would apply to the specific nation negotiating with the United States, but they would be *generalized* so as to apply to all nations.

GATT

But the Reciprocal Trade Act gave rise to only bilateral (two-nation) negotiations. A broader approach to tariff reduction and trade liberalization was obvi-

ously needed. This objective was to be sought through a proposed International Trade Organization (ITO). This organization was to foster international economic cooperation in general and to promote freer multilateral trade in particular. Out of much open debate by the representatives of some fifty-seven nations there evolved a charter for this proposed organization—a charter unacceptable to the United States Congress. American rejection spelled permanent defeat for the ITO.

However, before negotiations for the ITO charter were completed in 1948, a General Agreement on Tariffs and Trade (GATT) was signed in 1947 by twenty-three nations, including the United States. GATT is based upon three cardinal principles: (1) equal, nondiscriminatory treatment for all member nations, (2) the reduction of tariffs by multilateral negotiations, and (3) the elimination of import quotas. The nations participating in GATT have increased significantly in number, and the resulting tariff and quota agreements have done much to lower artificial trade barriers.

Economic integration: The Common Market

Another crucial development in trade liberalization has taken the form of economic integration. This entails (1) the removal of barriers to trade and to the making of payments between nations and (2) the free flow of labor and capital resources across national boundaries.

The most dramatic step in efforts to achieve European economic integration came in 1958 with the establishment of the European Economic Community (EEC), or the Common Market, as it is popularly called. The European Common Market, composed of France, West Germany, Italy, Belgium, the Netherlands, and Luxembourg, calls for (1) the abolishment of tariffs and import quotas on all products traded among the six participating nations over a twelve- to fifteen-year period beginning on January 1, 1958, and (2) the establishment of a common system of tariffs applicable to all goods received from nations outside the Common Market; and the plan envisions (3) the eventual free movement of capital and labor within the Market and (4) the creation of common policies with respect to a number of other economic matters of joint concern, for example, agriculture, transportation, and restrictive business practices. If fully realized, the Common Market has tremendous implications. The result will be a huge free-trade market with a population comparable to that of the United States—more than ample to remove any market limitations upon the achievement of mass-production economies by European industry. The aggregate national income of the Common Market nations was approximately $380 billion in 1968. The Common Market nations have achieved considerable progress in working toward their stated goals, particularly with respect to the first two objectives. Member nations were able to accelerate their scheduled internal tariff reductions so that they achieved the goal of intraregional free trade by July 1, 1968, $1\frac{1}{2}$ years before the earliest date originally contemplated. Common external tariffs for nonmember nations have also been accomplished.

Tangible evidence of the success of the Common Market is reflected in high rates of economic growth (Table 21·2) and a dramatic expansion of both internal and external trade. While it is impossible to determine with any degree of accuracy how much of the Common Market's economic success has been due to economic integration as such, one can plausibly argue that economic integration has been a major contributing factor in the European prosperity of the 1960s and 1970s. First, this integration generally promotes a more rational allocation of Europe's economic resources in accordance with the principle of comparative advantage. Second, integration of the national economies of Western Europe creates a large-scale mass market which is essential for European industries in realizing economies of large-scale production. More efficient production for a large-scale market permits European industries to realize the lower costs which small, localized markets have historically denied them. Indeed, it is this greater productive efficiency on the part of European firms that has contributed to the United States's balance of payments difficulties. All things considered, there can be little doubt that the Common Market as an

institution has been a significant factor in the buoyancy and expansion of the economies of its member nations.

The advantages and achievements of economic integration in Europe have been evident to nonmembers. In fact, the EEC nations began negotiations with four new prospective members—Great Britain, Denmark, Ireland, and Norway—in June of 1970. Assuming that admission is negotiated, the enlarged Common Market will have a combined GNP of almost two-thirds that of the United States. And it is quite likely that still other Western European nations will become a part of the Common Market in years ahead. Influenced by EEC's success, similar attempts at economic integration have taken place in Latin America, Africa, the Middle East, and Asia.

While economic integration is an important means of reducing trade barriers among members, serious problems can arise for nonmembers. For example, as the Common Market reduced internal tariffs toward zero and simultaneously established a common external tariff, it may have become more difficult for the United States and other free-world nations to sell in the Common Market. For example, *before* the establishment of the Common Market, American, German, and French automobile manufacturers all faced the same tariff in selling their products to, say, Belgium. However, with the establishment of internal free trade among EEC members, Belgian tariffs on German Volkswagens and French Renaults fell to zero, but an external tariff of, say, 25 or 30 percent still applies to all nonmember nations such as the United States. This obviously puts American firms and those of other nonmember nations at a serious competitive disadvantage. And, of course, to the extent that this disadvantage results in a growing mass market for European producers, they may realize greater economies of scale (lower unit costs) and find themselves increasingly able to compete with American manufacturers in the export market of nations outside the Common Market. On the other hand, the Common Market embodies a rapidly growing, but as yet relatively unsaturated, market for our manufactured goods. European incomes and living standards are rising, and the Common Market nations have entered the "high mass consumption" stage of their economic development. High Common Market external tariffs on imports from the United States will tend to make increasingly inaccessible to United States manufacturers a growing mass market for consumer durables and semidurables—those very products which American firms produce with such great efficiency. We shall see shortly that any shrinkage in exports to Europe tends to aggravate the United States's balance of payments problem.

The economic relationship between the United States and the Common Market also has crucial political overtones. Close economic ties are conducive to close political ties. But the persistence of substantial trade barriers between the EEC and the United States can result in a free world which is divided both economically and politically.

Trade Expansion Act of 1962

Against this background, it became increasingly evident in the early 1960s that, if the United States's economic isolation from the Common Market and potential political disunity were to be avoided, the United States should take the initiative to reduce trade barriers against the Common Market.

In the fall of 1962 Congress took a major step toward the achievement of close economic ties between the United States and the Common Market by passing the Trade Expansion Act. This act provides the President with broad powers to negotiate reciprocal tariff reductions. More specifically, the act gives the President authority to

1. Lower or eliminate entirely all tariffs on products where the Common Market and the United States together have 80 percent or more of the world's trade
2. Lower tariffs up to 50 percent on other goods over a five-year period.

The reductions were to be made by reciprocal negotiations and to embody "most-favored-nation" clauses, automatically extending the lower tariffs to many other countries.

The Trade Expansion Act explicitly acknowledged that the sweeping tariff reductions required for a close alignment of the Common Market and the

United States economies will entail certain costs. For example, a number of domestic industries, when relieved of tariff protection, will be faced with declining markets, falling profits, and unemployment. The act therefore provides for "trade adjustment assistance" to those who are adversely affected. Specifically, workers who lose their jobs because of increased import competition can get vocational training, relocation allowances, and cash payments up to $61 per week for as long as 78 weeks of unemployment. Adversely affected businessmen can get tax relief and loans and technical assistance for the modernization and reorganization of plants.

The "Kennedy Round"

The Trade Expansion Act was the legislative basis which permitted the United States to enter into the "Kennedy Round"[1] of tariff negotiations which, after some three years of effort, were concluded in June 1967.

There is some disagreement as to the overall success of the Kennedy Round negotiations. On the one hand, those strongly committed to free trade were disappointed that the authority given by the Trade Expansion Act to eliminate tariffs on products where 80 percent of world trade occurs between the United States and the Common Market was actually of little real consequence. The effectiveness of this provision was dependent upon an anticipated growth in Common Market membership—in particular, upon Britain's admission. France's veto of British membership simply meant that there were very few commodities for which United States–Common Market trade amounted to 80 percent of total world trade. On the other hand, there is no question that sizable tariff cuts were realized by the Kennedy Round. Estimates indicate that "the agreement covers more than $40 billion in world trade, that 70 percent of dutiable imports of the major participants is affected, that two-thirds of the tariff reductions were 50 percent or more, and that the nations making concessions account for 75 percent of world trade."[2] The tariff cuts negotiated in the Kennedy Round were to be put into effect in five equal annual installments beginning January 1, 1968. Tariffs cuts on industrial goods were larger than any previously negotiated. While the United States sought larger cuts on agricultural tariffs than those realized, a program was established to help the United States in the task of supplying food to the underdeveloped nations. The underdeveloped nations also benefited from the negotiations in that special efforts were made to reduce tariffs on products of particular interest to these nations without requiring full reciprocity.

In short, although the Kennedy Round perhaps did not fully measure up to early expectations, it was nevertheless a major step toward trade liberalization. On the bright side, we might look beyond the purely quantitative aspects of these tariff reductions and justifiably argue that the Kennedy Round's major achievement was in successfully sustaining the trend toward freer trade which began over three decades ago.

Table 44·2 provides us with a rough indication[3] of the extent to which import tariffs have been reduced under the Reciprocal Trade Act and GATT. Estimates are also included for the forthcoming tariff reductions negotiated at the Kennedy Round.

Protectionism revived?

Despite the long-term trend toward trade liberalization, protectionism still prowls the land. Indeed, pressures for greater import restrictions have been strong the past several years. A number of factors underlie these pressures for trade restrictions.

In the first place, pressures for protection are a backlash to the Kennedy Round. Many industries whose outputs and profits are being adversely affected by increased foreign competition are seeking

[1]So called because this sixth "round" of trade negotiations under GATT came about largely at the initiative of President Kennedy.

[2]William M. Roth, "What Happened in the Kennedy Round," *The Department of State Bulletin,* July 31, 1967, p. 123.

[3]These figures understate the importance of tariffs by not accounting for the fact that some goods are *excluded* from American markets because of existing tariffs. Then, too, average figures conceal the extremely high tariffs on particular items: watches, china, hats, woolens, scissors, wine, jewelry, glassware, and so forth.

TABLE 44·2 AVERAGE RATES OF DUTY UNDER UNITED STATES TARIFF LAWS, 1913–1970

Year	Tariff law	Duties collected, percent of value of dutiable imports
1913–1921	Underwood Law	27.0
1922–1929	Fordney-McCumber Law	38.5
1930–1933	Hawley-Smoot Law	52.8
1934	Reciprocal Trade Agreements Law	37.3
1947	GATT	15.3
1966	GATT, Trade Expansion Act	11.9
1970	GATT, Kennedy Round	7.0

Source: Walter Krause, *The International Economy* (Boston: Houghton Mifflin Company, 1955), p. 237, and U.S. Department of Commerce.

the restoration of protection, particularly in the form of import quotas. There are signs that organized labor—traditionally in the free-trade camp—is reevaluating its position in the face of unemployment caused by burgeoning imports. Secondly, it is contended, with some justification, that both the EEC and Japan discriminate against American imports. The Common Market's agricultural policies have been quite protective and therefore detrimental to American agricultural exports. Japan has maintained a rather tight system of barriers to the flow of both goods and capital into the Japanese economy. This feeling of trade discrimination against the United States is intensified by the belief that the United States is shouldering a disproportionately large share of the Free World's defense effort. Finally, it is very tempting to employ tariffs and other trade barriers to alleviate domestic unemployment problems. Although such action involves grave risks of retaliation and "trade wars," this temptation is especially great when—as in 1970 and 1971—macroeconomic policy seems unable to cope with rising unemployment and rising prices. It was in such a context, you will recall (Chapter 19), that President Nixon imposed a 10 percent surcharge on dutiable imports in August of 1971. In any event, there is no assurance whatever that the long-run trend toward freer trade will persist.

UNITED STATES BALANCE OF PAYMENTS DEFICIT

Perhaps the most publicized issue in international economics is the United States's balance of payments problem. Let us survey the background of this problem and then examine some of the suggested remedies.

Our changing payments position

For many years prior to 1950 the United States's balance of payments was characterized by a payments surplus. But the 1950s brought a marked change in America's payments position. Figure 44·1 reveals that, except for modest surpluses in 1957 and 1968, the United States has encountered payments deficits every year since 1949. Furthermore, these deficits have been very substantial since 1958. The ultimate consequence of these deficits has been a significant decline in American international gold reserves. Our gold stock, which totaled $25 billion in 1948, was less than $11 billion in early 1971. Why has this turnabout occurred? What can be done to correct our payments deficit?

Causes

A number of intertwined factors have given rise to our payments deficits.

1. Government military and economic aid Recall first that the United States's balance of payments problem has been quite unorthodox. Rather than arising from a trade deficit—that is, from an excess of imports over exports—our payments difficulties have occurred despite a trade surplus. The outflow of dollars from the United States in the form of financial transactions has exceeded our trade surplus. Government aid is one important segment of this dollar outflow. American economic grants and loans in the form of both military and economic aid amounted to $3.2 billion in 1970 and were an important contributor to our payments deficit.

One might think at first glance that American dollar aid would tend to increase our trade surplus and therefore not contribute to our payments deficit. But it has worked this way only to a limited degree. Some American aid dollars have been spent on American goods, thereby increasing our exports and our trade surplus. But other American aid dollars have been spent on, say, German and French goods, ultimately converging on the central banks of these countries and therefore not being respent on American exports. Thus foreign aid has entailed dollar outflows not fully matched by dollar inflows resulting from aid-induced expenditures on American exports. In this way aid has contributed to our payments deficit.

2. Private capital outflows This outflow of public dollars has been accompanied by substantial outflows of American private capital. Private capital outflows have been expanding since the mid-1950s. Growth in the outflow of long-term capital has occurred in response to the burgeoning profit opportunities available in the more rapidly expanding economies of the world, particularly those of Western Europe. Americans have found that the expected

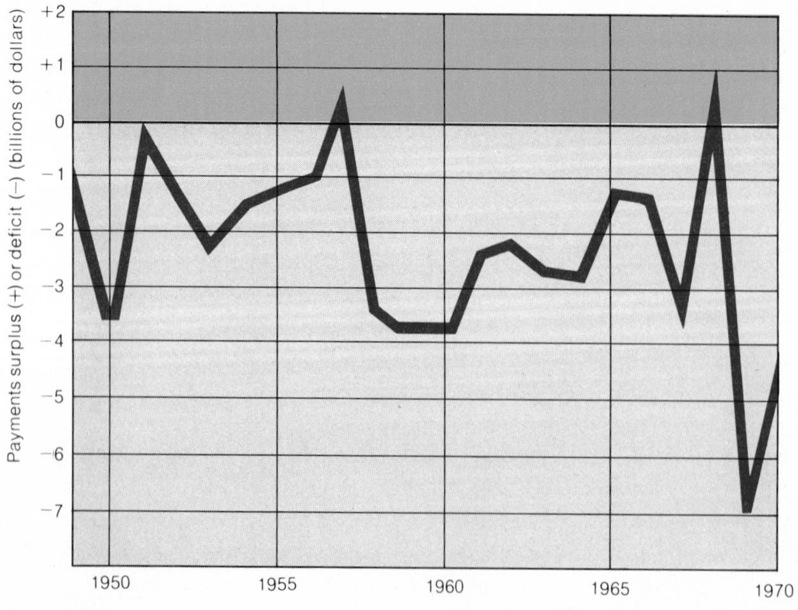

FIGURE 44 · 1 CHRONIC POSTWAR DEFICITS IN THE U.S. BALANCE OF PAYMENTS

Aside from 1957 and 1968, the United States has incurred a deficit in its balance of payments every year since 1949. The results have been a substantial decline in American gold reserves, diminished confidence in the dollar as a key currency, and a threat to the viability of the present international monetary system.

return on foreign investment has exceeded that on domestic investment, so they have invested abroad. In so doing, they have supplied the rest of the world with a growing quantity of American dollars.

The contribution of outflows of long-term American capital to our payments deficit is periodically intensified by sudden international shifts in short-term private capital. Short-term capital tends to be "hot money" in that it is highly responsive to interest rate differentials between nations. Thus, for example, in the spring of 1971 billions of dollars of short-term capital were shifted from the United States to Western Europe to take advantage of higher interest rates. Why were American interest rates lower than in Western Europe? Because the American and Western European economies were out of phase. Most European nations were in the mature stages of a strong period of economic expansion, and interest rates were high. But the United States had lowered interest rates, hoping to reduce the unemployment of the "inflationary recession" of 1970. The response by short-term investors was to shift their money capital from the United States to Europe in such amounts that the stability of the international monetary system was threatened.

Note in Table 43·1 that net capital outflows were $4.7 billion in 1970.

3. Foreign productivity increases The productivity of the nations of Western Europe and Japan has increased rapidly in recent years. This is partly a reflection of the success of postwar economic recovery programs. The economies of Western Europe and Japan have been rebuilt and strengthened with new and modern productive facilities, increasing the capacities of these nations to compete successfully with the United States in world markets. In the case of the Western European nations, productivity increases have been fostered by the transformation of Western Europe from a number of small, localized markets into a single, growing mass market through the Common Market. This has permitted European producers to realize greater economies of scale and lower unit costs and therefore to sell their products at lower prices. Rising productivity in Western Europe and Japan is also attributable to the fact that the United States has borne a large share of the free world's defense burden, freeing high-level manpower and other crucial resources to the task of modernizing the domestic industries of Japan and Western Europe (Chapter 37).

4. Domestic inflation American trade surpluses diminished in the 1960s—and threatened to give way to a trade deficit in 1971—because of domestic inflation. The prices of American export goods generally rose faster in the 1950s than did those of our closest competitors for world markets. Similarly, inflation in the United States during 1965–1969 contributed to a substantial deterioration in our payments position in the latter half of the 1960s. Inflation has tended to price American producers out of international export markets and has simultaneously made imported goods more attractive.

These two considerations—rapid productivity gains in Japan and the Common Market nations and domestic price rises in excess of those generally experienced by trading partners—have had the effect of narrowing our balance of trade surplus or, at least, of constraining its growth. Yet we had a *trade* surplus of $3.7 billion in 1970, as Table 43·1 indicates. But when the aforementioned public and private capital outflows are taken into account, this trade surplus translated into a payments *deficit*.

To summarize: In the immediate post–World War II period the United States enjoyed a trade surplus of such great magnitude that outflows of aid and private capital were quite easily covered. But the economic recovery and rapid productivity increases of Western Europe and Japan, coupled with American inflation, have caused the relative size of our trade surplus to fall from early postwar levels. At the same time, foreign economic and military aid has remained at a substantial level, and outflows of American investment capital have grown sharply. Thus our shrinking trade surplus has failed to cover our outflows of investment dollars and aid dollars. Foreign nations have used the extra dollars thus received to purchase American gold, or they have held these dollars as idle balances.

Cures: ad hoc measures

The changing world trade position of the United States obviously poses a problem. No nation can lose gold reserves indefinitely at rates that have averaged $1 billion or more per year in recent years. Some adjustments must be made in our international trade accounts to restore equilibrium. The crucial question involves the character of these adjustments.

The United States government has undertaken a variety of specific measures, largely in the form of controls, in the hope of correcting its payments problem. Let us briefly mention some of them. Overseas expenditures by the military have been scaled back where possible. Foreign aid has been "tied" to American goods; that is, aid recipients have been obligated to spend aid funds on American goods. Expenditures by government agencies have been subject to "Buy American" provisions. The amount of duty-free goods which American tourists can bring home from overseas was cut, and Congress has imposed a special tax on foreign travel. To reduce the outflow of American capital, Congress in 1963 enacted an "interest equalization tax" on American purchases of foreign stocks and bonds. In addition, moral suasion has been at work; the President requested American corporations and banks to restrict their capital flows going abroad in accordance with governmental guidelines. In 1968 mandatory limitations were imposed upon foreign investment by executive order.

While these measures may have ameliorated our payments problem to some degree, it is doubtful that their overall impact has been great so far. At least, our payments deficit persists at a seriously high level. Furthermore, since these ad hoc measures are obviously in the form of controls, they conflict with our commitment to the principle of free trade. For example, foreign aid grants or loans which are "tied" force recipients to buy American goods even though the recipients could perhaps purchase the same goods at a lower price from, say, Germany or France. "Buy American" provisions force government agencies to buy domestic goods and forgo equivalent goods produced abroad at lower prices. The interest equalization tax clearly hinders the flow of capital into its most productive uses. In short, many of these ad hoc measures distort the flow and pattern of world trade and investment away from those which are economically desirable. Yet as we shall see in a moment, large payments deficits for the United States cannot continue indefinitely without imperiling the functioning of the present international monetary system.

The imposition of a *10 percent tariff surcharge* by President Nixon in August of 1971 is perhaps the most dramatic attempt to control trade for the purpose of correcting our balance of payments deficit. By executive order all dutiable imports—roughly one-half of all American imports—became subject to an additional 10 percent tariff. For example, a Japanese tape recorder which was formerly purchased by an American importer for $200 will now cost him $220, and its retail price will also presumably rise by $20. By making imports relatively less attractive, it was hoped that American consumers would divert their spending from imported to domestic goods, thereby bolstering our balances of trade and payments. An intended side effect was that this diversion of expenditures would increase domestic employment. The risk of this policy, as noted earlier, is that other nations will retaliate, precipitating a "trade war." The net result could therefore be a declining volume of trade and the consequent loss of the gains from specialization according to comparative advantage, not to mention serious political divisiveness between the United States and its major trading partners.

Why embark upon such a precarious course? In the first place, our balance of payments situation deteriorated to crisis proportions in mid-1971; as noted earlier, our *trade* balance shifted from a surplus to a deficit. Drastic remedial action was therefore necessary. Secondly, the tariff surcharge was earmarked as a "temporary" measure, the presumption being that it would be suspended if our major trading partners reacted in ways that would be helpful to the United States in resolving its payments problem. Specifically, the United States hoped that Japan and the Common Market nations would resist actions that

would prevent the accompanying "floating" of the dollar from resulting in its actual devaluation. The surcharge was also looked upon as a device for pressuring our trading partners to assume a larger share of the free world's defense burden and to eliminate discriminatory barriers against American goods and capital. Hence, in a sense the tariff surcharge was established as a bargaining item; the implication was that "appropriate responses" by Western European nations and Japan—and subsequent improvement in the United States's payments position—would result in early termination of the tariff surcharge. Finally, given the recollections of the drastically adverse effects of trade warring in the 1930s and the fact that the dependence of Japan and EEC nations upon world trade is substantially greater than that of the United States in relative terms, the risk of a trade war is perhaps not as serious as might first appear.

Cures: basic measures

But our discussion of the causes of our balance of payments problem suggests more basic and perhaps less risky cures.

1. Increase American productivity A basic line of attack is for American producers to intensify their efforts to increase productivity as a means of making American goods more competitive in international markets. This is obviously more easily said than done. It implies the maintenance of full employment and a high level of net investment spending. It suggests increased activity in technological research by both industry and government. It demands farsightedness by labor and management in introducing automation and in eliminating obsolete work rules.

2. Restrict domestic inflation Given the causal role of domestic inflation in the United States's payments problem, it is obvious that a more effective use of monetary and fiscal policies to stabilize the price level would strengthen our position in world trade. However, recalling the Phillips curve dilemma, the vigorous application of monetary and fiscal policies to stabilize prices might contribute to unemployment (Chapter 22). Greater price stability with near-full employment may require that monetary and fiscal policies be supplemented with some form of "incomes policy," that is, a policy to control the size of the money income claims against the real output. The temporary wage-price freeze of 1971 is an extreme form of incomes policy and, indeed, its imposition was motivated in part by a desire to stabilize the prices of American goods so as to prevent further deterioration of our balances of trade and payments.

3. Redistribute aid and defense burdens Western Europe might well assume a larger share of the costs of the mutual defense effort and of economic aid programs designed to benefit the underdeveloped nations. The balance of payments problem of the United States stems in a sense from the fact that American military and economic assistance and capital outflows are considerably in excess of its trade surplus, causing an outflow of gold. European recovery and the resulting substantial shrinkage of the American trade surplus suggest that Europe can now share more fully in the free world's defense against communism and in the vital programs that assist the underdeveloped nations in improving their economic lot. This is not to suggest an overall cut in mutual defense spending or in economic assistance to less fortunate nations; rather, the aim is to redistribute the financial burden of these programs.

4. Devaluation Another fundamental means by which a nation might correct a balance of payments disequilibrium is to take steps to lower the value of its currency in relation to foreign currencies. Recall (Chapter 43) that devaluation has the effect of lowering all domestic prices relative to foreign prices. Hence, the exports of the nation that devalues tend to rise and its imports tend to fall, alleviating its payments deficit. Devaluation was in fact an important component of President Nixon's New Economic Policy in the late summer of 1971 (Chapter 19). We defer discussion of this dramatic devaluation until we analyze the international monetary system as it existed and functioned up to that time.

THE POSTWAR INTERNATIONAL MONETARY SYSTEM

It was well recognized at the end of World War II that the reconstruction of world trade would depend upon the establishment of a viable international monetary system. In order to lay the groundwork for such a system, an international conference of Allied nations was held at Bretton Woods, New Hampshire, in 1944. Out of this conference evolved a commitment to an "adjustable-peg" system of exchange rates. Furthermore, the conference created the International Monetary Fund (IMF) to make the new exchange rate system feasible and workable.

This international monetary system, emphasizing relative fixed exchange rates and managed through the IMF, has prevailed with modifications until recently. But, as we shall soon discover, the United States's floating of the dollar in August of 1971 dealt a serious blow to the system and set the stage for its thorough revision. Before discussing the floating of the dollar and speculating on possible consequences, let us examine the international monetary system that served the free world from World War II to the early 1970s. Significant components of that system may well be used in the new international monetary system that is evolving. And, in any event, it is important to understand why the postwar international monetary system ultimately broke down.

IMF and adjustable pegs

What is an adjustable-peg system of exchange rates? Why was it evolved? Consider the second question first. During the depressed 1930s various countries resorted to the practice of altering their exchange rates in the hope of stimulating domestic employment. In particular, many of them *devaluated* their currencies. For example, if the United States was faced with growing unemployment, it might *increase* the dollar price of pounds from \$2.40 for £1 to, say, \$3 for £1. This action would make American goods cheaper to the British and British goods dearer to Americans, increasing American exports and reducing American imports. The resulting increase in the net exports component of aggregate demand would stimulate output and employment. But the problem was that every nation can play the devaluation game, and most gave it a whirl. The resulting rounds of competitive devaluations benefited no one; on the contrary, they simply contributed to the demoralization of world trade. Nations at Bretton Woods therefore agreed that the postwar monetary system must provide for overall exchange rate stability whereby disruptive currency devaluations could be avoided.

What is an adjustable-peg system of exchange rates like? First, each member of the IMF is obligated to define its monetary unit in terms of gold (or dollars), thereby establishing par rates of exchange between its currency and the currencies of all other members. Each nation is further obligated to keep its exchange rate essentially stable vis-à-vis any other currency; that is, a nation is only allowed to vary its exchange rate 1 percent above and below its established par value. But how is this obligation to be fulfilled? After all, it would only be by chance that in a particular year any given nation would achieve an equilibrium in its balance of payments. And if they are not somehow countered, payments imbalances will be reflected in changes in the demand for or supply of a nation's currency and therefore in fluctuating exchange rates. How can a nation finance temporary payments deficits without having to let its exchange rate depreciate?

By two basic means. First, each member nation can establish a stabilization fund, affiliated with its central bank or treasury, which holds supplies of both foreign and domestic monies. These monies are used to augment the supply of or demand for any currency as required to avoid fluctuations in the rate of exchange. Secondly, the IMF plays a major role in stabilizing exchange rates. Specifically, the IMF is empowered to make short-term loans to nations faced with temporary, or short-run, balance of payments deficits. These loans are to be made out of currencies and gold contributed by the participating nations on the basis of size of national income, population, and volume of trade. The United States has

been the major contributor, providing about $5 billion, or roughly one-fourth of the total. If Great Britain or France, for example, faces a temporary shortage of dollars, it can borrow the needed dollars from the Fund by supplying its own currency as collateral. The dollars so acquired are in the form of a loan, not a grant, and must be repaid with interest in a relatively short period of time. Presumably in the near future the borrowing country's trade deficit with the United States will be corrected so that it can obtain the gold or dollars needed to retire its IMF loan.

While stabilization funds and IMF credit are the primary means of avoiding short-run fluctuations in exchange rates, the adjustable-peg system—as its name implies—provides for the orderly alteration of exchange rates to cope with international disequilibrium stemming from long-run, or fundamental, causes. It was recognized that if a nation's currency is overvalued in relation to other currencies, that nation will encounter severe difficulties in exporting. Hence, it will persistently be faced with a payments deficit. To cope with such situations the Fund allows each member nation to alter the value of its currency by 10 percent without explicit permission from the Fund in order to correct a deeply rooted balance of payments deficit. Larger exchange rate changes require the sanction of the Fund's board of directors. This procedure for changing exchange rates is more significant than first appears. By requiring approval of significant rate changes, the Fund attempts to guard against arbitrary and competitive currency devaluation prompted by nations seeking a temporary stimulus to their domestic economies or the solution to a payments deficit.

The objective of the adjustable-peg system is to realize a world monetary system which embraces the best features of both a fixed exchange rate system (such as the old international gold standard) and a system of freely fluctuating exchange rates. Short-run exchange rate stability—pegged exchange rates—stimulates trade and is conducive to the efficient use of world resources. Periodic exchange rate adjustments—adjustment of the pegs—made in an orderly fashion through the IMF and on the basis of permanent or long-run changes in a country's payments position, provide a mechanism by which international disequilibrium can be resolved by means other than changes in domestic levels of output and prices.

Gold and "key currencies"

The smooth operation of the world monetary system requires the existence of adequate monetary reserves or liquidity. We have noted that as nations incur short-run payments deficits, they need monetary reserves if exchange rates are to be kept stable while domestic adjustments in output and employment are avoided. What comprises the supply of monetary reserves internationally? Basically, two items: gold and certain "key currencies." The dollar has been the primary key currency, although the pound sterling functions in this capacity to a lesser extent.

As noted in Chapter 43, gold bullion is money internationally; gold is generally acceptable as a medium of exchange. But why has the dollar been a "key currency," that is, why is the dollar acceptable as money internationally? The answer has historical roots. The United States emerged from World War II as the free world's strongest economy; hence it became the center of international trade and finance. Furthermore, before and during the war the United States accumulated vast amounts of gold, and between 1934 and 1971 it maintained a policy of buying gold from and selling gold to foreign monetary authorities at a fixed price of $35 per ounce. Thus the dollar was convertible into gold on demand; the dollar came to be regarded as a substitute for gold and therefore "as good as gold."

The United States's position of leadership in the international economy imposes important responsibilities and constraints upon our international economic policy. In particular, we shall soon discover that the dollar's key currency role posed serious problems for the correction of our persistent balance of payments deficit.

Recent problems

Given the immensity of the problems associated with the rebuilding of international trade and finance after the war, there is no doubt that the present interna-

tional monetary system contributed significantly to the reconstruction and expansion of postwar trade. But certain fundamental weaknesses have developed in the system and have assumed serious proportions in recent years. In particular, two problems have plagued the international monetary system. The first has to do with the possibility of inadequate growth of monetary reserves. The second problem relates to the question of whether effective balance of payments adjustments are achieved under the system. This latter problem has special implications for the United States balance of payments deficit and the role of the dollar as a key currency.

Inadequate reserves

The viability of the present international monetary system presumes adequate reserves. As the system evolved, these reserves were composed of gold and key currencies, particularly the dollar. What are the sources of these reserves? And why might their growth have been inadequate?

The quantity of gold available as international monetary reserves is equal simply to the quantity produced, less the amount which goes into industrial uses (dentistry, jewelry) and the amount which is hoarded for speculative purposes. Because the price was held at $35 per ounce for some thirty-seven years and production costs have risen, gold mining became less and less profitable. As a result, additions to the world's stock of monetary gold have been, and presumably will continue to be, quite modest. Recent estimates suggest that at best the world's monetary gold stock will grow at only 2 percent per year in the foreseeable future.[4]

What about dollars? How have nations acquired dollars as international reserves? The answer here is peculiar, but of great significance. Foreign nations have acquired substantial dollar holdings as the direct result of the balance of payments deficits of the United States. That is, foreign nations have taken either gold or dollar balances from the United States in settlement for our payments deficits. These growing dollar reserves have been a more important source of international monetary reserves than have increases in the stock of gold. This brings us to the crux of the problem: Further expansion in the volume of world trade will require substantial increases in monetary reserves. And under postwar institutional arrangements, the future growth of world monetary reserves depended largely upon continued American payments deficits. The dilemma is obvious. The United States cannot continue to incur deficits indefinitely. But to the extent that the United States corrects its payments deficits, the growth of the world's monetary reserves—and therefore the prospects for continued expansion of world trade—will be diminished.

[4] *Economic Report of the President, 1968* (Washington), p. 181.

The adjustment problem

The other basic criticism of the postwar international monetary system is that it does not provide an effective means by which a nation can resolve a serious payments deficit. While the present system offers a procedure for orderly currency devaluation to correct a deeply rooted deficit, critics hold that in fact the system does not work effectively in this respect. Exchange rate "pegs" are rarely adjusted, and the system has in fact become one of rigid exchange rates. A nation's IMF commitment to stabilize its exchange rate and the availability of loans to help achieve this objective are both conducive to the deferring of exchange rate adjustments. In the meantime the nation's balance of payments deficit is likely to become more acute as speculative capital leaves the country in anticipation of devaluation.

PROPOSALS FOR REFORM

With these two problems—a potential reserve shortage and prolonged payments disequilibria—in mind, let us consider some recent proposals designed to bolster or restructure the current international monetary system. We shall examine three possible avenues of reform.

Increase the dollar price of gold

One frequently heard proposal for relieving the shortage of international monetary reserves is simply to raise the world price of gold. Given the key currency role of the dollar, the basic relationship which determines the monetary value of the world's gold stock is the dollar price of gold. Why not increase this price so as to transform the present amount of monetary gold into a greater dollar amount of reserves? After all, it is highly arbitrary for the price of gold to be at $35 per ounce and to have remained at that level for thirty-five years. By, say, doubling the price of gold to $70, the dollar value of existing international gold reserves would double! As a bonus, the higher gold price would stimulate the gold mining industry, and gold production would rise to augment international monetary reserves over time. If all nations alter the relation of their currencies to gold, rates of exchange and hence the flow of trade can remain undisrupted.

This proposal sounds wonderfully simple and logical. But there are serious problems involved. First of all, the United States has repeatedly stated that it would not increase the price of gold. It has done this in the interest of maintaining the effectiveness of the world monetary system. In other words, we have assured nations with whom we have incurred payments deficits that if they will hold larger dollar balances in the settlement of these deficits, they can rest assured that we will not raise the price of gold and thereby cut the value of their dollars in terms of gold. In short, nations such as Japan and Sweden, which have been willing to hold more dollars rather than aggravate our gold drain by insisting upon gold in settling our payments balance, would be penalized. Conversely, to increase the price of gold would be to reward those who have hoarded gold in anticipation of its price being raised. Thus by increasing the price of gold we would be rewarding those who, by hoarding gold, have contributed to the shortage of international monetary reserves. And it should be noted that the Soviet Union and South Africa are major producers and holders of gold; many people would find it quite objectionable to subsidize these two nations by raising the price of gold.

Secondly, if the United States were to alter the price of gold, this action might cast a pall of uncertainty over the future. If the price of gold is raised now, what is to prevent it from being raised again? And again? The usefulness of gold in the presently structured international monetary system might be undermined.

Finally, for centuries men have decried the absurdity and wastefulness of using gold as money. What folly—what a waste of resources—to dig gold out of the ground, refine and cast it, and put it back into the ground so that nations of the world can have an international medium of exchange. Why raise the price of gold and encourage such economically absurd activities? Why not move toward a credit-based monetary system?

Toward a managed system

This final question brings us to another kind of proposed reform. We noted in Part 3 that gold plays no significant role in the functioning of our domestic monetary system. The domestic money supply is based upon credit and not upon any commodity such as gold. The domestic money supply is managed by public authorities; confidence in the monetary system and therefore the effectiveness of the system depends upon how well money (credit) is managed. This system has the crucial advantage of permitting adjustment of the money supply in terms of the needs of the economy; the money supply is not restricted to the availability of some arbitrarily chosen commodity such as gold.

Triffin Plan A number of proposals over the years have suggested that the IMF be modified to make it a world central bank, a kind of "supercentral" bank. Professor Robert Triffin of Yale has put forward a far-reaching proposal of this type. Skirting the many technical details, it suggests that the IMF be made an international bank which would perform the same functions for the international economy that the

commercial banking system performs for a domestic economy, that is, accept deposits and make loans. Specifically, instead of holding key currencies as monetary reserves, surplus nations would be required to deposit a portion of these reserves in the IMF. On the basis of these deposits the IMF could *create* needed international monetary reserves by lending to deficit nations. In essence, the IMF's ability to provide needed monetary reserves would no longer be limited to the pools of currencies and gold received as the required subscriptions of its members. Rather, like a commercial banking system, the Fund could create credit (international monetary reserves) as required to meet payments deficits and finance a growing volume of world trade and investment. The advantage of such a system is quite clear: The availability of international monetary reserves would no longer depend upon the vagaries of world gold mining and the continuance of deficits in the balance of payments of key currency nations.

But the Triffin Plan does constitute a radical departure from existing international monetary arrangements. And its acceptance presumes a higher degree of international economic and political cooperation than nations have thus far been able to achieve. In particular, the effective functioning of a credit-(money) creating institution assumes a high degree of confidence in its management. What is to guarantee that the IMF will increase monetary reserves by the "right" amount? After all, an overexpansion of world monetary reserves might stimulate world trade to the extent that inflation occurs. Conversely, a failure to expand monetary reserves sufficiently could choke off the volume of trade and precipitate deflation and unemployment throughout the world. Is the "right" amount of reserves from the United States's point of view also the "right" amount for France, Britain, Japan, and New Zealand? The implication is clear: Nations must in effect agree to forgo some of their sovereignty over their domestic economies if the IMF is to be made a credit-creating world bank.

The Rio Plan and SDRs After several years of study and negotiation, the 106 members of the IMF endorsed a new plan at its 1967 meeting at Rio de Janeiro. The Rio Plan is designed to supplement gold and key currencies as international monetary reserves. The new plan is quite complex in its details;[5] only a terse summary is offered here.

As already noted, the Rio Plan provides for the creation of new international monetary reserves to supplement gold and key currencies. These new reserves are in the form of Special Drawing Rights, or, simply, SDRs. SDRs—popularly referred to as "paper gold"—are created at the initiative of the directors of the IMF, but only with the approval of an 85 percent majority of the voting power of Fund participants. Presumably, action to create SDRs will be initiated and approved only when there is a clear need to supplement international monetary reserves on a long-term basis. SDRs will be made available to Fund members in proportion to their IMF quotas and can be used, as gold is now used, to settle payments deficits or satisfy reserve needs; a nation which is short of foreign currencies can exchange its SDRs for needed currencies.

Perhaps the most remarkable characteristic of SDRs is that they are backed simply by the commitment of participating IMF nations to accept them in exchange for convertible currencies. Thus the value of this new reserve asset is much like the value of most domestic money in that participating nations agree to accept it as legal tender. Paper monetary reserves are not new in the international monetary system; the key currencies—dollars and pounds—now play this role. What is new about the SDRs is that they will represent a monetary reserve which is backed by the IMF nations as a group and which is created by the joint decisions of these nations.

The IMF decided to allocate some $9.5 billion of SDRs to member nations over the 1970–1972 period. Hence, SDRs have already provided a substantial increase in international monetary reserves and may well become the main source of future reserve growth. The introduction of SDRs as a new source

[5]See, for example, Thomas E. Davis, "The New International Monetary Plan in Perspective," *Monthly Review of Federal Reserve Bank of Kansas City,* February 1968, pp. 11–18.

of international reserves is particularly important because, as previously noted, the growth of international reserves of American dollars has been dependent upon United States balance of payments deficits. SDRs make it possible for the United States to achieve a balance of payments equilibrium without creating shortages of international monetary reserves.

Freely fluctuating exchange rates

Another proposal for reform of the international monetary system holds that nations should discard the objective of exchange rate stability and substitute a system of exchange rates which are free to fluctuate in response to changes in the demand for, and supply of, various currencies. Proponents of freely flexible exchange rates advance a number of arguments.

First and foremost, freely fluctuating rates would *automatically* and quickly correct balance of payments disequilibria. If a nation incurs a payments deficit, the international value of its currency will automatically fall or depreciate (Chapter 43). This decline will stimulate its exports and lower its imports, thereby correcting the original deficit. Stated differently, small and frequent changes in exchange rates would reduce the tendency for large balance of payments imbalances to accumulate. Secondly, the problem of inadequate monetary reserves would be largely resolved by establishing freely fluctuating exchange rates. Most reserves are currently held by the IMF and in stabilization funds for the purpose of keeping exchange rates stable when payments imbalances occur. Since payments imbalances would be quickly resolved under a system of fluctuating rates, this need for international reserves would obviously disappear.

But as we saw in Chapter 43, there are important objections to freely fluctuating exchange rates. Opponents allege, first, that fluctuating rates could seriously complicate the pricing of goods and services in world trade and could add to the uncertainty and risk of foreign trade. Fluctuating rates would therefore tend to reduce the volume of world trade. Speculative transactions might well accentuate exchange rate adjustments, causing a severe unsettling of world trade and investment. A basic purpose of the world monetary system is to stimulate trade; freely fluctuating exchange rates would work in the wrong direction. A second criticism is that fluctuating rates might precipitate trade controls. That is, a nation which loses world markets to a country whose currency is depreciating might turn to trade restrictions as a means of bolstering its own trade position. Finally, there is a political objection to freely fluctuating rates. Pegged rates have been an important stimulus to international cooperation and unity among free world nations; the adoption of fluctuating rates might induce nations to go their separate paths and thereby destroy this spirit of cooperation.

"FLOATING" THE DOLLAR

As part of his New Economic Policy, President Nixon on August 15, 1971, suspended the dollar's convertibility into gold. This startling announcement abrogated a policy to exchange gold for dollars at $35 per ounce which had existed for 37 years. This new policy severed the link between gold and the international value of the dollar, thereby "floating" the dollar and allowing its value to be determined by market forces. Such profound action was taken on the assumption that under the basically stable exchange rates of the postwar international monetary system the dollar had come to be substantially overvalued in relation to the currencies of our major trading partners—Japan and most of the Common Market countries. Hence, floating the dollar—that is, allowing its international value to be determined by supply and demand rather than by its convertibility price in terms of gold—is, in fact, a means of devaluing the dollar. Stated differently, convertibility to gold was suspended on the expectation that the free-market value of the dollar would settle at levels 5 to 15 percent below its previous value vis-à-vis the currencies of Japan and the EEC nations. We already know the immediate objectives of this devaluation. Exchange rates link the entire price structures of nations.

Therefore, a decline in the international value of the dollar means that all American goods will be cheaper to foreigners and, conversely, all foreign goods will be more expensive to Americans. In short, the devaluation of the dollar means that the United States's exports will rise and its imports will fall, tending to correct our payments deficit.

The United States's devaluation, coupled with the 10 percent import surcharge, raises some profound questions about the future course of world trade and the nature of the monetary system that will facilitate that trade. Most obviously, we have seen that the dollar—partly because of its convertibility into gold—has been the major key currency in the international monetary system. By the severing of the gold link and the devaluation of the dollar, the era of a world money system dominated by the American dollar may well be at an end. Indeed, what is the status of the postwar international monetary system with its emphasis upon stable exchange rates now that the value of the basic key currency is being allowed to fluctuate in accordance with market forces? Most experts agree that the floating of the dollar has dealt an extremely serious, if not fatal, blow to that system. It is quite evident that the postwar system will require drastic overhaul or may, in fact, be superseded by some new system. But the characteristics of the reforms or of a new system are anything but clear at this point in time. Reasonable guesses are that (1) the dollar and gold will play significantly less important roles in the new system and (2) provision for greater exchange rate flexibility will be incorporated in the new monetary system.

Consider the first point. While the dollar and gold will continue to be of significance, it is entirely possible that the German mark or the Japanese yen will also become a key currency. But reform may be more fundamental. In restructuring the international monetary system cooperating nations may choose to consider carefully the possibility of creating a managed international currency along the lines suggested by Triffin. Recall that the SDRs were a step in this direction. The new and severe international monetary crisis posed by floating the dollar could foster support for an international bank with money-creating capacity to meet the needs of an expanding volume of world trade.

Now the second point. It is also likely that the new monetary system will embody greater exchange rate flexibility. This does not mean that nations of the world are prepared to accept freely fluctuating exchange rates and the potentially inhibiting effect they may have upon the volume of trade. On the other hand, we have seen that a basic shortcoming of the postwar system under the IMF has been its inability to negotiate large enough changes in exchange rates to correct long-term balance of payments disequilibria. Fortunately, there are compromise options that might be capable of capturing the advantages of both exchange rate stability (a large and expanding volume of trade) and exchange rate flexibility (the resolution of balance of payments problems). One much-discussed option is a *crawling-peg* system of exchange rates. Skirting technical details, we can describe the crawling-peg proposal as permission for a nation faced with a chronic payments deficit to adjust the par value of its currency according to some specified formula. For example, if the par value of a currency could be changed by one-quarter of 1 percent each month, the par value of the currency of the deficit nation could be lowered by 3 percent per year. A similar adjustment could be made in ensuing years if the deficit persisted. The relatively small size of the adjustment per month and per year would preserve short-term exchange rate stability, discourage currency speculation, and be conducive to expanding trade. At the same time the crawling peg would provide enough flexibility to correct persistent payments deficits.

The search for a new, viable international monetary system will not be a simple matter. The United States's actions in floating the dollar and establishing the tariff surcharge impose painful adjustments upon other nations and simultaneously raise the specter of economic nationalism. Remember that the surcharge represents a sharp reversal of the United States's role as a champion of freer trade. Note, too, that to the extent America's exports are stimulated and its imports diminished by the floating of the dollar and the surcharge, our trading partners will experi-

ence the contractionary effects of slumping exports and rising imports. As monetary officials meet in the early 1970s for the purpose of reconstructing a workable international monetary system, the spirit of cooperation and mutual understanding that surrounded efforts to resolve the numerous monetary crises of the 1960s may be notable by its absence.

SUMMARY

1. In the 1929–1945 period the Great Depression and World War II severely disrupted the volume and pattern of world trade. The cold war posed serious obstacles to the rebuilding of international trade.

2. The immediate world economic problem after World War II was to achieve European economic recovery. A large flow of United States aid to Europe through UNRRA and the Marshall Plan contributed to this goal.

3. The reduction or elimination of artificial barriers to trade is a necessary condition for an expanding flow of world trade and finance. The Reciprocal Trade Agreements Act of 1934 was the beginning of a trend toward lower American tariffs. In 1947 the General Agreement on Tariffs and Trade was formed *a.* to encourage nondiscriminatory treatment for all trading nations, *b.* to achieve tariff reductions, and *c.* to eliminate import quotas. The Kennedy Round of tariff negotiations under GATT was based upon negotiating authority given the President under the Trade Expansion Act of 1962.

4. One of the remarkable international developments of the postwar period has been the move toward European economic integration in the form of the Common Market. Member nations recently achieved the complete elimination of internal tariff barriers and have established common external tariffs, whose levels have been and will be moderated as a result of various tariff reductions negotiated under the auspices of GATT. The EEC has also made substantial progress in freeing the intraregional movement of labor and capital resources. The Common Market nations have achieved substantial economic success, as reflected in rapidly growing GNPs, expanding per capita output, and a rising share of world trade.

5. For over two decades the United States has been faced with large and persistent balance of payments deficits. The growing productivity of Western Europe and Japan, American inflation, large outflows of investment capital, and a substantial American foreign aid program have all contributed to this deficit. American productivity increases, domestic restraints against inflation, a redistribution of the costs of Western military and economic aid programs, and devaluation of the dollar are basic remedial measures. A number of ad hoc policies—for example, the "tying" of foreign aid to American goods, a special tax on foreign travel, the "interest equalization tax" on the purchase of foreign securities, and the 1971 tariff surcharge—have been invoked to ameliorate the deficit.

6. The post-World War II international monetary system has been committed to an "adjustable-peg" system of exchange rates. In particular, the International Monetary Fund was created *a.* to make short-term foreign currency loans to help nations meet temporary payments deficits and *b.* to provide for an orderly adjustment of exchange rates to help correct fundamental payments deficits. As the world's monetary system evolved after the war, gold and certain "key currencies"—particularly American dollars and British pounds—have served as international monetary reserves.

7. Two serious and interrelated problems have plagued the international monetary system: *a.* the inadequate growth of international monetary reserves and *b.* the incapacity of nations—and the United States specifically—to achieve required balance of payments adjustments under the system. The reserve problem has its roots in the relatively small increase in the world's stock of gold and the fact that additional dollar reserves depend upon continuation of a United States payments deficit.

8. The adjustment problem stems from the fact that the adjustable-peg system of exchange rates encourages nations to forestall those exchange rate adjustments that are requisite to a balance of payments equilibrium. The problem of exchange rate devaluation has been particularly acute for the United States because the dollar has been a key currency in the international money market.

9. Three basic kinds of proposals have been offered to deal with the reserves and adjustment problems: *a.* Increase the dollar price of gold, *b.* develop a managed monetary system along the lines suggested by the Triffin Plan, or finally *c.* establish a system of freely fluctuating exchange rates.

10. The floating of the dollar in 1971 was a means of devaluation for the purpose of correcting the United States's balance of payments deficit. This devaluation, however, seriously disrupted the existing international monetary system to the extent that a thorough revision of that system, or the creation of an entirely new system, is a major problem facing free world nations in the 1970s.

QUESTIONS AND STUDY SUGGESTIONS

1. What factors underlay the disintegration of international trade? Explain the impact of each.

2. What were the character and size of American post–World War II economic aid? Describe and evaluate the Marshall Plan. What changes have occurred in the volume, character, and direction of American foreign aid since the end of that war?

3. Identify and discuss each of the following: *a.* The Hawley-Smoot Tariff Act of 1930, *b.* The Reciprocal Trade Agreements Act of 1934, *c.* GATT, *d.* The Trade Expansion Act of 1962, and *e.* the Kennedy Round.

4. What is "economic integration"? Why do many economists feel that European economic integration is an essential measure in reconstructing world trade? Use the "economies of scale" analysis of Chapter 26 to explain why the Common Market has enabled many European industries to compete more effectively in international markets.

5. Describe in detail the causes of the United States balance of payments deficit. In view of the fact that the United States is running a trade (export) surplus, how do you explain recent American gold outflows? How should this loss of gold be corrected?

6. Explain and illustrate:
a. "Policies that stimulate the domestic economy tend to cause a trade deficit."
b. "A balance of payments deficit imposes severe constraints upon domestic economic policies."

7. Identify and discuss the IMF, indicating its goals and its role in fostering an adjustable-peg system of exchange rates.

8. Explain why international monetary reserves have tended to become inadequate in recent years. How is the problem of achieving an adequate supply of international monetary reserves related to the United States balance of payments problem?

9. Critically analyze and discuss:
a. "America's payments deficits are the result of the dollar being overvalued. Therefore, the solution to its payments problem is simple: Increase the dollar price of gold."
b. "Balance of payments equilibrium will quickly result for all nations if their relative prices are in proper relationship to one another. The only systematic means of achieving these proper relationships is through a system of freely fluctuating exchange rates."

10. What is the Triffin Plan? What are SDRs? Comment: "The Triffin Plan and the creation of SDRs are steps toward the demonetization of gold."

11. What are the domestic and international consequences of "floating the dollar"? What effects has this decision had upon the postwar international monetary system? If you were participating in a revision of the international monetary system, what specific proposals would you offer?

12. Explain the "crawling-peg" system of exchange rates. What are the alleged advantages of this system?

SELECTED REFERENCES

Economic Issues, 4th ed., readings 84, 86, and 87.

Economic Report of the President, 1971 (Washington), chap. 5.

Kreinin, Mordechai E.: *International Economics: A Policy Approach* (New York: Harcourt Brace Jovanovich, Inc., 1971), chaps. 1–10.

Mikesell, Raymond F.: *Financing World Trade* (New York: Thomas Y. Crowell Company, 1969).

Snider, Delbert A.: *Introduction to International Economics,* 5th ed. (Homewood, Ill.: Richard D. Irwin, Inc., 1971), chaps. 13–21 and 25.

THE UNDERDEVELOPED NATIONS: A SPECIAL PROBLEM IN ECONOMIC GROWTH

It is exceedingly difficult for the typical American family, whose 1969 average income was $9,400, to grasp the simple fact that some two-thirds of the world's population persistently lives at the subsistence level. The average American is too busy waging a loud but losing battle against obesity or watching his color television set to acknowledge the abject poverty which characterizes much of our planet. A six-room suburban home, a new Buick, and a healthy bank account all tend to make the hunger, squalor, and disease which prevail in most nations of the world seem remote.

UNDERSTANDING THE UNDERDEVELOPED NATIONS

This ignorance and lack of concern cannot be condoned. We must

1. Identify the underdeveloped nations
2. Appreciate the attitudes of the peoples of the underdeveloped nations toward their economic circumstances
3. Understand the interest of the advanced nations in the development of these nations

Low per capita income

The underdeveloped nations of the world bear a common brand: poverty—low per capita incomes as compared with such industrially advanced countries as the United States, Great Britain, and Canada. Table 45·1 clearly identifies most of the underdeveloped nations. Of course, where one draws the line between "developed," "semideveloped," and "underdeveloped" is an arbitrary matter. Nevertheless, in Table 45·1 we can roughly envision these three classifications. Looking at the 1968 data, we might tag those nations with per capita incomes of $1,500 or more as developed, or advanced, nations. Included here, primarily, are the United States, Canada, Australia, New Zealand, and the countries of Western Europe. Next is the semideveloped group, whose per capita incomes vary from, say, $600 to $1,499 per year. This heterogeneous group includes one or two Latin American nations, several countries of Eastern and Southern Europe, and Japan, Ireland, and Israel. The rest of the world—including most of Asia, Africa, Latin America, and southeastern Europe—bear the designation "underdeveloped."

TABLE 45·1 NATIONAL INCOME PER CAPITA IN SELECTED COUNTRIES, 1958 and 1968

Country	1958	1968	Country	1958	1968
United States	$2,115	$3,578	Portugal	$216	$451
Sweden	1,391	2,905	Chile	328	449
Switzerland	1,195	2,294	Costa Rica	324	422
Canada	1,503	2,247	Jamaica	317	411
Iceland	965	1,972	Guatemala	236	276
Denmark	888	1,960	Brazil	139	271
France	853	1,927	Colombia	189	268
Norway	871	1,808	Philippines	193	250
Australia	1,126	1,807	Jordan	139	249
Luxembourg	1,077	1,750	China (Taiwan)	91	247
New Zealand	1,172	1,714	Peru	163	246
Belgium	936	1,696	El Salvador	207	244
West Germany	829	1,682	Dominican Republic	200	238
Netherlands	695	1,604	Honduras	177	230
United Kingdom	1,013	1,451	Syria	155	214
Soviet Union	940	1,351	Ghana	140	198
Finland	727	1,342	Ecuador	157	196
Italy	478	1,149	Paraguay	121	195
Israel	610	1,147	Morocco	158	185
Austria	588	1,146	Tunisia	160	181
Japan	290	1,122	Thailand	80	137
Ireland	464	808	Ceylon	118	132
Venezuela	630	803	Pakistan	62	121
Spain	305	663	Kenya	69	107
Greece	326	651	Sudan	80	97
Trinidad and Tobago	419	633	Indonesia	82	86
Cyprus	450	622	Haiti	75	81
Argentina	489	551	India	64	73
Mexico	272	511	Burma	53	67
Panama	322	502	Uganda	80	60
Malta	337	467	Congo (Leopoldville)	69	52

Source: United Nations, *Statistical Yearbook 1969* (New York, 1970), pp. 557–562.

We need not belabor the pitifully low per capita annual incomes evidenced in Table 45·1. However, the implications of the poverty reflected by these figures merit emphasis.[1]

The poverty of underdeveloped countries means that their people, on a broad average, have a life expectancy only about half that of the people of the highly developed countries. They suffer much of the time from malaria, dysentery, tuberculosis, trachoma, or other ills. . . . Their food supply is about one-third less, measured in calories, than that of the developed countries, and when account is taken of the needs of the human body for the relatively expensive "pro-

[1] Eugene Staley, *The Future of Underdeveloped Countries* (New York: Harper & Row, Publishers, Incorporated, for the Council on Foreign Relations, 1954), pp. 15–18.

tective" foods, such as milk and meat, the extent of malnutrition is found to be very great indeed. The opportunity to attend school is limited to a small minority. . . . Only one person in four or five, again on a broad average of underdeveloped countries, knows how to read or write. The supply of cloth for clothing, home furnishing, and other purposes is about one-fourth as great per person in underdeveloped as in highly developed countries. Nonhuman energy to supplement the labor of human beings in industry, agriculture, transport, and household tasks is less than one-twentieth as plentiful, measured in horsepower-hours per person. Incomes, on the average, are less than one-tenth as high.

Viewpoint of underdeveloped nations

The income disparities revealed in Table 45·1—great as they are—conceal the discontent harbored by the people of the underdeveloped nations. The bulk of these people are not resigned to their fate. Far from it. Most seek and feel they have a right to a better life. As they see it, poverty is not inescapable.

Two recent developments—one economic and the other political—have fanned the desire of the underdeveloped nations for material and social betterment:

1. The per capita income gap between the economically advanced nations and the underdeveloped nations has not merely persisted, but in many instances has widened. Among nations, the rich have been getting richer and the poor have been getting relatively poorer.[2]

This widening has intensified the discontent of the peoples of the underdeveloped countries. The equation for social unrest is no secret:

$$\text{Aspirations} - \text{standard of living} = \text{social unrest}$$

As the living standards of the advanced nations have improved, the economic goals and aspirations of the underdeveloped nations have increased accordingly. But their actual standard of living in most instances has shown meager growth. The differential—social unrest—has clearly been on the increase. One need only review the political and military crises of the post-World War II era to validate this point.

2. In recent years many of the underdeveloped lands have achieved, or are in the process of achieving, political independence. Accompanying this freedom from colonial status has been a tremendous upsurge of nationalistic spirit. The underdeveloped nations seek the economic independence, respect, and social status which they feel are due them as independent nations.

Viewpoint of advanced nations

Like it or not, the advanced nations, and the United States in particular, have a great stake in the future of the underdeveloped nations. This interest has several roots. The *humanitarian* aspect of this interest is obvious: many people take the position that the wealthier nations have a tremendous moral obligation to relieve the stark poverty of the less fortunate peoples. The *political-military* importance of the underdeveloped nations is also clear: The ideological conflict between the Western world and communism may well be won or lost according to the paths of development pursued by the underdeveloped countries. Then, too, for purely *economic* reasons the United States has a vital interest in these less advanced nations: In selfish terms, these nations provide us with vital raw materials and, simultaneously, with markets for a portion of our finished goods. Through trade with these nations all participants can reap a portion of the benefits of international specialization.

Dubious lessons of history

It is disarmingly tempting for the advanced nations to offer less fortunate nations a simple formula for economic development: "Do what we did." Such a formula is glib, inaccurate, and, to the informed citizens of poor nations, downright insulting. This advice is akin to advising an undernourished, one-legged youngster that he too can be quarterback for the Packers if he will just follow Bart Starr's training

[2] The grim jokes of the day mirror the widening economic gap between the United States and the underdeveloped nations:

Polish Communist party secretary: "Hear you've got a brother out of work in Detroit. Why don't you write him and tell him to come home?"

Warsaw automobile worker: "Sure, but who'd send us the food parcels?"

schedule. The simple fact of the matter is that the now advanced nations initiated their development in an environment vastly different from that currently faced by the underdeveloped countries. Witness the favorable setting for American economic development: abundant and diverse mineral resources, opulent sources of power, navigable rivers, fertile and free farmland, a temperate climate, a small but energetic and (for that time) intelligent labor force, and finally, the virtual absence of social and moral taboos on business and commerce. This is an environment ripe for economic growth.

Throw these characteristics into reverse and you have the typical underdeveloped nation: a niggardly resource base, a lack of power, low-quality land, a teeming and untrained population, and a host of fetishes narrowly circumscribing any existing spirit of enterprise. The spontaneous growth arising from the favorable environs of the North American continent is not likely to blossom forth in such a briar patch. In most cases growth, if and when it is to be achieved, must be forced by a degree of government planning and nurtured by the aid of the more advanced nations. This is not to imply that communism or socialism is the modern-day path to economic development, or to say foreign aid is the primary fountainhead of economic growth. We are saying that economic growth must be actively pursued and not merely awaited. We are also saying that many underdeveloped countries may not be able to pull themselves up by their own bootstraps without external assistance.

BREAKING THE POVERTY BARRIER

The avenues of economic growth are essentially the same for both advanced and underdeveloped nations:

1. Existing supplies of resources must be used more efficiently. This entails not only the elimination of unemployment but also the achievement of greater efficiency in the allocation of resources.

2. The supplies of productive resources must be altered—typically, increased. By expanding the supplies of raw materials, capital equipment, effective manpower, and technological knowledge, a nation can push its production possibilities curve to the right (Chapter 20).

Why have some nations been so successful in pursuing these avenues of growth while other countries have lagged far behind? The answer, as noted above, lies in differences in the physical and sociocultural environments of the various nations. Our plan of attack is to examine the obstacles in the underdeveloped countries to altering the quantities and improving efficiency in the use of (1) natural resources, (2) human resources, (3) capital goods, and (4) technological knowledge. Emphasis here will be upon the private sector of the economy. In addition, social and institutional impediments to growth will be illustrated. And finally, the roles of government and foreign aid in the development process will be analyzed.

Natural resources

A nation's endowments of natural resources constitute an obvious but crucial element in its capacity for economic development. Poor nations are frequently burdened with an adverse climate, a paucity of arable land, very scarce mineral resources, and few sources of power. An inadequate resource base poses a more serious obstacle to growth than does, say, a lack of capital goods or a qualitatively inferior labor force. The reason for this lies in the fact that there is little or nothing that can be done to overcome a weak resource base. Certainly swamps can be drained and jungles cleared, but the prospects here are usually very limited and the process exceedingly slow. As a matter of fact, faulty soil conservation practices and the application of wasteful technologies in mining often cause a premature shrinkage in an underdeveloped nation's natural resources. Then too, there is the ever-present possibility that technological improvements in the advanced nations will impair the economic value of the underdeveloped nation's natural resources. Witness the impact of synthetic rubber upon the natural rubber industries of Malaya and Indonesia.

The crucial limiting role of natural resources must be kept clearly in mind in programing the economic development of any nation. Though an inviting and pleasant mental exercise, it is flatly unrealistic for many of the underdeveloped nations to envision an economic destiny comparable to that of the United States, Canada, or the Soviet Union. Automated steel, automobile, and aluminum plants are simply not a part of the foreseeable economic futures of most underdeveloped nations. This is not, of course, to rule out future development for those underdeveloped nations plagued with severe scarcities of natural resources. Switzerland, Israel, and Japan, for example, have achieved relatively high levels of living despite narrow resource bases. At the same time, other nations with more affluent natural resources—for example, Bolivia—have not done so well. In almost all underdeveloped nations, despite the lack of natural endowments, there is ample room for growth. But it must be recognized that the relatively unaugmentable character of natural resources may set very real limits on this growth.

Employment of human resources

Three statements describe the typical underdeveloped nation's circumstances with respect to human resources:

1. It is overpopulated.
2. Disguised unemployment is widespread.
3. The quality of the labor force is exceedingly low.

Overpopulation Ironically, many of the nations with the most meager natural and capital resources have the largest populations to support. Table 45·2 compares the population of a few selected nations with that of the United States. In some of the underdeveloped countries the Malthusian population doctrine, rooted in the law of diminishing returns, is all too apparent. Population actually presses upon the food supply to the extent that per capita food consumption is pulled down perilously close to the subsistence level. In the worst instances it is only the despicable team of malnutrition and disease and the high death rate they provide which keeps incomes near subsistence.

TABLE 45·2 POPULATION PER SQUARE MILE OF SELECTED COUNTRIES, 1968

Country	Population per square mile
United States	55
Nigeria	177
Portugal	268
Philippines	312
Pakistan	325
India	416
Haiti	437
Ceylon	473
South Korea	803
Taiwan	972

Source: United Nations data.

It would seem at first glance that, since

$$\text{Per capita standard of living} = \frac{\text{consumer goods (food) production}}{\text{population}}$$

the standard of living could be raised simply by boosting consumer goods—particularly food—production. But in reality the problem is much more complex than this, because any increase in consumer goods production which initially raises the standard of living is likely to induce a population increase. This increase, if sufficient in size, will dissipate the increase in living standards, and subsistence living levels will again prevail.

But why does population growth tend to accompany increases in output? First, the nation's death rate will decline with initial increases in production. This decline is the result of (1) a higher level of per capita food consumption and (2) the basic medical and sanitation programs which almost invariably accompany the initial phases of economic development. Second, the birth rate will remain high or may even increase, particularly so as the medical and sanitation programs cut the rate of infant mortality. The cliché that "the rich get richer and the poor get children"

is uncomfortably accurate for many of the underdeveloped nations of the world. In short, an increase in the per capita standard of living may give rise to a population upsurge which will cease only when the standard of living has again been reduced to the level of bare subsistence.

In addition to the fact that rapid population growth can translate an expanding GNP into a stagnant or slow-growing GNP per capita, there are less obvious reasons why population expansion is an obstacle to development. On the one hand, large families reduce the capacity of a household to save, and this restricts the economy's capacity to accumulate capital. On the other hand, high birth rates result in a larger proportion of children in the population or, in other words, a smaller productive work force relative to total population.

Most authorities advocate birth control as the obvious and most effective means for breaking out of this dilemma. And breakthroughs in contraceptive technology in the 1960s have made this solution increasingly relevant. But the obstacles to this solution are typically great. Those nations which stand to gain most by accepting birth control as a release from this cycle of poverty are often the least willing, for religious and sociocultural reasons, and least able, for literacy reasons, to utilize the practice. Population growth in Latin America, for example, is among the most rapid in the world.

Caution: Not all underdeveloped nations suffer from overpopulation, nor is it to be concluded that a large population necessarily means underdevelopment. The points to note are (1) a large and rapidly growing population may pose a special obstacle to economic development, and (2) many of the underdeveloped and semideveloped nations are so burdened.[3]

Disguised unemployment Aside from the drag of overpopulation, the underdeveloped countries are faced with a serious underemployment problem. In contrast to the unemployment in advanced nations, the problem is not so much cyclical fluctuations—most underdeveloped nations are simply too poor to afford a business cycle!—but rather a chronic and large-scale overallocation of labor to agriculture.

How has this problem of disguised unemployment come about? The predominance of agriculture is common to virtually all the underdeveloped nations. It is very likely that two-thirds, four-fifths, or more of an underdeveloped nation's labor force will be engaged in agricultural pursuits. Much—possibly 25 to 30 percent—of this farm labor is underemployed, or surplus, labor,[4] that is, labor which contributes little or nothing to total agricultural output. In terms of our earlier discussion of the principle of diminishing returns, the agricultural "plant" (the fixed supply of arable land) of most underdeveloped nations is grossly overmanned, to the extent that the marginal product of one-fourth or one-third of the nation's agricultural labor force may be zero or even negative! This means that a large fraction of an underdeveloped nation's labor force might be reallocated from agricultural to industrial pursuits with little or no decline, and possibly an increase, in food production.

But as a matter of fact, this shift of human resources, which we recall is the earmark of a growing economy, has simply not come to pass. Why not? The most important and most obvious reason is that there are very few industrial jobs available in these underdeveloped nations to attract surplus labor from agriculture. The people of underdeveloped nations farm because there is nothing else to do. In addition, ignorance of alternative employments plus a host of religious and sociocultural factors may bind the worker to his land. It is apparently more pleasant to subsist while keeping busy (though unproductive) in familiar surroundings than to suffer the same fate in total idleness amidst the impersonal environment of a city. A final factor also retards any potential migration of surplus labor from agriculture to industry: The quality of the labor force may prohibit workers from accepting industrial employment even if it were readily available. A minimum level of training and education is necessary in operating the most simple ma-

[3]The interested reader should consult Clifford M. Hardin (ed.), *Overcoming World Hunger* (Englewood Cliffs, N.J.: Prentice-Hall, Inc., 1969).

[4]See Ragnar Nurkse, *Problem of Capital Formation in Underdeveloped Countries* (Fair Lawn, N.J.: Oxford University Press, 1967), p. 35.

chines; the labor forces of many underdeveloped nations have not as yet achieved that level. The result is that labor immobility is pronounced in most underdeveloped countries, and disguised unemployment persists.

Quality of the labor force Though long on numbers, the populations of the underdeveloped nations are pitifully short on quality. Malnutrition, the absence of proper medical care, and insufficient educational facilities all contribute to populations ill equipped for economic development and industrialization. Particularly vital is the absence of a vigorous entrepreneurial class willing to bear risks, accumulate capital, and provide the organizational requisites essential to economic growth. Closely related is the dearth of labor that is prepared to handle the routine supervisory functions basic to any program of development.

Capital accumulation

Most economists feel that an important focal point of economic development is the accumulation of capital goods. There are several reasons for this emphasis upon capital formation:

1. All underdeveloped countries do suffer from a critical shortage of capital goods—factories, machinery and equipment, public utilities, and so forth. There can be no doubt that better-equipped labor forces would greatly enhance the productivity of the underdeveloped nations and help to boost the per capita standard of living.

2. Increasing the stock of capital goods is crucial because of the very limited possibility of increasing the supply of arable land. If there is little likelihood of offsetting the law of diminishing returns in agriculture by increasing the supply of land, the obvious alternative is to counter its operation by better equipping the available agricultural manpower or by providing industrial capital to which this labor can be reallocated.

3. Once initiated, the process of capital accumulation can be cumulative. If capital accumulation can increase output ahead of population growth, a margin of saving will arise which permits further capital formation. In a sense capital accumulation can feed upon itself.

Let us first consider the prospects for underdeveloped nations to accumulate capital domestically. Then we shall examine the possibility of foreign capital flowing into them. In each case we are concerned with private capital; public investment will be considered later.

Domestic capital formation How does an underdeveloped nation—or any nation for that matter—accumulate capital? The answer: through the processes of saving and investing. A nation must save, that is, refrain from consumption, to release resources from consumer goods production. Investment spending must then occur to absorb these released resources in the production of capital goods. But the impediments to saving and investing are much greater in an underdeveloped nation than in an advanced economy.

The savings potential Consider first the savings side of the picture. The savings potential of the underdeveloped countries is low. Statistics indicate that the underdeveloped countries manage to save at best some 5 percent of their national incomes, while the advanced nations save about 10 percent. In explaining this point, it is important to distinguish between (1) the masses of people, who are unable or unwilling to save, and (2) the very wealthy, who can save, but who do not make their savings available for the accumulation of productive capital goods.

1. Saving is a luxury far beyond the reach of the masses of people in the underdeveloped nations; most consume their entire incomes to keep body and soul intact. Incomes are simply too low to permit the masses to save.

But this is only half the picture. There is serious doubt as to whether significant increases in per capita incomes will generate much saving. Most experts agree that the propensities of underdeveloped nations to consume—that is, their willingness to spend—depend not only upon their own levels of income but

also upon the relationship of their income levels to those of the advanced nations. Better communications, increased literacy, expanding hordes of American tourists, and in some instances, the presence of foreign troops have made the peoples of the underdeveloped nations increasingly aware of the superior consumption levels of the advanced nations. This whets the appetites of the poverty-ridden and intensifies their dissatisfaction with their own standard of living. New wants and higher aspirations lead to a high propensity to consume.[5] The underdeveloped nations, in short, are most anxious to consume, not save, any forthcoming increases in their national incomes.

2. This is not to say that no one saves in an underdeveloped nation. We have noted that saving might be as high as 5 percent of the national income. This saving stems from the highly unequal distribution of income which characterizes most of the underdeveloped nations. Ironically, both the poorest and the richest families of the world reside in the most underdeveloped countries. Those fortunate few with astronomical incomes—the tribal chieftains, the kings, the large landowners, and the religious leaders—do have ample capacity to save. Unfortunately, these high-income receivers frequently squander their wealth on luxury goods, trivialities, foreign travel, the hoarding of precious metals, or the purchase of existing properties in the form of land or urban real estate. The monetary saving which does occur often flows abroad for safekeeping or to take advantage of the more convenient saving outlets provided by the securities markets of the advanced nations. The important point is that those few who have the ability to save are often unwilling to do so or, if they are willing, do not make their saving available for investment in productive facilities.

Investment obstacles The investment side of the capital formation process abounds with equally serious obstacles. These obstacles serve to undermine the rate of capital formation even when a sufficient volume of savings is available to finance the needed investment. *The major obstacles to investment fall into two categories: the lack of investors and the lack of incentives to invest.*

Oddly enough, in some underdeveloped countries—Turkey and Pakistan, for example—the major obstacle to investment is simply the lack of businessmen who are willing to assume the risks associated with investment. This, of course, is a special case of qualitative deficiencies of the labor force previously discussed.

But even if substantial savings and a vigorous entrepreneurial class are present, an essential ingredient in capital formation—the incentive to invest—may be weak. And clearly a host of factors may combine in an underdeveloped nation to cripple investment incentives. Political and social instability—in particular, the fear of nationalization of industry—may dampen the incentive to invest. Similarly, very low incomes mean a limited domestic market for most nonagricultural goods. This factor is especially crucial when it is recognized that the chances of successfully competing with the mature industries of the advanced nations in international markets are typically nil. Then, too, the previously cited lack of trained administrative and operating personnel may be a vital factor in retarding investment. Finally, many of the underdeveloped countries simply do not have a sufficient accumulation of the *basic social capital,* that is, the public utilities, which are prerequisite to private investment of a productive nature. Poor roads, inadequate railways, little gas and electricity production, antiquated communications, unsatisfactory housing, and meager educational and public health facilities hardly provide an inviting environment for investment spending.

The absence of basic social capital presents more of a problem than one might first surmise. The dearth of social capital means that a great deal of investment spending which does not *directly* result in the production of goods and which may not be capable of bearing profits must take place prior to, and simultaneously with, productive investment in manufacturing machinery and equipment. Statistics for the advanced nations indicate that about 60 percent of gross investment goes for housing, public works, and public

[5] Ibid., p. 58.

utilities, leaving about 40 percent for directly productive investment in manufacturing, agriculture, and commerce.[6] These figures probably understate the percentage of total investment which must be devoted to social capital in the underdeveloped nations. The volume of investment required to initiate economic development may be much greater than it first appears.

There is one potential bright spot in this otherwise dismal picture: The possibility of accumulating capital through *nonfinancial investment,* or investment in kind. Given the prerequisite leadership and willingness to cooperate, capital can be accumulated by simply transferring surplus agricultural labor to the improvement of agricultural facilities or to the construction of basic social capital. If each agricultural village would allocate its surplus manpower to the construction of irrigation canals, wells, schools, sanitary facilities, and roads, significant amounts of capital might be accumulated at no sacrifice of consumer goods production. Nonfinancial investment simply bypasses the problems embodied within the financial aspects of the capital accumulation process. Such investment does not require consumers to save portions of their money income, nor does it presume the presence of an entrepreneurial class anxious to invest. In short, provided the leadership and cooperative spirit are present, nonfinancial investment is a promising avenue for the accumulation of basic capital goods.

External capital formation Can flows of private capital from the advanced to the underdeveloped nations avoid the obstacles to internal capital formation and thereby compensate for the paucity of investment spending in the underdeveloped nations? Most underdeveloped nations have received considerable assistance from such capital flows. But extreme caution is required lest we regard external capital as a panacea for economic underdevelopment. The obstacles to foreign flows of private capital are serious. Virtually all the deterrents to private domestic investment apply to foreign capital flows. In addition, there are certain unique barriers:

1. Underdeveloped countries frequently seek to make their economies more diversified. They want to develop home markets, on the one hand, and to reduce their dependence upon the economic well-being of the advanced nations, on the other. Foreign private capital, however, seeks out those industries which are currently the most profitable, that is, the ones which are now producing for the export market. In brief, while the underdeveloped nations strive for less dependence on world markets, flows of foreign private capital often tend to enhance that dependence.

2. The growing spirit of nationalism in the underdeveloped nations has made them increasingly reluctant to have their domestic economies dominated by foreign interests. Having won political independence, the typical underdeveloped nation seeks control over its own economic machinery. The result has been a maze of policies detrimental to the international flow of private capital into the underdeveloped regions. Discriminatory taxation, limits or prohibitions upon the withdrawal of profits, and cumbersome governmental regulations and red tape concerning incoming capital are some of the more common barriers. To this must be added the ever-present danger of confiscation which political instability entails. This is not to deny that considerable private foreign investment does occur. But relatively speaking, the flow is not large, and over the years it has failed to keep pace with the rising national incomes of the advanced nations.

Technological advance

Technological advance and capital formation are frequently part of the same process. Yet there are advantages in treating technological advance, or the accumulation and application of new ideas concerning methods of producing, and capital formation, or the accumulating of capital goods, as separate processes.

This is particularly so in discussing the underdeveloped countries. We view technological advance

[6] W. Arthur Lewis, *The Theory of Economic Growth* (Homewood, Ill.: Richard D. Irwin, Inc., 1955), p. 210.

in the industrially advanced nations as an essentially evolutionary process wherein researchers first inch forward the boundaries of technological knowledge. Then follows the financing and construction of the ever-larger amounts of complex capital equipment which the technological advance demands. But this picture is not accurate for the underdeveloped countries. The rudimentary state of their current technology puts these nations far from the frontiers of technological advance. There already exists a huge body of technological knowledge accumulated by the advanced nations which the underdeveloped countries might adopt and apply without undertaking the expensive tasks of research. For example, the adoption of modern crop rotation practices and the introduction of contour plowing require no additional capital equipment, and they may contribute very significantly to productivity. By raising grain storage bins a few inches above the ground, a large amount of grain spoilage can be avoided. Such changes may sound minor to people of advanced nations. However, the resulting gains in productivity can mean the difference between subsistence and starvation in some poverty-ridden nations.

In most instances the application of either existing or new technological knowledge entails the use of new and different capital goods. But within limits, this capital can be obtained without an increase in the rate of capital formation. That is, if the annual flow of replacement investment is rechanneled from technologically inferior to technologically superior capital equipment, productivity can be increased out of a constant level of investment spending. As a matter of fact, some technological advances may be *capital-saving* rather than *capital-using.* A new fertilizer, better adapted to a nation's topography and climate, might be cheaper than that currently employed. A simple metal plow which will last ten years may be cheaper in the long run than a technologically inferior wooden plow which requires annual replacement.

All this is not to deny that, before a nation's development program is far along, further technological progress will call for an expanding flow of investment in capital goods. However, even here we must keep in mind that the productivity increases which the most fundamental technological advances permit may provide an increase in the standard of living sufficient to generate a part of the saving prerequisite to meeting the nation's expanding capital goods requirements. By boosting incomes, basic technological advances may provide for the capital accumulation upon which still further technological progress depends. To a degree, technological advance and capital formation may feed upon one another. But we must guard against overoptimism even when this mutual reinforcement of technological and capital accumulation occurs. Remember that the lack of entrepreneurs, of qualified industrial labor, or of essential natural resources can block technological progress as effectively as can a dearth of capital equipment.

Social and institutional aspects

Purely economic considerations are not sufficient to explain the occurrence or the absence of economic growth. Massive social and institutional readjustments are usually an integral part of the growth process. Economic development entails not only changes in a nation's physical environment (that is, new transportation and communications facilities, new schools, new housing, new plants and equipment) but also drastic changes in the ways in which people think, behave, and associate with one another. Emancipation from custom and tradition is frequently the fundamental prerequisite of economic development. Possibly the most crucial but least tangible ingredient in economic development is "the will to develop." Economic growth may hinge upon "what individuals and social groups *want,* and *whether they want it badly enough to change their old ways of doing things* and to work hard at installing the new."[7]

A post-World War II (and pre-Castro) economic survey mission to Cuba provided an intriguing case study of the key role of social and institutional changes in economic growth. Cuba was found to

[7]Staley, op. cit., p. 218.

have a relatively high growth potential based upon excellent natural resources, an abundant supply of technical and industrial personnel, sufficient investment capital, and proximity to the vast United States market. Yet Cuba's actual rate of development had been meager. The cause for this poor showing lay in social and institutional barriers to growth.[8]

> Public administration was ineffective and often corrupt. The nation received much less than full value for monies invested in public works. These lacked a coherent plan related to development needs and were often left incomplete because of a change in administration. A mass of overly rigid labor regulations, erratically and politically administered, acted as a drag on enterprise, new and old. Like many other countries, Cuba has tried to legislate modern standards of social security without building up the productivity to sustain them. Agricultural experiment and extension services, mining, and other resource surveys, vocational training, current information on economic and social trends, and other potent aids to economic expansion were inadequate and poorly supported. The tax system was cumbersome and unjust, unnecessarily discouraging constructive initiative. . . . the public school system had been weakened and demoralized by maladministration and large-scale misappropriation of funds. . . .
>
> Commerce and manufacturing mostly followed the old pattern of high markups, low turnover, limited markets. Personnel management, with outstanding exceptions, was 25 to 50 years behind modern practice. This fact, the lack of competent and responsible trade union leadership, the sense of insecurity resulting from an unstable economy, and the lingering resentment in the ranks of labor over past abuses were largely responsible for the extremely bad labor relations which were probably the major obstacle to industrial development. . . .
>
> Though it [Cuba] has ample resources and opportunities, it is caught in a mesh of vicious circles. It could cut its way out if somehow improvement could be brought about in the organizing factors—government, business leadership, labor leadership—and if there could be a stronger sense of social cohesiveness and civic responsibility throughout the community. Here we are at the heart of the social problems of economic development.

[8]Ibid., pp. 208–210.

Because of the predominance of farming in the underdeveloped nations, the problem of achieving that institutional environment in agriculture which is most conducive to increasing production must be a vital consideration in any growth program. More specifically, the institutional problem of *land reform* demands attention in virtually all underdeveloped nations. But the needed reform may vary tremendously between specific nations. In some underdeveloped countries the problem assumes the form of excessive concentration of land ownership in the hands of a few wealthy families. This situation is demoralizing for the tenants, weakening their incentive to produce, and is typically not conducive to capital improvements. At the other extreme is the absurd arrangement whereby each and every family owns and farms a minute fragment of land far too small for the application of modern agricultural technology. An important complication to the problem of land reform lies in the fact that political considerations often push reform in that direction which is least defensible on economic grounds. Land reform may well be the most acute institutional problem to be resolved in initiating the process of economic development.

Crucial role of government

One of the most debated aspects of economic development concerns the role of government. What should be the size and nature of the role of an underdeveloped nation's government in the growth process? Such a complex question is not susceptible to a simple answer. Each case must be evaluated separately. The circumstances of one nation may call for vigorous, widespread, and persistent governmental action. In a neighboring nation, growth may best be achieved through major reliance upon private enterprise and the price system.

This much can be said with reasonable certainty: At least during the initial stages of economic growth we can expect government to play a more important role in the underdeveloped countries than did the governments of, say, the United States and Great

Britain in the initial phases of industrial development in those countries.[9] The economic development of Japan, Germany, and Soviet Russia have all entailed governmental sponsorship and/or direction of the growth process. As a matter of fact, economic development and the level of governmental participation in economic life are positively correlated.[10]

There are several closely related reasons for the expectation that government's role in the development of the underdeveloped nations is likely to be a major one. These reasons stem from the character of the obstacles facing these nations.

1. The absence of a sizable and vigorous entrepreneurial class, ready and willing to accumulate capital and initiate production, indicates that in many cases private enterprise is simply not capable of spearheading the growth process.

2. Many of the basic obstacles to economic growth center upon deficiencies of social goods and services. Sanitation and basic medical programs, education, irrigation and soil conservation projects, and the construction of highways and transportation-communication facilities are all essentially indivisible goods and services yielding widespread spillover benefits. These characteristics largely preclude their production by private enterprise and distribution to consumers through the price system. Government is the sole institution in a position to provide these goods and services in required quantities.

3. Government action may also be required to break through the saving-investment dilemma which impedes capital formation in the underdeveloped nations. We have noted that when the ability to save does exist, the desire to emulate the consumption standards of the advanced nations may make an underdeveloped nation's citizenry unwilling to save. And, when an entrepreneurial class exists, the deficiency of domestic markets and the temptation to invest in the advanced nations may similarly slow capital formation.

It may well be that only governmental fiscal action can provide a solution by forcing the economy to accumulate capital. The alternatives here are essentially twofold. One is to force the economy to save by increasing taxes. These tax revenues can then be channeled into top-priority investment projects. The problems of honestly and efficiently administering the tax system and achieving a relatively high degree of compliance with tax laws are frequently very great.

The other alternative is to force the economy to save through inflation; that is, the government can finance capital accumulation by printing and spending new money or by selling bonds to banks and spending the proceeds. The resulting inflation, you will recall, is the equivalent of an arbitrary tax upon the economy. There are serious arguments against the advisability of saving through inflation. In the first place, inflation tends to distort the composition of investment away from productive facilities to such items as luxury housing, precious metals and jewels, or foreign securities, which provide a better hedge against rising prices. Furthermore, significant inflation may reduce voluntary saving as potential savers become less willing to accumulate depreciating money or securities payable in money of declining value. Internationally, inflation may boost the nation's imports and retard its flow of exports, creating balance of payments difficulties.

4. Government is obviously in the key position to deal effectively with the social-institutional obstacles to growth. Population growth—in particular the persistence of high birth rates—is a basic problem which calls for the broad approach that only government can provide. The same can be said for the particularly crucial problem of land reform and the difficulties entailed in inducing the migration of labor from agriculture to industrial pursuits. And government is in an advantageous position to stimulate the will to develop, to change a "Heaven and faith will determine the course of events" philosophy to a "God helps those who help themselves" point of view.

[9]The student of history will recognize that the role of government was considerably greater in the development of the United States and Great Britain than most people recognize or care to admit.
[10]Charles P. Kindleberger, *Economic Development* (New York: McGraw-Hill Book Company, 1958), p. 139.

5. The underdeveloped nations seek *rapid* economic growth. The surging spirit of nationalism and the widening gap between the aspirations and the economic positions of the peoples of the underdeveloped nations constantly fan this passion to catch up with the advanced nations. The price system, you will remember, operates slowly, without certainty, and often with little regard for considerations of equity. It may be that government is the only mechanism through which the development process can be accelerated with certainty and with a reasonably equitable distribution of costs.

But all this must not blind us to certain potential problems and disadvantages which a governmentally directed development program may entail. If entrepreneurial talent is lacking in the private sector, can we expect men of quality to be present in the ranks of government? Is there not a real danger that government bureaucracy, not to mention outright maladministration and corruption, will prove an impediment, not a stimulus, to much-needed social and economic change? And, too, what of the tendency of centralized economic planning to favor the spectacular "showpiece" projects at the expense of less showy but more productive programs? Might not political objectives take precedence over the economic goals of a governmentally directed development program?

It must also be emphasized strongly that we are not here advocating socialism or communism as the most likely paths to opulence. The point to be made is that government might well be obligated by the environmental characteristics of an underdeveloped country to provide the incentive and the means of *initially* breaking the poverty barrier. With economic growth there may evolve a price system, an entrepreneurial class, and all the institutions and attitudes prerequisite to a strong private economy. Government may then relinquish its key role, assured that the private sector of the economy is capable of sustaining the growth process. Such has been the role of government in the economic development of Turkey and Japan.

ROLE OF THE ADVANCED NATIONS

Experience suggests that economic development depends primarily upon the capacity and will to develop that are present in a nation's economy. In virtually every case of significant and sustained economic growth, most of the initiative and means for development have been provided by that nation's domestic economy. Yet external aid can serve as a vital supplement to any country's development process and may be the deciding factor in the success or failure of its endeavor to grow.

As the most advanced industrial nation of the world, the United States has assumed a role of responsibility in assisting in the development of the underdeveloped countries. The United States, Canada, the nations of Western Europe, and Japan are the main free-world sources of economic assistance sufficient to help the underdeveloped nations break the poverty barrier and initiate economic growth. What are the ways in which American capitalism can assist the underdeveloped nations? And to what degree has each of these avenues of assistance been pursued?

The United States has aided the underdeveloped nations through a variety of American programs and through participation in international institutions designed to stimulate economic development.

Loans and grants

The most obvious way of assisting the underdeveloped nations is to extend credit or simply make outright grants to them. In this way the underdeveloped nations can obtain dollars without having to export; foreign aid permits the underdeveloped nations to offset their low domestic saving potential. Expenditure of foreign loans and grants on American capital goods and technical assistance permits the underdeveloped nations to expand their productive capacity without current curtailment of their domestic standard of living. This correctly implies the vital role which foreign aid can play in the early, crucial years

of an underdeveloped nation's growth program. Provided foreign capital is channeled into sufficiently productive uses, loan repayment can be made out of increases which occur in the underdeveloped country's national income. As noted at the outset of this chapter, there are humanitarian, political-military, and economic reasons underlying American aid to underdeveloped areas.

It is generally recognized that there is a need for both public and private financial assistance to the underdeveloped countries; private capital cannot be expected to do the job itself. This is so for two basic reasons:

1. Many of the underdeveloped nations lack the basic social capital—irrigation and public health programs and educational, transportation, and communications systems—prerequisite to the attraction of either domestic or foreign private capital. Foreign public aid is needed to tear down this major roadblock to the flow of private capital to the underdeveloped countries.

2. In those nations in which the political-military reasons for economic aid are most compelling, the climate for private capital is likely to be least appealing. That is, those nations which are the most undecided as to their ideological allegiance will attract little or no private capital from the West. But at the same time, keeping these nations in the free-world camp may well depend upon the amount of aid which they can obtain from the West.

After appraising other means by which the advanced nations have helped the underdeveloped nations, we shall discuss the quantitative aspects of American foreign aid.

The World Bank group

The United States has also been a major participant in the International Bank for Reconstruction and Development. The World Bank, as it is often called, grew out of the same Bretton Woods Conference which gave birth to the International Monetary Fund (IMF). Though its first loans in 1947 were for postwar reconstruction, the World Bank's major objective now is to assist underdeveloped nations in achieving growth. The 113 member nations have subscribed to the bank's $23 billion worth of capital stock roughly in proportion to their economic strength. The share of the United States is approximately one-third of the total. However, the World Bank not only lends out of its own capital funds but also (1) sells bonds and lends the proceeds and (2) guarantees and insures private loans.

Several characteristics of the World Bank merit comment.

1. The World Bank is in a sense a "last resort" lending agency; that is, its loans are limited to productive projects for which private funds are not readily available.

2. Because many World Bank loans have been for basic development projects—multipurpose dams, irrigation projects, health and sanitation programs, communications and transportation facilities—it has been hoped that the bank's activities will provide the basic social capital prerequisite to substantial flows of private capital.

3. The Bank has played a significant role in providing technical assistance to underdeveloped nations by helping them discover what avenues of growth seem most appropriate for their economic development.

The World Bank has met with at least limited success in promoting economic development. Since its operation began in 1947, the World Bank has lent about $17 billion to nations which can be classified as underdeveloped or semideveloped. Yet two basic criticisms have been levied at the bank. Some economists feel that it has been overly conservative in its lending policies; $17 billion spread over two and a half decades is a relatively small amount in view of the tremendous needs of the underdeveloped nations. Furthermore, the bank has only been mildly successful in stimulating the flow of private capital to the underdeveloped nations.

In recent years two World Bank affiliates have come into existence, functioning in areas where the World

Bank has been weak. The International Finance Corporation (IFC) has the primary function of investing in *private* enterprises in underdeveloped nations. The International Development Association (IDA) makes "soft loans" to the very poorest of the underdeveloped countries on much more liberal terms than does the World Bank.

Expanding the volume of trade

Some authorities contend that the simplest and most effective means by which the United States can aid the underdeveloped nations is by lowering trade barriers. "Trade, not aid," they say, will promote economic development. The easing of American protective tariffs and the elimination of import quotas will allegedly enable foreign nations to expand their national incomes through an increased volume of trade with the United States.

Though there is undoubtedly a kernel of truth in this view, it is easily exaggerated. It is true that some nations—for example, Iraq, Saudi Arabia, and Venezuela—need only obtain large foreign markets for their raw materials to achieve some measure of growth. Most underdeveloped nations, however, clearly need trade *and* aid. Their problem is not that of obtaining markets for the utilization of existing productive capacity or the sale of relatively abundant raw materials, but rather the more fundamental one of getting the capital and technical assistance needed to produce something for export! An expansion of international trade will help most of the underdeveloped nations, but it will not prove a panacea for the problems of most of them. Ironically, while condemning the trade restrictions of the industrially advanced nations, many of the underdeveloped nations have simultaneously invoked higher tariffs, import quotas, and exchange controls to encourage the growth of their domestic industries.

American economic stability

In absolute terms the United States is the leading trading nation of the world. Like it or not, many other nations—both underdeveloped and semideveloped—find their economies closely linked to the health of American capitalism. The old quip that "When Uncle Sam gets his feet wet, the rest of the world gets pneumonia" has some accuracy.[11]

A recession both in the United States and in Europe, though relatively mild, will typically cause serious suffering and hardship in the underdeveloped countries. Indeed in the 1958 recession the losses sustained by the underdeveloped countries by reason of the decline in raw-material prices by far outweighed any foreign aid given over several years.

How much aid?

How much aid must the advanced countries provide in order for the underdeveloped countries to achieve reasonable growth rates? Although such estimates are arbitrary, there is some concensus that total aid—public and private—of $15 to $20 billion per year will be needed in the early 1970s. The United Nations Conference on Trade and Development recommended in 1968 that the advanced nations should provide public and private capital flows equal to 1 percent of their GNPs. This "1 percent rule" would provide approximately $20 billion of assistance per year.

Actual capital flows have been significantly less—on the order of $12 or $13 billion per year. While the United States is the world's major provider of foreign aid in absolute terms, our record in relative terms is much less impressive. In 1970, for example, total American public aid was $3 billion. Most of this was in the form of development loans and technological assistance administered by our Agency for International Development (AID). A significant amount, however, took the form of grants of surplus food under the provisions of Public Law 480 (Chapter 36). Private capital flows to low-income countries augmented this aid by some $2 billion. On a relative basis, however, these amounts appear much less formidable. United States aid in recent years has been on the order of two-thirds or three-fourths of 1 percent of our GNP, significantly short of the 1 percent benchmark. And, in fact, total dollar aid has stabilized as the GNP has grown. Hence, total Amer-

[11] Alvin H. Hansen, *Economic Issues of the 1960's* (New York: McGraw-Hill Book Company, 1961), p. 136.

ican aid (public and private) has been a declining percentage of our GNP. Many other advanced and semiadvanced countries provide a larger percentage of their GNPs as aid to the low-income countries than does the United States. In relative terms, at least, one cannot say that American economic aid to the underdeveloped nations has been extravagant. As one authority has put it,[12]

> There is practically no danger that the United States government will spend more than our national interest requires on economic aid to underdeveloped countries. The danger is all the other way. Underdeveloped countries are not represented in Congress where the appropriation logs are rolled, and the compelling American interest in the advancement of the underdeveloped parts of the free world is less easy for statesmen to explain than for narrowmindedness and shortsightedness to obscure.

There is little doubt that the war in Vietnam, space exploration, the war on poverty, and urban and ecological problems have been highly competitive with our foreign aid program.

"Key countries" approach[13]

Assuming that domestic political considerations make unlikely any substantial increases in our foreign aid budget, is there any way to restructure or reorient our aid programs so as to increase their economic effectiveness? Some have argued that the basic flaw in the present program is that we spread a relatively modest amount of aid very thinly over some ninety-five or more recipient nations and territories, with the result that no significant growth is achieved anywhere. We are trying, it is argued, to do "too much for too many too soon." (The Russians, incidentally, concentrate the vast bulk of their aid on only ten or twelve nations.) Hence, it is contended that the United States should redistribute the bulk of its aid in the direction of a relatively few "key countries." The key countries would be those which

1. Have the greatest economic potential for achieving growth
2. Possess the "will to develop" as reflected in their willingness to initiate land and tax reform, establish sound fiscal and monetary policies, and maintain a stable, honest, and reasonably efficient government
3. Are strategic politically, geographically, or in terms of land and population size

Thus, for example, Brazil in South America, Turkey in the Middle East, and India in Asia might readily be labeled as key countries.

Advocates of the key country approach to American aid cite two potential merits of such a reorientation. First and foremost, this approach has a greater chance of success than our present one. Because they now will receive a substantially larger amount of aid, the key countries are in a better position to establish the conditions necessary for getting off dead center and into a process of self-sustaining economic growth. Furthermore, this approach puts the underdeveloped nations in a position in which they must display a will to develop and to make necessary institutional and policy changes in order to qualify as key countries. A second and more selfish merit is this: The economic achievements of the U.S.S.R. have favorably impressed many underdeveloped nations. The free world would benefit substantially if it were able to demonstrate by example to the uncommitted nations of the world that an underdeveloped country can achieve economic progress through nontotalitarian techniques.

The main weakness of the key countries approach lies in the fact that for a time many underdeveloped countries—the non-key countries—would receive less aid than they do now. But there are possible offsets: Assuming that the current key countries will achieve self-sustaining growth, aid to these advancing countries could be reduced in the future and reallocated to other nations, which could then be reclassified as key countries. That is, the nations which get less aid now would conceivably get a larger amount of aid in the long run. And, hopefully, those nations which develop successfully will be disposed to aid other underdeveloped countries.[14]

[12] Staley, op cit., p. 372.

[13] See Walter Krause, *Economic Development* (San Francisco: Wadsworth Publishing Company, Inc., 1961), chaps. 23 and 24.

[14] Other suggestions for improving our aid programs are found in the President's Task Force on International Development, *U.S. Foreign Assistance in the 1970s: A New Approach* (Washington, 1970).

Cautious optimism?

Have the underdeveloped countries made progress? In general, yes. During the 1960s the annual growth in real GNP for the underdeveloped countries averaged 5.2 percent, or about 2.7 percent per capita. These figures compare quite favorably with many of the economically advanced nations (Table 21·2). "What we are witnessing . . . is a vast transformation in which after centuries of stagnation much of the less-developed world has entered upon a period of real progress, which by any historical standard, can only be described as impressive."[15]

But this optimism must be tempered with caution. There are less encouraging considerations which must be noted. First, while some of the underdeveloped nations—for example, Pakistan and Taiwan—have realized rapid growth, others—Burma, India, and the Philippines—have made little or no progress on a per capita basis (Table 45·1). The growth picture, in short, is mixed. Second, a 3 percent increase in per capita income in an underdeveloped nation may mean only an extra $10 or $15 worth of goods and services per person per year, while the same 3 percent may translate into an additional $50 or $60 of output per person in an advanced country. In fact the absolute size of the income gap between the rich and the poor nations continues to widen even though growth rates for GNP are comparable.

Perhaps the main source of optimism is the great potentialities of the "Green Revolution," that is, the important technological breakthroughs in agriculture which have created new high-yield strains of rice and wheat for the underdeveloped countries. The main source of pessimism is that, despite breakthroughs in birth-control technology and awareness of the need to control population, the actual progress made to date in limiting population growth has been modest. Thus in the 1960s the GNPs of the advanced and the underdeveloped countries both grew on the average at about 5 percent. But because of more rapid population growth, the average *per capita* increase in the GNPs of the underdeveloped nations rose only 2.7 percent as compared with 3.9 percent for the advanced nations.[16] Population control may well be the *sine qua non* of rising living standards in the underdeveloped world.

[15] Committee for Economic Development, *Assisting Development in Low-Income Countries: Priorities for U.S. Government Policy* (New York: CED, 1969), p. 29.

[16] Ibid., p. 32.

SUMMARY

1. Most nations of the world are underdeveloped (low per capita income) nations. Spurred by ***a.*** the widening gap between their incomes and those of the advanced nations and ***b.*** the rising spirit of nationalism, the people of the underdeveloped nations are far from content with their current economic status.

2. Initial scarcities of natural resources and the limited possibility of augmenting existing supplies may impose a rigid limitation upon a nation's capacity to develop.

3. The presence of large populations in the underdeveloped countries contributes to low per capita incomes. In particular, increases in per capita incomes frequently induce rapid population growth, to the end that per capita incomes again deteriorate back to near-subsistence levels.

4. Disguised unemployment in the form of surplus agricultural labor exists in most of the underdeveloped nations. This underemployment stems from the absence of alternative job opportunities, on the one hand, and the occupational and geographic immobility of agricultural labor, on the other.

5. In the underdeveloped nations both the saving and investment aspects of the capital formation process are impeded by formidable obstacles. The vast majority of households in the underdeveloped nations receive incomes too small to permit them to save. Furthermore, little saving may be forthcoming out of incomes considerably higher than those currently received by this group. A high propensity to

consume accounts for this expectation. The very wealthy have considerable ability to save but prefer to spend lavishly or to invest their savings unproductively.

6. The absence of a vigorous entrepreneurial class and the weakness of investment incentives are the major obstacles to capital accumulation when money capital is readily available. Political and social instability, the lack of large domestic markets, shortages of operating and administrative personnel, and deficiencies of basic social capital all contribute to an uninviting environment for private investment. Some degree of capital accumulation can usually be achieved, however, through nonfinancial investment.

7. Discriminatory taxation, limits and prohibitions upon profit withdrawals, and a host of diverse government regulations are additional obstacles which impair the flow of private capital from the advanced to the underdeveloped nations.

8. Within limits the underdeveloped nations may achieve a degree of technological advance with little or no increase in their expenditures for research and capital accumulation. It must be acknowledged, however, that severe limitations may be imposed upon such advance by capital accumulation and the requirements of natural and human resources.

9. Appropriate alterations in the quantity and quality of a nation's economic resources will not guarantee economic growth. Appropriate social and institutional arrangements and, in particular, the presence of "the will to develop" are essential ingredients in economic development.

10. The role of government in the development of the underdeveloped nations is likely to be considerable. The nature of the obstacles to growth—the absence of an entrepreneurial class, the dearth of social capital, the saving-investment dilemma, and the presence of social-institutional obstacles to growth—and the fact that the underdeveloped nations seek rapid growth suggest the need for government action in initiating the growth process.

11. The United States can assist the underdeveloped nations in their quest for growth in several ways. *a.* We can extend aid in the form of grants, loans, and technical assistance directly through American programs and institutions—for example, AID—or indirectly through participation in international institutions—for example, the World Bank. *b.* By reducing its trade barriers, the United States can help the underdeveloped nations increase their national incomes through an expanding volume of international trade. *c.* Finally, the United States can help provide a world environment conducive to economic development by maintaining domestic economic stability. American economic aid to the underdeveloped nations has been modest in relative terms.

12. A number of American experts advocate a new "key countries" approach to our aid program in an effort to enhance its effectiveness in promoting self-sustaining growth in the underdeveloped nations.

QUESTIONS AND STUDY SUGGESTIONS

1. What are the major characteristics of an underdeveloped nation? List the major avenues of economic development available to such a nation. State and explain the obstacles which face the underdeveloped nations in breaking the poverty barrier. Now outline in detail the steps which an underdeveloped country might take to initiate economic development.

2. "The path to economic development has been clearly blazed by American capitalism. It is only for the underdeveloped nations to follow this trail." Critically evaluate.

3. "Economic inequality is conducive to saving, and saving is the prerequisite of investment. Therefore, greater inequality in the income distribution of the underdeveloped countries would be a spur to capital accumulation and growth." Critically evaluate.

4. "The spirit of nationalism sometimes aids and sometimes impedes the process of economic growth." Explain and illustrate.

5. "The underdeveloped nations are hurting themselves by seeking too quickly living standards and social legislation which their productive potential is now incapable of producing. They must resign themselves to 'less now' to get 'more later.' " To what degree is this position valid? What problems might its application entail?

6. "The advanced economies fear the complications which stem from oversaving; the underdeveloped countries bear the yoke of undersaving." Explain.

7. "The core of the development process involves changing human beings more than it does altering a nation's physical environment." Critically evaluate.

8. Much of the initial investment in an underdeveloped country must be devoted to basic social capital which does not directly or immediately lead to a greater production of goods and services. What bearing might this have upon the degree of inflation which results as government finances capital accumulation through the printing and spending of new money? Be specific.

9. "The nature of the problems faced by the underdeveloped nations creates a bias in favor of a governmentally directed as opposed to a decentralized development process." Do you agree? Substantiate your position. If you do agree, specify the implications of your position for the foreign aid programs of the United States.

10. What is the "key countries" approach to foreign aid? What are its advantages and disadvantages? Would you recommend such a reorientation of our present aid program?

11. Explain and evaluate: "Poverty and freedom cannot persist side by side; one must triumph over the other."

SELECTED REFERENCES

Economic Issues, 4th ed., readings 88, 89, 90, and 91.

Black, Lloyd D.: *The Strategy of Foreign Aid* (Princeton, N.J.: Van Nostrand Reinhold Company, 1968).

Commission on International Development, *Partners in Development* (New York: Frederick A. Praeger, Inc., 1969).

Maddison, Angus: *Economic Progress and Policy in Developing Countries* (London: George Allen & Unwin, Ltd., 1970).

Meier, Gerald M.: *Leading Issues in Economic Development,* 2d ed. (New York: Oxford University Press, 1970).

Schiavo-Campo, Salvatore, and Hans W. Singer: *Perspectives of Economic Development* (Boston: Houghton Mifflin Company, 1970).

Spiegelglas, Stephen, and Charles J. Welsh (eds.): *Economic Development: Challenge and Promise* (Englewood Cliffs, N.J.: Prentice-Hall, Inc., 1970).

36

THE ECONOMIC CHALLENGE OF SOVIET RUSSIA[1]

In November of 1957 Nikita Khrushchev declared economic war on the United States with these rather immodest assertions:

> We declare war upon you—excuse me for using such an expression—in the peaceful field of trade. We declare war. We will win over the United States. The threat to the United States is not the ICBM, but in the field of peaceful production. We are relentless in this and it will prove the superiority of our system.

This Soviet challenge—which, of course, has military, political, and sociocultural as well as economic aspects—is not simply a propaganda blast or an idle threat. It is a well-acknowledged reality. Furthermore, there is no serious doubt that Khrushchev's successors remain committed to this boast.

[1]This chapter is necessarily a brief survey of a very complex economy. Space simply does not permit a detailed analysis of many important and interesting aspects of Soviet economic life. The reader is urged to consult the highly recommended references cited at the end of the chapter and in the pages that follow.

We turn, then, in this final chapter to an analysis of this competing economy. We want to survey its institutions, understand its goals, evaluate its performance, and appreciate the challenge it poses for the West. There are two notable by-products of this endeavor. First, the Soviet economy is a fascinating case study in forced economic growth; the accomplishments and shortcomings of the Soviet system in vigorously pursuing economic growth provide invaluable lessons. Second, by examining an economy at the opposite end of the ideological spectrum, we cannot help but deepen our understanding of the capitalistic system.

INSTITUTIONS OF THE COMMAND ECONOMY

There are two outstanding institutional characteristics of the Soviet economy: (1) the public ownership of property resources and (2) central economic planning.

Public ownership

The Soviet constitution of 1936 makes the pervasiveness of public ownership of property resources quite clear:

Article IV. The economic foundation of the U.S.S.R. is the socialist system of economy and the socialist ownership of the instruments and means of production, firmly established as a result of the liquidation of the capitalist system of economy, the abolition of private ownership of the instruments and means of production, and the elimination of the exploitation of man by man.

Article V. Socialist property in the U.S.S.R. exists either in the form of state property (belonging to the whole people) or in the form of cooperative and collective-farm property (property of collective farms, property of cooperative societies).

The Soviet state owns all land, natural resources, transportation and communication facilities, the banking system, and virtually all industry. Most retail and wholesale enterprises and most urban housing are governmentally owned. In agriculture many farms are state-owned; most, however, are government-organized collective farms, that is, essentially cooperatives. The main exception to public ownership is the small plot of land which each collective farm family has set aside for its personal use: "Every household on a collective farm . . . has for its personal use a small plot of household land and, as its personal property, a subsidiary husbandry on the plot, a dwelling house, livestock, poultry, and minor agricultural implements. . . . " And, of course, clothing, household furnishings, and small tools and implements used by craftsmen are privately owned. Workers in rural areas and farmers typically own their homes, as do over one-third of all urban families.

Central economic planning

Despite a highly democratic constitution, in practice the government of Soviet Russia is a strong dictatorship. The Communist Party, although its membership includes only 4 or 5 percent of the total population, stands unchallenged. Indeed, the party and the government can be regarded as virtually synonymous.

As the constitution makes clear, the Soviet government, through economic planning, sets the objectives of the economy and directs resources toward the attainment of these goals:

Article XI. The economic life of the U.S.S.R. is determined and directed by the state national economic plan, with the aim of increasing the public wealth, of steadily raising the material and cultural standards of the working people, and of consolidating the independence of the U.S.S.R. and strengthening its defensive capacity.

In contrast with the decentralized market economy of the United States, that of the Soviet Union is a centralized, "command" economy which functions in terms of a detailed economic plan. The economy of the Soviet Union is government-directed rather than price-directed.

Circumscribed freedom

The dominant roles of public ownership and central planning correctly imply that it is not the free decisions of consumers and businessmen which determine the allocation of resources and the composition of total output in the Soviet Union. Yet we must recognize that, subject to the overall restraints imposed by the central planners, consumers and laborers have a degree of free choice.

The concept of consumer sovereignty as we know it does not exist in the Soviet Union. The preferences of individual consumers, as reflected in the size and structure of consumer demand, do *not* determine the volume and composition of consumer goods production in Soviet Russia; this determination is made by the government. However, consumers are free to spend their money incomes as they see fit on those consumer goods for which the central plan provides.

Similarly, although the Soviet Union has a history of compulsory job assignment, harsh labor codes, and, in the extreme, slave labor, much greater reliance has been put upon free occupational choice in recent years. But again, there are overall restraints imposed by the central plan. The composition of output as determined by the plan establishes the number and kinds of jobs available. Then the government planners set wage rates so as to attract the

needed number and types of workers to the various occupations. If the plan assigns great importance to steel and a low priority to shoes, jobs will be plentiful and wage rates established at a high level in the steel industry. Conversely, few jobs will be available and wages will be low in the shoe industry. In short, workers are largely free to change jobs in response to wage differentials; the differentials, however, are designed and manipulated to bring about an allocation of labor both geographically and occupationally which is consistent with the goals of the plan.

CENTRAL PLANNING

Perhaps the most dramatic feature of the Soviet economy is its use of central planning. In the Soviet Union the means of answering the Five Fundamental Questions is central planning. Choices made primarily through the market in our economy must be consciously made by bureaucratic decision in the U.S.S.R. The overall character of the Soviet Five- and Seven-year Plans has been succinctly described in these words:[2]

> The Soviet economic plan is a gigantic, comprehensive blueprint that attempts to govern the economic activities and interrelations of all persons and institutions in the U.S.S.R., as well as the economic relations of the U.S.S.R. with other countries. To the extent that the plan actually controls the development of events, all the manifold activities of the Soviet economy are coordinated as if they were parts of one incredibly enormous enterprise directed from the central headquarters in Moscow.

Now let us probe below the surface. What are the goals of the plans? How are the plans constructed and implemented? What problems does central planning entail?

Planning goals

The Soviet government—in reality the Communist Party—sets the basic objectives for the Russian economy. These objectives have varied somewhat as succeeding Five-year Plans have been formulated, but emphasis has been upon rapid economic growth through the development of heavy industry. The attainment of a high level of military strength is a closely correlated goal. Lip service is invariably accorded the goal of a higher standard of living for consumers, but the lower priority assigned to this goal means that it is frequently sacrificed to achieve the objectives of industrial expansion and military strength.

Basic planning problem: coordination

It is no simple matter to sweep away the market system, as the Soviet Union has done, and replace it with an effective central plan. After all, we have found that the market system is a powerful organizing force which coordinates millions upon millions of individual decisions by consumers, entrepreneurs, and resource suppliers and fosters a reasonably efficient allocation of resources. Is central planning a satisfactory substitute for the market?

The core of the planning problem is revealed by the input-output table (Table 34•1). Input-output analysis, you will recall, reveals the highly interdependent character of the various industries or sectors of the economy. Each industry employs the outputs of other industries as its inputs; in turn its outputs are inputs to still other firms. This means that a planning decision to increase the production of machinery by, say, 10 percent is not a single, isolated directive, but rather a decision which implies a myriad of related decisions for fulfillment. For example, in terms of Table 34•1, if planners do not make the related decisions to increase metal output by 6.5 units, fuel by 0.5 units, agricultural products by 1 unit, and to provide an extra 20 units of labor (not to mention additional second-round increases in all these inputs because 2.5 more inputs of machinery are also needed to increase machinery output!), bottlenecks will develop, and the planned increase in machinery output cannot be realized.

Let us look at the matter from a slightly different vantage point: Even if an internally consistent set of decisions—a perfectly coordinated plan—could be constructed by the central planners, the failure of any

[2] Harry Schwartz, *Russia's Soviet Economy,* 2d ed. (Englewood Cliffs, N.J.: Prentice-Hall, Inc., 1954), p. 146.

single industry to fulfill its output target would cause an almost endless chain of adverse repercussions. If iron mines—for want of machinery or labor or transportation inputs—fail to supply the steel industry with the required inputs of iron ore, the steel industry in turn will be unable to fulfill the input needs of the myriad of industries dependent upon steel. All these steel-using industries will be unable to fulfill their planned production goals. And so the bottleneck chain reaction goes on to all those firms which use steel parts or components as inputs.

It must be emphasized that our illustrative input-output table (Table 34·1) is a gross oversimplification of the problem of coordinating a command economy. There are now some 200,000 industrial enterprises producing goods in the Soviet Union. The central planners must see to it that all the resources needed by these enterprises to fulfill their assigned production targets are somehow allocated to them.[3]

> The literally billions of planning decisions that must be made to achieve consistency result in a complex and complete interlocking of macro-and micromanagement. . . . The number of planned interconnections increases more rapidly than the size of the economy, and since 1953 the Soviet economy has doubled in terms of national production. . . . Even with the most sophisticated mathematical techniques and electronic computers, the task of interrelating demands and factor inputs for every possible item by every possible subcategory becomes impossible for the central planners alone.

Coordination techniques

Despite the gargantuan character of the coordination problem, Soviet central planning has worked, and in some respects has functioned remarkably well. It is certainly legitimate to inquire: Why? What techniques do Soviet planners employ to achieve the level of coordination sufficient to make central planning workable? The answers lie substantially in the way the plans are constructed and implemented.

1. Planning by negotiation Given the overall economic objectives established by the Communist Party, it is the task of the State Planning Commission, or *Gosplan,* to construct a detailed economic blueprint designed to bring about the realization of these goals. In formulating a plan, the Gosplan collects voluminous amounts of statistical data from a host of subordinate ministries, each of which is concerned with the operation of certain industries. From these data, a tentative plan is constructed. The plan is then submitted to the various units of the Soviet administrative hierarchy for study, evaluation, and criticism. This criticism, it must be noted, concerns the specific details of the economic plan and not the overall goals which the plan seeks.

Let us illustrate this procedure. Note, first, that there are two obvious organizational alternatives for a planned economy: geographical (regional) and functional (industrial). All enterprises in a given region may be grouped for planning purposes, or all enterprises in a given industry may be grouped for planning regardless of their location. Over time the Soviet Union has used both alternatives and mixtures of the two. Currently the emphasis is upon the industrial approach, and a number of countrywide ministries—for example, the ministries of construction, machine tools, automobiles, tractors, and so forth—are subordinate to Gosplan in the planning hierarchy. The important point is that relevant segments of the overall plan are submitted to the subordinate agencies, which exercise operational control. Thus the plans are evaluated at the industry-wide level, by the trusts and combines—that is, groups of plants which are combined for administrative purposes—and ultimately by the individual plants or enterprises. At each level the plan is analyzed, suggestions are made for revision, and perhaps alterations are proposed in production goals or planned allocations of inputs. These evaluations are passed back up the planning hierarchy to Gosplan. Taking into account those suggestions and criticisms which it feels are worthy, Gosplan then draws up a final plan. When rubber-stamped by the party and the government, this becomes the Five- or Seven-year Plan.

The point to be emphasized is this: By breaking the overall plan into its component parts and subjecting these detailed segments to considerable critical ex-

[3] Barry M. Richman, *Soviet Management* (Englewood Cliffs, N.J.: Prentice-Hall, Inc., 1965), p. 17.

amination by subministries, combines, and plants, the Gosplan is able to establish a final plan which is more realistic and workable than would otherwise be the case. Soviet planners apparently recognize their limitations in obtaining and digesting masses of detailed information. The "down-and-up" evaluation of the tentative plan by the administrative hierarchy and its subsequent revision is aimed at obtaining on-the-spot knowledge and an understanding of immediate, detailed facts and circumstances which a relatively small group of planners could not otherwise grasp. To the extent that the resulting plan is more realistic and feasible, the chance is less that problems of coordination—in particular, bottlenecks—will arise to jeopardize plan fulfillment.

2. The priority principle A second means of making central planning workable is embodied in the priority principle of resource allocation. Not all production goals established by Gosplan are held to be of equal importance. The goals of certain "leading links" sectors or industries (machinery, chemicals, steel) are given high priority; other industries (agriculture, automobiles) in effect are assigned low priorities. Thus, when bottlenecks arise in the actual operation of the national plan, resources or inputs are shifted from low-priority to high-priority sectors of the economy. Coordination and plan fulfillment are sacrificed in low-priority production in order to maintain coordination and fulfill production targets in high-priority sectors. This accounts for the unevenness with which the goals of the various central plans have been fulfilled. Planned increases in housing and consumer goods are typically sacrificed to realize the planned increases in industrial and military goods production.

3. Reserve stocks To some extent coordination problems—bottlenecks and the chain reactions they precipitate—can be avoided by drawing upon reserve stocks of various inputs. Inventories, in other words, are used as a cushion or buffer to resolve specific bottlenecks or input deficiencies before they can trigger a serious chain of production shortfalls.

Although all these techniques contribute in varying degrees to the workability of Soviet central planning, they by no means ensure a high degree of efficiency. There is a great amount of evidence gathered from Soviet sources to indicate that bottlenecks do occur with rather alarming regularity:[4]

> The Byelorussian Tractor Factory, which has 227 suppliers, had its production line stopped 19 times in 1962 because of the lack of rubber parts, 18 times because of ball bearings, and 8 times because of transmission components. The pattern of breakdowns continued in 1963. During the first quarter of 1963 only about one-half of the plant's ball bearing and rubber needs were satisfied, and only half of the required batteries were available. One supplier shipped 19,000 less wheels than called for in the contract. In total, they were short of 27 different items. . . .
>
> It is not surprising that 90 enterprises out of 100 surveyed in the Chelyabinsk region blamed their underfulfillment of production plans in 1962 on supply deficiencies.

Executing the plan: control agencies

The proof of the pudding is in the eating. Setting up detailed production goals and making some provision for their internal balance are one thing; achieving those objectives may be something else again.

The Soviet government is not inclined to sit back, after each industrial plant and farm has been assigned its production targets, and hope for favorable results. On the contrary, an abundance of control agencies supervises the carrying out of each plan. Most obvious, of course, is the Gosplan and the various subordinate planning groups affiliated with it. These administrative units keep a running check on the progress of the plan. The Central Committee of the Communist Party and a variety of subordinate party organizations function as watchdog agencies by uncovering, reporting, and helping to correct deviations from the plan. The control functions of the infamous secret police are well known. And, too, a less formal type of control is exercised through a much-publicized program of "criticism and self-criticism," whereby the Soviet citizenry is encouraged to register complaints concerning deviations from, and violations of, the plan.

[4] Ibid., p. 123.

Perhaps the most vital enforcement agency is the state banking system, or *Gosbank.* The Gosbank with its thousands of branches supervises the financial aspects of each plant's production activities and in this manner has a running account of each plant's performance. More precisely, this supervision—"control by the ruble"—works something like this: The government establishes prices on all resources and finished products. For a greatly simplified example, the Leningrad Machine Tool Plant may require 1,000 tons of steel and 100 workers to produce 5,000 units of output per year. If steel costs 60 rubles per ton and each worker is paid 1,000 rubles per year, the total cost of the 5,000 units of output will be 160,000 rubles. Gosplan then directs the Gosbank to make this amount of credit available to the plant over the course of the year. Now, because all the plant's financial transactions—both receipts and expenditures—must be completed through the use of checks, the Gosbank will have an accurate record (in effect, a running audit) of the plant's progress, or lack thereof, in fulfilling the production targets assigned by the Five-year Plan. Should the plant achieve its assigned output at an expense less than 160,000 rubles, it will have overfulfilled its production goal. Inefficient, wasteful production will cause the plant to exhaust its bank credit before its production goal is reached. Either eventuality will be reflected in the plant's account with the Gosbank.

Incentives

How are the various economic units motivated toward fulfillment of the Five-year Plan? A combination of monetary and nonmonetary incentives, on the one hand, and coercive techniques, on the other, are employed to this end.

Monetary incentives The Soviet government relies heavily upon monetary incentives to obtain the maximum productive effort from labor. In particular, wages are geared to skill and productivity. The resulting wage differentials are considerable. Great emphasis is put upon piecework, more so than in the United States. Probably as much as four-fifths of the Soviet labor force works under a piecework plan of one sort or another. Elaborate systems of bonuses and premiums induce workers to exceed normal production rates. Most competent observers conclude that wage incomes in the Soviet Union are as unequally distributed as in the United States. Keep in mind, too, that Soviet income receivers, though not free to determine the portion of total output which is to take the form of consumer goods, are able to spend their incomes as they wish on the consumer goods which the Gosplan makes available to them. This means that differences in money incomes are generally reflected in real income differentials.

Nonmonetary incentives A variety of nonmonetary inducements also exist to stimulate labor to greater productivity. A rather comprehensive system of awards and decorations exists to cite exemplary workers. These are closely correlated with material rewards. For example, a "Hero of Socialist Labor" is likely to be accorded certain tax exemptions, monthly bonuses, low rental on state housing, free use of transportation facilities, government-supplied vacations at a Crimean resort, and so forth. The real standard of living of the average Soviet worker is about one-third that of his American counterpart, so that the value of such benefits is considerable. Much publicity accompanies these awards. A member of the "Order of Lenin" may enjoy fame and prestige comparable to that of a professional baseball player or movie star in the United States. In addition, "socialist competitions" are encouraged by the party, pitting the productive capacities of various groups of workers against one another.

The labor unions to which the vast majority of Soviet workers belong bear little or no resemblance to their American counterparts. In effect, Russian labor unions are functionaries of the state whose basic goals are to encourage a high rate of productivity among their members in carrying out the economic plan, to train new workers, to aid in the solution of labor discipline problems, and to administer the social security system. Wage rates are set by the government. Collective bargaining as we know it does not exist, and strikes simply do not occur. Soviet labor

unions do, however, prevent undue exploitation of their members by plant managers eager to fulfill their assigned production quotas. They also play an active role in providing recreational and cultural programs for workers.

Coercion Monetary and nonmonetary inducements are duly supplemented by a variety of coercive techniques. Indeed, Article XII of the Soviet constitution of 1936 flatly states that "Work in the U.S.S.R. is a duty and a matter of honor for every able-bodied citizen, in accordance with the principle 'He who does not work, neither shall he eat.'" But labor discipline has at times been very poor: absenteeism, tardiness, and worker indifference are common problems. The rate of labor turnover has also been a major problem. Plant managers frequently "pirate" the personnel of one another to ensure a labor force adequate for fulfillment of their output targets. Workers seem very willing to change jobs, however slight the resulting improvement in their standard of living might be.

Soviet authorities have taken action to cope with such problems. Fines, pay reductions, dismissal, eviction from state housing, the freezing of workers to their jobs, and discriminatory treatment with respect to social insurance benefits all hang over the head of the bungling, the lazy, the indifferent, and the overly mobile worker. In extreme cases "spies" and "wreckers" may be subject to the wrath of the secret police and assigned to "correctional labor camps" in Siberia or similarly remote areas.

Comparable monetary and nonmonetary inducements and compulsory techniques bear upon plant managers. High salaries, bonuses, awards, and promotion await those who fulfill their production targets. Failure exposes the plant manager to investigation and reassignment to a less palatable position. A good many plant managers are party members and therefore inspired by party doctrines.

Planning and prices

Let us now look at the way in which prices have been traditionally used in Soviet planning. Then we shall examine some important microeconomic shortcomings of Soviet planning and some recent reforms designed to meet these problems.

To say that the Soviet system is a command economy rather than a market economy is not to say that prices have no role to play in the centrally planned system. Although Soviet prices are not employed as a guiding mechanism in determining the structure of output, they are used in implementing the production objectives established by the state. *Soviet prices are government-manipulated to aid in the achievement of state-established goals; capitalistic prices are market-established and induce the fulfillment of individually determined goals.*

Actually, the function of prices in the Soviet Union has differed considerably between the production process, on the one hand, and the sale of final products to consumers, on the other. In the first instance prices are simply accounting devices which facilitate checking the efficiency with which products are manufactured. In the latter case prices are employed as rationing devices to distribute products to consumers without the use of government rationing.

Producer prices In producing, say, a television set, a Soviet plant will be faced with certain governmentally established prices for component parts, labor, and other needed resources. And, similarly, government will determine the price of the final product. Generally speaking, the basic principle in establishing these prices is that a plant or industry of average efficiency should realize total receipts from its production which will just cover its total costs; that is, it should break even. If production is less efficient than that deemed average by the plan, losses will result. Greater-than-average efficiency will result in unplanned profits.[5] In short, the prices of resources and components are used as accounting costs to assess the efficiency with which various plants and industries operate. Except for the fact that capitalistic prices are market-determined rather than govern-

[5]For the most part, these profits will accrue to the government as revenue from state-owned enterprises. A part may be used to expand the industry, if such expansion is consistent with the objectives of the plan. Another portion may be shared by the plant's workers and executives as a bonus for their efficiency.

ment-determined, this role of the Soviet price system parallels that of its capitalistic counterpart. But here—for two reasons—the similarity ends.

In the first place, in a capitalistic economy losses call for a contraction of output and a release of resources by the affected industry; profits signal industry expansion and the absorption of resources. Not so in the Soviet Union. Expansion and contraction of industry are determined by the government, not the price system. Therefore a relatively inefficient industry which is considered vital by the state may be expanded despite losses. Similarly, a highly efficient, profit-realizing industry may be purposely contracted by state planning.

Secondly, market-determined input prices in a capitalistic system reflect the relative scarcity of resources and their value in alternative uses. Thus, to minimize money costs in the production of a product is to minimize real costs, that is, to get a given good produced with a minimum sacrifice of alternative goods (Chapter 27). But in the Soviet Union prices are governmentally determined and therefore do not accurately reflect the relative scarcity of resources. Hence, the minimization of money costs in a Soviet enterprise does not mean that real costs of production are being minimized.

Consumer prices Whereas prices in the production process are essentially accounting devices used to gauge plan fulfillment, the prices of finished goods are established to serve as rationing devices. In other words, the government attempts to set consumer goods prices at levels which will clear the market so there will be no persistent shortages or surpluses. As a result, the price of television sets which is used for accounting purposes may vary considerably from the price which is charged consumers who purchase them. The difference typically takes the form of a sales tax or what the Russians call a turnover tax.

To illustrate: Suppose the accounting price of a finished television set is 1,500 rubles. This price is used by the Gosplan in judging the efficiency of the assembly plant. But because of the low priority assigned to consumer goods, consumer demand in the Soviet Union has persistently exceeded the available supply of consumer goods. This means that, if shortages and government rationing are to be avoided, the price charged by the state in selling television sets to consumers must be higher than the accounting price. Suppose the government estimates that the consumer price of television sets must be 3,000 rubles to bring the quantity demanded into balance with the quantity of television sets currently available. This is accomplished by adding a 100 percent turnover tax to television sets. At this price the market will be cleared and government rationing avoided.

Turnover taxes—which, incidentally, are the major source of government revenue in Russia—vary widely among various products. High turnover taxes on particularly scarce goods greatly discourage their consumption and force the amounts demanded into accord with the skimpy quantities allowed by the plan. Lower rates on consumer staples—for example, potatoes and other vegetables—available in relative abundance encourage their consumption. In general, the greater the relative scarcity of a product, the higher the turnover tax placed upon it. The total prices of such products will necessarily be higher and purchases discouraged. Lower tax rates on more abundant products give them lower relative prices and encourage their consumption. In this way inflation-causing income is taxed away, and the pattern of consumer spending is forced into rough accord with the planned composition of consumer goods output.[6]

RECENT PROBLEMS AND REFORMS

Let us now review some of the operational difficulties of Soviet planning and summarize recent economic reforms designed to resolve these problems.

Microeconomic problems

As the Soviet economy has grown and become more sophisticated and complex, detailed central planning has become more and more difficult and unworkable.

[6]For an authoritative discussion of Soviet pricing see Morris Bornstein, "The Soviet Price System" in Morris Bornstein (ed.), *Comparative Economic Systems: Models and Cases* (Homewood, Ill.: Richard D. Irwin, Inc., 1965), pp. 278–309.

Specifically, rather severe microeconomic problems have arisen.

In the first place, lacking a genuine price system to communicate the wants of consumers and producers, central planners have frequently directed enterprises to produce goods for which there is little or no demand. The result is unwanted inventories of unsalable goods. Secondly, the major "success indicator" for Soviet enterprise managers has been the quantity of output; the enterprise's main goal is to fulfill or overfulfill its assigned production target. Production costs and product quality are secondary considerations at best. Indeed, planners have found it very difficult to state a quantitative production target without unintentionally eliciting ridiculous "distortions" in output. Example: If an enterprise manufacturing nails has its production target stated in terms of weight (tons of nails), it will tend to produce all large nails. But if its target is a numerical one (thousands of nails), it will be motivated to produce all small nails! Furthermore, the Soviet press persistently denounces the poor quality of both consumer goods and many producer goods. Least-cost production is virtually impossible in the absence of a system of genuine prices which accurately reflect the relative scarcity of the various resources. Finally, Soviet enterprise managers have been highly resistant to innovation. Managers are more concerned with "bargaining" for realistic production targets and fulfilling their output goals so that they can achieve bonuses. New production processes invariably mean higher and often unrealistic targets, underfulfillment, and loss of bonuses.

Reforms: Libermanism

The Soviet government responded to these problems by introducing important reforms in the last half of the 1960s. The reforms stem in large measure from the proposals of Professor E. Liberman of Kharkov University. His plan calls for the introduction of a modified "profit motive" as the primary success indicator in an enterprise; for greater decentralization of decision making and greater autonomy for enterprise managers; and for some degree of "planning from below."

Under the new reforms, enterprises can take orders from customers (retailers or other enterprises) which specify the types (colors, sizes, styles) and amounts of each product. This "planning from below" provides "direct links" to consumer or producer demand and is obviously designed to bring about a better matching of output with the structure of demand. Management also negotiates with other firms for the purchase of needed inputs. Furthermore, the management of each enterprise has restricted authority in setting prices, including rates of pay for its labor force.

The enterprise's major success indicator will no longer be physical output, but rather "profits" calculated in relation to the fixed and working capital of the enterprise. The management and labor force of an enterprise will receive bonuses in direct relation to the size of their profits. This reorientation of goals means that enterprises will be penalized for the production of goods which are unsalable because they are of shoddy quality or, in the case of producer goods, do not fit the input requirements of purchasing enterprises. That is, enterprises must now be concerned not only with production, but also with the sale of output. Moreover, the new emphasis upon profitability means that greater attention must be paid to production costs.

These new reforms have been extensive; it is estimated that one-half of the Soviet Union's industrial production is carried on by enterprises operating under them. And it is clear that the reforms constitute a significant departure from traditional Soviet planning. Nevertheless, it would be premature to interpret the reforms as a trend toward capitalism as we know it. The major goals of the Soviet economy and the priorities attached to these goals are still determined by the central planners. It is significant that the plans of all enterprises working under the new system are reviewed by the planning authorities to assure their conformity with overall national goals and priorities.

As a matter of fact, the long-term viability of the Liberman reforms depends upon the ability of the Soviets to resolve certain problems posed by the reforms themselves. One problem stems from the simple fact that the new reforms are not enthusiasti-

cally embraced by all members of the Soviet economic and political hierarchy. "Old line" central planners correctly envision their authority and positions of power being eroded by any permanent and widespread decentralization of decision making. A second problem is a technical one: The realization of allocative efficiency depends upon sweeping price reforms which will make Soviet prices more accurately reflect the relative scarcity of inputs. The minimization of the money cost of producing any given output will reflect a minimization of real or opportunity costs only if resource prices are accurate indicators of relative scarcity. It is not at all clear that Soviet planners will be able to achieve, much less maintain over time, a new price structure based upon resource scarcity. Finally, one might question the workability of an economy which is "half command and half market." That is, will an economy comprised of a centrally planned segment, operating along the lines of traditional prereform planning, and a segment with greater decentralization, operating according to the profit orientation of Libermanism, encounter severe internal inconsistencies which will force the Soviet government to make a choice between the old and the new?

SOVIET ECONOMIC GROWTH

In view of our forgoing discussion of the Soviet Union's microeconomic problems, it is fair to say that the system has been quite unsuccessful in realizing the goal of allocative efficiency. But we know there are other goals in terms of which an economy's performance might be judged. The alternative and essentially macroeconomic goal which has been paramount with the Soviet leadership is *rapid* economic growth. Soviet Russia has pursued with great vigor the goal of rapid growth and the political-military strength derived therefrom. These two concepts of efficiency may be in conflict in certain important ways.[7] In particular, it is the fact that Soviet planning seeks very rapid growth which results in highly ambitious production targets and the overcommitment of resources. And ambitious targets and overcommitted resources are the source of many of the coordination problems discussed earlier. In any event, we know that the Soviet economy has performed well in terms of the objective of growth. Let us now consider the rate of growth achieved by the Soviet Union, the sources of this growth, and the prospect of its maintenance.

[7]The interested reader should consult Albert O. Hirschman, *The Strategy of Economic Development* (New Haven, Conn.: Yale University Press, 1959).

Growth comparisons

Authoritative estimates put the Soviet GNP at about one-half that of the United States. Figure 46·1 shows this relationship and indicates the relative composition of the national outputs of the two nations. Experts also agree that the Soviet growth rate has generally exceeded that of the United States. During the 1950s the Soviet GNP expanded at about 6 or $6\frac{1}{2}$ percent per year as compared with 3 or $3\frac{1}{2}$ percent for the United States. But Soviet growth performance slackened to about 5 percent per year in the 1960s, and projections for the 1970s suggest possible further deterioration to 4 or $4\frac{1}{2}$ percent. The latter figures are quite close to the full-employment growth rate of the United States. In short, the substantial growth rate advantage which the Soviet Union enjoyed in the 1950s and the early 1960s has tended to diminish and disappear.

Sources of Soviet growth

Let us first pinpoint certain factors which have contributed to high Soviet growth rates.

1. Natural resource base The Soviet Union has a generous and varied natural resource base. Although differing significantly in composition, it is not inaccurate to say that the natural resource endowments of the U.S.S.R. are roughly comparable to those of the United States. The major exception to this generalization is agricultural resources. Most of Russia's most fertile soil lies in regions susceptible to drought and short growing seasons.

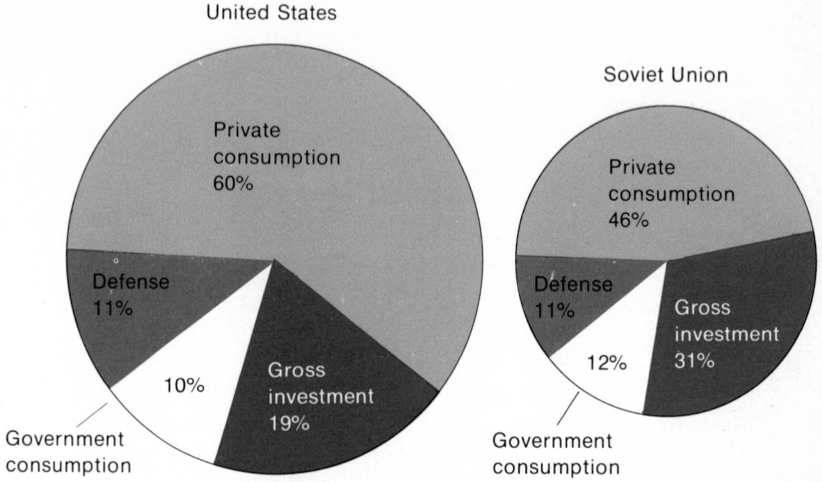

FIGURE 46·1 SIZE AND COMPOSITION OF GNP IN THE UNITED STATES AND THE SOVIET UNION.

Soviet Russia's GNP is roughly one-half the size of the United States's GNP. As compared with the United States, the Soviet Union puts relatively greater emphasis on investment goods than consumer goods. [Stanley H. Cohn, "Soviet Growth Retardation: Trends in Resource Availability and Efficiency," in Joint Economic Committee, *New Directions in the Soviet Economy* (Washington, 1966), p. 106.]

2. Totalitarianism and allocation It follows from the fact that the Soviet Union is a totalitarian state that the government can and does exercise tight political control over the allocation of resources. That the government has, with little hesitation of reservation, exerted a strong and often brutal "will to develop" is reflected in its efforts to indoctrinate, regiment, push and prod its citizenry, and to structure its institutions to the overriding goal of economic growth. The Soviet economy has aptly been described as "totalitarianism harnessed to the task of industrialization and economic growth."[8] To be more specific, we may say that the will to develop has been expressed most explicitly in the high-volume and growth-oriented composition of Soviet investment. The Soviet Union devotes almost one-third of its total output to investment as compared with one-fifth for the United States (Figure 46·1). Furthermore, the composition of Soviet investment has put emphasis upon those industries most crucial to the growth process. Retail and wholesale distributional facilities, for example, have been largely ignored in favor of steel, petroleum, chemicals, and machine tools.

3. Surplus farm labor You will recall from Chapter 45 that it is characteristic of underdeveloped countries to have a sizable amount of surplus or underemployed labor in agriculture. This was true of the Soviet Union at the time of the revolution. Under central planning much of this low-productivity farm labor was shifted to newly created industries, where its productivity was substantially higher. In 1925, 84 percent of the Soviet labor force was in agriculture;

[8]Robert W. Campbell, *Soviet Economic Power,* 2d ed. (Boston: Houghton Mifflin Company, 1966), p. 9.

currently about 30 percent are so employed. The result of this reallocation has been significant increases in the Soviet GNP.

4. Technological gap Rapid expansion in Soviet production has stemmed in good measure from the adoption of the superior technological knowledge pioneered by the Western nations. The Soviet Union has eagerly, unashamedly, and quite effectively borrowed and skillfully applied the superior techniques of other nations. In this manner the U.S.S.R. has quickly and very inexpensively bridged a long period of research and development activity in many key industries.

5. Full employment The Soviet economy's growth rate, unlike those of the United States and other capitalistic nations, has benefited in that since about 1930 Soviet economic planning has virtually eliminated cyclical unemployment. Unlike the United States, the Soviet Union has *not* had to count years of zero or negative growth due to recession in calculating its long-term rate of growth.

Retarding factors

Why has the Soviet growth rate diminished? What growth-retarding forces have been at work?

1. Diversion of resources A frequently cited reason for the slowing down of Soviet growth is that expanding defense expenditures in the 1960s and early 1970s have diverted resources from more growth-effective uses. In particular, growing defense outlays have caused declines in both the quantity and quality of industrial investment. Rising defense expenditures have become an "onerous burden" upon the Soviet economy because of their direct competitiveness with civilian investment and therefore economic growth. Furthermore, the "policy of channeling superior management and the best scientists and engineers into defense research and production denies prime innovative resources to civilian oriented investment"[9] and has adversely affected technological progress and the quality (productivity) of investment in the civilian sector.

The "onerous-burden hypothesis" may apply not only to the military, but also to the consuming sector:[10]

> Soviet leaders are finding it increasingly difficult to reject or postpone the satisfaction of consumers' wants. Revolutionary enthusiasm, it is said, no longer is sufficient to make sacrifices of consumer welfare acceptable either to the population at large or to many Communist Party members and leaders. The very sizeable improvements that have been made in consumer welfare in recent years have not relieved universal dissatisfaction with living conditions, but rather may have whetted the general appetite for further gains.

2. Replacement investment A less spectacular point of a more technical nature is that, as the size and age of the Soviet Union's stock of capital increases, replacement investment necessarily increases. That is, a growing proportion of gross investment must be for depreciation, leaving a smaller share as net investment to contribute to growth. Other things being the same, an increasing volume of gross investment is required to maintain a constant rate of growth.

3. Closing of technological gap While a technological gap remains between the Soviet Union and the West, it is quite clear that the gap has narrowed appreciably and in some instances may have been eliminated. And it is significant that the closing of the gap has generally occurred more fully in heavy industry than in sectors of the Soviet economy less crucial to growth. The important point is that, as the USSR has drawn abreast technologically, windfall productivity gains from technological borrowing have diminished, and the Soviet Union is increasingly faced with the highly resource-absorbing task of pushing forward its own technological frontiers.

4. Labor shortage Whereas much of the Soviet Union's earlier growth was attributable to shifts of

[9]Stanley H. Cohn, "General Growth Performance of the Soviet Economy," in Joint Economic Committee, *Economic Performance and the Military Burden in the Soviet Union* (Washington, 1970), p. 12.

[10]Terence E. Byrne, "Recent Trends in the Soviet Economy," in ibid., p. 5.

surplus labor from agriculture to industry, the Soviet Union is finding it increasingly difficult to make additional labor shifts without significantly imperiling the output of an already troubled agricultural sector. The overall picture in the Soviet Union is one of labor scarcity, and this is particularly so in certain skills and in certain cities and regions. This shortage is partly the consequence of the ambitiousness of the central plans and is undoubtedly aggravated by widespread malutilization of the labor force. It is interesting that the Soviet Union has recently imported workers from Eastern European satellite nations to ease its labor shortage. The basic point is that the relatively easy means of increasing GNP by employing more labor inputs is less available to the Soviets; they are faced with the more demanding task of expanding their GNP by increasing labor productivity, that is, output per worker.

5. Agricultural drag By Western standards Soviet agriculture is something of a monument to inefficiency and now constitutes a drag upon economic growth, engulfing as it does over 30 percent of the labor force. The low productivity of Soviet agriculture is attributable to many factors: the relative scarcity of good land; the neglect of agriculture as reflected in scarcities of farm capital and the limited use of chemical fertilizers; serious errors in planning and administration; the failure to construct an effective incentive system; and vagaries in rainfall and length of growing season. Given the relatively large size of the agricultural sector, a poor growing season can have highly adverse effects upon the Soviet growth rate. For example, the poor harvest of 1969 was a major factor in pulling that year's growth rate down to 2.3 percent.

6. Planning problems As suggested earlier, there are forces at work in the U.S.S.R. which have tended to reduce the relative efficiency of Soviet planning and thereby to retard the growth rate. These planning problems are closely linked to the development of the Soviet economy itself. Early planning under Stalin was not unlike the wartime planning of Western nations: A limited number of key production goals were established, and resources were centrally directed toward the fulfillment of these goals regardless of costs or consumer welfare. But the past success of such "campaign planning" has resulted in an industrially advanced economy. This new, more modern economy is vastly different from that of the earlier period of war-economy planning. The proliferation and realignment of priorities have already been noted. In short, planning techniques which were more or less adequate for the Stalinist era of limited production goals are decreasingly relevant and less workable in the more sophisticated economy of the 1970s. With growth the economy, and therefore planning, became decidedly more complex. Neither labor nor capital is as relatively abundant as it was a scant decade or so ago. The expansion of a relatively few standard product lines with a blatant disregard for costs is relatively simple; production of a much larger variety of products, each of which is more complex, within a context of growing cost-consciousness is quite a different matter. To state the situation quite simply, the Soviet economy has tended to outgrow its planning mechanisms. As we have seen, this fact has posed serious questions concerning the allocative efficiency of the system and its capacity to sustain its growth rate. Whether the Liberman reforms of the late 1960s with their emphasis upon "profitability" and decentralization will be capable of overcoming these planning problems remains to be seen.

Possible accelerating factors

But we must not embrace too readily the view that the Soviets have reached the end of the road in terms of growth. There are factors which suggest that the Soviet Union may be able to revitalize its growth record. Two general reminders are in order before we examine these specific growth-accelerating factors.

In the first place, we must acknowledge that there exists no generalization in the economics of growth to indicate that, once realizing the take-off into economic growth, a nation will achieve vigorous expansion—a kind of economic adolescence—for a time,

only to face middle age and an inevitable hardening of the economic arteries. Such vague biological analogies are of doubtful relevance to economic growth. There is no reason to anticipate an *automatic* or *inevitable* retardation of Soviet growth.

Secondly, we must not fall into the delusion that growth rates are unimportant. One often hears the consoling assertion that, because the United States has a GNP roughly twice that of the Soviet Union, there is no cause to be alarmed about the fact that the Soviet growth rate exceeds ours. This is simply not true. It must be clearly recognized that *any* growth rate differential favorable to the U.S.S.R., despite its smaller GNP base, implies an inevitable catching up in terms of absolute GNPs.

Consider now a number of specific factors which suggest that the Soviet growth rate can be maintained.

1. GNP increments An already rapidly expanding economy is in a most advantageous position to sustain its growth even in the face of insistent new demands upon its resources. The Soviet Union is now realizing annual increments in its GNP perhaps on the order of $20 to $25 billion per year. A 6 percent growth rate compounded will double the Soviet GNP in a scant twelve years! Increases of this size certainly provide the potential out of which rising demands from consumers, the military-space effort, and the foreign aid program *might* be met.

2. Education and technology It must also be recognized that the Soviet regime has historically put great emphasis upon education and research and development activity. One of the great accomplishments of the Soviet government has been its transformation of a basically illiterate rural population into a literate industrial labor force of considerable quality. Furthermore, it is well known that Soviet education and manpower policies are closely linked to economic objectives:[11]

> Science and technology are particularly recognized as the foundation of national strength; and consequently, they receive emphasis on all levels of the educational effort. . . . The quality of Soviet professional training in scientific, engineering, and applied fields today is, on substantive grounds, comparable to that offered in the West . . . in recent years the number of higher education graduates in the sciences and various applied fields—engineering, agriculture, and medicine—has exceeded substantially (by a factor of 2 or 3 to 1) the rate of training such specialists in the United States.

This educational effort provides a solid foundation for a Soviet research and development effort which is comparable to that of the United States in absolute terms, larger than the United States's as a percentage of GNP, and perhaps more farsighted in terms of distribution between basic and applied research. It is not irrelevant to note that new knowledge—technological progress—has a habit of sweeping aside impediments to economic expansion. The important point for our purposes is that future Soviet expansion may well reap a substantial output harvest from past investments in human capital and research and development activity.

3. Planning techniques Against the tendency of Soviet planning to become less efficient in the face of an increasingly complex economy must be set the likelihood of significant breakthroughs in the techniques and mechanics of central planning. Accelerated interest is evident in the application of advanced mathematical techniques and computers as means to achieve greater balance and coordination in planning. The Liberman reforms are ample evidence that the keynote in Soviet planning today is flexibility and experimentation.

4. Forced growth Finally, we must not lose sight of the fact that the ability of the Soviet leadership to mobilize human resources and to exercise wide discretion in determining the composition of output has been a key factor in past growth. The role of the Soviet government as a mechanism for *forcing* growth is likely to be sustained. Growth accomplishments are partly explainable in terms of eco-

[11] Nicholas DeWitt, "Education and the Development of Human Resources: Soviet and American Effort," in Joint Economic Committee, *Dimensions of Soviet Economic Power* (Washington, 1962), pp. 267–268.

nomic policy, and there is every reason to suspect that growth-oriented policies will remain the major, if not the sole, cornerstone of Soviet planning. In brief, the totalitarian system has advantages in the area of economic growth which cannot be taken lightly.

Future growth

It is no easy matter to balance the growth-inhibiting and growth-accelerating forces against one another and make an unqualified prediction as to future Soviet growth. In any event, a continued decline in Soviet growth, if this indeed proves to be the case, is little cause for complacency in the United States. Needless to say, it would be extremely shortsighted to base either our domestic economic policies or our international political strategy upon the assumption that long-term Soviet growth will decline by any substantial amount. The Soviet economic challenge and its manifold implications are not to be underestimated.

GENERAL EVALUATION

Our discussion thus far has centered upon central planning and the growth performance which planning has fostered. A more complete evaluation of the Soviet system calls for the consideration of several other accomplishments and shortcomings.

Accomplishments

1. Education Though circumscribed by Communist doctrine and shaped in terms of government goals, Soviet Russia has made tremendous strides in increasing the quantity and quality of education. Free public education has been a high-priority goal of the Soviet regime from the outset. Much has also been done to encourage cultural pursuits, again within limits imposed by the party.

2. Economic security In keeping with socialist tradition, the Soviet Union has developed a quite complete system of social insurance. Medical care is virtually free and disability and sick leave benefits are provided, as are maternity benefits. Rental payments are heavily subsidized and amount to only about 4 or 5 percent of a worker's income. Retirement pensions are available for industrial workers and have recently been extended to collective farmers. Although the size of benefit payments are not overly generous by American standards, they are sufficient in terms of the Soviet standard of living.

Shortcomings

Generally speaking, the major shortcomings of the Soviet system are the offspring of its accomplishments. Two major points merit emphasis.

1. Standard of living The costs of rapid industrialization and economic growth have been great, and have been borne for the most part by consumers. This is reflected both in the quantity and quality of Soviet consumer goods. Living standards are much lower than in the United States:[12]

> Soviet city life is similar to life in Western cities fifty years ago. People live in crowded apartments, use public transportation, wear drab clothing, and eat a starchy diet. . . . Soviet rural life compares with still earlier European experience, though the presence of large machinery and trucks makes for noncomparability. The general pattern in both city and country is still "old fashioned," yet elements of modernization run all through it.

Improvements in the Soviet standard of living have been significant in the last decade. But as far as the consumer is concerned, the Soviet Union is far from being a society of abundance.

2. Freedom The decisions which determine the overall economic, political, social, and cultural environment are made by the Soviet dictatorship. Only within governmentally prescribed limits is individual freedom tolerated. Consumers and wage earners are "free" to choose from the goods and jobs planners

[12] Clair Wilcox, Willis D. Weatherford, Jr., Holland Hunter, and Morton S. Baratz, *Economies of the World Today,* 2d ed. (New York: Harcourt, Brace & World, Inc., 1966), pp. 45–46.

decide to provide. In general, artists and writers must conform to the party line in their creative efforts.

Viewed in broader perspective, it must be emphasized that the Soviet Union is a dictatorship based ultimately upon coercion, terror, or the effective threat thereof. Though there has been a general relaxation of the tensions which surrounded Stalinist tyranny, the threat of force is omnipresent. Elections are a farce, the press is essentially a propaganda organ of the government, and the role of the secret police in maintaining allegiance and conformity continues to be substantial.[13]

Implications

Of this there is no doubt: The Soviet economic challenge injects an element of urgency to the economizing problem in American capitalism. The goals of sustained economic stability and adequate growth (Parts 2 to 4) take on new, critical dimensions in view of rapid Soviet economic expansion. In particular, a prolonged depression would seriously impair our chances of meeting the economic challenge of the Soviet Union. Certainly the question of achieving efficiency in the allocation of resources through the mechanism of the price system becomes increasingly acute (Part 5). American capitalism must continuously appraise the allocative efficiency of the market mechanism and the balance between private and social goods. This obviously entails a detailed reexamination of specific problem areas and existing public policies designed to cope with those problems (Part 6). And clearly the military, political, and economic significance of the less developed nations of the world calls for a farsightedness in our international trade and aid policies and practices which historically has been highly elusive (Part 7).

The role of American capitalism in the political, economic, and sociocultural affairs of the world can continue to be the dominant one. An awareness of economic principles, problems, and policies can play a central role in preserving that dominance.

[13]For a short study of the history and strategy of communism the reader should consult Andrew Gyorgy, *Communism in Perspective* (Boston: Allyn and Bacon, Inc., 1964). Andrei D. Sakharov's *Progress, Coexistence, and Intellectual Freedom* (New York: W. W. Norton & Company, Inc., 1968), is also of great interest. Sakharov, who was largely responsible for the development of Russia's atomic bomb, appeals to the party to democratize the Soviet system.

SUMMARY

1. The vivid contrast which the Soviet economy provides to American capitalism, the economic challenge it presents to the Western world, and the rapid economic growth achieved in Soviet Russia are important reasons for studying the Soviet economic system.

2. Virtually complete public ownership of property resources and central economic planning are the outstanding institutional features of the Soviet economy.

3. The major goals of the Five- and Seven-year Plans, as determined by the government, have been rapid industrialization and growth and military strength.

4. The basic problem of central planners is to achieve coordination or internal consistency in their plans so as to avoid bottlenecks and the chain reaction of production failures which they cause. The evaluation of preliminary plans by the administrative hierarchy, the assignment of priorities to planned goals, and reserve stocks are used to prevent or alleviate coordination problems in the U.S.S.R.

5. Many agencies check upon the actual execution of the Five-year Plans—the planning hierarchy, the Communist Party and its numerous officials, and the secret police. The most important of these agencies is the Gosbank, which exerts "control by the ruble."

6. In the production process, governmentally determined prices on resources and components and on finished products serve as accounting devices to evaluate the efficiency of production. In consumer goods markets, prices are adjusted through the turnover tax to ration products to consumers, that is, to balance the amount demanded with available supplies.

7. As the Soviet economy has become more complex, certain microeconomic problems—the production of unwanted goods, a distorted product-mix, and

resistance to innovation—have developed. The Liberman reforms of the 1960s, emphasizing profitability of production, "planning from below," and greater decentralization of decision making, have been adopted in response to these problems.

8. Although the Soviet GNP is only one-half as large as the United States's, the Soviet GNP has been growing more rapidly than ours. A generous natural resource base, great emphasis upon capital formation, the transfer of surplus agricultural labor to industry, the adoption of superior production techniques from the West, and the planning away of cyclical unemployment are factors which have contributed to this high growth rate.

9. A number of factors suggest a future decline in the Soviet growth rate: a diversion of resources from growth-inducing uses, the growth of replacement investment, a partial closing of the technological gap, a shortage of industrial labor, the stagnation of agriculture, and mounting planning problems attributable to the increasing complexity of the Soviet economy.

10. Other factors suggest that the Soviet growth rate is maintainable: large annual GNP increments are now available to meet new demands on resources, past investments in education and research may overcome growth obstacles, new techniques may substantially improve the efficiency of central planning, and the Soviet government will continue to force growth through its allocative decisions.

11. In addition to proving the feasibility of central planning and achieving a high growth rate, the Soviet Union has made significant advances in education and has established a comprehensive social security system. On the other hand, the Soviet standard of living is not enviable by Western standards, and freedom is closely circumscribed by party objectives.

QUESTIONS AND STUDY SUGGESTIONS

1. "So long as a central planning board, as opposed to society as a whole, sets the economic goals, there can be no freedom of occupational or consumer choice." Explain.

2. Compare the sources of insecurity which face an American and a Soviet steelworker.

3. "It has become increasingly difficult for thoughtful men to find meaningful alternatives posed in the traditional choices between socialism and capitalism, planning and the free market, regulation and laissez faire, for they find their actual choices neither simple nor so grand."[14] Explain and evaluate.

4. Compare the institutional framework of the Soviet economy with that of American capitalism. Contrast the manner in which production is motivated in these two economic systems.

[14]Robert A. Dahl and Charles E. Lindblom, *Politics, Economics and Welfare* (New York: Harper & Row, Publishers, Incorporated, 1953), p. 1.

5. How does Soviet planning attempt to cope with the Five Fundamental Questions which all economies must face? Discuss the problem of coordination. What mechanisms do Soviet planners use to avoid and correct problems of coordination? Explain: "Soviet planning problems mainly arise from the fact that the command economy is rooted in the logic of haste."

6. Evaluate carefully the level of efficiency which has been achieved in Soviet economic planning. Discuss the background and character of the Liberman reforms.

7. Compare the size, composition, and rate of growth of the GNPs of the United States and the Soviet Union. What have been the major sources of Soviet economic expansion? Do you feel that the Soviet Union will be able to sustain its past growth performance? Explain.

8. Carefully contrast the role of the price system in Soviet Russia and the United States. Explain the use of turnover taxes.

9. How is the number of automobiles to be produced determined in American capitalism? In the Soviet Union? How are these decisions implemented in the two economies?

SELECTED REFERENCES

Economic Issues, 4th ed., readings 92, 93, 94, and 95.

Bornstein, Morris, and Daniel R. Fusfeld (eds.): *The Soviet Economy,* 3d ed. (Homewood, Ill.: Richard D. Irwin, Inc., 1970).

Campbell, Robert W.: *Soviet Economic Power,* 2d ed. (Boston: Houghton Mifflin Company, 1966).

Cohn, Stanley H.: *Economic Development in the Soviet Union* (Boston: D. C. Heath and Company, 1970).

Joint Economic Committee, *Economic Performance and the Military Burden in the Soviet Union* (Washington, 1970).

Nove, Alec: *The Soviet Economy,* rev. ed. (New York: Frederick A. Praeger, Inc., 1965).

Sherman, Howard J.: *The Soviet Economy* (Boston: Little, Brown and Company, 1969).

INDEX

(Continued from front cover)

NATIONAL INCOME AND RELATED STATISTICS FOR YEARS, 1948–1970

National income statistics are in billions of current dollars. Details may not add to totals because of rounding.

			1948	1949	1950	1951	1952	1953	1954	1955	1956	1957
THE SUM OF	1	Personal consumption expenditures	$173.6	$176.8	$191.0	$206.3	$216.7	$230.0	$236.5	$254.4	$266.7	$281.4
	2	Gross private domestic investment	46.0	35.7	54.1	59.3	51.9	52.6	51.7	67.4	70.0	67.8
	3	Government purchases of goods and services	31.6	37.8	37.9	59.1	74.7	81.6	74.8	74.2	78.6	86.1
	4	Net exports	6.4	6.1	1.8	3.7	2.2	.4	1.8	2.0	4.0	5.7
EQUALS	5	Gross national product	257.6	256.5	284.8	328.4	345.5	364.6	364.8	398.0	419.2	441.1
LESS	6	Capital consumption allowances	14.5	16.6	18.3	21.2	23.2	25.7	28.2	31.5	34.1	37.1
EQUALS	7	Net national product	243.1	239.9	266.9	307.2	322.3	338.9	336.6	366.5	385.2	404.0
LESS	8	Indirect business taxes	18.9	22.4	25.4	29.2	30.9	34.2	33.5	35.5	34.4	37.9
EQUALS	9	National income	224.2	217.5	241.1	278.0	291.4	304.7	303.1	331.0	350.8	366.1
LESS	10	Social security contributions	5.2	5.7	6.9	8.2	8.7	8.8	9.8	11.1	12.6	14.5
	11	Corporate income taxes	12.5	10.4	17.8	22.3	19.4	20.3	17.7	21.6	21.7	21.2
	12	Undistributed corporate profits	13.5	13.1	11.1	11.8	12.0	10.5	11.0	14.8	13.2	12.7
PLUS	13	Transfer payments	17.3	18.9	22.3	20.1	21.2	23.0	25.5	27.4	29.7	33.4
EQUALS	14	Personal income	210.2	207.2	227.6	255.6	272.5	288.2	290.1	310.9	333.0	351.1
LESS	15	Personal taxes	21.1	18.6	20.7	29.0	34.1	35.6	32.7	35.5	39.8	42.6
EQUALS	16	Disposable income	189.1	188.6	206.9	226.6	238.3	252.6	257.4	275.3	293.2	308.5
LESS	17	Personal consumption expenditures	173.6	176.8	191.0	206.3	216.7	230.0	236.5	254.4	266.7	281.4
	18	Interest paid by consumers	2.2	2.4	2.9	3.1	3.5	4.3	4.6	5.1	5.9	6.4
EQUALS	19	Personal saving	13.4	9.4	13.1	17.3	18.1	18.3	16.4	15.8	20.6	20.7
	20	Real gross national product (in 1958 dollars)	323.7	324.1	355.3	383.4	395.1	412.8	407.0	438.0	446.1	452.5

RELATED STATISTICS			1948	1949	1950	1951	1952	1953	1954	1955	1956	1957
	21	Consumer price index (1967 = 100)	72.1	71.4	72.1	77.8	79.5	80.1	80.5	80.2	81.4	84.3
	22	Index of industrial production (1967 = 100)	43.3	40.9	47.4	51.4	53.3	57.7	54.3	61.1	63.2	63.7
	23	Supply of money (in billions of dollars)	111.5	111.2	116.2	122.7	127.4	128.8	132.3	135.2	136.9	135.9
	24	Unemployment (in millions)	2.3	3.7	3.4	2.1	1.9	1.9	3.6	2.9	2.8	2.9
	25	Unemployment as a % of the civilian labor force	3.8	5.9	5.3	3.3	3.1	2.9	5.6	4.4	4.2	4.3
	26	Total consumer credit outstanding (in billions of dollars)	14.4	17.4	21.5	22.7	27.5	31.4	32.5	38.8	42.3	45.0

6	1947	1948	1949	1950	1951	1952	1953	1954	1955	1956	1957	1958	
.4	$160.7	$173.6	$176.8	$191.0	$206.3	$216.7	$230.0	$236.5	$254.4	$266.7	$281.4	$290.1	1
.6	34.0	46.0	35.7	54.1	59.3	51.9	52.6	51.7	67.4	70.0	67.8	60.9	2
.0	25.1	31.6	37.8	37.9	59.1	74.7	81.6	74.8	74.2	78.6	86.1	94.2	3
.5	11.5	6.4	6.1	1.8	3.7	2.2	.4	1.8	2.0	4.0	5.7	2.2	4
.5	231.3	257.6	256.5	284.8	328.4	345.5	364.6	364.8	398.0	419.2	441.1	447.3	5
.9	12.2	14.5	16.6	18.3	21.2	23.2	25.7	28.2	31.5	34.1	37.1	38.9	6
.6	291.1	243.1	239.9	266.9	307.2	322.3	338.9	336.6	366.5	385.2	404.0	408.4	7
.7	20.1	18.9	22.4	25.4	29.2	30.9	34.2	33.5	35.5	34.4	37.9	40.6	8
.9	199.0	224.2	217.5	241.1	278.0	291.4	304.7	303.1	331.0	350.8	366.1	367.8	9
.0	5.7	5.2	5.7	6.9	8.2	8.7	8.8	9.8	11.1	12.6	14.5	14.8	10
.1	11.3	12.5	10.4	17.8	22.3	19.4	20.3	17.7	21.6	21.7	21.2	19.0	11
.6	8.0	13.5	13.1	11.1	11.8	12.0	10.5	11.0	14.8	13.2	12.7	10.5	12
.5	17.2	17.3	18.9	22.3	20.1	21.2	23.0	25.5	27.4	29.7	33.4	37.8	13
.7	191.3	210.2	207.2	227.6	255.6	272.5	288.2	290.1	310.9	333.0	351.1	361.2	14
.7	21.4	21.1	18.6	20.7	29.0	34.1	35.6	32.7	35.5	39.8	42.6	42.3	15
.0	169.8	189.1	188.6	206.9	226.6	238.3	252.6	257.4	275.3	293.2	308.5	318.8	16
.4	160.7	173.6	176.8	191.0	206.3	216.7	230.0	236.5	254.4	266.7	281.4	290.1	17
.4	1.8	2.2	2.4	2.9	3.1	3.5	4.3	4.6	5.1	5.9	6.4	6.5	18
.2	7.3	13.4	9.4	13.1	17.3	18.1	18.3	16.4	15.8	20.6	20.7	22.3	19
.6	309.9	323.7	324.1	355.3	383.4	395.1	412.8	407.0	438.0	446.1	452.5	447.3	20

6	1947	1948	1949	1950	1951	1952	1953	1954	1955	1956	1957	1958	
.5	66.9	72.1	71.4	72.1	77.8	79.5	80.1	80.5	80.2	81.4	84.3	86.6	21
.6	41.6	43.3	40.9	47.4	51.4	53.3	57.7	54.3	61.1	63.2	63.7	59.3	22
.0	113.1	111.5	111.2	116.2	122.7	127.4	128.8	132.3	135.2	136.9	135.9	141.1	23
.3	2.3	2.3	3.7	3.4	2.1	1.9	1.9	3.6	2.9	2.8	2.9	4.7	24
.9	3.9	3.8	5.9	5.3	3.3	3.1	2.9	5.6	4.4	4.2	4.3	6.8	25
.4	11.6	14.4	17.4	21.5	22.7	27.5	31.4	32.5	38.8	42.3	45.0	45.1	26

(Continued on back cover)